THE SAGE HANDBOOK OF
COUNSELLING & PSYCHOTHERAPY

FIFTH EDITION

EDITED BY **TERRY HANLEY & LAURA ANNE WINTER**

$\bigcirc$SAGE

Los Angeles | London | New Delhi
Singapore | Washington DC | Melbourne

SAGE was founded in 1965 by Sara Miller McCune to support the dissemination of usable knowledge by publishing innovative and high-quality research and teaching content. Today, we publish over 900 journals, including those of more than 400 learned societies, more than 800 new books per year, and a growing range of library products including archives, data, case studies, reports, and video. SAGE remains majority-owned by our founder, and after Sara's lifetime will become owned by a charitable trust that secures our continued independence.

Los Angeles | London | New Delhi | Singapore | Washington DC | Melbourne

THE SAGE HANDBOOK OF
COUNSELLING &
PSYCHOTHERAPY

Los Angeles | London | New Delhi
Singapore | Washington DC | Melbourne

SAGE Publications Ltd
1 Oliver's Yard
55 City Road
London EC1Y 1SP

SAGE Publications Inc.
2455 Teller Road
Thousand Oaks, California 91320

SAGE Publications India Pvt Ltd
B 1/I 1 Mohan Cooperative Industrial Area
Mathura Road
New Delhi 110 044

SAGE Publications Asia-Pacific Pte Ltd
3 Church Street
#10-04 Samsung Hub
Singapore 049483

Acquisitions Editor: Susannah Trefgarne
Editorial Assistant: Bali Birch-Lee
Production Editor: Zoheb Khan
Copyeditor: Sarah Bury
Proofreader: Derek Markham
Indexer: KnowledgeWorks Global Ltd.
Marketing manager: Ruslana Khatagova
Cover Design: Naomi Robinson
Typeset by KnowledgeWorks Global Ltd.
Printed in the UK

At SAGE we take sustainability seriously. Most of our products are printed in the UK using FSC papers and boards. When we print overseas we ensure sustainable papers are used as measured by the PREPS grading system. We undertake an annual audit to monitor our sustainability.

© Editorial arrangement, Terry Hanley and Laura Winter 2023;

Chapter 1.1 © Terry Hanley 2023.
Chapter 1.2 © Laura Anne Winter 2023.
Chapter 1.3 © Terry Hanley 2023.
Chapter 1.4 © Laura Anne Winter and Terry Hanley 2023.
Chapter 1.5 © Laura Anne Winter and Terry Hanley 2023.
Chapter 2.1 © Dwight Turner 2023.
Chapter 2.2 © Léonie Sugarman 2023.
Chapter 2.3 © Martin Milton 2023.
Chapter 2.4 © Esther Ingham 2023.
Chapter 2.5 © Sam Hope 2023.
Chapter 2.6 © Lesley Dougan 2023.
Chapter 2.7 © Cemil Egeli and William West 2023.
Chapter 2.8 © Ohemaa Nkansa-Dwamena and Yetunde Ade-Serrano 2023.
Chapter 2.9 © Liz Ballinger 2023.
Chapter 2.10 © Silva Neves and Dominic Davies 2023.
Chapter 3.1 © India Amos 2023.
Chapter 3.2 © William B. Stiles 2023.
Chapter 3.3 © Biljana Van Rijn 2023.
Chapter 3.4 © Andrew Reeves 2023.
Chapter 3.5 © Lucy Johnstone 2023.
Chapter 3.6 © Julia Lyons 2023.
Chapter 3.7 © Gabriel Wynn 2023.
Chapter 3.8 © Rachel Tribe and Claire Marshall 2023.
Chapter 3.9 © India Amos 2023.
Chapter 3.10 © India Amos 2023.
Chapter 3.11 © Chris Rose 2023.
Chapter 3.12 © Mary Creaner 2023.
Chapter 3.13 © Linda Finlay 2023.
Chapter 3.14 © Clare Symons 2023.
Chapter 3.15 © Peter Jenkins 2023.
Chapter 3.16 © Sobhi Girgis 2023.
Chapter 3.17 © John McLeod 2023.
Chapter 3.18 © Daisy Best and Helen Nicholas 2023.
Chapter 3.19 © Julie Prescott and Chathurika Kannangara 2023.
Chapter 3.20 © Anne Guy 2023.
Chapter 3.21 © Colin Feltham 2023.
Chapter 4.1 © Ishba Rehman 2023.
Chapter 4.2 © Mani Mehdikani, Julie Scheiner and Loren Whyatt 2023.
Chapter 4.3 © Steven Barnes, Julie Prescott and Jerome Carson 2023.
Chapter 4.4 © Edith Maria Steffen and Evgenia (Jane) Milman 2023.
Chapter 4.5 © Soha Daru 2023.
Chapter 4.6 © Tony White 2023.
Chapter 4.7 © Denis O'Hara 2023.
Chapter 4.8 © Gabriel Wynn 2023.
Chapter 4.9 © Joachim Schnackenberg 2023.
Chapter 4.10 © Soha Daru 2023.
Chapter 4.11 © Stephen Palmer and Rowan Bayne 2023.
Chapter 4.12 © Tracie Holroyd 2023.
Chapter 4.13 © Julia Lyons 2023.
Chapter 4.14 © Charlotte Conn, Aashiya Patel and Julie Prescott 2023.
Chapter 4.15 © Divine Charura and Penn Smith 2023.
Chapter 4.16 © Cate Campbell 2023.
Chapter 4.17 © Rosaleen McElvaney 2023.
Chapter 4.18 © Andrew Reeves 2023.
Chapter 4.19 © Christiane Sanderson 2023.
Chapter 5.1 © John Boorman, Eric Morris and Joe Oliver 2023.
Chapter 5.2 © Mark Linington and Victoria Settle 2023.
Chapter 5.3 © Claire Pollitt 2023.
Chapter 5.4 © Dr Heather Sequeira and Dr Jill Mytton 2023.
Chapter 5.5 © Sunil Lad and Jenika Patel 2023.
Chapter 5.6 © Michaela Swales and Christine Dunkley 2023.
Chapter 5.7 © Nick Totton 2023.
Chapter 5.8 © Catherine Kerr and Liz Royle 2023.
Chapter 5.9 © Ladislav Timulak 2023.
Chapter 5.10 © Emmy van Deurzen 2023.
Chapter 5.11 © Liz Ballinger 2023.
Chapter 5.12 © Faisal Mahmood and Emma Flax 2023.
Chapter 5.13 © Dominic Davies and Silva Neves 2023.
Chapter 5.14 © Elizabeth Robinson and Catherine Edmunds 2023.
Chapter 5.15 © Ruth Williams 2023.
Chapter 5.16 © Lionel Bailly 2023.
Chapter 5.17 © Adam J. Scott and Kate Adam 2023.
Chapter 5.18 © Stephen Palmer 2023.
Chapter 5.19 © Fiona Stirling and John McLeod 2023.
Chapter 5.20 © Keith Tudor 2023.
Chapter 5.21 © David Winter 2023.
Chapter 5.22 © Christine Kupfer, John McLeod and Mick Cooper 2023.
Chapter 5.23 © Jessica Yakeley 2023.
Chapter 5.24 © Richard J. Brown, Sara Bardsley and Vanessa Herbert 2023.
Chapter 5.25 © Dwight Turner 2023.
Chapter 5.26 © Konstantina Kolonia and Helen Kyritsi 2023.
Chapter 5.27 © Val Wosket and Peter Jenkins 2023.
Chapter 5.28 © Guy Shennan 2023.
Chapter 5.29 © Charlotte Sills and Keith Tudor 2023.
Chapter 6.1 © Kathryn Geldard and Rebecca Yin Foo 2023.
Chapter 6.2 © Kathryn Geldard and Rebecca Yin Foo 2023.
Chapter 6.3 © Anne Hayward and Ken Laidlaw 2023.
Chapter 6.4 © Cate Campbell 2023.
Chapter 6.5 © Rudi Dallos 2023.
Chapter 6.6 © Stephen Paul 2023.
Chapter 6.7 © Kate Anthony and Stephen Goss 2023.
Chapter 6.8 © Zehra Ersahin 2023.
Chapter 6.9 © Maxine Rosenfield 2023.
Chapter 6.10 © Stephen Goss, DeeAnna Merz Nagel and Kate Anthony 2023.
Chapter 7.1 © Shira Baram 2023.
Chapter 7.2 © Kirsten Amis 2023.
Chapter 7.3 © Elaine Kasket 2023.
Chapter 7.4 © David Goss 2023.
Chapter 7.5 © Gareth Williams 2023.
Chapter 7.6 © Zubeida Ali and Satinder Panesar 2023.
Chapter 7.7 © Alex Coren 2023.
Chapter 7.8 © Charlotte Conn and Aashiya Patel 2023.
Chapter 7.9 © Jenika Patel and Sunil Lad 2023.
Chapter 7.10 © Zsófia Anna Utry and Stephen Palmer 2023.

Apart from any fair dealing for the purposes of research or private study, or criticism or review, as permitted under the Copyright, Designs and Patents Act, 1988, this publication may be reproduced, stored or transmitted in any form, or by any means, only with the prior permission in writing of the publishers, or in the case of reprographic reproduction, in accordance with the terms of licences issued by the Copyright Licensing Agency. Enquiries concerning reproduction outside those terms should be sent to the publishers.

Library of Congress Control Number: 2022935614

British Library Cataloguing in Publication data

A catalogue record for this book is available from the British Library

ISBN 978-1-5297-8109-0
ISBN 978-1-5297-8108-3 (pbk)

CONTENTS

List of Figures and Tables x
About the Editors xi
Contributors xii
Preface to the Fifth Edition xxvii
Acknowledgements xxix

PART I: COUNSELLING AND PSYCHOTHERAPY IN CONTEXT 1

1.1 What are counselling and psychotherapy? 2
Terry Hanley

1.2 The social and political context of counselling and psychotherapy 8
Laura Anne Winter

1.3 What do people come to counselling and psychotherapy for? 14
Terry Hanley

1.4 What are the training routes in counselling and psychotherapy? 19
Laura Anne Winter and Terry Hanley

1.5 Where do counsellors and psychotherapists work? 23
Laura Anne Winter and Terry Hanley

PART II: SOCIAL JUSTICE AND INTERSECTIONALITY 29

2.1 Intersectionality, power and privilege 30
Dwight Turner

2.2 Age 34
Léonie Sugarman

2.3 Counselling and psychotherapy in the context of the climate and environmental crisis 39
Martin Milton

2.4 Disability 45
Esther Ingham

2.5 Gender 50
Sam Hope

2.6 Neurodivergence 56
Lesley Dougan

2.7 Religion and spirituality 62
Cemil Egeli and William West

2.8 Race, culture and ethnicity – what is your story? 67
Ohemaa Nkansa-Dwamena and Yetunde Ade-Serrano

2.9 Social class 74
Liz Ballinger

2.10 Sexuality 79
Silva Neves and Dominic Davies

PART III: CORE THERAPEUTIC AND PROFESSIONAL SKILLS — 85

3.1 Contracting and therapeutic beginnings — 86
India Amos

3.2 The client–therapist relationship — 91
William B. Stiles

3.3 Assessment — 97
Biljana van Rijn

3.4 Risk: assessment, exploration and mitigation — 104
Andrew Reeves

3.5 Formulation — 110
Lucy Johnstone

3.6 Using outcome and process measures — 116
Julia Lyons

3.7 Confidentiality, recordkeeping, and notetaking — 123
Gabriel Wynn

3.8 Working with interpreters — 129
Rachel Tribe and Claire Marshall

3.9 Therapeutic middles — 136
India Amos

3.10 Therapeutic endings — 142
India Amos

3.11 Personal and professional development — 147
Chris Rose

3.12 Clinical supervision — 153
Mary Creaner

3.13 Ethics in practice — 159
Linda Finlay

3.14 Complaints: learning, prevention and procedures — 165
Clare Symons

3.15 Therapy and the law — 171
Peter Jenkins

3.16 Mental health law — 177
Sobhi Girgis

3.17 Integrating research and practice — 184
John McLeod

3.18 Leadership: therapists as leaders — 190
Daisy Best and Helen Nicholas

3.19 Social media and professionalism — 196
Julie Prescott and Chathurika Kannangara

3.20 Knowledge of psychopharmacology — 201
Anne Guy

3.21 Critical thinking skills in counselling and psychotherapy — 208
Colin Feltham

PART IV: WHAT DO PEOPLE COME TO THERAPY FOR? — 213

4.1 Adult sexual violence: rape and sexual assault — 214
Ishba Rehman

4.2 Alcohol-related difficulties — 220
Mani Mehdikani, Julie Scheiner and Loren Whyatt

4.3	Anxiety and panic	226
	Steven Barnes, Julie Prescott and Jerome Carson	
4.4	Bereavement and loss	233
	Edith Maria Steffen and Evgenia (Jane) Milman	
4.5	Chronic physical health problems	238
	Soha Daru	
4.6	Counselling for drug-related problems	245
	Tony White	
4.7	Depression	251
	Denis O'Hara	
4.8	Eating disorders	257
	Gabriel Wynn	
4.9	Hearing voices	263
	Joachim Schnackenberg	
4.10	Low self-esteem	269
	Soha Daru	
4.11	Managing stress	275
	Stephen Palmer and Rowan Bayne	
4.12	Obsessive-compulsive disorder	282
	Tracie Holroyd	
4.13	Personality disorders	288
	Julia Lyons	
4.14	Phobias	294
	Charlotte Conn, Aashiya Patel and Julie Prescott	
4.15	Post-traumatic stress disorder	300
	Divine Charura and Penn Smith	
4.16	Sex and relationship problems	307
	Cate Campbell	
4.17	Sexual abuse in childhood	313
	Rosaleen McElvaney	
4.18	Suicide and self-harm	318
	Andrew Reeves	
4.19	Working with survivors of domestic violence	325
	Christiane Sanderson	

PART V: THEORIES AND APPROACHES — 331

5.1	Acceptance and Commitment Therapy	332
	John Boorman, Eric Morris and Joe Oliver	
5.2	Attachment-based psychoanalytic psychotherapy	338
	Mark Linington and Victoria Settle	
5.3	Cognitive analytic therapy	345
	Claire Pollitt	
5.4	Cognitive behavioural therapy	352
	Heather Sequeira and Jill Mytton	
5.5	Compassion focused therapy	359
	Sunil Lad and Jenika Patel	
5.6	Dialectical behaviour therapy	365
	Michaela Swales and Christine Dunkley	
5.7	Ecotherapy	372
	Nick Totton	
5.8	Eye movement desensitisation and reprocessing (EMDR)	378
	Catherine Kerr and Liz Royle	

5.9	Emotion-focused therapy *Ladislav Timulak*	385
5.10	Existential therapy *Emmy van Deurzen*	391
5.11	Feminist therapy *Liz Ballinger*	397
5.12	Gestalt therapy *Faisal Mahmood and Emma Flax*	403
5.13	Gender, sex and relationship diversity therapy *Dominic Davies and Silva Neves*	409
5.14	Interpersonal psychotherapy *Elizabeth Robinson and Catherine Edmunds*	415
5.15	Jungian analytical psychology *Ruth Williams*	421
5.16	Lacanian therapy *Lionel Bailly*	427
5.17	Mindfulness based cognitive therapy *Adam J. Scott and Kate Adam*	431
5.18	Multimodal therapy *Stephen Palmer*	436
5.19	Narrative therapy *Fiona Stirling and John McLeod*	444
5.20	Person-centred therapy *Keith Tudor*	450
5.21	Personal construct therapy *David Winter*	456
5.22	Pluralistic therapy *Christine Kupfer, John McLeod and Mick Cooper*	462
5.23	Psychoanalytic therapy *Jessica Yakeley*	468
5.24	Psychodynamic interpersonal therapy *Richard J. Brown, Sara Bardsley and Vanessa Herbert*	474
5.25	Psychodynamic therapy *Dwight Turner*	480
5.26	Schema therapy *Konstantina Kolonia and Helen Kyritsi*	485
5.27	The skilled helper model *Val Wosket and Peter Jenkins*	492
5.28	Solution-focused brief therapy *Guy Shennan*	498
5.29	Transactional analysis *Charlotte Sills and Keith Tudor*	503

PART VI: LIFESPAN, MODALITIES AND TECHNOLOGY 511

6.1	Counselling children *Kathryn Geldard and Rebecca Yin Foo*	512
6.2	Counselling young people *Kathryn Geldard and Rebecca Yin Foo*	517
6.3	Counselling older people *Anne Hayward and Ken Laidlaw*	523
6.4	Couple therapy *Cate Campbell*	530

6.5	Systemic family therapy *Rudi Dallos*	535		6.8	Videoconferencing therapy *Zehra Ersahin*	554
6.6	Group therapy *Stephen Paul*	541		6.9	Counselling by telephone *Maxine Rosenfield*	560
6.7	Electronically delivered text therapy *Kate Anthony and Stephen Goss*	549		6.10	Wider uses of technologies in therapy *Stephen Goss, DeeAnna Merz Nagel and Kate Anthony*	565

PART VII: SETTINGS 573

7.1	Working in schools *Shira Baram*	574		7.6	Working in primary care *Zubeida Ali and Satinder Panesar*	605
7.2	Working in colleges and universities *Kirsten Amis*	580		7.7	Short-term therapy *Alex Coren*	610
7.3	Working with the media *Elaine Kasket*	587		7.8	Workplace therapy *Charlotte Conn and Aashiya Patel*	617
7.4	Working with neuroscience and neuropsychology *David Goss*	592		7.9	Working in forensic settings *Jenika Patel and Sunil Lad*	622
7.5	Private practice *Gareth Williams*	598		7.10	Coaching *Zsófia Anna Utry and Stephen Palmer*	627

Postscript: How might counselling and psychotherapy change over the coming years?   **633**

Index   634

LIST OF FIGURES AND TABLES

FIGURES

Figure 2.6.1	Divergent, diverse and typical	58
Figure 3.3.1	An abbreviated assessment form at Metanoia Counselling and Psychotherapy Service (MCPS)	100
Figure 3.6.1	Some suggested dos and don'ts of using measures	118
Figure 3.6.2	Common measures	122
Figure 3.13.1	Ethics	160
Figure 3.15.1	Therapy and the law web resources	176
Figure 4.2.1	The cycle of change (Prochaska and DiClemente, 1982)	223
Figure 4.12.1	The OCD cycle	283
Figure 4.15.1	Four-stage pathway of working with PTSD	303
Figure 5.1.1	Core processes in Acceptance and Commitment Therapy	335
Figure 5.2.1	The Circle of Security™	339
Figure 5.3.1	An example of dysfunctional reciprocal roles and procedures	346
Figure 5.3.2	Example of a partial SDR	348
Figure 5.4.1	Beck's Negative Cognitive Triad	353
Figure 5.5.1	Three system model	360
Figure 5.18.1	Natalie's structural profile	442
Figure 5.18.2	Natalie's desired structural profile	442
Figure 5.27.1	Adaptation of the skilled helper model as single session formulation	494
Figure 5.29.1	Structural diagram of a personality	505
Figure 6.2.1	The proactive counselling process	521
Figure 6.3.1	Timeline of Lynda Green	527
Figure 6.5.1	Mapping of family and professional systems	539
Figure 7.5.1	A values-based approach to practice	599
Figure 7.5.2	Yogic symbol of the heart	601

TABLES

Table 3.20.1	Psychiatric drugs, their effects and withdrawal reactions	204
Table 4.11.1	Michael's modality profile	279
Table 4.15.1	Summary of PTSD diagnostic criteria	301
Table 4.18.1	Factors associated with higher risk	320
Table 5.6.1	Five functions of dialectical behaviour therapy	368
Table 5.18.1	John's full modality profile (or BASIC ID chart)	439
Table 5.18.2	Frequently used techniques in multimodal therapy and training	441
Table 6.6.1	Summary of differences for therapists between individual and group therapy	543
Table 6.6.2	Effective group therapy treatments	545
Table 6.6.3	Yalom's curative factors	546

ABOUT THE EDITORS

Terry Hanley is a Professor in Counselling Psychology at the University of Manchester. He is a HCPC Registered Counselling Psychologist and a Fellow of both the BPS and the Higher Education Academy. Terry works on a Doctorate in Counselling Psychology programme and has a particular interest in training therapists in humanistic approaches of therapy and research skills. In addition to editing *The SAGE Handbook of Counselling and Psychotherapy*, he is a co-author of *Introducing Counselling and Psychotherapy Research* (Sage, 2013) and lead editor of text *Adolescent Counselling Psychology* (Routledge, 2013). He has worked as a therapist with young people and young adults for a number of third-sector organisations, as a football therapist with the organisation Freedom from Torture, and as a clinical supervisor for staff at Bury Involvement Group. He has been researching web-based therapy with children and young people for over 20 years and has a growing interest in surfing therapy and the use of artificial intelligence in the caring professions. Follow him on twitter @drterryhanley. https://research.manchester.ac.uk/en/persons/terry.hanley

Laura Anne Winter is a HCPC Registered Counselling Psychologist and BPS Chartered Psychologist. She currently works at the University of Manchester as a Senior Lecturer in Education and Counselling Psychology and is the Programme Director for the Doctorate in Counselling Psychology and the Associate Director for Equality, Diversity, and Inclusion for the School in which she is based. Laura's research and writing has focused on social justice, equality, and related issues in counselling and psychotherapy, psychology, and education. Her clinical practice has been based in NHS, third sector, and University counselling service settings. For Laura's publications, see https://research.manchester.ac.uk/en/persons/laura.winter

CONTRIBUTORS

Kate Adam, BSc (Hons), PostGrad Dip, Reg. MBACP, MSc, Post MSc Dip, CPsychol, AFBPsS, Reg. HCPC, RAPPS, is a Chartered Consultant Counselling Psychologist, Applied Practice Supervisor and Associate Fellow of the British Psychological Society. Kate works as a Psychological Services Lead and Senior Occupational Health Manager within the Civil Service, supporting officers. Kate has several specialist interests, including psychological trauma and resilience, personality disorders, eating disorders, supervision and service design. She has an interest in evidencing best practice, evaluating interventions and is currently studying at the University of Leicester.

Yetunde Ade-Serrano is a chartered and registered Counselling Psychologist who works primarily in Independent Practice. She is a mentor, visiting lecturer, clinical supervisor, and an external examiner on Counselling Psychology training programmes. Her clinical interests include self-exploration and growth, Black women's identity, African Psychology and Spirituality, and working with Race and Difference across Cultures.

Zubeida Ali is a BACP accredited counsellor and clinical supervisor. She is employed by an NHS mental health trust and works in an IAPT setting where she is the Professional and Clinical Lead for Counselling as well as a practising counsellor. She is IAPT qualified, having undertaken both the IAPT Person Centred Counselling for Depression and Counselling for Depression Supervision training. Zubeida has worked in the field of primary care counselling for over 20 years, and in that time, through her involvement and roles within both BACP (Health Care Division) and the North West Psychological Professions Network (Workforce Executive), has ensured that the role of NHS counsellors has remained high on the agenda. This experience has informed the content of her chapter in this book.

Kirsten Amis is an accredited counsellor, a clinical supervisor and was a mental health nurse before teaching counselling for 26 years. Kirsten authored the BACP-approved route to registration, sits on the Scottish Government College and University Mental Health Advisory committee and the BACP University and Colleges Division executive committee. She was also a member of the 2021 QAA Subject Benchmark Statement panel for counselling and psychotherapy. Kirsten has authored three textbooks on counselling and working therapeutically with risk. She is currently the Mental Health Lead, managing the counselling service in a large, inner-city college, and it is that work which has informed the content of her chapter in this book.

India Amos is a HCPC registered Counselling Psychologist and Lecturer in Counselling and Psychotherapy at the University of Salford, Manchester, UK. India continues her research in the field of Transpersonal Psychology, using arts-based research methods. She is on the editorial board for the British Psychology Society's (BPS) *Qualitative Methods in Psychology Bulletin* (www.bps.org.uk/member-microsites/qualitative-methods-psychology-section).

Kate Anthony is a Fellow of the BACP, ISMHO and ACTO, and is CEO and co-founder of the Online Therapy Institute. Her doctoral thesis 'Developing Counselling and Psychotherapy in the Age of Technology and the Internet' was awarded by Middlesex University in 2010. She is author or co-editor of five textbooks on the field, and has contributed many articles and chapters over the last 25+ years. Her core MSc training was with Greenwich University, and she also has a BSc (Hons) in Psychology. Kate's renowned Certified Cyber Therapist course is available at www.kateanthony.net

Lionel Bailly is a Practicing Analyst of the Association Lacanienne Internationale (Paris) and an Academic Associate of the British Psychoanalytical Society. He is Honorary Senior Lecturer at University College London Psychoanalysis Unit where he is particularly involved in the doctoral school. He trained in medicine and psychiatry at the Salpêtrière Hospital in Paris, and before moving to the UK was head of the Child and Adolescent Bio-Psychopathology Unit of the Henri Rouselle Centre at St Anne Hospital (Paris). He is the author of *Lacan* in the Beginner's Guide Series (One World Press, 2009).

Liz Ballinger has been involved in counselling in a range of roles for almost 30 years. Before she retired from the University of Manchester, she acted as Programme Director for the MA in Counselling and as Deputy Director for the Professional Doctorate in Counselling, delivered in Manchester and Nairobi, Kenya. Her belief in the importance of the social context in the shaping of human experience has led her to an ongoing critique of therapy, and a related interest in the relationship of both gender and social class to therapeutic processes and outcomes.

Shira Baram is a counsellor and psychotherapist who works with children and young people (CandYP) and adults in private practice, third sector organisations and schools. Shira is an MBACP member and Co-Chair of the BACP Expert Reference Group in School Based Counselling (SBC), which has representatives from all four nations of the UK. Its objectives are to increase the access to SBC and to produce evidence and research related to the benefits for schools and CandYP. Shira is also a qualified mindfulness therapist and secondary school teacher. She is currently completing a Certificate in Therapeutic Play Skills with the Play Therapy UK (PTUK) for professional development and to increase her expertise in non-directive play skills with CandYP.

Sara Bardsley has been qualified as a Clinical Psychologist since 2016 and works with individuals who have long-term physical health problems, including medically unexplained symptoms, who present frequently at health services as a way of managing their ongoing distress. She regards Psychodynamic Interpersonal Therapy as an invaluable approach when working with individuals who present with complex physical and emotional health difficulties.

Steven Barnes is a Postdoctoral Researcher at the University of Social Sciences and Humanities (Uniwersytet SWPS) in Katowice, Poland. Steven's research and publications focus primarily on digital interventions for mental health (primarily in the field of adolescent anxiety disorders) in terms of efficacy and self-directed engagement, as well as the value of digital spaces as pedagogical tools. Steven's work also encompasses investigations surrounding the benefits of supported living for people with severe and enduring mental illness.

Rowan Bayne is Emeritus Professor of Psychology and Counselling at the University of East London where he was a core tutor on the postgraduate diploma in counselling and psychotherapy for 32 years. His recent books include: *Psychology for Social Work Theory and Practice* (with Paula Nicolson, Palgrave Macmillan, 4th ed., 2014), *Applied Psychology: Research, Training and Practice* (edited with Gordon Jinks, Sage, 2nd ed., 2013), *The Counsellor's Guide to Personality: Understanding Preferences, Motives and Life Stories* (Palgrave Macmillan, 2013) and *Getting Old: A Positive and Practical Approach* (with Carol Parkes, Routledge, 2021).

Daisy Best is a Counselling Psychologist with North Yorkshire Psychological Therapies Ltd. Daisy was employed in the NHS where she worked as an Acting Deputy Head of a psychology department. She was the Programme Director for a Doctorate in Counselling Psychology and is currently the Director of an independent psychology practice. She has undertaken and delivered training in leadership and has written a chapter for *Leadership and Diversity in Psychology* (McIntosh, Nicholas and Huq, Routledge, 2019). Daisy has led on numerous funded and voluntary projects and celebrates the range of opportunities available for all to engage in leadership.

John Boorman, DClinPsych, is a Clinical Psychologist for South London and Maudsley NHS Trust and co-director of Greenheart Psychological Services, an ACT and contextual based therapy provider. He is also Visiting Lecturer in the University of Hertfordshire's Clinical Psychology Department. John regularly delivers Acceptance and Commitment Therapy (ACT) training for a range of National Health Service, University and private organisations. He is currently on the committee board for the British Association of Behavioural and Cognitive Psychotherapies (BABCP) ACT Special Interest Group, which promotes the dissemination and training of ACT throughout the UK. His research interests include using ACT and contextual behavioural approaches with children, young people and their families.

Richard J. Brown is a Professor of Clinical Psychology at the University of Manchester and Honorary Consultant Clinical Psychologist with Greater Manchester Mental Health NHS Foundation Trust, where he runs the Functional Neurological Disorders service. He has used Psychodynamic Interpersonal Therapy (PIT) in clinical practice for many years and delivers teaching, supervision and research on the approach. He is a founder member of PIT-UK.

Cate Campbell is a sex, relationships and trauma therapist and supervisor. She delivers therapist training and has written courses and lectured with the Relate Institute and Foundation for Counselling and Relationship Studies, been a visiting lecturer at University College London and run CBT training in further education. She has written four books: *Sex Therapy: The Basics*

(Routledge, 2022), *Contemporary Sex Therapy* (Routledge, 2020), *Love and Sex in a New Relationship* (Routledge, 2018) and *The Relate Guide to Sex and Intimacy* (Vermiliion, 2015). https://orcid.org/0000-0003-1977-9053

Jerome Carson is Professor of Psychology at the University of Bolton. Jerome worked for 32 years in the National Health Service as a clinical psychologist. He has worked clinically with individuals, groups and families. In 2006 he started working in the recovery field and this gives him his main research inspiration today. He has published widely in over 300 publications and is co-editor of Mental Health and Social Inclusion and Social Work and Social Sciences Review. His other research interests are positive psychology, alcohol addiction, bereavement and autoethnography. Most of his work these days is spent supervising PhD, MSc and BSc students, although he also does some teaching and research.

Divine Charura is a Professor of Counselling Psychology at York St John University (UK). He is a Practitioner Psychologist and Counselling Psychologist and is registered with the Health and Care Professions Council in England. Divine is also an Honorary Fellow of the United Kingdom Council for Psychotherapy and an Adult Psychotherapist. Divine's research and therapeutic interest is in psychological trauma across the lifespan. Divine has co-authored and edited numerous books in psychology and psychotherapy. These include Love and Therapy: In Relationship (2015, Routledge) and Black Identities + White Therapies: Race, Respect and Diversity (2021, PCCS). For Divine's other publications, see https://ray.yorksj.ac.uk/profile/2104

Charlotte Conn is a Lecturer of Psychology at the University of Bolton, Bolton, Lancashire, teaching Psychology, Psychotherapy and Counselling from Foundation year right through to Master's level. She is a BACP Registered practitioner in person-centred counselling and currently works with an Employee Assistance Programme counselling East Lancashire Hospital Trust staff. Her counselling experience outside her current work ranges from counselling within sixth forms to helplines and GP surgeries with a specific focus on children and young people. She uses this experience to inform both her counselling and teaching practice, which has helped her to write the chapter on workplace therapy.

Mick Cooper is Professor of Counselling Psychology at the University of Roehampton and a chartered psychologist. Mick is author and editor of a range of texts on person-centred, existential and relational approaches to therapy, including *Working at Relational Depth in Counselling and Psychotherapy* (with Dave Mearns, 2nd ed., Sage, 2018), *Pluralistic Counselling and Psychotherapy* (with John McLeod, Sage, 2011) and *Integrating Counselling and Psychotherapy: Directionality, Synergy, and Social Change* (Sage, 2019). Mick has led a series of research studies – both qualitative and quantitative – exploring the processes and outcomes of humanistic counselling with young people, and has published in a range of leading international psychotherapy journals. Mick is the father of four children and lives in Brighton on the south coast of England.

Alex Coren, former Director of Psychodynamic Studies in the Department for Continuing Education, Oxford University, has written and taught extensively on the topic of short-term therapeutic interventions, with a focus on the application of process-led techniques and understanding to briefer and more protocol-driven therapeutic modalities. Prior to training as a psychoanalytic psychotherapist, where he worked in secondary and tertiary education, he was a psychiatric social worker in adult and child mental health settings. His books include *A Psychodynamic Approach to Education* (Sheldon Press, 1997) and *Short Term Psychotherapy* (Palgrave, 2010).

Mary Creaner, DPsych, is an Assistant Professor and Research Coordinator with the Doctorate in Counselling Psychology and Director of the MSc in Clinical Supervision, Trinity College Dublin, Ireland. Mary is an accredited therapist and clinical supervisor with the Irish Association for Counselling and Psychotherapy (IACP), and a member of the American Psychological Association (APA). Mary's research interests include clinical supervision practice and training, adult learning and psychotherapy research, and she presents her research nationally and internationally. https://orcid.org/0000-0003-1097-0417

Rudi Dallos is Emeritus Professor of Clinical Psychology at the University of Plymouth where he continues to engage in research and research supervision. He works in private practice, offering family therapy and clinical supervision and consultation. His recent publications include *Don't Blame the Parents* (OU Press, 2019), *Systemic Therapy and Attachment Narratives* (2nd ed., Routledge, 2021) and he is working on the fifth edition of *An Introduction to Family Therapy* (4th ed., OU Press, 2015).

Soha Daru is a HCPC registered Counselling Psychologist working in a Clinical Health Psychology department in the NHS. She is also a Lecturer on the MA Counselling and Psychotherapy course at the University of Leeds. Her research interests include health psychology, pluralistic approaches to therapy, working with trauma, self-esteem, culture, and diversity.

Dominic Davies is the founder of Pink Therapy. He has been in practice as a psychotherapist, clinical sexologist and clinical supervisor for almost 40 years, pioneering in the UK the development of working with Gender, Sex and Relationship Diversities (GSRD) as a new specialist field of clinical practice. Dominic adopts a norm-critical, kink-knowledgeable and sex-positive stance in his work. Dominic is a Fellow of both the National Council for Integrative Psychotherapy and the National Counselling Society. He directs an international training programme for qualified mental health professionals in GSRD therapy worldwide. Dominic has won several awards for his sexual freedom and mental health work. Most recently he was awarded a gold medal for being one of 50 worldwide Distinguished Sexual and Gender Health Revolutionaries and was also honoured by the Program in Human Sexuality at the University of Minnesota.

Emmy van Deurzen is an existential psychotherapist and philosopher who has written 18 books, which have been translated into as many languages. She is the founder director of the New School of Psychotherapy and Counselling and the Existential Academy in London and a visiting professor with Middlesex University.

Lesley Dougan is a white, cisgender, neurodivergent (ND) counsellor, supervisor and trainer in private practice on the Wirral. She is programme lead for the MA Counselling and Psychotherapy Practice at Liverpool John Moores University. She has over 25 years' experience in mental health, specialising in working with ND children, young people and adults and their families. She has a passion for social justice and intersectionality. She is currently completing a Professional Doctorate in Counselling and Psychotherapy Studies at the University of Chester.

Christine Dunkley, DClinP, is a consultant trainer with the British Isles DBT Training team. She worked in the NHS for 30 years as a medical social worker and psychological therapist. She is an international trainer and author, and was awarded a Fellowship by the UK Society for DBT in 2016. She served on the special reference group for personality disorders at UCL and has researched the communication of emotional pain in patients at risk of suicide.

Catherine Edmunds initially worked as a primary school teacher before setting up a community project for The Salvation Army, working with vulnerable families. This led to her retraining as a counsellor and child psychotherapist. She completed her Master's in Integrative Psychotherapy with The Northern Guild (Newman University) and went on to work in CAMHS. Catherine is an IPT-A and IPT therapist, supervisor and trainer. She works part-time in private practice and in adult secondary care as a Senior Psychological Therapist. She is committed to developing IPT and IPT-A within her local area through training, research and clinical work. Catherine is also the joint Deputy Chair for IPT UK.

Cemil Egeli is a senior lecturer in counselling and programme leader for the counselling skills (BA Combined Hons) programme at the University of Chester. He is studying for a PhD at the University of Warwick using autoethnographic and biographical methods to explore the experiences of students coming from mixed cultural and dual heritage backgrounds. He has an interest in spirituality and religion as well as music and the arts. He works as a counsellor and previously worked as a secondary school music teacher.

Zehra Ersahin, CPsychol, is a HCPC registered Counselling Psychologist, and lecturer of Clinical Psychology at the Social Sciences University of Ankara (SSUA). She is experienced in clinical research and supervision in various mental health care settings. Her research has primarily focused on exploring the mental health needs of vulnerable groups and young people accessing online therapy. She has an active interest in online therapeutic presence, diversity and spirituality. She is the director of the Spiritual Care and Counselling Department of SSUA, and a member of the executive committee of the Society for Intercultural Pastoral Care and Counselling based in Germany.

Colin Feltham is Emeritus Professor of Critical Counselling Studies, Sheffield Hallam University. He has written or edited over 30 books. He has taught critical thinking at Manchester University and humanistic psychology at the University of Southern Denmark. He is a member of Critical Therapy Antidote.

Linda Finlay is an existentially orientated, relational Integrative Psychotherapist in private practice in the United Kingdom. She also teaches psychology and counselling at the Open University. She has published numerous books and articles, including her three latest textbooks: *The Therapeutic Use of Self* (Sage, 2021), *Practical Ethics in Counselling and Psychotherapy* (Sage, 2019), and *Relational Integrative Psychotherapy* (Wiley, 2015). Her particular research interests include applying existential and hermeneutic phenomenological approaches to investigate experiences of disability and trauma. She is currently Editor of the *European Journal for Qualitative Research in Psychotherapy* (www.EJQRP.org). Website: http://lindafinlay.co.uk/

Emma Flax, MSc, MA, is a UKCP registered individual and group gestalt psychotherapist. She currently works as a student counsellor at the University of Sheffield, having previously run a successful private psychotherapy practice in Sheffield for over 10 years. Emma's first career, informed by a MSc in Cultural Geography and social research methods, was spent working as a research analyst and consultant in a business/consumer focused environment.

Kathryn Geldard lectures as guest lecturer at Queensland University of Technology, Australia. Her academic career includes programme leadership of Counselling at Sunshine Coast University, development of the Master of Counselling Degree and research regarding adolescent peer counselling and collaborative development of culturally sensitive adolescents' peer support programmes with Australia's First Nation people. She has authored textbooks founded on her extensive clinical counselling background with children, young people, and their families. Kathryn continues to write and publish in the field, consult with organisations, and supervise clinicians.

Sobhi Girgis, MMedSci, MRCPsych LLM (Mental Health Law), is a Consultant Psychiatrist and Responsible Officer of Sheffield Health and Social Care NHS Foundation Trust and Honorary Senior Clinical Lecturer at Sheffield University. He is trained in both General Adult and Forensic Psychiatry. He is the member of the Mental Health Act Operational Group in his NHS Trust. He is a member of the Parole Board of England and a Medical Member of the First Tier Tribunal (Mental Health). He is also employed by the Care Quality Commission (CQC) as a Second Opinion Appointed Doctor.

David Goss is a chartered counselling psychologist. He is a lecturer in counselling psychology at the University of Roehampton and director of Zence Consultancy. Clinically, he has his own private practice, has worked as a senior psychologist in the NHS and spent several years as the clinical lead for a neurological charity counselling service. His publications relate to discussions on integrating counselling (psychology) and neuroscience, although he is interested in a wide range of areas relating to human existence and wellbeing. He is currently exploring research relating wellbeing to urban farming, decision making, intuition, mindfulness and Zen Buddhism.

Stephen Goss, PhD, is Research Development Director at the Online Therapy Institute and Head of Clinical Evaluation and Investigation at Limbic AI. He is a consultant in service development and provides online clinical and research supervision worldwide on pluralism, online services and especially regarding technological and other innovations in practice. His publications include *Evidence Based Counselling and Psychological Therapies* (Routledge, 2000), *Technology in Counselling and Psychotherapy* (Palgrave, 2003) and *The Use of Technology in Mental Health* (CC Thomas, 2016). He is also a Consulting Editor of the *British Journal of Guidance and Counselling*, which he co-edited until 2020.

Anne Guy, UKCP (Reg), MBACP (Accred), is a psychotherapist in private practice, having previously worked as a lecturer at the University of Roehampton. She is a member of the Council for Evidence-Based Psychiatry, the secretariat co-ordinator for the All-Party Parliamentary Group for Prescribed Drug Dependence and an associate member of the Institute for Psychiatric Drug Withdrawal. She is the lead editor for the *Guidance for Psychological Therapists: Enabling Conversations with Clients Taking or Withdrawing from Psychiatric Drugs*, created in collaboration with leading UK therapy organisations and academics.

Anne Hayward, MSc, is a Lecturer at Exeter University Medical School, where she teaches on mental health treatments and medical communication. She is an accredited BABCP therapist and an integrative counsellor, and has worked in IAPT services as the lead therapist for older adults. Currently, she is researching 'Older clients' experience of counselling and psychotherapy' under the mentorship of Professor Laidlaw.

Vanessa Herbert is a Clinical Psychologist employed by Greater Manchester Mental Health NHS Foundation Trust and works in diabetes medicine. She completed a year-long specialist placement in Psychodynamic Interpersonal Therapy (PIT) in 2016 as part of the University of Manchester Clinical Psychology Doctorate programme. She uses PIT clinically, alongside other therapy approaches. Her research interests include the interpersonal experience of healthcare in people with long-term health conditions and understanding the barriers to empathy in healthcare systems.

Tracie Holroyd, MBACP (Accred), Eagala Advanced/Mentor, International Trainer, Director of Tamworth Counselling Services (TCS) Ltd and CHOICES (Community Help Offering Counselling and Equine Services) cic. Tracie has over 20 years' experience working with Local Education Authorities to implement counselling services in Pupil Referral Units (PRUs) and residential units in several authorities, working with young people with emotional and behavioural issues. TCS Ltd also provides Eagala sessions, bespoke training, critical incident management and employee assistance programmes. Tracie has gained a wealth of knowledge and experience in working with children, young people and adults with a variety of issues, including obsessive compulsive disorder (OCD).

Sam Hope (sam-hope.co.uk) is a therapist, writer and trainer with a background working in domestic violence and sexual violence services and with LGBTQA+ clients. Sam is the author of *Person-Centred Counselling for Trans and Gender Diverse Clients: A Practical Guide* (Jessica Kinglsey Publishers, 2019). They have an MA in Trauma Studies which focused on the complexities of gender-based violence.

Esther Ingham is a Counselling Psychologist. As an individual who acquired disability (incomplete spinal cord injury at C7), I have been fascinated by how I have since been variously constructed, understood and discriminated against as (dis)abled and (in)valid. These experiences have all in some way informed both my research and practice. I do not profess that this qualifies me to speak for anyone other than myself, as I am acutely aware there are as many experiences of disability as there are disabled individuals. However, there are some important common issues relating to disability that I feel I can help to acknowledge, consider and address.

Peter Jenkins is a counsellor, supervisor, trainer and researcher. He has been a member of both the BACP Professional Conduct Committee and the UKCP Ethics Committee. With 40 years' experience in the field of student counselling, he has also run postgraduate counsellor training at several UK universities. He has published a number of books on the legal aspects of therapy, including *Professional Practice in Counselling and Psychotherapy: Ethics and the Law* (Sage, 2017). His Sage website provides access to a range of free resources on legal and ethical issues in counselling and psychotherapy, including video clips and articles for download: https://us.sagepub.com/en-us/nam/author/peter-jenkins

Lucy Johnstone is a consultant clinical psychologist, author of *Users and Abusers of Psychiatry* (2nd ed., Routledge, 2000) and co-editor of *Formulation in Psychology and Psychotherapy: Making Sense of People's Problems* (2nd ed., Routledge, 2013) and *A Straight-Talking Guide to Psychiatric Diagnosis* (PCCS Books, 2014). She is the former Programme Director of the Bristol Clinical Psychology Doctorate and was lead author of the *Good Practice Guidelines on the Use of Psychological Formulation* (Division of Clinical Psychology, 2011.) She is also lead author, with Professor Mary Boyle, of the BPS publication *The Power Threat Meaning Framework* (2018). She has many years clinical experience in Adult Mental Health settings, and is an experienced conference speaker, lecturer and trainer.

Chathurika Kannangara is an Associate Professor in Psychology at the University of Bolton. She is a BACP registered Counselling Practitioner and a BPS Charted Psychologist. She is leading the MSc Counselling and Positive Psychology programme at the University of Bolton. Her research interest and recent publications are in the area of positive psychotherapy, wellbeing and resilience.

Elaine Kasket is a psychologist, author, speaker and Honorary Professor of Psychology at the University of Wolverhampton. She writes both academic material and public-facing work, including blogs, journalism, fiction and general non-fiction. Her latest book is *All the Ghosts in the Machine: The Digital Afterlife of Your Personal Data* (Robinson, 2019). Elaine appears frequently in print and online media worldwide and contributes to programmes for the BBC. She is a TEDx speaker, onstage storyteller, frequent podcast guest, and host of the podcast *Still Spoken*. She is currently writing *Exposed*, an exploration of privacy and technology across the life span.

Catherine Kerr, CPsychol, AFBPsS and EMDR Europe Approved Consultant, has many years' experience of working with a wide range of people across a variety of sectors. She specialises in working with the continuum of psychological and physiological reactions resulting from crisis and trauma. Cath's research explored the reasons why some EMDR trained therapists choose not to integrate this therapy into their practice to work with PTSD. She co-authored *Integrating EMDR into Your Practice* with Liz

Royle (Springer, 2010). She is a Director of KRTS International Ltd and currently works with organisations providing consultancy and training for employees who experience psychological trauma in the workplace.

Konstantina Kolonia, BA (Hons), MSc, DPsych, CPsychol, SchemaAdvCert, is a Principal Counselling Psychologist and an Advanced Schema Therapist, Supervisor and Trainer. She is specialised in personality disorders and trauma and over the last 20 years has worked extensively in various adult mental health settings in the NHS, as well as the forensic and voluntary sectors in London and Hertfordshire. Konstantina is currently working in community settings (Hertfordshire Partnership NHS Trust). She is an affiliate to the Schema Therapy UK and a member of the International Society of Schema Therapy (ISST).

Christine Kupfer has studied social and medical anthropology, education sciences, psychology and pluralistic counselling. Her research projects include a study on children's mental health in India, a citizen science project on depression, ethnographic work with Ayurveda patients to understand their conceptualisations of health and healing, research on Rabindranath Tagore, and her ongoing project, the 'Dark Side of Meditation'. She has published articles and book chapters on her research and has written a book on philosophical anthropology and transcultural education.

Helen Kyritsi, BSc (Hons) Psychology, DClinPsy, is a Consultant Clinical Psychologist in South West London. She has been leading psychological services in the NHS, where she contributes towards service development for people with severe mental health difficulties. With over 20 years' experience, mainly working in community mental health teams in London and Devon, Helen has developed a specialist interest in the treatment of childhood abuse, complex trauma and personality disorders. Helen is an Advanced Accredited Schema Therapist and Supervisor, a member of the International Society for Schema Therapy and an affiliate of the Schema Therapy UK training programme.

Sunil Lad is a Consultant Counselling Psychologist employed by Northamptonshire Healthcare Foundation Trust. He leads psychology provision in a number of secured environments where healthcare is offered in prison establishments. He has experience of working in a range of prison settings, from young offenders to high secure prison, and with those convicted of sexual offences. He mainly practices Compassion Focused Therapy in his practice as well as Cognitive Analytic Therapy. He is also National Clinical Director for Health and Justice in NHS England.

Ken Laidlaw is a clinical psychologist with world-leading expertise in the psychology of ageing, cognitive behavioural therapy for older people and attitudes to ageing. He is a Professor of Clinical Psychology at the University of Exeter. Professor Laidlaw is widely published in peer-reviewed academic journals and is the author of the influential book *Cognitive Behaviour Therapy for Older People: An Introduction* (Sage, 2015). He has been responsible for developing manuals for various clinical trials and led the development of a cross-cultural Attitudes to Ageing Questionnaire (AAQ), which was trialled in no fewer than 20 countries across the world.

Mark Linington is an attachment-based psychoanalytic psychotherapist, teacher and supervisor with The Bowlby Centre and the CEO and Clinical Director at the Clinic for Dissociative Studies in London. He worked for 12 years in the NHS with people with intellectual disabilities. He has written on the application of attachment theory to clinical work with people who have experienced trauma, including using the Circle of Security™ and McCluskey models for understanding attachment.

Julia Lyons (nee Noble) is a Chartered Counselling Psychologist based in the North of England. She is currently working in the National Health Service with individuals who present frequently to medical settings and who have complex and enduring difficulties. Julia has a keen research interest in using outcome measures to support practice and in the areas of personality disorder and complex trauma, maintaining a critical perspective towards diagnosis. She has also lectured on the University of Manchester Counselling Psychology doctorate programme.

Faisal Mahmood, MSc, MA, PhD, is a UKCP registered individual and group gestalt psychotherapist, BACP registered accredited counsellor and UKCP approved clinical supervisor. He currently works as Head of Counselling and Psychotherapy at Newman University, Birmingham. He has over 20 years' clinical experience working with clients in a wide range of settings, such GP surgeries, hospitals, voluntary sector and private practice. Faisal runs a private practice based in Solihull, where he offers individual, couples and group therapy as well as individual and group supervision. He also facilitates personal development groups and offers a range of CPD training events.

Claire Marshall is a Chartered Psychologist with an extensive background in management, teaching, research and psychological work in clinical, academic and civic settings. She is currently the Interim Programme Director at the University of East London, teaching primarily on the Doctorate in Counselling Psychology but also on the MSc Humanitarian Intervention. She has addressed critical mental health issues for organisations and individuals, implementing psychosocial interventions through researching, planning and evaluating programmes for a range of clients in clinical and field settings. She holds various clinical posts, including being consulted by solicitors to provide medical legal reports.

Rosaleen McElvaney, PhD, is a Clinical Psychologist and Psychotherapist with over 25 years working in the field of child sexual abuse. She is Principal Psychotherapist with Children's Health Ireland in St Clare's specialist child sexual abuse unit and Assistant Professor of Psychotherapy in Dublin City University. She has published extensively in international journals and her books include *Helping Children to Tell about Sexual Abuse: Guidance for Helpers* (Jessica Kingsley, 2016). She is a Fellow of the Psychological Society of Ireland.

John McLeod is Visiting Professor of Counselling at Abertay University, Dundee, and the Institute for Integrative Counselling and Psychotherapy, Dublin. He has published widely on a range of issues in counselling and psychotherapy research and practice and is committed to the development of flexible and responsive approaches to collaborative practice that enable clients to access their personal and cultural strengths and resources. The main focus of his work in recent years has been on finding ways that psychotherapy might contribute to a more constructive and sustainable relationship between human beings and the planet.

Mani Mehdikani is a Senior Psychological Therapist (Primary Care speciality, NHS) and a Consultant Clinical Psychologist (Homelessness speciality, with Change Grow Live). His post-qualification career has been mainly in the addictions field, and he has taught on this topic at several Clinical Psychology Doctorate training courses in the Northwest of England. He is a member of the British Psychological Society and the Association of Clinical Psychologists, and is registered with the Health and Care Professionals Council. Mani has postgraduate qualifications in Evolutionary Psychology (MPhil) and Personality Disorders (PGDip), is an accredited EMDR therapist and a Non-Alcoholic Trustee on the General Service Board of Alcoholics Anonymous Great Britain.

DeeAnna Merz Nagel, LPC, LMHC, BCC is a licensed psychotherapist and board-certified coach in the United States. In addition to her specialisations in telemental health and online coaching, she teaches the ethical integration of alternative and psychospiritual approaches in practice. DeeAnna is co-founder of the Online Therapy Institute and provides training, consultation and clinical supervision across the globe. Her most relevant publications regarding online delivery of services include *Therapy Online: A Practical Guide* (Sage, 2009) and *Coaching Online: A Practical Guide* (Routledge, 2021).

Evgenia (Jane) Milman practises psychology, teaches and conducts research examining how making meaning of difficult life experiences influences mental health following grief and trauma. She is a postdoctoral fellow at Western University and a faculty member at the Portland Institute for Loss and Transition. Dr Milman has authored dozens of research publications and book chapters on grief. She serves as the chair of the Distance and Online Education committee at the Association for Death Education and Counselling (ADEC) and is honoured to serve on the advisory board for the Tragedy Assistance Program for Survivors (TAPS).

Martin Milton, CPsychol, FBPsS, UKCP Reg, is Professor of Counselling Psychology at the School of Psychotherapy and Psychology at Regents University London. He also runs an independent practice in psychotherapy and supervision. Martin's interests include eco-therapy and the therapeutic aspects of the natural world. In this regard, Martin is on the Advisory Board of The Sacred Nature Initiative and has previously contributed to the Education committee of the Jane Goodall Institute UK and on Bristol Zoo's Advisory Group on the Social Sciences. He also served a term on the editorial board of the journal *Ecopsychology*. Martin Chairs the BPS Division of Counselling Psychology Environmental and Climate Crisis Workstream.

Eric Morris, PhD, works as the Director of the La Trobe University Psychology Clinic, in Melbourne, Australia. He is a clinical psychologist and researcher with a long-term interest in Acceptance and Commitment Therapy and contextual behavioural science. Eric researches ACT as an intervention for people with serious mental illness, caregivers, and in the workplace. He is the co-author of *ACTivate Your Life: Using Acceptance and Mindfulness to Build a Life that is Rich, Fulfilling and Fun* (Robinson, 2015), and a co-editor of *Acceptance and Commitment Therapy and Mindfulness for Psychosis* (with Louise Johns and Joseph Oliver, Wiley, 2013).

Jill Mytton, MSc, CPsychol, DPsych, is a Chartered Counselling Psychologist. She is currently a research supervisor and associate of the University of Salford, where she is carrying out a large-scale research study into the mental wellbeing of those who leave cultic groups. In addition to contributing chapters to three books, including this one, she is co-author with Windy Dryden of *Four Approaches to Counselling and Psychotherapy* (Routledge, 2017). Windy Dryden was the course tutor on her MSc Counselling degree. She has taught and provided clinical supervision in CBT on several diploma and doctorate courses.

Silva Neves is a College of Sexual and Relationship Therapists (COSRT) accredited and UKCP registered psychosexual and relationship psychotherapist, a trauma psychotherapist and a clinical supervisor. He is a Pink Therapy Clinical Associate. Silva specialises in GSRD (Gender, Sexuality and Relationship Diversities) and works extensively with LGBTQ+ people. Silva is a Course Director for CICS (Contemporary Institute of Clinical Sexology) and speaks internationally. Silva is a member of the editorial board for the leading journal *Sex and Relationship Therapy*. Silva is the author of *Compulsive Sexual Behaviours: A Psycho-Sexual Treatment Guide for Clinicians* (Routledge, 2021). Website: www.silvaneves.co.uk

Helen Nicholas, Counselling Psychologist, HCN Psychology, is a registered practitioner psychologist, accredited EMDR therapist and runs an independent practice in Somerset, UK. She has taught on the British Psychological Society (BPS) Division of Occupational Psychology leadership and development programme and has held several voluntary leadership positions within the BPS, such as BPS trustee, chair of the Division of Counselling Psychology and the Southwest of England Branch. Helen was the (Interim) Head of Department at a UK university and sits on the HCPC fitness to practice panels. She has co-edited a book on leadership and diversity in psychology.

Ohemaa Nkansa-Dwamena is a BPS chartered Counselling Psychologist and an HCPC registered practitioner psychologist. She is a lecturer on the counselling psychology programme at City, University of London, an external examiner and a clinical supervisor. She works primarily in independent practice with former clinical positions in the NHS, higher education and third sector settings. Her research and clinical interests include intersectionality, multiple identity negotiation, and culture and diversity in the therapeutic process.

Denis O'Hara is a Chartered Psychologist with the British Psychological Society, Program Director of the Master of Counselling program at the University of Queensland, and Adjunct Professor of Counselling at Griffith University and the University of the Sunshine Coast. He is a member of the Psychotherapy and Counselling Federation of Australia (PACFA) and the British Association of Counselling and Psychotherapy (BACP). His research interests include hope studies, chronic problems of the self, self-differentiation and psychotherapy integration.

Joe Oliver, PhD, is a Consultant Clinical Psychologist and director for Contextual Consulting, an ACT based consultancy in the UK. He is joint-director for the University College London Cognitive Behavioural Therapy in Psychosis Post Graduate Diploma, while also holding a post in the NHS. He is a consultant and regularly trains professionals both nationally and internationally. His research interests are in the use of contextual CBTs to enhance workplace wellbeing and also with people with distressing psychosis. Joe is co-editor of the textbook *Acceptance and Commitment Therapy and Mindfulness for Psychosis* (Wiley, 2013) and co-author of the ACT self-help book, *ACTivate Your Life* (Robinson, 2015).

Stephen Palmer, PhD, is a counselling, health and coaching psychologist. Academic posts include Professor of Practice, University of Wales Trinity Saint David (UWTSD), and Adjunct Professor of Coaching Psychology at Aalborg University. He is director of the National Academy of Coaching Psychology. He is Co-chair of the Association for Rational Emotive Behaviour Therapy and President of the International Society for Coaching Psychology. He has written/edited 60 books, including *The Beginner's Guide to Counselling and Psychotherapy* (Sage, 2015), *Brief Cognitive Behaviour Therapy* (with Curwen and Ruddell,

Sage, 2018), *Handbook of Coaching Psychology* (with Whybrow, Routledge, 2019) and *Introduction to Coaching Psychology* (with O'Riordan, Routledge, 2021).

Satinder Panesar studied at the University of Derby and has a MA in Integrative Counselling. She is an accredited, registered member of the BACP and UKCP. Satinder is a Punjabi-speaking Integrative Psychotherapist who has worked in the Third Sector, NHS Greater Glasgow and Clyde and private sector over the past 25+ years nationally, and has an interest in working with Trauma, Tradition and Culture. She is also a Clinical Supervisor, Trainer and Executive Coach. Satinder is a member of the BACP Healthcare Executive, whose aim is to promote and support excellence in healthcare counselling/psychotherapy and supervision.

Aashiya Patel is an associate lecturer at the University of Bolton, teaching Psychology and Counselling from foundation to postgraduate level. Aashiya is a BACP registered practitioner working with a particular interest in supporting clients to overcome trauma. This interest developed through experience providing workplace therapy for frontline personnel, such as paramedics, police and Her Majesty's Prison and Probation Service, and she utilises her experience to inform her counselling and teaching practice. Aashiya's current practice involves counselling NHS staff in East Lancashire. Other experience includes counselling vulnerable women and young adults across several refuge centres as well as families and children within a genetic counselling service.

Jenika Patel is an HCPC registered Counselling Psychologist. She is employed by Northamptonshire Healthcare Foundation Trust in Secured Services in a Category C prison. She has worked in forensic, prison services, substance misuse and community mental health teams. Jenika has developed a specialist interest in the role of trauma resulting from multiple and complex factors that impact and influence people's lived experiences. She holds the Postgraduate Diploma in Compassion Focused Therapy and has training in Sensorimotor Psychotherapy and Internal Family Systems.

Stephen Paul is a psychotherapist and group therapist. He is co-editor of *The Therapeutic Relationship Handbook* (with Divine Charura, McGraw Hill, 2014), *Love and Therapy* (Karnac, 2015) and co-author of *An Introduction to the Therapeutic Relationship* (Sage, 2015). In the mid-1970s, he introduced group therapy to a Liverpool psychiatric hospital. He was later Head of a hospital group therapy unit and then Head of a therapeutic school in Newcastle. He was director of The Centre for Psychological Therapies at Leeds Metropolitan University until 2012, where he taught group therapy for 19 years. Stephen now writes, works with MA students, and practises therapy, supervision and coaching.

Claire Pollitt is a Chartered Clinical Psychologist working in a community mental health team based in South Manchester. Claire qualified as a Cognitive Analytic Therapy (CAT) practitioner in February 2015 and routinely uses this therapeutic model in her work. Claire has a keen interest in compassion focused therapy, and finds that its imagery work and focus on compassionate behaviours, complement the revision stage of CAT, where the client is seeking to form more positive and helpful ways of relating to themselves and others.

Julie Prescott is Head of Psychology at the University of Law, Manchester. Julie's research looks at how digital innovations can support mental health. She has published widely in peer-reviewed journals, books and book chapters, and has recently published *A New App for Identity Structure Analysis and Professional Development* (with G. Passmore, Palgrave, 2022) and *Digital Innovations in Mental Health* (IGI Global, 2022). Julie is the co-editor of *Mental Health and Social Inclusion*, she sits on the EAB for the *British Journal of Guidance and Counselling*, and is section editor for *JMIR* mental health, and a reviewer for several journals.

Andrew Reeves is a Professor in Counselling Professions and Mental Health at the University of Chester, a BACP Senior Counsellor/Psychotherapist and a Registered Social Worker. He has written extensively about working with risk in helping relationships and his primary research areas include mental health, risk, trauma and men's mental health. He teaches on doctoral programmes at the University of Chester in counselling and psychotherapy and psychological trauma. He is past-Chair of BACP and is a member of the Steering Group for Pluralistic Practice.

Ishba Rehman is a HCPC registered Counselling Psychologist working in the NHS and third sector organisations for eating disorders and sexual trauma. She is also a chartered Member of the British Psychological Society (BPS) and a Lecturer on the

Professional Doctorate in Counselling Psychology programme at the University of Manchester. Her research interests include mental health, trauma-informed approaches to therapy, diversity, intersectionality and social justice.

Elizabeth Robinson, a psychiatric nurse by background, received her Interpersonal Psychotherapy (IPT) training in 1997 from Professor John Markowitz and Kathleen Clougherty (both trained by Gerald Klerman, the originator of IPT). She was the principal IPT research therapist for two clinical studies; the latter, a brain imaging study of IPT in treatment resistant depression, was for her PhD at Durham University. She works as an IPT trainer/supervisor as part of the government initiative Improving Access to Psychological Therapies for IPT training for adults, and as a Senior Psychological Therapist in adult secondary care. She is the Chair of the Training Committee for IPT UK.

Chris Rose is a psychotherapist, supervisor and consultant in private practice, with extensive experience in higher education. She has had a long involvement with both groupwork and counselling and psychotherapy training, and is the author of *The Personal Development Group: The Student's Guide* (Karnac, 2008, currently being revised). Chris has also edited *Self Awareness and Personal Development: Resources for Psychotherapists and Counsellors* (Palgrave Macmillan, 2012) and *Psychogeography and Psychotherapy: Connecting Pathways* (PCCS, 2019).

Maxine Rosenfield, MRes, has worked has worked in private practice as a counsellor and supervisor for 30 years. Maxine pioneered the use of one-to-one and group phone work in counselling and supervision in the UK in the late 1990s. Maxine has been on the Board of the Australasian Association of Supervision since 2005, supporting the development of the profession in Australasia. Additionally, Maxine is a clinical member and accredited supervisor of the Psychotherapy and Counselling Federation of Australia (PACFA), and has been awarded Honorary Life Membership by PACFA for services to the field of counselling, psychotherapy and supervision.

Liz Royle, PhD, MA, MBACP (Accred), trained in Eye Movement Desensitisation and Reprocessing (EMDR) in 1999 and became an EMDR Europe Approved Consultant in 2007. She has published and presented internationally on the subjects of psychological trauma and EMDR. She was a founder member of the UK Psychological Trauma Society. Liz has used EMDR with a range of presentations from recent events through to complex trauma and dissociative disorders. She is now a director of KRTS International Ltd and her research interests include addressing barriers to therapy, stigma and cultural competence.

Christiane Sanderson is a retired senior lecturer in Psychology from the University of Roehampton with over 35 years' experience working with survivors of childhood sexual abuse, interpersonal trauma and domestic abuse. She has run consultancy and training for parents, teachers, social workers, nurses, therapists, counsellors, solicitors, the Catholic Safeguarding Advisory Committee, the Methodist Church, the Metropolitan Police Service, the NSPCC and the Refugee Council, and in prisons. She is the author of several books, including *Counselling Skills for Working with Shame* (2015), *Counselling Skills for Working with Trauma: Healing from Child Sexual Abuse* (2013), *Introduction of Counselling Survivors of Interpersonal Trauma* (2009), *Counselling Survivors of Domestic Abuse* (*2008*) (all published by Jessica Kingsley Publishers), and *The Warrior Within: A One in Four Handbook to Aid Recovery from Childhood Sexual Abuse and Sexual Violence* (4th ed., One in Four, 2010).

Julie Scheiner is a chartered Counselling Psychologist and supervisor. She has worked in the voluntary sector, the NHS and in private practice for several years. Julie has previously co-authored a book chapter and written several papers about the subject of equine assisted therapy, which is of special interest. She has been working with clients presenting with alcohol addiction for the past several years. She also teaches on a DCPsych programme and is passionate about the new generation of Counselling Psychologists.

Joachim Schnackenberg, PhD, is director of hearing voices and recovery at a psychiatric organisation (Diakonie Kropp) in Germany. Internationally, he is active as a freelance trainer, supervisor, consultant and researcher via the efc Institute (www.efc-institut.de). Part of the Hearing Voices Movement since 2000, He has been applying Experience Focused Counselling (EFC)/Making Sense of Voices in acute, community and long-term settings. Joachim is co-editor of *The Practical Handbook of Hearing Voices* (PCCS Books, 2021), which introduces most talk-based and many social action approaches to hearing voices. He is the first author of *Stimmenhören und Recovery* (Psychiatrie-Verlag, 2017), a German-language textbook on EFC in practice. Joachim is continuously learning from and inspired by voices and voice hearers.

Adam J. Scott is a chartered psychologist, mediator and a minister in the United Reformed Church. He is currently a member of staff at Northern College in Manchester, where he uses his ministerial and psychological experience to oversee the College's ministerial formation programme and teach reflective practice. Adam has research interests in psychological resilience, trauma resulting from spiritual abuse, the damage conversion practices can do to LGBTQ+ people, and the application of mindfulness for the improvement of wellbeing.

Heather Sequeira, CPsychol, PhD, has spent the past two decades studying trauma, PTSD and OCD. She is the founder of PTSD Trauma Workshops and PTSD Masterclass, an innovative BPS approved workshop for clinicians and therapists in PTSD. With an extensive experience of trauma and fiercely non-pathologising in her approach, her mission is to bring together client-centred values with current research relevant to real-world practice. Heather holds an Honorary Senior Research Fellowship at the University of Birmingham, works as a clinician for the NHS and has regular input into BPS CPD, Clinical Psychology Doctoral Training programmes and CBT Diploma Courses.

Victoria Settle (Tori) is currently the CEO of The Bowlby Centre in Islington, London. She is an attachment-based psychoanalytical psychotherapist and supervisor and registered with the UKCP. She has taught extensively at The Bowlby Centre, specialising in Infant Development, and she runs short courses on Attachment Theory for people who have trained in the caring professions and who have an interest in learning about attachment. She has also written papers on the relevance of Infant Observations on psychotherapy trainings, published in the *Journal of Attachment* and *The Psychotherapist*.

Guy Shennan is a solution-focused therapist, supervisor and consultant, who provides training in solution-focused practice across social care, health, therapy and education contexts in the UK and beyond. The second edition of Guy's book, *Solution-Focused Practice: Effective Communication to Facilitate Change*, was published in 2019. From 2014 to 2018 he was the chair of the British Association of Social Workers. In 2018, Guy co-founded the Solution-Focused Collective, which focuses on the application of solution-focused ideas for social change.

Charlotte Sills is a psychotherapist, supervisor and trainer in London. For many years she was Head of the Transactional Analysis (TA) Department at Metanoia Institute, UK, and has taught TA nationally and internationally. She has published widely in the field of psychotherapy, including co-authoring with Helena Hargaden *Transactional Analysis – A Relational Perspective* (Routledge, 2002) and, with Phil Lapworth, *An Introduction to Transactional Analysis* (Sage, 2006). She is also Professor of Coaching at Ashridge Business School.

Penn Smith is a Senior Lecturer in Counselling and leads the BA in Counselling and Mental Health and Postgraduate Diploma in Humanistic Counselling at York St John University (UK). She is a Chartered Psychologist and a registered Counsellor with the British Association for Counselling and Psychotherapy. Penn's research and therapeutic interest is in understanding and working with the impact of complex trauma on mental wellbeing and relationships, and mental health rehabilitation and recovery. She has worked across a range of organisations, including third sector and emergency services, working with children, young people and adults who have experienced trauma.

Edith Maria Steffen is an Associate Professor in Counselling Psychology at the University of Plymouth, UK, and maintains a private practice as an HCPC registered counselling psychologist. Her research is focused on continuing bonds in bereavement, sensory experiences of the deceased (SED) and meaning-oriented grief therapy. She has published numerous journal articles and book chapters, and in 2018 she was co-editor of *Continuing Bonds in Bereavement: New Directions for Research and Practice* (Routledge, 2018). Most recently, she has co-edited *The Handbook of Grief Therapies* for Sage (2022).

William B. Stiles is Professor Emeritus of Psychology, Miami University, Oxford, Ohio, USA, and Senior Research Fellow at Metanoia Institute, London, UK. He has been President of the Society for Psychotherapy Research and of Division 29 of the American Psychological Association. He has served as Editor of *Psychotherapy Research* and *Person-Centered and Experiential Psychotherapies*. He has written about psychotherapy, verbal interaction and research methods.

Fiona Stirling is a counselling lecturer at Abertay University, Dundee. Her interest in Narrative Practice informs both her therapeutic work and her research, which is currently focused on exploring the lived experience of self-injury. Fiona has published around this topic, utilising autoethnography, a research method which centres personal narrative as a tool for exploring wider social, cultural and political experiences. Narrative also underpins her approach to education, in which she aims to discover and celebrate student strengths, make space for new learner stories to emerge, and draw upon the lived wisdom of student communities to improve the learning experience.

Léonie Sugarman, PhD, is a Chartered Psychologist and Emeritus Professor of Applied Psychology at the University of Cumbria. She is an Honorary Fellow and former Vice President of the British Association for Counselling and Psychotherapy. She has published in the area of life-span development, including *Counselling and the Life Course* (Sage, 2004) and (jointly with Ruth Wright) *Occupational Therapy and Life Course Development* (Wiley, 2009). Now retired, for many years she held editorial roles with the *British Journal of Guidance and Counselling*.

Michaela Swales, PhD, is the Director of Training with British Isles DBT and Professor of Clinical Psychology at Bangor University, where she is Director of the PG Diploma in DBT, the only postgraduate qualification in Dialectical Behaviour Therapy in the world. She is an international expert in the training and implementation of DBT and editor of *The Oxford Handbook of Dialectical Behaviour Therapy* (Oxford University Press, 2019).

Clare Symons is Head of Research with the British Association for Counselling and Psychotherapy (BACP), having formerly worked as a trainer of counsellors and psychotherapists at the University of Leicester, as Editor of *Counselling and Psychotherapy Research* journal and as a counsellor in a variety of settings, including higher education and the voluntary sector. Her doctoral research examined complaints and complaining behaviour in counselling and psychotherapy. Clare's current research interests include raising and supporting professional standards and facilitating counsellors' therapeutic use of routine outcomes measures in practice.

Ladislav Timulak, PhD, is Professor in Counselling Psychology at Trinity College Dublin, Ireland. His main research interest is psychotherapy research, particularly the development of emotion-focused therapy (EFT). He has written or co-written eight books, more than 90 peer-reviewed papers, and various chapters in both his native language, Slovak, and in English. His most recent books include *Essentials of Descriptive-Interpretive Qualitative Research: A Generic Approach* (co-authored with Robert Elliott, American Psychological Association, 2021) and *Transdiagnostic Emotion-Focused Therapy* (co-authored with Daragh Keogh, American Psychological Association, 2021).

Nick Totton is a therapist and trainer with nearly 40 years' experience. Originally a Reichian body therapist, his approach has become broad based and open to the spontaneous and unexpected. He is deeply involved with ecopsychology and addressing climate change. Nick originated trainings, still active, in Embodied-Relational Therapy and Wild Therapy. He has written or edited 20 books so far, most relevantly *Wild Therapy* (PCCS Books, 2020) and *Vital Signs* (edited with Mary-Jayne Rust, Karnac Books, 2012). He has a grown-up daughter, lives in Sheffield with his partner and grows vegetables. He has a website at www.nicktotton.net

Rachel Tribe is based at the Centre for Psychiatry, Queen Mary University of London and the School of Psychology, University of East London. She is a trustee for three international mental health charities. She has published over 125 journal articles and book chapters and edited seven books. She has contributed to theory and practice within psychology and mental health. She regularly undertakes international and national training and consultancy work. She is the joint editor with Dr Jean Morrissey of three editions of *The Handbook of Professional, Ethical and Research Practice for Psychologists, Counsellors, Psychotherapists and Psychiatrists* (Routledge, 2020).

Keith Tudor, PhD, MSc, MA, BA(Hons), is Professor of Psychotherapy at Auckland University of Technology (AUT), Aotearoa New Zealand. Initially trained in Gestalt therapy in the 1980s, he is a Certified and Teaching and Supervising Transactional Analyst and is equally at home in transactional analysis and person-centred psychology. He has contributed a number of publications in each field. As co-Lead of the Group for Research in Psychological Therapies at AUT, he is currently focusing on research and academic supervision of Master's students and doctoral candidates. Email: keith.tusor@aut.ac.nz. He has a small, independent online practice as a therapist, supervisor and trainer.

Dwight Turner is the Course Leader in Humanistic Counselling and Psychotherapy in the School of Humanities and Social Sciences at the University of Brighton, UK. Having trained at the Centre for Counselling and Psychotherapy Education (CCPE), Dwight then completed his doctorate through the University of Northampton, where he utilised creative techniques such as active imagination, drawing and sand play to explore the unconscious and internalised phenomenological experience of being the other. Dr Turner is also a psychotherapist and supervisor in private practice, and an activist working towards greater inclusion for disadvantaged groups in the fields of counselling and psychotherapy.

Zsófia Anna Utry (She/Her) is a Coaching Psychologist and a member and honorary vice president representing the Hungarian Association for Coaching Psychology in the International Society for Coaching Psychology (ISCP). She is currently working towards her accredited status with the ISCP. In her career and professional development of coaching practice she is interested in accessibility, diversity, inclusion, disabilities, and neurodiversity at work, and how a pluralistic approach to coaching can improve outcomes for neurologically different people. She advocates for Universal Design for the workplace, and cares about sustainability and the future of the environment.

Biljana van Rijn is a Faculty Head of Research and Doctoral Programmes at Metanoia Institute in London, an academic, researcher, Transactional Analysis supervisor and psychotherapist, and a counselling psychologist. Biljana has established a research centre and a clinic at Metanoia Institute, supporting different research areas, offering practice training and specialising in teaching clinical assessment. Her own interests include qualitative research in psychotherapy and supervision and clinical practice issues. In addition to her research papers and publications on clinical assessment, she has recently edited *Working with Sexual Attraction in Psychotherapy Practice and Supervision: A Humanistic-Relational Approach* (Routledge, 2021).

William West is a Visiting Professor in Counselling and Spirituality at the University of Chester, UK, where he supervises a number of PhD and postdoctorate students who share his interests in spirituality, faith, diversity and culture. William is a Fellow of the British Association for Counselling and Psychotherapy. His most recent book, co-edited with Greg Nolan, is *Extending Horizons in Helping and Caring Therapies* (Routledge, 2021).

Tony White is a member of the Australian Psychological Society. In 1986, Tony qualified as a psychologist and has worked in private practice since then. During that time, he has also worked in a drug rehabilitation centre, a prison, at a homeless centre, in an association for people with psychosis, and undertaking trauma debriefing with St John Ambulance service. He has written numerous books and articles on drug and alcohol abuse, suicide, pedophilia, teenagers and general counselling. He has specialised in Transactional Analysis as an approach to psychotherapy, but also uses CBT and psychoanalysis among other approaches.

Loren Whyatt is an Assistant Psychologist in a substance misuse charity (Change Grow Live) and a trainee counsellor. She has several years' experience working on the frontline with people with mental health and addiction problems, both in inpatient and community environments, as well as more recent experience working with clients with substance misuse problems in a therapy setting. She currently works in a PHE-funded outreach project with clients experiencing co-existing problems related to homelessness, substance misuse and mental health.

Gareth Williams qualified as a counsellor in 2000. Before this he spent two years as a full-time volunteer at Lothlorien therapeutic community, completed a psychology degree and a Master's exploring shamanism. He loves his work, has studied a wide range of psychotherapies and has been a visiting teacher on the Doctorate in Counselling Psychology at the University of Manchester for 10 years. Gareth has currently been in private practice as a therapist, compassion-based mindfulness teacher and supervisor for seven years. His special interests include creativity, ecotherapy and spirituality. If you would like to contact him, www.garethwilliams.earth is the place to go.

Ruth Williams gained an MA in Jungian and Post-Jungian Studies at the Centre for Psychoanalytic Studies (now the Department for Psychosocial and Psychoanalytic Studies), University of Essex, UK. She is a Jungian Analyst-Analytical Psychologist, Integrative Psychotherapist and Supervisor based in London. She is a Training and Supervising Analyst at the Association of Jungian Analysts, London, and member of the International Association for Analytical Psychology, based in Zurich. She has a particular interest in working with dreams, the imagination and diversity, and works with many practising therapists and trainees. She has been in private practice for 30 years. See www.RuthWilliams.org.uk

David Winter is Professor Emeritus of Clinical Psychology at the University of Hertfordshire, UK, where he was previously Programme Director of the Doctorate in Clinical Psychology, and is Director of Postgraduate Programmes at Colombo Institute of Research and Psychology, Sri Lanka. He spent most of his working life practising as a clinical psychologist in the English National Health Service. He is a Fellow of the British Psychological Society, and has around 200 publications, primarily on personal construct psychology and psychotherapy research. His current research interests include personal construct analyses of radicalisation and of the impact of major adversity, including civil war and pandemics.

Val Wosket has worked as a therapist, supervisor and trainer in university, private practice and voluntary settings for over 25 years. She is a former teaching faculty member of the International Society for the Study of Trauma and Dissociation and author of *The Therapeutic Use of Self: Counselling Practice, Research and Supervision* (Classic Edition, Routledge, 2017), *Supervising the Counsellor and Psychotherapist: A Cyclical Model* (with Steve Page, Routledge, 2015) and *Egan's Skilled Helper Model: Developments and Applications in Counselling* (Routledge, 2006).

Gabriel Wynn is a lecturer in counselling psychology at the University of Manchester, UK. She is a BPS Chartered Counselling Psychologist and HCPC registered Practitioner Psychologist. She is also a BACP accredited counsellor/psychotherapist. Gabriel's research interests centre on the development of research methods to investigate how clinical language is used to protect clinician power structures. Beside her academic work, since 1994 Gabriel has held therapeutic roles in hospital and community settings in the private, public and social sectors. She has held psychology service operational and lead roles since 2006. Her clinical expertise lies in community-based care to help people overcome disordered eating.

Jessica Yakeley is a Consultant Psychiatrist in Forensic Psychotherapy, Director of the Portman Clinic, and Director of Medical Education, Tavistock and Portman NHS Foundation Trust. She is also a Fellow of the British Psychoanalytic Society and Editor of the journal *Psychoanalytic Psychotherapy*. Her particular fields of interest and research include antisocial personality disorder, violence, paraphilias, risk, and psychodynamic methods of teaching about the doctor–patient relationship. She has published numerous peer-reviewed papers and chapters, and six books, including *Working with Violence: A Contemporary Psychoanalytic Approach* (Palgrave, 2010), *The Oxford Specialist Handbook of Medical Psychotherapy* (Oxford University Press, 2016), and *Learning about Emotions in Illness* (Routledge, 2014).

Rebecca Yin Foo is an Educational and Developmental Psychologist, a member of the Australian Psychological Society (APS) and a Fellow of the College of Educational and Developmental Psychology (FCEDP). She has previous experience working with children and young people with cerebral palsy and related developmental disabilities and their families at the Cerebral Palsy League (CPL). As a private practitioner, she is currently working with children, young people and their families, supporting them in areas such as learning and cognition, anxiety, depression, anger, social skills, self-esteem, behaviour and parenting. Rebecca has co-authored books on counselling and enjoys supervising students and early career psychologists.

PREFACE TO THE FIFTH EDITION

THE AIM OF THE BOOK

The Sage Handbook of Counselling and Psychotherapy is now well into its second decade. For the first time, it is likely that some of its readers are younger than it itself. During this time, it has become a core text for those hoping to learn more about the fields of counselling and psychotherapy and has been adopted by courses across the United Kingdom and in numerous other places across the globe. The popularity and reach of the text can be attributed to the vast wealth of information held within its pages. It contains contributions from a wide array of authors, 116 to be exact, and includes an abundance of essential information for those working in the counselling and psychotherapy arenas. This includes content that is both general, taking a step back and reviewing the disciplines from afar, and specific, really focusing in on some important topics. We believe it has something for everyone.

With the above in mind, here lies the text's major aim. We hope that this *Handbook* is a resource that anyone interested in counselling and psychotherapy might want to dip into to learn more about these ever-evolving worlds. It provides contributions on a wide array of topics, and we hope that it is of interest and use to:

- those who are starting out on the journey to become a therapist
- trained therapists interested in finding out about new areas of development or contemporary debates
- those in allied professions that may find themselves overlapping with the fields of counselling and psychotherapy
- the general public interested in finding out more about the weird and wonderful world of therapy.

CHANGES TO THIS NEW EDITION

The fifth edition of the *Handbook* is very much an evolution of the previous edition, rather than a complete overhaul. In addition to updating its content to keep it at the forefront of developments, we have listened to feedback and taken the opportunity to reshape some of the overall structure of the book. Consequently, the book now has the following seven main sections:

1. Counselling and psychotherapy in context
2. Social justice and intersectionality
3. Core therapeutic and professional skills
4. What do people come to therapy for?
5. Theories and approaches
6. Lifespan, modalities and technology
7. Settings

Many of these sections echo those in the previous editions. We have, however, taken the opportunity to make some important changes. These include:

- Inviting and working with an even broader range of authors to ensure that those contributing to the text reflect a wide range of social and political identities, backgrounds, experiences and roles within the broad field of counselling and psychotherapy.
- Adding several new chapters, along with the updated chapters, in the section on social justice and intersectionality. Specifically, this is to provide more space for considerations of intersectionality as a frame (see Chapter 2.1),

- along with inviting all authors of revised chapters to consider this more fully in their contributions. New chapters are included in the context of the climate and ecological crises (2.3) and neurodivergence (2.6).
- Ensuring that we present (more accurately) the way in which counsellors and psychotherapists engage with diagnostic labels and medicalised language in section 4. We have asked authors to ensure that they focus on assessment and understanding, rather than aetiology for example, and we have encouraged the authors (who come from a wide range of backgrounds) to consider a range of understandings of distress in their chapters, along with a range of ways of working with presentations rather than having a sole focus on one single therapeutic approach.
- Adding new chapters to the core skills section of the book to reflect the world in which we are all working now. These include a new contribution on social media and professionalism (see Chapter 3.19) and a revised chapter on working with interpreters (3.8), which was previously considered in the section on specialisms in the fourth edition.
- Changing the way that the therapeutic approaches introduced in the book are categorised. To reflect the many overlaps between therapeutic approaches, we no longer divide these up into psychodynamic, cognitive behavioural, humanistic, narrative and integrative categories. We believe doing so has the potential to perpetuate artificial divides between approaches that might more accurately align to numerous approaches.
- Amplifying the place that the use of technology now has in therapeutic work. Historically, this was viewed in this book as a specialism. Given the impact of the Covid-19 pandemic, technologically mediated therapy and technologically supported therapy have become increasingly commonplace. As such, the number of chapters focusing on technology has increased and, to reflect that, it is no longer a specialism in the same way. It has also been moved into a distinct section alongside working with lifespan issues and different therapeutic modalities (in Part 6).
- Expanding the range of settings that are introduced. In the final section of the book, chapters on working in schools (7.1) and forensic settings (7.9) have been included. We hope that continuing to develop such content helps to reflect the wide range of working contexts to which therapists may be contributing their knowledge.

As with other editions of this *Handbook*, it includes contributions from numerous new authors who have been sought out to contribute chapters in their specialist areas. The chapters have therefore been written by individuals who are experts in their areas of knowledge and provide an informed insider view into the topic in question. Importantly, those that were present in previous editions have been revised and updated so that they contain the most up-to-date information for the reader.

Although there have been numerous changes to this edition of the *Handbook*, there is also a lot that remains the same. All the chapters are purposefully written to be engaging and digestible to a practitioner audience. Each aims to provide a succinct overview of the topic being examined, while also providing a wealth of information to nourish the appetite for learning about it. The chapters engage with theoretical, practical and research-focused elements, while also bringing this content to life with brief examples informed by real-world practices. Finally, for those who wish to continue their reading about the topics in question, further recommended reading is provided at the end of each chapter.

Overall, our hope is that this text provides the reader with an up-to-date, thorough and informed resource that can be utilised to enrich their understanding of the vast territories that are counselling and psychotherapy. We also very much hope that you find the content interesting and enjoyable.

ACKNOWLEDGEMENTS

The first acknowledgement of this book must go to Professor Colin Feltham. Colin, who played a core part in orchestrating all the earlier editions to the *Handbook*, has left an impressive legacy to the world of counselling and psychotherapy. Indeed, both of us have used a copy of earlier versions of this *Handbook* to scaffold our own learning about therapy, reaching out to it for information for assignments while we were studying and for helpful tips once in practice. Although Colin has moved on from the *Handbook* to engage in new writing tasks, he is still very much present within the pages. Some of this is very explicit, with Colin contributing an updated chapter focusing on critical thinking in counselling and psychotherapy. In addition, many of his words are still present in the introductory section of the book and Colin previously co-authored chapters 1.1, 1.3, 1.4 and 1.5, but preferred to relinquish authorship now. However, some of his contributions are more implicit. During the previous edition, Colin's support and guidance was essential in seeing this mammoth editing task to fruition. This experience also rumbled on beyond that one (sizeable) task and, much as the *Handbook* provided a scaffolding for our therapy training, working with Colin on the fourth edition provided a scaffolding for the development of this new edition. With this in mind, we thank Colin for both his guidance and for leaving us with such an important and valuable resource to take forward for new generations of counsellors and psychotherapists.

Secondly, we would like to wholeheartedly thank all the authors who have contributed to the creation of this version of the *Handbook*. It has been a pleasure to work with so many individuals and to read the chapters as they have developed for this new edition. To be involved in conversations about the new developments in the counselling and psychotherapy field has been a privilege and without these contributions, this resource would not exist.

Thirdly, it is important also to thank the individuals at SAGE who have supported us in the pulling together of the book: Susannah, Ruth, and Bali, in particular.

TERRY HANLEY

I have found this *Handbook* a bit of a beast to edit. It has taken hours of work and lots of brain power to pull together the final product that you are reading. As with many others, juggling work tasks during the pandemic brought with it real challenges. As such, it is important for me to acknowledge the people who have supported me along the way to get this task completed.

The people at the epicentre of the impact of this project are my close family. Becky for the many conversations about this book, for always being supportive, and for being my fellow traveller through all of the Schitt's Creek episodes when it's been good to turn off. My kids (and dog) for ensuring that I got plenty of distractions; Arthur with the hours and hours of hockey, Matilda with the evening explorations into the Netflix back catalogue, Wilfred with the football and Fortnite School, and Charlie for the many daily walks, to name but a few of the distractions (that I've enjoyed). My mum also needs a special mention for the hours of support, and well, just being brilliant.

Beyond the above, I would also like to thank my colleagues (Erica, Gabriel, Ish, and Jo) and all of the students on the Doctorate in Counselling Psychology programme at the University of Manchester. Being able to share and discuss ideas, supportively be challenged, and continue to learn alongside such fantastic others has been a real privilege. These conversations have informed the size, shape, and contents of this book from its conception to its eventual publication.

Finally, I would like to acknowledge the support of Laura, the co-editor of the *Handbook*. It's been a challenge, but we got there. Thanks for being the consistent sounding board that has been needed throughout this project.

LAURA WINTER

Editing this book is certainly a huge, and often hugely rewarding task. I have been so well supported by colleagues from Sage and my co-editor Terry that thankfully the enormity of the task has felt only mildly overwhelming on occasion!

Mostly, I have enjoyed the process of returning to chapters from the last edition, and in particular working with new authors on new topics, hopefully communicating something about the importance of these topics to the world of counselling and psychotherapy. A big thank you to Terry for holding all of this with me, and for putting up with me when I start sentences with 'I'm not sure about that…', which inevitably ends in more questions and more work!

My family have once again endured many conversations about where things are up to, and Jack deserves a special mention for all the many conversations about our progress on this tome (among other things). In the acknowledgements of the last edition of this book I mentioned Bump (who become Rosa during the process). I have now got a much busier world, with Rosa, Cerys, and Bump #3 (who became Owen during the final stages of editing this Handbook) to thank for reminding me that work will always come further down the priority list.

PART I

COUNSELLING AND PSYCHOTHERAPY IN CONTEXT

1.1 WHAT ARE COUNSELLING AND PSYCHOTHERAPY?

TERRY HANLEY

OVERVIEW AND KEY POINTS

When starting a book such as this, it is important to set some parameters for content that follows. This chapter therefore begins by providing a working definition of what is meant by the use of the terms 'counselling' and 'psychotherapy'. The chapter then:

- provides a brief overview of the historical developments related to psychotherapy and counselling in the United Kingdom (UK).
- introduces the major counselling and psychotherapy professional bodies in the UK.
- discusses how counselling and psychotherapy relate to a variety of allied professions, such as health interventions (psychiatry, psychology and mental health nursing), complementary medicines and other core professions.
- reflects upon the values that psychotherapists and counsellors commonly hold onto in the UK. These are discussed in relation to some core issues, such as professionalisation and evidence-based practice.

DEFINITIONS AND AIMS

It may seem odd that a profession cannot clearly define its central activity, but no consensually agreed definition of either counselling or psychotherapy exists in spite of many attempts across the decades in Britain, North America and elsewhere to arrive at one. The question of pinning down crucial distinctions arose in concrete terms in the UK in the first decade of the twenty-first century when the Health Professions Council (HPC: now the Health and Care Professions Council (HCPC)) initiated preliminary steps towards the legal protection of the titles 'counsellor' and 'psychotherapist'. This proved incredibly contentious, with attempts to load the former with wellbeing-associated tasks and the latter with competencies in addressing more severe psychological problems initially breaking down. Despite this, the desire to create a shared way of defining what counselling and psychotherapy are has however rippled on. The most recent development is the publication of the *Scope of Practice and Education* (ScoPEd) framework (ScoPEd Oversight Committee, 2022), a collaborative project proposed by six professional counselling and psychotherapy bodies.

For the purposes of this book, the following working definition is used as a starting point:

> Counselling and psychotherapy are mainly, though not exclusively, listening-and-talking-based methods of addressing psychological and sometimes psychosomatic problems, including deep and prolonged human suffering, situational dilemmas, crises and developmental needs, and aspirations towards the realization of human potential. In contrast to biomedical approaches, the psychological therapies operate largely without medication or other physical interventions and may be concerned not only with mental health but with spiritual, philosophical, social and other aspects of living. Professional forms of counselling and psychotherapy are based on formal training which encompasses attention to pertinent theory, research skills, clinical and/or micro-skills development, the personal development/therapy of the trainee, and supervised practice.

A brief definition of this kind offers some parameters but omits mention of the many, ever-expanding and often competing schools of therapy, the arenas, and the several professions in which they are practised. The contention advanced by this book's editors is that counselling and psychotherapy, in spite of partly different historical roots and affiliations, have much more in common than they have serious and demonstrable differences and that practitioners and the public stand to gain more from the assumption of commonality than from spurious or infinitesimal distinctions. It is often acknowledged that 'British counselling' much more closely resembles psychotherapy as practised in the United States of America and parts of Europe than it does the various kinds of guidance and mentoring that it is often confused with. The term 'psychotherapeutic counselling' adopted by the United Kingdom Council for Psychotherapy (UKCP) acknowledges this.

Practitioners in this field work with many different types of goal and expectation (see Hanley – Chapter 1.2, this volume), implicit and explicit, each of which may call for the use of somewhat different skills, but arguably little is to be gained practically from further controversy about professional titles and distinctions. However, optimal clarity about services for those seeking them should be an overriding aim.

DEVELOPMENT OF PSYCHOTHERAPY AND COUNSELLING IN THE UK

Sigmund Freud was developing psychoanalysis – often considered the grandparent of most of the diverse schools in existence today – in Austria in the late nineteenth and early twentieth centuries. He lived the last year of his life in London. Before Freud there were many kinds of psychologically oriented therapies, and many had already used the concept of an unconscious. However, Freud has come to mark the historical pivot when previous centuries of religious, philosophical, and pseudo-scientific theories and methods (from religious propitiation to shamanism, sleeping cures, magnetism, hypnotism, etc.) were challenged by serious aspirations to establish psychotherapy as a scientific discipline. Psychoanalysis is perched curiously between being perceived as a challenge to previous faith in reason (the Enlightenment) and as the new grand narrative capable of rationally explaining all the psychological ills of humanity. Freud is often (although not by all) ranked with Darwin and Marx as one of the most significant scientific thinkers at the dawn of the twentieth century.

Freud's work developed in many directions, with individuals such as Melanie Klein and Anna Freud pioneering work with younger individuals. As it grew, psychoanalysis moved through Europe and North America in the first few decades of the twentieth century, the International Psychoanalytical Association being established in 1910 and the British Psychoanalytic Society in 1924. The British Association of Psychotherapists (originally the Association of Psychotherapists) was founded in 1951. In spite of much public and medical resistance to psychoanalysis (which was originally radically counter-cultural), interest and support grew, partly in connection with the two world wars and the search for remedies for 'shell shock' (the predecessor of post-traumatic stress disorder (PTSD)) and other problems experienced by military personnel. Concern about scientology led in 1971 to the Foster Report, which had implications for psychotherapy, and in 1978 to the publication of the Sieghart Report on the statutory regulation of psychotherapists. During the 1980s, conferences regularly held at Rugby (organised by the British Association for Counselling (BAC)) led to the creation of the United Kingdom Standing Conference for Psychotherapy. The group, which contained member organisations from humanistic, cognitive-behavioural, integrative and other traditions, eventually saw the creation of the United Kingdom Council for Psychotherapy (UKCP) in 1993. In more recent years it has extended its membership categories to include 'psychotherapeutic counsellor' and more flexible routes to membership. Running somewhat parallel to these developments, the British Confederation of Psychotherapists (now the British Psychoanalytic Council (BPC)) was formed in 1992. Unlike the more open stance of the UKCP, this body only represents training institutions with a psychoanalytic affiliation.

The development of counselling is harder to trace, there being no single dominant figure like Freud, or monolithic theory like psychoanalysis. Hans Hoxter may, however, be credited as one outstanding individual for his part in creating the counselling movement, including bringing American training ideas to Britain. Further relevant historical information is available in Aldridge (2014). It is usually agreed that early American vocational guidance projects and associations (for example, Frank Parsons' Vocation Bureau in Boston in 1908) laid the foundations of counselling, and guidance, for the young. This certainly features in the early career of Carl Rogers, who is probably the closest to being the 'founder' of (non-directive) counselling in the 1940s. Another player is perhaps Rollo May, who, influenced by Alfred Adler, wrote what many consider to be the first counselling text in the 1920s (May, 1992). Both Rogers and May were instrumental, alongside others, such as Abraham Maslow and Charlotte Buhler, in leading developments in the field of humanistic psychology, a perspective at the core of many approaches of counselling. Subsequently, key humanistic psychologists led the way in considering the importance of 'cross-cultural' counselling (e.g., Clemmont Vontress) and extended thinking about the relationship between global spiritual practices and therapy (e.g., Roy Moodley). In contrast to the UK, in the United States of America counselling was originally closely linked with personnel management and the workplace. In general, it is true to say that counselling has *historical* roots in practical guidance and problem-solving issues, and was often agency-based rather than associated with private practice. However, in the UK, it is now mainly characterised as distinctly other than advice giving and as having a primarily client-centred, facilitative and therapeutic function.

Seminal events in the UK included the establishment of the National Marriage Guidance Council in 1938, the import of counselling training methods from the USA to the Universities of Reading and Keele in 1966 (to serve the pastoral needs of students), and the establishment of the Westminster Pastoral Foundation in 1969. The Standing Conference for the Advancement of Counselling in 1970 led to the formation of the British Association for Counselling in 1977, renamed the British Association for Counselling and Psychotherapy (BACP) in 2000. The BACP is by far the largest such body in the UK. It should be said that a great deal of cross-fertilisation between these developments and others in psychotherapy was taking place and the emergence of psychodynamic counselling, for example, demonstrates these close links.

Another significant development to consider in the therapeutic landscape of the UK is the growth of counselling psychology. Much as counselling and psychotherapy developed along different paths, counselling and psychology also appear to have run relatively parallel trajectories. Counselling psychology in the UK has therefore grown with the view of explicitly bringing together these different bodies of work (Woolfe, 2016). Its home has primarily been the Division of Counselling Psychology, which was created in 1994 within the British Psychological Society (BPS) after emerging as a special section in 1982 (Orlans and Van Scoyoc, 2009). Despite counselling psychology being a relative newcomer to the applied psychologies in the UK, the BPS itself being created in 1901, it has quickly emerged as a popular training option. Although, in theory, practice and research, there are many overlaps between the work of counselling psychologists and counsellors and psychotherapists (see Feltham (2013) for a critical review of this territory), counselling psychology was regulated separately by the HCPC along with the other applied psychologies (e.g., clinical psychology and educational psychology) in 2009. The title Counselling Psychologist is therefore now a protected title, with only those approved by the HCPC being eligible to use it.

Alongside these developments we should also note pertinent developments elsewhere. Originally the Association of Medical Officers of Asylums and Hospitals for the Insane (AMOAHI, founded 1841), the Royal College of Psychiatrists was so named in 1971. Significant mutual aid and voluntary organisations such as Alcoholics Anonymous (1935), the Samaritans (1953) and Cruse (1959) should also be included in this brief portrait, as should the parallel existence of the personal social services and its casework tradition, which closely mirrored developments in counselling and psychotherapy.

Theoretically, psychotherapy and counselling develop continuously, some might say all too prolifically, with significant departures from psychoanalytic theory and practice observable from its earliest days. Klein, Jung and Adler were among the earliest to break away from Freud, and similar schisms, factions and developments are in evidence throughout psychotherapeutic history. Hence there resulted the growth of what is still thought to be the more than 500 schools (also known as theoretical orientations, approaches, brand names) of therapy we have today (Prochaska and Norcross, 2018). The question of whether such proliferation is desirable and in clients' interests, or not, must be faced by thoughtful practitioners, and indeed the integrationist movement stemming from the 1980s represents a shared concern for convergence (Norcross and Goldfried, 2019). In addition to eclectic, integrative and pluralistic developments, attempts have been made at a comprehensive unification of psychotherapies (Magnavita and Anchin, 2013).

In contrast to the moves towards the integration of approaches, early twenty-first century tensions regarding statutory regulation sometimes appeared to be pushing the psychoanalytic, humanistic and cognitive-behavioural therapy (CBT) camps further apart (see House and Loewenthal, 2008; Parker and Revelli, 2008; Weatherill, 2004). But much of this was fuelled by professionalisation pressures, economic demands highlighting the advantages of time-limited models, and government requirements for evidence-based practice.

To end this section, it is notable that many of those involved in guiding these developments have been white men, often holding positions that gave them significant platforms. While we certainly do not wish to undermine the important roles that these individuals have had on the growth of these professions, it is important to hold a mirror up to the professions and acknowledge that this has been the case. In contrast, the roles of women and people of colour have typically not been recorded to the same extent, or they were not provided with the opportunity to influence in the same way. The ripples of such a history continue to spread and are likely to be long-lasting. Some of the chapters that follow demonstrate how the professions have responded/started to respond to the discriminatory practices and unconscious biases that are endemic within them.

ALLIED PROFESSIONS

Most, but not all, agree that counselling and psychotherapy are part of the health professions. Freud battled to have psychoanalysis recognised as separate from medicine and Rogers similarly battled with psychiatric and psychological colleagues, but the psychological therapies today concern themselves largely with mental health promotion and mental illness reduction even where these terms are not used and where additional or different aims are espoused, such as personal growth and development, psycho-education, psychopractice, etc. (see Brown and Mowbray, 2002). Counsellors are therefore often found in health and social care settings along with psychotherapists, clinical and counselling psychologists, psychiatrists and mental health nurses. A second group of related professionals includes social workers, probation officers, welfare officers, human resources personnel, career guidance workers, occupational therapists, speech and communication therapists, occupational and health psychologists, and so on. Teachers, nurses, priests and others in caring roles may have some closely related functions. Members of the above groups, sometimes known as the 'core professions', have been considered good candidates for counselling and psychotherapy training, and typical intakes to courses include members of all these groups.

Each professional group has its own professional body, history and traditions of training and supervision. Each has designated tasks that differ from those of others, depending on context and client group. Counselling and psychotherapeutic skills are used to degrees in all these professions and, where individual workers possess dual or multiple qualifications (for example, a social worker may be trained in family and systemic therapy), they may formally provide therapeutic services. However, BACP and other clinically oriented bodies strive to emphasise a distinction between casual, informal or untrained, and uncontracted use of *counselling skills*, and disciplined, contracted, ethically protected, formal counselling or psychotherapy.

The above-mentioned groups are also related to those involved in practising the so-called complementary therapies (often regarding their work as holistic or mind–body integrated), including acupuncture, homeopathy, reflexology, aromatherapy, Alexander technique, spiritual healing, osteopathy, naturopathy, Bach flower remedies, etc. Again, practitioners may sometimes have dual qualifications and practise both psychological therapy and somatic or sensual therapies alternately or simultaneously, having due regard for appropriate contracting (Sills, 2006). Debates about the rights of certain of these groups to aspire to professional status cannot be ignored, but nor can public scepticism. In relation to distinctions between the titles of those engaged in closely related therapeutic professions and their putatively distinctive skills and effectiveness, see Cheshire and Pilgrim (2004), Gask (2004), James and Palmer (1996) and Milton, Polmear and Fabricius (2011).

A BRIEF OVERVIEW OF THE VALUES OF COUNSELLING AND PSYCHOTHERAPY

The overarching values, and the professional ethics that stem from these, of counselling and psychotherapy were summed up in the concepts of integrity, impartiality and respect (Reeves and Bond, 2021). These have been developed and related by the BACP (2018) to tenets of moral philosophy: fidelity (honouring the trust placed in the practitioner); autonomy (the client's right to be self-governing); beneficence (concern for the greatest good); non-maleficence (to cause least harm); justice (concern for fairness); accountability and candour; and the practitioner's self-respect (self-knowledge and care of self). Such principles are not without problems, however, since in practice there sometimes are conflicts between, for example, the wishes of a client and possible damaging consequences. Also, it is sometimes the case that what may be professionally ethical and desirable will be challenged as socially undesirable or questionable by others. Hence, the goals of individual autonomy and self-actualisation, which are held by many writers as central values in psychotherapy (e.g., Hinshelwood, Holmes and Lindley, 1998), have been criticised by some sociologists as leading to an 'autonomy obsession', an undermining of social responsibility and a cultural insensitivity. It is therefore important to bear in mind that what we often call *professional ethics* (as advocated in professional codes) are not necessarily always coterminous with *social ethics*. Notably, at this juncture of the history of counselling and psychotherapy, contemporary societal pressures and political movements in the UK have led to an increase in writing and public debate around the role of the counselling professions in tackling social injustices (Winter and Charura, forthcoming).

All professional bodies in this field have their own codes of ethics and practice – BACP's *Ethical Framework for the Counselling Professions* (2018) being a mature example – usually addressing issues of safety, contracting, relationship-building, competence, confidentiality, boundaries, law, advertising, complaints, care of the self, and so on. Other examples include the UKCP's (2019) *Code of Ethics and Professional Practice*, the HCPC's (2016) *Standards of Conduct, Performance and Ethics* and the BPS's (2021) *Code of Ethics and Conduct*. Fewer specific prohibitions now exist than historically, although sexual contact with clients, exploitation of clients and breach of confidentiality are prohibitions shared by all professional bodies. Nevertheless, often genuine and valid differences in values do exist between members of different professional bodies and different theoretical affiliations.

Understanding and elaboration of the foundational philosophical assumptions of therapists are an area of theory and training that is taking a long time to mature (Bennett, 2005; Erwin, 1997; Feltham, 2010; Howard, 2000). Recent growth has been seen, however, in connections between psychotherapy and neuroscience, evolutionary science, and socio-economic and ecological disciplines. Advances have also been made in how counselling and psychotherapy are delivered, most clearly in technological media, with the Covid-19 pandemic acting as an evolutionary catalyst for such work (Hanley, 2021). Such developments continue to push the parameters of what might constitute the traditional value base(s) of counselling and psychotherapy and raise numerous questions for those working in this arena.

A final area that warrants special mention is the push for evidence-based practice (EBP). Despite the clear tension between many therapists' holistic positioning and the reductive nature of the methodologies commonly adopted in efficacy and effectiveness research, the EBP movement continues to gather momentum. Issues such as cost-effectiveness and clinical effectiveness are becoming increasingly commonplace and, in many practice settings, counsellors and psychotherapists have to understand the implications of such concepts upon their work. For those who are challenged by such a position, this can involve opting out of certain services all together, for others it can involve working pragmatically so as to embed 'evidence' into their ways of working (e.g., Hanley, Winter, Gordon and Scott, 2022). Whatever an individual's perspective, EBP has become a core area that therapists need to be aware of, with accrediting bodies incorporating research into syllabi and supporting the development of textbooks (e.g., Cooper, 2008; Midgely, Hayes and Cooper, 2017).

CONCLUSION

Despite counselling and psychotherapy having a presence in the UK for almost a century, they are still relatively new professions (if we are to use that term). The dialogues and debates that have surrounded the attempts to define their parameters over the years highlight what a charged and volatile arena it is. While some argue that this process of creating boundaries is counter to the fundamental values and ethics of the work that they undertake, others disagree with processes in which limited numbers of people make decisions for a profession or contest where the divisional lines are to be set. While it looks increasingly likely that professional bodies will set firmer boundaries, the nature of the work of counsellors and psychotherapists will inevitably remain continually difficult to regulate. For instance, individuals will no doubt develop new role titles to engage in activities that will look very similar in practice. Some of these might be embedded more fully within the allied professions noted above, while others may evolve into completely new professions themselves. We will have to continue to 'watch this space' to see how things unfold, but one thing's for sure, there will be many more challenges ahead.

REFERENCES

Aldridge, S. (2014) *A Short Introduction to Counselling*. London: Sage.
BACP (2018) *Ethical Framework for the Counselling Professions*. Rugby: British Association for Counselling and Psychotherapy.
Bennett, M. (2005) *The Purpose of Counselling and Psychotherapy*. Basingstoke: Palgrave.

BPS (2021) *Code of Ethics and Conduct.* Leicester: British Psychological Society.
Reeves, A. and Bond, T. (2021) *Standards and Ethics for Counselling in Action (5th ed).* London: Sage.
Brown, J. and Mowbray, R. (2002) Visionary deep personal growth. In C. Feltham (Ed.), *What's the Good of Counselling and Psychotherapy? The Benefits Explained.* London: Sage.
Cheshire, K. and Pilgrim, D. (2004) *A Short Introduction to Clinical Psychology.* London: Sage.
Cooper, M. (2008) *Essential Research Findings in Counselling and Psychotherapy: The Facts are Friendly.* London: Sage.
Erwin, E. (1997) *Philosophy and Psychotherapy.* London: Sage.
Feltham, C. (2010) *Critical Thinking in Counselling and Psychotherapy.* London: Sage.
Feltham, C. (2013) *Counselling and Counselling Psychology: A Critical Examination.* Ross-on-Wye: PCCS Books.
Foster, J. (1971) *Enquiry into the practice and effects of scientology.* London: HMSO.
Gask, L. (2004) *A Short Introduction to Psychiatry.* London: Sage.
Hanley, T. (2021) Researching online counselling and psychotherapy: The past, the present and the future. *Counselling and Psychotherapy Research*, 21(3), 493–497. https://doi.org/10/gk87gz
Hanley, T., Winter, L., Gordon, R. and Scott, A. (2022) A research-informed approach to counselling psychology. In G. Davey (Ed.), *Applied Psychology* (2nd ed.). London: Wiley.
HCPC (2016) *Standards of Conduct, Performance and Ethics.* London: Health and Care Professions Council.
Hinshelwood, R.D., Holmes, J. and Lindley, R. (1998) *The Values of Psychotherapy* (2nd ed.). London: Karnac.
House, R. and Loewenthal, D. (Eds) (2008) *Against and for CBT: Towards a Constructive Dialogue?* Ross-on-Wye: PCCS Books.
Howard, A. (2000) *Philosophy for Counselling and Psychotherapy: Pythagoras to Postmodernism.* Basingstoke: Palgrave.
James, I. and Palmer, S. (Eds) (1996) *Professional Therapeutic Titles: Myths and Realities.* Leicester: British Psychological Society.
Magnavita, J.J. and Anchin, J.C. (2013) *Unifying Psychotherapy: Principles, Methods, and Evidence from Clinical Science.* New York: Springer.
May, R. (1992) *The Art of Counselling.* London: Souvenir.
Midgely, N., Hayes, J. and Cooper, M. (2017) *Essential Research Findings in Child and Adolescent Counselling and Psychotherapy.* London: Sage.
Milton, J., Polmear, C. and Fabricius, J. (2011) *A Short Introduction to Psychoanalysis* (2nd ed.). London: Sage.
Norcross, J. and Goldfried, M. (2019) *Handbook of Psychotherapy Integration* (3rd ed.). New York: Oxford University Press.
Orlans, V. and Van Scoyoc, S. (2009) *A Short Introduction to Counselling Psychology.* London: Sage.
Parker, I. and Revelli, S. (Eds) (2008) *Psychoanalytic Practice and State Regulation.* London: Karnac.
Prochaska, J. and Norcross, J. (2018) *Systems of Psychotherapy: A transtheoretical analysis (9th ed).* New York: Oxford University Press
ScoPEd Oversight Committee (2022). *ScoPEd Framework: A shared framework for the scope and practice and education for counselling and psychotherapy with adults.* London: ScoPEd collaboration
Sieghart, P. (1978) Statutory Registration of Psychotherapists.: *A Report of a Professions Joint Working Party.* London: E. & E. Plumridge Ltd.
Sills, C. (Ed.) (2006) *Contracts in Counselling* (2nd ed.). London: Sage.
UKCP (2019) *Code of Ethics and Professional Practice.* London: United Kingdom Council for Psychotherapy.
Weatherill, R. (2004) *Our Last Great Illusion: A Radical Psychoanalytic Critique of Therapy Culture.* Exeter: Academic.
Winter, L.A. and Charura, D. (Eds) (Forthcoming) *The Handbook of Social Justice in the Psychological Therapies.* London: Sage.
Woolfe, R. (2016) Mapping the world of helping: The place of counselling psychology. In B. Douglas, R. Woolfe, S. Strawbridge, E. Kasket and V. Galbraith (Eds), *Handbook of Counselling Psychology* (4th ed., pp. 5–19). London: Sage.

> **RECOMMENDED READING**
>
> The major resource for additional material about the background and development of counselling and psychotherapy has to be the chapters that follow in this book. For instance, each of the theories that are presented in Part 5 begins with a *Background and Context* section. These are jam-packed with interesting information.
>
> In looking outside this text, there are numerous excellent introductory texts to counselling, psychotherapy and all of the variants that we discuss throughout this book. If you are after a smaller read, however, we would recommend the books in Sage's short introduction series (see reference list above for some examples). Finally, readers might also want to refer to Colin Feltham's critical reflection on the areas of counselling and counselling psychology.
>
> Feltham, C. (2013) *Counselling and Counselling Psychology: A Critical Examination*. Ross-on-Wye: PCCS Books.

1.2 THE SOCIAL AND POLITICAL CONTEXT OF COUNSELLING AND PSYCHOTHERAPY

LAURA ANNE WINTER

OVERVIEW AND KEY POINTS

This chapter focuses on introducing the social and political context to counselling and psychotherapy, as an important and deeply intertwined part of our work as therapists. I begin by considering what we mean by this context, and what the current landscape looks like at the time of writing in May 2022. I then move on to explore why this is important and relevant for counsellors and psychotherapists to consider. I suggest that a developing focus on the social and the political in our fields can only enhance and improve both the work that we do and the outcomes and experiences for the people we work with. The main points outlined in this chapter are:

- The social and political context encompasses global, national, and local systems in which our clients are embedded and are largely inextricable from.
- Research demonstrates the significant influence of the social and political context on individual psychological wellbeing and mental health.
- Counselling and psychotherapy professional ethics codes suggest that we should pay attention to the socio-political and ensure that our work enhances equality and fairness for those we work with.
- Our work as counsellors and psychotherapists can have political implications in challenging power structures: the personal is political.
- While historically an emphasis on the social and political has been at the margins in the psychotherapeutic fields, recent shifts towards acknowledging this in models and frameworks for therapeutic work are promising. However, we still have work to do if we wish to embrace a social justice agenda in actions as well as words.

INTRODUCTION

In an ecological sense, the social and political context refers to those systems in which an individual is embedded and from which an individual is mostly inseparable (Winter et al., 2016): things like our economic systems, our political climate in terms of, for example, electoral politics and policies, our education systems, healthcare, policing, and our family and community context (Bronfenbrenner, 1979). I think it is fair to say that we live in 'turbulent times' globally, and as I sat down to consider the opening section of this chapter on the social and political context of counselling and psychotherapy, hoping to outline and give examples of what we might mean by this context, I confess to initially finding myself a little stuck on where to start.

The climate and ecological crises are having significant impacts across the world, and this is only likely to increase over the coming years. Going back only 15 years or so, we experienced the global financial crisis of 2007/8, which saw numerous countries plunge into a subsequent period of recession, managed in many places with strict austerity policies and budget cuts for public services, which impacted those already marginalised in society the hardest. Furthermore, for many decades, wars have been ongoing across the globe, perhaps most notably in recent years those in Afghanistan, Iraq, Kurdistan, Lebanon, Palestine, Syria, and Ukraine. Since late 2019 and early 2020, the global Covid-19 pandemic has provided much of the backdrop to any discussion of our social and political climate, causing many deaths as well as short-term and long-term illness and disability, and significant disruption to daily lives and the functioning of societies, with the closure of schools, shops and reduced physical social contact for many. With this, we have seen an even bigger increase in what was already an increasing area of technology-mediated ways of both connecting/socialising and delivering healthcare, education, and services (such as counselling and psychotherapy). On a national level, at the time of writing, the 'cost of living crisis', connected to increased costs of food, gas and oil and, as a knock-on effect, most other products and services, and various political scandals at Westminster loom over the United Kingdom.

Interconnected with the broader issues described so far are those associated more closely with identity and what counsellors and psychotherapists have sometimes referred to as 'diversity and difference' (but see Lago, 2011, for a critique of how these terms might have been used). An emphasis on intersectionality and identity (Crenshaw, 1989: see also Turner, Chapter 2.1, this volume) is extremely important when looking at the social and political context. Indeed, this is considered in more depth in Part 2 of this volume. How we experience, and are impacted by, the social and political events and forces, such as the ones described above, will be influenced by, and is socially structured by, individual identity and experiences of oppression (Velez & Spencer, 2018), as is evident when we see the ways in which these crises disproportionately impact those already most marginalised and oppressed in our social structures. Racism, misogyny, homophobia, transphobia, ableism, and other prejudices all form part of our social and political context.

All these areas mentioned (and many not mentioned here too) form the backdrop to the daily work we do in counselling and psychotherapy. I hope to illustrate in this chapter why this context deserves more time and attention in mainstream publications and trainings in counselling and psychotherapy (though please note that this perspective is by no means new!). Furthermore, I aim to indicate in brief what a sufficient recognition of our social and political context might mean for the work of counsellors, psychotherapists, and allied professionals.

RELEVANCE FOR COUNSELLORS AND PSYCHOTHERAPISTS

CONNECTIONS BETWEEN THE SOCIO-POLITICAL CONTEXT AND WELLBEING

At a very basic level, significant amounts of research demonstrate the connection between all the aspects of the social and political climate mentioned above and our mental health and wellbeing, as well as many other areas not covered in this chapter. Researchers have begun to document the connection between the climate and ecological crises and individual psychological wellbeing and mental health, for example, by highlighting the prevalence and experience of climate change linked grief, anxiety, trauma, and worry (Panu, 2020; Sciberras & Fernando, 2022). The negative emotional and psychological impacts of poverty, inequality, and austerity politics have all been widely researched and reported. For example, on inequality, Wilkinson and Pickett, in their book *The Spirit Level*, outlined that mental health problems are much more common in more unequal societies

(Wilkinson & Pickett, 2009), and they followed this with a detailed examination of the connection between inequality and wellbeing in *The Inner Level* (Wilkinson & Pickett, 2019). Following the financial crisis in 2007/8 and subsequent implementation of austerity measures, researchers examined the impacts of this on individuals' wellbeing and concluded that austerity policies were related to feelings of humiliation and shame, fear and distrust, instability and insecurity, isolation and loneliness, and feelings of powerlessness and being trapped (McGrath et al., 2015). Research from several countries, including Ireland (Corcoran et al., 2015) and Greece (Branas et al., 2015), documented a correspondence between austerity-related events and suicides in the population. The psychological impacts of war, forced migration, having to leave your home and country and seek asylum or refuge elsewhere are well known and established (e.g., see Hajak et al., 2021; Summerfield, 2000). Recent research has evidenced the significant psychological impacts of the Covid-19 pandemic, for example in relation to the complex impacts of 'lockdown' (Sundarasen et al., 2020) and in relation to the psychological impacts of long-covid (Burton et al., 2022).

From this brief discussion, it is evident that a large amount of research and academic scholarship show the ways in which our social and political context can interact with and influences our experience of psychological wellbeing and mental health, which are of course core concerns for those in the field of counselling and psychotherapy.

ETHICAL, LEGAL AND PROFESSIONAL RESPONSIBILITIES

It might also be important for counsellors and psychotherapists to consider the social and political context because of our ethical and professional responsibilities. The British Association for Counselling and Psychotherapy's (BACP) *Ethical Framework* (BACP, 2018) outlines six Ethical Principles of Counselling and Psychotherapy. One of these is 'Justice,' which relates to 'the fair and impartial treatment of all clients and the provision of adequate services' (p. 9). This explicitly speaks of equality of opportunity, avoiding discrimination and ensuring a fair provision of counselling and psychotherapy services for all members of society. Similarly, the United Kingdom Council for Psychotherapy's (UKCP) *Ethical Principles and Code of Professional Conduct* (UKCP, 2019) speaks of 'social responsibility' and 'diversity and equalities' and psychotherapists are required to 'actively consider issues of diversity and equalities as these affect all aspects of your work' (p. 4) and must not allow prejudice to impact their relationships with clients. Statements can also be found in both the Health and Care Professions Council's (HCPC, 2016) and British Psychological Society's (BPS, 2021) ethical guidance documentation (see Winter, 2015, for a discussion of these issues in applied psychology ethical codes). Finally, counsellors and psychotherapists are required to consider their legal obligations in relation to the social and political context, and in particular in relation to equality. The Equality Act 2010 legally protects people from discrimination based on several 'protected characteristics', which relate to identity (age, disability, gender reassignment, marriage or civil partnership, pregnancy and maternity, race, religion or belief, sex, and sexual orientation). Clients might therefore be able to make complaints of discrimination under the Equality Act should issues arise in the service they receive.

THE PERSONAL IS POLITICAL

The final reason to highlight when considering the relevance of the social and political context of counselling and psychotherapy is summed up mostly straightforwardly in the well-known feminist activist phrase 'the personal is political'. This phrase has often been drawn upon in psychology and counselling (e.g., Milton, 2018; Winter, 2019), and is commonly attributed to Carol Hanisch (1970), who argued that personal problems are political problems and that the political can also be personal. This phrase, and what it means, has far broader implications and applications, but particularly of relevance to therapists and psychologists is that, Hanisch's focus was on women's therapy groups. Hanisch argued that women's therapy groups are often viewed as solely focused on individual wellbeing and therapeutic support, but in these spaces, the women were talking about problems rooted in politics, and the act of *the group itself was political*. In addition to the influence of the political context on individuals, counselling and psychotherapy have the potential to change power relations and to influence social and political structures, and thus the personal is political and the political can often be personal (Winter, 2019). Importantly, 'the personal is political' rests on a broader understanding of 'politics' as concerning power relations, rather than simply referring to traditional electoral politics (Hanisch, 2006; Winter et al., 2020).

SOCIAL JUSTICE, POWER, OPPRESSION AND STRUCTURALLY EMBEDDED ADVANTAGE

It is important to recognise that no discussion of the social and political context is complete without reference to issues of power, oppression, and structurally embedded advantage (or privilege, but see Abdi (2021) on language) in our society. A critical approach to counselling, psychotherapy, and psychology (which does just this) has a long history (Fox & Prilleltensky, 1997; Proctor et al., 2006; Smail, 1987). Counselling has been critiqued as taking an overly individualistic approach, reflected in our ways of working and models of therapy, which has all too often neglected the importance of wider social forces and therefore potentially helped to maintain inequalities and discrimination in our society (Smail, 1987). However, this critical view has historically often been on the margins, and such perspectives have not been widely integrated into counselling theory or core training approaches, despite even authors like Carl Rogers writing about the political implications of our work (Rogers, 1977). While many can acknowledge the obvious relevance of the social and the political to wellbeing and therapeutic work (as seen above), some have argued that we must try to avoid any significant impingement of the political into our work, which is a critique I touch briefly on below. More recently, however, a 'social justice agenda' has been developing momentum across these fields (Chung & Bemak, 2012; Cutts, 2013; Toporek et al., 2006). Social justice can be defined as being

> …both a goal of action and the process of action itself, which involves an emphasis on equity or equality for individuals in society in terms of access to a number of different resources and opportunities, the right to self-determination or autonomy and participation in decision-making, freedom from oppression, and a balancing of power across society. (Cutts, 2013: 9–10)

This sits alongside movements associated with decolonisation (Morgan, 2021) and liberation approaches to counselling and psychotherapy (Duran, Firehammer & Gonzalez, 2008). A social justice perspective relates to viewing individuals in their wider social and political contexts rather than in isolation. It encourages a consideration of the numerous potential social factors which might impact on individuals and trigger distress (rather than a consideration solely of the individual psychological factors). Importantly, it also urges practitioners to work towards *actively challenging and addressing inequality on micro (individual), meso (group or community) and macro (political and societal) levels* (Chung & Bemak, 2012; Winter et al., 2016). The call is to go beyond words and to acknowledge the social and political in all elements of our work.

SOCIAL JUSTICE AS POLITICAL

The values included in definitions of social justice, such as equality, democracy, and participation, are *normative* ideas, which, importantly, are translated into action through political systems. For example, (in)equality is put into practice and happens on various levels, most of which are structured by politics and politically driven systems. Different political systems and structures drive different levels and types of democracy, participation, and equality. I suggest that these normative ideas contained in definitions of social justice are therefore political, and social justice is therefore *necessarily* a political idea. It is clear, then, that different political opinions and ideologies will influence how different therapists understand and practise 'social justice'. Social justice is political. Nevertheless, social justice in counselling and psychotherapy, and acknowledging the social and political in our work, is fundamentally **not** about persuading clients to agree with our views on electoral politics, nor does it mean reducing everything to solely being about social or political factors. It simply means acknowledging their important role, and the social and political implications of the work that we are doing in the field.

CONCLUSION

I noted earlier in the chapter that approaches which take account of the social and political have largely been at the margins in counselling, psychotherapy, and psychology. These are, however, not new (e.g., see Proctor et al., 2006; Rogers; 1977; Smail, 1987) and in recent years we have seen some shifts towards approaches and models which are explicitly taking account of the social and political context in greater degrees. For example, the Power Threat Meaning Framework positions social and political power as vital to understanding clients' distress (Boyle & Johnstone, 2020); the pluralistic framework has encouraged us to consider the political (Cooper & McLeod, 2010); and authors writing from compassion-focused approaches have written about the psychological consequences of some of our political and social structures (Gilbert, 2018). These show a continuation of the discussions about politics and therapy, and a positive shift towards greater recognition of the importance of this. They provide some hope that counselling and psychotherapy can begin to embrace more socially just practices, supporting individuals' and community wellbeing through our work. However, this is still building, and we have a way to go before we can truly say that counselling and psychotherapy fully embrace the connections between our professions and the sociopolitical. Given the current social and political context outlined above, there is an urgent need for this.

REFERENCES

Abdi, M. (2021, June). Language is important: Why we are moving away from the terms 'allyship' and 'privilege' in our work. *MA Consultancy Ltd.* [Blog], accessed at https://ma-consultancy.co.uk/blog/language-is-important-why-we-will-no-longer-use-allyship-and-privilege-in-our-work

BACP (2018). *Ethical Framework for the Counselling Professions.* Rugby: British Association for Counselling and Psychotherapy.

Boyle, M. & Johnstone, L. (2020). *A Straight Talking Introduction to the Power Threat Meaning Framework: An Alternative to Psychiatric Diagnosis.* Ross-on-Wye: PCCS Books.

BPS (2021). *Code of Ethics and Conduct.* Guidance Published by the British Psychological Society. Leicester: British Psychological Society.

Branas, C.C, Kastanaki, A.E., Michalodimitrakis, M., Tzougas, J., Kranioti, E.F., Theodorakis, P.N., Carr, B.G. & Wiebe, D.J. (2015). The impact of economic austerity and prosperity events on suicide in Greece: a 30-year interrupted timeseries analysis. *BMJ Open*, 5(1), https://doi.org/10.1136/bmjopen-2014-005619

Bronfenbrenner, U. (1979). *The Ecology of Human Development: Experiments by Nature and Design.* Harvard University Press.

Burton, A., Aughterson, H., Fancourt, D. & Phillip, K.E.J. (2022). Factors shaping the mental health and wellbeing of people experiencing persistent COVID-19 symptoms or 'long COVID': qualitative study. *BJPsych Open*, 8(2), 1–8, https://doi.org/:10.1192/bjo.2022.38

Chung, R.C.-Y. & Bemak, F.P. (2012). *Social Justice Counseling: The Next Steps beyond Multiculturalism.* Thousand Oaks, CA: Sage.

Cooper, M. & McLeod, J. (2010). *Pluralistic Counselling and Psychotherapy.* London: Sage.

Corcoran, P., Griffin, E., Arensman, E., Fitzgerald, A.P. & Perry, I.J. (2015). Impact of the economic recession and subsequent austerity on suicide and self-harm in Ireland: An interrupted time series analysis. *International Journal of Epidemiology*, 44(3), 969–977, https://doi.org/10.1093/ije/dyv058

Crenshaw, K. (1989). Demarginalizing the intersection of race and sex: A Black feminist critique of antidiscrimination doctrine, feminist theory and antiracist politics. *University of Chicago Legal Forum*, 1(8), 139–167, accessed at https://chicagounbound.uchicago.edu/cgi/viewcontent.cgi?article=1052&context=uclf

Cutts, L.A. (2013). Considering a social justice agenda for counselling psychology in the United Kingdom. *Counselling Psychology Review*, 28(2), 8–16.

Duran, E., Firehammer, J. & Gonzalez, J. (2008). Liberation psychology as the path toward healing cultural soul wounds. *Journal of Counseling & Development*, 86(3), 288–295, https://doi.org/10.1002/j.1556-6678.2008.tb00511.x

Fox, D. & Prilleltensky, I. (Eds) (1997). *Critical Psychology: An Introduction.* London: Sage.

Gilbert, P. (2018). *Living Like Crazy* (2nd ed.). York: Anwyn House.

Hajak, V.L., Sardana, S., Verdeli, H. & Grimm, S. (2021). A systematic review of factors affecting mental health and well-being of asylum seekers and refugees in Germany. *Frontiers in Psychiatry*, https://doi.org/10.3389/fpsyt.2021.643704

Hanisch, C. (1970). *The personal is political.* In S. Firestone & A. Koedt (Eds.). Notes from the second year (pp. 76–78). New York, NY: Editors.

Hanisch, C. (2006). *The personal is political: The women's liberation movement classic with a new explanatory introduction*. Retrieved from www.carolhanisch.org/CHwritings/PIP.html 28th Sept. 2022

HCPC (2016). *Standards of Conduct, Performance and Ethics*. London: Health and Care Professions Council.

Lago, C. (2011). Diversity, oppression, and society: Implications for person-centered therapists. *Person-Centered & Experiential Psychotherapy*, 10(4), 235–247.

McGrath, L., Griffin, V., Mundy, E. & Psychologists for Social Change (2015). *The Psychological Impact of Austerity: A Briefing Paper*. UEL: Psychologists for Social Change. Accessed at https://repository.uel.ac.uk/item/856z6

Milton, M. (2018). *The Personal is Political: Stories of difference and psychotherapy*. London: Bloomsbury

Morgan, H. (2021). Decolonising psychotherapy: Racism and the psychoanalytic profession. *Psychoanalytic Psychotherapy*, 35(4), 412–428, https://doi.org/10.1080/02668734.2021.1990114

Panu, P. (2020). Anxiety and the ecological crisis: An analysis of eco-anxiety and climate anxiety. *Sustainability*, 12(19), 7836, https://doi.org/10.3390/su12197836

Proctor, G., Cooper, M., Sanders, P. & Malcolm, B. (2006). *Politicizing the Person-centred Approach: An Agenda for Social Change*. Ross-on-Wye: PCCS Books.

Rogers, C.R. (1977). *On Personal Power: Inner Strength and Its Revolutionary Impact*. London: Robinson.

Sciberras, E. & Fernando, J.W. (2022). Climate change-related worry among Australian adolescents: An eight-year longitudinal study. *Child and Adolescent Mental Health*, 27(1), 22–29.

Smail, D. (1987). *Taking Care: An Alternative to Therapy*. London: Constable.

Summerfield, D. (2000). War and mental health: A brief overview. *British Medical Journal*, 321, 232–235, https://doi.org/10.1136/bmj.321.7255.232

Sundarasen, S., Chinna, K., Kamaludin, K., Nurunnabi, M., Baloch, G.M., Khoshaim, H.B., Hossain, S.F.A. & Sukayt, A. (2020). Psychological impact of COVID-19 and lockdown among university students in Malaysia: Implications and policy recommendations. *International Journal of Environmental Research and Public Health*, 17(17), 6206, https://doi.org/10.3390/ijerph17176206

Torporek, R.L., Gerstein, L.H., Fouad, N.A., Roysircar, G. & Israel, T. (Eds) (2006). *Handbook for Social Justice in Counseling Psychology: Leadership, Vision, and Action*. London: Sage.

UKCP (2019). *Ethical Principles and Code of Professional Conduct*. London: United Kingdom Council for Psychotherapy.

Velez, G. & Spencer, M.B. (2018). Phenomenology and intersectionality: Using PVEST as a frame for adolescent identity formation amid intersecting ecological systems of inequality. *Child and Adolescent Development*, 161, 75–90, https://doi.org/10.1002/cad.20247

Wilkinson, R. & Pickett, K. (2009). *The Spirit Level: Why Equality is Better for Everyone*. London: Penguin.

Wilkinson, R. & Pickett, K. (2019). *The Inner Level: How More Equal Societies Reduce Stress, Restore Sanity, and Improve Everyone's Wellbeing*. London: Penguin.

Winter, L.A. (2015). The presence of social justice principles within professional and ethical guidelines in international psychology. *Psychotherapy and Politics International*, 13(1), 55–66.

Winter, L.A. (2019). Social justice and remembering 'the personal is political' in counselling and psychotherapy: So, what can therapists do? *Counselling and Psychotherapy Research*, 9(3), 179–181.

Winter, L.A., Burman, E., Hanley, T., Kalambouka, A. & McCoy, L. (2016). Education, welfare reform and psychological wellbeing: A critical psychology perspective. *British Journal of Educational Studies*, 64(4), 467–483, https://doi.org/10.1080/00071005.2016.1171823

Winter, L.A., Guo, F., Wilk, K. & Hanley, T. (2016). Difference and diversity in pluralistic therapy. In M. Cooper and W. Dryden (Eds), *The Handbook of Pluralistic Counselling and Psychotherapy*. London: Sage.

Winter, L.A., Hanley, T., Bragg, J., Burrell, K. & Lupton, R. (2020). 'Quiet activism in schools': Conceptualising the relationships between the personal, the political and the Political in education. *Cambridge Journal of Education*, 50(3), 391–408, https://doi.org/10.1080/0305764X.2019.1707511

> **RECOMMENDED READING**
>
> Chung, R.C.-Y. & Bemak, F.P. (2012). *Social Justice Counseling: The Next Steps beyond Multiculturalism.* Thousand Oaks, CA: Sage.
>
> This text comes from the counselling profession in the United States and gives a lovely applied introduction to the idea of social justice within counselling practice.
>
> Proctor, G., Cooper, M., Sanders, P. & Malcolm, B. (Eds.) (2006). *Politicizing the Person-centred Approach: An Agenda for Social Change.* Ross-on-Wye: PCCS Books.
>
> This collection from 2006 provides a great introduction to politics and social change in the person-centred field in particular.
>
> Winter, L.A. & Charura, D. (Forthcoming). *The Sage Handbook of Social Justice in the Psychological Therapies.* London: Sage.
>
> This text, due for publication later in 2023, provides a thorough introduction to social justice in psychology, counselling and psychotherapy in the UK, including providing clinical examples, theory and applied chapters and a range of perspectives from across the psychological professions.

1.3 WHAT DO PEOPLE COME TO COUNSELLING AND PSYCHOTHERAPY FOR?

TERRY HANLEY

OVERVIEW AND KEY POINTS

People attend counselling and psychotherapy for a wide variety of reasons. These vary from person to person and invariably mean that therapy will differ from relationship to relationship. In complicating things further, many therapeutic approaches, and the settings in which they are offered, have their own understanding of the purpose of therapy. As such, therapy can take on a multitude of forms and address a variety of goals. With this in mind, this chapter:

- provides a non-partisan range of therapeutic goals that people might have when they attend therapy.
- offers a reflection on how different theoretical models and approaches (such as those presented in Part 5 of this book) might influence the therapeutic work engaged in.
- offers a reflection on how different presenting issues (such as those presented in Part 4 of this book) might influence the therapeutic work engaged in.
- reflects upon how different organisational settings (e.g., those noted in Part 7 of this book) might influence the type of therapeutic work engaged in.

INTRODUCTION

Counselling and psychotherapy in the United Kingdom have developed organically and according to path dependency principles (Aldridge, 2011). Some critics have said they have flowed almost promiscuously into many areas of our lives, so that exactly what they are *for*, what their goals are, is not always clear. It is possible to state that the overall goal of therapy is to facilitate clients' own resourcefulness, insight, problem-solving capacities, happiness, and so on, but critics are entitled to question such global terms. As Sandler and Dreher (1996) convey well, it is far from clear to many psychoanalytic practitioners exactly what the legitimate scope and aims of their work are and should be. Freud himself expressed various aims for psychoanalysis at different times, such as symptom removal, making the unconscious conscious, restoring the capacity to love and work, helping clients to move from neurotic misery to ordinary unhappiness, and conducting research into the human psyche. Each of the contemporary 'schools' of therapy has its characteristic and sometimes conflicting aims – some being altogether wary of 'aim attachment' and some being explicitly goal-oriented and driven to reach and demonstrate successful outcomes. Currently, a broad distinction may be seen between short-term outcome-focused therapy (such as is found in Improving Access to Psychological Therapies (IAPT) programmes) and open-ended process-oriented therapy. Here we look at some of the range of actual and possible goals.

SUPPORT

The term 'supportive therapy' suggests that some clients may primarily need and benefit from a form of therapy that upholds current ego strength and/or coping skills and does not seek to challenge or uncover. Some may need long-term supportive therapy, while others require short-term support in crises. Support may be in the form of warm, non-judgemental listening and encouragement and, although most therapy does not become advocacy, on occasion supportive therapy or counselling may also lean in this direction. Such supportive work remains disciplined and professional and distinct from befriending or friendship. Its aim is to support the person through a difficult time and/or towards a position of independence or readiness for more challenging therapy.

PSYCHO-EDUCATIONAL GUIDANCE

A wide range of psychologically informed practices are to be found under this umbrella term. Appropriate information giving, administering of questionnaires, coaching, mentoring, provision of social skills, lifeskills training, assertiveness and relaxation training, marriage enrichment programmes, parent effectiveness training, relapse prevention programmes, stress inoculation training, emotional intelligence and positive psychology training are all examples. All aim to identify improvable behaviour and to teach personal skills in various areas of life. The goal is not to uncover presumed psychopathology, but to directly enhance cognitive, behavioural and interpersonal functioning, to assist clients in meeting developmental challenges and to equip them with concrete coping techniques and philosophies. Coaching, in particular, has grown in recent years.

ADJUSTMENT AND RESOURCE PROVISION

The idea that people may be helped simply to adjust to their circumstances has usually been severely criticised by counsellors and psychotherapists. However, it is probably a fact in at least some therapy settings (e.g., employee assistance programmes (EAPs)) that clients seek short-term adjustment-oriented help that may include elements of supportive therapy, problem-solving skills, assertiveness training, brainstorming solutions, *plus* the provision of contextual information (e.g., how an organisation works, how to complain about your boss harassing you, etc.) and other welfare-oriented information, such as that relating to welfare benefits, housing, childcare, pensions, etc. In such contexts, therapists may act *both* as non-directive facilitators *and* as providers of relevant information, and in some cases as brokers between individual client and organisations.

CRISIS INTERVENTION AND MANAGEMENT

These terms are used broadly here to include the intervention and support of professionals in the aftermath of large-scale (e.g., plane crash, bombing incident), small-group (e.g., bank raid) or personal disasters (e.g., road traffic accidents). Survivors and witnesses of critical incidents or breakdowns of many kinds are often offered immediate help, which includes debriefing, support, practical and active-directive help, referral to specialist resources, and gradual restoration of normal functioning. The aim is to provide sensitive, non-intrusive, psychologically strengthening help in the first instance, avoiding connotations of psychopathology. Crisis intervention is concerned primarily with restoration of the level of functioning that existed prior to the crisis.

PROBLEM SOLVING AND DECISION MAKING

For a certain proportion of clients, the purpose of entering counselling or psychotherapy is to examine a life situation or dilemma and come to a (probably quite early) resolution or decision. How to cope with nuisance neighbours and difficult relationships, whether to have a termination of pregnancy, when to retire and whether to live in sheltered accommodation, whether or not to have optional surgery, are some examples. The aim is to facilitate exploration of issues, feelings and practicalities; addressing anxiety and loss may be part of the process. In some approaches, a philosophy and techniques of problem solving may be imparted as a proactive tool for living.

SYMPTOM AMELIORATION

A symptom is a usually distressing or troublesome change of condition which manifests in a crisis, inability to function as normal, or apparently inexplicable somatic phenomena. A majority of people who seek or are referred to therapy for the first time want their symptoms to go away; they wish to return to their normal mode of functioning and self-image. Sometimes their goals are hazy or implicit; a depressed client may, for example, obviously want to be simply less (or not) depressed. Probably one of the greatest mismatches between clients' and (many) therapists' goals is that while the former seek symptom amelioration or elimination, the latter often have more ambitious agendas based on a belief in presenting problems as being merely the tip of an iceberg, as 'defence mechanisms' masking underlying, unconscious conflicts. Exceptions to this tend to be cognitive-behavioural therapists, whose main aim is the identification of problematic behaviour and its reduction or elimination in the most efficient time span; and practitioners who strive to respond to clients stated needs and stages of change (e.g., Burton, 1998; Hanley, Sefi and Ersahin, 2016).

INSIGHT AND UNDERSTANDING

Some clients, and many therapists, have as their primary goals the investigation of causes of problematic feelings, thoughts and behaviour. Both client and therapist may wish to pursue the search for historical causes and the reasons for persistently counterproductive behaviour in current life circumstances. ('Why did this happen to me? Why am I like this? *Aha! – now I see where this comes from.*') For some practitioners and clients, the goal of therapy may be the attainment of deeper and deeper insights or a state of continuous understanding of self, of how conflicts arise, of motivations, etc.

CURE

Almost all psychotherapists and counsellors avoid use of the term 'cure' and any client expectations that therapy will result in final and dramatic removal of suffering. This may be due to (1) clinical experience, as clients are very seldom dramatically, comprehensively or resolutely cured; (2) dislike of medical connotations, by which suffering and problems in living are not regarded as biological disturbances to be treated with medical interventions; or (3) resistance to engendering hopes of unrealistic outcomes (and perhaps the disappointment and even litigation that might accompany such expectations). However, at least one approach, primal therapy, conceptualises human problems in unitary terms as *neurosis* (a psychobiological state), for which it possesses *the cure*. Increasingly, too, the pressure from the evidence-based practice lobby and the influence of the National Institute for Health and Care Excellence (NICE) lead practitioners to speak explicitly in terms of specifically outcome-focused work.

SELF-ACTUALISATION

Under this heading may be included all aims towards becoming a better person, having greater self-awareness or self-knowledge, and attaining a state of fully functioning personhood. The range of goals subsumed here may include, for example, anything from 'I want to be more assertive/risk-taking/happy' to 'I want to try out everything life has to offer, I want to overcome all obstacles in my life and find the real me'. Concepts of individuation, maturation, finding the real self, being true to oneself and increasing self-awareness fit here. Most observers accept that the concept of an end-point – the fully functioning person – is somewhat mythical; self-actualisation suggests a continuous process, a valuing of the journey more than a need to reach a goal; and some are highly critical of this aim altogether (Weatherill, 2004).

PERSONALITY CHANGE

Eschewed by the more cognitive-behavioural and short-term approaches, hints at least of the possibility of quite far-reaching personality change are either found in or projected into certain forms of therapy. At an illusory level, the rather retiring, somewhat unattractive and untalented person may fantasise that therapy will compensatorily convert him or her into everything that he or she is not. However, a number of client claims and testimonies based on the dramatic disappearance of distressing symptoms or limitations ('Therapy completely changed/saved my life') have suggested major life changes as a desired outcome for some clients. Many, particularly humanistic, psychotherapists regard their work as 'life-transforming therapy'. This goal raises questions about the nature of the concept of 'personality' and what actually constitutes personality change.

DISCOVERY OF MEANING AND TRANSCENDENTAL EXPERIENCE

Particularly in the wake of the relative decline of formal religion and loss of spiritual and moral leaders and mentors, it seems that therapy has become for many an avenue for the exploration of existential, spiritual or metaphysical meaning and transcendental experience. The existential, humanistic and transpersonal approaches lend themselves most explicitly to such aspirations. This 'movement' has been gathering momentum in recent years and may well change the nature of at least some therapy practice (Moodley and West, 2015).

SYSTEMIC, ORGANISATIONAL OR SOCIAL CHANGE

In some forms of therapy, change within domestic partnerships, families, task groups and other groupings is clearly a goal. But counselling and psychotherapeutic skills as human relations skills (sometimes based on an understanding of unconscious conflicts, sometimes not) are also applied to conflict resolution within and between organisations. Experimentation with group counselling and therapy where more than a dozen or so participants are involved, and sometimes hundreds of members participate, has often had goals of conflict resolution and other aspects of social change.

CONCLUSION

It is important to note that the reason individuals attend therapy might also be reflected in the type of evaluation a service may look for (e.g., if an individual wants to feel less anxious, then reviewing this on an anxiety scale may seem logical). At times, however, the process of evaluation is set by the service and may not match so neatly with the client's wants or needs. These service goals are important to acknowledge, as they are often directly linked to funding, but they might compete with the opinions of the therapist or client (e.g., a service might exist to support people getting back to work, while it may be the workplace that is providing an individual significant difficulties). Such elements can take us back to what the purpose of therapy is in the first place. While TV programmes view it as a predominantly individualised activity, and counselling and psychotherapy can be criticised for this (Dryden and Feltham, 1992), it cannot be removed from the broader systems that it embedded. As such, individuals may find themselves in services that do not serve or meet their needs, and practitioners and services need to be mindful that mismatches can occur. In recent years, some organisations have seen the development of experts by experience groups (individuals who have used services) which sit alongside experts by profession (individuals who have been trained counselling and psychotherapy approaches and work for the services) to mediate some of the complexities here. Such groups help to create discussions between the way services are run and the way they are experienced by those seeking support from them. They are not a panacea by any means, but they may be helpful in sensitising services to important issues that might not otherwise be raised.

Finally, clients may change their goals over time, and the aims of therapy negotiated between therapist and client may change. It is not unusual for some clients to begin with modest goals and to find further, more ambitious or deeper aims to work on. It has been said that some therapists may be satisfied with the client *feeling better* as an aim, when a more enduring aim might be to *get better*. It has also to be remembered that the types of goal previously identified refer to avowed types of goal. We know that there are also 'shadow goals': some clients may wish to be in a 'sick role', to prove how incapable they are, to maintain a therapist's attention, etc.; some therapists may primarily wish to prove something to themselves, to hold power, to perpetuate a livelihood, to find vicarious intimacy. In spite of ethical codes or frameworks, requirements for training therapy, supervision and other safeguards, unhealthy covert goals cannot be eliminated altogether.

REFERENCES

Aldridge, S. (2011) Counselling: An Insecure Profession? *A Sociological and Historical Analysis*. Unpublished PhD thesis, University of Leicester.
Burton, M.V. (1998) *Psychotherapy, Counselling and Primary Health Care: Assessment for Brief or Longer-term Treatment*. Chichester: Wiley.
Dryden, W. and Feltham, C. (Eds) (1992) *Psychotherapy and its Discontents*. Buckingham: Open University Press.
Hanley, T., Sefi, A. and Ersahin, Z. (2016) From goals to tasks and methods. In M. Cooper and W. Dryden (Eds), *The Handbook of Pluralistic Counselling and Psychotherapy* (pp. 28–41). London: Sage.
Moodley, R. and West, W. (Eds) (2015) *Integrating Traditional Healing Practices into Counselling and Psychotherapy*. London: Sage.
Sandler, J. and Dreher, A.U. (1996) *What Do Psychoanalysts Want? The Problem of Aims in Psychoanalytic Therapy*. London: Routledge/Institute of Psycho-Analysis.
Weatherill, R. (2004) *Our Last Great Illusion: A Radical Psychoanalytic Critique of Therapy Culture*. Exeter: Academic.

RECOMMENDED READING

The websites of key organisations (e.g., the British Association for Counselling and Psychotherapy, the United Kingdom Council for Psychotherapy and the National Health Service) provide overviews of the type of issues people present with in counselling and psychotherapy. Many of these issues are also introduced in Part 4 of this text.

Feltham, C. (2010) *Critical Thinking in Counselling and Psychotherapy*. London: Sage.

A book that encourages counsellors and psychotherapists to critically reflect on all aspects of their work. This includes considering questions such as 'Are there limits to personal change in therapy?' and 'Does the client know best?'.

Hanley, T., Sefi, A. and Ersahin, Z. (2016) From goals to tasks and methods. In M. Cooper and W. Dryden (Eds), *The Handbook of Pluralistic Counselling and Psychotherapy* (pp. 28–41). London: Sage.

This chapter reflects upon how therapists might work with the different types of goal that clients present with. It specifically discusses how professionals might use the goals articulated by clients to guide the therapeutic approach adopted.

1.4 WHAT ARE THE TRAINING ROUTES IN COUNSELLING AND PSYCHOTHERAPY?

LAURA ANNE WINTER AND TERRY HANLEY

OVERVIEW AND KEY POINTS

This chapter provides a reflection on how individuals train in counselling and psychotherapy and considers the various possible routes and some of the issues to think about along the way. Counselling and psychotherapy are considered separately, with reference made to both the similarities and differences in the training routes, as well as a short mention of training in allied disciplines. The main points covered in the chapter are as follows:

- Starting training in any therapeutic field is a big decision and has significant implications which should be considered prior to starting a course. These include reflecting on your personal and emotional readiness, as well as considerations about how training and subsequent work in a therapeutic field will work in your life financially and in terms of the time required.
- Training in counselling can be done in a variety of settings, but increasingly takes place in universities on a full- or part-time basis. Courses usually incorporate both a professional and an academic training component and can be completed at undergraduate or postgraduate level.
- Training in psychotherapy is also completed in a variety of settings, and is typically done part-time over a number of years. Similar to counselling, this will usually involve completion of supervised therapeutic practice, personal therapy hours, theoretical training and academic assignments.
- Individuals might also choose to train in allied disciplines, for example counselling psychology, or as a Psychological Wellbeing Practitioner or High Intensity Cognitive Behaviour Therapist for the National Health Service Improving Access to Psychological Therapy (IAPT) Programme.

INTRODUCTION

BEFORE EMBARKING ON TRAINING

Beginning training in a new career is a big step, and becoming a counsellor or psychotherapist involves significant investment in terms of both time and money, as well as the emotional energy required. Reeves (2018) suggests that when considering beginning training in counselling or psychotherapy it may be useful to reflect on the following questions:

1. Does counselling or psychotherapy training fit into your existing set of skills or employment?
2. If not, are counselling and psychotherapy skills likely to enhance your work? If so, how?
3. Have you ever been a client for counselling or psychotherapy? If so, was this a positive experience (and what was particularly helpful)?
4. Have you ever thought of seeking counselling or psychotherapy for yourself but decided against it? If so, why?
5. Is there a danger that you are considering counselling or psychotherapy training instead of actually going to receive counselling or psychotherapy yourself?
6. Do you know what counselling and psychotherapy is? Have you done some research to find out more?
7. Are you at a point in your life where you want or need a change in direction? Have you thought that being a counsellor or psychotherapist would be 'worthwhile'?
8. Have you looked into the career prospects for counsellors and psychotherapists?
9. Do you understand the different types of counselling and psychotherapy, and have you thought about the ones that might interest you the most?

It is also important to spend some time considering any practical issues in making the decision about if and where to train in counselling or psychotherapy. For example, it is important to think about costs and how the training will be paid for, as well as managing how time can be managed if studying alongside work, family, or other commitments. Furthermore, many individuals find that they have a desire to become a 'therapist' or 'to help people' rather than having initial ambitions more specific than this. If this is the case, there are choices to be made about what specific therapeutic profession to train in, and further reflexive examination of your own motivations to train as a therapist are likely to be useful (and stand you in good stead going forward). The sections which follow give a brief introduction to training in counselling, psychotherapy and two allied professions in turn.

COUNSELLING TRAINING

Traditionally, counselling training was structured around several stages of development as a counsellor, and students studied at first at introduction, then at skills and finally diploma level in order to qualify. Training programmes were mostly found in Further Education (FE) establishments, independent providers and charities, or voluntary organisations. Increasingly, however, there has been a move to locate training programmes in Higher Education (HE) providers such as universities, and many courses moved to postgraduate level (either postgraduate diploma or Master's). Both of these training routes are still available, and there are also increasingly courses at undergraduate level based in HE. Further, there are options to complete undergraduate degrees which combine teaching on both 'psychology' as an academic discipline and practice in counselling skills (Smith, 2016). Reeves (2018: 31) suggests that the move towards degree or Master's level training in counselling represents a shift 'towards the professionalization of counselling'. He also raises the argument that increasing the academic requirements of training to be a counsellor may lose potentially talented therapists who have no academic background or ambition and some of the more relational quality at the core of counselling. However, some might argue that increasing the academic emphasis of training will increase the knowledge base and therefore skill of the counselling workforce. The shift towards university training may therefore be viewed as a positive or a negative thing, depending on who you speak to, but this clear change in training has significant implications for those wanting to become therapists. For example, the costs of training are likely to be much higher at university level. Training in counselling has typically been part-time over two or three years: structured across a day or evening per week, or at weekends. Some courses now run full-time, however, and undergraduate programmes are mostly full-time.

The particular content of the course will vary, as counselling programmes will adopt different core models of therapy: for example, some may be focused on a single approach such as the person-centred model (see Tudor – Chapter 5.20, this volume), while others may be focused on training individuals to be 'integrative' in their practice. Such courses typically use a particular integrative approach to harness the training, for example Egan's Skilled Helper Model (see Wosket and Jenkins – Chapter 5.27 this volume) or, more recently, McLeod and Cooper's Pluralistic Framework (Kupfer, McLeod and Cooper – Chapter 5.22, this volume). Most programmes, however, will include the following aspects.

THEORETICAL TRAINING

This will vary depending on the approach, but students will often be required to attend classes or seminars, and will need to engage in some self-directed study, such as reading books or articles on the theory behind the practice of counselling.

TRAINING IN THE PRACTICE OF COUNSELLING

This is typically done through observation of tutor-led demonstrations and triad work (Smith, 2016), where one student will act in the role of 'client', one as 'counsellor' and one as 'observer', often with the 'client' bringing real-life issues to consider. Practice training might also include working with actors, watching videos of 'experts' engaging in 'role play' scenarios, or working as a group to observe practice and provide feedback in 'fishbowl' scenarios.

SUPERVISED PLACEMENT WORK

Typically, counselling courses require that students complete 100 or 150 hours of supervised therapeutic practice. Placements can be located in various settings, including healthcare, education and the voluntary sector. These are almost always unpaid. Supervision of practice typically occurs at a set frequency/ratio to the client work, and aims to support the learning and development of the trainees' practice (see Creaner, Chapter 3.12, this volume, for more information on supervision).

PERSONAL DEVELOPMENT WORK

This varies across programmes but will often involve taking part in a 'personal development group' and engaging in your own personal therapy, as well as taking part in experiential group and self-reflexive activities on the course (Donati and Watts, 2005). You might be encouraged to keep a reflexive diary or log while you undertake your training.

ASSESSMENT

Assessment of work might include a mixture of academic written work, reflexive written work, write-ups of case work with clients, videoed skills work with peers, or feedback from placement supervisors. In addition to the four areas noted above, courses which are completed at postgraduate level will typically involve conducting a research project in the final year (see Hanley, Lennie and West (2013) for an introductory research text which includes examples of students' experiences of research).

A final consideration to note is whether or not the programme is 'accredited', and if so, with which professional organisation. In the UK, organisations such as the British Association for Counselling and Psychotherapy (BACP), the United Kingdom Council for Psychotherapy (UKCP), Counselling and Psychotherapy in Scotland (COSCA) or the British Association for Behavioural and Cognitive Psychotherapy (BABCP) all accredit training courses. Accreditation means that the organisation has deemed that the course meets their requirements in terms of curriculum and training.

PSYCHOTHERAPY TRAINING

There are many similarities between counselling training and training in psychotherapy, and therefore much of what was said above applies here. For example, psychotherapy training courses will involve teaching in theory, training in the practice of psychotherapy, and will include both supervised placement work and personal development work of some kind. Training in psychotherapy will usually involve completing a significantly greater number of hours of personal therapy (which necessarily comes with increased costs). Often training in psychotherapy is a longer process than in counselling, and courses will take four years or more. In contrast to counselling, there are fewer psychotherapy training programmes in the UK. Similarly, though, they are provided by a range of organisations, including privately owned providers, or FE/HE institutions. It also operates typically on a part-time basis and can sometimes be quite flexible in terms of students being able to plan their own learning. Therefore, training can sometimes take much longer than structured programmes based in HE, but can also fit around other commitments perhaps more easily.

All psychotherapy training in the UK is affiliated to a college of the UKCP. These colleges vary in terms of their model of therapy (e.g., there is a college for 'Humanistic and Integrative Psychotherapy' and one for 'Family, Couple and Systemic Therapists'). Therefore, just as with counselling training, those interested in training in psychotherapy have an initial decision of what model of therapy they wish to be trained to deliver. Interested readers are referred to Part 5 of this book which gives a brief introduction to a wide range of therapeutic theories and models.

TRAINING IN ALLIED PROFESSIONS

Outside the specific disciplines of counselling and psychotherapy, there are a number of 'allied professions' which involve similar work. Two of these are briefly discussed here.

Many individuals in England are now training as psychological therapists within the National Health Service Improving Access to Psychological Therapy Programme (IAPT). IAPT is a government-funded initiative which aims to respond to the need for greater access for talking therapies for common mental health problems in order to improve people's wellbeing and reduce the costs of poor wellbeing (Clark, 2012). As well as employing some counsellors to provide humanistic counselling (see Winter and Hanley – Chapter 1.5, this volume), IAPT has their own training path for 'Psychological Wellbeing Practitioners' (PWPs) and 'High Intensity Cognitive Behavioural Therapists'. Training programmes are run at various UK universities and students' time is split between teaching at the university and time on supervised placements. The training for PWPs is focused on providing cognitive-behavioural interventions for individuals who are diagnosed with anxiety or depression and are typically classed as having a 'mild to moderate' presentation. Qualified High Intensity CBT therapists provide interventions for individuals who are classed as having moderate to severe anxiety or depression. The training for both roles involves one-year postgraduate diplomas, and you will need to qualify and work as a PWP prior to progressing to the High Intensity CBT course.

The profession of 'counselling psychology' is a branch of applied psychology which combines the fields of psychology and counselling, and thus tries to bring together ideas about the use of scientific research as applied to practice (from psychology) and the emphasis on humanistic values and viewing the individual in a holistic way (from counselling) (Hanley, Sefi, Cutts and Lennie, 2013). Woolfe (2016: 6) reflects on the difference between counselling and psychotherapy and counselling psychology and describes it as a '…minefield of complexity. The difference between these two activities, if it exists, is not at all clear'. Nevertheless, an important difference exists between training pathways. In order to become a qualified counselling psychologist you need to have an academic background in psychology, a requirement which is typically met by an undergraduate degree in Psychology accredited by the British Psychological Society (BPS), or a postgraduate conversion programme if your first degree wasn't in Psychology. You will then need to train to doctorate level or its equivalent in counselling psychology (Jones Nielson and Nicholas, 2016). This is typically a three-year, full-time route, or a longer part-time programme based in a HE institution, which involves completing a doctoral level research project as well as training in counselling psychology theory and practice. Courses also require that trainees engage in personal development, similar to courses in counselling and psychotherapy. Programmes need to be accredited by the Health and Care Professions Council in order that graduates can use the protected title of 'counselling psychologist', and they are also often accredited by the BPS. An alternative training path run by the BPS is possible, called the 'Qualification in Counselling Psychology' (QCoP) (see Galbraith, 2016).

CONCLUSION

This chapter has given a brief introduction to the large area of training in counselling and psychotherapy. Training in a therapeutic field can be time-consuming and emotionally draining, and requires both a personal and a professional commitment. Training is often very busy and can be quite difficult, as you are required to develop your skills and knowledge in theory and practice, all alongside developing on a personal level (and sometimes doing research too!). Alongside all this work, hopefully training in counselling and psychotherapy is a rewarding process which leads to qualification and then satisfaction in subsequent employment!

REFERENCES

Clark, D.M. (2012). The English Improving Access to Psychological Therapies (IAPT) Program: history and progress. In R.K. McHugh and D.H. Barlow (Eds), *Dissemination and Implementation of Evidence-based Psychological Interventions* (pp. 61–77). Oxford: Oxford University Press.

Donati, M. and Watts, M. (2005). Personal development in counsellor training: towards a clarification of inter-related concepts. *British Journal of Guidance and Counselling*, 33(4), 475–484.

Galbraith, V.E. (2016). Engaging with academia and training programmes. In B. Douglas, R. Woolfe, S. Strawbridge, E. Kasket and V. Galbraith (Eds), *The Handbook of Counselling Psychology* (4th ed., pp. 74–92). London: Sage.

Hanley, T., Lennie, C. and West, W. (2013). *Introducing Counselling and Psychotherapy Research*. London: Sage.

Hanley, T., Sefi, A., Cutts, L. and Lennie, C. (2013). Historical context. In T. Hanley, N. Humphrey and C. Lennie (Eds), *Adolescent Counselling Psychology: Theory, Research and Practice*. London: Routledge.

Jones Nielson, J.D. and Nicholas, H. (2016). Counselling psychology in the United Kingdom. *Counselling Psychology Quarterly*, 29(2), 206–215.

Reeves, A. (2018). *An Introduction to Counselling and Psychotherapy: From Theory to Practice* (2nd ed.). London: Sage.

Smith, K. (2016). Learning from triads: training undergraduates in counselling skills. *Counselling and Psychotherapy Research*, *16*(2), 123–131.

Woolfe, R. (2016). Mapping the world of helping: the place of counselling psychology. In B. Douglas, R. Woolfe, S. Strawbridge, E. Kasket and V. Galbraith (Eds), *The Handbook of Counselling Psychology* (4th ed., pp. 5–19). London: Sage.

RECOMMENDED READING

Each of the major professional counselling and psychotherapy organisations has syllabi that courses need to comply with to retain continued accreditation. These can be found on the different organisations' websites (e.g., the BACP at www.bacp.co.uk, the UKCP at www.psychotherapy.org.uk). Similar documents can be found for those working in IAPT services (developed by the NHS) and counselling psychologists (developed by the HCPC and BPS). These documents, although not riveting reads, provide a useful overview of what programmes cover.

Bor, R. and Watts, M. (2017). *The Trainee Handbook: A Guide for Counselling and Psychotherapy trainees* (4th ed). London: Sage.

1.5 WHERE DO COUNSELLORS AND PSYCHOTHERAPISTS WORK?

LAURA ANNE WINTER AND TERRY HANLEY

OVERVIEW AND KEY POINTS

In the final chapter in this section we address the question 'where do counsellors and psychotherapists work?' In doing so, we provide a brief background and some context to employment options in counselling and psychotherapy. We discuss several *potential* areas for work, including voluntary agencies, educational settings, the National Health Service (NHS), private practice and workplace settings. Please note that this only covers a small number of areas of potential work. See Section 7 of this volume for contributions on additional areas, such as working in forensic settings. The key points covered within the chapter are as follows:

- Counsellors and psychotherapists find employment in a variety of settings and often will have several different roles rather than one single role as a therapist.

- Areas of growth in terms of employment in counselling and psychotherapy include educational and workplace settings.
- A large proportion of counsellors and psychotherapists in the UK work in the NHS, including within Improving Access to Psychological Therapies (IAPT) services.
- Seeing clients in private practice continues to be a common element of the workload of a counsellor or psychotherapist.

INTRODUCTION

In this chapter we take a brief look at the types of potential employment for those developing a career in counselling. We have chosen to include this section because the subject of employment, although of obvious interest to both those wishing to enter the profession and those already trained, is often not touched upon in textbooks. It is perhaps an open secret that, despite the huge growth of interest in counselling and therapy and the expansion of their training markets, it remains the case that relatively few full-time, paid jobs exist.

It has been variously estimated that the UK counselling workforce may be up to 70,000 or even that employees using counselling skills make up about 1.7% of total employment (half a million workers) (Aldridge, 2011). The British Association for Counselling and Psychotherapy has approximately 57,000 members at the time of writing and the United Kingdom Council for Psychotherapy (UKCP) has roughly 10,000 members. In 2020 (just before the beginning of the Covid-19 pandemic), UKCP conducted a survey of their membership and found that the majority (85%) worked in private practice, and that most members worked part-time as a psychotherapist or psychotherapeutic counsellor (58% worked 20 hours or less per week) (UKCP, 2020). Similarly, in 2021, the BACP conducted an Employment Survey with 2,857 respondents from their membership and found that of the qualified, registered respondents, 34.3% worked some unpaid hours each week and only 34.7% of respondents agreed that they could earn a living from their counselling work. The most common role reported was working in private practice, the third sector, or in an educational setting. Those respondents who had the highest number of paid hours per week were those who were in workplace settings, NHS IAPT services, universities, or secondary schools (BACP, 2021).

The reasons for this mixed picture of employment are not easy to specify but no doubt include: (1) the fact that much counselling stems from and remains attached to the voluntary sector and a great deal of counselling is still provided as an unpaid service (indeed, respondents reporting the lowest number of paid hours in the BACP survey were those working in the third sector); (2) the continuing emergence of counselling and therapy as valid and evidence-based forms of professional service deserving of some but limited statutory funding; and (3) their relatively 'soft' image in competition with the work of, for example, psychiatrists (Gask, 2004) and clinical psychologists (Cheshire and Pilgrim, 2004), and the feeling of being undervalued as professionals in for example NHS settings (Ryan, Duncan and Moller, 2019).

Alongside the number of relatively few full-time paid jobs, as reflected in the UKCP and BACP surveys, there are of course patterns of part-time and sessional (hourly paid) opportunities, private practice, counselling/therapy-related work (e.g., supervision, training/lecturing, consultancy, writing) and the use of counselling and therapeutic skills in other roles (e.g., social work, mentoring). Indeed, there is a growing literature on the use of counselling skills in professions outside counselling (McLeod and McLeod, 2015). In the sections which follow we discuss several specific areas of work for counsellors and psychotherapists.

VOLUNTARY AGENCIES AND THIRD SECTOR SETTINGS

These settings include those national organisations, such as Relate, Samaritans, Cruse, Kooth, Victim Support, Mind, and Turning Point, as well as local third-sector or charitable/voluntary agencies. Provision of local women's therapy centres, rape crisis centres, HIV/AIDS agencies, and family-oriented drug- and alcohol-related services is widespread. Many of these rely on a mixture of statutory funding, voluntary fundraising and donations. Some will concentrate on a specific client group – for example, there are agencies supporting those who have been impacted by cancer, or individuals with eating disorders – while others will have a more generic or broad remit for their work. Voluntary agencies and third-sector organisations often employ counsellors and psychotherapists in a mixture of voluntary and paid positions. The services are sometimes offered free at the point of access, or on a donation or sliding scale of fees basis. Typically, services will now offer a mixture of online, telephone and face-to-face individual or group support. Therefore, the work is not always purely or solely counselling or psychotherapy, but may include telephone helplines, befriending, advocacy, information, and advice giving, awareness raising, and so on.

EDUCATIONAL SETTINGS

Schools, further and higher education and special educational projects are some of the longest-established settings in which forms of counselling and therapy take place. Primary and secondary schools in the UK offer counselling services, although not consistently. The provision varies across the UK, with Wales and Northern Ireland presently committed to having counsellors in all secondary schools and England and Scotland having between 61% and 85% counsellors in schools (Hanley, Noble and Toor, 2017).

There is a developing interest in school-based counselling and opportunities for employment, as well as a large amount of research focused on evaluating the effectiveness of the services on students' psychological wellbeing and educational outcomes (Cooper, 2013; Cooper et al., 2021), and the experience of young people in such settings (Knight, Gibson and Cartwright, 2018), as well as their parents and carers (Longhurst et al., 2021). With recent UK government reports highlighting the need for mental health support and integrated services in education (Carter, 2015; Department of Health, 2015), this is a trend which, at least in the short term, is likely to increase. In addition to specific counselling services, schools also continue to offer therapeutic work and pastoral support by educational psychologists, behaviour support workers, mentors and teachers (for a discussion of working as a therapist in schools, see Baram – Chapter 7.1, this volume).

Counsellors and psychotherapists also work in Further Education (FE) and Higher Education (HE) settings. This is an example of a setting in which counselling has been offered successfully for decades. In the transitional and vulnerable period between adolescence and adulthood, issues of career uncertainty, susceptibility to emotional, interpersonal and sexual problems, drugs and alcohol, homesickness, and educational and financial pressures require sensitive help. Student counsellors may have relatively high caseloads of self-referred clients presenting a wide range of personal concerns. Turnover is often high since the work is often crisis-oriented and determined by the pressures of the academic calendar. However, student counsellors work in one of the few areas with a relatively good, clear structure of pay, working conditions and progression prospects (see also Amis – Chapter 7.2, this volume).

COUNSELLING IN THE NATIONAL HEALTH SERVICE (NHS)

Counsellors and psychotherapists might be employed in a variety of settings in the NHS, including:

- Primary care, where a single professional is responsible for the care of the individual, for example in General Practice (GP) surgeries, or dedicated mental health primary care settings (see also Ali and Panesar – Chapter 7.6, this volume).
- Specialist services, for example services directed specifically at women or men, at people with specific physical health problems, or with a dual diagnosis of a mental health disorder and a drug or alcohol dependency.
- Secondary care, where a team of professionals is responsible for the care of the individual, for example in community mental health teams or inpatient services.
- Improving Access to Psychological Therapy (IAPT) services. This is a government-funded initiative in England which started in 2008, initially serving only adults, and then extended to include a children and adolescent service in 2010. This initiative aimed to respond to the need for greater access for talking therapies for common mental health problems in order to improve people's wellbeing and reduce the costs of poor wellbeing (such as welfare benefits and medical costs) (Clark, 2012). IAPT employs the equivalent of just over 5,500 full-time therapists to work within a 'stepped care' system implementing evidence-based psychological therapies recommended by the National Institute for Health and Care Excellence (NICE) for common mental health problems, such as depression and anxiety (Improving Access to Psychological Therapies, 2015). Counsellors and psychotherapists are often found at step 2 or 3 of IAPT services, offering low- or high-intensity Cognitive Behavioural Therapy (CBT) or humanistic counselling.

In recent years the NHS has undergone significant changes as a result of political forces, initially since the 2010–15 Coalition Government of Conservatives and Liberal Democrats and subsequent Conservative Government. More recently, it has been significantly impacted throughout the Covid-19 pandemic. Often NHS services are now provided by non-statutory providers, such as private health care companies and third-sector organisations which compete to win the contracts for services. Furthermore, given the climate of 'austerity' in the UK, and the impacts of the Covid-19 pandemic, the cost-of-living crisis and the turbulent economic and social climate globally, there have been significant cuts to health services, which necessarily impacts the potential for employment in the sector.

PRIVATE PRACTICE

Private practice is traditionally the location for most long-term counselling and psychotherapy and is based typically in practitioners' own homes, and sometimes in purpose-rented offices and group premises (see also Williams – Chapter 7.5, this volume). Increasingly, private practice is also occurring (as with many counselling and psychotherapy services in all the areas discussed in this chapter) remotely via telephone or video-conferencing software (see Chapters 6.7, 6.8, 6.9 and 6.10, this volume, on therapy and technology). North American texts have been issuing warnings for some years that this is the practice sector most under threat from 'managed care' and from consumers' greater sophistication, awareness of outcome research and precarious personal finances. On the other hand, some now believe that NHS waiting lists, time-limited and often CBT-oriented treatment may encourage more people to use the services of independent practitioners. Small private practices probably compose an element of many counsellors' and psychotherapists' workloads, quite typically supplementing part-time incomes in other settings (Clark, 2002; Syme, 1994; Thistle, 1998). Apostolopoulou (2013) reflects on the tensions raised by countries' economic problems for counsellors and psychotherapists in private practice, noting that while psychological distress and need may have increased, people's ability to pay for therapy may have decreased.

EMPLOYEE COUNSELLING IN THE WORKPLACE

Increasingly, the workplace has been the site of developments in counselling and opportunities for employment (see also Conn and Patel – Chapter 7.8, this volume). Employee counselling, established in the USA for decades, has also grown considerably in Britain. Just as student retention is one of the motives behind provision of student counselling, so prevention of absenteeism is a motive behind employee counselling services. The therapy provided is typically short-term and time-limited. Employers' concerns include drug and alcohol abuse, stress at work, employee relations, management of change, redundancy, accidents in the workplace, etc. Many large companies provide their own in-house counselling and coaching provision, sometimes as part of occupational health; some refer out to individual counsellors or group practices; many contract the services of external employee assistance programme (EAP) providers. These EAP providers are private companies that will manage the counselling service for the organisation by receiving referrals and providing therapists to conduct assessments and therapeutic interventions. A systematic review of the research literature indicated that counselling in the workplace is generally effective at reducing psychological distress and has a significant impact on absence from work (McLeod, 2010). It did, however, note several methodological weaknesses in the research synthesised. A more recent systematic review similarly reported that workplace counselling enhanced both employees' levels of 'functioning' and increased attendance at work (Joseph, Walker and Fuller-Tyszkiewicz, 2018).

CONCLUSION

It is clear that such a short chapter can only provide an introduction to answering the question 'where do counsellors and psychotherapists work?' In addition to the settings mentioned above, therapy may be offered in a range of further statutory services, such as social and probation services, police services and prisons; private health care organisations; and religious and pastoral organisations, e.g., Jewish Care's Shalvata (Holocaust Survivors' Centre), Catholic Marriage Advisory Centres, etc. As mentioned earlier, while relatively few full-time salaried posts exist, many of these offer reasonable pay levels. Some statutory employers pay well, and EAP providers – where they offer more than occasional sessional (hourly) work – can offer relatively high remuneration. Otherwise, pecuniary rewards run from nothing (particularly for trainees and those working as volunteers in community agencies) to modest hourly pay, to average wages for caring professionals. In private practice, some practitioners have been known to generate quite high incomes, but a trend towards a probable relative decline in clients being seen predictably from twice to five times a week (as in traditional psychoanalysis) for some years, and the growth in short-term therapies, is likely to undercut high incomes for all but a very few. As can be seen from this chapter, however, there are significant opportunities for counsellors and psychotherapists in a range of diverse settings. These opportunities and settings will undoubtedly shift over time and new avenues will open up alongside some possibilities narrowing.

REFERENCES

Aldridge, S. (2011). *Counselling: An Insecure Profession? A Sociological and Historical Analysis*. Unpublished PhD thesis, University of Leicester.

Apostolopoulou, A. (2013). The impact of the economic crisis on the private practice of counselling and psychotherapy: how much are clients and therapists 'worth'? *European Journal of Psychotherapy & Counselling*, *15*(4), 311–329. https://doi.org/10.1080/13642537.2013.849274

BACP (2021). *Mapping the Workforce*. Rugby: British Association of Counselling and Psychotherapy. Accessed at https://www.bacp.co.uk/bacp-journals/therapy-today/2021/october-2021/mapping-the-workforce/

Carter, A. (2015). *Carter Review of Initial Teacher Training (ITT)*. London: Department for Education.

Cheshire, K. and Pilgrim, D. (2004). *A Short Introduction to Clinical Psychology*. London: Sage.

Clark, D.M. (2012). The English Improving Access to Psychological Therapies (IAPT) Program: history and progress. In R.K. McHugh and D.H. Barlow (Eds), *Dissemination and Implementation of Evidence-based Psychological Interventions* (pp. 61–77). Oxford: Oxford University Press.

Clark, J. (Ed.) (2002). *Freelance Counselling and Psychotherapy*. London: Brunner-Routledge.

Cooper, M. (2013). *School-based Counselling in UK Secondary Schools: A Review and Critical Evaluation*. Glasgow: University of Strathclyde.

Cooper, M., Stafford, M.R., Saxon, D., Beecham, J., Bonin, E., Barkham, M., Bower, P., Cromarty, K., Duncan, C., Pearce, P., Rameswari, T. and Ryan, G. (2021). Humanistic counselling plus pastoral care as usual versus pastoral care as usual for the treatment of psychological distress in adolescents in UK state schools (ETHOS): a randomised controlled trial. *The Lancet Child & Adolescent Health*, *5*(3), 178–189, https://doi.org/10.1016/S2352-4642(20)30363-1

Department of Health (2015). *Future in Mind: Promoting, Protecting and Improving Our Children and Young People's Mental Health and Wellbeing*. London: NHS England.

Gask, L. (2004). *A Short Introduction to Psychiatry*. London: Sage.

Hanley, T., Noble, J. and Toor, N. (2017). Policy, policy research on school-based counseling in United Kingdom. In J. Carey, B. Harris, S.M. Lee and J. Mushaandja (Eds), *International Handbook for Policy Research in School-Based Counseling*. Cham, Switzerland: Springer.

Improving Access to Psychological Therapies (2015). *2014 Adult IAPT Workforce Census Report*. Accessed at www.iapt.nhs.uk/silo/files/2014-adult-iapt-workforce-census-report.pdf

Joseph, B., Walker, A. and Fuller-Tyszkiewicz (2018). Evaluating the effectiveness of employee assistance programmes: a systematic review. *European Journal of Work and Organizational Psychology*, *27*(1), 1–15, https://doi.org/10.1080/1359432X.2017.1374245

Knight, K., Gibson, K. and Cartwright, C. (2018). 'It's like a refuge': young people's relationships with school counsellors. *Counselling and Psychotherapy Research*, *18*(4), 377–386, https://doi.org/10.1002/capr.12186

Longhurst, P., Sumner, A.L., Smith, S., Eilenberg, J., Duncan, C. and Cooper, M. (2021). 'They need somebody to talk to': Parents' and carers' perceptions of school-based humanistic counselling. *Counselling and Psychotherapy Research*, early online publication, https://doi.org/10.1002/capr.12496

McLeod, J. (2010). The effectiveness of workplace counselling: a systematic review. *Counselling and Psychotherapy Research*, *10*(4), 238–248. https://doi.org/10.1080/14733145.2010.485688

(Continued)

(Continued)

McLeod, J. and McLeod, J (2015). Research on embedded counselling: an emerging topic of potential importance for the future of counselling psychology. *Counselling Psychology Quarterly*, *28*(1), 27–43. https://doi.org/10.1080/09515070.2014.942774

Ryan, G., Duncan, C. and Moller, N.P. (2019). Counsellors in the National Health Service: a mixed-method study of efficacy and satisfaction from the counsellor perspective. *Counselling and Psychotherapy Research*, *19*(3), 338–348, https://doi.org/10.1002/capr.12221

Syme, G. (1994). *Counselling in Independent Practice*. Buckingham: Open University Press.

Thistle, R. (1998). *Counselling and Psychotherapy in Private Practice*. London: Sage.

UKCP (2020). *A Snapshot of How Our Members Work*. London: United Kingdom Council of Psychotherapy. Accessed at www.psychotherapy.org.uk/news/a-snapshot-of-how-our-members-work/

RECOMMENDED READING

See Part 7 of this handbook. This section provides introductions to a wide range of therapeutic contexts. It has numerous chapters that explicitly look at the different settings in which therapists might find themselves working.

The jobs pages on the websites associated with the major professional organisations (e.g., the BACP, UKCP and BPS). Each of these regularly provides updated postings of jobs available to counsellors, psychotherapists and psychologists. Reviewing these, and the specifications related to the different roles, can be incredibly helpful in gaining a view of the employment landscape for therapists.

McLeod, J. and McLeod, Julia (2015). Research on embedded counselling: an emerging topic of potential importance for the future of counselling psychology. *Counselling Psychology Quarterly*, *28*(1), 27–43.

This is an interesting and useful paper reflecting on the developing use of counselling skills by professions outside counselling and psychotherapy.

PART II

SOCIAL JUSTICE AND INTERSECTIONALITY

2.1 INTERSECTIONALITY, POWER AND PRIVILEGE

DWIGHT TURNER

OVERVIEW AND KEY POINTS

Intersectional approaches to difference, privilege, supremacy, and otherness are relatively new to the field of counselling and psychotherapy. That said, this introductory chapter to this section is therefore designed to offer the reader some of the basic ideas and theories that sit behind such an approach to understanding issues of power in the counselling and psychotherapy framework.

To approach this topic in as brief and yet as comprehensive a way as possible, it is therefore necessary to present the reader with a number of bullet points to provide direction for this chapter. The chapter will cover:

- the origins of intersectionality.
- understanding intersectional identity within a counselling and psychotherapy framework.
- ways of working with power dynamics in the counselling and psychotherapy arena.
- criticisms of intersectionality.
- ideas for further reading and research on intersectional identity.

INTRODUCTION

'Intersectionality' is a term coined by a number of black feminist theorists under the third wave of feminism from the 1970s and 1980s. A term solidified by Kimberley Crenshaw, Patricia Hill Collins, and a number of other theorists of colour, the idea which sits behind intersectionality is that one does not hold a singular identity at any given moment in time, but what we are ultimately is a number of different identities, some of which offer us a sense of privilege, some of which may lead us to feel marginalised and an outsider (Cho et al., 2013; Collins, 2019; Collins & Bilge, 2016; Crenshaw, n.d.).

According to Crenshaw, her ideas around intersectionality came out of the legal field, where she recognised that black women were liable to be discriminated against, not just because they were black and not just because they were women, but because they were black women, and that the legal framework of the day had no real understanding of how to work with both identities concurrently when considering issues of discrimination.

The idea has grown considerably since then. Audre Lorde (1984a, 1984b) clearly stated in one of her seminal works that we do not lead single issue lives, her perspective clearly being intersectional in its positioning of identity as being multi-faceted and multi-layered. An intersectional approach, according to Patricia Hills Collins (2008), the idea that we hold a number of intersecting identities which might mark us out to be an outsider, also has to include the idea that there are numerous ways in which one may feel or be oppressed. Collins recognised that the patriarchy, white supremacy and capitalism were a triumvirate of socially constructed ways of being that may lead an individual or a group to feel oppressed based upon their gender, sexuality, class, race, culture, disability or age or any other factor.

As we can see from this very simple beginning of Crenshaw's (n.d.) work, broadening this out to an idea where any one of us may hold multiple forms of identity recognises that actually difference and diversity and otherness are very complex creations and are far more nuanced than the legalese used in the global north. For example, whereas the Equalities Act of 2010 in the United Kingdom recognises that there are nine protected characteristics, it too takes a semi-intersectional approach when touching on, for example, issues of racism, where the Act recognises that for racism to exist one has to be marginalised on the basis of not one but two and possibly more intersecting characteristics, for example being seen as a British Jew, a Romany gypsy, a British Jamaican. The fact that these are not just singular, but multiple, characteristics, recognises a gentle intersectionality in understanding these ideas.

INTERSECTIONALITY AND THE OTHER

Explorations of otherness from an intersectional lens then allow us to recognise the idea that some of the identities that we all hold will mark us out as the other. For example, my own identity as a black male from an Afro-Caribbean background means that I have often had to walk as the other in a culture which is predominantly white European. Readers of this chapter may have their own experience of being the other, be it through their gender, their sexuality, their age, their religion, their size, their ability, or some other facet that culture has socially determined marks them out as an outsider. Given that, as previously mentioned, identity is multi-faceted, the sense that we are all an other in some way then becomes quite obvious to observe. Otherness is therefore nothing to be afraid of; it is a key facet of all out identities, and although our experience of otherness may be determined either from an early age or via the lens of our workplace or our social situation, the idea that we will all phenomenologically experience moments of being an outsider means that this is a common experience when we consider the social construction of identity.

INTERSECTIONALITY AND PRIVILEGE

Within common parlance, privilege is seen as something negative. The idea that while men should give up their privilege or that the wealthy should pay more tax because they have the privilege to do so, actually places privilege as something which the other does not have. To recognise the folly in these ideas, one also has to go back to the idea of a collective construction of identities, where some identities are actually going to hold privilege. Returning to my own simplistic example, the idea that I am male gives me a certain privilege as a man within a westernised patriarchal culture. As an academic writing this chapter, there is an intellectual or an elitism that I am party to, hence my being invited to write a chapter for this tome.

Privilege can also sit within the fact that somebody is upper class, white, a patriarch within their culture or religion, able-bodied, young, fertile – ideas that culture has decided mark us out as being worthy of attention and status. The fact that just some of these will resonate with the readers of this chapter means that in the same way that we all walk with a sense of outsiderness, we all also contain elements of privilege in our identity. When exploring issues of privilege with students, I often state two things: that (1) identity is fluid and therefore ideas of privilege and outsiderness are fluid as well; and that (2) ideas of privilege are based around the context of where we are, what we are doing and who is around us at any given moment in time. The fact that I am an academic at a university in the south of England may mark me as having a certain elite privilege, but place me in a Russell Group university, then the fact that I am an academic in a former polytechnic will probably mark me out as being an outsider.

INTERSECTIONALITY AND POWER

Haug (2008) recognised that structures of power are not hierarchical as such, but within a social constructionist framework that resonates from the centre outwards. This is important to recognise in that those with power, or those who have over-identified with their sense of privilege, will then define what is the other from their centrist ideal. Perfect examples of this emerge from Simone de Beauvoir's idea of the sociological construction of gender (de Beauvoir, 2010). She recognised that what it was to be a woman was socially defined out of what it was to be a man, meaning that certain behaviours, certain emotions and certain ways of being that were not desirable in a man were then cast out and deemed feminine or of woman. These ideas about identity and who defines identity then lead us down a line of who has the power to define and marginalise.

Returning to de Beauvoir's (2010) construct of identity, the marginalisation and the pathologisation of women for, say, hysteria in early psychodynamic theory is a perfect example of the defining of a sociological construction of behaviour out of a centrist patriarchal narrative. The other perfect example from a more contemporary standpoint to show how power works in these instances could involve the construction and abuses held within gay conversion therapy, with this again being an ideology posited by a heterosexual patriarchal narrative against the sexually oriented other. Power and the power to define are central to ideas of who we are when it comes to understanding the social constructions of identity. That these structures of identity also filter into psychotherapy, and that we all, on any journey towards self-discovery, need to understand these adaptations, recognises that we are all impacted by the patriarchal, white supremacist, capitalist triumvirate.

RELEVANCE TO COUNSELLING AND PSYCHOTHERAPY

One of the major criticisms of intersectionality is that it is considered to be a race to the bottom and that there is a certain effort made by practitioners to gather as many disadvantaged identities as possible and collate them so that they will sit in one big pot of depression (Collins, 2019). This sort of critique of intersectionality fails to recognise my earlier statement that actually we walk with both privilege and otherness all the time. It tries to fix into place the idea that actually we are *either or*, which is a very westernised way of understanding identity, the binary standpoint being around and grounded in philosophy for hundreds of years.

Theorists like Deleuze, Buber, Levinas and others, though, have taken issue with this very simplistic way of westernising human experience and recognise that the human experience is a lot more complex and nuanced than this, and that we learn not just from ourselves but from the many others around us (Buber, 2010; Deleuze, 1994; Levinas, 2006). Even Carl Jung, for all his so-called prejudices and flaws, saw that the shadow was the other and recognised that without difference we cannot truly know who we are (Jung, 1964; Stephens, 2001; von Franz, 1980).

Sigmund Freud, from another perspective, saw the importance of recognising the political in the experiences of our clients (Freud, 1930). His own experience, of his journey in fleeing Nazi Germany and Austria and coming to the United Kingdom, was based on his own sense of growing outsiderness in a political environment was becoming ever more fraught and dangerous for both himself and his family. In his book, *Civilisation and its Discontents* (1930), Freud wrote quite clearly about the political, and all of these philosophers that I have mentioned in this simple chapter have seen so much, experienced so much and written so much about how the political has informed and influenced them. It can sometimes feel as if psychotherapy and psychotherapists are in denial of this social construction of identity, within which the political framework resides.

The idea that counselling and psychotherapy should be apolitical has existed in the field for decades. Sadly, what this perspective fails to recognise is that many of the structures of oppression which our clients may present with in the counselling and psychotherapy room have often been not just defined but reinforced by the political structures of the day.

Michael was a 45-year-old Asian man who was born in East Africa. His family came to the UK in the early 2000s. Having previously had a fairly privileged life in East Africa, for his family it was quite a shock to the system to find themselves living a less privileged existence in the UK. In East Africa, Michael was sent to one of the best schools in his area, whereas in the UK, because of a lack of money, his family struggled to send him to a local comprehensive. Michael had presented in therapy with issues of depression and low mood, which has come to the surface after the sudden death of his father. When I explored what it was like for him to have lost his father, Michael, although feeling quite low, said he was quite angry with his father, and was glad that his father had passed away. A deeper exploration helped me to understand that for Michael, his father's choice to leave their East African home and their family was one that Michael had not agreed with. Although he was too young to say so at the time, he really wanted to stay with his friends and his relatives.

Michael talked about the difficulties of going to a school in a mainly white area of England where he was one of very few Asian children in his year group. Regularly picked on, bullied and marginalised, these were experiences which Michael felt very much on his own. He was unable to express to his parents how he felt because they made him believe that he had come to the UK to get the best education possible. Increasingly isolated and lonely, Michael struggled at school, barely doing enough to pass his GCSEs, to get his A levels and to scrape his way through university.

We looked a lot at the intersectional identities at play in our work together. For Michael, at school he was the other. He was marginalised by his peers and often also by his teachers. So, for Michael, there was already a racially cultural difference which marked him out as an outsider. Within this, though, there was also a class difference, because Michael's world was very much one of privilege before he had come to this country. In East Africa they lived with servants in a large house on the outskirts of a major city, yet when they arrived in the UK Michael's family found themselves living in council accommodation for the first couple of years while they established themselves. This only changed in the years just before Michael's father passed away. Ideas of power and privilege were therefore always in Michael's presentation.

This even appeared in the work between Michael and myself. As stated previously, Michael's background was one where he was of Asian origin. What he told me, after several sessions, was that he felt uncomfortable with me because I was a black man. We looked at the reasons why this might be. We also explored the idea that, for Michael, his family had had servants in East Africa who looked after him and helped raise him, and here, I was a black male psychotherapist and I was in a position of apparent power over him. This left Michael feeling incredibly uncomfortable and not really sure if he could continue to work with me.

My counter-transference within the therapeutic relationship with Michael was one of huge compassion for what he had been through in this country. I recognised that my ability to hold and manage my other identity, that of a therapist with authority, would help Michael to regain a sense of who he was, especially if he was able to reintegrate those qualities he saw and projected onto me.

The power of an intersectional approach recognises the social constructions of identity which are presented to us within a therapeutic context. In this client example, the varying layers of identity that Michael held at varying times included both a sense of privilege and outsiderness. His life was not a single-issue life, because a single-issue life, in a therapeutic context, suggests a splitting off from the internalised other, an other of either privilege or otherness. This simple example suggests that counselling and psychotherapy has an awful lot to offer when considering issues of privilege and otherness. It is the ideal framework through which to see the power dynamics at play in counselling and psychotherapy, and while in a formalised sense intersectional approaches to counselling and psychotherapy are still new and in their infancy, what they also have the chance to do is to present counsellors and psychotherapists with the words, knowledge and framework through which to work more comprehensively with issues that have been around since the days of Sigmund Freud.

REFERENCES

Buber, M. (2010). *I and Thou*. Eastford, CT: Martino Publishing.
Cho, S., Crenshaw, K. W., & Mccall, L. (2013). Toward a field of intersectionality studies: theory, applications, and praxis. *Signs: Journal of Women in Culture and Society*, *38*(4), 785–810.
Collins, P. H. (2008). *Learning from the Outsider Within: The Sociological Significance of Black Feminist Thought Social Problems, 33*(6), 14–32.
Collins, P. H. (2019). *Intersectionality as Critical Social Theory*. Durham, NC: Duke University Press.
Collins, P. H., & Bilge, S. (2016). *Intersectionality: Key Concepts*. Oxford: Polity Press.
Crenshaw, K. (n.d.). Demarginalizing the intersection of race and sex: a Black feminist critique of antidiscrimination doctrine, feminist theory and antiracist politics. *University of Chicago Legal Forum*, *1*(8), 139–167, accessed at https://chicagounbound.uchicago.edu/cgi/viewcontent.cgi?article=1052&context=uclf.
de Beauvoir, S. (2010). *The Second Sex*. New York: Alfred A. Knopf.
Deleuze, G. (1994). *Difference and Repetition*. London: Bloomsbury.
Freud, S. (1930). *Civilisation and Its Discontents*. London: Penguin.
Haug, F. (2008). Memory work. *Australian Feminist Studies*, *23*(58), 537–541. https://doi.org/10.1080/08164640802433498
Jung, C. G. (1964). *Man and his Symbols*. London: Picador.
Levinas, E. (2006). *Humanism of the Other*. Urbana, IL: University of Illinois Press.
Lorde, A. (1984a). Age, race, class and sex: women redefining difference. In *Sister, Outsider*. Trumansburg, NY: Crossing Press.
Lorde, A. (1984b). *Sister Outsider*. Trumansburg, NY: Crossing Press.
Stephens, B. D. (2001). The Martin Buber–Carl Jung disputations: protecting the sacred in the battle for the boundaries of analytical psychology. *The Journal of Analytical Psychology*, *46*(3), 455–491. www.ncbi.nlm.nih.gov/pubmed/12174548
von Franz, M.-L. (1980). *Projection and Re-Collection in Jungian Psychology*. Chicago: Open Court Publications.

RECOMMENDED READING

Romero, M. (2017). *Introducing Intersectionality*. Cambridge: Quality Books.

An excellent start point for any exploration of intersectionality, Romero explores some of the original ideas which underpin this means of thinking, together with some of the history of intersectionality.

Collins, P. H., & Bilge, S. (2016). *Intersectionality: Key Concepts*. Oxford: Polity Press.

This recent text takes some of the themes provided by Romero's book and expands upon them. Taking a legal, social constructionist, and moral angle on issues of privilege and otherness, Hills Collins explores intersectionality via the impact of ideologies such as patriarchy, white supremacy, and capitalism.

Turner, D. (2021). *Intersectional Privilege and Otherness in Counselling and Psychotherapy*. Abingdon, UK: Routledge.

This text brings intersectionality and its concepts into the world of counselling and psychotherapy, and makes accessible the challenges for therapists and lecturers in holding the multiple identities of our clients and our students. This text explores themes such as othering, privilege and otherness and how these are unconscious experiences as well as conscious ones.

2.2 AGE

LÉONIE SUGARMAN

OVERVIEW AND KEY POINTS

The population of the United Kingdom is ageing, and while counsellors and psychotherapists will increasingly need to engage with this under-represented group of clients, the issue of age has much wider relevance – for clients, therapists, and the therapeutic relationship. Age is an ever-present, but often unspoken, dimension of difference in therapy. Chronological age is frequently used as an expedient index of social age and, despite its ambiguous meaning and significance, is salient throughout life. Our age is used to structure economic, social, and political life, and affords us particular rights and obligations. Despite its limitations, we still use age as a guide in accommodating to the behaviour of others, in formulating our self-image, in interpreting our experience and in contemplating our past and our future. Therapists cannot escape age – their clients' or their own. Key points in this chapter include:

- Age is an often overlooked but nonetheless relevant dimension of difference in counselling and psychotherapy.
- Clients' age will influence, but not totally determine, their needs.
- Clients' and therapists' age will influence their responses to each other.

INTRODUCTION

The population of the UK is ageing. In 2014 the median age of UK residents reached 40 for the first time, and in 2015 those aged 65 or over comprised 17.8% of the total (up from 15% in 1984), with the fastest increase being in those aged 85 and over (Office for National Statistics, 2016). It is clear that counsellors and psychotherapists will increasingly need to engage with this under-represented group of clients (Improving Access to Psychological Therapies (IAPT), 2014). However, the issue of age has much wider relevance than this – for clients, therapists and the therapeutic relationship.

The age of the client, the age of the therapist and the difference between them are ever-present, but often unspoken, elements of the socio-cultural context of therapy, and a potentially significant dimension of difference. Age, while seemingly a straightforward personal characteristic indicating time lived since birth, is also a social marker that structures, knowingly or unknowingly, the way we interpret our experience, and organises the ways in which we perceive and interact with each other (Baars, 2012). By dividing the human life span into socially meaningful units, we translate calendar time into social time, producing an age-grade system in which life stages such as 'youth', 'midlife' and 'old age' imply not only chronological age, but also a cluster of socially defined rights, responsibilities, developmental tasks and preoccupations that reflect cultural traditions, laws, values and beliefs concerning age-appropriate behaviour (Carney and Gray, 2015).

In the face of uncertainty, age norms and assumptions about ageing can offer a subtle sense of security (Dannefer and Setterston, 2010) and a set of ready-made and compelling life goals against which to assess how well or poorly we are doing 'for our age'. At the same time, age norms and age-related goals can directly or indirectly restrict personal choice and serve as mechanisms of social control. Therapists may need to help clients disentangle whether, in striving for age-related targets, they are 'being themselves' or merely 'acting their age'. While the loosening of age norms is potentially liberating, it can leave us unsupported by social structures and more dependent on personal resources and skills (Wrosch and Freund, 2001). The disorder, discontinuity and uncertainties of a fluid life cycle may propel clients into therapy as much as might the constraints of rigid age restrictions and expectations.

The negative stereotype of old age as a period of loss encompassing declines in physical attributes and mental acuity, increasing dependence on others, absence of role identity and lack of respect from society (Kite and Wagner, 2002) has for some time been counterposed with notions of successful ageing that emphasise independence, productivity and self-maintenance – in effect, an 'anti-ageing' movement. However, this perspective can be criticised for failing to acknowledge the reality of bodily ageing (Clarke and Korotchenko, 2011) and as reflecting western, neo-liberal cultural values that place a moral obligation on older people to resist ageing through continual efforts at lifestyle maximisation and body optimisation (Lamb, 2014; Rudman, 2006). Such a discourse sustains ageism by promoting perpetual youthfulness as a goal, and draws attention away from the socially constructed nature of disadvantage in later life (Vincent, 2013).

There is a need for theorising about old age that goes beyond the binaries of success and decline. In this vein, Boudiny (2013) proposes strategies for the fostering of adaptability, redefinitions of what is meant by involvement with life, and policies that prioritise the agency of the client in decisions over long-term care. Liang and Luo (2012) seek to emphasise balance based on difference rather than uniformity in their concept of harmonious ageing, while Sandberg (2013) develops the notion of affirmative ageing that construes the changes of ageing in midlife and beyond not as decline, but as the continuous production of difference. From this perspective, the self is seen not as ageless, but as ageful (Andrews, 2000), and in the same way that difference is celebrated in axes such as race and gender, the importance of age is not ignored. This applies to therapists as much as clients, and is seen, for example, in senior therapists' reflections on their experience of ageing and its impact on their work and professional identity (Geller and Farber, 2015).

RELEVANCE FOR COUNSELLING AND PSYCHOTHERAPY

While universal themes such as attachment, separation, dependency, change and loss will permeate counselling and psychotherapy irrespective of the clients' age or life stage, they take on a different hue according to the psychosocial context of successive life stages (Jacobs, 2012). Clients of different ages and life stages have different psychological, cognitive and sensory capacities. Therapists working with children and young adolescents need to be sensitive to both their level of verbal and cognitive development and their level of emotional maturity, while with clients in late adulthood accommodation may need to be made for decreasing sensory capacity (notably sight and hearing) and/or the declining mobility and cognitive functioning that may – but does not inevitably – accompany the ageing process.

Similarly, some issues will occur more frequently for clients within a particular age range. The design and structure of therapy services may reflect this understanding of life stage, such that, despite anti-discrimination legislation, age may be used as a gateway to therapy-related opportunities and resources. While this is more expedient than individualised assessment of need, age and need are imperfectly correlated, and any presumed correspondence may be based on erroneous assumptions and outmoded patterns of social organisation. As such, age- or life-stage based services encourage the stereotyping of particular age groups as problematic, and inadvertently add to age separation and segregation (Bytheway, 2005). However, to deny differential treatment to particular groups identified primarily by age may be to ignore real differences in capacity, vulnerability and power.

Access to therapy is influenced by money and power (Pilgrim, 1997), and people in early and middle adulthood are most likely to be both economically active and in positions not only to purchase their own therapy, but also to determine who else receives therapy or other mental health services, and for what problems. In this regard, children and older adults are similar since the economic power of the very young and the very old is frequently either minimal or negative – although even here one must exercise caution since the assumption that all older people are inevitably impoverished is itself an ageist myth. Nonetheless, the very young and the very old do frequently lack direct economic power and, as a result, they also lack social power – both of which may be needed to gain access to appropriate counselling and psychotherapy.

Children and frail older adults are less likely to self-refer than those in the more socially powerful and (potentially) more economically active stages of the life course. In addition, it is also more likely that therapists working with these clients will have direct contact with family members or professionals who may well have instigated the referral process. It should always be asked whether the services provided are in the best interest of the clients or, for example, of parents and school teachers in the case of children, or children and healthcare professionals in the case of vulnerable older clients. While advocacy by others may be a legitimate response to clients' limited capacities, therapists need to be wary of ageism that defines reality on behalf of either the young or the old, and decides for them what interventions are required.

Although both therapists and clients will hold assumptions concerning the ageing process and what it means to be a particular age, there remains relatively little discussion of how such images and assumptions affect the therapeutic relationship (Kessler and Bowen, 2015).

Clients' age will influence how they perceive the therapist. Clients who are significantly older or significantly younger than their therapist may believe that 'the world is different now' and that the therapist, being of a different generation, cannot possibly understand them. Thus, older clients may consider a much younger therapist to be inexperienced and/or presumptive in assuming they have anything to offer, with transference issues reflecting their relationship with their children or grandchildren. Also, older clients may imbibe ageist assumptions that devalue their own lives and experiences and, as a consequence, question whether they are deserving of therapeutic time and resources. Children and adolescents, by contrast, may experience the therapist as an authority figure, and parental transference may be relevant, with clients re-experiencing and re-enacting with the counsellor aspects of the relationship they have or had with their parents.

Younger clients may remind therapists of themselves at that age, or bring therapists' own children to mind, while older clients may remind them of their parents or grandparents (Knight, 2004). Older clients may trigger a deep-seated unease in young and middle-aged therapists, possibly distorting their clinical judgement as they catch glimpses of problems and challenges that may lie ahead both for the therapists themselves and for their parents and grandparents (Semel, 2006). Dysfunctional emotional reactions include threat, disgust, fear, shame and guilt (Knight, 2004), whereby younger, healthy, cognitively alert therapists are threatened by the reminder that one day they too may be older, ill and cognitively impaired. They may experience shame at this reaction, guilt regarding their own youth and health in comparison to that of their clients, and disgust at the indignities of extreme old age.

Therapists will remember something of what it was like to be a child or adolescent, and draw on this experience in developing their relationships with younger clients. Such knowledge can be both a resource and a hindrance. Not only is each individual's experience unique, but we are all not only of our place, but of our time. Every generation or cohort is distinctive, having grown up in a particular economic, political and social environment, with particular shared experiences. This reduces the extent to which our own life experiences can be used as a basis for understanding those in later or earlier generations.

Therapists may identify readily with the issues faced by clients of a similar age to themselves and who present scenarios that mirror issues that they are also addressing. While this can facilitate the development of empathy, therapists need to be wary of over-identifying with clients who seem 'similar to me', or of projecting onto clients their own reactions and interpretations. Also, it cannot be assumed that clients see counsellors of the same age as 'like them'. Similarity of age may reinforce clients' sense of inadequacy – 'how come he/she is coping so well, whereas I need help?'

Therapists, like clients, will be embedded in a network of inter-generational relationships, and need, therefore, to be sensitive to their emotional reactions to clients of different ages, carefully considering their possible impact on the course of therapy (Terry, 2008). While all therapists will have experienced young, and possibly middle, adulthood, fewer will have personal knowledge of late adulthood. This brings the advantage that clients can be faced without interference from the therapist's direct experience of this life stage, but increases the scope for therapists to be prey to unsubstantiated stereotypes and unarticulated assumptions concerning later life. When making the journey into the unknown territory of the life of significantly older or significantly younger clients, therapists need to be wary of unwarranted interference from their own life experience, their stereotypes about different life stages, and the chauvinistic prioritisation of their own current life goals and values.

Ageism – stereotyping, prejudice and discrimination based on chronological age – affects all individuals from birth onwards (Bytheway, 2005). As with other forms of oppression, such as sexism and racism, it involves attributing characteristics to individuals simply by virtue of their membership of a particular group. As with other forms of oppression, it is reinforced by the structures of society, being used to restrict access to services, privileges, entitlements and responsibilities. As a form of oppression it is unique, however, in that its nature and particular impact on an individual fluctuates and changes across the life course.

Ageism is frequently discussed primarily in relation to the lives of older adults (for example, Nelson, 2011). While drawing attention to the prejudice and discrimination experienced by older people, this bias can serve both to obscure ageism directed at other age groups, and also blind us to ageism within ourselves. Seeing the concept of ageism as relevant only to older adults fosters a 'them' and 'us' view of 'the elderly' as a minority group. If older people or, indeed, children are seen as different and separate from the rest of society, then this can be used *per se* to justify different and separate treatment.

CONCLUSION

In sum, I propose that age is an ambiguous concept that in some ways is becoming less significant, but in other ways remains crucial. Age cannot by itself define individual lives (Rogoff, 2002), but therapists should remain mindful of how it can be both crucially important in their therapeutic work and, at the same time (almost), completely irrelevant.

REFERENCES

Andrews, M. (2000) Ageful and proud. *Aging and Society*, 20(6): 791–795.

Baars, J. (2012) Critical turns of aging, narrative and time. *International Journal of Ageing and Later Life*, 7(2): 143–165.

Boudiny, K. (2013) 'Active ageing': From empty rhetoric to effective policy tool. *Ageing and Society*, 33(6): 1077–1098.

Bytheway, B. (2005) Ageism. In M.L. Johnson, V.L. Bengtson, P.G. Coleman and T.B.L. Kirkwood (Eds), *The Cambridge Handbook of Age and Ageing*. Cambridge: Cambridge University Press.

Carney, G.M. and Gray, M. (2015) Unmasking the 'elderly mystique': Why it is time to make the personal political in ageing research. *Journal of Aging Studies*, 35(2): 123–134.

Clarke, L.H. and Korotchenko, A. (2011) Aging and the body: A review. *Canadian Journal on Aging/La Revue canadienne du vieillissement*, 30(3): 495–510.

(Continued)

(Continued)

Dannefer, W.D. and Settersten, R.A. (2010) The study of the life course: Implications for social gerontology. In W.D. Dannefer and C. Phillipson (Eds), *International Handbook of Social Gerontology*. London: Sage.

Geller, J.D. and Farber, B.A. (2015) Introduction: Reflections of senior therapists. *Journal of Clinical Psychology*, 71(11): 1049–1059.

Improving Access to Psychological Therapies (IAPT) (2014) *Older People*. London: IAPT. Accessed at www.iapt.nhs.uk/equalities/older-people/

Jacobs, M. (2012) *The Presenting Past: The Core of Psychodynamic Counselling and Therapy* (4th ed.). Buckingham: Open University Press.

Kessler, E.-M. and Bowen, C.E. (2015) Images of aging in the psychotherapeutic context: A conceptual review. *GeroPsych: The Journal of Gerontopsychology and Geriatric Psychiatry*, 28(2): 47–55.

Kite, M.E. and Wagner, L.S. (2002) Attitudes toward older adults. In T.D. Nelson (Ed.), *Ageism: Stereotyping and Prejudice against Older Persons*. Cambridge, MA: MIT Press.

Knight, B.G. (2004) *Psychotherapy with Older Adults* (3rd ed.). Thousand Oaks, CA: Sage.

Lamb, S. (2014) Permanent personhood or meaningful decline? Toward a critical anthropology of successful aging. *Journal of Aging Studies*, 29: 41–52.

Liang, J. and Luo, B. (2012) Toward a discourse shift in social gerontology: From successful aging to harmonious aging. *Journal of Aging Studies*, 26: 327–334.

Nelson, T.D. (2011) Ageism: The strange case of prejudice against the older you. In R.L. Wiener and S.L. Wilborn (Eds), *Disability and Aging Discrimination: Perspectives in Law and Psychology*. New York: Springer.

Office for National Statistics (2016) *Population Estimates for UK, England and Wales, Scotland and Northern Ireland: Mid-2015*. London: ONS. Accessed at www.ons.gov.uk/peoplepopulationandcommunity/populationandmigration/populationestimates/bulletins/annualmidyearpopulationestimates/latest

Pilgrim, D. (1997) *Psychotherapy and Society*. London: Sage.

Rogoff, B. (2002) How can we study cultural aspects of human development? *Human Development*, 45(4): 209–210.

Rudman, D.L. (2006) Shaping the active, autonomous and responsible modern retiree: An analysis of discursive technologies and their links with neo-liberal political rationality. *Ageing and Society*, 26: 181–201.

Sandberg, L. (2013) Affirmative old age: The ageing body and feminist theories on difference. *International Journal of Ageing and Later Life*, 8(1): 11–40.

Semel, V.G. (2006) Countertransference and ageism: Therapist reactions to older patients. In C.M. Brody and V.G. Semel (Eds), *Strategies for Therapy with the Elderly: Living with Hope and Meaning* (2nd ed.). New York: Springer.

Terry, P. (2008) Ageism and projective identification. *Psychodynamic Practice*, 14(2): 155–168.

Vincent, J. (2013) The anti-aging movement: Contemporary cultures and the social construction of old age. In M. Schermer and W. Pixtons (Eds), *Ethics, Health Policy and (Anti-) Aging: Mixed Blessings*. New York: Springer.

Wrosch, C. and Freund, A.M. (2001) Self-regulation or normative and non-normative developmental challenges. *Human Development*, 44(5): 264–283.

RECOMMENDED READING

Geller, J.D. and Farber, B.A. (2015) Introduction: Reflections of senior therapists. *Journal of Clinical Psychology*, 71(11): 1049–1059.

The introduction and opening paper of a special issue on senior therapists' reflections on their experience of ageing and its impact on work and professional identity.

Kessler, E.-M. and Bowen, C.E. (2015) Images of aging in the psychotherapeutic context: A conceptual review. *GeroPsych: The Journal of Gerontopsychology and Geriatric Psychiatry*, 28(2): 47–55.

A discussion of images of ageing with specific reference to counselling and psychotherapy.

Sugarman, L. (2004) *Counselling and the Life Course*. London: Sage.

Using the framework of the life course, this book considers both the distinctiveness and commonalities of working with clients at different points in the life span. It also encourages readers to reflect on their own life course and life stage.

2.3 COUNSELLING AND PSYCHOTHERAPY IN THE CONTEXT OF THE CLIMATE AND ENVIRONMENTAL CRISIS

MARTIN MILTON

OVERVIEW AND KEY POINTS

It is hard to know when climate change was *first* brought to people's attention, but it was certainly being discussed publicly 35 years ago when the US Senate had a two-day hearing on '*Ozone depletion, the greenhouse effect and climate change*' (Mooney, 2016). Since then, it, and the other associated environmental devastations, have gained greater prominence, both in people's everyday experience and culturally. Climate change has been recognised as a global emergency and has increasingly become part of contemporary discourses with an enormous canon of scientific literature, public protests and TV, film and social media communicating many of the issues. The climate and environmental emergency is a multi-dimensional, societal issue which intersects with other social justice issues (race, poverty and migration, to name just three). Thus, a relational lens is important when trying to understand the complexity of the issue and its impact on clients, on therapists and on society more broadly.

In this chapter, readers will be invited to consider the nature of climate change and environmental destruction as both physical phenomena and psychological ones. The chapter discusses some of the ways in which climate and environmental destruction is affecting people's physical, social and psychological lives, and therefore the ways in which psychologists, counsellors and psychotherapists may receive this in the consulting room.

The chapter will specifically consider five key points:

1. The ways in which the climate and environmental crisis affects people's personal lives, and the way therapists engage with clients.
2. The evidence of psychological distress related to climate change.
3. The importance of therapists taking climate change seriously and refraining from reducing everything down to internal processes or projections.
4. The use of green/nature prescriptions or the possibility of outdoor therapy.
5. The place of action in the therapeutic process.

INTRODUCTION

CLIMATE CHANGE

Terminology changes as meanings evolve. This can be due to time, learning and, of course, different perspectives and interests. The term 'climate change' has more recently taken prominence over the previously used concept of 'global warming', which too easily confused people ('How can the planet be warming when the extreme weather event we are suffering is an Arctic vortex?', etc.). Equally, the term was easily hijacked by those who wanted to discredit the science for profit. This chapter does not have the space to burrow down into these processes in great depth, but readers could see Klein (2014) for a discussion of the deliberate discrediting of credible climate science by those who stand to gain financially from the use of fossil fuels, etc.

The term 'climate change' has the advantage of referring to human-triggered climate, weather and associated events, which are having an effect the world over. The term covers events such as accelerating ice sheet and glacial melt (Chen, Wilson and Tapley, 2006), increased risk associated with drought (Cook, Mankin and Anchukaitis, 2018), ever-growing periods of widespread wildfires across Australia and parts of the United States (Lui, Stanturf and Goodrick, 2010), and an increase in extreme precipitation in Europe (Madsen et al., 2014). These are all manifestations of a complex change to the climate.

RELEVANCE TO COUNSELLING AND PSYCHOTHERAPY

The physical manifestations of climate change create difficulties for those who have to face them. For example, even the most comfortable among us can probably imagine the fear and despair when having to be evacuated from your flooded home or when you return to find your place of safety damaged beyond repair. We can empathise with the terror of having to flee from fast-paced wildfires, uncertain as to whether you, your family and friends or animal companions may make it out alive. These are just a couple of obvious traumas and studies have suggested that such events result in an array of 'mental injuries' (see Lawrance et al., 2021), such as somatic disorders (Escobar et al., 1992; Leon, 2004), post-traumatic stress disorder (Galea, Nandi and Vlahov, 2005) and depression (Marshall et al., 2007). The American Psychological Association (APA) produced a comprehensive report on the relationship between psychology and global climate change, providing evidence that the experience of unusual weather events and the uncertainty about future events is associated with mental health outcomes (American Psychological Association, 2009). Thus, there is a growing awareness that the impact of climate change is more insidious than simply straightforward.

It is also evident that people are affected by climate change indirectly. Studies note that despite one's home currently being safe, changing landscapes, increased temperatures and the viewing of images of environmental degradation have implications for human psychological distress (Doherty and Clayton, 2011). Albrecht et al. (2007) note that the observation of dramatic landscape alteration inflicted feelings of solastalgia, a sense of helplessness and lack of control over the unfolding process. Some experience grief associated with a sense of loss of the environment and uncertainty of the long-term sustainability of human life on Earth (Randall, 2009).

People exist in time, responding both to events that *have* happened and also to our awareness of what *may* happen. The social aspect of this process also creates psychological difficulties as people report a sense of overwhelming impotence when realising that their personal effort to mitigate against the effects of climate change, by driving less, consuming less red meat or giving up flying, does not equate to immediate relief to the environment (Kennedy-Woodard and Kennedy-Williams, 2022). We also hear of difficulty with dealing with anger in relation to leaders who appear to recognise the urgency of the crisis yet fail to deliver policy that would change things (Kennedy-Woodard and Kennedy-Williams, 2022). Constant awareness about damage to the environment can also be expressed by eco-anxiety, which is characterised by severe worry about the future (Nobel, 2007). Similarly, individuals who have high exposure to ecological events through media or through their work become aware and greatly concerned about the state of the planet and may feel anxious (Searle and Gow, 2010).

Thus, climate change is having an impact on a wide range of people the world over and may be a factor in the distress that clients experience and bring to therapy (Milton, Gimalova and Simmons, 2020).

ENGAGING WITH CLIMATE CHANGE

With its long history of prioritising lived experience, relational thinking, and the emotional impact of life, applied psychology, counselling and psychotherapy can offer important insights to help us think about individual and social resilience in the face of the climate and environmental emergency. It is also argued that psychology has a significant role to play in the amelioration of the climate crisis itself (see Uzzell, 2021).

Sadly, despite their epistemological and ontological commitments, counselling and psychotherapy have not offered as much as they might. This may be partly as they remain embedded, to some degree, in contemporary political and economic perspectives that view humans through a more dichotomous or binary lens which results in us being seen as separate from nature (Kesebir and Kesebir, 2017). This facilitates what Klein (2014) has called a 'gig and dig' mindset, a view that allows the exploitation of the planet (and those that inhabit it) in favour of economic growth. This attitude and a sense of separateness underpins the rampant loss of biodiversity and habitat, extinction of species, pollution and climate change (Adams, 2005).

However, many argue that even if difficult, counselling and psychotherapy potentially have huge contributions to make to people in light of climate change and environmental destruction. Many schools of therapy take a relational stance to understanding people and the distress they bring to therapy which can be utilised to understand the impact of the climate emergency. Relational perspectives recognise that we exist in relation to the world around us – existential therapy reminds us of this in its focus on being-in-the-world, systems theory of the impact of communication and interactional power on members of a system, and some psychodynamic theorists outline in detail the interactions between an individual and the world around them, and the psychic damage that occurs in relation to environmental trauma.

It is important that we note the useful contributions that do exist. These include Searles (1972: no page), who challenged the over-reliance on internal formulations in psychoanalysis and noted that too often psychotherapy 'relegates the world to being a mere backdrop'. From another psychodynamic perspective, Samuels (1993) noted the profound relationship we have to place, and therapists such as Blair (2011), Rust (2004) and Moss (2012) show how our physical and mental health is intimately linked to nature and a healthy environment. Writings like these help us consider ways in which therapeutic practice can contribute to individual, group and community resilience as we live through, and try to mitigate, the worst of human induced climate change.

We may be seeing the counselling and psychotherapy professions mobilising to contribute to one of the most important psycho-cultural phenomena of our lifetimes.

THERAPEUTIC PRACTICE

Like many traumatising and power-related experiences, understanding climate-related distress as meaningful matters. So, when a therapist meets with a client and starts to hear what brings them to therapy, it is important that climate change is understood as a real and distressing matter. The climate and environmental crisis need to be taken seriously in the context of the client's life and presenting issue/s.

Counselling and psychotherapy have long recognised that fundamental to good work is the need for an ethos of unconditional positive regard (see Rogers, 1957). This fundamental orientation facilitates trust and hope, allowing the client to face their fears and explore them. It is this relational effort that allows deeper exploration and may facilitate more finely attuned formulations of a client's difficulties, that take into account personal psychology, emotional responsiveness and 'real' factors (see Cohn, 1989). This is very important when we are working with the direct and indirect impacts of climate change and environmental devastation.

While we sometimes see assessment and formulation discussed as an early part of the process, therapists should be mindful of their formulation throughout the work, as the twists and turns of the therapeutic journey frequently elucidate new and meaningful understandings that can be of assistance to the client – emotionally and in terms of their behavioural, relational and existential possibilities (for more on this, see Johnstone – Chapter 3.5, this volume). This is helpful as it allows for a blank canvas and for a personalised view of the client and their experience to be developed early, and is something that can be returned to throughout the work. The relationship between the personal and the contextual (i.e., climate-related material as a projection of their inner world as well as a response to a crisis) is often important.

A therapist who can escape slavish adherence to singular models, explore the meanings of the personal and the contextual, and the relationship between them, is of assistance to the client as attunement is enhanced. Where it is understood that the climate and environmental crisis is related to the client's difficulties, the therapist and client can consider what type of therapeutic intervention is likely to be useful. Gone should be the days when clients are subjected to a therapist's routine manner of practice, or exclusively subjected to relentless analyses of internal matters.

Equally, the recognition of the climate and the environment crisis, and nature more broadly, may lead to more helpful contexts for the therapeutic work to be undertaken in. While there are limits to anyone's practice and availability (clients as well as therapists), a truly relational and attuned therapy will allow us to consider not only content, but context. Going beyond what I have previously referred to as 'environmentally aware therapy' (Milton, 2010) is ecotherapy, which allows clients and therapists to discuss nature, maybe deciding to add a 'nature prescription' as an adjunct the work, or maybe undertaking some – or all sessions – outdoors in nature (see Harkness, 2019; Jordan, 2015).

Unlike with many historical traumas where understanding the experience of chaos, manipulation or abuse may be considered the primary task of therapy, where a client's experience is related to climate change, there is often space for action to be considered too. Action may help clients by affording them a chance to move from guilt and complicity, to feeling they have agency and are more in touch with choice. Of course, action along with others, whether it be joining a litter picking crew, writing to one's MP or attending Extinction Rebellion meetings, may break the isolation and overwhelmed feeling so many report in relation to the climate and environmental emergency.

CONCLUSION

In conclusion, therefore:

1. The climate and environmental crisis is more than simply headline news and political policy; it affects people's personal lives and, for psychologists, counsellors and psychotherapists, the way we engage with clients (see American Psychological Association, 2009; Doherty and Clayton, 2011; Randall, 2009).
2. There is growing evidence that people are finding climate change – the reality of it and the awareness of it – psychologically distressing (see Lawrance et al., 2021). Therefore, it is, and will continue to be, something that therapists encounter in their work.
3. An emerging literature suggests that, as with other socio-political phenomena, clients are helped when therapists take the objective facts of climate change seriously and refrain from reducing everything down to internal processes or projections.
4. Therapists should consider the use of green/nature prescriptions as an adjunct to therapy, or the possibility of outdoor therapy.
5. Therapists should also consider action in the therapeutic process. A growing literature suggests that there are helpful aspects to acting in relation to the climate and environmental crisis (Kennedy-Woodard and Kennedy-Williams, 2022).

REFERENCES

Adams, W. W. (2005). Ecopsychology and phenomenology. *Existential Analysis: Journal of the Society for Existential Analysis, 16*(2), 269–283.

Albrecht, G., Sartore, G. M., Connor, L., Higginbotham, N., Freeman, S., Kelly, B., … & Pollard, G. (2007). Solastalgia: The distress caused by environmental change. *Australasian Psychiatry, 15*(suppl.1), 95–98.

American Psychological Association (2009). *Psychology & Global Climate Change: Addressing a Multifaceted Phenomenon and Set of Challenges*. Washington, DC: APA. Available at www.apa.org/images/climate-change-booklet_tcm7-91270.pdf (downloaded on 22 January 2020).

Blair, L. (2011). Ecopsychology and the person-centred approach: Exploring the relationship. *Counselling Psychology Review, 26*(1), 43–52.

Chen, J. L., Wilson, C. R., & Tapley, B. D. (2006). Satellite gravity measurements confirm accelerated melting of Greenland Ice Sheet. *Science, 313*, 1958. doi: 10.1126/science.1129007

Cohn, H. W. (1989). The place of the actual in psychotherapy. *Free Associations, 1*(18), 49–61.

Cook, B. I., Mankin, J. S., & Anchukaitis, K. J. (2018). Climate change and drought: From past to future. *Current Climate Change Reports, 4*, 164–179. https://doi.org/10.1007/s40641-018-0093-2

Doherty, T. J., & Clayton, S. (2011). The psychological impacts of global climate change. *American Psychologist, 66*(4), 265.

Escobar, J. I., Canino, G., Rubio-Stipec, M., & Bravo, M. (1992). Somatic symptoms after a natural disaster: A prospective study. *The American Journal of Psychiatry*, *149*(7), 965–967.

Galea, S., Nandi, A., & Vlahov, D. (2005). The epidemiology of post-traumatic stress disorder after disasters. *Epidemiologic Reviews*, *27*(1), 78–91.

Harkness, C. (2019). *The Nature of Existence: Health, Wellbeing and the Natural World*. London: Red Globe Press.

IPCC (2014). *Climate Change 2014: Synthesis Report (AR5)*. Geneva: Intergovernmental Panel on Climate Change.

Jordan, M. (2015). *Nature and Therapy: Understanding Counselling and Psychotherapy in Outdoor Spaces*. Hove: Routledge.

Kennedy-Woodard, M., & Kennedy-Williams, P. (2022). *Turn the Tide on Climate Anxiety: Sustainable Action for Your Mental Health and the Planet*. London: Jessica Kingsley.

Kesebir, S., & Kesebir, P. (2017). A growing disconnection from nature is evident in cultural products. *Perspectives on Psychological Science*, *12*(2), 258–269.

Klein, N. (2014). *This Changes Everything: Capitalism vs. the Climate*. New York: Penguin.

Lawrance E., Thompson, R., Fontana, G., & Jennings, N. (2021). *The Impact of Climate Change on Mental Health and Emotional Wellbeing: Current Evidence and Implications for Policy and Practice*. Grantham Institute, Briefing paper 36, doi: https://doi.org/10.25561/88568

Leon, G. R. (2004). Overview of the psychosocial impact of disasters. *Prehospital and Disaster Medicine*, *19*(1), 4–9.

Lui, Y., Stanturf, J., & Goodrick, S. (2010). Trends in global wildfire potential in a changing climate. *Forest Ecology and Management*, *259*(4), 685–697.

Madsen, H., Lawrence, D., Lang, M., Martinkova, M., & Kjeldsen, T. R. (2014). Review of trend analysis and climate change projections of extreme precipitation and floods in Europe. *Journal of Hydrology*, *519*(Part D), 3634–3650.

Marshall, R. D., Bryant, R. A., Amsel, L., Suh, E. J., Cook, J. M., & Neria, Y. (2007). The psychology of ongoing threat: Relative risk appraisal, the September 11 attacks, and terrorism-related fears. *American Psychologist*, *62*(4), 304.

Milton, M. (2010). Coming home to roost: Counselling psychology and the natural world. In M. Milton (Ed.), *Therapy and Beyond: Counselling Psychology Contributions to Therapeutic and Social Issues*. Chichester: Wiley-Blackwell.

Milton, M., Gimalova, M., & Simmons, B. (2020). Counselling psychology and climate change: A survey of the DCoP membership. *Counselling Psychology Review*, *35*(2), 57–70.

Mooney, C. (2016). 30 years ago scientists warned Congress on global warming: What they said sounds eerily familiar. *The Washington Post*, 11 June, www.washingtonpost.com/news/energy-environment/wp/2016/06/11/30-years-ago-scientists-warned-congress-on-global-warming-what-they-said-sounds-eerily-familiar/ (accessed 15 December 2021).

Moss, S. M. (2012). *Natural Childhood*. London: National Trust.

Nobel, J. (2007). "*Eco-Anxiety: Something Else to Worry About.*" The Philadelphia Inquirer, April 9.

Randall, R. (2009). Loss and climate change: The cost of parallel narratives. *Ecopsychology*, *1*(3), 118–129.

Rogers, C. R. (1957). The necessary and sufficient conditions of therapeutic personality change. *Journal of Consulting Psychology*, *21*(2), 95–103. https://doi.org/10.1037/h0045357

Rust, M. J. (2004). Ecopsychology: Seeking health in an ailing world. *Resurgence Magazine*, February.

Samuels, A. (1993). 'I am a place': Depth psychology and environmentalism. *British Journal of Psychotherapy*, *10*(2), 211–219.

Searle, K., & Gow, K. (2010). Do concerns about climate change lead to distress? *International Journal of Climate Change Strategies and Management*, *2*(4), 362–379.

Searles, H. (1972). Unconscious processes in relation to the environmental crisis. *The Psychoanalytic Review*, *59*(3), 361–374.

Uzzell, D. (2021). Integrating the individual and the collective for a transformational response to the climate emergency. *Clinical Psychology Forum: Special Issue: Climate and Ecological Emergency*, *346*, 12–22.

RECOMMENDED READING

Counsellors and psychotherapists might find it helpful to review a range of relevant literatures (see many of the references listed in this chapter). It can be helpful to look at the geophysical processes underlying climate disruption (see IPCC, 2014) and it can also be useful to review the contributions that look at human's pro-environmental behaviours. But for many counsellors and psychotherapists, their first forays into the literature may be to look at the evidence for the psychological impact of climate change. In this regard, three particularly useful texts include:

American Psychological Association (2009). *Psychology & Global Climate Change: Addressing a Multifaceted Phenomenon and Set of Challenges.* Washington, DC: APA.

The report synthesises scientific literature and thinking on such topics as how people understand the risks of climate change, the psychological and contextual determinants of human behaviours that affect climate, the psychosocial impacts of climate change, the ways in which people adapt to and cope with threats related to climate change, the psychological factors that drive and limit action on climate change and the roles of psychologists (and other therapists) in responding to climate change.

Lawrance E., Thompson, R., Fontana, G., & Jennings, N. (2021). *The Impact of Climate Change on Mental Health and Emotional Wellbeing: Current Evidence and Implications for Policy and Practice.* Grantham Institute, Briefing paper 36, doi: https://doi.org/10.25561/88568

This document is a meta-analysis of the evidence on the psychological distress caused by, and in relation to, climate change and the associated costs incurred. The report notes increased rates of suicide (1% for every 1°C temperature rise), reduced population mental wellbeing, the ways that cases of psychological trauma caused by climate-driven disasters exceed those of physical injury, the ways in which extreme weather events are linked with post-traumatic stress disorder, depression and anxiety, and extreme distress. In addition, it reminds us that by straining limited resources, the climate crisis threatens to disrupt the provision of care for people with a mental illness diagnosis, and with fragile health systems, particularly our vulnerable populations.

Kennedy-Woodard, M., & Kennedy-Williams, P. (2022). *Turn the Tide on Climate Anxiety: Sustainable Action for Your Mental Health and the Planet.* London: Jessica Kingsley.

This up-to-date and accessible book looks at what we know about climate change (and as one of its chapter headings says – what we don't) before exploring the range of different emotions that people may feel in relation to it. Of particular note is the focus on moving from anxiety to action. It includes self-help exercises that a therapist might also be able to utilise in their practice.

2.4 DISABILITY

ESTHER INGHAM

OVERVIEW AND KEY POINTS

Disability is a psychological, philosophical, sociological and political issue that we cannot avoid. As practitioners, we have some ethical obligation to understand what assumptions and prejudices we bring to therapy, perhaps especially for/with individuals who may have experienced much 'treatment' and objectification, or been subject to prejudice/discrimination. Models of disability are used (consciously or otherwise) to understand and define (the implications of) impairment in a variety of contexts. They also reveal the many ways in which society enables and/or limits access to work/services/assets, and provide a framework from which we can gain understanding of disability issues and power play. An awareness of the various models of disability facilitates insight into attitudes, conceptions and prejudices of society that are (often unconsciously) used to inform organisations and individuals about how we relate to, interact with, manage, support and discriminate against people who live with the experience of disability.

- Disability is a complex issue; both to live with and to understand. Disabled people may, of course, want counselling for all/any of the reasons non-disabled people do, so for the therapist to assume centrality of issues of disability would be presumptuous. However, they may potentially also present extra issues in therapy that need consideration.
- Disability discourse has historically been dominated by the non-disabled. Disability also remains largely invisible in society despite the best efforts of the social disability movement. Unless we have some sort of personal experience, the majority of non-disabled people form their perceptions of disability largely from socially dominant models and media portrayal which still relies on negative stereotypes.
- The therapeutic practitioner is as susceptible to unconscious influence of negative constructions and attitudes towards disability as any other human in society. Becoming acquainted with the dominant models of disability can help with our personal critical reflection of our own attitudes and practice.
- I use the words 'disability' and 'disabled' to describe the experience of living with any condition of the mind and/or body that makes it difficult or impossible for the individual with the condition to perform certain activities, and restricts their interaction and/or participation with the world around them.

INTRODUCTION

Disability is a natural and inevitable part of human existence, yet it invokes different (often strong) feelings in us all. In order to explore issues relating to disability, it is necessary first to establish some clarity about what we are referring to. The *International Classification of Functioning, Disability and Health* (ICF) (World Health Organisaion, 2001) asserts that the term 'disability' refers to difficulties encountered in any (combination) of three areas of functioning: impairment, activity limitation and participation restriction. It can be physical and/or cognitive, congenital or acquired, and can be temporary, permanent or intermittent.

As a concept, disability can be ambiguous and is understood from numerous, often conflicting, epistemological perspectives. Whatever the context, a common component part of any discussion about disability is that issues of power and vulnerability cannot be avoided. Two questions are particularly pertinent: Who is responsible for the disability? And who is responsible for the solution? Until recently, models of disability have tended to be reductionist, static and time/culture bound, and consequently have invariably failed to give a complete account of the experience of disability (Watermeyer, 2012). From the perspective of the affected individual, much of the challenge of living with disability is often about managing the tensions caused by the various constructions of them as 'disabled'. Historically, western society has viewed disability as an incurable, tragic, individual medical issue. Economically, the consequences of disability in a capitalist society have reduced individuals to either needs- or work-based 'subjects', while aesthetically, the current cultural demands for physical 'perfection' and total independence render those living with any degree of physical/cognitive otherness utterly hopeless. Combined, these dominant constructions of disability subtly, but comprehensively, serve to brand disabled individuals in contemporary UK society as biologically inferior, socially devalued, unattractive and fundamentally disempowered (Shakespeare, 1994).

RELEVANCE TO COUNSELLING AND PSYCHOTHERAPY

Disability has historically been at the edge of awareness as an area for therapists to specifically consider, and any assessment or research in the area has been from a non-disabled perspective. Consequently, understanding of issues relating to disability has often been assumed only to relate to grief and loss, denial and/or depression (Parkinson, 2006). A link of inevitability has far too often been made that disabled individuals must be suffering some version of emotional distress, and that the disability fundamentally impinges on emotional and cognitive characteristics. This assumption is unhelpful, wrong, and maintains a notion that the individual is fundamentally deficient (in need of 'cure') and that the responsibility for change lies purely with them. It is now generally recognised that disability is not merely a medical issue, but also one of embedded societal oppression, and that this is perhaps a significant contributing factor as to why there are so few disabled researchers and practitioners in the field to challenge this one-dimensional, simplistic perspective (Oliver and Barnes, 2012). Other minority groups are becoming ever more demographically representative in counselling and psychotherapy research and training in the UK, with the result being that their presence in the learning environment can help uncover and challenge any significant omissions and negative attitudes and beliefs during the training process. However, this is still less common in discourses around disability, not least because of logistical issues which have prevented people with a disability from even accessing and being present in counsellor and psychotherapy training.

Disability issues inevitably impact on therapeutic practice. Of course, it is always possible that an individual may come to therapy with an issue unrelated to their experience of disability, although as practitioners we may not correctly identify it as such. Without some dedicated and specific consideration, there is a danger that practitioners will either over-emphasise disability and make it the root of all issues, or will ignore it altogether, which risks denying an integral part of an individual's experience of 'being-in-the-world'. To help balance and address this, I suggest all practitioners have ethical responsibility to take it upon ourselves to consider and critically reflect on our personal attitudes, prejudices and assumptions towards issues relating to disability. To inform this reflection, and potentially help (re)form our understanding, there follows a brief overview of the most dominant models of disability that are prevalent in our time.

MODELS OF DISABILITY

MORAL/RELIGIOUS MODEL

This age-old bias still pervades our everyday culture (Olkin, 2012). The moral/religious model is often associated with belief-systems in which disability is seen as punishment from God. Fundamentally, the model is based on the (superstitious) notion that disability represents the embodiment of evil, moral absence or a failure of faith, while biological wholeness/ability is somehow indicative of virtuousness and righteousness (Rosenburg, 2009). The presence of disability is blamed on the individual as the consequence of sin or immoral behaviour, and the accompanying shame can be spread to all those associated with the disabled person, sometimes leading to entire families being rejected from their communities.

Through this lens, disability can also be understood as a test of faith, whereby the disability is framed as an opportunity for redemption through resilience, endurance and patient faith and acceptance. 'Everything happens for a reason' can often be heard as popular non-disabled opinion in this context, serving to suggest that (dis)ability is a matter of merely adopting a different (better or superior) attitude akin to stoicism. With this understanding of disability as a moral and/or religious issue, any lack of healing or worsening of condition equates to having a lack of faith or weak moral fibre. This is potentially an extremely destructive association for the disabled individual as it mobilises assessment of personal issues of worth, ability and value which, in turn, become directly linked to effort and mindset. Disability thus becomes little more than a high-stakes (unasked for) opportunity for character development, whereby the responsibility lies solely with the individual to work hard to become a 'better person', have more faith or die.

(BIO)MEDICAL MODEL

The primary, most influential discourse since the mid-1800s (Lancet, 2009), the medical model assumes disability to be an abnormal failure or defect of the bodily system that necessarily causes disadvantage and must be treated – by first reducing the individual to what is 'wrong' in order to then fix, manage or minimise it. The model assigns significant power to 'expert' medical professionals, who objectively pathologise disability and dehumanise the affected individual by reducing them to a categorisation, dependent on diagnosis. Identified this way, the disabled individual becomes little more than a body in need of 'cure' and/or 'rehabilitation'. A lot of disabilities are not able to be cured or eliminated, so there is potential for the individual to be enduringly perceived to be of less worth, or evidence of failure in this context.

The medical model frames disability as a medical subordinate deviation from 'normal' and thus reinforces the notion that non-disabled people are somehow better or superior to people living with experience of disability. The model is often felt to be a 'model of limitations', which reduces the disabled individual to inferior (ideally passive) 'patient' (Smart and Smart, 2006), who is expected to obediently (and gratefully) spend time learning how to be helped by often dogmatic, even authoritarian, professionals. The focus on inability, limitation and dependency constructs disability as something pitiable, deviant and fundamentally disempowering in its denial of potential for independence, control and choice. It can create an assumption that a person with a disability is not fully legitimate (in-valid) and perpetually 'in need of help'. Simultaneously, it places total responsibility on the disabled individual to be compliant and personally motivated, and traps them within the medical establishment. There is a sinister expectation that the role of 'sick patient' must be played in a particular way in order to access help and support, and so, for those who experience their body as reconstructed within a medical discourse, their existence thus becomes restricted by the disciplines this imposes upon them as 'disabled' (Sullivan, 2005).

CHARITY/TRAGEDY MODEL

Mostly used (along with the medical model) by non-disabled people to define disability, the tragedy/charity model subtly infuses everyday life through media, language and culture. It potentially originates from the fear that some form of disability can (and through ageing, usually does) affect any/everyone, and that this fear is linked to a fundamental death anxiety present in all humans (Swain and French, 2000). The presence of disability then poses an overt existential confrontation to the (currently)able-bodied human.

The central tenet of the tragedy/charity model is that disabled people are victims of tragic circumstance to be pitied for their inevitable suffering (Oliver, 1996). They are assumed to be unhappy and unable to enjoy any worthwhile quality of life because of the limitations of their condition and, at its most extreme, the model theorises that disabled people would be 'better off dead' than living wretched lives. In this context, disabled people are believed to desire and aim for themselves to be 'normal', while the (more capable and resourced) non-disabled should assist in whatever way possible.

The tragedy/charity model apparently seeks to act to the benefit of the disabled individual by appealing to the philanthropy of those who are non-disabled and more privileged. While the overt positioning of the disabled individual as a tragic victim is often successful in providing much-needed services not funded by the state, it also perpetuates a negative and often offensive and misrepresentative stereotype of inevitably helpless individuals in need of care/management and unable to look after themselves. This serves potentially to lower the self-esteem and worth of people with a disability (there is an implicit expectation of gratitude and 'set of terms' imposed by the pitying and virtuous donor), and also risks a broader societal assumption that survival requires a 'culture of care' where segregation and institutionalisation is preferable to supported community integration.

It must also be acknowledged that disability as personal tragedy may be an appropriate understanding for some individuals, if associated with traumatic accident or illness.

LOSS MODEL

Drawing from the previous three models, the loss model (which is most prevalent in the counselling literature) assumes a state of psychological distress in the disabled person due to feelings of guilt, shame and loss. It conceptualises disabled people as needing 'special help' to engage in the real world, and suggests that there is a necessary process of psychological adjustment to go through in order to 'come to terms' with disability and individual limitations (Reeve, 2000). A failure to follow or express these predicted stages (usually anger, denial, mourning and adjustment) is thus viewed as evidence of being 'stuck in the process', rather than proof that the model may not always be appropriate. Consequently, subscribing to this model risks an oppressive positioning as there is no room to acknowledge possible emotional responses to discrimination and prejudice (Reeve, 2014).

SOCIAL MODEL

Challenging the medical perspective, and in attempt to reclaim some sense of power for affected individuals, the social model (the first to be developed by disabled people) serves to highlight the negative impact of the physical and social environment when it fails to accommodate the needs of disabled people – instead subjecting them to segregation, social isolation, discrimination and prejudice. Since the middle of the twentieth century, and inspired by identity activism, disability has become gradually redefined socio-politically as the detrimental consequence of a society that views limitations caused by impairments as defects or flaws, and thus as social devaluation. Simply put, it is society which disables people (Barnes, Mercer and Shakespeare, 2010). The model highlights the fundamental difference between 'impairment' – specific individual limitation – and the resultant 'disability' – the consequence of a society that does not cater for its environment to impairment. It is expressly concerned with identifying and addressing these 'barriers to participation' experienced as a result of various ableist social and environmental factors. This restructuring of disability as oppression of an individual with an impairment by their environment can empower disabled people to take control of what becomes essentially societal issues of social justice (Swain and French, 2008).

Some non-disabled people can find this conceptualisation of disability challenging as it involves a paradigm shift from 'cure' to 'care', and a focus on enabling and empowering that which has previously been seen to be hopeless and/or defective. Many disabled individuals find the model liberating as it recognises how the experience of disability shifts as the environment and context change, and consequently directly challenges the previously dominant notion that the issue is (within) the individual and solely their responsibility. However, there is also criticism that the social model doesn't acknowledge the often painful realities of living with impairment – not just disabled by society, but also the personal experience of living with physical/cognitive restrictions. To ignore this is to risk ignoring a major element of lived experience, as well as the potential for heightened existential awareness of the fragility of life. Also, within this model it can be unclear where issues of impairment end and disability begins.

PSYCHO-EMOTIONAL AND AFFIRMATION MODELS

Acknowledging the criticism that the social model ignores and delegitimises the emotional and individual experiences of disability (Thomas, 2007), the psycho-emotional model has extended the conceptualisation to include recognition of the psychological effort of being perpetually impacted by negative attitudes and prejudices within society, despite the risk this may aggravate and fuel the existing stereotypes of damaged and helpless disabled people. The affirmation model goes even further to validate expressions of anger as appropriate reactions to discrimination and marginalisation, and also celebrates individual differences in experience. It is a positive model of disability growing from disability identity culture, which celebrates the group identity as valuable, shared understanding of social barriers. The model directly challenges the non-disabled presumption that disability necessarily equates to personal tragedy and, as the name suggests, prioritises positive aspects of disability – asserting the view that many disabled individuals can (and do) lead full, satisfying lives. As a model that is not based on non-disabled presumptions of living with disability, there is a tendency for it to be rejected by mainstream (non-disabled) culture as unrealistic. Consequently, collective expressions of strength and pride (for example, in the disability arts movement) are sometimes reinterpreted (oppressively) as a lack of acceptance or (patronisingly) as an expression of courage and bravery (Swain and French, 2000).

HUMAN RIGHTS MODEL

The increasingly recognised and mobilised human rights model is important as it moves beyond conceptualisation and illustration of disability into a dynamic model of activism that offers a theoretical framework for disability public health policies that champion dignity and human rights (Deneger, 2017). Moving towards understanding disability from a human rights perspective necessarily rejects the privileging of 'normal' over 'abnormal', while also acknowledging and engaging with the 'dilemma of difference (of lived experience)'. As such, this model has capacity to validate individual differences (e.g., in relation to pain and suffering) alongside maintaining the importance of cultural identification (e.g., identity politics) without contradiction. It also focuses on issues relating to community membership and equitable access to resources, consequently comprehensively shifting the discourse from one of dependence to independence by employing both a rights-based perspective and a political voice.

REFERENCES

Barnes, C., Mercer, G., & Shakespeare, T. (1999). *Exploring Disability*. Cambridge: Polity Press.
Degener, T. (2017). A new human rights model of disability. In V. Della Fina, R. Cera & G. Palmisano (Eds), *The United Nations Convention on the Rights of Persons with Disabilities*. Cham, Switzerland: Springer. https://doi.org/10.1007/978-3-319-43790-3_2
Lancet, T. (2009). Disability: Beyond the medical model. *The Lancet*, 375(9704), 1793.
Oliver, C., & Barnes, C. (2012). *The New Politics of Disablement* (2nd ed.). Basingstoke: Palgrave Macmillan.
Oliver, M. (1996). *Understanding Disability: From Theory to Practice*. London: St Martin's Press.
Olkin, R. (2012). *What Psychotherapists Should Know about Disability*. New York: Guilford Press.
Parkinson, G. (2006). Counsellor's attitudes towards disability equality training (DET). *British Journal of Guidance & Counselling*, 34(1), 93–105.
Reeve, D. (2000). Oppression within the counseling room. *Disability & Society*, 15(4), 669–682.
Reeve, D. (2014). Counselling and disabled people: help or hindrance? In J. Swain, S. French, C. Barnes, & C. Thomas (Eds), *Disabling Barriers – Enabling Environments* (3rd ed.). London: Sage.
Rosenberg, M. (2009). Harm, liberty, and disability. *Disability Studies Quarterly*, 29(3), 8.
Shakespeare, T. (1994). Cultural representation of disabled people: dustbins for disavowal? *Disability and Society*, 9(3), 283–299.
Smart, J. F., & Smart, D. W. (2006). Models of disability: implications for the counseling profession. *Journal of Counselling Development*, 84(1), 29–40.
Sullivan, M. (2005). Subjected bodies: paraplegia, rehabilitation and the politics of movement. In S. Tremain (Ed.), *Foucault and the Government of Disability*. Michigan, MI: University of Michigan Press.
Swain, J., & French, S. (2000). Towards an affirmation model of disability. *Disability and Society*, 15(4), 569–582.
Swain, J., & French, S. (2008). *Disability on Equal Terms*. London: Sage.
Thomas, C. (2007). *Sociologies of Disability and Illness: Contested Ideas in Disability Studies and Medical Sociology*. Basingstoke: Palgrave Macmillan.
Watermeyer, B. (2012). Is it possible to create a politically engaged, contextual psychology of disability? *Disability & Society*, 27(2), 161–174.
World Health Organisation (2001). *ICF: International Classification of Functioning, Disability and Health*. Geneva: WHO.

RECOMMENDED READING

Wong, A. (Ed.) (2020). *Disability Visibility: First-Person Stories from the Twenty-First Century*. London: Vintage Books.

Compiled by activist Alice Wong, this is a vibrant collection of well-informed personal essays written by disabled people that gives insight into the vast diversity of disabled experience. With voices representing a broad spectrum of disabilities, it fiercely documents some of the difficulties encountered in everyday life, while also celebrating disability culture in our current society. A good starting point for engaging in disability discourse.

Oliver, M. (2009). *Understanding Disability: From Theory to Practice*. Basingstoke: Palgrave Macmillan.

Written by a leading academic in disability studies and a respected activist, this is an important collection of essays discussing current and enduring theories and polices that affect disabled people. It combines a mixture of personal experience and theoretical exploration and development across disciplines that provides excellent perspective for anyone wanting to understand key issues relating to disability.

Marks, D. (1999). *Disability: Controversial Debates and Psychosocial Perspectives*. London: Routledge.

Written by a psychotherapist who has been director of the MA in Disability Studies at Sheffield University, this book comprehensively reviews and critically engages with the debate around the social construction of disability. It provides a clear analysis of disability as it has been both historically and culturally constructed, and physically experienced.

2.5 GENDER

SAM HOPE

OVERVIEW AND KEY POINTS

This chapter gives an overview of the complexity of gender as a phenomenon that creates substantial social inequities. The many-layered ways gendered biases and assumptions show up in therapeutic work will be considered. The key points covered in this chapter are as follows:

- The social constructed nature of *both* gender *and* our ideas about biological sex are considered, and the reader is invited to reflect on the complexity of meanings attached to these ideas, moving away from oversimplistic binaries.
- The concept of intersectionality is highlighted, and the ways in which gender cannot be separated from classism, racism, colonialism and other social factors, pointing to the importance of considering these factors in the appreciation of gendered inequalities and how they play out in the therapy room.
- How sexism has influenced counselling theory is considered, and ways to challenge sexist thinking in the therapy room, including feminist and gender aware approaches to therapy.

INTRODUCTION

PRESENT-DAY INEQUALITIES, STRUCTURAL BIASES AND INTERSECTIONALITY

One way gender inequality is perpetuated is through bias. For example, a study found that scientists were 'significantly less likely to agree to mentor, offer jobs, or recommend equal salaries to a candidate if the name at the top of the resumé is Jennifer, rather than John' (Watts, 2014). We know this is a *structural bias* rather than simply people being biased towards their own group because women academics were also shown to be biased *against* women. Identical candidates were valued differently by both men and women depending solely on the assumed gender.

Concerns about gender inequality may depend on factors such as class, ethnicity, LGBTQIA+ status and disability. There have been many critiques of understandings of feminism that centre only the experiences and concerns of white, middle class, cishet women (Ahmed, 2017): cis being the accepted term for not trans, het (short for heterosexual) meaning not lesbian, gay, bi or asexual. Ahmed talks particularly about how women of colour are left out of feminist concerns and, given the economic disparities, this is entangled with issues of class and labour.

Kimberlé Crenshaw (1991) proposed the concept of *intersectionality* (see Turner – Chapter 2.1, this volume), originally to consider how black women's experiences of being *both* women *and* Black combined in ways that meant they were betrayed by separated conversations about racism and sexism. Crenshaw discusses the way racism impacts the discussion of violence against women in multiple ways: the disparity of media reporting of violence, with horrific crimes against women of colour going unreported, while crimes against white women perpetrated *by* men of colour were used to stir up racist discourse; and vast differences in prison terms and pursuing of prosecutions in favour of white victims. As Ahmed (2017: 34) says, 'It is a white female body that is assumed to be vulnerable and in need of protection from others'. Crenshaw also discusses the way white people have sexualised black people historically, and how this excludes black women from concern and exaggerates risk from black men, referring to civil rights-era white terrorism in which risk to white women was used to oppress and even lynch innocent black men.

Crenshaw highlights the difficulty, talking about the higher levels of gender-based violence against women within poor and marginalised communities and the complex social and environmental reasons for this, which get swept away by flattened feminist conversations in which violence happens equally to all women or obscured by people concerned that the connection between violence and *deprivation* will be used by racists to draw a false connection between violence and *race*. With respect to the rape of black women, race and gender converge so that the concerns of minority women fall into the void between concerns about women's issues and concerns about racism (Crenshaw, 1991: 1282). Other research confirms Crenshaw's assertion that gender-based violence happens to a much higher degree in areas of armed conflict and instability (OHCHR, 2021) and areas of poverty and social deprivation (Aaltonen et al., 2012).

Crenshaw (1991) also proposes intersectionality as a framework to look at other marginalisations, and indeed it has become a central organising principle for many feminists (Ahmed, 2017). Ahmed, who is a lesbian cis woman of colour, discusses the way black, lesbian and trans women have been excluded from womanhood and the feminist conversation.

Crenshaw's point that exclusion from safety structures and feminist inclusion increases risk of violence is also evidenced for trans youth: a large study from the US tells us that young trans people of all genders are at *significantly* higher risk of being the victims of sexual violence overall, and that risk goes up substantially in institutions where they face restroom and locker room restrictions, especially for trans girls (Murchison et al., 2019). Another study demonstrates that trans inclusive laws in no way negatively impact women's safety (Hasenbush, Flores and Herman, 2019), and yet the conversation around trans rights is often framed in terms of imagined threats to cis women's safety and rarely considers the safety of trans people. The mistreatment and disproportionate violence levelled at trans people of all genders, particularly misogyny-based violence targeted at trans women, is interwoven with sexism and ideas of 'appropriate' femininity and masculinity.

THE LEGAL AND SOCIAL BINARY

In Germany in 2019, the government introduced a third classification in addition to male and female that would allow intersex adults and children who are biologically outside the male/female binary to be registered as 'diverse'. When Germany brought in this change, intersex activists did not universally welcome the move, for many reasons, despite many pushing for legal change to allow both intersex and non-binary trans people to be legally accommodated appropriately in society. What would it mean for a child to be classified as 'other' in a society where the legal and social categories of male and female have so much importance? No other human difference is enshrined in European law, languages and social codes in quite the same way. How would a person address and talk about such a child? What labels and pronouns would be used? Which toilets would they be able to go into, as they grow up? What clothes would they be dressed in? And, more concerning still, in a country that has not yet fully outlawed medically unnecessary intersex genital surgery (known by some as intersex genital mutilation or IGM) on infants, might there be an expectation that children will eventually be assimilated into the legal categories of male and female via medical means? (Baars, 2018).

It should be noted here that not all cultures have seen gender as fixed or binary. In Turtle Island (indigenous American) culture, many tribes considered there to be more than two genders. Muxes of Juchitán, Mexico, Mashoga of Kenya and Hijras of India are all examples of culturally-specific ways of thinking about gender that go beyond a binary. Invariably, European colonialism marginalised and criminalised gender diversity and often used what might now be seen as LGBTQA+ positive attitudes to brand other cultures as inferior (Dozono, 2017).

When we speak of gender, gender identity and sex, we have a complex web of interlocking and overlapping terms, with variable meanings, and at the centre of much of this story is also a history of the unequal treatment of women, LGBTQA+ people and of colonised peoples. Butler (1999: 10) asserts that the category 'sex' is 'as culturally constructed as gender', and certainly the erasure of intersex people would seem to prove this. Ahmed (2017: 46) talks about gender as a 'path [that] is created by being followed and is followed by being created'. This path can take a therapist's thinking in particular directions without the therapist's awareness.

RELEVANCE TO COUNSELLING AND PSYCHOLOGY

GENDERED BIASES IN THEORY

Feminist critiques exist of many aspects of psychotherapeutic theory and its dominance by white, cishet, middle-class men. This section highlights examples of gender bias that may inform therapeutic work.

There is still a widely held belief that men and women have fundamentally different natures and aptitudes, and that accounts for the discrepancy. One popular body of research backing this idea is Baron-Cohen's theory that men have systematising and women have empathising brains, an idea that gained significant media attention and became popular in the 1990s. He also theorised that autism is more prevalent among boys because it is symptomatic of a highly systematising, non-empathising, 'extreme male' brain, but his work has been much criticised by feminist and autistic scholars as reflecting existing societal biases (Jack, 2011).

> On the Systemizing Quotient Test, testers are asked to rank their answers … to such questions as 'If I were buying a car, I would want to obtain specific information about its engine capacity' … Meanwhile, the Empathy Quotient test includes such prompts as 'I try to keep up with the current trends and fashions'… Clearly, these questions could easily reflect socialization as well as biology. (Jack, 2011)

When cultural bias is removed from the methodology, men are shown to have just as much empathy as women, but men *believe* women are more empathic and will downgrade their abilities if they realise they are being asked about empathy; this suggests the outcomes of men's ability (or not) to empathise are culturally determined by our shared beliefs about men and empathy (Jack, 2011). Milton (2012) has meanwhile demonstrated that autistic people do not, in fact, have lower empathy; neurotypical people display just as little ability to empathise with autistic people as autistic people do with neurotypical people; something known as the 'double empathy problem'. In addition, the significant prevalence of gay, bi, trans and gender non-conforming people across the gender spectrum who are also autistic (Dattard, 2020), and the emerging evidence that autistic women are going undiagnosed, misdiagnosed, and neglected by gender bias in the research contradicts the associations between autism and maleness, as well as highlighting troubling sexist stereotypes (Jack, 2011).

In a profession that has so many more women than men, it might be easy for therapists to believe in media-popular theories about women's naturally superior powers of empathy. This may play out in the therapy room in many ways – for instance, in terms of what we unconsciously expect of our male and female clients, including gender non-conforming ones, especially in relationship with others. There may be an assumption that women are better suited to caring (and primary parenting) roles than men, and we may hold biases against men who adopt these roles and women who refuse to.

This leads onto another area of research that has seen gender bias, and that is the centrality of parenting, and in particular mothering, in human development. Research by Booth-LaForce and Roisman (2014) shows that early attachment does not even predict attachment later in development, let alone adult attachment. Harris (1998) presents evidence that environmental factors rather than parenting factors are primary in child development. This echoes what Crenshaw (1991) highlighted about the impact of poverty and deprivation on conditions for women. Belsky at al. (2019), among others, demonstrate how postcode on day of birth is the biggest determining factor for lifelong mental health, as well as other health and attainment outcomes. Meanwhile Field (2016: 85) discusses how the 'working class woman is the subject of "expert" concern over the family functions' – Field is demonstrating the way systemic class and inequality issues are individualised by woman-blaming as a focus of understanding social problems. This echoes a common overall criticism of the therapy profession: that it individualises what are often in fact systemic problems (Bimrose, 1993).

Field (2016) suggests that emphasis on the importance and centrality of nuclear family bonds, and in particular maternal bonds, must be understood as part of a political desire to de-centre community, sociopolitical environment, poverty and worker conditions and a collective responsibility for social and emotional wellbeing. She speaks of the interrelatedness of different oppressions, for example, 'homophobia is tied up with women's oppression through dominant ideas about family life' (Field, 2016: 77), and charts oppressive ideas of 'family' back to the industrial revolution, giving early examples of how 'crime levels, prison overcrowding and social spending are blamed on sexual "immorality" and single parents, rather than poverty and poor housing' (p. 81). Her assertion is that the idealised family model is impossible for working-class people to live up to, and that is its function (pp. 65–94).

Therapists who focus on the importance of family and parenting, or uncritically hold in mind an idealised family with two heterosexual parents who take on the gender roles society expects, might unconsciously reinforce internalised shame carried by families that do not match this ideal.

Many of our European/Anglosphere theories are underpinned by assumptions of the centrality of a certain structure of nuclear family, but in Ugandan culture, for example, there are no distinct words for mother, grandmother, aunt, mother's cousin, and step relationships within the same family strata, and extended family and community are far more valued in child-rearing (Hume, 2008). How might this manifest in the therapy room? A therapist might find it easier to bring a focus onto a client's relationship with her 'absent mother' as the source of her problems than look at the wider field – the traumatising impact of living in a racist, anti-immigrant, misogynistic or classist society, for example.

UNLEARNING BIAS

Therapists may follow many different routes to increasing their awareness of the ways in which gender bias, gendered inequalities and gender stereotypes manifest in the therapy room.

'Gender Aware Therapy' (Good, Gilber and Scher, 1990) focuses on increasing awareness of how gender plays out in the therapy room, noticing stereotypes and redressing gendered differences in how therapists respond to clients. It focuses on developing competency and awareness.

According to Chaplin (1998), feminist counselling not only looks at awareness of gender but also *approach* – it is interested in dismantling hierarchies and dichotomies in general, so within the therapy room this might equally manifest as a way of equalising relations between feelings and cognitions as between masculinity and femininity – these things are not held in opposition, or one above the other, but as equal states all people flow between. Feminism has, historically, been interested in ways of going against the dominant paradigm, Ahmed's 'path well-trodden' (2017: 45–46) (for further discussion of feminist therapy, see Ballinger – Chapter 5.11, this volume).

Gender aware or feminist counselling is not just for women and gender minorities. Ahmed (2017: 25) discusses the 'gender fatalism' of the notion 'boys will be boys', a term often containing assumptions that men just can't help certain behaviours. Aware therapists balance understanding of the current conditions of gender and other social factors alongside a rejection that those conditions are inevitable, in understanding clients' navigation of masculinity. A young, working-class black man who is at increased risk of experiencing violence and police harassment may inhabit his masculinity differently from a young, middle-class, white man. A softly spoken gay man who was bullied through school for gender non-conformity might have a different relationship with notions of masculinity from a heterosexual man who has internalised strong beliefs about the correct ways to express masculinity that have gained him support and approval and feel congruent to him. A gay couple may still have to navigate gendered roles and expectations, but this will not neatly map onto heterosexual experiences.

These examples illustrate how gendered oppression has far-reaching and complex impacts. This is very definitely *not* to say 'sexism cuts both ways' – it is an unequal structure that demonstrably disadvantages women, just not in a simple, linear or binary way, and not in a way we can decontextualise from race, class, disability, cisheteronormativity and other unequal structures.

CONCLUSION

This chapter acknowledges that there are social and political impacts of gendered inequalities that will impact therapy clients in many and complex ways.

> To attend to women, we have to unlearn how we have learned to screen women out. We have to learn not to pass over her, just as we have been passed over. (Ahmed, 2017: 227)

The process of bringing unequal structures into conscious awareness is a painstaking one. It involves holding issues in mind that society has carefully taught the therapist to subtly overlook or not think about. Reading, listening to or viewing the words (therapy-related or otherwise) of women, and particularly marginalised women, can help take attention towards these overlooked structures and inequalities.

REFERENCES

Aaltonen, M., Kivivuori, J., Martikainen, P. & Salmi, V. (2012) Socio-economic status and criminality as predictors of male violence: does victim's gender or place of occurrence matter? *British Journal of Criminology* [Online], 52(6), 1192–1211. Available at http://dx.doi.org/10.1093/bjc/azs045

Ahmed, S. (2017) *Living a Feminist Life*. Durham, NC/London: Duke University Press.

Baars, G. (2018) New German Intersex Law: Third Gender but not as we want it. *Verfassungsbog.* Available at https://verfassungsblog.de/new-german-intersex-law-third-gender-but-not-as-we-want-it/

Belsky, D.W., Caspi, A., Arseneault, L., Corcoran, D.L., Domingue, B.W., Mullan Harris, K., Houts, R.H., Mill, J.S., Moffitt, T.E., Prinz, J.P., Sugden, K., Wertz, J., Williams, B. & Odgers, C.L. (2019) Genetics and the geography of health, behaviour and attainment. *Nature Human Behavior*, 3, 576–586. Available at https://doi.org/10.1038/s41562-019-0562-1

Bimrose, J. (1993) Counselling and social context. In R. Bayne & P. Nicolson (Eds), *Counselling and Psychology for Health Professionals*. London: Chapman and Hall.

Booth-LaForce, C. & Roisman, G.I. (2014) The Adult Attachment Interview: psychometrics, stability and change from infancy, and developmental origins: I. Introduction. *Monographs of the Society for Research in Child Development*, 79(3), 1–14. Available at https://doi.org/10.1111/mono.12110

Butler, J. (1999) *Gender Trouble*. London: Routledge.

Chaplin, J. (1998) *Feminist Counselling in Action*. London: Sage.

Crenshaw, K. (1991) Mapping the margins: intersectionality, identity politics, and violence against women of color. *Stanford Law Review*, 43(6), 1241–1299.

Dattard, L. (2020) Gender and sexuality in autism, explained. *Spectrum*, 18 September. Available at https://doi.org/10.53053/YBTA7630

Dozono, T. (2017) Teaching alternative and indigenous gender systems in world history: a queer approach. *The History Teacher*, 50(3), 425–447. Available at www.jstor.org/stable/44507259

Field, N. (2016) *Over the Rainbow: Money, Class and Homophobia (2nd ed.)*. Batley, UK: Dog Horn Publishing.

Good, G.E., Gilber, L.A. & Scher, M. (1990) Gender aware therapy: a synthesis of feminist therapy and knowledge about gender. *Journal of Counseling and Development*, 68, 376–380.

Harris, J.R. (1998) *The Nurture Assumption: Why Children Turn Out the Way They Do*. New York: The Free Press.

Hasenbush, A., Flores, A.R. & Herman, J.L. (2019) Gender identity nondiscrimination laws in public accommodations: a review of evidence regarding safety and privacy in public restrooms, locker rooms, and changing rooms. *Sexuality Research and Social Policy*, 16, 70–83.

Hume, P. (2008) Letter to the Editor: Re: African family. *Studies: An Irish Quarterly Review*, 97(385), 44–46.

Jack, J. (2011) 'The extreme male brain?': incrementum and the rhetorical gendering of autism. *Disability Studies Quarterly*, 31(3). Available at https://dsq-sds.org/article/view/1672/1599

Milton, D. (2012) On the ontological status of autism: the 'double empathy problem'. *Disability & Society*, 27(6), 883–887.

Murchison, G.R., Agénor, M., Reisner, S.L. & Watson, R.J. (2019) School restroom and locker room restrictions and sexual assault risk among transgender youth. *Pediatrics*, 143(6). https://doi.org/10.1542/peds.2018-2902.

OHCHR (2021) Women's human rights and gender-related concerns in situations of conflict and instability. *United Nations Office of the High Commissioner for Human Rights*. Available at www.ohchr.org/en/Issues/Women/WRGS/Pages/PeaceAndSecurity.aspx

Watts, A. (2014) *Why Does John Get the STEM Job rather than Jennifer?* Stanford University. Available at https://gender.stanford.edu/news-publications/gender-news/why-does-john-get-stem-job-rather-jennifer

RECOMMENDED READING

1. Fine, C. (2010) *Delusions of Gender: How Our Minds, Society, and Neurosexism Create Difference*. New York: W.W. Norton and Co.

Fine outlines the ways in which gender stereotypes reinforce not only behaviours but also the scientific search to essentialise gender difference.

2. Lorde, Audre (1984) *Sister Outside: Essays and Speeches*. Trumansburg, NY: Crossing Press.

A thought-provoking series of feminist essays bringing forward the experiences of marginalised women.

3. Serano, J. (2007) *Whipping Girl: A Transsexual Woman on Sexism and the Scapegoating of Femininity*. Berkeley, CA: Seal Press.

The perspective of a trans woman, highlighting the underlying disrespect for women and femininity at the heart of society's hostility towards trans women.

2.6 NEURODIVERGENCE

LESLEY DOUGAN

OVERVIEW AND KEY POINTS

My experience as a Neurodivergent therapist, client and educator informs this chapter. I begin by defining some of the key terms before considering how therapy can be impacted when either the therapist or client (or both) are Neurodivergent (ND). I will use '*Identity-first language*' (i.e., referring to Neurodivergent clients or therapists, as opposed to clients or therapists who are neurodivergent) throughout the chapter as advocated by the Human Rights Model of Disability, developed following the United Nations (UN) *Convention on the Rights of Persons with Disabilities* (United Nations, 2006). Identity-first language is essential because being neurodivergent 'informs every facet of a person's development, embodiment, cognition, and experience, in ways that are pervasive and inseparable from the person's overall being' (Walker, 2021: 87).

The chapter covers:

- neurodiversity, neurodivergence and neurotypicality.
- neurodivergence in relation to the different models of disability.
- neurodivergence in the context of counselling and psychotherapy.
- common experiences of neurodivergent people.
- neurodivergent affirming therapy.

INTRODUCTION

WHAT IS NEURODIVERSITY?

Neurocognitive functioning, both between and within individuals in any given society varies considerably (Doyle, 2020; Kapp et al., 2013). The term 'neurodiversity' encompasses the infinite differences within and between human minds (Singer, 1998). People whose processing fits within any society's concept of normalcy are Neurotypical (NT), whereas those whose processing diverges from the socially constructed 'norm' in any way are 'Neurodivergent' (ND). While having a different neurotype is not synonymous with a disability, many neurodivergent people face similar challenges and may be disabled by their neurotype (or society's responses to their neurotype). Neurodivergence manifests in many ways, which may not always be apparent to either the individual or to others. Some examples of ND processing include (but are not restricted to): ADHD, Autism, dyslexia, dyspraxia, dyscalculia, Tourette's syndrome, neurofibromatosis, synaesthesia, alexithymia, sensory processing sensitivity, rejection sensitive dysphoria.

MODELS OF DISABILITY

Given the association between neurodiversity and disability, and the discrimination faced by ND people, it is important to consider how we understand 'disability'. There are various models of disability. The Human Rights Model (sometimes referred to as the Empowerment Model) is contrasted here with the more commonly known Social, Medical, and Charity Models of disability.

The Human Rights Model (United Nations, 2006) of disability recognises that:

- Disability is a natural part of human diversity that must be respected and supported in all its forms.
- People with disabilities have the same rights as everyone else in society.
- Impairment must not be used as an excuse to deny or restrict people's rights.

The Medical Model centres the 'problem' with the individual, and what they can or cannot do because of their health condition, rather than society being centred around the needs of non-disabled people. Further, the Medical Model can be used to restrict the rights of disabled people, for example, the blanket 'Do Not Resuscitate Orders' placed on people with Learning Disabilities during the Covid-19 pandemic (Bloomer, 2021).

The Charity Model is a 'moralistic extension' of the Medical Model (Withers, 2012). Developed by non-disabled people, it frames disabled people as tragic and in need of support, while simultaneously highlighting 'inspirational individuals' who achieve 'despite' their disability. The false binary at the heart of the Charity Model enables non-disabled people to 'feel bad for disabled people's limited life chances and choose to help them – thereby making them 'good people' – and to be inspired by disabled people and realise how much more potential they have as someone who doesn't face the same limitations' (Ralph, 2017, n.p.). Both the Medical and Charity Models of disability are inconsistent with Human Rights (Degener, 2016).

The Social Model of disability is preferable to either the Medical or Charity Models. However, it is not without its faults. Namely:

- It advocates '*person-first*' rather than '*identity-first*' language.
- Many disabled people consider the Social Model of disability as ableist because it fails to see disabled people as the experts in their own lives, thereby enabling discrimination in favour of non-disabled people.
- Social Model interventions often fail to acknowledge the real impact of impairment on the lives of individuals (probably because of the insistence of '*person-first*' language).
- It tends to treat all disabilities the same.
- Its focus on society's barriers assumes that disabled people will access the services they need once the obstacles are removed.

RELEVANCE TO COUNSELLING AND PSYCHOTHERAPY

FROM PATHOLOGY TO NEURODIVERSITY: A PARADIGMATIC SHIFT

Historically, westernised socio-cultural-economic systems have been structured and developed around the needs of those in power, i.e., NT, able-bodied, white, cis-gender men. The mechanisms of power frame NT as the '*natural*', '*universally desirable human condition*' (Davies, 2016: 136). Normative counselling and psychotherapy practice has an implicit disablist attitudinal stance, i.e., it discriminates against disabled people (Moors, 2022). ND presentations are 'othered' or framed as 'difficulties' or 'deficits' by systems built around the needs of the NT majority. It is also worth remembering that other intersections of a neurodivergent person's identity, such as race, faith, gender identity, disability, age, socio-economic standing, sexuality, and relationships, add additional layers of oppression or marginalisation (see Turner – Chapter 2.1, this volume).

WHY IS CLARITY OF LANGUAGE IMPORTANT?

'Clarity of language supports clarity of understanding' (Walker, 2021: 31). Nevertheless, neurodiversity discourse is frequently misused and misunderstood, resulting in ND people being 'othered' by their NT peers. The image in Figure 2.6.1, explaining divergent, diverse and typical using shapes, is reproduced with the permission of Sonny Hallet, and communicates the nuances of neurodivergence so clearly.

NEURODIVERGENT MINDS – DIFFERENT NEUROTYPES

There is enormous variation in the way individuals experience and understand their ND; in the same way, there is considerable variation in the way individuals experience and understand their neurotypicality. For example:

- Some ND people will have received a formal neurodevelopmental diagnosis in childhood.
- Others go through life unaware that they are ND; some only realise after their child is diagnosed with a neurodevelopmental condition.
- Despite always knowing they have a neurogenetic condition, others, like myself, never (or take a long time to) connect the dots to realise they are ND.
- Some will recognise that they are ND without ever receiving a formal diagnosis from a professional.

All are valid.

ND people are a neurological minority or 'neurominority', whose processing and presentation diverge from the NT majority. ND people are disadvantaged across various life outcomes, including education, employment, relationships and health care (Doyle and McDowell, 2021), due to the fact that societal structures are largely designed by and for the needs of the NT, for example, hot-desking at work, artificial lighting at school or in the office, limited access to quiet space, assuming you need to sit still and give eye contact to be concentrating or listening, etc. Further, the recent emergence of Radulski's 'Critical Neuro Theory', which combines the concept of neurodiversity with critical disability approaches (including the Human Rights Model of disability) and Minority Group Model of Neurodiversity

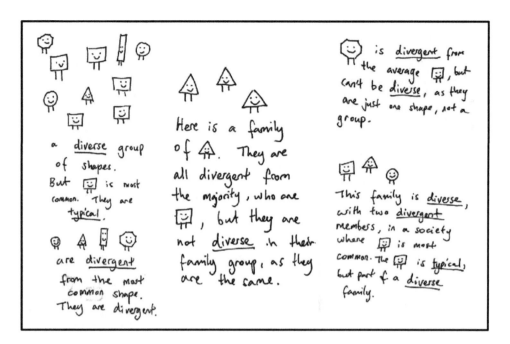

Figure 2.6.1 Divergent, diverse and typical

(Radulski, 2022), will play pivotal role in shifting the neurodiversity paradigm in the counselling profession.

An organismic psychological perspective is particularly helpful. When we permit ourselves to acknowledge the existence of a multiplicity of neurotypes and neurocognitive functioning in society (Goodley, 2016), we change our perspective to view neurodiversity through a similar lens to the one we use to make sense of flora and fauna in the context of biodiversity. Wynter (2003) refers to the 'archipelago of Human Otherness': just as a plant's ability to thrive is dependent on environmental conditions, the conditions which facilitate an individual to thrive (or actualise) will also vary considerably. Taking such an organismic perspective allows us to consider the equal importance of both homonomy and autonomy (Angyal, 1941; Tudor and Worrall, 2006) for ND trainees, therapists and clients, and the opportunity to view counselling and psychotherapy through a different lens.

COUNSELLOR CORE TRAINING AND CONTINUING PROFESSIONAL DEVELOPMENT

It is likely that your counselling training was 'normative' and did not cover neurodivergence, or perhaps it was covered in a tokenistic way, from a NT perspective, highlighting 'deficits' and emphasising the 'challenges' when working with ND people. The tutor team were probably all NT, and the training designed around NT norms and a 'right' 'way of being'. It is likely that neurodivergent trainees were on the receiving end of microaggressions, including being told they would not be good counsellors because of their idiosyncrasies, and perhaps experienced minority stress as a result (Meyer, 2003). Trainees who feel misunderstood by both tutors and peers may withdraw from training before qualifying.

Historically, continuing professional development (CPD) for working with ND clients (particularly Autistic clients) has emphasised the 'complexity' of such work. Understandably, some therapists may be reluctant to work with a ND person, feeling they lack competency (Raffensperger, 2009). If you are in the position of looking for CPD in this area, I would encourage you to do the following:

- Check whether ND trainers are delivering CPD on neurodiversity and counselling ND clients.
- Be wary of training that represents ND people as 'complex' (we are not).
- Be open to the fact that you may need to suspend NT viewpoints to enter the world of a ND client.

UNIVERSAL DESIGN WILL LEAD TO INCLUSIVE PRACTICE

The following section, informed by the lived experiences of ND therapists and clients, applies to all clients – ND or NT – and may alleviate some anxiety, while challenging therapy's 'neuro-normativity' (Huijg, 2020).

> We think we listen, but very rarely do we listen with real understanding, true empathy. Yet listening, of this very special kind, is one of the most potent forces for change that I know. (Rogers, 1980: 116)

When therapists are facilitative in 'acceptantly understanding the inner world of the other' (Rogers, 1977, cited in Kirschenbaum and Henderson, 1989: 382), the rest should fall into place. However, ND clients often report the opposite, with therapists invalidating minimising, misunderstanding, misrepresenting or denying their experience (Moors, 2022). Remember, the client *is* the expert on their own experience, regardless of whether they are NT or ND.

Common experiences of ND people include the following:

- Negative experiences of education (primary, secondary, FE or HE).
- Teachers or lecturers not appreciating their view on the world.
- Frequently feeling misunderstood.
- Difficulty fitting in with NT peers.
- Struggle with implicit social cues, especially when others use ambiguous language and either do not say what they mean or do not mean what they say.
- Processing/understanding information styles that differ from that of NT people.
- May have learned to people-please (or appease NT people to their own detriment).
- Plain speaking, which can come across as rude or abrupt by NT people.
- Sensory Perceptual Differences, which can appear to NT people as them 'over-reacting' to situations.
- Experiencing the emotions of others as if they are their own (echoemotica).
- Excessive neuronal activity leads to information overload and possible 'shut down', sometimes referred to as 'Intense World Syndrome'.
- Alexithymia (not being able to identify emotions experienced).
- Highly creative.
- Either appear to be a rule follower because conforming to rules reduces anxiety; or alternatively challenge the injustices of a NT status quo and are therefore less likely to conform.
- Passionate about social justice.
- Good at solving problems due to the ability of seeing patterns.
- The terms 'masking' and 'camouflaging' are often used interchangeably. However, they are, in fact, two distinct concepts focusing on internal and external processes (Radulski, 2022):
  - Masking refers being aware of your *internal* neurodivergent traits and concealing them.
  - Camouflaging refers to the way ND people attempt to adopt the NT norms.
- Having their way of being invalidated.
- Most people (both ND and NT) 'stim'. However, it is more frequent in the ND population and is unlikely to be conceptualised as stimming in the NT population.

To stim is to engage in any action that falls outside the boundaries of the social performance of normativity, and that provides some form of sensory stimulation in order to facilitate, intentionally or otherwise, some particular cognitive or sensorimotor process, or access to some particular state or capacity of consciousness or sensorimotor experience. (Walker, 2021: 102)

- Stimming can include (but this list is not exhaustive):
  - Bouncing your leg
  - Biting nails
  - Twirling hair
  - Clicking pens
  - Cracking knuckles
  - Whistling
  - Flapping hands
  - Rocking
  - Walking on tip toes
  - Twisting on an office chair
  - Repeating words or phrases of others (echolalia) or self-generated sounds (palilalia).

CONCLUSION

We can never know with certainty the neurotype of a new client, even if they have received a formal diagnosis (and does that even matter?). However, being responsive to all clients and their processing styles can make a considerable difference in clients feeling heard and understood. The following list is not prescriptive, but could be a useful starting point:

In your practice, consider:

- Adding details about you and the way you practise to your website using clean, unambiguous language. An up-to-date profile picture is essential.
- Let clients know that there is no expectation for eye contact and ask if they have a preferred way to be in the room. The view that eye contact conveys 'availability for psychological contact' (Stafford and Bond, 2020: 30) is an ableist misnomer.
- Adapting the pace of your speech depending on the individual client (my own internal metronome pace is 'andante', i.e., moderately slow).
- Speaking in short sentences rather than long monologues or leaving pauses between sentences to allow clients to process information.
- Adjusting the environment of the therapy space:
  o Can the lighting be dimmed?
  o Can the client access sunglasses or similar?
  o Does the therapy room have blinds or similar (to reduce distractions from outside)?
  o Are your clocks 'silent'? (Many clients are distracted by ticking clocks.)
  o Could outside noises interfere with sessions? (Many ND people experience gestalt auditory processing and have difficulty filtering relevant speech if the environment outside the therapy room is noisy.)
  o Do you have sensory items available to enable clients to 'stim'?
  o Do you have a blanket or throw for your clients if they need it (weighted or otherwise)?
  o Is there space in the room if a client needs to stand up, stretch or pace?
  o Minimise strong fragrances.
  o Is your therapy room close to a toilet? A potential combination of noise and smell may be distracting.

Most, if not all, clients thrive when there is consistency for their therapy, e.g., the room, the day, the time, their therapist, etc. After all, predictability can help to reduce anxiety.

REFERENCES

Angyal, A. (1941) *Foundations for a Science of Personality*. New York: Commonwealth Fund.

Bloomer, A. (2021) 'Blanket' DNACPR decisions for people with a learning disability were proposed at a local level. *Learning Disability Today*, 18 March. Available at www.learningdisabilitytoday.co.uk/care-quality-commission-report-on-do-not-attempt-cardiopulmonary-resuscitation-dnacpr-decisions (retrieved 27 March 2022).

Davies, K. (2016) How rude? Autism as a study in ability. In K. Runswick-Cole, R. Mallet and S. Simimi (Eds), *Re-thinking Autism: Diagnosis, Identity and Equality*. London: Jessica Kingsley.

Degener, T. (2016) Disability in a human rights context. *Laws*, 5(3), 35. https://doi.org/10.3390/laws5030035

Doyle, N. (2020) Neurodiversity at work: a biopsychosocial model and the impact on working adults. *British Medical Bulletin*, 135, 1–18. https://doi.org/10.1093/bmb/ldaa021

Doyle, N. and McDowell, A. (2021) Diamond in the rough? An 'empty review' of research into 'neurodiversity' and a road map for developing the inclusion agenda. *Equality, Diversity and Inclusion* [online], 41(3). https://doi.org/10.1108/EDI-06-2020-0172

Goodley, D. (2016) Autism and the Human. In K. Runswick-Cole, R. Mallet and S. Simimi (Eds), *Re-thinking Autism: Diagnosis, Identity and Equality*. London: Jessica Kingsley.

Huijg, D.D. (2020) Neuronormativity in theorising agency. In H.B. Rosqvist, N. Chown and A. Stenning (Eds), *Neurodiversity Studies: A New Critical Paradigm* (pp. 213–217). London: Routledge. doi: 10.4324/9780429322297-20

Kapp, S.K., Gillespie-Lynch, K., Sherman, L.E. and Hutman, T. (2013) Deficit, difference, or both? Autism and neurodiversity. *Developmental Psychology*, 49(1), 59–71. doi: 10.1037/a0028353

Kirschenbaum, H. and Henderson, V.L. (1989) *The Carl Rogers Reader*. Boston, MA: Houghton Mifflin.

Meyer, I.H. (2003) Prejudice as stress: conceptual and measurement problems. *American Journal of Public Health*, 93(2), 262–265.

Moors, H. (2022) *Ableism in therapy: a qualitative study of therapists' experiences as clients in personal therapy*. MA Dissertation, Liverpool John Moores University.

Radulski, B.M. (2022) Conceptualising autistic masking, camouflaging, and neurotypical privilege: towards a minority group model of neurodiversity. *Human Development*, 66, 113–127. doi: 10.1159/000524122

Raffensperger, M. (2009) Factors that influence outcomes for clients with an intellectual disability. *British Journal of Guidance & Counselling*, 37(4), 495–509.

Ralph, N. (2017) Understanding Disability: Part 4 – The Charity Model. *Drake Music* [Blog], 20 December. Available at www.drakemusic.org/blog/nim-ralph/understanding-disability-part-4-the-charity-model/ (retrieved 27 March 2022).

Rogers, C.R. (1980) *A Way of Being*. Boston, MA: Houghton Mifflin.

Singer, J. (1998) Odd People. In *The Birth of Community Amongst People on the Autism Spectrum: A Personal Exploration of a New Social Movement Based on Neurological Diversity*. An honours thesis presented to the Faculty of Humanities and Social Science, The University of Technology, Sydney.

Stafford, M.R. and Bond, T. (2020) *Counselling Skills in Action* (4th ed.). London: Sage.

Tudor, K. and Worrall, M. (2006) *Person-Centred Therapy: A Clinical Philosophy*. London: Routledge.

United Nations (2006) *UN Convention on the Rights of Persons with Disabilities*. New York: UN. Available at www.un.org/esa/socdev/enable/rights/convtexte.htm

Walker, N. (2021) *Neuroqueer Heresies: Notes on the Neurodiversity Paradigm, Autistic Empowerment, and Postnormal Possibilities*. Fort Worth, TX: Autonomous Press.

Withers, A.J. (2012) *Disability Politics and Theory*. Halifax, Nova Scotia: Fernwood Publishing.

Wynter, S. (2003) Unsettling the coloniality of being/power/truth/freedom: towards the human, after man, its overrepresentation – an argument. *CR: The New Centennial Review*, 3(3), 257–337.

RECOMMENDED READING

Association of Neurodivergent Therapists (ANDT), https://neurodivergenttherapists.com/ (established in 2021, ANDT is a group for ND therapists).

Although based in the UK, ANDT has a global reach. They organise monthly informal support for fellow ND therapists and trainees, facilitate structured discussions and organise training events.

Stark, E., Ali, D., Ayre, A., Schneider, N., Parveen, S., Marais, K., Holmes, N. and Pender, R. (2021) *Psychological Therapy for Autistic Adults* [online]. Oxford: Authentistic Research Collective. Available at https://www.authentistic.uk/ (retrieved 24 February 2021).

This is an exceptionally useful resource, written from lived experience. It contains a wealth of important information to consider when working therapeutically with neurodivergent people.

Walker, N. (2021) *Neuroqueer Heresies: Notes on the Neurodiversity Paradigm, Autistic Empowerment, and Postnormal Possibilities*. Fort Worth, TX: Autonomous Press.

Nick describes herself as a queer, transgender, flamingly autistic author and educator. Her work is challenging, informative and, as ND person, I find her writing deeply affirmative.

2.7 RELIGION AND SPIRITUALITY

CEMIL EGELI AND WILLIAM WEST

OVERVIEW AND KEY POINTS

Working with clients around issues relating to spirituality or religion presents a range of challenges and opportunities to counsellors and psychotherapists. It is apparent that clients do not always receive best practice in this area (Jenkins, 2010).

It is important to recognise that:

- Religion and/or spirituality remains an important part of many people's lives today.
- Engaging with spirituality and religion can contribute to people's health and wellbeing.
- Therapists need to be familiar with the challenges and benefits of working with their clients around their relationship with religion and spirituality.
- For many in the field, discussing religious or spiritual dimensions remains something of a taboo.

INTRODUCTION

It would be true to say that counselling and psychotherapy have an uneasy relationship with religion and spirituality and vice versa. At first glance, this might seem strange since both deal with profound questions relating to the human condition, in particular human suffering – how to make sense of it, how to deal with it and, above all, how to avoid or at least minimise it. However, if we reflect on the idea that the origins of modern counselling and psychotherapy lie in the Victorian era (McLeod, 2009) and, like modern medicine and psychology, early therapists sought to define their theory and practice as 'scientific'; if we then consider that to be 'scientific', indeed to be 'modern', at that time meant to be non- or, in some cases, anti-religious, then we see the challenges of putting religious and therapeutic systems alongside one another. Perhaps we are still reeling from the legacy of Freud, who saw analysis as a secular form of theology (Pound, 2007). Indeed, for some, therapy may, in some ways, be a replacement for religion in post-religious societies (Hofert, 2017).

BRITISH CONTEXT

Bullivant (2016) analysed data from the British Social Attitudes surveys and concluded that people in England and Wales who say they have no religion now significantly outnumber those who regard themselves as Christians (the largest religious group). However, Woodhead (2016) states that the new emergent group of non-religious or 'nones' may reject organised religion but that cannot be conflated with the growth of secularism or atheism. While the country may be growing in people who may define as non-religious, what this may mean in practice regarding their religiosity or spirituality is not clear.

GLOBAL PERSPECTIVE

While in Britain there is a growth of the non-religious population, the global trend is different. The World Population Review (2021) states that 85% of the global population identify with a religion. The Pew Research Center (2015) conducted a demographic study which predicts that most major religious groups will increase in number by 2050. They forecast that Christians will remain the largest group, while Islam will grow faster than any other of the larger religions and, by 2050, the number of Muslims will be roughly equal to the number of Christians throughout the world. There will also be increases in smaller religions, and people who are unaffiliated with religion (including atheists and agnostics) will be in decline globally. The role of religion and spirituality is set to remain strong on the world stage.

DEFINITIONS

There are a number of differing definitions, particularly of spirituality, but also of religion. There seems to be a developing consensus, reflected in most dictionary definitions, that spirituality relates to personal beliefs and religion to the organised group of believers, including places of worship, rituals and creeds. We shall use this distinction here. However, not everyone accepts these distinctions and from the viewpoint of therapeutic practice, it is always best to explore what words mean for clients.

In terms of definitions that are useful for therapy, Elkins et al.'s (1988) research into what people mean by 'spirituality' seems especially useful, with its focus on experience, John Rowan's (2005) transpersonal work reminds us that spirituality can involve changes in our sense of self, and John Swinton (2001) reminds us that it is about connections inside the person, between people and with creation. One of the key authors from a transpersonal viewpoint is Ken Wilber (2000), who presents a model that integrates Western secular therapy with Eastern ideas of spiritual development. His model has aroused sufficient criticism and strong support to suggest that it has value and it challenges us to think beyond a one size fits all for psychospiritual practice and to tailor our therapeutic response to the perceived (spiritual) and developmental needs of the individual client.

Pulling their ideas together, along with those of clients and colleagues, the following seems to be a useful composite description of some of the possible components of spirituality that are particularly relevant to therapy:

1. It is rooted in human experiencing rather than abstract theology, i.e., it helps to focus on spirituality as a human (and often embodied) experience and what this means to people.
2. It may involve feeling strongly connected to other people, animals, nature and the universe at large.
3. It may involve non-ordinary consciousness, i.e., in altered states of consciousness or trance states.
4. It deals with the meaning that people make of their lives.
5. It faces suffering, its causes and potentially its meaning to the individual.
6. It relates to God/Goddesses/divine/ultimate reality: these words are especially rich in meaning, and not always unproblematic.
7. It often uses the word 'soul' or 'higher self': these words often have powerful associations and meanings for people.
8. Techniques such as prayer, meditation, contemplation, mindfulness, yoga, Tai Chi, martial arts, music and creative arts can be used or experienced as spiritual practices (Egeli, 2019, 2021a; West, 2004, 2010).
9. It can include a range of activities, from sex to skateboarding (Carlisle, 2018; Mann, 2020; O'Connor, 2020).

Many people continue to have a plethora of experiences that they may or may not apply the word 'spiritual' to. Indeed, for some, therapy can itself be analogous to a spiritual pursuit (Rogers, 1980; Thorne, 2002).

RELEVANCE TO COUNSELLING AND PSYCHOTHERAPY

The training of therapists is intended to equip them to deal effectively with almost any issues raised by their clients. Inevitably, some of these client issues will raise questions relating to the therapist's own personal life and beliefs. So facing challenges arising from their clients' spiritual and religious beliefs should be par for the course. However, there is enough research around spirituality and therapy to show that a fair few therapists cannot rise to the challenges involved (Jafari, 2016; Jenkins, 2010) and neither can some of their supervisors (West, 2000b).

Any form of client assessment should naturally include questions relating to their religious upbringing and what religious or spiritual practices they have in their current life (Richards and Bergin, 2005; West, 2000a). This not only gives the therapist some very useful information (even finding out how unreligious or anti-religious a client might be is itself important) but also gives the client permission to discuss such issues if they see fit.

There are a number of ways of making sense of religion and spirituality within therapy. A detailed exploration of this topic is beyond the scope of this chapter. A few pointers, however, may be useful as a starting point.

1. DECOLONISATION AND CROSS-CULTURAL UNDERSTANDINGS

The pioneering writings of Roy Moodley (Moodley, 2006, 2007; Moodley and West, 2005) and Pittu Laungani (2007) could very well fit within decolonising discourse. They invite us to enlarge our cross-cultural understandings of what makes people suffer and of the creative role varying cultural, religious and spiritual factors can play in the relief of suffering. More recently, Nwoye (2015) calls for challenges to Eurocentric paradigms to psychopathology, which includes working with spiritualistic Africentric practices. McInnis (2021) calls for an African psychology perspective in therapy which can facilitate spiritual enlightenment.

Taking a decolonising or postcolonial perspective may be prudent (Charura and Lago, 2021). De Sousa

Santos (2008), talking epistemically, argues for cognitive justice through recognising the diversity of knowledge systems or an 'ecology of knowledges' which had been suppressed by western scientific thought. Counselling and psychotherapy somewhat plays into the modernist Eurocentric Cartesian view which separates mind and body (and ignores the spirit). Consequently, 'It would be a mistake to imagine that all clients reporting religious, spiritual or mystical beliefs or experiences would be understood or well received by their counsellors' (McLeod, 2009: 490).

2. RELIGION AS A SITE OF RESISTANCE, REFUGE AND PERSECUTION

It is important to understand the role religion may have for our clients in a broader political and social context. Using Christianity as an example, Malhorta (2012: 74) states that in the USA many African Americans have 'staged postcolonial resistance through an assertion of religion'. From a Latin American liberation theology perspective, Christianity has been a site of resistance to capitalism (Bell, 2001). From a UK viewpoint, Burrell (2021) writes, the growth of the Pentecostal community came partly as a response to the unwelcoming established churches Black people found themselves in.

We should also be aware of prejudices people may face due to their religion. For example, Inayat (2007) explores some of the vulnerabilities Muslim clients face due to the rising tide of Islamophobia, and Lowental (2021) investigates the invisibility of Jewishness and the ongoing presence of anti-semitism within psychology.

Both in the UK and across the world, people face discrimination, persecution and even death due to their religious beliefs and backgrounds (Amnesty, 2020; Ochab, 2020). It is important to be mindful of these wider societal factors and traumas when exploring religion with clients.

3. RELIGION AND SPIRITUALITY AS BOTH 'SOLUTION' AND 'PROBLEM'

Engaging with spirituality and religion can contribute to people's health and wellbeing. It can be a source of hope and a place of support, comfort and sanctuary in times of distress. Religion can conversely be the cause of suffering too. It may conflict with people's values and can be the source of tensions, guilt and shame. People may feel the need or pressure to conform or feel rejected or abandoned from religious groups. They may face spiritual abuse or addictions (Vaughn, 2000). Unfortunately, some religious groups can be discriminatory and issues such as homophobia are rife (Noblett, 2020).

4. RELIGION AND IDENTITY

Religion and spirituality can represent a key aspect of cultural identity for many people (Orbe and Harris, 2015). It ties into the client's personal values and, along with rituals and practices, it can be important when processing and negotiating changes and rites of passage across the lifespan. Religion and spirituality may be a source of support or tension for clients when working through life's journey.

A person's relationship with religion may be impacted by a range of intersecting social and personal factors. It may be helpful to clarify the role of spirituality and religion in their life. Just knowing that a client is Christian, Jewish or Muslim, for instance, is not enough. As Lipner (1993) suggests, religions are intrinsically plural and polycentric and there are liberal and traditional groupings in almost all religions.

From a mixed-race perspective, there are an increasing number of people who come from multi-faith backgrounds and do not neatly fit into one particular religious tradition. This can present tensions for people who sit between two or more religious traditions (Egeli, 2021b). If we are to engage with our clients, we must be aware of the nuances of their experience.

5. ETHICS

It is important to acknowledge a number of very crucial ethical issues when working with clients around issues to do with religion and spirituality. These include:

1. The respectful acceptance of clients' religious and spiritual beliefs and practices, however strange and unsettling they may appear to be, as it can be about recognising the diversity of knowledge and belief systems.
2. A recognition of the limits of both competence and the therapist's willingness to work in the area of religion and spirituality.

3. How, when spirituality is experienced in the therapy room, there is sometimes an apparent softening of boundaries between client and therapist and great care is then needed.
4. That self-awareness of the therapist with regard to their spiritual and religious beliefs and attitudes (including any countertransference issues) is an important underpinning of best practice in this area (Lannert, 1991; Wyatt, 2002).
5. That supervision of this part of therapeutic practice is especially important, even though some supervisors are reluctant to supervise or welcome therapeutic work around spirituality and religion (West, 2003).

CONCLUSION

The tensions between those of a religious or spiritual faith and the dominant, arguably secular, modern culture are unlikely to ease. Indeed, as counselling and psychotherapy continues its (somewhat tortuous) path towards professionalisation and forms of statutory accreditation, it may well embody some of these very tensions. Improvements in training and supervision are still, in our view, necessary before clients receive the help they are due with regards to religion and spirituality. This is especially important when taking cultural perspectives into account and adopting a more global or decolonising view.

REFERENCES

Amnesty International UK (2020) *China's Uighur Muslims: The Truth behind the Headlines*. Available at www.amnesty.org.uk/chinas-uighur-muslims-truth-behind-headlines?

Bell, D.M. (2001) *Liberation Theology after the End of History: The Refusal to End Suffering*. Abingdon, UK: Routledge.

Bullivant, S. (2016) *Contemporary Catholicism in England and Wales*. London: St Mary's University.

Burrell, R.R. (2021) Religion, therapy and mental health treatment in diverse communities: Some critical reflections and radical propositions. In D. Charura & C. Lago (Eds), *Black Identities and White Therapies: Race, Respect and Diversity*. Monmouth: PCCS Books.

Carlisle, G.C. (2018) Enlightened sexuality: exploring the implications of sacred sexuality. *Journal of Psychology and Theology*, *46*(1), 22–37. https://doi.org/10.1177/0091647117750654

Charura, D. & Lago, C. (Eds) (2021) *Black Identities and White Therapies: Race, Respect and Diversity*. Monmouth: PCCS Books.

Egeli, C. (2019) Tears from the void: The arts, the spiritual and the therapeutic. *Thresholds*, October. Available at www.bacp.co.uk/bacp-journals/thresholds/october-2019/tears-from-the-void/

Egeli, C. (2021a) Editorial: Towards a psychomusicology. *Journal of Critical Psychology, Counselling and Psychotherapy*, *21*(2), 6–10.

Egeli, C. (2021b) Counselling the Other. In C. Newnes (Ed.), *Racism in Psychology: Challenging Theory, Practice and Institutions*. London: Routledge. pp. 131–146.

Elkins, D.N., Hedstorm, J.L., Hughes, L.L., Leaf, J.A. & Saunders, C. (1988) Toward a humanistic-phenomenological spirituality. *Journal of Humanistic Psychology*, *28*(4) 5–18.

Hofert, K. (2017) Can psychotherapy replace the void left by religion in a modern post-religious society? First-person account. *British Journal of Psychiatry*, *211*(5), 273–273. doi:10.1192/bjp.bp.117.200964

Inayat, Q. (2007) Islamophobia and the therapeutic dialogue: Some reflections. *Counselling Psychology Quarterly*, *20*(3), 287–293. doi: 10.1080/09515070701567804

Jafari, S. (2016) Religion and spirituality within counselling/clinical psychology training programmes: A systematic review. *British Journal of Guidance and Counselling*, *44*(3) 257–267.

Jenkins, C. (2010) When the clients' spirituality is denied in therapy. In W. West (Ed.), *Exploring Therapy, Spirituality and Healing*. Basingstoke: Palgrave.

(Continued)

(Continued)

Lannert, J. (1991) Resistance and countertransference issues with spiritual and religious clients. *Journal of Humanistic Psychology*, *31*(4), 68–76.

Laungani, P. (2007) *Understanding Cross-Cultural Psychology*. London: Sage.

Lipner, J. (1993) The 'inter' of interfaith spirituality. *The Way*, *78*(Suppl.), 64.

Loewenthal, K.M. (2021) Invisible anti-semitism in psychology. In C. Newnes (Ed.), *Racism in Psychology: Challenging Theory, Practice and Institutions*. London: Routledge. pp. 16–25.

Malhotra, S. (2012). Postmodernity, Postcoloniality, and Religious Cultures. In D. Joy, J.F. Duggan (Eds), *Decolonizing the Body of Christ. Postcolonialism and Religions*. Palgrave Macmillan, New York. https://doi.org/10.1057/9781137021038_5

Mann, R. (2020) *Dazzling Darkness: Gender, Sexuality, Illness and God* (new revised ed.). Glasgow: Wild Goose Publications.

McLeod, J. (2009) *An Introduction to Counselling* (4th ed.). Maidenhead: Open University Press.

McInnis, E.M. (2021) The global system of white supremacy within UK clinical psychology: An African psychology perspective. In C. Newnes (Ed.), *Racism in Psychology: Challenging Theory, Practice and Institutions*. London: Routledge.

Moodley, R. (2006) Cultural representations and interpretations of 'subjective distress' in ethnic minority patients. In R. Moodley & S. Palmer (Eds), *Race, Culture and Psychotherapy*. London: Routledge.

Moodley, R. (2007) (Re)placing multiculturalism in counselling and psychotherapy. *British Journal of Guidance & Counselling*, *35*(1), 1–22.

Moodley, R. & West, W. (Eds) (2005) *Integrating Traditional Healing Practices into Counseling and Psychotherapy*. Thousand Oaks, CA: Sage.

Moodley, R., Aanchal, R. & Alladin, W. (2010) *Bridging East–West Psychology and Counselling: Exploring the Work of Pittu Laungani*. New Delhi: Sage.

Noblett, T. (2020) Report: The impact of coming out to religious parents. *Naz and Matt Foundation*. Available at www.nazandmattfoundation.org/reports

Nwoye, A. (2015) African psychology and the Africentric paradigm to clinical diagnosis and treatment. *South African Journal of Psychology*, *45*(3), 305–317.

Ochab, E.U. (2020) Persecuted Christians are not given much hope in 2020. *Forbes*, 18 February. Available at www.forbes.com/sites/ewelinaochab/2020/02/18/persecuted-christians-are-not-given-much-hope-in-2020/?sh=560ca6b16889

O'Connor, P. (2020) *Skateboarding and Religion*. London: Palgrave Macmillan.

Orbe, M.P. & Harris, T.M. (2015) *Interracial Communication: Theory into Practice* (3rd ed.). London: Sage.

Pew Research Center (2015) *The Future of World Religions: Population Growth Projections, 2010–2050*. Washington, DC: Pew Research Center. Available at www.pewforum.org/2015/04/02/religious-projections-2010-2050/

Pound, M. (2007) *Theology, Psychoanalysis and Trauma*. Canterbury: SCM Press.

Richards, P.S. & Bergin, A.E. (2005) *A Spiritual Strategy for Counselling and Psychotherapy* (2nd ed.). Washington, DC: American Psychological Association.

Rogers, C.R. (1980) *A Way of Being*. Boston, MA: Houghton Mifflin.

Rowan, J. (2005) *The Transpersonal: Spirituality in Psychotherapy and Counselling* (2nd ed.). London: Routledge.

Sousa Santos, B. de (2008) *Another Knowledge is Possible: Beyond Northern Epistemologies*. London: Verso.

Swinton, J. (2001) *Spirituality in Mental Health Care*. London: Jessica Kingsley.

Thorne, B. (2002) *The Mystical Path of Person-Centred Therapy: Hope beyond Despair*. London: Whurr.

Vaughn, F. (2000) *The Inward Arc: Healing in Psychotherapy and Spirituality*. Lincoln, UK: Shambala.

West, W. (2000a) *Psychotherapy and Spirituality: Crossing the Line between Therapy and Religion*. London: Sage.

West, W. (2000b) Supervision difficulties and dilemmas for counsellors and psychotherapists around healing and spirituality. In B. Lawton & C. Feltham (Eds), *Taking Supervision Forwards: Dilemmas, Insights and Trends*. London: Sage.

West, W. (2003) The culture of psychotherapy supervision. *Counselling and Psychotherapy Research*, *3*(2), 123–127.

West, W. (2004) *Spiritual Issues in Therapy: Relating Experience to Practice*. Basingstoke: Palgrave.

West, W. (Ed.) (2010) *Exploring Therapy, Spirituality and Healing*. Basingstoke: Palgrave.

Wilber, K. (2000) *Integral Psychology: Consciousness, Spirit, Psychology, Therapy*. London: Shambhala.

Woodhead, L.J.P. (2016) The Rise of 'No Religion' in Britain: The emergence of a new cultural majority. *Journal of the British Academy*, *4*, 245–261. https://doi.org/10.5871/jba/004.245

World Population Review (2021) *World Population Review*. Available at https://worldpopulationreview.com/country-rankings/religion-by-country

Wyatt, J. (2002) 'Confronting the Almighty God'? A study of how psychodynamic counsellors respond to clients' expressions of religious faith. *Counselling and Psychotherapy Research*, *2*(3), 177–184.

RECOMMENDED READING

Laungani, P. (2007) *Understanding Cross-Cultural Psychology*. London: Sage.

Nwoye, A. (2015) African psychology and the Africentric paradigm to clinical diagnosis and treatment. *South African Journal of Psychology*, *45*(3), 305–317.

These texts review spirituality and religion within a cross-cultural perspective.

Mann, R. (2020) *Dazzling Darkness: Gender, Sexuality, Illness and God* (new revised ed.). Glasgow: Wild Goose Publications.

Anglican priest Mann explores sexuality, gender, illness, God and being trans.

Rowan, J. (2005) *The Transpersonal: Spirituality in Psychotherapy and Counselling* (2nd ed.). London: Routledge.

This book offers a transpersonal perspective of spirituality in psychotherapy and counselling.

2.8 RACE, CULTURE AND ETHNICITY – WHAT IS YOUR STORY?
OHEMAA NKANSA-DWAMENA AND YETUNDE ADE-SERRANO

OVERVIEW AND KEY POINTS

This chapter presents an overview of the 'hamster wheel' exposure to racism in the United Kingdom evidenced in the lived experiences of people who have been impacted by racial discrimination. It defines key terms and highlights the necessity to appraise this subject area with a critical and intersectional lens. The foundation on which an experience can be encapsulated in an individual, or group, is not limited to single occurrences of incidences but is denoted by the persistent, unrelenting episodes of abuse. Discrimination in all its forms is historical; nonetheless, racial discrimination is a dynamic phenomenon with multiple facets.

This chapter addresses the following key areas:

1. Understanding the concepts of race, culture, and ethnicity.
2. Organisation, structural, systemic, and individual discrimination.
3. Racial trauma.
4. Recommendations for therapeutic practice and professional development.

INTRODUCTION

Race, culture, and ethnicity are not new concepts within the field of psychology. Rather than conceptualise these terms – Race, Culture and Ethnicity – in ways people may be accustomed to, we will instead set them within the context of current landscape in the UK.

We provide definitions for these terms as an introduction to the themes, recognising that although distinct, they interact on several levels. We do not endorse these designations due to the complexity of human identity and experience. Rather, we propose that no one ideology can adequately encompass the intricacy and conflicting components that constitute race, culture, and ethnicity.

In academic settings, definitions are often a guide to framing our understanding of the world, and the reality of race-related experiences manifests itself very differently from the constructed description. This is compounded by the interpretations made from these descriptions, which often depend on the experiences of the individual or group as 'we see things not as they are, but as we are' (Nin, 1961: 124). Hence, our starting point is to interrogate and explore people's experiences in relation to the specified themes.

Our stance aligns to the pluralistic values of Counselling Psychology where we give credence to the unique individual and group lived experiences as a guide to exploring the issues encountered in human interactions.

CONTEXTUALISING RACE, CULTURE AND ETHNICITY

Social sciences identify race as a categorisation of people who share visible biological characteristics and, in some sense, see themselves as a single group (or others describe them as such). Fernando (1991) argues that race is characterised by physical appearance and assumed to be genetically determined when, in actuality, it is a social construct. Despite what is known about race, most of the experience in the UK is epitomised by this physical characteristic (skin colour) that reduces the human experience of those from ethnic communities.

Sewell's (2009) definition utilises the term 'ethnicity' to describe common culture traits (e.g., language, locale, religion) that distinguishes individuals and groups of people. Omi and Winant (2014) assert that ethnicity theories are an account to understand race as socially constructed phenomenon. This is evidenced in the increasing use of ethnicity data in the UK.

Culture can be exclusive, referring only to race and ethnicity, or it can be inclusive, taking account of identity factors such as gender, sexual orientation, ability, age, religion, socio-economic status, and language (Daya, 2001; Pedersen, 2001). Culture, for some, is implicated as a tool in managing people within a social context (Abu-Lughod, 2006). Research has shown that culture is about shared systems of learning which are used by its members to interpret experiences (Wijsen, 1999). Cultural practices and interpretations can therefore be cumulative in nature. They occur between and within generations, which can transform over historical times. Therefore, culture is fluid: it is a moving entity that can be influenced by locality, time, events, and context.

The very essence of our comprehension of race, culture, and ethnicity must be viewed through the lens of intersectionality, giving due consideration to all elements of identity and experiences of privilege and oppression. Intersectionality proposes that all people are positioned within socially created categories of oppression and domination, such as race, culture, gender, and class, that are located within a historical context. Intersectionality considers the ways that identities related to multiple socially constructed categories create unique intersections of experiences, which are qualitatively different from the sum of individual identities (Cole, 2009; Crenshaw, 1989; Steinbugler, Press, and Días, 2006).

In the wake of the Covid-19 pandemic and the race-related killings both in the UK and the US, there has been a surge in conversation about race, culture, and ethnicity, but it predominately focused on race. Although there seems to be an openness to engage in dialogue and develop awareness, primarily, this often does not translate into action. The conversation tends to be stifled by defence mechanisms that desire to maintain power and privilege by employing technical methods of minimising experiences of racism (e.g., 'all lives matter', 'I do not see colour') while rationalising the harm being caused. One example is the current ongoing political debate around Critical Race Theory (CRT), with those in positions of power asserting that this tool, which is used to critically evaluate the experiences of racism, can be perceived as 'divisive' and 'contested as factual'. Another example is the Sewell Race Report (HM Government, 2021), which categorically denies the direct experience of racism and the impact of it on ethnic communities in all areas of life, including mental health. The controversy surrounding the Sewell Report was intensified by the internalised racist assumptions made by its authors. A further example of how people, institutions, and systems tend to minimise the experience of racism is situated in how the curriculum and the training of therapists advantages western and Eurocentric perspectives over and above other cross-cultural frameworks.

RACE CONTEXT IN THE UK

On a macro level, history has led to the inequity embedded in various structures, systems, and institutions built on colonialism, slavery, and power. In turn, this influences how we relate to one another, the opportunities that are available to people from ethnic communities, and access to mental health services.

Several reviews into racial equality and inequity have taken place in the UK, including ones that focus on racial inequality and mental health (e.g., The Sainsbury Centre for Mental Health report (2002), *The Lammy Review* (Lammy, 2017), *The McGregory-Smith Review* (2017), the Windrush Review (Williams, 2020), and the *Disparities in the Risk and Outcomes of Covid-19* report (Public Health England, 2020)), with the aim of providing actionable recommendations to improve experiences and outcome for people of colour. Some of the themes in these reports include:

- inequalities between ethnicities in educational attainment
- unequal treatment by the criminal justice
- evidence of bias and discrimination against people from ethnic communities in health and employment
- institutional ignorance and racism.

This highlights the longevity of these issues, the nature of the issues, and how the system maintains the occurrence of these issues.

In the practice of Counselling Psychology, counselling, and psychotherapy, institutional discrimination is revealed in curricula, training, supervision, clinical practice, development, provision, and evaluation of services. This is reflected in the comments made by the CEO of the British Psychological Society in 2020, where he states that the organisation is 'institutionally racist'. As a professional body responsible for setting practice standards for the psychology profession, it is disproportionately biased towards those who benefit from privileged positioning. The institutional racism inherent in organisational processes and procedures has meant ostracisations of people of colour and, in turn, the population they serve, rendering their experiences unseen, unheard, and unacknowledged. This directly contradicts the ethical requirements of the profession to do no harm, recognise, and take action against discrimination and intolerance (Johnson and Melton, 2020).

Interpersonal and individual levels of racism also exist in the UK context. These can be both overt (e.g., explicit racial slurs, racially motivated attacks, and murders) and covert (e.g., microaggressions) in nature. The latter is perhaps a less known and understood experience of racism but has a significant impact on the mental and physical health of people of colour.

Microaggressions, as coined by Pierce, Carew, Pierce-Gonzales, and Willis (1978: 66), was defined as 'subtle, stunning, often automatic and non-verbal exchanges which are put downs'. Microaggressions can be sub-categorised into microassaults, microinsults and microinvalidations. Sue and Constantine (2007) define the various terms as: (1) microassaults are conscious and intentional actions or slurs, such as using racial descriptions, displaying swastikas, or a black person being followed around by a security guard in a shop; (2) microinsults, on the other hand, are verbal and nonverbal communications that subtly convey rudeness and insensitivity and demean a person's racial heritage or identity. An example of this is an employee who asks a colleague who is black how they got their job, implying they may have landed it through an affirmative action or quota system; and (3) microinvalidations are communications that subtly exclude, negate, or nullify the thoughts, feelings, or experiential reality of a people of colour. For instance, white people asking where a black person was born, conveying the message that they are perpetual foreigners in their own land.

The effects of macro and interpersonal experiences of racism include psychological, physical, and health issues that activate racial trauma. We would highlight that racial trauma is distinct from other expressions of trauma because it is triggered solely on a person's race and ethnicity. Comas-Díaz, Hall, and Neville (2019: 1) state that:

> racial trauma, a form of race-based stress, refers to people of color and indigenous individuals' (POCI) reactions to dangerous events and real or perceived experiences of racial discrimination. Such experiences may include threats of harm and injury, humiliating and shaming events, and witnessing racial discrimination toward other POCI. Although like posttraumatic stress disorder, racial trauma is unique in that it involves ongoing individual and collective injuries due to exposure and re-exposure to race-based stress.

Our understanding of macro and interpersonal levels of racism is crucial to our reflexivity as practitioners. Ignorance around these issues mean practitioners can cause unintentional harm within the therapeutic relationship, by minimising, invalidating, or exacerbating the impact of racial trauma.

RELEVANCE TO COUNSELLING PSYCHOLOGY, COUNSELLING AND PSYCHOTHERAPY

Why does all this matter to the practice of therapists? It matters because race, culture and ethnicity permeate our contexts, clinical practice, supervision, research, training, continued professional development, service evaluation, service accessibility, and positioning as practitioners. The following case study and subsequent reflections explores these areas further and helps to situate the discussion on race, culture, ethnicity, and the therapeutic professions.

CASE STUDY

A male bi-racial client who self-referred to therapy saw his male Asian therapist for three months. He was hoping to have the space to explore his racial identity and the difficulties with challenging the stereotypical media portrayal of Asian men.

Sajid is a 35-year-old who presented as well educated and well groomed. Despite this, the therapist's impression was that Sajid came across as childlike. Sajid recounted prior experiences of therapy with a white male in the first few sessions, indicating that he had felt held by that therapist at a very vulnerable time of his life. However, he stated he was excited to be working with an Asian therapist since he was wanting to explore his racial identity, an area that he perceived was less accessible with his previous therapist.

In terms of his personal history, he recounted the environments he existed in and the experiences that often perceived him as the 'other', even though he did not see himself as such.

During therapy, Sajid elevated his therapist to a position of awe as he felt that their shared identity and experience cultivated a sense of safety. These positionings caused them both to make several assumptions about one another (e.g., the therapist made assumptions around relatedness to those from Asian backgrounds and Sajid made assumptions about the therapist's absolute ability to understand everything about him and his experience).

The manifestations of the emerging themes during therapy led to the ending of the therapeutic alliance – the relationship ruptured when the therapist shared the observation about Sajid's relatedness (or lack thereof) to women of a similar background.

POSITIONING AS PRACTITIONERS

Our positioning as practitioners in relation to the clients we work with and the contexts we work in are not devoid of the impact of race, culture, or ethnicity. The nuances of these aspects interplay with relational dynamics and the therapeutic lens. In the case study, the therapist took a knowing position due to the element of cultural and racial sameness, not acknowledging the idiosyncrasies of the client. He made assumptions about Sajid's experiences through a limited lens and his own experience as an Asian man. This meant that he missed the opportunity to see, hear, and validate Sajid's unique intersectional experience. This replicates people of colour not being seen as their full selves, limiting it to one aspect of life rather than the intersections of various elements that make up the person.

Within the profession, these are repeated narratives from clients of colour, who can experience therapy as invalidating and retraumatising. Often, this arises in a racially differing dyad. However, this case study highlights how the lack of awareness, even within the same communities, can minimise the client's experience and may cause undue harm. A lack of awareness around the therapist's positionality demonstrates a lack of understanding on how race, culture, and ethnicity influences positions of privilege and oppression.

The therapist's knowing position lacked the curiosity and criticality of how the client may have been shaped by his upbringing, social class, and race, among other facets. Furthermore, the therapist's racial positioning, based on his categorisation of Asian communities, meant that he projected onto Sajid his own developed beliefs of racial experiencing, thereby lacking cultural humility and curiosity.

TRAINING AND CONTINUED PROFESSIONAL DEVELOPMENT

> Awareness of race, culture and ethnicity is a fundamental element of good professional practice and an imperative segment of training. (Ade-Serrano and Nkansa-Dwamena, 2014)

As indicated in the case study, the absence of an awareness of race, culture, and ethnicity leads to unethical practice and perpetuates the culturally unattuned experiences people of colour can have within mental health services. Additionally, a lack of cultural sensitivity can have far-reaching consequences, particularly when a Eurocentric/western frame is adopted during training and continued professional development. This may include:

1. Alienating those from ethnic communities.
2. Retraumatisation of clients.
3. Early termination or unmendable ruptures within therapeutic relationships.
4. Ill-equipped practitioners who are unable to comprehend the dynamics of difference and power.
5. Personal and professional ignorance of practitioners' own identity construction.

Had the therapist engaged with training and continued professional development, it would have challenged his script on race, culture, and ethnicity, allowing for a level of congruence and modelling for Sajid. Individual self-development and awareness are at the heart of therapy and its training. It is an ongoing growth process. It should sync our exploration of ideals, values, understanding on issues related to race, culture, and ethnicity (our own and others) and form an integral part of our practice in a rich and meaningful way (Ade-Serrano and Nkansa-Dwamena, 2014).

SUPERVISION

Continued professional development and cultural curiosity can also be gained from a culturally informed supervisory space. A culturally framed supervision aids ethical practice, interrogates the practitioner's blind spots, and can help practitioners navigate cultural conflicts as well as unearth and challenge bias. We would argue that culturally appropriate supervision should be the standard not the exception.

In the presented case example, supervision may help to query the notion of sameness Sajid or the therapist purports to have, and potentially make use of a multi-perspective view of practice (see the seven eyed model of supervision; Hawkins and Shohet, 2020), which considers culture, contextual determinants, and intersectional identities and idiosyncratic life experiences, thereby widening the practitioner's scope of practice and lens. While assumptions about race, culture and ethnicity may serve as a doorway to curious interrogation, it can only have necessary impact when learning and development are applied in a meaningful way, personally and professionally.

CONCLUSION

To fully engage with race, culture, and ethnicity in counselling, psychotherapy, and psychology, and within our wider contexts, requires a multi-faceted understanding of intersectional experiences and identities, an understanding of the impact of historical legacies of discrimination, contextual determinants, and influences, in addition to an ongoing commitment to active anti-discriminatory practice. It also requires a meaningful examination of one's own positioning and lens. Outside any initial core training, it is the ethical responsibility of every practitioner, regardless of race, culture, or ethnicity, to engage with culturally appropriate continued professional development.

We offer some suggestions here to highlight areas of practice and ongoing development to be aware of, and to emphasise the pluralistic approach warranted when engaging with issues pertaining to the explored areas:

1. Culturally appropriate supervision needs to be sought and received, considering the triad of the therapeutic relationship and parallel processing.
2. Practitioners should consider the relevance of history and context, as it pertains to race, culture, and ethnicity.
3. The criticality of taking an intersectional approach to race, culture, and ethnicity.
4. Practitioners should consider their position and development of self in relation to race, culture, and ethnicity.
5. Practitioners should draw from cross-cultural frameworks which are not levelled against the Eurocentric/western frame.
6. Practitioners should engage with contextualised race, culture, and ethnicity research.
7. When assessing and formulating clients' narratives, bear in mind a need for cultural formulations grounded in the lived experiences of clients.
8. Practitioners need to be aware of organisational, structural, and systemic racism and its impact on relatedness and accessibility.
9. An awareness of the role of language in therapy and how this might inadvertently be wielded as a discriminatory tool.

REFERENCES

Abu-Lughod, L., 2006. Writing against culture. In E. Lewin (Ed.), *Feminist Anthropology: A Reader.* Oxford and Malden, MA: Blackwell.

Ade-Serrano, Y., and Nkansa-Dwamena, O., 2014. *Proposal to Include Race, Culture and Diversity in Counselling Psychology training.* London: unpublished.

British Psychological Society, 2020. *Annual conference. [Online].* Available at www.youtube.com/watch?v=vk8QGD6FhJQ (accessed 1 February 2022).

Cole, E., 2009. Intersectionality and research in psychology. *American Psychologist*, 64(3), 170–180.

Comas-Díaz, L., Hall, G.N., and Neville, H.A., 2019. Racial trauma: theory, research, and healing: introduction to the special issue. *American Psychologist*, 74(1), 1–5.

Crenshaw, K., 1989. Demarginalizing the intersection of race and sex: a black feminist critique of antidiscrimination doctrine, feminist theory, and antiracist politics. *University of Chicago Legal Forum*, 1(8), 139–167, accessed at https://chicagounbound.uchicago.edu/cgi/viewcontent.cgi?article=1052&context=uclf

Daya, R., 2001. Changing the face of multicultural counselling with principles of change. *Canadian Journal of Counselling*, 35(1), 49–62.

Fernando, S., 1991. *Mental Health, Race and Culture.* Basingstoke: Macmillan.

Hawkins, P., and Shohet, R., 2020. *Supervision in the Helping Professions.* Milton Keynes: Open University Press.

HM Government, 2021. *Commission on Race and Ethnic Disparities: The Report.* [The Sewell Report]. London: HM Government.

Johnson, M., and Melton, L.M., 2020. *Addressing Race-Based Stress in Therapy with Black Clients: Using Multicultural and Dialectical Behavior Therapy Techniques.* New York and London: Routledge.

Lammy, D., 2017. *The Lammy Review: An Independent Review into the Treatment of, and Outcomes for, Black, Asian and Minority Ethnic Individuals in the Criminal Justice System.* London: House of Commons.

McGregory-Smith, R., 2017. *Race in the Workplace: The McGregory-Smith Review.* London: House of Commons.

Nin, A., 1961. *Seduction of the Minotaur.* Athens, OH: Swallow Press/Ohio University Press.

Omi, M., and Winant, H., 2014. *Racial Formation in the United States* (3rd ed.). New York and London: Routledge.

Pedersen, P., 2001. Multiculturalism and the paradigm shift in counselling: controversies and alternative futures. *Canadian Journal of Counselling*, 35(1), 15–25.

Pierce, C., Carew, J., Pierce-Gonzalez, D., and Willis, D., 1978. An experiment in racism: TV commercials. In C. Pierce (Ed.), *Television and Education* (pp. 62–88). Beverly Hills, CA: Sage.

Public Health England, 2020. *Disparities in the Risk and Outcomes of Covid-19.* London: Public Health England.

Sewell, H., 2009. *Working with Ethnicity, Race and Culture in Mental Health: A Handbook for Practitioners.* London: Jessica Kingsley.

Steinbugler, A.C., Press, J.E., and Días, J.J., 2006. Gender, race, and affirmative action: operationalizing intersectionality in survey research. *Gender & Society*, 20(6), 805–825.

Sue, D.W., and Constantine, M.G., 2007. Racial microaggressions as instigators of difficult dialogues on race: implications for student affairs educators and students. *College Student Affairs Journal*, 26(2), 136–143.

The Sainsbury Centre for Mental Health, 2002. *Breaking the Circles of Fear: A Review of the Relationship between Mental Health and African and Caribbean Communities.* London: SCMH.

Wijsen, F., 1999. Beyond the fatal impact theory. In M. Amaladoss (Ed.), *Globalization and its Victims as Seen by its Victims.* Delhi: Vidyajyoti Education and Welfare Society.

Williams, W., 2020. *Windrush: Lessons Learned Review.* London: House of Commons.

RECOMMENDED READING

Ade-Serrano, Y., and Nkansa-Dwamena, O. (Eds), (2020). *Applied Psychology and Allied Professions: Working with Ethnic Minorities.* Leicester: BPS.

This book offers idiosyncratic insight through clinical, theoretical, and experiential lenses, prioritising unravelling of intersectional identities.

Turner, D. (2021). *Intersections of Privilege and Otherness in Counselling and Psychotherapy.* Abingdon, UK: Routledge.

This book explores the unconscious experience of privilege in the construction of otherness through the prism of intersectionality.

Eddo-Lodge, R. (2017). *Why I'm No Longer Talking to White People about Race.* London: Bloomsbury Publishing.

This book challenges individuals to interrogate their assumptions about skin colour and places the onus on white people to educate themselves, in addition to taking accountability for their words and behaviour.

2.9 SOCIAL CLASS

LIZ BALLINGER

OVERVIEW AND KEY POINTS

This chapter offers a summary of differing views concerning the nature of social class. The questioning of its contemporary relevance is countered by a review of evidence pointing to its continued importance as a key influence in people's lives. The low profile afforded to class within counselling literature is problematised and the salience of class to the therapeutic endeavour highlighted. Some recommendations are offered for consideration.

- A range of evidence points to the continuation of class both as a source of identity and as one of the most significant sources of social advantage/disadvantage.
- The literature points to a middle-class bias in both therapists and the client base.
- Counselling and psychotherapy have historically neglected the importance of class, despite its evident relevance to mental wellbeing and the counselling process.
- An appreciation of the importance of class is integral to developing a therapeutic approach which encompasses the social sources of distress and embraces social justice.

INTRODUCTION

THE SO-CALLED 'DEATH OF CLASS'

While Britain has been regarded as a peculiarly class-ridden society, the second half of the twentieth century saw a questioning of the continued significance of class. The scale and nature of economic, political and social change during that period were argued to have led to the demolition of old class barriers and its redundancy as a meaningful concept. Cannadine (2000: 14) wrote of class analysis being 'consigned to the waste paper basket of history', while other determinants of privilege, disadvantage and identity, such as race, sexual orientation and gender, became the focus of public and political attention.

As the twentieth century drew to a close, however, there were grounds for believing that class was back on the agenda. While economic and social change may have led to the erosion of 'traditional' class barriers, inequality remained and, indeed, was on the rise. By the turn of the century Britain had the third highest levels of inequality in the western world (Wilkinson and Pickett, 2010). The 2008 financial crisis ushered in economic recession and financial austerity programmes that deepened inequality further: Clark (2014) talked of an ensuing societal schism. At the time of writing, this is being graphically illustrated by the Covid-19 pandemic as the hardest hit, both in terms of physical and financial wellbeing, are those already worst off (e.g., Blundell et al., 2020). There have been growing signs of continuing class awareness among the general population (Evans and Mellon, 2016). All these developments are reflected in a resurgence of interest in both class and inequality in the economic and social sciences (e.g., Atkinson, 2015; Savage, 2015; Todd, 2021; Wilkinson and Pickett, 2010, 2018).

CLASS AS A CONCEPT

Class is 'sticky and complicated' to define (Beswick, 2020). It has attracted a range of different, often competing, understandings over time. However, two abiding central matters of concern can be identified: material inequality and its social manifestations. These two dimensions interact with other evident dichotomies, for example, the objective and subjective dimensions of class, academic and lay understandings, which have coloured its understanding differentially over time.

In terms of material inequality, an important official measure of class continues to be occupation, which is seen as connected with other potential measures, such as income, acquired wealth and vulnerability to poverty. Occupation was central to the 1911 Registrar General's Scale, the first official measure of class, which drew a divide between middle-class non-manual and working-class manual occupations. The National Statistics Socio-Economic Classification (NS-SEC) replaced this as the official measure, and socio-economic status, rather than class, is now the classification most widely used in class-based research. However, when we turn to subjective assessments of social positioning, the terms 'middle class' and 'working class' retain a contemporary currency in our identification of ourselves and others. This identification process involves a set of 'signs and signals', for example, accent, family background, vocabulary, education, housing and lifestyle, which are commonly viewed as indicative of class (Cannadine, 2000: 22).

Bourdieu, an increasingly important figure in class analysis, brought together material and social inequality in his depiction of class. He portrayed class as based on differential ownership of different forms of capital or 'properties capable of conferring strength, power and consequently profit on their holder' (Bourdieu, 1987: 4). The important forms of class capital are economic (income and wealth), social (networks and group membership) and cultural (ownership of valued knowledge and know-how). A fourth category, symbolic capital, refers to the possession of the accepted 'signs and signals' of class noted above.

Bourdieu's ideas informed the development of a new class model for contemporary Britain (Savage, 2015). Utilising an understanding of class as the crystallisation of different kinds of capital, it identifies seven classes: a wealthy elite; the established middle class: the technical middle class; new affluent workers; traditional working class; emerging sector workers; and the precariat. Bourdieu's notion of habitus, or the socialised norms guiding thinking, feeling, behaviour and practice, has also been gainfully employed in a small but growing area of study – the lived experience of class. Commentators such as Reay (2005), Savage, Bagnall and Longhurst (2005), McKenzie (2015) and Hanley (2016) have explored the powerful impact of social class on self-esteem, self-identity and emotional experiencing, as well as on the way we make sense of our world and interact with it. The class we are born into plays an important role in the shaping of what Reay calls our 'psychic landscape' and helps explain both how class of origin remains an important source of identity and the sense of internal conflict that can accompany social mobility (e.g., Hanley, 2016; O'Neill, 2019). It also helps explain why people's self-identification can be at odds with their current occupational status (Beswick, 2020).

THE CONTEMPORARY SIGNIFICANCE OF CLASS

As mentioned previously, despite the so-called 'death of class', evidence of significant inequality across a range of human experience points to its continuing power. Such inequality has repercussions across a whole range of measures, such as housing standards, transport, services and material goods. Vulnerability to unemployment and underemployment are patterned by socio-economic status. Reflecting its title, the precariat, as identified by Savage (2015), lives a precarious existence. Making up 15% of the population, members' lives are characterised by low incomes, negligible savings, rented housing, and movement between low paid, insecure work and unemployment. Generally, vulnerability to poverty increases as we descend the income scale, both for those in and out of work. In 2019–20, 22% of the population as a whole were living in relative poverty; the figure for children was 31%. Between 2015 and 2019, 13% of the population had been living with persistent poverty (Francis-Devine, 2021).

Similar inequality characterises the nation's physical health. There is a clear health gradient, with those in the strongest socio-economic positions tending to have the best quality of health and those in the lowest socio-economic positions the worst (Benzeval et al., 2014). Crucially for counselling and psychotherapy, research evidence points to continuing class differences in mental health (Elliot, 2016). High income and material standards of living are associated with relatively low rates of mental health problems; low income and poor living standards correlate with relatively high rates of mental health issues.

Importantly, class not only describes inequality, it prescribes it. Commentators talk of a 'sticky ceiling' and a 'sticky floor' restricting both upward and downward movement. In 2018–19, people from better-off backgrounds were 80% more likely to end up in professional occupations than those from working-class backgrounds. People from working-class backgrounds were twice as likely to end up in working-class occupations than those from professional backgrounds. Reflecting these intergenerational realities, those from working-class backgrounds ended up earning 24% less on average than those from professional backgrounds (Social Mobility Commission, 2019). It needs to be remembered that these figures are averages. The lived experience of class is inherently intersectional, that is, it is always entangled and indeed enmeshed with other sources of inequality and identity, such as race, gender, sexuality and disability (e.g., Tyler, 2020).

A final area of significance comes out of the small amount of research focusing specifically on people's identification with class. While some studies have demonstrated a general lack of personal identification with class (e.g., Savage et al., 2005; Skeggs, 1997), the same studies and others have demonstrated a general recognition of its continuing existence as a system. Interestingly, in a 2015 study, 43% of participants identified themselves as being conscious of their class, while 97% of participants placed themselves as either middle or working class when prompted to do so (Evans and Mellon, 2016). Other studies point to the importance of internalised class messages. The 'psychic landscape of class' is populated by notions of inferiority and superiority and is lived out in emotions such as envy, pride and shame (e.g., Sayer, 2005). The importance of class born into, or ascribed status, features heavily in such subjective accounts.

RELEVANCE TO COUNSELLING AND PSYCHOTHERAPY

Consideration of class issues would seem important at a number of levels to developing a therapeutic approach incorporating both an intersectional understanding and a commitment to social justice. Some of the challenges are for counselling and psychotherapy *per se* and their professional organisations. Others are more matters for consideration on the part of individual therapists, counselling organisations and training providers. Some straddle both areas. Here they are briefly addressed under a number of banner headings.

THE VALUE BASE OF COUNSELLING AND PSYCHOTHERAPY

Therapy's so-called 'class-blindness' can be contextualised within a long-running critique of counselling and psychotherapy, that of its rooting of psychological distress within individual psychology rather than social circumstance. This can and does lead to criticisms, from within and without, of political naïvety, social irrelevance and, indeed, political and social conservatism. The most active raising of class issues has taken place in the US (e.g., Liu, 2015). There continues to be an absence of a developed research interest or body of relevant literature concerning the differing dimensions of class and their relevance to counselling in contemporary Britain.

THE CLASS BASE OF COUNSELLORS AND COUNSELLING

While there is a lack of definitive evidence of the class base of counselling and psychotherapy, it is commonly perceived as a middle class one, leading to therapy 'being worryingly out of touch with the needs, the strengths and struggles of working-class people' (Trevithick, 1998: 116). It can be somewhat of a circular argument: if occupation is the measure, becoming a psychotherapist or counselling psychologist is inevitably an entrée into middle-classness. This is arguably less true for counsellors, although the drive towards the professionalisation of counselling can be viewed as a group attempt to gain middle-class status. While there is limited available information about therapists' class background, the expense and length of training, the move to university-based training and the educational qualifications required for entry pose inevitable barriers to access. On a positive note, some small-scale research found a strong level of personal identification with 'working-classness' among participating counsellors (Ballinger and Wright, 2007). Generally, however, the question of widening access to practise as well as paying attention to the class-awareness of counsellors in training would seem to be important areas for development.

THE CLASS BASE OF CLIENTS

A variety of factors are argued to contribute to a parallel middle-class bias in the client population, despite their reduced likelihood of mental health issues compared to their poorer counterparts. Again, evidence is incomplete here, reflecting in part the diversity of therapeutic settings and perhaps a continued failure to take class seriously. One well-documented setting, however, is the statutory health sector, where clear differences emerge in access to talking therapies. Those on lower incomes are less likely to be offered talking therapies and more likely to be prescribed medication when presenting with mental health issues (Rogers and Pilgrim, 2003). One proffered explanation is bias on the part of referrers, with 'downward classism' (Liu, 2015: 8) evident among referring medics. Other explanations focus on working-class reluctance to access therapy. Cited reasons have included: therapy's emphasis on the verbalisation of emotions and introspection; reduced expectations of emotional health; the greater deference to medical authority; and the desire for more practical solutions (e.g., Holman, 2014).

THE COUNSELLING RELATIONSHIP AND PROCESS

The middle-class character of the counselling body is regarded as potentially problematic here. It has been argued that social class can have a substantial impact on the quality of the counselling relationship. One area relates to an imbalance of power and status and its repercussions. Working-class clients have reported a sense of discomfort and inferiority when working with counsellors they perceived as middle class (Balmforth, 2009). On a parallel note, unacknowledged classism on the part of counsellors can lead to stereotyping and judgementalism, which is antithetical to the empathy and positive regard that is widely seen as fundamental to the counselling endeavour.

THE NATURE OF COUNSELLING ITSELF

The social, economic, cultural and political roots of distress raise questions over therapy's relevance, particularly to disadvantaged members of society. Moreover, Holman (2014) talks of a level of incompatibility between the inherently middle-class counselling habitus and that of working class clients. One result may be that working-class people may self-exclude; another may be the shaming experience of feeling negatively judged as inadequate and disempowered (Sayer, 2005). Such classism, albeit unconscious and unintended, can potentially stray into the field of victimisation of society's victims, constituting a form of what Bourdieu labels 'symbolic violence' over working-class lives. This would be antithetical to the concept of social justice, which hopefully underpins all therapeutic work.

CONCLUSION

The construction of a class-sensitive approach to counselling calls on the addressing of such issues sketched above. Any such approach would need to consider barriers to access, look at ways of drawing therapists from across the social spectrum, widen training to embrace more sociological understandings and promote class awareness. There remains the challenge of developing services tailored to best meet the needs of individuals across the social spectrum.

REFERENCES

Atkinson, A.B. (2015) *Inequality: What Can Be Done?* Cambridge, MA: Harvard University Press.

Ballinger, L. and Wright, J. (2007) Does class count? Social class and counselling. *Counselling and Psychotherapy Research*, 7(3), 157–163.

Balmforth, J. (2009) 'The weight of class': clients' experience of how perceived differences in social class between counsellor and client affect the therapeutic relationship. *British Journal of Guidance and Counselling*, 37(3), 375–386.

Benzeval, M., Bond, L., Campbell, M., Egan, M., Lorenc, T., Petticrew, M. and Popham, F. (2014) *How Does Money Effect Health?* York: Joseph Rowntree Foundation.

Beswick, K. (2020) Feeling working class: affective class identification and its implications for overcoming inequality. *Studies in Theatre and Performance*, 40(3), 265–274.

Blanden, J., Gregg, P. and Machin, S. (2005) *Intergenerational Mobility in Europe and North America*. A Report for the Sutton Trust. London: The Centre for Economic Performance.

Blundell, R., Costa Dias, M., Joyce, R. and Xiaonses, X. (2020) *COVID-19 and Inequalities*. London: Institute for Fiscal Studies. Available at https://ifs.org.uk/uploads (accessed 9 December 2021).

Bourdieu, P. (1987) What makes a social class? On the theoretical and practical existence of groups. *Berkeley Journal of Sociology*, 32, 1–17.

Cannadine, D. (2000) *Class in Britain*. London: Penguin Books.

Clark, T. (2014) *Hard Times: The Divisive Toll of the Economic Slump*. London and New Haven, CT: Yale University Press.

Elliot, I. (2016) *Poverty and Mental Health: A Review to Inform the Joseph Rowntree Foundation's Anti-Poverty Strategy*. London: Mental Health Foundation.

(Continued)

(Continued)

Evans, G. and Mellon, J. (2016) Social class: identity, awareness and political attitudes: Why are we still working class? *British Social Attitudes*, 33. Available at www.bsa.natcen.ac.uk/ media/39094/bsa33_social-class_v5.pdf (accessed 28 December 2021).

Francis-Devine, B. (2021) *Poverty in the UK: Statistics*. London: House of Commons Library. Available at https://commonslibrary.parliament.uk/research-briefings/sn07096/ (accessed 13 January 2022).

Hanley, L. (2016) *Respectable: The Experience of Class.* London: Allen Lane.

Holman, D. (2014) 'What help can you get talking to somebody?' Explaining class differences in the use of talking treatments. *Sociology of Health and Illness*, 36(4), 531–548.

Liu, W.M. (ed.) (2015) *The Oxford Handbook of Social Class and Counseling*. Oxford: Oxford University Press.

McKenzie, L. (2015) *Getting By: Estates, Class and Culture in Austerity Britain*. Bristol: Policy Press.

O'Neill, D. (2019) On being a working class academic. *Medium.* Available at https:// medium.com/@deirdreoneill_40170/on-being-a-working-class-academic-c57772392e62Reay (accessed 28 December 2021).

Reay, D. (2005) Beyond consciousness? The psychic landscape of social class. *Sociology*, 39(5), 911–928.

Rogers, A. and Pilgrim, D. (2003) *Mental Health and Inequality*. Basingstoke: Palgrave.

Savage, M. (2015) *Social Class in the Twenty-First Century*. London: Penguin Books.

Savage, M., Bagnall, G. and Longhurst, B. (2005) Local habitus and working-class culture. In F. Devine, M. Savage, J. Scott and R. Crompton (Eds), *Rethinking Class: Culture, Identities and Lifestyle*. Basingstoke: Palgrave Macmillan (pp. 95–122).

Sayer, A. (2005) *The Moral Significance of Class*. Cambridge: Cambridge University Press.

Skeggs, B. (1997) *Formation of Class and Gender: Beocming respectable*. London: Sage.

Social Mobility Commission (2019) *The State of the Nation, 2018–2019: Social Mobility in Great Britain.* Available at www.gov.uk/government/publications (accessed 25 December 2021).

Todd, S. (2021) *Snakes and Ladders: The Great British Social Mobility Myth*. London: Chatto & Windus.

Trevithick, P. (1998) Psychotherapy and working class women. In I. Bruna Seu and M. Colleen Heenan (Eds), *Feminism and Psychotherapy: Reflections on Contemporary Theories and Practice.* London: Sage (pp. 115–134).

Tyler, I. (2020) *Stigma: The Machinery of Inequality*. London and New York: Zed Books.

Wilkinson, R. and Pickett, K. (2010) *The Spirit Level: Why Equality is Better for Everyone*. London: Penguin.

Wilkinson, R. and Pickett, K. (2018) *The Inner Level: How More Equal Societies Reduce Stress, Restore Sanity and Improve Everyone's Well-Being*. London: Allen Lane.

RECOMMENDED READING

Savage, M. (2015) *Social Class in the Twenty-First Century*. London: Penguin Books.

This provides an accessible overview of understandings of social class and the differing dimensions of inequality in contemporary Britain.

Kearney, A. (2018) *Counselling, Class & Politics: Undeclared Influences in Therapy*. Ross-on-Wye: PCCS Books.

This version of the 1996 original has been edited by Gillian Proctor. It remains one of the strongest and most accessible introductions to issues of class blindness within counselling in the UK.

Liu, W.M. (Ed.) (2015) *The Oxford Handbook of Social Class and Counseling*. Oxford: Oxford University Press.

While the focus is class within the US, this is a superb, comprehensive source for reference across a wide range of counselling issues.

2.10 SEXUALITY

SILVA NEVES AND DOMINIC DAVIES

OVERVIEW AND KEY POINTS

The definition of sexuality is complex and multi-dimensional because our modern understanding of it intersects with biology, psychology, sexology, societal norms and, of course, social justice. Words we use shape how we think and, as terminology about sexuality identity changes fast, so is the way we think about it. It may be daunting for therapists who may feel out of their depth for not knowing the current terminology to use. Luckily, websites such as the charity organisation Stonewall offer an updated glossary of terms (see www.stonewall.org.uk/help-advice/faqs-and-glossary/list-lgbtq-terms).

This chapter covers the following key points:

- Sexuality is defined by desire, behaviours, and identity.
- The topic of sexuality is shrouded in myths which can perpetuate sexual shame, especially for those who do not fit within heteronormativity (the assumption that heterosexuality is only 'normal' and everything else is 'strange'). It is therefore a subject that needs to be addressed within the professions of psychotherapy and psychology, as well as social justice.
- Therapists need to be aware of the impact of heteronormativity and mononormativity (the assumption that monogamy is only 'normal' and everything else is 'strange') to help clients of all sexualities (including heterosexual people) more efficiently and remain ethical.
- Therapists who do not have sufficient knowledge in diverse sexualities may accidentally cause harm.

INTRODUCTION

DEFINING SEXUALITY, SEXUAL ORIENTATION, SEXUAL BEHAVIOURS

Barker and Iantaffi (2022: 39) define sexuality and sex:

Generally, the word 'sexuality' is used to refer to the sexual attractions and desires that we have, whereas the word 'sex' is used for the sexual practices we engage with. There's a sense that we *have* a sexuality, and that we *do* sex.

In his definition of sexual orientation, Moser (2016) points out that there are several characteristics to be considered:

1. **Lust** is a strong and persistent sexual attraction. We often refer to this as our orientation: who or what we lust after.
2. **Relative immutability**: sexual orientation is most commonly attributed (often retrospectively) as emerging during childhood or early puberty and remaining reasonably constant throughout one's lifetime.
3. **Flexibility**: despite its relative constancy, our sexual interests and sometimes our orientation, might change over time. For many of us, we don't have much control over what interests us or whether it might change, and for most people, it remains fairly fixed, but we should be aware of this flexibility working with clients.
4. **Consequences**: engaging with one's sexual orientation can have profound psychological and social consequences. The effects of denying a sexual orientation are generally detrimental to the mental health of a person and might in some circumstances lead to suicide.

One's sexual orientation is independent of gender, as Nichols (2021: 183) points out:

It refers to the gender of whom you are sexually and romantically attracted to. Sexual orientation doesn't change when people transition, but the label will change. In other words, someone assigned male at birth and attracted to women will be perceived as heterosexual before they transition, but once they are trans women – they are lesbians!

Sexuality comprises three elements: desire, behaviour, and identity. These are not always consistent. Jason is married to Lucy, and they have three children. Jason sometimes meets men for sex on Grindr and identifies as 'straight'. Bernadette is married to Mary. She identifies as an asexual, gay woman, Mary identifies as a dyke.

The identity labels (and pronouns) people choose to describe themselves should be respected. Some women who love women will prefer the term gay, and others will name themselves lesbian, dykes or queer. Using the term the client prefers to describe themselves demonstrates our respect for them.

A BRIEF HISTORY OF SEXUALITY

Human sexuality has been constructed in various ways across time and cultures. We are still less than 150 years into the scientific research in sexual diversity. There were periods of human history when what one did sexually and whom one loved meant very little and other times when variations meant a great deal. We are currently in a phase in human history where sexuality is seen as a matter of social justice regarding its involvement with the State and its legal system. While in Britain two people of the same sex can marry and adopt children, there are large parts of Poland where whole towns have declared themselves LGBT-Free Zones. We also see in countries ruled by Sharia law that LGBT people are executed, or in Chechnya placed in concentration camps. Various African countries have declared homosexuality illegal based on their Christian beliefs.

In the early 1980s, the conversations on sexuality took an unexpected turn when the epidemic of HIV and AIDS spread worldwide. Outside sub-Saharan Africa it decimated the gay male population. The progress in thinking about sexuality as a natural and vibrant part of being human was associated with disease. Everybody became afraid of sex, and promiscuity was synonymous with being careless and bringing chaos to society. People with religious beliefs took the opportunity to hail AIDS as God's answer to homosexuality. It was also at that time that clinicians cautioned the public of the danger of 'too much sex', which equated to casual sex with people who were not in committed partnerships. Carnes (2001 [1983]) was the first clinician to bring forth the idea of 'sex addiction' as a pathology of 'too much sex'. Now, neither the American Psychiatric Association's DSM-5 (APA, 2013) nor the World Health Organisation's ICD-11 (WHO, 2019) endorses the conceptualisation of 'sex addiction', yet it is a term – and a mindset – that is still popular. Thankfully, there is a growing number of clinicians who challenge this pathologising framework (Bering, 2013; Braun-Harvey and Vigorito, 2016; Donaghue, 2015; Ley, 2012; Neves, 2021).

Today, HIV is no longer a death sentence in the western world. The medical progress made it possible for people to live with HIV with the same life expectancy as those whose HIV status is negative. People who adhere to their medication as prescribed have an undetectable viral load, which means they can't transmit the virus to others (an important piece of medical information promoted as U=U, Undetectable equals Untransmittable). The advance of PrEP (Pre-Exposure Prophylaxis) means that people can avoid contracting HIV too, which has contributed to a major decrease in HIV infections. However, the stigma about HIV lives on.

The fight for social justice and the acceptance of the diversity of sexuality is not over. It is still legal to practise 'conversion therapy', or so-called 'reparative therapy' in many countries. This is underpinned by the belief that being other than heterosexual and cisgender is not natural and seeks 'to cure' people of their 'homosexuality' and transgender feelings. All the major psychology and psychotherapy organisations in the UK signed the *Memorandum of Understanding on Conversion Therapy (version 2)*, with the agreement that the practice is harmful and unethical, but the move to make it illegal has been a long and hard road with much opposition from religious groups. Sadly, 'conversion therapy' practices happen within the therapy room too. Bartlett, Smith and King (2009) asked therapists who were members of BACP, UKCP and BPS whether they have contracted to reduce same-sex attractions; 17% said they had done so, and 4% agreed to contracts trying to eliminate/cure someone of their same-sex attractions.

There are currently 71 countries upholding anti-gay laws, for which punishment varies from imprisonment to the death penalty, according to the Human Dignity Trust (n.d.). The UK Government's official statistics show that hate crime rose by 19% against LGB and 16% against trans people in 2019/20. Although we are now in the twenty-first century, it seems that there is still much need for social justice towards full acceptance of gender, sex and relationship diversities.

CONCEPTUALISING SEXUALITY

The fast-evolving field of contemporary sexology has helped us understand sexuality with modern conceptualisations, one of which is the biopsychosocial perspective (Barker, 2018). It is one that encourages us to think of sexuality from the dimensions of our biology (our body, our brain), our psychology (personal experiences and reflection) and our social construct (cultural messages, life circumstances). This model takes into consideration people's individual sense of their sexuality with cognitive and somatic experiences and how they relate their sexuality with the outside world. Indeed, much of people's distress that is related to their sexuality (and intimate relationships) stems from societal, familial and religious prohibitions inducing shame and a sense of 'being wrong'. The biopsychosocial model guides us in helping our clients understand the function of their sexual difficulties by tracing where and how they have learnt to think the way they do about their sexuality or sexual behaviours. Much of that understanding requires the therapist to equip themselves with the appropriate and contemporary knowledge of human sexuality and to commit to the social justice of busting harmful sex myths that cause distress. Some of the common sex myths, to name only a few, are:

1. Sex before marriage is bad.
2. Abortion is a sin.
3. Heterosexuality is the only 'normal' sexuality.
4. Being monogamous is the 'Gold Standard' of relationships.
5. Sex means vaginal intercourse.
6. Masturbation is wrong.
7. Watching pornography is bad.
8. In anal sex among men, the insertive partner is seen as more masculine.
9. There is something wrong with people who have too much casual sex.
10. There is something wrong with people who do not want sex.

Indeed, even today in the twenty-first century, it seems that self-acceptance of one's own sexuality is an act of defiance and social justice.

RELEVANCE TO COUNSELLING AND PSYCHOTHERAPY

SEXUAL ATTRACTION, DESIRE, AROUSAL AND BEHAVIOURS

The equal rights we have in the UK and in some other western countries do not mean that it is the end of stigma. In the UK, same-sex sexual activities are not considered a criminal offence anymore. 'Homosexuality' is no longer considered a mental health diagnosis. The law protects the LGBTQ+ communities. People identifying as LGBTQ+ can now legally get married. However, homophobia, biphobia, transphobia, sexism and racism have not disappeared. For example, if a trans person is married and seeks a gender recognition certificate, their spouse must give permission.

The Minority Stress Model (Meyer, 2003) identifies a specific type of chronic stress experienced by LGBTQ+ people, which include (1) experiences of prejudice, (2) expectation of rejection and discrimination, (3) hiding and concealing, and (4) internalised homophobia.

Minority stress, and indeed 'coming out', still exists because of ongoing prejudice (fear of holding hands, not being able to go on holiday anywhere in the world due to some countries anti-gay laws, being attacked, etc.). According to the Home Office statistics, there was an increase of 19% in sexual orientation hate crimes (15,835) in the year 2019–20 (Home Office, 2020). We know that these statistics are an underestimate because many people do not report homophobic incidents to the police. Stories of homophobia, biphobia and transphobia abound: a gay couple was told that the owner of the house they wanted to buy refused to sell it to them because the owner disagreed with their religious views. A lesbian couple posted on social media pictures of their bruised faces after being attacked for holding hands. A black trans woman was murdered for bringing shame to their family's community. Unfortunately, these are not one-off stories, they are happening consistently, across the globe.

Because of an increase in legal rights, it is a common mistake to ignore the specific intersection of needs of people on a sexual and gender diversity spectrum that does not strictly fit with cisgender heterosexuality. In the therapeutic context, the thought '*I work with them like any other human beings*', although a well-intentioned sentiment of equality, can actually erase the differences, specifically the facts that growing and living in a heteronormative world is not the same experience as one who is a cisgender heterosexual person, a cisgender gay person or black trans queer.

Because of the heteronormative world that we live in, it is easy for LGBTQ+ clients and heterosexual people who identify as 'kinky' to feel ashamed of their sexuality. The clinical trainings that counsellors and psychotherapists receive are usually heteronormative too and are not equipped enough to understand their clients' attraction, desires, arousal and sexual behaviours. It is difficult for therapists to help clients make sense of their sexuality through meaningful exploration if the therapists themselves are not aware of their heteronormative blind spots. In fact, the rich conversations about clients' sex lives are routinely missed. In assessments, the simple question '*how is your sex life?*' is not asked. It goes without saying that a thorough exploration of clients' erotic world is hardly ever considered as important and meaningful parts of their wellbeing. To address this, we now outline important areas for clinical consideration: attraction, desire, arousal, and behaviours or practices. We make suggestions for issues which therapists might encounter and areas for therapeutic consideration.

ATTRACTION

Who and what turns them on: specific genders, attitudes, physical attributes, personalities, specific activities like kink or vanilla, or specific objects (fetishes).

Example for consideration: Bisexuality is often erased. If the bisexual person is in a relationship with someone of a different sex, they are perceived as heterosexual, if they are with a same-sex partner, they are seen as gay. In both cases, a bisexual person remains bisexual, but their bisexuality is negated. This can have serious consequences for their mental health.

Intervention: Validating the client with their affirmation of their bisexuality identity and being curious about the minority stress caused by the erasure of bisexuality to offer a safe space to discuss those specific issues, a space that is not offered outside the consulting room.

DESIRE

The somatic and cognitive wanting of sexual and/or romantic contacts. Our brain is the main sexual organ, not only our genitals.

Morin (1995: 50) offers the concept of the Erotic Equation:

> Attraction + Obstacles = Excitement

This is easily observable when we notice that the very things that are not readily available are more exciting to get. Some of the obstacles that can make a sexual attraction more exciting are the prohibitions that our society impose on people's sex lives.

Example of consideration: It is common for people in long-term relationships to worry about the waning of sexual desire, believing that it might mean they are less attracted to each other.

Intervention: Explaining to clients that a lower sexual desire does not necessarily indicate an absence of attraction (or love) can reduce their distress. Introducing Morin's Erotic Equation can help with brainstorming how clients can create an 'obstacle' in their relationships to increase desire. For long-term relationships, it is usually learning to create a little bit of distance between partners (Perel, 2006).

AROUSAL

This is the physical change following sexual desire. While desire resides in the erotic mind, arousal can be observed in erections for men and the swelling of the clitoris for women. Gurney (2020: 61) discusses psychological arousal:

> It involves things like the environment, trust, safety, love, power play, how exciting you find different sexual acts, visual stimuli, the dynamic or connection between you and your partner, talking, attraction, passion, props, sensuality, closeness, eye contact, the role you take and much more.

Example of consideration: Too much of desire or arousal might be labelled as 'sex addiction', while absent sexual desire can be pathologised as 'low sexual desire disorder' when it could be asexuality. These are problematic thinking because they can encourage dubious and harmful clinical interventions. In the case of 'sex addiction', some popular addiction-oriented techniques to reduce urges, when applied to sexuality (or sexual urges), may be akin to aversion therapy, which can cause more distress for clients. In the case of asexuality, forcing Sensate Focus (a common sex therapy technique of step-by-step sensual touch, gradually leading to including genitals and breasts and designed to help reduce the anxiety associated with penetrative sex) could be a form of 'conversion therapy'.

Intervention: Helping clients being curious about their erotic processes non-judgementally. If a client expresses distress for having too much or too little sexual desire/arousal, it is best to help client understand the source of the distress: is it because they think their erotic process does not fit in the acceptable level of sexual expression deemed as 'normal' by society, or is it that their behaviours are unethical/hurtful to their partner(s)? In a non-judgmental manner, therapists can help clients find the meaning of their erotic conflicts and make conscious decisions about their sex lives based on honest self-awareness.

BEHAVIOURS/PRACTICES

The decision to act or not on sexual attraction, desire and arousal. Some behaviours are congruent with the person's self-identification of sexual orientation but not for everybody (in some circumstances, gay people marry in heterosexual relationships to hide and to protect themselves).

Example of consideration: Some sexual practices, or lifestyles such as BDSM (bondage, discipline, dominance and submission, sadomasochism) are notoriously misunderstood and pathologised as symptoms of unresolved trauma. Sprott and Williams (2019) assert that kink and fetishes can be part of people's sexual orientation for some, and be serious leisure activities for others. There is controversy because clinicians argue that some paraphilia classified as mental health disorders in the DSM-5 should be removed. These debates are welcome because they help with challenging preconceived ideas and expanding our understanding of sexuality. More needs to be done to understand other sexual behaviours (and orientations) to prevent harm.

Intervention: The first thing to do is for therapists to check their own erotic awareness, blind spots and biases so that they can avoid unchecked countertransference and unduly pathologise their clients. It is important to adopt the stance of diversity and sex-positivity, which means to accept that one person's turn-on can be another person's repulsion, and that it most important thing aspects of the client's wellbeing in psycho-sexual health is for them to have sexual behaviours that match their own values, thus reducing the feeling of shame about them.

CONCLUSION

It is common to hear clients' stories about not feeling understood by their previous therapists, not because they were bad therapists, but because they did not understand the nuance of sexuality and the breadth of the diversities of sexual orientations and sexual behaviours (Israel et al., 2008; King, 2015). This is mostly due to insufficient trainings on Gender, Sex and Relationship Diversities (GSRD) within core counselling and psychotherapy trainings. There is wide diversity even within heterosexuality, yet, therapists are not equipped to ask relevant questions about their clients' sexual desire, arousal and behaviours. The professions of counselling and psychotherapy need to be at the forefront of social justice and the human right to sexual health and sexual pleasure. Counsellors and psychotherapists need to be adequately trained in the knowledge of diverse sexualities to better serve clients.

REFERENCES

American Psychiatry Association (2013). *Diagnostic and Statistical Manual of Mental Disorders, Fifth Edition.* DSM-5. Arlington, VA: American Psychiatric Association.

Barker, M.J. (2018). *The Psychology of Sex*. Abingdon, UK: Routledge.

Barker, M.J. & Iantaffi, A. (2022). *How to Understand your Sexuality: A Practical Guide for Exploring Who You Are*. London: Jessica Kingsley.

Bartlett, A., Smith, G. & King, M. (2009). The response of mental health professionals to clients seeking help to change or re-direct same-sex orientation. *BMC Psychiatry*, 9, 11. Available at www.biomedcentral.com/1471-244X/9/11

Bering, J. (2013). *Perv: The Sexual Deviant in All of Us*. London: Transworld.

Braun-Harvey, D. & Vigorito, M.A. (2016). *Treating Out of Control Sexual Behavior: Rethinking Sex Addiction*. New York: Springer.

Carnes, P. (2001 [1983]). *Out of the Shadows: Understanding Sexual Addiction* (3rd ed.). Minnesota, MN: Hazelden.

Donaghue, C. (2015). *Sex Outside the Lines.* Dallas, TX: BenBella Books.

(Continued)

(Continued)

Gurney, K. (2020). *Mind The Gap: The Truth about Desire and How to Futureproof Your Sex Life*. London: Headline Publishing Group.

Home Office (2020). *Official Statistics: Hate Crime, England and Wales, 2019 to 2020*. London: Home Office. Available at www.gov.uk/government/statistics/hate-crime-england-and-wales-2019-to-2020/hate-crime-england-and-wales-2019-to-2020

Human Dignity Trust (n.d.). *LGBT – The Law: Map of Criminalisation*. [Website]. Available at www.humandignitytrust.org/lgbt-the-law/map-of-criminalisation/

Israel, T., Gorcheva, R., Burnes T.R. & Walther W.A. (2008). Helpful and unhelpful therapy experiences of LGBT clients. *Psychotherapy Research*, *18*(3), 294–305. doi: 10.1080/10503300701506920

King, M. (2015). Attitudes of therapists and other health professionals towards their LGB patients. *International Review of Psychiatry*, *27*(5), 396–404. doi: 10.3109/09540261.2015.1094033

Ley, D. (2012). *The Myth of Sex Addiction*. Lanham, MD: Rowman & Littlefield.

Memorandum of Understanding on Conversion Therapy, version 2 (MoU2). Available at www.cosrt.org.uk/wp-content/uploads/2017/10/MoU2_FINAL.pdf

Meyer, I.H. (2003). Prejudice, social stress, and mental health in lesbian, gay, and bisexual populations: conceptual issues and research evidence. *Psychological Bulletin*, *129*(5), 674–697. https://doi.org/10.1037/0033-2909.129.5.674

Morin, J. (1995). *The Erotic Mind: Unlocking the Inner Sources of Sexual Passion and Fulfillment*. New York: HarperCollins.

Moser, C. (2016). Defining sexual orientation. *Archives of Sexual Behavior*, *45*, 505–508. https://doi.org/10.1007/s10508-015-0625-y

Neves, S. (2021). *Compulsive Sexual Behaviours: A Psycho-Sexual Treatment Guide for Clinicians*. Abingdon, UK: Routledge.

Nichols, M. (2021). *The Modern Clinician's Guide to Working with LGBTQ+ Clients: The Inclusive Psychotherapist*. New York: Routledge.

Perel, E. (2006). *Mating in Captivity: Unlocking Erotic Intelligence*. New York: HarperCollins.

Sprott, R.A. & Williams, D.J. (2019). Is BDSM a sexual orientation or serious leisure? *Current Sexual Health Reports*, *11*, 75–79. https://doi.org/10.1007/s11930-019-00195-x

Stonewall (n.d.). *Glossary of LGBTQ+ Terms*. [Website]. Available at www.stonewall.org.uk/help-advice/faqs-and-glossary/list-lgbtq-terms

WHO (2019). *International Classification of Diseases (11th Revision)*. ICD-11. Geneva: World Health Organisation. Available at https://icd.who.int/en

RECOMMENDED READING

Morin, J. (1995). *The Erotic Mind: Unlocking the Inner Sources of Sexual Passion and Fulfillment*. New York: HarperCollins.

This book is a thorough guide to help readers explore their own erotic processes, including their turn-ons and fantasies.

Barker, M.J. (2018). *Rewriting the Rules: An Anti Self-Help Guide to Love, Sex and Relationships*. Abingdon, UK: Routledge.

This book is helpful in challenging common sex and relationship myths.

Lehmiller, J.J. (2018). *The Psychology of Human Sexuality* (2nd ed.). Oxford: Wiley-Blackwell.

This book is a thorough reference book on sexology, including sexuality, sexual orientations and sexual behaviours.

PART III

CORE THERAPEUTIC AND PROFESSIONAL SKILLS

3.1 CONTRACTING AND THERAPEUTIC BEGINNINGS

INDIA AMOS

OVERVIEW AND KEY POINTS

For anyone who is interested in the process of therapy, or who has contemplated undertaking a training course in counselling or psychotherapy, the question 'how does therapy start?' is likely to have been asked. Although it is acknowledged that different therapeutic approaches may have different priorities, and that it is not possible to predict the course of therapy as it progresses for each individual client, this chapter aims to offer an overview of some of the central elements that may be considered by a therapist at the outset of commencing any type of therapy.

This chapter presents discussion on the following:

- Receiving and managing client referrals.
- The establishment of initial psychological contact with the client and therapeutic contracting.
- The identification of appropriate therapy goals.

RECEIVING A REFERRAL AND MAKING AN ASSESSMENT

Pathways into counselling can be varied. A therapy referral may be received from a General Practitioner (GP) or Consultant Psychiatrist responsible for the client's care. Alternatively, the client may refer themselves for a therapeutic assessment or be invited to do so at their place of work. The extent of information contained within a referral can vary. It may include a description of the client's problem, the reason for the referral, relevant risk issues, or it may simply request a therapy assessment to be arranged.

Initial contact with the client may come in different forms. In fact, establishing with the client the most suitable means of communication is helpful. It could be said that this is the point where the therapy relationship begins. Whether the therapy is set to take place remotely or in person, the therapist has the opportunity to begin building rapport when making the first contact. Essential information regarding the date, time, location, and duration of the session requires communication, and a warmth and genuineness from the outset can communicate an accepting presence. Mearns, Thorne and McLeod (2013: 130) encourage practitioners to stay mindful of the question 'what process does the client have to go through to get to me…?' Barriers to accessing counselling are well documented. Chantler (2005: 252) reported from experience 'issues of childcare, lack of money, transport, speed of response, choice of counsellor in terms of ethnicity, location, preferred language for counselling and access for disabled women were all likely to influence the take-up of counselling'. Systemic interpretations of counselling attendance can help to inform practical ways of overcoming identified barriers. Reflecting on the necessary process clients may have had to engage with to access therapy with you is likely to stir an emotional response worthy of exploration in supervision.

Within the person-centred counselling tradition the therapist's receipt of prior information regarding a prospective client can be considered problematic (Mearns et al., 2013). Client information collected by another practitioner could be considered distracting, even detrimental to the process in which the primary aim is to receive the client with an open mind. In some cases, referral letters or notes might be consulted following the first session with the client. Individual therapists vary in their position on this subject. However, it might be worth considering what client information might be essential to know ahead of your first meeting, if any.

In most cases, it is the therapist's responsibility to assess the appropriateness of the referral, though for counselling trainees on placement, referrals are more commonly assessed by the counselling service provider to ensure their appropriateness (Rattray, 2018). The first session is likely to include an assessment of what has brought the client to therapy. This may involve an invitation to the client to share their personal story, describe their psychological symptoms, provide information on how they are currently coping, and from

CASE STUDY

Samira is a therapist working in a primary care service. She received a referral asking for a client, James, 39 years old, to be contacted for a therapeutic assessment. Attached to the referral was a detailed report from James's GP, which appeared to extensively outline James's personal history and previous therapy experience. As was routine for Samira, she chose not to consult the referrer's report until after the first session with James, as she was keen not to be influenced by the lens through which another practitioner may have viewed the client. James attended his first scheduled appointment and appeared immediately agitated and restless. Samira found it particularly difficult to aid James's self-disclosure. She wondered whether he was expecting to be asked a list of direct questions in the session, rather than being invited to openly explore his reason for attending therapy. Despite his evident frustration, James tolerated the remainder of the session and Samira agreed to meet James again at the same time the following week for an extended assessment. Shortly after the first session, Samira read the referral report and noticed the depth with which the referrer had detailed James's risk history.

The section entitled risk said the following:

> James has a significant history of suicide attempts. Aged 15 years, James took a serious substance overdose which required hospitalisation. James appeared to maintain a stable period of mental health between the ages of 26 and 38. However, four months ago James suffered the death of his brother and consequently took a second overdose, again requiring hospitalisation.

Would Samira have benefitted from knowing this information prior to meeting with James? What impact might it have made if Samira had been aware of James's significant suicide risk history? How might Samira have used the information? Would it have been important to be transparent with James about the knowledge she had regarding risk or otherwise? See Reeves (Chapter 3.4, this volume) for further discussion of risk assessment and management in therapeutic work.

where they draw their strength. It may include all or only some of these areas initially. See Van Rijn (Chapter 3.3, this volume) for further details on assessment in therapy. An assessment session can also be used to judge whether the form of therapy on offer is suitable for the prospective client. For example, in a Cognitive Behaviour Therapy (CBT) assessment, ascertaining the likelihood that the client will benefit from the proposed intervention is considered vital to avoid misallocation (Nakajima et al., 2021). It may be that the decision is made not to offer therapy, as perhaps there are other services better suited to meet the clients need/s, in which case the client may be referred on.

For person-centred therapists, the client is viewed as the expert in their own experience of the problem. Therefore, the therapy work requires a collaborative effort. The practitioner seeks to integrate their understanding of the client's social world and, with the client, develops a shared narrative from which to construct meaning (Saha, Beach and Cooper, 2008). Seeking this understanding hopefully provides a foundation that makes it possible to tailor interventions to the individual client and their unique socio-cultural experience (Lakes, López and Gallo, 2006). Trevino, Tao and Van Epps (2021) apply the analogy of a window to illuminate how opportunities for cultural exploration occur between therapists and clients in psychotherapy. They refer to 'cultural conversations … that communicate values, worldviews, and cultural beliefs' (p. 263), and explore how cultural conversations are likely to emerge, particularly for clients with marginalised identities, in initial therapy sessions. Part 2 in this volume explores some of these issues further.

Psychological contact is a mutual endeavour and refers to therapist and client's awareness and willingness to engage with one another. Rogers (1957) went as far as to say that therapy will be unable to occur unless the therapist and client are in psychological contact. Therefore, psychological contact is often considered a precondition of counselling. The therapist's congruence, empathic understanding and unconditional positive regard for the client facilitates the establishment and maintenance of psychological contact (Rogers, 1957). Assuming that psychological contact will exist has been questioned, and movement away from a dichotomous understanding of psychological contact as either being present or absent has been seen. For example, work by Prouty (2001) has highlighted instances in which psychological contact required for therapy can be supported with the use of pre-therapy techniques. Stiles (Chapter 3.2, this volume) explores the nature of the therapeutic relationship in more depth. Working together is the essence of collaboration, and this can be modelled from the outset. Putting this ethic into action requires the therapist to engage with the knowledge their client already possesses, to recognise the shared responsibility for identifying appropriate therapy goals, and the active participation of both the client and the therapist in therapy tasks.

THERAPY CONTRACTING

A therapeutic contract refers to the discussion and agreement of the decisions deemed relevant to the progression of therapy and is used as a way to capture and formalise such elements, affording security and clarity for both parties. Engagement in explicit contracting with the client ahead of their commitment to the therapeutic process ensures the practitioner's respect of their client's autonomy (British Association of Counselling and Psychotherapy, 2018; British Psychological Society, 2018). The client's decision to enter into therapy is a significant one and may feel daunting. With that in mind, what information might be helpful for the client to know? Orienting the client to the nature of the therapeutic process is key if the client is to be able to offer their informed consent. Informing the client of the extent of the practitioner's case notes, the therapist's therapeutic orientation and/or training, the alternative therapeutic approaches that are available to the client from other service providers, the length of therapy, the client's right to terminate sessions, and the therapist's fee for sessions further supports their awareness of the aims of therapy, and perhaps serves to normalise any fears they may have regarding their role in the relationship. Therapists at this stage may be curious of any questions the client may have and engaging with questions can again demonstrate therapeutic collaboration (Kazantzis and Kellis, 2012).

CONFIDENTIALITY

The client should be made aware of the limits of confidentiality at the earliest opportunity. While practitioners are encouraged and trained to do everything reasonable to limit the disclosure of confidential material, it is also important, in the spirit of fostering a trusting therapy relationship, that therapists take care to inform their clients of where the boundaries lie (Donner et al., 2008). Often, the therapy contract is laid down in a physical document and is signed by the client. Ahead of finalising the contract, it may be suitable to provide the client with a therapy leaflet or information sheet to be read outside the session. See Wynn (Chapter 3.7, this volume) for more information on confidentiality in therapy.

LENGTH OF THERAPY

The length of therapy refers to the number of sessions in which the client and therapist meet. Some therapy is open-ended, meaning that the number of sessions can be negotiated and reviewed at any time. This is most commonly the case in private practice (Carey, 2005). Other therapeutic contracts are time-limited and therefore adhere to a specified number of sessions. Short-term therapy is typically between 12 and 25 sessions, with brief therapy being six sessions or less (Shapiro et al., 2003). The term 'therapy duration' may also be considered in relation to the 'therapeutic hour' (usually 50 minutes) or the frequency of sessions, which may be negotiated collaboratively with the client (Öst et al., 2001). Typically, therapy sessions are scheduled once a week to maintain continuity, although the circumstances of the client may not enable this. Within some therapeutic traditions, therapeutic sessions may occur even more frequently than once a week. For example, within the psychoanalytic tradition, analysands may attend therapy two or more times per week.

THERAPY FEES

There are several ways to approach the issue of payment for therapy. Practitioners can set a fixed fee which is applied to all, or set a variable pay scale, dependent upon the client's financial circumstances. Therapists may choose to provide free therapy or open negotiations regarding payment. In addition, therapists may or may not accept fees from alternative sources other than the client, often referred to as third-party payment. Whatever approach is incorporated by the practitioner, it is paramount that fee policies are communicated clearly to the client before embarking on therapy. Research in this area presents an interesting picture. Clark and Sims (2014) report how many therapists continue to experience uncertainty around the practice of setting and collecting fees. The literature indicates that practitioners battle with a desire to help that clashes with the necessity to make a living (Holmes, 1998), guilt (Pepper, 2004), and ethical concerns about reducing fees for certain clients (Treloar, 2010), and charging clients for 'socially mediated trauma's' (Smith, 2020: 3).

Much of the literature suggests that client fees have little to no impact on therapeutic outcomes; however, it remains a therapist issue permeated with ambiguity. Within the psychoanalytic tradition, the exchange of money is viewed as being ripe with symbolic meaning and therefore may offer relevant information about the client to be utilised in therapy. Schonbar and Krueger (1986) encouraged therapists to approach the matter with honesty, forthrightness, and a lack of anxiety as it can provide a template for discussing other uncomfortable issues within the therapy setting, potentially serving as a model for the client.

IDENTIFYING THERAPY GOALS

Once a therapy contract has been agreed, there is a question of where to go next? The therapist may be transparent about what they have come to know about the client through their referral, or they may invite the client to disclose in their own terms what the client would like to focus on. The client has arrived with the intention to change something, but this intention may not be fully known or easily articulated. For some, the establishment of therapy goals ensures the stage is set for effective therapy (Gibson et al., 2020). Other therapies seek to pursue intentions and aims with the awareness that goals may not be precise (Jacobs, 2017). Often the development of therapy goals is employed with the aim of building a shared sense of therapeutic purpose with the client, translating aims into specific described changes. Throughout the duration of the therapy, there may be the development of short-term, between-session goals, and medium- or long-term goals which ultimately drive the path of therapy. Hanley, Sefi and Ersahin (2016) discuss the growing body of research related to goal-oriented therapy approaches. Collaborative goal setting within the therapy relationship can be understood as one way in which to support the notion of the client as an active component in the change process, who is able to identify the appropriate direction of therapy towards their desired goals. For example, within Acceptance and Commitment Therapy (ACT), goals which specify what the individual would like to avoid are considered to have far less utility than those goals which the therapist can support the client to move towards. Sometimes goals must be translated from what Harris (2009) refers to as 'dead person's goals' to 'living person's goals'. The goal of no longer wanting to feel depressed may usefully be translated into a 'living person's goal' by asking the client: 'Then what would you do differently? What would you start of do more of? And how would you behave differently with friends and family?' (Harris, 2009: 65). This could lead to the identification of how the client wants to live.

An awareness of the need to balance goal-directed working with the task of creating and maintaining an effective relationship with the client is always required. Integral to the role of the therapist is to consider the rationale for the therapeutic decisions they make as well as allocating time to reflect on their outcome. 'Looping back' on moments in therapy practice helps practitioners to evaluate what was effective, helpful or a hindrance in the setting up of therapy (Bager-Charleson, 2020).

REFERENCES

Bager-Charleson, S. (2020). *Reflective Practice and Personal Development in Counselling and Psychotherapy*. London: Sage.
British Association of Counselling and Psychotherapy (BACP) (2018). *Framework for the Counselling Professions*. Rugby: BACP.
British Psychological Society (BPS) (2018). *Code of Ethics and Conduct*. Leicester: BPS.

(Continued)

(Continued)

Carey, T. A. (2005). Can patients specify treatment parameters? A preliminary investigation. *Clinical Psychology & Psychotherapy*, *12*(4), 326–335.

Chantler, K. (2005). From disconnection to connection: 'race', gender and the politics of therapy. *British Journal of Guidance & Counselling*, *33*(2), 239–256.

Clark, P. and Sims, P. L. (2014). The practice of fee setting and collection: implications for clinical training programs. *The American Journal of Family Therapy*, *42*(5), 386–397.

Donner, M. B., VandeCreek, L., Gonsiorek, J. C. and Fisher, C. B. (2008). Balancing confidentiality: protecting privacy and protecting the public. *Professional Psychology: Research and Practice*, *39*(3), 369.

Gibson, A., Cooper, M., Rae, J. and Hayes, J. (2020). Clients' experiences of shared decision making in an integrative psychotherapy for depression. *Journal of Evaluation in Clinical Practice*, *26*(2), 559–568.

Hanley, T., Sefi, A. and Ersahin, Z. (2016). From goals to tasks to methods. In M. Cooper and W. Dryden (Eds), *The Handbook of Pluralistic Counselling and Psychotherapy* (pp. 28–41). London: Sage.

Harris, R. (2009). *ACT Made Simple: An Easy-to-Read Primer on Acceptance and Commitment Therapy*. Oakland, CA: New Harbinger Publications.

Holmes, J. (1998). Money and psychotherapy: object, metaphor or dream. *International Journal of Psychotherapy*, *3*(2), 123.

Jacobs, M. (2017). *Psychodynamic Counselling in Action* (5th ed.). London: Sage.

Kazantzis, N. and Kellis, E. (2012). A special feature on collaboration in psychotherapy. *Journal of Clinical Psychology*, *68*(2), 133–135.

Lakes, K., López, S. R. and Gallo, L. C. (2006). Cultural competence and psychotherapy: applying anthropologically informed conceptions of culture. *Psychotherapy: Theory, Research, Practice, Training*, *43*(4), 380–396.

Mearns, D., Thorne, B. and McLeod, J. (2013). *Person-Centred Counselling in Action*. London: Sage.

Nakajima, M., Dykiert, D., Wilkinson, P. and Midgley, N. (2021). How do therapists assess suitability? A qualitative study exploring therapists' judgements of treatment suitability for depressed adolescents. *Counselling and Psychotherapy Research*, 22, 503–513.

Öst, L.-G., Alm, T., Brandberg, M. and Breitholtz, E. (2001). One vs five sessions of exposure and five sessions of cognitive therapy in the treatment of claustrophobia. *Behaviour Research and Therapy*, *39*(2), 167–183.

Pepper, R. (2004). Raising fees in group therapy: some ethical and clinical implications. *Journal of Contemporary Psychotherapy*, *34*, 141–152.

Prouty, G. (2001). The practice of Pre-Therapy. *Journal of Contemporary Psychotherapy*, *31*(1), 31–40.

Rattray, S. (2018). *Counselling Placements: An Organisation's Guide*. Good Practice in Action 082. Rugby: British Association of Counselling and Psychotherapy. www.bacp.co.uk/media/4777/bacp-counselling-placements-organisations-guide-fs-gpia082-nov18.pdf

Rogers, C. R. (1957). The necessary and sufficient conditions of therapeutic personality change. *Journal of Consulting Psychology*, *21*(2), 95.

Saha, S., Beach, M. C. and Cooper, L. A. (2008). Patient centeredness, cultural competence and healthcare quality. *Journal of the National Medical Association*, *100*(11), 1275.

Schonbar, A. R. and Krueger, D. W. (1986). *The Last Taboo: Money as Symbol and Reality in Psychotherapy and Psychoanalysis*. New York: Bruner/Mazel.

Shapiro, D. A., Barkham, M., Stiles, W. B., Hardy, G. E., Rees, A., Reynolds, S. and Startup, M. (2003). Time is of the essence: a selective review of the fall and rise of brief therapy research. *Psychology and Psychotherapy: Theory, Research and Practice*, *76*, 211–235.

Smith, R. (2020). Consciously uncoupling from counselling practice. *Psychotherapy Politics International*, *18*(2), e1529. https://doi.org/10.1002/ppi.1529

Treloar, H. R. (2010). Financial and ethical considerations for professionals in psychology. *Ethics and Behavior*, *20*, 454–465.

Trevino, A. Y., Tao, K. W. and Van Epps, J. J. (2021). Windows of cultural opportunity: a thematic analysis of how cultural conversations occur in psychotherapy. *Psychotherapy*, *58*(2), 263–274.

RECOMMENDED READING

Trevino, A. Y., Tao, K. W. and Van Epps, J. J. (2021). Windows of cultural opportunity: a thematic analysis of how cultural conversations occur in psychotherapy. *Psychotherapy*, *58*(2), 263–274.

This study reports on the ways in which cultural conversations emerge in the first psychotherapy session and how clients and therapists engage in cultural conversations.

Devlin, A. S. and Nasar, J. L. (2012). Impressions of psychotherapists' offices: do therapists and clients agree? *Professional Psychology: Research and Practice*, *43*(2), 118–122.

Using photographs portraying a variety of different psychotherapy rooms, this paper investigates psychotherapists' evaluation of the quality of care, comfort in the setting and therapist qualities that they expected clients to experience. It contains recommendations of features likely to create a warm therapeutic office.

Hanley, T., Sefi, A. and Ersahin, Z. (2016). From goals to tasks to methods. In M. Cooper and W. Dryden (Eds), *The Handbook of Pluralistic Counselling and Psychotherapy* (pp. 28–41). London: Sage.

This chapter introduces a rationale for the incorporation of goal-setting work in therapy, different types of therapeutic goals as well as practical methods of how goal setting may be introduced to clients.

3.2 THE CLIENT–THERAPIST RELATIONSHIP

WILLIAM B. STILES

OVERVIEW AND KEY POINTS

Practitioners and researchers agree that the client–therapist relationship is a core aspect of counselling and psychotherapy. This chapter reviews three conceptual approaches to the relationship: psychodynamic, person-centred, and psychometric, all of which are considered in a context of responsive human interaction.

- Psychodynamic authors suggest the relationship encompasses (a) the real relationship, (b) the transference, and (c) the working alliance.
- Person-centred authors focus on three necessary and sufficient therapist-provided conditions in a healing relationship: (a) genuineness, (b) unconditional positive regard, and (c) accurate empathy.
- Psychometric authors conceptually and statistically distinguish components of the alliance: (a) the affective bond between client and therapist, (b) agreement on the goals of treatment, and (c) agreement on treatment tasks.

INTRODUCTION

The client–therapist relationship is among the most researched and conceptualised aspects of therapy, and the sprawling literature continues to expand (e.g.,

Norcross and Lambert, 2019; Norcross and Wampold, 2019; Watson and Wiseman, 2021). What follows is my personal selection and understanding.

Research and theory about the relationship takes place in the context of the repeated observation that sharply contrasting treatment techniques and theoretical approaches are similarly effective (Barkham and Lambert, 2021; Wampold and Imel, 2015), or 'Everybody has won and all must have prizes' (The Dodo, quoted by Carroll, 1946 [1865]; applied to comparative psychotherapy outcome research by Rosenzweig in 1936 and since then by many others).

The concept of the therapist–client relationship offers to resolve the paradox. Across diverse treatments and populations, the strength of the relationship has been the most consistent process correlate of treatment outcome (Flückiger et al., 2018). If the relationship is a major active ingredient or a necessary condition for progress, as some suggest, then it is understandable that many treatment approaches can be effective.

But what is the client–therapist relationship? One common feature is *responsiveness* (Stiles, 2021). Therapists responsively use and adjust the available tools to try to ensure that their client receives effective treatment. Therapists are being responsive when they choose treatments in response to presenting problems, plan treatments in response to clients' progress, formulate interventions in response to clients' requirements and capacity, and adjust interventions already in progress in response to subtle signs of uptake. Because of such responsiveness, no two minutes of therapy are the same, much less any two clients' treatments. Appropriate responsiveness means each treatment is bespoke, tailored for this client and this therapist at this time. Responsiveness is integral to relationships across conceptual approaches to treatment (Watson and Wiseman, 2021). In this chapter, I review how three illustrative conceptual approaches, psychodynamic, person-centred, and psychometric, have characterised the relationship.

PSYCHODYNAMIC CONCEPTS OF THE RELATIONSHIP

Psychodynamic theorists have focused on a distinction between the real relationship and the transference (Freud, 1958; Zetzel, 1956). Some have further distinguished the working alliance (Gelso and Carter, 1994; Greenson, 1965). Gelso and Carter (1994) offered the following relatively succinct version:

The real relationship is seen as having two defining features: genuineness and realistic perceptions. Genuineness is defined as the ability and willingness to be what one truly is in the relationship – to be authentic, open, and honest. Realistic perceptions refer to those perceptions that are uncontaminated by transference distortions and other defences. In other words, the therapy participants see each other in an accurate, realistic way (Gelso and Carter, 1994: 297).

The transference configuration … consists of both client transference and therapist counter-transference. … Transference is the repetition of past conflicts with significant others, such that feelings, attitudes, and behaviors belonging rightfully in those earlier relationships are displaced onto the therapist; and counter-transference is the therapist's transference to the client's material, both to the transference and the nontransference communications presented by the client. (Gelso and Carter, 1994: 297)

[The working] alliance may be seen as the alignment or joining of the reasonable self or ego of the client and the therapist's analyzing or 'therapizing' self or ego for the purpose of the work. (Gelso and Carter, 1994: 297)

Psychodynamic interest has focused on interpreting the transference as a way of understanding how past hurts can be manifested as problems in the present and how they may be re-experienced and acted out within the therapeutic relationship. The relationship may offer a safe context to resolve conflicts that have interfered with life outside therapy. Positive feelings for the therapist may also represent transference, and the analysing positive transference can be a path to insight (e.g., Brenner, 1979; see Messer and Wolitsky, 2010). From an object relations perspective, the therapist might serve as good internal object; internalising the therapist could be transformative in ways that do not require insight (Geller and Farber, 1993; Zuroff and Blatt, 2006).

Kohut (1971, 1977) distinguished mirroring transferences, in which the therapist is experienced as an extension of the self, as a twin, or as an appendage whose function is mainly to support the client's (unrealistically) grandiose views of the self, from idealising transferences, in which the client draws strength or reassurance from being associated with an idealised therapist's exaggerated virtues. Progress may come when the therapist fails to fulfil these unrealistic expectations. The client's resulting frustration brings the expectations into awareness, making it possible to examine and change them.

Manifestations of the transference in treatment can be dramatic, and observations of transference phenomena have figured centrally in the psychoanalytic literature since Freud's case studies of Anna O. and Dora (Breuer and Freud, 1957; Freud, 1953). Reliable measurement has proved more difficult, however. Probably the most sustained and best-known effort has been the work on the core conflictual relationship theme (CCRT) (e.g., Luborsky and Crits-Christoph, 1998). CCRT research assesses patients' stories of relationships, reasoning that a client's stories about relationships in or out of therapy are likely to manifest repeated patterns or themes that reveal the core conflicts.

PERSON-CENTRED CONCEPTS OF THE RELATIONSHIP

Whereas psychodynamic theorists may view the transference as a distorted fragment impinging on a distinct real relationship, person-centred theorists have tended to take a holistic, here-and-now perspective (Rogers, 1957, 1980). Yes, people may transfer attitudes and strong feelings from past relationships to present ones, but to consider these as unreal is to deny or derogate the immediacy of the client's actual experience. Rather than seeking to judge and interpret such experiences, the therapist's job is to understand and accept them. Fully experiencing, acknowledging, and stating ('symbolising') experiences allows them to be considered and re-valued in light of current reality (see Greenberg's (1994) commentary on Gelso and Carter (1994)). The value placed on any particular experience is up to the client, not the therapist or the theory. This conceptualisation directs attention not to the historical development of the client's problems but instead to the relationship conditions that the therapist provides within the therapy.

Rogers' (1957: 95) six therapist-provided 'necessary and sufficient conditions of therapeutic personality change' have been popularly reduced to three, which may be stated succinctly (my gloss, not Rogers') as: (1) be yourself; (2) trust the client; and (3) listen. Although these facilitative conditions, or attitudes, can be stated simply, they can be endlessly unpacked. Here is a sample of how Rogers did it:

> The first element [be yourself] could be called genuineness, realness, or congruence. The more the therapist is himself or herself in the relationship, putting up no professional front or personal façade, the greater is the likelihood that the client will change and grow in a constructive manner. This means that the therapist is openly being the feelings and attitudes that are flowing within at the moment.

> The second attitude of importance in creating a climate for change [trust the client] is acceptance, or caring, or prizing – what I have called 'unconditional positive regard.' When the therapist is experiencing a positive, acceptant attitude toward whatever the client is at that moment, therapeutic movement or change is more likely to occur.

> The third facilitative aspect of the relationship [listen] is empathic understanding. This means that the therapist senses accurately the feelings and personal meanings that the client is experiencing and communicates this understanding to the client. (Rogers, 1980: 115–116)

Easy to say, hard to do. From a practitioner's perspective, being genuine (and distinguishing this from self-serving disclosure), accepting the client (who may hold beliefs or engage in practices contrary to your personal principles), and understanding empathically (when the client tells endless bland stories) can be difficult and taxing. Under some circumstances, the conditions can seem contradictory. For example, if I disapprove (suicide, child molesters, etc.), can I listen empathically, and does being genuine demand that I disclose it? Fortunately, the theory suggests that perfect adherence is not required. Beneficial effects can be expected to the degree that the conditions are fulfilled. On the other hand, from the perspective of an external observer, the conditions may seem to merge into a general positive evaluation. Nevertheless, research on these three core conditions continues to accumulate (Elliott et al., 2018; Farber, Suzuki and Lynch, 2018; Kolden et al., 2018).

Some person-centred authors have described fully encountering the client as therapeutic work at *relational depth* (e.g., Mearns and Cooper, 2017; Schmid and Mearns, 2006). They suggest that therapy's power to transform proceeds from the therapist's ability 'to engage the client at a more fundamental, existential level', so that clients 'feel met at the deepest levels at which they experience themselves' (Schmid and Mearns, 2006: 178).

PSYCHOMETRIC CONCEPTS OF THE ALLIANCE

In a seminal conceptualisation, Bordin (1979) characterised the alliance as multidimensional, encompassing (a) the affective bond between client and therapist, (b) agreement on the goals of treatment, and (c) agreement on treatment tasks, or means of achieving those goals. Subsequent alliance researchers have constructed scales to assess the dimensions, for example, using ratings on items like 'I feel friendly towards my therapist' to measure bond or 'I am clear as to what my therapist wants me to do in these sessions' to measure agreement on tasks. Typically, investigators have administered a pool of such items and then grouped them into scales using factor analysis or related statistical techniques. Results have offered some support (i.e., the factors often appear to correspond to conceptual dimensions), though the factors tend to be substantially intercorrelated (e.g., Agnew-Davies et al., 1998).

Although some have used Bordin's (1979) concepts of bond, agreement on tasks, and agreement on goals (notably Horvath, 1994), researchers have not concurred on the boundaries of the alliance construct or on the number or names of the dimensions. Some have combined or re-labelled Bordin's dimensions, for example, combining agreement on tasks and agreement on goals as working strategy consensus (Gaston, 1991) or partnership (Agnew-Davies et al., 1998). Others have added dimensions, such as patient working capacity and therapist understanding and involvement (Gaston, 1991; Marmar, Weiss and Gaston, 1989), confident collaboration (Hatcher and Barends, 1996), or openness and client initiative (Agnew-Davies et al., 1998). Research has not consistently supported the differentiation of the varied dimensions, however, and many researchers have ignored the dimensional scores, using a single total or aggregate score to assess the alliance.

The alliance has sustained intense interest from researchers because of its replicated positive correlations with measures of psychotherapy outcome (Flückiger et al., 2018). Moreover, there is evidence that the often-observed differences in the effectiveness of different therapists may be attributable to their differing ability to form strong alliances (Baldwin, Wampold and Imel, 2007; Crits-Christoph et al., 2009).

Evaluative process measures like the alliance do not assess specific behaviours, but rather, judgements of whether the behaviours were well chosen and well executed under the circumstances. In other words, they concern appropriate responsiveness. Although such measures may assess whether or not the therapist did the right thing, the downside is that they do not specify what was right or wrong about it (Stiles, 2021). Thus, the replicated positive correlations amount to showing that good process predicts good outcome – sensible but not very informative.

Obtaining differentiated measurements of the alliance may require observational approaches (see Luborsky, 1976). Ribeiro et al. (2013) have developed an observational measure of the relationship based on the degree to which therapists work within (or outside) the client's therapeutic zone of proximal development, defined as the space between the client's current therapeutic developmental level and their potential therapeutic developmental level that can be reached in collaboration with the therapist. Observational coding systems have also been developed to provide more differentiated assessments of the alliance in family therapy (Escudero, Heatherington and Friedlander, 2010) and child therapy (McLeod and Weisz, 2005).

Training therapists to improve relationships forces therapists and trainers to confront the complexities. Crits-Christoph et al. (2006) have shown that therapists can be trained to improve alliances, with likely positive influences on outcomes. Safran and Muran (2000) designed a successful treatment around improving relationships (see, for example, Safran et al., 2014).

Some significant short-term fluctuations in the alliance have been described as *rupture–repair sequences* (Eubanks-Carter, Muran and Safran, 2010; Safran and Muran, 2000). Ruptures may occur when previously hidden negative feelings emerge or when the therapist makes a mistake or fails to act as the client expects or wishes. If the therapist recognises the rupture, it may offer an opportunity for therapeutic interpersonal learning, as ruptures in the therapy relationship may recapitulate the client's relationship difficulties outside therapy. More generally, recognising, acknowledging and overcoming relational difficulties can provide valuable experiential learning in the here-and-now of the session.

REFERENCES

Agnew-Davies, R., Stiles, W.B., Hardy, G.E., Barkham, M. and Shapiro, D.A. (1998) Alliance structure assessed by the Agnew Relationship Measure (ARM). *British Journal of Clinical Psychology*, 37: 155–172.

Baldwin, S.A., Wampold, B.E. and Imel, Z.E. (2007) Untangling the alliance–outcome correlation: Exploring the relative importance of therapist and patient variability in the alliance. *Journal of Consulting and Clinical Psychology*, 75: 842–852.

Barkham, M. and Lambert, M.J. (2021) The efficacy and effectiveness of psychological therapies. In M. Barkham, W. Lutz and L. Castonguay (Eds), *Bergin and Garfield's Handbook of Psychotherapy and Behavior Change* (7th ed., pp. 135–189). New York: Wiley.

Bordin, E.S. (1979) The generalizability of the psychoanalytic concept of working alliance. *Psychotherapy: Theory, Research, and Practice*, 16: 252–260.

Brenner, C. (1979) Working alliance, therapeutic alliance, and transference. *Journal of the American Psychoanalytic Association*, 27 (supplement): 137–157.

Breuer, J. and Freud, S. (1957) *Studies on Hysteria*. New York: Basic Books.

Carroll, L. (1946 [1865]) *Alice's Adventures in Wonderland*. New York: Random House.

Crits-Christoph, P., Gallop, R., Temes, C.M., Woody, G., Ball, S.A., Martino, S. and Carroll, K.M. (2009) The alliance in motivational enhancement therapy and counseling as usual for substance use problems. *Journal of Consulting and Clinical Psychology*, 77: 1125–1135.

Crits-Christoph, P., Gibbons, M.B.C., Crits-Christoph, K., Narducci, J., Schamberger, M. and Gallop, R. (2006) Can therapists be trained to improve their alliances? A preliminary study of alliance-fostering psychotherapy. *Psychotherapy Research*, 16: 268–281.

Elliott, R., Bohart, A.C., Watson, J.C. and Murphy, D. (2018) Therapist empathy and client outcome: An updated meta-analysis. *Psychotherapy*, 55: 399–410.

Escudero, V., Heatherington, L. and Friedlander, M.L. (2010) Therapeutic alliances and alliance building in family therapy. In J.C. Muran and J.P. Barber (Eds), *The Therapeutic Alliance: An Evidence-based Approach to Practice and Training* (pp. 240–262). New York: Guilford Press.

Eubanks-Carter, C., Muran, J.C. and Safran, J.D. (2010) Alliance ruptures and resolution. In J.C. Muran and J.P. Barber (Eds), *The Therapeutic Alliance: An Evidence-based Approach to Practice and Training* (pp. 74–94). New York: Guilford Press.

Farber, B.A., Suzuki, J.Y. and Lynch, D.A. (2018) Positive regard and psychotherapy outcome: A meta-analytic review. *Psychotherapy*, 55: 411–423.

Flückiger, C., Del Re, A.C., Wampold, B.E. and Horvath, A.O. (2018) The alliance in adult psychotherapy: A meta-analytic synthesis. *Psychotherapy*, 55: 316–340.

Freud, S. (1953) Fragments of an analysis of a case of hysteria. In J. Strachey (Ed. and trans.), *The Standard Edition of the Complete Psychological Works of Sigmund Freud* (Vol. 7, pp. 3–122). London: Hogarth Press (original work published 1905).

Freud, S. (1958) The dynamics of transference. In J. Strachey (Ed. and trans.), *The Standard Edition of the Complete Psychological Works of Sigmund Freud* (Vol. 12, pp. 99–108). London: Hogarth Press (original work published 1912).

Gaston, L. (1991) Reliability and criterion-related validity of the California Psychotherapy Alliance Scales – patient version. *Psychological Assessment*, 3: 68–74.

Geller, J.D. and Farber, B.A. (1993) Factors influencing the process of internalization in psychotherapy. *Psychotherapy Research*, 3: 166–180.

Gelso, C.J. and Carter, J.A. (1994) Components of the psychotherapy relationship: Their interaction and unfolding during treatment. *Journal of Counseling Psychology*, 41: 296–306.

Greenberg, L.S. (1994) What is 'real' in the relationship? Comment on Gelso and Carter (1994). *Journal of Counseling Psychology*, 41: 307–309.

Greenson, R.R. (1965) The working alliance and the transference neuroses. *Psychoanalysis Quarterly*, 34: 155–181.

Hatcher, R.L. and Barends, A.W. (1996) Patients' view of the alliance in psychotherapy: Exploratory factor analysis of three alliance measures. *Journal of Consulting and Clinical Psychology*, 64: 1326–1336.

Horvath, A.O. (1994) Empirical validation of Bordin's pantheoretical model of the alliance: The Working Alliance Inventory perspective. In A.O. Horvath and L.S. Greenberg (Eds), *The Working Alliance: Theory, Research and Practice* (pp. 109–128). New York: Wiley.

Kohut, M. (1971) *The Analysis of the Self*. New York: International Universities Press.

(Continued)

(Continued)

Kohut, M. (1977) *The Restoration of the Self*. New York: International Universities Press.

Kolden, G.G., Wang, C.-C., Austin, S.B., Chang, Y. and Klein, M.H. (2018) Congruence/genuineness: A meta-analysis. *Psychotherapy*, 55: 424–433.

Luborsky, L. (1976) Helping alliances in psychotherapy: The groundwork for a study of their relationship to its outcome. In J.L. Claghorn (Ed.), *Successful Psychotherapy* (pp. 92–116). New York: Brunner/Mazel.

Luborsky, L. and Crits-Christoph, P. (1998) *Understanding Transference: The Core-Conflictual Relationship Theme Method* (2nd ed.). Washington, DC: American Psychological Association.

Marmar, C.R., Weiss, D.S. and Gaston, L. (1989) Towards the validation of the California Therapeutic Alliance Rating System. *Psychological Assessment*, 1: 46–52.

McLeod, B.D. and Weisz, J.R. (2005) The therapy process observational coding system-alliance scale: Measure characteristics and prediction of outcome in usual clinical practice. *Journal of Consulting and Clinical Psychology*, 73: 323–333.

Mearns, D. and Cooper, M. (2017) *Working at Relational Depth in Counselling and Psychotherapy* (2nd ed.). London: Sage.

Messer, S.B. and Wolitsky, D.L. (2010) A psychodynamic perspective on the therapeutic alliance. In J.C. Muran and J.P. Barber (Eds), *The Therapeutic Alliance: An Evidence-based Approach to Practice and Training* (pp. 97–122). New York: Guilford Press.

Norcross, J.C. and Lambert, M.J. (Eds) (2019) *Psychotherapy Relationships that Work* (3rd ed., Vol. 1). New York: Oxford University Press.

Norcross, J.C. and Wampold, B.E. (Eds) (2019) *Psychotherapy Relationships that Work* (3rd ed., Vol. 2). New York: Oxford University Press.

Ribeiro, E.M., Ribeiro, A.P., Gonçalves, M.M., Horvath, A.O. and Stiles, W.B. (2013) How collaboration in therapy becomes therapeutic: The Therapeutic Collaboration Coding System. *Psychology and Psychotherapy: Theory, Research, and Practice*, 86: 294–314.

Rogers, C.R. (1957) The necessary and sufficient conditions of therapeutic personality change. *Journal of Consulting Psychology*, 21: 95–103.

Rogers, C.R. (1980) *A Way of Being*. Boston, MA: Houghton Mifflin.

Rosenzweig, S. (1936) Some implicit common factors in diverse methods of psychotherapy. *American Journal of Orthopsychiatry*, 6: 412–415.

Safran, J.D. and Muran, J.C. (2000) *Negotiating the Therapeutic Alliance: A Relational Treatment Guide*. New York: Guilford Press.

Safran, J.D., Muran, J.C., Demaria, A., Boutwell, C., Eubanks-Carter, C. and Winston, A. (2014) Investigating the impact of alliance-focused training on interpersonal process and therapists' capacity for experiential reflection. *Psychotherapy Research*, 24: 269–285.

Schmid, P.F. and Mearns, D. (2006) Being-with and being-counter: Person-centered therapy as an in-depth co-creative process of personalization. *Person-Centered and Experiential Psychotherapies*, 5: 174–190.

Stiles, W.B. (2021) Responsiveness in psychotherapy research: Problems and ways forward. In J.C. Watson and H. Wiseman (Eds), *The Responsive Psychotherapist: Attuning to Clients in the Moment* (pp. 15–35). Washington, DC: APA Books.

Wampold, B.E. and Imel, Z.E. (2015) *The Great Psychotherapy Debate: Research Evidence for What Works in Psychotherapy* (2nd ed.). New York: Routledge.

Watson, J.C. and Wiseman, H. (Eds) (2021) *The Responsive Psychotherapists: Attuning to Clients in the Moment*. Washington, DC: APA Books.

Zetzel, E.R. (1956) Current concepts of transference. *International Journal of Psychoanalysis*, 37: 369–376.

Zuroff, D.C. and Blatt, S.J. (2006) The therapeutic relationship in brief treatment of depression: Contributions to clinical improvement and enhanced adaptive capacities. *Journal of Consulting and Clinical Psychology*, 74, 130–140.

> **RECOMMENDED READING**
>
> Norcross, J.C. and Lambert, M.J. (Eds) (2019) *Psychotherapy Relationships that Work* (3rd ed., Vol. 1). New York: Oxford University Press.
>
> Norcross, J.C. and Wampold, B.E. (Eds) (2019) *Psychotherapy Relationships that Work* (3rd ed., Vol. 2). New York: Oxford University Press.
>
> A compilation of relationship elements that have demonstrated effectiveness.
>
> Watson, J.C. and Wiseman, H. (Eds) (2021) *The Responsive Psychotherapists: Attuning to Clients in the Moment*. Washington, DC: APA Books.
>
> Summaries of clinical and scientific thinking about therapeutic responsiveness by authors active in the field.
>
> Rogers, C.R. (1957) The necessary and sufficient conditions of therapeutic personality change. *Journal of Consulting Psychology*, 21: 95–103.
>
> The classic description of the necessary and sufficient therapist-provided relationship conditions for successful psychotherapy from a person-centred perspective.

3.3 ASSESSMENT

BILJANA VAN RIJN

OVERVIEW AND KEY POINTS

The aim of this chapter is to introduce and begin to explore the assessment process in counselling and psychotherapy. As well as suggesting a definition and aims of assessment, we will also consider a possible structure and ways of conducting the sessions, and revisit some of the ethical values and principles underlying it. I see assessment as a collaborative and reflective process, which at the beginning of therapy has a purpose of ensuring beneficence and integrity of the therapeutic engagement. I will illustrate different aspects of assessment by giving clinical vignettes for reflection.

The following are the chapter summary points:

- Assessment is a therapeutic process which is usually the most focused at the beginning of counselling and leads to a decision by the client and the counsellor about engaging in the counselling process. Its main aim is to ensure, as far as possible, that a client is entering into a counselling process that can be beneficial for them.
- An assessment session usually has a focus and a degree of structure. It contains some information gathering, clarification of the main issues the client is bringing to therapy, risk assessment and beginnings of the therapeutic agreement and formulation.
- Counselling contexts have implications for assessments decision and outcomes. Establishing personal or organisational limitations of the service

- and professional competence need to be a part of making decisions about assessment outcomes.
- Conducting assessments online has additional implications for practice. Issues such as confidentiality, legal issues and assessment of risk need to be given additional consideration.
- The therapeutic relationship starts to take shape within the assessment process. Reflection on its process and experience could be valuable within the session and a source of information about the future working alliance.

WHAT IS ASSESSMENT?

Assessment is a therapeutic process which, at the beginning of counselling, leads to a specific outcome, a decision by the client and the counsellor about engaging in the counselling process. This usually gives a particular intensity to the initial sessions and highlights the importance of structure and focus, to best support the client at the time when they are potentially entering into an unknown. Malan (1979) defined assessment in relation to its tasks of *finding out what the problem is, how it developed and what should be done about it*. This definition summarises the focus of the initial sessions and links assessment to formulation and treatment planning.

Historically, there has been an uneasy relationship between humanistic counselling and the idea of assessment, and concern that it would lead to labelling and taking power away from the client. These are legitimate considerations and ethical issues of sharing power, transparency and collaboration are essential in underpinning the assessment process.

WHY DO WE ASSESS?

The primary aims of assessment are linked to ensuring, as far as possible, that a client is entering into a counselling process that can be of benefit to them. That means that a counsellor needs to be able to develop an understanding of the core and the presenting issues for the client and make a decision about their ability to meet those needs. For this reason, an assessment session involves some gathering of information about the client and their circumstances.

CASE STUDY

Ellie is a woman in her late twenties. She recently had Cognitive Behaviour Therapy (CBT) at her local Improving Access to Psychological Therapy (IAPT) service. She found it helpful to talk to someone and is now looking for longer-term therapy. She described herself as 'a worrier', but this had recently got out of hand. She described becoming so anxious that she burst into tears at work and had to leave the office. Her job as a Personal Assistant in a demanding environment was relatively recent and she wanted to show that she was able to cope with it. Ellie has been off sick since that day and felt worried about going back to work. She was frequently thinking about dying and imagining her own funeral. She has been feeling very low in this period and spent most of the days sleeping. Ellie has a support network of friends and family, but she hasn't been using them. She lives alone and has avoided social contact while she was off sick. She also found it difficult to care for herself. Her General Practitioner (GP) has prescribed anti-depressants.

In this case study, Ellies's current circumstances seem to show that depression and anxiety were her primary issues. However, to understand her experience better, we might also want to find out how these problems developed and whether they have any resonances in her history.

Ellie's father was a gambler. He left home when she was two years old, and her mother ended up with a lot of his debt. They became homeless for a while and then had to move several times. Although Ellie doesn't remember much of that period, she remembers her mother's struggle to make ends meet. Ellie worried about her mum and tried to be a good daughter for her. She always did her best and worked hard at home and at school. Ellie didn't get on with her sister, whom she described as 'wild' when she was a teenager. Her mother and her sister both live nearby.

> Ellie's history suggests early roots to her anxiety and an adaptive strategy of working hard to maintain psychological security. It seemed that at this stage in her life and career, that strategy was breaking down.
>
> If this was your case, you might wish to consider how much support you or your service could provide for Ellie, and whether you might need to have contact with her GP if her depression intensified.
>
> An assessment session is also a beginning of a counselling relationship. If a counsellor is assessing her own clients, an assessment session will be a process by which some of the groundwork for the working alliance will be established.
>
> *Ellie seemed quiet in the assessment session. She responded to questions but did not elaborate on them. She seemed very polite and pleasant. The counsellor liked Ellie, but found it difficult to engage with her and started to feel very drowsy during the session. However, she felt able to work with her and thought that her own drowsiness related to Ellie's depression and psychological withdrawal. She thought that Ellie's internal world was probably very different from the face she presented to the world and that they needed to build trust and safety to allow her to express herself. She agreed with Ellie about the importance of working for a longer period.*

HOW TO CONDUCT AN ASSESSMENT SESSION?

An assessment session usually needs to have a focus and a degree of structure and contain a certain amount of information gathering. However, the session itself is not expected to follow a particular format but can be facilitated by the counsellor to meet these aims while providing space for the client to tell their story. A useful therapeutic stance during assessment might involve (Bager-Charleson and Van Rijn, 2011; Van Rijn, 2015):

- a balance between attentive listening and enquiry in order to both explore the relevant issues and gain information;
- a focus on core issues, without going too deeply into the painful emotional content, at the time when the therapeutic relationship is not established;
- establishing a therapeutic frame and boundaries.

It is often helpful to have a template for the assessment notes. You can use it to make notes during the session, or as a background to support you in structuring the session. Several templates are currently available and in print, or you can create your own. Figure 3.3.1 is an abbreviated assessment form at Metanoia Counselling and Psychotherapy Service (MCPS), with a brief rationale for each category and prompts (see Figure 3.3.1).

In considering how to structure an assessment session in your own practice, you need to consider your work context, experience, and the therapeutic approach.

ASSESSMENT CONTEXTS

Counselling assessments take place in different working environments and therapeutic contexts. Counsellors work in organisations where they might assess their own clients or conduct assessments in order to make referrals to other therapists within the service. Sometimes, assessments can be conducted remotely using video conferencing.

In organisational contexts, the expectations of an assessment session(s) are often more clearly defined and linked to the available services. Clients often have less choice about the type of counselling or counsellor they might see. The power imbalance could be perceived to be more in favour of the organisation. If you are conducting an assessment within an organisation, it is important to be familiar with the scope and the limitations of the service. This often relates to the length of therapy, sessional fees, and experience and qualifications of the counsellors. The scope of the service has implications for the clients who can be accepted by the service. The exclusion criteria, for example, might involve clients with addictions, with severe mental health issues such as psychosis, etc.

Assessments also take place in private practice, although they are often less formal and focus more on a mutual assessment between the therapist and the client. The power and the choice could be seen to be more in favour of the clients. However, in this context it is also important for a counsellor to ask themselves similar questions about what they can provide and their limitations. This could relate to personal limitations

Date of assessment:

Reference number:

Name:

Address and contact details:

DOB:

GP details:

Notes: *Make a note if the client was not taken into the service, signposting to other services.*

PRESENTING ISSUES AND CURRENT CIRCUMSTANCES:

Rationale: *To understand the main focus for counselling, client's motivation, functioning and social support.*

Prompts:

What brings the client into therapy at this stage in their life?

How is the client functioning in social situations and work?

What is their support network like?

FAMILY BACKGROUND AND PERSONAL HISTORY:

Rationale: *Historical and developmental issues that could have an impact on counselling, such as trauma, attachment issues and developmental difficulties.*

Prompts:

Factual information: who was around, order of birth in the family, broadly based personal history, relationship history.

COUNSELLING/PSYCHOTHERAPY HISTORY:

Rationale: *Finding out how the client's previous experience of counselling might impact on the new relationship.*

Prompts:

Where? How long for? Was it helpful?

Give information if the client is new to therapy.

Answer queries.

AIMS STATED:

Rationale: *Beginning to formulate the counselling agreement.*

Prompts: *What does the client want to achieve/focus on in counselling?*

STATE OF HEALTH:

Health/medication:

Alcohol intake:

Smoking:

Use of drugs:

Other:

Rationale: *Information about medical history, medication, and addictive behaviours.*

Prompts: *Enquire about the details and any recent changes.*

Figure 3.3.1 An abbreviated assessment form at Metanoia Counselling and Psychotherapy Service (MCPS)

that might become an obstacle to establishing a working alliance, such as a counsellor's unresolved personal issues. Limitations could also be professional, such as insufficient training or experience.

In both organisational and private practice settings, it is important to be familiar with mental health and emergency services, their provision and access requirements.

ONLINE ASSESSMENT

The Covid-19 pandemic, which started in 2019, impacted the delivery of counselling and psychotherapy in services as well private practice. As services moved to online provision, the professional bodies brought in guidance to support the therapists in this way of working (British Association for Counselling and Psychotherapy, 2019; British Psychological Society, 2020; UK Council for Psychotherapy, 2021).

These guidance documents highlight several issues relevant to clinical assessment:

- Legal issues, such as general data protection guidance (The General Data Protection Regulation and the Data Protection Act 2018). A client and a therapist could be located in different countries and legal systems. It is a good practice to ensure that you are familiar with these differences and how they might impact your ability to work with a client.
- Practical issues such as familiarity and digital competence.
- Professional and ethical issues: such as confidentiality, and protection from intrusion on both sides will need to be addressed in the online assessment.

Online contact is relationally different from meeting a client face to face. The pandemic has necessitated the development of online working, and in doing so facilitated professional development in this area. Conducting assessment online has benefits as well as limitations. One of the important benefits of online assessments is that they have a potential to improve access to therapy for clients who are housebound or unable to travel. On the other hand, working online can be very challenging for clients who do not have sufficient resources or equipment and don't have the digital skills or privacy in their living arrangements.

Online assessment impacts the therapeutic relationship by reducing all the non-verbal cues to the facial expressions captured by the camera, thus limiting the richness of contact and connection. On the other hand, there is a potential for an online disinhibition effect (Suler, 2004), which can lead clients to disclose more than they are ready for even during the assessment. It is important to take that on board in considering whether the client's presenting issues might be suitable for online working.

ASSESSMENT AND THE THERAPEUTIC RELATIONSHIP

The therapeutic alliance (Bordin, 1979) is an aspect of the therapeutic relationship related to collaboration between the therapist and the client, and their emotional connection. It has been widely researched as one of the common factors that is essential for successful outcomes (Lambert and Barley, 2002). As in any other relationship, both parties contribute to it, and research shows that clients are active in shaping the relationship (Bohart and Greaves Wade, 2013), as are the therapists (Baldwin et al., 2007). This process starts during the assessment when the newness and the intensity of the first meeting often highlight both the client's and the therapist's habitual ways of relating. Reflection on this process can support the establishment of a good working alliance.

Some interventions during an assessment can assist the therapist and the client in thinking about how they experience each other and their expectations of the therapeutic process. The pluralistic approach to therapy developed by Cooper and McLeod (2011) suggests that a meta-therapeutic dialogue would engage clients in talking about their expectations and preferences about directiveness, self-disclosure, focus of therapy, the amount of challenge, etc.

In an assessment session, as in any other time in counselling, we need to consider that a therapeutic relationship involves both individuals, their cultural background, preferences and histories. The counsellor and the client bring to it all of who they are, including our broad cultural contexts, personal background and attachment styles (Bowlby, 1982). Our personal context as well as the cultural field will impact both the assessment session and the future therapeutic process.

> **CASE STUDY**
>
> *In the assessment session with Ellie, from the way they related to each other, the counsellor reflected that Ellie might have an expectation that the counsellor would be leading the sessions. However, this was not how she usually worked. She approached this issue by asking Ellie what she thought would be helpful in their work together. Ellie said she wasn't sure how counselling was supposed to be but didn't want the counsellor to be silent all the time. They agreed that Ellie would bring anything she wanted to talk about, and the counsellor would offer her reflections and comments, but would not lead the sessions.*

ASSESSMENT OF RISK

Generally, the risk issues that therapists might come across include:

- a risk of the client's suicide and self-harm;
- violence and harm to others;
- safeguarding of vulnerable adults and child protection;
- mental health and crisis.

In the assessment session, the therapist usually starts with the recognition of the areas of risk and their potential severity, as well as the client's strengths or the protective factors in their life. Assessing risk is an important part of ethical practice and continues throughout the work with the client. Reeves (2015) reflects on the complexity of these issues and suggests five different contexts for thinking about them. These are linked to: situations and events, the therapeutic relationship, the context in which therapy takes place, professional issues, and risks linked to the wellbeing of the practitioner. This significantly widens the concept of risk assessment and places it in the context of the therapeutic process. We don't only need to reflect on the severity of risk the client presents with, but also the therapeutic relationship, our work environment and psychological readiness to take on a client (see also Reeves – Chapter 3.4, this volume). In online assessments it is important to consider that a client might be isolated and vulnerable, and to discuss safety arrangements with them (for example, who they might contact if they are distressed).

USING QUESTIONNAIRES IN ASSESSMENT

There is an increasing use of questionnaires for evaluation and monitoring of outcomes in current therapeutic practice. This is the case in the health services, but also in other organisations that provide counselling and psychotherapy. In my experience of running a service which routinely evaluates practice, clients are often more enthusiastic about their use than practitioners. In ongoing counselling, questionnaires can be used for feedback as well as supporting clients in monitoring their own wellbeing. Questionnaires in assessment can help practitioners develop an overview about the level of the client's distress (CORE Information Management Systems Ltd., 2007), or recognise symptoms of mental health issues such as anxiety (Spitzer et al., 2006) and depression (Kroenke et al., 2001). These questionnaires can support us in developing an awareness of risk, which clients often initially disclose in questionnaires. Therapists often have misgivings about a questionnaire format and structure, and it may take a while to feel at ease with integrating them into your own assessment practice.

I have found it useful to think about questionnaires as one of the many tools clients can use to communicate their personal experience, and I engage with them in the same way as any other aspect of our dialogue. It might be helpful to reflect on how you might approach using them in your assessments.

ETHICAL ISSUES

Ethical issues in the assessment process follow the general counselling principles and values reflected in the British Association for Counselling and Psychotherapy (BACP) *Ethical Framework for the Counselling Professions* (2018) and the United Kingdom Council for Psychotherapy (UKCP) *Ethical Principles and Code of Professional Conduct* (2009). Ethical considerations are at the heart of how we arrive at assessment decisions, issues of beneficence, therapist competence, and dealing with risk.

REFERENCES

British Association for Counselling and Psychotherapy (2018). *Ethical Framework for the Counselling Professions.* Lutterworth: BACP.

British Association for Counselling and Psychotherapy (2019). *Working Online in the Counselling Professions.* Lutterworth: BACP. Available at www.bacp.co.uk/media/2162/bacp-working-online-supplementary-guidance-gpia047.pdf

Bager-Charleson, S. and Van Rijn, B. (2011). *Understanding Assessment in Counselling and Psychotherapy.* London: Learning Matters.

Baldwin, S. A., Wampold, B. E., et al. (2007). Untangling the alliance–outcome correlation: Exploring the relative importance of therapist and patient variability in the alliance. *Journal of Consulting & Clinical Psychology*, 75(6): 842–852.

Bohart, A. C. and Greaves Wade, A. (2013). The client in psychotherapy. In M. Lambert (Ed.). *Bergin and Garfield's Handbook of Psychotherapy and Behaviour Change* (pp. 219–257). Hoboken, NJ: John Wiley & Sons.

Bordin, E. S. (1979). The generalizability of the psychoanalytic concept of the working alliance. *Psychotherapy: Theory, Research, Practice*, 16(3): 252–260.

Bowlby, J. (1982). *Attachment and Loss. Vol. 1. Attachment.* London: Hogarth Press and the Institute of Psycho Analysis.

British Psychological Society (2020). *Psychological Assessment Undertaken Remotely.* Leicester: BPS. Available at www.bps.org.uk/coronavirus (accessed 29 November 2021).

Cooper, M. and McLeod, J. (2011). *Pluralistic Counselling and Psychotherapy.* London: Sage.

CORE Information Management Systems Ltd (2007). *CORE Net.* Available at www.coreims-online.co.uk

Kroenke, K., Spitzer, R. L., et al. (2001). The PHQ-9: Validity of a brief depression severity measure. *Journal of General and Internal Medicine*, 16: 606–613.

Lambert, M. J. and Barley, E. D. (2002). Research summary on the therapeutic relationship and psychotherapy outcome. In J. C. Norcross (Ed.), *Psychotherapy Relationships that Work: Therapist Contributions and Responsiveness to Patients* (pp. 17–32). Oxford: Oxford University Press.

Malan, D. H. (1979). *Individual Psychotherapy and the Science of Psychodynamics.* [S.l.]. London: Butterworths.

Reeves, A. (2015). *Working with Risk in Counselling and Psychotherapy.* London: Sage.

Spitzer, R. L., Kroenke, R., et al. (2006). A brief measure for assessing generalized anxiety disorder: The GAD-7. *Archives of Internal Medicine*, 166: 1092–1097.

Suler, J. (2004). The online disinhibition effect. *CyberPsychology & Behavior*, 7(3), 321–326. https://doi.org/10.1089/1094931041291295

United Kingdom Council for Psychotherapy (2009). *UK Council for Psychotherapy, Ethical Principles and Code of Professional Conduct.* London: UKCP. Available at www.psychotherapy.org.uk/code_of_ethics.html

United Kingdom Council for Psychotherapy (2021). *UKCP Guidelines for Working Online/Remotely.* London: UKCP. Available at www.psychotherapy.org.uk/media/jrohoner/ukcp-guidelines-for-working-online-or-remotely-v1-0.pdf (accessed 29 November 2021).

Van Rijn, B. (2015). *Assessment and Case Formulation in Counselling and Psychotherapy.* London: Sage.

RECOMMENDED READING

Cooper, M. and McLeod, J. (2011). *Pluralistic Counselling and Psychotherapy.* London: Sage.

This book proposes an ethical and empowering therapeutic stance for practitioners of different orientations, which has a potential to develop therapists' responsiveness. Meta-therapeutic dialogue about the process of therapy is of particular relevance for assessments.

(Continued)

> (Continued)
>
> Van Rijn, B. (2015). *Assessment and Case Formulation in Counselling and Psychotherapy*. London: Sage.
>
> This book presents ways of working with assessments, diagnosis and formulation in reflective therapeutic practice and within different theoretical orientations.
>
> British Psychological Society (2020). *Psychological Assessment Undertaken Remotely*. Leicester: BPS. Available at www.bps.org.uk/coronavirus (accessed 29 November 2021).
>
> The guidelines developed by the professional bodies will support you when considering different aspects of conducting online assessments and in having current information in your practice.

3.4 RISK: ASSESSMENT, EXPLORATION AND MITIGATION

ANDREW REEVES

OVERVIEW AND KEY POINTS

Risk is present in all work we undertake as therapists: from risks about harm to the client, or others, through to risk of unhelpful therapy with a poor outcome for the client. Much of the literature, however, talks about risk from a binary perspective: risk is present, or it is not. In reality, of course, the task is not to determine whether risk is present or not, but rather to identify risks pertinent for that particular client and their situation, and to find ways, collaboratively, with the client in the context in which therapy is taking place, to work with it effectively. This chapter will consider risk from several different perspectives and explore ways in which it can be successfully engaged with.

- Risk, in different forms, is present in all therapeutic interactions and the task of the therapist is to identify those risks and work with them proactively, collaboratively with the client.

- While risk to 'self and others' is most commonly thought about by therapists in their work, other risks are present too. Risk can be considered from five primary perspectives: situational, relational, contextual, professional, and personal. All need the full attention of therapists during the process of therapy.

- The identification and management of risk has been subject to much consideration, with the development of many quantitative approaches to determine the presence and extent of risk. These are typically called 'risk assessment questionnaires', or similar.

- However, very few risk assessment tools have any meaningful efficacy in determining the extent of risk as it applies to the individual client. Rather, the imperative is for therapists to confidently and openly engage in a dialogue about risk with their clients.

- Working with risk, therefore, is always a collaborative process (assuming the client has capacity to engage in dialogue about their risk).

INTRODUCTION

When introduced to the concept of contracting in therapy, we are told that the contract not only informs and supports the therapeutic process, but also limits aspects of it too. Specifically, the contract is used to outline to clients the limits of confidentiality we can offer, typically limited by the potential for the client's suicide, or of harm to another, or through a statutory requirement, for example, terrorism. The term 'risk management' has seeped into popular parlance and is used in a variety of settings and contexts. However, in therapy, the notion of risk management implicitly seems to place the therapist in the position of *doing to* the client, as opposed to *doing with*. This chapter will explore the subtleties of risk, drawing together key practical considerations to help therapists work with risk confidently and effectively.

WHAT DO WE MEAN BY 'RISK'?

Too often in practice risk is viewed as a binary construct: a client is either at risk or is not. This is clearly a simplistic view of risk that does not pay attention to the multifaceted and dynamic processes that underpin it. Likewise, risk is almost always associated with harm whereas, in many instances, it might also talk of opportunity for change. If we consider the *Oxford English Dictionary* (OED, 2021) definition of risk as 'exposure to the possibility of loss, injury, or other adverse of unwelcome circumstance', that synonymous relationship with harm is clear; the second definition offered, however, says risk can also be 'bold or daring'.

The meaning of risk is often rooted in the perception of it rather than the actuality. For example, were I minded to undertake an ascent of Mount Everest, those around me might perceive the risk to be of loss, injury or even death, whereas for me it might be challenge, opportunity and a life-changing experience. Or, if I were struggling with an intensely painful, chronic health condition and were contemplating suicide, those around me might perceive my risk of suicide to be dangerous, to be avoided and prevented, whereas suicide might for me mean escape, relief and the end of pain. As each individual projects onto the risk situation their own experience of it, society does the same and we might all think of how attitudes to risk change over time.

Previously (Reeves, 2015) I have defined risk across five primary parameters: situational, relational, contextual, professional and personal.

- *Situational risks*: those that often relate to client presentation, such as risk of suicide, self-injury, violence to others, terrorism.
- *Relational risks*: those that typically refer to dynamics between therapist and client, such as sexual attraction, financial exploitation, unacknowledged or mismanaged transferential or countertransferential dynamics.
- *Contextual risks*: those that relate to the context in which therapy is located, such as an inconsistent or unequitable delivery of therapy, lack of clear ethical position, procedures of working practices inconsistent with the underpinning ethical principles of therapy.
- *Professional risks*: those that relate to the behaviour or actions of the therapist both inside and outside therapy, such as criminal prosecution, adverse publicity, therapist actions and behaviour while using social media.
- *Personal risks*: those that relate to the impact on the therapist of their work, such as vicarious trauma, relationship or family difficulties, meeting own needs in therapy as opposed to those of the client.

Using these parameters, as well as others, we can see how risk is a multi-layered presence in our work that includes risk of harm to the client, but not exclusively. For example, consider Lesley in the case study below.

The situation with Lesley demonstrates how risks can present in different forms, all with the potential for harm to either the client or the therapist. As such, we need to be mindful that risks can be present in a variety of ways and always be attentive to their presence.

> **CASE STUDY**
>
> Lesley is a 30-year-old female client. She sees a therapist working in private practice. She has a history of self-injury, although has not injured herself for several months. She talks of 'wanting to go to sleep but not wake up', but is clear that it is not her intention to act on her suicidal ideation. She has approached this particular therapist on a personal recommendation and has found them attentive, empathic and warm. On a couple of occasions Lesley has been unable to pay the agreed fee for therapy and her therapist has said it 'doesn't matter'. She sees this as evidence of her therapist's possible attraction to her.
>
> There are a number of risks identified in this brief scenario:
>
> - *Situational*: previous history of self-injury; expressed suicidal ideation (albeit without intent);
> - *Relational*: unexpressed sexual attraction to the therapist, and particularly in the context of other contracted boundaries not being adhered to (e.g., payment);
> - *Contextual*: therapy located in private practice (perhaps without written procedures for responding to client risk, etc.); vague contract in relation to payment (and potentially other factors);
> - *Professional*: the therapist's failure to manage issues of fee appropriately and the danger of what might be communicated to and experienced by the client; unacknowledged client attraction to the therapist;
> - *Personal*: currently possible rather than actual, but the mismanagement of the other four areas of risk has the potential to be personally damaging to the therapist at some point in the future.

PRESENTING RISKS IN THERAPY

Space does not allow for a comprehensive discussion of risks across all five parameters outlined. For the purposes of this chapter, we will focus on situational risks. There are several situational risks that most commonly present in therapy: risk of suicide, dangers associated with self-harm/injury, risk of harm to others, safeguarding and child protection, and mental health crisis.

RISK OF SUICIDE

For a fuller discussion of working with risk of suicide, see Reeves – Chapter 4.18, this volume. The potential for suicide is possibly the risk associated with the greatest degree of fear and anxiety for practitioners (Kottler, 2010; Panove, 1994; Reeves, 2015). The reality is, and this is perhaps where the greatest degree of anxiety sits, that working with suicide risk is an inherently unpredictable endeavour and organisational policies often fail in the face of such unpredictability, or at least do not provide the certainty that anxious practitioners or organisations go in search of.

DANGERS OF SELF-HARM/INJURY

For a fuller discussion of working with self-harm/injury, see Reeves – Chapter 4.18, this volume. While self-injury (cutting, burning, hair pulling, scratching, biting, etc.) and self-harm (eating disorders, reckless driving, over work, over exercise, lack of self-care) are typically conceptualised as ways in which clients (or indeed ourselves) cope with adversity and emotional turmoil, often when it has proved impossible to find alternative means of expression or the right words to articulate distress, the perceived danger can sit heavily on therapists' shoulders. It is important to determine the line between self-harm/injury as a mechanism for self-support and where it becomes potentially life-threatening, albeit in an unknown way to the client themselves.

RISK OF HARM TO OTHERS

The majority of therapists contract with their clients to act in the event of concern of harm, often meaning child protection. However, the risk of violence to others beyond child protection concerns is very present in therapy, but one, I suspect, for which we receive little training to determine. A look at the available literature identifies some information from psychiatry and clinical psychology, but there is very little literature for therapists in helping them to determine levels of risk of violence and indicators for concern. If there were a 'poor relation' in the hierarchy of risk and the attention and thought it attracts, it would be this. I have offered some thoughts previously on this (Reeves, 2015: 72–85).

CHILD PROTECTION AND SAFEGUARDING

Unlike the wider risk of violence to others, child protection and safeguarding concerns attract a great deal more attention and supportive literature. Child protection sits within a safeguarding frame, as does the protection of what used to be termed 'vulnerable adults', but is now defined as 'adults at risk', defined by the Office of the Public Guardian (2015: 4) as 'people [who] may be at risk of abuse or neglect due to the actions (or lack of action) of another person'.

A range of potential harm to vulnerable adults was also outlined: physical, domestic, sexual, psychological, financial or material, modern slavery, discriminatory, and organisational. While not all working procedures or therapeutic contracts will make explicit reference to breaking confidentiality to safeguard adults at risk, most will limit confidentiality when there is evidence of child protection concerns.

MENTAL HEALTH CRISIS

It is difficult to define clearly what is meant by a 'mental health crisis' as it could include many presentations that would not, in and of themselves, present an immediate cause for concern in therapy. For example, high levels of distress, due to anxiety or depression, might not be uncommon for many practitioners. However, some presentations are more likely to cause concern and be perceived as a risk for the client, such as an emerging psychosis, or where there is evidence the client is in such distress they are unable, temporarily, to take responsibility for their own actions and wellbeing (Reeves and Buxton, 2020). In such situations, many therapists would deem it appropriate to seek the input of other specialist services or, in extreme situations, may require that a statutory assessment under the Mental Health Act be undertaken.

RISK ASSESSMENT: QUANTITATIVE APPROACHES

In defining what we mean by risk and outlining some of the primary situational risks that might present in therapy, we are left with the core dilemma for many therapists: how to determine the *level* of risk and what action, subsequently, may be required; if another intervention is indicated, whether the client is able to consent to that intervention and, if not, how best to act while continuing to respect their autonomy, independence and wellbeing; finally, if another invention is indicated and the client is able to consent but refuses to do so, how the therapist should act then.

Many quantitative risk assessment tools have been developed to help 'apply science' to risk: the rigorous application of an evidence-based tool helps determine, objectively, the likelihood of the risk occurring (Surgenor, 2015). Due to the plethora of such tools developed by the risk assessment industry, there are too many to detail here. However, they draw on the research evidence that details risk factors (factors that make the risk more likely), while also working to identify protective factors (factors that make the risk less likely).

While such tools can be helpful in providing the practitioner with a structure in which to formulate an understanding of presenting risk, problems lie in their general lack of predictive capability. The Royal College of Psychiatrists (2020: 28) note that 'Current suicide risk assessment tools mainly use demographic risk factors (which may be as common in the general population) and have largely been developed without a solid empirical basis. … The reliance upon risk factor identification fails both clinicians and patients'.

It is important, therefore, to use such tools as a means of informing decision-making processes and judgements about risk, but not to allow them to direct such judgements. Additionally, such tools can be helpful in both structuring our thinking about risk and finding a way of beginning a discussion with our client about risk, particularly if we feel anxious about doing so.

RISK EXPLORATION: DISCOURSE-BASED APPROACHES

It is hard to overstress the importance of an open, transparent and respectful dialogue with clients about risk. This can trigger anxieties in professionals who fear that a discussion about risk, such as a question about suicide, might appear clumsy, insensitive or, at worst, increase risk by putting the thought of harm into the client's mind when it was not there before (there is no evidence for this fear). The unacknowledged countertransference (Leenaars, 2004) of working with risk is an important therapeutic consideration for therapists to attend to, in supervision, in therapy, with their manager and in their own self-reflections. Our philosophical position in relation to risk – our views and perspectives – can be powerfully informing in the work we do.

There are, of course, many ways in which such dialogues might be facilitated. Practitioners often look for a blueprint – a ready-made script – they can draw on at times of difficulty in sessions. This is impossible to provide, however, as a relational process is informed by the therapeutic relationship itself: the context in which that relationship is located, the nature of the therapist, the nature of the client, and the ways in which therapy-talk has been constructed between the two. The principle to follow, regardless of the risk being explored, is to be prepared to 'go there' and, as one therapist once described it, 'be brave'.

RISK MITIGATION: RESPONDING TO CONCERNS

Risk mitigation does not necessarily mean the eradication of risk, but rather for risk to be lessened sufficiently so that the threat of harm is reduced and the opportunity for change increased. Risk can sometimes also present opportunities for change, and it is important these are identified and worked with too; the nature of the risk will profoundly inform the response needed. Some situational risks, in virtue of working policy or legislation, will require action on behalf of the therapist. For example, child protection concerns might require a referral to social care agencies because of a child protection policy in place in the organisation, while concerns about the potential for a terrorist act will require a confidential referral to the police, in virtue of the legislative requirements in the UK: some risks demand certain actions.

However, other situational risks allow for a greater scope of response. Interventions should focus on the client's capacity and willingness to take responsibility for their own safety and wellbeing so that, between sessions, they can practise ways in which they can respond to distress differently and more proactively. Indications that a client is unable or unwilling to take such steps might point to a situation where additional or different interventions are required.

COLLABORATIVE POSITIVE RISK-TAKING

Unless a client is deemed temporarily not to have capacity to make informed decisions about their wellbeing, perhaps through high levels of distress or underlying or emerging mental health distress (e.g., psychosis), we need to work with the agency of the client to help safeguard their, and others', wellbeing. The reality is that for most clients with capacity, it will not be the therapist who keeps the client safe, or others safe, but the actions and willingness of the client to act to self-support when away from sessions.

I outline the value of crisis plans – or 'keep safe' plans – in Chapter 4.18 (this volume) in relation to working with suicide and self-harm/injury. These plans can be used in response to other risks too, including the risk of violence to others. The plan would be carefully negotiated and agreed in the session, with the aim being to help the client take responsibility for their emotional wellbeing and actions, initially between sessions (where the plan can then be reviewed), but also thereafter once the therapy has finished. It is important to keep several therapeutic considerations in mind when working with clients collaboratively around risk (Reeves, 2015: 145):

- The client has the capacity to understand the nature and extent of the risk as it presents.
- The client is willing and able to work collaboratively with the therapist around risk.
- The therapist understands the nature and extent of the risk as it presents.
- The therapist is willing and able to work collaboratively with the client around risk.
- Any actions and agreements are made within the context of any contract in place for therapy, or variations are clearly negotiated and agreed to beforehand and remain ethically informed.
- No expectations or agreements should disregard any existing policy or practice expectation around how to respond to risk situations.
- Any actions or agreements are regularly reviewed and fully explored in supervision and line management discussions, if appropriate.
- All actions and agreements are recorded, in writing or in a format accessible to the client, while respecting their confidentiality.

Such crisis plans relate to the wellbeing of the client, or to support them in managing potential violence to others. However, the wellbeing of others is also critical, and plans should not be used without careful consideration of the likely impact on other people. For example, therapists should not use plans as a means of managing child protection concerns or where violence is actual and ongoing. In such situations, therapists should act in accordance with their working policies and agreements made at the outset of therapy. In most circumstances, child protection concerns are likely to be raised with safeguarding leads (if working with children and young people) or social care departments. It is difficult to be too definitive with respect to actual or ongoing violence, as some settings will have a policy of breaking confidentiality to the police, whereas others will hold the client's confidentiality. It is important to be clear as to the organisation's expectations in such situations, or to have clearly thought about your own position if working independently.

If practitioners can support themselves – their anxieties and fears of 'getting it wrong' – in their work, they can also provide a safe and facilitative opportunity for clients not only to understand the nature of the risk they find themselves in more fully, but to use those opportunities to make important changes.

REFERENCES

Kottler, J. A. (2010). *On Being a Therapist* (4th ed.). San Francisco, CA: Jossey-Bass.

Leenaars, A. A. (2004). *Psychotherapy with Suicidal People: A Person-centred Approach*. Chichester: Wiley.

Office of the Public Guardian (2015). *Safeguarding Policy*. Birmingham: Office of the Public Guarding. Available at https://assets.publishing.service.gov.uk/government/uploads/system/uploads/attachment_data/file/934858/SD8-Office_of-the-Public-Guardian-safeguarding-policy.pdf

Oxford University Press (2021). *Oxford English Dictionary*. Oxford: Oxford University Press.

Panove, E. (1994). *Treating suicidal patients: What therapists feel when their patients make suicidal threats*. Unpublished thesis, University of Columbia.

Reeves, A. (2015). *Working with Risk in Counselling and Psychotherapy*. London: Sage.

Reeves, A. and Buxton, C. (2020). Crisis and trauma. In N. Moller, A. Vossler, D. W. Jones and D. Kaposi (Eds), *Understanding Mental Health and Counselling* (pp. 159–188). London: Sage.

Royal College of Psychiatrists (2020). *Self-Harm and Suicide in Adults: CR229*. London: Royal College of Psychiatrists. Available at www.rcpsych.ac.uk/docs/default-source/improving-care/better-mh-policy/college-reports/college-report-cr229-self-harm-and-suicide.pdf?sfvrsn=b6fdf395_10

Surgenor, P. W. G. (2015). Promoting recovery from suicidal ideation through the development of protective factors. *Counselling and Psychotherapy Research*, 15(3), 207–216.

RECOMMENDED READING

Reeves, A. (2015). *Working with Risk in Counselling and Psychotherapy*. London: Sage.

A text that considers a range of risks in therapy, including exploring the issue of positive risk-taking as well as using supervision to support practice.

Niolon, R. (2006). *Dangerous Clients: Assessment and Work Resources for Student and Professionals*. Available at www.psychpage.com/learning/library/counseling/danger.htm

A short, online summary of key factors to consider when assessing the risk of violence in clients.

Van Rijn, B. (2015). *Assessment and Case Formulation in Counselling and Psychotherapy*. London: Sage.

A helpful introductory text that discusses the key principles surrounding assessment and case formulation in practice.

3.5 FORMULATION

LUCY JOHNSTONE

OVERVIEW AND KEY POINTS

Formulation is a rapidly growing area of interest and practice within mental health, therapy and counselling. A formulation can be defined as an evidence-based summary, hypothesis or narrative that informs the intervention. Formulations can draw on a number of different therapeutic modalities, including integrative ones, and can be used in teams as well as in individual and family work. A number of best practice principles for formulation have been developed, and the relatively limited research to date suggests that it has many potential functions and benefits. The issue of how formulation relates to psychiatric diagnosis is a complex one. However, in the wake of controversy about diagnostic categories, we can expect formulation to play an increasingly central role in therapeutic activity across all settings.

- A formulation is a hypothesis about the reasons for a person's difficulties.
- Formulations can draw from a number of different therapeutic modalities.
- Team formulation is a popular and growing area of practice.
- Formulation is relevant to current debates about the validity of psychiatric diagnosis.

FORMULATION IN PRACTICE

Formulation is a core skill of the profession of clinical psychology, and also appears in the regulatory requirements for clinical, counselling, educational, health, forensic, occupational, sports and exercise psychologists (Health and Care Professions Council, 2009), as well as psychiatrists (Royal College of Psychiatrists, 2010) and mental health nurses (Nursing and Midwifery Council, 2010). The United Kingdom Council for Psychotherapy (UKCP) *Professional Occupational Standards* for cognitive, systemic and constructivist therapists also include formulation (UKCP, n.d.). It is also the subject of a growing number of books and articles (Corrie and Lane, 2010; Johnstone and Dallos, 2013; Ryan, 2020). The Division of Clinical Psychology (DCP) of the British Psychological Society (BPS) has issued *Good Practice Guidelines on the Use of Psychological Formulation* outlining criteria for best practice use with individuals, couples, families and teams across a range of settings and specialties (Division of Clinical Psychology, 2011).

The structure, content and emphasis of a formulation vary somewhat according to therapeutic modality (Johnstone and Dallos, 2013). Some traditions – for example, person-centred – do not use explicit formulations at all. This chapter will focus on the features that are common to formulations from all theoretical backgrounds. In this broad sense, a formulation can be defined as 'the tool used by clinicians to relate theory to practice' (Butler, 1998: 2); an evidence-based hypothesis or 'best guess' about the reasons for someone's difficulties that is used to inform the intervention and suggest ways forward. It provides a structure for developing a shared understanding or narrative which draws on two equally important kinds of evidence. The therapist or clinician brings knowledge derived from theory, research and clinical experience, while the client brings expertise about their own life and the meaning and impact of their relationships and circumstances. The core assumption underpinning the co-construction of a formulation is that '…at some level it all makes sense' (Butler, 1998: 2). This exploration of personal meaning within a trusting relationship is at the heart of formulation-based practice.

The term 'formulation' can be used in several senses. Formulation as an event, 'thing' or noun, in other words a specific summary, can be presented in a variety of different ways, from the 'reformulation' letters of Cognitive Analytic Therapy (CAT) to the diagrams favoured in Cognitive Behaviour Therapy (CBT). This is the form in which formulation is encountered by trainees and students. There are times and purposes for which a summary – a formulation as an event – may be useful, such as at the start and end of contact with counselling or mental health services. Appropriately adapted versions can be used for communication with other professionals, in letters to referrers, and so on. However, it is important to remember that any such summary arises out of formulation as a process; in other words, out of a conversation within a relationship. This is captured in the definition 'a process of ongoing collaborative sense-making' (Harper and Moss, 2003: 8). While it may be useful at some point, and for some purposes, to produce a written version, this is only a snapshot of an evolving story which is never complete and always open to revision.

In an even wider sense, formulation can be seen as an entire approach to mental health and therapeutic work. For most clinical psychologists, formulation is not just a specific activity or skill, but a whole way of thinking about people's distress and difficulties. All clinical and therapeutic encounters will be approached from the formulation-based assumption that even the most extreme expressions of confusion, despair and distress are, ultimately, meaningful communications about relationships and adversities.

A fictitious example of a formulation that might be developed in collaboration with a client over a period of weeks or months is offered below. The client, 'Matthew', aged 25, is experiencing feelings of low mood and desperation after the ending of a short-term relationship.

> You are currently feeling very low, stuck and hopeless because after a number of years of struggling against various difficulties, you seem to have reached a dead end in your life. When your girlfriend left, it seemed to confirm your deepest fear that no one would ever accept and love you, however hard you try.
>
> In our conversations, we have traced back the roots of your despair. Your early life was dominated by your father's violence and abuse towards your mother. This, along with his harsh parenting of you, meant that you were not able to develop a sense of security and self-worth. Although your parents eventually separated, and you are close to your mother, it is not surprising that you have been left with anxieties about relationships. You find it particularly difficult to deal with anger and conflict, because of your dread of turning out like your father.
>
> As a child, you were so pre-occupied with events at home that you found it hard to make friends, and some of your classmates took advantage of your lack of confidence by bullying you. Despite your academic ability, you hated school. You truanted and started using cannabis to cope with your fears and loneliness. This has left you unqualified for anything but low-paid jobs, which in turn leaves you short of money and lacking in purpose in your life. You feel excluded from society and conscious that you have not fulfilled your mother's hopes for you. In this context, you have come to see having a relationship as the only answer to your problems. When your last attempt did not work out, you were overwhelmed with self-blame and hopelessness. In constantly telling yourself that you are a useless failure, you seem to be re-playing your father's harsh criticisms, and being as hard on yourself as he was on you. Your childhood has left you with a deep need to be emotionally close to someone, and when this seems to be out of reach, you are once again overwhelmed by those earlier feelings of loneliness and hopelessness.
>
> Despite all this, you have many strengths. You are intelligent, and have a talent for music. You are sensitive and self-aware, with a good understanding of how you have come to be in this situation. You generally get on well with your mother, and you now have quite a few friends. You have shown great determination in surviving the challenges of your life, and you have already started to take steps towards overcoming your difficulties.

We can see that the formulation is personal to Matthew, while drawing on a body of evidence about the impact of bullying and witnessing domestic violence. The various factors are integrated into a coherent narrative through the central thread of their meaning to Matthew himself. The formulation suggests a personal pathway forward, which will include building on the trusting relationship with a therapist, understanding the impact of his particular life events, and processing the feelings from the past. We would hope that the formulation helps him to feel that his experiences are understandable, that he has many strengths and that, with support, he can eventually overcome his difficulties.

Formulation can have other uses and benefits, including: clarifying hypotheses and questions, providing an overall picture or map, noticing what is missing, prioritising issues and problems, selecting and planning interventions, minimising bias by making choices and decisions explicit, framing medical interventions, predicting responses to interventions, thinking about lack of progress, and ensuring that a cultural perspective is incorporated (Division of Clinical Psychology,

2011: 8). It can also be seen as an intervention in itself. Sensitively developed and shared, it can help the client to feel understood and contained, and strengthen the therapeutic alliance (Division of Clinical Psychology, 2011: 8). The meta-message of a formulation is: 'You are having an understandable response to an abnormal situation. Anyone else who had been through the same experiences might well have ended up feeling the same. You too can recover.'

BEST PRACTICE FORMULATION

As well as having potential uses and benefits, formulation can, like any other clinical activity, be carried out badly or unhelpfully. The *Guidelines* (Division of Clinical Psychology, 2011) list a number of criteria which are designed to reduce this risk. In keeping with the distinction between formulation as an event and formulation as a process, the criteria relate to content (e.g., the formulation should be expressed in accessible language, culturally aware, non-blaming, and inclusive of strengths and achievements) and also to process (e.g., formulating should be collaborative and respectful of the client's views about accuracy and helpfulness) (Division of Clinical Psychology, 2011: 29–30). Therapists are expected to take a reflective stance which helps to avoid formulating in insensitive, non-consenting or disempowering ways (Division of Clinical Psychology, 2011: 21).

Three additional best practice criteria deserve consideration. The first is that formulation should consider 'the possible role of trauma and abuse' (Division of Clinical Psychology, 2011: 29). 'Trauma' here is defined, in keeping with the literature on trauma-informed practice, as including a wide range of adversities, such as sexual, physical and emotional abuse, neglect, bullying, witnessing or being a victim of domestic violence, and so on. A large and growing body of research confirms that a range of traumas and adversities play a causal role across all mental health presentations, including anxiety, low mood, eating distress, mood swings and 'psychosis' (www.acestoohigh.com). Trauma-informed formulations help to ensure that this knowledge is integrated into interventions.

A trauma-informed approach recognises that services may be not only unhelpful but retraumatising through disempowering and coercive practices (Fallot and Harris, 2009). This leads to the principle that formulations developed within service settings should consider the 'possible role of services in compounding the difficulties' (Division of Clinical Psychology, 2011: 29).

A third principle is the requirement to include 'a critical awareness of the wider societal context within which formulation takes place' (Division of Clinical Psychology, 2011: 20). The intention is to minimise the individualising tendency of medical and (some) psychotherapeutic models, which, by locating the difficulties primarily within the person, implicitly convey a message of blame and deficit (Johnstone, 2014).

FORMULATION AND DIAGNOSIS

Formulation is used in many health settings to place diagnoses of cancer, learning disability, stroke, dementia, and so on within a holistic context. The use of diagnosis raises different issues in psychiatry, where the debate about the validity of categories such as 'schizophrenia', 'personality disorder' and 'bipolar disorder' is heated and ongoing. This raises the question of whether, in mental health work, formulation should be used as an addition to, or an alternative to, psychiatric diagnosis. The Division of Clinical Psychology (DCP) *Guidelines* (2011: 17) state that 'best practice formulations … are not premised on psychiatric diagnosis. Rather, the experiences that may have led to a psychiatric diagnosis (low mood, unusual beliefs, etc.) are themselves formulated'. The argument is that if a psychosocial formulation can provide a reasonably complete explanation for the experiences that have led to a psychiatric diagnosis, then there is no place or need for a competing hypothesis that says 'and by the way, it is also because she has schizophrenia'. A comprehensive, evidence-based formulation makes the diagnosis redundant. This contrasts with the training curriculum for psychiatrists, who are required to 'demonstrate the ability to construct formulations of patients' problems that include appropriate differential diagnoses' (Royal College of Psychiatrists, 2010: 25).

It is important to distinguish between psychiatric formulation – an addition to diagnosis – from psychological formulation – an alternative to diagnosis. They look different and have different implications in practice. In the case of Matthew, the contrast is between something like 'Clinical depression triggered by the breakup of a relationship' as opposed to 'Experiencing a loss which has brought earlier unresolved hurts and rejections to the surface'. While both versions can be seen as a welcome widening of the gaze of the biomedical model of distress, the first may simply facilitate a main focus on the 'illness' that the life events have apparently 'triggered', along with medication as the main or only intervention. Only the second fully conveys the message that: 'Your problems are a meaningful and understandable emotional response to your life circumstances.'

FORMULATION IN TEAMS

Team formulation is the process of facilitating a group or team of staff to develop a shared formulation about a service user (Johnstone, 2013). This is now common practice in mental health services and also in many older adult (Dexter-Smith, 2015), learning difficulty (Ingham, 2015), child and adolescent (Milson and Phillips, 2015), forensic (Lewis-Morton et al., 2015) and health (Cole, 2013) settings. Ideally, these meetings are a standard feature in the weekly timetable across all parts of the service. The facilitator's role is to reflect, summarise, clarify and encourage creativity and free-thinking about the service user under discussion, not to provide solutions. In this way, the team can develop a shared formulation about the service user's difficulties and any 'stuck points' in their work with them.

Clinicians have reported a number of benefits from the practice of team formulation, including, over time, promoting culture change towards more psychosocial perspectives (British Psychological Society, 2007; Kennedy et al., 2003).

FORMULATION AND RESEARCH

At present, practice has outstripped research. The evidence for formulation as a specific intervention is limited (Cole, Wood and Spendelow, 2015), although there is extensive research into the theoretical content and psychological principles on which it is typically based (e.g., attachment theory, developmental psychology, CBT, and so on). The questions of whether or not formulation, either in its individual or its team versions, promotes recovery, improves outcomes, reduces the need for medication and admissions, and so on, remain open. Other things being equal, we can assume that clinical practice based on an explicit, shared and agreed hypothesis is likely to be more effective than the alternative. However, more investigation is needed to establish the most effective ways of developing, using and sharing these co-constructed 'best guesses'.

Client reports about individual formulation are mixed. Some describe it as increasing understanding and trust, as empowering, as a relief, and as enabling them to move forward ('It just all made sense. I got it because … it was true'; 'It was bang on, so I trusted that she understood'; 'I think if you know the reason something's happening it automatically becomes more controllable') (Redhead, Johnstone and Nightingale, 2015: 7, 10). Formulation has been found to enable people to recognise the ways they are inadvertently maintaining their problems, and to choose more helpful ways of reacting (Tyrer and Masterton, 2019). Others have reported experiencing it as saddening, frightening or overwhelming (Morberg Pain, Chadwick and Abba, 2008).

Clearly, sharing a formulation is a potentially powerful experience that should be carried out thoughtfully and sensitively, so that the emotional impact is experienced as, overall, helpful, even if there is a degree of distress at reaching core insights. Studies into staff perceptions of team formulation suggest that it is highly valued by multidisciplinary teams (Cole et al., 2015; Hollingworth and Johnstone, 2014). A recent trial into rehabilitation wards using team formulation resulted in patients feeling less criticised by staff and reporting improvements in ward atmosphere (Berry et al., 2015). An overview of the small number of existing studies into team formulation identified staff themes of improving staff communication, collaboration and functioning; changing and challenging ways of thinking, including the medical model; and increasing psychological awareness and focusing on the service user's needs (Bealey, Bowden and Fisher, 2021).

FUTURE DIRECTIONS IN FORMULATION

In the last few years, formulation has grown from a relatively specialised professional term to become common currency within statutory services and therapeutic training and practice. It is no coincidence that this is happening in the wider context of the controversy about psychiatric diagnosis, which is the foundation of mental health theory and practice. In the face of this potential threat, formulation, in its psychiatric version, is increasingly being promoted as an answer to the shortcomings of diagnosis. If diagnosis is 'insufficient in conceptualising psychopathology in any individual patient', formulation can be co-opted to fill the gaps (Craddock and Mynors-Wallis, 2014). It should be noted that views about diagnosis in relation to formulation do not align in any simple way with professional background or discipline, and psychiatrist members of the Critical Psychiatry Network have joined with clinical psychologists to urge us to 'Drop the language of disorder' in favour of a narrative or formulation-based approach (e.g., Kinderman et al., 2013).

Psychological formulation is, essentially, about listening to someone's story. As such, every counsellor or therapist will already be 'formulating', or co-constructing meanings, since this is the heart of all good practice. However, reflecting on this evolving story in an explicit shared form can be a powerfully validating and transformative experience for client and therapist, as well as for teams. Only time will tell whether formulation practice will also bring about a much-needed shift away from primarily biomedical to psychosocial models in mental health services as a whole.

REFERENCES

Bealey, Bowden, G. and Fisher, P. (2021). A systematic review of team formulations in multidisciplinary teams: Staff views and opinions. *Journal of Humanistic Psychology*, Online first, 7 September, 1–28. doi: 10.1177/00221678211043002

Berry, K., Haddock, G., Kellett, S., Roberts, C., Drake, R. and Barrowclough, C. (2015). Feasibility of a ward-based psychological intervention to improve staff and patient relationships in psychiatric rehabilitation settings. *British Journal of Clinical Psychology*, 55(3), 236–252. doi: 10.1111/bjc.12082.

British Psychological Society (2007). *New ways of working for applied psychologists in health and social care: Working psychologically in teams*. Leicester: British Psychological Society.

Butler, G. (1998). Clinical formulation. In A. S. Bellack and M. Hersen (Eds), *Comprehensive clinical psychology* (pp. 1–23). Oxford: Pergamon.

Cole, S. (2013). Using integrative formulation in health settings. In L. Johnstone and R. Dallos (Eds), *Formulation in psychology and psychotherapy: Making sense of people's problems* (2nd ed., pp. 243–259). London: Routledge.

Cole, S., Wood, K. and Spendelow, J. (2015). Team formulation: A critical evaluation of current literature and future research directions. *Clinical Psychology Forum*, 275, 13–19.

Corrie, S. and Lane, D.A. (2010). *Constructing stories, telling tales: A guide to formulation in applied psychology*. London: Karnac.

Craddock, N. and Mynors-Wallis, L. (2014). Psychiatric diagnosis: Impersonal, imperfect and important. *British Journal of Psychiatry*, 204, 93–95.

Dexter-Smith, S. (2015). Implementing psychological formulations service-wide. *Clinical Psychology Forum*, 275, 43–47.

Division of Clinical Psychology (2011). *Good practice guidelines on the use of psychological formulation*. Leicester: British Psychological Society. Available at www.bpsshop.org.uk/Good-Practice-Guidelines-on-the-use-of-psychological-formulation-P1653.aspx

Fallot, R.D. and Harris, M. (2009). *Creating cultures of trauma-informed care*. Washington, DC: Community Connections.

Harper, D. and Moss, D. (2003). A different chemistry? Re-formulating formulation. *Clinical Psychology*, 25, 6–10.

Health and Care Professions Council (2009). *Standards of proficiency: Practitioner psychologists*. London: HCPC.

Hollingworth, P. and Johnstone, L. (2014). Team formulation: What are the staff views? *Clinical Psychology Forum*, 257, 28–34.

Ingham, B. (2015). Team formulation within a learning disabilities setting. *Clinical Psychology Forum*, 275, 33–37.

Johnstone, L. (2013). Using formulation in teams. In L. Johnstone and R. Dallos (Eds), *Formulation in psychology and psychotherapy: Making sense of people's problems* (2nd ed., pp. 216–242). London: Routledge.

Johnstone, L. (2014). *A straight-talking introduction to psychiatric diagnosis*. Ross-on-Wye: PCCS Books.

Johnstone, L. and Dallos, R. (Eds) (2013). *Formulation in psychology and psychotherapy: Making sense of people's problems* (2nd ed.). London: Routledge.

Kennedy, F., Smalley, M., and Harris, T. (2003). Clinical psychology for in patient settings: principles for development and practice. *Clinical Psychology Forum*, 30, 21–24.

Kinderman, P., Read, J., Moncrieff, J. and Bentall, R.P. (2013). Drop the language of disorder. *Evidence-based Mental Health*, 16(1), 2–3.

Lewis-Morton, R., James, L., Brown, K. and Hider, A. (2015). Team formulation in a secure setting: Challenges, rewards and service-user involvement. *Clinical Psychology Forum*, 275.

Milson, G. and Phillips, K. (2015). Formulation meetings in a Tier 4 CAMHS inpatient unit. *Clinical Psychology Forum*, 275.

Morberg Pain, C., Chadwick, P. and Abba, N. (2008). Clients' experience of case formulation in CBT for psychosis. *British Journal of Clinical Psychology*, 47(2), 127–138.

Nursing and Midwifery Council (2010). *Standards for competence for Registered Nurses*. London: NMC.

Redhead, S., Johnstone, L. and Nightingale, J. (2015). Clients' experiences of formulation. *Psychology and Psychotherapy: Theory, Research and Practice*, 88(4), 453–467.

Royal College of Psychiatrists (2010). *A competency-based curriculum for specialist core training*. London: RCP. Available at www.rcpsych.ac.uk/docs/default-source/training/curricula-and-guidance/general_psychiatry_curriculum_march_2019.pdf?sfvrsn=9e53c99a_6

Ryan, P. (2020). *Enhancing clinical case formulation: Theoretical and practical approaches for mental health practitioners*. Abingdon, UK: Routledge.

Tyrer, R. and Masterson, C. (2019). Clients' experience of change: An exploration of the influence of reformulation tools in Cognitive Analytic Therapy. *Clinical Psychology and Psychotherapy*, 26(2), 167–174. https://doi.org/10.1002/cpp.2339

United Kingdom Council for Psychotherapy (n.d.). *Professional occupational standards: For the information of commissioners, trainers and practitioners*. London: UKCP.

RECOMMENDED READING

Corrie, S. and Lane, D.A. (2010). *Constructing stories, telling tales: A guide to formulation in applied psychology*. London: Karnac.

The authors discuss formulation and its relationship to narrative and story-telling, both within and beyond therapeutic settings.

Johnstone, L. and Dallos, R. (Eds) (2013). *Formulation in psychology and psychotherapy: Making sense of people's problems* (2nd ed.). London: Routledge.

The editors give a comprehensive overview of definitions, principles, practice and debates, illustrated by formulating two case histories from a range of therapeutic perspectives.

Division of Clinical Psychology (2011). *Good practice guidelines on the use of psychological formulation*. Leicester: British Psychological Society.

These are useful guidelines for formulation produced by the British Psychological Society and are freely available online.

3.6 USING OUTCOME AND PROCESS MEASURES

JULIA LYONS

OVERVIEW AND KEY POINTS

Outcome and process measures are increasingly becoming a routine part of counselling and psychotherapy services. This chapter provides an overview of this topic by answering the following questions: What are outcome and process measures? Who might want to use them? When can we use them? And how can we implement them into practice?

- Outcome and process measures can be useful for practitioners, services and research.
- Consideration of which measures to use and how they can be implemented may enhance the usefulness of the information gathered.
- Brief measures may be one way of making measures a routine part of practice.
- Guidance documents are available to practitioners wishing to use these approaches in their work.

WHAT ARE OUTCOME AND PROCESS MEASURES?

OUTCOME MEASURES

Outcome measures in counselling and psychotherapy aim to systematically assess one or more aspects of client functioning. There are different types of outcome measure, such as global outcome measures, symptom checklists, and diagnostic and screening instruments. Global outcome measures measure general wellbeing and are applicable to all clients regardless of clinical setting, mode of therapy or specific problems. Symptom checklists, diagnostic and screening instruments look for the presence of particular symptoms or conditions.

PROCESS MEASURES

Process measures are a way of monitoring how a client experiences therapy. There is substantial evidence that the relationship between practitioner and client contributes significantly to outcome, regardless of the model of therapy (Lambert, 2007). These measures aim to frequently track the therapeutic alliance as therapy progresses. This information can then be used to inform practice through methods such as feedback, supervision and deliberate practice (Prescott, Maeschalck and Miller, 2017).

GOAL-BASED OUTCOME MEASURES

Goal-based outcome measures are a way of recording at the beginning of therapy what the client and practitioner want to achieve from therapy and thereafter tracking progress towards these goals (Law, 2013). One of the key advantages of goal-based outcome measures is their focus on what the client views as important rather than more traditional outcome measures which adopt an external viewpoint to consider distress (Hanley, Sefi and Ersahin, 2016).

WHO MIGHT BE INTERESTED IN PROCESS AND OUTCOME MEASURES?

COUNSELLORS AND PSYCHOTHERAPISTS

During routine clinical practice therapists continually assess the progress of their clients. For the most part, therapists assess outcomes in an informal manner based on client reports and clinical judgement (Hatfield and Ogles, 2004). However, it is increasingly recognised that the use of formal assessment can provide additional validation for clinical judgement (Prescott et al., 2017). Research has shown process and outcome measures can actually improve outcomes in therapy, and monitoring client-based outcomes in combination with systematic feedback and deliberate practice has been observed to increase the effectiveness of therapists (Goldberg et al., 2016).

Organisations representing counselling and psychotherapists advocate the use of these measures, with the British Association for Counselling and Psychotherapy

(BACP) dedicating resources to choosing and using routine outcome measures in practice (BACP, 2021). Research has shown that some of the benefits of such an approach for clinicians include: facilitating a dialogue with clients; reducing the likelihood of dropout; improving the speed with which good outcomes are achieved; improving the quality of information gained by covering potential gaps in assessment and/or review; and improving identification of worsening symptoms (Bickman et al., 2011; Ekqvist and Kuusisto, 2020; Lambert and Shimokawa, 2011; Lambert et al., 2003; Noble, 2016).

COMMISSIONING SERVICES

Other stakeholders with an interest in the results from process and outcome measures are those in charge of commissioning services. The nature of therapy is that it takes place behind closed doors and this can mean it is difficult for organisations to assess its impact. In the current climate, where there is limited funding available for counselling and mental health resources, services have to find ways of justifying their worth to continue their existence or face severe budget restrictions. Using measures is one of many ways to assess service quality. Naturally, this could make some practitioners a little nervous, feeling their practice might be scrutinised, or that the application of measures is reductionist and thus opposed to the philosophy of more humanistically oriented therapies. These are valid concerns. However, there are benefits of pooling data. For example, the UK's National Health Service (NHS) Improving Access to Psychological Therapies (IAPT) service uses routine outcome data to secure funding and improve services (NHS Digital, 2021).

EVIDENCE-BASED PRACTICE AND RESEARCH

Measures are also valuable to inform research and create an evidence base for our work. Both outcome and process measures can be used to help answer the question 'what works for whom?' They can objectively assess the client's progress by collecting data systematically throughout the client's duration in therapy. If these data are collected for a large number of clients, then researchers can apply statistical tests to analyse the data and look to see if there are general patterns which may inform practice, for example, whether particular modalities (humanistic, psychodynamic, cognitive behavioural therapy) are more effective with certain client groups, whether clients continue to improve after therapy has finished, or identify effective therapy components across modalities. Initiatives such as the BACP Student Counselling Outcomes, Research and Evaluation (SCORE) project have been commissioned to develop a shared UK national database of outcome measure data (Broglia et al., 2021).

WHEN DO WE USE OUTCOME AND PROCESS MEASURES?

One valid question is, having decided to use measures, what considerations might need to be made before implementing them with clients? Key concepts in this domain include the importance of obtaining *informed consent* from clients and looking at the *validity* and *reliability* of the tool you are intending to use before implementing the measure with clients. An explanation of these concepts is given below.

INFORMED CONSENT

Informed consent is a concept most practitioners will be familiar with due to its application to therapy more generally, but it also applies to using measures specifically. The BACP *Ethical Framework* states that data gathering and measuring must be conducted in the full knowledge of the client (BACP, 2019). This includes explaining how long the data will be kept and its purpose, and who has access to the data. If clients refuse, then it should be made clear that this will not affect their therapy. It is considered best practice to obtain written consent.

VALIDITY AND RELIABILITY

When selecting an outcome measure it is important that it has been validated for its intended purpose, as a poor measure can provide inaccurate information about symptom severity and client progress. Bantjes et al. (2018) highlight some of the difficulties of using routine outcome measures with a patient population with different cultural demographics from the population that was used to develop and test the measure. Furthermore, the concept of reliability is important. Some measures are intended for one-off use only, whereas others are designed for repeated application. Practitioners can check the reliability and validity of a measure by obtaining the reference journal paper (often widely available by searching online). These papers outline the research on which the measure was based and include information about the population it was designed for and its conditions of use.

AT WHAT POINTS DURING THERAPY DO WE USE MEASURES?

To answer this question, Law (2014) recommends reflecting on what useful information might be gained from measures from the perspective of both the practitioner and the client. In general, assessment measures may be used to gain a better understanding of the presenting problem, and the goals or aims of therapy. During therapy, measures can be used to gain more information on the client's level of engagement, the therapeutic alliance, and track symptoms and goals. At the end of therapy, measures can help to assess whether further support is needed, evaluate the overall experience and benchmark client's progress over time. The application of a chosen measure should correspond to generating the information you are interested in finding out.

HOW OFTEN SHOULD WE USE MEASURES?

The balance between getting enough useful information through the measure process and not drowning a client in paperwork needs to be carefully considered. Gelkopf, Mazor and Roe (2021) found that clients do not complete all therapy measures in real-world settings. This can pose a challenge to understanding the effectiveness of an intervention, as typically those clients who complete measures have better attendance and are more motivated in therapy, which can bias its reported effectiveness. Therefore, to get the clearest picture possible, Miller, Hubble and Chow (2020) recommend completing measures that are brief and quick to administer and score at every session. By this approach, in the event of an unplanned ending there are pre- and post-measures for comparison.

HOW CAN OUTCOME AND PROCESS MEASURES BE IMPLEMENTED INTO PRACTICE?

See case example below for a template for how measures can be introduced into practice. Once established, Law and Wolpert (2014) provide guidelines when using measures routinely (Figure 3.6.1).

Do	Make sure you have the measures you need ready before the session.
Do	Always explain why you are asking anyone to fill out a measure.
Do	Look at the answers.
Do	Discuss the answers with clients.
Do	Share the information in supervision.
Do	Always use information from the measures in conjunction with other clinical information.
Don't	Give out a measure if you think the person doesn't understand why they are being asked to complete it.
Don't	Use any measure if you don't understand why you are using it.
Don't	Insist on someone filling out measures if they are too distressed.
Don't	See the numbers generated from measures as an absolute fact.
Don't	See your clinical judgement as an absolute fact.

Figure 3.6.1 Some suggested dos and don'ts of using measures

Adapted from Duncan Law and Miranda Wolpert, *Guide to Using Outcomes and Feedback Tools with Children, Young People and Families* (2014), used with permission

CASE STUDY

Harris University Counselling Service (HUCS) are keen to use measures for the benefit of their students, practitioners and the service. HUCS use a project team consisting of practitioners to evaluate widely used measures and decide which measures the service will adopt. The service decides to use CORE-OM, ORS and SRS at every session (see recommended measures at the end of this chapter). These measures are explained to students at assessment and informed consent is gained. During the course of therapy, practitioners share interpretation of the measures with their clients to inform progress of therapy and use the measures as part of their clinical information in supervision. The service routinely evaluates their outcome measures in context and shares the data at monthly team meetings, which generates wider discussion. The service contributes their data to the BACP SCORE project to build evidence for the sector.

WHAT OUTCOME OR PROCESS MEASURES SHOULD I USE?

There is no universally accepted measure of outcome, and there is a vast array of outcome measures – at one count, 1,430 were identified (Froyd, Lambert and Froyd, 1996). It is generally accepted that it is helpful if there is some consistency across measures in order to enable meaningful interpretation across individuals and services. As a result, numerous organisations, including the BACP, the IAPT initiative based throughout the United Kingdom, and the Child Outcomes Research Consortium (CORC+), offer guidance on recommended measures to use in practice (see Figure 3.6.2 and recommended reading at the end of the chapter).

In recent years, ultra-brief measures have been developed after research suggesting that the majority of clinicians do not consider any measure taking longer than five minutes to complete, score and interpret to be practical (Brown, Dreis and Nace, 1999). Short measures can be used to provide real-time feedback and are therefore available for immediate treatment modification to prevent clients dropping out of therapy or suffering a negative outcome (Prescott et al., 2017). By using ultra-brief methods, measure evaluation can become a routine part of therapy.

CONCLUSION

The direction of travel indicates outcome and process measures are fast becoming a requirement at counselling and psychotherapy services. However, researchers have highlighted the dangers of measures being implemented without acknowledging clinical judgement (Gelkopf et al., 2021). When measures are perceived or experienced as part of top-down or tick-box culture, they may undermine or even harm the therapeutic alliance (Greenhalgh, 2009). However, when implemented with due consideration, these measures can be used in ways to improve the therapeutic alliance and learn more about our clients. Law and Wolpert (2014) recommend that these measures are implemented with an ethos of discovering more about the therapeutic process and the client, without neglecting the surrounding context, and that the results of the measures are used collaboratively to enhance shared decision making. Strengths and limitations of measures should be acknowledged as part of this process, and full discussion of these outcomes should take place before any interpretation. The development of brief measures and initiatives by organisations aiming to facilitate consistency in measures and collate large amounts of data could herald exciting new discoveries for the profession and opportunities for improvement in practice.

REFERENCES

Bantjes, J., Hunt, X., Tomlinson, M. & Smit, A. (2018). A case study of lessons learnt from implementing a routine outcome monitoring system for psychotherapy in a South African community clinic. *South African Journal of Psychology, 48*(2), 193–205.

Barkham, M., Bewick, B., Mullin, T., Gilbody, S., Connell, J., Cahill, J., Mellor-Clark, J., Richards, D., Unsworth, G. & Evans, C. (2013). The CORE-10: a short measure of psychological distress for routine use in the psychological therapies. *Counselling and Psychotherapy Research, 13*(1), 3–13.

Bickman, L., Kelley, S. D., Breda, C., de Andrade, A. R. & Riemer, M. (2011). Effects of routine feedback to clinicians on mental health outcomes of youths: results of a randomized trial. *Psychiatric Services, 62*, 1423–1429.

British Association for Counselling and Psychotherapy (2019). *Ethical guidelines for research in the counselling professions.* Lutterworth: BACP. Available at www.bacp.co.uk/media/3908/bacp-ethical-guidelines-for-research-in-counselling-professions-feb19.pdf

British Association for Counselling and Psychotherapy (2021). *Good research practice.* Lutterworth: BACP. Available at www.bacp.co.uk/events-and-resources/research/good-research-practice/

Broglia, E., Ryan, G., Williams, C., Fudge, M., Knowles, L., Turner, A., Dufour, G., Percy, A., Barkham, M. & SCORE Consortium (2021). Profiling student mental health and counselling effectiveness: lessons from four UK services using complete data and different outcome measures. *British Journal of Guidance & Counselling, 49*, 1–19.

Brown, J., Dreis, S. & Nace, D. K. (1999). What really makes a difference in psychotherapy outcome? Why does managed care want to know? In M. A. Hubble, B. L. Duncan & S. D. Miller (Eds), *The heart and soul of change: What works in therapy* (pp. 389–406). Washington, DC: American Psychological Association.

Duncan, B. L., Miller, S., Sparks, J. A., Claud, D. A., Reynolds, L. R., Brown, J. & Johnson, L. D. (2003). The Session Rating Scale: preliminary psychometric properties of a 'working' alliance measure. *Journal of Brief Therapy, 3*(1), 3–12.

Duncan, B. L., Sparks, J., Miller, S. D., Bohanske, R. & Claud, D. (2006). Giving youth a voice: a preliminary study of the reliability and validity of a brief outcome measure for children, adolescents, and caretakers. *Journal of Brief Therapy, 5*, 66–82.

Ekqvist, E. & Kuusisto, K. (2020). Changes in clients' well-being (ORS) and state hope (SHS) during inpatient substance abuse treatment. *Nordic Studies on Alcohol and Drugs, 37*(4), 384–399.

Froyd, M. J., Lambert, M. J. & Froyd, J. E. (1996). A review of practices of psychotherapy outcome measurement. *Journal of Mental Health, 5*(1), 11–16.

Gelkopf, M., Mazor, Y. & Roe, D. (2021). A systematic review of patient-reported outcome measurement (PROM) and provider assessment in mental health: goals, implementation, setting, measurement characteristics and barriers. *International Journal for Quality in Health Care, 33*(1), pmzz133.

Goldberg, S. B., Babins-Wagner, R., Rousmaniere, T., Berzins, S., Hoyt, W. T., Whipple, J. L., Miller, S. D. & Wampold, B. E. (2016). Creating a climate for therapist improvement: a case study of an agency focused on outcomes and deliberate practice. *Psychotherapy, 53*(3), 367–375.

Greenhalgh, J. (2009). The applications of PROs in clinical practice: what are they, do they work, and why? *Quality of Life Research, 18*(1), 115–123.

Hanley, T., Sefi, A. & Ersahin, Z. (2016). From goals to tasks to methods. In M. Cooper & W. Dryden (Eds), *The handbook of pluralistic counselling and psychotherapy.* London: Sage.

Hatfield, D. R. & Ogles, B. M. (2004). The use of outcome measures by psychologists in clinical practice. *Professional Psychology: Research and Practice, 35*(5), 485.

Kroenke, K., Spitzer, R. K. & Williams, J. B. (2001). PHQ-9: validity of a brief depression severity measure. *Journal of General Internal Medicine, 16*, 606–613.

Lambert, M. (2007). Presidential address: what we have learned from a decade of research aimed at improving psychotherapy outcome in routine care. *Psychotherapy Research, 17*(1), 1–14.

Lambert, M. J. & Shimokawa, K. (2011). Collecting client feedback. *Psychotherapy, 48*(1), 72.

Lambert, M. J., Whipple, J. L., Hawkins, E. J., Vermeersch, D. A., Nielsen, S. L. & Smart, D. W. (2003). Is it time for clinicians to routinely track patient outcome? A meta-analysis. *Clinical Psychology: Science and Practice*, *10*(3), 288–301.

Law, D. (2013). *Goals and goal-based outcomes (GBOs): Some useful information*. London: CAMHS Press.

Law, D. (2014). General guidance on using forms in therapy. In D. Law & M. Wolpert (Eds), *Guide to using outcomes and feedback tools with children, young people and families* (pp. 45–52). London: CORC.

Law, D. & Wolpert, M. (2014). *Guide to using outcomes and feedback tools with children, young people and families*. London: CORC. Available at www.corc.uk.net/media/1950/201404guide_to_using_outcomes_measures_and_feedback_tools-updated.pdf

Miller, S. D. & Duncan, B. L. (2004). *The Outcome and Session Rating Scales: Administration and scoring manuals.* Chicago, IL: Author.

Miller, S. D., Duncan, B., Brown, J., Sparks, J. & Claud, D. (2003). The Outcome Rating Scale: a preliminary study of the reliability, validity, and feasibility of a brief visual analog measure. *Journal of Brief Therapy*, *2*(2), 91–100.

Miller, S. D., Hubble, M. A. & Chow, D. (2020). *Better results: Using deliberate practice to improve therapeutic effectiveness*. Washington, DC: American Psychological Association.

NHS Digital. (2021). *Psychological therapies: Reports on the use of IAPT services.* London: NHS Digital. Available at https://digital.nhs.uk/data-and-information/publications/statistical/psychological-therapies-report-on-the-use-of-iapt-services/june-2021-final-including-reports-on-the-iapt-pilots-and-quarter-1-data-2021-22/outcomes

Noble, J. N. (2016). Evaluating one's own practice while training: a systematic case study design in a further education setting. *Counselling and Psychotherapy*, *16*(4), 235–243.

Prescott, D. S., Maeschalck, C. L. & Miller, S. D. (2017). *Feedback-informed treatment in clinical practice: Reaching for excellence*. American Psychological Association.

Spitzer, R. L., Kroenke, K., Williams, J. B. & Löwe, B. (2006). A brief measure for assessing generalized anxiety disorder: the GAD-7. *Archives of Internal Medicine*, *166*, 1092–1097.

RECOMMENDED READING

MindEd – the MindEd website project (www.minded.org.uk).

Specific resources to support counsellors and psychotherapists to facilitate the integration of process and outcome measures into their practice.

Law, D. & Wolpert, M. (2014). *Guide to using outcomes and feedback tools with children, young people and families*. London: CORC. Available at www.corc.uk.net/media/1950/201404guide_to_using_outcomes_measures_and_feedback_tools-updated.pdf

A practical and accessible guide to using outcome and process measures to inform clinical practice with children and young people, but principles are applicable to general practice.

Prescott, D. S., Maeschalck, C. L. & Miller, S. D. (2017). *Feedback-informed treatment in clinical practice: Reaching for excellence*. American Psychological Association.

An in-depth approach to selection, application and implementation of outcome and process measures, including discussion of future directions for the field.

Below are some of the recommended measures (in alphabetical order) by BACP, IAPT and CORC+ which also fulfil criteria of being brief and simple to administer. For more information on measure recommendations check out the organisations' websites.

Outcome measures

Clinical Outcomes in Routine Evaluation (CORE-10) (Barkham et al., 2013).

CORE-10 is designed as a short screening measure of psychological distress where session-by-session change monitoring is required. The 10-item questionnaire includes items covering depression, anxiety, trauma, physical problems and risk. It also assesses general functioning, social functioning, close relationships and the self.

Generalised Anxiety Disorder (GAD-7) (Spitzer et al., 2006).

The GAD-7 was designed as a seven-item screening tool for generalised anxiety disorder, although it also monitors symptoms of panic disorder, social anxiety and post-traumatic stress disorder.

Outcome Rating Scale (Miller et al., 2003) and Child Outcome Rating Scale (Duncan et al., 2006).

The ORS for ages 13 years and over and the CORS for children under 13 years provide a brief measure of global distress suitable for assessing treatment outcome. These very brief four-item measures take only a few minutes to complete and score.

Patient Health Questionnaire (PHQ-9) (Kroenke et al., 2001).

This measure contains nine items and is designed to measure symptoms of depression in primary care. It can be used to monitor changes in symptoms over time and indicates depression severity.

Process measures

Session Rating Scale (SRS) (Duncan et al., 2003) and Child Session Rating Scale (CSRS) (Miller & Duncan, 2004).

The SRS for ages 13 years and over and the CSRS for children aged under 13 years are brief four-item measures. They were developed as a self-report working therapeutic alliance measure designed specifically for every session clinical use.

Figure 3.6.2 Common measures

3.7 CONFIDENTIALITY, RECORDKEEPING, AND NOTETAKING

GABRIEL WYNN

OVERVIEW AND KEY POINTS

Counsellors and psychotherapists must collect, use, store, dispose of, and sometimes share confidential information about service users. In management roles we are likely to also handle confidential data about staff and organisational functions. Careful recordkeeping forms part of the overall integrity of services we offer our clients, colleagues, and the public.

This chapter provides an overview of our responsibilities in handling people's personal data legally and ethically. The chapter is organised over three key areas:

- **Confidentiality, data protection and information sharing** focuses on our legal obligations under the United Kingdom General Data Protection Regulation (UK-GDPR) and national safeguarding legislation.
- **Recordkeeping** focuses on management of personal data at regional, organisational and practitioner levels.
- **Notetaking** focuses on good practice in style and content of clinical documentation.

CONFIDENTIALITY, DATA PROTECTION AND INFORMATION SHARING

CONFIDENTIALITY AND THE LAW

Assurance of confidentiality is fundamental to forming and maintaining trusting relationships and is therefore a cornerstone of ethical practice for counsellors and psychotherapists. Under UK common law (which means, law established by prescient rather than Act of Parliament), information shared with counselling professionals in confidence should not be disclosed without consent, good justification or legal authority (UK Caldicott Guardian Council 2021). On the other hand, practitioners should not give assurance of total confidentiality to people they work with, but instead explain the limits of confidentiality verbally and in written agreement documents. Examples of required disclosures include order by a court, Child and Family Court Advisory Service (CAFCASS) or other legal authority. Other examples include emergency and life-threatening situations, drug trafficking and money laundering, serious crimes, female genital mutilation (FGM), and other child and adult protection and safeguarding concerns.

MAKING REQUIRED AND VOLUNTARY DISCLOSURES

Some counselling agencies will have a relevant policy that details the steps that must be taken when a staff member either becomes privy to information they are required to disclose or receives a mandatory request for service user information. The policy ought to be followed alongside line management advice. Short of having an established procedure to follow, therapists ought to seek the advice of their Data Protection lead or supervisor. A record of the request and information supplied should be kept in the service user record. Response deadlines should be heeded. It is good practice, where possible, to inform the person that specific information must be disclosed when it is unlikely to cause undue distress or other detriment to them or others if they know this. It is also good practice to request that recipients of confidential information also treat it as confidential (British Association for Counselling and Psychotherapy (BACP), 2018).

In situations where voluntary disclosure of confidential information is requested (e.g., by police, lawyers, housing associations, education providers, occupational health, benefits administrators, and so on), service user consent is always required even if they finished therapy some time ago. The service user is likely to know about or even to have initiated the information request. It can be significantly helpful to service users when we comply with such requests following a conversation with them about their disclosure wishes.

We will now review our responsibilities under UK-GDPR, then move on to look at sharing information under statutory safeguarding duties.

THE INFORMATION COMMISSIONER'S OFFICE

Following UK's withdrawal from the European Union in 2020, GDPR was retained in law as UK-GDPR 2021, alongside an amended version of the Data Protection Act 2018. Responsibility for enforcing UK-GDPR lies with the Information Commissioner's Office (ICO). The ICO is an independent authority that upholds information rights in the public interest. It promotes openness by public bodies, and data privacy for individuals, who are also called 'data subjects'. 'Data controllers' include therapy services and sole traders who collect, store and use personal information about service users, staff and volunteers electronically either directly or as a third party; and exercise professional judgement in the processing of this personal data; and have a direct relationship with data subjects; and make decisions about these individuals as a result of processing their data. As data controllers, we must register with the ICO and carry out associated responsibilities. If we plan to send, receive or store personal data outside the UK, we must first be aware of applicable restrictions. If we use email or text messaging for marketing or fundraising, we must also abide by UK Privacy and Electronic Communications Regulations (PECR) 2003. Infringements of UK-GDPR or PECR are liable for substantial fines. It is advisable for therapy services and private practitioners to obtain legal advice about complying with UK-GDPR.

INDIVIDUAL DATA RIGHTS

Under UK-GDPR, individuals have legal rights in relation to how their personal data is handled. Therapy providers must make available a Privacy Notice that informs service users, staff and volunteers of these rights, and where they can complain about data handling. Further information and Privacy Notice template can be found at the GDPR website (https://gdpr.eu/privacy-notice/).

Individual data rights are extensive. Some are briefly explained here. A full list and further elucidation can be found on the ICO website (https://ico.org.uk/).

The right to be informed means we must be transparent with people about the purposes for processing their personal data, retention periods and with whom data will be shared.

The right of access means, when asked, we must promptly give people copies of the data we hold about them, for example if they make a 'Subject Access Request' (SAR).

The right to rectification means we must correct any erroneous or incomplete information if requested.

The right to erasure, or the 'right to be forgotten', means we must delete personal information at the request of the data subject if it is no longer necessary for the purpose for which it was collected, or where the person withdraws lawful consent.

The right to data portability means we must create records in a way that personal data can be transferred easily and securely across different information technology (IT) systems.

SEVEN PRINCIPLES OF UK-GDPR

Therapy providers must create, follow and periodically update a data protection policy that details how they comply with UK-GDPR; how personal data is used and shared (including, where applicable, for research); individual data rights; and the names and contact details for people in the organisation accountable for information governance. UK-GDPR principles are summarised here. Readers should visit the ICO website to obtain full details and compliance requirements.

a. **Lawfulness, fairness and transparency**: Six legal bases exist for processing personal data *lawfully* under UK-GDPR Article 6. Where consent is the legal basis, the provider should explain the data subject's right to withdraw consent. Where the legal basis is a statutory or contractual requirement, the possible consequences to the person of failing to provide necessary data should be explained (e.g., the provider cannot proceed with treatment, or a prospective employer cannot offer a post). A further ten legal bases exist for processing 'special category' (also known as 'sensitive') data in UK-GDPR Article 9(2), which is any information that reveals or infers a person's health (which may include disability, pregnancy, or gender reassignment); sex life or sexual orientation; racial or ethnic origin; political opinions; trade union membership; religious or philosophical views; and genetic or biometric data. Therapy providers commonly must process 'special category' data and are generally limited to consent as the legal condition for this. Professional bodies may provide additional guidance to their members on applicable Article 9(2) conditions (e.g., BACP). Rules also apply to processing information about criminal offences. Before starting any new project or service, therapy providers should conduct a Data Protection Impact Assessment (DPIA), including a map of data flows and legal bases for processing. ***Fairness*** and ***transparency*** mean we honestly explain to people how and why we handle their data.

b. **Purpose limitation**: Personal data is used only for intended purposes, which are identified, documented and reviewed in the Privacy Notice.
c. **Data minimisation**: Data processed is adequate and relevant to the intended purpose and limited to what is necessary.
d. **Accuracy**: Data is correct and up to date. Any challenges to data accuracy are noted and considered.
e. **Storage limitation**: Data is kept only as long as needed, in line with documented retention periods.
f. **Integrity and confidentiality (security)**: Data is kept safe from unauthorised disclosure.
g. **Accountability**: Practices and practitioners are responsible for complying with UK-GDPR.

SAFEGUARDING

A range of legislation in England, Scotland, Wales and Northern Ireland mandates recordkeeping and reporting processes for safeguarding children and adults at risk of harm. Training in child and adult safeguarding is generally mandatory for employed staff across the health and social care sectors in the UK. Mental health practitioners working in all other sectors should ensure they are appropriately trained and prepared to record and report information about children and adults at risk of harm in line with organisational policies and advice from local safeguarding boards. Failure to record, analyse or share information with relevant authorities in a timely manner can have serious consequences for the health and safety of children and adults at risk of harm.

UK-wide guidance on recordkeeping and information sharing for safeguarding children can be found in *Safeguarding Children and Young People: Roles and Competencies For Healthcare Staff* (Royal College of Nursing, 2019), and for safeguarding adults in *Adult Safeguarding: Roles and Competencies for Healthcare Staff* (Royal College of Nursing, 2018). Statutory guidance on child safeguarding in England can be found in *Working Together to Safeguard Children* (Department for Education, 2018). Welsh statutory guidance for safeguarding children is found in *Working Together to Safeguard People Volume 5 – Handling Individual Cases to Protect Children at Risk* (Welsh Government 2019a), and safeguarding adults in *Working Together to Safeguard People: Volume 6 – Handling Individual Cases to Protect Adults at Risk* (Welsh Government, 2019b). In Scotland, the multi-agency children's wellbeing framework *Getting it Right for Every Child* is in development (Scottish Government, 2021). Guidance on safeguarding adults in Scotland can be found at *Support and Protection Revised Code of Practice* (Scottish Government, 2014). Northern Ireland guidance can be found in *Understanding the Needs of Children in Northern Ireland* (UNOCINI, 2011) and *Adult Safeguarding Prevention and Protection in Partnership* (Department of Health, Social Services and Public Safety [NI], 2015).

Practitioners working in educational settings and independent training providers in England with people aged up to 18 must follow statutory guidance around recordkeeping detailed in *Keeping Children Safe in Education* (Department of Education, 2021).

CALDICOTT GUARDIANS

The provision of safe and effective care is supported by appropriate information sharing between relevant agencies. In the UK, eight Caldicott Principles complement individual data rights and should be applied by staff in health and social care organisations, when a balance must be struck between protecting patient confidentiality and sharing information to promote continuity of care, or patient and public safety. In law, by 2023 all directly-provided and contracted NHS and adult social care organisations are encouraged to appoint a Caldicott Guardian, who is a specially trained senior health professional who advises staff on complying with the Caldicott Principles. These include:

- Justify the purpose(s) for using confidential information.
- Use confidential information only when necessary.
- Use minimum necessary confidential information.
- Access to confidential information should be on a strict need-to-know basis.
- Everyone with access to confidential information should be aware of their responsibilities.
- Comply with the law.
- The duty to share information is as important as the duty to protect patient confidentiality.
- Inform patients about how their confidential information is used.

More information about Caldicott Guardian responsibilities is provided by the National Data Guardian (2021).

RECORDKEEPING

In this section we briefly look at organisational responsibilities for staff recordkeeping knowledge and training, and IT system developments in the public and private sectors.

RECORDS AS INFORMATION ASSETS

Therapy providers may hold records for different categories of confidential personal information, including but not limited to:

- **Clinical** (patient referrals, treatment and discharge; team meeting and supervision notes; research)
- **Staff and volunteers** (recruitment, management, training, occupational health)
- **Organisational** (databases, reports and audits, emails, meeting minutes, accidents and incidents, complaints)
- **Financial** (procurement, contracts, accounting and payroll, customer payments and receipts)
- **Premises** (visitor logs, CCTV)

Information contained in these records is an organisational 'asset'. The lifecycles of all types of information assets, from creation, through use, storage and appraisal to deletion, should be tracked in an organisational register. More information on maintaining information asset registers can be found on the ICO website.

TRAINING AND CERTIFICATION

It is advisable that all practitioners undertake training in clinical recordkeeping. Basic certification can be accessed for free from e-Learning for Healthcare (https://portal.e-lfh.org.uk/). Clinical managers with responsibility for organisational data protection, information governance and Caldicott Guardians should complete more advanced training. Organisations in England that control NHS patient data must complete an annual self-assessment to measure performance against the National Data Guardian's security standards through the Data Security and Protection Toolkit (www.dsptoolkit.nhs.uk/). This includes online security certification administered through the National Cyber Security Centre (www.ncsc.gov.uk/cyberessentials/overview). Organisations registered with the Care Quality Commission (CQC) are assessed on their compliance with Health and Social Care Act 2008 (Regulated Activities) Regulations 2014. Key lines of enquiry in CQC inspections include the maintenance of accurate, complete and detailed service user records, staff employment records and management of regulated activities (Care Quality Commission, 2021).

IT SYSTEMS

Across the UK, publicly-funded mental health services currently use a range of different IT systems for storage, reporting and analysis of patient data. Following decades of failed NHS England initiatives to create interoperable Electronic Health Records (EHR) systems, the NHS England (2019) *Long Term Plan* and the UK Health and Care Bill 2021 sets out how, by 2022, Clinical Commissioning Groups (CCGs) will be absorbed by Integrated Care Systems (ICSs). ICS regional management bodies are charged with integrating primary and specialist care, physical and mental health services, and social care. This work includes the development of Local Health and Care Records (LHCR) to support cohesive care across services. Regardless of the data management system in operation, NHS child and adult mental health and learning disability services in England are required to make monthly data submissions to NHS Digital Mental Health Services Data Set (MHSDS). This national dataset re-uses clinical and operational data for secondary purposes, including commissioning, service improvement and service design.

For private practitioners, educational settings and third sector providers, the marketplace is rapidly expanding for branded, customisable 'practice management system' software packages that organise and store patient records in secure cloud servers. These systems enable some reporting and analysis of patient data. Some packages include inbuilt video call platforms, and can handle appointment booking and reminders, and payments and invoicing.

NOTETAKING

Service user records are likely to contain information from several sources, including our process notes. The suggestions made here around style, content and structure for clinical notes ought to be considered alongside service- and sector-specific policies, and guidance from local healthcare trusts and professional regulatory bodies.

STYLE

Accuracy, precision and clarity: Notes should provide a reliable account of our work. Facts should be clearly differentiated from opinions. Quotes from service users can be indicated by notations such as 'X said...'. Assumptions or judgements (either positive or negative) should be avoided. Specific and quantitative descriptors are superior to vague terms such as 'mild' or 'significant', or colloquial terms such as 'struggling', 'upset' or 'challenging', which do not provide a clear picture of a person's situation. Abbreviations and acronyms which might not be understood by a future reader are best written in full. It is a good habit, before saving notes, to proofread them as if we were another professional seeking to understand the person's treatment, and as if we were the person we are writing about.

Conciseness and relevance: The minimum necessary information should be included for the note's function, for example, to record relevant therapeutic issues discussed or decisions made. While information unrelated to the purpose of therapy is best omitted, if information is provided by the service user that indicates we may have a statutory responsibility to take protective action, we should seek advice from managers or the local safeguarding board around appropriate documentation.

Anti-discriminatory: Culturally competent practitioners not only actively avoid stereotyping or using stigmatising labels in documenting their work, but go further by seeking to be alert to differences, power inequalities and historical legacies that impact how people interact with each other. Personal biography deeply impacts our perceptions of self and others. Furthermore, organisational culture is not neutral – it may reinforce attitudes that can be subtly detrimental to minoritised people, or alternatively may promote the skills, knowledge and values that support social justice in therapeutic practice (Okitikpi and Aymer, 2010).

Timeliness and chronology: Practitioners should plan sufficient time into each clinical day to immediately complete notes. Leaving notes for 'later' is an unwise strategy, because nuances of important conversations can be quickly forgotten or documentation omitted entirely. Colleagues may require up-to-date information about our work with service users. It is wise to briefly document most or all contacts with service users, including incidental phone calls, text messages and emails (excluding data about other people) (NHSx, 2021). All contact with other professionals about our service users should likewise be documented. Notes should be stored in chronological order within an individual record, with identifiers that assist targeted search and retrieval.

Individually separated: When working with families, couples or groups, it is good practice to keep separate process notes for each individual. Difficulties around protecting confidentiality can arise when our notes cover work conducted with more than one person if we must respond to a SAR from one of those individuals.

Redactions and corrections: Where clinical notes are found to have been entered in error or contain inaccurate information, we have a duty to promptly correct them. Where notes require adjustment, the original note should be crossed out but kept in the file, with the correction signed and dated (Mathioudakis et al., 2016). Where notes have been entered on the wrong person's file, this must be noted along with the date and signature of the person crossing out the note.

Signed, dated and time stamped: Indicate who wrote the note and when it was entered into the record.

CONTENT AND STRUCTURE

What we might include in our session notes, and how we might organise them, varies by professional context. When working in services, we should follow managerial direction and service recordkeeping policies to support service-wide consistency in recordkeeping. When in private practice, our professional membership organisations and registration bodies are likely to offer guidance around responsible notetaking. It is helpful to occasionally review the guidance and refresh our notetaking habits accordingly, to avoid the risk of personal proclivities degrading the quality of our records. General content areas covered in clinical and process notes might include: assessment reports, formulation and reformulation; treatment plans and updates; psychometric tests and outcome measures; risk assessments and how concerns are followed up and resolved; session notes, including service user ideas, concerns and expectations of therapy, session focus, and next steps; rationale for all clinical decisions, including therapeutic approach and methods; summaries of multidisciplinary or multiagency meetings, and implementation of recommendations arising from care plan reviews; and assessment of the impact of interventions and therapeutic support on service user experience and therapy outcomes. It may also be important to include notes about family and carer involvement and consultation. Practice transparency, service user engagement and self-care can be enhanced if we show our clinical notes to service users where helpful or requested (Esch et al., 2016).

REFERENCES

British Association for Counselling and Psychotherapy (2018). *Ethical Framework for the Counselling Professions.* Lutterworth: BACP. Available at www.bacp.co.uk/events-and-resources/ethics-and-standards/ethical-framework-for-the-counselling-professions/

Care Quality Commission (2021). *Regulation 17: Good Governance.* Rochester, UK: CQC. Available at www.cqc.org.uk/guidance-providers/regulations-enforcement/regulation-17-good-governance

Department for Education (2018). *Working Together to Safeguard Children.* London: DfE. Available at https://assets.publishing.service.gov.uk/government/uploads/system/uploads/attachment_data/file/942454/Working_together_to_safeguard_children_inter_agency_guidance.pdf

Department for Education (2021). *Keeping Children Safe in Education.* London: DfE. Available at https://assets.publishing.service.gov.uk/government/uploads/system/uploads/attachment_data/file/1021914/KCSIE_2021_September_guidance.pdf

Department of Health, Social Services and Public Safety [NI] (2015). *Adults Safeguarding Prevention and Protection in Partnership.* Belfast: DHSSPS. Available at www.health-ni.gov.uk/sites/default/files/publications/dhssps/adult-safeguarding-policy.pdf

Esch, T., Mejilla, R., Anselmo, M., Podtschaska, B., Delbanco, T. & Walker, J. (2016). Engaging patients through open notes: An evaluation using mixed methods. *BMJ Open*, 6:e010034. doi:10.1136/bmjopen-2015-010034

Mathioudakis, A., Rousalova, I., Gagnat, A.A., Saad, N. & Hardavella, G. (2016). How to keep good clinical records. *Breathe*, 12(4), 369–373. doi: 10.1183/20734735.018016

National Data Guardian (2021). *Guidance about the Appointment of Caldicott Guardians, their Role and Responsibilities Published by the National Data Guardian for Health and Social Care.* London: NDG. Available at https://assets.publishing.service.gov.uk/government/uploads/system/uploads/attachment_data/file/1013756/Caldicott_Guardian_guidance_v1.0_27.08.21.pdf

NHS England (2019). *The NHS Long Term Plan.* London: NHS England. Available at www.longtermplan.nhs.uk/wp-content/uploads/2019/08/nhs-long-term-plan-version-1.2.pdf

NHSx (2021). *Records Management Code of Practice.* London: NHS. Available at www.nhsx.nhs.uk/information-governance/guidance/records-management-code/

Okitikpi, T. & Aymer, C. (2010). *Key Concepts in Anti-discriminatory Social Work.* London: Sage.

Royal College of Nursing (2018). *Adult Safeguarding: Roles and Competencies for Healthcare Staff.* London: RCN. Available at www.rcn.org.uk/professional-development/publications/pub-007069

Royal College of Nursing (2019). *Safeguarding Children and Young People: Roles and Competencies for Healthcare Staff.* London: RCN. Available at www.rcn.org.uk/professional-development/publications/pub-007366

Scottish Government (2014). *Adult Support and Protection Revised Code of Practice.* Edinburgh: Scottish Government. Available at www.gov.scot/publications/adult-support-and-protection-revised-code-of-practice/documents/

Scottish Government (2021). *Getting it Right for Every Child.* [Website]. Edinburgh: Scottish Government. Available at https://webarchive.nrscotland.gov.uk/20210417140438/https://www.gov.scot/policies/girfec/

UK Caldicott Guardian Council (2021). *The Common Law Duty of Confidentiality.* Available at www.ukcgc.uk/duty-of-confidentiality

UNOCINI (2011). *Understanding the Needs of Children in Northern Ireland.* Belfast: UNOCINI. Available at www.health-ni.gov.uk/sites/default/files/publications/dhssps/unocini-guidance.pdf

Welsh Government (2019a). *Working Together to Safeguard People Volume 5 – Handling Individual Cases to Protect Children at Risk.* Cardiff: Welsh Government. Available at https://gov.wales/sites/default/files/publications/2019-05/working-together-to-safeguard-people-volume-5-handling-individual-cases-to-protect-children-at-risk.pdf

Welsh Government (2019b). *Working Together to Safeguard People: Volume 6 – Handling Individual Cases to Protect Adults at Risk.* Cardiff: Welsh Government. Available at www.northwalessafeguardingboard.wales/document/working-together-to-safeguard-people-volume-6-handling-individual-cases-to-protect-adults-at-risk/

> **RECOMMENDED READING**
>
> Mitchells, B. and Bond, T. (2021). *Confidentiality & Record Keeping in Counselling & Psychotherapy* (3rd ed.). London: Sage.
>
> This definitive handbook for counsellors and psychotherapists covers the legal bases and good practices that support confidentiality, recordkeeping, information and ethics. It includes dilemma scenarios for reflection and applied learning.
>
> NHSx (2021). *Records Management Code of Practice*. London: NHS. Available at www.nhsx.nhs.uk/information-governance/guidance/records-management-code/
>
> Useful for clinical managers with responsibility for recordkeeping and data management in organisations which work within or under contract to NHS organisations in England, or in social care or other local authority-funded services working jointly with the NHS, this guide covers record management obligations, organising and storing records, and the record lifecycle, with useful links to other relevant guidance.
>
> Rye, J. (2020). *Setting Up and Running a Therapy Business: Essential Questions and Answers* (2nd ed.). Abingdon, UK: Routledge.
>
> A guide to many of the practical aspects of working as a sole trader, this book includes consideration of data storage standards, UK-GDPR and relevant client agreements.

3.8 WORKING WITH INTERPRETERS

RACHEL TRIBE AND CLAIRE MARSHALL

OVERVIEW AND KEY POINTS

> And in my situation especially, I know that language will be a crucial instrument, that I can overcome the stigma of my marginality, the weight of presumption against me, only if the reassuringly right sounds come out if my mouth… (Hoffman, 1999: 123)

An appreciation of the intertwined relationship between culture, language and experience is crucial if psychotherapy is to address issues of inclusion, social justice and provide equality of access to psychotherapeutic services. The inability to speak fluently in English does not preclude the need to access psychological and psychotherapeutic services. Priebe, Giacco and El-Nagib (2016), in a review for the World Health Organisation, noted that language barriers were deemed to be one of the most significant factors in restricting access to mental health services for migrants who had limited language proficiency in the language of their new country. In a systematic review, Ohtani et al. (2015) found that language barriers lead to an under-utilisation of mental health services.

Key points in this chapter include:

- More than 300 languages are reportedly spoken in British schools (British Council, 2021).
- In the United Kingdom, data estimates that 7.7% of the population are non-native English speakers (Statistica, 2021).
- A lack of opportunities, gender politics, social isolation, pre-migration trauma, cognitive decline in later life or other reasons are factors that could contribute to a reduction in a person's fluency when speaking English (Gerskowitch and Tribe, 2021; Shah, 2017).
- Equalities legislation and professional codes promote best practice and outlaw discrimination, therefore clinicians' readiness and skill in working with interpreters in a clinical setting are essential.
- The rich, multicultural tapestry of contemporary Britain means there will always be residents who are not fluent in the English language who may require access to counselling and psychotherapy, and considering the barriers to access this might pose is an important endeavour for clinicians.

WORKING WITH INTERPRETERS: THERAPEUTIC DISCOURSE

The role of interpreters in mental health is a skilled and complex task (Chang et al., 2021; Kuay et al., 2015; Resera, Tribe and Lane, 2014). Working with an interpreter and across language and culture requires active consideration of these factors. Working with an interpreter may initially be challenging to practitioners, and it requires adjustments, but it will lead to a number of positive outcomes (Tribe and Thompson, 2009). The provision of an interpreter within a therapy session ensures that potential service users who are not fluent English speakers are not denied access to services (Gerskowitch and Tribe, 2021). Additional outcomes may include practitioners adopting a questioning stance to their work, encouraging reflective practice, which may lead to an expansion and enriching of many aspects of therapeutic practice and an enlarged clinical repertoire.

Practitioners may be reminded of the central role of language in creating versions of selves, of ill-health and of 'recovery', and of the ways wellbeing and mental health are linguistically and culturally located. White et al. (2021) argue that many people fail to recognise the validity or 'languaging' of other people's understandings of their distress or mental health. They refer to this as an 'epistemic injustice'. This can be further problematised when issues of power and privilege are present and can be consciously or unconsciously played out in the therapeutic encounter. These issues require active and ongoing consideration by practitioners. The socially constructed nature of the therapeutic discourse itself contains power differentials (Harper and Speed, 2014), wherein dominant, expert-led perceptions may come to define the process of therapy. The client's reduced access to articulating for themselves because they are not fluent in English adds a further layer to these dynamics.

In terms of therapeutic discourse and best practice, the British Association of Counselling and Psychotherapy (BACP) (2019) and the British Psychological Society (BPS) (2017) have produced guidelines on working with interpreters. The BPS (2020) produced additional, brief guidance on working virtually with an interpreter.

WORKING WITH INTERPRETERS: QUALITY OF CARE IN MENTAL HEALTH PROVISION

It has been demonstrated that quality of care is negatively affected when patients with limited English proficiency (LEP) are not provided with interpreters (Chang et al., 2021; Karliner et al., 2007). Legislation in Britain, including the Equality Act 2010 (HM Government, 2010), requires equity of service provision. The Mental Health Act 1983 (amended 2007) (HM Government, 2007) guidance recommends that qualified interpreters should be used in this context. The Mental Health Act White Paper 2021 notes that disproportionate numbers of people from minoritised ethnic communites are being detained in psychiatric facilties and that changes need to be made. Moreover, a wide range of benefits of working with a professional interpreter have been reported, including clients who reported feeling more understood, and improved clinical care has been documented, although this is a contested area. Karliner et al. (2007), in a systematic review, noted that using a professional interpreter can improve care that approaches or equals that for patients without language barriers. Chang et al. (2021) noted that expanding interpreters' roles beyond merely 'linguistic conversion' and including cultural information may improve the therapeutic alliance and interpreter-facilitated interventions. That clinicians may be ambivalent about working with interpreters has been acknowledged by practitioners in the UK (Tribe and Tunariu, 2009). Reasons for this may include anxiety at having a third person in the room, which can give rise to feelings of being observed and possibly judged, and/or experience of a change in the therapeutic context and the associated relational dynamics (Tribe and Thompson, 2017).

MODELS OF INTERPRETATION

Tribe (2020) distinguishes four modes of interpretation:

1. Linguistic mode.
2. Psychotherapeutic/constructionist.
3. Advocate.
4. Cultural broker.

Each mode of working lends itself better to different contexts. In the *Psychotherapeutic/constructionist mode*, the interpreter is primarily concerned with the intended meaning and feeling-content being conveyed, rather than word-for-word interpretation. Similarly, *in cultural broker mode*, the interpreter interprets not only the spoken word but also relevant cultural and contextual variables. **These two modes are the most relevant for psychotherapists**. In the *advocate (or sometimes 'health advocate') mode*, an interpreter has a wider role and is there to advocate not only for the individual client, but also for a specific section of the community. The *linguistic mode* is used when (as far as is possible) word-for-word interpretation is required, for example in a police statement.

Interpreters make a substantial contribution in enabling therapeutic interventions to take place. In alliance with the clinician, they also play a key role in building trust, facilitating mutual respect, communicating affect, and often negotiating complex systems-of-meanings between two cultural worlds (Angelelli, 2004; Tribe, 1999). The contribution interpreters make to health and social care services, such as counselling and psychotherapy, often goes unrecognised. Interpreters have voiced concerns and dissatisfaction with clinicians for not acknowledging their professional skills and status (Granger and Baker, 2003). Acknowledgement by clinicians of the interpreters' role as complex and crucial would help to create a constructive and collaborative environment, which in turn may also safeguard from incidental misunderstandings (Resera et al., 2014).

WAYS OF WORKING

Language represents one of the fundamental components of psychotherapeutic work, in terms of the cathartic effect of talking and being listened to and witnessed by a skilled practitioner. Language actively constructs realities of what is possible, what is marginalised or denied, and modes of relating (McNamee and Gergen, 1992). Language and culture stand in a mutual, reciprocal and interactive relationship with one another. Working with an interpreter concentrates attention on the dynamic relationships between the construction of reality, particularly through a cultural lens. Culture shapes the delivery of our spoken language as well as a range of non-verbal behaviours, including facial expressions, gestures and eye contact. These non-verbal behaviours form part of psychotherapeutic practice. The interpreter may be able to assist the clinician to engage with the client's intended message behind gestures or expressions, adding nuance to the therapist's understanding and minimising misunderstandings.

Languages are not directly interchangeable. What may be said in a few words in one language may take several sentences for the meaning to be accurately conveyed in another language. For example, there is no word which defines the gender of a cousin in English, no equivalent word for 'mind' in Swiss German and no words for 'please' and 'thank you' in Finnish. Similarly, the term 'burn-out' does not exist in either of the Sri Lankan languages and there is no word for 'menopause' in Somali. When these words are used, interpreters will have to think carefully about how to convey the corresponding meaning of a 'missing' word. Many of the words used within mental health settings in Britain will be drawn from a western or ethnocentric perspective. The debate about the appropriateness of using this model uncritically and indiscriminately across cultures is outside the scope of this chapter, the interested reader is referred to Charura and Lago (2021), Fernando (2017) and Tribe (2014).

THE IMPORTANCE OF A FIRST LANGUAGE: THE MOTHER TONGUE

The processing of emotions through a mother tongue versus a subsequent language a person has learned is beginning to be understood (de Zuleta, Gene-Cos and Grachev, 2001; Tribe and Keefe, 2009). It appears that emotions that were experienced or stored in a person's mother tongue tend only to be fully accessible when that language is deployed. Emotions are in some ways culturally and linguistically mediated (Tsai, 2007). So, the clinician needs to grasp the cultural context in which such memories have been initially represented. This makes employing an interpreter all the more important. A client's inability to communicate effectively can be isolating and prevent them from accessing or meaningfully engaging with talking therapy. The need to seek support might feel like a vulnerability, causing someone to retreat into themselves or rely on habitual, individualised ways of dealing with distress. This might even lead to resisting offers of therapeutic support. The combined contribution of these two aspects highlights the crucial importance of working with interpreters and cultural brokers.

CHANGED DYNAMICS

The presence of an interpreter in the clinical session will shape the dynamics of the therapeutic encounter. 'Clarification of the interpreter's role and the session structure improved provider–interpreter collaboration, with two perceived benefits: improved assessment through elicitation of clinically relevant information and stronger therapeutic alliance through "emotion work"' (Chang et al., 2021: 353). This can be beneficial, although at times it can generate challenges. For example, some clinicians have argued that the presence of interpreters:

- adds to the complexity of therapy process (Leanza et al., 2014)
- can contribute to clinicians feeling a greater detachment from the service users, as well as feeling less powerful and less effective in their work (Raval, 1996).

Working with interpreters has at the same time been reported as crucial for the depth, quality and outcome of therapy (e.g., Tribe and Tunariu 2009). It has also been shown to increase clients' understanding of their situation and the care options offered, to enhance trust in the process and to improve rapport with the health professional (Raval, 1996).

A case example will now be presented to exemplify some of the issues that clinicians might consider when working with interpreters.

CASE STUDY

Ali has been referred to you by his GP, who says that he is 'suffering from' 'post-traumatic stress disorder' after arriving from Syria, having experienced multiple distressing events prior to leaving his country and during his journey by air and land across numerous countries. Ali mentions that he came to the UK via the 'Jungle' in Calais, six months ago and would benefit from 'talking therapy'. Ali now has full refugee status and is legally entitled to live and work in the UK. He is attending English classes. He previously worked as an architect in Syria. The GP notes that Ali will require an interpreter for the work.

How would you go about preparing yourself for working with Ali through an interpreter? Please consider why you selected these particular preparations?

KEY PRACTICE ISSUES

- Psychotherapists who have not trained in working with interpreters should undertake a training course. If this is not feasible, for example if you will be working with an interpreter unexpectedly, read the relevant guidelines (e.g., Tribe and Thompson, 2017). Also, allocate time to consider the issues or discuss them with a more experienced colleague in advance of your first session with an interpreter.
- Consider attending deaf awareness training in advance of working with a British Sign Language Interpreter (BSLI).
- Check the interpreter is qualified and appropriate for the consultation and speaks the mother tongue of the service user (rather than a second or third language).

- Allocate 10–15 minutes in advance of the meeting to enable the interpreter to brief you on any cultural issues which may have a bearing on the session.
- Interpreters may not have had experience of psychotherapy before and it may be useful to clarify the purpose of the meeting.
- Be mindful of confidentiality and trust issues when working with someone from a small language community (including the Deaf community) as the client may be anxious about being identifiable and mistrustful of an interpreter's professionalism.
- State clearly to both the interpreter and client that you alone hold clinical responsibility for the meeting, including any risk or safeguarding issues that might arise.
- Create a good atmosphere where client and interpreter both feel able to ask for clarification if anything is unclear.
- Be respectful to your interpreter; they are an important member of the team who makes your work possible.
- Match for gender and age, when appropriate. Do not use a relative and never use a child as an interpreter.
- Interpreters should undergo language testing to ensure that they have the requisite experience and expertise to handle the interpreting task.
- Be aware of the wellbeing of your interpreter and the possibility of your interpreter suffering from vicarious traumatisation. Consider what support they will be offered.
- At the end of the session, allocate 10–15 minutes to debrief the interpreter about the session and offer support and supervision as appropriate.

With thanks to the British Psychological Society (BPS) for permission to adapt the above from the BPS guidelines for *Working with Interpreters in Health Settings* (2017).

RESEARCH EVIDENCE

Zafirah, Dyer and Hamshaw (2020), in a small-scale study on the impact of compassion fatigue on mental health sign language interpreters working with children, found compassion fatigue was prevalent. They noted that preventative factors included: receiving support, having professional experience and obtaining compassion satisfaction from their work. Most interpreters have not undergone training in mental healthcare or received clinical supervision to minimise susceptibility to vicarious trauma (Splevins et al., 2010).

In studying the emotional impact of interpreting in mental health, Doherty, MacIntyre and Wyne (2010) found that of the 18 participating interpreters:

- 67% reported experiencing difficulties with ruminating about the narratives shared by the service users in the session
- 33% stated interpreting for service users with mental health problems had an impact on their personal lives.

Psychotherapists should be aware of their duty of care to interpreters and offer a briefing and debriefing session.

Mirza et al. (2020) noted that:

- interpreters reported difficulties with the technicalities of interpretation, while health providers were more concerned about the content of communication
- 84% of interpreters and 54% of health providers in a study conducted in the USA were interested in undertaking additional training.

The value of undertaking specialist professional training and related continuing professional development (CPD) on interpretation and language support by interpreters and psychotherapists remains an important issue. Undertaking training can improve practice and enhance the skill base of interpreters and psychotherapists. The establishment of a good working alliance between client, interpreter and clinician is paramount. Interpreters deserve respect and support from the practitioners they work with. Without them, the therapy work cannot take place. Developing skills and confidence in working with an interpreter will enhance the clinical repertoire of psychotherapists and ensure that psychotherapy is accessible to all members of our community.

REFERENCES

Angelli, C.V. (2004). *Medical Interpreting and Cross-Cultural Communication*. Cambridge: Cambridge University Press.

British Association for Counselling and Psychotherapy (2019). *Working with Interpreters in the Counselling Professions*. Lutterworth: BACP. Available at www.bacp.co.uk/members/info_sheets

British Council (2021). *Language Trends 2021: Language trends in primary and secondary schools in England*. London: British Council.

British Psychological Society (BPS)(2017). *Working with Interpreters in Health Settings: Guidelines for Psychologists*. Leicester: BPS. Available at www.bps.org.uk/content/working-interpreters-health-settings

British Psychological Society (BPS)(2020) *Working with interpreters online or via the telephone*. Leicester: BPS

Chang, D.F. et al. (2021). Rethinking interpreter functions in mental health services. *Psychiatric Services*, 72(3), 353–357.

Charura, D. & Lago, C. (2021). *Black Identities + White Therapies*. Monmouth: PCCS Books.

Department of Health and Social Care (2021). *Reforming the Mental Health Act*. London: DoHaSC.

de Zuleta, F., Gene-Cos, N. & Grachev, S. (2001). Differential psychotic symptomatology in polygot patients: Case reports and their implications. *British Journal of Medical Psychology*, 74, 277–292.

Doherty, S.M., MacIntyre, A.M. & Wyne, T. (2010). How does it feel for you? The emotional impact and specific challenges of mental health interpreting. *Mental Health Review Journal*, 15(3), 31–44.

Fernando, S. (2017). *Institutional Racism: Psychiatry & Clinical Psychology: Race Matters*. London: Palgrave Macmillan.

Gerskowitch, C. & Tribe, R. (2021). Therapists' experience of working with interpreters in NHS setting: Drawing upon a psychoanalytic theoretical framework to contextualise the findings of an IPA study. *British Journal of Psychotherapy*, 37(2), 301–318.

Granger, E. & Baker, M. (2003). The role and experience of interpreters In R. Tribe & H. Raval (Eds), *Undertaking Mental Health Work Using Interpreters*. London: Routledge.

Harper, D. & Speed, E. (2014). Uncovering recovery: The resistible rise of recovery and resilience. In J. Moncrieff, M. Rapley & E. Speed (Eds), *De-medicalizing Misery II: Society, Politics and the Mental Health Industry* (pp. 40–57). London: Palgrave.

HM Government (2007). *Mental Health Act (1983 amended 2007)*. London: HMSO. Available at www.mentalhealthcare.org.uk/mentalhealthact (accessed 8 October 2021).

HM Government (2010). *Equality Act 2010*. London: HMSO. Available at www.legislation.gov.uk (accessed 20 May 2016).

Hoffman, E. (1990). *Lost in Translation*. London: Penguin.

Karliner, L.S., Jacobs, E.A., Chen, A.H. & Mutha, S. (2007). Do professional interpreters improve clinical care for patients with limited English proficiency? A systematic review of the literature. *Health Service Research*, 42, 726–754.

Kuay, J., Chopra, P., Kaplan, I. & Szwarc, J. (2015). Conducting psychotherapy with an interpreter. *Australasian Psychiatry*, 23(3), 282–286.

Leanza, Y., Miklancic, A., Bolvin, I. & Rosenberg, E. (2014). *Working with Interpreters: Cultural Consultation: Encountering the Other in Mental Health Care*. New York: Springer.

McNamee, S. & Gergen, K. (Eds) (1992). *Therapy as a Social Construction*. London: Sage.

Mirza, M., Harrison, E., Bentley, J., Chang, H.-C. & Birman, D. (2020). Language discordance in mental health services: An exploratory survey of mental health providers and interpreters. *Societies*, 10, 66. doi:10.3390/soc10030066

Ohtani, A., Suzuki, T., Takeuchi, H. & Uchida, H. (2015). Language barriers and access to psychiatric care: A systematic review. *Psychiatric Services*, 66(8), 798–805.

Priebe, S., Giacco, D. & El-Nagib, R. (2016). *Public Health Aspects of Mental Health among Migrants and Refugees: A Review of the Evidence on Mental Health Care for Refugees, Asylum Seekers and Irregular Migrants in the WHO*. Geneva: World Health Organisation.

Raval, H. (1996). A systemic perspective on working with interpreters. *Clinical Child Psychology and Psychiatry*, 1, 29–43.

Resera, E., Tribe, R. & Lane, P. (2014). An introductory study into the experiences of interpreters and counsellors working with refugees and asylum seekers. *International Journal of Culture & Mental Health*, 8(2), 192–206.

Shah, A. (2017). Mental capacity and ageing. In P. Lane & R. Tribe (Eds), *Anti-discriminatory Practice in Mental Health for Older People.* London: Jessica Kingsley.

Splevins, K., Cohen, K., Bowley, J. & Joseph, S. (2010). Vicarious post traumatic growth amongst interpreters. *Qualitative Health Research*, 20(12), 1705–1715.

Statistica (2021). *Statistica.com* [Website]. Available at www.statistica.com (accessed 30 October 2021).

Tribe, R. (2020). Working with migrants through an interpreter. In D. Bhugra (Ed.), *Oxford Textbook of Migrant Psychiatry.* Oxford: Oxford University Press.

Tribe, R. (1999). Bridging the gap or damming the flow? Bicultural Workers, Some observations on using interpreters when working with refugee clients, many of whom have been tortured. *British Journal of Medical Psychology*, 72, 567–576.

Tribe, R. (2014). Culture, Politics and Global Mental Health: Deconstructing the global mental health movement: Does one size fits all? *Disability and the Global South*, 1,2, 251–265.

Tribe, R. & Keefe, A. (2009). Issues in using interpreters in therapeutic work with refugees. What is not being expressed? *European Journal of Psychotherapy and Counselling*, 11(4), 409–424.

Tribe, R. & Thompson, K. (2009). Exploring the three way relationship in therapeutic work with interpreters. *International Journal of Migration, Health and Social Care*, 5(2), 13–21.

Tribe, R. & Thompson, K. (2017). *BPS Guidelines for Working with Interpreters in Health Settings*. Leicester: British Psychological Society.

Tribe, R. & Tunariu, A.D. (2009). Mind your language? Working with interpreters in health care settings and therapeutic encounters. *Journal of Sex and Relationship Therapy*, 24, 74–84.

Tsai, J.L. (2007). Ideal affect: Cultural causes and behavioural consequences. *Perspectives on Psychological Science*, 2, 242–259.

White, R., Fay, R., Chiumento, A., Giurgi-Onca, C. & Phipps, A. (2021). Communication about distress and wellbeing: Epistemic and ethical considerations. *Transcultural Psychiatry*, 59(4), 413–424.

Zafirah, N.K., Dyer, A. & Hamshaw, R.J.T. (2020). The impact of compassion fatigue on mental health sign language interpreters working with children: A thematic analysis. *Journal of Interpretation*, 28(2), 7.

RECOMMENDED READING

Tribe, R. & Thompson, K. (2017). *BPS Guidelines for Working with Interpreters in Health Settings*. Leicester: British Psychological Society.

These guidelines provide a range of information about working with interpreters, including the relevant legislation, conducting a language needs assessment, training and related issues, preparation, written translations, psychometric assessment and recommendations for improvements in the future.

Tribe, R. & Raval, H. (Eds) (2003/2014). *Working with Interpreters in Mental Health*. London: Brunner-Routledge.

This edited book gives an insight into the issues and challenges facing interpreters and professionals working with interpreters. It is informed by theoretical, research and clinical considerations, and helps practitioners

(Continued)

> (Continued)
>
> to develop better ways of working in partnership with interpreters to assist service users who require an interpreter.
>
> Department of Health (n.d.). *Working with Interpreters in Mental Health* [Film]. Available at the University of East London website at www.uel.ac.uk/psychology/staff/racheltribe.htm or at www.youtube.com/watch?v=k0wzhakyjck
>
> This 10-min film made for the Department of Health. It provides introductory information for mental health professionals who are working with interpreters.

3.9 THERAPEUTIC MIDDLES

INDIA AMOS

OVERVIEW AND KEY POINTS

The process of therapy is a fluid and multidimensional one. It may not be entirely straightforward to pinpoint when exactly the beginning of therapy moves into becoming the middle phase. However, the middle of therapy can be referred to as the 'work phase' and is characterised by those therapy tasks which seek to facilitate the client's psychological change congruent with their identified goals. In addition, the writing and storing of case notes constitutes an important element of therapeutic engagement and is discussed by Wynn (Chapter 3.7, this volume). The management of client risk has not been discussed in this chapter. Nevertheless the ongoing management of risk is an integral part of the middle of therapy, as well as the beginning and the end! Readers are referred to Reeves (Chapter 3.4, this volume) for an expanded discussion regarding the management of risk.

This chapter presents discussion on the following:

- Managing and maintaining the relationship
- Reviewing therapeutic work
- Managing attendance
- Ruptures and resolutions
- Use of the supervisory relationship.

MANAGING AND MAINTAINING THE RELATIONSHIP

The middle phase of therapy continues its focus on the quality of the relationship. The applied nature of this relationship is commonly conceptualised as the working or therapeutic alliance (Bordin, 1979), which has been said to consist of three elements:

1. Agreement between therapist and client on the *goals* of therapy (what therapy is trying to do).
2. Agreement on the *tasks* of therapy (how therapy is done).
3. The therapist–client *bond* (consisting of trust and acceptance).

(Bordin, 1979)

Counselling and psychotherapy can involve the application of a variety of different skills that are understood as being effective for psychological change to occur.

While a psychodynamic psychotherapist may focus more explicitly on the transference and countertransference that arises through the relationship, in Cognitive Behavioural Therapy (CBT) the work may be more centred on the client's current problems and what serves to maintain those difficulties in the present. There are chapters in this *Handbook* which are dedicated to the discussion of individual therapeutic orientations, and readers are directed towards those specific chapters for further detail regarding the nature of different types of therapy. Regardless of the therapy orientation, it is the relationship that has been found to be one of the most consistent predictors of therapy outcome (Flückiger et al., 2018). Therefore, conceptualising the therapist as the facilitator of the therapy process invites attention towards the therapists' way of 'being', perhaps more so that the therapists' way of 'doing'.

SKILLS: ACTIVE LISTENING AND REFLECTING FEELINGS

The act of listening may seem like a straightforward one, but it serves several important therapeutic purposes that may be easily overlooked. Actively listening to clients is essential if the therapist is to attempt to step into the perceptual world of the client. When the therapist offers the client all of their attention, the client may respond positively by interacting on an increasingly authentic level, perhaps becoming more likely to disclose how they are feeling. The therapist may also incorporate reflective listening, in which they reflect or restate back to the client their understanding of the client's experience. The therapist may reflect the client's exact words, communicating understanding of the feelings the client has expressed. At other times, the therapist may check out if they have understood an underlying feeling that may be on the edge of the client's awareness (Preston, 2008). Alternatively, the therapist may pick up on the client's feeling and reflect that back to them. For example, 'You are feeling angry about that?', or 'It sounds like the idea of that is scary for you?' Reflecting the feeling of the meaning evident in the client's words can reinforce, to the client, that they have been heard and, perhaps more importantly, understood. When there has been a misunderstanding on the part of the therapist, the technique of reflecting enables the client to clarify what it is they mean.

Paraphrasing can also be a useful tool in addition to reflection (Egan, 2006). Paraphrasing involves the provision of a concise statement of the client's message from the counsellor to accurately capture the essence of what the client has disclosed. An example in response to the client saying 'I do not know if lying around in bed all day is good for my mood, but I cannot find any reason to get up and do anything' might be for the therapist to paraphrase by saying 'It sounds like you know what might help with your low mood, but are finding it hard to see the reason to get out of bed at the moment'. As therapists listen, they are selecting what to respond to as well as monitoring their own thoughts, feelings, images and embodied felt senses. Therapists commonly use their body as an instrument in therapy, continuously drawing on their bodily responses to clients to gain insight into the client's experience. Cozolino (2004) formalised the helpful concept of 'shuttling' to describe the therapist's process of moving their awareness between themselves and their client. The therapist may choose to 'shuttle down' into their bodies if they feel distant or distracted away from their client. It may lend itself well to the exploration of why it may be difficult for the therapist to listen to their client effectively. Alternatively, therapists may choose to 'shuttle up' into their minds when feeling confused by client material.

REVIEWING THE WORK AND MONITORING

It is considered good practice for therapists to periodically review their therapeutic work with clients (British Association of Counselling and Psychotherapy, 2018). A review may contain a discussion of the client's expectations of therapy, a review of their therapeutic goals, inviting the client to reflect on those aspects of therapy which they have found helpful or unhelpful, or to negotiate the focus of the remainder of the therapy sessions. How therapists may approach conducting a review of therapy can differ. Therapy reviews may be completed via informal or formal methods. Some therapists may prefer to stipulate from the outset that a review session will take place at a specific point in the therapy, so the client is aware ahead of time. Others may prefer to informally review the therapeutic process as it develops. Eliciting feedback from the client can serve to reinforce the client's development and has been found to promote therapy attendance (Swift et al., 2012). Collaboration in therapy ensures that power is shared within the relationship and reviewing therapeutic work provides an opportunity for the practitioner to 'check out' any assumptions they may have made about the client's experience of the process.

Reviewing the therapy process can be supported through employment of metacommunication. Metacommunication can be defined as communication about communication (Cooper and Spinelli, 2012). It is the practice of drawing attention to and dialoguing specifically about the therapist–client interaction and communication. Rennie (1998) identifies four forms or purposes of metacommunication. These include:

- The therapist reveals the purposes of their own communication.
- The therapist reveals the impact of the client's communication.
- The therapist enquires into the purposes behind the client's communication.
- The therapist enquires into the impact on the client of the therapist's own communication.

An example of metacommunication may involve the therapist saying: 'When I put that to you, how did you find yourself reacting to it? or 'When you said that I found myself feeling…'. These acts of metacommunication serve to promote congruence in the therapy relationship, as the counsellor is transparent about the intentions of their communication and genuinely curious about the client's reactions. Metacommunication within this form of therapy is integral as it offers the opportunity of an ongoing dialogue between the client and the therapist about what the client is finding helpful or unhelpful about therapeutic sessions. In the context of CBT, Wills and Sanders (2013: 35) refer to metacommunication as 'a type of mindfulness-in-action' as it brings the focus into the here and now and offers the opportunity to reflect on what is occurring in the moment. As a result of these exchanges, helpful insight can be gained that may be used to further inform the client's psychological formulation. Deepening or even modifying the formulation which provisionally seeks to inform the therapeutic work may result (see Johnstone – Chapter 3.5, this volume).

REPAIRING RUPTURES TO THE THERAPEUTIC RELATIONSHIP

Therapy reviews can serve to maintain the reciprocal relationship necessary between client and therapist. With that in mind, reviewing the work may likely occur in the event of an impasse or rupture in the relationship (Safran, Muran and Eubanks-Carter, 2011).

A rupture in the therapeutic alliance can be considered as a moment of interpersonal tension between the therapist and client. In some cases, a major breakdown in the therapy relationship might take place. Of course, in any relationship, disturbances, conflicts, mistakes and misunderstanding can occur, and the therapy relationship is no different. Ruptures have been conceptualised as important and critical junctures within the therapy process and can occur at any time. Perhaps they may emerge as a single momentary event, over several sessions, or appear as a recurrent theme throughout the duration. Safran and Muran (2000), two prolific authors in this area, identified two types of rupture that may arise: *withdrawal* ruptures and *confrontation* ruptures. A withdrawal rupture may be indicated by the client offering minimal responses in sessions, or even falling silent completely. Signs of a confrontation rupture may include the direct expression of anger, resentment, frustration or discontent with the therapist or therapeutic process. It is important for the therapist to work constructively with alliance ruptures as the successful resolution or negotiation of alliance ruptures within therapy can foster growth and insight for the client and therapist.

The multicultural counselling literature highlights the ways in which systems of power and oppression influence the therapeutic process and can contribute harm to clients if not attended to. Cultural ruptures which can be related to microaggressions in individual and group therapy, have received attention in the literature (Miles et al., 2021). Evidence suggests that the repair of ruptures in the therapy relationship is related to positive outcomes in therapy (Okamoto and Kazantis, 2021). Some even go as far as to say that the negotiation of ruptures in the relationship is at the heart of the change process (Safran and Muran, 2000). Ruptures offer an insight into the interpersonal patterns of the client, which may be a source or maintenance factor in their psychological distress. So, too, do ruptures draw therapists' attention to their own process, which it is necessary to explore in supervision. Experience of a rupture within the therapy can therefore offer moments of potentially productive exploration of interpersonal patterns in sessions (Safran and Segal, 1990). The case example below highlights the importance of supervision when identifying a potential rupture and considering a client's non-attendance at therapy.

CASE STUDY

Verity is a psychotherapist currently engaged in fortnightly supervision with Jasmine. In their last supervisory session, Verity brought one of her current clients to be discussed. Verity used a pseudonym to protect the anonymity of her client when in supervision – she referred to them as Frances. Frances had started therapy with signs of mixed anxiety and depression. Frances had reported having a chaotic childhood, moving to several different foster families through their teens. Verity reported how she was becoming increasingly concerned by Frances's sporadic attendance at therapy – they were either turning up late to appointments or not attending at all. Verity reported that their relationship felt increasingly distant, and that Frances appeared less and less inclined to explore their psychological distress. This week, in supervision, Verity reports the same thing: Frances was 30 minutes late for their most recent appointment and therefore the only thing they were able to explore in the session was their attendance. Verity confided in Jasmine her consideration over whether to discharge Frances from therapy as they were no longer engaging. Verity reflected on how the situation was making her feel. She expressed feeling irritated by Frances's behaviour, and unsure of why this was occurring week after week as Frances had not opened up about what was preventing them from attending sessions. With support from her supervisor, Verity cast her mind back to the beginning of therapy and the initial six sessions with Frances, all of which they attended. It was only after Verity had to cancel their seventh therapy session at short notice because she needed to attend an urgent hospital appointment that Frances's attendance pattern appeared to change. Jasmine and Verity paused at this point to consider how that event may have impacted Frances, and subsequently their attendance.

Is it possible that a rupture occurred in the relationship between Verity and Frances? How might the scenario presented in the case study be worked with?

An empathic engagement with the client is essential to facilitate the client's disclosure and exploration of difficult feelings. Rogers' (1957) core conditions may be considered particularly relevant here as the therapist's unconditional positive regard and empathy can enable the client to work through the challenging terrain of the relationship. This can help clients to experience first-hand that the surfacing of difficult feelings within the context of therapy relationships does not necessarily destroy them, or indeed destroy the self (Safran and Kraus, 2014). Metacommunication skills are implicated again here, as resolving a rupture often can involve self-disclosure on the part of the therapist – sharing their observations and checking out their understanding of the client's experience. This is best communicated in a tentative and exploratory fashion that emphasises the subjectivity of the remarks made.

MANAGING ATTENDANCE

Clients may cancel the therapy session ahead of schedule or not attend on the day without giving notice. This is commonly recorded as the client 'Did Not Attend' (DNA). Some organisations in which psychotherapists may work will have cancellation and attendance policies which will indicate how matters of non-attendance must be managed.

Swift et al. (2012) concluded that there are six practices that may help to reduce the premature termination of therapy: educating the patient about therapy duration; clarifying the therapist's role; clarifying patterns of change; attending to clients' preferences; strengthening and supporting the client's hope; and assessing the progress of treatment. The importance of a clear agreement of a therapeutic contract between the therapist and client, should serve to promote the client's attendance (see Amos – Chapter 3.1, this volume). Offering clients their choice of appointment time and providing simple reminders could be two effective ways of increasing therapy attendance (Oldham et al., 2012).

When clients do not attend therapy consistently, questions related to their 'readiness' can be raised, although it is important to go beyond evaluating the client's motivation to reflect on the obstacles that may be faced by clients seeking help (Chantler, 2005; Inayat, 2007), and consider how service design aimed at overcoming practical barriers can support client's access to the therapy space (for example, see Johnson, 2011).

SELF-REFLECTION AND SUPERVISION

There is an ethical obligation for counsellors to receive supervision for their therapeutic work (BACP, 2018; UK Council for Psychotherapy, 2019). Clinical supervision offers a space for reflection upon therapeutic practice and, as a result, enables the development of skills essential for competent practice. Driscoll (2006) considers the use of experiential learning to develop further knowledge as one function of supervision. It is suggested that the exploration of personal feelings that can surface because of client work serves an important role if therapists are to work towards moment-to-moment provision of empathy, acceptance and genuineness. Reflexive practice can be considered an active process in which the practitioner purposefully explores their experiences (Willig, 2019). They may seek to create possible explanations for their experience, while remaining open to alternative possibilities, even if fundamental beliefs and values are brought into question (Scaife, 2010). A practitioner's reflection on their practice may take place within the context of supervision or on their own. It may be conducted using a structured model aimed at specifically supporting the development of reflexive practice (Johns, 2004; Mezirow, 1981; Nayak, 2019), or there may be no framework at all and simply involve the self-reflection of the therapist to themselves. Casement (1985) developed the notion of the 'internal supervisor' after noticing how trainees of counselling and psychotherapy would initially rely heavily on their supervisor for guidance in their therapeutic work. Over time trainees would gradually begin to emulate their supervisors, having internalised the qualities they observed. At this point, trainees were said to have developed the capacity to utilise perspectives and insights that are available to them as they work with their clients, both separately and autonomously from their supervisors.

Regardless of the method, the aim of reflexivity is to draw attention to the ways in which practitioners themselves may influence what emerges within the therapy relationship. See Creaner (Chapter 3.12, this volume) for a more in-depth discussion of the forms and purposes of clinical supervision.

REFERENCES

Bordin, E. S. (1979). The generalisability of the psychoanalytic concept of the working alliance. *Psychotherapy*, *16*, 252–260.

British Association of Counselling and Psychotherapy (BACP) (2018). *Ethical framework for the counselling professions.* Lutterworth: BACP.

Casement, P. (1985). *On learning from the patient.* London: Tavistock.

Chantler, K. (2005). From disconnection to connection: 'Race', gender and the politics of therapy. *British Journal of Guidance & Counselling*, *33*(2), 239–256.

Cooper, M., & Spinelli, E. (2012). A dialogue on dialogue. In L. Barnett & G. Madison (Eds), *Existential psychotherapy: Vibrancy, legacy and dialogue* (pp. 141–157). London: Routledge.

Cozolino, L. (2004). *The making of a therapist.* New York: W.W. Norton.

Driscoll, J. (2006). *Practising clinical supervision: A reflective approach for healthcare professionals.* Oxford: Elsevier Health Sciences.

Egan, G. (2006). *Essentials of skilled helping: Managing problems, developing opportunities.* Pacific Grove, CA: Brooks-Cole.

Flückiger, C., Del Re, A. C., Wampold, B. E., & Horvath, A. O. (2018). The alliance in adult psychotherapy: A meta-analytic synthesis. *Psychotherapy*, *55*(4), 316–340.

Inayat, Q. (2007). Islamophobia and the therapeutic dialogue: Some reflections. *Counselling Psychology Quarterly*, *20*(3), 287–293.

Johns, C. (2004). *Becoming a reflective practitioner*. Oxford: Wiley-Blackwell.

Johnson, C. (2011). Disabling barriers in the person-centered counseling relationship. *Person-Centered & Experiential Psychotherapies*, *10*(4), 260–273.

Mezirow, J. (1981). A critical theory of adult learning and education. *Adult Education Quarterly*, *32*(1), 3–24.

Miles, J. R., Anders, C., Kivlighan III, D. M., & Belcher Platt, A. A. (2021). Cultural ruptures: Addressing microaggressions in group therapy. *Group Dynamics: Theory, Research, and Practice*, *25*(1), 74.

Nayak, S. (2019). Black feminist diaspora spaces of social work critical reflexivity. In L. Wroe, R. Larkin & R. A. Maglajlic (Eds), *Social Work with Asylum Seekers, Refugees and Undocumented People: Going the extra mile* (pp. 41–56). London: Jessica Kingsley.

Okamoto, A., & Kazantzis, N. (2021). Alliance ruptures in cognitive-behavioral therapy: A cognitive conceptualization. *Journal of Clinical Psychology, 77*(2), 384–397.

Oldham, M., Kellett, S., Miles, E., & Sheeran, P. (2012). Interventions to increase attendance at psychotherapy: A meta-analysis of randomized controlled trials. *Journal of Consulting and Clinical Psychology, 80*(5), 928–939.

Preston, L. (2008). The edge of awareness: Gendlin's contribution to explorations of implicit experience. *International Journal of Psychoanalytic Self Psychology, 3*(4), 347–369.

Rennie, D. L. (1998). *Person-centred counselling: An experiential approach.* London: Sage.

Rogers, C. R. (1957). The necessary and sufficient conditions of therapeutic personality change. *Journal of Consulting Psychology, 21*(2), 95.

Safran, J. D., & Kraus, J. (2014). Alliance ruptures, impasses, and enactments: A relational perspective. *Psychotherapy, 51*(3), 381.

Safran, J. D., & Muran, J. C. (2000). Resolving therapeutic alliance ruptures: Diversity and integration. *Journal of Clinical Psychology, 56*(2), 233–243.

Safran, J. D., Muran, J. C., & Eubanks-Carter, C. (2011). Repairing alliance ruptures. *Psychotherapy, 48*(1), 80.

Safran, J. D., & Segal, Z. V. (1990). *Interpersonal process in cognitive therapy.* New York: Jason Aronson.

Scaife, J. (2010). *Supervising the reflective practitioner: An essential guide to theory and practice.* London: Routledge.

Swift, J. K., Greenberg, R. P., Whipple, J. L., & Kominiak, N. (2012). Practice recommendations for reducing premature termination in therapy. *Professional Psychology: Research and Practice, 43*(4), 379.

UK Council for Psychotherapy (UKCP) (2019). *UKCP code of ethics and professional practice.* London: UKCP.

Willig, C. (2019). Ontological and epistemological reflexivity: A core skill for therapists. *Counselling and Psychotherapy Research, 19*(3), 186–194.

Wills, F., & Sanders, D. (2013). *Cognitive behaviour therapy: Foundations for practice.* London: Sage.

RECOMMENDED READING

Clarkson, P. (2003). *The therapeutic relationship* (2nd ed.). London: Whurr.

This book explores Clarkson's conceptualisation of five different modalities of client–therapist relationships which may be considered effective in therapy. It presents an integrative principle upon which similarities and differences between therapeutic approaches are considered.

Eubanks, C. F., Sergi, J., & Muran, J. C. (2021). Responsiveness to ruptures and repairs in psychotherapy. In J. C. Watson & H. Wiseman (Eds), *The responsive psychotherapist: Attuning to clients in the moment* (pp. 83–103). Washington, DC: American Psychological Association.

This text explores therapeutic responsiveness to rupture–repair cycles in therapy relationships.

Nayak, S. (2019). Black feminist diaspora spaces of social work critical reflexivity. In L. Wroe, R. Larkin & R. A. Maglajlic (Eds), *Social work with asylum seekers, refugees and undocumented people: Going the extra mile* (pp. 41–56). London: Jessica Kingsley.

This chapter explores a Black feminist diasporic approach to critical reflexivity in social work. It offers a framework transferable to reflective practice in counselling.

3.10 THERAPEUTIC ENDINGS

INDIA AMOS

OVERVIEW AND KEY POINTS

The fact that the therapy relationship will end is inevitable from the outset of therapy, and therefore requires specific attention from practitioners. Whether it is the ending of an individual therapy session or bringing a therapy relationship to a final close, the end of therapy can be hugely significant for the client as well as the therapist. In this chapter, the significance of ending therapy is elucidated as well as drawing attention to the multiple ways in which therapeutic endings can manifest. The kind of interactions considered relevant to the end of therapy will be discussed, and the question of what constitutes a 'good' ending will be considered.

This chapter presents discussion on the following:

- The importance of therapy endings.
- Therapy tasks, including relapse prevention and reviewing therapeutic work.
- Planned versus unplanned endings.
- Considering referrals.
- Managing the impact of endings.

PREPARING FOR ENDING

Whether the client and therapist have been working together long term or have had engaged in brief therapy, it is likely that the client's relationship with the therapist has played a significant role in their efforts to change. It is understandable that drawing a therapeutic relationship to a close can evoke a strong emotional reaction for the client as well as for the practitioner. For some, the termination process has been referred to as the resolution to the ultimate alliance rupture (Eubanks-Carter, Muran and Safran, 2010), characterised by an opportunity for transformation (Quintana, 1993).

Providing ample time to prepare for the ending is considered an essential part of the therapeutic process. It is often the case within time-limited therapy that periodic reminders of how many sessions are remaining are offered to the client. In open-ended therapy, the question of when to end therapy is something to be negotiated between client and therapist. Research has shown that clinicians are generally poor at gauging their client's experience of the alliance (Norcross, 2010). Clinical tools such as the Session Rating Scale (SRS) (Johnson, 1995) and Outcome Rating Scale (ORS) (Miller and Duncan, 2000) have been developed to gain client feedback on their perception of the alliance and their progress in therapy and can be usefully employed to determine an answer to the question: 'What is a good outcome in psychotherapy?'. Symptom reduction could be seen as an indicator of effective psychotherapeutic work. Indeed, most outcome research aimed at investigating the effect of therapies does so by measuring the reduction of symptoms in clients (Cuijpers, 2019). Other research has illuminated the diversity in client-defined outcomes. A study by Binder et al. (2010), conducting in-depth interviews with former psychotherapy clients, found four categories of outcomes were deemed most important: (a) establishing new ways of relating to others; (b) less symptomatic distress or change in patterns of behaviour that used to bring suffering; (c) better self-understanding and insight; and (d) accepting and valuing oneself. In relation to his objective for clients, Carl Rogers (1961: 171) stated that clients 'seem to move toward more openly being a process, a fluidity, a changing … they are in flux, and seem more content to continue in this flowing current'. For therapists and clients working together without pre-determined criteria as to when to stop, the question of when to end is crucial. In a research study by Råbu, Binder and Haavind (2013) about negotiation of endings in open-ended therapy, one of the overarching themes that emerged related to the shared ideal of reaching a consensus about ending therapy. This agreement seemed to be based largely on an embodied, sensed affect as opposed to the use of arguments or metacommunication exclusively. This study highlighted how both parties within the relationship tended to be careful, considerate and sensitive about the other's feelings and reactions about ending.

In many therapeutic approaches, space is commonly left for both parties to reflect upon their work together, acknowledge the client's progress in therapy, and to explore feelings about ending the process. This requires that time is afforded for this exploration to take place in advance of the final session. For example, counsellors have reported the necessity to plan endings with clients from the onset of short-term counselling (Ling and Stathopoulou, 2021). Therapy sessions may become less frequent as the ending moves closer, perhaps moving from weekly to fortnightly (although this is not always the case or possible in some services).

THERAPEUTIC ENDING TASKS

There are several areas which can be explored towards the end of therapy. Assisting clients to integrate their experience of therapy, as well as reinforce positive changes made, is often considered to be one of the primary tasks at this stage. Summarising the work and the client's attainment of goals is also a central task undertaken at the end of therapy (whether articulated as such or not). At the beginning of therapy, specific goals for the client may have been agreed upon. While it is possible that the therapeutic work and the client's goals may have been regularly reviewed throughout the duration of therapy, the impending ending of therapy offers the opportunity to look explicitly at what the client has achieved and why this change has occurred. Attention may also be given to any specific areas in which the client might benefit from strengthening their skills. These might be considered some of the tasks associated with ending. For many therapists, it is important that clients themselves reflect on their process of change. After all, the client is responsible for any changes made. It is useful to facilitate their recognition of this, as it may go some way in embedding the positive changes observed.

Summarising any new coping strategies or techniques developed can be useful, as well as considering under what circumstances the client might seek to implement these methods in the future. The term 'relapse prevention' refers to the identification and prevention of the return of any old habits, or ways of living, that cause the client psychological distress. In Cognitive Behavioural Therapy (CBT), a more specific structure towards relapse prevention may take place. The last number of sessions may be used specifically to explore, with the client, how they might seek to maintain their progress and manage any setbacks. Of course, the client is likely to experience difficult events and painful feelings again in their lives beyond therapy. Helping the client to spot any warning signs related to the return of their difficulties can better equip them to manage any stress which may arise. The therapist may also offer information regarding the support that is available to the client beyond the end of therapy. Often it is recommended that the practitioner make the client aware of the invitation to return or to be re-referred to the service if the need arises (Gelso and Woodhouse, 2002).

Therapists might use specific techniques to encourage discussions related to the client's movement out of therapy. For instance, a goodbye letter to the client from the therapist may include a thoughtful account of the client's original problems and their developing resolution over the course of sessions. Positive achievements may be noted as well as the acknowledgement of difficulties and unresolved feelings. In some therapies, such as Cognitive Analytic Therapy (CAT) (see Pollitt–Chapter 5.3, this volume), letter writing is considered a central feature. Known as a reformulation letter, the therapist writes to the client an account of their life history, drawing attention to personal meanings and emotions, in addition to showing how present ways of living represent the strategies developed to cope with early life. As with all psychological formulations, it is emphasised that the explanation is provisional and therefore open to revision by clients. Therapeutic letters are intended to extend the work of therapy beyond the sessions themselves and have been identified by clients as cementing the therapeutic relationship (Hamill, Ried and Reynolds, 2008).

Sometimes therapists may offer a follow-up appointment. This may be between six and eight weeks after therapy is finished. The decision to invite the client back after a period can reassure the client that the therapeutic relationship, while professional, was genuine, and that a final session to 'check-in' with the client's progression is of interest to the therapist. Holmes (2012) notes how some clients may not opt for a follow-up appointment. Some clients find that following therapy they discover themselves to be much more independent in managing their distress than they may have anticipated. The idea of returning to therapy may be considered as a threat to their new-found freedom, and therefore they may not accept the invitation.

PLANNED VERSUS UNPLANNED ENDINGS

Ending what is likely to have been a close and significant relationship can be a powerful experience. Themes of loss and/or separation can arise (Holmes,

2010). Feelings of abandonment may appear (Salberg, 2010). In the case that grief, loss and abandonment have already been key themes throughout the therapy, there can be important processing potential at this juncture. The use of the word 'termination' to describe the ending of therapy, according to Schlesinger (2005: 4), suggests a mutually agreed ending of therapy, associated with the 'opportunity to work through' the thoughts and feelings brought up by the impending end. This description conveys that, for therapists, the ending is an active and integral part of therapy with its own processes and outcomes. Endings that are not mutually agreed have been given various labels. These include 'imposed', 'forced' or 'unplanned' endings. If the therapist changes for the client, the term being 'transferred' may be heard.

It is perhaps idealistic to expect all therapeutic relationships to come to a planned and well-managed ending. Sometimes the end of therapy is forced, meaning it was not foreseen. An unplanned ending can occur for a variety of reasons. It may be enforced by the client or the therapist. The client may drop out of therapy for an unknown reason, or an adverse event may render the client or therapist unable to continue. Additionally, the client may behave in a manner which is considered incompatible with the requirements of the service. Robson (2008) highlights the possible reasons for unexpected endings caused by the therapist, including changes in employment status or personal circumstances or ill-health or death. It is possible too that therapists may be held accountable for conduct that violates professional standards, leading to a break down in therapy relationships (see Richardson et al., 2008). It may be agreed between the client and therapist to end the therapy prematurely, or external factors may influence when it is forced to finish. For example, in some circumstances clients may be discharged for poor attendance (see Amos – Chapter 3.9, this volume).

Reeves (2010) has written extensively about his experience of an unplanned ending due to his client's suicide. As with any unplanned ending, it is vital that this type of sudden ending be considered, and plans made for the appropriate management in its event. Supervision is of the utmost importance in the event of any ending, unplanned or otherwise. Davis (2008) referred to the potential for therapists to feel anger when a client chooses to end therapy prematurely, as a sense of incompleteness to the work may arise. However, it is important for the therapist to remain mindful of their own vulnerabilities. The following case study depicts a counsellor processing their experience of an unexpected ending with a client.

CASE STUDY

AN UNPLANNED ENDING

Kenny works for a voluntary counselling agency, where policy stipulates therapists can offer eight sessions to clients. He has been working with client, Jaheda, for a month. She had sought therapy after being made redundant and being forced to sell her house. She reported feeling low in mood and less interested in socialising with friends. Therapy appeared to be going well. Their last session together was two weeks ago and since then Jaheda has stopped attending sessions and has not contacted the service to explain. Kenny felt confused about why Jaheda had decided to stop coming in and he wondered why she may have chosen this. In line with service protocols, Kenny sent Jaheda a letter to acknowledge her non-attendance and invite her to contact the service to discuss what action to take. When Jaheda did not respond to the letter within the allocated time, or return for sessions, Kenny was forced to discharge her from therapy in accordance with the service policy. In supervision, Kenny reflected on his feeling of sadness that Jaheda had not continued with therapy. He expressed a feeling of disappointment in himself, reflecting on the question of 'did I do enough?' With support from his supervisor on the content, Kenny chose to write Jaheda a therapeutic letter to acknowledge the ending of their therapeutic engagement. The letter summarised the issues they had discussed in therapy, and the progress that was made.

The case study above describes an unplanned ending which occurred because of the client's choice. Let's consider a different type of ending which may have occurred for Kenny and Jaheda.

CASE STUDY

AN IMPOSED ENDING

Jaheda and Kenny had been seeing each other for seven sessions. In that time, Jaheda appeared to have benefited greatly from exploring the impact of her changing employment status and was feeling more confident about making future career plans. Over the course of sessions Jaheda had begun to talk increasingly about her hopes of finding a girlfriend, and the anxiety she felt in relation to dating. Kenny considered this to be an important exploration for Jaheda within the broader context of her presentation and, despite her original presenting issues already being addressed, could see the advantage of continuing sessions with her. Jaheda requested to extend sessions, but this request could not be facilitated by the agency. Kenny and Jaheda had a final session together before ending therapy.

These examples have offered an insight into two ways in which the therapeutic relationship may end. It may be worth considering what impact either of these scenarios may have on the practitioner and client, and how they might be managed.

MAKING A REFERRAL ONWARDS

In some cases, it might be considered that the client is not yet ready to engage in therapy, and so sessions are stopped for that reason. Alternatively, it may be considered that the client requires a different form of therapy, or possibly in a different setting. Or the client may be 'stepped up' to a more intensive course of psychological therapy because of a lack of significant gains being achieved within the context of the current treatment.

Dryden (2008) draws attention to the expectation therapists often apply to themselves, thinking that they should be able to work with any client who seeks their help. There can be a pressure on qualified and trainee therapists, who may be seeking client contact hours to complete their training or needing to sustain a certain income. Dryden (2008) reminds us, however, to stay mindful of whether we can offer the client the best help possible, or whether another therapist may be a better alternative at that time. Working within our professional competence is an ethical commitment (British Association of Counselling and Psychotherapy, 2018) and practitioners may, in some cases, perceive that a client needs help that sits outside their professional limits of ability. Therefore, in this event, they may see the benefit in making onward referrals for clients.

MANAGING THE IMPACT OF THERAPEUTIC ENDINGS

Schlesinger (2005) has argued that therapists tend to have excessively high expectations when it comes to therapeutic endings, that practitioners often imagine endings to be more streamlined than is often possible. Therapists can often be left with a lot of unanswered questions in the event of an unplanned ending, finding it difficult not to know 'the end of the story'. As has been explored in this chapter, when clients do not return to therapy a multitude of thoughts and feelings can surface for the therapist, including worry, guilt, anger, confusion, relief, frustration and sadness. These feelings can be addressed within the context of supervision and, as has been reiterated throughout these last three chapters, approaches to reflexive practice can help practitioners to find optimal ways to support themselves when the end of therapy is prematurely initiated by the client. Endings which are forced due to external factors, like the alternative scenario in the case study detailed above, can also feel like an unsatisfactory ending.

Endings can be difficult. When the ending is unplanned it can be particularly difficult for the therapist and can require some attention within supervision. How endings are made sense of may depend on our theoretical orientation or worldview. However, it is likely that the aspects of ending discussed in this chapter will resonate with practitioners from across the spectrum of therapeutic approaches.

REFERENCES

Binder, P., Holgersen, H. and Nielsen, G. (2010). What is a "good outcome" in psychotherapy? A qualitative exploration of former patients' point of view, *Psychotherapy Research*, *20*(3), 285–294. doi: 10.1080/10503300903376338

British Association of Counselling and Psychotherapy (BACP) (2018). *Ethical framework for the counselling professions*. Lutterworth: BACP.

Davis, D. (2008). *Terminating therapy: A professional guide to ending on a positive note*. New York: John Wiley & Sons.

Dryden, W. (2008). Tailoring your counselling approach to different clients. In W. Dryden and A. Reeves (Eds), *Key issues for counselling in action* (2nd ed., pp. 117–131). London: Sage.

Cuijpers, P. (2019). Targets and outcomes of psychotherapies for mental disorders: an overview. *World Psychiatry*, *18*(3), 276–285.

Eubanks-Carter, C., Muran, J. C. and Safran, J. D. (2010). Alliance ruptures and resolution. In J. C. Muran and J. P. Barber (Eds), *The therapeutic alliance: An evidence-based guide to practice* (pp. 74–94). New York: Guilford Press.

Gelso, C. J. and Woodhouse, S. S. (2002). The termination of psychotherapy: what research tells us about the process of ending treatment. In G. S. Tryon (Ed.), *Counseling based on process research: Applying what we know* (pp. 334–369). Boston, MA: Allyn & Bacon.

Hamill, M., Ried, M. and Reynolds, S. (2008). Letters in cognitive analytic therapy: the patient's experience. *Psychotherapy Research*, *18*(5), 573–583.

Holmes, J. (2010). Termination in psychoanalytic psychotherapy: an attachment perspective. In J. Salberg (Ed.), *Good enough endings: Breaks, interruptions, and terminations from contemporary relational perspectives* (pp. 63–82). Abingdon, UK: Routledge.

Holmes, J. (2012). *Storr's art of psychotherapy* (3rd ed.). Abingdon, UK: Taylor & Francis.

Johnson, L. D. (1995). *Psychotherapy in the age of accountability*. New York: W.W. Norton.

Ling, L. S. and Stathopoulou, C. H. (2021). An exploration of ending psychotherapy: the experiences of volunteer counsellors. *Counselling and Psychotherapy Research*, *21*(3), 729–738.

Miller, S. D. and Duncan, B. L. (2000). *The outcome rating scale*. Author.

Norcross, J. C. (2010). The therapeutic relationship. In B. L. Duncan, S. D. Miller, B. E. Wampold and M. A. Hubble (Eds), *The heart and soul of change: Delivering what works in therapy* (2nd ed., pp. 113–141). Washington, DC: American Psychological Association.

Quintana, S. M. (1993). Toward an expanded and updated conceptualization of termination: implications for short-term, individual psychotherapy. *Professional Psychology: Research and Practice*, *24*, 426–432.

Råbu, M., Binder, P. E. and Haavind, H. (2013). Negotiating ending: a qualitative study of the process of ending psychotherapy. *European Journal of Psychotherapy & Counselling*, *15*(3), 274–295.

Reeves, A. (2010). *Counselling suicidal clients*. London: Sage.

Richardson, S., Cunningham, M., et al. (2008). *Broken boundaries: Stories of betrayal in relationships of care*. London: Witness.

Robson, M. (2008). Anticipating and working with unplanned endings. In W. Dryden and A. Reeves (Eds), *Key issues for counselling in action* (2nd ed., pp. 199–210). London: Sage.

Rogers, C. (1961). *On becoming a person: A therapist's view of psychotherapy*. Boston, MA: Houghton-Mifflin.

Salberg, J. (2010). Historical overview. In J. Salberg (Ed.), *Good enough endings: Breaks, interruptions, and terminations from contemporary relational perspectives*. Abingdon, UK: Routledge.

Schlesinger, H. J. (2005). *Endings and beginnings*. New York: The Analytic Press.

> **RECOMMENDED READING**
>
> Duncan, B., Miller, S. and Sparks, J. (2004). *The heroic client: A revolutionary way to improve effectiveness through client directed, outcome informed therapy*. San Francisco, CA: Jossey-Bass.
>
> A thought-provoking read which advocates for the client's voice in all aspects of therapy. It includes discussion of the use of formal feedback tools before ending individual therapy sessions as a way in which to guide future interactions.
>
> Vasquez, M. J., Bingham, R. P. and Barnett, J. E. (2008). Psychotherapy termination: clinical and ethical responsibilities. *Journal of Clinical Psychology*, 64(5), 653–665.
>
> This article outlines 12 recommendations for proactively addressing the end of therapy.
>
> Bolton, G., Howlett, S., Lago, C. and Wright. J. (2004). *Writing cures: An introductory handbook of writing in counselling and therapy*. London: Routledge.
>
> This book contains a chapter on the integrative use of writing by clients and therapists in Cognitive Analytic Therapy, which includes reference to goodbye letters.

3.11 PERSONAL AND PROFESSIONAL DEVELOPMENT

CHRIS ROSE

OVERVIEW AND KEY POINTS

Counselling and psychotherapy are relational experiences embedded in particular contexts, which are capable of profoundly changing both client and therapist. Personal and professional development, inextricably entwined, demand the therapist's long-term commitment to understanding how their own self engages with the other. It implies a growth in flexibility and creativity, in the capacity to reflect and to embrace ambiguity and difference. This chapter looks at:

- How we conceptualise the nature of both 'self' and 'development', shaped by socio-political and cultural contexts.
- The important contribution made by the training environment for present and future development.
- The fundamental importance of learning from the client and from supervision.
- The paradox that experience and confidence brings an increased appreciation of human complexity and our own limitations.

INTRODUCTION

In the context of counselling and psychotherapy, the personal and the professional are inextricably bound together, with no easy distinctions to be made. For every professional decision – which modality to train in, for example – there is a personal story that drives it. In trying to describe the professional therapist, we very quickly use relational qualities such as integrity, compassion, humility and wisdom. Developing personally means developing professionally and vice versa: there is no way to rinse the personal out of a profession that is based upon the ways in which humans relate at depth.

It is now accepted wisdom that the relational qualities of the therapist are more important in determining outcome than any other variable (Rønnestad and Skovholt, 2013; Skovholt and Jennings, 2004). This has assumed even greater significance as our understanding of therapy as a relational process has grown more complex. This has moved from the belief that the therapist could deal with their own difficulties through personal therapy and then provide a clear space to concentrate upon the client, to an acknowledgement that emotions will inevitably transfer from client to therapist and vice versa in the process of therapy, to a recognition that whatever is happening in the room is a joint creation of client and therapist. This appreciation of the co-constructed nature of any therapeutic relationship has meant that self-reflexivity has become increasingly incorporated into training textbooks, with a plethora of 'reflection points' and exercises; the challenge is to whole-heartedly engage with this key aspect of therapy. It is a democratic and universal requirement, with no exceptions!

WHAT IS THE SELF THAT WE ARE REFLECTING ON?

What do we mean by a 'self'? Our seeming obsession with 'self' – self-determination, self-expression, self-awareness, self-sufficiency, self-fulfilment – has arisen in a particular historical, socio-political and economic context. Western society promotes a definition of the self as unitary, capable of autonomous self-willed action to shape individual fortunes. Other cultures, if they are able to withstand the colonising onslaught of globalisation, may hold different views about the importance and definition of 'self'. It is important, therefore, to pause to reflect on what we mean when we use the word.

Any attempt to interrogate 'oneself' about intimate matters – feelings, desires, dilemmas, for example – reveals a variety of internal views, tensions, conflicts and paradoxes rather than one consistent voice. In addition, it is easy to recognise that our behaviour can radically change according to circumstance. If we attempt to explain this using the concept of 'role', there is the implicit existence of an actor – a 'true self' putting on different emotions, attitudes and behaviours, depending on the performance. In this version of the self, there are costumes to be discarded, layers to be peeled away to reveal the person within. Self-exploration and awareness here implies a type of archaeological excavation, revealed in phrases such as 'deep down', 'beneath it all' and the 'inner person'. What is concealed deep within becomes reified as 'authentic' whereas the more superficial layers are thought to be the product of social conditioning, and somehow less pure or unchanging.

The 'true self' is a phrase associated with Winnicott (1965), who is perhaps one of the most well-known theorists across all modalities of counselling and psychotherapy. Much of his writing does indeed lend itself to this topographical version of the self, but has also been used to support an intersubjective definition of self – which is a testament both to the subtleties of his work and the complexity of defining a person. His much quoted saying, 'there is no such thing as a baby' challenges us to acknowledge that 'baby' requires mother, father, ancestors and context. There is no self without other, for we are created in interaction. Despite the western contemporary insistence on autonomy and individuality, people become who they are in the context of others. The social, cultural, political, economic, historical and physical environments shape and give meaning to our lives. The powerful forces of family, class, society, race, religion, age, gender and physical ability teach us how to experience life and what sense to make of it. It is the patterns of responses that we learn in these complex multi-layered experiences that make us who we are.

Rather than a solid core, this version of self is an interpersonal, intrapersonal process. It is created moment to moment in our interactions with others, with past, present and imagined futures, with our internal dialogues. We can move from joy to despair, from compassion to cruelty, persecutor to victim, and so forth. The more we know about ourselves, the more we are able to recognise the paradoxical and sometimes disturbing range of our multiple selves.

It is our capacities to reflect, imagine and create meaning that create the sense of a unitary self. Life is generally chaotic, messy and confused. It is often only in retrospect that we 'understand' what is happening, through selecting and editing the complexity into a coherent narrative. Self-reflection can weave and hold together our multiple selves into a seemingly coherent unity.

Ideas about the self as multiple are well established within counselling and psychotherapy. Configurations of self (Mearns and Thorne, 2007), sub-personalities (Rowan, 1989), the internal society (Hermans, 2014) and the internal group (Rose, 2012) are examples of this way in which the complexity of human experience has been grappled with. Thinking about the self as multiple rather than unitary opens up new avenues for personal development while inviting a more complex appreciation of what development might mean.

WHAT DOES DEVELOPMENT MEAN?

Development as a hopeful vision of constant improvement may have been dismantled intellectually in postmodernism but still colours much of our thinking. We want to be 'more' confident, competent, knowledgeable, authoritative, loveable, wise, compassionate, effective, and so forth. It is important for any counsellor and psychotherapist to have chosen their own list of adjectives – in other words, to have thought seriously about what 'developing' might mean for them.

Psychotherapy and counselling attract clients largely because they offer the possibility of change; perhaps that is what attracts therapists also. Despite the mantra that we all are OK, we are aware that certain ways of living and relating are not. There is a difficult balance between these often less than conscious imperatives to improve and the recognition that as humans we cannot attain perfection. What constitutes 'good enough'?

For many clients, the therapist is the model of psychological health. They are imagined to have successful long-term, loving relationships, to be surrounded by friends and family and bolstered by financial security. The therapist's own self-definition often does not match this image – and may even be tinged with shame that it falls short.

There is, however, the argument that our own struggles are the very stuff that enables us to do the work we do, as expounded, for example, by Jung's archetype of the 'wounded healer' (Jung, 2014). This is part of a widespread discourse across centuries and cultures that links suffering with wisdom. But does personal development require that our own wounds be 'healed' so that we can help others? Or is it the case, as Adams (2014) points out, that there is no such thing as the 'Untroubled Therapist' and personal development involves letting go of any illusion that we can be cleansed and freed from our personal struggles? Just as it is helpful to let go of the idea of a unitary self, so it is important to move away from seeing development as a linear, unidirectional movement. We need more complex, dynamic multidimensional images.

Personal and professional development, I suggest, implies a growth in flexibility and creativity, in the capacity to reflect, and in the tolerance of ambiguity and difference, a widening of what can be seen, heard and understood both cognitively and emotionally. Taking the idea of the 'internal group' as an example, what might this involve?

Using the idea of the self as a group, the driving force of development is identifying, listening to and responding imaginatively to the voices that populate our thoughts. It means giving a place not only to those more clearly articulated internal voices, but also to those in the background, to some as well as psyche. The more we can discover about our group members, the more it becomes possible to develop a coherent but flexible and creative internal conversation. The internal facilitator, who is a central character in this process of group development, has tough but vital tasks: finding a place for the many voices, however negative or difficult; drawing boundaries; shaping a nuanced and considered group discourse.

This process is fluctuating, uneven, circuitous and rarely smooth. Just as in other groups, the internal group has periods of stagnation, often leading into crisis and instability, which may go on to provide the impetus for genuine change. The relationship between discomfort and growth is an everyday part of therapy. Where are the clients who come into counselling because they are comfortable and think they would like to shake themselves up? Aren't we driven to change by discomfort?

Experiences that disturb both how we feel and how we think can produce long-lasting changes. To learn something new that is not trivial involves a letting go of previous attitudes and ideas. Training courses destabilise and deskill us in the process of expanding our understandings and emotional tolerance. Challenging clients push us into new territories of intellectual and experiential learning. Changes in personal circumstances require us to develop new resources. Personal and professional development, like all worthwhile learning, costs us something before it rewards us.

CONTEXT

We are who we are in the context of the environments that we inhabit – personal, physical, socio-political, environmental, and so forth. The context is not the backdrop to the play, but is seamlessly integrated into who we are and who we might become. It shapes our thoughts, attitudes and emotions and the opportunities that are available to us. Development means struggling wherever possible beyond some of these constraints in order to genuinely hear, see and respect those who are other or different.

The ways in which we have learnt to protect ourselves are parts of the self that all of us are fearful of letting go, even when they have ceased to serve us well. These have been effective in previous contexts, which is why they are so embedded; so much a part of ourselves that there will be aspects that we cannot recognise without the mirror that others hold up to us. Trying to become aware of how we behave, how we relate to others and to the world is a constant challenge for the therapist, and the context within which this challenge is set is always moving. Global movements, pandemics, political instabilities, technological advances and the climate emergency are part of the larger shifting scene within which changes in personal circumstances and work environments render it impossible to complete the work of personal and professional development (PPD).

The end is out of sight, but the beginning is often to be found in the context of training.

TRAINING...

The challenge of self-reflection may be encountered for the first time in the context of training, which in itself presents a dilemma. Training inevitably involves some form of assessment and judgement, in whatever style it is carried out. Students are simultaneously challenged intellectually, exposed to new ideas and theories, and asked to examine their own experiences, attitudes and ways of being. In some instances, the combination provides an enormously powerful and effective stimulus to learning, but often the reality of needing to 'pass' constricts these possibilities.

In a context of assessment, it can be difficult for the training course to provide and the student to experience that crucial balance of security and challenge that is needed for meaningful personal learning. Already stretched intellectually and emotionally by theories and practice, it is a step too far for some students to relax their grip on the version of themselves that they are familiar with.

The relationship with authority – being instructed to self-reflect or being required to have personal therapy – can strangle self-exploration and openness, and this often comes at a time before the student has examined the issue of authority in their own lives. This may be compounded by the students' need for guidance and clarity in models and practice to navigate the new ideas and experiences they are encountering. Trainers and supervisors play a highly influential part in the students' development, often with phases of idealisation/denigration.

The counterbalance to all this is the huge potential for personal development that training offers. It has very particular characteristics that may lay down foundations, positive and negative, for future development. Intellectual stimulus in combination with relational challenges and peer support in learning groups and particularly PPD groups (Godward, Dale and Smith, 2020; Rose, 2008) provides fertile grounds for self-awareness, as does writing personal and/or learning journals (Wright and Bolton, 2012).

Here it becomes possible for students to identify and work with their core personal issues that they consider to be dominant in their lives. Aponte and Kissil (2016) call these the 'signature themes' that need identifying in order to understand their impact, real and potential, upon the client work.

...AND BEYOND

Having completed the task of qualification and found work as a therapist, it becomes possible and necessary to take ownership of one's own self-development. There is a continued controversy concerning the value and importance of personal therapy in training, but at least 80% of therapists enter into it at some point and consider it to be valuable (McLeod and McLeod, 2014). The demands of client work bring home the message that no single model can adequately respond to human complexities, and that drawing upon the self is vital.

Whatever is happening in the therapy room is a joint creation, so it is no surprise that learning for the client will involve learning for the therapist also. Evidence from a survey of more than 4,000 psychotherapists from 20 different countries put 'experience in therapy with clients' as the major impact upon their professional development. The supervisory relationship is ranked next in order, demonstrating its central role throughout training and beyond (Orlinsky et al., 2001, cited in Rønnestad and Skovholt, 2003).

Many other avenues for PPD encountered in training continue to be highly valued by experienced counsellors: further study, learning and PPD groups, journalling, for example. In addition, many find themselves learning through teaching and supervising others.

Any therapist who works over a long time-span will experience blows to their own self-worth – clients who fail to attend, to respond, to move on, who attack and denigrate, who self-harm or even kill themselves. How the therapist responds to these experiences is critical.

> [A]s practitioners feel more confident and assured as professionals with the passing of time, also they generally see more clearly the limitations in what they can accomplish. Fuelling this process of increased realism are the 'series of humiliations' which therapists experience over time. If these 'blows to the ego' are processed and integrated into the therapists' self-experience, they may contribute to the paradox of increased sense of confidence and competence while also feeling more humble and less powerful as a therapist. (Rønnestad and Skovholt, 2003: 38)

In addition to these 'humiliations', time spent working intimately with the distress and trauma of others takes its toll. Exhaustion and burnout can be avoided or mitigated with space for reflection, along with supportive but challenging supervision and peer relationships (Skovholt and Trotter-Matheson, 2016; Vetere and Stratton, 2016). Donna Orange (2016) talks about her own internal support group of writers and philosophers, whom she values for their sustaining wisdom.

HOW

The rationale – the 'why' of PPD – is clearly established. The 'how' is hugely varied, individual, idiosyncratic and, above all, creative. PPD is a particular type of learning, and therapists have different learning styles and ways of engaging and challenging their multiple selves. Groups, journals, art, sport, academic learning, dance, reading, writing, singing, movement, nature and more can all provide rich ground for new learning. The list is extensive, and McLeod and McLeod (2014) offer a comprehensive survey.

The key ingredients in whatever format are curiosity, imagination, reflexivity and an engagement with others. The 'others' might be internal voices, self-dialogues, colleagues, friends, strangers or a sense of the transcendent. A monologue is rarely the vehicle for significant learning. We need interruptions and challenges to enlarge our thinking and experiencing.

CONCLUSION

It has become part of the accepted wisdom that as therapists we can only engage with our clients' worlds to the degree that we can engage with our own. Our own 'signature themes' may never disappear but the more we have acknowledged and explored them, the better able we are to recognise their presence in our client work, use them creatively or, at the very least, mitigate their impact.

With experience it becomes increasingly obvious that the personal and the professional cannot be split apart. Decisions to join a professional organisation, to subscribe to a particular ethical code, to be an active or passive member, are all personal decisions that are open to self-scrutiny and further understanding. The demand for integrity has to be like the lettering in the stick of rock, running throughout the person of the therapist, their practice and their organisation.

Above all, experience brings an increased sensitivity both to the complexities of human experience and to the limits of therapy and the therapist. Any simplistic or reductionist accounts of the human condition are antithetical to personal and professional development. An increased confidence as a therapist is accompanied by the appreciation of the limitations of therapy and therapists. The more we know, the more we realise how little we know.

Intellectual effort, emotional engagement and creativity stand out as the vital qualities that fuel PPD. It is a lifelong process that requires a commitment to learning and self-reflection, and although that might sound dull and worthy, this paradoxically comes hand in hand with an appreciation that we need to take ourselves less seriously! Having fun has got to be somewhere on the list of PPD activities!

REFERENCES

Adams, M. (2014) *The Myth of the Untroubled Therapist*. London and New York: Routledge.
Aponte H.J. and Kissil, K. (Eds) (2016) *The Person of the Therapist Training Model: Mastering the Use of Self*. New York: Routledge.
Hermans, H.J.M. (2014) Self as a society of I-positions: a dialogical approach to counselling. *Journal of Humanistic Counselling*, 53: 134–159.
Godward, J., Dale, H. and Smith, C. (2020) *Personal Development Groups for Trainee Counsellors: An Essential 'Companion*. London and New York: Routledge.
Jung, C.G. (2014) *The Practice of Psychotherapy* (2nd ed.). London: Routledge.
McLeod, J. and McLeod, J. (2014) *Personal and Professional Development for Counsellors, Psychotherapists and Mental Health Practitioners*. Maidenhead: Open University Press.
Mearns, D. and Thorne, B. (2007) *Person Centred Counselling in Action* (3rd ed.). London: Sage.
Orange, D. (2016) *Nourishing the Inner Life of Clinicians and Humanitarians*. Abingdon, UK, and New York: Routledge.
Rønnestad, M.H. and Skovholt, T.M. (2003) The journey of the counselor and therapist: research findings and perspectives on professional development. *Journal of Career Development*, 30(1): 5–44.
Rønnestad, M.H. and Skovholt, T.M. (2013) *The Developing Practitioner: Growth and Stagnation of Therapists and Counsellors*. New York: Routledge.
Rose, C. (2008) *The Personal Development Group: The Student's Guide*. London: Karnac.
Rose, C. (Ed.) (2012) *Self Awareness and Personal Development: Resources for Psychotherapists and Counsellors*. Basingstoke: Palgrave Macmillan.
Rowan J. (1989) *Subpersonalities: The People Inside Us*. London: Routledge.
Skovholt, T.M. and Jennings, L. (2004) *Master Therapists: Exploring Expertise in Therapy and Counselling*. New York: Allyn and Bacon.
Skovholt, T.M. and Trotter-Matheson, M. (2016) *The Resilient Practitioner: Burnout Prevention and Self-care Strategies for the Helping Professions*. London and New York: Routledge.
Vetere, A. and Stratton, P. (Eds) (2016) *Interacting Selves: Systemic Solutions for Personal and Professional Development in Counselling and Psychotherapy*. London and New York: Routledge.
Winnicott, D.W. (1965) *Maturational Processes and the Facilitating Environment*. London: Hogarth Press.
Wright, J. and Bolton, G. (2012) *Reflective Writing in Counselling and Psychotherapy*. London: Sage.

RECOMMENDED READING

McLeod, J. and McLeod, Julia (2014) *Personal and Professional Development for Counsellors, Psychotherapists and Mental Health Practitioners*. Maidenhead: Open University Press.

A comprehensive, research-based exploration of the why and hows of PPD, including extensive learning tasks.

Rose, C. (Ed.) (2012) *Self Awareness and Personal Development: Resources for Psychotherapists and Counsellors*. Basingstoke: Palgrave Macmillan.

This book offers a range of approaches to explore multiple selves, including music, the written word, visual imagery, the natural environment, transcendence and embodiment.

Wright, J. and Bolton, G. (2012) *Reflective Writing in Counselling and Psychotherapy*. London: Sage.

This book illustrates the varied ways that reflective writing can be used within different modalities and forms of counselling, with examples and suggestions for self-exploration.

3.12 CLINICAL SUPERVISION

MARY CREANER

OVERVIEW AND KEY POINTS

It is widely accepted that clinical supervision is an essential professional activity in counselling and psychotherapy training to facilitate supervisee professional development and client welfare (Bernard and Goodyear, 2019). Supervision is also a mandated career-long requirement by many professional organisations for their practising members (e.g., British Association for Counselling and Psychotherapy (BACP)). Depending on the professional organisation, various supervision criteria (i.e., ratio of supervision hours to client hours, format and frequency of supervision sessions, etc.) need to be met for accreditation/re-accreditation purposes. Hence, supervision plays a central role in the career-span of the counsellor and therapist. With reference to this background, this chapter provides an overview of the following:

- The purpose of supervision in counselling and therapy.
- Negotiating the supervision relationship and working alliance.
- Feedback and evaluation in supervision.
- Opportunities and challenges in supervision.

THE PURPOSE OF SUPERVISION IN COUNSELLING AND THERAPY

Historically, supervision in the counselling/therapy tradition was seen as a logical application of the therapy approach being taught, to the supervisee's professional development (Carroll, 2007). As specific supervision models (e.g., Hawkins and McMahon, 2020; Page and Wosket, 2001) inevitably evolved, there has been a shift to understanding supervision as a learning endeavour focused on the practice being undertaken rather than solely on the person of the supervisee (Carroll, 2007). Embedded in many supervision models is what Falender and Shafranske (2004: 3) refer to as the 'pillars' of supervision, namely: the supervisory relationship (the working alliance), inquiry (focus on what is happening in supervision and therapy) and educational praxis (personalised educational interventions to facilitate supervisee learning).

There are many definitions and descriptions of clinical supervision available, due in part to different perspectives arising from the context in which supervision is offered, part due to the complexity of the supervision relationship, and part due to the inadequate conceptualisation of supervision (Milne et al., 2008). Nonetheless, most agree that the main purposes are to advance supervisee professional development, safeguard client welfare and provide for gatekeeping in the profession (Bernard and Goodyear, 2019).

The primary functions of supervision, as outlined by Proctor (1987), are three-fold, specifically: (1) a normative function which promotes accountability, quality control and ethical best practice; (2) a formative function to facilitate learning and competency development within the profession; and (3) a restorative function to buffer the potential stresses of the work (and training), provide support and foster an attitude of self-care. This framework remains a useful resource for the supervisor in holding the primary foci of supervision in the foreground. It is also an accessible framework for the supervisee to reflect on their learning needs as they prepare for supervision (Creaner, 2014).

Depending on what aspects of practice are brought to supervision for reflection, and the learning needs of the supervisee therein, the emphasis may vary across these three functions at a given time. However, all three functions need to be accommodated within the frame of good supervision. For example, the BACP (2018: 23) propose that 'good supervision is much more than case management' and requires attention to the relational circumstance in which it occurs. In contrast, supervisors may be overly supportive or protective of the relationship at the expense of appropriately challenging the supervisee or providing corrective feedback as the need arises (Heckman-Stone, 2004). Hence, there is a need for supervisors to balance between the three functions of supervision and ensure that each is attended to proportionately in the context of the supervision relationship.

NEGOTIATING THE SUPERVISION RELATIONSHIP AND WORKING ALLIANCE

The supervision relationship may be considered as the pivot on which all supervision endeavours flourish or flounder. Of all of the constructs discussed in relation to supervision, the *relationship* has received considerable attention in the literature (Bernard and Goodyear, 2019). A frequently cited framework within the supervision relationship is that of Bordin's (1983: 37–38) 'working alliance', which comprises 'mutual agreements' between the supervisee and the supervisor with reference to the 'goals' or what is to be accomplished in supervision (e.g., skills development, case conceptualisation); the 'tasks' or methods used for the attainment of the supervision goals (e.g., listening to recordings of client sessions, role play); and the 'bonds' or mutual investment by both the supervisor and supervisee in the supervision process. In other words, setting up a supervision relationship requires teasing out an overall working agreement so that the boundaries of supervision with reference to the relationship, roles, responsibilities and rights of all parties are clear from the outset (see Creaner, 2014, for a learning agreement template).

Agreement on the goals of supervision will naturally be influenced by a variety of factors and the developmental level of the supervisee will elicit particular areas for discussion. For example, in the training situation, the agreement of goals will need to accommodate requirements of the training course (e.g., programme learning outcomes) and their professional accreditation criteria. Similarly, in the case of qualified practitioners, accreditation/re-accreditation criteria will also need to be explicit. Other factors for consideration include the theoretical approach in which the supervisee is training or practising, the context of the client work (e.g., trauma work), the context of the organisation (e.g., a health service), the professional/ethical context (e.g., code of ethics, inclusive practice), and so forth.

With reference to agreement on the tasks of supervision, Bordin (1983) suggests that these are inextricably linked to the specified goals of supervision and the means or methods by which these goals can be facilitated. A variety of methods and interventions (e.g., feedback, critical reflection, monitoring client outcome, etc.) are available and good supervision provides for multiple methods (Milne et al., 2008). Different supervisors will have different styles and, likewise, supervisees will have individual learning preferences. Optimally, the tasks of supervision need to be negotiated and personalised within supervision (see Wallace and Cooper, 2015, on *supervision personalisation forms*). Such negotiation and individualisation can contribute to a sense of mutuality in the supervision process and enrich the supervisory bond (Bordin, 1983).

In addition to agreeing on the goals, tasks and bonds of supervision, the agreement should also refer to the practicalities of the work (e.g., frequency and length of supervision sessions, arrangements in the case of emergencies). Clear agreements serve the interests of the supervisor, the supervisee and their client, and need to be reviewed regularly as the supervision relationship develops and the learning needs of the supervisee evolve (Bernard and Goodyear, 2019).

THE IMPACT OF THE SUPERVISION RELATIONSHIP

Many positive and negative consequences have been attributed to the quality of the supervisory relationship. On the positive side, good supervision relationships have been seen to contribute to skills development, self-awareness and confidence building (Weaks, 2002; Wheeler and Richards, 2007). In addition, good supervision enhances supervisee satisfaction (Weaks, 2002), encourages the disclosure of practice issues (Sweeney and Creaner, 2014) and promotes culturally sensitive practice (Soheilian, et al., 2014).

Although many studies indicate that the majority of supervisees (both trainee and qualified) experience supervision as useful and growth promoting (e.g., Weaks, 2002; Wheeler and Richards, 2007), this is not always the case. Research has demonstrated that negative consequences are frequently experienced by supervisees and the impact of such experiences include decreased disclosure (Sweeney and Creaner, 2014), supervisee distress, feelings of inadequacy and perceived negative impacts upon their clients (Chircop Coleiro, Creaner and Timulak, 2022). While negative experiences may also bring the opportunity to openly discuss the difficulty and deepen the supervision alliance, this is unlikely to happen in the absence of a psychologically safe environment (Page and Wosket, 2001).

As discussed by Ellis and colleagues (2014), poor supervision can range from inadequate to harmful supervision. In the former, inadequate supervision refers to instances when 'the supervisor fails to provide the minimal level of supervisory care as established by their discipline or profession' (e.g., supervisors not attending to the normative, formative and restorative aspects of supervision) (Ellis et al., 2014: 437). Harmful supervision arises from 'supervisory practices that result in psychological, emotional, and/or physical harm or trauma to the supervisee' (e.g., boundary violations whereby the supervisee feels shamed, pathologised, etc.) (Ellis et al., 2014: 440).

In a cross-cultural comparative study (Ellis et al., 2015) between supervisees in the Republic of Ireland (RI) (n=149) and the United States (US) (n=151), the results indicated that, at some stage in their career, 92.4% (RI) and 86.4% (US) of the supervisees received inadequate supervision (e.g., no supervision contract, client work not monitored) and that 51.7% (RI) and 39.7% (US) of the supervisees had experienced harmful supervision (e.g., supervisor was abusive). Of further note in this study was that supervisees did not always identify inadequate or harmful supervision as such, indicating that supervisees may need further information on what they have a right to expect from supervision. Considering the negative impact of such experiences on the supervisees, and the unknown impact on their clients, supervisees need to be actively supported in expressing and addressing any difficulties they may encounter, particularly in the training context, where power differentials are salient (Chircop Coleiro et al., 2022; Ellis et al., 2015; Knox et al., 2021).

FEEDBACK AND EVALUATION IN SUPERVISION

Both trainee and qualified supervisees welcome and seek frequent, clear, direct and balanced feedback which offers guidance for further development (Heckman-Stone, 2004; Weaks, 2002). Ambiguous feedback and a lack of balance between affirming and corrective feedback are seen as contributing factors to poor supervision (Chircop Coleiro et al., 2022). From the perspective of a supervisor, providing feedback and evaluation are often seen as challenging tasks, especially if the supervisee demonstrates resistance to receiving feedback (Carroll, 2014). However, as feedback is a key intervention in supervision and a means by which learning is advanced (Milne et al., 2008), supervisors and supervisees need to openly address the challenges that providing feedback may present. Supervisees may also be encouraged to provide regular feedback to their supervisors and seek routine feedback from their clients, optimally through objective outcome measures (see Zhu and Luke, 2021).

Within supervision, all feedback is a statement of evaluation, whether formative or summative. Evaluation is what ultimately distinguishes supervision from counselling or therapy and is an essential element of all supervision (Bernard and Goodyear, 2019), whatever the developmental level of the supervisee. Hence, evaluation is intrinsic to reflective supervision 'where review is central to growth' and includes both evaluation of the work done and also planning for continuing development (Carroll, 2014: 53).

While widely endorsed as a necessity in supervision, particularly in training, little is empirically known about the process or effect of evaluation on the supervisees or on outcomes for their clients. Even less is known about the evaluative process with qualified and more experienced practitioners. Although evaluation may not be an explicit feature in the supervision of qualified practitioners (though best practice would suggest that it ought to be explicit in the supervision contract), it is an ever present phenomenon. Beyond training, many professional organisations require reports from supervisors for accreditation and re-accreditation purposes (e.g., BACP).

Evaluation is also linked to the gatekeeping function of supervision, wherein the monitoring of ethical, legal and professional practice for client welfare is a constant responsibility of supervisors across the career-span of supervisees (Bernard and Goodyear, 2019). It is therefore important for supervisors to critically reflect on and make explicit what is being evaluated, when that evaluation will occur, how the evaluation will be delivered and how evaluation of supervision can be elicited. In addition, such criteria need to be explicitly and collaboratively discussed at the outset and form part of the supervision contract (Falender and Shafranske, 2004).

OPPORTUNITIES AND CHALLENGES IN SUPERVISION

SUPERVISOR TRAINING

As mentioned, developments in supervision have contributed to conceptualising supervision as a professional activity in its own right, requiring professional competencies which are different from those of the counsellor/therapist (American Psychological Association (APA), 2014). Along with this understanding, increased focus is being placed on supervisor training. As a consequence, increasingly professional organisations and health services are requiring their supervisors to undertake training and supervision competence frameworks are being developed. For example, BACP recently developed a *Supervision Competence Framework* comprising eight core competence domains (e.g., the supervisory relationship; equality, diversity and inclusion; individual needs of the supervisee) based on a wide-ranging review of supervision research literature (BACP, 2021). In addition, professional organisations are providing supervision practice guidelines (e.g., APA, 2014), and supervision training curricula (e.g., BACP, 2021).

TECHNOLOGY, SOCIAL MEDIA AND SUPERVISION

The use of technology in clinical supervision is not a new phenomenon (e.g., live supervision, bug-in-ear). As technology and web-based activity has become a facet of everyday life, it is not surprising that it has been readily adopted in the supervision domain, as evident in the increasing literature focusing on the use of web technology (e.g., email, video-conferencing) in supervision. This development is partly driven by pragmatic factors (e.g., access to supervisors in rural communities) along with the flexibility and decreased costs of travel that technology provides (Rousmaniere, 2014). More recently, online supervision has also been driven by the challenges of meeting face to face during the Covid-19 pandemic and related public health restrictions (Watters and Northey, 2020). However, as with face-to-face counselling and psychotherapy, there are a number of ethical, legal, professional and practical considerations with reference to the use of internet technology in supervision, for example, issues of confidentiality with regard to the security of communication channels, the implications of providing supervision outside one's professional jurisdiction and/or the country of the supervisee, competence in the use of technology for both the supervisor and supervisee (Renfro-Michel, Rousmaniere and Spinella, 2016). Again, as with other aspects of supervision, the use of technology needs to be accommodated within the supervision contract and also needs to include contingency plans, as relevant, in the event of emergencies, technological breakdowns, and so forth (Rousmaniere, 2014).

Within this arena, the use of social media has also become ubiquitous in recent years and also presents a further area for clarification in supervision with reference to supervisor's and supervisee's social media presence (Creaner, 2020). This conversation may be included in the initial contract and address such areas as the supervisor's policy on accepting social media 'friend' requests from supervisees, the ethics of online searches for supervisor/supervisee/client information and the ethical implications of social media contact with clients (APA, 2014).

SUPERVISION RESEARCH

While the quantity and quality of supervision research has increased in recent decades, many gaps remain in our knowledge and understanding of supervision. For instance, and by no means exhaustive, we need to understand more fully the impact of good and poor supervision on supervisee and client outcomes. In seeking a robust evidence base, we also need to understand more fully how developmental, contextual and cultural factors influence and affect the supervision process. Furthermore, the area of supervisor training, competency development and evaluation are pertinent areas of inquiry.

Considering the multiplicity of variables and factors inherent in the supervision relationship and the counselling/therapy relationship, it is a challenging area of inquiry. Repeatedly, we hear from those who undertake supervision research, particularly systematic reviews (e.g., Kühne et al., 2019; Wheeler and Richards, 2007) and meta-analyses (e.g., Chircop Coleiro et al., 2022), of the difficulties concerning the lack of methodological rigour in studies, the lack of a clear conceptualisation of supervision and the diversity of measures employed make it difficult to draw conclusions across studies that could inform practice (Wheeler, Aveline and Barkham, 2011). Nonetheless, these challenges present many opportunities for further development. Wheeler and colleagues (2011) envisioned a research agenda for supervision being developed, so that a common set of measures are agreed and supervision practitioners and researchers collaborate in the research endeavour.

CONCLUSION

As supervision seeks to collaboratively and critically reflect on practice, an opportunity is also presented to critically reflect on the quality of supervision provided. The fact that there is wide acceptance of its usefulness and effectiveness in counselling and therapy may potentially inhibit critical reflection on the times when it is not experienced as useful or effective. As every encounter between a supervisor and supervisee is a unique experience, each supervisory relationship will also be a unique experience. Hence, the challenge to supervisors is to flexibly engage with the person of the supervisee to facilitate professional development, scaffold and promote best practice, provide support and, in light of the inherent hierarchy, work towards a collaborative, growth-enhancing and equal relationship.

REFERENCES

American Psychological Association (2014) *Guidelines for Clinical Supervision in Health Service Psychology*. Washington, DC: APA. Available at www.apa.org/about/policy/guidelines-supervision.pdf (accessed 15 January 2022).

Bernard, J.M. and Goodyear, R.K. (2019) *Fundamentals of Clinical Supervision* (6th ed.). Upper Saddle River, NJ: Pearson.

Bordin, E.S. (1983) A working alliance based model of supervision. *Counseling Psychologist*, 11: 35–41.

British Association for Counselling and Psychotherapy (2018) *Ethical Framework for the Counselling Professions*. Lutterworth: BACP. Available at www.bacp.co.uk/events-and-resources/ethics-and-standards/ethical-framework-for-the-counselling-professions/ (accessed 10 January 2022).

British Association for Counselling and Psychotherapy (2021) *Supervision Competence Framework and Training Curriculum*. Lutterworth: BACP. Available at www.bacp.co.uk/events-and-resources/ethics-and-standards/competences-and-curricula/supervision-curriculum/ (accessed 10 January 2022).

Carroll, M. (2007) One more time: what is supervision? *Psychotherapy in Australia*, 13(3): 34–40.

Carroll, M. (2014) *Effective Supervision for the Helping Professions*. London: Sage.

Chircop Coleiro, A., Creaner, M. and Timulak, L. (2022) The good, the bad, and the less than ideal in clinical supervision: a qualitative meta-analysis of supervisee experiences. *Counselling Psychology Quarterly*, https://doi.org/10.1080/09515070.2021.2023098

Creaner, M. (2014) *Getting the Best Out of Supervision in Counselling and Psychotherapy: A Guide for the Supervisee*. London: Sage.

Creaner, M. (2020) The role of social media in counselling and psychotherapy. In R. Tribe and J. Morrissey (Eds), *Handbook of Professional and Ethical Issues for Psychologists, Counsellors and Psychotherapists* (3rd ed., pp. 117–128). Abingdon, UK: Routledge.

Ellis, M.V., Berger, L., Hanus, A.E., Ayala, E.E., Swords, B.A. and Siembor, M. (2014) Inadequate and harmful clinical supervision: testing a revised framework and assessing occurrence. *The Counseling Psychologist*, 42: 434–472.

Ellis, M.V., Creaner, M., Hutman, H. and Timulak, L. (2015) A comparative study of clinical supervision in the Republic of Ireland and the United States. *Journal of Counseling Psychology*, 62(4): 621–631.

Falender, C.A. and Shafranske, E.P. (2004) *Clinical Supervision: A Competency-based Approach*. Washington, DC: American Psychological Association.

Hawkins, P. and McMahon, A. (2020) *Supervision in the Helping Professions* (5th ed.). Maidenhead: Open University Press.

Heckman-Stone, C. (2004) Trainee preferences for feedback and evaluation in clinical supervision. *The Clinical Supervisor*, 22(1): 21–33.

Knox, S., Goertz, M., Mak, T.W., Pinto-Coelho, K.G. and Hill, C.E. (2021) Immediacy in supervision: supervisees' perspectives on positive and negative events. *Journal of Psychotherapy Integration*. http://dx.doi.org/10.1037/int0000270

(Continued)

(*Continued*)

Kühne, F., Maas, J., Wiesenthal, S. and Weck, F. (2019) Empirical research in clinical supervision: a systematic review and suggestions for future studies. *BMC Psychology*, 7(1): 1–11.

Milne, D., Aylott, H., Fitzpatrick, H. and Ellis, M.V. (2008) How does clinical supervision work? Using a 'best evidence synthesis' approach to construct a basic model of supervision. *The Clinical Supervisor*, 27(2): 170–190.

Page, S. and Wosket, V. (2001) *Supervising the Counsellor: A Cyclical Model* (2nd ed.). Hove: Brunner-Routledge.

Proctor, B. (1987) Supervision: a co-operative exercise in accountability. In M. Marken and M. Payne (Eds), *Enabling and Ensuring: Supervision in Practice* (pp. 21–34). Leicester: National Youth Bureau, Council for Education and Training in Youth and Community Work.

Renfro-Michel, E., Rousmaniere, T. and Spinella, L. (2016) Technological innovations in clinical supervision: promises and challenges. In T. Rousmaniere and E. Renfro-Michel (Eds), *Using Technology to Enhance Clinical Supervision* (pp. 3–19). Alexandria, VA: American Counseling Association/Wiley.

Rousmaniere, T.G. (2014) Using technology to enhance clinical supervision and training. In C.E. Watkins and D. Milne (Eds), *International Handbook of Clinical Supervision* (pp. 204–237). New York: Wiley.

Soheilian, S., Inman, A.G., Klinger, R., Isenberg, D. and Kulp, L. (2014) Multicultural supervision: supervisees' reflections on culturally competent supervision. *Counselling Psychology Quarterly*, 27(4): 379–392.

Sweeney, J. and Creaner, M. (2014) What's not being said? Recollections of nondisclosure in clinical supervision while in training. *British Journal of Guidance and Counselling*, 42: 211–224.

Wallace, K. and Cooper, M. (2015) Development of supervision personalisation forms: a qualitative study of the dimensions along which supervisors' practices vary. *Counselling and Psychotherapy Research*, 15(1): 31–40.

Watters, Y. and Northey, W.F. Jr (2020) Online telesupervision: a competence forged in a pandemic. *Journal of Family Psychotherapy*, 31(3–4): 157–177.

Weaks, D. (2002) Unlocking the secrets of 'good supervision': a phenomenological exploration of experienced counsellors' perceptions of good supervision. *Counselling and Psychotherapy Research*, 2(1): 33–39.

Wheeler, S., Aveline, M. and Barkham, M. (2011) Practice-based supervision research: a network of researchers using a common toolkit. *Counselling and Psychotherapy Research*, 11(2): 88–96.

Wheeler, S. and Richards, K. (2007) The impact of clinical supervision on counsellors and therapists, their practice and their clients: a systematic review of the literature. *Counselling and Psychotherapy Research*, 7(1): 54–65.

Zhu, P. and Luke, M.M. (2021) A supervisory framework for systematically attending to outcomes in clinical supervision. *International Journal for the Advancement of Counselling*. doi:10.1007/s10447-021-09455-9

RECOMMENDED READING

Bernard, J.M. and Goodyear, R.K. (2019) *Fundamentals of Clinical Supervision* (6th ed.). Upper Saddle River, NJ: Pearson.

This comprehensive text covers all aspects of supervision theory and practice for supervisors.

Carroll, M. (2014) *Effective Supervision for the Helping Professions*. London: Sage.

This is an accessible text which considers supervision from the learning, ethical, professional and organisational perspectives.

Creaner, M. (2014) *Getting the Best Out of Supervision in Counselling and Psychotherapy: A Guide for the Supervisee*. London: Sage.

Drawing on supervision research and best practices, this book explores the supervisory learning relationship and provides resources for supervisors and supervisees to optimise their supervisory experience.

3.13 ETHICS IN PRACTICE

LINDA FINLAY

OVERVIEW AND KEY POINTS

Ethics are embedded in every moment of therapeutic practice as we strive to be competent, respectful, boundaried professionals. Ethics involve integrity and duty of care, with the client's interests prioritised but with attention also paid to the self-care we therapists require in our daily work. Ethics are challenging, yet endlessly fascinating, with few clear-cut rules beyond the guidance provided by professional frameworks.

- Ethics draw on personal values, professional standards and legal requirements.
- What is ethical for one person may be regarded as unethical by another.
- Ethical therapists aim to maintain an attitude of continuous reflexive awareness and questioning of the broader relational and social context.
- We exercise our professional judgements as best we can in the light of our professional theories, frameworks and guidelines.

INTRODUCTION

Ethics envelop us. Rather than being remote philosophical principles enshrined in professional codes, they are intricately woven into the personal and professional values which shape our work and give it meaning (Finlay, 2019).

Many of the chapters in this volume grapple with ethical concerns. The importance of appropriate contracting (consent and confidentiality), respect for difference and diversity, recognition of potentially problematic power dynamics – all these issues occupy central places in most professional-ethical guidelines. Similarly, when therapists contemplate appropriate beginnings and endings, and when they collaborate in therapeutic alliance, they implicitly (sometimes explicitly) engage ethics.

This chapter focuses on *ethics-in-practice* and how therapists might engage professional guidelines in thoughtful, reflexive (self-aware) ways. The first two sections consider what ethics comprise and how the formal ethical frameworks laid down by professional bodies may be embraced. A final section discusses ethical dilemmas from everyday practice.

WHAT ARE ETHICS?

Ethics include the values, morals and principles we commit to, and which guide our professional actions. I see them nested in the space between personal values, professional standards and legal requirements (Figure 3.13.1).

Professional ethical frameworks highlight the protection of clients' interests, safety and welfare. They seek to ensure that clients receive a service based on a reasonable standard of care and competence (Reeves and Bond, 2021). Ethical principles often straddle personal and professional elements, as in the British Psychological Society (BPS) guidelines, where 'respect', 'competence', 'responsibility' and 'integrity' are highlighted (BPS, 2021).

Ethics-in-practice, however, address more than dry philosophical imperatives and often raise complex questions. Simply following a few clear-cut rules is rarely sufficient to make our practice ethical. What is ethical for one person isn't necessarily ethical for another: for example, what one therapist might consider being appropriately 'boundaried' might be seen by another as too loose or too restricting.

In addition, professional principles and values may clash in practice. Ethical dilemmas are not just about 'right' or 'wrong'. A therapist may be torn between breaking confidentiality to inform others that a client feels suicidal (*duty of care*, *non-maleficence*), while desperately wanting to *respect the client's confidence* and their right to choose to take their own life (*right of autonomy*). Or a therapist, while valuing professional *humility*, might still seek to give clients hope through confidence rooted in self-assured *expertise*. And in certain situations, a therapist might well be torn between prioritising the *client's interest* versus attending to their own *self-care* (Finlay, 2019).

Figure 3.13.1 Ethics

The concept of 'relational ethics', which sees ethics in terms of relationship rather than directives, may be helpful here. Relational ethics involve being human and being responsive, respectful and receptive to the other (Finlay, 2019). Much depends on the individuals involved and the meanings of the specific situation. A therapist who asks lots of questions might be regarded by some clients as invasive and intrusive. But their questioning could also be read as proof of genuine interest. Similarly, encouraging a client to do more self-care might be received as evidence of caring concern or could be interpreted as critical blaming. A client may view the holding of a time boundary as either harsh or safe. All depends on how the intervention is experienced relationally.

Ethics-in-practice should therefore be understood in the vibrant immediacy of the relevant relational context – one which embraces both respect for the individuals involved and the specific social circumstances of their encounter. Similarly, if relational concerns are critical to professional action, there must be room for individual judgement, intuition and creativity in actual moments of relating.

To give an example: a therapist confronted a dilemma when her client refused to work online when the Covid-19 pandemic lockdown hit. The therapist wanted to respect her client's choice and their long-standing relationship, so rather than accept the client's choice to end therapy, she invited her client for a session outside to 'walk and talk' (Cooley and Robertson, 2020) and discuss issues of technology and future options. With extra support and teaching, the client became comfortable with the technology and therapy resumed online.

Being an ethical professional means recognising and taking responsibility for one's own clinical decisions, undertaken as they are in particular individual, relational, institutional and cultural contexts. We professionals must reflect on and apply our own personal and professional standards sensitively and appropriately, thinking them through responsibly, perhaps in dialogue with others (such as supervisors). It's about trying to be a 'good enough therapist' who is *reflexive* (critically self-aware) (Finlay, 2019).

The guidance offered by professional ethical codes is an important starting point.

WORKING WITH PROFESSIONAL FRAMEWORKS

Most, if not all, professional-ethical codes of practice explicitly or implicitly agree that:

> The therapist is responsible for acting in a competent, respectful, boundaried way, with integrity, and in the best interest of their client. (Finlay, 2019: 17)

However, professional guidelines cannot encompass the full diversity of our practice across different contexts nor can they legislate for all eventualities. Guidelines must always be interpreted and applied.

In the United Kingdom, professional bodies tend to favour *ethical frameworks* which act as **aspirational mission statements** and outline 'principles' (e.g., autonomy, justice, beneficence), 'values' (e.g., respect, integrity, honesty) and 'standards' (e.g., confidentiality, recordkeeping, relationship-building). These frameworks may best be seen as a compass, rather than a map; direction not route.

Codes of conduct are different. They are more directive, describing behavioural rules that are professionally required or prohibited. While not law, as such, they carry professional weight regarding complaints or disciplinary hearings and are relevant in civil and criminal law (Mitchels and Bond, 2010).

The British Association for Counselling and Psychotherapy (BACP), for instance, provides detailed guidelines, together with numerous additional resources, videos and legal practice guides. Their 'Good practice in action' resources offer valuable information on many aspects of practice, including confidentiality, contracting, recordkeeping and choosing a supervisor. Their foundational document, *Ethical Framework for the Counselling Professions* (BACP, 2018), aims to foster an ethical resourcefulness that is responsive to diverse contexts. It starts with a section on 'Our commitment to clients', then lists how we should put clients first, work to professional standards, show respect, build appropriate relationships, maintain integrity, and demonstrate accountability and candour (see the box below).

Throughout the longer BACP framework document, attention is paid to the values, principles and moral qualities we strive to uphold, including care, diligence, empathy and humility. The final section on good practice offers more detailed guidelines, together with information relevant to supervision, training/education, research and self-care (Finlay, 2019).

Respect (for others' choices, autonomy, difference and dignity) is one of the fundamental ethical principles promoted across professional guidelines. For instance, the *Code of Ethics and Conduct* of the British Psychological Society states that:

> Respect … provides the philosophical foundation for many … other ethical principles. Respect for dignity recognises the inherent worth of all human beings, regardless of perceived or real differences in social status, ethnic origin, gender, capacities, or any other such group-based characteristics. This inherent worth means that all human beings are worthy of equal moral consideration. (BPS, 2021)

EXCERPT FROM THE BACP'S *ETHICAL FRAMEWORK FOR THE COUNSELLING PROFESSIONS*

… [A]s members or registrants of BACP, we take being trustworthy as a serious ethical commitment. We have agreed that we will:
1. **Put clients first by:**
    a. making clients our primary concern while we are working with them
    b. providing an appropriate standard of service to our clients
2. **Work to professional standards by:**
    a. working within our competence
    b. keeping our skills and knowledge up to date
    c. collaborating with colleagues to improve the quality of what is being offered to clients
    d. ensuring that our wellbeing is sufficient to sustain the quality of the work
    e. keeping accurate and appropriate records

(Continued)

(*Continued*)
3. **Show respect by:**
   a. valuing each client as a unique person
   b. protecting client confidentiality and privacy
   c. agreeing with clients on how we will work together
   d. working in partnership with clients
4. **Build an appropriate relationship with clients by:**
   a. communicating clearly what clients have a right to expect from us
   b. communicating any benefits, costs and commitments that clients may reasonably expect
   c. respecting the boundaries between our work with clients and what lies outside that work
   d. not exploiting or abusing clients
   e. listening out for how clients experience our working together
5. **Maintain integrity by:**
   a. being honest about the work
   b. communicating our qualifications, experience and working methods accurately
   c. working ethically and with careful consideration of how we fulfil our legal obligations
6. **Demonstrate accountability and candour by:**
   a. being willing to discuss with clients openly and honestly any known risks involved in the work and how best to work towards our clients' desired outcomes by communicating any benefits, costs and commitments that clients may reasonably expect
   b. ensuring that clients are promptly informed about anything that has occurred which places the client at risk of harm or causes harm in our work together, whether or not clients are aware of it, and quickly taking action to limit or repair any harm as far as possible
   c. reviewing our work with clients in supervision
   d. monitoring how clients experience our work together and the effects of our work with them.
   (BACP, 2018)

It is important to remember that all professional frameworks evolve over time as ideas change about what is 'right'. They aim to remain responsive to new ways of thinking/working and acknowledge changing landscapes of practice (e.g., responding to new digital working practices and updating guidance on respecting diversity, and promoting equality and inclusiveness). Professional and legal requirements can also change (such as revised data protection laws).

Given this changing professional context, it is important for practitioners to be familiar with up-to-date versions of their relevant professional guidelines. The regular review of new guidelines and their meaning for your own work context is expected of you (Reeves and Bond, 2021). It is also important to use supervision (and other opportunities) for ethical explorations with colleagues, and to evaluate actions taken. For instance, you might reflect on an intervention and ask if you would act similarly with other clients or if colleagues would condone your actions.

However, no practice or course of action becomes unethical simply because it is controversial or if other practitioners say they would have reached different conclusions (BACP, 2018). The sheer messiness and complexity of our day-to-day practice mean there are no clear-cut ethical recipes. Our responsibility is to think through (carefully and reflexively) the specific circumstances and implications of our actions (Finlay, 2019).

ETHICAL DILEMMAS IN PRACTICE

To emphasise the complexity of ethics-in-practice, consider the following everyday dilemmas. (The italicised terms highlight key ethical principles at stake.)

> **Dilemma 1** – At the end of a hard-working day, you are about to relax with a glass of wine. You are interrupted by a long text message from a client saying he is feeling desperate after a traumatic work encounter. He requests an urgent, brief *Zoom* conversation that evening. Do you oblige?

Discussion: The primary ethical dilemma concerns the need to hold professional *boundaries* (Amis, 2017) versus the client's need for *kind/*

empathetic responses. The importance of your own *self-care* and need for time off is challenged by the pull you might feel to 'rescue'. Without the usual safe therapy frame, you could well be less focused and grounded, and an off-the-cuff session could prove counterproductive. The fact that you are tired and drinking alcohol is also relevant: The United Kingdom Council for Psychotherapy (2019) offers the following guidance in their *Code of Ethics*: 'Ensure that you do not work with clients if you are not able to do so for physical or mental health reasons, or when impaired by the effects of drugs, alcohol or medication.' Thoughtful caution is required and consideration of alternatives: say, a compassionate text message the following morning or the offer of an emergency session sometime soon.

Dilemma 2 – In your first trimester of pregnancy, you are experiencing anxiety, morning sickness and indigestion. These feelings impact sessions occasionally. Should you take sick leave? Should you disclose your pregnancy to clients? Might you share your morning sickness issues? You are particularly concerned about the needs of one client who is grieving the death of her own child.

Discussion: There are three priorities here: your need for *self-care*, your *duty of care* to your clients, and whether or not you can still work *competently* and be sufficiently present to your clients and their needs.

If your morning sickness interrupts the therapeutic work, then you might well need to take some time off. Many therapists would not want to *self-disclose* their pregnancy or share similar personal information; much depends on the nature of your relationship with your clients (Marais and McBeath, 2021). It may also make a difference if you are working online, where your pregnancy might be less obvious. Ultimately, you need to consider the possible impact on your clients, particularly the one who is grieving the death of her child. If you do self-disclose, you need to make sure that clients don't get unduly drawn into caring for you. Clients could be impacted eventually by your maternity leave, so they will need some preparation for a *planned break* in therapy (which may include a temporary replacement therapist).

Dilemma 3 – A supervisee has disclosed that she feels uncomfortable with the attentions she is receiving from her own therapist. It began when they attended the same conference, and the therapist gave her a lift in his car. He later took her out for a meal and confided personal problems to her.

Discussion: This situation is concerning and needs action. Our professional codes recommend maintaining appropriate personal and professional boundaries with clients and this therapist would appear to have crossed the line. The social-therapy *dual relationship* (Gabriel, 2005) risks harm to the client, outweighing any supposed benefits. Guidance from the UKCP (2019) is clear: 'Be aware of the *power* [my emphasis] imbalance between the practitioner and client and avoid dual or multiple relationships which risk confusing an existing relationship and may impact adversely on a client.'

At the very least, some discussion with the supervisee of the nature of appropriate/inappropriate therapeutic boundaries is needed. It is part of the supervisor's role to enhance the *professional development* of the supervisee towards ensuring their best possible practice for clients and you have a role to play to encourage dialogue between the supervisee and her therapist.

The supervisee also needs to know her rights, and that you both might have a formal malpractice *complaint* to bring to his professional organisation. In discussion with your own supervisor (and/or professional body), you have a duty to consider taking your concerns *respectfully* to the therapist directly, although your *recordkeeping* and breaking *confidentiality* (Mitchels and Bond, 2021) – legal and ethical concerns – would need to be negotiated transparently.

The UKCP guidelines remind us that we have wider responsibilities:

37. Challenge questionable practice in yourself or others, reporting to UKCP potential breaches of this Code, and activating formal complaints procedures especially where there may be ongoing harm to clients, or you have significant grounds for believing clients to be at risk of harm.

Dilemma 4 – At the end of an emotional session, your client asks for a hug. Do you give it?

Discussion: This question reaches into the heart of personal and professional *boundaries* (Amis, 2017). The answer depends on many things, including the specific relationship involved, the wider context and what the hug might mean to both parties. Would the contact of a hug be healing for the client and in their long-term interests? If so, some therapists might consider offering the hug. However, it is important to explore the client's needs and what the hug would represent. Not giving the hug could prove more therapeutic if it encouraged the client to find their own self-soothing responses. If either person perceived the hug as confusing, invasive or sexually suggestive, it would be a violation. Ethnicity, religion, gender, age, sexuality and issues of authority/*power* need to be considered. In addition, social norms given the *cultural context* will play their part. This context also includes the therapist's theoretical framework: therapists working in psychoanalytic and cognitive-behavioural contexts, for instance, are less likely to use touch than are humanistic and body oriented practitioners (Finlay, 2019).

Dilemma 5 – Newly qualified, you are creating a professional website to promote your private practice. Your web-developer recommends emphasising your expertise and marketing yourself on Facebook, using client testimonials. Do you follow that advice?

Discussion: The presence of social media poses huge challenges to therapists seeking to maintain *boundaries* between their personal and professional digital presence. Is there a risk that without careful 'privacy settings' your professional marketing opens up access to your personal life (via tags, photos, blogs)?

It is also important to represent yourself accurately, *professionally* and with *integrity*. Acceptable marketing practice varies in different organisations/cultures, but it is always problematic to claim experience or training you don't have. The UKCP (2019), for instance, lays down the following guidelines which might limit your marketing claims:

11. Provide in your advertising, and on request, a clear and honest statement of the qualifications relevant to your field of practice … and advertise your services accurately and in a responsible and professional manner, without exaggeration ….

13. Not make any claims which you cannot demonstrate to be true or include testimonials from clients in any advertising. …

23. Offer only the forms of therapy in which you have had adequate training or experience.

24. Understand the limits of your competence and stay within them in all your professional activity, referring clients to another professional when appropriate. This includes recognising that particular client groups, such as children and families, have needs which not all practitioners are equipped to address.

CONCLUSION

Our goal of being an ethical (i.e., respectful, competent, boundaried) professional is expressed in the integrity and duty of care we enact where clients' interests are prioritised and sufficient attention is paid to therapist self-care.

What makes ethics challenging – and fascinating – is that there are few clear-cut rules for what makes practice ethical. What is ethical for one person may not necessarily be seen as ethical by another. The answer to almost every ethical question and dilemma is 'It depends…'.

If we can maintain an attitude of reflexive questioning that recognises and respects broader relational and social contexts, we are some ways towards being ethical. As practitioners, we are usually left trying to exercise professional judgement as best we can, in the light of professional theories and practice guidelines. If we do this sensitively and thoughtfully, and with caring, humane intention, we go a long way towards the goal of being ethical practitioners.

ACKNOWLEDGEMENTS

I am grateful to Sage for allowing me to reproduce material from Finlay (2019) *Practical Ethics in Counselling and Psychotherapy: A Relational Approach.*

REFERENCES

Amis, K. (2017) *Boundaries, Power and Ethical Responsibility in Counselling and Psychotherapy.* London: Sage.
British Association for Counselling and Psychotherapy (BACP) (2018) *Ethical Framework for the Counselling Professions.* Lutterworth: BACP. Available at www.bacp.co.uk/events-and-resources/ethics-and-standards/ethical-framework-for-the-counselling-professions/
British Psychological Society (BPS) (2021) *Code of Ethics and Conduct.* Leicester: BPS. Available at www.bps.org.uk/guideline/bps-code-human-research-ethics-0

Cooley, S.J. and Robertson, N. (2020, July) *The Use of Talking Therapy Outdoors*. London: British Psychological Society. Available at www.researchgate.net/publication/345978052_The_use_of_talking_therapy_outdoors

Finlay, L. (2019) *Practical Ethics in Counselling and Psychotherapy: A Relational Approach*. London: Sage.

Gabriel, L. (2005) *Speaking the Unspeakable: The Ethics of Dual Relationships in Counselling and Psychotherapy*. London: Routledge.

Marais, G. and McBeath, A. (2021) Therapists' lived experience of self-disclosure. *European Journal for Qualitative Research in Psychotherapy*, *11*, 72–86.

Mitchels, B. and Bond, T. (2010) *Essential Law for Counsellors and Psychotherapists*. Los Angeles, CA: Sage.

Mitchels, B. and Bond, T. (2021) *Confidentiality and Record Keeping in Counselling and Psychotherapy* (3rd ed.). London: Sage.

Reeves, R. and Bond, T. (2021) *Standards and Ethics for Counselling in Action* (5th ed.). London: Sage.

United Kingdom Council for Psychotherapy (UKCP) (2019) *Code of Ethics and Professional Practice*. London: UKCP. Available at www.psychotherapy.org.uk/media/bkjdm33f/ukcp-code-of-ethics-and-professional-practice-2019.pdf

RECOMMENDED READING

Amis, K. (2017) *Boundaries, Power and Ethical Responsibility in Counselling and Psychotherapy*. London: Sage.

A short readable text which highlights key ethical issues.

Reeves, R. and Bond, T. (2021) *Standards and Ethics for Counselling in Action* (5th ed.). London: Sage.

This book examines ethical issues and guidance in depth, providing many examples and online resources.

Finlay, L. (2019) *Practical Ethics in Counselling and Psychotherapy: A Relational Approach*. London: Sage.

This book examines relational dynamics and practical ethical issues arising in practice.

3.14 COMPLAINTS: LEARNING, PREVENTION AND PROCEDURES

CLARE SYMONS

OVERVIEW AND KEY POINTS

Complaints in counselling, psychotherapy and related psychological therapies are handled by a number of different organisations and professional bodies that relate to these activities as they define them. In addition, the literature relating to complaints often does not distinguish between counselling and psychotherapy. The terms 'counselling', 'psychotherapy' and 'therapy' are therefore used interchangeably throughout this chapter. Additionally, although formal complaints can be made by clients about their therapists, they are also brought by therapists about their supervisors, trainees about their trainers, and by therapists about other therapists. For ease I will largely refer to complaints brought by clients in this chapter.

Having a formal complaint made by a client is something that most therapists would likely prefer not to have to face. However, taking time to consider the areas of practice that can be problematic and how to address these may offer opportunities to improve practice in a way that protects clients and also minimises the risk of triggering a complaint. In this chapter I will cover:

- Findings from research relating to incidence of complaints and the kinds of issues arising in practice that can cause difficulty.
- How learning from complaints research can support responsive practice, including repair of alliance ruptures.
- What to expect in formal complaints processes.

COMPLAINTS RESEARCH

Complaints in counselling and psychotherapy is an area that has received little research attention, perhaps partly due to the ethical complexity of undertaking such sensitive material. That said, complaints potentially hold considerable information about what has gone wrong in therapy from the point of view of those who have complained, meaning that there is a considerable amount that can be learned that could improve practice. Much of what we do know about complaints comes either from studies that are now largely out of date or from reports or magazine articles written and published by relevant professional bodies, which may be more recent but can lack detail.

It is difficult to estimate the prevalence of therapist misconduct, but numbers of complaints compared with membership numbers can give some indication of incidence. An analysis of complaints received by the British Association for Counselling and Psychotherapy (BACP) showed that the total complaints received represented at its highest level not more than 0.17% – or an incidence of less than two complaints for every 1,000 members of the total membership within the period researched (Symons et al., 2011). It should be noted that this research is now somewhat dated, and these figures may have changed. More recent figures in BACP's report from the Public Protection Committee (BACP, 2021) show that the proportion of members with concerns raised about their conduct was 0.34%, indicating that the rate of complaints has risen over time, but remains low overall. Similarly, the Health and Care Professions Council (HCPC) shows that 0.72% of their registered practitioner psychologists were subject to fitness to practise concerns being raised against them in the 12-month period up to March 2019 (HCPC, 2019), while the United Kingdom Council for Psychotherapy's (UKCP) figures are broadly similar at 0.78% in 2020 (UKCP, 2021). Although it appears that the rate of complaints against psychological therapists is increasing over time, the rate overall remains low.

Although such figures might prove reassuring for therapists, there is some evidence that poor practice or malpractice is under-reported by clients (Symons et al., 2011). This may, in part, be due to clients' difficulties in feeling able to bring a formal complaint (Bowie, McLeod and McLeod, 2016), due to, for instance, lack of information about how to complain, feeling responsible for the failure of therapy, or feeling so depleted and harmed by the therapy that it does not feel possible to start a formal process (Symons, 2012). Research shows that, unsurprisingly, clients are harmed by experiences of poor practice that lead to complaints, with one qualitative study stating that 28.2% described a worsening of symptoms (Scholten et al., 2018), but clients also report that unhelpful therapy that does not give rise to a complaint can have a negative effect om wellbeing in the medium term (Bowie et al., 2016).

What is happening in therapy that gives rise to complaints or causes such harm to clients? When it comes to the aspects of practice that give rise to complaints, research and reports from professional bodies in counselling and psychotherapy indicate similar findings. Analysis of complaints against counsellors made to the BACP (Khele, Symons and Wheeler, 2008) showed that complaints were made about counsellor responsibility (which included managing breaks and endings as well as financial, sexual and emotional exploitation), failure to practice in an anti-discriminatory manner, confidentiality, boundaries, contracts and counsellor competence. The highest proportion of upheld complaints was in the area of boundaries. More recently, publication of the annual report of the UKCP's Professional Conduct Committee (UKCP, 2021) states that the root cause of complaints received the previous year were most frequently related to breaches of confidentiality and boundaries, but also included failure to adequately explain the terms and conditions of therapy (linked to contracting), dual relationships and poor management of endings, as well as other issues, including sexual exploitation. Similarly, a breakdown of calls from members of the public accessing the BACP's advice and support line (BACP, 2021) shows that boundaries, confidentiality, endings and recordkeeping are all areas that give cause for concern, although other areas also feature, including fees, client access to records and social media concerns.

LEARNING FROM COMPLAINTS

A difficulty with complaints is that they arise after things have gone irreparably wrong, and therefore after the potentially harmful practice has occurred. Regulatory organisations and the Professional Standards Authority (PSA), an oversight body for regulators in counselling and psychotherapy, are increasingly interested in how to learn from what has been raised in complaints – what has gone wrong in the past – in order to reduce and prevent harm (Professional Standards Authority, 2017) – sometimes called upstream prevention of complaints. While the PSA document relates specifically to regulators and professional bodies, the principle of learning from complaints in order to improve practice with clients to protect them from what might go wrong is also relevant to individual practitioners. Identifying from complaints reports and research the areas that give rise to complaints and cause difficulties in practice presents us with an opportunity reflect on these aspects of our own practice and to consider aspects of our work with clients that would benefit from further development. This is not about practising defensively – seeking to avoid complaints because of the therapist's fear and concern about these processes – but instead about an ethical approach to practice which recognises that every practitioner has areas of weakness in their practice and that every client brings unique challenges to the work that can create difficulties for the therapist.

In research, clients who experienced unhelpful therapy have indicated that their therapists did not work collaboratively by discussing what they hoped to get from the therapy or whether it was proving helpful, and instead seemed to follow their own agenda rather than that of the client (Bowie et al., 2016). These findings are supported more widely in the research literature, which demonstrate that therapists may not address failures in treatment, even when this is recognised (Stewart and Chambless, 2008) and that even identifying lack of progress for clients in the first instance can prove difficult for therapists (Hatfield et al., 2010). With this in mind, it seems more helpful – and a way of seeking to prevent harm in therapy – for the therapist to be proactive about seeking feedback from their clients about how the therapy is progressing and whether it is meeting the client's needs, listening carefully to their views and being prepared to modify practice accordingly, rather than relying solely on their own assessment of progress.

Even in cases where we are proactive about eliciting feedback from clients, ruptures – defined as 'a tension or breakdown in collaborative relationship between patient and therapist' (Safran et al., 2002: 236) – can occur. Research has identified that ruptures happen in 11–38% of therapy sessions (Safran et al., 2002), may be intrinsic to therapeutic work (Barrett et al., 2008), and that unrepaired ruptures may result in poor outcomes (McLaughlin et al., 2014). However, working to repair such ruptures and seeking to overcome difficulties in the therapeutic relationship is associated with more positive outcomes for clients, can be experienced as therapeutic and healing in itself and can foster a stronger therapeutic alliance (McLaughlin et al., 2014).

A challenge in working with and repairing ruptures is that they can produce powerful and difficult feelings for therapists, including guilt, confusion and feeling deskilled and incompetent. Recommended ways of responding to ruptures include open acknowledgement by the therapist of the difficulty and working with the client to explore and understand it. Such an approach means reflecting honestly on our practice and potentially asking difficult questions of ourselves and our work, tolerating uncertainty and ambiguity. We need to be open to considering that our responses can cause harm or have unintended consequences and be on the lookout for this, however much doing so might make us feel uncomfortable. Reflecting on practice in this way requires humility, to recognise our potential for making harmful mistakes. And where we identify those mistakes, it requires candour, the commitment to admitting them openly to our clients and in supervision.

FORMAL COMPLAINTS PROCESSES

Before bringing a complaint to an organisation, the client is usually advised to attempt to resolve the situation with the counsellor. This should provide the counsellor with an opportunity to listen fully and to consider how best to resolve the issue and, as highlighted in the previous section, it is essential that therapists are alert, open and receptive to their clients bringing such concerns if there is to be any possibility of repairing the relationship. However, it is important to remember that many clients might not feel able to voice their concerns to their counsellor, or may have attempted to do so but found that their counsellor responded defensively or without properly considering their concerns.

If the rupture, conflict or dispute can't be resolved with the counsellor, it may then escalate into a formal complaint. The details of complaints procedures vary across organisations and professional bodies, but broad principles that they share are set out here. Nonetheless, it is important to refer to your own regulatory body's professional conduct procedures for specific details of how it would process a complaint.

If the counsellor works within an organisational setting, in the first instance, resolution of the complaint would be encouraged within that organisation, following their complaints procedure, including any appeals process. In cases where the complaint made to the organisation cannot be resolved satisfactorily and the process has been exhausted, or if the counselling takes place where there is no such organisational process available (e.g., with a practitioner in private practice), the client might choose to make a formal complaint to a relevant professional body.

Formal complaints can be made to a professional body that a counsellor is a member of. Complaints usually relate to a therapeutic service provided to the complainant, such as therapy itself or possibly supervision or training. However, in some cases, complaints can be brought for other reasons, such as when a therapist is convicted of a crime and it is considered to be in the public interest for the professional body to investigate whether this has any impact on their standing as a member. Complaints can usually be brought by the person who received the therapeutic service, but in some circumstances complaints can be brought by someone representing the client, for example a parent or guardian representing a child who has received counselling.

Generally, complaints must be made in writing to the relevant professional body and the complainant will be asked to include all relevant details about themselves, the practitioner and about the nature of their complaint. When the complaint is received by the professional body, preliminary checks will be undertaken to ensure that it includes the necessary information to proceed with a complaint process, and also to check whether, for example, the person complained about is a member of the body complained to. After this point, the professional body may conduct a preliminary check, sometimes called a *threshold test*. This seeks to assess whether the complaint would represent a failure to uphold professional standards if it were upheld. If this test is not met, then the complaint is closed at that point. If the test is met, then the complaint is taken forward, meaning that the person complained about is informed about the complaint and invited to respond to the allegations in writing, usually within a set period of time.

At this point there may be various possible outcomes, which depend on the specific procedures within each professional organisation. Minor or technical allegations of misconduct may be dealt with by issuing a letter of advice to the member, provided they accept that they have not upheld professional standards. Alternatively, the accounts from both the complainant and the member might be considered by an assessment panel. At this point, the case might be dismissed, but there can sometimes be a range of other options available, such as consensual disposal where the member and the professional body agree to resolve the complaint without going to a full hearing. Alternatively, the assessment panel might decide that the complaint should proceed to a full hearing, sometimes called an adjudication panel, a practice hearing, or a disciplinary hearing.

When a complaint case goes to a full hearing, again, the details of how this is conducted will vary across different organisations and the process may also vary depending on the seriousness of the allegation and whether it represents serious professional misconduct or is more about the professional service received. Whatever the level of seriousness, details of the case are brought to a panel of adjudicators who consider all the information and evidence, and both the client and therapist attend a hearing with the panel. Both client and counsellor are usually allowed to attend with a representative to support them. The panel considers the complaint and evidence presented and then makes a decision about the outcome.

If the complaint is upheld, there may be sanctions for the member. These range from developmental sanctions, which might include conditions about working such as a requirement for additional supervision or further training, to more severe sanctions, such as suspension or withdrawal of membership or registration. Upheld complaints and sanctions are normally published on the professional body's website or other professional journal.

If a formal complaint it brought against you, this is likely to be distressing and challenging both personally and professionally. There are practical steps that it is important to take, such as informing your insurer and informing and seeking support from your supervisor. It is vital to respond to the complaint promptly and within the time limit set by the professional organisation. Although it might prove challenging at a time that might feel wounding and uncertain, it is important to reflect honestly and non-defensively on your practice and on the allegations made by the client so that you can respond in a way that demonstrates ethical thinking and an ability to recognise errors and mistakes and instances where you may have fallen below what is expected in professional standards. Responding in this way, with candour and humility, and taking appropriate responsibility for your part in the therapeutic relationship, is more likely to be looked on more favourably than a defensive response that seeks to put all blame on the client.

CONCLUSION

Complaints research demonstrates that the likelihood of a therapist having a formal complaint made against them to a professional body is low, but concern for protection of the public and to improve the standard of practice that we offer all clients means that there is enormous potential value in learning from complaints. Common areas of difficulty in practice that can give rise to complaints include boundaries, contracting and confidentiality, so it seems prudent to be particularly mindful about these areas in clinical practice. However, ruptures can occur throughout therapeutic work, leading to poor outcomes if they are not addressed and repaired. A proactive way of working that invites feedback from clients, along with authentic and honest reflection on our mistakes and areas of weakness in practice, may go some way in helping to prevent ruptures or the possibility of complaints.

REFERENCES

BACP (2021) *Public Protection Committee: 2020 Annual Report*. Lutterworth: British Association for Counselling and Psychotherapy. Available at www.bacp.co.uk/news/news-from-bacp/2021/12-march-public-protection-committee-annual-report-published/ Accessed February 2022.

Barrett, M.S., Wee-Jhong, C., Crits-Cristoph, P. & Gibbons, M.B. (2008) Early withdrawal from mental health treatment: Implications for psychotherapy practice. *Psychotherapy Theory, Research, Practice, Training*, 45(2), 247–267.

Bowie, C., McLeod, J. & McLeod, J. (2016) 'It was almost like the opposite of what I needed': A qualitative exploration of client experiences of unhelpful therapy. *Counselling and Psychotherapy Research*, 16(2), 79–87.

Hatfield, D., McCullough, L., Frantz, S.H.B. & Krieger, K. (2010) Do we know when our clients get worse? An investigation of therapists' ability to detect negative client change. *Clinical Psychology and Psychotherapy*, 17, 25–32.

HCPC (2019) *Protecting the Public: Promoting Professionalism. Fitness to Practise Annual Report 2019*. London: Health and Care Professions Council. Available at www.hcpc-uk.org/about-us/insights-and-data/ftp/fitness-to-practise-annual-report-2019/ Accessed February 2022.

Khele, S., Symons, C. & Wheeler, S. (2008) An analysis of complaints to the British Association for Counselling and Psychotherapy, 1996–2006. *Counselling and Psychotherapy Research*, 8(2), 124–132.

McLaughlin, A.A., Keller, S.M., Feeny, N.C., Youngstrom, E.A. & Zoellner, L.A. (2014) Patterns of therapeutic alliance: Rupture–repair episodes in prolonged exposure for PTSD. *Journal of Consulting and Clinical Psychology*, 82, 112–121.

(Continued)

(Continued)

Professional Standards Authority (PSA) (2017) *Right-Touch Reform: A New Framework for Assurance of Professions. A Summary: Harm Prevention. Can We Reduce the Amount of Harm?* London: Professional Standards Authority for Health and Social Care. Available at www.professionalstandards.org.uk/publications/detail/right-touch-reform-a-new-framework-for-assurance-of-professions

Safran, J.D., Muran, J.C., Samstag, L.W. & Stevens, C. (2002) Repairing alliance ruptures. In J.C. Norcross (Ed.), *Psychotherapy Relationships That Work: Therapist Contributions and Responsiveness to Patients* (pp. 235–254). New York: Oxford University Press.

Scholten, S., Velten, J., Kintscher, M. Pataki, A. & Magraf, J. (2018) Beschwerden über Psychotherapie und ihre Auswirkungen auf Patienten und Patientinnen [Complaints about psychotherapy and their impact on patients]. *Psychotherapie, Psychosomatik, Medizinische Psychologie*, 68, 9–10, 423–427.

Stewart, R.E. & Chambless, D.L. (2008) Treatment failures in private practice: How do psychologists proceed? *Professional Psychology: Research and Practice*, 39, 176–181.

Symons, C. (2012) *Complaints and Complaining in Counselling and Psychotherapy: Organisational and Client Perspectives.* Unpublished PhD thesis, Institute for Lifelong Learning, University of Leicester.

Symons, C., Khele, S., Rogers, J., Turner, J. & Wheeler, S. (2011) Allegations of serious professional misconduct: An analysis of the British Association for Counselling and Psychotherapy's Article 4.6 cases, 1998–2007. *Counselling and Psychotherapy Research*, 11(4), 257–265.

UKCP (2021) *UKCP Professional Conduct Committee Annual Report 2020.* London: United Kingdom Council for Psychotherapy. Available at www.psychotherapy.org.uk/about-ukcp/how-we-are-structured/ukcp-committees/professional-conduct-committee/

RECOMMENDED READING

It is essential that you familiarise yourself with the ethical code or framework from your relevant professional body as well as their formal complaints or professional conduct processes and ensure that you keep up to date with any reviews and changes. These documents are publicly available and easily accessed on the professional bodies' websites. In addition, it can be useful to supplement your understanding of ethical thinking by studying the ethical codes of other related professional bodies.

BACP (2021) *Good Practice across the Counselling Professions 004: What Works in Counselling and Psychotherapy Relationships.* Lutterworth: British Association for Counselling and Psychotherapy. Available at www.bacp.co.uk/events-and-resources/ethics-and-standards/good-practice-across-the-counselling-professions/gpacp004-what-works-in-counselling-and-psychotherapy-relationships/

This open access resource offers a digest of quantitative research about what works in counselling relationships, including findings from working with and repairing alliance ruptures.

Richardson, S. (2008) *Broken Boundaries: Stories of Betrayal in Relationships of Care.* London: Witness.

This book brings together accounts by seven women who experienced betrayal of trust and exploitation by different healthcare providers, including counsellors and psychotherapists. At times, this is a harrowing read but also thought-provoking and a valuable prompt to reflecting on the potential to do harm in therapy.

3.15 THERAPY AND THE LAW

PETER JENKINS

OVERVIEW AND KEY POINTS

Therapists are discovering that they increasingly need to have at least a basic working knowledge of the law, whatever their reservations about the legal system or the law itself. This chapter sets out some of the main parameters of the interface of counselling and psychotherapy and the law in the United Kingdom. The main points of reference relate to the civil law in England and Wales, with the law in Scotland and Northern Ireland operating in distinct, but still broadly parallel, ways. The emphasis will be on describing the key trends and professional issues to be considered by practitioners, rather than setting out the precise detail, which can be followed up in the references and resources supplied. The chapter briefly sets out:

- How legal principles applying to counselling and psychotherapy are mediated by the practitioner's context for practice, employment status and client group.
- Legal aspects of managing professional relationships with clients.
- Legal obligations and options in handling risk.
- Legal principles applying to the management of sensitive information.
- Developments regarding the statutory regulation of therapists.

MAKING LINKS BETWEEN PSYCHOTHERAPEUTIC PRACTICE AND THE LAW

Therapists often look for general principles, and even for absolute certainty, when encountering the law. While, as practitioners, we try to encourage our clients and colleagues to contain, stay with and *work through* ambiguity and uncertainty, our own strong preference is very often to have clear and very definite answers to the professional dilemmas which we face. The following example might illustrate this process at work.

CASE STUDY

Paul did some unpaid weekly counselling sessions for a small voluntary agency. He became concerned about his client, Sarah, who seemed to be increasingly depressed and self-absorbed, to the extent that her pre-teenage sons, who were involved in illicit drug-taking and joy-riding, seemed to her to be 'running wild' and almost beyond her control as a single parent. The senior counsellor at the agency was unable to provide any clear guidance on how he should respond to the risks he perceived for the sons, given that there was no specific evidence of child abuse. Any attempt to explore her problematic relationship with her sons, or to express his own anxiety about this situation as a counsellor, seemed to produce little response from her, possibly due to her somewhat depressed emotional state. However, Paul's supervisor was increasingly concerned about the client and the risk to the sons' welfare. His supervisor felt strongly that Paul should make contact with social services to report this as a safeguarding issue, given the apparent reluctance or inability of the client to take any action herself.

From a professional and ethical point of view, a therapist's first point of reference should be with regard to their code of ethics, such as the British Association for Counselling and Psychotherapy's *Ethical Framework for the Counselling Professions* (BACP, 2018). This case contains a classic dilemma, namely of promoting client autonomy versus protecting the welfare of the client and also of third parties. From a legal point of view, the practitioner's responses will be framed by a number of key factors, which are highly specific and will vary according to:

- the *context* in which the therapist practises
- the therapist's *employment* status
- the nature of the *client group*.

The interaction of these key factors provides a clue to the complexity of the law as it relates to counselling and psychotherapy. Exploring the possible options and responses to particular legal dilemmas is often highly specific, as general principles have to be applied carefully to this particular counsellor, working in this setting, on this employment basis, with the client group. Thus, there may well be differences between the safeguarding requirements faced by therapists working in a statutory setting and those for a counsellor, such as Paul, who is counselling in a voluntary agency. Alternatively, a counsellor such as Paul, who is either directly employed, or who is seen by the law to approximate to 'employed' status, may have little real discretion in deciding how to respond to issues of client or third-party risk, due to agency policy. A therapist in private practice, on the other hand, generally has substantially greater freedom of action in deciding how best to work with these issues. Therapists working with children, or with adults experiencing mental health problems, may similarly face certain pressures to act, which are *not* obligatory when working with other client groups, who are deemed to be less vulnerable.

The resulting combination of legal pressures means that therapists often encounter a wider and more varied range of legal issues than do other comparable professionals, such as social workers or mental health practitioners. Therapists need, therefore, to consider carefully how well they are prepared for recognising and responding to such professional dilemmas, which necessarily carry a *legal* element as well as an ethical or a professional set of choices (Bond, 2015).

LEGAL ASPECTS OF MANAGING PROFESSIONAL RELATIONSHIPS WITH CLIENTS

The discussion above has emphasised the *variability* of the law as applied to different psychotherapeutic situations.

The following sections now provide a brief outline of more general legal principles, which will need to be adapted to a range of specific situations. The core of counselling and psychotherapy work consists of the therapeutic relationship and its essential boundaries. These mark it as being distinct from other professional stances, such as teaching or social work, or other helping relationships, such as friendship or mentoring. From a legal perspective, the key factors relating to the therapist's therapeutic relationship with clients are framed by the concepts of:

- contract
- duty of care
- liability.

DEFINING A CONTRACT

Counsellors and therapists often use the term 'contract' in a rather loose way, referring to a set of arrangements guiding contact with the client, the purpose of the counselling and psychotherapy, and arrangements for supervision and recording. While the use of formal written agreements with clients may be considered a hallmark of good practice, these documents may not be considered to constitute a contract in a proper legal sense. A legal contract requires the fulfilment of a precise set of conditions (Jenkins, 2007: 27):

- *capacity* for the parties involved, i.e., not mentally disordered or under 18 years of age
- a firm *offer* and unequivocal *acceptance*
- a clear *intention* of both parties to create a legally binding agreement
- a contract that is supported by *consideration*, i.e., an exchange of goods or services for payment.

Many therapeutic contracts would *not* meet all these conditions, particularly regarding payment, as much counselling or therapy is provided *without* charge to the client, for example in schools, in the National Health Service (NHS), or by voluntary agencies. In private therapy or supervision practice, however, the agreement would, in all likelihood, constitute a legal contract. As a result, a therapist, supervisor, supervisee or client could take legal action for breach of a contract in the small claims section of the county court should there be an alleged breach of the contract.

Rather than applying a legal contract as such, therapists may be using a document which is actually better termed a consent form, or a working agreement. This can be useful and necessary for setting out the limits to confidentiality, for example. In this way, a client may give their advance consent to their general practitioner being contacted if they become suicidal. The counsellor then has substantial protection in law against any later charge of breach of confidence from an aggrieved client. Consent forms, or working agreements, are also important in documenting the client's *informed consent* to therapy.

DUTY OF CARE

Not all counsellors or psychotherapists will be covered by the law of contract. However, therapists will be subject to a duty of care towards their *client*, and supervisors will be similarly bound to their *supervisees*. The following fictitious vignette illustrates some features of this crucial part of the law relating to psychotherapeutic practice.

> **CASE STUDY**
>
> Niki was a newly qualified psychotherapist working in the NHS with clients who had been subjected to extensive domestic violence, and who often had previous histories of experiencing serious childhood sexual abuse. Interested in trauma work, Niki began experimenting by using some radical hypnotic techniques with a client after attending a week-long workshop in the USA. Unfortunately, the client's mental condition began to deteriorate rapidly soon afterwards and she was admitted for psychiatric treatment. Following this, she then brought a civil case against Niki as her former psychotherapist for breach of duty of care, alleging that the psychotherapeutic techniques had caused her lasting psychological damage and resultant substantial loss of earnings.

Action of this kind is brought under tort law, for the infliction of non-intentional harm, and requires the fulfilment of the following conditions:

- the existence of a duty of care between practitioner and client
- breach of that duty
- resultant foreseeable harm to the client as a direct result of the breach.

For counselling and psychotherapy clients, the alleged harm will normally be *psychological* rather than physical in nature. However, the law sets a very high threshold for such damage. It requires that the alleged harm meets the diagnostic criteria for a psychiatric illness, such as clinical depression, generalised anxiety disorder, or post-traumatic stress disorder, rather than simply taking the form of the more everyday human emotions of anger, distress or disappointment.

CASE LAW CONCERNING THERAPISTS

Many therapists are somewhat apprehensive of being sued by their clients, particularly when the latter are very aggrieved about some aspect of the therapy provided. However, the relative lack of reported cases in the UK suggests that the law actually presents very formidable barriers to clients successfully winning this type of case. Derived from medical case law, therapists subject to this type of action will be judged according to the *Bolam test*, namely whether their actions were consistent with the 'practice of competent respected professional opinion'. Relying on the evidence of expert witnesses, the judge needs to decide whether the therapist was working *within* the parameters of their chosen approach, such as psychodynamic, person-centred or other method. In practice, it is very difficult for clients to prove that the therapist's actions directly *caused* their psychological damage. In the case of Niki above, the client's *prior* history of abuse and possible evidence of psychiatric treatment *in the past* may well be used in court to invalidate her claim or, at the very least, reduce any damages eventually awarded to her.

LIABILITY

Therapists are often keen to assume a professional duty of care towards their clients, as this is consistent with their overall professional stance and their obligations under a code of ethics. From a legal point of view, liability is defined in rather narrower terms and takes specific forms, which are determined by the therapist's *employment* status rather than simply by the existence of a therapeutic relationship with the client. Liability can take the form of:

- *personal* liability, where a therapist doing paid private work holds *direct* responsibility for any non-intentional harm caused to the client

- *vicarious* liability, where an *employer* holds liability for the work of employees and volunteers.

Returning to the points made earlier, Niki's liability would be primarily determined by her status as an employee of the NHS Trust. The client would need to sue her *and* the NHS Trust together. To that extent, a psychotherapist in Niki's position would be 'protected' by their employer, which may have its own legal department and extensive experience in responding to claims and litigation. There remains a strong case, nevertheless, for therapists to keep their own professional indemnity insurance, rather than rely totally on the goodwill of their employer. Holding such insurance gives the therapist access to independent legal advice and, if necessary, separate legal representation in court, should this be necessary.

The barriers against clients succeeding in this case remain substantial. It needs to be remembered that clients also have access to a non-legal route of redress, namely by bringing a *complaint* against the therapist, either to the therapist's employer, or to their professional association, such as BACP or United Kingdom Council for Psychotherapy (UKCP). Given the shift towards establishing accessible and user-friendly complaints procedures by therapists' organisations, it is probably much more likely that counsellors and psychotherapists will face at least one serious professional or organisational complaint during their working career, rather than undergo actual litigation in court.

LEGAL OBLIGATIONS IN HANDLING RISK

Therapists often express real concern about the ethical tension and conflict existing between their obligations towards the client and those towards other members of society, who may be put at risk by the client's actions. In fact, the concept of risk can take a number of forms:

- Risk to the *client*, via deliberate self-harm, actual or attempted suicide.
- Risk to a *third party*, such as child abuse, domestic violence, serious crime or terrorism.
- Risk to the *therapist*, via assault or stalking.

Therapists subscribe to an ethical commitment to promote the client's autonomy and to protect their wellbeing. This may come into conflict with real or imagined *legal* obligations, particularly when counterbalanced against an expectation that therapists should avoid harm to the client or others, by breaking client confidentiality if necessary. This might be in order to take preventative action by alerting the authorities concerned, for example, in the case of suspected child abuse.

As discussed below, therapists have a duty of trust and confidence towards clients. There are few overriding, absolute legal requirements to break confidentiality, and these concern instances of terrorism and drug money laundering. Therapists may be required by their contract of employment or agency policy to report suspected child abuse, or threatened client self-harm or suicide, when working for statutory agencies such as health, education and social services. However, even these requirements need to be carefully balanced against the therapist's duty of trust and confidentiality towards the client.

In fact, in situations involving non-terrorist crime, therapists (outside Northern Ireland) have the *right*, but not necessarily a *duty*, to break confidentiality in the wider public interest. A therapist *could*, therefore, contact the police to report criminal activity by a client, such as an undetected murder, or a credible threat of revenge towards a former partner, or to report a client who was stalking the therapist her/himself. From an ethical, professional and therapeutic point of view, any such decision to report clearly needs to be prefaced wherever possible by discussion with the client, and consultation with a supervisor and experienced colleagues. However, the law will generally support such action if taken in a measured, responsible and accountable manner, as evidenced by the statutory provision for 'whistleblowing' facilities in the workplace.

LEGAL PRINCIPLES APPLYING TO THE MANAGEMENT OF SENSITIVE INFORMATION

Therapists learn a great deal of highly sensitive information about clients during the course of their work. In terms of the law, therapists owe a duty of confidence to clients, where this would be a reasonable expectation. This duty can also be assumed to apply in the case of a contract for the psychotherapeutic work (see earlier). The legal protection for client confidentiality has been further strengthened by statute, such as the client's right to *respect* for privacy under human rights legislation, and, more emphatically, by the provisions of the General Data Protection Regulation and the Data Protection Act 2018. These require therapists to adopt transparent forms of recordkeeping which are consistent with the fundamental rights of citizens to know and, wherever appropriate, to have substantial access to such records.

ACCESS BY THIRD PARTIES TO CLIENT RECORDS

Part of the therapist's role in managing sensitive client data has been to limit unauthorised access by other interested parties, such as the partner of a client undergoing therapy. There has been a rising interest by external agencies in requiring access to client records, for use in legal proceedings. These agencies include:

- *solicitors* representing clients in legal proceedings, such as litigation for workplace stress
- *police officers* seeking evidence for a prosecution in the case of alleged child abuse
- *courts* requiring the surrender of counselling and psychotherapy records, including personal and supervision notes, to assist the court in its deliberations.

Counsellors and psychotherapists do not possess legal privilege, unlike solicitors, and cannot simply refuse to comply with court-ordered demands for notes, except at the risk of being held in contempt of court. Practitioners faced with court-authorised demands for the release of client records need to take legal advice, but are faced with the reality that client confidentiality is outweighed by the wider public interest. Therapists, trainers and professional associations need to take fuller account of this issue, where client and therapist confidentiality is ultimately provided with limited protection by the law, that is when the law itself declares an interest in accessing client secrets confided within the therapy session (see Wynn – Chapter 3.7, this volume).

STATUTORY REGULATION OF THERAPISTS

Therapists' organisations have been heavily engaged in lobbying for the statutory regulation of counselling and psychotherapy over the past few decades. These moves were ultimately unsuccessful, as signalled by a clear government decision *not* to implement statutory regulation for counselling and psychotherapy (Department of Health, 2011). Professional standards are managed by a combination of voluntary and statutory registers relying on professional self-regulation, overseen by the Professional Standards Authority for Health and Social Care. There is a certain degree of statutory regulation of the talking therapies, but it is partial and resembles a 'patchwork quilt'. There is limited and highly selective legal protection of Title, but only for some practitioners, such as Counselling, Clinical and Educational Psychologists, and Arts, Play and Music Therapists, who are all regulated by the Health and Care Professions Council (HCPC). In terms of Practice, adoption counselling is regulated by the Adoption and Children Act 2002 and infertility counselling by the Human Fertilisation and Embryology Act 1990.

LEGAL BAN ON CONVERSION THERAPY

In October 2021, the government opened a consultation on proposals to ban talking conversion therapy in England which was intended to change clients' sexual orientation or transgender status (HM Government, 2021). The proposed legislation intends to introduce 'a new criminal offence and to ensure that conversion therapy is recognised appropriately when it is the motivation for an existing crime', thereby providing 'a robust, effective and proportionate policy' (HM Government, 2021: 3). This legal ban would apply to all clients under age 18, and to all clients over age 18 who had not provided informed consent to such therapy. This proposed legislation, if enacted, would represent a far-reaching incursion of the law into therapeutic practice, with markedly severe penalties (Jenkins and Esses, 2021).

CONCLUSION

Therapists need to be familiar with the broad outline of the civil law and the specific ways in which it impacts on their practice. In reality, the relationship of the law to counselling and psychotherapy is mediated by a number of factors, such as the therapist's context for practice, employment status and client group. Therapists need to be aware of the principles underlying contracts, if in private practice or undertaking client work for a fee, and to work within the parameters of accepted professional norms in discharging their duty of care to clients. The process of managing risk presents a number of challenges to therapists, where there are relatively few absolute requirements to break client confidentiality. Data protection law has subjected therapists' recordkeeping to wider principles of public transparency, access and accountability. While the law is generally supportive of client confidentiality, therapists must normally comply with court-authorised demands for access to client records in the public interest. Government policy does not currently support statutory regulation of therapists, but favours reliance on a complex combination of voluntary and statutory registers and professional self-regulation.

Psychologists Protection Society Seminar in June 2014 on 'Records as Evidence':

www.theprofessionalpractitioner.net/index.php/cpd-activities/14-cpd-activity-records-as-evidence

Counselling Mind-Ed (free online training material, on legal and ethical aspects of working with children and young people, such as applying the law, recordkeeping and safeguarding): www.minded.org.uk

British Association for Counselling and Psychotherapy legal resources (linked to the *Ethical Framework* (BACP, 2021): www.bacp.co.uk/ethics/newGPG.php

Figure 3.15.1 Therapy and the law web resources

REFERENCES

BACP (2018) *Ethical Framework for the Counselling Professions*. Lutterworth: British Association for Counselling and Psychotherapy.
Bond, T. (2015) *Standards and Ethics for Counselling in Action* (4th ed.). London: Sage.
Department of Health (2011) *No Health Without Mental Health*. London: HMG.
HM Government (2021) *Banning Conversion Therapy Government Consultation*. Command Paper 535. HMSO: London. Available at www.gov.uk/government/consultations/banning-conversiontherapy
Jenkins, P. (2007) *Counselling, Psychotherapy and the Law* (2nd ed.). London: Sage.
Jenkins, P. and Esses, J. (2021) *Thoughtful Therapists: Scoping Survey for Government Equalities Office Consultation on Conversion Therapy*. Available at https://thoughtfultherapists.org/scoping-survey-pdf

RECOMMENDED READING

Daniels, D. and Jenkins, P. (2010) *Therapy with Children: Children's Rights, Confidentiality and the Law* (2nd ed.). London: Sage.

This book provides a detailed discussion of the rights of children and young people, based on case studies drawn from school-based counselling.

Jenkins, P. (2007) Supervision in the dock? In K. Tudor and M. Worrall (Eds), *Freedom to Practise*. Volume 2: *Developing Person-centred Approaches to Supervision* (pp. 176–194). Ross-on-Wye: PCCS Books.

This chapter suggests a framework for distinguishing ethical and legal aspects of the supervisor's 'duty of care' to supervisees and clients.

Jenkins, P. (2017) *Professional Practice in Counselling and Psychotherapy, Ethics and the Law*. London: Sage.

This student textbook analyses the key components of professional practice, based on the BACP *Ethical Framework for the Counselling Professions* (2016).

3.16 MENTAL HEALTH LAW

SOBHI GIRGIS

OVERVIEW AND KEY POINTS

The care of people with mental disorders is regulated by a host of legal provisions, and not restricted to a specific mental health law. Detention in hospital could be effected by part 2 'civil' or part 3 'criminal' of the Mental Health Act (MHA) 1983, the Mental Capacity Act (MCA) 2005 or the Children Act (1989), among other legislations. Deprivation of liberty and enforcing treatment undoubtedly constitute serious encroachments on personal autonomy. Thus, the legal framework includes clear safeguards against the misuse of such powers. In 2007, significant changes were made to the MHA 1983, including the introduction of Community Treatment Orders (CTO). The Code of Practice of the MHA was revised in 2015 to provide stronger protection of people who come under compulsory powers. It puts emphasis on the compliance with the Human Rights Act (HRA) 1998, the Equality Act 2010 and the Care Act 2014.

- Most countries have their own specific mental health law, including devolved nations within the United Kingdom.
- Detention in hospital for treatment of mental disorder could be effected by a number of legal provisions, and not restricted to MHA 1983.
- There are several safeguards to ensure lawful and fair treatment of people with mental disorders.
- Legal frameworks and clinical practice need to comply with HRA 1998, the Equality Act 2010 and the Care Act 2014.

INTRODUCTION

The care of people with mental disorder is regulated by a host of legal provisions arising from, among other sources, Acts of Parliament, secondary legislation, Case Law, the European Convention on Human Rights (ECHR), the HRA 1998 and judgments made by the European Court of Human Rights (ECtHR).

Detention in hospital is a significant encroachment on personal liberty. Most countries have a specific mental health law to regulate the use of such powers and stipulate sufficient safeguards against their misuse. Devolved UK administrations have slightly different mental health laws.

Provisions for detention in hospital are also available through other legislation, for example, the MCA 2005, the Children Act 1989, the Criminal Procedure (Insanity) Act 1964 as amended by the Criminal Procedure (Insanity and Unfitness to Plead) Act 1991, and the Homicide Act 1957. The Criminal Justice Act 2003 enables the courts to add treatment requirements to a community sentence, for example, mental health, drug treatment, or alcohol treatment requirements.

Legal provisions dealing with issues of capacity have developed over the years through case law. These were eventually codified by the MCA 2005. The latter was amended to include clear procedures and safeguards regarding deprivation of liberty. A clearer test for deprivation of liberty has been introduced through a recent Supreme Court judgment – the 'Cheshire West' case.

MENTAL HEALTH ACT 1983 (AS AMENDED BY MHA 2007)

The Act deals with the care and treatment of people with mental disorders. The 2007 amendment widened the definition of mental disorder and abolished the previous four categories (mental illness, mental impairment, severe mental impairment, and psychopathic disorder). Mental disorder is defined in the Act as 'any disorder or disability of the mind'. Learning disability is only considered to be a mental disorder for the purpose of detention for treatment if it is associated with abnormally aggressive or seriously irresponsible behaviour. Dependence on alcohol or drugs *per se* is not considered a mental disorder and patients cannot be detained solely because of their dependence. However, psychiatric disorders arising from alcohol or drug misuse constitute mental disorders, for example, intoxication, withdrawal, or alcoholic psychotic disorder. The 2007 amendment abolished the 'treatability' criteria for some mental disorders. Instead, it created an 'appropriate medical treatment' test, which applies to all mental disorders. No longer can Electro-Convulsive Therapy (ECT) be given to a capacious adult without their consent unless it is a lifesaving treatment.

Patients can be detained in hospital under 'civil' sections (Part II of the Act) or 'criminal sections', which are issued by a Court or Ministry of Justice (Part III of the Act). Part IV regulates consent to the treatment of mental disorder, while Part V deals with appealing against detention and CTO. Clinicians have been given new powers to impose certain conditions on patients on their release from detention and the ability to recall patients back to hospital.

The Act opened the door for professionals other than doctors, including psychologists, to become 'Approved Clinicians (ACs)' or 'Approved Mental Health Professionals (AMHPs)'. The 'Responsible Clinician (RC)' is the AC with overall responsibility for the care of patients coming under compulsion. AMHPs carry out the functions that used to be the preserve of the 'Approved Social Worker (ASW)'.

MEDICAL TREATMENT UNDER MHA

The medical treatment of mental disorders includes nursing care, psychological intervention, and specialist mental health habilitation, rehabilitation, and care. The 2007 amendment explicitly included psychological intervention within the definition.

The Act defines appropriate medical treatment for mental disorder as 'medical treatment which is for the purpose of alleviating or preventing a worsening of a mental disorder or one or more of its symptoms or manifestations' (section 145(4) of the Mental Health Act). This can include treatment of physical health problems only if such treatment is part of, or ancillary to, treatment for mental disorder (e.g., treating wounds self-inflicted because of mental disorder). Sections 57, 58 and 58A set out types of medical treatment to which special rules apply, including, in many cases, the need for a certificate from a 'Second Opinion Appointed Doctor (SOAD)' approving the treatment. Under section 63, detained patients may be given medical treatment for any kind of mental disorder, if they consent to it, or if they have not consented to it, but the treatment is given by or under the direction of the AC in charge of such treatment (unless sections 57, 58 or 58A apply). Psychological therapies and other forms of medical treatments, which, to be effective, require the patient's cooperation, are not automatically inappropriate simply because a patient does not wish to engage with them. Such treatments would remain appropriate and available if they continue to be clinically appropriate and would be provided if the patient agrees to engage.

PART II OF THE MHA 1983

This part deals with 'civil detentions', that is, not through the criminal justice system. Section 2, lasting for up to 28 days, is for assessment or assessment followed by treatment. Section 3, lasting for up to six months, is for treatment. It can be renewed at regular intervals, initially for six months, then annually. Admission under sections 2 or 3 requires two medical recommendations and an application by an AMHP. Section 4 allows urgent detention for up to 72 hours, when only one medical recommendation could be secured. Section 5 deals with application for a 'holding' power order that allows a nurse or a doctor to keep a patient already in hospital to facilitate assessment for detention under sections 2 or 3. Section 7 concerns application for a guardianship order. Section 17 regulates granting leaves of absence. Section 20 deals with renewal of detention, while section 23 regulates discharge from detention.

PART III OF THE MHA 1983

These are orders made by a criminal court in relation to offenders or by the Ministry of Justice in relation to sentenced or unsentenced prisoners who need psychiatric treatment in hospitals. Section 37 is a Hospital Order imposed by the Magistrates or Crown Court. It operates in the same way as its civil counterpart s. 3. A Restriction Order under s. 41 can be attached to s. 37 only by the Crown Court. Section 41 aims at protecting the public from serious harm. Under s. 41, leave of absence and transfer between hospitals will require Ministry of Justice permission. Discharge can only be ordered by a Mental Health Tribunal or the Ministry of Justice. Section 38 Interim Hospital Order allows the court to remand convicted offenders to hospital for a trial of treatment before deciding to sentence them to a Hospital Order. The courts also have other powers to remand offenders, prior to conviction, to hospital for preparation of reports (s. 35) or treatment (s. 36). Section 47 is used by the Ministry of Justice to transfer a serving prisoner to hospital. A Restriction Order s. 49 (similar to s. 41) is usually attached to s. 47. Remanded prisoners in urgent need for treatment can be transferred to hospital under ss. 48/49.

PART IV OF THE MHA 1983

This regulates medical treatment of mental disorder and issues of consent. Treatment with medication, after the first three months of their first administration under detention (s. 58), requires the patient's consent *or* the agreement of a SOAD. In urgent cases, the RC can authorise treatment pending compliance with certification by an SOAD (s. 62). New safeguards have been introduced for ECT (s. 58A). Capacious patients cannot be given ECT without their consent unless it is lifesaving.

SAFEGUARDS FOR DETAINED PATIENTS

Patients must be given information on their detention and any safeguards. All detained patients and patients under CTOs have a new right of access to an Independent Mental Health Advocate (IMHA). Patients can appeal against detention or CTO to the Mental Health Tribunal or the Hospital Managers. The MHA gives significant powers to the nearest relative (NR), including objecting to detention in hospital for treatment (s. 3), ordering discharge of the patient, and applying for review of the patient's detention by a tribunal.

REFORM OF MHA 1983

In 2017, the Government announced its intention to reform the MHA. Professor Simon Wesley conducted an independent review and published his report, *Modernising the Mental Health Act: Increasing Choice, Reducing Compulsion*, in December 2018, making 154 recommendations. The Government carried out a consultation in 2021 and published its response as a White Paper in August 2021, accepting most of the review's recommendations. Following a further consultation on the White Paper, the Government promised a bill when the 'parliamentary time allows'. The White Paper set plans to tighten the admission criteria and raise the threshold for compulsory detention, reduce the use of CTOs, strengthen the safeguards available to people who come under the MHA by giving more frequent access to the mental health tribunal and to enhance support from family members and independent advocates. Also, patients would be given statutory rights to make advance choices about their future mental health care and treatment. The bill will limit the scope of using the MHA for people with learning disability and autistic spectrum disorders. Measures will be introduced to improve the experiences of people from 'BAME' groups. A Draft Mental Health Bill was published in June 2022.

COMMUNITY TREATMENT ORDER (CTO)

The 2007 amendment introduced CTO – a new regime to apply compulsory powers in the community. The RC can impose certain conditions on patients on their release from detention and recall patients back to hospital if treatment in hospital is required. An RC can recall the patient to hospital for up to 72 hours, where treatment can be given. If a longer period of care is needed, the CTO can be revoked, initiating a new six-month period of detention in hospital. In general, treatment cannot be enforced in the community, except when physical force is required to administer emergency treatment to people lacking capacity.

GUARDIANSHIP ORDERS

If the welfare of people with mental disorder is the main focus rather than the treatment of the mental disorder, patients can be placed under guardianship in the community rather than be detained in hospital. The Local Authority most often takes the role of the Guardian.

POWERS OF ENTRY AND POLICE POWERS (S. 135 AND S. 136)

Section 135 allows an AMHP to apply to a magistrate for a warrant authorising a police officer to enter specific premises, by force if necessary, if there is reasonable cause to suspect that someone with a mental disorder:

- has been or is being ill-treated, neglected, or kept otherwise than under proper control on the premises; or
- is living there alone and unable to care for themselves.

The police also have powers under s. 136 in relation to people they find in a non-residential place who appear to be suffering from mental disorder and to be in immediate need of care or control. People will then be taken to a 'place of safety' where their mental health is assessed within 24 hours.

AFTERCARE (S. 117)

Patients detained for treatment are entitled to appropriate services, according to their needs, when they leave hospital. Section 117 places an obligation on Clinical Commissioning Groups (CCGs) and Local Authorities (LAs) to provide those services free of charge. Section 117 was significantly amended by the Care Act 2014 to ensure that care plans are patient-centred.

CRIMINAL PROCEDURE (INSANITY) ACT 1964 (AS AMENDED)

People whom the court accepts to be 'legally insane' are given the special verdict of 'not guilty by reason of insanity'. They can be admitted to hospital for treatment in a similar way to s. 37. The law was amended in 1991 to cover people who are 'unfit to plead'. Those people cannot have a full trial, but their case will be subject to a 'trial of facts'. The jurors will decide whether the person has committed the act or the omission. The person can be admitted to hospital for treatment but can also be given guardianship, a community sentence or absolute discharge.

POLICE AND CRIMINAL EVIDENCE ACT (PACE) 1984

This legislation recognises the vulnerability of people with mental disorder when they come into contact with the police. If a police constable thinks, or is told in good faith, that a detained person is 'mentally disordered', an interview cannot be conducted in the absence of an 'appropriate adult'.

HOMICIDE ACT 1957 (AS AMENDED BY THE CORONERS AND JUSTICE ACT 2009)

This legislation introduced the partial defence of 'diminished responsibility' to a charge of murder. This defence is available to people suffering from a mental disorder which substantially impairs their mental responsibility for the killing. They receive a conviction of manslaughter rather than murder and are invariably sentenced to a hospital order with restriction. The test for diminished responsibility has been modernised by the Coroners and Justice Act 2009.

COMMUNITY CARE LAW

There has been a plethora of successive Acts covering community care. The National Assistance Act 1948, a key piece of legislation, followed the establishment of the National Health Service (NHS). It abolished the workhouses and kick-started the modern system of social benefits. Much legislation followed dealing with community care in a piecemeal manner. In the 1980s there was a shift of care from psychiatric institutions to the community, with the closure of asylums. The National Health Service and Community Care Act 1990 defined the responsibilities of health and LAs in providing community care services. The NHS no longer has the primary responsibility for the provision of non-hospital services for those requiring long-term care. The Act required LAs to assess the care needs of people whom they are either obliged or empowered to assist.

The Care Act 2014 is the biggest change to community care law in 60 years. It brought together several existing laws and introduced new duties to LAs to ensure that wellbeing, dignity, and choice are at the heart of health and social care. Relevant professionals (particularly those involved in discharging or treating patients in the community) should also consider the general responsibilities of LAs under Part 1 of the Act (e.g., duty to promote wellbeing, promote integration and cooperation duties). The Act significantly amended the duties of LAs and CCGs under s. 117 of the MHA 1983.

MENTAL HEALTH UNITS (USE OF FORCE ACT) 2018

This piece of legislation was passed to improve practice around the use of restrictive interventions, such as restraining, seclusion, long-term segregation, and rapid tranquilisation.

MENTAL CAPACITY ACT 2005

This is a 'codifying' Act, as it did not create new legal principles but enshrined in statute common law principles concerning people lacking mental capacity and those who take decisions on their behalf. It replaced existing statutory schemes for enduring powers of attorney and court of protection receivers with reformed and updated provisions. The Act is underpinned by five key principles: presumption of capacity, supporting individuals to make their own decisions, not equating unwise decisions with lack of capacity, acts done on behalf of people lacking capacity must be in their best interest, and lastly, these acts should be the least restrictive of their basic rights and freedoms.

The MHA 2007 amended the MCA 2005 to introduce Deprivation of Liberty Safeguards (DoLS), a legal framework for depriving people who lack capacity of their liberty if that is in their best interests. The safeguards apply to people who are either in a hospital or in registered care homes. DoLS contain detailed requirements about when and how deprivation of liberty may be authorised. The legislation also provides detailed arrangements for renewing and challenging the authorisation of deprivation of liberty. Specifically, DoLS were introduced to prevent human rights breaches identified by the judgment of the ECtHR in the 'Bournewood' judgment.

In March 2014, the Supreme Court made a judgment in a case best known as 'Cheshire West'. The judgment established the 'acid test' to decide whether there is deprivation of liberty. The Court asserted that people who lack capacity enjoy the same human rights enjoyed by everybody else. Patients lacking capacity to consent to admission to a psychiatric hospital where the regime amounts to deprivation of liberty, and who are objecting to being there, cannot remain 'informally'. Those patients cannot be detained under DoLS either. The MHA could be a more appropriate legal framework.

In 2019, the UK parliament passed a new legislation to replace Deprivation of Liberty Safeguards with a new scheme, Liberty Protection Safeguards (LPS). This will apply to England and Wales. The aim is to create a new simplified legal framework. Liberty Protection Safeguards will apply to all settings, including domiciliary settings, and will extend to 16- and 17-year-olds. There were plans to enact the Mental Capacity (Amendment) Act 2019 in October 2021. This was delayed to April 2022 and has since been further pushed back. There is no set date to enact the legislation at the time of writing.

HUMAN RIGHTS ACT 1998

The UK was a co-signatory of the European Convention on Human Rights (ECHR) at its inception in 1950. The HRA 1998 gives further effect in UK law to the rights contained in the ECHR. It makes available in UK courts a remedy for breach of Convention rights, without the need to go to the ECtHR. Some of the rights are absolute, some are qualified (by the needs of society), and some are limited (by other legislation). The relevant ECHR articles are listed below.

The current Conservative Government is planning to repeal the HRA 1998 and to introduce a British Bill of Rights. A consultation was due to be launched in December 2015 but, at the time of writing, this has not been conducted.

ECHR ARTICLES

Article 2 Right to life (absolute)

Article 3 Prohibition of torture (absolute)

Article 4 Prohibition of slavery and forced labour (absolute)

Article 5 Right to liberty and security (limited)

Article 6 Right to a fair trial (limited)

Article 7 No punishment without law (absolute)

Article 8 Right to respect for private and family life (qualified)

Article 9 Freedom of thought, conscience and religion (qualified)

Article 10 Freedom of expression (qualified)

Article 11 Freedoms of assembly and association (qualified)

Article 12 Right to marry (limited)

EXAMPLES OF RELEVANCE OF THE HRA 1998

Article 5 allows the detention of people with 'unsound mind' on the basis of objective medical evidence. This principle underpins the process of detaining people with mental disorder under the MHA. Medical recommendations provide the necessary 'objective medical evidence'. Article 5 also requires speedy review by a 'court'. Following the Winterwerp case, the mental health tribunals were given the power to discharge patients to ensure compliance with article 5.

Article 6 underpins the proceedings of the tribunals and the entitlement of patients to free legal representation in connection with the review, by a tribunal, of their detention. Article 8 protects the right of detained people to privacy of their correspondence and contact with family and friends. Article 3 guards against any intervention that could be considered as 'inhumane or degrading'.

SOME LEGAL ISSUES RELEVANT TO COUNSELLORS AND PSYCHOTHERAPISTS

The current MHA made it possible for registered practitioner psychologists to become ACs and AMHPs. Psychological treatment has been explicitly included in the definition of 'medical treatment'. As such, appropriate medical treatment can theoretically be limited to psychological treatment, for example, in a personality disorders unit. Psychological treatment for detained patients is provided under the authority of the RC (s. 63).

It is interesting that treatment is considered as 'available' even if a detained patient refuses to engage. This poses an ethical dilemma for the therapist. If psychological treatment is the main form of treatment for a detained patient, admission to a particular unit is only possible if such intervention is available in that unit.

Following the Cheshire West case, there has been increased attention to the issues of capacity, best interest, whether the patient is objecting to admission or treatment, and whether there is deprivation of liberty. Psychologists and counsellors should regularly contribute to the decision-making process around those issues.

It is unlawful for a public authority to act in a way which is incompatible with a Convention right, for example, the right to respect for private and family life. Under s. 6 of the HRA 1998, individual therapists would fall under the definition of public authority if they were working for an organisation whose functions are of a public nature, for example, an NHS hospital or a private hospital providing NHS treatment.

REFERENCES

Department of Health (2015) *Mental Health Act 1983: Revised Code of Practice*. London: HM Stationery Office.

Department of Health and Social Care (2018) *Modernising the Mental Health Act: Increasing Choice, Reducing Compulsion*. Final Report from the Independent Review. 6 December. London: Department of Health and Social Care. Last updated 14 February 2019. Available at www.gov.uk/government/publications/modernising-the-mental-health-act-final-report-from-the-independent-review

Department of Health and Social Care (2021) *Consultation Outcome: Reforming the Mental Health Act*, Published 24 August 2021. Available at https://www.gov.uk/government/consultations/reforming-the-mental-health-act/reforming-the-mental-health-act

Department of Health and Social Care (2021) *Consultation Outcome: Reforming the Mental Health Act*, Published 24 August 2021. Available at https://www.gov.uk/government/consultations/reforming-the-mental-health-act/reforming-the-mental-health-act

Department of Health and Social Care (2022) *Draft Mental Health Bill*. Published June 2022. Available at https://assets.publishing.service.gov.uk/government/uploads/system/uploads/attachment_data/file/1093555/draft-mental-health-bill-web-accessible.pdf

STATUTES

Care Act 2014 c.23

Children Act 1989 c.41

Coroners and Justice Act 2009 c.25

Criminal Justice Act 2003 c.44

Criminal Procedure (Insanity) Act 1964 c.84

Criminal Procedure (Insanity and Unfitness to Plead) Act 1991 c.25

Equality Act 2010 c.15

European Convention on Human Rights 1950: Convention for the Protection of Human Rights and Fundamental Freedoms, Rome, 4. XI.1950 available at www.echr.coe.int/Documents/Convention_ENG.pdf

Homicide Act 1957

Human Rights Act 1998

Mental Capacity Act 2005 c.9

Mental Health Act 1983 (as amended by MHA 2007) c.20

Mental Health Units (Use of Force Act) 2018 c.27

National Assistance Act 1948 c. 29 (Regnal. 11 and 12 Geo 6)

National Health Service and Community Care Act 1990 c. 19

Police and Criminal Evidence Act (PACE) 1984 c. 60

CASES

Bournewood case: HL v UK 45508/99 (2004) ECHR 471

P v Cheshire West & Chester Council; P & Q v Surrey County Council [2014] UKSC 19

Winterwerp v Netherlands 6301/73 (1979) ECHR 4

RECOMMENDED READING

Department of Health (2015) *Mental Health Act 1983: Revised Code of Practice*. London: HM Stationery Office.

The revised code is a well-written account of the principles of mental health law and their application in clinical practice. It is a statutory document for all health and social care staff in England.

Jones, R. (2018) *Mental Capacity Act Manual* (8th ed.) London: Sweet & Maxwell.

The book provides an up-to-date account of the legal framework of mental capacity and deprivation of liberty safeguards.

P v Cheshire West & Chester Council; P & Q v Surrey County Council [2014] UKSC 19.

The judgment is hugely influential in mental capacity law. It introduced a clear test for deprivation of liberty and clarifies for the first time that people with learning disability are entitled to the same degree of human rights as anybody else.

3.17 INTEGRATING RESEARCH AND PRACTICE

JOHN MCLEOD

OVERVIEW AND KEY POINTS

This chapter explores how knowledge from research can be used to enhance the quality of therapy services that are available to clients. The aims of the chapter are to:

- provide an overview of developments in research on the process and outcomes of counselling and psychotherapy
- identify the key skills and knowledge required to be a research-informed practitioner
- discuss critical issues and debates within this field, and their implications for the future of counselling and psychotherapy research and practice.

INTRODUCTION

The principle of evidence-based practice, widely adopted within the health and social care professions, has contributed to pressure for counselling and psychotherapy practice to be research-informed. Therapy service providers and consumer groups increasingly expect research evidence about the effectiveness of different therapy approaches to be available. Research also functions to support therapist learning and development, and to provide clients with opportunities to present their perspective on what has been helpful or unhelpful in the therapy they have received.

It is possible to differentiate between two broad areas of focus for therapy research: outcome and process. Outcome research seeks to establish the effectiveness of different therapy interventions. Process research examines the ways in which different activities and factors contribute to outcome.

Counselling and psychotherapy process research began with the pioneering work of Carl Rogers and his colleagues in the 1940s, into the 'necessary and sufficient conditions' for therapeutic change. Since that time, a wide range of methods for studying therapy process have been developed. Some studies have used quantitative methods, such as questionnaires or rating scales completed by clients and therapists at the end of therapy sessions, or coding systems applied by raters to analyse recordings of sessions. Other process research makes use of qualitative methods, such as interviews with clients and therapists, and analysis of patterns of narrative and discourse in transcripts of therapy sessions. An important recent development has been the availability of unobtrusive physiological monitoring techniques to investigate embodied processes in sessions.

The largest single body of research into the process of therapy has centred on the question of the characteristics of facilitative client–therapist relationships, for example using the Working Alliance Inventory to invite clients and therapists to record their perceptions of the strength of *bond*, *task* and *goal* dimensions of the relationship. This research has produced convincing evidence that the strength of the working alliance early in therapy and successful resolution of ruptures in the alliance are significant predictors of eventual good outcome in therapy. Other psychotherapy process research has used qualitative methods to examine the client's experience of the therapy process, and the ways that different ways of using language (e.g., metaphors, questions, silence) influence therapy interactions. There is also extensive research into the nature of psychoanalytic processes in therapy, such as the role of transference and countertransference.

Outcome research (also described as 'efficacy', 'effectiveness' or 'evaluation' studies) has the primary aim of finding out how much a particular counselling or therapy intervention has helped or benefited the client. Findings from follow-up studies, in which client symptoms are measured at the start and end of therapy, consistently indicate that around two-thirds of clients improve, with one-third remaining the same or deteriorating after treatment. The limitation of this kind of research design are readily apparent: it is possible that all, or some, of the clients who improved might have done so even if they had not received therapy. In response to this methodological critique, many outcome studies have employed the strategy of the randomised controlled trial (RCT), in which clients are assessed prior to receiving therapy and are randomly allocated to different treatment conditions. Within this design, it can be assumed that any differences in outcome between the treatment groups at the end of therapy are attributable to the effects of therapy, because all other factors have been held constant. From the 1970s, many hundreds of RCTs have been carried out into the impact of different therapy approaches on different client populations. Once a number of RCTs have been conducted, it is possible to look at whether a consistent pattern emerges regarding the relative effectiveness of competing therapy models with particular client groups. This procedure involves the use of a technique for systematic review of outcome literature, known as meta-analysis.

Although there is no doubt that RCTs represent a powerful tool for examining the effectiveness of counselling and psychotherapy, it is also clear that there are many challenging methodological issues associated with the use of this approach within the domain of research in counselling and psychotherapy. In essence, the critical factor is that the technical requirements of a good randomised trial mean that the clients who are recruited to the study, and the therapy that is provided for them, may be rather different from therapy that occurs in routine practice. As a result, RCT findings may lack relevance for everyday practice. By contrast, practice-based or naturalistic outcome studies, where all clients receiving therapy from an agency or a clinic complete brief symptom scales at each session, are more faithful to the conditions of everyday therapy (Holmqvist, Philips and Barkham, 2015).

In recognition of the fact that therapy is a complex phenomenon, there is widespread acknowledgement across the psychotherapy research community that it is necessary to make use of the different types of knowledge and insight offered by a diversity of research methodologies – a principle that has been described as *methodological pluralism* (Slife and Gantt, 1999). Recent years have seen the emergence and increasing application of an ever-expanding repertoire of research approaches, including many varieties of qualitative, quantitative and mixed methods studies, as well as systematic case studies, economic cost–benefit analyses, studies co-produced by researchers and service users, personal experience research such as autoethnography, ecological data collection in everyday life settings, and use of techniques from neuroscience.

ESSENTIAL RESEARCH SKILLS AND KNOWLEDGE

In order to be adequately research-informed, therapists need to have a sufficient overview of the field of counselling and psychotherapy research as a whole, in order to be able to find their way around the available literature. Brief introductory accounts of the history and current status of therapy research can be found in McLeod (2019). More detailed discussion of specific areas of therapy research can be found in Barkham, Castonguay and Lutz (2021) and Gelo, Pritz and Rieken (2015).

Beyond a general map of the territory of therapy research, it is essential to be able to locate and critically analyse research articles, and understand the purposes and methodological procedures associated with a range of core types of research articles: systematic reviews of research findings; qualitative, interview-based research; quantitative outcome research; systematic case study research; and personal experience research. Further information on these approaches is available in Bager-Charleson and McBeath (2021) and Vossler and Moller (2015).

Learning about how therapy research is carried out is most effective, in terms of leaving a career-long curiosity and interest in research on the part of the learner, when it is delivered by teachers who are also therapists and able to talk about how research findings have influenced their own work with clients, and learners are able to participate in actual research studies (Gelso, Baumann and Chui, 2013). The therapy research textbook by McLeod (2022) has been written to support this kind of model of apprenticeship learning.

There is an understandable degree of caution in therapists, around sticking to hard-won ideas, skills and methods that have served them well in the past. As a consequence of these factors, the majority of therapists are reluctant to change their practice in the light of knowledge that they may have gleaned from reading research studies. The *points of contact* model suggests that, rather than aiming to be explicitly research-informed across the whole of one's practice, it is more realistic to think in terms of a specific, limited number of points of contact between research and practice (McLeod, 2016). For example, with most of their clients, a therapist may operate at a satisfactory level of effectiveness. However, they may become aware that there are some skills, such as broaching difference or engaging in self-disclosure, that are awkward to use or trigger negative client responses. In these instances, it may be useful to look closely at the relevant research literature for indications of alternative ways of deploying that skill – and then use training, deliberate practice and supervision to become more competent and comfortable with it. Another type of point of contact between research and practice is when a therapy clinic or agency notices that certain groups of clients are not being well served, or there are difficulties with structural aspects of the service, such as waiting lists or risk management. In these scenarios, the research literature is likely to provide a variety of strategies and options that the agency might try out or consider. A point of contact perspective does not assume that research evidence will necessarily produce a clear-cut answer to a practice dilemma (although this can sometimes happen). Instead, the literature offers new ways of thinking about a problem, and examples of what has worked or not worked, in different contexts.

An area of therapy practice that can be challenging for both individual clinicians and therapy services as a whole is how to handle situations in which the therapist and client identify with different cultural and ethnic traditions and backgrounds. These situations can lead not only to misunderstanding between therapist and client, but can also evoke painful and hard-to-talk-about emotions, memories and trauma associated with experiences of racism, oppression, colonialism and white privilege. Research into culturally-sensitive and culturally-adapted therapy, and the experience of clients and therapists, allows readers to stand back from their own individual experience, acquire a broader perspective, and learn from the experience of others. Examples of studies that have the potential to provide such insights include Dos Santos and Dallos (2012), Gandhi (2021), Tarabi, Louloupoulou and Henton (2020) and Ward (2005).

RESEARCH THAT CAN BE INTEGRATED INTO PRACTICE

Research on counselling and psychotherapy is conducted for a variety of purposes. Many studies are carried out by full-time researchers based in universities and research centres, with the aim of contributing to policy-making and the development of academic theory and knowledge. However, there are also excellent studies carried out by researchers who are primarily therapy practitioners, and activities that involve therapists directly using research techniques and tools within their work with clients. Examples of this kind of practice-near research include professional knowledge studies, investigating one's own practice, and the application of client feedback and monitoring techniques.

Professional knowledge studies. One of the ways in which therapists develop and maintain competence is through sharing what they have learned through informal and informal communities of practice. Professional knowledge research takes this a step further by collecting and analysing therapist experiences, using interviews, surveys and other methods (McLeod, 2022). Involvement in professional knowledge research is meaningful for both trainees and seasoned practitioners, because it speaks directly to their interests and concerns. It is also possible to be a research participant, by being willing to be interviewed or completing a survey, or initiating such a study within one's own professional community. Studies that exemplify the range and scope of professional knowledge research include Bimont and Werbart (2018), Mjelve, Ulleberg and Vonheim (2020) and Tummala-Narra et al. (2018).

Investigating one's own practice. Although ethical and boundary issues need to be sensitively handled, there are many ways in which practitioners can use research methods to analyse and document their own training and practice, ranging from autoethnography (Råbu et al., 2021) to analysis of case records (Clement, 1994). A particularly valuable approach to using one's own practice for research purposes is through conducting a systematic case study research (McLeod, Thurston and McLeod, 2014) based around: (1) the construction of a rich dataset on the case, drawn from a range of different sources of information; and (2) the analysis of case data by a group or team of researchers (usually including the therapist, and sometimes also including the client). The case study method is making an increasingly significant contribution to the evidence base for counselling and psychotherapy (Fishman, 2017). Practitioners are in a good position to collect and write up case studies based on their own work with clients, as well as using involvement in case study inquiry groups to enhance personal and professional development. Examples of different styles of systematic single-case investigations where the therapist is also the main researcher include Blunden (2020), Fleet et al. (2016) and Pass (2012).

Using feedback and monitoring tools in work with clients. One of the most important shifts in counselling and psychotherapy practice over the last 20 years has been the growing use of brief process and outcome monitoring scales completed by clients at every session, as a means of tracking change and facilitating collaborative dialogue with clients around whether therapy is meeting their needs (Lambert, 2017). The first wave of research into this technique provided consistent evidence that this way of collecting feedback had a meaningful positive impact on the outcomes of therapy, particularly for client whose improvement had stalled. Subsequent research suggested that the picture was more complicated, with the effective use of feedback tools depending on successful negotiation of a range of contextual factors, including therapist attitude and competence (Solstad et al., 2021) and appropriate choice of feedback tool. The use of feedback and monitoring tools to enhance client engagement in therapy therefore represents a situation in which practitioners need to have a sufficient understanding of not only the specific techniques that are available, but also the underlying issues and processes that are evoked when such instruments are administered.

Although the approaches to counselling and psychotherapy research discussed above are explicitly oriented towards the needs and interests of practitioners, and the opportunities that are open to them, it is important to note that they almost always involve some degree of collaboration with university-based researchers, for instance in the context of studying for a postgraduate qualification, or as part of a practice research network (Barkham, 2014). In addition, there is an increasing use of research designs that embed focused qualitative or case study projects into large-scale randomised trials (Fishman et al., 2017).

CONCLUSION

It is essential to acknowledge the limitations of research into counselling and psychotherapy. Compared to a field such as biomedical science, or even a single sector of that field, such as cancer care, the number of active psychotherapy researchers is significantly smaller (McLeod, 2017).

The existence of schools of therapy, each with its own theoretical perspective, presents further difficulties for the psychotherapy research community in respect of researcher allegiance effects and overall research strategy. Researcher allegiance refers to the tendency for researchers conducting supposedly rigorous and well-controlled scientific outcome studies to report results that favour the therapy approach in which they have been trained, at the expense of whatever approach to which it has been compared (Luborsky et al., 1999). Further criticism of therapy research has focused on the ways in which the views and experiences of service users, and members of minority groups, are not sufficiently reflected in published studies (McPherson et al., 2020; Smith et al., 2021).

While it is essential to be aware of the limitations of contemporary research in counselling and psychotherapy, it is also clear that it has the potential to represent a distinctive and essential source of information for practice. It is widely acknowledged that research training needs to be incorporated into counsellor and psychotherapist training programmes, and that updating research should be made available through continuing professional development. The central or core research competency that needs to be acquired during basic training is the ability to read and critically appraise the contribution that research articles and reviews can make to practice. Beyond this, trainees need to know about the strengths and weaknesses of different methods for evaluating therapy outcomes, and to be helped to develop their own position in relation to ongoing debates about the nature of evidence-based practice and the relative effectiveness of different therapy interventions for particular disorders. Finally, it is not possible to appreciate the research process without experiencing it first-hand and actually *doing* a research study of some kind (McLeod, 2022).

REFERENCES

Bager-Charleson, S., & McBeath, A. (Eds) (2021). *Enjoying Research in Counselling and Psychotherapy: Qualitative, Quantitative and Mixed Methods*. London: Palgrave Macmillan.

Barkham, M. (2014). Practice-based research networks: Origins, overview, obstacles, and opportunities. *Counselling and Psychotherapy Research*, *14*(3), 167–173.

(Continued)

(*Continued*)

Barkham, M., Castonguay, L., & Lutz, W. (Eds) (2021). *Bergin and Garfield's Handbook of Psychotherapy and Behavior Change* (7th ed.). New York: Wiley.

Bimont, D., & Werbart, A. (2018). 'I've got you under my skin': Relational therapists' experiences of patients who occupy their inner world. *Counselling Psychology Quarterly*, *31*(2), 243–268.

Blunden, N. (2020). 'And we are a human being': Coproduced reflections on person-centred psychotherapy in plural and dissociative identity. *Psychotherapy and Politics International*, e1578.

Clement, P.W. (1994). Quantitative evaluation of 26 years of private practice. *Professional Psychology: Research and Practice*, *25*, 173–176.

Dos Santos, O., & Dallos, R. (2012). The process of cross-cultural therapy between white therapists and clients of African-Caribbean descent. *Qualitative Research in Psychology*, *9*(1), 62–74.

Fishman, D.B. (2017). The pragmatic case study in psychotherapy: A mixed methods approach informed by psychology's striving for methodological quality. *Clinical Social Work Journal*, *45*(3), 238–252.

Fishman, D., Messer, S.D., Edwards, D.J.A., & Dattilio, F.M. (2017). *Case Studies within Psychotherapy Trials: Integrating Qualitative and Quantitative Methods*. New York: Oxford University Press.

Fleet, D., Burton, A., Reeves, A., & DasGupta, M.P. (2016). A case for taking the dual role of counsellor-researcher in qualitative research. *Qualitative Research in Psychology*, *13*(4), 328–346.

Gandhi, R.S. (2021). Being brown: An autoethnographic exploration of internalised colonisation. *Psychodynamic Practice*, *27*(2), 127–143.

Gelo, O.C.G., Pritz, A., & Rieken, B. (Eds) (2015). *Psychotherapy Research: Foundations, Process, and Outcome*. New York: Springer.

Gelso, C.J., Baumann, E.C., Chui, H.T., et al. (2013). The making of a scientist–psychotherapist: The research training environment and the psychotherapist. *Psychotherapy*, *50*, 139–149.

Holmqvist, R., Philips, B., & Barkham, M. (2015). Developing practice-based evidence: Benefits, challenges, and tensions. *Psychotherapy Research*, *25*(1), 20–31.

Lambert, M.J. (2017). Maximizing psychotherapy outcome beyond evidence-based medicine. *Psychotherapy and Psychosomatics*, *86*(2), 80–89.

Luborsky, l., Diguer, L, Seligman, D.A., Rosenthal, R.,. Krause, E.D., Johnson, S., Halperin, G., Bishop, M,. Berman, J.S., & Schweizer, E. (1999). The researcher's own therapy allegiances: A "wild card" in comparisons of treatment efficacy. *Clinical Psychology: Science and Practice 6*, 95–106.

McLeod, J. (2016). *Using Research in Counselling and Psychotherapy*. London: Sage.

McLeod, J. (2017). Science and psychotherapy: Developing research-based knowledge that enhances the effectiveness of practice. *Transactional Analysis Journal*, *47*(2), 82–101.

McLeod, J. (2019). *An Introduction to Counselling and Psychotherapy* (6th ed.). Maidenhead: Open University Press.

McLeod, J. (2022). *Doing Research in Counselling and Psychotherapy* (4th ed.). London: Sage.

McLeod, Julia, Thurston, M., & McLeod, J. (2014). Case study methodologies. In A. Vossler and N. Moller (Eds), *The Counselling and Psychotherapy Research Handbook*. London: Sage.

McPherson, S., Rost, F., Sidhu, S., & Dennis, M. (2020). Non-strategic ignorance: Considering the potential for a paradigm shift in evidence-based mental health. *Health*, *24*(1), 3–20.

Mjelve, L.H., Ulleberg, I., & Vonheim, K. (2020). 'What do I share?' Personal and private experiences in educational psychological counselling. *Scandinavian Journal of Educational Research*, *64*(2), 181–194.

Pass, E.R. (2012). Combining expressive writing with an affect- and attachment-focused psychotherapeutic approach in the treatment of a single-incident trauma survivor: The case of 'Grace'. *Pragmatic Case Studies in Psychotherapy*, *8*(2), 60–112.

Råbu, M., McLeod, J., Haavind, H., Bernhardt, I.S., Nissen-Lie, H., & Moltu, C. (2021). How psychotherapists make use of their experiences from being a client: Lessons from a collective autoethnography. *Counselling Psychology Quarterly*, *34*(1), 109–128.

Slife, B.D., & Gantt, E.E. (1999). Methodological pluralism: A framework for psychotherapy research. *Journal of Clinical Psychology*, *55*(12), 1453–1465.

Smith, K., McLeod, J., Blunden, N., Cooper, M., Gabriel, L., Kupfer, C., … & Winter, L.A. (2021). A pluralistic perspective on research in psychotherapy: Harnessing passion, difference and dialogue to promote justice and relevance. *Frontiers in Psychology*, 3728.

Solstad, S.M., Kleiven, G.S., Castonguay, L.G., & Moltu, C. (2021). Clinical dilemmas of routine outcome monitoring and clinical feedback: A qualitative study of patient experiences. *Psychotherapy Research*, *31*(2), 200–210.

Tarabi, S.A., Loulopoulou, A.I., & Henton, I. (2020). 'Guide or conversation?' The experience of second-generation Pakistani Muslim men receiving CBT in the UK. *Counselling Psychology Quarterly*, *33*(1), 46–65.

Tummala-Narra, P., Claudius, M., Letendre, P.J., Sarbu, E., Teran, V., & Villalba, W. (2018). Psychoanalytic psychologists' conceptualizations of cultural competence in psychotherapy. *Psychoanalytic Psychology*, *35*(1), 46–59.

Vossler, A., & Moller, N. (Eds) (2015). *The Counselling and Psychotherapy Research Handbook*. London: Sage.

Ward, E.C. (2005). Keeping it real: A grounded theory study of African American clients engaged in counseling at a community mental health agency. *Journal of Counseling Psychology*, *52*(4), 471–481.

RECOMMENDED READING

Carey, T.A., & Stiles, W.B. (2016). Some problems with randomized controlled trials and some viable alternatives. *Clinical Psychology and Psychotherapy*, *23*, 87–95.

A thoughtful discussion of the challenges involved in conducting therapy research in a manner that is faithful to the complexity of practice.

McLeod, J. (2022). *Doing Research in Counselling and Psychotherapy* (4th ed.). London: Sage.

Detailed guidelines on how to carry out, and critically evaluate, all of the main types of counselling and psychotherapy research study.

Patel, T. (2020). Research in therapeutic practice settings: Ethical considerations. In R. Tribe & J. Morrissey (Eds), *The Handbook of Professional Ethical and Research Practice for Psychologists, Counsellors, Psychotherapists and Psychiatrists* (3rd ed., pp. 191–205). London: Routledge.

Research in counselling and psychotherapy is highly ethically sensitive, because it involves collecting data from individuals who may be emotionally vulnerable. This chapter provides an informative and accessible guide to ethical principles and procedures for addressing such dilemmas.

3.18 LEADERSHIP: THERAPISTS AS LEADERS

DAISY BEST AND HELEN NICHOLAS

OVERVIEW AND KEY POINTS

This chapter introduces leadership, the attributes associated with good leadership and how these align with the training and experience of therapists' leadership skills. Compassionate leadership fits well with the values of therapists, so this is explored alongside self-awareness and social justice. The authors make a case for leadership as an applied concept, attainable for all therapists regardless of context or role. This chapter suggests:

- Therapists have a wide range of transferable skills suitable for leadership positions.
- Emotional intelligence is essential in leadership.
- Self-awareness and compassion are important in leadership roles.
- Therapists can learn about their own managerial and leadership style through personal and professional development.
- Therapists can create a variety of opportunities to develop as a leader at work, in their professional bodies, organisations and personal life.

WHAT IS LEADERSHIP?

Leadership has many components and is ever evolving. For example, it is no longer only where one person directs the roles and responsibilities of others. Effective leadership can also be measured by how the 'group membership' is fostered within the team (Rhodes, 2016). The ability to work alongside others, encourage shared goals and nurture collective ideas, underpinned by an ethical framework, is what makes psychologists, counsellors and therapists ideal leaders.

Leadership differs from management in that leaders don't necessarily have overall responsibility for an organisation or the people within it. For example, within a domestic violence counselling service, the manager is expected to have some or all responsibility for the staff, budget, and the effective running of the service. The leader may facilitate a domestic violence awareness programme for survivors, organise fundraising activities, and plan self-care activities for staff. Therefore, managers are leaders, but leaders are not always managers.

Our conceptualisation of leadership may depend on our own experiences of leaders and line managers in our past, and represents a diverse field (McIntosh, Nicholas and Huq, 2019). The research on leadership has included personality trait theories, where key personality traits have been attributed to leaders. For example, extraversion has been shown to be the most important trait of effective leaders (Judge et al., 2002) alongside cognitive ability, conscientiousness and emotional stability (Tagger, Hackett and Saha, 1999). There are also theories about transformational leadership (Bass, 1999), where leaders are inspirational and develop their 'followers' into leaders. The literature on leadership presents a plethora of research on specific managerial styles (e.g., authoritarian, laissez-faire, democratic) and the important qualities leaders need to have to be effective within their teams. The expectations put on leaders is ever growing and they are often expected to display qualities, behaviours and excellence in so many areas that it may be daunting to those wanting to gain some experience in this area. More often, within organisations there is a need to develop leaders who have specific skills, expertise and abilities, which may include succession planning and future proofing teams. For therapists, leading a team often runs alongside their clinical workload.

There does not seem to be a standardised approach to leadership. In the United Kingdom, the clinical leadership competency framework outlines 'leadership competencies that clinicians need to become more actively involved in the planning, delivery and transformation of health and social care services' (NHS Leadership Academy, 2011: 6). The original NHS leadership framework was criticised for being reductionist, not specific enough to the situation or task, and that it focused on training rather than development. However, it did serve to highlight some of the personal qualities and behaviours that effective leaders should aspire towards. Most of these skills are already included in the training that therapists receive, and therefore the authors are very much in favour of outlining the transferable skills that are important. Within therapy training, an emphasis on personal development and self-awareness is standard and forms part of many professional and regulatory body competences (British Association for Counselling and Psychotherapy (BACP), 2018; Health and Care Professions Council (HCPC), 2015; UK Council for Psychotherapy (UKCP), 2017). This includes how to act with integrity, the importance of professional and personal development, and managing emotions, which are all important qualities of a leader. Another transferable skill is working with others. Therapists build and maintain relationships, encourage contributions and work well within teams. Managers of therapeutic services also need to manage their teams, team resources, as well as the performance of their staff. Improving and critically evaluating services, facilitating change, making decisions and evaluating the impact of changes made are all key to managing a therapeutic service.

CHARACTERISTICS OF A LEADER (AND OF A THERAPIST)

COMPASSION

With an increased demand for mental health services and a reduction in resources, pressure on services is increasing (The Kings Fund, 2015), and have been worsened by the Covid-19 pandemic (British Medical Association, 2021). It is therefore more vital than ever that staff wellbeing is considered and supported by leaders. Leadership approaches that are interpersonal and socially attuned are more likely to enhance wellbeing (Rhodes, 2016). One form of this type of leadership style is compassionate leadership.

Compassion is fundamental to our work as therapists and has been described as '…a basic kindness, with a deep awareness of the suffering of oneself and of other living things, coupled with the wish and effort to relieve it' (Gilbert, 2013: xiii). In a compassionate leadership context, it has also been described as 'attending, understanding, empathising and helping' (Atkins and Parker, 2012, cited in West et al., 2017: 3; and West, 2021: 5–6). Therefore, the aim of being 'aware' in order to 'relieve' suffering is seen in a compassion-focused approach to therapy and compassionate leadership. Attending, which requires the ability to actively listen and to pay attention to what is being said (and not said), is a core skill that we learn during training. We demonstrate this by summarising and clarifying without judgement and with empathy. The process of being understood is empowering as we show that we are making sense of and valuing an individual's experience, thus enhancing self-efficacy and others' ability to solve problems for themselves. We provide an empathic environment where the individual can feel sufficiently safe to trust, and therefore take risks to change. In our helping role, we work collaboratively to generate solutions. Thus, the overlap between the skills required to be a compassionate therapist and compassionate leader is evident.

Compassionate leadership is an approach that allows for innovation without blame or bullying when the outcome is not successful. Also, it provides the experience of 'psychological safety' in which people can speak out and feel 'empowered' to develop and deliver new ways of working for the benefit of services (West et al., 2017). This approach is consistent with how we work with our clients, in that we place value on their experiences and recognise their autonomy in their journey towards their goals, all from a foundation of the core conditions of empathy, unconditional positive regard and congruence (Rogers, 1961). Compassionate leadership, therefore, allows for individual and organisational growth within a supportive and nurturing context (West, 2021).

SELF-AWARENESS

Self-awareness, generated via self-reflection and personal development, is core to our clinical practice. Being aware of our power in the therapeutic dyad is essential in ensuring optimum equality and collaboration. Awareness of the potential of our power in leadership roles can also prevent others from being harmed when we are in pursuit of our own direction, ensuring 'the same power that allows you to lift the people onto your shoulders treads none underfoot' (Rhodes, 2016: 7). It has been argued that becoming a leader, and therefore gaining a position associated with power, can result in a move towards superiority which risks oppressing others (Taylor, 2021). Awareness of our own emotional intelligence, behaviour towards others and ability to reflect upon our interactions could eradicate this risk. As Taylor (2021: 44) identifies, 'empathic and conscientious people should be encouraged to take up positions of power', illustrating the importance of qualities inherent in our professions that align with a reflective philosophy.

SOCIAL JUSTICE

Social justice is integral to the core values or our work as therapists and is therefore important when considering how we can lead on increasing equality and reducing discrimination. This can be undertaken via activism, training others about injustice and providing therapeutic interventions to those impacted by oppression. It is of equal importance for therapists to ensure models of leadership are 'leaderful' where power is dispersed rather than held by one individual or group (Hargons et al., 2017). Therapists can change societal values, influence policies and engage in community consultation (Tribe, 2019), while also being conscious of their power and privilege (Winter, 2019).

CREATING LEADERSHIP OPPORTUNITIES

With the skills for leadership already within the grasp of therapists, we can begin to consider the opportunities for all to become involved in leadership. Some examples of how we can create these opportunities are provided here. Many therapists already possess a range of 'business' related skills, including managing budgets and finite resources, evaluating services, applying for funding and writing policies. Furthermore, using creativity and innovation for marketing and social media campaigns are opportunities in which leadership can be exercised.

Both authors have held leadership positions, one within a psychology academic department and one within an NHS psychology service. Making the transition between therapist and manager can be challenging. Our split roles of psychologist in a clinical setting and in a leadership and managerial role needed skills in time management, conducting staff reviews and appraisals, performance reviews, return-to-work interviews, monitoring staff wellbeing, involvement in mental health campaigns, teaching roles, planning, and developing services. Within the NHS, leaders at a Band 8 practitioner psychologist level need to demonstrate knowledge of legislation, policy, the ability to support staff who may experience distressing situations, using clinical governance mechanisms to support clinical practice, carrying out research, auditing, evaluating therapy services and safeguarding.

Your role may include being a mentor, coach, compassionate listener, container to hold staff anxieties or difficulties, and the ability to focus on staff resilience levels. You may also need to get involved in mediation if human resources are involved in a performance review. These tasks are usually part of other roles that you will need to carry out, such as clinical practice, carrying a workload, research and lecturing in academia.

Consultant roles and head of NHS services can take many years of experience to gain. However, there are other leadership roles that are attainable for early career therapists who would like to become involved in leadership projects and gain valuable leadership experience to apply for these roles in future. Leadership skills can be learnt and, as therapists, we can be leaders in a variety of settings. We can plan and facilitate a therapy group, lead a conference symposium and sit on a committee with your regulatory or professional body. Therapists can also experience leadership responsibilities and make an impact through supervision and mentoring others.

Supervision can be in formal settings, such as where the supervisor is clinically responsible for the trainee, in consultant settings, such as mentoring, coaching, consultation amd peer supervision, or as a tutor–tutee relationship in academia. It is important to separate your role as a line manager/tutor and your clinical supervisory responsibilities, keeping an eye on the dual relationship. Being supervised by your line managers can pose multiple relationship and ethical issues (Tromski-Klingshirn and Davis, 2007). Although supervision may not be a regulatory requirement, it is seen as essential in the continuing professional development of psychologists (British Psychological Society, 2017a; HCPC, 2015) and therapists. Responsibility for supervising those in training provides us with opportunities to lead by example. Leadership in this context can include supporting the trainee to apply theory to practice, including developing an understanding of the application of ethical codes and working with them to nurture their own style of working. In contributing to the development of our future colleagues, we can provide a collaborative space in which trainees/students can learn as well as contribute to service development and innovation.

Mentoring can be seen more as guiding and influencing the mentee, and mentoring relationships are personal in nature, involving direct interaction. Mentoring represents an integrated approach whereby the mentor supports the mentees' development. This can include psychological, practical and emotional support as well as direct guidance on the job role and career development. Some key characteristics of the mentoring relationship of clinical medical students (Dimitriadis et al., 2012; Meinel et al., 2011), for example, showed that higher performance students were more likely to be involved in the formal mentoring programme, that the mentoring relationship was mutually satisfying for mentor and mentee, and that the mentoring relationship played a key role in the students' professional development. The mentoring and supervisory relationship can be long lasting and has many benefits for both the supervisor and supervisee (Nicholas and Goodyear, 2020).

Therapists may facilitate groups in their clinical practice that are either therapeutic, psycho-educational or both. We may be responsible for designing the format of a group and then supporting others to take over the leadership of it. Organising, planning, promoting, facilitating, delegating and supporting others in their role are all aspects of effective leadership. Equally, we may lead on specific projects, such as the management of a waiting list or the delivery of a stakeholder event. One of the authors led a project aimed at promoting counselling psychology as part of her role as Training Coordinator for the British Psychological Society, Division of Counselling Psychology. This entailed applying for funding, managing the budget, recruiting a film maker and carrying out interviews with Counselling Psychologists across the UK. She travelled to interview them and worked with the film maker to produce a short film that is available on YouTube (British Psychological Society, 2017b). She used this project to reflect upon and put into action her learning from a Leadership Development Programme that she was attending at the time.

As advocates for mental health awareness, we can lead on campaigns that help to raise awareness of mental health and the services that provide support. Our capacity to work effectively in building relationships may involve working with a range of stakeholders, including the local community, people who access services, trustees, or managers of the organisation we work with and national organisations that can support the work we are doing. We may be well suited to leading committees where we pay close attention to collaboration and a wider understanding of the impact of decisions made on the diversity of the community that the committee is designed to serve (Fassinger and Shullman, 2017).

Finally, during our own training or once we qualify, there are many opportunities for us to engage in research where we can have an impact on policies which, ultimately, help to change or create services and interventions for people. We are driven towards making an impact and publishing research that can be used directly to influence and promote change, which is one way to do this. One of the authors, for example, used their research to contribute to an All-Party Parliamentary Group Inquiry aimed at influencing future service provision for survivors of domestic violence.

Leadership is not just about managing staff and teams, it includes the wellbeing of staff, improving wellbeing at work, helping staff to manage stress and ensuring employee engagement. Research by Young and Bhaumik (2011) outlined demographic, attitudinal and behavioural characteristics associated with 'optimal' employee experiences. Their findings showed that organisations with a higher-than-average retention rate, including those with good relationships between managers and employees, resulted in lower average absences. Those with a higher-than-average employee engagement, where senior managers delivered on their promises, also had lower-than-average absences. It is therefore important that as a leader and manager you consider the relationship you have with your staff, the promises you make (ensuring that these can be kept by you) and how you monitor employee engagement.

Leadership roles often cause you to be in the middle between senior management and the demands and expectations they will place on you and the employees. Both parties may have different needs and be focused on different aspects of their role. For example, within academia, staff (lecturers) will be very focused on their teaching and research responsibilities, with little time to consider retention rates, the marketing of courses and the financial constraints of the university. Senior management may be focusing on balancing staff to student ratios, the financial cost to the department and the direction that the university chancellor is focusing on. As the middle person, this can be difficult to manage and will depend on your own coping strategies, resilience levels and personality.

CONCLUSION

This chapter has highlighted the transferable skills therapist have that are essential in leadership. Many of the skills are learnt during training or in our work as clinicians. It is important to be strategic in your approach to a leadership position and to identify the skills you will need and currently may not have, for example, business development, strategic planning, finance and budgeting. Look out for mentoring and 'buddy' schemes within your organisation, discuss career opportunities with your line manager and perhaps include some of these in your annual appraisal so that there is commitment from your organisation to support you. There are many business-related courses available online. As part of our own personal and professional development, seeking out leadership opportunities, upskilling ourselves and engaging in new challenges has been very rewarding.

REFERENCES

Atkins, P., & Parker, S. (2012). Understanding individual compassion in organisations: the role of appraisals and psychological flexibility. *Academy of Management Review*, 37(4), 524–546.

Bass, B.M. (1999). Two decades of research and development in transformational leadership. *European Journal of Work and Organisational Psychology*, 8(1), 9–32. https://doi.org/10.1080/135943299398410

British Association for Counselling and Psychotherapy (2018). *Ethical Framework for the Counselling Professions*. Lutterworth: BACP. Available at www.bacp.co.uk/media/3103/bacp-ethical-framework-for-the-counselling-professions-2018.pdf

British Medical Association (2021). *The Impact of COVID-19 on Mental Health in England: Supporting Services to Go beyond Parity of Esteem*. London: BMA. Available at bma-the-impact-of-covid-19-on-mental-health-in-england.pdf (accessed 9 November 2021).

British Psychological Society (2017a). *Practice Guidelines and Policies* (3rd ed.). Leicester: BPS. Available at https://www.bps.org.uk/guidelines-and-policies

British Psychological Society (2017b). *Why Counselling Psychology?* YouTube. www.youtube.com/watch?v=JcDKz5J-90s&t=7s

Dimitriadis, K., von der Borch, P., Stormann, S., Meinel, F.G., Moder, S., Reincke, M., & Fischer, M.R. (2012). Characteristics of mentoring relationships formed by medical students and faculty. *Medical Education Online*, 17, 1–9.

Fassinger, R.E., & Shullman, S.L. (2017). Leadership and counseling psychology: What should we know? Where should we go? *The Counselling Psychologist*, 45(7), 927–964.

Gilbert, P. (2013). *The Compassionate Mind*. London: Constable.

Hargons, C., Mosley, D., Falconer, J., Faloughi, R., Singh, A., Stevens-Watkins, D., & Cokley, K. (2017). Black Lives Matter: A call to action for counselling psychology leaders. *The Counselling Psychologist*, 45(6), 873–901. doi: 10.1177/0011000017733048

Health and Care Professions Council (2015). *Standards of Proficiency: Practitioner Psychologists*. London: HCPC. Available at www.hcpc-uk.org/resources/standards/standards-of-proficiency-practitioner-psychologists/

Judge, T.A., Bono, J.E., Ilies, R., & Gerhardt, M.W. (2002). Personality and leadership: A qualitative and quantitative review. *Journal of Applied Psychology*, 87(4), 765–780.

McIntosh, M., Nicholas, H., & Huq, A.H. (Eds) (2019). *Leadership and Diversity in Psychology: Moving beyond the Limits*. Abingdon, UK: Routledge.

Meinel, F.G., Dimitriadis, K., von der Borch, P., Stormann, S., Niedermaier, S., & Fischer, M.R. (2011). More mentoring needed? A cross-sectional study of mentoring programs for medical students in Germany. *BMC Medical Education*, 11(68), 1–11. https://doi.org/10.1186/1472-6920-11-68

Nicholas, H., & Goodyear, R. (2020). Supervision of a sample of clinical and counselling psychologists in the UK: A descriptive study of their practices, processes and perceived benefits. *The European Journal of Counselling Psychology*, 9(1), 39–48.

NHS Leadership Academy (2011). *Clinical Leadership Competency Framework*. London: NHS Institute for Innovation and Improvement. Available at www.leadershipacademy.nhs.uk/wp-content/uploads/2012/11/NHSLeadership-Leadership-Framework-Clinical-Leadership-Competency-Framework-CLCF.pdf

Rhodes, E. (2016). The psychologist guide to… leadership. *The Psychologist*, 9 May. Leicester: British Psychological Society. Available at www.bps.org.uk/psychologist/psychologist-guide-leadership

Rogers, C. (1961). *On Becoming a Person: A Therapist's View of Psychotherapy*. Boston, MA: Houghton-Mifflin.

Tagger, S., Hackett, R., & Saha, S. (1999). Leadership emergence in autonomous work teams: Antecedents and outcomes. *Personnel Psychology*, 52, 899–926. https://onlinelibrary.wiley.com/doi/epdf/10.1111/j.1744-6570.1999.tb00184.x

Taylor, S. (2021). The problem of pathocracy. *The Psychologist*, 8 October. Leicester: British Psychological Society.

The Kings Fund (2015). *Briefing Paper: Mental Health under Pressure*. London: The Kings Fund. Available at www.kingsfund.org.uk/sites/default/files/field/field_publication_file/mental-health-under-pressure-nov15_0.pdf

Tribe, R. (2019). Social justice, leadership and diversity. In M. McIntosh, H. Nicholas & A.H. Huq (Eds), *Leadership and Diversity in Psychology: Moving Beyond the Limits*. Abingdon, UK: Routledge

Tromski-Klingshirn, D.M., & Davis, T.E. (2007). Supervisees' perceptions of their clinical supervision: A study of the dual role of clinical and administrative supervisor. *Counselor Education and Supervision*, 46(4), 294–304. https://doi.org/10.1002/j.1556-6978.2007.tb00033.x

UK Council for Psychotherapy (2017). *UKCP Standards of Education and Training: The Minimum Core Criteria Psychotherapy with Adults*. London: UKCP. Available at www.psychotherapy.org.uk/media/03olj3jw/ukcp-adult-standards-of-education-and-training-2017.pdf

West, M. (2021). *Compassionate Leadership: Sustaining Wisdom, Humanity and Presence in Health and Social Care.* London: The Swirling Leaf Press.

West, M., Eckert, R., Collins, B., & Chowla, R. (2017). *Caring to Change: How Compassionate Leadership Can Stimulate Innovation in Health Care.* London: The Kings Fund. Available at www.kingsfund.org.uk/sites/default/files/field/field_publication_file/Caring_to_change_Kings_Fund_May_2017.pdf

Winter, L.A. (2019). Power and privilege in psychology: Can we have egalitarian leadership. In M. McIntosh, H. Nicholas & A.H. Huq (Eds), *Leadership and Diversity in Psychology: Moving Beyond the Limits*. Abingdon, UK: Routledge.

Young, V., & Bhaumik, C. (2011). *Health and Well-Being at Work: A Survey of Employees.* Department for Work and Pensions Research Report No. 751. London: Department for Work and Pensions. Available at https://assets.publishing.service.gov.uk/government/uploads/system/uploads/attachment_data/file/214526/rrep751.pdf

RECOMMENDED READING

Chen, P.Y. & Cooper, C.L. (Eds) (2014). *Wellbeing: A Complete Reference Guide*. Vol. III *Work and Wellbeing*. Hoboken, NJ: Wiley Blackwell.

This book has a wealth of evidence-based research and practice-based knowledge for leaders who are open to reflecting on their organisations, their own and staff work–life balance and looks at how they can promote wellbeing in their organisations and in their teams.

McIntosh, M., Nicholas, H., & Huq, A.H. (Eds) (2019). *Leadership and Diversity in Psychology: Moving Beyond the Limits*. Abingdon, UK: Routledge.

Leadership comes with both opportunities and challenges. This book presents the personal and honest accounts of practitioner psychologists in leadership roles, working with diverse client groups and using differing leadership skills and styles. It is an insightful, reflective and informative book.

West, M.A. (2021). *Compassionate Leadership: Sustaining Wisdom, Humanity and Presence in Health and Social Care.* London: The Swirling Leaf Press.

The book provides excellent resources and opportunities for leaders to reflect on their own organisation and ways of developing a more compassionate way of working. Issues such as inclusivity, psychological safety and self-care, which align perfectly with our values, are explored.

3.19 SOCIAL MEDIA AND PROFESSIONALISM

JULIE PRESCOTT AND CHATHURIKA KANNANGARA

OVERVIEW AND KEY POINTS

> Social networks are creating new ethical problems. Counsellors need ethical guidelines and procedures to minimise the negative impact of their public stance, as someone taking a public position needs to take time to determine how this will affect their professional life. (Haeny, 2014: 1)

As the opening quote highlights, consideration and guidance is needed for counsellors using social media, as well as technology more generally. This chapter will consider how counsellors can safely use, and benefit from the use of, social media, while remaining professional in their use. The key areas of consideration are:

- Social media is public and publishing online leaves a digital footprint, even when the content is deleted. Therefore, caution is required when engaging in social media platforms both on a personal and professional level.
- Professional boundaries need to be maintained at all times. This is inclusive of when a counsellor is using social media for personal reasons. Your personal use of social media in terms of what you say, like and share may impact a person's judgement of you as a counsellor. Therefore, be mindful in what you post and say on social media at all times.
- A clear distinction between a counsellor's personal and professional online presence is advised. As the previous two points highlight, boundaries between the professional and the personal can often blur online. Therefore, even if you feel you have clearly separated the two, still be mindful of your use.
- Counsellors can, and indeed have the right to, use social media, but they do need to remain mindful of this use and should not have an online presence that compromises their professionalism, their work with clients or engage in content that has an adverse effect on the profession.
- The Golden Rule is if in doubt, do not post it, share it or comment on it! Always remain professional and think of any potential impact of your post/comments.

INTRODUCTION

Social media use is a popular online activity and has become a norm. Social media comes in many forms, including blogs, forums, platforms for photo-sharing, chat apps, social gaming and social networks sites (SNS). Current social media platforms include: TikTok, Twitter, Instagram, Facebook, Snapchat, YouTube, LinkedIn, Reddit, WhatsApp and Pintrest. Recent estimates suggest there are over 2.95 billion global SNS users (Tankovska, 2020). According to UK data, in January 2021 there were 53 million active social media users, equating to 77.9% of the UK population. These statistics emphasise the popularity of social media and SNS use across the population (Statista Research Department, 2021). Despite the public nature of posting on SNS and social media platforms, social media platforms are often used as modern mechanisms through which individuals may access support and services, including mental health support and services (e.g., Brown, Rathbone and Prescott, 2021; Prescott, Rathbone and Brown, 2020). Social media has the potential to provide support and access to a wide audience, but the use of social media can pose new ethical problems for counsellors and therapists (Frankish et al., 2012; White and Hanley, 2022). Indeed, the British Association of Counsellors and Psychotherapists (BACP) acknowledge this need for guidance and have provided information for counsellors on the BACP website in order to help counsellors understand and navigate social media in an ethical way (BACP, 2021a). Please take a look at this guidance for further information on this topic before you engage in social media as a professional. The Health and Care Professionals Council (HCPC) also provides its members with guidance, as well as some case study examples, on using social media (HCPC, 2021). The UK Council for Psychotherapy (UKCP) also has some guidelines for members that readers may find useful (UKCP, 2021).

The more we use technology, the more the boundaries between our professional and personal selves are likely to blur. Professionals need to be mindful of the blurring of boundaries online as social media can feel like a safe space in which to express your personal opinions. However, your personal thoughts and opinions may differ from those you as a professional would like to be associated with, and they may also not be opinions and thoughts that other counselling professionals want to be associated with the profession more generally. All content on social media needs to be professional. It is advised that you set any settings within a platform to the most secure limit to control who can view your personal social media platforms as well as limit who can access the images and photos that others may post of you. Through making your accounts secure, you are taking as much control as possible of the content that is posted on your accounts.

REMEMBER! If in any doubt – do not post!

Also be mindful of resharing and reposting/retweeting posts and content with thread messages. The content in a thread may also have implications for yourself and bring into question your professionalism. Therefore, you need to make sure you read the whole thread before you reshare. So, even if an opinion is not that of the person sharing the information or related to the counselling profession, it may be perceived as such. For example, retweeting an interesting post and the comments in the thread may be viewed as the counsellor's opinion. Remember that being professional includes images, language use, behaviour as well as your associations, likes and dislikes on social media.

WAYS OF WORKING

Although we want to advise caution when sharing online, we also want to highlight the benefits of being a counselling professional who utilises social media. It is common practise for many counsellors and psychotherapists to carry out their therapy activities in a private sphere. Practitioners are now starting to use social media to reach and influence the wider world. If applied mindfully, social media can help to inform, educate the public, destigmatise mental health, as well as normalise and promote therapy – all great things! The mindful use of social media can be a powerful tool when applied appropriately, and we suggest reflecting on the following in your social media usage: purpose, audience, boundaries, control and ethical practice. Setting a purpose for your use of social media is important and can enable you to consider your audience, set boundaries and control any potential ethical issues or concerns that may be raised.

PURPOSE

While social media can be beneficial for the counselling profession and individual practitioners, it is important to evaluate the use of social media. The first step is to define the purpose of why you are engaging in social media as a practitioner. The following questions could be useful to consider:

1. What am I going to achieve?
2. What do I want to achieve?
3. Who is the target audience?
4. What is the age group of the target audience?
5. What is the best social media platform for the intended purpose?
6. What is the unique advantage of using social media for the intended purpose?

EXAMPLES

If a practitioner would like to establish their presence in association to a certain therapeutic or theoretical modality, they might like, for instance, to write blogs on certain topics or in a certain area. Blogging would potentially allow the practitioner to share this information with their own clients for the sole purpose of benefiting their clients, making this a good reason for using social media. Therefore, thinking back to the six questions above, first, the blog has the purpose of providing clients with information, allowing clients to be more informed on a topic or subject matter, the target audience are the clients and any other interested participant of the blog. The audience is potentially the practitioner's client group and followers of the blog. This will provide an opportunity for a therapist to provide clients with additional information about a specific issue or an area of concern that is relevant to the client, or a specific therapeutic approach that will be applied with the client.

Another example may be a therapist who uses positive psychotherapy in their own practice, as one of the contemporary modalities of practice, writing blogs on this topic and sharing the content or link on social media. This will give the practitioner an opportunity to share additional information about a therapeutic modality that will be used in sessions with their clients. This will also allow the professional to demonstrate and publicise their professional expertise.

AUDIENCE

To further elaborate, once a social media platform has been considered by a counselling practitioner as a tool enabling a certain purpose to be achieved, the target audience to be reached is the next step that needs careful attention. When sharing the information on social media, different platforms appear to be more popular among different age groups and professions, etc. For example, Facebook is now less popular among young groups (under 40s), with younger ages preferring Snapchat, Instagram and TikTok. If a practitioner would like to share content with young people, then these platforms may need to be considered. As an example, a short TikTok video to raise awareness on cyberbullying will be effective when working with young people, where such a resource can be used to provide additional information in support of therapy.

A further example could be when a practitioner wants to publicise a recent research paper with fellow professionals working in counselling sector. When considering counselling professionals as the target audience, suitable social media platforms would be LinkedIn and Twitter instead of, say, Facebook. Certain social media forums, such as LinkedIn, identify as being more professional and more suitable for work within professional boundaries. Twitter is also viewed as a way to publicise professional material, such as sharing articles and opinions. If a practitioner would like to share research or practice-related articles that benefit the clinical work of other practitioners in the field, using Twitter is a way to reach out to professionals.

EXAMPLE

Sarah is a counselling practitioner who is also an active researcher. Sarah uses Twitter and LinkedIn to connect with other professionals in the sector by sharing her research publications. Sarah considers this to be an opportunity to contribute to the counselling practice sector by sharing the most recent scientific information and tools that would help other practitioners. Sarah also directs those of her clients who are interested in learning more about the approaches she uses during her therapy sessions towards these social media posts, which her clients find informative.

As discussed above, careful consideration of purpose and the desired target audience will impact the outcome of social media engagement. For instance, a practitioner who is willing to dedicate time to educate the general population about suicide as a topic of concern should carefully decide which social media platforms will optimise and achieve the targeted objective. In such a scenario, Facebook and Twitter may better serve the purpose, compared to LinkedIn. To reach out to the general population, the social media platform chosen must be more person-oriented, easily accessible, and perhaps brief, hence Twitter and Facebook might be the most appropriate platforms.

The purpose of the examples above is to achieve greater awareness, to enhance the professional profile of a counsellor and the profession, and to provide an educational tool for a practitioner's own clients, such as a blog about building resilience or general mental health. However, social media engagement needs to be carefully selected in line with ethical frameworks.

BOUNDARIES, CONTROL AND ETHICAL PRACTICE

It is important to highlight the mindful use of social media. Keeping a log of social media posts is crucial. If needed in the future, you can always go back to the log and check what has been posted. It is also important to maintain boundaries and control over your professional and personal presence on social media, to keep them separate while maintaining professionalism on both. As an example, if you decide to create a Facebook group for your professional work and this group is created using your personal Facebook account, be mindful that the readers, clients and the general public may easily access your personal Facebook account and information. It is always advisable to use a separate social media account for professional practice. This will help in maintaining the boundary between your personal and professional lives. When posting on social media, you can also control the level of engagement with the audience for that post, such as whether the audience can post comments or like them, etc. Some of these controls and boundaries are highlighted and discussed in the *Good Practice in Action 040* guide, published by BACP (2021b).

EXAMPLE (POOR PRACTICE)

Rebecca, a counselling practitioner, uses social media to inform clients about the benefits of mindfulness in improving wellbeing. She maintains a Facebook group where all clients who are interested can join and access the information on the group. However, Rebecca has not realised that in creating a professional Facebook group that was originally linked to her personal Facebook account, she had allowed clients to access some content on her personal account. She started to receive friend requests from clients that she did not want to accept because it would impact her boundaries between her personal and professional life. She then had to go back to her clients to explain that she would not be accepting Facebook friend requests from her clients, which put her in an uncomfortable position. She could have avoided this problem by creating a separate professional Facebook account and forming a group linked to the same account.

RESEARCH EVIDENCE

There is an increasing acceptance of technology in all aspects of our lives, and social media usage is growing, as the statistics previously mentioned indicate. Social media can be a great way to connect with people. The connection social media can provide can enable people to find and access support, including support for mental health and emotional needs (i.e., Brown et al., 2021; Prescott, Rathbone and Brown, 2020; Prescott, Rathbone and Hanley, 2020). There are several benefits to digital mental health technologies, including ease of access, the broadening of access and reach, increased efficiency, decreased costs and the potential to reduce the stigma surrounding mental health (Prescott, 2021). However, with the increase of social media use in general, as well as for therapeutic support, there is a potential danger for counselling professionals using social media to blur the professional and personal boundaries (Au, 2018). According to Au (2018: 478), when using social media, there is going to be an inevitable spill-over between professionals' personal and professional roles: 'it is, thus, unreasonable to have professionals maintain a professional identity all the time'.

Other things to consider when engaging with online activity is your own technology proficiency and the rules under the General Data Protection Regulation (GDPR). The BACP provides guidance on GDPR, which provides information on consent, an explanation of rights under the GDPR, descriptions of special category and criminal offence data as well as guidance on protecting children's data (British Association for Counselling and Psychotherapy, 2021c).

CONCLUSION

Hopefully this chapter has made you think about your own social media and SNS use so you can continue to use it in a positive way. Don't forget that counselling practitioners can use social media to manage impressions, share resources and communicate with other professionals. Social media can be a valuable platform to reach and engage people, as we have hopefully emphasised throughout this chapter. Be mindful in your use as a professional resource as well in your personal life, take on board the guidance available to help you maintain boundaries and remain professional online. Be 'savvy' users and make sure you have some understanding of the technology and the platforms you are engaging with.

REFERENCES

Au, A. (2018). Online physicians, offline patients: Professional identity and ethics in social media use. *International Journal of Sociology and Social Policy*, 38(5/6), 474–483. https://doi.org/10.1108/IJSSP-08-2017-0102

British Association for Counselling and Psychotherapy (2021a). *Guidance on the Use of Social Media: Information for Members*. [Website]. Lutterworth: BACP. Available at www.bacp.co.uk/membership/membership-policies/social-media/

British Association for Counselling and Psychotherapy (2021b). *Good Practice in Action 040, Commonly Asked Questions: Social Media, Digital Technology and the Counselling Professions*. [Website]. Lutterworth: BACP. Available at www.bacp-social-media-audio-video-counselling-professions-commonly-asked-questions-gpia040.pdf

British Association for Counselling and Psychotherapy (2021c). *FAQs about GDPR: A Quick Guide to the New General Data Protection Regulation*. [Website]. Lutterworth: BACP. Available at www.bacp.co.uk/about-us/contact-us/gdpr/

Brown, G., Rathbone, A.L., & Prescott, J. (2021). Social media use for supporting mental health (SMILE). *Mental Health Review Journal*, 26(3), 279–297. doi 10.1108/MHRJ-10-2020-0079

Haeny, A.M. (2014). Ethical considerations for psychologists taking a public stance on controversial issues: The balance between personal and professional life. *Ethics & Behavior*, 24(4), 265–278. https://doi.org/10.1080/10508422.2013.860030

Health and Care Professions Council (2021). *Standards: Meeting Our Standards: Communication and Using Social Media*. [Website]. London: HCPC. Available at www.hcpc-uk.org/standards/meeting-our-standards/communication-and-using-social-media/

Frankish, K., Ryan, C., Harris, A. (2012). Psychiatry and online social media: potential, pitfalls and ethical guidelines for psychiatrists and trainees. *Australasian Psychiatry*, 20(3), 181–187. doi:10.1177/1039856212447881

Prescott, J. (2021). *Digital Innovations in Mental Health*. Hershey, PA: IGI Global.

Prescott, J., Rathbone, A.L., & Brown, G. (2020). Online peer to peer support: Qualitative analysis of UK and US open mental health Facebook groups. *Digital Health*, 6, 1–17, https://doi.org/10.1177/2055207620979209

Prescott, J., Rathbone, A.L., & Hanley, T. (2020). Online mental health communities, self-efficacy, and transition to further support. *Mental Health Review Journal*, 25(4), 329–344. doi 10.1108/MHRJ-12-2019-0048

Statista Research Department (2021). Active social media users in the United Kingdom 2021. *Statista.com* [Website], 7 September. Available at www.statista.com/topics/3236/social-media-usage-in-the-uk/#topicHeader__wrapper. (accessed October 2021).

Tankovska, H. (2020). Number of social network users worldwide from 2017 to 2025. *Statista.com* [Website]. Available at www.statista.com/statistics/278414/number-of-worldwide-social-network-users/ (accessed October 2021).

UK Council for Psychotherapy (2021). *Security and Confidentiality Guidelines*. [Website]. London: UKCP. Available at www.psychotherapy.org.uk/media/1ptnp1jt/ukcp-security-and-confidentiality-guidelines-2018.pdf

White, E., & Hanley, T. (2022). Therapist + Social Media = Mental health influencer? Considering the research focusing upon key ethical issues around the use of social media by therapists. *Counselling and Psychotherapy Research*, early view, 1–5. https://doi.org/10.1002/capr.12577

RECOMMENDED READING

British Association for Counselling and Psychotherapy (2021). *Good Practice in Action 040, Commonly Asked Questions: Social Media, Digital Technology and the Counselling Professions*. [Website]. Lutterworth: BACP. Available at www.bacp-social-media-audio-video-counselling-professions-commonly-asked-questions-gpia040.pdf (accessed October 2021).

This guide provides BACP members with a current look at the BACP's ethical framework and the use of social media and technology. It provides guidance on how professionals might use social media as a professional and how you might use it in client care.

> British Association for Counselling and Psychotherapy (2022). *Good Practice in Action 047, Commonly Asked Questions: Working Online in the Counselling Professions*. [Website]. Lutterworth: BACP. Available at www.bacp-working-online-gpia047-apr20.pdf (accessed October 2021).
>
> This fact sheet was last updated in 2022 so it provides current information and guidance on working online with a focus on the ethical considerations and challenges that working online poses. This is particularly relevant due to the Covid-19 pandemic and the move towards counselling provision online.
>
> Tribe, R., & Morrissey, J. (2020). The Handbook of Professional, Ethical and Research Practice for Psychologists, Counsellors, Psychotherapists and Psychiatrists (3rd ed.). Abingdon, UK: Routledge: https://doi.org/10.4324/9780429428838
>
> The third section of this book focuses on clinical considerations and responsibilities. Within this section, Chapter 10 by Mary Creaner considers the role of social media in counselling and psychotherapy.

3.20 KNOWLEDGE OF PSYCHOPHARMACOLOGY

ANNE GUY

OVERVIEW AND KEY POINTS

Psychiatric drugs such as antidepressants and antipsychotics were prescribed to over a quarter of the UK population in 2017–18 (Taylor et al., 2019). The proportion is likely to be even higher among people in psychological therapy. Historically, psychological therapists (here abbreviated to 'therapists') were trained to avoid all discussion of psychiatric medications as being the province of medics. It is now recognised, however, that there are five appropriate opportunities for us to support clients as they navigate decisions and experiences around taking or withdrawing from these drugs:

- To support the ethical principle of working with informed consent which underpins contracting – how might taking such drugs impact any proposed therapy? This may be aided by the provision or signposting of medical *information* about drugs (as distinct from giving medical *advice*).
- To explore clients' understanding of what's 'wrong' with them and how they understand such drugs to work. To consider the implications of this for the therapeutic process which is focused on 'what happened' to them.
- To explore their experience of taking such drugs in terms of both helpful and unhelpful effects.
- To help identify and prevent possible withdrawal reactions, again by signposting relevant information (e.g., on how withdrawal can be managed to minimise the possibility of withdrawal reactions being triggered).
- To therapeutically support a client who is experiencing withdrawal reactions.

Therapists educated in the latest evidence on psychiatric drugs are then equipped to decide if, when and how to use that information for the benefit of their clients when such opportunities present.

INTRODUCTION

Psychiatric drugs are prescribed more often today than at any other time in our profession's history. An analysis by Public Health England (PHE) established that in 2017–18, 26% of the UK adult population was prescribed a psychiatric drug, with around 17% being prescribed antidepressants (Taylor et al., 2019). The steep rise in prescriptions (which have broadly doubled in the last 20 years (Kendrick, 2015)) means that most therapists now work with clients who have either taken or are taking psychiatric drugs. Evidence also continues to emerge that such drugs are associated with physical dependence and, as a result, can be difficult to withdraw from. Withdrawal reactions are often being mistaken for the return of the original issue for which the drug was prescribed, and people are sometimes being put back on them unnecessarily (Davies and Read, 2019).

In response to this situation, the main UK accrediting bodies for psychological therapy and a group of leading academics and practitioners worked together to create guidance to give therapists explicit permission to learn about the latest evidence on psychiatric drugs to enable informed, evidence-based conversations with clients. Much of the following content is therefore drawn from that guidance (Guy, Davies and Rizq, 2019; Rizq, Guy, with Stainsby, 2020), which is endorsed by the British Association for Counselling and Psychotherapy (BACP), the United Kingdom Council for Psychotherapy (UKCP), the British Psychological Society (BPS) and the National Counselling Society (NCS).

The guidance aims to empower and support conversations that may already be taking place with clients. You will need to decide for yourself whether, and to what extent, you wish to use it in the context of your therapeutic work. This decision will depend on your modality, setting, and the individual needs of your clients. The client's agency, as always, should be supported and respected at all times. Clients should be encouraged to discuss withdrawal from prescribed psychiatric drugs with a knowledgeable prescriber who can give medical advice, oversee and manage any withdrawal process appropriately. While guidance advocates the importance of informed client choice based on full information about potential benefits and risks, it does not advocate telling clients to take, not take, stay on or withdraw from psychiatric drugs. These decisions should be made by the prescriber and client.

SUPPORTING INFORMED CONSENT AND SHARED DECISION MAKING

Although there is no specific ethical guidance on how therapists should respond to issues relating to taking or withdrawing from psychiatric drugs, there are relevant general ethical principles provided by the main professional accrediting bodies which include:

- working with informed consent
- respecting a client's best interests
- keeping knowledge and skills up to date
- demonstrating accountability and candour
- working respectfully with colleagues.

The rapid growth of scientific and medical knowledge can make it difficult for any professional guidance to keep up. This means there is scope for differences of opinion among those providing care for the client, so these issues have the potential to raise ethical questions that relate to boundaries of professional competence, modality and role. For example, clients may ask you for medical advice and information and you can quickly find yourself drawn into discussions about drug choice, dosage and frequency. It is important, therefore, to distinguish between providing medical *advice* and providing medical *information*. Discussing scientific evidence, sharing information from a reputable source, or offering a different perspective where appropriate with clients differs substantially from offering a diagnosis, prescribing drugs or advising withdrawal. It is important to be clear about this distinction with clients and it can bear repeating. Clients requiring advice on psychiatric drugs should *always* be referred to their medical practitioner or a knowledgeable prescriber. But helping a client to understand the potential advantages and disadvantages of taking prescribed psychiatric drugs *during therapy* can be thought of as part of your responsibility to ensure your client's informed consent for the work you do together. This is different from the prescriber's responsibility to inform the client about the physiological and psychological effects of their prescribed drugs. It can, of course, be helpful for you to support this process too where appropriate, for example by directing clients to relevant sources of information.

EXPLORING UNDERSTANDING OF WHAT'S WRONG AND HOW DRUGS WORK

HOW ARE PSYCHIATRIC DRUGS UNDERSTOOD TO WORK?

Moncrieff (2020) summarises that despite decades of intensive research into various neurotransmitters, genetics and neural networks, a definitive cause of any form of mental distress has yet to be determined. In the light of this uncertainty, two models for drug action have been proposed. The 'disease-centred' model of drug action assumes that psychiatric drugs reverse (or partially reverse) an underlying abnormality or disease process that is presumed to give rise to the symptoms of a disorder. This is closely related to theories that some mental health conditions arise from 'chemical imbalances' in neurotransmitters in the brain. Consequently, many people have been told that there is a biological reason for their depression (such as a biochemical change in the brain or a genetic factor).

As there is little dependable evidence to support the above model, the 'drug-centred' model has more recently been proposed. This highlights that psychiatric drugs produce an altered global state that involves physiological, psychological and behavioural changes. These changes are superimposed on, and interact with, symptoms of mental 'disorders' in ways a person may experience as either helpful or unhelpful. An example of this is the effects of a benzodiazepine on anxiety. Benzodiazepines reduce arousal and induce a state of calmness and relaxation. This may be experienced as a relief for someone suffering from anxiety, but it does not mean that the person returns to their 'normal' or pre-symptomatic state. Moreover, it is accompanied by sedation and mental clouding, which may be problematic. Because they alter normal bodily functions, all drugs have adverse effects and may do more harm than good, especially if prescribed in the long term. Psychiatric drugs are likely (to varying degrees) to impair and suppress aspects of a person's mental and emotional functioning. Individuals have to decide and periodically re-evaluate whether the overall effects of a drug are preferable to the original distress or difficulties they experienced.

THE MAIN PSYCHIATRIC DRUGS: POSSIBLE ADVERSE EFFECTS AND WITHDRAWAL REACTIONS

You may wish to familiarise yourself with some of the main psychiatric drugs, their common uses, adverse effects and withdrawal reactions. Table 3.20.1 offers a summary of this information. For more information see section 4 in Guy, Davies and Rizq (2019).

A combination of prescribed drugs and psychotherapy is often cited as being a superior intervention to the use of drugs or therapy alone, particularly with depression. Overall, evidence that such a combination is superior to either intervention given alone is not conclusive. The assumptions behind this research, that antidepressants are effective, and that antidepressants and psychotherapy provide distinctive, additive mechanisms against depression, have not been proven.

EXPLORING CLIENTS' UNDERSTANDING

Understandably, some clients do not wish to experience strong feelings of distress and might assume that drugs will quickly and with little effort bring them relief. Therapists will need to consider not only the implicit and explicit messages received by clients regarding psychiatric drugs, but the beliefs and meanings associated with these, as they could prevent them from accepting an alternative view of what could help. In these and many other situations, you will need to sensitively explore the beliefs and meanings held by the client, taking into account their particular experiences as well as any unrealistic expectations they may have about psychiatric drugs.

The British Psychological Society (BPS) takes the view that:

> clients and the general public are negatively affected by the continued and continuous medicalisation of their natural and normal responses to their experiences; responses ... which do not reflect illnesses so much as normal individual variation ... This misses the relational context of problems and the undeniable social causation of many such problems. (BPS, 2011)

EXPLORING OUR OWN UNDERSTANDING AND BELIEFS

The disease-centred model of drug action is closely linked to the biomedical or 'medical model' approach in healthcare. Its continued dominance means it is likely to shape the attitudes, beliefs and values of therapists from all psychotherapeutic backgrounds and to influence practice in a variety of different ways. Before thinking about how to integrate knowledge of psychiatric drugs into your work, it may be useful to think about your relationship to the 'medical model' and its place in your practice. This will help you to consider whether and to what extent it contributes to any beliefs you may have about prescribed psychiatric drugs.

Some therapists work in settings that privilege a biomedical framework, requiring them to use the language of psychiatric classification, standardised assessment and manualised 'clinical' techniques, which fits more closely with the 'disease-centred' model that emphasises notions of deficiency, symptomatology and medicalisation (sometimes referred to as the 'what's wrong with you' approach). Other therapists work in settings that

Table 3.20.1 Psychiatric drugs, their effects and withdrawal reactions

Drug class	Effects that may be perceived as adverse	Possible withdrawal reactions
Benzodiazepines and Z-drugs Benzodiazepines: Used for anxiety, sedation, alcohol withdrawal (e.g., Temazepam, Diazepam) Z-Drugs: Used for insomnia (e.g., Zopiclone) Pregabalin, Gabapentin: Used for anxiety, chronic pain (e.g., Lyrica, Neurontin)	Sedative Significant risk of dependence Drowsiness and impaired cognitive ability	Sweating, nausea, dizziness, abdominal cramps Anxiety, agitation, insomnia, muscle stiffness Tingling, electric shock type feelings. Risk of epilepsy Panic attacks, poor memory Hallucinations, delusions Nightmares
Antidepressants Used for depression and anxiety (e.g., Fluoxetine, Paroxetine)	Sedative SSRIs/SNRIs: nausea, drowsiness, insomnia Sexual dysfunction Anxiety and agitation Emotional blunting Suicidality	Anxiety Nausea, dizziness, insomnia Mood changes Hallucinations Vivid dreams Confusion
Stimulants Used for attention deficit hyperactivity disorder (e.g., Ritalin)	Insomnia Growth suppression in children	Tearfulness, irritability, emotional lability
'Mood stabilisers' Used for bipolar affective disorder (e.g., Lithium, Tegretol)	Sedative Drowsiness, tremor, lethargy, decreased ability to learn new information, prolonged reaction time, poor memory, reduced spontaneity Weight gain Reduced emotional responses Toxic state: levels have to be regularly monitored	No physical withdrawal effects Relapse or rebound of mania
Anti-psychotics Used for psychotic disorders (including schizophrenia), acute mania, sedation (e.g., Chlorpromazine, Haloperidol, Olanzapine, Risperidone)	Sedative Dampened emotional responses and motivation Dizziness, sexual dysfunction, weight gain Cardiovascular effects Akathisia and extra-pyramidal effects Tardive dyskinesia Anticholinergic effects: dry mouth, blurred vision, constipation Restlessness Suicidality	Nausea, headache, tremor Sleep disturbance, irritability, aggression, depression Possibility of 'supersensitivity psychosis', particularly when withdrawing from clozapine Rebound psychosis

N.B. More than one psychiatric drug can be prescribed at any one time. Also, some drugs classed primarily as 'psychiatric' may be used to treat physical health conditions.

privilege theoretical frameworks emphasising the psychological, systemic and psychosocial aspects of experience thought to underpin emotional distress (more akin to a 'what happened to you' approach). You may find it useful to reflect on the professional framework and language used in your practice setting, and how it may affect your beliefs and attitudes about prescribed drugs.

Therapeutic modalities are also important. Within the humanistic and psychodynamic traditions, distress is regarded as having potential value and purpose. Rather than being seen as 'pathological' (and of little use), it can be regarded as an opportunity for change and transformation. By contrast, cognitive behavioural approaches focus mainly on removing symptoms of distress by altering patterns of cognition, emotion and behaviour that may be maintaining emotional suffering. How might your theoretical position shape your understanding of psychological distress and how, in turn, might it influence your perspective on the use of prescription drugs?

Finally, we should consider the influence of our personal experience: Do I have any experience of taking prescribed psychiatric drugs myself? Am I aware of any family members or friends who have taken prescribed drugs?

There are a range of ways you might use knowledge on this issue, and while your theoretical position may mean you will not routinely choose to give or signpost information, just knowing enough to highlight the potential effects of these drugs could make a material difference to your clients.

EXPLORING THE EXPERIENCE OF TAKING PSYCHIATRIC DRUGS AND THEIR AFFECTS ON THE THERAPEUTIC RELATIONSHIP

As we have seen, prescription psychiatric drugs act on the brain to alter mood and consciousness, sometimes helping to control reactions to emotional distress by numbing, sedating or tranquilising a person. While some clients will find the effects of psychiatric drugs helpful, they can significantly impact the therapeutic relationship and process. Some of the possible effects on thinking, feeling and behaviour are listed below.

Effects on thinking may include:

- poor memory or concentration
- confusion or losing track of ideas
- difficulties in making links or structuring thought
- problems staying focused
- inability to retain insights over time.

Effects on feeling may include:

- emotional withdrawal, being less able or willing to connect with themselves or others
- being uninvolved, distanced, 'not really there'
- an inability to reconnect with feelings relating to past experiences
- suppressed anger, sadness or fear.

Effects on behaviour may include:

- passivity
- uncooperativeness or overcompliance
- denial of responsibility
- apparently poor motivation and/or attendance
- repetitive speech or behaviour
- disengagement from work or social activities.

You will need to bear in mind that many of the effects listed here can also be part of the experience of emotional distress. You may therefore wish to consider exploring with your client whether any perceived effects could have been evident before they took the prescribed drug.

HELPING TO IDENTIFY AND PREVENT POSSIBLE WITHDRAWAL REACTIONS BY SIGNPOSTING RELEVANT INFORMATION

Despite limited evidence for the benefits of prolonged treatment, some people are advised to continue taking psychiatric drugs long after their problem has subsided. During therapeutic work, however, clients may consider coming off them. They might think about moving to therapy alone or even ending all interventions if they are feeling better. Some may be concerned about possible harmful effects or feel their drugs have not helped them. Whatever the motivation, the process of withdrawal may not be an easy one. It requires planning and preparation and may take some time.

WHAT IS WITHDRAWAL?

When a person takes a psychiatric drug, their body views it as foreign and tries to counteract its effects by adapting to it. This means that, over time, higher doses may be needed to achieve the same effect ('tolerance'). It also means that when a drug that has been taken for some time is stopped, the body's adaptations are no longer opposed by the drug's presence. This can lead to the unpleasant sensations and experiences that are called 'withdrawal' – these can be severe and last for weeks, months or even years.

The process of withdrawal itself can also take months or years, rather than days or weeks. A rushed or unplanned withdrawal process is unlikely to succeed, particularly if a drug has been taken for a long time. Withdrawal is usually achieved by 'tapering', i.e., the slow reduction over time of a drug that is managed by a prescriber who is likely to be following a proven, recommended protocol. It is important to remind clients of the risks of any abrupt discontinuation or reduction of a psychiatric drug, and the need to bear in mind that a knowledgeable prescriber should offer specific tapering advice. As this is an emerging area of knowledge, therapists should remember that not all prescribers will necessarily be aware of the need for, and how to plan, a slow reduction. Clients may need signposting to relevant information that will give them the confidence to ask for a prescriber's support with this (e.g., Royal College of Psychiatrists, 2019).

IDENTIFYING WITHDRAWAL REACTIONS

Some of the main reactions are listed in Table 3.20.1. It is possible that someone might experience some of these even if they just miss a dose or two. Hearing a client say 'I must really need these pills as I feel it if I haven't taken them' would be an opportunity to consider raising the possibility that what is being experienced is withdrawal rather than the re-emergence of an underlying issue.

SUPPORTING A CLIENT THROUGH WITHDRAWAL – THE 'COMBINED WISDOM' APPROACH

Although there is a lack of formal research into which therapeutic strategies best support withdrawal, there is a three-stage 'combined wisdom' approach derived from the experience of those working with this client group. This covers:

- How to help someone prepare to withdraw.
- What support is helpful or unhelpful during withdrawal.
- What to do after withdrawal is complete.

More detail on this approach can be found in section 6 of Guy, Davies and Rizq (2019).

CONCLUSION

At the time of writing, less than 3% of the UK population has access to services which support safe withdrawal from prescribed drugs (Guy et al., 2020). Patients are understandably turning in increasing numbers to online sources of information and peer support (White, Read and Julo, 2021). While moves are afoot for the NHS to start offering services, given current pressures, it is unlikely these will be consistently available in the immediate future. In the meantime, therapists can play an important role in helping their clients understand the effects of the drugs they are prescribed, and we should all consider ourselves empowered to educate ourselves further on the subject.

REFERENCES

British Psychological Society (2011) *Response to the American Psychiatric Association DSM-5 Development*. Leicester: BPS. Available at https://dxrevisionwatch.files.wordpress.com/2012/02/dsm-5-2011-bps-response.pdf (accessed 22 February 2022).

Davies J., & Read J. (2019) A systematic review into the incidence, severity and duration of antidepressant withdrawal effects: are guidelines evidence-based? *Journal of Addictive Behaviors*, 97: 111–121.

Guy, A., Brown, M., Lewis, S., & Horowitz, M. (2020) The 'patient voice': patients who experience antidepressant withdrawal symptoms are often dismissed, or misdiagnosed with relapse, or a new medical condition'. *Therapeutic Advances in Psychopharmacology*, 9 November. doi:10.1177/2045125320967183

Guy, A., Davies, J., & Rizq, R. (Eds) (2019) *Guidance for Psychological Therapists: Enabling Conversations with Clients Taking or Withdrawing from Prescribed Psychiatric Drugs*. London: APPG for Prescribed Drug Dependence.

Kendrick, T. (2015) Long-term antidepressant treatment: Time for a review? *Prescriber*, 26(19), 5 October, 7–8.

Moncrieff, J. (2020) *A Straight-talking Introduction to Psychiatric Drugs: The Truth about How They Work and How To Come Off Them* (2nd ed.). Ross-on-Wye: PCCS Books.

Rizq, R., Guy, A., with Stainsby, K. (2020) *A Short Guide to What Every Psychological Therapist Should Know about Working with Psychiatric Drugs*. London: APPG for Prescribed Drug Dependence.

Royal College of Psychiatrists (2019) *Stopping Antidepressants*. London: RCP. Available at www.rcpsych.ac.uk/mental-health/treatments-and-wellbeing/stopping-antidepressants

Taylor, S., Annand, F., Burkinshaw, P., Greaves, F., Kelleher, M., Knight, J., Perkins, C., Tran, A., White, M., & Marsden, J. (2019) *Dependence and Withdrawal Associated with Some Prescribed Medicines: An Evidence Review*. London: Public Health England.

White, E., Read, J., & Julo, S. (2021) The role of Facebook groups in the management and raising of awareness of antidepressant withdrawal: Is social media filling the void left by health services? *Therapeutic Advances in Psychopharmacology*, 11. https://doi.org/10.1177/2045125320981174

RECOMMENDED READING

Guy, A., Davies, J., & Rizq, R. (Eds) (2019) *Guidance for Psychological Therapists: Enabling Conversations with Clients Taking or Withdrawing from Prescribed Psychiatric Drugs*. London: APPG for Prescribed Drug Dependence.

Rizq, R., Guy, A., with Stainsby, K. (2020) *A Short Guide to What Every Psychological Therapist Should Know about Working with Psychiatric Drugs*. London: APPG for Prescribed Drug Dependence.

These guides are both available for free download at www.prescribeddrug.info

Moncrieff, J. (2020) *A Straight-talking Introduction to Psychiatric Drugs: The Truth about How They Work and How to Come Off Them* (2nd ed.). Ross-on-Wye: PCCS Books.

This book provides a very accessible summary of evidence that both therapists and some clients may find helpful.

Davies, J. (2021) *Sedated*. London: Atlantic Books.

This book provides a more in-depth consideration of the social and political role played by psychiatric drugs.

3.21 CRITICAL THINKING SKILLS IN COUNSELLING AND PSYCHOTHERAPY

COLIN FELTHAM

OVERVIEW AND KEY POINTS

It isn't self-evident what critical thinking is or what place it has in therapy. Since the term itself has now become ubiquitous and easily misunderstood, we should unpack it and rethink its applications. Readers may be familiar with the terms 'critical theory', 'critical psychology', 'critical race theory', 'critical pedagogy', 'critical thinking therapy', and so on, which overlap but also depart from each other. The following is a working definition of critical thinking:

> Approaching all relevant traditions, practices, texts and questions and one's own personal and cultural assumptions with a degree of sceptical analysis, with an associated effort to articulate the grounds for criticism, and to make possible alternative proposals.

This chapter covers the following:

- A rationale for and definition of critical thinking is given. Suggestions are made as to its application at different points in therapists' careers.
- An outline of some basics of critical thinking is offered, with examples of key terms and their significance in the field of therapy.
- Potential uses and benefits of critical thinking are raised, along with cautions and conclusions.

INTRODUCTION

We all think critically to some extent, insofar as we constantly evaluate our world. By adulthood, we all have idiosyncratic thinking habits, some of which serve us well and some that probably do not. Everyone training in therapy is obliged to demonstrate critical-analytical thinking in order to satisfy academic course requirements. But already at this early point in the chapter, I have omitted an instance of critical thinking. Before anyone begins to train as a therapist, discerning thought has gone into these questions:

- Is therapy a good career move for me?
- Do I have the necessary qualities for this field?
- Are the costs of training warranted by the likely future rewards?
- Do psychological therapies offer reasonable explanations for personal distress, or are sociology, politics, philosophy, or religion better explainers?

How much explicit evaluation of this kind precedes training is unknown, but these questions already throw up at least two items of basic critical thinking: (1) affect heuristic, and (2) sunk costs. The first refers to emotional investment – 'I like people, I like working with them, I feel good about helping people, using the theories I have read about'. The second applies to mid-training realities – 'Having spent money on a course, I have invested in it financially as well as emotionally, and this itself probably renders radical critical thinking about the wisdom of my career choice less likely'. Mature practitioners are deeply invested in the field, and livelihood and family commitments are usually intertwined. *Enjoying* the practice of therapy, the engagement with clients, may paradoxically disincline us from examining its fundamentals lest this causes cognitive dissonance.

Many texts explicate the essentials of critical thinking. It is worth noting three particular books in particular:

1. *Thinking Fast and Slow*, by Daniel Kahneman (2011).
2. *The Scout Mindset*, by Julia Galef (2021).
3. *Rationality*, by Stephen Pinker (2021).

Kahneman (2011) and Galef (2021) rely on a more or less binary model. For Kahneman, fast thinking is the kind of necessary, rapid thought process required situationally, contrasted with slow thinking, which is more deliberative and calculating. Fast thinking is often necessary and sometimes faulty, but can be corrected by slow, data-informed thought. Galef uses the metaphors of soldier and scout mindset, the former being a defensive and combative approach, the latter being open-minded and mapping the terrain. Soldiers use motivated reasoning, usually enemy-focused, while scouts want to discover what actually is. Pinker's book (2021) is perhaps more nuanced, looking at probability and randomness, but also gives a central place to critical thinking. We could 'lose ourselves' unprofitably in these texts, and even more so in the analytical philosophy that often implicitly underpins them. Presumably, we wish to identify and utilise those aspects of critical thinking that help to improve us as psychological practitioners.

WHO NEEDS CRITICAL THINKING?

As a young adult, you might weigh up career choices, say between therapy or accountancy. Settling on therapy, you would have to choose among courses and the professional titles they lead to. You might have to choose among theoretical orientations, say psychoanalytic, humanistic or CBT. These resemble consumer choices involving considerable time, money and long-term prospects. Ideally, your decisions would be reached by dispassionate calculation, but as we know from house purchases, we also have to factor in availability, affect, and possible child-driven matters like local schools and transport. Whatever research we put in, acute affect can trump it, for example, if we fall in love with someone, or with a house, and follow through in spite of emerging counter-evidence.

Trained, qualified and with some professional, clinical experience, we are faced with daily challenges with clients. We all have areas of relative inexperience or ignorance, and these may challenge us to refer some clients elsewhere, to rapidly educate ourselves and gain necessary supervisory inputs, or to believe that our primary clinical orientation will carry us through any doubts. Therapy being intrapsychically and interpersonally demanding, we may decide sometimes to re-enter our own therapy in order to address unresolved issues or blind spots. Decision-making operates in all these cases, influenced by external pressures and personal resources. Decisions often involve some anxiety (Guy, 1987).

Within each clinical session, multiple challenges can arise. Is the work going well, facilitated by good rapport and other therapeutic relationship factors, or are glitches, ethical questions or uncertainties present? How do our own personality factors help or hinder in the moment during therapy, and how well can we identify and address each client's idiosyncratic needs? Big moments of risk (say, to self-disclose or not, or to try a novel technique) come and go. Practitioners are aware of their own moods, fluctuating energy and preoccupations, that can sometimes prevent optimal therapeutic functioning. The kinds of critical thinking required in all these instances require time for reflection, for supervision and continuing professional development. Too much self-doubt is unhelpful, but so too is insufficient self-questioning.

Much therapy is based on unconditional positive regard and 'credulous listening', which centre clients' own accounts of their personal difficulties. Yet clients have their own blind spots, defences and resistance against change. A part of the therapist's mind is likely to contain unspoken questions about the client's narrative, and this is based on critical thinking. The therapist weighs up these factors, and decides when and how to address such dissonance, using judicious timing and sensitive choice of words and tone. The personal values held by client and therapist sometimes differ (politics is one example) and the therapist must suspend their own beliefs in these instances, even where they may deem the client to be mistaken.

Research skills are covered elsewhere in this book (see McLeod – Chapter 3.17, this volume), but let us note here the large overlaps between reflecting on clinical work, reading up on aspects of that work, and higher-level therapist education (postgraduate courses) requiring specific research projects. A doctoral research project demands specific cognitive and writing skills and empirical work, but has to be rooted in personal interest, that is, in genuine inquisitiveness that sustains the project.

There is another set of critical thinking challenges likely to arise during the course of a therapist's career. This includes philosophical, political and religious questions. While some therapists have explicit anchorage in a religious or spiritual practice, others have none, and these identities may sometimes be challenged by clients with 'clashing positions'. Similarly (and perhaps increasingly), we may have polarised political positions. By this, I do not mean only our voting sympathies, but the identity politics of feminism, multiculturalism, sexuality and gender, and associated positions.

There is reason to believe that most therapists do not think 'philosophically' but many have existential preoccupations, and questions of free will, authenticity, meaning and death are thrown up by some clients. While some training touches on all these matters, none can be anything like comprehensive. How can I help this client come to terms with health and death anxiety? What do I, a Muslim woman therapist, need to think about with my atheist male client? To what extent do I, a white therapist, want or need to immerse myself in critical race theory in order to help my non-white clients? At a more macro-level, we may sometimes wonder if money is better spent on social improvements than on individual therapy.

CRITICAL THINKING BASICS

Awareness that something is often better evaluated than taken for granted is a first step. Close reading and *accurate comprehension* is important to prevent falsely caricaturing others' ideas. Generating *alternative hypotheses* and explanations is next. *Gathering evidence* to support and refute different positions follows. This can be done reflectively (mentally), by reading, or on paper, using *brainstorming* and dividing views by columns. The well-known Johari window may be used to identify *blind spots*, those areas that may not even occur to us without some external stimulation.

Motivated reasoning leads us to look for evidence that will only confirm that we already believe, in other words the kind of *confirmation bias* that bedevils much research. The *irrational primacy effect* is the tendency to stick with those beliefs we encounter early on, instead of remaining open to countervailing evidence. It is quite common, for example, to be fascinated with 'deep' theories and dismiss those that chime with commonsense (Chater, 2019). *Jumping to conclusions* is a cognitive and clinical error sometimes found among medical and psychological practitioners, for example, leading to premature and incomplete diagnoses. In many situations we are inclined to *cherry-pick*, or select and discard data based on its attractiveness or otherwise.

Models of brief therapy grew out of a critique of the *over-determination* of open-ended, often very long-term therapy in which time was arguably wasted on irrelevant details. *Either-or thinking* can become a trap, for example if the client is trying to decide whether to end or persist in an unhappy marriage, when sometimes temporary disengagement, compromise or patience may pay off. A *false equivalence* may be drawn between so-called 'conversion therapy' (often a religiously motivated, abusive programme claiming to change the sexual orientation of gay people) and ethical, professional psychological therapy.

Appeal to authority and tradition is a common phenomenon. Explicitly or implicitly, students are often encouraged to believe relatively uncritically in the theories of the founders of therapeutic theories or their disciples. A similar trend is found in *appeal or submission to obfuscatory language*. For example, postmodernist writing is often dense, obscure and hard to challenge, yet exercises in deconstructing its texts have proven enlightening (e.g., Pluckrose and Lindsay, 2021). An obverse of appeal to authority is the *ad hominem error* of critiquing an author instead of her or his ideas.

There can be strength in enthusiastic passions, for example in the belief that we are holistic beings who are self-healing and we are damaged by expert advice or drugs, or alternatively that we must submit ourselves to professional expertise. However, we can become entrenched rather than strengthened, and it is wise to review our beliefs and practices when we reach a point of *shutting out new evidence*. The 'truth' is often nuanced and can vary from case to case. A related error is sticking with what we find easy rather than what we find challenging or complicated. There are also temptations towards clinical *optimism bias*, encouraging a client's (premature) *flight into health*.

Sometimes we encounter a challenge to our beliefs that deserves to be resisted or refuted. Cultural and ethical fads arise which impinge on the world of therapy and demand change. But change is not necessarily always good. Deciding on *when to do battle* is also part of the remit of critical thinking. Therapy has been subject at various times to uncritical beliefs in epidemic traumatic childhood, satanic abuse, multiple selves, and so on. In our own moment, an emphasis on evidence-based practice seems axiomatically compelling and has boosted the reputation of CBT but has also undermined confidence in humanistic and psychodynamic approaches.

For busy practitioners, it is everyday clinical matters that are paramount. Yet behind the streams of clients on waiting lists and those actively being seen, large questions remain and someone must address them.

What is meant by mental health and its problems? What are the main causes of distress and how are these best addressed? What is the overall burden of such distress? Which are the most cost-effective means of addressing this, and what alternatives should be considered? We cannot simply dismiss non-psychotherapy avenues to understanding and resolution. We naturally ask to what extent capitalism causes or exacerbates distress, but we should also (I believe) continue to investigate biological causes. Nor, arguably, should we imagine that any panacea is forthcoming or that human life can ever be free from suffering. Such large questions may appear academic or beyond the clinician's expertise, but everyday encounters with clients constitute relevant data. Critical thinking in its incarnation of simple curiosity is a universal property.

CAUTIONS

Having stressed the importance of critical thinking, we should also pause to put it into perspective. Excessive evaluation is not always helpful. The practice of therapy depends to a large extent on the affective qualities of intuition, warmth and empathy, which are to be valued. The *paralysis of analysis* or over-emphasis on cognitive rumination is best avoided. To quite an extent, critical thinking can be made into a habit rather than an artificial, periodic exercise. The spontaneity and improvisation central to good therapy should not be sacrificed to unhelpful doubt, and even nihilism, that can be generated by excessive critical thinking. Critical thinking focusing on either trivial or grandiose matters is probably best avoided.

KEY ISSUES FOR THERAPY

'How can we do this better?' always has to be an overriding concern. But there is a difference between doing therapy better and more helpfully addressing questions of mental health. A psychotherapeutic tradition, simply because it has persisted for a century, is not necessarily the best way to research and resolve all mental health problems, and the forms of distress change across time and place. The plurality of models isn't *necessarily* helpful; nor are the professional fixtures of accreditation, supervision and ethics. Questioning these does not equate to abandoning them, but modifications across time are necessary.

The range of critical thinking applied to therapy extends from asking 'does it help at all?' through 'is private practice equitable?' to 'how many sessions are optimal?' and 'is the Power-Threat-Meaning-Framework, for example, sound?', and all that lies between. Tradition has to be examined but so too do novel theories and methods. Psychoanalysis has been dubbed 'the impossible profession' but it is probably fairer to say that all therapy and counselling is complex, challenging and in need of constant evaluation. All practitioners and trainers have a responsibility to tackle the questions impinging on their areas of practice, but therapists are not detached philosophers. Indeed, therapy being partly informed by an affective and psychodynamic epistemology adds a layer of complexity and potential richness. Critical thinking can be used to proudly defend the contributions of therapy.

CONCLUSIONS

Critical thinking may sound like an unnecessary academic burden, yet without it we might not have advanced much from the 1950s. Hans Eysenck was hated in his time but his severe criticism regarding lack of evidence for the effectiveness of psychotherapy served to fuel needed further research (Eysenck, 1952). Jeffrey Masson's severe criticisms helped to tighten ethical frameworks and complaints procedures (Masson, 1989). If it were not for the critical thinking of Albert Ellis and Aaron Beck, who became impatient with the psychoanalytic approach in which they had trained, we might have no CBT today. Critical thinking underpins progress and the appellation *critico-creative* thinking nicely sums this up.

Given the new cultural challenges with which therapists are faced, it is incumbent on us to encourage full-spectrum critical thinking, sometimes called viewpoint diversity, in order to arrive at more balanced evaluations of best practice. Remember too that many aspects of therapeutic theory are critical of common, unreflective ways of being. For example, psychoanalysis suggests that we often deceive ourselves unconsciously and act against our own best interests (Jacobs, 2000). Ambitious readers may wish to consult Baggini (2019) on the many non-Eurocentric traditions of thinking that cast light in a multicultural society. The question also remains to be tested as to therapy as a free speech forum, based on the Freudian invitation from 1895 to 'free association', contrasted with aspects of today's hate speech laws. This critical thinking issue potentially arises both in-session and as a matter for professional bodies' policies.

REFERENCES

Baggini, J. (2019) *How the World Thinks: A Global History of Philosophy*. London: Granta.
Chater, N. (2019) *The Mind is Flat: The Illusion of Mental Depth and The Improvised Mind.* London: Penguin.
Eysenck, H. J. (1952) The effects of psychotherapy: an evaluation. *Journal of Consulting Clinical Psychology*, 16: 319–324.
Galef, J. (2021) *The Scout Mindset: Why Some People See Things Clearly and Others Don't*. New York: Portfolio/Penguin Random House/London: Piatkus.
Guy, J. D. (1987) *The Personal Life of the Psychotherapist*. New York: Wiley.
Jacobs, M. (2000) *Illusion: A Psychodynamic Interpretation of Thinking and Belief*. London: Whurr.
Kahneman, D. (2011) *Thinking Fast and Slow*. New York: Farrar, Straus and Giroux.
Masson, J. M. (1989) *Against Therapy*. London: Fontana.
Pinker, S. (2021) *Rationality: What it is, Why it Seems Scarce, What it Matters.* London: Penguin.
Pluckrose, H. and Lindsay, J. (2021) *Cynical Theories: How Activist Scholarship Made Everything about Race, Gender and Identity*. Durham, NC: Pitchstone.

RECOMMENDED READING

Dryden, W. and Feltham, C. (Eds) (1992) *Psychotherapy and its Discontents*. Buckingham: Open University Press.

This gathered together the main objections to therapy from the 1950s to the 1990s by eminent critics from outside and within the profession.

Feltham, C. (2010) *Critical Thinking in Counselling and Psychotherapy*. London: Sage.

One of the first texts to examine the specific areas ripe for critique in this field, this book contains 60 topics to which critical thinking applies, and it remains valid today.

Forshaw, M. (2012) *Critical Thinking for Psychology: A Student Guide*. Chichester: Wiley.

A comprehensive guide to applied critical thinking for all students of psychology, including counselling psychologists at various levels.

PART IV

WHAT DO PEOPLE COME TO THERAPY FOR?

4.1 ADULT SEXUAL VIOLENCE: RAPE AND SEXUAL ASSAULT

ISHBA REHMAN

OVERVIEW AND KEY POINTS

Sexual violence is a term used to describe any kind of unwanted/non-consensual sexual act or activity. It affects many women, men and children throughout the world and often has adverse consequences for the individuals, their families, and the wider communities. Sexual violence can take many forms, such as sexual harassment and exploitation, sexual assault and rape, intimate partner violence, genital mutilation, etc. This chapter covers sexual violence with a focus on adult experiences of rape and sexual assault (for a contribution on sexual abuse in childhood, see McElvaney – Chapter 4.17, this volume). It is, however, important to note that sexual violence affects people irrespective of gender, sexuality, age, class, culture, religion, etc. The key points addressed in this chapter are:

- Sexual assault does not always involve physical violence or injury. It can cause psychological distress that may implicate an individual's psychosocial and emotional wellbeing and in turn hinder their functioning in important areas of life.
- Individuals vary in their responses to experiences of sexual violence, with some reporting high levels of acute stress following the event and others reporting high levels of chronic stress that may result in the development of post-traumatic stress disorder (PTSD).
- Therapists may come across clients where sexual violence is the primary presentation or where it emerges in the client's narrative of other presenting difficulties. When assessing experiences of sexual violence, therapists need to understand the client's subjective experience rather than making assumptions or generalisations about their experience and the resulting impact on their lives.
- There are various reflective and evidence-based models that therapists can draw on to help formulate collaboratively with the client their experience of sexual violence.
- Developing a shared understanding of the client's experience of sexual violence and associated difficulties can facilitate the therapist in offering support that is appropriate to the client's context, needs and expectations.

ASSESSMENT AND UNDERSTANDING

DEFINITIONS

Terms such as 'survivor' or 'victim' are often used across the literature on sexual violence and trauma. Hence, for the purpose of this chapter, I will be using these terms in various instances. However, when referring to those who have experienced sexual violence (in a therapeutic context), it is important to use the terminology that fits the individual's understanding of their experience.

The World Health Organisation (Krug et al., 2002) describes sexual violence as 'any sexual act, attempt to obtain a sexual act, unwanted sexual comments or advances, or acts to traffic, or otherwise directed, against a person's sexuality using coercion, by any person regardless of their relationship to the victim, in any setting, including but not limited to home and work'. Sexual violence can lead to devastating consequences for the individual(s) physiological, psychological, social and emotional wellbeing. 'Sexual assault' and 'rape' are often used when describing sexual violence. These terms are at times misunderstood and therefore used improperly in various contexts. Using the two terms synonymously may conceal important differences between two crimes which have distinct legal ramifications.

The term 'rape' has been in legal use for several decades, although 'sexual assault' came into legal use to define crimes of sexual violence in the mid-late 1900s. In the United Kingdom, the Sexual Offences Act 2003 c42 is an important piece of legislation that provides a legal framework for understanding the terms 'sexual assault' and 'rape' (Khan, 2004). Therapists working with victims and perpetrators of sexual trauma should make themselves familiar with these definitions and their legal ramifications.

Sexual assault:

1. Person A commits the offence if:

    (a) A intentionally touches another person B,
    (b) The touching is sexual,
    (c) B does not consent to the touching, and
    (d) A does not reasonably believe that B consents.

2. Whether a belief is reasonable is to be determined having regard to all the circumstances, including any steps A has taken to ascertain whether B consents.

Rape:

1. Person A commits the offence if:

    (a) A intentionally penetrates the vagina, anus or mouth of another person (B) with his penis,
    (b) B does not consent to the penetration, and
    (c) A does not reasonably believe that B consents.

2. Whether a belief is reasonable is to be determined having regard to all the circumstances, including any steps A has taken to ascertain whether B consents.

UNDERSTANDINGS AND RESPONSES TO SEXUAL VIOLENCE

Sexual assault and rape can be experienced by anyone across their life span, and all have a legal right to protection. Much of the research on the aetiology of sexual violence focuses on the offenders' perspective. It considers theories of personality, cognition and genetics alongside environmental variables. Research focusing on the victim's perspective relies on the victims' responses to experiences of sexual violence. It considers why some victims experience acute symptoms while others develop more chronic post traumatic symptomology in relation to their experience of sexual violence. This section focuses on the understandings of sexual violence from the perspective of the victim, and then importantly goes on to consider how clients who are victims may respond to sexual violence.

Unfortunately, victims of sexual assault and rape are (at times and by some) perceived as being responsible for the violence they have experienced by exposing themselves to environments that may be risky or unsafe (Amnesty International, 2005). Such perceptions may contribute to feelings of shame and guilt among victims and may in turn lead them to withhold important information from others (including the police or helping professionals). Therefore, crimes of sexual violence are often underreported, and their intensity and severity minimised. A survey of UK residents found over half of the respondents (56%) thought that in some of the situations the victim should take responsibility for being subjected to sexual violence (Havens, 2010).

Individuals vary greatly in their responses to sexual violence, with a significant proportion experiencing symptoms of trauma that can be understood as PTSD or Complex PTSD (C-PTSD) (see Charura and Smith – Chapter 4.15, this volume). Recent estimates show that a vast majority (94%) of those experiencing sexual assault or rape develop acute post traumatic symptoms, with many enduring symptoms of PTSD that may last months, years, or even a lifetime (Bisson and Andrew, 2007; Rothbaum et al., 1992). Early responses to sexual violence often include a sense of physical disgust, shock, denial, tearfulness, anxiety, social withdrawal, etc. These can be understood as normal reactions to a highly distressing event that violates an individual's sense of safety and integrity. In addition, many victims of sexual violence also report long-term difficulties with mood (anxiety, depression, irritability and anger), shame/guilt, flashbacks, nightmares, substance misuse and thoughts/behaviours consistent with self-harm (Skinner and Taylor, 2004).

FORMULATION

The impact of sexual violence on an individual can be varied and complex, based on a combination of factors, such as those discussed previously. It is important to understand the varying nature of individual responses to experiences of sexual violence and to tailor support that fits their needs. The first thing to bear in mind when offering therapeutic services to victims/survivors of sexual violence is to consider the legal aspects associated with offering therapy in the context of a criminal investigation (which may lead to prosecution and/or trial). Individuals may vary in their attempts to seek justice for the crime(s) committed against them and may wish to do this at different stages in the therapeutic process (or once therapy has concluded). Therapists working with victims/survivors of sexual violence should respect client autonomy and consider the implications of offering therapy in a pre-trial context that takes into account the Crown Prosecution Service's (CPS) *Provision of Therapy to Vulnerable or Intimidated Witnesses prior to Criminal Trial: Practical Guidance* (2011).

Prior to any therapeutic engagement with victims/survivors of sexual violence, therapists must ensure they have the necessary skills and organisational support to provide a safe therapeutic space for the client. In the initial stages of the assessment process, therapists should also consider the nature of sexual violence and its associated physical health risks. Liaising with medical professionals (following appropriate consent from the client) can be useful. Given the complex nature of experiencing following sexual violence, therapists should have an understanding of mental health issues such as depression, anxiety, trauma and dissociation. In addition, appropriate knowledge and training in safeguarding (adults and children) helps in managing the client's risk to self and others.

To determine the individual's suitability for treatment, therapists must first seek to assess their 'window of tolerance'. The concept of 'window of tolerance' is of great relevance to sexual trauma assessment and the process of recovery. It is the space/window within which an individual feels safe and able to deal with everyday stressors without feeling overwhelming anxiety, fatigue or a sense of loss of control (O'Shea Brown, 2021). It is important to assess the client's window of tolerance in the initial stages of therapy. This may be followed by increasing the client's awareness of symptoms through psychoeducation and experiential learning. Grounding/relaxation and emotional regulation techniques are often helpful in increasing a client's window of tolerance and facilitating subsequent application of interventions.

Assessment of sexual violence should be aimed at gaining a detailed account of an individual's presenting difficulties, including the nature, duration and severity of symptoms (both physiological and psychological) and their impact on the client's functioning in important areas of life (interpersonal, social, occupational, etc.). Any predisposing factors of relevance to the client's experience and coping must also be considered. Additionally, therapists should also assess family and environmental factors when understanding the individual's response to sexual violence and the intensity of their post traumatic symptoms. Other factors that may exacerbate the individuals' difficulties associated with sexual trauma include stigma, misconceptions and inadequate social support. Hence, carrying out a detailed assessment and subsequent formulation that considers these complexities is of key importance.

There are various therapeutic approaches that are utilised to formulate clients' experiences of sexual violence. Selecting a suitable approach should be achieved through a collaborative process that considers therapist competence in that model and client needs and expectations. When formulating client experiences of sexual trauma, there is no evidence to suggest that one therapeutic approach is better than another. Most services across the UK offer a combination of experiential, humanistic and cognitive behaviourally oriented approaches. Some of the approaches found to be helpful in supporting victims of sexual violence include trauma focused cognitive therapies, Eye Movement Desensitisation and Reprocessing (EMDR), Acceptance and Commitment Therapy (ACT), Cognitive Analytical Therapy (CAT) and Dialectical Behaviour Therapy (DBT).

It is common for victims/survivors of sexual violence to experience feelings of powerlessness and helplessness at the time of the incident. Many may continue to have such feelings long after the incident (for varying lengths of time). Therapists should take this into account when assessing and formulating the nature, severity and implications of sexual violence experienced by the client. Therapists should also share information about therapeutic approaches suited to the client's needs and encourage client autonomy in making informed decisions regarding their choice of treatment.

WAYS OF WORKING WITH VICTIMS OF ADULT SEXUAL VIOLENCE

A range of relational and evidence-based frameworks and approaches to treatment have been found to be effective in the treatment of trauma resulting from sexual violence. An assessment of the client's 'window of tolerance' (discussed previously) should inform the selection of therapeutic approach taken. It is useful to conceptualise recovery from sexual trauma as a staged process whereby treatment is tailored appropriately to the client's stage of recovery. The first stage relies on the establishment of safety, the second stage focuses on retelling the narrative of the traumatic incident(s), and the final stage is aimed at reconnecting with others

(Herman, 2015). A specific therapeutic approach that may be useful for the client in one stage of therapy may be of minimal use or even counterproductive to the same client in a different stage. For example, some cognitive approaches such as Trauma Focused Cognitive Behavioural Therapy – CBT(TF) – rely heavily on the nature of trauma memory and its appraisal. This may be particularly difficult for victims of sexual violence in the early stages of therapy.

Regardless of the therapeutic approach taken, it is often helpful to initiate the treatment process with psychoeducation and stabilisation (using grounding and relaxation techniques). This can be useful in increasing the client's 'window of tolerance' and in turn facilitate subsequent processing of trauma memories associated with the client's experience of sexual violence. A particular focus of trauma-focused therapies is to allow the trauma memory to be integrated into the individual's life story rather than something that defines their existence. Some clients will benefit from managing post traumatic symptoms of hypervigilance, nightmares, flashbacks, dissociation, event related mood changes, etc. Others may want to focus more on their self-esteem and social and interpersonal difficulties. Therefore, it is important for therapists to avoid a 'one size fits all' approach and tailor therapeutic support in line with the client's subjective experience and needs.

CASE STUDY

Zara is a 22-year-old university student reporting sexual assault by an acquaintance on her way back from a social event, two years ago. She described being in a state of complete shock and denial in the initial aftermath of the incident. Zara reported becoming more aware of what had happened a few weeks later, which led to feelings of guilt and shame stemming from a sense of disappointment and personal responsibility for being subjected to sexual violence. During assessment, Zara described experiencing hypervigilance, marked anxiety in social situations and recurring flashbacks/nightmares about the incident, which affected her wellbeing. She also explained how she was finding it difficult to maintain interpersonal relationships, particularly those that required intimate contact.

Following the initial assessment, it was collaboratively agreed that any interventions involving recall of the traumatic incident may lead to high levels of distress for Zara. Hence, the initial sessions were largely focused on developing an effective therapeutic relationship, offering psychoeducation related to sexual violence/PTSD and practising grounding and relaxation techniques. Zara responded well to these interventions. She found the grounding and relaxation skills (supplemented with visualisation) helpful in reducing the post traumatic symptomology associated with her experience of sexual violence.

After eight sessions, Zara felt more able to speak about the incident. As Zara began to explore the incident, several questions presented themselves: 'Why me? What did I do to deserve this? Was it my fault? Why didn't anyone come to help?' It was important at this stage in therapy to focus on reappraising the situation so Zara no longer felt responsible for the sexual violence directed towards her.

As this case was due to go to trial, all therapy offered was in a pre-trial context. Zara was made aware of the associated legal aspects. Following the tenth session, Zara felt more able to manage her anxiety and other symptoms associated with the sexual trauma. An ending was therefore collaboratively agreed. Four months later, the trial took place, although the perpetrator was not convicted due to insufficient evidence. Zara reportedly felt disappointed as she contacted the therapist to inform her of the decision.

Zara demonstrated a willingness to re-engage in therapy to continue working on her post traumatic symptoms (flashbacks, nightmares, hypervigilance). Another 10 sessions (informed by Trauma Focused CBT) were offered and contracted for. The sessions focused on facilitating Zara to develop a detailed understanding of her trauma and management of the post traumatic symptomology.

Another key concept closely linked to the 'window of tolerance' is 're-traumatisation'. It is the conscious or unconscious reminder of past trauma that results in a re-experiencing of the initial traumatic event(s). Therapists working with victims/survivors of sexual violence must have an understanding of re-traumatisation and how it may be triggered by a situation, an attitude or expression, or by certain environments that replicate the dynamics (loss of power/control/safety) of the original trauma (Zgoda, Shelly and Hitzel, 2016).

Evaluation of therapy for victims/survivors of sexual violence can be done using qualitative feedback from the client during and after therapy. Using standardised tools can also be helpful in diagnosis and assessment of PTSD symptomology associated with the client's experience(s) of sexual violence. Standardised outcome measures such as Impact of Events Scale – Revised (IESR-R) and PTSD Checklist (PCL-5) are often used across therapeutic services in the UK (government, private and third sector) in order to determine the nature and severity of PTSD symptoms. The Dissociative Experiences Scale (DES II) may also be used to assess the client's extent of disconnection from their thoughts, feelings, memories or sense of identity. However, it is important to note that dissociation is a less common symptom of PTSD.

THE JOURNEY TO RECOVERY

As with their responses to experiences of sexual violence, individuals also vary greatly in their journeys to recovery. These can be influenced positively or negatively by environmental factors and the responses they receive from professionals and services. It is therefore imperative that therapists understand the complex nature of sexual violence and associated distress that victims experience. An awareness of the misconceptions, societal views, media influence and legal issues in the context of sexual violence is also important, particularly for those supporting victims/survivors of sexual trauma. Therapists should also aim to consider aspects that go beyond the client's experience of sexual violence. These include sensitivity to the socio-cultural norms and role expectations that may influence the client's pre- and post-sexual violence views, and dictate responses of friends, families and services. It is also important for therapists to understand how various markers of identity (e.g., gender, race/ethnicity, sexual orientation, physical ability) and their complex intersections (and how the society views them) can exacerbate the oppression victims of sexual violence may experience.

VICARIOUS TRAUMA AND COMPASSION FATIGUE

Therapists supporting victims/survivors of sexual violence may themselves be at an increased risk of developing symptoms of acute and/or chronic traumatic stress. The term 'vicarious trauma' is used to describe the process through which traumatic stress is transferred to therapists because of exposure to client narratives of trauma (Figley, 2002). Vicarious trauma left unchecked can result in disturbances in therapist thoughts and beliefs around trust, safety, control and power (Kadambi and Truscott, 2004). There are different types of stress that impact those supporting survivors of trauma: traumatic stress or secondary traumatic stress, which can be understood as 'compassion fatigue'. It is therefore imperative that therapists working with individuals who have experienced sexual violence are mindful of their own health and wellbeing. Therapists should seek to prioritise their own self-care alongside supporting their clients in their journeys to recovery.

REFERENCES

Amnesty International (2005). *Stop violence against women: How to use international criminal law to campaign for gender-sensitive law reform.* London: Amnesty International.

Bisson, J., & Andrew, M. (2007). Psychological treatment of post-traumatic stress disorder (PTSD). *Cochrane Database of Systematic Reviews*, (3). doi: 10.1002/14651858.CD003388.pub3

Crown Prosecution Service (2011). *Provision of Therapy to Vulnerable or Intimidated Witnesses prior to Criminal Trial: Practice Guidance.* London: CPS.

Figley, C.R. (Ed.) (2002). *Treating Compassion Fatigue*. London: Routledge.

Haven. (2010). *Wake up to rape: Research summary report*. London: Haven http://www.womensgrid.org.uk/archive/2010/02/21/wake-up-to-rape-research-summary-report-of-haven-commissioned-survey/

Herman, J.L. (2015). *Trauma and Recovery: The Aftermath of Violence – From Domestic Abuse to Political Terror*. London: Hachette.

Kadambi, M.A., & Truscott, D. (2004). Vicarious trauma among therapists working with sexual violence, cancer and general practice. *Canadian Journal of Counselling and Psychotherapy*, *38*(4).

Khan, A. (2004). Sexual Offences Act 2003. *The Journal of Criminal Law*, *68*(3), 220–226.

Krug, E.G., Dahlberg, L.L., Mercy, J.A., Zwi, A.B., & Lozano, R. (2002). *World Report on Violence and Health*. Geneva: World Health Organisation.

O'Shea Brown, G. (2021). Trauma and the body. In G. O'Shea Brown, *Healing Complex Posttraumatic Stress Disorder: A Clinician's Guide* (pp. 77–90). Essential Clinical Social Work Series. New York: Springer.

Rothbaum, B.O., Foa, E.B., Riggs, D.S., Murdock, T., & Walsh, W. (1992). A prospective examination of post-traumatic stress disorder in rape victims. *Journal of Traumatic Stress*, *5*(3), 455–475. doi: 10.1002/jts.2490050309

Skinner, T., & Taylor, H. (2004). *Providing Counselling, Support and Information to Survivors of Rape: An Evaluation of the 'STAR Young Persons' Project*. London: Home Office.

Zgoda, K., Shelly, P., & Hitzel, S. (2016). Preventing retraumatization: A macro social work approach to trauma-informed practices and policies. *The New Social Worker*, 17 October.

RECOMMENDED READING

Ehlers, A., & Clark, D.M. (2000). A cognitive model of posttraumatic stress disorder. *Behaviour Research and Therapy*, *38*(4), 319–345. doi: 10.1016/S0005-7967(99)00123-0

This paper offers an understanding of the 'cognitive model of PTSD'. The model has been designed in line with the key clinical features of PTSD and offers a framework of PTSD treatment by identifying the main targets for change.

Foa, E.B., Rothbaum, B.O., & Steketee, G.S. (1993). Treatment of rape victims. *Journal of Interpersonal Violence*, *8*(2), 256–276. doi: 10.1177/088626093008002006

This article reviews a range of psychological interventions utilised when working with post-rape sequelae. The article also offers suggestions for improvements in the assessment of PTSD (resulting from rape) and for predicting treatment response in victims/survivors of rape.

Raja, S. (2012). *Overcoming Trauma and PTSD: A Workbook Integrating Skills from ACT, DBT, and CBT*. Oakland, CA: New Harbinger Publications.

This is a self-help workbook with integrated skills from ACT, DBT and CBT. It offers various skills, strategies and interventions that clinicians can draw upon and recommend to those overcoming trauma and PTSD.

4.2 ALCOHOL-RELATED DIFFICULTIES

MANI MEHDIKANI, JULIE SCHEINER AND LOREN WHYATT

OVERVIEW AND KEY POINTS

Many clients who present with alcohol-related difficulties may initially come to therapy for help with problems other than their alcohol use. For them, everything else is the *real* problem (their trauma, family problems, social services, etc.) and if you as the therapist could just help them with these other problems, then everything will be fine and they can go back to normal, healthier levels of drinking (Flores, 2004). In fact, many alcoholics have an alcohol *solution* rather than an alcohol problem. Even in the case of those who are not psychologically dependant on alcohol, it is possible that the client is there to see you somewhat reluctantly, perhaps pushed into attending the appointment by a concerned partner, family member or GP, or mandated to engage with alcohol treatment by the courts. When working with clients with alcohol problems, the therapist has the task of balancing respect for client autonomy with their duty of beneficence. Counsellors cannot be completely non-directive as there are clear ethical and moral implications to (metaphorically) hold hands with a client while they drink themselves to ruin and death (Flores, 2004). Working with clients with alcohol problems requires a combination of empathy and confrontation (as the goal rather than the style of communication). Accurate empathy may be hard to attain for many therapists as alcoholics often have to deal with moral dilemmas that are sometimes hard for non-addicts to fathom (Diamond, 2000).

In undertaking therapy or counselling with people with alcohol-related problems there are several key issues that should be considered, which we cover in this chapter:

- What do we mean by 'alcohol-related difficulties'? This term can be ambiguous and can refer to a range of client difficulties, including heavy drinking, binge drinking, dependency, etc.
- What is the client's phase in their alcohol treatment and recovery journey?
- How motivated or resistant is the client about making changes to their drinking?

ASSESSMENT AND UNDERSTANDING

How and why to undertake assessment may depend to some extent on whether the alcohol problem is heavy or excessive drinking or the manifestation of 'addiction'. If it is suspected that a client is physically dependent on alcohol, and they experience severe withdrawal symptoms when they do not drink alcohol, the therapist or counsellor must never advise the client to stop drinking suddenly. However, care must be taken to communicate clearly that the advice not to stop suddenly is not the same as *permission* to continue drinking. It is important that the client is made aware that in some cases withdrawal from alcohol can be life-threatening.

Before delving into the mechanics of the assessment process, it is worth pausing to consider a few things even before that first meeting. The therapist or counsellor should carefully reflect on their own attitudes, prejudices and biases, along with some of the common myths (Velleman, 2011) around this topic. For example:

- What is your *theory* of the problem – a disease, a habit or something else?
- What is your position on labels such as *alcoholic* or *addict*?
- Is full recovery conceptually available? Or a never-ending journey?
- What are your views on control, choice and responsibility in heavy drinking?
- Are alcohol problems 'self-inflicted'?
- What is your view on mutual aid and networks of recovery, such as SMART Recovery or 12 Step approaches such as Alcoholics Anonymous (AA)?

The therapist's own attitude towards alcohol use is also important and you are unlikely to approach this topic from a completely neutral stance. Your views about alcohol are likely to have been shaped by factors such as your own past experiences with it, whether and how much you drink, your religious beliefs, your societal and cultural context, among other factors.

ASSESSMENT

The settings and context in which you see clients with alcohol-related difficulties are important. In some settings, such as specialist alcohol treatment centres, assessing for alcohol use is a routine part of the work of the clinic and may be undertaken by other staff before clients are seen by the therapist. In other settings, such as private practice, assessment may be opportunistic, with the client ostensibly attending for some other problem (low mood, anxiety, etc.) but presenting with signs of problematic alcohol use (e.g., appearing intoxicated, displaying symptoms of withdrawal or smelling strongly of alcohol).

During assessment, the therapist will methodically go over every life domain (e.g., physical and mental health, sleep, memory function, relationships, employment, finances, housing, etc.) where alcohol might have a problematic impact. By identifying alcohol as a problem in one or more of these domains, the client will also reveal their core values and the therapist can use these to skilfully develop discrepancy (Miller and Rollnick, 2013).

Besides aiding motivation, the assessment has several other functions:

- the client's history and start of their alcohol problems
- their previous treatment history
- possible co-morbid psychiatric difficulties
- polysubstance use
- physical and psychological dependency, including using screening such as the Alcohol Use Disorders Identification Test (AUDIT) and the Severity of Alcohol Dependence Questionnaire (SAD-Q)
- risks and safeguarding needs
- the client's goals around their drinking.

FORMULATION

According to Mace and Binyon (2005), what distinguishes formulations (i.e., from diagnostic approaches) is that they are interactive processes that help provide an exploratory summary focusing on what is unique about a person, and aid in the understanding of the person's responses to their illness. They often include past difficulties and experiences in relation to alcohol addiction and what factors may have contributed to this. Formulations may be akin to a jigsaw puzzle in terms of understanding what has brought a client to their current place, what is going on in a client's life now, when the difficulties began (e.g., a distinction should be made between when the client started drinking and when they or others began to see it as a problem), and key experiences and relationships in a client's life.

WAYS OF WORKING

THEORETICAL MODELS OF AND INTERVENTIONS FOR ALCOHOL-RELATED PROBLEMS

Formulations are *theory*-driven. Theoretical models that inform alcohol-related difficulties are far too numerous to list comprehensively and to be delved into here in any detail, but can be broadly 'classified into behavioural, cognitive, psychodynamic, humanistic, systemic, motivational, disease, and social and environmental' (National Institute for Health and Care Excellence, 2011). Among the earliest were 'old-fashioned' Freudian theories (focusing on *regressive* or *defensive* functions of alcohol use). Later, neo-Freudians made important contributions to this area, for example the *self-medication hypothesis*, which posits a role for affect regulation and the idea that a substance is selected because it helps 'repair' a particular emotional impairment (i.e., stimulants for impulsiveness or analgesics for anger, etc.) (Khantzian, 1997). Flores (2004) and Weegmann and Khantzian (2018) have underscored several psychodynamic and related traditions and some of these are enumerated, and key points briefly summarised, below:

> **Kleinian** approach – derived from the work of Melanie Klein, this posits that addiction to substances like alcohol can recreate early primitive *paranoid-schizoid* ways of functioning. Alcohol use in this context is seen as a form *psychic evasion*, viewed as being ultimately anti-growth or anti-maturation. The client often undergoes a 'wavering of positions', oscillating between insight into the harms they cause and rejecting change often within and between therapy sessions. This aligns with the notion of *ambivalence* in motivational approaches (see below).
> **Kohutian** approach – from the work of Heinz Kohut on self-psychology, this rests on the impact of early disturbances in parenting with respect to

empathy and narcissism (here not seen as selfishness but aligning with AA's view of the 'inflated ego' and interpreted as clients trying to obtain the needs they were not able to obtain from others or *selfobjects*). In this context, alcohol can be viewed as a comforting selfobject and an ultimately failed attempt at self-repair.

Bowlbian approach – based on the work of John Bowlby. It has been suggested that if, as children, individuals are exposed to unhelpful attachment experiences, they are more likely to develop maladaptive strategies for managing distress, such as avoidance or anxiety, and as adults, these individuals may turn to external sources, such as alcohol or other substances, to manage emotions. Key elements of this approach (highlighted by Flores, 2004) include:

a) Clients may see alcohol as both *secure base* and *safe haven*.
b) The insight that for an alcohol-dependent client to form a healthy attachment to their therapist and the treatment they must first detach (or *de*-attach) themselves from their substance. It is partly for this reason that in the initial phase of the work the therapist is likely to be viewed by the client as both *helper* and *depriver* (Reading, 2002).
c) The client's attachment pattern can help organise their treatment, including giving the therapist insights into early caregiver relationships and experiences, how they might self-regulate, how transference might manifest during the work, etc.
d) The suggestion that if attachment disturbance occurred at an early *sensitive* stage and/or was severe, then even the best therapy is limited in its curative effects. It is suggested that in such cases, the expected attachment information that the client's early neural networks had been primed to receive did not materialize, leading to permanent changes to their neural architecture. In extreme cases, the best the client can hope for might be in finding a long-term or even life-long facilitating environment (e.g., AA); in such cases, encouraging clients to attend mutual aid networks as an adjunct to therapy is not just desirable but is instead a vital therapeutic task.

Cognitive and behavioural approaches – a number have been highlighted in the NICE guidelines for alcohol use (NICE, 2011):

Social Behaviour and Network Therapy (SNBT) – clients with alcohol problems do not exist in a vacuum but are established in social networks. When a person drinks heavily, the people around them are usually affected in some way. Relationships can impact on or be impacted by excessive alcohol consumption and become damaged or fragmented. Systematic approaches, such as BCT (see below) or SBNT, offer support to both the person who is drinking problematically and their significant others, and aim to improve communication and understanding between them and help to build a network that is supportive and encouraging of positive change (Copello et al., 2013).

Behavioural Couples Therapy (BCT) – this approach is predicated on the view that alcohol problems are often maintained by a set of vicious cycles of communication (e.g., circular communication: 'I drink because you nag' / 'I nag because you drink') and behaviours (e.g., a drinking bout leads to a partner becoming upset and bringing up past such episodes; this leads to an argument and withdrawal of caring behaviours, leading to a new drinking bout) in the client's primary relationship. The aim of this approach is to help a couple break the above cycles and replace them with 'virtuous' ones.

Cognitive Behavioural Therapy (CBT) – in the national UK guidelines (NICE, 2011), these can refer to any of three approaches which are broadly similar in terms of theoretical assumptions. In addition, these overlap greatly with the counselling approach suggested by Velleman (2011), both in terms of the techniques used and in the notion that many clients may be helped towards 'controlled' or 'sensible' drinking, rather than abstinence being seen as the only viable drinking goal for all. As Velleman has noted, the latter goal is often easier than the former and therapists should be upfront and honest with their client if they believe the latter's goal for drinking is unrealistic. These approaches are listed below:

a) **'Standard' CBT** – similar to the CBT approaches used with other difficulties (e.g., anxiety disorders), with certain modifications to account for special features of alcohol use. Like other CBT approaches, there is an emphasis on how our problems are often shaped by our appraisal of reality, the role played by the interconnectedness of our cognitions, emotional states and behaviours (with alcohol here seen as a form of *chemical avoidance*) and by a range of cognitive biases. In addition, this approach may incorporate other elements, including *alcohol-related* and *permission giving* beliefs, *expectancy* effects and *intentionality*, etc.

b) **Relapse Prevention** – the key organising principle here is the *abstinence violation effect*. This argues that what differentiates a lapse from a relapse is the person's appraisal of a failed attempt to remain abstinent (or to stick with a sensible drinking plan). The above effect is more likely to be triggered if the person's *failure* cognitions are deemed to be internal ('*I* am a failure'), global ('I fail at *everything*') and stable ('I *always* fail').

c) **Coping Skills Training** – as noted in key guidance (NICE, 2011), this is rooted in the approach pioneered by a landmark study of alcohol treatments (Project MATCH (Project MATCH, 1993)) and includes practical and experiential skills-based training (e.g., drink refusal skills).

Parenthetically, when working with clients with comorbid mental health problems, such as anxiety or depression, therapists should treat their alcohol misuse first, as often simply stopping or even reducing alcohol use can lead to substantial improvements in mood.

EMBEDDING THE WORK WITHIN THE RECOVERY JOURNEY

The techniques used and interventions offered to clients will depend on what stage they are at in their recovery journey, and on their stage in the cycle of change (Prochaska and DeClemente, 1982; see Figure 4.2.1).

Recovery can be broken down into four phases (adapted from Flores, 2004):

1. **Pre-recovery** – often the phase when the therapist first encounters the client, who may either be in the *pre-contemplative* or *contemplative* stage of change. The therapist's aim at this phase should be to use motivational approaches first to tip the client into an ambivalent state and then to resolve this by developing discrepancy.

2. **Desistence** – in this the shortest part of the journey (lasting 2–3 weeks), the client begins to make changes to reduce or stop their alcohol use; desistence (which often requires a form of

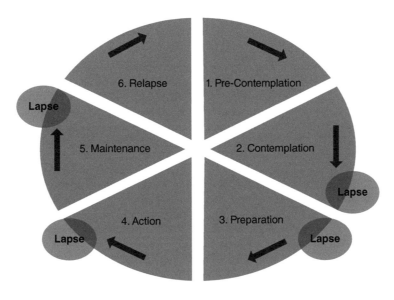

Figure 4.2.1 The cycle of change (Prochaska and DiClemente, 1982)

detoxification) should be the client's decision and any attempt to 'push' the client towards this stage is less likely to lead to lasting changes.
3. **Early-stage abstinence** – once detoxified, clients may need to tackle their psychological dependence on alcohol. In terms of the effort expected from clients, this is perhaps the hardest and steepest climb on their recovery journey (typically lasting 6–12 months) and this is also where the risks around lapses and relapse are at their greatest. The therapeutic part of the work should ideally begin at no earlier than the mid-point of this phase.
4. **Late-stage recovery** – clients become increasingly (over the course of around five years) able to control their own choices and take responsibility for their recovery. Here, an important part of the process for many clients is continuing engagement with networks of recovery (e.g., AA, SMART Recovery).

Effective interventions when working with alcohol problems, particularly in the early stages of recovery, should include a motivational element. The therapist should see the main purpose of the intervention as motivating and gently guiding clients towards positive change around their drinking.

MOTIVATIONAL INTERVIEWING

As noted earlier, many alcohol-using clients are (for a variety of reasons) at best ambivalent and at worst resistant regarding the need for change. Motivational interviewing (MI) is an important technique when working with clients with alcohol problems or other addictions. Although not considered therapy as such, it can be used alongside other interventions as a means of facilitating treatments and instigating change (Miller and Rollnick, 2013). While there are a variety of techniques that are used, Miller and Rollnick, MI's founders, suggest it is its 'spirit' that requires most attention:

1. **Collaboration** – therapist and client meet as equals with the therapist aiming to create a therapeutic relationship that is conducive but not coercive to change.
2. **Evocation** – the therapist does not attempt to instil motivation in the client, but instead draws out the motivation that is already within them.
3. **Autonomy** – responsibility for change lies with the client and is not imposed by the therapist.
4. **Compassion** – the therapist demonstrates acceptance of the client's struggle, offers compassionate care, and a commitment to supporting the client.

CASE STUDY

MOLLY – A CASE STUDY IN RECOVERY AND RELAPSE PREVENTION

Molly, a female client in her late 30s, came to therapy as she had been struggling with her recovery for several years having made several attempts at abstinence. Molly referred to herself as a 'party animal', but also recognised the importance of staying sober given that she wanted to start her own family. Molly had been through several treatment facilities for detox and joined AA and several other programmes. In working with Molly, it was important to recognise her triggers for drinking, the reasons behind these, the function the drinking served for her and to explore the 'party animal' persona that Molly felt was an important part of her identity. In terms of formulation, Molly understood that the drinking and party persona was also related to being able to self-regulate her emotions, so when she felt up/down/good/bad, drinking always helped to self-soothe and self-regulate.

Molly took the stance that if she should relapse, this would form part of her therapy so that we could further understand her triggers to drinking. It transpired that the persona of 'party animal' developed over time to hide a multitude of disordered attachments with her immediate family, all of whom could be described as 'functioning alcoholics', given that they may not have always been emotionally available to her.

During sessions, Molly was able to explore the fractured nature of her attachments with her family and how alcohol functioned as a way of dealing with the pain of absent parents. She developed healthier relationships outside her party self through AA and mutual aid. Leaving behind her party lifestyle also meant severing ties with friendships where alcohol was the mainstay and developing healthier ways of relating. The therapeutic relationship has been central to bringing about change for Molly, by providing a safe space to explore the pain of dysfunction in her life, which at times also played out in our therapeutic relationship in unexpected ways.

CONCLUSION

Although often existing on a continuum, this problem is still poorly defined. Some therapy models all but deny the existence of addiction, while others see a distinction between alcoholism and alcohol abuse; but even here, at what point might the latter become the former (in AA vernacular 'when does a cucumber become a pickle?') (Flores, 2004)? The theoretical models that can inform such difficulties are far too numerous to list, never mind do any justice to, in this slim treatise. Nonetheless, working therapeutically with clients with alcohol-related problems (regardless of the model) can be both challenging and rewarding. A key challenge can be clients' defences around their alcohol use, often manifesting as resistance or ambivalence. Interventions such as MI suggest that motivation to change is neither a stable nor an inherent property located in the person. However, helping clients move along the cycle of change may be only the first step in a long, and perhaps lifetime, recovery journey.

REFERENCES

Copello, A., Orford, J., Hodgson, R. & Tober, G. (2013). *Social Behaviour and Network Therapy for Alcohol Problems.* London: Routledge.

Diamond, J. (2000). *Narrative Means to Sober Ends: Treating Addiction and its Aftermath.* New York: Guilford Press.

Flores, P.J. (2004). *Addiction as an Attachment Disorder.* Oxford: Jason Aronson.

Khantzian, E.J. (1997). The self-medication hypothesis of substance use disorders: a reconsideration and recent applications. *Harvard Review of Psychiatry*, 4(5), 231–244.

Mace, C. & Binyon, S. (2005). Teaching psychodynamic formulation to psychiatric trainees. Part 1: Basics of formulation. *Advances in Psychiatric Treatment*, 11, 416–423.

Miller, W.R. & Rollnick, S. (2013). *Motivational Interviewing: Helping People Change* (3rd ed.). New York: Guilford Press.

National Institute for Health and Care Excellence (NICE) (2011). *Alcohol-use Disorders: Diagnosis, Assessment and Management of Harmful Drinking (High-risk Drinking) and Alcohol Dependence.* CG115. London: NICE.

Prochaska, J. & DiClemente, C. (1982). Transtheoretical therapy: toward a more integrative model of change. *Psychotherapy: Theory, Research and Practice*, 19(3), 276–288.

Project MATCH (Matching Alcoholism Treatment to Client Heterogeneity) (1993). *Alcoholism, clinical and experimental research*, 17(6), 1130–1145. https://doi.org/10.1111/j.1530-0277.1993.tb05219.x

Reading, B. (2002). The application of Bowlby's attachment theory to the psychotherapy of addictions. In M. Weegman & R. Cohen (Eds), *The Psychodynamics of Addiction* (pp. 3–12). London: Whurr.

Velleman, R. (2011). *Counselling for Alcohol Problems* (3rd ed.). London: Sage.

Weegman, M. & Khantzian, E.J. (2018). 'Dangerous desires and inanimate attachment': modern psychodynamic approaches to substance misuse. In P. Davis, R. Patton & S. Jackson (Eds), *Addiction: Psychology and Treatment* (pp. 69–83). Chichester: John Wiley & Sons.

RECOMMENDED READING

Flores, P.J. (2004). *Addiction as an Attachment Disorder.* Oxford: Jason Aronson.

This text presents a compelling case for the application of attachment theory, along with related approaches such as self-psychology and the 12 Steps, to understanding addictions as a person's ultimately counterproductive attempt at self-repair in the context of affect regulation.

Miller, W.R. & Rollnick, S. (2013). *Motivational Interviewing: Helping People Change* (3rd ed.). New York: Guilford Press.

(Continued)

> (Continued)
>
> This is a comprehensive guide to motivational interviewing, written by its originators.
>
> Velleman, R. (2011). *Counselling for Alcohol Problems* (3rd ed.). London: Sage.
>
> This book offers a practical guide to working with clients with alcohol-related problems.

4.3 ANXIETY AND PANIC

STEVEN BARNES, JULIE PRESCOTT AND JEROME CARSON

OVERVIEW AND KEY POINTS

This chapter covers the features of anxiety and panic, guidance for assessment, and pertinent theoretical models for understanding the conditions. Resulting clinical interventions are discussed alongside a relevant case study. Key reading and research are also recommended. This chapter suggests that anxiety conditions:

- are intrusive, enduring and multifaceted, varying in presentation.
- encompass several manifestations: generalised anxiety disorder (GAD) and panic disorder (PD) are the most frequently occurring.
- are frequently relapsing conditions (often linked to ongoing stressors and/or poor treatment adherence (Glenn et al., 2013).
- have a pathology resulting in reduced treatment-seeking – diagnosis rates likely underestimate the size of the anxious population (Kessler and Greenberg, 2002).
- can precipitate long-term physical, social and occupational disability, and premature mortality if untreated (Lenze and Wetherell, 2011).

ASSESSMENT AND UNDERSTANDINGS

ANXIETY AND PANIC: AN OVERVIEW

The onset of anxiety disorders is complex and multifaceted but can be broadly considered as the outcome of a combination of biological and psychological vulnerabilities and/or environmental experiences and triggers (Locke et al., 2015). Biological markers include heritability, with studies indicating a multigenic contribution towards neurotic or anxious predisposition, particularly where parents have a severe psychiatric disorder (Ayano et al., 2021). Psychological factors include the persistent tendency towards elevated risk perception and lack of attentional control. Environmental factors (e.g., learning/experience) may contribute to reinforce psychological vulnerabilities. In the case of specific disorders such as panic disorder, a clearly identifiable experience may provoke psychological symptom onset (e.g., growing perception of danger of somatic symptoms).

Generalised anxiety disorder (GAD) leads to excessive anxiety and worry (apprehensive expectation) about a range of stimuli, rather than a single event/situation. Individuals experiencing GAD may be (as with other anxiety disorders) unusually sensitive to perceived threat and demonstrate distorted representations of potential risk. Anxiety is frequent and GAD sufferers may report difficulties remembering a time without these feelings. Anxieties are often difficult to control, disproportionate to actual risk, and excessive, creating significant distress and impaired functioning. Individuals may also become restless, easily fatigued, irritable, have sleep disturbances, and/or have difficulty concentrating. As GAD symptoms tend to be less intense than in other anxiety disorders (e.g., panic disorder), the condition is often under-recognised. Difficulties in diagnosis and chronic and enduring negative outcomes associated with untreated GAD are noted in the literature (Greener, 2014).

In comparison to GAD, symptoms of panic disorder (PD) are often more intense with less gradual onset. Panic attacks are distinct experiences of intense anxiety and fear, accompanied by a range of somatic symptoms (e.g., palpitations/accelerated heart rate, sweating, difficulty breathing, nausea) and a strong perception of danger/fear of dying, with an urge to escape. While panic attacks may result from an identifiable environmental trigger, they may occur unexpectedly. PD sufferers will have experienced more than one spontaneous attack, occurring alongside persistent concern of future attacks and associated avoidance behaviours.

PD often occurs alongside other anxiety conditions (e.g., agoraphobia). Fear and avoidance across a range of situations associated with agoraphobia is implicated in panic attack recurrence. When considering the distinction between these two conditions, panic may not be present in all agoraphobia cases, with attacks described as 'expected' (associated with a specific fear) or 'unexpected' (occurring with no apparent trigger) rather than 'situationally bound' – people may often experience both types. Notably, PD sufferers often report anticipatory anxiety of future panic attacks (a 'fear of fear'), or a significant change in behaviour following previous attacks. There may also be extraneous causes of panic attacks (such as substance use) or panic arising from other medical conditions (e.g., hyperthyroidism).

Interventions for anxiety and panic should be based on a detailed assessment and analysis of symptoms in addition to other associated problems, including:

- A detailed history of the problem and the nature of its emergence
- identification of clear goals for therapy
- use of appropriate measurement inventories to assess progress.

Several strategies exist for dealing with these difficulties. For instance, the above can be discussed with the client within a cognitive-behavioural framework.

THEORETICAL EXPLANATIONS OF GAD AND PD

GENERALISED ANXIETY DISORDER

Cognitive models of GAD all share a focus on the central concept of worry (Dugas et al., 1998). Developments in understanding GAD support the need to categorise it as a chronic and disabling disorder, identifiable even if coexisting other anxiety conditions and present for at least six months. Dugas et al.'s conceptual model represented the considerable advancement in understanding GAD and forms the basis for the treatment approach as recommended by the Department of Health in the United Kingdom (IAPT, 2007). The central component of this model is 'intolerance of uncertainty' – a tendency to hold negative beliefs regarding uncertainty and its implications.

These negative beliefs:

- often consist of hypothetical worrying ('what if?' thinking), producing behavioural responses deemed appropriate to perceived risk
- may induce repeated checking, reassurance seeking, poor/lack of ability to delegate, procrastination or avoidance
- play an important role in the development and maintenance of worry and the disorder.

Beliefs regarding worry can be examined using cost–benefit analyses – individuals may hold beliefs about worry as having both positive attributes (e.g., 'worrying helps me solve problems') and negative attributes (e.g., feeling overwhelmed/unable to control worry). While both positive and negative beliefs require targeting during therapy, Dugas et al. (1998) point to positive appraisals of worry in reinforcing experiences of anxiety.

Problem orientation:

- refers to an individual's response to a problem
- as a higher order metacognitive activity, does not refer to a specific skill or skillset, but a wider orientation to problems (Ladouceur et al., 1998)
- may remain negative despite adequate knowledge of problem-solving skills
- appears to be linked to intolerance of uncertainty (e.g., viewing problems as threatening or doubting ability to solve them with a positive outcome).

Cognitive avoidance:

- incorporates both emotional and cognitive features
- has implications for GAD treatment through the integration of methods (where appropriate) usually used in phobia treatment, such as exposure protocols.

PANIC DISORDER

CASE STUDY

Ian was a 56-year-old man with one grown-up daughter. The client had self-referred after a relapse of anxiety and depression. While he had worked in finance in early-adulthood, he had switched careers to become a London taxi driver. He was now living in a housing association flat. His symptoms rendered him too ill to work regularly and his acute anxiety stopped him leaving the flat much. Earlier in life he had always had girlfriends, but now he was largely isolated. He had a long-standing friend who visited him less and less frequently, feeling that Ian had given up and wasn't trying hard enough to get better. His daughter had also reduced her visits.

This was a complete contrast to when I first met Ian some 30 years earlier. Then he was married. His wife had recently given birth to their daughter. They lived in their own semi-detached house in a London suburb. Ian travelled to work every day in the City of London, where he had worked in finance since he was 18. Despite attending a grammar school, he had no intention of going to university and wanted to earn money and enjoy the good life. For years he had done exactly that. His first bout of mental ill-health led to a short-term admission in a private psychiatric unit. In retrospect, this was a portent of what was to come later.

Always a very smart dresser in designer clothes and with his hair cut in expensive salons on King's Road in Chelsea, the sight presenting me on this referral was a complete contrast. His weight had ballooned. His clothes looked unkempt. The flat was unclean. He was also a heavy smoker. He was now frightened of even going out the front door. When he did so, he became very panicky and was desperate to return home. He felt certain he was going to have a heart attack and constantly monitored his symptoms, often seeking reassurance. Persuading him to go out for a walk (graded exposure therapy) was very difficult. He was now a 'nervous wreck'. What had happened to the young businessman I had met 30 years previously?

Ian's life was now ruled by fear. He had many of the symptoms of PD. The most prominent of these were sweating, palpitations, shaking, depersonalisation and a fear of dying. His days were wracked by anxiety. How had it come to this? His descent paralleled that of some people with problems of psychosis. How could anxiety and depression have such a profound effect on a previously high-functioning individual?

The cognitive behavioural model of panic (Clark, 1986) proposes that panic attacks occur as a result of misinterpreting somatic signals, when the danger associated with bodily sensations is exaggerated (e.g., misinterpreting heart palpitations as an impending heart attack or misinterpreting shakiness as evidence of loss of control and insanity).

Triggers for panic attacks may be:

- external (e.g., environmental – panic attacks occurring in a feared situation)
- internal (bodily sensations, thoughts, mental images)
- both.

If the individual interprets a trigger as threatening, they may then become apprehensive, leading to a range of bodily sensations which may be interpreted as catastrophic. This catastrophic interpretation itself elevates perceptions of threat, in turn exaggerating the bodily sensations and further catastrophic interpretation. This cycle continues, culminating in panic attack.

Once an attack is established, the individual then develops further responses which serve to maintain the problem, for example:

- Selective attention: hypersensitivity to physical symptoms indicative of threat-detection (e.g., worry or panic, leading sufferers to notice them more).
- Safety behaviours: used to prevent feared catastrophic outcomes (e.g., sitting down to prevent collapse). These provide alternative explanation for why feared events did not happen.
- Avoidance behaviours: restricting contact with anxiety-inducing stimuli reduces opportunities to discover that feared outcomes do not actually occur.

The cognitive model proposes that PD develops as a result of triggering pre-existing learnt assumptions about physical symptoms (e.g., as always indicative of major problems). These assumptions may have several origins, such as parental response to illness, perceived medical mismanagement, and/or sudden death of significant others. They may be relatively stable (Beck, 1976) but become more pertinent when triggered by personal events (e.g., own illness, a first panic attack).

WAYS OF WORKING WITH ANXIETY AND PANIC

For both anxiety and panic, cognitive-behavioural approaches and protocols employing conditioning and learning techniques have proven effective (Craske and Barlow, 2007). Initially, clients are educated on the principles guiding the approach and the rationale for the treatment plan based on their difficulties. This process must begin from the onset of treatment, ideally (and particularly for PD) with client involvement. For GAD, the formulation may be progressively developed during treatment. In all cases, recommended outcome measures should be used to monitor session-by-session progress.

FOR GENERALISED ANXIETY DISORDER

Education: Treatment often begins by educating the client about the normal features of anxiety (Dugas et al., 1998). This should include:

- Explaining the above model and the central role of worry. Anxiety and worry should be explained as extreme outcomes of an otherwise normal phenomenon.
- Either following or alongside psychoeducation, clients are instructed to keep a 'worry diary', to help recognise the types and triggers of their worry. Worries can be classified as either worries about current problems or about hypothetical situations.

Modifying beliefs about worry: Identifying and reconsidering beliefs about symptoms is central to GAD treatment. Irrational beliefs about worry (positive and negative) may be modified using behavioural experiments, for example reducing intolerance of uncertainty by targeting avoidance, checking behaviours or reassurance seeking. Clients are first aided in identifying behaviours used to increase feelings of certainty, but which conversely increase worry. Such experiments, often given for homework, may include visiting an unknown restaurant without checking it beforehand. Internal behaviours, such as thought control, can be similarly abandoned. For instance, positive beliefs about worry can be challenged through non-judgemental discussion (Robichaud, Koerner and Dugas, 2019), or by encouraging clients to exaggerate and 'lose control' of their worry, so that anticipated and feared consequences can be disconfirmed. Uncontrollability of worry can be challenged by setting aside distinct 'worry-periods' (e.g., 15 minutes). Worries outside this period must then be set aside until the next timeslot. The outcomes of these experiments can then be recorded.

Problem-solving training: Robichaud, Koerner and Dugas (2019) posit two dimensions of problem-solving: (1) problem-solving orientation; and (2) problem-solving skills. Orientation may be improved by encouraging clients to conceptualise worries as opportunities rather than threats, while skills can be improved by determining clear step-by-step methods for identifying and dealing with problems and decision-making.

Imaginal cognitive exposure: The roles of avoidance, thought suppression and neutralisation are explained to clients, who are then helped to identify core fears associated with worry. Scenarios can be used to expose clients to worry until anxiety levels reduce. It is important that scenarios do not include neutralisation (e.g., self-reassuring statements) and that core fears are addressed without resorting to extremes. These can be repeated as homework tasks.

Relaxation training: Given the restlessness and tension experienced in GAD, progressive and applied relaxation techniques can be beneficial not only as a stand-alone approach (in which instance they should adhere to a standard protocol (e.g., CBT) and be delivered over 12–15 weeks – see NICE, 2011), but also as a preparatory tool to assist clients with aspects of treatment which might involve engaging with worry (e.g., belief modification or imaginal cognitive exposure). Caution should be used to ensure that proper use of relaxation techniques does not become a further source of worry.

FOR PANIC DISORDER

Education about anxiety: Given the tendency towards catastrophic misinterpretations of bodily symptoms in PD, education is a first stage in treatment. Clients can be given clear information on anxiety and panic to assist with making sense of natural bodily responses to perceived threat and how, in the context of real danger, these represent a functional and adaptive response. Experiments such as the 'paired-associates task' (Clark et al., 1988) can be used to determine whether attention alone impacts symptom experience.

Dealing with misinterpretations of physical symptoms: Clients are enabled to identify thoughts associated with concerns about physical symptoms and develop alternative interpretations of them. Once these are established, evidence for each perspective should be considered and a behavioural experiment agreed (e.g., running vigorously to test beliefs regarding the dangers of high heart-rate). While therapists should be directive in engaging clients to consider their thoughts regarding symptoms, alternative views need to be elicited from the client.

Dealing with avoidance: Once beliefs regarding the dangers of physical symptoms reduce, clients should resume avoided behaviours in a graduated manner. These experiments can be used to continue to challenge maladaptive beliefs about worry (e.g., expectations of fainting).

Reducing safety behaviours: Safety behaviours help to explain how, despite the repeated failure of feared consequences manifesting during panic attacks, clients nonetheless continue to believe in their probability. Safety behaviours should be gradually reduced as clients become more confident in alternative perspectives regarding their symptoms.

Relapse prevention: Consideration of the patterns of unhelpful behaviours together with discussion and reconsideration of long-standing assumptions regarding the dangers of physical symptoms should occur towards the end of treatment, with a view to maintaining positive change.

ALTERNATIVE PERSPECTIVES

It is perhaps impractical to address the global demand for treatment via in-person care models alone (Torous et al., 2021). There is therefore increasing interest in digital mental health technologies (DMHT) (e.g., smartphone apps, virtual reality, social media and chatbots) to extend mental health support (Torous et al., 2021). Benefits include ease of access, reach, increased cost-efficiency, and the potential to reduce stigma. However, the digital divide should not be overlooked, nor should the prospect that DMHTs may be more appealing to certain demographics (e.g., young people), which should be considered in their design and development.

An abundance of smartphone apps exist to support mental health issues, although there is a dearth of research in their evaluation. An insight paper representing leaders in mHealth research, industry and health care systems globally (Torous et al., 2019: 97) argued the need for consensus on standards, principles and practices in research and evaluation of smartphone apps, with no formal guidelines or criteria currently in place to regulate either their development or evaluation. A recent meta-review found apps for anxiety and depression hold more clinical advantages than apps developed for other mental health issues, but that research is needed to recommend them (Lecomte et al., 2020).

THERAPEUTIC GAMES

Therapeutic games (TGs) show potential in helping to meet the increasing demand for mental health provision. A recent systematic review suggests that TGs have significant potential in reducing anxiety levels in adolescents (Barnes and Prescott, 2018). Web-based environments and games afford a flexible and personal approach to learning, providing the learner with immediate feedback in environments adaptable to individual needs (Charlier et al., 2016). Therapeutic games may be beneficial for numerous mental health issues, including reducing psychopathological symptoms associated with gambling disorders (Tárrega et al., 2015) and as an effective preliminary treatment to CBT for bulimia (Giner-Bartolomé et al., 2015). They can achieve clinically measurable improvements and behavioural changes (Baranowski et al., 2013) and can engage hard-to-reach groups (e.g., adolescents) in accessing mental health support. Gaining feedback from potential users is paramount when designing TGs to increase not only engagement and usage, but also their therapeutic efficacy (Barnes and Prescott, 2022).

REFERENCES

Ayano, G., Betts, K., Calderon Maravilla, J., & Alati, R. (2021). The risk of anxiety disorders in children of parents with severe psychiatric disorders: a systematic review and meta-analysis. *Journal of Affective Disorders, 282*(1), 472–487. doi: 10.1016/j.jad.2020.12.134

Baranowski, T., Buday, R., Thompson, D., Lyons, E. J., Shirong-Lu, A., & Baranowski, J. (2013). Developing games for health behaviour change: getting started. *Games for Health, 2*(4), 183–190. doi: 10.1089/g4h.2013.0048

Barnes, S., & Prescott, J. (2018). Empirical evidence for the outcomes of therapeutic video games for adolescents with anxiety disorders: systematic review. *JMIR Serious Games, 6*(1), e3. doi: 10.2196/games.9530. PMID: 29490893

Barnes, S., & Prescott, J. (2022). Therapeutic Gaming for Adolescent Anxiety: Development and Evaluation of a Mobile Intervention. In J. Prescott (Ed.), *Digital Innovations for Mental Health Support* (pp. 187–227). IGI Global. https://doi.org/10.4018/978-1-7998-7991-6.ch009

Beck, A. T. (1976). *Cognitive Therapy and the Emotional Disorders.* New York: International Universities Press.

Charlier, N., Zupancic, N., Fieuws, S., Denhaerynck, S., Zaman, K., & Moons, P. (2016). Serious games for improving knowledge and self-management in people with chronic conditions: a systematic review and meta-analysis. *Journal of American Medical Informatics Association, 23*(1), 230–239. doi: 10.1093/jamia/ocv100. PMID: 26186934

Clark, D. M. (1986). A cognitive approach to panic. *Behavior Research and Therapy, 24*(4), 461–470. doi: 10.1016/0005-7967(86)90011-2

Clark, D. M., Salkovskis, P. M., Gelder, M. G., Koehler, C., Martin, M., Anastasiades, P., et al. (1988). Tests of a cognitive theory of panic. In I. Hand & H. U. Wittchen (Eds.), *Panic and phobias 2.* Berlin: Springer-Verlag.

Craske, M. G., & Barlow, D. H. (2007). *Mastery of Your Anxiety and Panic (Therapist Guide)* (4th ed.) Oxford: Oxford University Press. doi: 10.2196/17458

Dugas, M. J., Gagnon, F., Ladouceur, R., & Freeston, M. H. (1998). Generalised anxiety disorder: a preliminary test of a conceptual model. *Behaviour Research and Therapy, 36*, 215–226.

Giner-Bartolomé, C., Fagundo, A. B., Sánchez, I., Jiménez-Murcia, S., Santamaría, J. J., Ladouceur, R. Menchón, J. M., & Fernández-Aranda, F. (2015). Can an intervention based on a serious videogame prior to cognitive behavioural therapy be helpful in bulimia nervosa? A clinical case study. *Frontiers in Psychology, 6*, 982. doi: 10.3389/fpsyg.2015.00982

Glenn, D., Golinello, D., Rose, R. D., Roy-Byrne, P., Stein, M. B., Sullivan, G., Bystritsky, A., Sherbourne, C., & Craske, M. G. (2013). Who gets the most out of cognitive-behavioral therapy for anxiety disorders? The role of treatment dose and patient engagement. *Journal of Consulting and Clinical Psychology, 81*(4), 639–649. doi: 10.1037/a0033403

Greener, M. (2014). Managing generalised anxiety disorder. *British Journal of Mental Health Nursing, 3*(3), 100–104. doi: 10.12968/bjmh.2014.3.3.100

IAPT (2007). *The Competencies Required to Deliver Effective Cognitive and Behavioural Therapy for People with Depression and with Anxiety Disorder: Improving Access to Psychological Therapies.* London: Department of Health.

Kessler, R. C., & Greenberg, P. E. (2002). The economic burden of anxiety and stress disorders. *Neuropsychopharmacology: The fifth Generation of Progress, 67*, 982–992.

Ladouceur, R., Blais, F., Freeston, M. H., & Dugas, M. J. (1998). Problem solving and problem orientation in generalized anxiety disorder. *Journal of Anxiety Disorders, 12*(2), 139–152. doi: 10.1016/S0887-6185(98)00002-4

(Continued)

(Continued)

Lecomte, T., Potvin, S., Corbière, M., Guay, S., Samson, C., Cloutier, B., Francoeur, A., Pennou, A., & Khazaal, Y. (2020). Mobile apps for mental health issues: meta-review of meta-analyses. *JMIR Mhealth Uhealth, 8*(5), e17458

Lenze, E. J., & Wetherell, J. L. (2011). A lifespan view of anxiety disorders. *Dialogues in Clinical Neuroscience, 13*(4), 381–399. doi: 10.31887/DCNS.2011.13.4/elenze

Locke, A. B., Kirst, N., & Shultz, C. G. (2015). Diagnosis and management of generalized anxiety disorder and panic disorder in adults. *American Family Physician, 91*(9), 617–624. PMID: 25955736

NICE (2011). *Generalised Anxiety Disorder and Panic Disorder (with or without Agoraphobia) in Adults: Management in Primary, Secondary and Community Care.* Clinical Guideline 113. London: NICE.

Robichaud, M., Koerner, N., & Dugas, M. J. (2019). *Cognitive Behavioral Treatment for Generalized Anxiety Disorder: From Science to Practice* (2nd ed.). Abingdon, UK: Routledge.

Tárrega, S., Castro-Carreras, L., Fernández-Aranda, F., Granero, R., Giner-Bartolomé, C., Aymamí, N., Gómez-Peña, M., Santamaría, J. J., Forcano, L., Steward, T., Menchón, J. M., & Jiménez-Murcia, S. (2015). A serious videogame as an additional therapy tool for training emotional regulation and impulsivity control in severe gambling disorder. *Frontiers in Psychology, 6*, 1721. doi: 10.3389/fpsyg.2015.01721

Torous, J., Bucci, S., Bell, I. H., Kessing, L. V., Faurholt-Jepson, M., Whelan, P., Carvalho, A. F., Keshavan, M., Linardon J., & Firth, J. (2021). The growing field of digital psychiatry: current evidence and the future of apps, social media, chatbots, and virtual reality. *World Psychiatry, 20*(3), 318–335 doi:10.1002/wps.20883

RECOMMENDED READING

Robichaud, M., Koerner, N., & Dugas, M. J. (2019). *Cognitive Behavioral Treatment for Generalized Anxiety Disorder: From Science to Practice* (2nd ed.). Abingdon, UK: Routledge.

A step-by-step formulation for GAD treatment is covered, emphasising the central role of intolerance of uncertainty.

Wells, A. (1997). *Cognitive Therapy of Anxiety Disorder: A Practice and Conceptual Guide.* Chichester: Wiley.

This book provides models, cases and treatment interventions across the anxiety disorders, clearly connected with cognitive theory and application to therapy delivery.

Clark, D. A., & Beck, A. T. (2011). *Cognitive Therapy of Anxiety Disorders: Science and Practice.* New York: Guilford Press.

This book covers thinking and research on anxiety treatment and instruction in assessment, cognitive restructuring and evidence-based intervention using accessible case studies.

4.4 BEREAVEMENT AND LOSS

EDITH MARIA STEFFEN AND EVGENIA (JANE) MILMAN

OVERVIEW AND KEY POINTS

Bereavement and loss, while universally shared human experiences, can affect us in vastly differing ways. A multitude of factors may influence how grief is experienced by different individuals and how they may present in counselling and psychotherapy. The diversity of possible client presentations is increasingly matched by a diversity of available therapeutic approaches, and this chapter outlines how some contemporary grief therapy approaches may be drawn on when working with a client who struggles with their grief.

- The majority of grievers cope with their loss without the need for therapy; however, 10–20% of grievers continue to struggle significantly and may require specialist intervention.
- A range of models of grief can be applied when assessing and formulating grieving clients.
- Meaning-oriented grief therapy integrates narrative and emotion-focused techniques within a humanistic and existential approach that seeks to help clients reconstruct meaning that has been shattered by their loss.
- Exposure-based interventions have been found to be particularly effective with more complicated and traumatic grief presentations.

ASSESSMENT AND UNDERSTANDING

Despite the widely held belief that grief is characterised by substantial distress that gradually dissipates, there is considerable diversity in how people experience grief and how it evolves over time. In fact, only 10% of grievers seem to experience what has been termed *common grief*, thus titled because it corresponds with the commonly accepted description of grief: initially highly distressing and gradually diminishing to pre-death levels approximately 18 to 24 months following the loss (Galatzer-Levy and Bonanno, 2012). By contrast, the majority of grievers (46–66%) appear to experience relatively stable levels of functioning following the loss, while the remaining 10–20% of grievers tend to experience ongoing, severe grief. Grievers can also present with many other complications following their loss, such as sleep disturbance, problems with eating, substance abuse and suicide ideation (Casey, 2011; King, 2004; Kovandzic, Vieraitis and Yeisley, 1998; Prigerson et al., 1999). Some frequently given diagnoses include depression, post-traumatic stress disorder (PTSD), and now also prolonged grief disorder (PGD) (Lundorff et al., 2017; Rheingold et al., 2012; Stroebe, Schut and Stroebe, 2007). Prolonged grief disorder has recently been included in the DSM-5-TR and the ICD-11 (Prigerson et al., 2021; World Health Organisation, 2019). While the pathologisation of grief remains controversial, there is some consensus that 10–20% of grievers struggle significantly more and for longer (Lundorff et al., 2017). Several alternative terms have been used to refer to these presentations, most prominent among these is *complicated grief* (CG) (for a comprehensive review of terminology and history see: Milman, Neimeyer and Boelen, 2021). Among the problems compiled under these labels are ongoing, profound separation distress, characterised by persistent yearning and preoccupation with the deceased as well as other difficulties that can be broadly categorised as emotional distress (e.g., numbness) and difficulties re-engaging in life following the loss (e.g., identity confusion).

Apart from these more complicated trajectories, grievers may also report *post-traumatic growth* (PTG), which entails positive personal change beyond mere recovery of pre-death functioning. Post-traumatic growth is characterised by positive developments in one's perception of identity, relationships, future and/or spirituality (Tedeschi and Calhoun, 2008). Of note, growth does not simply represent the absence of psychological struggle (Calhoun et al., 2010; Neimeyer, Bottomley and Bellet, 2018). Instead, post-loss growth has been shown to be greatest among grievers experiencing intermediate levels of distress and complications, while the least growth appears to occur among grievers with the lowest or the highest levels (Currier, Holland and Neimeyer, 2012).

Just as there is a wide variety of ways in which grieving clients may present, there is a great diversity of theoretical frameworks, or models of grief, to conceptualise different grief phenomenologies and trajectories. Many of these are directly linked with specific therapeutic orientations. One of the most well-known models of grief goes back to Freud's psychoanalytic *grief work hypothesis* (Freud, 1917), suggesting that the bereaved need to go through a painful process of *decathexis*, i.e., working through the loss and relinquishing the attachment to the deceased to free themselves up for new relationships (also often referred to as 'letting go and moving on'). This modernist model dominated western bereavement scholarship and practice for most of the twentieth century, and its basic premise can be found in other western models, such as the still popular although empirically unfounded *stages of grief* (Kübler-Ross and Kessler, 2005). In recent decades, different understandings, such as the postmodern and cross-culturally informed *continuing bonds* perspective (Klass, Silverman and Nickman, 1996; Klass and Steffen, 2018), have challenged the 'breaking bonds' dictum, and there is now increasing acknowledgement and acceptance of bereaved people staying connected with the deceased beyond death (Steffen, in press). More recent psychoanalytic and attachment-informed approaches to grief no longer promote detachment from the deceased (e.g., Hagman, 2016; Kosminsky and Jordan, 2016), and even the more positivist cognitive-behavioural and exposure-based approaches now view a helpful ongoing relationship with (the memories of) the deceased as a worthy goal of grief therapy (e.g., Iglewicz et al., 2020). Other models of grief that have contributed to a changed perspective are the Two-Track Model of Bereavement (TTMB) (Rubin, 1999) and the Dual Process Model (DPM) (Stroebe and Schut, 1999). The TTMB views the grief journey to involve both a biopsychosocial functioning track and a relationship track. The DPM suggests that the bereaved oscillate between a 'loss orientation' and a 'restoration orientation', providing useful frameworks for mapping and negotiating the challenges faced by the bereaved. The concepts of *disenfranchised grief* (Doka, 1989) and, more recently *suffocated grief* (Bordere, 2019) have highlighted the need for a contextualised understanding of grief, as embedded in wider socio-cultural and socio-political systems and narratives. Furthermore, research into the role that meaning plays in grief has been particularly influential (Neimeyer, in press). A profound loss can shatter our assumptive worlds (Janoff-Bulman, 1992), and grievers find themselves needing to reconstruct the meaning of their worlds (Neimeyer, 2001).

WAYS OF WORKING WITH GRIEF: USING A MEANING-ORIENTED APPROACH

Sally, a 63-year-old schoolteacher from London who lost her father to suicide three years previously, presents to therapy with feelings of stuckness in her grief. She says she finds it difficult to understand her father's actions and struggles with feelings of sadness and bitterness as well as shame, leading her to avoid thinking and talking about this 'dirty secret', which, however, always remains at the back of her mind in a 'Pandora's Box'. She says the man who killed himself was somehow a 'different father' from the one she thought he was, making it hard to know who to grieve. In addition, images of what he might have looked like at the time of death haunt her daily.

In working with Sally, an approach grounded in meaning reconstruction therapy is proposed, which posits that grief often involves 'reconstructing a world of meaning that has been shattered by the loss' (Neimeyer, 2001). It incorporates narrative and emotion-focused elements and focuses on meaning-making in terms of the *event story* of the death, the *back story* of the relationship with the deceased (i.e., the continuing bond) and the *personal story* of the self (Neimeyer, in press). Working with Sally, all three dimensions are interwoven in her grief experience due to the event of suicide profoundly hampering the development of a continuing bond with her father and how she views herself in relation to him and a society in which suicide is still a taboo, leading to disenfranchised grief.

First, the therapeutic relationship and therapists' empathic attunement to the client is central in this humanistic approach. Simultaneously, focused and structured interventions are offered. While the traumatic aspect of the death suggests the primary importance of processing the *event story*, Sally may not be ready for this initially. The Meaning in Loss protocol (Neimeyer, Milman and Steffen, 2022) includes an early focus on the *back story* through a narrative technique entitled 'Introducing the Deceased' (Hedtke, 2012), and on the *personal story* through a narrative technique entitled 'Chapters of Our Lives' (Neimeyer, 2014). This allows Sally to bring her father into the therapy room as a person, and to create a map of her life through chapter headings, locating her relationship with her father within it and how and where the suicide changes the narrative, thus facilitating some initial sense-making of this difficult-to-grasp event.

Once Sally is ready for more focused work on the traumatic aspects of the *event story*, the slow and detailed narrative retelling of the death and its circumstances can be proposed (Neimeyer, 2012), followed by reflexive exploration of the possible meanings of the event. In Sally's case, *directed journaling* (Lichtenthal and Neimeyer, 2012) is proposed as homework after the retelling session, and this enables her for the first time to access and express anger she has been holding towards her father, something she describes as liberating.

With these traumatic aspects of the death now appearing less haunting, the therapeutic emphasis shifts towards more in-depth working on the relationship with the deceased, for example addressing 'unfinished business' through chair work or letter-writing (Neimeyer, 2012). Both techniques allow clients to address the deceased directly and, through imaginal dialogue, receive the deceased's responses. For Sally, it becomes eye-opening to find her father revealing life-long vulnerabilities in these exchanges, which she recognises as originating in his complicated childhood. Realising he was not simply the 'strong man' of her childhood desire and learning about his inability to manage his own emotions, something he had hidden from her, she is now beginning to view his suicide as somewhat more intelligible. In the sense-making process, Sally starts to reconfigure not only her father but also herself, as her self-narrative, interwoven with his, also needs to be adapted, with unmet needs from her own childhood having emerged, casting a different light on her own life course and sense of self.

It is noteworthy that following this process of dialoguing and reflecting, Sally begins to notice happier memories of her father, for example remembering a song he used to whistle. She says it is as if her father is again available to her, having been locked away in 'Pandora's Box' for years. While she is still sad that he was not always the father she needed, the father he was able to be and the love he was able to give is now more present to her, in sometimes unexpected and surprising ways. It is this dynamic aliveness and realness of the continuing bond that can be the outcome of such therapeutic engagement. Sally's case is a true example of this.

ALTERNATIVE PERSPECTIVES

The meaning reconstruction approach, while integrating from a number of other therapies, is only one of many grief therapy approaches available to practitioners. In addition to general grief approaches, there is a growing body of literature on how to work with specific populations or circumstances. Interested readers are referred to the *Handbook of Grief Therapies* (Steffen, Milman and Neimeyer, in press) for more information.

In the following, we would like to focus specifically on exposure-based therapies, as grievers presenting to therapy frequently find themselves stuck in their grief due to the traumatic aspects of the event. For example, grief that occurs in violent circumstances is often characterised by persistent and disruptive imagery of the death, as is the case with Sally, who is plagued daily by images of what her father might have looked like after his suicide. Such imagery is understood to develop as a result of the griever's difficulty tolerating and thereby processing the horrific details of the death event (McFarlane, 1992). Exposure-based therapies are designed to facilitate emotional and cognitive processing of such aversive aspects of the death, gradually bolstering the griever's tolerance for these details and to facilitate meaning making of the death.

There is considerable variety in how exposures are carried out, depending in part on the client's distress tolerance. Some therapeutic approaches, chiefly Prolonged Exposure, do not prioritise accommodating the client's distress tolerance. Instead, this intervention maximises the vividness of the retelling by instructing clients to close their eyes for full immersion in the image being recounted and directing clients to focus on emotionally or viscerally evocative details so as to heighten awareness of these details (Foa et al., 2007).

By contrast, other therapeutic approaches, particularly EMDR, meaning-oriented therapies and Restorative Retelling, are designed to decrease the likelihood of being emotionally overwhelmed, and thus prevent potential dissociative reactions, flashbacks and panic attacks. For example, using the Restorative Retelling protocol with Sally would entail preparatory work exploring the positive qualities in Sally's relationship with her father, because strengthening the continuing bond in this way can buffer the distress of recounting images of her father's death. Furthermore, Restorative Retelling is designed to create psychological distance from the death by externalising death imagery via drawing. Specifically, Sally would be asked to draw the death scene, focusing on her father's face and then describe what she has drawn. As the name suggests, Restorative Retelling also includes a restoration component, wherein Sally is encouraged to explore the role she would have wanted to play in her father's dying: 'I know you weren't there when your dad died, but if you could, where would you want to put yourself in his dying moments? What would you be doing?' In response, Sally might imagine rescuing her father or offering him care to relieve his pain or fear. Furthermore, redirecting her focus away from the death itself, the therapist might gently begin exploring with Sally, 'How might your dad feel about you releasing these images of his lifeless face and the story of his suicide?'

Clinically, the existence of diverse grief trajectories and additional complications highlight the need for grief therapists to understand and accommodate specific grief presentations. For example, a depressed griever might benefit from approaches that prioritise meaningful reengagement in daily living (Meichenbaum and Myers, 2016). Grievers who feel they are coping well, in accordance with the resilience grief trajectory, may benefit from a normalising therapeutic encounter that provides an opportunity to reflect on what has been helpful and problem-solve emerging challenges, such as navigating the griever's evolving interpersonal needs. Therapists may also need to consider how to foster positive bereavement outcomes. Of course, how a clinician tailors therapy to any particular grief presentation depends on their theoretical and epistemological approach to grief therapy. Nevertheless, being well informed about diverse grief presentations ensures that the clinician can make decisions regarding which aspects of the grief experience to target in therapy.

REFERENCES

Bordere, T. (2019). Suffocated grief, resilience, and survival among African American families. In M. H. Jacobsen & A. Petersen (Eds), *Exploring grief: Towards a sociology of sorrow* (pp. 188–204). Abingdon, UK: Routledge.

Calhoun, L., Tedeschi, R., Cann, A., & Hanks, E. (2010). Positive outcomes following bereavement: Paths to posttraumatic growth. *Psychologica Belgica*, *50*(1–2).

Casey, L. (2011). *Review into the needs of families bereaved by homicide.* London: Ministry of Justice.

Currier, J. M., Holland, J. M., & Neimeyer, R. A. (2012). Prolonged grief symptoms and growth in the first 2 years of bereavement: Evidence for a nonlinear association. *Traumatology*, *18*(4), 65.

Doka, K. J. (1989). *Disenfranchised grief: Recognizing hidden sorrow.* Lanham, MD: Lexington Books.

Foa, E., Hembree, E., & Rothbaum, B. (2007). *Prolonged exposure therapy for PTSD: Emotional processing of traumatic experiences (Treatments that work). Therapist guide.* Oxford: Oxford University Press.

Freud, S. (1957). Mourning and melancholia. In J. Strachey (Ed.), *The standard edition of the complete psychological works of Sigmund Freud* (Vol. XIV, pp. 252–268). London: Hogarth Press. (Original work published 1917.)

Galatzer-Levy, I. R., & Bonanno, G. A. (2012). Beyond normality in the study of bereavement: Heterogeneity in depression outcomes following loss in older adults. *Social Science & Medicine*, *74*(12), 1987–1994.

Hagman, G. (2016). *New models of bereavement theory and treatment: New mourning.* London: Routledge.

Hedtke, L. (2012). Introducing the deceased. In R. A. Neimeyer (Ed.), *Techniques of grief therapy: Creative practices for counseling the bereaved* (pp. 253–255). New York: Routledge.

Iglewicz, A., Shear, M. K., Reynold, C. F., III, Simon, N., Lebowitz, B., & Zisook, S. (2020). Copmplicated grief therapy for clinicians: An evidence-based protocol for mental health practice. *Depression and Anxiety*, *37*(1), 90–98. https://doi.org/10.1002/da.22965

Janoff-Bulman, R. (1992). *Shattered assumptions: Towards a new psychology of trauma.* New York: Free Press.

King, K. (2004). It hurts so bad: Comparing grieving patterns of the families of murder victims with those of families of death row inmates. *Criminal Justice Policy Review*, *15*(2), 193–211.

Klass, D., Silverman, P. R., & Nickman, S. L. (Eds) (1996). *Continuing bonds: New understandings of grief.* London: Taylor & Francis.

Klass, D., & Steffen, E. M. (2018). *Continuing bonds in bereavement: New directions for research and practice.* Abingdon, UK: Routledge.

Kosminsky, P., & Jordan, J. R. (2016). *Attachment informed grief therapy.* New York: Routledge.

Kovandzic, T. V., Vieraitis, L. M., & Yeisley, M. R. (1998). The structural covariates of urban homicide: Reassessing the impact of income inequality and poverty in the post-Reagan era. *Criminology, 36*(3), 569–600.

Kübler-Ross, E., & Kessler, D. (2005). *On grief and grieving: Finding the meaning of grief through the five stages of loss.* New York: Simon & Schuster.

Lichtenthal, W. G., & Neimeyer, R. A. (2012). Directed journaling to facilitate meaning making. In R. A. Neimeyer (Ed.), *Techniques of grief therapy* (pp. 161–164). New York: Routledge.

Lundorff, M., Holmgren, H., Zachariae, R., Farver-Vestergaard, I., & O'Connor, M. (2017). Prevalence of prolonged grief disorder in adult bereavement: A systematic review and meta-analysis. *Journal of Affective Disorders, 212*, 138–149.

McFarlane, A. C. (1992). Avoidance and intrusion in posttraumatic stress disorder. *The Journal of Nervous and Mental Disease, 180*(7), 439–445.

Meichenbaum, D., & Myers, J. (2016). Strategies for coping with grief. In R. A. Neimeyer (Ed.), *Techniques of grief therapy: Assessment and intervention* (pp. 117–123). New York: Routledge.

Milman, E., Neimeyer, R. A., & Boelen, P. A. (2021). Problematic grief. In H. S. Chapple & H. L. Servaty-Seib (Eds), *Handbook of Thanatology* (3rd ed.). Minneapolis, MN: Association of Death Education and Counseling.

Neimeyer, R. A. (Ed.) (2001). *Meaning reconstruction and the experience of loss.* Minneapolis, MN: American Psychological Association.

Neimeyer, R. A. (Ed.) (2012). *Techniques of grief therapy.* New York: Routledge.

Neimeyer, R. A. (2014). Chapters of our lives. In B. E. Thompson & R. A. Neimeyer (Eds), *Grief and the expressive arts: Practices for creating meaning.* New York: Routledge.

Neimeyer, R. A. (in press). Grief therapy as a quest for meaning. In E. M. Steffen, E. Milman, & R. A. Neimeyer (Eds), *The handbook of grief therapies.* London: Sage.

Neimeyer, R. A., Bottomley, J. S., & Bellet, B. W. (2018). Growing through grief: When loss is complicated. In K. J. Doka & A. Tucci (Eds), *When grief is complicated* (pp. 95–111). Washington, DC: Hospice Foundation of America.

Neimeyer, R. A., Milman, E., & Steffen, E. (2022). The Meaning in loss group: Principles, processes and procedures. In R. A. Neimeyer (Ed.), *New techniques of grief therapy: Bereavement and beyond.* New York: Routledge.

Prigerson, H. G., Boelen, P. A., Xu, J., Smith, K. V., & Maciejewski, P. K. (2021). Validation of the new DSM-5-TR criteria for prolonged grief disorder and the PG-13-Revised (PG-13-R) scale. *World Psychiatry, 20*(1), 96–106. https://doi.org/https://doi.org/10.1002/wps.20823

Prigerson, H. G., Bridge, J., Maciejewski, P. K., Beery, L. C., Rosenheck, R. A., Jacobs, S. C., … Brent, D. A. (1999). Influence of traumatic grief on suicidal ideation among young adults. *American Journal of Psychiatry, 156*(12), 1994–1995.

Rheingold, A. A., Zinzow, H., Hawkins, A., Saunders, B. E., & Kilpatrick, D. G. (2012). Prevalence and mental health outcomes of homicide survivors in a representative US sample of adolescents: Data from the 2005 National Survey of Adolescents. *Journal of Child Psychology and Psychiatry, 53*(6), 687–694.

Rubin, S. S. (1999). The Two-Track Model of Bereavement: Overview, retrospect and prospect. *Death Studies, 23*(8), 681–714. doi:10.1080/074811899200731

Steffen, E. M. (in press). Grief therapies for our times: A pluralistic proposition. In E. M. Steffen, E. Milman, & R. A. Neimeyer (Eds), *The handbook of grief therapies.* London: Sage.

Steffen, E. M., Milman, E., & Neimeyer, R. A. (Eds) (in press). *The handbook of grief therapies.* London: Sage.

Stroebe, M., & Schut, H. (1999). The dual process model of coping with bereavement: Rationale and description. *Death Studies, 23*, 197–224.

(Continued)

(Continued)

Stroebe, M., Schut, H., & Stroebe, W. (2007). Health outcomes of bereavement. *The Lancet*, *370*(9603), 1960–1973.

Tedeschi, R. G., & Calhoun, L. G. (2008). Beyond the concept of recovery: Growth and the experience of loss. *Death Studies*, *32*(1), 27–39.

World Health Organisation (2019). *International classification of diseases 11th revision ICD-11 beta draft 2017*. Geneva: WHO. https://icd.who.int/dev11/lm/en

RECOMMENDED READING

Neimeyer, R. A. (Ed.) (2012). *Techniques of grief therapy*. New York: Routledge.

This book contains a large assortment of easy-to-follow brief grief therapy technique descriptions, stemming from a range of different therapies and addressing a multitude of issues and presentations.

Servaty-Seib, H. L., & Chapple, H. S. (Eds) (2022). *Handbook of thanatology: The essential body of knowledge for the study of death, dying, and bereavement* (3rd ed.). Minneapolis, MN: Association for Death Education and Counseling.

This latest edition of the *Handbook of thanatology* constitutes an authoritative source of knowledge in all areas of death studies, thus enabling therapists to draw on a wider understanding of the issues involved.

Steffen, E. M., Milman, E., & Neimeyer, R. A. (Eds) (in press). *The handbook of grief therapies*. London: Sage.

This state-of-the-art volume comprises a compilation of introductory chapters to leading grief therapy approaches as well as a series of chapters on specific populations and presenting issues in grief.

4.5 CHRONIC PHYSICAL HEALTH PROBLEMS
SOHA DARU

OVERVIEW AND KEY POINTS

A chronic physical health problem is a long-term, persistent health condition lasting a few months to years (NHS, 2021b). Chronic physical health problems can have life-changing consequences on individuals' physical and mental health, quality of life and overall functioning (Megari, 2013). People with these health problems have an increased risk of developing depression, anxiety and other psychological problems (The King's Fund, 2012). It is important for us as psychological therapists to consider the link with mental health, understanding chronic physical health problems and ways to work with it. In this context, this chapter aims to cover the following:

- What chronic physical health problems are.
- A few ways to assess and understand these problems.
- A case example to illustrate a chronic physical health problem.
- Ways of working with chronic physical health problems using Acceptance and Commitment therapy (ACT) and Cognitive Behavioural therapy (CBT).

ASSESSMENT AND UNDERSTANDING

WHAT ARE CHRONIC PHYSICAL HEALTH PROBLEMS?

A chronic physical health problem is a long-term, enduring health condition requiring ongoing management over a period of years (NHS, 2021b). It is a problem that cannot currently be cured but can be managed with the help of medication and/or other therapies (NHS, 2021b). Various terms are used to describe chronic health problems, including chronic disease (Centers for Disease Control and Prevention, 2021), chronic condition (NHS, 2021b), chronic illness (National Institute of Mental Health (NIMH), 2021), and long-term physical health problems (National Institute for Health and Care Excellence (NICE), 2022). There exists tremendous variation in the illnesses, which are included under the general term 'chronic disease', as well as differences in the duration in which an illness must be present to be classified as a chronic or long-term condition. The time usually lasts from over three months (National Centre for Health Statistics, 2011), to over a year (Anderson, 2010; National Centre for Health Statistics, 2010) to lasting decades in nature (NHS Data Model and Dictionary, 2022). The causes and risk factors for chronic disease can sometimes be linked to lifestyle (Benziger et al., 2016) and underlying genetic, socio-economic, cultural, political and environmental determinants (World Health Organisation, 2005). More than 15 million people in England (approximately 30% of the population) have a chronic physical condition (Department of Health, 2011, 2012). These conditions are more common in people aged over 60 and in more deprived groups, although anyone can be affected by them (Department of Health, 2012). Although more up-to-date statistics are unavailable, these figures indicate the extent to which people experience these conditions and the importance of attending to them.

Chronic health problems include a broad range of conditions, including the following (NIMH, 2021; NHS, 2021b):

- Non-communicable diseases (e.g., cancer, arthritis, diabetes, asthma, and cardiovascular disease).
- Communicable diseases (e.g., Human Immunodeficiency Virus (HIV)/Acquired Immunodeficiency Syndrome (AIDS)).
- Ongoing impairments in structure (e.g., vision and hearing impairment, joint disorders, etc.).

Other chronic health problems include Parkinson's disease, irritable bowel syndrome (IBS) and chronic back pain (NIMH, 2021; NHS, 2021b). Many people also struggle with 'medically unexplained symptoms' where chronic physical symptoms are experienced with no clear biological cause (e.g., multiple sclerosis, chronic fatigue syndrome and fibromyalgia) (NHS, 2021c.). Symptoms such as fatigue, persistent pain and gastric problems can lead to significant emotional distress.

Chronic physical health problems can have a life-changing impact on individuals' wellbeing, quality of life and functioning level (Megari, 2013) and can present its own challenges. Living with a chronic health condition can involve various changes and adjustments, and have a negative impact on work, relationships, finances and one's identity (Larsen, 2021). It might accompany numerous losses, such as a loss of the person they once were (loss in identity), loss of health, independence and relationships, and losing their source of income or employment (Thompson and Kyle, 2021). The condition can also restrict daily activities or those one formerly enjoyed (Centers for Disease Control and Prevention, 2021). Having chronic health problems might lead to social isolation, low self-esteem, stigma, discrimination and impaired social relationships (Hämmig, 2019; Molina and Simon, 2014; Stinson and Fisher, 2020; Trindade et al., 2018). One may feel exhausted, frustrated or worried when experiencing pain or flare ups and undergoing medical tests and treatments (Mental Health Foundation, 2022).

It is not surprising, then, that mental health problems are fairly common among those who struggle with chronic physical health problems (NIMH, 2021). Research shows that people with a long-term physical health condition are two to three times more likely to experience mental health problems than the general population (The King's Fund, 2012). There is an increased risk of developing depression or anxiety and of it worsening over time (Doherty and Gaughran, 2014). Further, mental health problems can make it more difficult for people to cope with their physical health condition (Dempster, Howell and McCorry, 2015), leading to a vicious cycle. People with mental health problems are also at higher risk of developing physical illness and have higher mortality rates (Doherty and Gaughran, 2014).

Many mental health problems can be considered long-term conditions in themselves, for example schizophrenia and depression (NHS, 2021b). It might be difficult to draw a distinction between 'mental' and 'physical' health due to the overlap between the two domains. People have also noticed similarities between long Covid, myalgic encephalomyelitis (ME) and fibromyalgia (Wong and Weitzer, 2021). Long Covid includes symptoms experienced from Covid-19 which are usually more severe, persistent and enduring (NHS, 2021a). Long Covid is also associated with a whole host of problems involving multiple body systems, much like other chronic diseases that often go unrecognised and undiagnosed (DuLong, 2022; O'Rourke, 2022). The case example in the next section details some of these symptoms.

ASSESSING CHRONIC PHYSICAL HEALTH AND RELATED MENTAL HEALTH PROBLEMS

Incorporating a 'patient-centred approach' to assessing and managing chronic health problems is needed as patients' (or clients') perspectives are taken into account to better understand the condition and its impact on their life (Forestier et al., 2019). This is sometimes assessed by interviews or patient reported measures which are described below. Roth and Pilling (2015) have developed a competence framework for working with chronic health problems, including core knowledge and professional skills, and psychological interventions to work with this population. They encourage undertaking a comprehensive biopsychosocial assessment by assessing the client's physical and psychological problems, impact on functioning, coping strategies employed, physical and mental health history and understanding contact with and from other health professionals. They recommend helping the client to articulate their goals while engaging them in the assessment process throughout.

Various outcome measures are used to supplement this process of information gathering. For instance, patient reported outcome measures (PROMs) are a broad range of health-related outcome measures consisting of a direct report by clients. PROMs include the assessment of symptoms, clients' functional ability, health-related quality of life, and the impact on various psychological, physical and social domains (Forestier et al., 2019). More general mental health outcome measures, such as the Patient Health Questionnaire (PHQ9), Generalised Anxiety (GAD7) and Beck's depression inventory are used to measure depression, anxiety and mental wellbeing. The Long-Term Conditions Questionnaire (LTCQ) is a 20-item measure to understand the impact of long-term health conditions on individuals' lives as well as the support they might need (Potter et al., 2021). The Warwick-Edinburgh Mental Wellbeing Scales (WEMBS) is a subjective wellbeing measure to understand how people experience and evaluate certain domains and activities in their lives (Warwick Medical School, 2021). The Valued Living questionnaire has 10 valued domains of living, for instance, family, friends, education, work, parenting, physical care, recreation, spirituality, etc. (Hayes, 2019). The measure taps into these domains by asking people to rate their importance, which can help to focus on certain areas to manage the condition. However, as with any outcome measure, the ones mentioned may not capture the complexity of the chronic health condition owing to the diversity of symptoms. Most questionnaires may not therefore cover all dimensions of individuals' experience of their health condition.

CASE STUDY

Sam is a 35-year-old man who developed symptoms of long Covid after contracting Covid-19 a year ago. He spent a week recovering in intensive care, which was a very traumatic experience as he witnessed several people dying and didn't know whether he would see his family again. He describes this experience as 'coming out of a warzone'. Sam still experiences flashbacks and nightmares from this time and has been suffering from severe fatigue, brain fog, body aches, heart palpitations, breathlessness, neurological symptoms and concentration and memory difficulties. He lives with his partner and formerly worked as a manager in a company but is now unemployed due to the impact of long Covid on his life.

When Sam realised he was not recovering from the symptoms of Covid-19 two months after getting it, he contacted several doctors and underwent tests and scans only to find out they were all normal. Sam initially wondered if it was 'all in his head', although he still experienced severe difficulties in retaining information, struggled to do daily tasks, including walking, showering and cooking, and as a result lost his confidence and developed low mood and anxiety. His family and friends did not understand why he was still struggling, which placed a strain on many of his relationships. His workplace expected him to get back to work as his tests were normal and he no longer had Covid-19. He found it difficult to socialise and meet people due to severe fatigue, pain and anxiety, and he felt very isolated as a result.

As people did not believe him or understand that he was still unwell, this reinforced his high expectations and self-critical thoughts about getting over the illness. He often felt angry and disappointed with himself for being unable to cope. Sam pushed himself to complete tasks, such as making important phone calls or going shopping for groceries, which only resulted in him staying in bed and feeling exhausted for days after. This was not only draining but also demotivating, and he couldn't be bothered to do anything anymore.

Sam is struggling financially as he lost his job and is currently fighting for financial support from the government. He feels stuck in a vicious loop of isolation, low mood, anxiety, uncertainty, and a long list of physical health issues. It was only recently that Sam received a diagnosis of long Covid from his GP, which resulted in limited access to psychological support, pulmonary rehabilitation and physiotherapy appointments. However, he still struggles with its physical, psychological and social impact.

The next section will detail ways of working with chronic physical health problems. Sam's example will be discussed in further detail while alluding to the interventions used.

WAYS OF WORKING WITH CHRONIC PHYSICAL HEALTH PROBLEMS

Managing a chronic health problem usually requires regular multidisciplinary monitoring from various healthcare professionals (Forestier et al., 2019), such as GPs, physiotherapists, neurologists, cardiologists, nurses and psychological therapists. From the viewpoint of counselling and psychotherapy, a few approaches have been evidenced to be helpful in managing chronic physical health problems, including Acceptance and Commitment Therapy (ACT) and cognitive behavioural therapy (CBT). Although one might argue whether an intervention belongs to one approach rather than another (pacing, for instance), they are still evidenced as being helpful for people experiencing chronic health issues.

ACCEPTANCE AND COMMITMENT THERAPY

Acceptance and Commitment Therapy (ACT) is consistent with Buddhist tenets (Fung, 2015) and aims to help clients to accept their thoughts and feelings by embracing them (Harris, 2006) and moving towards their inherent values (Hayes, 2019). The value of ACT in the management of chronic health problems is evidenced by various studies (Graham et al., 2016; Kuba and Weissflog, 2017). Some of the interventions used are outlined below (Harris, 2019):

- **Recognising what works (or doesn't)**: Many people with chronic physical health problems have tried numerous techniques to overcome their difficulties. Some of these strategies have worked, whereas others might not have done. In Sam's example, he used to push himself both mentally and physically to engage in tasks, and doing so ended up in him feeling demotivated and exhausted for days after. Recognising whether and how these strategies have worked in the short term or long term, and exploring their associated costs, helped Sam to understand their workability (or lack of workability).

- **Accepting difficult thoughts and emotions**: Chronic physical health problems can be accompanied by a host of upsetting thoughts and feelings, including relief, anger, grief, etc. For instance, Sam was worried about being able to cope, and felt frustrated with himself and those around him. This resulted in him being overly critical of himself and getting angry with the people around him. By accepting his feelings, Sam learned to acknowledge them rather than dwelling on them. This involved visualisation exercises, such as imagining that the negative emotions are like a big wave which then recedes back into the sea. In counselling sessions, it is equally important for therapists to be validating and accepting of clients' struggles and current capacities.
- **Mindfulness**: This includes contacting the present moment by non-judgementally observing one's thoughts, emotions, physical sensations, etc. To illustrate, Sam had upsetting thoughts, such as 'I am useless', 'I am disappointing others', and during these times, he tried saying to himself 'I am having the thought that I am useless'. Rather than automatically internalising the thought, he learned simply to observe the thought. Sam also engaged in breathing and relaxation exercises, which helped calm the body and relieve some of his anxiety.
- **Living according to one's values**: Connecting to things that are important to clients can help them refocus and feel better. ACT encourages reflecting on one's values and choosing to do something that takes them towards living their values. In Sam's example, he valued feeling useful, productive and supporting his family. When he engaged in relatively manageable tasks, such as tidying parts of his room and drying the dishes after a meal, it gave him a sense of usefulness and being able to help his family.

COGNITIVE BEHAVIOURAL THERAPY

The efficacy of cognitive behavioural therapy (CBT) for managing chronic physical health problems is evidenced by various studies (Hadley and Novitch, 2021; O'Dowd et al., 2006). Some of the interventions used include behavioural activation, pacing of behaviour to avoid prolongation or exacerbation of fatigue or pain flares, assertive communication, and understanding and challenging maladaptive beliefs about the health condition.

- **Cognitive restructuring or finding alternatives**: This involves identifying thinking biases such as catastrophising, jumping to conclusions or engaging in 'all or nothing thinking'. In Sam's case, he believed not completing certain tasks in a day meant he was 'useless' or a failure. He compared himself to how he used to be before contracting Covid and had high expectations from himself which didn't match his current circumstances. This 'all or nothing thinking' was exhausting in itself as it was very demanding on his physical and emotional wellbeing. Over time, Sam tried to have a more balanced view of the situation by looking at alternative ways to perceive the situation, for example, 'I am trying my best considering my personal circumstances'.
- **Pacing**: People might avoid doing things due to fatigue, pain or low mood, as in Sam's example. CBT suggests attempting to engage in activities despite these difficulties by pacing activities, rather than trying to do a lot at once, and taking breaks in between them. These activities can range from doing light stretching, to exercising and socialising. On some days, Sam wasn't able to do much at all, and by pacing and being patient with himself, he would do as much as he could without pushing himself beyond capacity. He prioritised tasks and engaged in them without getting exhausted for days after. This also gave him a sense of achievement and accomplishment as he was accepting what he could and couldn't do. Although he still had 'good days' and 'bad days', pacing helped him to feel both physically and mentally better.

CONCLUSION

To conclude, the interventions described in this chapter can be useful with individuals struggling with chronic physical health problems. However, it is important to tailor them to specific needs and background. In Sam's situation, he was also referred for trauma-focused therapy for the flashbacks and nightmares he experienced. While counselling clients with chronic physical health problems, it is also useful to take a biopsychosocial approach, which considers sleep problems, diet, medication management, relationships, etc.

REFERENCES

Anderson, G.F. (2010). *Chronic care: making the case for ongoing care*. Princeton, NJ: Robert Wood Johnson Foundation.

Benziger, C.P., Roth, G.A., & Moran, A.E. (2016). The global burden of disease study and the preventable burden of NCD. *Global Heart*, *11*(4), pp. 393–397. https://doi.org/10.1016/j.gheart.2016.10.024

Centers for Disease Control and Prevention (2021). *About Chronic Diseases*. Washington, DC: Available at www.cdc.gov/chronicdisease/about/index.htm (accessed 13 March 2022).

Dempster, M., Howell, D., & McCorry, N. K. (2015). Illness perceptions and coping in physical health conditions: A meta-analysis. *Journal of Psychosomatic Research*, *79*(6), 506–513. https://doi.org/10.1016/j.jpsychores.2015.10.006

Department of Health (2011). *Ten Things You Need to Know about Long-term Conditions*. London: DH [Website]. Available at www.dh.gov.uk/en/Healthcare/Longtermconditions/tenthingsyouneedtoknow/index.htm (accessed 13 March 2022).

Department of Health (2012). *Report: Long-term Conditions Compendium of Information* (3rd ed.). London: DH. Available at www.gov.uk/government/publications/long-term-conditions-compendium-of-information-third-edition (accessed 10 March 2022).

Doherty, A. M., & Gaughran, F. (2014). The interface of physical and mental health. *Social Psychiatry and Psychiatric Epidemiology*, *49*(5), 673–682. https://doi.org/10.1007/s00127-014-0847-7

DuLong, J. (2022). *How Long Covid Concerns are Ramping up Progress on Other Chronic Diseases*. Available at https://edition.cnn.com/2022/03/22/health/long-covid-chronic-illness-autoimmune-wellness/index.html (accessed 13 March 2022).

Forestier, B., Anthoine, E., Reguiai, Z., Fohrer, C., & Blanchin, M. (2019). A systematic review of dimensions evaluating patient experience in chronic illness. *Health and Quality of Life Outcomes*, *17*(1), 1–13. https://doi.org/10.1186/s12955-019-1084-2

Fung, K. (2015). Acceptance and commitment therapy: Western adoption of Buddhist tenets?. *Transcultural Psychiatry*, *52*(4), 561-576. https://doi.org/10.1177/1363461514537544

Graham, C. D., Gouick, J., Krahé, C., & Gillanders, D. (2016). A systematic review of the use of Acceptance and Commitment Therapy (ACT) in chronic disease and long-term conditions. *Clinical Psychology Review*, *46*, 46–58. https://doi.org/10.1016/j.cpr.2016.04.009

Hadley, G., & Novitch, M. B. (2021). CBT and CFT for chronic pain. *Current Pain and Headache Reports*, *25*(35). https://doi.org/10.1007/s11916-021-00948-1

Hämmig, O. (2019). Health risks associated with social isolation in general and in young, middle and old age. *PLoS One*, *14*(7). https://doi.org/10.1371/journal.pone.0219663

Harris, R. (2006). Embracing your demons: An overview of acceptance and commitment therapy. *Psychotherapy in Australia*, *12*(4), 2–8.

Harris, R. (2019). *ACT Made Simple: An Easy-to-read Primer on Acceptance and Commitment Therapy*. Oakland, CA: New Harbinger Publications.

Hayes, S. (2019). Acceptance and commitment therapy: towards a unified model of behavior change. *World Psychiatry*, *18*(2), 226–227. https://doi.org/10.1002/wps.20626

Kuba, K., & Weissflog, G. (2017). Acceptance and commitment therapy in the treatment of chronic disease. *Psychotherapie, Psychosomatik, Medizinische Psychologie*, *67*(12), 525–536. https://doi.org/10.1055/s-0043-118742

Larsen, P. D. (2021). *Lubkin's Chronic Illness: Impact and Intervention*. Burlington, MA: Jones & Bartlett Learning.

Megari, K. (2013). Quality of life in chronic disease patients. *Health Psychology Research*, *1*(3). https://doi.org/10.4081/hpr.2013.e27

Mental Health Foundation (2022). *Long-term Physical Conditions and Mental Health*. London: MHF. Available at www.mentalhealth.org.uk/a-to-z/l/long-term-physical-conditions-and-mental-health (accessed 19 March 2022).

(Continued)

(Continued)

Molina, K. M., & Simon, Y. (2014). Everyday discrimination and chronic health conditions among Latinos: The moderating role of socioeconomic position. *Journal of Behavioral Medicine*, *37*(5), 868–880.

National Center for Health Statistics (2010). *Health, United States: With Special Feature on Death and Dying.* Available at https://www.cdc.gov/nchs/data/hus/hus10.pdf (accessed 25 September 2022).

National Center for Health Statistics (2011). *Health, United States: With Special Feature on Socioeconomic Status and Health.* Available at https://www.cdc.gov/nchs/data/hus/hus11.pdf (accessed 25 September 2022).

National Institute for Health and Care Excellence (NICE) (2022). *Depression in Adults with a Chronic Physical Health Problem: Recognition and Management.* London: NICE. Available at www.nice.org.uk/guidance/cg91/ifp/chapter/depression-and-long-term-physical-health-problems (accessed 10 March 2022).

National Institute of Mental Health (NIMH) (2021). *Chronic Illness and Mental Health: Recognizing and Treating Depression.* London: NIMH. Available at www.nimh.nih.gov/health/publications/chronic-illness-mental-health (accessed 13 March 2022).

NHS (2021a). *Long-term Effects of Coronavirus (Long COVID).* London: NHS. Available at www.nhs.uk/conditions/coronavirus-covid-19/long-term-effects-of-coronavirus-long-covid/ (accessed 13 March 2022).

NHS (2021b). *Long-term Physical Health Condition.* London: NHS. Available at www.datadictionary.nhs.uk/nhs_business_definitions/long_term_physical_health_condition.html (accessed 13 March 2022).

NHS (2021c). *Medically unexplained symptoms.* Available at https://www.nhs.uk/conditions/medically-unexplained-symptoms/ (accessed 25 September 2022).

NHS Data Model and Dictionary (2022). *Long Term Physical Health Condition.* Available at https://www.datadictionary.nhs.uk/nhs_business_definitions/long_term_physical_health_condition.html (accessed 25 September 2022).

O'Dowd, H., Gladwell, P., Rogers, C. A., Hollinghurst, S., & Gregory, A. (2006). Cognitive behavioural therapy in chronic fatigue syndrome: A randomised controlled trial of an outpatient group programme. *Health Technology Assessment*, *10*(37), 1–121.

O'Rourke, M. (2022). *COVID Long Haulers are Calling Attention to Chronic Illnesses: But Society is Not Prepared for the Growing Crisis of Long COVID.* Available at www.scientificamerican.com/article/covid-long-haulers-are-calling-attention-to-chronic-illnesses/ (accessed 13 March 2022).

Potter, C. M., Peters, M., Cundell, M., McShane, R., & Fitzpatrick, R. (2021). Use of the Long-Term Conditions Questionnaire (LTCQ) for monitoring health-related quality of life in people affected by cognitive impairment including dementia: Pilot study in UK memory clinic services. *Quality of Life Research*, *30*(6), 1641–1652. https://doi.org/10.1007/s11136-021-02762-z

Roth, A. D., & Pilling, S. (2015). *A Competence Framework for Psychological Interventions with People with Persistent Physical Health Conditions.* London: UCL. Available at www.ucl.ac.uk/drupal/site_pals/sites/pals/files/migrated-files/Physical_Background_Doc.pdf (accessed 13 March 2022).

Stinson, D. A., & Fisher, A. N. (2020). Self-esteem and health. In K. Sweeny, M. L. Robbins & L. M. Cohen (Eds), *The Wiley Encyclopedia of Health Psychology*, [Online first], 2 September, 615–621. https://doi.org/10.1002/9781119057840.ch112

The King's Fund (2012). *Long-term Conditions and Mental Health: The Cost of Co-morbidities.* London: The King's Fund. Available at www.kingsfund.org.uk/sites/default/files/field/field_publication_file/long-term-conditions-mental-health-cost-comorbidities-naylor-feb12.pdf (accessed 13 March 2022).

Thompson, S. C., & Kyle, D.J. (2021). The role of perceived control in coping with the losses associated with chronic illness. In J. H. Harvey & E. D. Miller (Eds), *Loss and Trauma* (pp. 131–145). New York: Routledge.

Trindade, I. A., Duarte, J., Ferreira, C., Coutinho, M., & Pinto-Gouveia, J. (2018). The impact of illness-related shame on psychological health and social relationships: Testing a mediational model in students with chronic illness. *Clinical Psychology & Psychotherapy*, *25*(3), 408–414. https://doi.org/10.1002/cpp.2175

Warwick Medical School (2021). *The Warwick-Edinburgh Mental Wellbeing Scales – WEMWBS*. Warwick: Warwick Medical School. Available at https://warwick.ac.uk/fac/sci/med/research/platform/wemwbs/ (accessed 31 March 2022).

Wong, T. L., & Weitzer, D. J. (2021). Long COVID and myalgic encephalomyelitis/chronic fatigue syndrome (ME/CFS): a systemic review and comparison of clinical presentation and symptomatology. *Medicina*, *57*(5), 418. https://doi.org/10.3390/medicina57050418

World Health Organisation (2005). *Chronic Diseases and Their Common Risk Factors*. Geneva: WHO. Available at www.who.int/chp/chronic_disease_report/media/Factsheet1.pdf (accessed 13 March 2022).

RECOMMENDED READING

Harris, R. (2019). *ACT Made Simple: An Easy-to-read Primer on Acceptance and Commitment Therapy*. Oakland, CA: New Harbinger Publications.

This book offers a guide to ACT for physical and mental health issues.

Moore, P., & Cole, F. (2010). *The Pain Toolkit: For People Living with Persistent Pain*. London: NHS. Available at www.nhs.uk/Planners/yourhealth/Documents/The%20pain%20toolkit%20-%20Oct%2010%20-%20READ.pdf

This book provides a CBT toolkit for people experiencing chronic pain.

Owen, R. (2013). *Living with the Enemy: Coping with the Stress of Chronic Illness Using CBT, Mindfulness and Acceptance*. New York: Routledge.

This is a self-help book on coping with chronic physical health issues using CBT and ACT principles.

4.6 COUNSELLING FOR DRUG-RELATED PROBLEMS

TONY WHITE

OVERVIEW AND KEY POINTS

This chapter covers an explanation of common drugs and the unique characteristics of clients who are drug users. It provides an assessment of a client using the stages of change model, which shows the client's current motivation for change and some common aspects of working with drug users to assist them to change their use. This includes things like harm minimisation, assessing if a client's drug use is problematic and the types of things that can trigger a person to relapse. Finally, there is an example of working with a drug user who is self-medicating.

The chapter covers the following key points:

- The three categories of drugs.
- A drug user's level of motivation for change.
- Basic techniques when working with drug users.
- Problem drug use due to self-medication.

ASSESSMENT AND UNDERSTANDING

What types of drugs are commonly reported by clients in drug counselling? Mehdikhani et al. (see Chapter 4.2, this volume) discuss alcohol, so that will not be discussed in this chapter. The most commonly used drugs that clients present with in drug counselling are:

1. Depressants, which slow the messages between the brain and the body and can make one feel relaxed and calm (downers). Depressants include: cannabis or marijuana, which is by far the most commonly used illicit drug; benzodiazepines (benzos), which include minor tranquillisers such as valium, but also xanax and librium; and opiates, most commonly heroin and morphine.
2. Stimulants, which speed up the messages between the brain and the body and make the person feel alert, awake and confident (uppers). Stimulants include: amphetamines, including methamphetamine or ice; cocaine; ecstasy or MDMA.
3. Hallucinogens, which change one's sense of reality and senses, such as taste, vision and smell, which can be distorted. Hallucinogens include: cannabis or marijuana; LSD; magic mushrooms or psilocybin.
4. Inhalants, where one breathes in the vapours to give an immediate 'high'. These include petrol, glue, paint thinner, laughing gas and vegetable oil sprays.

These are the most common types of drugs that are reported to counsellors in drug counselling settings and the drugs that are referred to in this chapter.

COMMON ISSUES SEEN WHEN WORKING WITH CLIENTS WHO USE DRUGS

DRUGS AND BREAKING THE LAW

The first point about these drugs is that in many countries around the world most of these drugs are illegal. In countries like the UK, drugs such as cocaine, cannabis, LSD, and heroin are illegal to use. Not only that, but in many societies drug use is also a moral issue. Using drugs is often viewed by mainstream society as being 'bad', sinful or an immoral thing to do. This means the drug counsellor is working with a group of people who are prepared to break the rules, both the laws of the land and the moral rules about what is regarded as good and bad behaviour. The drug counsellor has a client population who are 'under socialised' in this way and are prepared to behave in non-conformist ways.

The drug-using client is also going to be part of the drug-using subculture of that society. Some of them have only a small involvement in that subculture, whereas others are very heavily involved and spend a lot of their time with other people in that group. What this means is that the drug counsellor is going to have clients who are sometimes heavily involved in the drug 'scene' and are involved, at times, in quite significant levels of drug dealing. Some clients will be involved in drug dealing of varying degrees. This can leave the drug counsellor in a difficult position. They must communicate to the client that they do not want to know any specific information about any nefarious activities which they may do. You are simply there to counsel them about their drug use and other emotional difficulties they have.

If the counsellor is working in a drug rehabilitation centre, then of course they are working with drug users each day. However other groups, such as the prison population, the homeless and sex workers, will also have a high percentage of people who can also have drug use problems. Even the general counsellor who is not specialising in drug problems will quite often come across drug use and abuse by clients, even from those groups that are considered to be the pillars of the society, like the professions.

DRUG USERS AND LYING

Another problem for the drug counsellor is getting accurate information from the client. The most common problems that clients present with are things like depression, anxiety, relationship problems, and so on. These are the 'bread and butter' of the general counsellor's work. The first thing one does with a client is to assess their depression and anxiety by asking questions about its severity, frequency, duration, and so on. The same applies for the drug counsellor, where one needs to get a reasonable estimate of the current use of the person, and indeed their history of use. Unfortunately, this is sometimes harder to do than with non-drug use problems.

There is a saying in the addictions field: 'If you don't want to be lied to about a person's drug use, then don't ask them the question.' Lying and deception is endemic in the drug scene; everybody does it. However, it should be noted that the vast majority of clients lie to their counsellors (not only those using drugs). Farber, Blanchard and Love (2019) cite research which indicates that 90% of clients will lie at some point to their counsellor about a whole variety of topics, for a variety of reasons. I would suggest that it is even more typical among drug users and in the drug scene. First, clients lie out of simple necessity. It is not illegal to be depressed, whereas it is illegal to use drugs, so one has to lie about their drug use, or they are going to get caught pretty quickly. One does not have to lie about their depression.

By the time some drug-using clients get to the counsellor, the lying may be habitual and ingrained, especially about a topic like their current drug use. When the client answers the question about their current and historical drug use, the counsellor takes it for what it is and keeps an open mind that more information on this topic may come to light at a later session.

The lying and deception is often as much to themselves as to the counsellor. I was recently working with a woman who had a pattern of significant methamphetamine use (please note this is a composite, fictionalised case). Then one day she reported that she had stopped using, which I wasn't expecting but it was good news. A couple of sessions later she disclosed that she had recently gone to a psychiatrist who had prescribed her significant amounts of dexamphetamines for her ADHD and she was now taking those everyday.

As it turns out, her drug taking hadn't stopped, but only changed. However, in her mind she was no longer taking drugs but was taking prescribed medication. She wasn't lying to me but lying to herself. This is common for regular drug users. The idea of being an addict, either the alcoholic or the junkie drug addict, is a very unpleasant one. These words carry with them strong negative connotations. To clearly acknowledge that you are an alcoholic or a junkie is a very unpleasant and difficult thing to do. Once done, the person can feel significant shame or self-loathing as a consequence of seeing themselves like this.

Much has been written about the addict's denial of their addiction. One of the main milestones in the treatment of an addict is when they finally give up their denial and accept that they are an alcoholic or a drug addict. Massella (1990: 79) states that denial is the 'primary symptom of chemical dependence'. Goulding (1985: 116) says that 'The hardest problem we face in the treatment of the alcoholic is the resolution of, or breakdown of, denial'. It is denial that is seen to protect the person from the threat of inadequacy. The woman mentioned above was in denial about her drug taking, which allowed her to preserve some sense of self-respect, self-esteem and to avoid the shame and self-loathing. She wasn't lying to me about her drug use, she was lying to herself.

DRUG COUNSELLING AND STRESS LEVELS

The most common problems that confront the general counsellor are things like depression, anxiety, insomnia, relationship problems, and so on. In this sense, drug counselling is more 'blood and guts' therapy compared to the 'average' type of counselling. The counsellor is dealing with more dramatic types of problems; one could say more destructive types of problems. For the person who has had a 10-year career of using drugs, then they have done well if they do not have some kind of criminal record, some kind of virus from the drug use, a sexually transmitted disease, experienced an overdose or have some other kind of bodily damage due to the drug use.

If someone has a 10-year career of anxiety or depression, they will have not have these. If one has depression, that won't give them a virus or an overdose. Having anxiety does not increase one's chances of getting a criminal record. In this sense, one can say that the stakes are less high or less dramatic for counselling non-drug-using clients. Drug-using clients tend to be more destructive than 'average' clients. Drug-using clients generally live with higher levels of stress, and hence the counsellor is more likely to have higher stress levels from the workplace.

ASSESSMENT OF THE CLIENT WITH THE STAGES OF CHANGE MODEL

The stages of change model is a very widely used way of assessing drug-using clients. It assesses the client's current motivation level for using or stopping using drugs. It comes from the work of Prochaska and DiClemente (1992), who propose five stages of change.

For each stage, there are different types of treatment that should be used.

PRECONTEMPLATION

Precontemplation is sometimes known as the 'happy user' stage and this person has no intention of changing their drug use in the foreseeable future. They are currently quite happy and satisfied with how they use drugs. This can result from defence mechanisms like denial and resistance, a lack of knowledge about the risks in drug taking, rebelliousness about drug taking, and some feel resigned or overwhelmed about their drug taking and believe there is no hope of giving up.

CONTEMPLATION

At the contemplation stage the happy user now becomes an 'unhappy user' for some reason. They become unhappy about using drugs. It can be the financial cost, fears of health problems, their drug use is causing relationship difficulties, they dislike the idea of being addicted, and so on. Some people can stay in this stage for a long period of time as they have an interest in changing but little commitment to do it. There is a lot of thinking about their drug use and very little of doing anything about it. They have made the decision to change and are planning and thinking how to put it into effect.

PREPARATION

Typically, preparation is a short stage. The person reaches the point of intending to change in the near future and there are small changes in behaviour. The person will then either move onto the next stage (action) or return to the contemplation stage. Their planning to stop is now serious and they are clearly thinking about how to put it into effect.

ACTION

In the action stage, the person is now in the process of changing their behaviour but they are in the early stages, usually less than six months. A lot of energy is being put into maintaining abstinence, developing new ideas, activities and friends to replace the drug use. Those who seek out professional help often have already started changes in their lives and drug use. This person will either move onto the next stage or return to a previous stage.

MAINTENANCE

People in the maintenance stage have now given up their drug use for a relatively long time (over six months and up to five years). The client's focus is on maintaining their lifestyle changes and this new lifestyle now becomes the norm. However, relapse can and does occur, and then the person can move back to any of the previous stages. Or the relapse is a temporary aberration, and the person reasonably quickly restores the stage of maintenance. The longer the person stays in maintenance, then relapses are less frequent and less intense until long periods of abstinence begin to occur.

WAYS OF WORKING WITH CLIENTS WHO ARE USING DRUGS

This section describes some of the most common aspects of working with drug users.

INFORMATION

The drug counsellor must make sure the user has accurate information about drugs, what they are and how they work. For example, knowing the three categories of drugs described at the beginning of this chapter and that they can either slow down or speed up the central nervous system. Bibliotherapy is useful here to give the drug user some reading material on the basics of drugs and their effects. Many government health agencies have an array of pamphlets for this purpose that are easy to understand.

HARM MINIMISATION

Harm minimistation includes providing information to the client about how to use drugs more safely. It covers issues such as:

- Infections – most commonly HIV and hepatitis C. What they are and how to reduce the chances of catching any viruses, especially for injecting drug users.
- Overdoses – How to reduce the possibility of an overdose. Overdose is most likely to occur when a combination of drugs is used in one drug-taking session. This mainly includes the depressants, such as the opiates, benzodiazepines and cannabis. Using these drugs in combination in particular can lead

to overdose. Other advice is don't use drugs alone and what to do if someone you are with overdoses, including some basic first aid.
- Dangers specific to various drugs – for example, with ecstasy one must be careful that the body does not overheat and the drug user needs to keep hydrated. Hallucinogens can potentially lead to psychosis. Inhalants have a propensity to cause brain damage.
- Mental health – information highlights the problems that can occur if a person has a history or propensity for mental health problems. This is especially so with the hallucinogens. The longer term effects of drugs such as cannabis can result in ongoing depression.
- Dangers of injecting drug use – how to inject safely.
- Do not get drugs on credit.
- Safe sex practices.

RECREATIONAL AND PROBLEM DRUG USE

The majority of people who use drugs suffer few negative effects and do not develop a drug addiction. However, how does someone ascertain if their drug use is a problem or not? One way of describing this is with what are called the four Ls:

> Liver – Health problems caused by the drug use.
> Lover – Relationship problems caused by the drug use.
> Livelihood – Financial problems caused by the drug use.
> Legal – Legal problems caused by the drug use.

In this case, the counsellor works with the client to define what they see as significant health, relationship, financial or legal problems that are the result of their drug use. Doing so allows them to gain a greater sense of that line between recreational and problem drug use. For example, if a man's wife has told him she will leave him unless he stops smoking marijuana, that does indicate a significant relationship problem generated by his drug use. If she only complains spasmodically and at times joins him in his smoking, then that is much less of a relationship problem. What percentage of the weekly income is spent on drugs and what is acceptable? Is that 5%, 20% or 50%? Such discussions allow the client to define the line between recreational use and dysfunctional drug use in these four areas.

TRIGGERS

This is a common technique for working who someone who is wanting to avoid using drugs. It allows them to identify the high-risk situations where they are more likely to use. These are situations where they can be 'triggered' into using again. These situations can relate to feelings, thoughts, people, places and events. The client can construct four lists to identify their triggers.

1. FEELINGS

Feelings can include both good and bad moods, such as:

> I got the job, so I had to celebrate
> I had a day off work
> I get stressed out
> I feel anxious or depressed

2. THOUGHTS

The things you say to yourself that make you want to use:

> I am no good and an alcoholic
> Just one drink, that won't hurt
> Tomorrow I will not drink for a week

3. PEOPLE

Anyone you are with which results in an increased desire to use:

> When I am with my drinking friends
> After I have seen my mother, I need a drink
> My wife nags me so much I just need to relax

4. WHERE AND WHEN

Places and events where you are more likely to use:

> On Christmas day
> At the football
> With a cup of coffee
> As I sit down to watch television at night

Undertaking exercises such as these allow the person to identify high-risk situations. Those situations can then be avoided altogether or prepared for in some way.

IN this way, the client is afforded more protection against a relapse.

The examples above, of techniques for working with clients using drugs, adopt the cognitive behavioural therapy approach. They work with the person's specific behaviours and their faulty thinking patterns that can lead to problem drug use, for example by identifying the person's triggers. The psychodynamic approach is different because it seeks out early childhood traumas and works with resolving the feelings about the trauma which the person experienced. Its focus is not the behaviours and thoughts, but the deeper feelings from the trauma the person has experienced. The case study below gives an example of how this psychodynamic approach can work.

CASE STUDY

Self-medication is a common reason for problem drug use. The person experiences some feelings like depression or anxiety, and they discover that by using a drug it relieves the distress. They become addicted because they need to use the drug each day to continue feeling the relief from the distress. A 36-year-old woman presented with habitual marijuana use most days of the week. She uses the drug to 'medicate' her anxiety and insomnia, usually by smoking at night when the children are asleep.

When she was 7 years old her mother died, and her father was cold and aloof as a parent. She has two siblings, with whom she has long-term, acrimonious relationships. In essence, when her mother died, she became emotionally isolated with no close affectionate relationships in her life. As one can imagine, this sense of abandonment was traumatic for her and she has been plagued with abandonment anxiety for most of her life.

The client reports that marijuana has always eased her anxiety and allows her to sleep. She has been a bad insomniac for many years, but the intoxication allows her to sleep through a full night without waking up. Trauma debriefing is used to treat the original trauma of abandonment. The client is asked to recount the facts of the trauma, which is what happened when her mother died and what has happened subsequent to that. As the client reports the facts, often feelings surface. When they do, the counsellor encourages the expression of these feelings and for the client to speak the words that go with those feelings. In this way, the emotions and the trauma are worked through (for more information on working with trauma, see Charura and Smith – Chapter 4.15, this volume).

There can often be a layering of feelings. When reporting her mother's death, at first the client felt and expressed her anger at being abandoned by her. After a few times of doing this, she began to experience a great sadness at the loss of her mother. A few sessions later, she finally experienced her great fear at being abandoned and now she was all on her own. With the recounting of the trauma and the working through of the emotions about the trauma, the feelings subside. Once this happens, the marijuana use is less necessary as the client does not need to 'medicate' the feelings away anymore.

REFERENCES

Farber, B. A., Blanchard, M. and Love, M. (2019). *Secrets and Lies in Psychotherapy*. Washington, DC: American Psychological Association:

Goulding, R. L. (1985). Alcoholic dependency and denial. In L. Kadis (Ed.), *Redecision Therapy: Expanded Perspectives* (pp. 113–116). Watsonville, CA: Western Institute for Group and Family Therapy.

Massella, J. D. (1990). Intervention: Breaking the addiction cycle. In D. C. Daley and M. S. Raskin (Eds), *Treating the Chemically Dependent and their Families*. Newbury Park, CA: Sage.

Prochaska, J. O. and DiClemente, C. C. (1992). Stages of change in the modification of problem behaviours. In M. Herson, R. M. Eisler and P. M. Miller (Eds), *Progress in Behaviour Modification 28*, 183–218.

> **RECOMMENDED READING**
>
> White, T. (2013). *Working with Drug and Alcohol Users*. London: Jessica Kingsley Publishers.
>
> Part 2 of this book covers techniques used in drug counseling in a comprehensive way.
>
> Marsh, A. and Dale, A. (2006). *Addiction Counselling*. Melbourne: IP Communications.
>
> The books is a comprehensive statement about the CBT approach to addictions counselling.
>
> Thombs, D. L. (1999). *Introduction to Addictive Behaviors* (2nd ed.). London and New York: Guilford Press.
>
> This book gives a good coverage of the different models and approaches to addiction and methods of treatment.

4.7 DEPRESSION

DENIS O'HARA

OVERVIEW AND KEY POINTS

Depression is one of the most common and pervasive of mental health conditions with 5–12% of the world population being depressed at any given time (Dattani, Ritchie and Roser, 2021). While there is evidence for the increase in the incidence of depression globally, this increase has escalated during the Covid-19 pandemic (Leech et al., 2021). Depression comes in many forms and in varying degrees of intensity. For some, depression comes and goes relatively quickly, and for others, it is experienced as a lifetime struggle. While the various forms of depression have symptoms or characteristics in common, there is also variety in its expression. Depression is also often part of a complex web of other mental health problems, resulting in different combinations of comorbidity. In this respect, depression can be thought of as a problem in its own right, but also a signal that a person is experiencing a complexity of mental health problems which interrelate, making both diagnosis and treatment challenging.

The key points explored in this chapter are:

- Depression is expressed in different ways and in varying degrees of severity and is often associated with other mental health conditions.
- It is a complex condition with various causes and associated individual personal vulnerabilities.
- Given the fact that there are multifactorial causes for depression, counsellors and psychotherapists are required to consider a wide range of factors in any psychological assessment.
- Several well-researched psychotherapeutic models have been developed to work therapeutically with those who are depressed.

ASSESSMENT AND UNDERSTANDING

Even though depressive states have been recognised for millennia, the term 'depression' is a relatively new one, only coming into common usage in the twentieth century. Historically, depression was referred to as 'melancholia' and described a state of lowered mood and life energies. The word 'depression' comes from the Latin verb *deprimere*, 'to press down', and it is this usage which gradually became the typical reference within medicine. It should be noted, however, that depression as understood in western countries, is not necessarily a recognised concept in other countries. In many Eastern languages, for example, there is no directly equivalent word for depression. In such societies, what might be identified as depression in western diagnostic manuals would more typically be understood as dysfunctional social and behavioural characteristics, rather than as a specified condition (American Psychiatric Association (APA), 2013; World Health Organisation (WHO), 2019).

The fifth edition of the *Diagnostic and Statistical Manual of Mental Disorders* (DSM-V) (APA, 2013) sets out a list of criteria which, when appropriately identified, constitute a diagnosis of depression. The following list, while not representing the full set of criteria, constitutes the key features of what is referred to as 'major depressive episode'. They include:

A. Five or more of the following symptoms have been present during the same two-week period, represent a change from previous functioning, and include either depressed mood or loss of interest or pleasure.

- Depressed mood
- Marked diminished interest or pleasure
- Significant weight loss or weight gain
- Insomnia or hypersomnia
- Psychomotor agitation or retardation
- Fatigue or loss of energy
- Feelings of worthlessness or excessive guilt
- Diminished ability to concentrate
- Recurrent thoughts of death or suicidal ideation

B. The symptoms cause clinically significant distress or impairment in social, occupational, or other important areas of functioning. (APA, 2013)

There are other criteria which refer to the need to assess if symptoms are due to other medical or mental health conditions. It should also be noted that in the DSM-V revision, the two-month exclusion of bereavement from the onset of the depression as a diagnostic caveat has been withdrawn.

Depression has no single cause. Unlike pathogenic diseases, there is no blood test which will identify a pathogen for depression. Rather, there are multiple factors involved in its development and any assessment approach should consider psychological, social and biological factors and vulnerabilities, such as:

- Genetic factors
- Early life attachment problems
- Temperament type
- Negative attributional style
- Interpersonal factors
- Stressful life events (Hankin et al., 2009).

Recently, research attention has been given to the potential influence of genes on the development of depression. While there is emerging evidence that genes do play a role in an individual's susceptibility to depression, genes are not a singular causal determinant. Rather, it is highly likely that genes play a mediating role in the complex of factors which together predispose an individual to depression (Dunn et al., 2015; Poulton, Moffitt and Silva, 2015; Shadrina et al., 2018). Increasingly, research is demonstrating the inextricable link between biology and environment in the aetilogy of depression (Kendler et al., 2020; Weissman, 2020).

The most significant aspects of environment long identified are the attachment relationship, and a secure and safe environment. Secure attachment relationships with parents and caregivers provide for the individual a sense of safety and a secure emotional base from which to explore the world. When attachment relationships are confused or disrupted, it can limit an individual's capacity to feel emotionally secure and to form other healthy relationships. Studies have demonstrated that insecure attachment in children and adolescence can lead to depression well into early adulthood (Agerup et al., 2015; Spruit et al., 2020). Moreover, there is evidence that the wider home context, which provides a safe and supportive environment, limits the likelihood of depression developing in children and adolescents (Cuijpers et al., 2015). Notably, adolescent depression is acknowledged as a predictor of ongoing adult mental health problems (Naicker et al., 2013). As early life relationships form the foundation for a healthy sense of self, others and the world, any disruptions in these relationships make a person more vulnerable to developing depression.

Personality temperament can also be a vulnerability factor in developing depression (Behn, Herpertz and Krause, 2018; de la Parra, Dagnino and Behn, 2021). Different temperament schemes have in common a trait-based view of personality, which is theorised to be developed from both genetic and environmental factors. A number of studies have demonstrated a link between certain temperament sub-types and depression (Marijnissen et al., 2002).

A separate but related vulnerability to depression is attributional style. Attributional style refers to how people explain or attribute meaning to life events. Individual events can be explained in several different ways, leading to either positive or negative conclusions. As is the case with personality temperaments, individuals have a tendency to perceive the world in certain predisposing ways and, as a result, interpret their experiences through cognitive filters. Those with a positive attributional style tend to construct meaning of events in ways that maintain a positive psychological frame. Alternatively, others are more inclined to interpret life events in more customarily negative ways. Evidence suggests that those who are oriented towards a more negative attributional style are more susceptible to depression (Romens et al., 2011; Rubenstein et al., 2016).

Interpersonal factors are also identified as a vulnerability factor in the development of depression. Such factors as communication skills, social relating, coping style and social supports, when well developed, act as buffers against low mood. Those individuals who rate poorly on interpersonal communication and relating and who have limited social support are much more susceptible to depression (O'Shea, Spence and Donovan, 2013). Those who are able to employ positive coping strategies when confronted by life stressors have been shown to be less likely to become depressed (Adler, Conklin and Strunk, 2013).

The different vulnerabilities to depression can function as individual factors but quite often interrelate and combine to increase an individual's susceptibility to depression. One of the overarching vulnerabilities is life stress. This is because stress can act as a catalyst for responding negatively to experiences. While many life experiences can act as stressors in a person's life, a specific form of stress is trauma. Traumatic experiences come in different forms, from single events like a car accident, to multiple traumatising development experiences, such as emotional and sexual abuse. Ultimately, there is no one variable which explains how depression is initiated and developed in humans. Future studies are likely to provide a clearer understanding of the complex interplay of genes, biological, cognitive/emotional, relational and environmental factors in this challenging mental health condition.

There are a range of assessment instruments for depression that are routinely used to assist in assessment and case formulation. The most important of these is the clinical interview, followed by standardised tests.

WAYS OF WORKING WITH DEPRESSION

As is well known, there are many different approaches to psychotherapeutic change. While counsellors and psychotherapists can facilitate significant positive change in clients via a singular theoretical approach, it is more common to include a variety of approaches, adjusting therapy to clients' needs. As many counselling and psychotherapy theories are well supported by research, it is important to consider their respective contributions to the understanding of the change process.

Psychodynamic approaches pay special attention to interpersonal factors, and how attachment issues and early life experiences influence individuals' unconscious view of self, others and the world. A central focus is the identification of recurring conflictual relationship themes and the emotions related to these themes. The aim of therapy is to help the client make conscious the relational patterns and emotional states experienced and to explore how they function and the meaning they hold (Barkham et al., 2017; Fonagy et al., 2020).

Humanistic approaches highlight the importance of subjective and intersubjective experiences and emotional states with a focus on the here-and-now. An important feature of such approaches is the high value placed on the person's subjective and embodied experience. From this perspective, depression is first seen as an experience reflective of conflict between different parts of the self, an incongruence between the real and ideal self. When there is a discrepancy between one's ideal view of self, as possibly portrayed by primary others, and one's actual or real self, the inner dialogue between these different self-portrayals can lead to conflict, resulting in depression (Elliott, 2012; Sanders and Hill, 2014).

Cognitive-behavioural approaches pay particular attention to the vulnerabilities associated with personality temperaments, cognitive attributions, and the impact of stress on biological and psychological coping. The aim of therapy is to identify and realign an individual's attributional style and strengthen coping strategies through psychoeducational means. Therapeutic strategies are also designed to respond to biological and behavioural weaknesses through behaviour management (Gilbert, 2009, 2021).

CASE STUDY

Travis is a 27-year-old single male who lives in a shared flat with a male friend from his university days. He is a qualified engineer who works with a building and design firm. Until recently Travis has enjoyed work, but over the past couple of months he has found it a struggle to go to work due to feeling very flat in mood, fatigued and lacking in interest in any of his normal social pursuits. Travis has also experienced a shift in his sleeping pattern, tending to wake in the early hours of the morning and struggling to go back to sleep. Of late, his flat mate noticed a marked shift in Travis's social interactions, both at home and with friends. While he was never overly gregarious, Travis is now withdrawn, often turning down invitations to social outings with friends.

One of the first priorities in working with Travis from a humanistic perspective is to privilege his experience and story and to facilitate the therapeutic relationship. Attention would be paid to felt experience both in terms of emotional states and physiological experience. Felt experiences are seen as potential points of access for both the client and the therapist to identify incongruencies between different internal dialogues and lived experience. In the case of Travis, one inner voice may berate him for not taking his career more seriously by pursuing faster advancement in his firm or at least a higher, postgraduate, qualification. The other voice may defend against this demand, taking the view that he had already worked hard to get his engineering degree and a good job and now deserved to slow down and enjoy the fruits of his labour, travelling and enjoying a social life. The task of the therapist is to assist Travis to observe the intensity of this conflict split and to explore the physical and emotional impact it is having on him. It is common in depressive states for there to be a strong self-critical voice which is often associated with shame and self-loathing. The circular nature of the inner conflict split serves to make the sufferer feel stuck with no hope of resolution. This experience is usually associated with overwhelming emotions, which also serve to disable the individual from taking action to resolve the situation.

Within humanistic theory, conflict splits are understood to arise from different aspects of the self. The *ideal self* in the above example promotes a driven sense of career advancement while the *real self* argues for a balanced life experience. The challenge for the individual is to step outside the inner struggle and to become aware of the priorities and values of the real or actual self and to live in a fashion which is genuine and congruent with it. As in the above case, the therapist's task is to help the client get in touch with his or her authentic self and associated desires and in so doing regain hope in a positive future (O'Hara, 2013; Sanders and Hill, 2014).

ALTERNATIVE PERSPECTIVES

Different therapies approach and enact effective change processes in a variety of ways. Another approach to Travis's struggles is Acceptance and Commitment Therapy (ACT) (Harris, 2019). ACT is founded in behavioural and cognitive approaches but has a less pathologising view of the human condition than many other therapies, and as such is not dissimilar to humanistic approaches in holding the view that human social and psychological struggles are not primarily symptoms of mental illness but struggles in living authentically. According to ACT, the human psyche naturally attends to negative experiences, often leaving us with a sense of shame and cognitive confusion. Change occurs when we accept and are present to our experiences, observe our thoughts rather than be captured by them, and live and act according to our core values. The key principles of ACT are:

- contact and connection with the present moment
- expansion and acceptance (enhance a transcendent sense of self)
- cognitive defusion
- the Observing Self
- values clarification
- committed action (Hayes, Strosahl and Wilson, 2016).

A therapist working from an ACT perspective would seek to help Travis identify the ways in which he moves towards and away from healthy action. The therapist would explain that unpleasant experiences are part of life and not something intrinsically to fear and withdraw from. Travis would be encouraged to be present to uncomfortable emotions and experiences with a view to observing them and accepting their existence rather than necessarily trying to change them directly or to hide from any associated negative thoughts. It would be explained that 'thoughts are just thoughts' and we can defuse negative thoughts by deciding to notice them without being directed by them. Values clarification is another important aspect of ACT because healthy committed action arises from clarifying our core values.

When we clarify our values and are able to be present in the moment while observing our thoughts and accepting ourselves, healthy change is made possible. For Travis, this would entail being present to his fear of social engagement, by being present to his experience, by defusing negative thoughts and by deciding to act according to his core values.

When considering working with someone struggling with depression, it is critically important to consider not just the theory or theories informing your work, but the way of working that will most benefit the individual client.

REFERENCES

Adler, A. D., Conklin, L. R. and Strunk, D. R. (2013). Quality of coping skills predicts depressive symptom reactivity over repeated stressors. *Journal of Clinical Psychology*, *69*(12), 1228–1238.

Agerup, T., Lydersen, S., Wallander, J. and Sund, A. M. (2015). Associations between parental attachment and course of depression between adolescence and young adulthood. *Child Psychiatry and Human Development*, *46*, 632–642.

American Psychiatric Association (2013). *Diagnostic and Statistical Manual of Mental Disorders* (5th ed.) DSM-5. Washington, DC: American Psychiatric Association.

Barkham, M., Guthrie, E., Hardy, G. E. and Margison, F. (2017). *Psychodynamic-Interpersonal Therapy: A Conversational Model*. London and Thousand Oaks, CA: Sage.

Behn, A., Herpertz, S. C. and Krause, M. (2018). The interaction between depression and personality dysfunction: state of the art, current challenges, and future directions. Introduction to the Special Section. *Psykhe (Santiago)*, 1–12. https://doi.org/10.7764/psykhe.27.2.1501

Cuijpers, P., Weitz, E., Karyotaki, E., Garber, J. and Andersson, G. (2015). The effects of psychological treatment of maternal depression on children and parental functioning: a meta-analysis. *European Child & Adolescent Psychiatry*, *24*(2), 237–245.

Dattani, S., Ritchie, H. and Roser, M. (2021). Mental health. *Our World in Data* [Online]. Available at: https://ourworldindata.org/mental-health

de la Parra, G., Dagnino, P. and Behn, A. (2021). *Depression and Personality Dysfunction: An Integrative Functional Domains Perspective*. Cham, Switzerland: Springer.

Dunn, E. C., Brown, R. C., Dai, Y., Rosand, J., Nugent, N. R., Amstadter, A. B. and Smoller, J. W. (2015). Genetic determinants of depression. *Harvard Review of Psychiatry*, *23*(1), 1–18.

Elliott, R. (2012). *Emotion focused therapy*. In P. Sanders (Ed.), The Tribes of the Person-centred Nation: An Introduction to the Schools of Therapy Associated with the Person-centred Approach. Ross-on-Wye: PCCS Books.

Fonagy, P., Lemma, A., Target, M., O'Keeffe, S., Constantinou, M. P., Ventura Wurman, T., Luyten, P., Allison, E., Roth, A., Cape, J. and Pilling, S. (2020). Dynamic interpersonal therapy for moderate to severe depression: a pilot randomized controlled and feasibility trial. *Psychological Medicine*, *50*(6), 1010–1019.

Gilbert, P. (2009). *Overcoming Depression* (3rd ed.). London: Constable Robinson.

Gilbert, P. (2021). *Depression: From Psychology to Brain State*. York: Annwyn House.

Hankin, B. L., Oppenheimer, C., Jenness, J., Barrocas, A., Shapero, B. G. and Goldband, J. (2009). Developmental origins of cognitive vulnerabilities to depression: review of processes contributing to stability and change across time. *Journal of Clinical Psychology*, *65*(12), 1327–1338.

(Continued)

(Continued)

Harris, R. (2019). *ACT Made Simple: An Easy-to-read Primer on Acceptance and Commitment Therapy* (2nd edition). Oakland, CA: New Harbinger Publications.

Hayes, S. C., Strosahl, K. D. and Wilson, K. G. (2016). *Acceptance and Commitment Therapy: The Process and Practice of Mindful Change*. New York: Guilford Press.

Kendler, K. S., Ohlsson, H., Sundquist, J. and Sundquist, K. (2020). The rearing environment and risk for major depression: A Swedish National High-Risk Home-Reared and Adopted-Away Co-Sibling Control Study. *American Journal of Psychiatry*, *177*(5), 447–453.

Leach, C., Finning, K., Kerai, G. and Vizard, T. (2021). *Coronavirus and Depression in Adults, Great Britain*. London: Office for National Statistics. [Online]. Available at www.ons.gov.uk/peoplepopulationandcommunity/wellbeing/articles/coronavirusanddepressioninadultsgreatbritain/julytoaugust2021

Marijnissen, G., Tuinier, S., Sijben, A. E. S. and Verhoeven, W. M. A. (2002). The temperament and character inventory in major depression. *Journal of Affective Disorders*, *70*(2), 219–223.

Naicker, K., Galambos, N. L., Zeng, Y., Senthilselvan, A. and Colman, I. (2013). Social, demographic, and health outcomes in the 10 years following adolescent depression. *Journal of Adolescent Health*, *52*(5), 533–538.

O'Hara, D. J. (2013). *Hope in Counselling and Psychotherapy*. London: Sage.

O'Shea, G., Spence, S. H. and Donovan, C. L. (2013). Interpersonal factors associated with depression in adolescents: Are these consistent with theories underpinning interpersonal psychotherapy? *Clinical Psychology and Psychotherapy*, *21*, 548–558.

Poulton, R., Moffitt, T. E. and Silva, F. A. (2015). The Dunedin Multidisciplinary Health and Development Study: Overview of the first 40 years, with an eye to the future. *Social Psychiatry Psychiatric Epidemiology*, *50*(5), 679–693.

Romens, S. E., MacCoon, D. G., Abramson, L. Y. and Pollak, S. D. (2011). Cognitive style moderates attention to attribution-relevant stimuli. *Cognitive Therapy and Research*, *35*, 134–141.

Rubenstein, L. M., Freed, R. D., Shapero, B. G., Fauber, R. L. and Alloy, L. B. (2016). Cognitive attributions in depression: Bridging the gap between research and clinical practice. *Journal of Psychotherapy Integration*, *26*(2), 103–115.

Sanders, P. and Hill, A. (2014). *Counselling for Depression*. London: Sage.

Shadrina, M., Bondarenko, E. A. and Slominsky, P. A. (2018). Genetics Factors in Major Depression Disease. *Front. Psychiatry 9*(334). doi: 10.3389/fpsyt.2018.00334

Spruit, A., Goos, L., Weenink, N., Rodenburg, R., Niemeyer, H., Stams, G. J. and Colonnesi, C. (2020). The Relation Between Attachment and Depression in Children and Adolescents: A Multilevel Meta-Analysis. *Clinical child and family psychology review*, *23*(1), 54–69. https://doi.org/10.1007/s10567-019-00299-9

World Health Organisation (2019). *International Classification of Diseases* (11th Revision). ICD-11. Geneva: World Health Organisation. Available at https://icd.who.int/en

RECOMMENDED READING

Busch, F. N., Rudden, M. and Shapiro, T. (2016). *Psychodynamic Treatment of Depression*. Washington, DC: American Psychiatric Publishing.

This book provides a comprehensive overview of depression, especially in terms of biological and psychological vulnerabilities. The authors explore key psychodynamics principles and approaches to the treatment depression.

> Gilbert, P. (2009). *Overcoming Depression* (3rd ed.). London: Constable Robinson.
>
> Paul Gilbert provides a thorough and detailed examination of depression, with particular attention to cognitive-behavioural approaches to treatment and an emphasis on compassion-focused strategies.
>
> Sanders, P. and Hill, A. (2014). *Counselling for Depression: A Person-centred and Experiential Approach to Practice*. London: Sage.
>
> This book provides a fresh review and outline of the central features of humanistic and experiential approaches to working with depression. Emphasis is placed on practitioner competencies and on the value of research evidence.

4.8 *EATING DISORDERS*

GABRIEL WYNN

OVERVIEW AND KEY POINTS

Eating disorders are complex behavioural and emotional problems with potentially serious, and in some cases, life-threatening medical consequences. However, with caringly delivered evidence-based therapy, people with even severe eating disorders can recover and live full lives. This chapter focuses on anorexia, bulimia and binge eating disorder, which share core features, including episodic or prolonged dietary restraint; fear of weight gain and/or a desire to lose weight; and undue self-worth placed on control of eating, body weight and shape. Anorexia refers to mental and physical illness driven by obsessive desire to lose and suppress weight to below healthy norms. Bulimia is a syndrome comprised of periods of dietary restriction followed by episodic binge eating then attempts to purge food from the digestive tract. Binge eating disorder is similar to bulimia but without purgatory behaviour. It is not uncommon for a person to remain eating disordered over time due to the enduring presence of core maintaining factors, while their symptoms migrate through different diagnoses.

The key points addressed in this chapter are:

- Eating disorders are directly caused and maintained by core behavioural and cognitive processes.
- Certain family, demographic and social risk factors predispose some people to developing eating disorders.
- The good clinician is alert to the possibility of trauma comorbidity with people presenting for eating disorders treatment, and sensitively tailors their approach to the unique background and needs of the individual and their support network.

ASSESSMENT AND UNDERSTANDING

This section looks at screening and assessment along with maintaining and predisposing factors for eating disorders.

Initial screening for eating disorders can be carried out with tools such as the Eating Attitudes Test (EAT-26) (Garner et al., 1982). Following detection, use of evidence-based assessment questionnaires helps build a thorough picture of the nature, extent and effects of eating disorder symptoms. The Eating Disorders Examination (EDE) (Fairburn, Cooper and O'Connor, 2008) is a semi-structured interview schedule for people aged 14+ that directs clinical information gathering and scores for severity of eating disorder features. Clinicians are also well advised to screen for trauma (Brewerton, 2019) using tools such as the Life Events Checklist and Interview for DSM-5 (LEC-5) (Weathers et al., 2013). Following this, further screening may be advisable for post-traumatic stress and dissociation.

MAINTAINING FACTORS

We now look at core maintaining behavioural and cognitive factors and some of their physiological consequences.

MAINTAINING BEHAVIOURS

Intermittent or sustained deliberate dietary restriction with the aim of weight suppression is the primary maintaining behaviour in all eating disorders. Weight loss in adults to below body mass index 18, and in children and adolescents below the 10th percentile of those their age, leads to anorexia. Insufficient energy intake can cause reproductive hormone insufficiency, which in women may disrupt the menstrual cycle (amenorrhoea) and over time lead to bone loss (osteoporosis). While anorexia is a rare condition, it is estimated that up to 20% of people with anorexia die from system failure related to medical complications or suicide (Mitchell, Pomeroy and Adson, 1997).

Anorexia has two subtypes. In the 'binge-purge' subtype, binge eating and compensatory self-induced vomiting or laxative misuse are present. In the 'restrictive,' subtype, these behaviours are mostly absent. Binge eating occurs in all eating disorders except restrictive anorexia. Strong feelings of hunger or deprivation caused by dietary restriction lead to episodes of unrestrained eating, when thousands of calories may be consumed over a few hours. Binges are commonly followed by feelings of regret or shame, because an idealised state of rigid dietary self-control has been broken. People may attempt to reverse eating by making themselves sick, or to disrupt the digestive process by misusing laxatives. Self-induced vomiting leaves food in the stomach to be digested (Fairburn, 2008). Habitual vomiting can cause cardiac, gastrointestinal, dental and reproductive complications (Herzog and Eddy, 2007). Laxative misuse is entirely ineffectual in preventing energy absorption and poses serious health risks (Roerig et al., 2010). The ineffectiveness of purging in preventing energy absorption helps explain why weight in people with binge-purge eating patterns tends to fluctuate within normal ranges.

MAINTAINING COGNITIONS

People with eating disorders disproportionately invest self-worth in unsustainable or unhealthy weight or eating goals at the expense of more constructive aims in life. Morale and dignity are progressively diminished by negative health, emotional and relational consequences arising from pursuit of thinness. Fear of becoming fat generally intensifies with weight loss, becoming delusional at lower weights. Extreme hunger causes preoccupation with thoughts about food. Brain energy depletion causes cognitive rigidity, perseveration, indecisiveness, impaired concentration, anxiety, irritability, obsessiveness, ritualistic habits and social withdrawal. These cognitive changes serve to further maintain the eating disorder (Fairburn, 2008).

PREDISPOSING FACTORS

We now look at some family issues linked to the development of eating problems, and then explore demographic and social risk factors.

FAMILY

Eating disorders tend to aggregate in families. Family personality and behavioural influences may account for this. Perfectionism (Fairburn et al., 1997, 1999), exactness and obsessive-compulsive traits (Kaye et al., 1991; Lilenfeld et al., 1998) are risk factors in anorexia and bulimia. Parental alcohol problems (Fairburn et al., 1997) and depression (Fairburn et al., 1998) are risk factors for bulimia and binge eating. Parental body dissatisfaction and dieting pose long-term risks for all eating disorders (Haynos et al., 2016). Incest has been correlated with development of eating disorders (Wonderlich et al., 1996).

DEMOGRAPHIC

Eating disorders occur predominantly in women. Euro-American research around diagnosis and treatment of eating disorders predominantly focuses on psychopathology in white females. Popular eating disorder measures and treatment approaches may therefore be limited in their sensitivity to risk factors and symptomology for ethnically and racially minoritised women (Kelly et al., 2012). Eating disorders in women of colour may in some cases be more characterised by weight concern and purging as forms of self-control, than by dietary restriction for modifying shape or weight (Perez et al., 2021;

Serier, Smith and Yeater, 2018). Sexual minority youth (e.g., lesbian, gay, bisexual) report higher prevalence of eating disorders than heterosexual peers (Watson et al., 2016). In gender minority youth (e.g., transfeminine, transmasculine, genderqueer), gender incongruence and body dysphoria are associated with greater eating disorder symptomology than that experienced by cis-gendered peers (Diemer et al., 2015; Nowaskie et al., 2021; Roberts et al., 2021). Males and people of ethnically and racially minoritised background with eating disorder symptoms may be less likely than white females to receive a professional referral for specialist treatment (Andersen, 2014; Becker et al., 2003).

SOCIAL

Social risk factors can be broadly subdivided into fashion-generated body image dissatisfaction and forms of abuse driven by social inequalities.

It is generally accepted that cultures idealising female thinness and weight consciousness predispose girls and women to developing eating disorders. While these cultures are not limited to Europe and North America (Nasser, 1997), white middle-class Euro-American women have for centuries been 'expected to look and dress in ways that immobilize them' (Rothblum, 1994: 58). Beauty advertising created by and for women serves as psychological corsetry when women and girls adopt slimness virtue-signalling and fat-shaming of self and others. A survey conducted by the UK House of Commons Women and Equalities Commission (2021) found that social media advertising promoting diets, beauty products and cosmetic surgery are closely associated with poor body image in viewers. This report found anxieties were exacerbated during Covid-19 lockdown, possibly due to people spending more time watching social media content and less time engaged in social activity.

Taking these observations further, women's bodies have for centuries been subject to controls more violent than dieting. Unequal societies systemically generate unrecognised and unreported forms of gender- and race-based coercion and abuse of minoritised members. Casualties of these systems are compelled through shame or fear to keep quiet about what has been done to them – to 'wear the mask that grins and lies' (Dunbar, 2021: 157). People who speak out against abuse can be accused of complicity in their own mistreatment, or be expected to challenge the irremediable structures that permitted the abuse they have suffered.

Gender-sensitive adverse childhood experiences, including sexual abuse, are risk factors for all eating disorders, particularly bulimic forms, which function to regulate trauma-related emotional distress (Micali et al., 2017). Suppressed anger is associated with eating disorders (Waller et al., 2003). While anger is a natural response to abuse, and also to insufficient protection from abuse, notions of acceptable feminine behaviour quash anger (Cox, Stabb and Bruckner, 1999). Complex emotional responses to traumatic experiences can sometimes be overlooked or pathologised by mental health practitioners (Brewerton, Alexander and Schaefer, 2018).

WAYS OF WORKING WITH PEOPLE WITH EATING DISORDERS

This section looks at recommended approaches, formulation and treatment for eating disorders.

RECOMMENDED APPROACHES

The National Institute for Health and Care Excellence (NICE) (2017) advises self-help as the first step for bulimia and binge eating disorder (e.g., Fairburn, 2013) and outpatient therapies as the first step in the treatment of anorexia, including eating disorder-focused cognitive behaviour therapy (CBT-ED) (Fairburn, 2008) and Maudsley anorexia nervosa treatment for adults (MANTRA) (Schmidt, Wade and Treasure, 2014; for a self-help version called cognitive interpersonal therapy, see Schmidt, Startup and Treasure, 2019). Family-based approaches (FT-AN, FT-BN) (Lock and Le Grange, 2012) are recommended for children and young people, with respect to Gillick competence. A shortcoming of all these approaches is their neglect of commonly comorbid post-traumatic symptoms in eating disorders presentations.

For adults and children with low weight or other co-existing health or psychiatric difficulties, assessment and treatment should also be provided by appropriately trained medics in line with MARSIPAN guidance (Royal College of Psychiatrists, 2012, 2014). There is little scientific evidence that psychotropic medications are helpful in the treatment of anorexia. There is some evidence that selective serotonin reuptake inhibitors may be helpful in reducing binge eating in adults (NICE, 2017).

Specialist dietitians can provide advice and support with refeeding people with anorexia, and for metabolic conditions including diabetes, and digestive issues such as coeliac and irritable bowel syndromes. The outpatient therapist must collaborate closely with allied professionals, and promptly refer on to more intensive services where indicated.

FORMULATION AND TREATMENT

Formulation enables a collaborative, evolving understanding between the person seeking help and therapist of how specific behaviours and thoughts maintain specific problems. Formulation also promotes agreement about the changes required to achieve the person's goals. Early psychoeducation helps the person, and their family where helpful, to understand how their weight control efforts are counterproductive to emotional and physical wellbeing.

Following initial formulation, it is helpful to position behavioural change first, with the aim of restoring regular eating patterns. With children and adolescents, the therapist may teach parents to actively manage their child's eating at family mealtimes, and then gradually transition control back to the child (Lock and Le Grange, 2012). Regular eating gradually reverses emaciation and malnutrition in anorexia and eliminates hunger and deprivation as primary causes of binge eating in bulimia and binge eating disorder. Purging typically self-resolves with the cessation of binge eating. Improved energy intake naturally ameliorates psychological problems, including depression and anxiety. Then effective work can be done on the key cognitive task of replacing weight control with more meaningful expressions of personal value. Good therapy will devote time to helping people build and strengthen generative ties with meaningful others, because healthy long-term relationships supply a potent basis for self-worth and recovery from emotional ill health. Developing tolerance of strong moods and difficult events with minimal eating disturbance is another important task of recovery. An effective course of eating disorders therapy may take six weeks to 12 months to complete, while therapy encompassing trauma work may take longer.

CASE STUDIES

A TRAUMA-INFORMED APPROACH

Kiefer is a 33-year-old trans man of mixed Irish and Tobagoan heritage. Kiefer was cut off as a child from his Black Tobagoan extended family and rarely saw his father, who moved to Canada when Kiefer was 5 years old. Kiefer was subject to racialised harassment through secondary school, which his white mother did not fully acknowledge or deal with proactively. As a prepubescent girl, Kiefer was sexually abused by an adult male friend of his mother's. Kiefer was not believed when he later told his mother what her friend had done to him. Kiefer developed anorexia at age 14, which evolved to bulimia when he was 16. Kiefer now believes his eating disorder expressed his wish to suppress breast development and menstruation. He kept his eating disorder a secret from his mother and younger sister, and later from the medics handling his transition, who did not assess for eating disorders or trauma. Kiefer's mother and sister were indifferent to Kiefer's transition and did not offer support when he experienced painful post-surgical complications.

Kiefer's drive to reduce body fat through starvation resolved following transition. As he adopted regular eating patterns, the bulimia spontaneously remitted. However, through his 20s Kiefer drank alcohol and took cocaine regularly, and continued to experience episodic binge eating. He entered therapy after he verbally abused his partner Jessa in a drunken row, for which he felt intense remorse. Early in therapy Kiefer's therapist conducted a trauma assessment. The results informed their formulation and priorities for trauma-informed eating disorders therapy. Kiefer explained his therapy goal as:

> By resolutely reconstructing myself, I survived racial and gender ambiguity and disintegration in my late teens. I must now face my legitimate anger about being an unprotected child, whose wounds were not recognised. I want to care for myself in ways I was not cared for, without using drugs or food for comfort. I must learn not to reject or hurt Jessa, who loves me better than anyone else in my life.

Kiefer established new stress-relieving routines to avoid episodic binge eating and committed to not drinking alcohol at home. The therapist conducted four joint sessions with Kiefer and Jessa to help them explore and deepen trust in their relationship. The therapist rounded out Keifer's therapy with a course of narrative exposure therapy (Schauer, Neuner and Elbert, 2011). Kiefer documented his entire life story. The therapist paid empathic witness to Kiefer's pain throughout this work, which he found healing. The process also validated his significant personal creativity and emotional resourcefulness. Follow-up appointments were held at three, six and 12 months. Over this time, Keifer reconnected with family members in Tobago. He continued to integrate his life experiences with regular compassion-focused meditation practice.

REFERENCES

Andersen, A.E. (2014). Diagnosis and treatment of males with eating disorders. In A.E. Andersen (Ed.), *Males with Eating Disorders* (pp. 133–162). London: Routledge.

Becker, A.E., Franco, D.L., Speck, A. & Herzog, D.B. (2003). Ethnicity and differential access to care for eating disorder symptoms. *International Journal of Eating Disorders*, 33, 205–212. doi: 10.1002/eat.10129

Brewerton, T.D. (2019). An overview of trauma-informed care and practice for eating disorders. *Journal of Aggression, Maltreatment & Trauma*, 28(4), 445–462. doi: 10.1080/10926771.2018.1532940

Brewerton, T.D., Alexander, J. & Schaefer, J. (2018). Trauma-informed care and practice for eating disorders: Personal and professional perspectives of lived experiences. *Eating and Weight Disorder: Studies of Anorexia, Bulimia and Obesity*, 2, 329–338. doi: 10.1007/s40519-018-0628-5

Cox, D., Stabb, S. & Bruckner, K. (1999). *Women's Anger: Clinical and Developmental Perspectives*. London: Routledge.

Diemer, E., Grant, J.D., Munn-Chernoff, M., Patterson, D.A. & Duncan, A.E. (2015). Gender identity, sexual orientation, and eating-related pathology in a national sample of college students. *Journal of Adolescent Health*, 57(2), 144–149. doi: 10.1016/j.jadohealth.2015.03.003

Dunbar, P.L. (2021). *The Complete Poems of Paul Laurence Dunbar*. Corby, UK: Mint.

Fairburn, C.G. (2008). *Cognitive Behavior Therapy and Eating Disorders*. New York: Guilford Press.

Fairburn, C.G. (2013). *Overcoming Binge Eating* (2nd ed.). New York: Guilford Press.

Fairburn, C.G., Cooper, Z., Doll, H.A. & Welch, S.L. (1999). Risk factors for anorexia nervosa: Three integrated case-control comparisons. *Archives of General Psychiatry*, 56(5), 468–476.

Fairburn, C.G., Cooper, Z. & O'Connor, M.E. (2008). Eating Disorder Examination (EDE 16.0D). In C.G. Fairburn (Ed.), *Cognitive Behavior Therapy and Eating Disorders* (pp. 265–308). New York: Guilford Press.

Fairburn, C.G., Welch, S.L., Doll, H.A., et al. (1997). Risk factors for bulimia nervosa: A community-based case-control study. *Archives of General Psychiatry*, 54, 509–517.

Fairburn, C.G., Welch, S.L., Doll, H.A., et al. (1998). Risk factors for binge eating disorder: A community-based, case-control study. *Archives of General Psychiatry*, 55, 425–432.

Garner, D.M, Olmsted, M.P., Bohr, Y. & Garfinkel, D.E. (1982). Eating Attitudes Test: Psychometric features and clinical correlates. *Psychological Medicine*, 12(4), 871–878. doi: 10.1017/S0033291700049163

Haynos, A.F., Watts, A.W., Loth, K.A., Pearson, C.M. & Newmark-Stzainen, D. (2016). Factors predicting an escalation of restrictive eating during adolescence. *Journal of Adolescent Health*, 59, 391–396. doi: 10.1016/j.jadohealth.2016.03.011

Herzog, D.B. & Eddy, K.T. (2007). Diagnosis, epidemiology and clinical course of eating disorders. In J. Yager and P.S. Powers (Eds), *Clinical Manual of Eating Disorders* (pp. 1–30). Washington, DC: American Psychiatric Publishing.

(Continued)

(Continued)

House of Commons Women and Equalities Commission (2021). *Changing the Perfect Picture: An Enquiry into Body Image*. London: House of Commons. Available at https://committees.parliament.uk/publications/5357/documents/53751/default/

Kaye, W.H., Gwirtsman, H.E., George, D.T. & Ebert, M.H. (1991). Altered serotonin activity in anorexia nervosa after long-term weight restoration. *Archives of General Psychiatry*, 48(6), 556–562.

Kelly, N.R., Mitchell, K.S., Gow, R.W., Trace, S.E., Lydecker, J.A., Bair, C.E. & Mazzeo, S. (2012). An evaluation of the reliability and construct validity of eating disorder measures in white and black women. *Psychological Assessment*, 24(3), 608–617. doi: 10.1037/a0026457

Lilenfeld, L.R., Kaye, W.H., Greeno, C.G., et al. (1998). A controlled family study of anorexia nervosa and bulimia nervosa. *Archives of General Psychiatry*, 55, 603–610.

Lock, J. & Le Grange, D. (2012). *Treatment Manual for Anorexia Nervosa: A Family-based Approach* (2nd ed.). New York: Guilford Press.

Micali, N., Martini, M.G., Thomas, J.J., Eddy, K.T., Kothari, R., Russell, E., Bulik, C.M. & Treasure, J. (2017). Lifetime and 12-month prevalence of eating disorders amongst women in mid-life: A population-based study of diagnoses and risk factors. *BMC Medicine*, 15(12). doi: 10.1186/s12916-016-0766-4

Mitchell, J.E., Pomeroy, C. & Adson, D.E. (1997). Managing medical complications. In D.M. Garner and P.E. Garfinkel (Eds), *Handbook of Treatment for Eating Disorders* (2nd ed., pp. 383–393). New York: Guilford Press.

Nasser, M. (1997). *Culture and Weight Consciousness*. London: Routledge.

National Institute for Health and Care Excellence (NICE) (2017). *Eating Disorders: Recognition and treatment*. [Clinical Guidance NG69]. London: NICE. Available at www.nice.org.uk/guidance/ng69

Nowaskie, D.Z., Filipowicz, A.T., Choi, Y. & Fogel, J.M. (2021). Eating disorder symptomology and transgender patients: Differences across gender identity and gender affirmation. *International Journal of Eating Disorders*, 54, 1493–1499. doi: 10.1002/eat.23539

Perez, M., Perko, V., Yu, K.Y., Hernandez, J.C., Ohrt, T.K. & Stadheim, J. (2021). Identifying central symptoms of eating disorders among ethnic and racial minority women. *Journal of Abnormal Psychology*, 130(7), 748–760. doi: 10.1037/abn0000695

Roberts, S.R., Salk, R.H., Thoma, B.C., Romito, M., Levine, M.D. & Choukas-Bradley, S. (2021). Disparities in disordered eating between gender minority and cisgender adolescents. *International Journal of Eating Disorders*, 54, 1135–1146. doi: 10.1002/eat.23494

Roerig, J., Steffen, K., Mitchell, J. & Zunker, C. (2010). Laxative misuse. *Drugs*, 70(12), 1487–1503.

Rothblum, E.D. (1994). 'I'll die for the revolution but don't ask me not to diet': Feminism and the continuing stigmatization of obesity. In In P. Fallon, M.A. Katzman & S.C. Wooley (Eds), *Feminist Perspectives on Eating Disorders* (pp. 53–76). New York: Guilford Press.

Royal College of Psychiatrists (2012). *Junior MARSIPAN: Management of Really Sick Patients under 18 with Anorexia Nervosa*. London: Royal College of Psychiatrists.

Royal College of Psychiatrists, Royal College Physicians, Royal College of Pathologists (2014). *MARSIPAN: Management of Really Sick Patients with Anorexia Nervosa* (2nd ed.). London: Royal College of Psychiatrists.

Schauer, M., Neuner, F. & Elbert, T. (2011). *Narrative Exposure Therapy: A Short Term Treatment for Traumatic Stress Disorders* (2nd ed.). Gottingen, Germany: Hogrefe.

Schmidt, U., Startup, H. & Treasure, J. (2019). *A Cognitive Interpersonal Therapy Workbook for Treating Anorexia Nervosa*. Abingdon, UK: Routledge.

Schmidt, U., Wade, T.D. & Treasure, J. (2014). The Maudsley model of anorexia nervosa treatment for adults (MANTRA): Development, key features, and preliminary evidence. *Journal of Cognitive Psychotherapy*, 28(1), 48–71. doi: 10.1891/0889-8391.28.1.48

Serier, K.N., Smith, J.E. & Yeater, E.A. (2018). Confirmatory factor analysis and measurement invariance of the Eating Disorder Examination Questionnaire (EDE-Q) in a non-clinical sample of non-Hispanic White and Hispanic women. *Eating Behavior*, 31, 53–59. doi: 10.1016/j.eatbeh.2018.08.004

Waller, G., Babbs, M., Milligan, R., Meyer, C. Ohanian, V. & Leung, N. (2003). Anger and core beliefs in the eating disorders. *International Journal of Eating Disorders*, 34(1), 118–124. doi: 10.1002/eat.10163

Watson, R.J., Adjei, J., Saewye, E., Homma, Y. & Goodenow, C. (2016). Trends and disparities in disordered eating among heterosexual and sexual minority adolescents. *International Journal of Eating Disorders*, 50(1), 22–31. doi: 10.1002/eat.22576

Weathers, F.W., Blake, D.D., Schnurr, P.P., Kaloupek, D.G., Marx, B.P., & Keane, T.M. (2013). *The Life Events Checklist for DSM-5 (LEC-5)*. Washington, DC: US Department of Veteran Affairs. Available at www.ptsd.va.gov

Wonderlich, S., Donaldson, M.A., Carson, D.K., Staton, D., Gertz, L., Leach, L.R. & Johnson, M. (1996). Eating disorders and incest. *Journal of Interpersonal Violence*, 11(2), 195–207. doi: 10.1177/088626096011002004

RECOMMENDED READING

Fairburn, C.G. (2008). *Cognitive Behavior Therapy and Eating Disorders*. New York: Guilford Press.

This landmark text details transdiagnostic theory and individual cognitive behavioural treatment protocol for adults and adolescents with eating disorders.

Lock, J. & Le Grange, D. (2012). *Treatment Manual for Anorexia Nervosa: A Family-based Approach* (2nd ed.). New York: Guilford Press.

Lock and Le Grange's family therapy approach is better-known as the 'Maudsley model'.

BEAT (2019). Best practice in the engagement and empowerment of families and carers affected by eating disorders. July. Available at https://beat.contentfiles.net/media/documents/family-empowerment-guidance-1_fP1wHWr.pdf

This paper proposes a series of best practice standards for adoption by all health care providers offering eating disorder services.

4.9 HEARING VOICES

JOACHIM SCHNACKENBERG

OVERVIEW AND KEY POINTS

The experience of hearing voices has long been pathologised and problematised in western mental health services. It was assumed to be a key symptom of a diagnosis of schizophrenia or psychosis, which were in turn conceptualised and assumed to be primarily biological in origin. As a consequence, hearing voices was not considered to be an experience that was understandable and meaningful within the person's life context and was best attempted to be eradicated, ideally with the help of antipsychotic medication. Counselling was explicitly not considered to be helpful for people who were distressed by their experience of hearing voices, seeing visions or having unshared realities.

This pathologising and problematising understanding of hearing voices, seeing visions and having unshared realities has been questioned in recent decades and it is now clear in the specialised research and practice communities that it is not the voices, visions or unshared realities that are a problem in themselves, nor that they are symptoms of an illness. They are just what they are: experiences. Instead, it is the way that the experiencer and people around them relate to the experience of voices, visions and unshared realities that can determine whether a person can become overwhelmed by the experience or not. The less avoidant a person and the people around them relate to the experience and associated feelings and thoughts the less overwhelmed the person will be by the experience and the less likely they will be given a mental health diagnosis (Schnackenberg, Iusco and Debesay, 2021). It is now also well established that hearing voices, seeing visions and having unshared realities and being distressed by the experience regularly occurs within a person's life context, with the impact of, and relationship to trauma – and not faulty biology – being a much more likely contributor to the development and ongoing distress associated with these experiences (Van Os et al., 2018; Varese et al., 2012).

Hearing voices is also not confined to a particular diagnosis, such as psychosis or schizophrenia, as was long believed. Instead, it occurs across diagnoses (Waters and Fernyhough, 2017) and none, as most people who hear voices never have any contact with mental health services and find their own way of coping with the experience (Parker, Schnackenberg and Hopfenbeck, 2021). Another key practice experience for some practitioners has been that approaches that are helpful in relation to voices can easily be adapted to working with visions, other sensory experiences and unshared realities. However, to ease readability, this chapter will focus on hearing voices. It will outline some key understandings and ways of working when people are distressed by the experience of hearing voices:

- What is it like to hear voices?
- Recognising and assessing distress in relation to the voice hearing experience.
- Current conceptualisations of hearing voices.
- Ways of working with hearing voices.

ASSESSMENT AND UNDERSTANDING

WHAT IS IT LIKE TO HEAR VOICES?

It is important to understand that although it is likely in mental health and psychotherapeutic or counselling services that clients who present with voices are distressed by their experience, this is not, in fact, the case for the majority of people. As a result, most voice hearers are not using mental health or counselling services.

There may be different ways for a non-voice hearer to try to get an understanding of what the experience is like and how it is both very different and yet not so different from the experiences of people who have not yet heard voices. The obvious and first port of call should of course be to simply ask and take seriously what voice hearers themselves say about what the experience is like. This has not been and continues not to be the norm in mental health and counselling services.

There are additional ways of gaining an understanding of this experience in a more general sense (not specific to an individual client). Two are introduced here.

a) The hearing voices exercise
This exercise, or a variant of it, was first invented by a well-known voice hearer who recovered from a diagnosis of chronic schizophrenia, Ron Coleman. It is best experienced as part of a hearing voices training, although if all are voluntarily agreed it could be tried out among colleagues too. Key to it is that everyone should only partake voluntarily after the exercise has been explained beforehand. In this exercise, two people attempt to have a conversation about an ordinary everyday subject, while one person has one or two or even more people speaking into their ears at the same time. It is important to include a fair degree of nasty and personalised comments about the person who is hearing these 'voices', such as 'loser', 'waste of space', 'failure' and even stronger nasty comments. It is helpful if the participants in this exercise can try to keep going for about 2–4 minutes and also informally or formally debrief about what it was like afterwards. Engaging in a reflection afterwards, where one imagines having this very same or a type of this kind of experience

over longer periods, that is, hours, days, weeks, months, years, can help to increase awareness of the impact of the experience on various aspects of daily life. This may include the ability to communicate or think clearly, how one feels about oneself and the world, how possible it is to engage in work and relationships, and so on. The reflection will highlight the central role that voices can play in understanding a person's current distress. It will suddenly become clear how little influence one can end up feeling about one's own behaviour, communication or even thinking.

b) Relating to one's own experience of conflict

It may also be helpful to remember or focus on what it is like for us to be experiencing unresolved conflicts in our own minds. We may, for example, have had a strong disagreement with our boss or our partner and the conflict remains unresolved. We might still be feeling really wronged or strongly intimidated by the other party. If, and when, we carefully observe what happens in our own minds once we have left the actual conflicting communication, we may discover that we are carrying on having the argument with the other party in our heads. We may be putting arguments forward against what we feel they are saying or feel they had actually wanted to say without saying it. We may become quite verbally or physically abusive in our minds towards the other side in response. Or we may be feeling so scared and intimidated that we are experiencing ourselves as just a small vulnerable child that would ideally just like to hide away. Hearing voices can feel very similar to having such a conflict going on in one's mind the whole time. Understanding how tiring, energy zapping and all-consuming such unresolved conflicts can make us feel may give a little taste of what it can be like to hear voices all or some of the time. It is no surprise, then, that voice hearers can recount the experience as being potentially all-consuming, overwhelming, frightening, threatening and as something that is best not to look at too closely.

HOW TO RECOGNISE AND ASSESS WHETHER SOMEONE IS HEARING VOICES AND DISTRESSED BY THE EXPERIENCE

In practice, it can be both very easy and difficult to spot whether someone might be hearing voices. It may also be important to remember that many voice hearers will not call their voice hearing experience 'voices', but something else, because of the stigma associated with it both in society and among mental health professionals. They will often understandably fear being declared 'mad' and in 'need of medication', 'non-understandable', 'non-curable' and/or in need of them to be taken to hospital or to stay in hospital until they do not complain of their voice hearing experience anymore. As a result, many voice hearers have developed alternative language instead, such as having telepathic abilities, being in contact with God, gods, spirits, the CIA, animals, etc. They may also describe it as having inner parts, the subconscious, their own thoughts, etc. It is then normally helpful to use the kind of vocabulary and language used by the person having these experiences. A person who is distressed by the experience will often speak of it as them being under some kind of control or influence by something outside their own will.

Once it is clear that the person hears voices and wants to explore and speak about the experience a little more, it is important to note that there are few good, standardised assessments available that might give a detailed understanding of the experience. Research tools commonly used to assess the impact of different approaches mostly remain fairly superficial in their ability to gain an in-depth understanding.

Therefore, in practice, one of the main tools developed within the Hearing Voices Movement (HVM) (a civil rights movement led by a voice hearer and active professionals that engages in social action and proposes new and non-pathologising ways of approaching the experience), the semi-structured Maastricht Interview (Romme and Escher, 2000), might represent one of the best ways of gaining a good understanding of the potentially far-reaching impact and relevance of the experience within the voice hearer's life context. It explores the nature of the experience, the personal history in relation to the voices and the experience in everyday life (for more detail, see Romme and Escher, 2000; Schnackenberg et al., 2021).

It can also be a particularly useful way of bringing increasing order into what can often feel like an overwhelming chaos produced by the experience of hearing voices. The central focus on hearing voices and their role in a person's life will regularly also make clear (in combination with the experience of the hearing voices exercise described above) how experiences like anxiety, depression, seemingly disjointed thinking, having non-shared realities, etc. can frequently be seen as being strongly connected with the experience of hearing voices. For example, a voice hearer may find it difficult to think clearly, if voices are constantly interrupting their flow of thought. It is also not hard to understand that a person may end up feeling that they are the devil if a voice constantly tells them that the world is going to end because of them.

CONCEPTUALISATIONS OF HEARING VOICES

As indicated above, hearing voices was for a long time conceptualised as a largely passive experience caused by hypothesised (never well evidenced) biological illness processes. It was even defined as being beyond a person's own control, meaning the person could ultimately only hope that professionals would find a suitable medication that would subdue the voices or get rid of them. In this context, it is also not surprising that both within society and among mental health professionals there often exists a great fear and/or helplessness. Commanding voices are often considered to be particularly dangerous. This kind of mindset and practice is still widespread, and changes come about only slowly. However, there are now many talk-based individual and group approaches, as well as social action initiatives, available. These have been developed and propelled forward by people with lived experience and professionals who are particularly interested in moving beyond a still dominant biologising paradigm of chronic illness towards a truly recovery-focused way of working (Parker et al., 2021).

As indicated above, it is now clear that hearing voices in itself is never actually the main problem or decider on whether a person feels distressed by the experience, as had long been believed and is still widely practised. It is instead the nature of the relationship and the degree of constructiveness in how both voice hearer and accompanying persons relate to the experience that will decide on whether a person feels the need for support or not. Just how far the discussion has come may be best highlighted with the example of a person hearing commanding voices telling them to kill themselves. This would have normally been an automatic reason for the people around them to be alarmed and possibly to make sure the person goes into hospital, with an assumption that nothing good could come out of this experience.

However, approaching this same experience with a new mindset can now lead to understanding that the voice can be used positively, and in some approaches can even be actively worked with to understand that the voice may only intend to encourage the voice hearer to change their life for the better (Romme et al., 2009). Killing oneself could, for example, come to be understood as an encouragement to try to significantly change the way that the person goes about living their life – when they are actually unhappy with it. Killing another person could turn out to be a call to significantly change the nature of an unhelpful relationship. The HVM approach therefore advocates for an awareness that voices, too, just like people, do communicate by using metaphors, symbols and exaggerations. And just like in person-to-person communication, the use of metaphors, symbols and exaggerations is more likely to be employed by a person/voice when they feel that they have got something vitally important to say that has not yet been heard properly by the other party. It makes sense that strong expressions of communication are used at that point, to get through to the other side (Schnackenberg et al., 2021).

The different ways of understanding and normalising the experience of hearing voices across different approaches therefore includes conceptualising them as being expressions of dissociation or even being able to cause dissociation; they might be metaphors, exaggerations or symbols; they could also be considered part of a subconscious process; they express unwanted emotions and thoughts; or they could also be experiences that are not ultimately important to clearly define, as it might be more important to go with the understanding of the voice hearer themselves (Parker et al., 2021).

WAYS OF WORKING WITH HEARING VOICES

The degree of change in both research and practice in relation to hearing voices taking place in recent years has been breath-taking. Accordingly, a variety of new approaches is available. These include community and social action initiatives, many of which are spearheaded by people with lived experience. Group-based approaches have also developed, of a self-help nature and co-led with a professional, and professionally led groups. There are also several new individualised approaches, with some developed from existing approaches, and some seemingly entirely or largely new. These include cognitive behavioural approaches, mindfulness, compassion-focused therapy, experience-focused counselling (EFC) *aka* Making Sense of Voices (MsV), as well as creative approaches, such as the use of drama and music therapy. Some of these approaches have already acquired a fairly robust classic evidence base, some have a developing evidence base, and some are mostly anecdotal. All have in common that they have gone into areas long thought not possible, spurred on, largely, by a desire to improve the life and mental health service experience of people who are distressed by their hearing voices experience (Parker et al., 2021).

As different people prefer different styles of working, it may be good to be familiar with more than one approach and use them eclectically, depending on the client's preference at a given time. It should be clear that all these approaches should be engaged with as part of a trusting and safe feeling relationship. A fairly comprehensive overview can be found in *The Practical Handbook of Hearing Voices* (Parker et al., 2021). Training and supervision in many of these approaches would be helpful and advisable before engaging in them.

In the following, EFC is used to demonstrate a case example, as it encompasses many of the assumptions of other approaches and goes even further in its ways of working and conclusions. It is also the main approach advocating the possibility of working with voices independently of any given mental health diagnosis.

EXPERIENCE-FOCUSED COUNSELLING

While the classic evidence base is still developing, though promising, EFC/MsV represents an approach that is particularly endorsed by many in the Hearing Voices Movement. A usual EFC approach, though it should always be adapted to the individual needs of the person who has the voice hearing experience, might look as follows:

Starting assumption: hearing voices are not a symptom of a disease, but a normal, human experience that can be understood in the context of life events. Voices are often found to be positive in intention or can at least be used positively. The process should be as client-led as possible. There are four main tools available, alongside the regular focus on improving one's ways of relating to the voices. These are:

1. The **Maastricht Interview (semi-structured)**: open conversation about the voices and experiences with a focus on subjective meaning and context of the experience.
2. The **Maastricht Report**: a written report of the contents of the interview using the language of the voice-hearing person.
3. The **Maastricht Construct**: a collaborative client-led process seeking a subjective and meaningful explanatory model regarding the voice-hearing experience in the context of the voice hearer's life and based on the interview and report.
4. The **use of constructive talking with voices**: indirect or direct dialogue of the person or accompanying person with the voices is possible with the aim to find out what the voices want to say and what potentially positive function they may have in a person's life.

CASE STUDY

Ruth, 38, has been given a diagnosis of an eating disorder (anorexia) and body dysmorphic disorder. She has been hearing voices since she was a child but never told anyone about them out of fear of being declared insane. She has had various psychiatric hospital stays as well as experiences of psychotherapy, and continues to have ongoing struggles with eating and her body image. While she has, on the surface, become a successful person – holding down a job, engaging in various social projects, and is married with children – she also continues to experience regular depths of self-loathing and despair and has actively attempted to take her life on several occasions.

As part of the Maastricht Interview, it becomes clear that she hears 10 voices, most of these have remained the same since her childhood. As she allows herself to consider the possible positive meaning of the voices as part of the Maastricht Construct process, she is starting to ask the voices – with support by the EFC professional – what they want. All the voices make clear that they want her to live a life free of the fears, self-loathing and shame associated with her traumatic experiences, which she has been slow to acknowledge

(Continued)

(Continued)

out of an understandable fear of being emotionally overwhelmed. They say they want her to be free of being overwhelmed by feelings of shame and guilt. Specifically, three of the voices introduce themselves as guardians of a truth about her personal experiences that are too unbearable for Ruth to look at so far. They do feel that she could hear this truth, although they do also acknowledge that Ruth has decided that she is not ready to hear it (yet). Other voices are cautioning Ruth not to go to certain traumatic memories as it would be too much for her to bear. Still others encourage her to live her life freely and assertively.

REFLECTIVE NOTE:

During further discussions with Ruth, it becomes clear that the voices can be seen as a mirror of the various feelings, inner movements, dynamics, inner conflicts, etc. that Ruth experiences. These are very akin to what survivors of long-standing interpersonal trauma might be describing, even without voices. It is thus for Ruth to identify and decide whether and which aspect she would like to work on next. This may include practising her assertiveness skills, making decisions led less by fear than thus far, learning to accept feelings of shame and guilt rather than avoiding them, and thus being less overwhelmed by them, etc.

REFERENCES

Parker, I., Schnackenberg, J. & Hopfenbeck, M. (2021). *The Practical Handbook of Hearing Voices: Therapeutic and Creative Approaches*. Monmouth: PCCS Books.

Romme, M. & Escher, S. (2000). *Making Sense of Voices*. London: Mind Publications.

Romme, M., Escher, S., Dillon, J., Corstens, D. & Morris, M. (Eds) (2009). *Living with Voices: 50 Stories of Recovery*. Monmouth: PCCS Books.

Schnackenberg, J.K., Iusco, O.-M. & Debesay, S. (2021). Experience focused counselling (Making Sense of Voices). In I. Parker, J. Schnackenberg & M. Hopfenbeck (Eds), *The Practical Handbook of Hearing Voices. Therapeutic and Creative Approaches*. Monmouth: PCCS Books.

Van Os, J. (2018). *Environmental factors in schizophrenia*. Talk given at the conference, 'Schizophrenie im Dialog' ('Schizophrenia in Dialogue'), RWTH Aachen University, Germany, 11 January.

Varese, F., Smeets, F., Drukker, M., Lieverse, R., Lataster, T., Viechtbauer, W., Read, J., van Os, J. & Bentall, R.P. (2012). Childhood adversities increase the risk of psychosis: A meta-analysis of patient-control, prospective- and cross-sectional cohort studies. *Schizophrenia Bulletin*, 38(4), 661–671.

Waters, F. & Fernyhough, C. (2017). Hallucinations: A systematic review of points of similarity and difference across diagnostic classes. *Schizophrenia Bulletin*, 43(1), 32–43.

RECOMMENDED READING

Parker, I., Schnackenberg, J. & Hopfenbeck, M. (Eds) (2021). *The Practical Handbook of Hearing Voices: Therapeutic and Creative Approaches*. Monmouth: PCCS Books.

This edited book offers the most comprehensive overview of the various psychosocial approaches and directions that have been developed in recent years to work in non-medical ways with voice hearers.

> Romme, M. & Escher, S. (2000). *Making Sense of Voices*. London: Mind Publications.
>
> This book lays out the theoretical and practical foundation of the individual approach of the Hearing Voices Movement (EFC aka MsV).
>
> Romme, M., Escher, S., Dillon, J., Corstens, D. & Morris, M. (Eds) (2009). *Living with Voices: 50 Stories of Recovery*. Monmouth: PCCS Books.
>
> This edited book summarises many of the theoretical and practical insights in relation to the role of voice hearing in recovery, exemplified with 50 inspiring personal stories of voice hearers recovering from the distress associated with voice hearing.

4.10 LOW SELF-ESTEEM

SOHA DARU

OVERVIEW AND KEY POINTS

Self-esteem is a significant part of our daily life and interactions and reflects the experiences we have with our social surroundings, such as those with friends, family and at work. High self-esteem enables us to persevere in times of difficulty, promotes resilience (Liu et al., 2014), while also predicting wellbeing and success in domains such as health, work and relationships (Orth and Robins, 2014). Conversely, low self-esteem is associated with various mental health problems, such as depression, suicidal tendencies, eating disorders, anxiety, violence and substance abuse (Henriksen et al., 2017). Considering the link with mental health, understanding the concept of low self-esteem and ways to work with it is important for us as psychological therapists. In this context, this chapter aims to cover the following:

- What is self-esteem?
- A few ways to assess and understand it.
- Conceptualisation of Fennell's (1997) model of low self-esteem.
- A case example to illustrate understanding and managing low self-esteem.
- Ways of working with low self-esteem using approaches such as cognitive behaviour therapy (CBT), Acceptance and Commitment Therapy (ACT) and compassion-focused therapy (CFT).

ASSESSMENT AND UNDERSTANDING: WHAT IS SELF-ESTEEM?

The 'self' encompasses one's emotions, thoughts, behaviours, sensations and urges (Oliver and Bennett, 2020). The word 'esteem' originates from 'estimate', denoting evaluation or judgement (Oliver and Bennett, 2020). According to Rosenberg (1965), self-esteem indicates self-respect, self-acceptance and satisfaction with oneself. Others argue that self-esteem reflects how people feel about themselves (Webb, 2019), or the degree to which they evaluate themselves positively compared to others (Harter, 1999). Taking into account a cultural worldview, as well as factors such as age, ethnicity, gender etc., is crucial when understanding and assessing self-esteem (Harris and Orth, 2020). For instance, cultural differences might underlie how self-esteem is constructed and to what extent people evaluate themselves positively (Salzman, 2018). Further, authors disagree on the extent to which self-esteem fluctuates or remains relatively stable across time (Schiraldi, 2016). Various studies discuss the causes of low self-esteem, although Lachmann (2013) captures these briefly to include disapproving authority figures, uninvolved or preoccupied caregivers, bullying, trauma, unhelpful belief systems, and unrealistic messages from society and the media.

The phrase self-esteem is related to a few others and is sometimes used interchangeably with terms such as self-worth, self-concept, self-evaluation, self-confidence, self-efficacy and self-appraisal (Brown and Marshall, 2006). However, many authors differentiate between these terms (Webb, 2019), for example, self-confidence and self-competence are seen as superordinate to self-esteem (Brown and Marshall, 2006). Some use the term 'state' self-esteem when referring to self-worth, indicating that these feelings are less enduring when compared to global self-esteem, which is more lasting (Leary, et al. 1995). Another related term, self-compassion, will be discussed in a later section of this chapter.

ASSESSING SELF-ESTEEM

The most commonly used self-report scale to assess or measure low self-esteem is the Rosenberg Self-Esteem Scale, developed by Morris Rosenberg (1965). It measures global self-esteem and assesses positive and negative feelings about the self, including feeling valued and worthy (Rosenberg, 1965). It is a 10-item scale where the items are answered using a four-point Likert scale format ranging from strongly agree to strongly disagree.

Other scales measuring self-esteem include the Self-Esteem Inventory (Coopersmith, 1967), the Self-Perception Profile (Harter, 2012), and the Self-Description Questionnaire (Marsh, 1990).

FENNELL'S COGNITIVE BEHAVIOURAL MODEL OF LOW SELF-ESTEEM

Fennell's cognitive behavioural model of low self-esteem (Fennell, 1997) is based on Beck's (1976) original cognitive model of emotional disorders. The model proposes that innate factors (such as temperament) and life experiences influence an individual's perceptions about themselves, others and the world. These perceptions (also called core beliefs) impact how people make sense of their life experiences. In people with relatively low self-esteem, there could be a general feeling of inadequacy or more specific beliefs such as 'I am unworthy', 'I am not good enough', 'I am worthless' or 'I am unlovable' (Fennell, 1997). Such beliefs lead to the development of certain rules or dysfunctional assumptions which permit maintaining self-esteem only as long as they are met (Fennell, 2005). If these rules are not met, the beliefs are activated and maintained. Activation of these beliefs leads to negative predictions, which trigger anxiety and may lead to various maladaptive behaviours, such as avoidance, safety-seeking behaviours (Salkovskis, 1991), aggression and substance abuse (Fennell, 2005). In the case where negative predictions are disconfirmed and the outcome is positive, this information is potentially dismissed or ignored instead of signalling that the core belief might be incorrect. The consequence is confirmation of the core belief. This leads to self-criticism or hopelessness and depressed mood, which may be temporary or become persistent and severe. In this manner, the cycle perpetuates, and depressions seeks to fuel it. The following case example illustrates this.

CASE STUDY

Maya is a 33-year-old mother of a young boy aged 4. She lives with her partner and son and describes her partner as being 'supportive'. She works part-time as a support worker and has recently enrolled on a training course to be a professional counsellor. Maya contacted a therapist soon after starting her counselling training as she was struggling with the course and questioning her decision to train as a therapist. She described feeling anxious and low in mood a lot of the time and had difficulty sleeping. During the first few counselling sessions, Maya shared a few childhood experiences of neglect, bullying and lack of validation. She had developed core beliefs such as 'I am a failure' and 'I am not good enough'. To cope with these distressing beliefs, she had subconsciously created certain rules or assumptions, which were, 'I have to be in control in order to relax' and 'I need to complete tasks perfectly to be good enough'. Maya and her counsellor discussed how these rules served a protective feature and were developed to protect her self-esteem. Maya recognised that she had come up with these standards, which she felt she must achieve to remain comfortable with herself (Fennell, 1997). This impacted her ability to complete her coursework as she put a lot of pressure on herself to succeed, leading to her feeling overwhelmed and wanting to leave the course. When her standards of being in control and completing tasks perfectly were not met, this would activate her core belief and trigger low mood and anxiety, which further confirmed the core belief, 'I am not good enough, I am a failure because I can't even complete my assignment'. She also felt guilty for not being able to spend quality time with her son and partner. Her energy levels were impacted, and she often struggled to sleep at night. Her core beliefs were also triggered when she made mistakes or did not do something perfectly. This led to negative predictions (e.g., 'I will never be able to achieve anything'), which demotivated her from continuing the course. To cope with this, Maya engaged in safety behaviours (e.g., over-preparation). However, over-preparing fuelled the negative predictions ('I need to complete tasks perfectly to be good enough') and further maintained the vicious cycle of anxiety. At times when her course tutors praised her for her work, she discounted this by telling herself 'this was an easy task, anyone could have achieved it'. In this manner, positive or neutral information was skewed to fit the core beliefs 'I am not good enough' and 'I am a failure'.

The next section will detail ways of working with low self-esteem, starting with cognitive behavioural therapy (CBT), and proceeding to Acceptance and Commitment Therapy (ACT) and compassion-focused therapy (CFT). Maya's example will be discussed in further detail while alluding to the interventions used.

WAYS OF WORKING WITH LOW SELF-ESTEEM

COGNITIVE BEHAVIOURAL THERAPY

The efficacy of CBT for low self-esteem is evidenced by various studies (Beattie and Beattie, 2018; Kolubinski et al., 2018). Fennell's (1997) model, described above, helps clients to increase awareness of the processes that fuel their negative self-belief and maintain safety/avoidance behaviours. This is followed by stepping back to question these unhelpful thoughts rather than accepting them as a true reflection of the person having them (Fennell, 2016). Clients can then be encouraged to test out old perspectives via behavioural experiments and consider whether new perspectives might be useful. Some of these interventions are briefly described below (Fennell, 2016):

- **Gaining awareness**: The first step is helping clients understand what their anxious predictions and self-critical thoughts are and observing the precautions they take to avoid the predictions from happening. Taking Maya's example, her counsellor suggested recording these thoughts, the corresponding emotions, bodily sensations and situational context by writing them down. This helped Maya to follow it through in a systematic way and reflect on whether she was engaging in biases such as jumping to conclusions, catastrophising, blaming herself or expecting perfection from herself.
- **Cognitive restructuring or finding alternatives**: This entails questioning the predictions and self-critical thoughts by writing down alternative ones as well as how strongly the client believes them. Taking Maya's example again, her therapist encouraged her to ask herself: 'What evidence suggests what I am predicting? What alternative views exist? What is the evidence for these alternative views? What is the worst that can happen and how might I deal with it?' Maya then reflected on other ways to view the situation and considered 'letting go' of control because making mistakes did not necessarily mean that she was not good enough or had failed; it meant she was human and was trying her best. This shift was a process that took a few sessions.
- **Testing out predictions**: Maya was then supported to test out these predictions and to keep a diary to log the alternatives. These 'experiments' involved treating herself kindly and behaving in line with her new perspective. Over time, Maya was able to feel more

at ease with the course and did not put as much pressure on herself to do well. She worked with her therapist to create a better study–work–life balance which led to more fulfilment.
- **Identifying one's good qualities, skills, talents, achievements and the small things people might be discounting**: Maya started recording a 'positives portfolio' by keeping an account of her positive qualities as well as examples of how she demonstrated them. Over time, she tried to focus on the positives within her and attempted to bring this to her attention when she felt anxious or low.

ACCEPTANCE AND COMMITMENT THERAPY

Acceptance and Commitment Therapy (ACT), one of the third-wave CBT interventions, was developed by Steven Hayes in 1986 (Harris, 2011), and appears to be consistent with some of the core principles of Buddhism (Fung, 2015). ACT interventions aim to change the function of distressing events and an individual's relationship to their emotions and cognitions through strategies such as acceptance of thoughts and feelings, contacting the present moment and self-compassion (Gloster et al., 2020). A body of research indicates that suppressing unwanted thoughts leads to them emerging more frequently and intensely (Hayes-Skelton and Eustis, 2020; Neff and Tirch, 2013). In line with this, ACT proposes that rather than replacing negative emotions with positive ones, positive feelings can be produced by embracing the negative (Harris, 2019). Lastly, the approach involves making choices to move towards a direction which is congruent with clients' values and committing to making changes that are consistent with these values (Hayes, Strosahl and Wilson, 1999). Some of the strategies used to enable this process include the following (Harris, 2019):

- **Recognising what has worked (or not)**: ACT encourages recognising past attempts to overcome difficulties, and how they have worked in the short term or long term, and exploring their associated costs. This can entail understanding what the client has done to avoid negative thoughts and feelings.
- **Recognising struggle is the problem**: If the client tries to control how they are feeling, they will remain in a vicious cycle which increases their suffering (Harris, 2019). One of the commonly used metaphors is that of quicksand: the more one struggles with it, the faster they are sucked under it. ACT encourages recognition of this with a view to accept thoughts and feelings as outlined below. Using Maya's example, ACT encourages thoughts and feelings to *just be* there instead of challenging them.
- **The process of defusion**: This involves learning to avoid battling with cognitions, memories and sensations, and not giving them one's complete attention or holding on to them. After naming the cognition, Harris (2019) suggests 'neutralising' it by observing the thought as if it were an object, for example describing its size, volume, texture, location, speed, movement, etc. This is followed by 'playing around' with the thought and modifying its auditory, visual and kinaesthetic properties, for instance saying it quickly or in a different tone or voice. This can allow the self-critical thought (e.g., 'I'm not good enough') to be experienced and reduce its power.
- **Mindfulness**: This is the process of non-judgemental observation of processes that occur both internally (in the mind and body) and externally. Engaging in mindfulness skills by contacting the present moment can include the following: coming back to one's body by changing posture, engaging in a form of movement, or altering breathing, and engaging with the environment by noticing the five senses (e.g., what the client can see, feel, taste, smell and hear). These skills can be drawn on outside the therapy room and clients can be encouraged to reflect on how they might apply them to various situations in their lives.

COMPASSION-FOCUSED THERAPY

Compassion-focused therapy (CFT) is a form of psychotherapy developed by Paul Gilbert. Gilbert proposed that compassion towards the self and others is fundamental to promote psychological and emotional healing and is also helpful in relieving feelings of shame and self-criticism which are common with low self-esteem (Gilbert, 2009). Compassion is a 'sensitivity to suffering in self and others, with a commitment to try to alleviate and prevent it' (Gilbert, 2014: 19). Some authors believe that ACT overlaps with a few conceptualisations of self-compassion (Neff and Tirch, 2013). The usefulness of CFT for managing low self-esteem is very relevant given the self-compassionate attitude to oneself and has been evidenced in various studies (Krieger et al., 2019; Rose, McIntyre and Rimes, 2018; Thomason and

Moghaddam, 2021). Further, self-compassion is associated with resilience, optimism, happiness, productivity and motivation (Tiwari et al., 2020). However, CFT has been described as an approach instead of a new form of therapy and has slightly different exercises and ways to develop self-compassion. Some of the exercises which CFT encourages are mentioned below (Irons and Beaumont, 2017):

- **Compassion-focused imagery exercises**: These employ guided imagery to calm the mind and body. For example, imagining oneself in a safe and calming place can help soothe distressing feelings and self-critical thoughts.
- **Soothing breathing**: This is being attentive towards one's breathing pattern and rhythm, and 'slowing down' in one's body as one breathes. This can help soothe physical sensations related to self-criticism, anxiety or low mood.
- **Body scan**: This builds on to the soothing breathing and involves not only focusing on one's breath, but slowly scanning the body from the top down (or the other way around) to notice any signs of tension stored in the body. This is followed by imagining the tension is leaving the body and feeling a sense of gratefulness for this release.
- **Compassionate letter writing**: This involves writing a letter to oneself in a non-judgemental way and having empathy or validating one's suffering and pain.

To conclude, while this chapter has discussed a few approaches to working with low self-esteem, it is important to tailor them to clients' specific needs and background.

REFERENCES

Beattie, S. & Beattie, D. (2018). An investigation into the efficacy of a cognitive behavioural therapy group for low self-esteem in a primary care setting. *The Cognitive Behaviour Therapist*, 11. https://doi.org/10.1017/S1754470X18000168

Beck, A. T. (1976). *Cognitive Therapy and The Emotional Disorders*. New York: International University Press.

Brown, J. D. & Marshall, M. A. (2006). The three faces of self-esteem. In M. H. Kernis (Eds), *Self-esteem, Issues and Answers: A Sourcebook of Current Perspectives* (pp. 4–9). New York: Psychology Press.

Coopersmith, S. (1967). *The Antecedents of Self-esteem*. San Francisco, CA: W. H. Freeman.

Fennell, M. J. (1997). Low self-esteem: A cognitive perspective. *Behavioural and Cognitive Psychotherapy*, 25(1), 1–26. https://doi.org/10.1017/S1352465800015368

Fennell, M. J. (2005). Low self-esteem. In *Encyclopedia of Cognitive Behavior Therapy* (pp. 236–240). Boston, MA: Springer.

Fennell, M. (2016). *Overcoming Low Self-esteem: A Self-help Guide Using Cognitive Behavioural Techniques* (2nd ed.). London: Hachette.

Fung, K. (2015). Acceptance and commitment therapy: Western adoption of Buddhist tenets? *Transcultural Psychiatry*, 52(4), 561–576. https://doi.org/10.1177/1363461514537544

Gilbert, P. (2009). Introducing compassion-focused therapy. *Advances in Psychiatric Treatment*, 15(3), 199–208. https://doi.org/10.1192/apt.bp.107.005264

Gilbert, P. (2014). The origins and nature of compassion focused therapy. *British Journal of Clinical Psychology*, 53(1), 6–41. https://doi.org/10.1111/bjc.12043

Gloster, A. T., Walder, N., Levin, M. E., Twohig, M. P. & Karekla, M. (2020). The empirical status of acceptance and commitment therapy: A review of meta-analyses. *Journal of Contextual Behavioral Science*, 18, 181–192. https://doi.org/10.1016/j.jcbs.2020.09.009

Harris, R. (2019). *ACT Made Simple: An Easy-to-read Primer on Acceptance and Commitment Therapy*. Oakland, CA: New Harbinger Publications.

Harris, R. (2011). *The Confidence Gap: A Guide to Overcoming Fear and Self-Doubt*. Boston, MA: Trumpeter Books.

(Continued)

(Continued)

Harris, M. A. & Orth, U. (2020). The link between self-esteem and social relationships: A meta-analysis of longitudinal studies. *Journal of Personality and Social Psychology*, 119(6), 1459–1477. http://dx.doi.org/10.1037/pspp0000265

Harter, S. (1999). *The Construction of the Self: A Developmental Perspective*. New York: Guilford Press.

Harter, S. (2012). *Self-perception Profile for Adolescents: Manual and Questionnaires*. Denver, CO: University of Denver.

Hayes, S. C., Strosahl, K. D. & Wilson, K. G. (1999). *Acceptance and Commitment Therapy: An Experiential Approach to Behavior Change*. New York: Guilford Press.

Hayes-Skelton, S. A. & Eustis, E. H. (2020). Experiential avoidance. In J. S. Abramowitz & S. M. Blakey (Eds), *Clinical Handbook of Fear and Anxiety: Maintenance Processes and Treatment Mechanisms* (pp. 115–131). Washington, DC: American Psychological Association. https://doi.org/10.1037/0000150-007

Henriksen, I. O., Ranøyen, I., Indredavik, M. S., & Stenseng, F. (2017). The role of self-esteem in the development of psychiatric problems: a three-year prospective study in a clinical sample of adolescents. *Child and Adolescent Psychiatry and Mental Health*, 11(1), 1–9. https://doi.org/10.1186/s13034-017-0207-y

Irons, C. & Beaumont, E. (2017). *The Compassionate Mind Workbook: A Step-by-step Guide to Developing Your Compassionate Self*. London: Robinson.

Kolubinski, D. C., Frings, D., Nikčević, A. V., Lawrence, J. A. & Spada, M. M. (2018). A systematic review and meta-analysis of CBT interventions based on the Fennell model of low self-esteem. *Psychiatry Research*, 267, 296–305. https://doi.org/10.1016/j.psychres.2018.06.025

Krieger, T., Reber, F., von Glutz, B., Urech, A., Moser, C. T., Schulz, A. & Berger, T. (2019). An internet-based compassion-focused intervention for increased self-criticism: A randomized controlled trial. *Behavior Therapy*, 50, 430–445. https://doi.org/10.1016/j.beth.2018.08.003

Lachmann, S. (2013). 10 sources of low self-esteem. *Psychology Today*, 24 December. Available at www.psychologytoday.com/gb/blog/me-we/201312/10-sources-low-self-esteem (accessed 22 January 2022).

Leary, M. R., Tambor, E. S., Terdal, S. K. & Downs, D. L. (1995). Self-esteem as an interpersonal monitor: The sociometer hypothesis. *Journal of Personality and Social Psychology*, 68(3), 518–530. https://doi.org/10.1037/0022-3514.68.3.518

Liu, Y., Wang, Z., Zhou, C. & Li, T. (2014). Affect and self-esteem as mediators between trait resilience and psychological adjustment. *Personality and Individual Differences*, 66, 92–97. https://doi.org/10.1016/j.paid.2014.03.023

Marsh, H. W. (1990). Self Description Questionnaire-I. *Cultural Diversity and Ethnic Minority Psychology*. APA PsycTests. https://doi.org/10.1037/t01843-000

Neff, K. & Tirch, D. (2013). Self-compassion and ACT. In T. B. Kashdan & J. Ciarrochi (Eds), *Mindfulness, Acceptance, and Positive Psychology: The Seven Foundations of Well-being* (pp. 78–106). Oakland, CA: New Harbinger Publications.

Oliver, J. & Bennett, R. (2020). *The Mindfulness and Acceptance Workbook for Self-Esteem: Using Acceptance and Commitment Therapy to Move Beyond Negative Self-Talk and Embrace Self-Compassion*. Oakland, CA: New Harbinger Publications.

Orth, U. & Robins, R. W. (2014). The development of self-esteem. *Current Directions in Psychological Science*, 23(5), 381–387. https://doi.org/10.1177/0963721414547414

Rose, A., McIntyre, R. & Rimes, K. A. (2018). Compassion-focused intervention for highly selfcritical individuals: Pilot study. *Behavioural and Cognitive Psychotherapy*, 46, 583–600. https://doi.org/10.1017/S135246581800036X

Rosenberg, M. (1965). *Society and the Adolescent Self-Image*. Princeton, NJ: Princeton University Press. https://doi.org/10.2307/2575639

Salkovskis, P. M. (1991). The importance of behaviour in the maintenance of anxiety and panic: A cognitive account. *Behavioural and Cognitive Psychotherapy*, 19(1), 6-19. https://doi.org/10.1017/S0141347300011472

Salzman, M. B. (2018). Culture and Self-Esteem. In *A Psychology of Culture* (pp. 43–54). Boston, MA: Springer.

Schiraldi, G. R. (2016). *The Self-esteem Workbook*. Oakland, CA: New Harbinger Publications.

Thomason, S. & Moghaddam, N. (2021). Compassion-focused therapies for self-esteem: A systematic review and meta-analysis. *Psychology and Psychotherapy: Theory, Research and Practice*, 94(3), 737–759.

Tiwari, G. K., Pandey, R., Rai, P. K., Pandey, R., Verma, Y., Parihar, P., Ahirwar, G., Tiwari, A. S. & Mandal, S. P. (2020). Self-compassion as an intrapersonal resource of perceived positive mental health outcomes: A thematic analysis. *Mental Health, Religion & Culture*, 23(7), 550–569. https://doi.org/10.1080/13674676.2020.1774524

Webb, J. (2019). The difference between self-esteem, self-worth, self-confidence and self-knowledge. *PsychCentral* [Blog], 19 May. Available at https://psychcentral.com/blog/childhood-neglect/2019/05/the-difference-between-self-esteem-self-worth-self-confidence-and-self-knowledge#1 (accessed 7 January 2022).

RECOMMENDED READING

I would recommend the below texts for the three approaches to working with self-esteem described here:

CBT: Fennell, M. (2016). *Overcoming Low Self-esteem: A Self-help Guide Using Cognitive Behavioural Techniques* (2nd ed.). London: Hachette.

ACT: Harris, R. (2019). *ACT Made Simple: An Easy-to-read Primer on Acceptance and Commitment Therapy*. Oakland, CA: New Harbinger Publications.

CFT: Irons, C. & Beaumont, E. (2017). *The Compassionate Mind Workbook: A Step-by-step Guide to Developing Your Compassionate Self*. London: Robinson.

4.11 MANAGING STRESS

STEPHEN PALMER AND ROWAN BAYNE

OVERVIEW AND KEY POINTS

Over the past four decades, there has been an increase in the media coverage given to stress. Items include news about employees successfully suing their employers in the courts for occupational stress and the associated clinical disorders that accompany it. The Health and Safety Executive (n.d.) have been recommending stress prevention programmes at work, so employers have been under mounting pressure to take action at both the individual and organisational levels. With all this attention at work, in the media, on radio and television, plus the numerous self-help books, it is not surprising that we often hear people saying 'I'm stressed', yet from a counselling perspective the practitioner needs to unpack this statement before they can start to address the presenting problem. Stress, *per se*, is not a recognised clinical condition, and from a purely academic cognitive perspective, it could be argued that it does not exist! However, the client is likely to believe it is a clinical condition, similar to anxiety or depression.

Key factors discussed in this chapter include:

- There are a number of theories of stress which can inform counselling practice.
- Perceptions of the activating event or situation can largely influence whether or not a situation is perceived as a challenge or stress scenario. Intermediate and core beliefs can influence perceptions.
- Depending upon the presenting problem, multimodal, solution-focused, problem-solving and cognitive behavioural therapeutic approaches easily adapt to the field of stress counselling and management.
- Employers may use interventions at the individual level to reduce stress, such as stress counselling, employee assistance programmes and stress management training, and at the organisational level, such as tackling potential hazards (e.g., demands, bullying, work patterns and the working environment).

ASSESSMENT AND UNDERSTANDING

THEORIES OF STRESS

The definition of stress can vary as it depends upon the theory from which it is derived, and then the theory can underpin and inform practice (i.e., interventions at both individual and/or organisational levels). The Health and Safety Executive (HSE) (n.d.) defines stress as *'the adverse reaction people have to excessive pressures or other types of demand placed on them'*. It is a useful definition, as it distinguishes between the right amount of pressure being fine and too much pressure (which depends upon the person) being unacceptable in the workplace.

In the field of counselling, practitioners are likely to adapt their counselling approach to assisting clients presenting as stressed or having to tackle what they perceive as stressful situations, such as job interviews, giving presentations at work and high work demands. Therefore, their assessment may be based on their usual approach. Although this may be helpful in many cases, if the approach does not focus on modifying the situation and/or the perceptions of the situation, or how the person responds to stress, then the client may still report that they are distressed unless over the course of time the situation has changed.

The basic theories of stress can be summarised under three headings: stimulus, response and interactive variables. These will now be briefly examined. The **stimulus** variable or engineering approach conceptualises stress as a noxious stimulus or demand that is externally imposed upon a person, which can lead to ill health. In this model, stress can also be caused by too much or too little external stimulation. The **response** variable or physiological approach is based on Selye's (1956) triphasic model, involving the initial alarm reaction (sympathetic-adrenal medullary activation), the stage of resistance (adrenal-cortical activation) and the stage of exhaustion (final reactivation of the sympathetic-adrenal medullary system) leading to 'diseases of adaptation'. This response process is known as the **general adaptation syndrome**. Both the stimulus variable and response model are based on the stimulus–response paradigm (SR) and largely disregard the importance of perceptions and beliefs which may exacerbate, moderate or inhibit the activation of the stress response in any given situation. From a counselling perspective, interventions focus on removing the noxious stimulus or demand, developing strategies to balance periods of rest and activity and/or physiological based techniques, such as relaxation.

It is recommended that the **interaction** between the external and internal worlds of the person or client needs to be included in any practice-based theory of stress. The interactive variable or psychological approach to stress attempts to overcome the deficiencies of the earlier models. There have been a number of proposed psychological theories: the interactional and the transactional. The interactional theories centre on the fit between the person and their environment, often known as the 'Person–Environment Fit' theory. Possible interventions include assessment to see if the person fits the job or role, and any possible adaptation or skills training to enhance the fit. Others focus on the interactive nature of job demands and decision latitude. Possible interventions include increasing the ability of the person to make their own decisions.

Transactional theories of stress focus on the cognitive and affective aspects of a person's interactions with their environment and the behavioural coping styles they may adopt or lack. One of the most well-known theories is that of Richard Lazarus (Lazarus, 1976; Lazarus and Folkman, 1984), who defined stress as resulting from an imbalance between demands and resources. Lazarus asserts that a person evaluates a particular incident, demand or ongoing situation. This initial evaluation, known as primary appraisal, involves a continuous monitoring of the environment and analysis of whether a problem exists. If a problem is recognised, then the stress response may be activated and unpleasant feelings and emotions may be experienced. The next stage, secondary appraisal, follows when the person evaluates their resources and options. Unlike the earlier models of stress, the important issue is whether the person recognises that a problem exists. Once recognised, *if* the demands are greater than the resources, *only then* does stress occur. If the resources are greater than the demands, then the person may view the situation as a challenge and not a stress scenario. If the person is too inexperienced to recognise that a particular problem exists, then this is not considered as a stress scenario. This is an important distinction as, ironically, it is the subjective and not the objective assessment of any scenario that may trigger the stress response. From a counselling perspective, strategies can include reappraising the initial perceptions of a situation or problem, seeking and developing practical solutions and, if necessary, modifying any intermediate or core beliefs that are hindering the person from tackling the situation, especially if it is a reoccurring or ongoing problem.

WAYS OF WORKING WITH STRESS

As previously noted, a counsellor can just apply their usual counselling approach to assisting a client to tackle a challenging problem or stress scenario. Some approaches can very easily adapt to the transactional theories of stress, including cognitive behavioural therapy (Sequeira and Mytton – Chapter 5.4, this volume), rational emotive behavioural therapy (REBT) (Ellis et al., 1997), multimodal therapy (Palmer and Dryden, 1995; Palmer – Chapter 5.18, this volume), and problem-solving and integrative therapy (Milner and Palmer, 1998). Interestingly, the evidence-based solution-focused, cognitive behavioural coaching approach (SF-CBC), which has developed over the past two decades in the coaching psychology field, can also be used for stress counselling as it seeks to address both the practical and cognitive aspects of any stress scenario, in a similar way as integrative counselling, developed by Milner and Palmer (1998). However, in counselling literature, the integrative SF-CB approach has not been researched or explored to the same extent.

When developing stress management programmes for the client, the counsellor will be influenced by the needs of the client, who may require stress counselling/management for a current problem or preventative stress management to help cope with daily hassles and general stress reduction, or a combination of both. If the person is stressed by a current problem, then interventions based on solution-focused, problem-solving and rational-emotive and cognitive-behavioural methods are generally effective. Although relaxation and distraction techniques may have some benefit for symptom management, they may not necessarily help the person to reappraise or resolve the problem or stress scenario. If the problem resolves itself over the course of time, then non-directive counselling may appear to be just as effective as more prescriptive or focused approaches. However, one of the cognitive behavioural therapeutic approaches (e.g., CBT, REBT) is often considered to be the psychological therapy of choice for the majority of stress-related problems, symptoms and conditions, such as performance anxiety, work-related phobias, panic and somatic complaints. Surviving a difficult life event may in itself lead to an increase in self-efficacy, which will help the person adaptively appraise, and thereby manage, similar events in the future.

In counselling, a thorough assessment of the problem or presenting issue and the client's symptoms may guide the counsellor towards the appropriate interventions to use. Whether or not the counsellor uses their usual approach or takes a solution-focused, problem-solving, cognitive behavioural or multimodal approach, assessment is still important. Palmer and Dryden (1995) have found using the multimodal assessment procedures developed by Lazarus helpful (see Palmer – Chapter 5.18, this volume). This involves close examination of the seven modalities that comprise the entire range of personality: Behaviour, Affect (i.e., emotion), Sensation, Imagery, Cognition, Interpersonal, Drugs/biology. This is known by the acronym, BASIC ID. An in-depth questionnaire can be used to assist this assessment process (Lazarus, 2019), although it is not essential for brief counselling. By assessing each modality, it may become apparent that a client, for example, avoids doing certain useful behaviours, feels anxious, has physical tension, catastrophic imagery, stress-inducing thoughts, passive-aggressive behaviour, and is taking medication for headaches. Once the assessment of each modality is finished, a series of research-based techniques and interventions can be discussed, the rationale explained to the client and the most useful interventions applied. Technique selection may depend on which modality the client may be more sensitive to. Therefore, in the previous example, if a client's catastrophic imagery appears to trigger high levels of stress and anxiety, then coping imagery may become the desired intervention. Furthermore, clients suffering from specific stressors, such as financial problems, do not necessarily find the interpersonal and emotional strategies as helpful as those clients with relationship difficulties. These factors need to be considered when developing an individualised stress management programme for the client.

Taking into account the stress research and interactional theories of stress, there is a variety of objectives in an intervention, for example: to solve the problem, to alter the way the client responds, to help the client reappraise the stressor, to help the client change the nature of the stressor.

Understandably, some people can become stressed and anxious about impending events or tasks that they find challenging, such as giving presentations at work, job interviews, wedding speeches, submitting important assignments and/or taking exams. They may have chosen to avoid these activities for some years. Unfortunately, the downside of avoidance is that they have not necessarily increased the relevant skills required for the task if they are called upon to do them. For example, instead of putting themselves forward to prepare and give presentations at work or college, they let their colleagues volunteer instead. However, on some occasions they have been told by their manager to give an important presentation within the month and it becomes unavoidable. This is when they may request a one-off stress counselling session to assist them with their high levels of distress at the impending assignment.

> **CASE STUDY**
>
> Michael was asked by his manager to give a presentation at the next team meeting. Michael found giving presentations 'very stressful' and had avoided them as far as possible. However, on this occasion he was unable to evade giving the presentation as he believed that it could impact upon his promotion prospects. Table 4.11.1 is an example of how a modality profile (based on the multimodal approach) was used, listing the relevant 'problems' in the second column with the various techniques and strategies to tackle his performance anxiety in the third column. The techniques are principally taken from the rational-emotive cognitive behavioural approach.

ALTERNATIVE PERSPECTIVES

As discussed previously, there are many different approaches to helping clients tackle stress. The previous section highlighted how multimodal and cognitive behavioural approaches can be used to tackle stress. In this section, we consider a different approach.

Lyubomirsky (2010) suggested a systematic way of matching clients and interventions (in her case for increasing happiness), which is consistent with the concept of preference. In modified form, it is to reflect on what it would be like to do an intervention for, say, several days and to rate it on criteria of feeling natural, enjoyment and doing it to please others or because it is fashionable. Obviously, the first two criteria indicate trying that intervention and the second two are warning signs.

The following list is of preferences and examples of interventions that, given normal development, will meet the criteria. In the list, X refers to a source of stress. These interventions and others are also ways of developing preferences and non-preferences (Bayne, 2013; Myers and Kirby, 1994). Two important assumptions in preference theory are that each person's preferences have a higher ceiling for development than their opposed non-preferences, and thus, in a good enough environment, develop more than their non-preferences, and that this is desirable.

Extraversion – Talking about X

Introversion – Quiet reflection about X

Sensing – Check details relevant to X (e.g., what was actually said or happened)

Intuition – Brainstorm about X or an aspect of X and summarise the main issues

Table 4.11.1 Michael's modality profile (Palmer, Cooper and Thomas, 2003)

Modality	Problem	Proposed technique
Behaviour	Procrastination: avoids writing the presentation by doing other tasks, such as tidying up files	Use time management techniques to challenge unhelpful beliefs about being 'a failure'
Affect/Emotional	Feels increased anxiety	Use feeling identification to ascertain helpful (concern) versus unhelpful (anxiety) emotions
Sensory	Feels sick before giving presentation	Use relaxation techniques before presentation
Imagery	Can only see myself delivering a poor presentation	Use coping imagery
Cognitive/thoughts/ideas	I must give an excellent presentation (demandingness), or I will never get promoted (all or nothing) and I will be a failure (label)	Dispute unhelpful beliefs by identifying thinking errors and employing appropriate thinking skills, including self-acceptance training Complete an Enhancing Performance Form
Interpersonal	Has poor communication skills	Practise and develop communications skills
Drugs/ biological	Experiences palpitations and drinks excessive coffee as a way to relax	Reduce caffeine intake by alternating drinks with decaffeinated coffee

Thinking – Analyse X, do a cost–benefit analysis, create a flow chart

Feeling – Empathise with other people involved (if any), clarify if any of your core values are relevant to X

Judging – Make a plan about X or an aspect of X, do it as a list of actions and consider doing one of them

Perceiving – Gather more information relevant to X

Calm – Stay relaxed, think of all the potential benefits of a decision you may take about X

Worrying – Think of more worries and risks relating to X and the precautions and preparations you can take to reduce them.

If the interventions which fit your client's preferences don't work well enough, Kroeger, Thuesen and Rutledge (2002: 252–253) suggest a 'good stretch', by which they mean a brief switch to using your non-preferences. Obviously, this approach could be attacked as not falsifiable, as 'having it both ways'. However, trying interventions consistent with preferences first and usually, and the emphasis on brevity in trying 'a good stretch', are sound counter-arguments.

Preference theory sometimes explains, in a constructive way, why generally effective interventions fail. For example, some people enjoy a calm, familiar and pleasing setting, and letting their minds drift – exercise as 'a moving meditation' – while others want lots of stimulation, variety and speed – exercise as 'absorbing action' (Brue, 2008). Similarly, counsellors may have a go at using preference theory to refine something that happens naturally: varying their way of relating to clients with different personalities, for example, being more organised and detailed with clients who prefer both Sensing and Judging, showing their expertise through rationales and explicit use of theory with people who prefer both Intuition and Thinking, being warmer with clients who prefer Feeling, more playful (but still professional) with clients who prefer both Sensing and Perceiving, and more patient with clients who prefer Worrying.

This is not asking counsellors to be inauthentic. Rather, it offers the beginnings of a clearer account of how to be what Lazarus (1993: 404–407) called an 'authentic chameleon'. Dryden has also commented helpfully on this concept: that counsellors 'cannot be all things to all clients … your personality and temperament limit how much you can vary' and that it tends to be referred clients 'whom the referrer thinks need a robust and no nonsense counsellor, rather than clients who need a lot of gentle coaxing' (Dryden, 2011: 41). In other words, use your preferences most but non-preferences sometimes, including when being empathic with clients whose personality is very different from your own and when your own development allows. If not, referral is a positive and ethical option.

CASE STUDY

Blossom was sleeping badly. She was worried about her brother's imminent wedding and anticipating a stressful day that she would make worse just by being there. She decided that poor sleep was making everything else worse so she searched the internet for ideas, finding two authoritative books: Rosenberg (2014) and Wiseman (2014). She tried walking more, increasing speed and distance gradually, but found it boring and too regimented; and she tried not using her computer later in the evening, but found that frustrating.

In counselling, she identified three aspects of 'the wedding problem': that she was boring (because introverts are boring); that because she finds small talk 'excruciatingly tedious' people give up on her and walk away; and that in order to be healthy and well balanced she'd have to change her personality, but she didn't know how to.

Blossom challenged and replaced each of these beliefs and found that appreciating herself as an introvert also meant that she felt more confident socially: she became less worried about other people's reactions to her and more interested in how she felt in them. She said: 'It's such a relief to learn that I'm not antisocial and that I don't have some deep personality defect – I just need more time to myself than some people and lots of peace and quiet!' Thus, Blossom became much more accepting of an element of her real self (which is not always so easy to do) and, more subtly, no longer criticised herself for not having the opposite quality, for being an 'unsuccessful extravert'.

She took a further step, assertively expressing her needs by giving herself time to recover from periods of being sociable. Thus, at her brother's wedding, she escaped (her term) and read for an hour between dinner and dancing, and even enjoyed the social part more as a result. And, before the wedding day, she explained to her brother what she was doing and why. This direct talk with her brother was unusual for Blossom and she rehearsed it first, following the guidelines in Dickson (2012). The image of a tree bending in the wind, then coming upright again – part of the skill of persisting with a key phrase in the face of strong pleas and emotional requests – proved particularly helpful.

Blossom decided to work more on directly developing her non-preference for extraversion with a friend who was a socially skilled introvert (or possibly an extravert).

REFERENCES

Bayne, R. (2013) *The Counsellor's Guide to Personality: Understanding Preferences, Motives and Life Stories.* Basingstoke: Palgrave Macmillan.
Brue, S. (2008) *The 8 Colors of Fitness.* Delroy Beach, FL: Oakledge Press.
Dickson, A. (2012) *A Woman in Your Own Right: Assertiveness and You* (2nd ed.). London: Quartet.
Dryden, W. (2011) *Counselling in a Nutshell* (2nd ed.). London: Sage.
Ellis, A., Gordon, J., Neenan, M. and Palmer, S. (1997) *Stress Counselling: A Rational Emotive Behaviour Approach.* London: Cassell (now published by Sage Publications).

Health and Safety Executive (HSE) (n.d.) *Work-related Stress and How to Manage It*. London: HSE. Available at www.hse.gov.uk/stress/overview.htm

Kroeger, O., with Thuesen, J.M. and Rutledge, H. (2002) *Type Talk at Work*. New York: Dell Publishing.

Lazarus, A.A. (1993) Tailoring the therapeutic relationship, or being an authentic chameleon. *Psychotherapy*, 30, 404–407.

Lazarus, C.N. (2019) *MLHI-3: Multimodal Life History Inventory*. Champaign, IL: Research Press.

Lazarus, R.S. (1976) *Patterns of Adjustment*. New York: McGraw-Hill.

Lazarus, R.S. and Folkman, R. (1984) *Stress, Appraisal, and Coping*. New York: Springer.

Lyubomirsky, S. (2010) *The How of Happiness: A Practical Guide to Getting the Life You Want*. London: Piatkus.

Milner, P. and Palmer, S. (1998) *Integrative Stress Counselling: A Humanistic Problem-focused Approach*. London: Cassell (now published by Sage Publications).

Myers, K.D. and Kirby, L.K. (1994) *Introduction to Type Dynamics and Type Development*. Palo Alto, CA: CPP.

Palmer, S., Cooper, C. and Thomas, K. (2003) *Creating a Balance: Managing Stress*. London: British Library.

Palmer, S. and Dryden, W. (1995) *Counselling for Stress Problems*. London: Sage.

Rosenberg, R.S. (2014) *Sleep Soundly Every Night, Feel Fantastic Every Day: A Doctor's Guide to Solving Your Sleep Problems*. New York: Demos Health.

Selye, H. (1956) *Stress of Life*. New York: McGraw-Hill.

Wiseman, R. (2014) *Night School: The Life-changing Science of Sleep*. London: Pan Books.

RECOMMENDED READING

Dickson, A. (2012) *A Woman in Your Own Right: Assertiveness and You* (2nd ed.). London: Quartet.

This is the best practical book on assertiveness, for all genders.

Lynn, S.J., O' Donohue, W.T. and Lilienfeld, S.O. (Eds) (2015) *Health, Happiness, and Well-Being: Better Living through Psychological Science*. London: Sage.

The book includes literature reviews, with some attention to applications, by leading researchers on 'chilling out' (meditation, relaxation and yoga), sleep, exercise, happiness and other areas of psychology relevant to managing stress.

Nicolson, P. and Bayne, R. (2014) *Psychology for Social Work Theory and Practice* (4th ed.). Basingstoke: Palgrave Macmillan.

This book includes detailed practical guidelines for some generally effective methods of managing stress: assertiveness, strengths, expressive writing and preference theory.

4.12 OBSESSIVE-COMPULSIVE DISORDER

TRACIE HOLROYD

OVERVIEW AND KEY POINTS

This chapter will define and explore the concepts and various, but not inclusive, obsessions (intense, uncontrollable, recurring thoughts, images, and fears), compulsions (repetitive actions) and behaviour patterns of obsessive-compulsive disorder, hereinafter referred to as OCD. The key points that this chapter will cover are:

- The different ways that OCD can manifest itself.
- Therapeutic interventions when working with clients suffering with OCD.
- The cycle of OCD.
- Identifying the characteristics of OCD.

ASSESSMENT AND UNDERSTANDING

OCD is a serious and intrusive mental health disorder which can impact on daily life in such a way that it is debilitating to the sufferer. OCD is considered to be an anxiety disorder, which is a mental health disorder, and for some, the biggest challenge is to accept this type of 'label'. OCD sufferers can be resistant to such a label, and this can then impede the process of gaining professional support either through their GP or by accessing therapy. For some, the need for a diagnosis can have a negative impact, in that they might find it unhelpful or too distressing to acquire.

Those with OCD may experience shame in and guilt about their behaviours, as they can access rational thoughts that conflict with the compulsions and repetitive behaviour patterns they complete, which they know are irrational. They may even know that their fear from their instructive thoughts is unfounded.

For those who do present in the counselling room, it is important for us, their therapist, to remember the courage it has taken for them to engage in therapy. For most, the compulsions and obsessive behaviours are probably having such an impact on their life that they can no longer either hide their behaviours or conduct themselves in the way in which they strive to do.

The World Health Organisation's *International Classification of Diseases* (ICD-11) (2019) states that for a definite OCD diagnosis to be made, obsessional symptoms, or compulsive acts, or both, must be present on most days for at least two successive weeks and be a source of distress or sufficient to interfere with activities. The obsessional symptoms should have the following characteristics:

a) They must be recognised as the individual's own thoughts or impulses.
b) There must be at least one thought or act that is still resisted unsuccessfully, even though others may be present which the sufferer no longer resists.
c) The thought of carrying out the act must not in itself be pleasurable (simple relief of tension or anxiety is not regarded as pleasure in this sense).

According to OCD UK (OCD UKa, n.d.), 'If a person's trait does not cause anxiety or impact or disorder in their life, then it is unlikely to be OCD, although a health professional will need to conduct an assessment to confirm a diagnosis or not'.

Some of the ways in which OCD can manifest are as:

- rituals
- contamination
- intrusive thoughts
- hoarding
- order and symmetry
- sensorimotor OCD
- avoidance
- sexual thoughts or behaviours.

This list is not exhaustive, although these are the most common types, as OCD compulsions can arise and manifest themselves to absolutely anything.

The actions and rituals of a sufferer of OCD are commonly performed in their belief that they dispel a deep-rooted fear. This can be known or unknown to the individual. Even if known to themselves, having an understanding does not alleviate the compulsive behaviour, as sufferers are, as previously stated, aware of the irrational thoughts, but have no other way to eradicate them unless they perform their routine. The routine does momentarily ease the distress they were feeling, but it does not last as the intrusive thoughts reappear, and the cycle begins again (see Figure 4.12.1).

OCD behaviour is the irrational belief that sufferers can control a situation or outcome by completing certain patterns, caused by the intrusive thoughts. Examples of intrusive thoughts are:

- 'If I click the lights in a particular order, it will stop any harm to my family.'
- 'If I wash my hands, I will not die from any germs.'
- 'I must check the switches around the house, in a certain order and a certain number of times to ensure those I love are safe.'

Another trait of an OCD sufferer is gaining reassurance by completing certain behaviours. This can be repetitive: 'have I turned out the lights?', 'did I lock the door?' Some individuals may experience violent intrusive thoughts, and they create a belief that thinking something may make it more likely to happen. A stereotypical perspective of OCD is a person with the compulsion to wash their hands, due to fear of contamination. While others without OCD wash their hands when they think it is required, depending on their environment, because they are dirty and then they see that they are clean, the OCD sufferer will wash their hands until they 'feel' clean or it satisfies the intrusive thoughts and compulsions. And when the ritual is completed, the compulsion is satisfied and their thoughts are that all is OK in their world and with their loved ones, until the next intrusive thought, creating the compulsion and the cycle begins again.

A compulsion can be either overt (i.e., checking that the switches are all turned off, which, when repeated, can be seen by others) or covert, when an action is not seen by others (i.e., counting or repeating words or phrases). An overt compulsion can manifest as washing hands or face, having items in a certain order or repeating patterns of behaviour that can be seen by others. They are enacted physically and externally of the sufferer. In contrast, a covert compulsion, or 'cognitive compulsion', as they can be referred to, is an internal action, and a process of mental actions. Examples of these actions are compulsive visions, thoughts and ideas, and counting numbers to try to irradiate the negative intrusive thoughts.

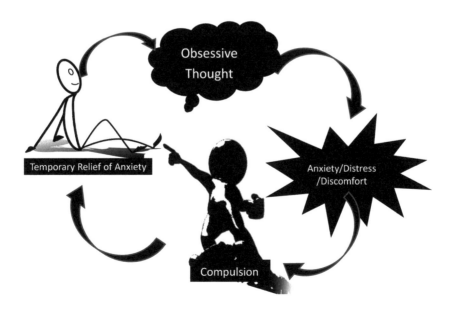

Figure 4.12.1   The OCD cycle

Let us briefly consider the impact that the Covid-19 pandemic, which started in 2020, and the severity in which it affected those who previously suffered with OCD. Those who had previously had a compulsion to ritually wash their hands for fear of contamination, initially felt more accepted in society – this was their 'norm'. Unfortunately, for some this increased their fears of contamination and created more intense thoughts, behaviour patterns and compulsions. The external rationale and enforcement from humanity, that the world was not a safe place, thus increased the sufferer's anxiety and the creation and introduction of more coping strategies, in the form of further compulsions and intrusive thoughts.

The impact on an OCD sufferer's life can be so significant that they are unable to engage in everyday life. For example, someone might have a bathroom ritual that takes three hours to perform each morning and evening. If this ritual is interrupted or they believe that they have not completed it in the 'correct' order, they may be compelled to return to the beginning of their pattern of behaviour. This could take half a day and would therefore have an impact on all areas of life: with family, friends and work.

Although each person's experience of compulsive and intrusive thoughts and symptoms are unique to themselves, the presence of anxiousness is generic. The magnitude of an OCD sufferer's experiences is hard to imagine for those people who have never experienced OCD. Some degree of OCD tendencies become evident to most people when a person experiences stresses in their life. It is believed that childhood trauma or bullying can be a cause (Matthews et al., 2008). Also, having a natural tendency to be neat and to like to have everything in order can be a personality trait that evolves into OCD, although it is not conclusive that this can happen. The fundamental motivation of an OCD sufferer is one of fear, which creates anxiety and the need to control situations and outcomes, and the belief that their rituals can affect the outcomes. It can be quite damaging to the therapeutic relationship to express the idea that we all have OCD-type symptoms as it understates the distress that they encounter daily and the significant impact it has on a person's daily functions.

As each person who suffers with OCD experiences it differently, and with less or greater magnitude, there is no list of obsessions or compulsions, nor is there enough research and evidence to give a definitive answer on the reasons for the development of the symptoms. Instead, practitioners can work with clients to develop an individualised understanding of the development of the problem, integrating psychological theory and research knowledge as appropriate (see Johnstone – Chapter 3.5, this volume). It is believed that there are several theories on how OCD can develop and, as with many mental health issues, it is likely that OCD is a consequence of a combination of factors.

The National Institute of Mental Health (NIMH) (n.d.) states that the following factors could all contribute to the cause of OCD:

- **Brain function**: Researchers have shown that people with OCD have altered connections in the frontal cortex of the brain, which leads to the changed behaviour.
- **Genetics**: Studies with twins and other families have shown that people have a higher risk of developing OCD if they have a first-degree relative who already has it (Pauls et al., 2014).
- **Personality**: Researchers believe that personality traits such as neat, methodical people with high standards are more vulnerable to develop OCD.
- **Personal experience**: There have been studies conducted that show a correlation between childhood trauma and OCD symptoms (Matthews et al., 2008), however, more research is needed.

WAYS OF WORKING WITH OCD

The most well-known therapeutic intervention is cognitive behavioural therapy (CBT) (see Sequeira and Mytton – Chapter 5.4, this volume) and Exposure and Response Prevention (ERP). CBT is a goal-oriented, problem-solving theory which will assist in the client in gaining insight to their thoughts, beliefs and attitudes. The therapist's role is to reframe their thinking process and to support clients in finding effective coping strategies.

Exposure therapy is a model that can treat anxiety disorders, and as a core feature of OCD is anxiety, it can be beneficial (Kaplan and Tolin, 2011). The therapist replicates the client's trigger situations within the session and together, therapist and client explore the thoughts, compulsions and behaviours in the here-and-now, without the intention to cause any harm. The therapist and the client can then create alternative coping strategies in the moment. This can also assist the client to experience the overwhelming urges and then, with the therapist's support, gain evidence that these compulsions can subside without them needing to undertake the previous negative coping strategies of their rituals.

Depending on the intensity of the compulsions, intrusive thoughts and behaviours, an OCD sufferer can influence the therapeutic approach utilised. This is also dependant on the theoretical training and qualifications of the therapist.

Working with an OCD sufferer whose rituals have been embedded for some years can lead to various modalities being introduced. As certain compulsive behaviours and thought patterns change and coping strategies are adopted, alternative intrusive thoughts, compulsions and behaviours can emerge, creating another cycle of OCD.

Polyvagal Theory can educate the OCD sufferer in the coregulation of the autonomic nervous system (Dana, 2018). A Polyvagal-trained therapist will assist the client to identify the three states of our nervous system (Ventral Vagal, Sympathetic and Dorsal) and mapping these states can reduce shame and self-criticism and allows for curiosity. Experiencing these different states within the session can allow clients the sense of organisation and aids clients to connect and disconnect from each state. This model suggests that those suffering with OCD are operating from their sympathetic state, whereby they are hypervigilant, fearful, and have a sense of impending danger – they are in the fight, flight or freeze mode. Understanding and experiencing these three nervous states can then allow the client to access the Ventral Vagal. In this state, we are co-regulated and self-regulated – we are looking for connection, with self, others, and the world. We are in the moment and are able to stay focused. We are resourceful, compassionate to ourselves and others, flexible and resilient. and therefore are able to think more rationally and overcome the irrational compulsions created by the intrusive thoughts that have no rationale.

Another alternative approach is the experiential Equine Assisted Growth and Learning Association (EAGALA) model. This intervention is a solution-oriented approach, where the client works with a mental health professional (MH), an equine specialist (ES) and horses. It is 100% ground-based (i.e., does not involve getting on and riding the horses) and no previous horse knowledge or horsemanship experience is required. Horses offer the unique opportunities for clients to discover their inner strength, beyond traditional talk therapy. Horses are large and powerful and it's hard to ignore their presence, much like a seemingly life issue like the compulsions an OCD sufferer experiences. Since horses are highly sensitive, and survive by paying close attention to their environment, they respond to the feeling state and body language that clients express. Participants in this therapy have to work to connect with a horse and to find a way to develop a relationship with the horse based on trust, just as we do in our personal lives – trust in others and trust in oneself. An OCD sufferer has got to trust that they can override the immense discomfort without the need to fulfil their compulsions. Horses' actions can be a metaphor in the clients' life story. They can see what is at the heart of the challenge or issue and it can have a profound experience, more than simply talking about it with a therapist. With the support of the EAGALA team, clients understand how the stories that they have told themselves have kept them from moving forward and learn to make decisions that lead to changing behaviours.

The case study below provides a fictional example of working with a client with OCD.

CASE STUDY

Myles initially presented in therapy with generalised anxiety. During his initial session he makes a passing comment regarding his OCD tendencies. This might easily have been disregarded as it is a sweeping comment, which Myles dismisses because he has learnt techniques to deal with it. Playing it down as he did could have been due to potential embarrassment or shame, or a lack of understanding of the impact it was having on him. Exploring different aspects of his life, Myles shares his love of adrenaline and being a thrill-seeker, which seems to contradict his thoughts and feelings of being fearful, and concerns of what others maybe thinking of him. Working through to gain more understanding of what the meaning of OCD is, Myles passes this off as simply meaning

(Continued)

(Continued)

that he is a 'neat freak' and likes to wash his hands, perhaps a little more often than others he has observed. Myles offers other historical information that can be attributed to his OCD, such as being bullied during childhood. However, any further information regarding this experience cannot be something that can be recalled regarding this experience.

After a few sessions, Myles comes to therapy with the intention of working on his OCD. It is only then that he realises how much more the behaviours are embedded in his behaviour. Further exploration reveals other habits that have been developed, such as only walking on certain paths, doors having to be shut in a certain order, and the feeling of dirt on his hands, meaning that he must wash them frequently. Myles found that journaling had been helpful in the past, but it was not something he was currently doing. Revisiting this might be useful. Instead of relying on memory, he would be able to gain a more accurate account of thoughts, beliefs and behaviour patterns.

More sessions were attended and focused upon uncovering further information on many different aspects of his life. During these sessions, CBT techniques were used to reframe his thought processes and to develop coping strategies. He restarted journaling, and worked to develop a deeper understanding of what it means for him to trust others, before attempting to apply this to himself in his everyday life. The optimum six sessions leads to positive outcomes in the pre- and post-General Anxiety Disorder (GAD) and Patient Health Questionnaire (PHQ-9) assessment tools. Myles, who reported feeling less anxious and that he had some revised and refreshed coping strategies, decided to finish attending sessions.

Despite Myles' progress, he experienced another life trauma and was left feeling fearful. He noticed an increase of intrusive thoughts and compulsions, and his old need of feeling in control re-emerged, something that he wasn't feeling before this new traumatic event. He returns to therapy. Initially, as with his first series of sessions, he did not immediately refer to his OCD being present. He did, however, make another passing comment that he knew that other things were buried deep down inside himself, but he was not prepared to go there at that time. Further sessions therefore focused primarily upon his anxiety, and the triggers to this.

Then the global pandemic occurred. Imagine how someone like Myles with OCD might experience this, with the virus spreading and the need to regularly wash hands becomes the 'norm'. The contamination appears to be everywhere, and OCD symptoms could magnify beyond anything experienced before. The intrusive thoughts, fear, paranoia and the compulsions become insatiable. The compulsion to wash hands and face is so frequent that it leaves hands raw and inflamed. Thoughts that everything and everyone are contaminated impact on basic needs, such as eating and drinking, which become such an issue that Myles becomes physically unwell. He has the compulsion to remove all his clothing if he goes outside, for fear of the contamination, and he sometimes insists that those around him also comply. He has constant thoughts and feelings that germs are penetrating all areas of the safe, sanitised environment that has been created. There is immense pressure on not only himself but on all those around him. The thoughts of death, which for Myles has been one of his underlying fears, return and he feels it is his responsibility to keep everyone safe.

While in therapy, Myles was supported to reframe and rationalise these thoughts, and normalise the situation, exploring factual information and linking it to times when these thoughts were not present. He was encouraged to find practical interventions (e.g., how to create and maintain items free from contamination) that would enable him to eat and drink. Myles struggled with any challenges to his thought process and was unable to make use of previously successful coping strategies, which would have eased the pattern of his OCD behaviour if only he could have implemented them. Some of these strategies might seem obvious to others, but Myles's overwhelming sense of fear inhibited his ability to think logically and rationalise his intrusive thoughts and implement these strategies. It could be a long process for Myles to learn how to control his invasive thoughts and compulsions.

For those with OCD, any traumatic event or not feeling in control of a situation may trigger old and new OCD tendencies. For clients like Myles, experiencing acceptance, being heard and understood, in an emotionally safe and non-judgemental space, will allow them, at their own pace, to delve deeper into their OCD and the unique experience and impact it has on them, their life and relationships. It can also help them to find alternative ways to curb their intrusive thoughts and overcome their compulsions in their own way.

CONCLUSION

Obsessive-compulsive disorder is a recognised mental health problem that can affect sufferers in a variety of ways, and in difference degrees of severity. It is believed that 1.2% of the population (12 in every 1000) will suffer with OCD at some point in their lives (OCD UKb, n.d.). Therapeutic interventions working in conventional and non-conventional models can be beneficial to individuals experiencing OCD.

REFERENCES

Dana, D. (2018). *The Polyvagal Theory in Therapy: Engaging the Rhythm of Regulation.* New York: W.W. Norton.

Kaplan, J.S. & Tolin, D.F. (2011). Exposure therapy for anxiety disorders. *Psychiatric Times*, 28(9). https://psychiatrictimes.com/anxiety/exposure-therapy-anxiety-disorders

Matthews, C.A., Kaur, N. & Stein, M.B. (2008). Childhood trauma and obsessive-compulsive symptoms. *Depression & Anxiety*, 25(9), 742–751.

MIND (n.d.). *Causes of Obsessive-Compulsive Disorder*. [Website]. Available at www.mind.org.uk/…/obsessive-compulsive-disorder-ocd/causes-of-ocd

National Institute of Mental Health (NIMH) (n.d.). *What is Obsessive-Compulsive Disorder (OCD)?* London: NIMH. Available at: www.nimh.nih.gov/health/topics/obsessive-compulsive-disorder-ocd

OCD UKa (n.d.) *Diagnosing OCD.* https://www.ocduk.org/ocd/diagnosing-ocd/

OCD UKb (n.d.). Occurences of OCD. https://www.ocduk.org/ocd/how-common-is-ocd/

Pauls, D., Abramovitch, A., Rauch, S., et al. (2014). Obsessive–compulsive disorder: an integrative genetic and neurobiological perspective. *National Review of Neuroscience*, 15, 410–424. https://doi.org/10.1038/nrn3746

World Health Organisation (2019). *International Statistical Classification of Diseases and Related Health Problems (11th Revision)*. (ICD-11). Geneva: WHO. Available at www.who.int/standards/classifications/classification-of-diseases

RECOMMENDED READING

OCD Action – www.ocdaction.org.uk

For those who would like to find out more about OCD, this easy-to-read and informative site is for anyone wanting to gain further understanding from professionals working with those affected by OCD.

Dana, D. (2018). *The Polyvagal Theory in Therapy: Engaging the Rhythm of Regulation.* New York: W.W. Norton.

An engaging book written in such a way that links the cognitive and the polyvagal theoretic approach to assist with life's traumas.

Thomas, L.A. & Lytle, M.H., with Dammann, B. (2016). *Transforming Therapy through Horses: Case Stories Teaching the EAGALA Model in Action*. Santaquin, UT: EAGALA.

The unique way this experiential model comes to life and the application of the model is broken down with case studies and theory so readers can get a true feel of how the process works within an EAGALA session.

4.13 PERSONALITY DISORDERS

JULIA LYONS

OVERVIEW AND KEY POINTS

The term 'personality disorders' is problematic for many practitioners and individuals who have been labelled as having a personality disorder. The field has been heavily criticised for its outdated classification system, methods of diagnosis and treatment. This chapter aims to acknowledge the controversy surrounding this topic while providing a comprehensive overview of the subject, because every counsellor or psychotherapist is likely to encounter individuals with personality difficulties in their work. There is a prevalence of 4–15% in the general population for individuals meeting the criteria for a personality disorder (Coid et al., 2006), and research has shown that individuals with personality disorders have poor treatment outcomes (Hasin et al., 2011). It is important that practitioners have an understanding of personality disorders in order to inform counselling and psychotherapy. The key points addressed in this chapter are:

- Personality disorders represent one of the most controversial topics within medical and mental health settings due to problems with diagnosis and concerns over associated stigma for the individual.
- Personality disorders represent a core difficulty in how individuals relate to themselves and others.
- The field of personality disorders is in a state of flux. There is a strong pull from practitioners and the research community to move away from a categorical diagnostic view to a more dimensional one, in which maladaptive traits are on a continuum.
- Research indicates that there is still far to go before effective interventions are developed for personality disorders. Long-term approaches incorporating whole-team perspectives are currently recommended.

ASSESSMENT AND UNDERSTANDING

The causes of personality disorders are not fully known, although it is accepted by many that a biopsychosocial model is likely to be the most informative. There is some agreement in the field that personality disorder has its roots in childhood and adolescence (Newton-Howes, Clark and Chanen, 2015), becoming clinically recognisable in the transition between childhood to adulthood, yet it is not usually diagnosed before the age of 18 years, due to a lack of a method to differentiate between personality disorder traits and turbulent, yet common, adolescent behaviour. Cicchetti (2014) proposes equifinality in the development of personality disorders, meaning that a number of pathways, rather than a single trajectory, can lead to a personality disorder. This model suggests a complex interplay of biological predispositions to particular temperaments in association with developmental experiences in early life activate in response to adverse life events, and consequently manifest in personal and interactional difficulties (Bateman, Gunderson and Mulder, 2015).

It is important to consider a brief history and the current personality disorder classification system as the context partly explains some of the controversy around diagnosis and stigma that individuals with these difficulties experience today. Personality disorder was not regarded as a diagnosis until the nineteenth century when Schneider (1923) described a group of 'psychopathic personalities'. In his writings, he alluded to a core aspect of personality disorders, the inability to form and sustain functional and healthy interpersonal relationships. Schneider (1923) described nine personality types using only his clinical experience. Surprisingly, these nine categories remain largely consistent through to the modern day. The *Diagnostic and Statistical Manual of Mental Disorders* (DSM-5) (American Psychiatric Association, 2013) contains 10 categories of personality disorders divided into three clusters. Cluster A (odd or eccentric) includes the paranoid, schizoid and schizotypal categories. Cluster B (dramatic, emotional or erratic) contains the anti-social, borderline, histrionic and narcissistic categories. Cluster C (anxious or fearful) covers the avoidant, dependent and obsessive-compulsive categories.

To meet the criteria for a personality disorder in DSM-5 (American Psychiatric Association, 2013) individuals have significant impairment in self and interpersonal functioning, and one or more pathological personality traits. These impairments are relatively stable across time and consistent across situations, and are not better understood as normal within individuals' culture or environment, or due to the effects of a substance or general medical condition. Although this definition captures the core features of personality disorder, it has been criticised as having a strong subjective element, assuming there is a clear differentiation between 'normal' and 'abnormal' personality. In recent years, this definition has also been criticised for locating individuals' difficulties within themselves rather than as a reflection of wider circumstances.

The other main diagnostic system, the *International Classification of Diseases* (ICD-11) (World Health Organisation, 2021) made a radical reconceptualisation to personality disorder classification in its most recent edition. The WHO has moved away from personality disorder categories and instead uses dimensions of severity – mild, moderate and severe. There is also an additional category of personality difficulty for individuals who do not meet criteria for disorder but whose personality affects health status. Following assessment of severity, clinicians can specify one or more domain traits: negativity, affectivity, anankastia, detachment, dissociality and disinhibition. A borderline personality pattern has also been included. However, this revision is not without controversy – with the publication of ICD-11 it is likely that more patients than before will be told they have a personality disorder. An explicit aim of the WHO remit for the ICD working group was to increase the diagnosis of personality disorder, on the basis that only around 8% of patients in the UK receive this diagnosis, despite suggestions that prevalence of personality disorder is about 40–90% for inpatients and outpatients with psychiatric disorders (Tyrer et al., 2019). Their aim was that by increasing the prevalence of diagnosis and making personality disorders more commonplace, then this would reduce the stigma for individuals (Watts, 2019). There are strong indications that this might not be the case. In a systematic review investigating personality disorder diagnosis and different clinical populations, a diagnosis was associated with negative effects on identity and hope (similar to a diagnosis of psychosis) and did not provide functional utility (such as access to treatments) (Perkins et al., 2018). Furthermore, Watts (2019) argues that clinicians in overstretched services may see personality disorder diagnosis as a barrier to treatment and this will exacerbate discrimination against those from lower socio-economic status groups who are more likely to meet diagnostic criteria for a personality disorder (Coid et al., 2006).

Given the difficulties with diagnosis and classification, some may wonder why practitioners and researchers are trying to identify individuals with personality disorders. However, research has found that individuals with personality disorders have poor treatment outcomes in both mainstream psychological and physical health settings (Hasin et al., 2011). Individuals with a diagnosis of personality disorder have high rates of mortality (Fok et al., 2012). These high rates of mortality are partially accounted for by increased rates of suicide (Hiroeh et al., 2001), with rates of attempted suicide reported to be around 5–10%. However, individuals with personality disorder are also at increased risk for physical health conditions, such as heart disease, which might be contributed to by difficulties in interpersonal interactions, preventing effective communication with healthcare professionals. Furthermore, lifestyle choices commonly associated with personality disorders, such as alcohol and drug misuse, and smoking, may also increase mortality (Frankenburg and Zanarini, 2004).

WAYS OF WORKING WITH INDIVIDUALS DIAGNOSED WITH PERSONALITY DISORDERS

Individuals diagnosed with personality disorders often present to practitioners as requesting help from clinical symptoms (such as chronic depression or self-harm) rather than looking for an intervention for their personality difficulties (Tyrer, Reed and Crawford, 2015). This can mean there is often a reoccurrence of symptoms, as Tyrer et al. (2015) suggest that personality disorders underlie the development and maintenance of comorbid mental health and social difficulties. Furthermore, improvement in symptoms following an intervention is difficult to distinguish from core personality change.

ASSESSMENT

Assessment of personality disorder is usually completed using an assessment instrument for personality disorders and/or a semi-structured interview, typically taking between one and two hours. A review by Clark et al. (2018) identified 23 validated instruments for the diagnosis of personality disorder, and it has been highlighted that the absence of fast and reliable assessment methods may be one of the reasons why few individuals with personality disorder receive a formal diagnosis. Bateman et al. (2015) pointed out a lack of a standardised assessment procedure results in stereotyped thinking by practitioners, where individuals who self-harm are automatically given a diagnosis of borderline personality disorder, and those who have a history of aggression or with a criminal record are assigned with anti-social personality disorder.

Difficulties in assessment have also led some practitioners to be reluctant to diagnose individuals with personality disorders, regarding it as a diagnosis of exclusion, whereby individuals are beyond help or extremely difficult to work with. Tyrer et al. (2015) suggest that practitioners reluctant to diagnose tend to fall into one of two camps: either practitioners dismiss personality disorders as a non-diagnosis which has no firm underlying construct, or they believe personality disorders should be dealt with by specialist services. Part of the difficulty in assessment is that no one questions the existence of personality but the line between 'normal personality' and 'personality disorders' is not clearly defined. In addition, the core relational deficit as a central feature of the disorder means that assessment of personality disorder is partly through interaction, rather than any individual symptom.

FORMULATION

Many see formulation as an essential element of working with individuals with personality disorders, as it provides a way of conceptualising an individual's difficulties within their unique life experiences, moves away from the associated stigma and bridges across diagnosis. The British Psychological Society recommends practitioners conduct a needs-based formulation (Jarrett, 2006). This process involves placing the individual's experiences in a contextual and explanatory framework that can help the individual and others around them to develop awareness of their behaviours, thoughts and emotions. This tool can then be used to inform any subsequent interventions.

INTERVENTION

The interventions offered are usually therapeutic and pharmacological. Therapeutic interventions have traditionally included a broad range of approaches, from more structured behavioural approaches, such as dialectical behaviour therapy, to more unstructured approaches, such as long-term psychoanalytic psychotherapies. Personality disorder interventions were typically given in long-term intensive therapeutic community inpatient centres. However, a lack of robust outcomes together with the changing structure of healthcare services, in response to resource constraints, has led to many of these services being revised. Currently, the United Kingdom National Institute for Health and Care Excellence (NICE) guidance recommends a combination of individual and group approaches, alongside other services, such as social services and drug and alcohol rehabilitation (NICE, 2009). An array of interventions has been developed from each of the main paradigm models specifically for personality disorders. These include dialectical behaviour therapy (from the behaviourist paradigm) (Linehan, 1993), mentalisation-based treatment and transference-focused psychotherapy (from the psychodynamic paradigm) (Bateman and Fonagy, 1999; Clarkin et al., 2001), and schema-focused therapy (from the cognitive paradigm) (Young, Klosko and Weishaar, 2003).

However, despite the creation of these specialist interventions, problems with providing them remain. Specialist interventions require trained specialists to deliver them, and often much commitment from the individual. In addition, research has shown that these interventions impact on symptoms but do not significantly improve interpersonal functioning (Bateman et al., 2015). Furthermore, when these interventions are compared with each other, and other therapies that are planned with personality disorders in mind, then there is little difference in the effectiveness between them (Noble, 2015). The case example below outlines two therapeutic approaches with an individual diagnosed with 'borderline personality disorder'.

CASE STUDY

INDIVIDUAL WITH DIAGNOSIS OF 'BORDERLINE PERSONALITY DISORDER'

Sarah is 27 years old and has a diagnosis of borderline personality disorder. She experienced a chaotic childhood and started self-harming at the age of 11. She has had several intense friendships and romantic partners, but these have not lasted long term, and usually end suddenly, after which she has felt overwhelming emotions and has attempted suicide on four occasions.

PSYCHOLOGICAL INTERVENTION

A practitioner providing an intervention for Sarah could start by developing a shared formulation with her, which acknowledges the traumatic experiences that led to the diagnosis of a personality disorder and the current impact this is having on Sarah's life. This could then lead to working through Sarah's difficulties and her desired outcomes using a specialised intervention (see examples below). During this process, a practitioner would pay close attention to the relational dynamics occurring in the therapeutic relationship, as this could give an indication of Sarah's interpersonal patterns and be a useful opportunity to develop new ways of communicating.

SPECIALIST INTERVENTION: DIALECTICAL BEHAVIOUR THERAPY

Conceptualisation of distress: Dialectical behaviour therapy (DBT) (Linehan, 1993) views borderline personality disorder as a biosocial disorder, citing that there is biological evidence to suggest that some individuals have a heightened sensitivity to emotion, experience emotions more intensively and have a slower return to emotional baseline. This is paired with a social environment in which the individual's coping mechanisms and responses to this emotional dysregulation are invalidated. As a result, individuals experience intense emotional states, which they feel unable to regulate.

What does the approach do? DBT is a structured, manualised method combining behavioural change and acceptance-based approaches in four areas: distress tolerance, emotion regulation, interpersonal effectiveness and mindfulness. This is implemented through an intensive programme of group skills training, individual therapy and immediate telephone support. Typically, DBT programmes last for 12–18 months. See Swales and Dunkley (Chapter 5.6, this volume) for a discussion of DBT.

SPECIALIST INTERVENTION: MENTALISATION BASED TREATMENT

Conceptualisation of distress: Mentalisational based treatment (MBT) suggests that individuals lack robust awareness of mental states of self and others (known as mentalisation) often as a result of experiencing trauma/neglect/lack of emotional availability from others (particularly attachment figures) in early life. This results in difficulties in emotional expression, appropriately communicating distress and understanding the intentions of others (Bateman and Fonagy, 1999).

What does the approach do? In sessions, therapists aim to activate the attachment system and provide a relational context to explore the mind of the other, increasing their ability to mentalise. It is a manualised approach taking place over 12–18 months, ideally offered twice per week, with sessions alternating between group and individual treatment.

ALTERNATIVE PERSPECTIVES

Due to practitioners and researchers raising concerns over-defining pathological personality, there is a growing body of practitioners who prefer to use other terms, such as complex trauma, to acknowledge individuals' previous history and wider context. The #TraumaNotPD movement reframes one category of personality disorder, borderline, as a form of complex trauma, evidenced by a robust literature connecting childhood trauma and the psychosocial environment with identity disturbance and interpersonal difficulties (Giourou et al., 2018).

The recent changes to personality disorder classification systems in ICD-11 (WHO, 2021) suggests the field is moving away from rigid categories to acknowledge that individuals fall on a spectrum of universal personality traits, a theory well established in personality research (Matthews, Deary and Whiteman, 2009). Hengartner et al. (2014) have evaluated the personality disorder literature and propose four dimensions. These are emotional dysregulation versus stability, extraversion versus introversion, antagonism versus compliance and constraint versus impulsivity. Within such an approach, all individuals (including those within the general population) have degrees of these traits, and individuals diagnosed with personality disorder may fall towards the extremes of these traits.

Similarly, interventions for individuals with personality disorders are moving towards looking at the common factors within interventions rather than advocating for particular approaches (Weinberg et al., 2011), since most approaches demonstrate similar outcomes. Bateman et al. (2015) highlight that one of the main unanswered questions for the future of interventions for personality disorder, given the high prevalence rates in the population and need for services, is whether interventions should be given by all practitioners who receive training to become personality disorder informed, or whether it remains the domain of specialist practitioners.

After a long history of stagnation in diagnostic and intervention approaches in regards to personality disorder, these debates and questions highlight that the field has moved into a dynamic and exciting era of development.

REFERENCES

American Psychiatric Association (2013). *Diagnostic and statistical manual of mental disorders* (5th ed.). DSM-5. Washington, DC: American Psychiatric Publishing.

Bateman, A. and Fonagy, P. (1999). Effectiveness of partial hospitalization in the treatment of borderline personality disorder: a randomized controlled trial. *American Journal of Psychiatry*, 156, 1563–1569.

Bateman, A. W., Gunderson, J. and Mulder, R. (2015). Treatment of personality disorder. *The Lancet*, 385, 735–743.

Cicchetti, D. (2014). Illustrative developmental psychopathology perspectives on precursors and pathways to personality disorder: commentary on the special issue. *Journal of Personality Disorders*, 28(1), 172–179.

Clark, L.-A., Shapiro, J. L., Daly, E., Vanderbleek, E. N., Oiler, M. R. and Harrison, J. (2018). Empirically validated diagnostic and assessment methods. In W. J. Livesley (Ed.), *Handbook of personality disorders* (2nd ed.). New York: Guilford Press.

Clarkin, J. F., Foelsch, P. A., Levy, K. N., Hull, J. W., Delaney, J. C. and Kernberg, O. F. (2001). The development of a psychodynamic treatment for patients with borderline personality disorder: a preliminary study of behavioral change. *Journal of Personality Disorders*, 15, 487–495.

Coid, J., Yang, M., Tyrer, P., Roberts, A. and Ullrich, S. (2006). Prevalence and correlates of personality disorder in Great Britain. *The British Journal of Psychiatry*, 188, 423–431.

Fok, M. L.-Y., Hayes, R. D., Chang, C.-K., Stewart, R., Callard, F. J. and Moran, P. (2012). Life expectancy at birth and all-cause mortality among people with personality disorder. *Journal of Psychosomatic Research*, 73(2), 104–107.

Frankenburg, F. R. and Zanarini, M. C. (2004). The association between borderline personality disorder and chronic medical illnesses, poor health-related lifestyle choices, and costly forms of health care utilization. *The Journal of Clinical Psychiatry*, 65, 1478–1665.

Giourou, E., Skokou, M., Andrew, S. P., Alexopoulou, K., Gourzis, P. and Jelastopulu, E. (2018). Complex posttraumatic stress disorder: the need to consolidate a distinct clinical syndrome or to reevaluate features of psychiatric disorders following interpersonal trauma. *World Journal of Psychiatry*, 8(1), 12.

Hasin, D., Fenton, M. C., Skodol, A., Krueger, R., Keyes, K., Geier, T., Greenstein, E., Blanco, C. and Grant, B. (2011). Personality disorders and the 3-year course of alcohol, drug and nicotine use disorders. *Archives of General Psychiatry*, 68, 1158–1167.

Hengartner, M. P., Ajdacic-Gross, V., Rodgers, S., Müller, M. and Rössler, W. (2014). The joint structure of normal and pathological personality: further evidence for a dimensional model. *Comprehensive Psychiatry*, 55, 667–674.

Hiroeh, U., Appleby, L., Mortensen, P. B. and Dunn, G. (2001). Death by homicide, suicide, and other unnatural causes in people with mental illness: a population-based study. *The Lancet*, 358, 2110–2112.

Jarrett, C. (2006). Understanding personality disorder. *The Psychologist*, 19, 402–404.

Linehan, M. M. (1993). *Skills training manual for treating borderline personality disorder.* New York: Guilford Press.

Matthews, G., Deary, I. J. and Whiteman, M. C. (2009). *Personality traits* (3rd ed.). Cambridge: Cambridge University Press.

Newton-Howes, G., Clark, L.-A. and Chanen, A. (2015). Personality disorder across the life course. *The Lancet*, 385, 727–734.

NICE (2009). *Borderline personality disorder: The NICE guideline on treatment and management.* Clinical Guidelines 78. London: National Collaborating Centre for Mental Health. (www.nice.org.uk/guidance/CG78/).

Noble, J. (2015). *A systematic review of interventions and their effectiveness to prevent recurrent self-harm in individuals diagnosed with borderline personality disorder using quantitative primary research.* Paper presented at the International Society for the Study of Personality Disorders, Montreal, Canada.

Perkins, A., Ridler, J., Browes, D., Peryer, G., Notley, C. and Hackmann, C. (2018). Experiencing mental health diagnosis: a systematic review of service user, clinician, and carer perspectives across clinical settings. *Lancet Psychiatry*, 5, 747–764.

Schneider, K. (1923). *Die psychopathischen Persönlichkeiten.* Berlin: Springer.

Tyrer, P., Reed, G. M. and Crawford, M. J. (2015). Classification, assessment, prevalence, and effect of personality disorder. *The Lancet*, 385, 717–726.

Tyrer, P., Mulder, R., Kim, Y. R. and Crawford, M. J. (2019). The development of the ICD-11 classification of personality disorders: an amalgam of science, pragmatism, and politics. *Annual Review of Clinical Psychology*, 15, 481–502.

Watts, J. (2019). Problems with the ICD-11 classification of personality disorder. *The Lancet Psychiatry*, 6(6), 461–463.

Weinberg, I., Ronningstam, E., Goldblatt, M. J., Schechter, M. and Maltsberger, J. T. (2011). Common factors in empirically supported treatments of borderline personality disorder. *Current Psychiatry Reports*, 13(1), 60–68.

World Health Organisation (2021). *International statisitical classification of diseases and related health problems* (11th ed.). ICD-11. Geneva: WGO. Available at https://icd.who.int/

Young, J. E., Klosko, J. S. and Weishaar, M. E. (2003). *Schema therapy: A practitioner's guide.* New York: Guilford Press.

RECOMMENDED READING

Watts, J. (2019). Problems with the ICD-11 classification of personality disorder. *The Lancet Psychiatry*, 6(6), 461–463.

This paper provides a brief overview on current debates within the field and highlights areas of current practice which may lead to further stigma for individuals diagnosed with personality disorders.

Editorial (2015). Rethinking personality disorder series. *The Lancet*, 385(9969), 664, 717–743.

This series of three papers challenges popular opinion that personality disorder diagnosis is permanent and untreatable and provides evidence for effective interventions.

Paris, J. (2015). *A concise guide to personality disorders.* Washington, DC: American Psychological Association.

This book reviews what is known and unknown about personality disorders, and its applications to clinical practice.

4.14 PHOBIAS

CHARLOTTE CONN, AASHIYA PATEL AND JULIE PRESCOTT

OVERVIEW AND KEY POINTS

Phobias can have a debilitating impact on an individual's everyday life due to the fear felt upon experiencing the stimulus. Research has been able to provide a variety of psychological approaches and treatments for someone experiencing a phobia. Treatments ultimately reduce the fear and allow the individual to live more comfortably. Ongoing clinical research and outcomes continue to develop approaches and treatments to increase the effectiveness of existing treatments. This chapter will address the following:

- An outline of phobias and their diagnoses, particularly relating to specific phobia, social phobia and agoraphobia.
- Differing psychological approaches and their steps towards treatment, including the person-centred approach, psychodynamic/psychoanalytical therapy and cognitive behavioural therapy (CBT).
- A case study looking at steps within the CBT approach of graded exposure to needle phobias.
- A rationale for virtual reality to be utilised as an alternative approach to phobias.

ASSESSMENT AND UNDERSTANDING

The term 'phobia' is defined as an intense yet unrealistic fear of an object, place or situation. The object, place or situation that provokes this immediate fear response is referred to as the phobic stimulus. When people suffer from phobias, the presence of a phobic stimulus can induce feelings of extreme terror or anxiety and can lead to a person feeling out of control of their own body. Other symptoms include panic attacks, an overwhelming sense of imminent danger or even a sense of impending death.

People who struggle with phobias may avoid the stimulus altogether, which can significantly impair their daily functioning, thus leading to distress. The fear experienced may vary based on the proximity to the phobic stimulus. However, in some cases sufferers of phobias may experience 'anticipatory anxiety', which in simple terms is the fear of fear itself.

To receive a diagnosis of a phobic *disorder*, a person must meet the relevant diagnostic criteria. For example, the phobic stimulus must almost always prompt an immediate phobic response, such as fear, anxiety or dread, and should typically lead to avoidance of the feared stimulus. The fear or anxiety must be disproportionate to the actual danger posed by the phobic stimulus and must cause significant impairment or distress in occupational, social or other important areas of functioning. The symptoms should not be better explained by other mental disorders and these symptoms must be present for at least six months prior to diagnosis (American Psychiatric Association, 2013). If a person meets these criteria, then they may be diagnosed with a phobic disorder. Phobias which are undiagnosed, however, are common among the general population.

Although phobic disorders fall within a larger group of mental health problems known as anxiety disorders, they can be divided in to three categories:

- Specific phobia
- Social phobia
- Agoraphobia.

SPECIFIC PHOBIA

A specific phobia is characterised by a person being disproportionately fearful, anxious or avoidant of a specific object or situation. These phobias generally develop in childhood or adolescence and can be a completely unique experience to the individual. Children may express these phobias through freezing, crying or clinging to another person and some people may find that specific phobias become less severe as they get older.

Some examples of these are:

- Situational phobias such as visiting the dentist, travelling on airplanes or enclosed spaces.
- Body-based phobias such as injections, blood, vomit or medical procedures.
- Animal phobias such as spiders or other insects, rodents or dogs.
- Natural environment phobias such as storms, water or heights.

According to the *Diagnostic and Statistical Manual of Mental Disorders* (American Psychiatric Association, 2013), the average individual with this condition fears three or more objects or situations. The amount of fear or anxiety may vary based on proximity to stimulus as well as environmental factors such as the presence of others or duration of exposure. Often, people who struggle with specific phobias adapt their lives in ways to avoid the stimulus, for example, a person with a situational phobia of airplanes may only travel abroad via alternative forms of transport, if at all.

SOCIAL PHOBIA

A social phobia, also known as social anxiety disorder, is characterised by a person being disproportionately fearful, anxious or avoidant of social situations. Although it is common for people to feel nervous or awkward in certain social situations, a person diagnosed with social phobia will experience more severe symptoms, such as panic attacks or extreme distress.

A social phobia can lead to impairment in daily activities such as:

- meeting unfamiliar people
- speaking to authority figures
- initiating a conversation
- consuming food or drink in the presence of others
- public speaking or other public performances.

People with social phobia may find themselves experiencing anticipatory anxiety prior to the social situation and may also fear being scrutinised by others. In some cases, people experiencing social phobia fear causing offence to others in social situations by doing or saying something wrong. Due to the cognitive ideation of being humiliated, rejected, embarrassed or offending others, social phobia can lead to difficulty in forming or maintaining relationships and in some cases can lead to extreme isolation. It can also affect self-esteem and confidence, with an overall impact on daily functioning.

AGORAPHOBIA

Agoraphobia is characterised by a person being disproportionately fearful, anxious or avoidant of a wide range of places or situations. It is often misunderstood as simply a fear of open spaces. However, it is more complex than this and involves places or situations that can cause a person to feel helpless, embarrassed or trapped.

According to the DSM (American Psychiatric Association, 2013), diagnosis of agoraphobia requires a person to experience disproportionate fear or anxiety in response to two or more of the following situations or spaces:

- Being outside of their home alone
- Being in enclosed spaces such as a shop, cinema or classroom
- Being in open spaces such as parks, open markets or parking lots
- Standing in a crown or queuing
- Using public transport such as buses or trains.

Sufferers of agoraphobia may believe that being present in a certain place or situation will lead to something awful happening. They may feel that leaving the place or situation may become difficult or that if the anxiety intensifies, they may be unable to escape. Some people may feel unsafe in certain places or situations as they believe help may be unavailable should they require it. For example, they may worry they will be helpless if they were to experience a panic attack or incontinence. Due to a fear of being embarrassed, helpless or trapped, they may struggle to leave their homes altogether, which can seriously impact daily functioning.

WHY DO PEOPLE EXPERIENCE PHOBIAS?

There is no consensus in the literature regarding why phobias develop as no one theory accounts for the development and maintenance of all phobias. Nevertheless, there is rich empirical evidence to suggest that environmental, genetic, cultural and behavioural factors may all contribute to the development of phobias. For example, some literature suggests that phobias may have a genetic link with evidence from twin studies suggesting the development of the same phobia despite separate upbringings (Van Houtem et al., 2013). Additionally, the learning theory of phobia development suggests that principles of classical and operant conditioning may lead to the development and maintenance of phobias (Coelho and Purkis, 2009). For example, being bitten by a dog may lead to a specific animal phobia or experiencing bullying in school or the workplace may lead to social phobia. Nevertheless, this theory does not account for people who develop phobias despite no previous experiences with the stimulus. It is possible that in some cases, a combination of factors leads to the development of phobic disorders and the growing body of evidence informs treatments and ways or working.

WAYS OF WORKING WITH PHOBIAS

Many counselling and psychotherapy models tackle an individual's phobia with the intention of ridding the phobia or at the very least lessening the impact of fear. The way this is approached differs between each intervention and its theory and methods.

This part of the chapter intends to acknowledge the most widely and commonly used phobia interventions. However, it is not an exhaustive list, and there are many variations of approaches and treatments available for phobias, including biological and pharmaceutical approaches.

PSYCHOANALYTICAL THERAPY

- Freud, the founder of the psychoanalytical approach, theorised that phobias could be caused by several instinctual and unconscious drivers, but ultimately believed that all phobias began in childhood.
- Initially, Freud believe phobias were due to undischarged sexual tension.
- Later, he perceived phobic anxieties as due to unresolved inner conflict, connecting to the concept of 'displacement', meaning phobias are a result of repressed memories, or through 'projecting' these painful feelings onto an alternative object.
- Early treatment was through the psychodynamic model of deep exploration through free association, transference and dream interpretation.

- Recent psychoanalysts have coined an approach to phobias through 'Panic Focused Psychodynamic Psychotherapy' (PFPP) (Busch et al., 2012), which is a less directive therapeutic approach from the therapist over 12 weeks compared to the open-ended sessions typically adopted in psychoanalytical therapy. PFPP is also a symptom-focused therapy, with a set of defined techniques to allow the patient to take control of the session but also to rapidly face their phobic anxieties.

PERSON-CENTRED COUNSELLING

- Rogers, the founder of person-centred counselling, believed every individual has the humanistic ability to grow but the conditions surrounding them may not be enabling the individual to achieve that growth (Rogers, 1951). Should the conditions be supportive, then our actualising tendency means that we would move towards growth and development.
- Within person-centred counselling, for psychological change to occur in therapy then the six necessary and sufficient conditions need to be met. These include the commonly referred to 'core conditions' (though Rogers' did not use this term), or the therapist-focused conditions of demonstrating empathy, providing unconditional positive regard and being congruent (genuine) with the client.
- Rogers also believed a non-directive stance from the therapist was vital as the client is the expert on themselves and therapists are to sit in the client's position with them rather than divert them away.
- Offering the necessary and sufficient conditions rather than techniques enables the client to feel in control of their sessions and to resolve issues through the exhaustion of difficult feelings throughout the talking therapy.
- More recent person-centred therapists argue that Rogers' requirements for the client to be in a 'state of incongruence' relates directly to the client being in a state of anxiety. Therefore, despite the lack of tailored interventions within the theory, the therapy is still effective for anxieties and thus effective for relating to issues such as phobias (Elliot, 2013).

COGNITIVE BEHAVIOURAL THERAPY

- Cognitive behavioural therapy (CBT), as coined by Beck (1967), is a therapy that takes direct actions to focus on the interconnected problematic behaviours and thoughts.
- CBT therapists believe the onset of a phobia is due to either classical or operant conditioning, where the client associates a thought or behaviour with a negative reinforcement to a stimuli/situation/object, etc.
- When that situation is encountered again, the client may then be left with negative automatic thoughts, which can then lead to a phobic behaviour (i.e., running away, panic attacks, fainting, etc.).
- CBT is more of a directive therapy than person-centred therapy (PCT) and is *typically* short term when working with phobias.
- For phobias, the CBT therapist may use graded exposure to introduce slowly the feared stimuli to the client until the unhelpful thoughts and behaviours are counteracted.
- Recently, the use of technology simulations have improved the CBT efficacy for phobias. Specifically, virtual reality has been utilised as an additional phase in exposure therapy, with vast improvements in its efficacy (Botella et al., 2017).

CASE STUDY

Sally has a severe phobia of needles, which causes her to faint at the sight of them. She is having surgery soon and will have to be on blood thinner injections for weeks afterwards. After cancelling and rearranging her surgery several times, her doctor recognised that her needle phobia required specialist therapy due to the health implications it was causing. Her GP referred her to a CBT therapist.

Sally was assessed and talked about all the times she had bad reactions to needles. She discussed with the CBT therapist how she faints at the sight of needles, even when watching television programmes. Sally has been petrified of needles for as long as she can remember, but as the assessment continued, she particularly remembered a time she was in hospital as a child and had a blood test. After the blood test, as she stood up to receive her certificate of bravery, she suddenly fainted. When she awoke, medical staff were surrounding her and she was violently sick. This then spiralled into fainting and humiliation whenever vaccinations were required. She soon recognised that if she did not have the injections, she would not faint; her CBT therapist recognised this as her having developed avoidance behaviours.

Sally and her therapist set a goal for her to be able to have her surgery and inject herself with the blood thinners. The therapist educated Sally on the nature of exposure therapy and demonstrated that Sally would need to be actively involved in tasks for it to take full effect. Her negative associations with needles and the resulting avoidance behaviours were outlined, followed by a description of how gradual exposure to needles will eventually reduce the anxiety surrounding them to achieve 'habituation'. Examples from Sally's avoidance behaviours were used to inform the habituation and graded exposure process.

To create a systematic process, situations surrounding needles were discussed and Sally rated each of them with a score from 0 to 8. The first step would be the situation where she feels the fear the least, to ensure realistic and practical goals were being set. It was agreed that Sally would do the first three steps without any other assistance. Sally then planned her exposure with guidance from a worksheet provided by the CBT therapist. She decided her first step would be to look at a cartoon drawing of a needle. She then rated her anxiety before, during and after the exposure. This was repeated with the detail of the needle becoming more and more lifelike until she felt her anxiety had reduced enough for her to be able to look at a real needle. She continued with the CBT sessions throughout, although once she got to this stage, the homework was reviewed and planned for further developments. Sally felt she needed assistance with the next steps of graded exposure. Together, Sally and her therapist watched someone else getting an injection until habituation occurred; they then continued to work on this until ultimately Sally could inject herself without significant avoidance behaviours.

ALTERNATIVE APPROACHES – VIRTUAL REALITY EXPOSURE THERAPY

Traditional forms of therapy for phobias are often costly and pose several risks. For example, for some phobias, sessions may need to be held in public. There is then a risk to patient confidentiality, and this also opens up the possibility of the session being interrupted or impacted by uncontrollable circumstances, which could include weather or other people. There is also the possibility of additional expenses such as travel. An alternative approach to phobia treatment that can overcome some of these issues is the use of virtual reality (VR) as a therapeutic approach, through a process of virtual reality exposure therapy (VRET). Research has found that VRET can provide an immersive and an interactive experience for clients and this can be conducted privately as well as inexpensively. Due to the potential versatility of virtual reality, VR can allow a therapist to determine the environment suitable for a client as well as generate relevant scenarios. This gives the client a very personal and unique experience, and it also allows the therapist to have some control over variables that would otherwise not be possible in a natural setting.

In exposure therapy, clients are presented with stimuli through either in vivo exposure (IVE) or imaginal exposure (IE). Both methods have advantages and disadvantages. In vivo exposure (IVE) involves live exposure to a stimulus. This method is often utilised to treat specific phobias or anxieties where live stimuli is easy to introduce, such as arachnophobia (fear of spiders), acrophobia (fear of heights), as well as social anxiety. Although IVE is an extremely effective method in the treatment of phobias, there are many phobias, such as aviophobia (fear of flying) and social anxiety, which may require sessions to be conducted in public, such as with an anxiety in public speaking. Such anxieties would pose a risk to patient confidentiality if conducted with live stimuli. In addition, they could become expensive, especially if several exposure sessions are required and live stimuli may introduce uncontrollable variables that may influence the overall effect of the treatment, as previously mentioned. Some people may also feel that IVE is too aversive, and this could lead to people dropping out of treatment or not seeking treatment at all. Imaginal exposure (IE) can address several of the limitations of IVE, since people are tasked with generating the stimulus in their imagination rather than confronting a live version of the stimulus. However, this has the problem that a person may not be able to, or unwilling to, generate a vivid imaginal representation of something they fear.

Due to the potential issues and drawbacks to these treatments, therapists have been seeking alternatives since the 1990s in the form of VR technology. VR technology includes a wide range of configurations, including head-mounted displays (HMDs), external projection setups such as the CAVE Automatic Virtual Environment, and simulators, all of which vary in terms of technical specifications (e.g., display resolution, tracking accuracy and field of view). Generally, VRET replaces the live stimuli of an IVE session with a realistic virtual stimulus. Due to the realistic and immersive virtual environment that VR affords, the fear-inducing stimulus will have the desired effect as IVE. Since VR is limited to the user's visual and auditory senses, it may sometimes incorporate tactile stimuli through an apparatus (e.g., force feedback gloves, toy spiders) to allow VR users to feel objects with their hands.

The virtual environment offers the potential to be customised to the patient's individual needs, allowing VRET to offer an unparalleled level of control for the therapist to manipulate factors that could not be controlled in a standard IVE session. Therapists can then tailor the sessions based on the patient's needs as well as providing a safe and confidential environment.

Early interest in the use of VRET was impacted by the limits of technology at the time as it was expensive, uncomfortable and the technology was low quality, which often led to simulator sickness. It was also limited due to the technical competencies of the therapist as it was often the case that the use of the technology required special training to operate. These limitations ultimately restricted the use and research of VR-based psychotherapy. However, with more recent advances in VR technology, and due to the more widespread and commercial uptake of VR through gaming systems, more and more people have the technical skills to utilise and engage this technology for therapeutic means. Both the HTC Vive and Oculus Rift VR head-mounted devices (HMD) are lighter and powerful enough to render high-quality visual and auditory stimuli. Both of these head-mounted VR devices are integrated with major digital distribution services such as Steam (https://store.steampowered.com/vr/). Steam has attracted both small, independent developers and large, professional developers to create high-quality VR programs. A renewed interest in VR has led to more mobile VR, a less powerful yet inexpensive version of computer-based VR that could run on smartphones utilising a cardboard headset.

REFERENCES

American Psychiatric Association and American Psychiatric Association. DSM-5 Task Force. (2013). *Diagnostic and Statistical Manual of Mental Disorders: DSM-5* (5th ed.). Washington, DC: American Psychiatric Association.

Beck, A.T. (1967). *Depression.* Harper and Row: New York.

Botella, C., Fernandez-Alvarez, J., Guillen, V., Garcia-Palacios, A. and Banos, R. (2017). Recent progress in virtual reality exposure therapy for phobias: a systematic review. *Current Psychiatry Reports*, 19(7), 42.

Busch, F. N., Milrod, B. L., Singer, M. B. and Aronson, A. C. (2012). *Manual of Panic Focused Psychodynamic Psychotherapy – Extended Range.* Abingdon, UK: Taylor and Francis.

Coelho, C. M. and Purkis, H. (2009). The origins of specific phobias: influential theories and current perspectives. *Review of General Psychology*, 13(4), 335–348. https://doi.org/10.1037/a0017759

Elliot, R. (2013). Person-centered/experiential psychotherapy for anxiety difficulties: theory, research and practice. *Person-Centered and Experiential Psychotherapies*, 12(1), 16–32.

Rogers, C. R. (1951). *Client-Centered Therapy.* Boston, MA: Houghton Mifflin.

Van Houtem, C. M. H. H., Laine, M. L., Boomsma, D. I., Ligthart, L., van Wijk, A. J. and De Jongh, A. (2013). A review and meta-analysis of the heritability of specific phobia subtypes and corresponding fears. *Journal of Anxiety Disorders*, 27(4), 379–388.

RECOMMENDED READING

American Psychiatric Association and American Psychiatric Association. DSM-5 Task Force. (2013). *Diagnostic and Statistical Manual of Mental Disorders: DSM-5* (5th ed.). Wadhington, DC: American Psychiatric Association.

The DSM-5 identifies the aforementioned types of phobias and provides examples as well as diagnostic criteria to illustrate the differences between them.

Marks, I. M. (2013). *Fears and Phobias.* London: Academic Press.

This book provides further insight into several of the areas covered in this chapter, such as types of phobia and treatments.

Miloff, A., Linder, P., Hamilton, W., Reuterskiold, L., Andersson, G. and Carlbring, P. (2016). Single-session gamified virtual reality exposure therapy for spider phobia vs. traditional exposure therapy: study protocol for a randomized controlled non-inferiority trial. *Trials*, 17(60). https://doi.org/10.1186/s13063-016-1171-1

This journal article highlights the efficacy of new and upcoming practices in virtual reality and graded exposure to phobias.

4.15 POST-TRAUMATIC STRESS DISORDER

DIVINE CHARURA AND PENN SMITH

OVERVIEW AND KEY POINTS

From our professional experience, we have noted that for many clients accessing therapy, the profound psychological distress they present with often arises from the combined impact of life's stress, existential challenges, or experiences of trauma. The American Psychological Association (APA) define trauma as 'an emotional response to a terrible event like an accident, rape, or natural disaster' (APA, 2022). Furthermore, for some, post-traumatic stress may ensue following a one-off traumatic experience or multiple experiences over time. Given the magnitude of the subject area of psychotraumatology, and the word limitation of this chapter, our focus will be on a relational approach to conceptualising and working with trauma, and in particular post-traumatic stress. To start with, however, we offer a definition of post-traumatic stress disorder.

This chapter outlines the following:

- Definitions and relational conceptualisation of post-traumatic stress disorder (PTSD)
- Offers a case study from therapeutic practice and a model of working from a relational perspective with PTSD from assessment to ending
- Offers an illustration of the types of skills and strategies the approach utilises in working with PTSD.

ASSESSMENT AND UNDERSTANDING POST-TRAUMATIC STRESS DISORDER

Post-traumatic stress disorder (PTSD) was first officially defined in 1980 when the American Psychiatric Association published the third edition of the *Diagnostic and Statistical Manual of Mental Disorders* (DSM III) (APA, 1980). Rather than outline and repeat the criteria for both the DSM-5 and the *International Classification of Diseases 11th Revision* (ICD-11) for PTSD in this chapter, all of which are available in the diagnostic manuals in detail, we will focus on the core symptoms for PTSD common to both the ICD-11 (WHO, 2019) and the DSM-5 (APA, 2013) criteria.

These are:

- Intrusions or re-experiencing of the event (such as intrusive memories; repetitive play in which the events or aspects of it are expressed; nightmares, flashbacks, or distress triggered by reminders of the event or events).
- Avoidance (such as avoiding thoughts, feelings, or memories of the event or events; or avoiding people, places, conversations, or situations that are associated with the event or the events).
- Arousal and reactivity or sense of current threat (such as irritability, being overly vigilant, being easily startled, concentration problems, or sleep problems).

In Table 4.15.1, we offer a summary of the PTSD diagnostic criteria. The criteria presented in this chapter is in line with the DSM-5 (APA, 2013) criteria applying to adults, adolescents and children older than 6 years.

Having presented a summary of the diagnostic criteria for PTSD, we acknowledge that the presentation of more complex responses to trauma have been argued to fit in a separate category of Complex Post Traumatic Stress Disorder (cPTSD) (Herman, 1992). These types of traumatic experiences involve additional cognitive, emotional, behavioural, relational, and characterological changes beyond the symptoms of PTSD, thereby implying a need for adapted models of understanding and treatment (Dyer and Corrigan, 2021; Karatzias et al., 2019).

DIVERSITY OF PRACTICE GUIDELINES AND MODALITIES FOR WORKING WITH PTSD

There are several primary unimodal approaches recommended for PTSD. The evidence for their effectiveness

Table 4.15.1 Summary of PTSD Diagnostic criteria

PTSD (DSM-5; APA, 2013)	PTSD (ICD-11; WHO, 2019)
A. **Exposure to actual or threatened death, serious injury, or sexual violence in one (or more ways)** i.e., direct exposure; witnessing trauma; learning that a relative or friend was exposed to trauma; experiencing repeated or extreme exposure to aversive details of trauma.	• Exposure to extremely threatening or horrific event or series of events.
B. **Re-experiencing of intrusive symptoms** i.e., distressing memories; nightmares; dissociative reactions such as flashbacks; or emotional or distress or physiologic reactivity after exposure to traumatic reminders. C. **Avoidance of stimuli associated with the event** i.e., trauma-related thoughts or feelings or external reminders. D. **Negative changes in cognitions and mood that began or worsened after the trauma** i.e., memory loss; overly negatives thoughts and assumptions about oneself or the world; exaggerated blame of self or others for causing the trauma; feeling isolated. E. **Alterations in arousal and reactivity that began or worsened after the trauma** i.e., irritable behaviour or aggression; reckless or destructive behaviour; hypervigilance; exaggerated startle response, difficulty concentrating; difficulty sleeping.	• Re-experiencing • Avoidance • Persistent perceptions of heightened current threat.
F. **Duration**. Symptoms last for more than 1 month.	• Must last at least several weeks.
G. **Functional significance**. Symptoms cause clinically significant distress or functional impairment (e.g., social, occupational).	• Significant impairment in personal, family social educational, occupational, or other important areas of social functioning.
H. **Exclusion**. Symptoms are not due to medication, substance misuse, or other illness.	

in PTSD populations has been well established in gold-standard meta-analyses and randomised control trials (RCTs). These, for example, include therapies such as cognitive behavioural therapy (CBT), cognitive processing therapy (CPT), cognitive therapy (CT), Prolonged Exposure Therapy (PE), Narrative Exposure Therapy (NET), and Eye Movement Desensitisation and Reprocessing (EMDR) (Dyer and Corrigan, 2021). There have continued to be developments in different modalities in addition to these, for example psychodynamic psychotherapy for post-traumatic stress disorder, which considers the impact of trauma on the psyche and on ego function; and other orientations that focus on specific imaginative and resource-oriented techniques or draw on humanistic-existential principles around reframing a new self-concept following trauma and developing the capacity for post-traumatic growth (Murphy, Elliott and Carrick, 2019).

In addition to these, there is a plethora of literature which has highlighted the centrality of the therapeutic relationship in working with PTSD and complex or relational trauma (Dyer and Corrigan 2021; van der Kolk, 2014). This contemporary body of literature and research primarily argues that longer-term work with PTSD requires deeper therapeutic relationships and trust for the client to feel safe, contained, and psychologically held to enable them to process their trauma (Lord, 2019). Thus, the section that now follows will offer the relational protocols that we are proposing can inform therapists of diverse modalities in working with PTSD. Additionally, the case study we offer illuminates the ways in which this happens in practice.

RELATIONAL PRINCIPLES, ASSUMPTIONS AND CENTRAL IDEAS

A relational approach explores the role relationships play in understanding self and maintaining who we are (Finlay, 2016; Paul and Charura, 2014). As human beings we all have an inner drive for connection and attachment with others. The relational approach posits trauma happens in and through relationships and it can therefore also be argued that processing trauma, change, and growth can occur through the co-creation of the therapeutic relationship. Through the co-construction of shared meaning, the aim of therapy is to increase awareness of an individuals' way of relating to self and other (intellectual insight) and how this relates to PTSD. A safe and supportive relationship can provide the opportunity for an individual to experience a positive 'self with other' experience as well as develop a new and more productive model of relating (Finlay, 2016; Paul and Charura, 2014). Individuals who experience PTSD can often lose trust in self and in others, making it difficult to connect on a relational level (van der Kolk, 2014). Shame and self-blame/doubt can be particularly toxic and difficult to confront in the presence of another. It is no surprise, therefore, that it takes time to address experiences of PTSD.

RELATIONAL WAYS OF WORKING WITH PTSD

In this section we will focus on a relational approach which can be applied in all modalities. To preserve confidentiality of the clients we work with, the following case study is a fictitious composite but is based on our own experiences and those of the individuals we have worked with.

CASE STUDY

Sam is a 30-year-old who presents for therapy with symptoms of PTSD (see Table 4.15.1). In the assessment phase of the therapy, Sam describes to the therapist numerous traumatic experiences from childhood through to adulthood, including childhood abuse, neglect, and bereavement. A 'recent experience' has triggered the re-experiencing of intrusive symptoms, exacerbated by media coverage of a high-profile case involving survivors of abuse. Sam describes that when intrusive memories of the traumatic experiences emerge, distressing nightmares, flashbacks, and panic set in. As a result, Sam has withdrawn from social contact, feels isolated, and overwhelmed. This has resulted in what Sam describes as a 'dark cloud' and 'low mood'. Sam is now signed off work due to the magnitude of the impact of the re-experiencing and intrusive suicidal ideation.

In discussing this case study, we will offer a brief four-stage pathway/strategy, which includes: (i) Assessment; (ii) Case formulation and treatment planning; (iii) Therapeutic treatment; and (iv) Ending and reintegration (Figure 4.15.1).

At the centre of this proposed four-stage pathway of working with PTSD, as noted in Figure 4.15.1, are skills central to the therapeutic process, which include contracting, asserting the importance of confidentiality, holding boundaries, naming limitations, and potential contraindications of engaging in trauma therapy. Of equal importance is the capacity of the therapist and client to engage in an ethical, collaborative, therapeutic relationship in which there is trust, commitment, containment, and openness. For illustrative purposes to each stage, we will offer an example of a psychological approach, but this model can be adapted accordingly to each practitioner's way of working. In our practice of working with PTSD, we include for example a three-step recovery plan

Pause for reflection on the therapeutic approach

Given Sam's presentation as described in the above case example, how would you approach working with Sam from your own therapeutic modality?

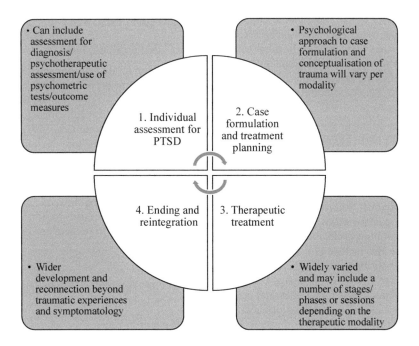

Figure 4.15.1 Four-stage pathway of working with PTSD

(Herman, 1992/1997) and we will expand on this in the sections that now follow. We commence here with an exploration of what is included in assessment and move through the stages to ending and re-integration.

ASSESSMENT

In trauma therapeutic work, the assessment process is an important part of conceptualising the client's experience and in formulating an understanding of the therapeutic work that will ensue.

A relational approach to assessment from a trauma-informed perspective focuses on 'what happened to you' rather than 'what is wrong with you'. It is also holistic, meaning that assessment is of the bio-psycho-social-sexual-spiritual domains to ensure that it captures the diversity of PTSD experiences. It begins with an invitation to share the trauma narrative or experience and gathers information that includes:

- an understanding of the person's conceptualisation of their life at present – 'the here and now' – as impacted by the trauma – 'the there and then' (this could include DSM-5 Criterion A & B)
- an exploration and identification of the changes that they notice in themselves and in the ways of relating with self and others post-trauma (this could include DSM-5 Criterion C & D)
- a perception of the impact of trauma on psychological functioning and social activities of daily living (this could include DSM-5 Criterion E & G)
- a discussion of how long they have been experiencing symptoms and difficulties (this could include DSM-5 Criterion F)
- an assessment of risk to self and/or other.

Assessment is a continual process and can be revisited as new information emerges and changes in the therapeutic relationship and the client's life occur. As part of

Pause for reflection on assessment

What would be your therapeutic approach to assessment with Sam?

assessment, depending on the professional's approach, numerous psychometric PSTD assessment screening and outcome measures may be used. In other orientations, however, the focus is on the therapeutic relationship and functionality reported by the client over time rather than pathologising or interpreting their experiences based on measures.

CASE FORMULATION AND TREATMENT PLANNING

Several mental health professionals use formulation as a key therapeutic tool that enables a greater understanding of an individual's difficulties (see Johnstone – Chapter 3.5, this volume). Information collected might include presentation, experiences of trauma, exploring what maintains the trauma cycle, and identifying protective factors. It may also include any other information that enables both patient/client and therapist to make links with regards to emotions, thoughts, behaviours, memories, and functionality. From a relational perspective, formulation is conducted in collaboration with the patient/client and is an organic process that can change over time, hence, if new information comes to light interventions can be refocused accordingly. Through this process both the therapist and patient/client can make sense of the PTSD experiences and begin to identify what maintains certain behaviours and responses to engage in the therapy, process the trauma, and make changes in the future. At this stage, the plan and goals for therapy are collaboratively set. Processing trauma requires openness and trust in the therapeutic relationship; thus, the treatment plan offers a map of how to navigate the terrain of difficult traumatic process. Processing in this context includes stabilisation, grounding, and developing a capacity for tolerance of heightened emotional arousal that will inevitably emerge in the process. In line with this, Herman (1992/1997) offered three fundamental milestones which can be considered in treatment planning. These are namely: (i) establishing safety; (ii) reconstructing the trauma narrative; and (iii) restoring relational connection.

THERAPEUTIC TREATMENT

(I) ESTABLISHING SAFETY

Establishing a safe environment can be a complex and time-consuming process and often involves rebuilding the patient/client's ego functions, as well as key discussions around their capacity for self-care and self-soothing strategies (Herman, 1992/1997). Trauma can have a devastating effect and ranges from experiencing single overwhelming events to more complex and prolonged psychological pain. Thus, the therapist's commitment to the task of ensuring safety is crucial to PTSD work. Setting appropriate boundaries and working within the patients/client's capacity to tolerate and manage emotional dysregulation is therefore key when establishing safety.

(II) RECONSTRUCTING THE TRAUMA NARRATIVE

> The conflict between the will to deny horrible events and the will to proclaim them aloud is the central dialectic of psychological trauma. (Herman, 1992/1997: 1)

Traumatic events typically occur outside everyday shared reality, often leaving individuals with a sense that they are harbouring the unspeakable. These secret parts of self, by their very definition, are meant to be kept unknown and unseen by others. In addition, an example of a defence to trauma experiences may be the repression of the trauma and associated memories. However, triggers such as visual, audio, or sensory reminders may result in the emergence of these memories or experiences in consciousness. The discomfort of denial and constant battle to dampen down the re-experiencing of trauma/PTSD symptoms can lead individuals to seek the language to express their pain, bear witness to their lived experience, and feel understood. Many agree that trauma memory processing is a vital part of working therapeutically with individuals presenting with PTSD.

Pause for reflection on formulation and treatment planning

What would be your approach to formulation and treatment planning with Sam?
What alternative approach to formulation and treatment planning could you take?

The action of retelling a trauma narrative in a safe environment can therefore produce a change in the dysfunctional processing of traumatic memories (Herman, 1992/1997; Paul and Charura, 2014).

(III) RESTORING RELATIONAL CONNECTION

Restoring relational connection which allows for a shared understanding and the possibility of finding compassion through working tentatively with felt experiences requires a flexible approach that embodies hope for a future where change, acceptance, and connection can not only be tolerated but also embraced. Being received in this way goes beyond the process of 'speaking your truth' and offers an opportunity for working through traumatic experiences, bodily responses, or felt senses (van der Kolk, 2014) in the 'here and now', thus enabling a restoration for relational connection with self and other. In the process of working through traumatic material/memories, it is important for therapists to deeply respect the patient/client's trauma experience, the impact on personality, and relationships while valuing their difference and diversity (Charura and Lago, 2021).

ENDING AND REINTEGRATION

Working through an ending stage of therapy could explore strategies for dealing with any pervasive feelings of anxiety, boredom, emptiness, avoidance, unconscious fantasies about the ending of trauma therapy, and/or experienced loss. In some cases, it also requires working through and challenging compulsions to repeat destructive behaviours. An ending phase addresses re-integration and relapse prevention strategies which may include a re-evaluation of functionality, or the capacity for re-engaging in inter/personal relationships. It also includes re-framing the traumatised self in a way that is more congruent with a meaningful and new functional self and a healthy identity (Paul and Charura, 2014). Additionally, it is good practice, where an unplanned ending emerges, or where the practitioners' competences are not aligned with helping individuals presenting with PTSD, that they refer to other services.

There is a growing body of literature that highlights the concept of post-traumatic growth (Greenblatt-Kimron, 2021; Nuccio and Stripling, 2021). It is worth stressing that both of us, as authors and clinicians, have worked with clients who also have reported post-traumatic growth, and this continually gives us hope in our work with those who have experienced trauma. While our chapter is drawn from a relational approach, which can be applied to a range of modalities, we would like to conclude by acknowledging how PTSD presents in a range of different ways in different individuals and thus approaches to treatment also must be diverse in contemporary society.

Pause for reflection on the therapeutic environment and therapeutic process

- What might you do to ensure you establish a safe therapeutic environment for Sam?
- How might you support Sam with the process of reconstructing or reframing the trauma narrative?
- Reflect on how you may develop a relational connection with Sam and what some of the challenges may be?

Pause for reflection on reintegration, relapse prevention, and ending therapy

- How might you support Sam with the process of reintegration and relapse prevention?
- What might you do to ensure a good ending to the therapeutic relationship with Sam? (also reflect on what some of the changes might be?)

REFERENCES

American Psychiatric Association (1980) *Diagnostic and Statistical Manual of Mental Disorders* (3rd ed.). DSM-III. Washington, DC: American Psychiatric Publishing.

American Psychiatric Association (2013) *Diagnostic and Statistical Manual of Mental Disorders* (5th ed.). DSM-5. Washington, DC: American Psychiatric Publishing.

American Psychological Association (2022) *Trauma*. [Website]. Available at: www.apa.org/topics/trauma.

Charura, D. and Lago, C. (Eds) (2021) *Black Identities and White Therapies: Race, Respect and Diversity.* Ross-on-Wye: PCCS Books.

Dyer, K. F. W. and Corrigan, J.-P. (2021) Psychological treatments for complex PTSD: A commentary on the clinical and empirical impasse dividing unimodal and phase-oriented therapy positions. *Psychological Trauma: Theory, Research, Practice, and Policy*, *13*(8), 869–876. https://doi.org/10.1037/tra0001080

Finlay, L. (2016) *Relational Integrative Psychotherapy: Processes and Theory in Practice*. Chichester, UK: Wiley.

Greenblatt-Kimron, L. (2021) World assumptions and post-traumatic growth among older adults: The case of Holocaust survivors. *Stress and Health: Journal of the International Society for the Investigation of Stress*, *37*(2), 353–363. https://doi.org/10.1002/smi.3000

Herman, J. L. (1992) Complex PTSD: A syndrome in survivors of prolonged and repeated trauma. *Journal of Traumatic Stress*, *5*(3), 377–391. https://doi.org/10.1002/jts.2490050305

Herman, J. L. (1992/1997) *Trauma and Recovery: The Aftermath of Violence – From Domestic Abuse to Political Terror.* New York: Basic Books.

Karatzias, T., Hyland, P., Bradley, A., Fyvie, C., Logan, K., Easton, P., Thomas, J., Philips, S., Bisson, J. I., Roberts, N. P., Cloitre, M. and Shevlin, M. (2019) Is self-compassion a worthwhile therapeutic target for ICD-11 Complex PTSD (CPTSD)? *Behavioural and Cognitive Psychotherapy*, *47*(3), 257–269. https://doi.org/10.1017/S1352465818000577

Lord, S. A. (Ed.) (2019) *Reflections on Long-term Relational Psychotherapy and Psychoanalysis: Relational Analysis Interminable.* Abingdon, UK: Routledge.

Murphy, D., Elliott, R. and Carrick, L. (2019) Identifying and developing therapeutic principles for trauma-focused work in person-centred and emotion-focused therapies. *Counselling & Psychotherapy Research*, *19*(4), 497–507. https://doi.org/10.1002/capr.12235

Nuccio, A. G. and Stripling, A. M. (2021) Resilience and post-traumatic growth following late life polyvictimization: A scoping review. *Aggression and Violent Behavior*, *57*. https://doi.org/10.1016/j.avb.2020.101481

Paul, S. and Charura, D. (2014) *An Introduction to the Therapeutic Relationship in Counselling and Psychotherapy.* London: Sage.

van der Kolk, B. A. (2014) *The Body Keeps the Score: Brain, Mind, and Body in the Transformation of Trauma.* Harmondsworth: Penguin.

World Health Organisation (2019) *ICD-11: International Classification of Diseases* (11th revision). ICD-11. Geneva: WHO. Available at https://icd.who.int/

RECOMMENDED READING

Finlay, L. (2016) *Relational Integrative Psychotherapy: Processes and Theory in Practice*. Chichester, UK: Wiley.

This essential book outlines a relational therapy model that prioritises the client and allows for diverse approaches to be integrated within a strong therapeutic relationship.

Paul, S. and Charura, D. (2014) *An Introduction to the Therapeutic Relationship in Counselling and Psychotherapy*. London: Sage.

This key book offers a practical and practice-based evidence guide to all aspects of the therapeutic relationship in counselling/psychotherapy and examines the issues impacting on the therapeutic relationship across a range of models of practice.

van der Kolk, B. A. (2014) *The Body Keeps the Score: Brain, Mind, and Body in the Transformation of Trauma*. Harmondsworth: Penguin.

This highly recommended book explores the devastating effect of trauma on individuals, their families and future generations. Moving away from standard talking and drug therapies, it offers a contemporary paradigm for mind, brain and body treatment.

4.16 SEX AND RELATIONSHIP PROBLEMS
CATE CAMPBELL

OVERVIEW AND KEY POINTS

Functional sexual difficulties can impact relationships, and poor relationships can affect sexual functioning. Relationship therapists need the ability to offer non-judgement and enabling counselling with a sexual focus. It's helpful to have an understanding of psychosexual therapy in order to assess clients' needs and refer appropriately when required.

- In the UK, sex therapy is a biopsychosocial discipline interested in medical, psychological and contextual influences on people's problems.
- Relationship and contextual issues can often be addressed by therapists with a general awareness of sexual issues.
- Clients with sexual 'dysfunctions' are better referred to qualified psychosexual therapists.
- Treating clients' anxiety and helping them to self-validate is as important as addressing the presenting sexual problem.

ASSESSMENT AND UNDERSTANDING

RESEARCH

Research into sexual problems is extensive. Pharmacological solutions are constantly sought, and sex therapy has become increasingly academic and professionalised in the past couple of decades. Three famous studies which have organised the development of sex therapy are:

- Zoologist Alfred Kinsey's reports (Kinsey, Pomeroy and Martin, 1948; Kinsey et al., 1953), which blew to smithereens formerly restrictive ideas about sexuality. They demonstrated, for instance, that married people had affairs, enjoyed kink and that sexual orientation exists on a continuum. The Kinsey Institute in Indiana continues sexual research to this day.
- Sex researchers Masters and Johnson's (1966) detailed laboratory studies into sexual response using live human subjects for the first time. They demonstrated the body's journey from arousal to

orgasm. Their later (1970) research led to the development of sex therapy with couples using sensate focus, based on a CBT model.
- Shere Hite's (1976) survey of 3,000 women's sexuality confirmed Masters and Johnson's finding that clitoral stimulation was required for female orgasm, even if it occurred indirectly. That most women were dissatisfied with their sex lives, and that few men understood what aroused women, led to much more interest in sex therapy generally.

BACKGROUND AND CONTEXT

Although researchers Masters and Johnson developed sex therapy with *couples*, sexual problems have become increasingly medicalised, individualised and pathologised (Tiefer, 2010). Treating the issues successfully is often a matter of managing and normalising anxiety and changing unhelpful thinking and beliefs.

SEXUAL PROBLEMS

Those who present for sex therapy either have a recognised sexual problem or an issue related to sex which requires exploration. Those referred to a qualified psychosexual therapist generally have a 'sexual dysfunction', as defined in the American Psychiatric Association's *Diagnostic and Statistical Manual (DSM)* (2013). According to the latest version, *DSM 5*, to qualify as a 'dysfunction', symptoms must have existed for at least six months, occur in at least three-quarters of sexual experiences and cause distress. The 'dysfunctions' mainly relate to arousal difficulties, pain/sensation and issues with orgasm.

LOSS OF DESIRE Although some medication, notably SSRI antidepressants, abnormal hormone levels or aversive menopausal symptoms often lead to loss of desire, context is often a major contributory factor. Basson's (2000) research established that most women in relationships lasting more than 10 years, and around a third of men, experience responsive rather than spontaneous desire. Desire follows, rather than precedes, arousal and is also affected by circumstances and beliefs, Basson discovered. Moreover, spontaneous desire usually returns in a new relationship. Suggesting that couples schedule sex for times when they're able to feel relaxed addresses this, although some couples' erroneous belief that sex *ought* to be spontaneous often needs to be tackled. A similar limiting belief that sex shouldn't be affected by everyday stress means that many couples present with concerns about the infrequency of their sexual encounters, often believing they are abnormal rather than just tired. Busy lives, lack of privacy, infertility, difficult pregnancy, bereavement, work difficulties and financial worries are among the reasons sex becomes a rare event. Normalising this, and pointing out that we live in a sexualised society where it can *seem* that everyone else is highly sexually active, can help restore confidence. Becoming aware of times when sexual interest occurs, or is even possible, and situations when sexual interest is closed down, has also been demonstrated to have a major impact on improving frequency (Bancroft et al., 2009).

Frequently, another problem co-exists which has led to one partner avoiding sex and the other then giving up attempts to initiate, finally losing interest themselves. Sometimes, couples collude to avoid sex, developing a pursuer–distancer dynamic, whereby the distancer claims low desire yet feels desired, and the pursuer is able to claim high libido while avoiding sex. Couples often exchange roles if the low libido partner begins to show sexual interest.

ERECTILE DIFFICULTY Erectile difficulty (ED), involving the inability to get or keep an erection, is probably the other sexual issue people are most aware of, especially since the introduction of PDE-5 inhibitors, drugs like Viagra, which improve blood flow to the penis. In order to determine whether to refer to a psychosexual therapist, it is important to assess whether the ED is constant, how long it has existed and whether it is situational. For instance, has it just started with a new partner, after taking recreational drugs or drinking alcohol? If masturbation and morning erections are unaffected and the ED is recent, the cause may be psychological and a talking therapy may be sufficient. However, ED which has developed gradually and is constant may be an early sign of cardiovascular disease or diabetes, and should be medically checked. Some prescribed and recreational drugs can also affect erections, as can low testosterone levels and other conditions, so it is wise to advise clients to consult their GP. Nonetheless, even when organic causes are treated, anxiety may remain. For those without medical problems, just one or two incidents of ED may cause so much worry that it starts occurring regularly. ED can be associated with other concerns, such as fear of pregnancy, relationship problems, loss of attraction or recent ejaculation. Sometimes, there are unrealistic expectations, such as someone of middle-age anticipating erections will remain as hard and reliable as they were as a teenager, or a partner may be particularly demanding or critical.

EARLY EJACULATION Also known as premature ejaculation, early ejaculation (EE) is often assumed to be associated with lack of maturity or nervousness and is expected to diminish with experience. However, some people do always ejaculate very quickly following stimulation. Those who ejaculate before penetration or as soon as they penetrate have diagnosable EE, but anyone who thinks they have EE will benefit from psychoeducation.

Many of those with EE are unable to recognise the point of inevitability, beyond which ejaculation becomes inevitable. Sex therapists can offer exercises to help identify this and to practise lasting longer. GPs may offer local anaesthetics and SSRIs.

DELAYED EJACULATION At the other end of the spectrum are those who find it difficult to ejaculate despite adequate stimulation, and may fake orgasm to end intercourse or withdraw and masturbate to climax. Loss of desire or attraction are often assumed by the partner, but delayed ejaculation (DE) can happen during periods of stress too. Recreational drugs or prescribed medication may also be implicated. Sometimes there is fear of pregnancy or other psychological concerns, such as believing sex is dirty, or worry about hurting the partner. Some people with an unusual masturbatory technique, which makes penetrative sex unsatisfying, have always had DE.

As with most sexual issues, DE is only a problem if the couple see it as one, so it is important to determine what has brought them into therapy, the health of the relationship and their expectations of sex. The opportunity to improve confidence in a sex therapy programme, to de-emphasise the importance of penetration and orgasm and to improve intimacy can all help.

FEMALE ORGASMIC DISORDER Also known as anorgasmia, some people may never have had an orgasm, may be finding it harder to climax or feel the quality of their orgasm has changed, perhaps due to medication, following illness or surgery. The rhythmic contraction of the uterus during orgasm may contribute to pleasure and be missed following hysterectomy, for instance.

Sometimes what is perceived as adequate stimulation is far from it, especially when couples expect intercourse to result in climax. A mere 20–30% of women say they can climax with intercourse alone (Shirazi et al., 2017), with the overwhelming majority needing additional clitoral stimulation. As these are self-reports, the true figure may be even lower, as the ability to orgasm through intercourse is so highly valued (Frith, 2015). However, many women are not distressed if they don't orgasm at every sexual encounter, but may develop response pressure in their effort to please partners with their climax. Some women who have experienced childhood sexual abuse or intimate partner abuse may feel guilty about their orgasms or have become accustomed to withholding during sex with an abusive partner.

PAIN Numerous medical conditions can cause pain associated with intercourse, or pain can just be present in the pelvic area. Involuntary tightening of the pelvic floor in women, so that intercourse is impossible, may follow some sort of trauma or occur spontaneously. Known as vaginismus, it is often treated by attempts to insert different sizes of 'trainers' or fingers into the vagina and learning to relax the pelvic floor. Some therapists concentrate more on any fears which may be associated with penetrative sex or on treating psychological trauma. Most women with vaginismus enjoy sex in other respects and are orgasmic, so it is ethical to ensure both partners actually wish to have intercourse before attempting treatment.

Some people need help when anal sex is painful. This is often due to insufficient relaxation and preparation, but penetration may not be realistic if there are haemorrhoids or other bowel conditions. Stimulation with fingers and tongue, using appropriate protection, may still be possible, although clients may need help adjusting to this reality.

PORNOGRAPHY Many clients say their sex education was inadequate and largely acquired through watching pornography, which has given them an unrealistic view of their own bodies and of partnered sex. For some, ED and DE are also being seen in association with excessive use of pornography or sexual chat rooms. The 'click and load' suspense associated with online porn may contribute to some of the problematic effects, ultimately requiring increasingly unusual visual stimulation to obtain the desired effect (Birchard, 2015). This is controversial, as accurately researching the physical effects of online sexual behaviours is difficult (Dwulit and Rzymski, 2019). However, it is often clients themselves who make the association between pornography use and problems with partnered sex.

Despite no independent evidence to support this, masturbation and pornography are seen as damaging by numerous online 'no fap' communities, which seek to 'reboot' brains through abstention from masturbation (Fernandez, Kuss and Griffiths, 2021). This fuels controversy over whether or not sexual dependency is real. Nonetheless, therapists continue to be approached by clients who claim that sexual compulsion and problems, particularly related to the time spent online, are threatening their relationship. Partners often feel considerable shame and perceive the behaviour as worse than an affair (Hall, 2015), so help is sought for both the problem itself and the relationship. A common therapy approach is to experiment with abstinence while strengthening the relationship and treating any underlying trauma which the sexual behaviour is being used to avoid. Clients sometimes also attend a 12-step group such as Sex Addicts Anonymous (https://saauk.info).

IDENTITY Although issues with sexual and gender identity are frequently encountered in therapy, all clients may feel differently positioned by their sexual problems, with many being unable to identify how they express their sexuality except through intercourse (Campbell, 2022), something which can be usefully explored in therapy.

WAYS OF WORKING WITH SEX AND RELATIONSHIP PROBLEMS

Psychosexual therapists, as they are known in the UK, work directly with presented sexual problems, as well as contributory attitudes and beliefs and relationship consequences. Some specialise in particular dysfunctions, work with individuals or couples, with sexual dependency or with identity issues related to sexuality and gender.

SEXUAL FOCUS

The work involves assessing and clarifying the presented issues to determine the best approach and whether referral to a specialist sex or trauma therapist is needed. If not, much of the work may involve the clients' attitude to sex and intimacy. Sometimes the couple's beliefs about sex and relationships can be looked at to determine how they are interfering with sexual expression. Genograms (family trees) can provide a useful tool to explore attitudes to sex and bodies in each partner's family of origin. Identifying the, often conflicting, sexual scripts that may be enacted between the couple can enable them to begin the process of change.

Sexual avoidance may begin following some new sort of commitment, such as an engagement, marriage, moving in together, buying a home or starting a family. As commitment grows, so may fears of rejection or loss or of being found lacking if they become too close. Therapists are alert to the couple's unconscious dynamic and ways they collude to sidestep intimacy, often arguing or becoming busy as they start to feel too close or developing incompatible sexual appetites, such as the pursuer–distance presentation described above. Work on differentiation, whereby each partner can self-validate, is necessary to allow intimacy and effective affect regulation. Shame may be associated with underlying trauma which is evoked by closeness and may be treated with both partners present or in individual therapy, particularly Transactional Analysis, Eye Movement Desensitisation and Reprocessing (EMDR) and Internal Family Systems Therapy. Exploring the parts of themselves that feel sexual and those that don't can benefit most couples.

CASE STUDY

SEXUAL FOCUS

Fatima and Louise presented with a history of arguing related to Fatima's poor timing of sexual initiation. Fatima felt personally assaulted by Louise's rejections and Louise felt stifled. It emerged that Fatima believed that if she wasn't being sexual with Louise, she had 'wasted' the difficult coming out to her family, who had initially disapproved of her sexuality. Louise, meanwhile, felt that there was no room for her own sexual expression and was experiencing Fatima as controlling. The therapist suggested they pause sex and work on consent, establishing how to approach one another and how to refuse sexual advances more kindly. With the emphasis on intimacy, they were able to work on what was possible rather than what wasn't and were better able to express their own needs.

PSYCHOSEXUAL THERAPY

A core cognitive behavioural therapy (CBT) approach is often employed using additional skills as appropriate. This begins with an initial assessment to determine the nature of the problems and whether sex therapy is likely to be suitable. If so, the work continues with individual history-taking sessions, which also offer an opportunity for psychoeducation, stabilising, safeguarding and establishing a therapeutic relationship. One partner may bring or send the other to be fixed, but often both have sexual problems, or one partner may be exacerbating the other's difficulties through undue criticism or their own avoidant strategies.

With a detailed history for both partners, the therapist is able to identify how the couple may have reached this point and what circumstances, beliefs or behaviours are maintaining their problems. A meeting to discuss the therapist's formulation of their issues is usually fascinating for the couple, who can then decide whether to continue with treatment. As CBT is a stepped approach, the couple may step off at any stage, with some having already changed as a result of the history-taking experience.

Those who continue into therapy are given exercises to undertake individually and together which include graduated exposure to threatening intimacy. There may also be specific exercises to improve confidence in erections, manage pain, delay ejaculation or induce orgasm. Throughout, reference to the history taking and formulation can assist the therapist in anticipating and treating blocks to progress, but all exercises are treated as experimental. The therapist benefits from more information when the couple feels experiments have gone badly and the couple are encouraged when they go well.

CASE STUDY

SEX THERAPY

Bryn and Elena were keen to start a family, but Bryn had started to lose his erection. He had no problems with masturbation, so the therapist wondered if he was secretly worrying about a pregnancy. He admitted feeling concerned, as he had a poor relationship with his own father. With trauma therapy as a potential back up if necessary, the couple started sensate focus experiments and Bryn was given exercises to improve confidence in his erections. This helped him to feel more in control, and the increased intimacy that resulted from sensate focus made him feel closer to Elena. This encouraged him to believe they'd be good parents. Despite the return of reliable erections relatively quickly, the couple remained in therapy for several more sessions as they felt it was so beneficial for their relationship overall.

Some couples with extreme anxiety begin with gentle clothed touch and talking exercises before the therapist judges they are ready for naked sensate focus experiments. These initially involve the couple touching one another non-sexually for their own interest without commenting on how they are finding this. This helps them to differentiate and mindfully concentrate on their own experience, rather than becoming anxious that they are not pleasing one another. The couple agree to no sexual contact other than that prescribed by the therapist, who gradually introduces more varied touch and experimentation. While the couple's over-arching goal may be to fix their presenting problem, the focus is on the steps to achieve this which are entirely dedicated to learning rather than achieving outcomes. As sexual touch is introduced, each partner remains responsible for their own sexual experience, showing the other what they would like if necessary, and accepting that each encounter may not end with orgasm.

When this process is approached slowly and experimentally, couples usually find their own sweet spot, realising they are less interested in their original goals than they are in the relaxed intimacy they have discovered. In practice, couples may be satisfied with their progress long before the goals are reached and step off the programme, or they continue and feel their expectations have been exceeded. They usually tell the therapist when they feel ready to end, and are offered a follow-up appointment to pick up on any remaining issues to have emerged. Often, however, they use the session to celebrate their renewed relationship.

REFERENCES

American Psychiatric Association (2013) *Diagnostic and Statistical Manual of Mental Health Disorders*, (5th ed.). DSM-5. Washington, DC: APA.

Bancroft, J., Graham, C. A., Janssen, E. & Sanders, S. A. (2009) The dual control model: current status and future directions. *Journal of Sex Research*, 46(2–3), 121–142.

Basson, R. (2000) The female sexual response: a different model. *Journal of Sex and Marital Therapy*, 26(1), 51–65.

Birchard, T. (2015) *CBT for Compulsive Sexual Behaviour*. Hove, UK: Routledge.

Campbell, C. (2022) *Sex Therapy: The Basics*. Abingdon, UK: Routledge.

Dwulit, A. D. & Rzymski, P. (2019) The potential associations of pornography use with sexual dysfunctions: an integrative literature review of observational studies. *Journal of Clinical Medicine*, 8(7), 914. www.ncbi.nlm.nih.gov/pmc/articles/PMC6679165/ (accessed 14 February 2022).

Fernandez, D. P., Kuss, D. J. & Griffiths M. D. (2021). The pornography 'rebooting' experience: a qualitative analysis of abstinence journals on an online pornography abstinence forum. *Archives of Sexual Behaviour*, 50, 711–728.

Frith, H. (2015) *Orgasmic Bodies*. Basingstoke: Palgrave Macmillan.

Hall, P. (2015) *Sex Addiction: The Partner's Perspective*. Hove, UK: Routledge.

Hite, S. (1976) *The Hite Report: A Nationwide Study on Female Sexuality*. London: Collier Macmillan.

Kinsey, A. C., Pomeroy, W. B. & Martin, C. E. (1948) *Sexual Behavior in the Human Male*. Philadelphia, PA: W. B. Saunders.

Kinsey, A. C., Pomeroy, W. B., Martin, C. E. & Gebhard, P. (1953) *Sexual Behavior in the Human Female*. Philadelphia, PA: W. B. Saunders.

Masters, W. & Johnson, V. E. (1966) *Human Sexual Response*. Boston, MA: Little Brown & Co.

Masters, W. & Johnson, V. E. (1970) *Human Sexual Inadequacy*. New York: Bantam Books.

Shirazi, T., Renfro, K., Lloyd, E. & Wallen, K. (2017) Women's experience of orgasm during intercourse: question semantics affect women's reports and men's estimates of orgasm occurrence. *Archives of Sexual Behavior*, 47(3), 605–613.

Tiefer, L. (2010) Still resisting after all these years: an update on sexuo-medicalization and on the new view campaign to challenge the medicalization of women's sexuality. *Sexual and Relationship Therapy*, 25(2), 196–198.

RECOMMENDED READING

Barker, M.-J. (2018) *Rewriting the Rules* (2nd ed.). Abingdon, UK: Routledge.

A different way of looking at taken-for-granted attitudes to sex, love and relationships.

Campbell, C. (2020) *Contemporary Sex Therapy*. Abingdon, UK: Routledge.

A comprehensive explanation of the core CBT approach to psychosexual therapy.

Weiner, L. & Avery-Clark, C. (2017) *Sensate Focus in Sex Therapy*. Abingdon, UK: Routledge.

An illustrated guide to sensate focus with a detailed commentary.

4.17 SEXUAL ABUSE IN CHILDHOOD

ROSALEEN MCELVANEY

OVERVIEW AND KEY POINTS

This chapter will discuss child sexual abuse (CSA) and how it impacts on the individual across the lifespan. I discuss the key issues to focus on while engaging in an assessment and formulation with clients who have a history of CSA and will use a fictitious client, Julie, to illustrate how one might work with a client in counselling or psychotherapy. Key points include:

- Each individual is unique in terms of how they experience CSA and how it impacts on their lives.
- A comprehensive assessment of need, using an ecological lens and drawing on a range of developmental theories, will help identify how best to support individuals in recovering from this trauma.
- It may be useful to focus on three key domains of functioning: interpersonal relatedness, sense of self and affect regulation.
- A range of theoretical models and techniques can be useful in addressing issues related to CSA.

ASSESSMENT AND UNDERSTANDING

Child sexual abuse (CSA) is regarded as the most potent of childhood adversities in terms of adult psychopathology (Lamoureax et al., 2012). Most definitions refer to sexual activity in the context of a relationship where there is an imbalance of power and coercion is used to engage a child in sexually inappropriate behaviour. The behaviours may range from exposing children intentionally to sexual material to inappropriate touching of genital body parts to attempted or actual penetration. It is widely accepted that abuse in childhood has potentially long-term consequences. These can continue into adulthood and may include anxiety, depression, eating difficulties, substance misuse and dependency, personality difficulties, heart disease, liver disease, cancer and acute stress (Toth and Cicchetti, 2013). Not all children experience negative psychological outcomes. Indeed, there is a growing body of literature indicating that many adults report post-traumatic growth arising from experiences of abuse (Tedeschi and Calhoun, 2004). Some children do not show short-term effects but experience difficulties later, in adolescence or adulthood. Many manage to 'block it out' either consciously or unconsciously but, over time, ways of being in the world that were adaptive responses to the abuse experience in childhood become maladaptive as the adult engages with the challenges of adulthood. We know that most people who have been abused do not tell until adulthood, depriving them of the opportunity to reflect with others on what happened, to be reassured that it was not their fault, and to come to terms with the impact of such experiences. As most children have been sexually abused by someone known to their family, there can be significant fallout in extended families when adults disclose sexual abuse from childhood.

It is important to bear in mind that psychological impact is cumulative – subsequent experiences of trauma will exacerbate earlier difficulties. Sexual abuse does not happen in isolation; often children experience some form of physical abuse, sometimes neglect and always emotional abuse. In addition, childhood abuse is a significant risk factor for later victimisation, thus it is important to enquire about all experiences of victimisation when meeting a client with a history of child abuse. Finally, early child abuse can impact both the structure and function of the brain, that is, the size and shape of specific areas of the brain and how these parts of the brain work in terms of emotional and cognitive functioning, evidenced through the use of neuro-imaging technology (van der Kolk, 2014). The abused child may experience difficulties encoding emotionally overwhelming information, affecting the amygdala (the part of the brain that facilitates emotional processing), leading to later difficulties in emotional experiencing. Parts of the frontal lobe of the brain can be impaired from chronic abuse, resulting in difficulties with problem-solving and decision-making when faced with a conflict. Many adults, particularly those who have not spoken of their abuse experiences with others, continue to experience these difficulties in adulthood, which may be exacerbated as a result of avoidant behaviour patterns that protect the individual from experiencing distress but also inhibit their experiencing of positive emotions.

The initial assessment informs the therapist's formulation about what the client's presenting difficulties are, what may have contributed to these difficulties and how we might help the client overcome these difficulties. An understanding of the client's unique developmental and family history helps to build a picture of this unique individual's vulnerabilities and protective factors that can mediate the psychological fallout from experiences of abuse (Toth and Cicchetti, 2013). This in turn will help us understand this client, what they need now and how we might help them in resolving their difficulties. As CSA is fundamentally an interpersonal experience and the family context plays a significant role in the healing process, a systemic or ecological lens is needed to fully understand the impact. Intrapersonal factors that influence how an individual is impacted by CSA may include temperament, personality, self-esteem, sense of efficacy and agency, intelligence and problem-solving skills. Interpersonal factors may include attachment style, current relationships with family or peers, whether supportive or conflictual. Family factors may include parental mental health or family stability. At the community or social level, involvement in social activities can mediate the impact, while living in a volatile neighbourhood may exacerbate the child's difficulties. While we have no specific evidence of the impact of not telling, in therapeutic services we do see how keeping the secret has negatively influenced people's relationships with themselves and others as they navigated their way through childhood, adolescence and adulthood. The extent of support the individual has been able to draw on, both intrapersonally and interpersonally, will strongly determine how they have been impacted by such experiences and the extent to which they will benefit from therapy.

I find it helpful to focus on the client's phenomenology, their lived experience of the world, in terms of three key domains of functioning: interpersonal relatedness, self-identity and emotion regulation.

INTERPERSONAL RELATEDNESS

The breach of trust that is inherent to the experience of CSA impacts the child in terms of their capacity for relatedness. In adulthood, this may manifest as difficulties with trust and expectations of others that impact on maintaining healthy, meaningful relationships. The client may be overly trusting, lacking an awareness of their own boundaries and how these intersect with others' or they may be overly suspicious of others, slow to trust and open up to others for fear of being hurt again. Similarly, difficulties with trust can be experienced in peer relationships, friendships, work relationships and intimate and sexual relationships. Adults may seek out or avoid conflict, be overly submissive or aggressively assertive, operating from internal working models that are indiscriminate or that assume others cannot be trusted.

SENSE OF SELF

The experience of abuse is one where the child often feels powerless. This can impact on a child's sense of agency and autonomy, important processes for the development of a sense of self. The stigmatisation associated with abuse may result in the child feeling ashamed and embarrassed, which may be exacerbated by many years of keeping silent about the experience. Trauma shatters a child's assumptions about themselves and the world around them; in particular, the assumption that they are intrinsically good, and that they deserve to be treated with respect. Adults who have experienced childhood abuse engage in more negative thinking about themselves and about the world than individuals who have not experienced childhood trauma.

AFFECT REGULATION

The emotionally overwhelming nature of CSA, the difficulty in making sense of the experience, presents a challenge to a developing child's capacity for regulating their feelings, in particular their capacity to tolerate intense negative emotional states. This may manifest itself along a spectrum from extreme avoidance of strong feelings to emotional outbursts, reflecting extreme sensitivity (hypervigilance and hyperarousal). Avoiding talking about or thinking about what happened can be a coping strategy that works well for many. In the extreme, this is manifested as dissociation, an unconscious protective mechanism to help us avoid having to confront intolerable emotional pain. However, this avoidance results in a narrowing of emotional repertoire, preventing many from engaging meaningfully in life and relationships. An over-attentiveness to others can represent an intense need for predictability and control in order to feel safe. This continuous state of alertness can impact on the individual's physical wellbeing. Individuals struggle to find ways to manage their emotions, to self soothe, which can result in them numbing themselves to avoid feeling anything. To reduce tension, they may resort to self-harming behaviour, such as cutting, eating difficulties, substance abuse or aggressive behaviour.

It can be useful to use psychometric tests, such as the Trauma Symptom Inventory (TSI) (Briere, 1995), to gather information about trauma-specific difficulties. The TSI is a self-report measure (100 questions), which lists symptoms or experiences that are typically associated with trauma. Clients are asked to indicate whether, and the degree to which, they experienced these difficulties in the previous six months. Standardised norms are available so that clients' scores can be compared with others who have experienced trauma. The 10 clinical scales include: anxiety, depression, anger/irritability, intrusive experiences (such as flashbacks), avoidance and dissociation, sexual difficulties and self-identity difficulties, and tension-reduction behaviours that attempt to reduce internal tension (self-harm, angry outbursts, suicidal feelings). The results can provide an opportunity to talk about some of the more painful and embarrassing difficulties that clients experience, as well as providing a baseline measure that can be used to evaluate any changes in symptoms or experiences over time.

WAYS OF WORKING WITH CLIENTS WHO HAVE EXPERIENCED SEXUAL ABUSE IN CHILDHOOD

Julie (28 years) presents for therapy following a series of arguments with her fiancé. Julie is ambivalent about getting married, constantly postponing the decision. She and her fiancé are experiencing difficulties with intimacy in that Julie has become avoidant in recent months. Julie finds this surprising as she has never had any difficulty with sex. However, she was sexually abused by an uncle between the age of 8 and 10. Julie presents with significant low self-esteem issues; she sees herself as fundamentally flawed. She copes with emotional pain by avoidance. Julie has recently begun to suffer from panic attacks and has been encouraged to attend therapy, although she is ambivalent about how this could help.

In my first meeting with Julie, I will begin the process of developing a formulation by simply giving her the space to tell me about herself and what brought her to therapy. I will be listening out for information that helps me make sense of her story, why she may be experiencing her current difficulties and how she tells her story. I will be curious and reflective, encouraging a similar stance in her, and I will emphasise collaboration: we will try to understand Julie better together. I will also be paying attention to my own experience of Julie, how it is to be with her and what emotions she evokes in me – how I respond to her and her story.

I draw on a range of theoretical models in my work. The humanistic approach, which emphasises empathy, unconditional positive regard, and congruence, helps me build a strong therapeutic relationship with Julie. Drawing on a cognitive-behavioural approach, I will try to help Julie gain more mastery over her anxious feelings and panic attacks. This may result in her feeling more empowered, strengthen the collaborative nature of our relationship, and give her more hope that therapy will help her – all important predictors of successful outcome in therapy. I will use psychoeducation to inform Julie of the dynamics of sexual abuse and hopefully help her understand that many of her reactions to this experience are commonly experienced by others who have been sexually abused. This may help with potential feelings of isolation, shame and self-blame. An emotion-focused approach will help me focus on helping Julie process her feelings about what happened through experiencing her emotions in the room with me, and help her transform painful maladaptive emotions into more adaptive life-affirming emotions.

While it is often the symptoms (anxiety, relationship difficulties) that bring clients for help, focusing on these may not be enough to lead to longer-lasting change. A psychodynamic approach supports me in taking a 'not-knowing' stance, fostering curiosity and reflective capacity. I will try to give Julie the opportunity to re-experience unconscious internal conflicts through the transference with me, so that she can work through such conflicts in the here and now, through the vehicle of the therapeutic relationship.

Given Julie's reported difficulties with self-esteem and her struggle with intimacy and commitment, I am interested in particular in Julie's attachment style and interpersonal functioning. My aim is for therapy to be a corrective emotional experience for Julie. I may offer interpretations that help her gain insight into how her early relationships and early trauma get re-enacted in her current life and current relationships. This may help Julie understand interpersonal communication styles that are unhelpful and the defence mechanisms she uses to protect herself from the overwhelming anxiety that threatens to overcome her.

THERAPEUTIC RELATIONSHIP

While the therapeutic relationship is important for all clients, it holds particular significance for those who have experienced childhood abuse as theirs is an interpersonal wound that involves a breach of trust. Healing takes place through the therapeutic relationship. I will want to create the right environment, where Julie will learn to trust me so that she can share her innermost thoughts and feelings, feel understood and met in an authentic encounter where she is not judged, no matter how abhorrent her story. Depending on Julie's personality and emotional processing style, this may require providing a warm, caring, authentic and non-judgemental presence. However, Julie may find such an approach threatening and unbearable to tolerate. A cognitive-behavioural focus on the working alliance may suit better, where the attention is on shared goal setting, transparency and collaboration. At some point it will be important for me to take a neutral stance, to enable her to project onto me those intolerable feelings, such as shame and being judged, to experience the negative transference. Julie might then experience me as the withholding therapist, the abuser or the neglectful parent. I will need to pay attention to my countertransference, how it is to be experienced as withholding or abusive, if I am to help Julie work through unresolved conflicts as I try to hold the limits of the therapeutic frame and provide a safe and containing experience for Julie. I will need to use my own supervision to keep me on the right path, both inviting Julie's transference reactions and acknowledging whatever strong emotions get triggered in me through this relationship to ensure that I can stay present and bear witness to her intense emotional pain. I may fall into a trap of being the 'rescuer', wanting to protect Julie from her own pain. My own emotional processing style will impact on my ability to facilitate her in expressing her emotions.

DEVELOPING A SENSE OF SELF

The experience of being valued and respected will hopefully help Julie to feel a greater sense of self-worth. After all, this is how we develop our sense of self, through being loved and cared for by our primary caregivers. I may ask Julie to perform 'homework' exercises that will boost her experience of herself as competent, capable of experiencing pleasure and being cared for. In sessions, I will help Julie focus on her emotions and experience her embodied self. We will explore how her avoidant way of being in the world may stop her feeling connected to herself, physically, emotionally and spiritually. Trauma-focused cognitive-behaviour therapy (TF-CBT) techniques can be useful to help Julie explore unhelpful automatic thoughts and negative self-statements about herself and the world that serve to reinforce her negative self-image (Deblinger et al., 2015). Through processes of gradual exposure, talking about and processing the trauma, I can facilitate Julie to modify these unhelpful beliefs and assumptions, to gain self-mastery over her psychological difficulties, to build her repertoire of coping skills and to reduce the symptoms of trauma. CBT can foster empowerment and a sense of agency for Julie – aspects of self that are essential components of self-esteem.

Exploring Julie's story may also reveal issues of self-blame and shame, interlinked concepts in the context of CSA (McElvaney et al., 2021). I will try to help Julie make sense of what has happened, drawing on my own knowledge and experience of working in this field – why it happens, how it happens, how common it is, how it can impact on people. This may bring some comfort to her, knowing that she is not alone in having these difficult thoughts and feelings. It may help her understand that sexual abuse is never a child's fault; that no matter what a child does, the responsibility lies with the abuser. Knowing that others have been through these experiences, have felt the same way, have had the same crazy thoughts and have gone on to experience healing may give hope to Julie who may feel stuck in repeated patterns. Being treated with warmth and respect will also help Julie feel pride in herself, the antidote to shame.

MANAGING FEELINGS

Most trauma literature indicates that emotional processing of the traumatic experience is necessary to overcome the psychological impact of the abuse. Coping mechanisms that were effective in the past may no longer work. The manner in which experiences are encoded into the memory systems may result in visceral patchy memories that are fragmented and difficult to make sense of, experienced as flashbacks and causing considerable distress. This may be due to a combination of the child being emotionally overwhelmed at the time and a lack of ability to understand what is happening (van der Kolk, 2014). Memories can be activated or triggered by innocuous events or experiences. Julie's pending marriage may have triggered fears that have been out of her awareness and now demand attention.

Emotion-focused therapy for trauma (Paivio and Pascual Leone, 2010) aims to reduce intrusive symptoms (such as nightmares or flashbacks), change maladaptive perceptions of self and others and reduce avoidance. It is through engagement with our experiences that we are able to address our unresolved emotions and find better, more adaptive ways of being in the world. Change processes in emotion-focused therapy focus on developing and maintaining a safe therapeutic relationship, bringing memories into the here and now so that the associated painful emotions can be experienced, expressed and transformed into more productive and constructive ones. My hope is that Julie's emotional repertoire will expand to enable her to engage more fully in her life.

CONCLUSION

It is important in any therapeutic work to consider the client's environment outside the therapeutic space, how current relationships or family issues impact on the change process and what social supports can be harnessed for Julie. The issue of whether Julie's uncle may be a risk to other children will need to be addressed, which may involve liaison with child protection services. It may also be necessary for Julie and her fiancé to engage in couples therapy. Childhood experience of trauma impacts on how couples communicate, their expectations of each other, how they seek or avoid intimacy (McIntosh, 2019). In the interests of good ethical practice and collaboration, it is important that we monitor our work with clients, constantly checking in with them as to what they find helpful and what they find unhelpful. Collaboration, respect, transparency and authenticity are the trademarks of trauma-informed therapy. Recovering from the impact of childhood sexual abuse can be a long and difficult journey for many clients. The task of the therapist is to share that journey; sometimes to lead, sometimes to follow and sometimes to travel alongside, but always to be present.

REFERENCES

Briere, J. (1995). *Trauma Symptom Inventory (TSI) Professional Manual*. Lutz, FL: Psychological Assessment Resources, Inc.

Deblinger, E., Mannarino, A., Cohan, J. A., Runyon, M. K. & Heflin, A. H. (2015). *Child Sexual Abuse: A Primer for Treating Children, Adolescents, and Their Non-offending Parents* (2nd ed.). Oxford: Oxford University Press.

Lamoureux, B. E., Palmieri, P. A., Jackson, A. P. & Hobfoll, S. E. (2012). Child sexual abuse and adulthood interpersonal outcomes: Examining pathways for intervention. *Psychological Trauma: Theory, Research, Practice and Policy*, *4*(6), 605–613. http://doi.org/10.1037/a0026079

(Continued)

(Continued)

McElvaney, R., Lateef, R., Collin-Vezina, D., Alaggia, R. & Simpson, M. (2021). Identifying shame in child sexual abuse disclosure. *Journal of Interpersonal Violence*, https://doi.org/10.1177/08862605211037435

MacIntosh, H. (2019). *Developmental Couple Therapy for Complex Trauma: A Manual for Therapists.* New York: Routledge.

Paivio, S. C. & Pascual-Leone, A. (2010). *Emotion-focused Therapy for Complex Trauma: An Integrative Approach.* Washington, DC: American Psychological Association.

Tedeschi, R. G. & Calhoun, L. G. (2004). Target article: 'Posttraumatic growth': Conceptual foundations and empirical evidence. *Psychological Inquiry*, 15(1), 1–18.

Toth, S. L. & Cicchetti, D. (2013). A developmental psychopathology perspective on child maltreatment. *Child Maltreatment*, 18(3), 135–139.

van der Kolk, B. (2014). *The Body Keeps the Score: Brain, Mind, and Body in the Healing of Trauma.* Harmondsworth: Penguin and New York: Viking.

RECOMMENDED READING

Sanderson, C. (2013). *Counselling Skills for Trauma.* London: Jessica Kingsley.

An accessible rich resource of knowledge and skills essential for practitioners.

Paivo, S. C. & Pascual-Leone, A. (2010). *Emotion-focused Therapy for Complex Trauma: An Integrative Approach.* Washington, DC: American Psychological Association.

Part One provides the theoretical and research base for the EFTT model, while Part Two outlines how the model is put into practice.

MacIntosh, H. (2019). *Developmental Couple Therapy for Complex Trauma: A Manual for Therapists.* New York: Routledge.

A manual that provides copious case vignettes to help the therapist navigate work with traumatised couples.

4.18 *SUICIDE AND SELF-HARM*

ANDREW REEVES

OVERVIEW AND KEY POINTS

Working with suicide and self-harm in therapy can be both challenging and demanding. The demands of organisational working, meeting the requirements of procedural or policy expectations, in addition to responding empathically and appropriately to a potentially highly distressed client, require commensurate skill. Knowing how best to respond to a client's potential suicidal intent or self-harm, or helping a client to begin to explore these potentially highly shameful aspects of their experience, require that the therapist is aware of both their client's process and their own.

- Suicide and self-harm, while relatively simply defined, represent complex responses to life difficulties and crisis.
- The risk of suicide, or the presence of self-harm, can easily become the focus for therapy. Instead, the therapeutic encounter should provide clients with opportunities to understand the meaning of their thoughts and actions in the context of their difficulties.
- While an assessment of the risk and protective factors is important, a therapeutic exploration of those factors is more likely to provide insight for the therapist and client alike into levels of risk.

ASSESSMENT AND UNDERSTANDING

UNDERSTANDING SUICIDE

The World Health Organisation (WHO) defines suicide simply as: '…the act of deliberately killing oneself' (World Health Organisation, 2021). Beyond this simple definition it is important to remember that suicide itself is not a single process of deciding to end one's life with subsequent action, but rather can present in different ways. For some, suicide is a response to unimaginable emotional turmoil or life crisis (e.g., terminal illness), where a plan is considered and moved towards. For others, suicide is an ever-present consideration; some clients say that knowing they can end their life is the only way in which they manage to live. For others, often young people particularly, suicide can be an impulsive act in response to a situation, where there had been no previous thoughts about suicide, but with the person then propelled quickly and unexpectedly to a suicidal crisis. Therapists can helpfully reflect on these differences when working with suicide risk.

UNDERSTANDING SELF-HARM

Babiker and Arnold (1997: 2) define self-harm as: 'an act which involves deliberately inflicting pain and/or injury to one's body, but without suicidal intent', while the National Institute for Health and Care Excellence (NICE) states that self-harm is 'self-poisoning or injury, irrespective of the apparent purpose of the act' and that 'self-harm is an expression of personal distress, not an illness, and there are many varied reasons for a person to harm him or herself' (NICE, 2004: 7).

Babiker and Arnold's definition draws out a distinction between self-harm and suicidal ideation when they state 'but without suicidal intent'. A generally held view is that self-harm is usually used as a coping strategy against profound or overwhelming feelings of distress (anger, hurt, rage, low self-esteem) and is a means of living rather than dying (Royal College of Psychiatrists, 2010). It can be helpful therapeutically to consider differences between self-harm and self-injury (Reeves, 2015).

> **Self-harm** can include behaviours with indirect and deferred consequence, such as over-exercise, eating disorders, smoking, alcohol and drug use, and sexual risk-taking, for example.
> **Self-injury** can include behaviours with direct and immediate consequence, such as cutting, burning, banging, ingesting dangerous substances (including of medication), for example.

This is not simply a semantic difference, but rather focuses on the differences in *communication* of the action – with immediate or deferred impact – and also the potential understanding and insight of the client into the nature of the behaviour. For example, while a client may understand for themselves that cutting is a form of self-injury, they may not necessarily think of over-exercise as a potentially equally damaging behaviour.

One of the helpful aspects of differentiating between self-injury and self-harm is that it provides us all with an opportunity to understand the motivating factors. We may not all cut ourselves at times of distress, but there may be times where we self-harm: through overwork, excessive spending, over- or under-eating, disregarding physical ill-health and pushing on regardless (Reeves, 2015). In terms of self-harm, the behaviour itself is an unhelpful defining criterion that can distract from understanding the driver behind it (e.g., anxiety, rage, hurt, powerlessness, etc.).

ASSESSING SUICIDE AND SELF-HARM

Assessing risk demands psychological contact and a willingness and ability to remain connected with the client. The predominant approach to assessing risk in the UK continues to be informed by risk factors (factors that make risk more likely), and the research evidence is heavily weighted to this information (see Table 4.18.1).

Understanding factors associated with a higher risk can help contextualise the presentation of the individual's experience. However, is important that therapists engage openly with their clients about suicide, asking such questions as:

- Have you ever thought about harming yourself or killing yourself in response to how you are feeling?
- Have you made any plans about how you might kill yourself?
- What has helped you not kill or harm yourself? How do you support yourself at difficult times?
- On a scale of 1–10, with 1 being the best and 10 being the worst, how would you rate your feelings and thoughts about suicide or self-harm now?

While some clients may talk openly about their suicidal thoughts or self-harming, many will not talk about them at all, or will perhaps allude to them through metaphor or imagery (Reeves et al., 2004). Likewise, contrary to the myths of self-harm being 'attention-seeking', the

Table 4.18.1 Factors associated with higher risk

Gender, e.g., males generally present with greater risk across age groups

Age, e.g., males across the age span, but particularly 15–59, and the over 75 years

Relationships: single, widowed, divorced, separated

Social isolation

Psychopathology including:

schizophrenia

mood disorders, including depression

psychosis

post-traumatic stress disorder

affective disorders, including bipolar

affective disorder

organic disorders

personality disorders, e.g., sociopathy, aggression

Alcohol and drug use

Hopelessness

Occupational factors, e.g., unemployment, retirement

History of childhood sexual or physical abuse

Adult sexual assault

Specific suicide plan formulated

Prior suicide attempt and/or family history of suicide or suicide attempts

Physical illness, e.g., terminal illness, biochemical, hormonal

Bereavement or recent trauma

Significant and unexplained mood change

Self-harm

(Reeves, 2010; and based on Appleby et al., 2015; Battle, 1991; Battle, Battle and Trolley, 1993; Bernhard and Bernhard, 1985; Gilliland, 1985; Hazell and Lewin, 1993; Hersh, 1985; Ruddell and Curwen, 2008; Williams and Morgan, 1994)

overwhelming majority of self-harm is hidden, often not coming to the attention of treating or helping organisations.

Assessment approaches will be strongly informed by working context and the theoretical orientation of the therapist, as has been discussed in other chapters. Fundamentally, however, the therapist must attend to two critical considerations when working with risk, which an assessment can help inform:

1. The level of risk the client is currently experiencing and whether they can work in therapy safely.
2. The nature of the risk (whether that be through suicidal ideation, self-harm, or both) and the meaning that might have for the client. This is the central therapeutic premise in working with risk but can only be undertaken if the therapist (and client) are satisfied with the answer to (1), above.

WAYS OF WORKING WITH SUICIDE AND SELF-HARM

Much is written about how suicide might present in therapy, with less written about *how* therapists might respond to suicide potential or self-harm. How a therapist responds to the disclosure of self-harm, or the possibility of suicide, can profoundly shape the formulation and understanding of the focus of therapy. The therapist will, in virtue of the fact that they are human too, already have a 'position' on suicide and self-harm: it is a subject that rarely leaves people feeling neutral. Likewise, therapists may intellectually understand why an individual may self-harm, but then may experience a very different response in therapy, with a client perhaps showing a cut or burn or providing a description of their self-harming behaviour. The intellectual niceties around suicide and self-harm evaporate quickly when contextualised by a client with whom we have developed a close relationship. The potential for therapists to feel angry, hurt, rejected, attacked or undermined by their client's suicide potential or self-harm is high.

As was discussed in Chapter 3.4 (this volume), a predominant view about risk in mental health services is that best practice is informed through the application of risk assessment tools. Such tools – questionnaires and other psychometric instruments – proport to help identify people at higher risk of suicide and self-harm by identifying known risk factors. However, as the Royal College of Psychiatrists (2020: 28) state:

> Current suicide risk assessment tools mainly use demographic risk factors (which may be as common in the general population) and have largely been developed without a solid empirical basis. ... The reliance upon risk factor identification fails both clinicians and patients.

Rather, and particularly so for counsellors and psychotherapists (and other helping professionals where the relationship is central), a dialogic approach to working with suicide and self-harm is much more relevant and important. As Shneidman (1998: 6) states:

> Our best route to understanding suicide is not through the study of the structure of the brain, nor the study of social statistics, nor the study of mental diseases, but directly through the study of human emotions described in plain English, in the words of the suicidal person. The most important question to a potentially suicidal person is not an inquiry about family history or laboratory tests of blood or spinal fluid, but 'where do you hurt?' and 'how can I help you?'

Shneidman's assertion here superbly articulates a primary 'working with' focus: 'where do you hurt?' and 'how can I help you?'. Once satisfied that the client can work safely in therapy, the focus of therapy should be an exploration of the distress underpinning and informing the risk, rather than simply a continuation of a two-dimensional risk management strategy.

CHALLENGES

There are many ways in which therapists might 'act out' their otherwise unacknowledged responses to risk in a therapy session. Most common is denying they have a 'response' at all: 'I am fine in working with self-harm, it really doesn't bother me', or perhaps 'I believe that every client has a right to kill themselves if they wish, so it is not for me to get involved'. Both examples, on the surface, might appear to be acceptable. However, I would argue that it is essential for us as therapists to be impacted by our client's potential suicide or self-harm. Anaesthetising ourselves against such pain has the potential to parallel the client's experience of themselves, and potentially undermines the empathy and insight required to offer emotional support.

Leenaars (2004: 101–102) outlines several ways in which such responses might hinder work with clients at risk, particularly when the therapist's response includes guilt, anger, anxiety, or fear. For example:

- Underestimation of the seriousness of the suicidal action (or intent).
- Absence of a discussion of suicidal thoughts (or intent).
- Allowing oneself to be lulled into a false sense of security by the client's promise not to repeat a suicide attempt (or act on suicidal thoughts).
- Disregard of the 'cry for help' aspect of the suicidal attempt (or thoughts), and concentration exclusively on its manipulative character.
- Exaggeration of the client's provocative, infantile and aggressive sides.
- Denial of one's own importance to the client.
- Failure to persuade the client to undergo (or continue with) counselling or psychotherapy.
- The feeling of lacking the resources for the evaluation required by a particular client.
- Exaggerated sense of hopelessness in response to the client's social situation and abuse of drugs/alcohol.
- Being pleased with the client's claims to have all problems solved after only a brief period of time.
- Feeling upset when the client shows resistance after only a brief course of inquiry, despite the therapist's initial profound commitment.

Regardless of length of post-qualifying experience or therapeutic orientation, therapists can find themselves silenced by suicide potential, not exploring with the client the meaning of their suicidal thoughts, and thus not considering with the client the degree of intent and thus the level of risk (Reeves et al., 2004).

The same is true when working with self-harm. In some instances, therapists will only focus on the self-destructive aspect of self-harm (as opposed to that part of the behaviour that facilitates coping) and view this as counter to growth and development. Self-harm can often provoke powerful responses in the therapist, including anger, a sense of being attacked by it, revulsion, and hopelessness. The more insight a therapist can have into their own process, the more they will be able to connect with their client's process.

The feelings and responses outlined to both suicide potential and self-harm are not wrong: they are understandable human reactions to another's profound distress. However, they become potentially harmful when they are unacknowledged and unsupported. The more a therapist can reflect on their own process – their feelings, thoughts, reactions and behaviours in response to suicide potential or self-harm – the clearer and more collaborative the therapeutic formulation will be.

ENGAGING WITH SUICIDE AND SELF-INJURY

Suicide potential and self-harm demand the therapist not only *works with* these issues from a therapeutic position, but also *responds to* these issues in virtue of the risk that may be present. The task is therefore twofold: providing space for meaning-making and change, while also ensuring the client's safety. Consider the client Sam, below.

CASE STUDY

Sam is a 52-year-old male client. He attends for counselling because of depression, but on further exploration Sam talks of sometimes 'wanting to be out of the way', as well as punching walls when angry. He is socially isolated but is a member of a local faith group, with whom he spends time during the week. When he feels particularly lonely he drinks, but recognises this is not helpful. He experienced a close bereavement 12 months previously.

The therapist faces an immediate challenge here, regarding the ambiguous nature of Sam's statement 'wanting to be out of the way', and whether this refers to suicidal thinking. At some stage, it will be important for the therapist to ask Sam about this, perhaps by saying, '…when you say you "want to get out of the way", Sam, I wonder if you mean finding space for yourself, or if these are thoughts about ending your life…?' If Sam's thoughts are about suicide, these need to be contextualised by the other risk factors present in this scenario:

- Gender (male is a high-risk group)
- Age (52 sits in the highest-risk age group for suicide in men)

- Self-injury (punching the wall when angry)
- Social isolation
- Use of alcohol
- Bereavement
- Implied ideation ('I want to be out of the way').

There are protective factors (that make suicide less likely) too, however, which also need to be considered:

- Attending counselling
- Some social contact
- Attending a community group (faith group)
- Self-injury (paradoxically, it helps provide an outlet for feelings, albeit self-destructively)
- Some insight (awareness of the impact of alcohol).

A judgement about Sam's level of risk needs to be made, informed by protective and risk factors but, most importantly, through dialogue with Sam directly about how he takes care of himself and how he has managed not to end his life up to this point. In such a situation, a crisis plan, or 'keep safe' plan, might be collaboratively developed, which provides Sam with a structured way of thinking about his risk and how he can respond to that when away from sessions. I have written more about such plans elsewhere (Reeves, 2015: 53–54), but they might include:

- The actual risk being considered (e.g., thoughts of taking an overdose)
- The times when the risks are likely to be at their highest (e.g., at night)
- 'Red flags' the client might be aware of that could trigger such thoughts (e.g., when they are alone)
- Factors that make the feelings worse, being as specific as possible (e.g., alcohol or drugs)
- Factors that make the feelings better, being as specific as possible (e.g., being around people)
- Who is available to offer informal support (e.g., family, friends)
- Who is available to offer formal support (e.g., a crisis team, accident and emergency, a telephone helpline), ensuring details such as telephone numbers are recorded on the plan
- What might make accessing support less likely (e.g., not wanting to wake someone up)
- What might make accessing support more likely (e.g., agreeing contact with someone in advance)
- Intrapersonal mechanisms for self-care (e.g., meditation, breathing techniques, distraction, etc.)
- A date for review (which will usually be the next session).

CONSIDERATIONS FOR SELF-HARM

Many clients who self-harm do not necessarily wish to talk about their harm specifically, but rather concentrate on the factors that shape how their feel. If clients do wish to focus on their self-harm, exploration on the meaning of their self-harm, rather than spending time on the behaviour itself, can be helpful. I have written in more detail elsewhere (Reeves, 2013) about the importance of a relational approach in helping the client to find words for feelings that are otherwise expressed through injury. Different approaches all have something to offer here: I have given a specific example using a narrative approach to help in meaning-making (Reeves, 2013). Likewise, in the same text, I have also offered an overview of a more cognitive-behavioural approach when clients wish to find strategies to stop self-harming, including alternatives to self-harm.

CONCLUSION

There is a strong temptation for therapists to determine a 'good outcome' based on the mitigation of risk. Likewise, with self-harm, therapists can be inadvertently drawn into using the behaviour of self-harm as a barometer of 'success', that is, a reduction in self-harm = effective therapy; an increase in self-harm

= ineffective therapy. Things are never that binary. Undoubtedly, and as has been discussed here, responding to risk is a critical consideration in ensuring the client's capacity to make use of therapy safely. However, a client's sense of a 'good outcome' for them might not necessarily include the eradication of suicidal ideation or the elimination of self-harm. Enabling the client to be able to consider their experience of therapy – and of the therapeutic relationship – will help ensure therapy remains client-focused rather than risk-driven.

REFERENCES

Appleby, L., Kapur, N., Shaw, J., Windfuhr, K., Hunt, I.M., Flynn, S., While, D., Roscoe, A., Rodway, C., Ibrahim, S. and Tham, S. (2015) *National Confidential Inquiry into Suicide and Homicide by People with Mental Illness.* Manchester: Centre for Mental Health and Safety, University of Manchester.

Babiker, G. and Arnold, L. (1997) *The Language of Injury: Comprehending Self-Mutilation.* Leicester: British Psychological Society.

Battle, A.O. (1991) *Factors in assessing suicidal lethality.* Paper presented at the Crisis Center Preservice Volunteer Training, University of Tennessee College of Medicine, Department of Psychiatry, Memphis, TN.

Battle, A.O., Battle, M.V. and Trolley, E.A. (1993) Potential for suicide and aggression in delinquents at juvenile court in a southern city. *Suicide and Life Threatening Behaviour*, 23(3): 230–243.

Bernhard, J.L. and Bernhard, M.L. (1985) Suicide on campus: response to the problem. In E.S. Zinner (Ed.), *Coping with Death on Campus* (pp. 69–83). San Francisco, CA: Jossey-Bass.

Gilligand, B.E. (1985) *Surviving college: teaching college students to cope.* Paper presented at the Symposium on Suicide in Teenagers and Young Adults, University of Tennessee College of Medicine, Department of Psychiatry, Memphis, TN.

Hazell, P. and Lewin, T. (1993) An evaluation of postvention following adolescent suicide. *Suicide and Life Threatening Behaviour*, 23(2): 101–109.

Hersh, J.B. (1985) Interviewing college students in crisis. *Journal of Counseling and Development*, 63: 286–289.

Leenaars, A.A. (2004) *Psychotherapy with Suicidal People: A Person-centred Approach.* Chichester: Wiley.

NICE (2004) *Self-Harm: The Short-term Physical and Psychological Management and Secondary Prevention of Self-harm in Primary and Secondary Care.* London: National Institute for Health and Clinical Excellence.

Reeves, A. (2010) *Counselling Suicidal Clients.* London: Sage.

Reeves, A. (2013) *Challenges in Counselling: Self-harm.* London: Hodder Education.

Reeves, A. (2015) *Working with Risk in Counselling and Psychotherapy.* London: Sage.

Reeves, A., Bowl, R., Wheeler, S. and Guthrie, E. (2004) The hardest words: exploring the dialogue of suicide in the counselling process: a discourse analysis. *Counselling and Psychotherapy Research*, 4(1): 62–71.

Royal College of Psychiatrists (2010) *Self-harm, Suicide and Risk: Helping People Who Self-harm.* College Report CR158. London: Royal College of Psychiatrists.

Royal College of Psychiatrists (2020) *Self-Harm and Suicide in Adults: CR229.* London: Royal College of Psychiatrists. Available at www.rcpsych.ac.uk/docs/default-source/improving-care/better-mh-policy/college-reports/college-report-cr229-self-harm-and-suicide.pdf?sfvrsn=b6fdf395_10

Ruddell, P. and Curwen, B. (2008) Understanding suicidal ideation and assessing for risk. In S. Palmer (Ed.), *Suicide: Strategies and Interventions for Reduction and Prevention* (pp. 84–99). London: Routledge.

Shneidman, E.S. (1998) *The Suicidal Mind.* Oxford: Oxford University Press.

Williams, R. and Morgan, H.G. (Eds) (1994) *Suicide Prevention: The Challenge Confronted.* London: HMSO.

World Health Organisation (2021) *Suicide.* Geneva: World Health Organisation. Available at www.emro.who.int/health-topics/suicide/feed/atom.html

RECOMMENDED READING

Leenaars, A. (2004) *Psychotherapy with Suicidal People: A Person-centred Approach*. Chichester: Wiley.

This book offers a broad account of the range of issues therapists face when working with suicidal clients, additionally including explanations for suicidal thinking.

Reeves, A. (2015) *Working with Risk in Counselling and Psychotherapy*. London: Sage.

This book discusses therapeutic work with suicide risk and self-harm, as well and other areas of risk (e.g., violence to others and safeguarding). It looks at the concept of positive risk-taking in therapy.

Shneidman, E.S. (1998) *The Suicidal Mind*. Oxford: Oxford University Press.

This is a seminal text from a key suicidologist, providing a critical evaluation of our understanding of suicide, as well as challenging preconceived ideas and intervention approaches.

4.19 WORKING WITH SURVIVORS OF DOMESTIC VIOLENCE
CHRISTIANE SANDERSON

OVERVIEW AND KEY POINTS

Working with survivors of domestic abuse (DA), while highly rewarding, can be extremely challenging and demanding. To fully understand the impact and long-term effects of DA, therapists need to view such abuse within the context of complex trauma in which bodily and psychological integrity is threatened and the attachment system is compromised (Sanderson, 2010, 2013). When working with survivors of DA, practitioners need to be aware of the the Power Threat Meaning Framework (PTMF) (Johnstone and Boyle, 2018) and the principles of a trauma-informed practice (TIP) model alongside their preferred model, which titrates the therapeutic process through an approach consisting of three phases – stabilisation, processing and integration – to promote post-traumatic growth (Herman, 1992a; Sanderson, 2013). In addition, clinicians need to be mindful of the impact of bearing witness to clients' experiences of DA to minimise vicarious traumatisation. This chapter outlines that:

- To work with survivors of Domestic Abuse (DA) counsellors need to be aware of the spectrum of DA behaviours, and understand that these are not confined to physical abuse but include coercion and control, emotional and psychological abuse, neglect, as well as physical, sexual, financial and spiritual abuse, and that men, women and those who are transgender are at risk of DA.
- It is essential that counsellors contextualise DA within a PTM framework and through a trauma lens in which prolonged coercion and control give rise to a range of psychobiological symptoms which are normal reactions to trauma rather than indices of individual pathology or personality disturbance.
- Counsellors need to validate and legitimise the DA experiences, restore reality and avoid pathologising survivors by contextualising DA within a psychobiological as well as a socio-political framework.
- Counsellors need to be mindful of the safety of the survivor and any dependents through continuous risk assessment, and balance this with safety

planning and restoring survivors' autonomy to make their own choices.
- Practitioners need to view symptoms and behaviours as responses, or adaptations, to prolonged threat and the misuse of power and control rather than evidence of the survivors' pathology.

ASSESSMENT AND UNDERSTANDING

Counsellors need to be mindful of the safety of the survivor and any dependents through continuous risk assessment, and balance this with safety planning and restoring survivors' autonomy to make their own choices. Assessment of DA is often complicated, with many survivors being too scared or ashamed to disclose their abuse, making it difficult to identify. Alongside this, the distortion of reality and the belief that they are complicit in their abuse generates fears of not being believed, or being judged, or being controlled or coerced by professionals, including counsellors (Dutton, 1992).

Many survivors enter therapy not able to talk about their abuse either through sheer terror, shame or fear of re-traumatisation. It is crucial that practitioners adopt a sensitive approach to enable disclosure (British Medical Association, 2007; Sanderson, 2013) and ensure confidentiality. Some survivors may enter therapy as a result of legal proceedings or referral from children's services, but may be reluctant to engage as they do not feel entirely safe and fear potential repercussions for having reported the abuser.

As children in DA environments are considered to be at risk, it will be necessary to implement safeguarding procedures and conduct a risk assessment for both the survivor and any dependent children or vulnerable adults.

Many therapists get caught up in safeguarding procedures and risk assessment yet neglect to assess the impact DA has had on the survivor and their clinical needs. It is critical that counsellors assess for the degree of traumatisation and trauma symptoms, especially dissociation (Sanderson, 2013). The systematic and repeated use of DA leads to complex trauma (Herman, 1992b), including the range of symptoms seen in PTSD, especially the sub-type of PTSD with prominent dissociative symptoms. It is also frequently comorbid with depression, anxiety, self-harm or substance misuse as a way of medicating the abuse, somatisation disorder or dissociative disorder (Sanderson, 2013). It is critical to assess the survivor's readiness for therapy and to assess for these in order to create a comprehensive formulation and care plan.

The new Domestic Abuse Act 2021 has created a statutory definition of DA, alongside how partners must be related or known to each other, new legal procedures with special provision for victims of DA in family proceedings, DA protection orders, a guarantee that all survivors will be in priority need for housing and will keep a secure tenancy in social housing if they need to escape an abuser, and the appointment of a Domestic Abuse Commissioner. The Domestic Abuse Act 2021 defines domestic abuse as any form of '…physical or sexual abuse, violent or threatening behaviour, controlling or coercive behaviour, economic abuse, psychological, emotional or other abuse' whether a single event or a course of conduct that occurs when both the abuser and the victim are aged 16 or over, who are personally connected to each other. It also includes new criminal offences, including post-separation coercive control, non-fatal strangulation, threats to disclose private sexual images, and a ban on abusers using a defence of 'rough sex' (Home Office, 2021).

Controlling or coercive behaviour is typically seen in the early stages of abusive relationships, which can escalate into physical violence. For example, Sarah's abuse was initially subtle, with her partner wanting to spend as much time with her as possible yet isolating her from her friends. This masked his pathological jealousy and restricted her contact with the outside world. He started to monitor her phone and became verbally abusive in referring to her as fat and undesirable. He would often use sex as a way of controlling her either by withholding it or forcing her to perform degrading sexual acts. The aim was to force her to surrender, obliterate any sense of self-agency and engender mental defeat (Sanderson, 2013). Over time, Sarah was trapped in a cycle of abuse from which she was too afraid to escape and which led to post-traumatic stress disorder (PTSD) and dissociative states.

Controlling and coercive behaviour is commonly seen in female perpetrators of DA, entailing constant criticism of the partner's masculinity or femininity and their behaviour, which becomes a source of shame. For example, with Charles, this manifested in repeated verbal aggression from his wife alongside micro-managing his behaviour, monitoring his phone calls, text messages and emails, as well as tracking his car satellite navigation system. This would often be accompanied by threats of suicide if he did not comply or submit to her demands.

The dynamics of DA are a subtle and gradual escalation of coercion and control, starting with loving care and attention, or 'love bombing', to entrap the partner, which escalates into the increased use of threats, intimidation and violence in order to dominate and ensure total submission. These dynamics are part of the cycle of abuse (Herman, 1992b; Sanderson, 2008) in which the tension-building phase leads to an assault, followed by the conciliation or honeymoon phase. The intermittent reinforcement in this cycle ultimately leads to traumatic bonding (Dutton and Painter, 1981), dissociation and 'betrayal blindness' as the survivor tries to manage the cognitive dissonance inherent in the oscillation between love and hate, affection and brutalisation, caring and dehumanisation (Sanderson, 2008, 2013).

Although perpetrators of DA are not homogeneous, there are a number of commonalities, such as the need to control and dominate through the use of coercion, control, threat and violence. Abusers also commonly display pathological jealousy, which indicates insecure attachment and fear of abandonment or rejection, underpinning the need to control and dominate (Dutton, 2007; Sanderson, 2013).

WAYS OF WORKING WITH SURVIVORS OF DA

Therapists need to be aware of the impact of complex trauma on relational functioning to minimise the replication of abuse dynamics in the counselling process (Herman, 1992b). In this, they need to establish a safe and secure base in which to develop a sensitively attuned therapeutic relationship (Pearlman and Courtois, 2005). Survivors of DA find it difficult to trust and can oscillate between hostility and extreme neediness. Practitioners need to be mindful that trust is not finite and that survivors may regularly test the commitment of the therapist, which can create ruptures in the therapeutic relationship. Therapists must understand these within the context of the survivor's experience and not personalise such ruptures or reject, shame or punish the survivor (Sanderson, 2015). Instead, they must provide an authentic human relationship to counteract and undo the effects of dehumanisation and facilitate post-traumatic growth.

CORE THERAPEUTIC GOALS

- Validate and legitimise the DA.
- Provide a secure and safe space to establish a sensitively attuned therapeutic relationship in which to develop trust and restore relational worth.
- Use psychoeducation to raise awareness of DA, minimise shame, self-blame and restore reality.
- Reframe symptoms, feelings, thoughts and behaviours as adaptations to threat and prolonged misuse of power and control, which aided their survival.
- Implement a trauma-informed practice (TIP) approach and to titrate the therapeutic process through a trauma-informed practice model which focuses on stabilisation, processing and integration.
- Identify existing resources and cultivate these.
- Facilitate autonomy to enable survivors to make their own choices and post-traumatic growth.

In addition, counsellors need to consider the fundamental principles of TIP (Herman, 1992a; Sanderson, 2013), which emphasises a phased approach alongside their own therapeutic model. The principles in the PTM framework underpin trauma-informed practice and the core principles that guide the treatment (Harris and Fallot, 2001; Quiros and Berger, 2013), namely those of safety, trustworthiness, collaboration, choice and empowerment.

In order to manage power dynamics ethically, it is essential to reduce the intrinsic structural power in the therapeutic encounter by acknowledging and discussing power dynamics and the rights and responsibilities of both parties. This needs to be supported by a sharing of power and knowledge through psychoeducation and promoting equality, autonomy, agency and choice to mitigate reinforcing powerlessness and helplessness. Alongside sharing power, practitioners must be able to modulate control dynamics by encouraging survivors to take control in their lives as well as the therapeutic space, and be willing to relinquish control by not being too directive or expecting clients to work at a pace that suits them rather than what is manageable. To ensure that survivors feel safe, practitioners need to promote choices in where the survivor sits, the positioning of the chairs, and the physical space between practitioner and client. Survivors need to be able to see the door and feel that they have a choice in how closely the chairs are positioned, and at which angle. Many survivors feel uncomfortable sitting directly opposite the practitioner as this elicits shame and may replicate the scrutiny of the abuser during the abuse, and may feel more comfortable if the chairs are placed at an angle, or side by side, at least initially. This also helps to regulate eye contact as it is often under the gaze of others that shame is induced. Trauma wise practitioners (TWPs) need to be mindful that the intensity of eye gaze and eye contact can be triggering and lead to dissociation. Trauma wise practitioners are encouraged to share the regulation of this with each client to find the optimal distance that feels safe for them.

In addition, survivors need to feel that they have a choice in whether to talk or not to talk, and to find a way of regulating silence. While therapeutic silences can be very fruitful opportunities to reflect and access feelings, for many survivors silence is experienced as punitive and is reminiscent of the abuse. It is essential that practitioners regulate the silence appropriately, and that prolonged silences do not trigger or activate shamed or dissociative states. The shame associated with child sexual abuse (CSA) is easily evoked in prolonged silence and survivors may interpret this as judgement or rejection and abandonment.

The fundamental principles of a TIP model are to titrate the therapeutic process into three phases consisting of: (1) stabilisation, (2) processing and (3) integration.

Stabilisation consists of psychoeducation, grounding skills and affect regulation to widen the window of tolerance and increase distress tolerance (Sanderson, 2022). Psychoeducation enables survivors to link physiological responses to their abuse and see these as normal reactions to trauma rather than a loss of their sanity (Sanderson, 2013). Alongside this, developing skills such as mindfulness and grounding techniques enable survivors to regain control of trauma reactions and come back into the body to live in the present without being catapulted back into the terrifying past (van der Kolk, 2014). This needs to be supported by enabling survivors to access a range of sources that can offer support, such as police, advocacy, housing and specialist support groups.

Once survivors have gained mastery over their trauma reactions, they can move into phase two to process flashbacks, intrusive memories, nightmares and traumatic experiences. In exploring the trauma and developing a more coherent narrative, the survivor can begin to gain meaning and make sense of his or her experience and restore reality (Sanderson, 2013, 2022). As survivors process their experiences and gain meaning, they can move into the final phase and begin to integrate mind, body and brain, and reconnect sensations, feelings and thoughts, and experience post-traumatic growth. While these phases are not linear, and not all survivors experience post-traumatic growth, many are able to restore control over their symptoms and regain a sense of agency and autonomy.

A fundamental goal throughout the three phases is the building and maintenance of a therapeutic relationship in which the survivor can learn and practise relational skills (Pearlman and Courtois, 2005). This is pivotal to rebuilding relational worth and to discover more authentic ways of relating, in which needs, feelings and thoughts can be expressed without fear of being punished or humiliated. It is through the therapeutic relationship that the survivor can begin to reconnect to self and others with renewed trust (Sanderson, 2013). This will enable the survivor to restore reality and challenge distorted perceptions, especially those imposed by the abuser. In addition, therapists need to restore power and control to the survivor so that they can regain autonomy and self-agency to make their own choices, including whether to leave or not. If the survivor is working towards leaving the abusive relationship, counsellors need to support this by implementing careful safety planning to minimise the risk of further violence (Sanderson, 2008; Women's Aid Federation, 2009).

While some survivors of DA enter therapy immediately after being traumatised, many survivors remain silent for many years as they are too ashamed to talk about their experiences until trust has been established. In such cases, therapists need to work on two parallel levels, one which focuses on the DA experience in the past and the other in the present to alleviate current stress and symptoms.

CASE STUDY

Sophie met and married her partner when they both had successful careers but wanted to start a family as soon as possible. They had three children in quick succession with Sophie taking a career break to look after the children. Sophie's husband was extremely charming, a seemingly caring and loving husband, and doting father. Shortly after the birth of the third child, a son, Sophie's husband began to express concerns about Sophie's mothering and her mental health, and started to control and intimidate her. Despite the lack of any evidence to substantiate these concerns, he escalated his coercive behaviour to the point of instigating custody proceedings.

> When Sophie entered therapy she suffered from a number of PTSD symptoms, including hypervigilance, hyperarousal, flashbacks and extremely negative beliefs about herself and her relational worth. The first phase of the therapeutic process focused on providing a place of safety for Sophie to regain some control over her PTSD symptoms and her life. This necessitated a degree of psychoeducation to understand her DA experiences and to validate and legitimise her experiences, restore reality and challenge the false beliefs imposed on her by her husband. Through the mastery of grounding skills she was able to re-regulate her trauma responses, develop affect regulation and increase her window of tolerance. From this she was able to process her abuse experiences and integrate these. Over time she was able to restore trust and belief in herself, gain meaning and purpose in life, and begin her journey to post-traumatic growth. The therapeutic setting became a sanctuary or holding environment for Sophie to just 'be', rather than having to be hypervigilant or feel overpowered or controlled by someone else, and it allowed her the autonomy to make her own decisions or choices without fear of abuse.

It is difficult to evaluate the outcome of the therapeutic process when working with survivors of DA as this will vary enormously. For some survivors, the goal is to leave their partner, while for others it might be acquiring the skills necessary to manage the DA. Essential for all is validating the abuse, restoring control over trauma symptoms through affect regulation and widening the window of tolerance to allow for processing and integration of the trauma and facilitate post-traumatic growth (Sanderson, 2013).

There are a number of therapeutic challenges inherent in working with survivors of DA, not least the need for flexibility and the ability to tolerate uncertainty. In addition, bearing witness to DA can impact on practitioners and lead to vicarious traumatisation and secondary traumatic stress (Sanderson, 2013). To minimise this, and to avoid being overwhelmed by the enormity of DA, counsellors need to ensure that they have access to professional and personal support so that they can enable survivors to move towards living life more authentically, with greater self-agency and equality, without the fear of further abuse.

REFERENCES

British Medical Association (2007) *Domestic Abuse*. London: BMA.

Dutton, D.G. (2007) *The Abusive Personality: Violence and Control in Intimate Relationships* (2nd ed.). New York: Guilford Press.

Dutton, D.G. and Painter, S.L. (1981) Traumatic bonding: the development of emotional attachment in battered women and other relationships of intermittent abuse. *Victimology: An International Journal*, 6, 139–155.

Dutton, M.A. (1992) *Empowering and Healing Battered Women: A Model for Assessment and Intervention*. New York: Springer.

Harris, M. and Fallot, R.D. (2001) Trauma-informed inpatient services. *New directions for mental health services*, (89), 33–46. https://doi.org/10.1002/yd.23320018905

Herman, J.L. (1992a) *Trauma and Recovery*. New York: Basic Books.

Herman, J.L. (1992b) Complex PTSD: a syndrome in survivors of prolonged and repeated trauma. *Journal of Traumatic Stress*, 5, 377–392.

Home Office (2021) *Domestic Abuse Act 2021*. London: Home Office. Available at www.legislation.gov.uk

Johnstone, L. and Boyle, M. (2018) The power threat meaning framework: an alternative nondiagnostic conceptual system. *Journal of Humanistic Psychology*, 0022167818793289.

Pearlman, L.A. and Courtois, C.A. (2005) Clinical applications of the attachment framework: relational treatment of complex trauma. *Journal of Traumatic Stress*, 18, 449–459.

(Continued)

(Continued)

Quiros, L. and Berger, R. (2015) Responding to the sociopolitical complexity of trauma: an integration of theory and practice. *Journal of Loss and Trauma*, 20(2), 149–159.

Sanderson, C. (2008) *Counselling Survivors of Domestic Abuse*. London: Jessica Kingsley Publishers.

Sanderson, C. (2010) *Introduction to Counselling Survivors of Interpersonal Trauma*. London: Jessica Kingsley Publishers.

Sanderson, C. (2013) *Counselling Skills for Working with Trauma: Healing from Child Sexual Abuse, Sexual Violence and Domestic Abuse*. London: Jessica Kingsley Publishers.

Sanderson, C. (2015) *Counselling Skills for Working with Shame*. London: Jessica Kingsley Publishers.

Sanderson, C. (2022) *The Warrior Within: A One in Four Handbook to Aid Recovery from Childhood Sexual Abuse and Sexual Violence* (4th ed.). London: One in Four.

van der Kolk, B. (2014) *The Body Keeps the Score: Brain, Mind, and Body in the Healing of Trauma*. Harmondsworth: Penguin.

Women's Aid Federation (2009) *The Survivor's Handbook* (revised ed.). London: Women's Aid Federation. Audio version (2008). Both available at www.womensaid.org.uk

RECOMMENDED READING

British Medical Association (2007) *Domestic Abuse*. London: BMA.

This is an excellent resource that introduces the nature of domestic abuse (DA) and its medical, psychological and social impact on individuals. It also includes advice on how to facilitate disclosure and guidance on how to access other support services.

Herman, J.L. (1992) *Trauma and Recovery*. New York: Basic Books.

This is a classic text that examines the nature and dynamics of DA and how this impacts on survivors. It is an in-depth exploration of how DA affects psychobiological and psychosocial functioning.

Sanderson, C. (2022) *The Warrior Within*: A One in Four Handbook to Aid Recovery from Childhood Sexual Abuse and Sexual Violence (4th ed.). London: One in Four.

Although aimed at survivors of childhood sexual abuse and sexual violence, this has a new chapter on Domestic Violence and is packed with psychoeducation and exercises that practitioners can use when working with clients.

PART V

THEORIES AND APPROACHES

5.1 ACCEPTANCE AND COMMITMENT THERAPY

JOHN BOORMAN, ERIC MORRIS AND JOE OLIVER

OVERVIEW AND KEY POINTS

Acceptance and Commitment Therapy (ACT) is a contextual cognitive behavioural treatment that aims to strengthen clients' flexible responding to their internal experiences (feelings, thoughts, urges) in order to help them engage in actions and choices guided by personal values.

- The main aim is to help clients live a rich and meaningful life in accordance with their values.
- This is achieved by strengthening clients' skills in mindfully discriminating thoughts and feelings, in order to reduce unhelpful responding and foster psychological acceptance of this internal content.
- ACT also seeks to reduce clients' entanglement with what it terms the 'conceptualised self' (e.g., self-stories) in order to increase flexible perspective taking on psychological distress.
- Therapy seeks to help clients engage in specific patterns of committed behavioural action, which are directly linked to what they consider important.
- ACT has been found to be as effective as other CBTs at treating anxiety, depression, addiction and somatic health problems.

BRIEF HISTORY

Acceptance and Commitment Therapy (ACT, pronounced as a single word 'act') is part of an evolution of behavioural and cognitive psychotherapies that emphasise mindfulness and acceptance. These mindfulness-based interventions include, among others, dialectical behaviour therapy (DBT) (Linehan, 1993) and mindfulness-based cognitive therapy (Segal, Williams and Teasdale, 2002). ACT sits within the wider science of human understanding known as Contextual Behavioural Science (Hayes, Barnes-Holmes and Wilson, 2012). One of the aims is to foster treatment development through a proposed reticulated model (Hayes et al., 2013), which describes how clinical practitioners and basic science researchers can engage in a mutually beneficial relationship in order to build a more progressive, unified psychology.

ACT is based on the scientific philosophy of functional contextualism. Functional contextualism defines the goal of science to be the prediction and influence of behaviour, with precision, scope and depth, using empirically based concepts and methods. Behaviour is understood and influenced on the basis of function rather than form, and all actions are considered to occur within a specific context (e.g., historical, situational, environmental, social, cultural and verbal influences). What is considered 'true' in this pragmatic philosophy are ways of speaking that allow for 'successful working'. Concepts or rules that do not point to what to *do* (as a therapist or scientist) are discarded. ACT incorporates elements of both the first (behaviour therapy) and second (cognitive therapy) 'waves' of CBT, while introducing new elements such as mindfulness, acceptance, and defusion from thoughts.

ACT was originally developed by the American psychologist Steven Hayes, who, along with other colleagues, looked to expand upon the behaviour analytic principles first put forward by B.F. Skinner regarding verbal behaviour. At its inception in the late 1970s and early 1980s, ACT was originally called 'comprehensive distancing', a concept first suggested by Beck, where the therapy goal was to assist clients to develop healthy distancing from problematic thoughts and mental processes. Then followed a period spanning over 15 years when attention was centred on empirical development of a therapeutic model. Central to the model was the concurrent development of a behavioural account of human language and cognition, known as relational frame theory (RFT) (Hayes, Barnes-Holmes and Roche, 2001). Finally, the therapy model and procedures were comprehensively explicated in the first ACT manual in 1999 (Hayes, Strosahl and Wilson, 1999), and updated in a new edition (Hayes, Strosahl and Wilson, 2012).

BASIC ASSUMPTIONS

ACT takes the view that psychological pain is both universal and normal and is part of what makes us human. ACT therefore challenges the assumption put forward in many mainstream models of psychopathology, and perhaps by society in general, that psychological health is equated with the absence of pain, or conversely, that the presence of pain is indicative of faulty or abnormal processes (biological or psychological).

Drawing upon literature into thought/emotion suppression and how humans cope with pain, ACT argues that attempts to control, avoid and/or escape from distressing thoughts and feelings can result in life restrictions and diminished functioning. A core assumption of ACT is that psychological problems are maintained by excessive avoidance of painful experiences (thoughts, feelings, memories, etc.).

Based on the research into RFT, ACT demonstrates how everyday language processes have the ability to amplify normal psychological pain. The ACT model of psychopathology assumes that psychological suffering can occur when private experiences become the dominant source of behavioural regulation and contact with other environmental contingencies are diminished. The emphasis in ACT is therefore not to alter the frequency or form of distressing internal experiences (although naturally this will occur over the course of an ACT intervention), but rather to change the relationship (function) the client has with these experiences. This is perhaps where ACT differs most from other behavioural and cognitive approaches, which primarily look to change the form or frequency of thoughts and feelings.

The emphasis on changing the function of internal experiences (rather than their frequency or form) is always in the service of assisting clients to take actions consistent with valued life directions. Values differ from goals, which are concrete and time limited, in that they are seen as life directions that don't have an end point. Examples of valued areas that clients might find important could include relationships, family, work/education, spirituality, and health. A basic assumption in ACT is to take a pragmatic view to clients solving their problems, focusing on what works to help them move towards their values, as opposed to what is right or true. This stance, also known as the *pragmatic truth criterion*, is taken from the philosophy of functional contextualism.

ORIGINS AND MAINTENANCE OF PROBLEMS

Relational Frame Theory (RFT) describes how psychological distress is maintained through normal language processes. RFT views the core of human language and cognition as the learned ability to relate anything to anything (or arbitrarily), mutually and in combination. In this way, potentially any internal or environment stimulus (e.g., sights, sounds, smells, memories) has the capacity to induce painful thoughts and emotions. Research into RFT has shown that relational responding is a basic and learned aspect of language that serves important functions in the outside world, for example problem solving or prediction, but can be problematic when this method of learning is over-applied to private experiences (Hayes et al., 2001). Importantly, relational responding has the capacity to transform the functions of any property (physical or mental) and modifies other behavioural processes, such as classical and operant conditioning. Smoking may be taken as an example to explain this process. If a smoker is asked to imagine a cigarette, they may note its formal physical properties, such as its colour (e.g., white), its shape (e.g., a cylinder) and its contents (e.g., contains tobacco). In addition to the physical properties, however, a cigarette can also acquire informal or arbitrary properties through the human ability to relate anything to anything (relational responding). For example, a cigarette can also be viewed as something that is 'dependable', or like a 'good friend' who is always there in times of crisis. From an RFT perspective, as 'cigarette' and 'best friend' are brought into a relational frame of coordination, some of the functions of the cigarette are transformed and share the functions noted in a best friend. Importantly, these functions have the potential to dominate over other sources of behavioural regulation, such as health warnings.

Based upon RFT, ACT essentially sees human psychological problems in terms of a lack of psychological flexibility, which is fostered by two core processes, termed experiential avoidance and cognitive fusion.

Experiential avoidance occurs when an individual is unwilling to stay in contact with certain thoughts, feelings and physical sensations, and also tries to alter the content of these internal experiences, even when this causes behavioural or emotional harm. While engaging in such acts of avoidance can often serve to ameliorate problems in the short term, it has the potential to lead to long-term suffering. ACT views experiential avoidance as a central process in the origin and maintenance of psychological problems, the use of which is supported by folk psychology and mainstream culture (e.g., advice to 'just get over it', 'move on', etc.). ACT highlights how significant energy can be expended in attempts to escape, avoid or otherwise control these events, and proposes psychological acceptance as the healthy and adaptive alternative.

Cognitive fusion occurs when individuals fail to notice a distinction between the contents of their thoughts and themselves as the *thinker*, and become *fused* with their thoughts. According to RFT, cognitive fusion becomes a source and maintenance process of psychological problems when people are unhelpfully guided more by the literal content of their thoughts than by what they directly experience in their environment. Clients are often asked to notice and observe the ebb and flow of their private experiences, in an attempt to create a helpful distance and space from their minds (*defusion*) to respond differently. ACT also focuses on helping clients to be in more direct contact with their actual experiences, rather than with what their thoughts are telling them is happening.

Hayes's (1989) research on verbal behaviour suggests that inflexible or unhelpful actions are frequently maintained by rigid verbal rules or beliefs, such as attempts to seek social recognition (e.g., reassurance seeking), and/or inaccurate descriptions of how thoughts and feelings work (e.g., beliefs about thought suppression, 'just get over it', etc.). Furthermore, the presence of these verbal rules can dominate to such an extent that people do not learn from their experience, especially if it does not fit with their own verbal rules. This research suggests that therapists may be more effective adopting an experiential learning approach, using metaphors and exercises that help the client to notice their own experience, rather than providing more or different verbal rules that could carry the risk of maintaining inflexibility.

While ACT does not ignore or neglect biological and social factors that can cause, influence and maintain psychological distress, it places greater emphasis on the person and how they interact with their physical and internal environments (or contexts). The ACT therapist is part of the context of the client and vice versa; the focus for the ACT therapist is on creating a therapeutic context that helps the client pragmatically change their behaviour, in the service of their chosen values.

THEORY OF CHANGE

The main therapeutic goal of ACT is to increase an individual's psychological flexibility. ACT attempts to increase a person's psychological flexibility by:

- using acceptance and mindfulness processes to develop more flexible patterns of responding to their own psychological struggles
- reducing the impact of thoughts and self-conceptualisations (self-stories) on behaviour
- helping the client to be in contact with their own (actual) experiences
- increasing frequency and variety of values-based behaviours.

ACT endeavours to help clarify what areas are important or of value in a client's life (e.g., family, relationships, work/education, etc.) and to notice what barriers (e.g., unhelpful responses to negative thoughts, avoidance patterns) are preventing them from consistently moving towards these values. The focus therefore is not on controlling or reducing painful thoughts or feelings, but rather on directing behaviour change according to what is important to the individual.

Through acceptance and mindfulness techniques, clients are taught to become more aware and notice their internal mental, physical and emotional processes. This is in the service of allowing clients the opportunity to directly observe such processes without attempting to judge or change them. Once clients become more aware of their own private experiences, they then have the opportunity to make more informed choices on whether to be guided by such thoughts or feelings. Through developing the skills of acceptance, mindfulness and a flexible perspective taking, an alternative choice is available: to be able to engage in behaviours that are consistent with their deepest values, while 'making room for' experiences.

SKILLS AND STRATEGIES

ACT therapists often adopt an experiential approach to therapeutic change through the use of metaphors and exercises carried out in the session. The aim is to help clients come into direct contact with their learning histories, as opposed to the verbal descriptions of these experiences. By noticing how their minds work and exploring the results of sensible but unworkable

Figure 5.1.1 Core processes in Acceptance and Commitment Therapy

strategies, clients are encouraged to consider whether an alternative stance of being more in the present, while holding thoughts and feelings lightly and being in touch with personal values, may produce greater life vitality. The ACT therapist does not try to convince the client of this; the arbiter is the client's own lived experience of the workability of such an approach.

Within ACT there are six core processes; these are viewed as positive psychological skills as opposed to techniques or methods for avoiding and controlling psychological pain (see Figure 5.1.1). None of these six processes is an end in itself. Rather, ACT views them as methods and strategies for increasing psychological flexibility and allowing values-based actions. The six core therapeutic processes of ACT are:

- *Acceptance*. The aim is to actively accept what is there, without defence or judgement. The focus is on approaching whatever painful thought or feeling shows up as opposed to avoiding, distracting or controlling these. Experiential acceptance can be thought of as an alternative to experiential avoidance.
- *Defusion*. The aim is to help clients notice the processes of thinking in order to see the functional impact this can have on their behaviour. Clients are invited to step back and create distance from their thoughts to allow information from the environment to help shape and guide their behaviour.
- *Contacting the present moment*. This is achieved through the use of a variety of approaches, including mindfulness, whereby the therapist helps the client to make contact with the here-and-now. Fundamentally, the aim is to assist the client to notice their internal private content (thoughts, feelings, bodily sensations) with a non-judgemental stance, that is without judging, evaluating or critiquing them.
- *Self as context or flexible perspective taking*. Helping the client to become aware that they have a place or self from which they can observe difficult thoughts and feelings, without being caught up with

them. Clients learn for themselves how this sense of their self remains constant, and has been with them throughout all of their life experiences.

The final two core ACT processes are known as the approach or activation strategies:

- *Values*. Clarifying with the client what areas are really important in their life. Once the client has identified particular values as important, the ACT practitioner asks the client to evaluate whether their behaviour is in accordance with these.

- *Committed action*. Clients are invited to engage in any behaviour change strategies that enable them to flexibly persist in taking values-based actions.

ACT also draws heavily on traditional behaviour analysis in using functional analysis and therapeutic techniques derived from learning theory. ACT is not simply a collection of techniques. Rather it is a therapeutic model: practitioners flexibly introduce a variety of strategies in a formulation-based way to the areas/domains most in need of attention. A case example is provided to help illustrate some of ACT's core therapeutic processes.

CASE STUDY

Jill is a 25-year-old woman who presented with anxiety, relationship and work-related difficulties. She reported these problems had been ongoing for the past four years and led to her experiencing a significant amount of distress. Jill was plagued by thoughts of being worthless and a failure. She avoided going into work as she was fearful of being scrutinised by her colleagues, who would realise she was incompetent. This left her with debilitating symptoms of anxiety, including palpitations and difficulty concentrating. She also struggled to maintain personal relationships outside work, reporting her inability to trust others led to the breakdown of several intimate relationships. After completing an assessment, her therapist suggested that certain behavioural avoidance patterns (not going into work, distracting herself by isolating herself from her friends and drinking excessive amounts of alcohol) were strategies employed to cope with the verbal rules about herself in comparison to others. However, these behaviour patterns led to her feeling low, worthless and resulted in prolonged periods of struggle.

Jill was helped to identify alternative ways of responding to her distress, which included noticing how thoughts (verbal rules) about herself and others led to avoiding people. A central metaphor was introduced, the *quick sand metaphor* (Hayes et al., 1999), which describes how a client's struggle, while understandable, can often have the paradoxical effect of worsening distress. This metaphor also helped Jill make sense of her difficulties and understand her behavioural patterns in a different context, which included the short-term relief gained from avoiding people also served to move her away from sources of comfort. Jill was invited to let go of this struggle through learning to sit with this discomfort in session. She gradually started to accept these thoughts and feelings as being a normal, yet painful part of her experiences. After working to strengthen these processes, Jill realised that relationships and work were vitally important and she did not want to let the struggle with her verbal content get in the way of being with others. She chose to make several behavioural commitments, including going into work and socialising more with her friends, while continuing to notice and let go of her struggle when painful thoughts and feelings showed up. This created a greater sense of joy for Jill as she was living a life which was important to her.

RESEARCH

The empirical development of ACT has pursued a somewhat different path from some other behavioural and cognitive psychotherapy research. Initially, a significant amount of time was spent gaining empirical support for the basic theory behind ACT (RFT), before the focus shifted onto conducting outcome research on the therapeutic model. Research into RFT has yielded over 400 studies over a 30-year period. In addition to both the basic (RFT) and outcome (evaluating the effectiveness of ACT) research, a great deal of attention has also focused on examining the specific ACT process (e.g., acceptance, experiential avoidance, cognitive defusion, values) and how these may influence outcomes such as life satisfaction and wellbeing. Studies investigating these processes have identified that changes in levels of experiential avoidance can have an indirect effect on an individual's level of psychological distress (A-Tjak et al., 2015).

The outcome research into the efficacy of ACT has developed significantly. To date, ACT has over 325 randomised controlled trials (RCTs) conducted with a diverse range of conditions, including psychosis, anxiety, depression, substance misuse, smoking cessation, borderline personality disorder, epilepsy and weight loss (Hayes, 2019). ACT has been shown to be as effective as established psychological treatments (CBT) for anxiety, depression, substance misuse, pain and somatic problems (A-Tjak et al., 2015; Gloster et al., 2020).

The American Psychological Association has listed ACT to be an evidence-based treatment for the treatment of chronic pain, psychosis, addictions and anxiety and depression.

REFERENCES

A-Tjak, J.G.L., Davis, M.L., Norina, N., Powers, M.B., Smits, J.A.J. and Emmelkamp, P.M.G. (2015) A meta-analysis of the efficacy of Acceptance and Commitment Therapy for clinical relevant mental and physical health problems. *Psychotherapy and Psychomatics*, 84, 30–36.

Gloster, A., Walder, N., Levin, M., Twohig, M. and Karekla, M. (2020) The empirical status of Acceptance and Commitment Therapy: A review of meta-analyses. *Journal of Contextual Behavioral Science*, 18, 181–192.

Hayes, S.C. (Ed.) (1989) *Rule-Governed Behavior: Cognition, Contingencies, and Instructional Control*. New York: Plenum.

Hayes, S.C. (2019) *State of the ACT evidence*. Association for Contextual Behavioral Science. Retrieved from http://contextualscience.org/state_of_the_act_evidence (accessed 10 May 2022).

Hayes, S.C., Barnes-Holmes, D. and Roche, B. (2001) *Relational Frame Theory: A Post-Skinnerian Account of Human Language and Cognition*. New York: Kluwer.

Hayes, S.C., Barnes-Holmes, D. and Wilson, K.G. (2012) Contextual Behavioral Science: Creating a science more adequate to challenge the human condition. *Journal of Contextual Behavioral Science*, 1, 1–16.

Hayes, S.C., Long, D.M., Levein, M.E. and Follette, W.C. (2013) Treatment development: Can we find a better way? *Clinical Psychology Review*, 33, 870–882.

Hayes, S.C., Strosahl, K. and Wilson, K.G. (1999) *Acceptance and Commitment Therapy: An Experiential Approach to Behavior Change*. New York: Guilford Press.

Hayes, S.C., Strosahl, K. and Wilson, K.G. (2012) *Acceptance and Commitment Therapy: The Process and Practice of Mindful Change* (2nd ed.). New York: Guilford Press.

Linehan, M.M. (1993) *Cognitive-Behavioral Treatment of Borderline Personality Disorder*. New York: Guilford Press.

Segal, S.V., Williams, M.G. and Teasdale, J.D. (2002) *Mindfulness-Based Cognitive Therapy for Depression*. New York: Guilford Press.

RECOMMENDED READING

Harris, R. (2019) *ACT Made Simple: An Easy-to-read Primer on Acceptance and Commitment Therapy* (2nd ed.). Oakland, CA: New Harbinger.

This easy-to-read introduction into the ACT model offers the interested reader a step-by-step guide on how to use ACT clinically.

Oliver, J., Hill, J. and Morris, E. (2015) *ACTivate Your Life: Using Acceptance and Mindfulness to Build a Rich, Meaningful, and Fun Life*. London: Robinson.

An accessible, highly practical self-help book, which introduces the reader to the ACT processes and how they can be applied to problems of depression, anxiety, anger and self-esteem.

Luoma, J.B., Hayes, S.C. and Walser, R.D. (2007) *Learning ACT: An Acceptance and Commitment Therapy Skills-Training Manual for Therapists*. Oakland, CA: New Harbinger.

An excellent book which, complete with videos, helps the budding ACT practitioner develop their existing learning and practical understanding of how to implement ACT.

Association for Contextual Behavioral Science: www.contextualpsychology.org.

5.2 ATTACHMENT-BASED PSYCHOANALYTIC PSYCHOTHERAPY

MARK LININGTON AND VICTORIA SETTLE

OVERVIEW AND KEY POINTS

Attachment-based psychoanalytic psychotherapy is a form of psychotherapy provided to individuals, couples, families and groups which uses both attachment theory and psychoanalytic theory as a way of understanding people, their relationships and their difficulties. It makes use of those aspects of psychoanalytic theory which elucidate the nature of the internal world but it locates attachment needs, rather than sexual or aggressive drives, at the heart of development.

The central premise of attachment-based psychoanalytic psychotherapy is that in order to explore safely, we all need to feel securely attached. This means that our clients, as *care seekers*, cannot begin to explore their internal and external worlds until they feel safe in their relationship with us as their psychotherapist or *caregiver*. This is arguably the most important contribution that attachment has made to the practice of psychoanalytic psychotherapy. This premise can be understood by applying the Circle of Security™ (Powell et al., 2014) model to attachment-based psychoanalytic psychotherapy with adults (see Figure 5.4.1).

Key points include:

- Difficulties in our current relationships stem from our patterns of attachment, which have been shaped by our earliest relationships to our primary

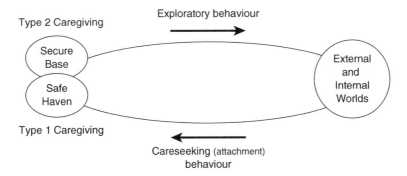

Figure 5.2.1 The Circle of Security™

Adapted from Powell, B., Cooper, G., Hoffman, K. and Marvin, B. (2014). *The Circle of Security Intervention: Enhancing Attachment in Early Parent–Child Relationships*. New York: Guilford Press.

caregivers. Our preverbal experience makes up the core of our developing self.
- These patterns of attachment are not necessarily fixed and later relationships can offer us the opportunity to transform our sense of self.
- Our sense of attachment security is influenced by how we think about and reflect on our relational experiences as well as the experiences themselves.
- The client's relationship to their psychotherapist is primary and it supplies both a secure base from which to explore and a safe haven to find comfort and soothing.
- A sense of felt security, generated through sensitive attunement on the part of the psychotherapist, enables us to access disavowed or dissociated experiences.
- Accessing and reflecting on these previously unverbalised feelings and thoughts gives us a stronger and more integrated self-narrative.
- Acknowledgment of the impact of real experiences in the external world; both with caregivers and in society, including the traumatic experience of discrimination.

BRIEF HISTORY

The early thinking of the object relations school of psychoanalysis influenced John Bowlby but he profoundly disagreed with the dominant psychoanalytic belief that infants' responses relate to their internal fantasy rather than to real-life events. He set out to develop a theory of motivation and behaviour control built on science rather than Freud's psychic energy drive theory model, and for this he was effectively ostracised from the psychoanalytic community.

In 1951, Bowlby put forward the hypothesis that 'the infant and young child should experience a warm, intimate, and continuous relationship with his mother (or permanent mother substitute) in which both find satisfaction and enjoyment' (Bowlby, 1951: xi), the lack of which may have significant and irreversible mental health consequences.

Bowlby collaborated with social worker and psychoanalyst James Robertson in making the 1952 documentary film *A Two-Year-Old Goes to the Hospital*, which filmed the effects of separation on children in hospital and was instrumental in a campaign to alter hospital restrictions on visits by parents. Bowlby's work, coupled with Robertson's films, caused a practical revolution in hospital visiting by parents, hospital provision for children's play, educational and social needs and the use of residential nurseries.

Bowlby's attachment theory was finally written in three volumes (Bowlby, 1969, 1972, 1980).

In the 1970s, in collaboration with Bowlby, Mary Ainsworth developed a research tool called the *Strange Situation*, which enabled observers to classify young toddlers as either *securely* or *insecurely* attached to their primary attachment figure (Ainsworth and Bell, 1970). She observed that there were differences in the attachment behaviour of the toddlers which depended upon the patterns of communication between the caregiver and the toddler. The insecurely attached toddlers were then divided into two groups, whose main patterns of attachment were either avoidant (I don't expect you to meet my needs so I won't seek you out – in response to dismissive caregiving) or ambivalent (if I push I may get my needs met so I will seek you out persistently, but I don't trust that you are there so I will push you away too – in response to preoccupied caregiving).

In the 1980s, the theory of attachment was developed further by Mary Main, who made two major contributions to the thinking on attachment. First, she discovered a third category of insecure attachment, which she described as *disorganised* and which she linked to high levels of fear (being frightening or being frightened) in both the children and their caregivers (Main and Solomon, 1990). Second, she devised the *Adult Attachment Interview* (AAI), which enabled observers to classify the adults' verbal descriptions of their childhood experiences of attachment (Main, Kaplan and Cassidy, 1985). The key aspect of this development was that the attachment behaviour observed directly and described by Bowlby and Ainsworth could now be studied at a representational level.

In the 1990s, studies were conducted by Peter Fonagy and Miriam and Howard Steele in London. Their key contribution was their 'Reflective-Functioning' subscale, which essentially was used to measure parents' capacity to think about their own thinking – with correlations between this capacity and attachment outcomes in the Strange Situation (Fonagy, Steele and Steele, 1991). They observed that the more parents were able to reflect on their own and their infants' mental states, the more likely the infants were to be securely attached to them.

Attachment-based psychoanalytic psychotherapy is attentive to the type of caregiving needed (McCluskey, 2005). If the client is approaching the psychotherapist in a state of fear and/or distress, the client needs type 1 caregiving. Type 1 caregiving (the provision of a 'safe haven') is characterised by soothing, comforting and the attuned regulation of feelings. When the client has become soothed they will return to their natural human state of exploratory behaviour. In this state, the client needs the support of type 2 caregiving, which recognises, validates and encourages the competency of the client in their exploration of their internal and external worlds.

In the last decade or so, exciting new connections have been made between psychoanalysis, attachment theory and neuroscience, and there is a burgeoning of literature exploring how the brain has evolved to learn, unlearn and relearn through being a secure attachment to a reliable caregiver.

Attachment theory has provided fresh insights into how we might understand and work with dissociation in all its forms and how an attachment-based approach could work effectively with clients who have suffered severe trauma.

BASIC ASSUMPTIONS

- There is an inner world, conscious and unconscious, developed in relationships with others, most significantly in our early relationships with attachment figures.
- Aspects of these early caregiving relationships become internalised and working models for future relationships.
- Trauma experienced by these caregivers can be passed on intergenerationally to the infant as part of these internal working models.
- Trauma disrupts attachment relationships and emotional development.
- We form attachment relationships from infancy through childhood and adulthood and into old age.
- Our sense of self is continuously shaped by inter-subjective experience.
- What happens in reality, in the external world, profoundly impacts our sense of attachment security.
- The self develops in relationship to differing cultural, social and political contexts and is impacted by the inequality of power relations.
- Trauma disrupts attachment relationships and emotional development.
- We continuously re-enact our working models of relationship and re-engage these internal working models throughout life.
- Understanding is co-created within the therapy relationship, making what was previously unconscious available to consciousness.
- The psychotherapist's own attachment history and ways of relating will be highly influential in the effectiveness of the psychotherapy.

ORIGIN AND MAINTENANCE OF PROBLEMS

Attachment-based psychoanalytic psychotherapy understands the majority of our emotional and relational problems as originating in experiences of chronically insecure relationships with caregivers. These experiences can occur with detrimental consequences at different periods across the life cycle from pre-birth through to early adulthood (although consistently insecure experiences at a younger age are likely to be more negatively significant for later life). These insecure, sometime traumatised, aspects of caregiving, which are sometimes present across the generations in families, are transmitted physically, non-verbally and verbally to the infant, child and adolescent. The characteristics of these three main insecure forms of caregiving – preoccupied, dismissive, frightened/frightening (Cassidy and Shaver, 1999; Karen, 1994) – are expressed in forms of intrusiveness, high emotionality, neglect, emotional unresponsiveness and abuse. These different forms of insecure caregiving lead to the adaption of three broad complementary categories of attachment patterns: ambivalent, avoidant or disorganised (Cassidy and Shaver, 1999; Karen, 1994). The purpose of these attachment patterns (which are forms of careseeking) is to maximise the responsiveness and availability of the caregiver, given the way they relate.

These repeated experiences in caregiving relationships become working models of relationships internalised in our body and mind. These (insecure) working models of relationships, which are usually mostly outside our conscious awareness, operate as templates for expectations and ways of relating in our later relationships with peers and adult caregivers. We repeat these patterns of relating unless we have an opportunity to experience other more secure ways of relating.

Features of these patterns of relating include:

- How effectively we seek help from caregivers, including as adults with peers. When we have had insecure caregiving-careseeking experiences we are likely to have difficulties in obtaining and receiving help from caregivers in a way that effectively meets our needs.
- The way we experience our feelings in ourselves, how we communicate our feelings to others and our ability to regulate these feelings in ourselves and with others. The regulation of feelings means the ability to bring feelings into a tolerable range (see the Window of Tolerance model in Seigel, 1999).
- Our internal sense of our self as a person, including how we judge ourselves, our knowledge of our competencies and our relationship with our body.
- How we interact in peer relationships, including our ability to play easily and creatively with others, and develop and share common interests (Heard and Lake, 1997) and be romantically, physically and sexually intimate.

Such patterns of relating, originating in a person's past childhood relational experiences, are understood to emerge in the psychotherapeutic relationship (transference). The psychotherapist will utilise their internal responses (countertransference) to such, often unconscious, material to understand more about the nature of the person's attachment patterns.

THEORY OF CHANGE

Put briefly, the theory of change is that if our clients can feel secure in their attachment to us as psychotherapists and we can, in turn, offer attuned responses, we can enable our clients to develop a greater capacity to think about themselves, both in and out of a relationship.

It is important that, within the therapeutic relationship, the psychotherapist is able to be contingent – they need to respond well to the client's spontaneous gestures or initiatives. If the psychotherapist can attune to the emotional world of the client, then feelings that would in the past have threatened to overwhelm the state of the client can be contained safely and digested by the client with the aim of being integrated into the self. Once the psychotherapist has regulated the anxiety, fear or anger expressed by the client, then exploration can safely be started, attachment wounds can be mourned and enlivenment and companionable interest sharing can follow.

Through free association, dreams, transference re-enactments, sharing of countertransference and patterns in our client's developmental history, together we can begin to make sense of our client's experiences and the primary task of becoming more securely attached can begin. This process of formulating how our clients think and feel enables them to understand how their inner world impacts on their everyday life.

SKILLS AND STRATEGIES

Attachment-based psychoanalytic psychotherapy views the psychotherapeutic session as a unique intersubjective encounter occurring moment by moment in a form that is asymmetrically co-created by the two (or more) participants (Aron, 1996).

The key strategy of this form of psychotherapy is to provide the appropriate form of secure caregiving that will, first, enable the regulation of fear and distress and, second, facilitate reflective and narrational exploration. Secure caregiving is understood to have two broad forms (Heard, Lake and McCluskey, 2009). In order to fulfil this strategy, the attachment-based psychoanalytic psychotherapist employs a number of integrated skills:

1. **The skill of empathic attunement** (McCluskey, 2005; Stern, 1985, 1995). This skill is used predominantly non-verbally and to a large extent is outside verbal conscious awareness, but occurs in the domain of implicit relational knowledge (Stern, 2004).
2. **Attentiveness and responsiveness to fear**, with its range of responses of fight, flight, freeze and collapse. Fear (which includes its range of associated feelings, such as nervousness, anxiety, panic and distress) is understood as arising from an accurate appraisal of the *current* environment. For example, meeting a psychotherapist for the first time is realistically likely to arouse anxiety. It is also understood as arising from *past trauma* (most especially attachment trauma) from which the person has not yet recovered.
3. **The provision of secure caregiving** to increase the experience of safety and security in the relationship, with the intention of achieving the outcome of relief from distress and the increase of the natural instinct to exploration both internally and externally. Throughout this work the psychotherapist must be attentive to both the real here-and-now relationship and the links with past experiences of relating (both their own and the client's).
4. **The use of countertransference and understanding of trauma-based enactments**. Attachment-based psychoanalytic psychotherapists learn to attune to their own physiological and emotional responses when working with a client. These responses often have a connection to the unconscious emotional and relational experiences of clients. Sometimes such material is enacted in some form by the therapist and client, which then requires careful exploration.
5. **The facilitation of mourning**. Mourning, while culturally influenced, is also an evolved process that supports the recovery from loss and trauma. It includes the experience and expression of feelings and the enactment of relational behaviours (clinging, searching, withdrawing). The individual's attachment experience will significantly influence the form of their mourning. An attachment-based psychoanalytic psychotherapist helps the client to mourn by recognising and validating the client's experiences of loss and/or trauma. The therapist pays particular attention to the emotional and relational aspects of these real-life events and helps the client over time to construct a reflective narrative of these distressing experiences.

RESEARCH

Attachment theory is one of the most researched psychological and relational theories. Its origins are firmly rooted in empirical longitudinal studies of attachment relationships (Grossmann, Grossmann and Kindler, 2005; Main, Hesse and Kaplan, 2005; Sroufe et al., 2005; Steele and Steele, 2005) as well as many other smaller-scale study projects. There are important overlaps with research in three interrelated disciplines: neuroscience (Schore, 1999), infant and child development (Beebe and Lachmann, 2002; Stern, 1985, 1995) and trauma (Herman, 1992; van der Hart, 2006; van der Kolk, 2014). All of these different aspects of scientific human social research significantly influence the practice of attachment-based psychoanalytic psychotherapy. Furthermore, there is a growing development of research on psychotherapy generally, predominantly utilising outcome measures, but also looking to include explorations of the significance of the quality of the relationship on the psychotherapy (for example, at the United Kingdom Council for Psychotherapy (UKCP) Research Council; Rowland and Goss, 2000). Finally, there is a growing edge of research regarding the clinical application of attachment theory in psychotherapy (McCluskey, personal communication; The Bowlby Centre, 2012).

REFERENCES

Ainsworth, M. D. S. and Bell, S. M. (1970). Attachment, exploration, and separation: Illustrated by the behavior of one-year-olds in a strange situation. *Child Development, 41*, 49–67.

Aron, L. (1996). *Meeting of Minds: Mutuality in Psychoanalysis*. New York: The Analytic Press.

Beebe, B. and Lachmann, F. (2002). *Infant Research and Adult Treatment: Co-constructing Interactions*. New York: The Analytic Press.

Bowlby, J. (1951). *Child Care and the Growth of Love; based by permission of the World Health Organization on the report 'Maternal Care and Mental Health'*. Harmondsworth: Penguin.

Bowlby, J. (1969). *Attachment and Loss*. Vol. 1: *Attachment*. Harmondsworth: Penguin.

Bowlby, J. (1972). *Attachment and Loss*. Vol. 2: *Separation: Anxiety and Anger*. Harmondsworth: Penguin.

Bowlby, J. (1980). *Attachment and Loss*. Vol. 3: *Loss: Sadness and Depression*. Harmondsworth: Penguin.

Cassidy, J. and Shaver P. R. (Eds) (1999). *Handbook of Attachment: Theory, Research, and Clinical Applications*. New York: Guilford Press.

Fonagy, P., Steele, H. and Steele, M. (1991). Maternal representation of attachment during pregnancy predicts the organisation of infant-mother attachment at one year of age. *Child Development, 62*, 891–905.

Grossmann, K., Grossmann, K. E. and Kindler, H. (2005). Early care and the roots of attachment and partnership representation: The Bielefeld and Regensburg Longitudinal Studies. In K. E. Grossmann, K. Grossmann and E. Waters (Eds), *Attachment from Infancy to Adulthood: The Major Longitudinal Studies* (pp. 98–136). New York: Guilford Press.

Heard, D. and Lake, B. (1997). *The Challenge of Attachment for Caregiving*. London: Karnac.

Heard, D., Lake, B. and McCluskey, U. (2009). *Attachment Therapy with Adolescents and Adults: Theory and Practice Post Bowlby*. London: Karnac.

Herman, J. L. (1992). *Trauma and Recovery: From Domestic Abuse to Political Terror*. New York: Basic Books.

Karen, R. (1994). *Becoming Attached: First Relationships and How They Shape Our Capacity to Love*. Oxford: Oxford University Press.

Main, M., Hesse, E. and Kaplan, N. (2005). Predictability of attachment behavior and representational processes at 1, 6, and 19 years of age: The Berkeley Longitudinal Study. In K. E. Grossmann, K. Grossmann and E. Waters (Eds), *Attachment from Infancy to Adulthood: The Major Longitudinal Studies*. New York: Guilford Press, pp. 245–304.

Main, M., Kaplan, N. and Cassidy, J. (1985). Security in infancy, childhood, and adulthood: A move to the level of representation. In I. Bretherton and E. Waters (Eds), *Growing points of attachment theory and research. Monographs of the Society for Research in Child Development, 50* (1–2, Serial No. 209), 66–104.

Main, M. and Solomon, J. (1990). Procedures for identifying infants as disorganized/disoriented during the Ainsworth Strange Situation. In M. T. Greenberg, D. Cicchetti and E. M. Cummings (Eds), *Attachment in the Preschool Years: Theory, Research, and Intervention* (pp. 121–160). Chicago, IL: University of Chicago Press.

McCluskey, U. (2005). *To Be Met as a Person: The Dynamics of Attachment in Professional Encounters*. London: Karnac.

Powell, B., Cooper, G., Hoffman, K. and Marvin, B. (2014). *The Circle of Security Intervention: Enhancing Attachment in Early Parent–Child Relationships*. New York: Guilford Press.

Rowland, N. and Goss, S. (2000). *Evidence-based Counselling and Psychological Therapies: Research and Applications*. London: Routledge.

Schore, A. N. (1999). *Affect Regulations and the Origin of the Self: The Neurobiology of Emotional Development*. Hillsdale, NJ: Lawrence Erlbaum Associates.

Siegel, D. (1999). *The Developing Mind: How Relationships and the Brain Interact to Shape Who We Are*. New York: Guilford Press.

(Continued)

(Continued)

Sroufe, A. L., Egeland, B., Carlson, E. A. and Collins, W. A. (2005). *The Development of the Person: The Minnesota Study of Risk and Adaptation from Birth to Adulthood*. New York: Guilford Press.

Steele, M. and Steele, H. (2005). Understanding and resolving emotional conflict: The London Parent–Child Project. In K. E. Grossmann, K. Grossmann and E. Waters (Eds), *Attachment from Infancy to Adulthood: The Major Longitudinal Studies* (pp. 137–164). New York: Guilford Press.

Stern, D. N. (1985). *The Interpersonal World of the Infant: A View from Psychoanalysis and Developmental Psychology*. New York: Basic Books.

Stern, D. N. (1995). *The Motherhood Constellation: A Unified View of Parent–Infant Psychotherapy*. New York: Basic Books.

Stern, D. N. (2004). *The Present Moment in Psychotherapy and Everyday Life*. New York: W. W. Norton.

The Bowlby Centre (2012). *The Spine of the Relational World*. London: The Bowlby Centre.

Van der Hart, O. (2006). *The Haunted Self: Structural Dissociation and the Treatment of Chronic Traumatization*. New York: W. W. Norton.

Van der Kolk, B. (2014). *The Body Keeps the Score: Mind, Brain and Body in the Transformation of Trauma*. Harmondsworth: Penguin.

RECOMMENDED READING

Bowlby, J. (1988). *A Secure Base: Clinical Applications of Attachment Theory*. London: Routledge.

This book presents the most fundamental aspects of attachment theory and helps to bridge the gap between theory and practice.

Duschinsky, R. (2020). *Cornerstones of Attachment Research*. Oxford: Oxford University Press.

An essential book for understanding historic and contemporary research into attachment.

McCluskey, U. and O'Toole, M. (2020). *Transference and Countertransference from an Attachment Perspective*. London: Routledge.

This book is an in-depth exploration of the detailed dynamics of attachment-based systems and their application in professional caregiving.

5.3 COGNITIVE ANALYTIC THERAPY

CLAIRE POLLITT

OVERVIEW AND KEY POINTS

Cognitive analytic therapy (CAT) was proposed as a formal psychotherapy model in the 1980s by Anthony Ryle, who viewed conceptual integration as key to the development of a comprehensive psychological theory. CAT integrated both cognitive and analytic ideas within its early framework, particularly drawing on personal construct theory and object relations theory. In later years, it also incorporated concepts from Vygotsky and Bahktin. These significant and influential ideas were revised and harmonised to form a coherent model of psychological functioning, which has explanatory power in relation to psychopathology, and creates a sound framework for therapeutic intervention.

CAT proposes that through early social experiences, we develop a repertoire of reciprocal roles (RRs), which become internalised as working models for conducting relationships. They are reciprocal in that any role we occupy can only be understood in relation to the complementary role of another. During interaction both social parts are learnt, and we can enact these both towards ourselves and others, while creating expectancy that the other person will occupy the alternate position. When these RRs are activated, they manifest as repeating patterns (reciprocal role procedures), which are observable in how we relate to others, and form the basis of self-management and self-regulation.

The key points of CAT are as follows:

- CAT aims to develop client self-reflective capacity and recognition of problematic roles and procedures, in order to revise them.
- CAT is transdiagnostic and has been applied to a wide array of clinical difficulties.
- CAT is commonly used within a 16-session individual therapy format, or 24 sessions for more complex presentations.

BRIEF HISTORY

The evolution of CAT theory can be traced by the emergence of three psychological models, outlined below.

The procedural sequence model (PSM) (Ryle, 1982) was informed by Kelly's view of cognitive processes (Kelly, 1955). Kelly proposed that people develop models of reality based on 'constructs', which are understood in polarity to each other (e.g., 'hot' in relation to 'cold') and shape our expectations and behaviours. Kelly thought that, like scientists, people develop constructs based on observation and experimentation, and that we make amendments according to our findings. Ryle developed this idea by introducing the concept of 'procedures', which combine cognition, affect and behaviour in a sequential pattern. Procedures consist of an appraisal and action, followed by an evaluation of consequences and either confirmation or revision. Ryle suggested that psychological distress can be accounted for by a restricted range of procedures that were dysfunctional and/or resistant to revision.

With the introduction of the concept of RRs, the procedural sequence object relations model (PSORM) (Ryle, 1985) incorporated the psychoanalytic premise of an internal world. However, this was not based upon instincts, 'phantasy' and reified internal objects, as in the work of Klein (1946). Ryle shared Fairburn's (1986) perspective on the importance of external relationships in shaping an individual's inner world, with reciprocal roles deriving from internalised interactions with key carers. The influence of wider culture was later emphasised with Leiman's (1992) reflections on the work of philosopher Bakhtin (1986), who proposed that thought itself is dialogical, mirroring the person's conversation with key carers and society. The stability of the reciprocal role is maintained by the individual seeking and eliciting the complementary response in others. This notion incorporates the psychoanalytic concepts of transference, countertransference and projective identification. However, CAT demystifies these processes, making them observable and applicable outside the confines of the therapeutic relationship.

Seeking to account for the difficulties observed in borderline personality disorder (BPD), the multiple self states model (MSSM) (Ryle, 1997) extended CAT theory by introducing the concept of three interdependent levels of psychological functioning. Ryle proposed that in BPD there is damage to all levels. Level one relates to the degree to which the individual has a multiplicity of healthy reciprocal roles. Level two relates to how higher-order procedures, which are meta-cognitive in nature, continuously select and integrate within the repertoire of RRs according to the context and the individual's aims and values. Level three relates to conscious self-awareness and self-reflective capacity, which is itself seen as a procedure originating from internalised interactions with attentive caregivers.

BASIC ASSUMPTIONS

- CAT is collaborative, emphasising the importance of joint activity and conceptual tools (e.g., diagrams and therapeutic letters) in supporting the client to develop a self-reflective capacity.
- CAT involves the therapist's active use of self (including emotional responses), to build a shared understanding of the client's roles and procedures, and to avoid enacting these unhelpfully within the therapeutic relationship.
- The client is an active participant in change, engaging in self-monitoring and testing out what has been learnt within therapy in their 'everyday' lives.
- Therapy is time-limited and uses this constraint to mobilise and focus the therapy.

ORIGIN AND MAINTENANCE OF PROBLEMS

DYSFUNCTIONAL RECIPROCAL ROLES AND PROCEDURES

The internalisation of destructive or limited RRs is seen as a primary source of distress, interpersonal problems and self-management difficulties. For example, if an individual has received parenting that is harsh and critical, they may internalise the following reciprocal role (see Figure 5.3.1).

The top 'pole' signifies the parental position, while the bottom reflects the lived experience of the

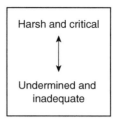

Figure 5.3.1 An example of dysfunctional reciprocal roles and procedures

individual. Both parts are internalised, and may be enacted in three keys ways:

- Self to self – sets perfectionist standards and becomes self-critical if these aren't met.
- Self to other – sets unrealistic standards of others and becomes critical if these aren't met.
- Other to self – 'invites' others to be critical towards them through their rigidity and negative judgement. Demonstrates a cognitive bias towards perceiving others as attacking.

The more limited the individual's repertoire of roles, the stronger the 'pull' of reciprocation is likely to be. Outlined below are further examples of problematic RRs:

- mocking to humiliated
- smothering to stifled
- controlling to dominated
- rejecting to 'thrown away' and defective
- withholding to deprived
- abandoning to vulnerable and alone.

Problematic procedures are those that are self-limiting, have negative consequences or fail to reduce distress/meet the individual's emotional needs. They may have originated as adaptive responses to early life experiences, which have since become outdated and unhelpful. For example, an individual who has been mistreated by a parent could understandably develop a placatory procedure. However, during adulthood such behaviour may leave them vulnerable to further mistreatment. Problematic procedures are resistant to revision either because of their circularity (traps), because of false polarised choices (dilemmas), or because of the abandonment of appropriate goals due to maladaptive beliefs (snags).

An illustration of each is given in relation to the case example:

- Dilemma – Either I am anxiously striving for perfection, or I feel guilty and become self-critical.
- Trap – To avoid feeling like a failure and being criticised by myself and others, I avoid situations and activities where I feel unsure of myself. This avoidance undermines my development and my confidence, leaving me feeling more like a failure and self-critical.
- Snag – Feeling inadequate, I sabotage good things in my life as if I do not deserve them.

DIMINISHED RR INTEGRATION AND SELF-REFLECTIVE CAPACITY IN BPD

CAT proposes that in BPD presentation, at level one, there is a very limited repertoire of RRs, possibly formed through extreme experiences of abuse and neglect. At level two, higher-order procedures concerned with integration and selection within the reciprocal role repertoire are incomplete or disrupted. This is thought to occur due to trauma-induced dissociation and/or exposure to incoherent, neglectful or contradictory experiences. Dissociation initially occurs as a response to unmanageable external threat but is re-triggered with memories or perceived repetitions of the threat. This process can lead to RRs and their procedures becoming partially dissociated, so that when in one role the person has limited awareness of or access to alternates. These partially dissociated RRs, known as self-states, are thought to account for the rapid changes in being that can be seen in BPD, with the noted lack of sequential awareness of what has led to the sudden shift. This dysfunction results in further impairment at level three, which relates to self-awareness and capacity for self-reflection.

THEORY OF CHANGE

The CAT process involves building a reformulation of the client's difficulties, with the subsequent recognition and revision of problematic RRs and procedures. The therapist and client agree a list of target problems. The procedures which are seen as maintaining these are named as target problem procedures, and these become the focus for change.

The CAT theory of change is influenced by Vygotsky's (1978) work on sign mediation and the zone of proximal development (ZPD). Vygotsky suggested that meaning is formed through shared activity, whereby joint signs (such as those found in language) are created through repeated parental responses to the child's gestures and verbal expressions. Once internalised, these signs enable the development of psychological tools, which in turn shape the mind's capacities. A memory mnemonic is an example of such a tool. CAT therefore emphasises the co-creation of psychological tools in the form of a therapeutic letter and a sequential diagram of the reciprocal role repertoire. Once internalised, these tools can represent the client's inner world, thereby facilitating self-reflection and subsequent change.

Vygotsky described the ZPD as the distance between the individual's actual developmental level and the level of current potential development (determined through problem-solving ability with more-capable others). Growth occurs when the individual is working within their ZPD, where the task is experienced as challenging, but not so novel or demanding that it cannot be accomplished by the individual themselves with appropriate support. Through repetition, the aided task becomes one that the individual can perform independently. In CAT, this concept helps the therapist identify the optimal conditions for effective therapeutic intervention by informing the appropriate pace of therapy, the required level of therapist guidance and likely achievable 'exits' to problematic procedures.

SKILLS AND STRATEGIES

REFORMULATION

Reformulation involves building a joint understanding with the client of their difficulties and how these are being maintained by problematic RRs and procedures. This process involves the creation of a sequential diagrammatic reformulation (SDR) and a prose reformulation letter.

From assessment, the therapist begins mapping the client's reciprocal roles and procedures with them to form the SDR. This is amended and elaborated upon as the client develops new understandings about themselves. Such joint activity, characterised by curiosity, care and persistence in understanding the client's inner world, can subsequently be internalised to form the basis of a healthy self-management procedure. The SDR is based on descriptions of the client's relationship history, functional analysis of current behaviours and observations of interactions within the therapeutic relationship. It is designed to provide the client with perspective on their difficulties, to help generate 'exits'. Figure 5.3.2 describes a partial SDR for the aforementioned case example.

An initial reformulation letter is typically read aloud to the client around session four. The letter also outlines target problems and procedures, but it has the added value of placing these in a historical context, framing

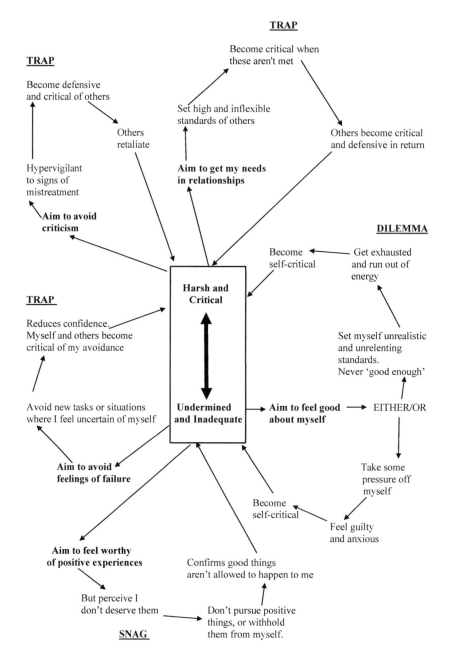

Figure 5.3.2 Example of a partial SDR

them as survival modes that once had appropriate and protective functions. It aims to connect past neglect, abuse and trauma with the current RRs and procedures of the client, in a manner which conveys warmth and understanding for the person's struggle. This can provide a powerful means of validation and normalisation, which strengthens the therapeutic relationship early in the alliance.

RECOGNITION

Having built an understanding of their RRs and procedures, the client is encouraged to recognise them as they occur, as a prerequisite to revision. The therapist may introduce personalised self-monitoring diaries or mindfulness practice to facilitate this skill development between sessions. In each session, the client rates their target problem in terms of how rapidly they noticed the associated problematic procedure, and later how effectively it was addressed. The SDR tool is used in every session to assist the client to recognise RRs and procedures as they occur, both in the narratives of their life which they bring to therapy and within the therapeutic relationship.

REVISION

Revision involves the client amending problematic RRs and procedures by finding 'exits' to replace them with healthier patterns of relating to themselves and others. Various change methods from other therapies may be utilised, generating therapeutic richness and flexibility. However, methods must be carefully selected and applied to ensure that they are theoretically consistent with CAT and are reformulation-driven.

Outlined below are several change methods and examples of their possible application within CAT:

- Assertiveness skills – addressing dilemma related to either 'I am a bully or a victim'.
- Self-soothing skills – addressing a self-harm procedure in which the function of the behaviour is to manage feelings of distress.
- Use of empty chair technique or non-send letters – to process past losses related to dilemma of 'I get involved with others and get hurt, or I am in control but totally alone'.
- Psychoeducation and cognitive restructuring – reducing shame in sexual abuse victims who have a self-sabotage snag, based upon feeling non-deserving.

In the case example, change methods could include a behavioural experiment, to test out the impact of positive self-encouragement versus self-criticism on motivation levels. Thought-challenging diaries and psychoeducation around thought biases can be employed to address the tendency to perceive others as critical, while assertiveness practice may include saying 'no' to excessive work demands. The intervention may also include helping the client to extend their social and recreational interests, in order to establish activities outside those based upon 'self-improvement', and to address avoidance of situations where they feel unconfident or 'non-deserving'.

Irrespective of other methods employed, within CAT the therapeutic relationship is the major vehicle of change. The therapist's key role is to resist the pull to adopt the expected reciprocal role. Regular CAT supervision is important, and therapists must be aware of how their own RRs and procedures may collude with those of the client. Through direct experience of acknowledging and exploring RRs through the therapeutic relationship, the client can negotiate new ways of being. These new behavioural styles, and a positive experience of the therapist, can form the basis of healthier RRs and procedures to be practised outside the therapeutic relationship. Research indicates that good therapy outcomes are associated with therapists who recognise problematic enactments within the therapy relationship and collaboratively work with the client to resolve them (Bennett, Parry and Ryle, 2006; Daly et al., 2010).

In the case example, possible enactments could include the client avoiding homework tasks when they feel unable to perform them perfectly, experiencing the therapist as critical and acting defensively or becoming attacking due to perceiving that not enough has been achieved.

ENDING

The ending is explicitly used to address unresolved grief issues, unhelpful procedures related to managing loss and RRs characterised by rejection or abandonment. To facilitate the transition, the client is either offered a follow-up at one month (16-session CAT) or four follow-ups over six months (24-session CAT).

Both the therapist and client exchange 'goodbye letters'. Their key function is to facilitate the expression of feelings regarding therapy ending, and to keep the experience and learnt 'exits' active in the client's mind following therapy completion.

Both letters can include:

- naming of 'exits' with specific examples applied during therapy
- acknowledgement of challenges that the client found particularly difficult
- significant moments within the therapeutic relationship, such as resolving reciprocal role enactments
- naming possible feelings of disappointment in relation to initial hopes for change
- naming of thoughts and feelings in relation to ending, and its meaning in the context of the client's history
- naming of possible problematic RRs and procedures that may be triggered by ending, with possible 'exits'
- indications for future work, particularly during the follow-up period.

RESEARCH

The current CAT research base is largely dominated by practice-based evidence (PBE) with complex clinical populations (Hallam et al., 2021). Taylor and Hartley (2021) suggest that this reflects CAT's roots as a pragmatic approach established principally through clinical endeavour, with clinicians carrying out studies alongside their routine practice. Citing the strengths and weakness of PBE, the authors advocate for a pluralistic research methodology, with a focus on fostering greater collaboration between clinicians and research institutions.

Evidence to date suggests that such investment in CAT research would be justified. In a meta-analysis of 25 studies providing pre-post treatment outcomes, Hallam et al. (2021) found that CAT resulted in large pre-post improvements in global functioning, moderate to large improvements in interpersonal functioning and large reductions in depressive symptoms. These effects were maintained at follow-up or were improved on in the case of interpersonal functioning. Analysis of nine randomised controlled trials (RCTs) in the review demonstrated small to moderate, significant post-therapy gains relative to comparators. While acknowledging methodological limitations, the authors state that these findings signify that CAT is helpful for a variety of clinical presentations.

Furthermore, a review by Calvert and Kellet (2014) indicated that CAT has specific utility for treating people given a diagnosis of personality disorder, with 11 of the 25 studies being focused on these individuals. The authors state that these studies (eight assessed as high quality, with two being RCTs) suggest that CAT can produce positive outcomes for this client group, both in routine clinical practice and under trial conditions. In this context, CAT has been included as a potential treatment in the National Institute for Health and Care Excellence (NICE) guidelines for *Borderline Personality Disorder* (NICE, 2009). Positive outcomes were also indicated for anorexia nervosa by two high-quality RCTs in the study.

Overall, research findings to date appear encouraging, indicating that a coordinated strategy to extend the breadth and depth of the CAT evidence base is merited (Calvert and Kellet, 2014).

REFERENCES

Bakhtin, M.M. (1986) *Speech Genres and Other Late Essays.* Austin, TX: University of Texas Press.

Bennett, D., Parry, G. and Ryle, A. (2006) Resolving threats to the therapeutic alliance in cognitive analytic therapy of borderline personality disorder: a task analysis. *Psychology and Psychotherapy: Theory, Research and Practice*, 79: 395–418.

Calvert, R. and Kellett, S. (2014) Cognitive analytic therapy: a review of the outcome evidence base for treatment. *Psychology and Psychotherapy: Theory, Research and Practice*, 87: 253–277.

Daly, A.M., Llewelyn, S., McDougall, E. and Chanen, A.M. (2010) Rupture resolution in cognitive analytic therapy for adolescents with borderline personality disorder. *Psychology and Psychotherapy: Theory, Research and Practice*, 83: 273–288.

Fairburn, F.W. (1986) *Psychoanalytic Studies of the Personality*. London: Tavistock.

Hallam, C., Simmonds-Buckley, M., Kellett S., Greenhill, B. and Jones, A. (2021) The acceptability, effectiveness, and durability of cognitive analytic therapy: systematic review and meta-analysis. *Psychology and Psychotherapy: Theory, Research and Practice*, 94: 8–35.

Kelly, G.A. (1955) *The Psychology of Personal Constructs*. New York: W.W. Norton.

Klein, M. (1946) Notes on some schizoid mechanisms. In M. Klein, P. Heiman, S. Isaacs and J. Riviere (Eds), *Developments in Psychoanalysis*. London: Hogarth.

Leiman, M. (1992) The concept of sign in the work of Vygotsky, Winnicot and Bakhtin: further integration of object relations theory and activity theory. *British Journal of Medical Psychology*, 67: 97–106.

NICE (2009) *Borderline Personality Disorder: Treatment and Management*. Clinical Guideline 78. London: National Institute for Health and Clinical Excellence.

Ryle, A. (1982) *Psychotherapy: A Cognitive Integration of Theory and Practice*. London: Academic Press.

Ryle, A. (1985) Cognitive theory, object relations and the self. *British Journal of Medical Psychology*, 58: 1–7.

Ryle, A. (1997) *Cognitive Analytic Therapy and Borderline Personality Disorder: The Model and the Method*. Chichester: John Wiley.

Taylor, P.J. and Hartley, S. (2021) Reformulating the relationship between cognitive analytic therapy and research: navigating the landscape and exploring new directions. *Psychology and Psychotherapy: Theory, Research and Practice*, 94: 1–7.

Vygotsky, L.S. (1978) *Mind and Society: The Development of Higher Psychological Processes*. Cambridge, MA: Harvard University Press.

RECOMMENDED READING

Colbridge, C., Brummer, L. and Coid, P. (2017) *Cognitive Analytic Therapy: Distinctive Features*. London: Routledge.

An introductory text outlining the distinctive features of the approach.

Ryle, A. and Kerr, I. (2020) *Introducing Cognitive-Analytic Therapy: Principles and Practice of a Relational Approach to Mental Health* (2nd ed.). Chichester: John Wiley & Sons.

This text provides a comprehensive overview of CAT theory.

Wilde McCormick, E. (2017) *Change for the Better: Personal Development through Practical Psychotherapy* (5th ed.). Los Angeles, CA: Sage.

A self-help book providing plenty of case material.

5.4 COGNITIVE BEHAVIOURAL THERAPY

HEATHER SEQUEIRA AND JILL MYTTON

OVERVIEW AND KEY POINTS

Cognitive behaviour therapy (CBT) is a popular and well-researched form of psychotherapy that focuses on how our thoughts, feelings and behaviours are interconnected. CBT presumes that how we (1) act and how we (2) think can have a strong effect on (3) how we feel, and vice versa. This causal sequence can be harnessed to help us change our thoughts, feelings and behaviour for the better.

The invitation of CBT is to experiment with alternative perspectives.

- CBT requires a solid meaningful therapeutic relationship where there is a strong emphasis on collaborative working, self-empowerment and equality.
- CBT is practical, action-oriented, rational and aims to help the client gain independence and effectiveness in dealing with real-life issues.
- CBT is the most researched and scientifically validated of any of the 'talking therapy' approaches.
- The main focus of CBT is on thinking, behaving, feeling and communicating in the here-and-now with an emphasis on promoting 'realistic' and 'helpful' thinking and actions.
- CBT helps people learn effective self-helping skills that can stay with them for life.

BRIEF HISTORY

Around the middle of the twentieth century, two eminent American psychologists, Albert Ellis and Aaron Beck, became dissatisfied with the psychoanalytic approach in which they were trained. Ellis went on to develop rational emotive behaviour therapy (REBT) and Beck to develop what has become the most-used cognitive approach to therapy today. Both of these therapeutic approaches echo the ideas of the Greek, Roman and Eastern philosophers who argued that the way we think about our world and ourselves plays an important role in our emotions and behaviours. Gautama Buddha once observed, 'We are what we think. All that we are arises with our thoughts, with our thoughts we make the world' and Stoic philosopher Epictetus noted, 'What disturbs people's minds is not events but their judgements on events'.

Aaron Beck had noticed that the thoughts and dreams of his depressed clients were focused on unrealistic negative ideas, and in 1963 and 1964 he published two seminal papers on the relationship between thinking and depression (Beck, 1963; Beck et al., 1964). Specifically, Beck identified that people struggling with depression presented with what he termed the Negative Cognitive Triad: a negative view of (1) themselves, (2) the world and (3) the future (see Figure 5.4.1). Within psychotherapy this observation represented a groundbreaking shift from traditional psychoanalytic and behavioural ideas by positing the centrality of thinking in our understanding of psychological distress.

Beck's CBT is arguably the most influential approach within CBT and from the original Beckian methods many other forms of CBT have evolved (Wills, 2021) for example, REBT (Ellis, 2011), meta-cognitive therapy (Wells, 2013), schema therapy (Jacob and Arntz, 2013; Young, Klosko and Weishaar, 2003) and 'Third Wave' cognitive behavioural approaches (Kahl, Winter and Schweiger, 2012).

For more than 50 years, CBT has delivered an evidence-based way to understand and treat psychological difficulties and has grown into what is arguably the most influential and widely validated psychotherapeutic model in the world. It has been extended and adapted to the treatment of many forms of psychological (and body-based) problems. Based on a solid foundation of neurological and behavioural research (David, Cristea and Hofmann, 2018; Fordham et al., 2021), there is a large body of clinical evidence supporting its efficacy, with issues including (but not limited to) depression, generalised anxiety disorder, anorexia, obsessive-compulsive disorder (OCD), post-traumatic stress disorder (PTSD), phobias, personality disorders, schizophrenia and psychosis (Naeem et al., 2016; Papola, 2021; Wykes, 2014). In addition, there is evidence that CBT can aid the impact management of physical diseases such as multiple sclerosis, chronic fatigue syndrome, cancer and chronic pain (van Beugen et al., 2014;

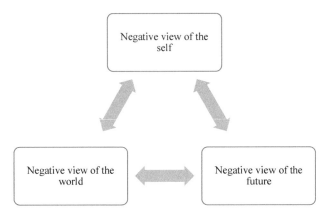

Figure 5.4.1 Beck's Negative Cognitive Triad

White, 2001). CBT has an established evidence base for use in individual face-to-face therapy, group therapy and family therapy.

BASIC ASSUMPTIONS

COGNITION

Human beings have cognitions. This means that we process information coming through our senses and make interpretations and evaluations about that information. In this way, we interact with our life experiences and develop our own *individualised* meanings about our perceptions and experiences. The central role of cognition in our psychosocial and emotional health is the most basic assumption of CBT (Bennett-Levy et al., 2004).

In this way, our emotional and behavioural responses to events in our lives (e.g., a traumatic life event or loss of a relationship) depend not on the event alone, but on the personal interpretation that we give to that event. This explains why people can undergo exactly the same event but experience vastly different emotional responses to the same situation.

Take an example: two people are turned down at the same job interview with similar feedback. Person One attaches the following meaning to this event:

> 'It's really disappointing that they did not offer it to me, but the feedback indicates that I did not sell my skills sufficiently to prove my worth in the job. If I practise this for future interviews, it will improve my chances of getting a similar position next time.'

In contrast, Person Two attaches a different meaning to the event:

> 'Just typical. Being rejected is more proof that I am worthless. Everyone can see that I am useless so it's not even worth trying again.'

In this fictional example, the two people place very different personal meaning on the same event. The different meanings cause (1) different emotional responses and (2) different behavioural actions. It is important to note that the meanings or appraisals that people place on life experiences can be positive or negative, helpful or unhelpful and accurate or distorted. The model CBT suggests that mental health issues, such as depression or generalised anxiety, are maintained or made worse by negatively biased and distorted ways of thinking. It is held that the meanings ascribed to experiences depend to a large extent on a person's prior life experiences (particularly early childhood experiences).

BEHAVIOUR

Behaviours are also an integral part of changing or maintaining our psychological states and how we feel. For example, responding to not getting a job offer with avoidance behaviours, such as watching daytime TV and spending prolonged time on social media, is likely to lead to further low mood, increased physiological anxiety and a decrease in self-belief. On the other hand, if the person talks the situation through with a supportive friend and takes some small steps to practise interview skills (behaviour/actions), it is likely that they will start to grow in self-confidence (cognitions/beliefs about the self) and begin to feel more upbeat and positive in their mood.

INTERACTING SYSTEMS

CBT goes beyond just considering the way we think or behave, but it takes the view that experiences are interactions between various systems within the person and their environment.

According to Kennerly, Kirk and Westbrook (2016), contemporary CBT commonly identifies four 'internal' systems. These are:

- cognition
- affect, or emotion
- behaviour
- physiology.

Within CBT, these systems are seen to be interrelated with each other, plus the persons, broader life experiences (environment/social environment). This is illustrated by Padesky and Mooney's 'five-system framework' (see Greenberger and Padesky, 2016). Using this framework, it is intuitive to see how by changing what we think (cognition), we create a causal sequence or 'domino-effect' on how we act (our behaviour), our physical reactions (physiology) how we feel (our emotions). By making a change to one element, we can change the whole framework, including the wider environment/social environment and vice versa.

ORIGIN AND MAINTENANCE OF PROBLEMS

Beck's original cognitive model proposed that it is distorted and negatively biased thinking that underlies psychological disturbance. This is because distorted and negatively biased thinking prevents a person from dealing with aversive life events in the most resilient and effective way possible.

Beck identified a number of 'logical errors' that characterise such Negative Automatic Thoughts (NATS):

- *Arbitrary inference*: people sometimes draw conclusions about events without any supporting evidence.
- *Dichotomous or black-and-white thinking*: thinking in extreme terms. For example, using the words 'never' and 'always' rather than 'sometimes' (e.g., I never look attractive; my friend Helen always looks fantastic), or placing experiences in one of two opposite categories, such as beautiful and ugly.
- *Maximisation and minimisation*: events are evaluated as much more or much less important than they really are. A normally calm mother losing her temper one day with her child may exaggerate the event (maximisation) and conclude that she is a very bad mother with poor childcare skills (minimisation).
- *Catastrophising*: assuming a negative outcome and jumping to the conclusion that this would lead to a chain of worst possible outcomes. For example, 'If I get nervous during my sales presentation I will forget what I am saying. This means that I will not make the sale, I will get fired and never get another job like this one. I won't be able to pay the mortgage so lose the house, and my young family will be homeless.'
- *Emotional reasoning*: we assume that our emotions reflect the way things actually are. For example, if we feel ignored by a friend, then we assume that we were actually ignored rather than looking for a range of alternative explanations (e.g., 'she did not see me' or 'she has stuff on her mind'). Instead, we assume 'I *feel it*, therefore it is true'.
- *Mind reading*: assuming what is going on for others without checking it out. For example, 'My boss did not acknowledge my report so she obviously thinks it's not up to scratch'.
- *Fortune telling*: assuming that things will turn out badly without trying it out. For example, 'It's not worth me asking Alisha for a date as she is bound to turn me down'.

As identified by Wills (2021), everyone experiences these types of distorted thoughts at times. However, at times of psychological stress, distorted thinking becomes more prevalent and plausible. This in turn, can increase a person's attention to negative aspects of their experience (negative attention bias) which further adds to the convincing nature of the distorted unhelpful pattern of thought.

SCHEMAS

Schemas are the unspoken rules or underlying core beliefs which we all hold about the self, others and the world. Schemas are generally learned through, and are consistent with, our early/childhood experiences. They include enduring patterns of memories, perceptual patterns, bodily sensations and emotions, which act as non-conscious templates to filter incoming information. When an event occurs, our schemas determine not only what we look at, what we remember and how we interpret information, but also how we regulate our emotions in response to events.

Schemas can be adaptive and healthy or unhelpful and unhealthy. Unhelpful schemas tend to be negative, rigid and absolute. When unhealthy schemas are activated, they affect all the stages of information processing. Thus, a person with the schema 'I am worthless' will tend to distort incoming information to match this belief. More likely, realistic or helpful information (that could discount this belief) may be ignored or distorted: 'My friend only said something nice because she wants something from me'.

When unhealthy schemas are activated, the individual tends to be prone to Negative Automatic Thoughts (NATs). For example, a person struggling with anxiety may automatically and repeatedly think 'I can't cope with this', and a person suffering with depression may think 'I'm useless, I'll never be able to do this, I give up'. Although people with positive mental health can also experience such automatic thoughts, they are more frequent and disruptive in people with mental health problems.

Aaron Beck and other researchers have produced extensive updates to Beck's original work, incorporating perspectives from clinical, cognitive, biological and evolutionary perspectives (Beck and Bredemeier, 2016; Beck and Haigh, 2014). For example, in the Unified Model of Depression (Beck and Bredemeier, 2016), genetic predispositions and early experiences and/or trauma both contribute to the development of information-processing biases (e.g., attentional and memory biases) and biological reactivity to stress (e.g., amygdala, hypothalamic-pituitary-adrenal (HPA) axis, cortisol). The authors indicate how the combination of early experiences, cognitive biases and stress reactivity can gradually lead to the development of the 'Negative Cognitive Triad' (i.e., depressogenic beliefs about the self, world and future). In turn, these beliefs heighten the impact of stressful or negative life events (such as physical disease, relationship loss, etc.) by influencing the meaning placed on the experience by the individual. As Beck and Bredemeier (2016) go on to describe, once the 'depression programme' is activated, negative thoughts tend to trigger corresponding emotions (e.g., sadness) and behavioural responses (e.g., withdrawal). Furthermore, they highlight that interventions that target predisposing, precipitating or resilience factors can reduce risk and alleviate symptoms.

THEORY OF CHANGE

Change in CBT usually means alleviation or reduction of the emotional problems through the intentional adjustment of how we think and behave in response to our environment (including our social environment). Cognitions and behaviours are the primary target for change, although the emotional and physiological aspects are also clearly acknowledged (Hofmann et al., 2012). It is important to note that another key active ingredient in therapy is a sound therapeutic alliance, and in recent years there has been an increased focus on the role of collaboration between the client and the therapist in bringing about change.

Psychoeducation: The process of change begins with psychoeducation about the cognitive-behavioural model (i.e., that the client's inner cognitive world causally affects emotions and behaviours). The emphasis is on individually conceptualising the client's problems in relation to the cognitive model and providing some early symptom relief. The process continues with the therapist helping the client to set goals, identify and challenge cognitive errors, automatic thoughts and schema and strategies for behavioural change. Ultimately, the client is helped to become 'their own therapist' and relapse management is emphasised.

Formulation and case conceptualisation: This is a shared understanding of the client's problems built collaboratively by client and therapist and used to conceptualise the client's problems. A formulation is a tentative hypothesis about the origins and maintenance of the client's difficulties and is conceptualised in terms of:

- The client's current thinking patterns by assessment of their information processing, automatic thoughts and schema.
- Precipitating factors – a consideration of current stressors will help an understanding of what has precipitated the present difficulties. These might be related to home, work, family or friends, and examples would include loss, illness, traumatic events or life changes.
- Predisposing factors can include past traumatic events, childhood experiences, genetic vulnerability and personality factors.

The formulation leads to identification of personalised strategies and practical and psychological skills that will empower the client to make the desired changes (Kuyken, Padesky and Dudley, 2008). This collaborative understanding of the client's issues is developed and refined on an ongoing basis as more information and understanding is acquired through the therapeutic process.

SKILLS AND STRATEGIES

Beck maintained from the early days of the development of cognitive behaviour therapy that the context of a sound therapeutic relationship was very necessary, although not sufficient, to bring about change (Beck et al., 1979). The core conditions described by Rogers (1957) of empathy, unconditional positive regard and congruence have to be in place to facilitate the effective use of CBT techniques. There is now strong empirical support that CBT techniques need the context of a sound therapeutic alliance to be most effective (Beck and Dozois, 2011; Dobson, 2022; Leahy, 2008; Okamoto et al., 2019) Therapists and clients need to be able to work in a collaborative way with their clients, 'joining forces' against the problem, enabling clients to become their 'own therapist'. This stance, known as Collaborative Empiricism, empowers clients by giving them a say in their own therapeutic process and it fosters self-efficacy.

CBT uses a variety of skills and strategies to bring about change. Techniques are chosen on the basis of the case formulation and in collaboration with the client (Padesky, 2020). Cognitive strategies are central to this approach and are used to help the client identify, examine, reality test and modify automatic thoughts, errors in information processing and schema. They include:

- Socratic questioning: a form of challenging dialogue using systematic questioning and inductive reasoning.
- Cost–benefit analysis: looking at the advantages and disadvantages of holding a particular belief.
- Alternative perspectives: for example, viewing their problem from the perspective of a close relative.
- The use of automatic thought diaries to help clients identify and understand how thoughts influence their emotions and behaviour.
- Emotional regulation strategies, such as distraction, reappraisal and labelling.
- Reality testing: looking at evidence 'for' and 'against' the dysfunctional and distorted thoughts.
- Cognitive rehearsal: practising coping with difficult situations either in role play with the therapist, in imagination or in real life.

CBT advocates Action Plan Assignments to encourage clients to practise their newly learned skills in the 'real world' and thus to enhance the therapeutic process. Beck and Dozois (2011) suggest that completion of Action Plans (previously known as 'homework') increases the sense of mastery of new strategies and offers the client an increased sense of control over life challenges. These practised skills can equip the client against relapse.

RESEARCH

CBT approaches have undergone the most extensive scientific scrutiny and empirical validation of any of the psychotherapeutic approaches and is regarded as the current gold standard of psychotherapy (David et al., 2018).

Thousands of well-controlled studies on the effectiveness of CBT have been conducted across a wide range of client problems so we have good understanding of its average overall effects (Fordham et al., 2021). For example, Hofmann et al. (2012) conducted a review of 106 meta-analyses (studies that combine and analyse the results from multiple similar studies to obtain a superior understanding of how well a treatment works). Hofmann et al. found that CBT has the most extensive support for anxiety disorders, hypochondriasis, body dysmorphic disorder, bulimia, anger control problems and general stress. Likewise, Tolin (2010) finds cognitive therapies to be superior over alternative therapies for clients with anxiety and depressive disorders, and argues against claims of treatment equivalence with other psychotherapeutic models. Evidence of effectiveness is also well established for substance use disorder, personality disorders, bipolar disorder, psychosis and many other mental health issues (Hofmann and Asmundson, 2011; Windgassen et al., 2016).

There is also an increasing body of neuroscientific research indicating that a positive response to CBT is correlated with changes in the activity of relevant brain regions (such as those associated with emotional regulation) and is associated with the way that the brain processes and reacts to emotional stimuli (Beevers et al., 2015; Chalah and Ayache, 2018; Katayama et al., 2020). Although it is not yet clear whether these neurobiological changes are a cause or a consequence of recovery with CBT, these neuroscientific studies are furthering our level of understanding regarding the possible mechanisms of how CBT can bring about changes in mental health.

CBT has evolved into a very diverse field. It is now best understood not as one approach but as many different therapies with shared concepts, principles and theories. It can be regarded as a huge family of interventions with proven efficacy for treating a wide range of mental health conditions. These range from mild everyday issues to the most challenging and serious of mental health problems. CBT integrates clinical, emotional, cognitive, biological and evolutionary perspectives into our understanding of mental health. Above all, it is the empathic therapeutic relationship coupled with methods of scientifically proven efficacy that make it among the most useful and far-reaching methods of psychological intervention.

REFERENCES

Beck, A.T. (1963). Thinking and depression. 1. Idiosyncratic content and cognitive distortions. *Archives of General Psychiatry*, 9, 324–333.

Beck, A.T., Allport, F.H., Beck, A.T., Bruner, J.S., English, H.B. and E.A.C., Festinger, L. and Sarbin, T.R. (1964). Thinking and depression. *Archives of General Psychiatry*, 10(6), 561–571.

Beck, A.T. and Bredemeier, K. (2016). A unified model of depression: integrating clinical, cognitive, biological, and evolutionary perspectives. *Clinical Psychological Science*, 4(4), 596–619.

Beck, A.T. and Dozois, D.J.A. (2011). Cognitive therapy: current status and future directions. *Annual Review of Medicine*, 62, 397–409.

Beck, A.T. and Haigh, E.A.P. (2014). Advances in cognitive theory and therapy: the generic cognitive model*. *Annual Review of Clinical Psychology*, 10(1), 1–24.

Beck, A.T., Rush, A., Shaw, B. and Emery, G. (1979). *Cognitive Behavioural Therapy of Depression*. New York: Guilford Press.

Beevers, C.G., Clasen, P.C., Enock, P.M. and Schnyer, D.M. (2015). Attention bias modification for major depressive disorder: effects on attention bias, resting state connectivity, and symptom change. *Journal of Abnormal Psychology*, 124(3), 463–475.

Bennett-Levy, J., Butler, G., Fennell, M., Hackman, A., Meuller, M. and Westbrook, D. (Eds) (2004). *Oxford Guide to Behavioural Experiments in Cognitive Therapy*. Oxford: Oxford University Press.

Chalah, M.A. and Ayache, S.S. (2018). Disentangling the neural basis of cognitive behavioral therapy in psychiatric disorders: a focus on depression. *Brain Sciences*, 8(8), 150. http://dx.doi.org/10.3390/brainsci8080150

David, D., Cristea, I. and Hofmann, S.G. (2018). Why cognitive behavioral therapy is the current gold standard of psychotherapy. *Frontiers in Psychiatry*, 9, 4. doi: 10.3389/fpsyt.2018.00004

Dobson, K. (2022). Therapeutic relationship. *Cognitive and Behavioral Practice*, 29(3), 541–544. https://doi.org/10.1016/j.cbpra.2022.02.006

Ellis, A. (2011). *Rational Emotive Behavior Therapy*. Washington, DC: American Psychological Association.

Fordham, B., Sugavanam, T., Edwards, K., Stallard, P., Howard, R., Das Nair, R., *et al.* (2021). The evidence for cognitive behavioural therapy in any condition, population or context: a meta-review of systematic reviews and panoramic meta-analysis. *Psychological Medicine*, 51(1), 21–29. doi:10.1017/S0033291720005292

Greenberger, D. and Padesky, J. (2016). *Mind Over Mood: Change How You Feel by Changing the Way You Think* (2nd ed.). New York: Guilford Press.

Hofmann, S.G. and Asmundson, G.J.G. (2011). The science of cognitive behavioral therapy. *Behavior Therapy*, 44, 199–212.

Hofmann, S.G., Asnaani, A., Vonk, I.J.J., Sawyer, A.T. and Fang, A. (2012). The efficacy of cognitive behavioral therapy: a review of meta-analyses. *Cognitive Behavioural Therapy and Research*, 36(5), 427–440.

Jacob, G.A. and Arntz, A. (2013). Schema therapy for personality disorders: a review. *International Journal of Cognitive Therapy*, 6(2), 171–185.

(Continued)

(Continued)

Kahl, K.G., Winter, L. and Schweiger, U. (2012). The third wave of cognitive behavioural therapies. *Current Opinion in Psychiatry*, 25(6), 522–528.

Katayama, N., Nakagawa, A., Kurata, C., Sasaki, Y., et al. (2020). Neural and clinical changes of cognitive behavioural therapy versus talking control in patients with major depression: a study protocol for a randomised clinical trial. *BMJ Open*, 10, e029735. doi: 10.1136/bmjopen-2019-029735

Kennerly, H., Kirk, J., and Westbrook, D. (2016). *An Introdcution to Cogntive Behaviour Therapy (3rd edition)*. London: Sage

Kuyken, W., Padesky, C.A. and Dudley, R. (2008). The science and practice of case conceptualization. *Behavioural and Cognitive Psychotherapy*, 36(6), 757.

Leahy, R.L. (2008). The therapeutic relationship in cognitive-behavioral therapy. *Behavioural and Cognitive Psychotherapy*, 36(6), 769.

Naeem, F., Khoury, B., Munshi, T., Ayub, M., Lecomte, T., Kingdon, D. and Farooq, S. (2016). Brief Cognitive Behavioral Therapy for Psychosis (CBTp) for schizophrenia: literature review and meta-analysis. *International Journal of Cognitive Therapy*, 9(1), 73–86.

Okamoto, A., Dattilio, F.M., Dobson, K.S. and Kazantzis, N. (2019). The therapeutic relationship in cognitive-behavioral therapy: essential features and common challenges. *Practice Innovations*, 4(2), 112–123. https://doi.org/10.1037/pri0000088

Padesky, C. (2020). Collaborative case conceptualization: client knows best. *Cognitive and Behavioral Practice*, 27(4), 392–404, https://doi.org/10.1016/j.cbpra.2020.06.003

Papola, D., Ostuzzi, G., Tedeschi, F., Gastaldon, C., Purgato, M., Del Giovane, C., et al. (2021). Comparative efficacy and acceptability of psychotherapies for panic disorder with or without agoraphobia: systematic review and network meta-analysis of randomised controlled trials. *The British Journal of Psychiatry*, 1–13. doi:10.1192/bjp.2021.148

Rogers, C.R. (1957). The necessary and sufficient conditions of therapeutic personality change. *Journal of Consulting Psychology*, 21(2), 95–103.

Tolin, D.F. (2010). Is cognitive-behavioral therapy more effective than other therapies? A meta-analytic review. *Clinical Psychology Review*, 30(6), 710–720.

van Beugen, S., Ferwerda, M., Hoeve, D., Rovers, M.M., Spillekom-van Koulil, S., van Middendorp, H. and Evers, A.W.M. (2014). Internet-based cognitive behavioral therapy for patients with chronic somatic conditions: a meta-analytic review. *Journal of Medical Internet Research*, 16(3), e88.

Wells, A. (2013). Advances in metacognitive therapy. *International Journal of Cognitive Therapy*, 6(2), 186–201.

White, C.A. (2001). Cognitive behavioral principles in managing chronic disease. *Western Journal of Medicine*, 175(5), 338–342.

Wills, F. (2021). *Beck's Cognitive Therapy: Distinctive Features* (2nd Edition). London: Routledge.

Windgassen, S., Goldsmith, K., Moss-Morris, R. and Chalder, T. (2016). Establishing how psychological therapies work: the importance of mediation analysis. *Journal of Mental Health*, 25(2), 93–99.

Wykes, T. (2014). Cognitive-behaviour therapy and schizophrenia. *Evidence-based Mental Health*, 17(3), 67–68.

Young, J., Klosko, J. and Weishaar, M. (2003). *Schema Therapy: A Practitioner's Guide*. New York: Guilford Press.

> **RECOMMENDED READING**
>
> Beck, J. (2020). *Cognitive Behavior Therapy: Basics and Beyond* (3rd ed.). New York: Guilford Press.
>
> A comprehensive yet accessible roadmap to the practice of CBT. It offers an excellent integration of theory, research and clinical examples.
>
> Leahy, R.L., Holland, S.J. and McGinn, L.K. (2011). *Treatment Plans and Interventions for Depression and Anxiety Disorders*. London and New York: Guilford Press.
>
> This book includes indispensable tools for treating the most common clinical problems. It provides concise, easy-to-understand theory and excellent practical interventions, plus 74 reproducible worksheets.
>
> Persons, J.B. (2012). *The Case Formulation Approach to Cognitive-Behavior Therapy*. London and New York: Guilford Press.
>
> This is an insightful and reflective book, committed to individualised treatment within an evidence-based framework.

5.5 COMPASSION FOCUSED THERAPY

SUNIL LAD AND JENIKA PATEL

OVERVIEW AND KEY POINTS

Compassion focused therapy (CFT) was originally developed for people with chronic and complex mental health problems.

- CFT uses an understanding of evolution, attachment theory and the care giving system in order to help others to learn to soothe themselves.
- CFT adopts a biopsychosocial approach to therapy by integrating wisdoms from different schools of therapy.
- CFT uses techniques such as soothing breathing and compassionate imagery to change physiology and patterns of thinking and behaviour so people are not reacting from the threat systems.

BRIEF HISTORY

CFT was developed by Paul Gilbert after observing the difficulties many of his clients had in feeling reassured and less distressed following standard therapy interventions. While able to shift from an overly self-critical and self-blaming perspective, some clients would reflect: 'I now know that I'm not to blame for being abused as a child, but I still *feel* like I'm to blame, that there's something bad or toxic about me'. Upon further inquiry, many clients describing this experience emphasised that the inner voice tone that was present when trying to bring alternative cognitive perspectives was frequently laden with contempt, hostility and disappointment.

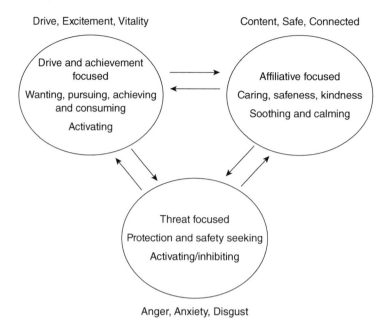

Figure 5.5.1 Three system model

(Gilbert, P., *The Compassionate Mind* (2009), reprinted with permission from Constable & Robinson Ltd)

So, CFT interventions began simply by helping clients to practise cultivating supportive and warm emotional tones alongside coping strategies and alternative thoughts. When encouraged to practise a more warm, caring voice tone, many struggled, finding this type of positive effect blocked, alien or even anxiety-provoking. Research has found that many people find that kindness and care can feel uncomfortable and be easily dismissed (Gilbert et al., 2014; Pauley and McPherson, 2010), so CFT involves understanding the blocks, fears and resistances to both compassionate motivation and affiliative feelings in the change process.

BASIC ASSUMPTIONS

CFT is grounded by insights from evolutionary psychology that stress the importance of understanding our brains and emotions in the context of how they have been shaped over millions of years (Gilbert, 2014). From this perspective, we can see that we have very old (in evolutionary terms) parts of our brains – referred to as our 'old brain' – that we share with other animals. Our old brains include basic *motives* to pursue food and reproductive opportunities, to care for our offspring and be oriented by status, basic *emotions* (e.g., anxiety, anger, disgust) and *behaviours* (e.g., fight/flight/freeze). However, during the last million years or so, our ancestors evolved along a line that led to a rapid expansion of complex cognitive abilities, including the capacity to imagine, plan, ruminate, mentalise and self-monitor. These new psychologies brought wonderful things into the world: art, literature, medicines and a capacity to work on complex problems facing our species. However, these same abilities (known as 'new brain' abilities) can also, in certain circumstances, create problems for us. For example, if a zebra is chased but then escapes from a lion, it will begin to calm down and return to what it was doing prior to being chased (e.g., eating grass). However, if we escape a lion that is chasing us, it is unlikely we would calm down quickly and return to eating our lunch. Rather, under conditions of high, old-brain emotion (e.g., anxiety), our new brains are shaped and influenced. It is likely that we would start to ruminate about what might have happened if the lion had caught us or worry about whether it will still be there later. In turn, these new-brain patterns of thinking and imagining send signals to our old brain, keeping the threat going. As a result, through no fault of our own, we can easily get caught up in 'loops in the mind' that can drive much of our distress.

CFT takes a scientific approach through the lens of evolution. In order to recognise this, CFT states that there are three systems that organise our motives, thinking, emotions and physiological processes in the body (Gilbert, 2009, 2014; Panksepp, 1998), which are qualitatively different from each other. These are:

1. A threat system which has the motives to avoid harm, injury and loss. It is associated with certain protective behaviours (e.g., flight, fight, freeze and submit responses) and emotions (such as anger, anxiety and disgust). This system can often be dominant and directs attention to the nature of the threat, and creates 'better to be safe than sorry' styles of thinking (e.g., overgeneralising, catastrophising) which facilitate quick responses.
2. A drive/excitement system which has the motives to acquire social and non-social resources promoting survival and reproduction. When these resources are attained, this system can leave us experiencing positive emotions and feelings, such as excitement, joy and elation, which may make it more likely that we engage in similar behaviours in the future.
3. A soothing system which has the motives to rest and digest when not defending against threats or needing to pursue resources. It is sometimes referred to as the 'rest and digest' system, and is linked to a number of physiological responses (e.g., part of the parasympathetic system) that are associated with calming and slowing the body down. It is hypothesised that, over time, this system was adapted in mammals to be linked to the experience of attachment and caring, and may therefore be linked with a 'tend and befriend' motivation.

With this understanding of evolution, CFT overlaps with well-established literatures (e.g., Attachment Theory; Bowlby, 1969), modern neuroscience and physiological research, highlighting the powerful role that caring has upon how the brain matures and gene expression (e.g., Belsky and Pluess, 2009; Cozolino, 2007). As infants and children, turning towards caring and support from others when distressed can have a powerful impact on reducing our distress and helping us to feel safe; similarly, as adults, turning towards friends and loved ones can have similar calming effects. So working with the systems that are involved in the affiliative regulation of emotion is essential in therapy (Gilbert, 2014), and helping people to find ways to access this externally (i.e., with other people) and internally (e.g., through self-soothing, reassurance and compassion) can be an important therapeutic task.

ORIGINS AND MAINTENANCE OF PROBLEMS

CFT takes a biopsychosocial approach to understanding the origin and maintenance of problems. And that the sources of suffering can range from inheriting genes that may make one vulnerable to physical or mental health difficulties to adverse life experiences including abuse, bullying neglect and poverty.

CFT therefore emphasises the importance of *social shaping* – that our experiences in life shape our biology and, consequentially, our psychology. From this perspective, the 'version' of us in the world today is just one of thousands of different versions that could have emerged, if we had had a different set of experiences. To this end, we often ask everyone to consider how they might be different today if they had been raised by their neighbours rather than in their house or by their family. This is an important tenet of CFT as it helps us to understand that the ways we have learnt to cope and the ways problems have developed are 'not our fault'. This may help the process of clients deshaming aspects of themselves that they had little control over, and help them to learn to take responsibility for how they would like to manage these in the future.

From this perspective, psychological problems can be maintained through a variety of processes, many of which link to various 'loops in the mind' and understandable safety strategies developed to manage fears in the external (i.e., other people) and internal (i.e., arising inside of us) world. For example, to manage concerns that others might reject, criticise or harm us (e.g., physically), we may develop strategies linked to hypervigilance, avoidance or aggression. To manage internal fears linked to feeling our emotions/memories are overwhelming, or to concerns that we are inferior or a failure, we may develop protective strategies linked to experiential avoidance, repression and/or self-criticism and rumination to manage these. Unfortunately, while all of these strategies can be helpful in the short term, they tend to link to a variety of unintended consequences over time, including keeping the threat going (and, therefore, the initial 'problem').

THEORY OF CHANGE

In CFT, the individual is supported to explore how their threat systems have developed through key experiences, leading to responses which mean that some emotions are fused together, avoided or over engaged in so that they become overwhelming and difficult to manage. CFT helps clients to think about the three main functions of emotion: threat protection defence, resource and reward seeking, and resting settling, safeness and contentment. Within therapy, clients learn about the link between the autonomic nervous system and other physiological systems and their abilities to emotionally regulate. It is this understanding, which compassion helps to change, that has a long-term physiological impact (Cozolino, 2017; Schore, 2019; Steffen et al., 2020).

The intention, behaviour and thinking associated with the caring motivation of compassion is different from other motives, such as competitive self-interest, cooperation, or threat and self-protection (Gilbert, 1989/2016). Importantly, however, increased sensitivity to suffering by itself can be associated with increased distress and depression (Gilbert et al., 2019). Hence, within CFT, these feelings are focused on and strategies of how they are managed are developed.

CFT seeks to facilitate change via the development of a compassionate mind and in building compassionate capacity to engage with one's difficulties. CFT uses a standard definition of compassion as 'a sensitivity to the suffering of self and others, with a commitment to try to alleviate or prevent it'. There are *two key psychologies* that underpin this definition. The first involves developing the ability to notice and turn *towards* and engage *with* suffering (as opposed to avoiding or dissociating from it). Given that engaging with distress and suffering is often difficult, the first psychology of compassion often involves a form of strength and courage to do this.

The second psychology of compassion involves developing wisdom and dedication to find ways to alleviate and prevent suffering. This requires practice in developing skills and techniques that will aid our ability to manage suffering and advance our wellbeing.

Within therapy, the client begins to adopt the idea to live to be helpful, not harmful, to self and others, and becomes more sensitive to the ease with which we can inadvertently be harmful. In CFT, practices are fostered that recruit the care-giving system to help build an inner secure base through breathing and compassion practices. In therapy blocks, fears and resistances are worked with as inhibitors due to the threat system being recruited. The therapist is not there to 'fix things gone wrong', but rather to help people re-pattern through learning skills and developing awareness and insight into our brains and how we have been socially shaped.

SKILLS AND STRATEGIES

Psychoeducation is used in CFT through guided discovery and Socratic questioning to collaboratively develop a formulation and develop insight into the individual's difficulties. Using this information, the practices that the client may not have developed through their life are introduced. Practices that cultivate feeling supported are introduced, inviting a sense of safeness, which the client can then practise. In order to further develop awareness and separate conflicting emotions that are experienced for unprocessed events, chair work or the multiple selves exercise are used as a way to develop insight. An important aspect of the practices is to support clients, where the safeness is cultivated through a compassionate image which counteracts self-criticism and shame that leads to distress (Gilbert, 2020).

CFT has a number of key steps to help clients to become more sensitive to distress and suffering, and to develop skills to help manage and alleviate this. These include:

- Developing an empathetic and compassionate understanding of how our brains develop and function, and how, for the individual, their affect regulation systems have been sensitised by various experiences in life, consequently protective strategies have emerged and how these have led to a number of unintended consequences.
- Developing a greater awareness of, and ability to engage in and manage, unhelpful threat and drive-system processes.
- Developing capacity to experience positive affect and an inner physiology linked to the soothing-affiliative system that can help in the regulation of the threat system.
- Building the desire and commitment (motivation) to engage with and acquire the skills to alleviate distress by using a variety of trans-therapeutic, multi-modal interventions.

'Jane' sought therapy for help with persistently high levels of anxiety. She described being burnt out from work and feeling isolated because she was experiencing anxiety when she was in company with others.

She described symptoms of anxiety (e.g., that others would not like her or would want to harm her), which led to her avoiding social situations, feeling isolated and being low in mood.

Jane reported that she had witnessed domestic violence between her parents. Both her parents regularly drank alcohol, which often led to violence towards her mother. Her father would often be out of work, so the family struggled financially. Jane had few memories of her parents caring for her or showing any affection. As the eldest child, she also wanted to protect her younger siblings and would try to distract them and take care of them when her father was being abusive. At school she struggled to make friends and isolated herself from others, but was able to escape her difficulties through reading. She did well at school and felt that she got praise by achieving well and getting good grades.

Jane became focused on work as this was the area where she felt a sense of achievement and felt good about herself. However, the unintended consequence was that it helped her to become distracted and to avoid difficult and painful emotions until they appeared again. She often avoided mixing socially and would experience anxiety when having to go into social situations.

We formulated her difficulties through the lens of the three-system model, as well as longitudinally through a threat-based formulation (see Dale-Hewitt and Irons, 2015). This helped her to link how early experiences have led to the development of key fears and threats in the 'here-and-now', and how she learnt to use developed protective strategies to manage these. We recognised how these safety strategies can sometimes lead to unintended consequences that drive self-criticism, shame, loneliness and distress. Jane found this helpful, as it provided an initial opportunity to understand that many of her struggles were understandable in the context of her life experiences and were attempts to manage threats in the world and survive.

As therapy progressed, we formulated 'loops in the mind' (e.g., worrying about what others would think about her, leading to panic and anxiety symptoms and then isolating herself), and how her three systems were being activated.

ATTENTION TRAINING AND MINDFULNESS

We explored with Jane how attention can be thought about as a spotlight – where it focuses, it 'lights up'. She was able to recognise that certain patterns were well rehearsed, and she would get stuck in the threat-based concerns (e.g., memories, worries, images). We practised attention training and mindfulness exercises, and over time she described feeling more able to be aware of when her attention was caught up by her threat system, and to find ways to redirect this in helpful ways.

As time progressed, we learnt that her threat system was easily triggered by other people and led to avoidance behaviours that made her feel better and switched off the threat system, as a warning signal to potential harm. We started to recognise that as a child she picked up on cues where violence could occur and learnt how to avoid this so that she would feel safe, acknowledging that people raising their voices and certain facial expressions from men would trigger her threat system.

SOOTHING RHYTHM BREATHING

Like other approaches, CFT uses the emerging 'science of breathing', which suggests that certain types of breathing rhythm (e.g., slower, smoother, deeper) are associated with various helpful benefits in therapy, partly through giving rise to physiological changes (e.g., increased heart rate variability) that may help to regulate threat processing. Using these insights, Jane learned how to practise a 'soothing breathing rhythm', and how to utilise this to help regulate occasions in which she began to spiral into highly anxious, threat-based states. This was particularly helpful when engaging in social interactions where she could feel herself getting anxious and panicky.

IMAGERY

Within CFT, compassion can be experienced in three directions or flows. Through the use of imagery, this was generated and cultivated with Jane in the following ways:

- Self to others (e.g., developing his ideal compassionate self, and using this to direct compassion to others close to her).
- Other to self (e.g., developing an ideal compassionate figure who can give her warmth, care, emanating wisdom and strength at times of difficulty).
- Self to self (e.g., exploring her memories of victimisation and harm and developing a compassionate understanding of the distress, which led to her reducing blame and self-criticism and, consequently, distress).

Jane initially struggled when thinking about a warm and caring other who could give her compassion, as she felt that if people were nice to her then she would be vulnerable and could be harmed, like her mother was. As therapy progressed, she saw how this was understandable, and was linked to the unpredictable nature in which she had learnt about relationships (e.g., although she was never attacked, she held shame that she did not intervene or protect her mother). Over time, she was able to develop her compassionate mind, and this was strengthened by practising the multiple selves exercise, where we were able to separate emotions of shame, sadness and fear and recognise how they led to feeling overwhelmed and confused. We also used her compassionate image and multiple selves to help restructure trauma-like memories of domestic violence. Finally, we used a variety of the skills to help her tolerate some of his 'here-and-now' anxiety, and, crucially, develop the courage to step back from some of her safety strategies and facilitate exposure.

RESEARCH

In recent years the evidence of the effectiveness of CFT has been growing for a wide range of clinical populations, such as with inpatients (Heriot-Maitland et al., 2014) with a range of presentations, for example pain (Penlington, 2019), trauma (Au et al., 2017) and psychosis. It is also effective in forensic psychotherapy (Ribeiro da Silva et al., 2021). In a meta-analysis of 21 studies, Kirby, Tellegen and Steindl (2017) found differences in depression, anxiety and psychological distress following a CFT intervention.

REFERENCES

Au, T., Sauer-Zavala, S., King, M., Petrocchi, N., Barlow, D. and Litz, B. (2017). Compassion based therapy for trauma related shame and posttraumatic stress: initial evaluation using a multiple baseline design. *Behavior Therapy*, 48(2), 207–221.

Belsky, J. and Pluess, M. (2009). Beyond diathesis-stress: differential susceptibility to environmental influences. *Psychological Bulletin*, 135(6), 885–908.

Bowlby, J. (1969). *Attachment and Loss*. Vol.1: *Attachment*. London: Hogarth.

Cozolino, L. (2007). *The Neuroscience of Human Relationships: Attachment and the Developing Brain*. New York: W.W. Norton.

Dale-Hewitt, V. and Irons, C. (2015). Compassion focused therapy. In D. Dawson and N. Moghaddam (Eds), *Formulation in Action: Applying Psychological Theory to Clinical Practice* (pp. 161–183). Berlin: De Gruyter.

Depue, R. A. and Morrone-Strupinsky, J. V. (2005). A neurobehavioural model of affiliative bonding. *Behavioural and Brain Sciences*, 28, 313–395.

Gilbert, P. (1989/2016). *Human Nature and Suffering (2nd Edition)*. London: Routledge.

Gilbert, P. (2009). *The Compassionate Mind*. London: Constable & Robinson.

Gilbert, P. (2014). The origins and nature of compassion focused therapy. *British Journal of Clinical Psychology*, 53(1), 6–41.

Gilbert, P. (2020). Compassion: from its evolution to psychotherapy. *Frontiers of Psychology*, 11. doi: 10.3389/fpsyg.2020.586161

Gilbert, P., Basran, J., MacArthur, M., and Kirby, J. N. (2019). Differences in the semantics of prosocial words: an exploration of compassion and kindness. *Mindfulness* 10, 2259–2271.

Gilbert, P., McEwan, K., Catarino, F., Baião, R. and Palmeira, L. (2014). Fears of happiness and compassion in relationship with depression, alexithymia, and attachment security in a depressed sample. *British Journal of Clinical Psychology*, 53(2), 228–244.

Heriot-Maitland, C., Vidal, J., Ball, S. and Irons, C. (2014). A compassionate-focused therapy group approach for acute inpatients: feasibility, initial pilot outcome data, and recommendations. *British Journal of Clinical Psychology*, 53(1), 78–94.

Kirby, J., Tellegen, C. L. and Steindl, S. (2017). A meta-analysis of compassion based interventions: current state of knowledge and future directions. *Behavior Therapy*, 48(6), 778–792.

Panksepp, J. (1998). *Affective Neuroscience*. Oxford and New York: Oxford University Press.

Pauley, G. and McPherson, S. (2010). The experience and meaning of compassion and self-compassion for individuals with depression or anxiety. *Psychology and Psychotherapy: Theory, Research and Practice*, 83, 129–143.

Penlington, C. (2019). Exploring a compassion-focused intervention for persistent pain in a group setting. *British Journal of Pain*, 13(1), 59–66.

Ribeiro da Silva, D., Rijo, D., Brazão, N., Paulo, M., Miguel, R., Castilho, P., Vagos, P., Gilbert, P. and Salekin, R. (2021). The efficacy of the PSYCHOPATHY.COMP program in reducing psychopathic traits: a controlled trial with male detained youth. *Journal of Consulting and Clinical Psychology*, 89(6), 499–513.

Schore, A. N. (2019). *Right brain psychotherapy*. New York: Norton.

Steffen, P. R., Foxx, J., Cattani, K., Alldredge, C., Austin, T., and Burlingame, G. M. (2020). Impact of a 12-week group-based compassion focused therapy intervention on heart rate variability. *Appl. Psychophysiol. Biofeedback*. 46, 61–68 doi: 10.1007/s10484-020-09487-8

RECOMMENDED READING

Gilbert, P. (2009). *The Compassionate Mind*. London: Constable & Robinson.

This is a comprehensive text on the nature of the human mind, distress and suffering, and how compassion may help. It includes various exercises to practise and try out.

Gilbert, P. (2010). *Compassion Focused Therapy: The CBT Distinctive Features Series*. Hove: Routledge.

A small but useful guide for therapists interested in using CFT. It takes the reader through the key steps of the therapeutic process, including assessment, formulation and key CFT interventions.

Kolts, R. (2016). *CFT Made Simple: A Clinician's Guide to Practicing Compassion Focused Therapy*. Oakland, CA: New Harbinger.

This is a helpful book for therapists wanting to learn about using CFT. It is full of useful examples and case dialogues.

5.6 *DIALECTICAL BEHAVIOUR THERAPY*

MICHAELA SWALES AND CHRISTINE DUNKLEY

OVERVIEW AND KEY POINTS

Dialectical behaviour therapy (DBT) is a behavioural treatment developed originally to reduce suicidal and self-harm behaviours for clients with a diagnosis of borderline personality disorder. Therapists work in teams and model a dialectical approach to problem solving, combining traditional cognitive-behavioural therapy (CBT) change strategies with mindfulness and Zen-inspired acceptance practices. There are five modalities to the programme of treatment, aimed at redressing clients' skills and motivational deficits. In summary:

- DBT is a psychological therapy nested in a comprehensive programme of care delivered by a team of therapists working in a consultation team.
- The overarching goal in DBT is 'a life worth living'.
- Therapists rank problem behaviours by order of severity.
- Therapy addresses skills deficits by teaching skills.
- Therapy takes a dialectical approach to problem solving, balancing mindfulness and acceptance with behavioural change strategies.

BRIEF HISTORY

Dialectical behaviour therapy (DBT), developed by Marsha Linehan, evolved from the application of behaviour therapy to the treatment of suicidal behaviours. Linehan began working with suicidal women and subsequently identified that a diagnosis of borderline personality disorder (BPD) occurred frequently in this group. Subsequently, she has described her own journey to recover from suicidal and self-harming behaviours, and how these experiences influenced the development of the treatment (Linehan, 2020). The first clinical trial of DBT (Linehan et al., 1991) was also the first randomised controlled trial demonstrating efficacy for any treatment for clients with a BPD diagnosis. This brought about a new therapeutic optimism about the possibility of recovery for this population. The treatment manuals were published in 1993 (Linehan, 1993a, 1993b) and a training programme began the same year. Since then, there have been multiple research trials, and clinical programmes have sprung up around the world. DBT is a principle-driven treatment (Swales and Heard, 2017: Chapter 1) that focuses on the treatment of specific behaviours, most commonly suicidal and self-harm behaviours.

BASIC ASSUMPTIONS

The three core philosophical perspectives of DBT are: behaviourism, Zen and dialectics. In this radical behaviourist approach, DBT therapists conceptualise the diagnostic criteria for BPD as a series of behaviours. These covert and overt behaviours can be changed using the principles of learning theory. Once clients no longer experience the internal behaviours of the diagnosis (e.g., sense of emptiness) and do not engage in the readily observable behaviours (e.g., suicide attempts), then the diagnosis no longer applies.

Linehan translated the problems described by the diagnosis of BPD into five separate systems of dysregulation, each of which is targeted for change within the treatment:

- Emotional dysregulation (affective lability and problems with anger)
- Interpersonal dysregulation (chaotic relationships and fears of abandonment)
- Self-dysregulation (identity disturbance and sense of emptiness)
- Behaviour dysregulation (suicidal and impulsive behaviours)
- Cognitive dysregulation (paranoid ideation and transient dissociated states).

DBT conceptualises that a client's inability to regulate emotion drives disturbances in all the other domains. In turn, disruption in each domain impacts on the others, further intensifying the emotion dysregulation. Suicidal, self-harm and impulsive behaviours are either a natural consequences of extreme dysregulation or attempts to reregulate affect. By translating the diagnostic 'symptoms' into these systems of dysregulation and identifying behaviours within each system, DBT was ahead of the proposed changes to both *Diagnostic and Statistical Manual of Mental Disorders* (4th edition) (DSM-IV; American Psychiatric Association, 1994) and the *International Classification of Diseases* (10th revision; ICD-10) (World Health Organisation (WHO), 2010) to move away from categorical classifications systems (the latest editions are DSM-5; American Psychiatric Association, 2013; and ICD-11; World Health Organisation, 2016).

In her early work, Linehan encountered problems in applying behaviour therapy to this client group. Often clients did not complete homework or agreed tasks. Their presentation altered from week to week, driving numerous changes in treatment direction. Sometimes they failed to return to sessions at all. Linehan hypothesised that clients struggle to engage with the therapy because the relentless focus on change invalidates their experiences of themselves and their capabilities. Tensions build as the therapist pushes harder for change while the client believes it impossible or undeserved. To mitigate the impact of a persistent change-focused agenda, Linehan sought an acceptance-based counterpoint. If the learning theorists were experts in the science of change, who were the experts in the art of acceptance? She turned to the ancient philosophy of Zen and the practice of mindfulness. This thread of acceptance weaves throughout the therapy, informing the attitudes, strategies and skills that comprise the elements of DBT.

How can such contrasting strategies of change and acceptance form a cohesive therapy? Linehan's answer is to house them within an overarching dialectical philosophy. Dialectics emphasises the interconnectedness and wholeness of reality such that multiple perspectives are not only possible, but encompass truth. For DBT therapists, oppositional views on problems and solutions are an opportunity find a synthesis that respects the wisdom in each perspective. Embracing dialectics in this way helps defuse the tensions that develop in therapy where the client has intense emotional pain and change is difficult and slow.

ORIGIN AND MAINTENANCE OF PROBLEMS

Linehan's biosocial theory of the development of BPD suggests that the disorder occurs as a result of an ongoing transactional process between emotional vulnerability in the individual and an invalidating environment. Features of emotional vulnerability include a highly sensitive nervous system with low threshold for emotional reactions. Once activated by emotional stimuli, responses are fast, extreme and slow to return to a baseline position. Linehan likens the effect to a burn victim, missing a layer of 'emotional skin', so every interaction is painful. Invalidating environments compound the problem, so a chain reaction occurs, intensifying the effects on both the environment and the individual until full BPD is evident.

An 'invalidating environment' is one which negates or dismisses the individual's internal experiences and behavioural responses regardless of their actual validity. Emotions are dismissed, as in 'what are you scared of? Just do it', or criticised, such as 'you're over-reacting', or simply ignored. The individual learns to ignore her own internal responses, instead searching the environment for cues on how to respond. For example, a child of alcoholic parents stops attending to internal cues of hunger, as food only arrives when her parents are sober. Instead she searches for signals in her parents that they might offer food, and her 'hunger' feelings become redundant. When ignored over time, emotions become bewildering and unmanageable. The environment struggles to provide an effective response to emotional volatility and may inadvertently reinforce dysfunctional behaviour. For example, an individual may repeatedly say, 'I can't bear it' when a demand is made on her, and is told, 'just get on with it'. Then she self-harms and the demand is removed. Even the most caring environment may become invalidating in an attempt to suppress dysfunctional behaviour. Linehan provides a no-blame model, looking at the incremental, transactional development of problems rather than ascribing a single cause.

The result of this transactional process is a skills deficit within the individual: clients cannot up-regulate physiological arousal when required, and when emotionally aroused cannot turn attention away from the stimulus. Information processing is impaired, preventing the organisation of behaviour in the service of her short- or long-term goals. Consequently, clients engage in mood-driven behaviour, which may be impulsive or destructive, and at times they shut down or freeze. Self-harming or suicidal thoughts and behaviours may function to regulate affect in the short term by providing an escape from the cycle or may change an emotional state. Consequences in the environment (e.g., caregiving or rejection by others) can act to increase or reduce the likelihood of further repetitions of the behaviour in a constantly evolving set of actions and reactions. In summary, DBT conceptualises clients' problems as arising from both capability and motivational deficits that are addressed in the five modalities of a comprehensive DBT programme (see Table 5.6.1).

THEORY OF CHANGE

DBT therapists work towards helping their clients achieve a 'life worth living' by reducing behaviours that interfere with the accomplishment of this goal, while increasing and strengthening skills. The change process begins with the client entering a phase of pre-treatment, in which goals are identified and commitment is obtained. Table 5.6.1 shows the five functions of DBT and the modes through which they are delivered in a standard outpatient programme.

DBT is a team treatment where a community of therapists treats a community of clients. A client in DBT has individual therapy with their primary therapist, and must attend a separate skills training component of the

Table 5.6.1 Five functions of dialectical behaviour therapy

Function	Modes in standard outpatient DBT
Enhance client capabilities	Skills training group
Improve motivational factors	Individual one-to-one therapy
Assure generalisation to the natural environment	Telephone coaching
Enhance therapist capabilities	Weekly therapist consultation meeting
Structuring the environment	Case management, family/marital/community interventions

programme. The primary therapist also provides out-of-session help to generalise skills – usually via telephone coaching. The individual therapists and skills trainers all attend a weekly therapists' consultation meeting to maintain adherence to the treatment, and to share multiple perspectives on solving clients' problems.

Each modality of therapy has its own target hierarchy. Within individual therapy, behaviours are addressed in the following order:

- Life-threatening behaviour, for example, suicidal or homicidal actions, non-suicidal self-injury, and urges to harm self or others.
- Therapy-interfering behaviour, including behaviours that prevent the therapist from delivering therapy or the patient from receiving it. For example, missing sessions, repeatedly saying 'I don't know'.
- Quality of life-interfering behaviour, including severe destabilising conditions. For example, behaviours leading to homelessness or unemployment. Also, behaviours that are part of other comorbid conditions, such as major depressive disorder or bulimia nervosa.

At the start of therapy a unique 'target hierarchy' is drawn up for each client, with specific behaviours to be changed. This may be modified during the course of treatment.

The predominant mechanism of change in DBT is behavioural rehearsal. Clients track their target behaviours on a diary card and in each individual session a behavioural chain and solution analysis is conducted on the most severe target behaviour on the card. Events preceding and following the target behaviour are analysed to identify controlling variables of that specific incident. New, more skilful, behaviours are rehearsed in session (Heard and Swales, 2015).

SKILLS AND STRATEGIES

The primary skill of the DBT therapist is to maintain a dialectical approach, welcoming tensions that arise, seeking out the validity in both sides of the argument, and moving towards synthesis. The therapist models how to relinquish black-and-white thinking by looking for new perspectives and finding a 'both/and' position. Therapists validate the functional and logical components of clients' behaviours before highlighting dysfunctional aspects. For example, if the client says, 'I know people are repulsed by my scarring, so I hide at home', the therapist will validate, 'Yes, some people might be repulsed by scarring, and staying home makes sense when you want to avoid that response. Are there any other, less isolating ways to solve this?' Each problem situation is viewed as a practice opportunity for new skills, and in particular those learned in the skills training sessions (see above). The therapist favours consulting with the client on how to manage problems in her environment, rather than instructing the environment on how to manage the client.

A range of dialectical strategies is used, the main one being the balance between acceptance and change that the therapist weaves seamlessly into the solution analyses of the clients' targeted behaviours. The therapist moves back and forth between a reciprocal style of communication and an irreverent off-beat manner, keeping an eye on the flow of the session and altering styles strategically to maintain therapeutic momentum.

The weekly consultation meeting is where therapists apply the principles of the therapy to themselves. Beginning with a mindfulness practice, the emphasis is then on 'therapy for the therapist' – being alert to signs of burnout, seeking out the validity in opposing opinions to ensure nothing is being missed and working towards comprehensive, dialectical solutions to any problems presented. An observer ensures the team adheres to the model.

The four skills training modules in DBT are mindfulness, emotion regulation, interpersonal effectiveness and distress tolerance (Linehan, 1993b, 2015). Mindfulness is considered a core skill. Therapists teach clients to turn the spotlight of their attention away from distressing stimuli, to identify what would be effective and to take action when needed. Together they acknowledge that change is inevitable, and that each situation that cannot be changed must be tolerated until natural change occurs. The therapist and client are encouraged to use skilful means and evaluate the outcome without judgement, slowly shaping more effective behaviour (Dunkley and Stanton, 2013). In emotion regulation, they are taught to identify emotions and their function, and how to act opposite to an unjustified emotion and to problem-solve and tolerate justified emotion (Dunkley, 2021). In interpersonal effectiveness, they learn to assess their priorities in a given situation, to make skilful requests or decline unwanted invitations. In distress tolerance, they learn to get through a crisis without making it worse, and accept distressing situations that cannot be changed immediately or in the longer term.

CASE STUDY

Sara is a 23-year-old client of the community mental health team. She lives alone and has taken three serious overdoses in 12 months. She cuts her arms and binge drinks. She started in DBT two months ago, having had four sessions of pre-treatment with her therapist, Zac. Together she and Zac identified her goal to go to college to study Art.

In pre-treatment Zac explained how Sara's behaviours are often a way to manage uncomfortable emotions. He described how developing new skills could reduce the behaviours that are preventing her from getting to college. Sara and Zac meet every Tuesday for her individual DBT therapy session.

Each day Sara fills in her diary card, keeping track of the behaviours that she and Zac placed on her target hierarchy. Also on her diary card is a list of all the skills she is learning in the skills training group. Each time she practises a skill she circles it on her card.

Sara attends the skills training group every Thursday with nine other patients. She has completed two sessions of mindfulness and a six-week module of interpersonal effectiveness. Skills trainers Jo and Gwen teach a new skill and set homework one week, then take feedback the following week to assess their clients' learning. The three modules – interpersonal effectiveness, emotion regulation and distress tolerance – are taught on a rolling programme with two sessions of mindfulness between modules.

During weekly individual therapy with Zac, Sara knows they will focus on the highest priority incident from her diary card that week. If Sara has recorded an incident of cutting her arm, then together she and Zac analyse the steps leading up to and following the cutting and actively rehearse more skilful solutions. If Sara tries a solution and it doesn't work, Zac helps analyse what went wrong; sometimes she has misapplied a skill or needs to combine two or three skills together. Last week she had urges to cut herself following a row with a neighbour, so Zac role-played the scenario with her, so that she could practise her interpersonal effectiveness skills. Afterwards he reminded her that if she was struggling to use the skill she could call him (using telephone consultation) to get some additional skills coaching.

RESEARCH

Since the first research trial (Linehan et al., 1991), most studies have been conducted on women with a diagnosis of BPD presenting with recurrent suicidal behaviour. A recent Cochrane review identified 24 randomised controlled trials investigating the impact of the treatment for people in this specific population (Storebø et al., 2020).

In summary, the trials demonstrated that DBT is efficacious in reducing symptoms of BPD and self-harm, and improving psychosocial functioning. Other studies have demonstrated DBT decreases hospital stays and improves treatment retention (Koons et al., 2001; Linehan et al., 1991, 2006; Verheul et al., 2003). DBT has also been shown to be cost-effective, in part because of its impact on reducing unscheduled care (Krawitz and Miga, 2019).

DBT has also been tested for efficacy with other client groups. DBT adapted for adolescents by including parents in the skills training component of the treatment has been proven efficacious in two trials, one in the US and one in Norway (McCauley et al., 2018; Mehlum et al., 2014, 2016). Initial trials of DBT for children also look promising (Perepletchikova et al., 2017). Two trials of DBT for women with both BPD and substance dependence demonstrated benefits in decreasing substance misuse (Linehan et al., 1999, 2002). There is also an emerging evidence base for the use of DBT with adults with a diagnosis of binge-eating disorder and bulimia nervosa (Chen et al., 2008; Telch, Agras and Linehan, 2001). Studies in inpatient settings, although not randomised, have also demonstrated the usefulness of DBT in managing behavioural disturbance (Bohus et al., 2004). Early work by Lynch in adapting DBT for older adults with comorbid depression and personality disorder (Lynch et al., 2003, 2007) has subsequently evolved into a distinct but related treatment, Radically-Open DBT (RODBT), which targets emotional overcontrol that may be seen in recurrent depression and in anorexia nervosa (Lynch, 2018a, 2018b). Given its effectiveness in tackling emotion regulation difficulties, recent studies have also endorsed the group skills component of DBT as a transdiagnostic intervention for people with common mental health disorders (Delaquis et al., 2021). A comprehensive overview of all adaptations of the treatment can be found in the *Oxford Handbook of Dialectical Behaviour Therapy* (Swales, 2019).

REFERENCES

American Psychiatric Association (1994) *Diagnostic and Statistical Manual of Mental Disorders* (4th ed.). DSM-IV. Washington, DC: APA.

American Psychiatric Association (2013) *Diagnostic and Statistical Manual of Mental Disorders* (5th ed.). DSM-5. Washington, DC: APA.

Bohus, M., Haaf, B., Simms, T.M.F.L., Schmahl, C., Unckel, C., Lieb, K. and Linehan, M.M. (2004) Effectiveness of inpatient dialectical behavioral therapy for borderline personality disorder: a controlled trial. *Behaviour Research and Therapy*, 42, 487–499.

Chen, E.Y., Matthews, L., Allen, C., Kuo, J.R. and Linehan, M.M. (2008) Dialectical Behaviour Therapy for clients with binge-eating disorder or bulimia nervosa and borderline personality disorder. *International Journal of Eating Disorders*, 41(6), 505–512.

Delaquis, C.P., Joyce, K.M., Zalewski, M., Katz, L.Y., Sulymka, J., Agostinho, T. and Roos, L.E. (2021) *Dialectical behaviour therapy skills groups for common mental health disorders: a systematic review and meta-analysis*. https://doi.org/10.31234/osf.io/rpu9h

Dunkley, C. (2021) *Regulating Emotion the DBT Way: A Therapists Guide to Opposite Action*. Abingdon, UK: Routledge.

Dunkley, C. and Stanton, M. (2013) *Teaching Clients to Use Mindfulness Skills: A Practical Guide*. London: Routledge.

Heard, H.L. and Swales, M.A. (2015) *Changing Behavior in DBT®: Problem Solving in Action*. New York: Guilford Press.

Koons, C.R., Robins, C.J., Tweed, J.L., Lynch, T.R., Gonzalez, A.M., Morse, J.Q., Bishop, G.K., Butterfield, M. and Bastian, L.A. (2001) Efficacy of dialectical behavior therapy in women veterans with borderline personality disorder. *Behavior Therapy*, 32, 371–390.

Krawitz, R. and Miga, E.M. (2019) Cost-effectiveness of dialectical behaviour therapy for borderline personality disorder. In M. Swales (Ed.), *Oxford Handbook of Dialectical Behaviour Therapy*. Oxford: Oxford University Press.

Linehan, M.M. (1993a) *Cognitive Behavioral Treatment of Borderline Personality Disorder*. New York: Guilford Press.

Linehan, M.M. (1993b) *Skills Training Manual for Borderline Personality Disorder*. New York: Guilford Press.

Linehan, M.M. (2015) *DBT® Skills Training Manual*. New York: Guilford Press.

Linehan, M.M. (2020) *Building a Life Worth Living: A Memoir*. New York: Random House.

Linehan, M.M., Armstrong, H.E., Suarez, A., Allman, D. and Heard, H. (1991) Cognitive behavioral treatment of chronically suicidal borderline patients. *Archives of General Psychiatry*, 48, 1060–1064.

Linehan, M.M., Comtois, K.A., Murray, A.M., Brown, M.Z., Gallop, R.J., Heard, H.L., Korslund, K.E., Tutek, D.A., Reynolds, S.K. and Lindenboim, N. (2006) Two-year randomized controlled trial and follow-up of dialectical behavior therapy vs therapy by experts for suicidal behaviors and borderline personality disorder. *Arch Gen Psychiatry*, 63(7), 757–766. doi: 10.1001/archpsyc.63.7.757.

Linehan, M.M., Dimeff, L.A., Rynolds, S.K., Comtois, K.A., Shaw-Welch, S., Heagerty, P. and Kivlahan, D.R. (2002) Dialectical behavior therapy versus comprehensive validation plus 12-step for the treatment of opioid dependent women meeting criteria for borderline personality disorder. *Drug and Alcohol Dependence*, 67, 13–26.

Linehan, M.M., Schmidt, H., Dimeff, L.A., Craft, J.C., Kanter, J. and Comtois, K.A. (1999) Dialectical behavior therapy for patients with borderline personality disorder and drug-dependence. *The American Journal on Addictions*, 8(4), 279–292.

Lynch, T.R. (2018a) *Radically Open Dialectical Behaviour Therapy: Theory and Practice for Treating Disorders of Overcontrol*. Oakland, CA: New Harbinger Publications.

Lynch, T.R. (2018b) *The Skills Training Manual for Radically Open Dialectical Behavior Therapy: A Clinician's Guide for Treating Disorders of Overcontrol*. Oakland, CA: New Harbinger Publications.

Lynch, T.R., Cheavens, J.S., Cukrowicz, K.C., Thorp, S., Bronner, L. and Beyer, J. (2007) Treatment of older adults with co-morbid personality disorder and depression: a dialectical behavior therapy approach. *International Journal of Geriatric Psychiatry*, 22, 131–143.

Lynch, T.R., Morse, J.O., Mendelson, T. and Robins, C.J. (2003) Dialectical behavior therapy for depressed older adults: a randomized pilot study. *American Journal of Geriatric Psychiatry*, 11(1), 33–45.

McCauley, E., Berk, M.S., Asarnow, J.R., Adrian, M., Cohen, J., Korslund, K., Avina, C., Hughes, J., Harned, M., Gallop, R. and Linehan, M.M. (2018) Efficacy of dialectical behavior therapy for adolescents at high risk for suicide: a randomized clinical trial. *JAMA Psychiatry*, 75(8), 777–785.

Mehlum, L., Ramberg, M., Tormoen, A., Haga, E., Diep, L.M., Laberg, S., *et al.* (2016) Dialectical behaviour therapy compared with enhanced usual care for adolescents with repeated suicidal and self-harming behaviour: outcomes over a one-year follow-up. *Journal of the American Academy of Child and Adolescent Psychiatry*, 55(4), 295–300.

Mehlum, L., Tormoen, A., Ramberg, M., Haga, E., Diep, L.M., Laberg, S., *et al.* (2014) Dialectical behaviour therapy for adolescents with recent and repeated self-harming behaviour – first randomized controlled trial. *Journal of the American Academy of Child and Adolescent Psychiatry*, 53, 1082–1091.

Perepletchikova, F., Nathanson, D., Axelrod, S.R., Merrill, C., Walker, A., Grossman, M., Rebeta, J., Scahill, L., Kaufman, J., Flye, B., Mauer, E. and Walkup, J. (2017) Randomized clinical trial of dialectical behavior therapy for preadolescent children with disruptive mood dysregulation disorder: feasibility and outcomes. *Journal of the American Academy of Child and Adolescent Psychiatry*, 56(10), 832–840.

Storebø, O.J., Stoffers-Winterling, J.M., Völlm, B.A., Kongerslev, M.T., Mattivi, J.T., Jørgensen, M.S., Faltinsen, E., Todorovac, A., Sales, C.P., Callesen, H.E., Lieb, K. and Simonsen, E. (2020) Psychological therapies for people with borderline personality disorder. *Cochrane Database of Systematic Reviews*, Issue 5, Art. No. CD012955. doi: 10.1002/14651858.CD012955.pub2. (accessed 25 October 2021).

Swales, M.A. (ed.) (2019) *Oxford Handbook of Dialectical Behaviour Therapy*. Oxford: Oxford University Press.

Swales, M.A. and Heard, H.L. (2017) *Dialectical Behaviour Therapy: Distinctive Features*. (2nd ed.). London: Routledge.

Telch, C.F., Agras, W.S. and Linehan, M.M. (2001) Dialectical behavior therapy for binge eating disorder. *Journal of Consulting and Clinical Psychology*, 69(6), 1061–1065.

Verheul, R., van den Bosch, L.M.C., Koeter, M.W.J., De Ridder, M.A.J., Stijnen, T. and van den Brink, W. (2003) Dialectical behaviour therapy for women with borderline personality disorder: 12-month, randomised clinical trial in The Netherlands. *British Journal of Psychiatry*, 182(2), 135–140.

World Health Organisation (1994) *International Classification of Diseases* (10th ed.) ICD-10. Geneva: WHO.

World Health Organisation (2016) *International Classification of Diseases* (11th ed.) ICD-11. Geneva: WHO.

RECOMMENDED READING

Linehan, M.M. (2015) *DBT® Skills Training Manual*. New York: Guilford Press.

This book contains instructions, clinical examples and teaching points for the delivery of the full skills training programme, and includes a link to download all the handouts in electronic format.

Linehan, M.M. (1993) *Cognitive Behavioral Treatment of Borderline Personality Disorder*. New York: Guilford Press.

This is the original text explaining Linehan's underpinning theory of DBT and the core components of treatment.

Heard, H.L. and Swales, M.A. (2015) *Changing Behavior in DBT®: Problem Solving in Action*. New York: Guilford Press.

This book provides further exploration of the problem-solving strategies used in DBT, including the common pitfalls in treatment delivery and how to avoid them.

5.7 ECOTHERAPY

NICK TOTTON

OVERVIEW AND KEY POINTS

Ecotherapy (also ecopsychology, ecopsychotherapy, nature therapy, nature-assisted therapy, outdoor therapy) is an umbrella term for several approaches combining psychological therapy with green environments. It believes that spending time outdoors around growing things and living creatures is inherently good for us, and works to amplify this effect through various exercises and techniques, and through a therapeutic relationship in the outdoors. Most ecotherapists also believe that our civilisation suffers from a 'nature deficit', an alienation from the rest of life at the root of many of our cultural ills, including global heating and other environmental emergencies, and hope to heal the culture as well as the individual. Some have tried to define differences, or even an opposition, between ecotherapy and ecopsychology. Others see these differences as factitious, or at least so nuanced and full of exceptions as to be unhelpful. This chapter will treat the two terms as interchangeable.

Ecotherapy:

- takes an ecosystemic view of human problems
- largely happens outside the therapy room in green surroundings
- avoids '*using*' the other-than-human as is normal to our culture, encouraging clients to find their own way into relationship with other-than-human beings
- often has a spiritual attitude of reverence for living systems
- at times directly engages with environmental politics.

BRIEF HISTORY

Many people have independently contributed to the development of ecotherapy and ecopsychology, but if there is a founding figure it is the American psychologist Theodore Roszak, through his book *Voices of the Earth: An Exploration of Ecopsychology* (Roszak, 2002 [1993]) and the collection he co-edited (Roszak, Gomes and Kanner, 1995). A number of others, mostly in the USA, have since taken the work in a variety of directions (there is no central organisation or authority). The best known of these include Joanna Macy, John Seed, David Abram, Andy Fisher and Bill Plotkin. It is indicative of the unusual origins of ecotherapy/ecopsychology that many are not actually psychotherapists or counsellors. In the United Kingdom, significant figures include Mary-Jayne Rust (2020), Hilary Prentice, David Key, the late Martin Jordan (2014; Jordon and Hinds, 2016) and Nick Totton (2014, 2021).

True to its philosophy, ecotherapy has grown like a forest rather than a plantation, with few rules, organisations and institutions. To switch metaphors, it resembles a complex river delta, with many water courses flowing side by side, branching and braiding until it is impossible to identify which is which. Although Roszak's ecopsychology is a crucial component, many ecotherapists have come through other routes: adventure and outdoor therapy and bushcraft, art and art therapy, spirituality, horticulture, permaculture, ecology, environmental activism, and of course counselling and psychotherapy, have all led people to the practice of ecotherapy.

The large and growing field of animal-assisted therapy (AAT) is closely associated and in some ways overlaps with ecotherapy. AAT (also known as animal-facilitated therapy) originally based itself on the perceived benefits for sick or disturbed children from being around animals (see the discussion below of biophilia). However, it has become apparent that many animals, especially perhaps dogs and horses, are highly sensitive to human emotional fields, and in fact may actively seek to take part in the therapeutic process (Dunning, 2017). Equine therapy, in particular, with both children and adults, has become very popular in recent years (Karol, 2007; Kohanov, 2001).

References to 'ecotherapy' both in the popular media and in research papers quite frequently concern only the beneficial effects of being in green spaces and lack any psychotherapeutic element. This should be distinguished from the ecotherapy being discussed here, where the therapeutic relationship runs three ways between client, therapist and the other-than-human.

BASIC ASSUMPTIONS

A striking aspect of ecotherapy is its heterogeneity, mirroring the diversity of the ecosystems which are central to its practice. It is therefore difficult to make realistic generalisations about the whole field, but here are some positions which probably all ecotherapists share, although to varying degrees.

Ecotherapy's philosophical foundations are in ecology, deep ecology (Sessions, 1995) and ecosystemic thinking (Bateson, 1980). It situates human beings *within*, rather than above or beyond, the whole web of life forms on this planet, and identifies our sense of separateness from the rest of life as the source of many of our problems. Hence, a powerful source of healing is immersion in the 'wild', in the other-than-human (Totton, 2021), and ecotherapy seeks to offer opportunities for this, trying to balance familiarity and adventure, safety and risk, at the level which works best for each individual or client group (Totton, 2021).

Important to many ecotherapists is Edward O. Wilson's concept (1990) of *biophilia*: the hypothesis that humans have an innate attraction towards other life forms, which, given the opportunity, expresses itself as love and nurturing. We often see this clearly in small children's love and awe of other animals. Yet of course, we also often see cruelty and destructiveness, and these two strands continue into adulthood, with the love and awe perhaps often increasingly masked. Ecotherapy practitioners are accustomed to noticing and nurturing the small signs of biophilia in many of their clients who have hardened against other life forms, until eventually a breakthrough may reconnect them with their childhood love for the other-than-human, and their grief about its loss.

Ecotherapists have employed many mainstream therapy concepts to help make sense of our difficult relationship with the rest of the living world. These include attachment theory (Jordan, 2009), addiction (Glendinning, 1995; Maiteny, 2012), perversion (Hoggett, 2013), and eating disorder (Rust, 2005). However, these connections sometimes function as productive analogies rather than direct theoretical links. A more central concept is *ecosystemic thinking* (Bateson, 1980; Keeney, 1979; Totton, 2021).

To think ecosystemically about a person is to see them not as an isolated individual, but as an open system nested within other open systems, and with yet other open systems nested within them. This complex field of being is always present in the therapy room; when therapist and client meet, a new field is created from their relationship. And at any moment the creative spark of growth can come from anywhere in the field. This way of experiencing the therapeutic nexus is at the heart of ecotherapy, and a key way that working outdoors can influence working in the therapy room.

ORIGIN AND MAINTENANCE OF PROBLEMS

It follows from the biophilia hypothesis that many psychological problems either originate in, or are exacerbated by, alienation from the other-than-human. Among the conditions where this link can convincingly be argued are anomie and the experience of meaninglessness (Hay, 2005), depression (Kidner, 2007; Macy, 1995), addiction (Seifert, 2014; Wilshire, 1999), and compulsive consumption (Kanner and Gomes, 1995; Rust, 2008).

Most ecotherapists also agree that there are specific psychological consequences from the conscious or semi-conscious awareness of environmental catastrophe (Bodnar, 2008; Rust, 2008). These can range between frantic anxiety, despair, numbness and 'manic defences' such as drinking, drugging, compulsive consumption and promiscuity. Sometimes as an ecotherapy client reconnects with their love for other-than-human life, the destruction of global ecosystems hits them like a hurricane, and they need deep support in assimilating this reality and moving towards some sort of reparative action.

THEORY OF CHANGE

Ecotherapy sees immersion in and engagement with the other-than-human world, the world of 'nature' and 'wildness', as having an inherently transformative tendency. This is partly because spending task-free time outdoors tends to stimulate relaxation and spaciousness, through what has been termed 'soft fascination' (Kaplan, 1995; Kaplan and Kaplan, 1989): phenomena like clouds, leaves and running water capture our involuntary attention through a complexity which gives pleasure without demanding cognitive processing, facilitating a meditative state. A quite different sort of ecotherapy emphasises task, quest and achievement – for example, climbing and trekking – as a way towards empowerment and individuation (Gillis and Ringer, 1999).

There is also a relational ecotherapy. In many ways, the therapist's role changes from dyadic partner to witness and accompanier of the client's journey into relationship with the other-than-human. It can be striking how, so to speak, the burden of transference lifts, and a more equal, adult-to-adult relationship becomes possible between therapist and client (Berger, 2007): the transferential focus shifts to tree, or animal, or plant, or river (Totton, 2021). Very often, the client experiences a unique degree of non-judgemental acceptance from the other-than-human – what in person-centred work would be termed 'unconditional positive regard'. We can treat this as a projection of the client's own healthy core or, from a more spiritual viewpoint, accept that the experience is meaningful in its own terms and that we can receive love and acceptance from the other-than-human. Either way, the experience is profound. It can also teach practitioners who experience it how to offer their clients a deeper level of acceptance.

SKILLS AND STRATEGIES

A number of practices have been developed towards ecotherapy's goal of reconnecting clients with the living world around them. Here are a few examples.

THERAPEUTIC GARDENING

The therapeutic content here can range from an opportunity for exercise and to experience the calming and grounding effects of working in a garden, perhaps with individual or group therapy happening alongside this, to much more radical fusions of the two. The Natural Growth Project, a trailblazing scheme set up by the Medical Foundation for the Victims of Torture, was established on 30 allotments and in a large garden (for those too disabled by torture to manage an allotment). Those on the allotments were visited weekly by a psychotherapist and a gardener.

> The therapist's role is not to co-ordinate activities but rather to reflect on the experience of the client through the contact with nature. Using nature as a metaphor, it is possible very quickly to access deeply traumatic events and to work on the most difficult feelings, and the life cycle embodied in nature carries the promise of healing. (Linden and Grut, 2002: 12)

SOLO/VISION QUEST

A core element of wilderness and adventure therapy is the 'solo': a period of time spent in the wild outdoors on one's own. An irreducible aspect of this is *survival*, physical and psychological – testing oneself against the wild. For ecotherapy, there is also an aspect of *encounter*, opening oneself to being touched and changed by the wild.

The 'solo' structure is also central to spiritual practices of the wild, such as the Native American Vision Quest, and there has been a fruitful interplay between these approaches and ecotherapy. The original vision quest involved going naked and fasting into the wild for four days, taking only a blanket and sacred pipe. Contemporary western versions are often more moderate, perhaps only a day or less, but are still serious undertakings.

Some stay close to the original: Caswell (2007) describes a vision quest in Death Valley consisting of four days of preparation ('severance'), four days of fasting alone in a wild landscape (the 'threshold'), and four days of group work to interpret and understand the threshold experience ('incorporation'). In the altered state induced by fasting, solitude and 'severance', every event takes on meaning, as the other-than-human is set free to speak to us and we are set free to listen. 'The exterior landscape and its creatures are an inseparable part of the interior landscape, the landscape of the spirit and the heart' (Caswell, 2007: 609).

MEDICINE WALK

A variation on the vision quest is the Medicine Walk (Foster and Little, 1988). Rather than sitting on one spot, one moves through a landscape holding a question about one's life, and attending to what one encounters as a message about one's question. A full-scale medicine walk lasts at least from dawn to sunset, alternating walking and resting, and participants are encouraged to fast. The medicine walk can be used as part of the preparation for a vision quest or some other rite of passage. It can also be used in a smaller-scale way in an individual therapy session or as part of an ecotherapy workshop, often with a walker and a witness/accompanier.

MAKING CONTACT

A key technique for the more relational forms of ecotherapy is to let oneself be drawn towards a particular being or landscape element – an animal, bird, plant, tree, rock, water, or cave, for example – and find a way to enter into contactful relationship with it. This might involve sitting with it, observing it, touching it, smelling it, climbing on or into it, vocalising to or with it or having a silent conversation with it, dancing with it, sleeping and dreaming by it – the options are enormous, once one has taken the key step of allowing the possibility of relating.

This is clearly a form of play, offering an opportunity to re-enter the world of childhood, where the whole environment is alive and intelligent. Many people who adventure in this way find themselves returning with gifts and messages from the other-than-human, which can then be worked with and understood over time.

NATURE ART

A further way of developing contact with the other-than-human is to make art (Atkins and Snyder, 2017; Siddons Heginworth, 2011): to draw or paint or sculpt, to make structures and patterns in particular locations out of what one finds there (Berger and Lahad, 2013), to create masks to represent one's connection with magical beings.

RESEARCH

There is considerable evidence, both quantitative and qualitative, for the positive effect that spending time outdoors in green environments has on psychological and physical wellbeing. As well as research on the general benefits (Mind, 2013), this includes work focused on:

- Recovery from illness and surgery (Ulrich, 1984)
- Children and young people (Louv, 2010)
- The elderly (Gigliotti, Jarrott and Yorgason, 2004; Watts and Hsieh, 2010)
- Mental patients (Wilson et al., 2008)
- Addiction (Black, 2015; Cornille et al., 1987)
- Depression (Gonzalez et al., 2010)
- Asylum seekers (Linden and Grut, 2002)

Some of this work (notably Linden and Grut, 2002) is focused specifically on ecotherapy proper, while some of it simply reports on the beneficial effects of being in or able to see green spaces.

Perhaps the best meta-study so far of ecotherapy is Annerstedt and Währborg (2011), which analysed three meta-analyses, six pieces of research classified as high evidence grade, and 29 classified as low to moderate evidence grade. The study concluded that 'a rather small but reliable evidence base supports the effectiveness and appropriateness of NAT [Nature-Assisted Therapy] as a relevant resource for public health. Significant improvements were found for varied outcomes in diverse diagnoses, spanning from obesity to schizophrenia' (Annerstedt and Währborg, 2011: 371).

Another valuable, if more discursive, research survey is Chalquist (2009), which argues *for* ecotherapy rather than taking a neutral position. Jordan and Hinds (2016) is another useful resource, focused mainly on mental health-oriented approaches and research. Finally, David Key and Margaret Kerr have provided several papers of qualitative research around their training model, the Natural Change Project (Key, 2015; Key and Kerr, 2012), and also a critique of quantitative research which advocates a new research model specifically for ecotherapy and ecopsychology (Kerr and Key, 2011; Key and Kerr, 2011).

REFERENCES

Annerstedt, M. & Währborg, P. (2011) Nature-assisted therapy: systematic review of controlled and observational studies. *Scandinavian Journal of Public Health*, 39(4), 371–388. https://doi.org/10.1177/1403494810396400

Atkins, S. & Snyder, M. (2017) *Nature-Based Expressive Arts Therapy: Integrating the Expressive Arts and Ecotherapy*. London: Jessica Kingsley.

Bateson, G. (1980) *Mind and Nature: A Necessary Unity*. London: Fontana/Collins.

Berger, R. (2007). Nature therapy: Developing a framework for practice. *Unpublished doctoral dissertation*, University of Abertay, Dunde, Scotland.

Berger, R. & Lahad, M. (2013) *The Healing Forest in Post-crisis Work with Children: A Nature Therapy and Expressive Arts Program for Groups*. London: Jessica Kingsley.

Black, M. (2015) *'The Trees Were Our Cathedral': A Narrative Enquiry Into Healing from Addiction through a Relationship with Nature*. Dissertation, Faculty of the California Institute of Integral Studies. http://pqdtopen.proquest.com/doc/1757513031.html?FMT=ABS (accessed 8 June 2016).

Bodnar, S. (2008) Wasted and bombed: Cinical enactments of a changing relationship to the earth. *Psychoanalytic Dialogues*, 18(4), 484–512.

Caswell, K. (2007) Hunger on the mountain. *Janus Head*, 9(2), 605–624.

Chalquist, C. (2009) A look at the ecotherapy research evidence. *Ecopsychology*, 1(2), 64–74.

Cornille, T., Rohrer, G., Phillips, S. & Mosier, J. (1987) Horticultural therapy in substance abuse treatment. *Journal of Therapeutic Horticulture*, 2(1), 3–8.

Dunning, A. (2017) *The Horse Leads the Way: Honoring the True Role of the Horse in Equine Facilitated Practice*. Shrewsbury: YouCaxton.

Foster, S. & Little, M. (1988) *The Book of the Vision Quest*. New York: Prentice-Hall.

Gigliotti, C., Jarrott, S. & Yorgason, J. (2004) Harvesting health: Effects of three types of horticultural therapy activities for persons with dementia. *Dementia*, 3(2), 161–180.

Gillis, H.L. & Ringer, M. (1999) Adventure as therapy. In J.C. Miles & S. Priest (Eds), *Adventure Programming* (pp. 29–37). State College, PA: Venture Publishing.

Glendinning, C. (1995) Technology, trauma, and the wild. In T. Roszak, M.E. Gomes & A.D. Kanner (Eds), *Ecopsychology: Restoring the Earth, Healing the Mind* (pp. 41–54). San Francisco, CA: Sierra Club Books.

Gonzalez, M.T., Hartig, T., Patil, G.G., Martinsen E.W. & Kirkevold, M. (2010) Therapeutic horticulture in clinical depression: A prospective study of active components. *Journal of Advanced Nursing*, 66(9), 2002–2013.

Hay, R. (2005) Becoming ecosynchronous, part 1: The root causes of our unsustainable way of life. *Sustainable Development*, 13, 311–325.

Hoggett, P. (2013) Climate change in a perverse culture. In S. Weintrobe (Ed.), *Engaging with Climate Change: Psychoanalytic and Interdisciplinary Perspectives* (pp. 56–71). London: Routledge.

Jordan, M. (2009) Nature and self: An ambivalent attachment? *Ecopsychology*, 1(1), 26–31.

Jordan, M. (2014) *Nature and Therapy: Understanding Counselling and Psychotherapy in Outdoor Spaces*. London: Routledge.

Jordan, M. & Hinds, J. (2016) *Ecotherapy: Theory, Research and Practice*. London: Palgrave.

Kanner, A.D. & Gomes, M.E. (1995) The all-consuming self. In T. Roszak, M.E. Gomes & A.D. Kanner (Eds), *Ecopsychology: Restoring the Earth, Healing the Mind* (pp. 77–91). San Francisco, CA: Sierra Club Books.

Kaplan, R. & Kaplan, S. (1989) *Experience of Nature*. New York: Cambridge University Press.
Kaplan, S. (1995) The restorative benefits of nature: Towards an integrative framework. *Journal of Environmental Psychology*, 16, 169–182.
Karol, J. (2007) Applying a traditional individual psychotherapy model to equine-facilitated psychotherapy (EFP): Theory and method. *Clinical Child Psychology and Psychiatry*, 12, 77–91.
Keeney, B.P. (1979) Ecosystemic epistemology: An alternative paradigm for diagnosis. *Family Process*, 18, 117–129.
Kerr, M.H. & Key, D.H. (2011) The Ouroboros (Part 1): Towards an ontology of connectedness in ecopsychology research. *European Journal of Ecopsychology*, 2, 48–60.
Key, D.H. (2015) Transpersonal patterns in the Natural Change Project. *Self & Society*, Summer 43(2), 106–119.
Key, D.H. & Kerr, M.H. (2011) The Ouroboros (Part 2): Towards an intersubjective-heuristic method for ecopsychology research. *European Journal of Ecopsychology*, 2, 61–75.
Key, D.H. & Kerr, M.H. (2012) The Natural Change Project. In M.-J. Rust & N. Totton (Eds), *Vital Signs: Psychological Responses to Ecological Crisis* (pp. 239–250). London: Karnac.
Kidner, D.W. (2007) Depression and the natural world: Towards a critical ecology of psychological distress. *International Journal of Critical Psychology*, 19(Spring), 123–143.
Kohanov, L. (2001) *The Tao of Equus*. Novato, CA: New World Library.
Linden, S. & Grut, J. (2002) *Healing Fields: Working with Psychotherapy and Nature to Rebuild Shattered Lives*. London: Frances Lincoln.
Louv, R. (2010) *Last Child in the Woods: Saving Our Children from Nature-deficit Disorder*. Chapel Hill, NC: Algonquin Books.
Macy, J. (1995) Working through environmental despair. In T. Roszak, M.E. Gomes & A.D. Kanner (Eds), *Ecopsychology: Restoring the Earth, Healing the Mind* (pp. 240–259). San Francisco, CA: Sierra Club Books.
Maiteny, P.T. (2012) Longing to be human: Evolving ourselves in healing the earth. In M. J Rust & N. Totton (Eds.), *Vital signs: Psychological responses to ecological crisis* (pp. 47–60). London: Karnac.
Mind (2013) *Feel Better Outside, Feel Better Inside: Ecotherapy for Mental Wellbeing, Resilience and Recovery*. London: Mind.
Roszak, T. (2002 [1993]) *Voices of the Earth: An Exploration of Ecopsychology*. Grand Rapids, MI: Phanes Press.
Roszak, T., Gomes, M.E. & Kanner, A.D. (Eds) (1996) *Ecopsychology: Restoring the Earth, Healing the Mind*. San Francisco, CA: Sierra Club Books.
Rust, M.-J. (2005) Ecolimia nervosa? *Therapy Today*, 16(10), 11–15.
Rust, M.-J. (2008) Climate on the couch: Unconscious processes in relation to our environmental crisis. *Psychotherapy and Politics International*, 6(3), 157–170.
Rust, M.-J. (2020) *Towards an Ecopsychotherapy*. London: Confer.
Seifert, A.-R. (2014) Cultivating new lives: An ethnographic pilot study of eco-therapy provision for people with alcohol-related problems in Northern Ireland. *Anthropology in Action*, 21(1), 4–12.
Sessions, G. (Ed.) (1995) *Deep Ecology for the 21st Century: Readings on the Philosophy and Practice of the New Environmentalism*. Boston, MA: Shambhala.
Siddons Heginworth, I. (2011) *Environmental Arts Therapy and the Tree of Life*. Exeter: Spirit's Rest Books.
Totton, N. (2014) The practice of Wild Therapy. *Therapy Today*, 25(5), 14–17.
Totton, N. (2021) *Wild Therapy: Undomesticating Inner and Outer Worlds* (2nd ed.). Monmouth: PCCS Books.
Ulrich, R. (1984) View through a window may influence recovery from surgery. *Science*, 224(4647), 420–421.
Watts, C. & Hsieh, P.-C. (2010) The use of horticulture-based programs to promote engagement for older adults with dementia. *Therapeutic Recreation Journal*, 49(3), 257.
Wilshire, B. (1999) *Wild Hunger: The Primal Roots of Modern Addiction*. Lanham, MD: Rowman & Littlefield.
Wilson, E.O. (1990) *Biophilia*. Cambridge, MA: Harvard University Press.
Wilson, N., Ross, M., Lafferty, K. & Jones, R. (2008) A review of ecotherapy as an adjunct form of treatment for those who use mental health services. *Journal of Public Mental Health*, 7(3), 23–35.

> **RECOMMENDED READING**
>
> Roszak, T., Gomes, M.E. & Kanner, A.D. (Eds) (1996) *Ecopsychology: Restoring the Earth, Healing the Mind*. San Francisco, CA: Sierra Club Books.
>
> This is the classic text of ecotherapy and ecopsychology: an anthology of substantial and often theoretical writings, which did a great deal to establish the field. It is US focused.
>
> Rust, M.-J. & Totton, N. (2012) *Vital Signs: Psychological Responses to Ecological Crisis*. London: Karnac.
>
> This is a more recent collection showcasing varied approaches to theory and practice. It is largely, though not entirely, UK focused.
>
> Buzzell, L. & Chalquist, C. (2009) *Ecotherapy: Healing with Nature in Mind*. San Francisco, CA: Sierra Books.
>
> This is an anthology of short pieces from a wide variety of sources, addressing different aspects and practices. It is US focused.

5.8 EYE MOVEMENT DESENSITISATION AND REPROCESSING (EMDR)

CATHERINE KERR AND LIZ ROYLE

OVERVIEW AND KEY POINTS

Eye Movement Desensitisation and Reprocessing (EMDR) has developed considerably over the last 30 years and is recognised by the National Institute for Health and Care Excellence (NICE, 2005) for the effective treatment of post-traumatic stress disorder (PTSD). In her core texts, Shapiro states that EMDR shares key elements of traditional approaches. A unique aspect of EMDR is its use of Dual Attention Bilateral Stimulation (DABS), in the form of eye movements, tapping or tones, to process disturbing memories.

- The theoretical underpinning of EMDR is the Adaptive Information Processing model.
- This posits that the brain has an innate healing process that can be stimulated by DABS.
- It is believed that present dysfunction is caused by maladaptively stored memories of distressing events.
- EMDR unhooks the negative emotions from a memory, enabling recall with an ecological validity of distress, and facilitates links to adaptive memory networks.
- This EMDR treatment protocol consists of an eight-phase structure.

BRIEF HISTORY

EMDR was developed by American psychologist Francine Shapiro in 1987 in something of a chance breakthrough. While out walking and experiencing some disturbing thoughts, she realised that her thought patterns were somehow improving. She noticed that, when she was affected by negative reflections, her eyes spontaneously moved from side to side. At the same time, her disturbing thoughts lost their negative emotional charge. She hypothesised that there was a link between these two events, testing her theory on colleagues before embarking on rigorous research. Her first clinical study concentrated on the treatment of veterans of the Vietnam War and survivors of sexual assault (Shapiro, 1989). Clinical input was gathered from trained practitioners around the world, leading to a refinement of the model. Originally called Eye Movement Desensitisation (EMD), in 1990 the approach was renamed EMDR to incorporate the cognitive and emotional restructuring elements. Subsequent extensive research has further developed the principles, protocols and procedures. This evolution from a simple desensitisation technique has led to the need for a consensus definition. This, together with the need to maintain the integrity of the EMDR therapy approach, has led to clarification of definitions and language.

There are three categories of EMDR therapy as endorsed by the Council of Scholars Steering Committee:

- **Category 1 – EMDR Psychotherapy**: this can be conceptualised as having three parts: (1) history-taking and preparation, (2) memory reprocessing, and (3) reevaluation and reconsolidation. This is not necessarily a linear structure, and parts occur concurrently and consecutively over the duration of treatment.
- **Category 2 – EMDR Treatment protocols**: these are intended to treat specific disorders or symptoms, or address special clinical situations, either for individuals or groups. They are consistent with the definition of EMDR therapy and can be used as a stand-alone approach or as part of a more comprehensive psychotherapy. *The standard eight phase treatment protocol is the basis of most training and will be the focus of this chapter.*
- **Category 3 – EMDR-derived Techniques**: these are shorter protocols and procedures that use core elements of EMDR therapy. They can be used as either a stand-alone brief intervention or as a supplement to EMDR therapy (Laliotis et al., 2021).

BASIC ASSUMPTIONS

EMDR is underpinned by the belief that the brain has the same self-healing capacity as the body. Just as the body fights infection and strives for physical balance, so the brain strives to move on from traumatic events and regain psychological balance. *It is posited that the DABS used within EMDR triggers this innate healing process.*

Many psychotherapeutic approaches hold that the majority of our adult belief systems are rooted in childhood experiences. The Adaptive Information Processing (AIP) model of EMDR (Shapiro, 2001, 2007, 2018) similarly suggests that most psychopathology has its roots in distressing past experiences that have been maladaptively stored. This prevents the correct processing of associated thoughts, images, emotions and physical sensations, thus remaining intrusive, easily triggered and leading to current dysfunctions. Such maladaptively stored memories are not able to link to more adaptive memory networks. An example of this is someone who, as a child, was humiliated in a classroom situation. The associated shame, beliefs of defectiveness and physical feelings, such as blushing and anxiety, are kept alive and easily triggered even as an adult. This may lead to social anxiety or general feelings of low self-esteem. There is no emotional link with adaptive information, such as 'I was a child – the teacher was the one who was defective for allowing this'. EMDR seeks to link the old negative belief to a more positive one that can be believed both intellectually and emotionally. This is then strengthened with the processed memory. AIP theory suggests that the mind will not accept a positive cognition that is not ecologically valid. Therefore, it would not be possible to install 'It's not my fault' when processing a road traffic accident where the client was drink-driving and entirely to blame. Another example of an invalid positive cognition would be 'I'm safe' where the client faces ongoing danger. In such cases, a more adaptive positive cognition may be 'I can learn from this' or 'I can make changes'.

ORIGIN AND MAINTENANCE OF PROBLEMS

EMDR case conceptualisation takes a three-pronged approach. It aims to locate the *past events* that underpin the current dysfunction. These may be obvious or very subtle and can even include pre-verbal events. In cases of multiple traumatic events, the clinician will aim to cluster memories that share a common aspect. An example could be a common belief, such as 'I am worthless', or a theme, such as multiple incidents of sexual abuse. Where possible, they will be aiming for a generalisation effect, whereby targeting one memory in cluster processes many others simultaneously.

The clinician will next process *current situations* that exacerbate the problem. Finally, they will target *future events* where a different response is desired. Often once the past events have been processed, the present triggering events and the anticipation of future dysfunction have largely resolved, although some clients may need help in learning new skills, such as assertiveness. Having changed long-standing beliefs can mean they need support in creating their new life.

A useful analogy here is that of a weed. The client can be helped to remove the head of the weed, effectively managing symptoms and making state changes or EMDR can be used to target the 'touchstone' memory, the earliest occurrence of a negative belief. By processing this, the root of the weed is removed, thus making trait changes.

THEORY OF CHANGE

As with other psychotherapies, there is not a definitive answer to how EMDR works. DABS (particularly via eye movements) is viewed as the mechanism of change in EMDR. Questions have been raised about the necessity of this aspect of EMDR, but research has shown a moderate and significant enhancing effect of eye movements (Lee and Cuijpers, 2013). Varied theories have emerged relating to how DABS effects change.

Eye movements are theorised to reduce the vividness of emotional images by interfering with working memory processes (van den Hout et al., 2014). Put simply, desensitisation occurs due to the inherent limitations of viseo-spatial and central executive working memory resources.

Many studies have investigated the neurobiological mechanisms of DABS. Neuro-imagery studies of EMDR consistently show that DABS can facilitate the activation of areas of the frontal lobes (Bergmann, 2010). Increased interhemispheric communication potentially enhances the retrieval of episodic memories which, once processed, can be properly consolidated and stored (Propper and Christman, 2008).

Another theory is that DABS links into the same processes that occur during Rapid Eye Movement (REM) sleep (Stickgold, 2002) when the brain is most active in sifting through the day's events and laying down new memories. In the authors' opinion, this would better explain the forging of adaptive links that occur as the brain naturally seeks to extract learning and gain insight from each new experience.

There are ongoing studies into the brain processes underpinning EMDR (Cuijpers et al., 2020) but the evidence seems to support Shapiro's (2018) view of there being many mechanisms.

During processing, the images, sounds and thoughts related to the target can change. Clients may remember further details or associate to other related instances as memory networks are activated. There may be changes in emotions and somatic sensations, with these rising, peaking then falling away or changing. The overall effect will be to reduce the disturbance and for the client to spontaneously and naturally begin to have more adaptive thoughts and emotions about the event.

SKILLS AND STRATEGIES

The EMDR treatment protocol consists of an eight-phase structure, including history-taking and treatment planning, preparation, assessment, reprocessing, strengthening, body scan, closure, and re-evaluation (Laliotis et al., 2021; Shapiro, 2001).

PHASE 1: HISTORY-TAKING (AND TREATMENT PLANNING)

The clinician takes a full client history and explores current symptoms, goals and preferences for therapy. The case is conceptualised in accordance with AIP theory. It is determined which memories to target and in what order. Safety factors and the client's current level of functioning are explored, and it is crucial to screen for dissociative disorders and poor ego strength as the standard EMDR protocol is not appropriate for these presentations.

PHASE 2: PREPARATION

While maintaining fidelity within the standard protocol, this is not at the expense of building a solid therapeutic alliance and ensuring the client has a safe space to make sense of their distress. The therapeutic relationship is strengthened and a clear explanation of EMDR processing given. The client must understand the process and have fears or expectations addressed. In phase 2, different forms of DABS are tested and the clinician checks that the client can maintain dual awareness between past distress and their present safety.

This balance of 'a foot in the past and a foot in the present' provides the optimal state for processing.

Self-soothing, affect management and stabilisation techniques are taught so that both clinician and client are confident that any disturbance can be tolerated. DABS can be used to stimulate positive memory networks and are often introduced in this phase. The clinician can enhance the client's inner resources, such as states of calm, self-compassion and strength, with DABS.

In EMDR Psychotherapy, phases 1 and 2 may run concurrently and may take several weeks, particularly for complex trauma.

PHASE 3: ASSESSMENT

Here, the client is helped to identify the components of the target memory in a structured way. This includes:

- A target image representing the worst aspect of the memory.
- An associated negative belief about the self (the negative cognition) that is a currently held, irrational and negative thought (e.g., I am in danger, I am helpless).
- The emotions and body sensations that arise when the memory is accessed.
- A positive cognition that the client would prefer to believe about themselves both now and in respect to the target memory. This helps activate any adaptively stored material.

The clinician establishes baseline measures so that subsequent progress can be checked. The Subjective Units of Disturbance (SUD) scale is used to measure the total disturbance and the Validity of Cognition (VOC) scale measures how much the client believes the positive cognition at an emotional, not an intellectual, level.

Drawing out the components in this way activates the memory ready for reprocessing.

PHASE 4: REPROCESSING – PREVIOUSLY KNOWN AS DESENSITISATION

Now the clinician provides DABS while the client processes the memory.

As AIP posits that the DABS stimulates the brain's innate healing process, the clinician needs to intervene minimally. Their role is to reassure the client and maintain optimal levels of arousal for effective processing. Clients are asked to just notice whatever comes up during processing and the clinician will take very brief feedback between sets of DABS in order to oversee the process. Occasionally processing gets stuck, and the clinician will have a range of interventions to facilitate the return to processing.

At the end of phase 4, the SUD for the target will be reduced to 0 or 1 out of 10 or an ecologically valid level.

PHASE 5: STRENGTHENING – PREVIOUSLY KNOWN AS INSTALLATION

The clinician helps the client to re-evaluate the suitability of the positive cognition, then, using DABS, integrates this with the targeted memory, thereby strengthening and enhancing associations to positive memory networks. The VOC scale is used to evaluate the effectiveness of the positive cognition.

PHASE 6: BODY SCAN

The clinician checks for any residual somatic disturbance that may be raised when the client holds the original memory in mind while considering the positive cognition. They help the client to scan for tension, discomfort or unusual sensations that need to be processed with DABS.

PHASE 7: CLOSURE

Not every target is fully processed in a single session, so the clinician needs to be able to contain the remaining disturbance and stabilise the client before they leave the session.

Whereas in phase 4, discussion was deliberately avoided so as not to interfere with processing, now there is an opportunity for debriefing and exploration of insights gained. The clinician may close with a relaxation exercise and will help the client to identify helpful self-care strategies for the week ahead. Processing will continue for some time after the session, so clients are asked to keep a log to note any new thoughts, feelings, behaviours, dreams or memories that arise in between sessions. This information is crucial for the next phase of the protocol.

PHASE 8: RE-EVALUATION

Re-evaluation is done at the beginning of every session following a reprocessing session. The client's experiences in the week are reviewed and the previous reprocessing targets reassessed. This review feeds into the consideration of subsequent targets and the overall treatment plan. As therapy progresses, the clinician and client will review whether all the necessary targets have been processed in relation to the past, present and future approach.

The following composite case study illustrates a typical EMDR processing session for a single adult trauma.

CASE STUDY

Adam was diagnosed with post-traumatic stress disorder (PTSD), as defined in the *Diagnostic and Statistical Manual of Mental Disorders* (5th edition; American Psychiatric Association, 2013) (DSM-5), following a road traffic collision (RTC). A diagnostic assessment carried out by a clinical psychologist recommended 12 sessions of EMDR treatment protocol.

Thorough history-taking revealed no earlier associated trauma. Adam was taught several self-soothing and grounding techniques to help him manage his levels of arousal. It was important that this, and a good therapeutic relationship, were in place prior to addressing the traumatic material.

The reprocessing session began with phase 3 – the assessment of the target memory, drawing out:

- The image representing the worst aspect of the memory – coming around a blind bend into a queue of stationary traffic.
- The negative belief – 'I'm in danger' – in keeping with the currently held, irrational fear that was blighting his life.
- The emotions and body sensations of fear, a tight chest and clenching stomach.

Adam rated these as 8/10 on the SUD scale. He wanted to believe that he was safe, and it was over, but this only rated a 2/7 on the VOC scale.

Adam was asked to hold these components of the memory in mind and the clinician began phase 4 with DABS. In between each set of eye movements, Adam was asked for short feedback on what he noticed. This is summarised below:

- Anxiety rising and recalling more details of the moment of impact.
- Tension felt throughout his body as though bracing for impact.
- Remembering the screams from an injured driver.
- Remembering feeling trapped in his vehicle and seeing broken glass glinting in the sunlight.
- His thought that another car could come around the corner and plough into him and his anxiety peaked at that point.
- Memory of emergency services' sirens.
- Memory of someone coming to help and comfort him.
- Feeling relief and a sense of being protected by their presence behind his vehicle.
- Remembering other drivers standing at the side of the road – at this point he spontaneously said aloud 'it had already happened – it wasn't my fault'. It was only then that he realised he had felt responsible for the accident. This was a massive insight for him, and he experienced a surge of relief.
- He thought about how his specific car had saved him from serious physical injuries and how his choice had protected him.
- His thoughts continued to realise how many elements generally contributed to his road safety, then and now, – his driving experience, and road awareness. He felt a sense of some control and a resulting inner calm.
- His calmness increased as DABS continued.

> Once his SUD had reduced to an ecologically valid 0, Adam was asked what words best went with that memory now. It was natural and easy for him to say, 'I'm safe now'. The clinician installed this positive cognition with DABS and checked there was no residual somatic disturbance. The session was closed with a debriefing of his experience of the processing and a relaxation exercise.
>
> When Adam returned, the next session began with the re-evaluation and consideration of next steps.

EMDR is sometimes wrongly viewed as rigid and formulaic. The eight phases can be viewed as a cradle holding a wide range of therapeutic skills. How individual clinicians take a history and stabilise a client will vary, depending on their therapeutic background and experiences. The clinician must build understanding and control by teaching containment, emotional tolerance, grounding strategies and providing psychoeducation. Only then should they consider addressing the processing of the traumatic memories. Consequently, EMDR is more fluid than would first appear and is not always a linear process. As well as the strong relational aspect, clinicians should be culturally competent and informed about innovative strategies and working with special populations (Nickerson, 2016).

RESEARCH

EMDR is recommended as one of the therapeutic approaches for the effective treatment of PTSD and much research has been focused in this area (NICE, 2005). However, further studies have suggested the effectiveness of EMDR for many other presentations (Valiente-Gómez et al., 2017). Maxfield (2019) analyses randomised controlled trials that preliminarily show the effectiveness of EMDR for issues such as psychosis, major depressive disorders, obsessive-compulsive disorder, substance use disorder, and pain. Shapiro (2001) refers to trauma in terms of large 'T', the major, obvious traumatic incidents, and small 't' traumas. The latter are 'those experiences that give one a lesser sense of self-confidence and assault one's sense of self-efficacy' (Parnell, 2007: 4). Where small 't' trauma is posited to be at the root of dysfunction, EMDR may also be beneficial. Examples include social anxiety and low self-esteem.

Fidelity to the protocol is important and training and supervision are vital in this. Further details of recognised training providers can be found at EMDR Association UK and Ireland (www.emdrassociation.org.uk), EMDR Europe (www.emdr-europe.org) and EMDR International Association (www.emdria.org).

REFERENCES

American Psychiatric Association (2013). *Diagnostic and Statistical Manual of Mental Disorders* (5th ed.). DSM-5. Washington, DC: APA.

Bergmann, U. (2010). EMDR's neurobiological mechanisms of action. *Journal of EMDR Practice and Research*, 4(1), 9–24.

Cuijpers, P., van Veen, S. C., Sijbrandij, M., Yoder, W. and Cristea, I. A. (2020). Eye movement desensitization and reprocessing for mental health problems: a systematic review and meta-analysis. *Cognitive Behaviour Therapy*, 49(3), 165–180. https://doi.org/10.1080/16506073.2019.1703801

Laliotis, D., Luber, M., Oren, U., Shapiro, E., Ichii, M., Hase, M., La Rosa, L., Alter-Reid, K. and Tortes St. Jammes, L. (2021). What is EMDR therapy? Past, present, and future directions. *Journal of EMDR Practice and Research*, 15(4), 187–201. doi:10.1891/EMDR-D-21-00014

Lee, C.W. and Cuijpers, P. (2013). A meta-analysis of the contribution of eye movements in processing emotional memories. *Journal of Behavior Therapy and Experimental Psychiatry*, 44, 231–239.

(Continued)

(Continued)

Maxfield, L. (2019). A clinician's guide to the efficacy of EMDR therapy. *Journal of EMDR Practice and Research*, 13(4), 239–246.

National Institute of Clinical Excellence (2005). *Post Traumatic Stress Disorder (PTSD): The Management of PTSD in Adults and Children in Primary and Secondary Care. Clinical Guideline 26*. London: NICE.

Nickerson, M. (2016). *Cultural Competence and Healing Culturally-based Trauma with EMDR Therapy: Innovative Strategies and Protocols*. New York: Springer.

Parnell, L. (2007). *A Clinician's Guide to EMDR: Tools and Techniques for Successful Treatment*. New York: W.W. Norton.

Propper, R. and Christman, S. (2008). Interhemispheric interaction and saccadic horizontal eye movements: implications for episodic memory, EMDR, and PTSD. *Journal of EMDR Practice and Research*, 4, 269–281.

Shapiro, F. (1989). Efficacy of the eye movement desensitization procedure in the treatment of traumatic memories. *Journal of Traumatic Stress Studies*, 2, 199–223.

Shapiro, F. (2001). *Eye Movement Desensitization and Reprocessing: Basic Principles, Protocols and Procedures* (2nd ed.). New York: Guilford Press.

Shapiro, F. (2007). EMDR, adaptive information processing, and case conceptualization. *Journal of EMDR Practice and Research*, 1, 68–87.

Shapiro, F. (2018). *Eye Movement Desensitization and Reprocessing: Basic Principles, Protocols and Procedures* (3rd ed.). New York: Guilford Press.

Stickgold, R. (2002). EMDR: a putative neurobiological mechanism of action. *Journal of Clinical Psychology*, 58, 61–75.

Valiente-Gómez, A., Moreno-Alcázar, A., Treen, D., Cedrón, C., Colom, F., Pérez V. and Amann B.L. (2017). EMDR beyond PTSD: a systematic literature review. *Frontiers in Psychology*, 8. https://doi.org/10.3389/fpsyg.2017.01668

van den Hout, M.A., Eidhof, M.B., Verboom, J., Littel, M. and Engelhard, I.M. (2014). Blurring of emotional and non-emotional memories by taxing working memory during recall. *Cognition and Emotion*, 28(4), 717–727.

RECOMMENDED READING

Royle, E. and Kerr, C. (2010). *Integrating EMDR into your Practice*. New York: Springer.

This book helps novice practitioners integrate EMDR into their current practice, whatever their theoretical orientation.

These next two books detail the history, development and basic principles of this therapeutic approach, and explore some innovative strategies and protocols.

Nickerson, M. (2016). *Cultural Competence and Healing Culturally-based Trauma with EMDR Therapy: Innovative Strategies and Protocols*. New York: Springer.

Shapiro, F. (2018). *Eye Movement Desensitization and Reprocessing: Basic Principles, Protocols and Procedures* (3rd ed.). New York: Guilford Press.

5.9 EMOTION-FOCUSED THERAPY

LADISLAV TIMULAK

OVERVIEW AND KEY POINTS

Emotion-focused therapy (EFT) is a humanistic-experiential treatment building on the traditions of person-centred and Gestalt therapy, integrating research-informed developments in this and other forms of therapy. The basic premise of EFT is that the core chronic painful feelings (maladaptive emotion schemes), which shape the client's emotional processing of their interaction with their environment, need to be accessed and transformed in therapy. Thus, EFT is:

- a form of research-informed humanistic-experiential therapy
- a therapy that focuses on the transformation of chronic painful emotion by accessing underlying emotion schemes and transforming them with adaptive emotions
- a therapy that values the therapeutic relationship, which it views as pivotal in bringing about lasting therapeutic change in clients
- a therapy that is a form of research-informed treatment for depression, complex trauma eating disorders, anxiety disorders and couple distress.

BRIEF HISTORY

Emotion-focused therapy (EFT) is primarily associated with the work of Leslie (Les) Greenberg (2011, 2015). It has strong roots in the research tradition of client-centred therapy. Greenberg's mentor, Laura Rice, was a student of Carl Rogers, and Rice's work on the evocative functions of empathy in client-centred therapy significantly informed the early development of emotion-focused therapy. Greenberg also trained in Gestalt therapy and his couples work was further influenced by systemic training. Greenberg's early interest in the subject of emotion in psychotherapy (e.g., Greenberg and Safran, 1987) resulted in a research programme that led first to the development of a model for couples therapy, initially named *emotionally-focused couple therapy*, in collaboration with his student Sue Johnson (Greenberg and Johnson, 1988) and later, to the development of an individual therapy modality (initially named *process-experiential therapy* (Greenberg, Rice and Elliott, 1993) and subsequently renamed *emotion-focused therapy* (Greenberg, 2015; Greenberg and Paivio, 1997). The rich tradition of process research on EFT means that in EFT virtually all therapist interventions are informed by research-based observations. The research on EFT also includes a number of randomised clinical trials (RCTs) (for an overview of process and outcome research in EFT see Timulak et al., 2018). Development in the area of couples work was mainly furthered by Sue Johnson (2019) and her collaborators, although Greenberg has also, in collaboration with Rhonda Goldman, made a return to research and writing in this area (Greenberg and Goldman, 2008). Current practice of EFT is well summarised in the American Psychological Association's bestseller, *Learning Emotion-focused Therapy* (Elliott et al., 2004) and in several other books describing EFT work with depression (Greenberg and Watson, 2006), complex trauma (Paivio and Pascual-Leone, 2010) and emotional distress more generally (Elliott and Greenberg, 2021; Greenberg, 2015; Timulak, 2015; Timulak and Keogh, 2022).

BASIC ASSUMPTIONS

Emotion-focused therapy (EFT) is a neo-humanistic treatment that relies on a constructivist epistemology (Greenberg, 2011). According to Greenberg (2011: 32), 'people are seen as constantly synthesizing conscious experience out of many levels of processing'. These levels of processing include sensorimotor, emotion schematic and conceptual processing. In EFT, Rogers' concept of congruence between experience and symbolised awareness is replaced by a concept of coherence between various levels of processing (Greenberg, 2011). As within Rogers' theory, people are seen as striving for adaptive functioning in the context of interaction with their environment. According to Greenberg (2011: 35), 'people are dynamic self-organizing systems in constant interaction with the environment ... [while] ... affect regulation is seen as a core aspect of motivation'. Indeed, in EFT (Elliott et al., 2004; Greenberg, 2011, 2015) emotions are seen as important sources of information that tell us whether our interaction with the environment is adaptive, promoting survival and growth. Emotions inform us about the extent to which our needs are met (Greenberg, 2011, 2015; Timulak, 2015).

EFT differentiates between various aspects of emotional experience. For instance, it differentiates between primary, secondary and instrumental emotions (Greenberg and Safran, 1987). Within this framework, primary emotions are the very first reactions we feel in response to a situation (e.g., fear when we are threatened). Secondary emotions are usually emotional responses to primary emotions or accompanying thoughts (e.g., I do not like my fear, so I become angry). Instrumental emotions are emotions deliberately expressed in order to influence others (e.g., crocodile tears engaged in to elicit comfort from others). EFT theory recognises also a distinction between adaptive and maladaptive emotions (assessed on the basis of whether they inform or do not inform adaptive action; see Greenberg, 2015) and focuses as an intervention on accessing chronic primary maladaptive emotions in order that they can be transformed in therapy though the accessing of primary adaptive emotions. EFT theory also recognises different levels of emotional arousal (Warwar and Greenberg, 1999) and there is a focus in therapy on attaining an optimal level of emotional arousal in order that emotions are not only talked about, but are actually accessed, experienced and expressed within the therapy session. It is also understood that maladaptive emotion schemes (the usual way in which we process certain emotions) can only be transformed in therapy when those emotions are activated within the session. EFT theory also distinguishes between productive and unproductive in-session emotional experiencing; while primary, adaptive emotions are perceived as being productive, the experiencing of maladaptive primary emotions is regarded as productive only if such emotion is experienced in a way that is not overwhelming, is owned and is well differentiated so it could be transformed in therapy (Greenberg, Auszra and Herrmann, 2007).

ORIGIN AND MAINTENANCE OF PROBLEMS

An important part of our processing of interactions with the environment occurs through schematic processes. In EFT, these schematic processes are called emotion schemes (Greenberg, 2011). Psychopathology occurs either when information contained in these emotion schemes is not symbolised in the individual's awareness, or when emotion schemes are maladaptive (Greenberg et al., 1993; Greenberg and Watson, 2006). Psychopathology thus develops (1) out of non-optimal awareness of emotions, or (2) out of problematic emotional processing based in maladaptive emotion schemes which results in chronic painful feelings. The origins of these types of problematic processing typically lie in early development; for example, when the emotional support provided to the individual was suboptimal, or when emotional experiences were so difficult (traumatic) that they disrupted the formation of healthy ways of interacting with the individual's environment. Even later in a person's development, significant traumatic experiences may impact on the quality of emotional/conceptual processing of interactions with the interpersonal and social environment, and may lead to non-optimal or limited use of own capacities. Similarly, biological vulnerabilities and their interplay with the (social) environment may be responsible for the formation of problematic emotion schemes.

THEORY OF CHANGE

Therapeutic change in EFT is based on (1) increasing the client's awareness of the richness of information contained in emotions, and (2) on the reworking of problematic emotional schemes, particularly through the use of adaptive emotional experiences to counteract maladaptive ones. Therapy thus focuses on bringing an optimal level of emotional arousal (e.g., overcoming emotional avoidance), on broadening awareness of emotional experiences, on regulating dysregulated emotions, on transforming chronic maladaptive emotions (schemes) through the experiencing of adaptive emotions in the context of maladaptive emotions, and finally on meaning-making that takes into account the wealth of information contained in the emotional experience (Greenberg, 2011, 2015).

The process of change can also be understood in terms of a productive sequence of emotional experiencing that is facilitated in therapy (Pascual-Leone and Greenberg, 2007; Timulak, 2015) that starts with (1) problematic, secondary, global undifferentiated distress (e.g., I feel hopeless, helpless, down, etc.) and emotional/behavioural avoidance (e.g., I do not want to feel the pain, I am afraid of situations that may bring it); followed by (2) the accessing of core painful (maladaptive) feelings (e.g., I feel worthless, unlovable) which are sparked by the client's interaction with the environment (e.g., they do not love me) and problematic self-treatment (e.g., it is all my fault); (3) the identification of unmet needs (e.g., I want to feel loved and accepted); and responded to by (4) experiences of adaptive emotions such as compassion (e.g., I feel loved) and healthy protective anger (e.g., I deserve to be loved), in turn gradually leading to grieving (e.g., it is sad what I had to go through, but I can let go of it now) and a sense of empowerment (e.g., I feel stronger inside now).

SKILLS AND STRATEGIES

Therapeutic work in EFT is embedded in the therapist's provision of a Rogerian authentic, caring and unconditional relationship. The default position of the therapist is one of empathic attunement to the client's affective experience, a position very similar to that found in person-centred therapy. The therapist facilitates the client's exploration by empathic exploration and empathic understanding-focused interventions. The therapist's empathy is, however, more active than would be the case in person-centred therapy, with the therapist using empathic responses to evoke emotional experience, refocus the client on emotional processes, or empathically conjecture as to the nature of the client's emotional experience (Elliott and Greenberg, 2021; Elliott et al., 2004). All of these strategies are employed with the goal of promoting access to the client's emotional experience.

The EFT therapist's work is also influenced by case conceptualisation (Goldman and Greenberg, 2015) that mainly focuses on identifying the primary maladaptive emotion schemes that need to be accessed and transformed through the use of experiential tasks (see below). Timulak and Pascual-Leone (2015) offer a framework that can inform EFT therapist strategy; conceptualisation within this framework focuses on identifying painful triggering situations; the client's self-treatment in the context of these situations; the client's typical secondary emotions in those situations (global distress); the client's apprehension and avoidance of the situations that bring painful feelings; the client's core painful maladaptive feelings (i.e., loneliness, shame and fear) in those triggering situations; and the unmet needs embedded or contained in core painful, primary maladaptive feelings. The therapy then focuses on accessing these painful primary feelings and facilitating the articulation of unmet needs (e.g., to be loved, accepted and/or safe); the articulation of which typically invites adaptive experiential responses from the client (typically compassion and protective anger) that lead to emotional transformation.

EFT is also a 'marker'-driven therapy, which means that when certain markers present themselves in the session (e.g., self-criticism), the therapist introduces experiential tasks, during which the therapist actively guides the client to access their emotional experience, own it, regulate it if needed and transform it if needed. Experiential tasks (see Elliott et al., 2004) include for instance: *systematic evocative unfolding* (in which the client is guided to recall in a slow-process situations that troubled him or her in order to get a sense of what it was within that situation that sparked an unexpected or problematic reaction); *clearing a space* (an emotional regulation-promoting task); *experiential focusing* (a task that allows the client to access emotional experience and symbolise them in awareness); *two chair dialogue for self-criticism* (in which the client enacts problematic self-treatments such as self-criticism in order to transform the maladaptive schemes); *two chair dialogue for self-interruption* (an imaginary dialogue in which the client accesses previously avoided emotional experience); and *empty chair dialogue* (in which the client engages in an imaginary dialogue with a [significant] other in order to identify emotional injuries in relation to that other and in order to transform the underlying maladaptive emotion schemes rooted in such injuries). In short-term therapies, approximately 50% of the time is spent in various experiential tasks, predominantly self–self or self–other chair dialogues.

To illustrate the nature of therapeutic work in EFT, I will use a case presented by McNally, Timulak and Greenberg (2014; also McNally, 2012).

CASE STUDY

The client, Jane (pseudonym), sought out therapy for depression. She presented with many somatic symptoms related to emotional distress, and she reported feeling down, irritable and profoundly hopeless. As therapy proceeded, it emerged that Jane felt ostracised from, and judged by, her family of origin (in particular, she felt judged by her mother). She also married at a young age, and her husband had been abusive. She felt very guilty for not having being able to protect her children from her abusive husband. Although she was now remarried, she also felt let down by her current husband. She was very self-critical of herself (e.g., *There is something wrong with me; Nobody loves me; I let down my children; I am a bad mother; I am a bad daughter*); felt shamed and alone and still felt traumatised by the abusive attacks of her ex-husband. She was very avoidant of her core painful feelings and, despite her presenting irritability, was not able to stand up for herself without feeling tremendous guilt.

In therapy, Jane was able to access her pain in the context of soothing responses from her therapist. For instance, in session 12 she touched on the pain of missing her children when she had to withdraw from an abusive situation. In a two chair dialogue, with the judging/critical part of herself in the Critic chair (e.g., voicing judgement and criticism about how she failed to protect her children) and the impacted, ashamed part of herself in the Experiencer chair, Jane describes her pain thus:

Jane [speaking from the Experiencer chair to the Critic chair]:
I used to come home every night from work and go into their (Jane's children) empty rooms (sniffs) and walk around as though I was lost (sighs). I used to have this ache in my heart all the time, that I wanted them there with me (crying) and I couldn't have them (sniffs)
Therapist: What was that ache like? Seems like you're feeling...
Jane: (sniffs) It just...
Therapist: Right now...
Jane: (sniffs) It was like a – a physical hurt, ah (sniffs) and it hurt so much and I used to – without thinking about it – set the table and call them (Jane's children) for dinner – and I'd realise that they were not there (sniffs)...

...
Therapist: Mm-hm it really tore you apart.

One session prior to this exchange, she touched on the vulnerability she felt in the presence of her husband, a sense of not feeling loved. In an empty chair dialogue with her imagined husband in the other chair, she articulated what she needed from her husband when feeling unloved, overlooked and uncared for (Unmet Need):

Jane: I still need you (client's husband) there – to protect me (crying) – even though I might – come across that I don't need it all the time, I still need you there to protect me – I want – you once – to put me ahead of everybody else (sniffs)...
Therapist: So I want to be ahead – (C. sigh) – of (C. sniff) everyone – else.
Jane: I want to be number one in your life – ah – not after everybody else – (sniff)...

When enacting her husband's response to this unmet need (Jane was asked to sit in the other chair and witness the expressed pain and unmet need), Jane unexpectedly communicated a very caring and loving response, which she (sitting back in 'her' chair and asked to feel how it was like to get this response) in turn experienced as very soothing.

In session 12 she was also able to stand up to the judgement she had always felt from her mother (e.g., for failing as a daughter, as a wife and a mother of her own children). In the empty chair dialogue with her imagined mother, she stood up for herself (Protective Anger):

Jane: I have to live up to these expectations (her mother's expectations) (sniffs)... I don't want to do it anymore, it's too hard (sniffs). I want to get off of it, I don't want to do it anymore, it's hard (sniffs) I feel hurt... I don't deserve it.

....

Jane: Ah, I'd like you (client's mother) just to accept me for myself, even if I'm not that good all the time (sniffs)...
Therapist: Mm-hm, so you want to be accepted.
Jane: I want to be accepted for myself (sniffs).

This expression left Jane feeling calm and empowered, and the session appeared to be quite pivotal in the overall case.

RESEARCH

Emotion-focused therapy is particularly well researched in terms of process research and as a treatment for depression, with research indicating that it was somewhat more effective than classical person-centred therapy and comparably effective to cognitive-behavioural therapy (a summary of these studies can be found in Elliott et al., 2021 and Timulak et al., 2018. Research studies also assessed the efficacy of EFT in the treatment of complex trauma stemming from child abuse (a summary of that work can be found in Paivio and Pascual-Leone, 2010). More recently, it was studied for anxiety disorders (e.g., Shahar, Bar-Kalifa and Alon, 2017; Timulak and McElvaney, 2018) and eating disorders (Glisenti et al., 2021). The couples' version of EFT (Greenberg and Goldman, 2008; Greenberg and Johnson, 1988; Johnson, 2019) is also one of the most researched couples therapies in the world.

REFERENCES

Elliott, R. and Greenberg, L. (2021). *Emotion-focused counselling in action*. London: Sage.

Elliott, R., Watson, J. C., Goldman, R. N. and Greenberg, L. S. (2004). *Learning emotion-focused therapy: The process-experiential approach to change*. Washington, DC: American Psychological Association.

Elliott, R., Watson, J. C., Timulak, L. and Sharbanee, J. (2021). Research on humanistic-experiential psychotherapies: updated review. In M. Barkham, W. Lutz and L. G. Castonguay (Eds), *Bergin and Garfield's handbook of psychotherapy and behavior change* (7th ed.). Hoboken, NJ: John Wiley & Sons.

Glisenti, K., Strodl, E., King, R. and Greenberg, L. (2021). The feasibility of emotion-focused therapy for binge-eating disorder: a pilot randomised wait-list control trial. *Journal of Eating Disorders*, 9(1), 1–15.

Goldman, R. N. and Greenberg, L. S. (2015). *Case formulation in emotion-focused therapy*. Washington, DC: American Psychological Association.

Greenberg, L. S. (2011). *Emotion-focused therapy*. Washington, DC: American Psychological Association.

Greenberg, L. S. (2015). *Emotion-focused therapy: Coaching clients to work through their feelings* (2nd ed.). Washington, DC: American Psychological Association. (The first edition published in 2002.)

(Continued)

(Continued)

Greenberg, L. S., Auszra, L. and Herrmann, I. R. (2007). The relationship among emotional productivity, emotional arousal and outcome in experiential therapy of depression. *Psychotherapy Research*, *17*, 482–493.

Greenberg, L. S. and Goldman, R. N. (2008). *Emotion-focused couples therapy: The dynamics of emotion, love, and power*. Washington, DC: American Psychological Association.

Greenberg, L. S. and Johnson, S. M. (1988). *Emotionally focused therapy for couples*. New York: Guilford Press.

Greenberg, L. S. and Paivio, S. C. (1997). *Working with emotions in psychotherapy*. New York: Guilford Press.

Greenberg, L. S., Rice, L. N. and Elliott, R. (1993). *Facilitating emotional change: The moment by moment process*. New York: Guilford Press.

Greenberg, L. S. and Safran, J. D. (1987). *Emotion in psychotherapy: Affect, cognition, and the process of change*. New York: Guilford Press.

Greenberg, L. S. and Watson, J. (2006). *Emotion-focused therapy for depression*. Washington, DC: American Psychological Association.

Johnson, S. M. (2019). *The practice of emotionally focused couples therapy: Creating connections* (3rd ed.). Abingdon, UK: Routledge.

McNally, S. (2012). *Transforming emotion schemes in emotion-focused therapy*. Unpublished dissertation. Trinity College, Dublin.

McNally, S., Timulak, L. and Greenberg, L. S. (2014). Transforming emotion schemes in emotion-focused therapy: a case study investigation. *Person-Centered & Experiential Psychotherapies*, *13*, 128–149.

Paivio, S. C. and Pascual-Leone, A. (2010). *Emotion-focused therapy for complex trauma: An integrative approach*. Washington, DC: American Psychological Association.

Pascual-Leone, A. and Greenberg, L. S. (2007). Emotional processing in experiential therapy: Why 'the only way out is through'. *Journal of Consulting and Clinical Psychology*, *75*, 875–887. doi: 10.1037/0022-006X.75.6.875.

Shahar, B., Bar-Kalifa, E. and Alon, E. (2017). Emotion-focused therapy for social anxiety disorder: results from a multiple-baseline study. *Journal of Consulting and Clinical Psychology*, *85*(3), 238.

Timulak, L. (2015). *Transforming emotional pain in psychotherapy: An emotion-focused approach*. London: Routledge.

Timulak, L., Iwakabe, S. and Elliott, R. (2018). Clinical implications of quantitative, qualitative and case study research on emotion-focused therapy. In L. S. Greenberg and R. N. Goldman (Eds), *Clinical handbook of emotion-focused therapy*. Washington, DC: American Psychological Association.

Timulak, L. and Keogh, D. (2022). *Transdiagnostic emotion-focused therapy: A clinical guide to transformation of emotional pain*. Washington, DC: American Psychological Association.

Timulak, L. and McElvaney, J. (2018). *Transforming generalized anxiety: An emotion-focused approach*. Abingdon, UK: Routledge.

Timulak, L. and Pascual-Leone, A. (2015). New developments for case conceptualization in emotion-focused therapy. *Clinical Psychology & Psychotherapy*, *22*, 619–636.

Warwar, S. and Greenberg, L. S. (1999). *Client emotional arousal scale–III*. Unpublished manuscript, York University, Toronto, Ontario, Canada.

> **RECOMMENDED READING**
>
> Elliott, R. and Greenberg, L. S. (2021). *Emotion-focused counselling in action*. London: Sage.
>
> This is an excellent introduction to EFT for students. It provides a thorough description of the experiential tasks used in EFT, written in a student-friendly manner.
>
> Timulak, L. (2015). *Transforming emotional pain in psychotherapy: An emotion-focused approach*. Abingdon, UK: Routledge.
>
> This is a relatively short presentation of EFT through the lens of emotion transformation. The book uses plenty of clinical examples.
>
> Timulak, L. and Keogh, D. (2022). *Transdiagnostic emotion-focused therapy: A clinical guide to transformation of emotional pain*. Washington, DC: American Psychological Association.
>
> This is the latest thinking of the author of this chapter on EFT for depression, anxiety, and related difficulties using a transdiagnostic framework.

5.10 EXISTENTIAL THERAPY

EMMY VAN DEURZEN

OVERVIEW AND KEY POINTS

Existential therapy is a philosophical form of counselling and psychotherapy, with long roots into philosophy and with over a century of development. There are many forms of existential therapy, including the four that are usually recognised:

1. An analytical version, *Daseinsanalysis* (Binswanger, Boss).
2. A meaning-based approach, called Logotherapy (Frankl, Längle).
3. An existential/humanistic or existential/integrative approach (Yalom, Schneider).
4. An existential-phenomenological approach (Laing, van Deurzen, Spinelli).

Each of these varied forms of existential therapy seeks to establish a direct engagement with people's difficulties, in order to make sense of them without needing to pathologise them. Existential therapists accept that human existence is intrinsically difficult. They aim to enable people to tackle their problems in living, by gaining greater understanding.

Existential therapy therefore always:

- engages with the big questions
- emphasises paradoxical concepts like freedom and responsibility
- focuses on the way in which purpose, values and beliefs shape our lives
- reminds people of the limits of the human condition
- inspires people to regain their passion for life.

BRIEF HISTORY

Existential therapy finds its origins in applied philosophy. The original idea of philosophy, literally the love of wisdom, was to actively search for the secret of a well-lived life. Hellenistic philosophers used the Socratic method of dialectical discussion to reveal and unravel the truth about personal and universal issues and dilemmas. This practice fell into desuetude but was revitalised at the beginning of the twentieth century when a number of psychiatrists began applying the thinking of existential philosophers such as Kierkegaard, Nietzsche and Heidegger to their clinical work (Deurzen, 2010; Deurzen et al., 2019). Karl Jaspers, Ludwig Binswanger and Medard Boss were the first to formulate some principles for existential psychotherapy (May, Angel and Ellenberger, 1958). Their work, based mainly in Germany and Switzerland, was known as *Daseinsanalysis* or existential analysis.

Authors such as Paul Tillich (1952) and Rollo May (1969) spread the approach more widely in the United States. Their influence on the human potential movement and on humanistic psychotherapy and counselling was extensive. There are obvious existential elements in approaches such as person-centred therapy and Gestalt psychotherapy, while Irvin Yalom (1980), James Bugental (1981) and Alvin Mahrer (1996) have made direct contributions to the development of existential/humanistic forms of psychotherapy in North America. More recently, Kirk Schneider has taken existential therapy into a more spiritual direction (Schneider and Krug, 2017).

In Europe, existential psychotherapy was further developed by Victor Frankl's (1964 [1946]) logotherapy, which is a largely meaning-driven approach, which has now spread more widely around the world. More recently, Alfried Längle has added further layers of practice to logotherapy, calling it existential analysis (Längle and Wurm, 2016). In the United Kingdom, the work of R.D. Laing (1960) was much inspired by the existentialist writing of Jean-Paul Sartre (1956 [1943]). It facilitated the flourishing of existential psychotherapy in the UK, which was firmly established from 1988 with the founding of the Society for Existential Analysis, together with its journal *Existential Analysis*. A number of training courses at the Philadelphia Association, Regent's University, Roehampton University and the New School of Psychotherapy and Counselling, at the Existential Academy, were developed and the existential-phenomenological approach characteristic of the UK is now widespread across Europe and beyond. A number of noteworthy publications made the existential approach better known (see Cohn, 1997; Deurzen, 2010, 2012, 2015, 2021; Deurzen and Adams, 2016; Deurzen and Arnold-Baker, 2018; Deurzen et al., 2019; Deurzen, 2021; Spinelli, 2014). Existential-phenomenological therapy has been adopted by many psychotherapists across the world, as became evident at the first World Congress for Existential Therapy in London in 2015, and the second World Congress in Buenos Aires in 2019. The third World Congress is held in Athens in 2023.

BASIC ASSUMPTIONS

Existential therapy helps people in coming to terms with their lives in all their complexity rather than just addressing psychological or relationship problems.

Many problems are the natural and inevitable consequence of the challenges and limitations of the human condition, such as death, loneliness, failure, weakness, guilt, anxiety, poverty, illness and futility. The objective is not to cure people of pathology, which is an unhelpful and misleading concept borrowed from the medical model, but rather to assist them in coming to terms with the contradictions, dilemmas and paradoxes of their everyday existence. The following concepts are distinctive for existential therapy:

1. Anxiety is a valuable instrument in helping us become more aware of the demands of reality. It is a form of life energy and when embraced can help live life to the full.
2. Human beings often feel alone but are never in complete isolation. We are always in a given world, with other people and in a situation, which affects our experience.
3. Problems need to be seen in their cultural, social and political context.
4. We all tend to hide away and deceive ourselves about life and our own position in it. Facing the truth and aiming for a more authentic way of being are important goals.
5. The concept of 'self' is a relative one. It is only as I act in the world and connect to objects, people and ideas in the world, that I create a sense of self. There is no such thing as a solid, immutable self. We are in constant transformation and flux and can change and redefine ourselves.

6. Existential therapists work with what is unknown and hidden. They do not accept the idea that there is an inner place called 'the unconscious'. Nor is there such a thing as absolute truth. They explore multiple interpretations of reality at different levels of existence in dialogue with their clients.
7. People need purpose and meaning in life. Tuning into personal yearnings and longings helps finding a life project, in line with beliefs and values.
8. Vitality comes from accepting both positives and negatives in life. There can be no life without death and no health without illness, no happiness without unhappiness (Deurzen, 2009).
9. We live in time. We recollect ourselves from the past. We present ourselves in the now and project ourselves into the future. We ask ourselves whether what we do makes sense in relation to eternity. All these dimensions of time are equally important. Temporality is a core aspect of existential work.
10. We live in space, on four different dimensions. The four worlds model describes these as follows. A. We are embodied in a physical world where we interact with material objects. B. We are with other people in a social world. C. We relate to ourselves in our private, intimate, inner world. D. We adopt and form theories and ideas that give meaning to life at a spiritual or ideological level.

ORIGIN AND MAINTENANCE OF PROBLEMS

Life is intrinsically problematic as tensions are created at all levels. Every day we encounter problems of all sorts. We need to build confidence in our ability to tackle and solve these problems and improve our competence in dealing with increasingly tougher situations. We find pleasure in the vitality that comes with a resolute and courageous attitude to living.

Sometimes we might try to make things easier for ourselves by escaping from reality and living with illusions. One of the ways in which we deceive ourselves is by imagining that we can't change. We can learn to embrace our freedom and responsibility and make our own choices and changes in life.

Sometimes people feel so overwhelmed that they withdraw from the world completely, in isolation or chaos, losing their foothold in social/cultural reality and giving up their remaining strength and *joie de vivre*.

One of our constant causes for concern is the presence of others. We might see our fellow human beings as potential threats and as untrustworthy. Our destructive interactions or avoidance of interaction with others can become a self-fulfilling prophecy of doom.

We often live with regret over what happened yesterday, in fear of what may be demanded of us tomorrow and in guilt over what we have not yet accomplished today. We are quite capable of emotionally paralysing ourselves in this manner. Working with moods and feelings is central to existential therapy and is done by tracing the values that are at the root of feelings, using the so-called emotional compass (Deurzen, 2012).

Some people are in situations that significantly restrict or constrict their outlook and their freedom of action. Genetic, developmental, accidental, class, cultural or gender factors can all generate apparently insurmountable obstacles. Everyone's life presents numerous difficulties that have to be accommodated, resolved or overcome. Some people manage to surmount substantial initial disadvantages or adversity, whereas others squander their advantage or flounder in the face of minor misfortunes.

Every problem has several solutions. Facing the situation and putting it in perspective is always possible, given some time and with some assistance, and this will lead to finding new ways of viewing and engaging with the problem.

Existential therapy encourages resolute living, which is based in the capacity to meet whatever may come with steadfastness and in a spirit of adventure.

THEORY OF CHANGE

Change takes place continuously in life. We spend much energy trying to keep things the same. When aiming for stability and safety we may find it difficult to allow changes to happen, even when this could be beneficial. We may fear the process of transformation that everything in this world is subject to and fend it off.

When clients come to therapy, they do so because they want to find the strength and confidence to allow changes for the better to happen in their lives. They need the therapist to help them to be steady when confronting their fears and doubts, so as to find a way through.

The objective of existential work is to enable clients to become more open to their own experience in all its paradoxical reality. They will become more tolerant of their anxiety and more understanding of themselves by self-reflection. They gain awareness of their worldview and interpretation of reality, reshaping their story and thus their future as well.

Becoming aware of strengths, talents and abilities is as important as to explore the darker side of experience. Hidden passions and yearnings bring new energy for change.

For those who are in a situation of crisis, which is a moment of danger and loss, the challenge is to find new opportunities instead of being thrown into a state of confusion. Existential therapy explores new paths and new directions, ensuring that the crisis is a point of breakthrough rather than breakdown (Laing, 1960).

Even when circumstances are dire or unfair, it is still possible to find courage and create new ways of improving your fate, perhaps by finding new meaning in it.

SKILLS AND STRATEGIES

The existential approach is not in favour of techniques, as these hamper human interaction at a deep, direct and real level. The therapeutic encounter consists of an authentic human exchange, in dialogue. Skills are drawn largely from the method of phenomenology, the scientific study of human consciousness. But we might also use other philosophical methods, such as logic, dialectics, hermeneutics and maieutics. These will be described and illustrated by the example of a fictitious existential therapy client called Millie. Millie is a young woman in her early twenties who seeks therapy when she feels frozen and incapacitated by constant fear and anxiety, which is stopping her living a normal life.

When Millie arrives for therapy, she finds herself in a welcoming conversation with her existential therapist, who freely asks questions as well as answering them. The therapist may think of this conversational strategy as a Socratic dialogue, where the client is helped to pinpoint inner knowledge, she was not previously aware of. Millie will be encouraged to trace a deep personal sense of her predicament and articulate this. Millie's therapist will help her discover paradoxical realities that have confused her in her life. Millie will find her therapist very real in the dialogue. The relationship between them will be up for constant scrutiny. The dynamic between them is open to honest appraisal. This will help Millie to become more reflective about the way in which she responds and relates to the outside world and its challenges. Her way of being will never be pathologised. She will soon begin to feel freer in her descriptions of what matters to her, as her therapist becomes an ally. Together they will ponder how Millie makes sense of her world and how she can look at things from new angles. In this way she will soon start to see the conflicts and troubles she is dealing with as something temporary and situational rather than permanent. She sees it is possible to understand and confront reality.

Existential therapists encourage an attitude of openness and directness. Millie and her therapist speak in everyday language. She is not mollycoddled but will be treated with utmost respect and care. Millie will start focusing on strengths she had already developed and can learn to master further. She will soon get used to becoming tougher on herself than she has been in the past. Millie will then be more curious about her difficulties and where they come from, tracking the circumstances that created them. As the situation is elucidated, Millie will gain strength and take courage in being able to understand things better. She can begin to take charge of the process and be in the world in a much more determined way. She will get continuous feedback from her therapist when she forgets to notice her own progress. She will get bolder at experimenting. She will recognise what gives her safety and comfort in unfamiliar situations and build confidence that she can follow her own purpose and direction. She will learn to move forward, as if she is learning to ride a bike by keeping her eyes on where she is going, to stay in tune with the forces of gravity.

In line with phenomenological principles, Millie's therapist will help her to make explicit her assumptions about the world. She will get to know her values and beliefs, until a clear worldview emerges. Sometimes the therapist will help her confront contradictions. At other times the therapist might point to consequences or implications of her beliefs or ideas. In this way Millie may discover that she is much more judgemental of other people and herself than she realised. She will find that this tendency to dismiss herself and others is part of what gets her into trouble and confusion. Initially the therapist will just stay with Millie's usual mode of being, but soon will challenge it and invite Millie to experiment with new ways of being. They will speak about her past, her present and her future. They will explore her relationship to herself in her inner world. They will examine how she is with others, and how she is when alone. In this process she will come to know herself from many different angles. She will remember more and more about the talents and abilities she has hidden away and that she was afraid of developing.

Her existential therapist will not tell her how to be but will draw her out of hiding. Her therapist will help her look at problems in a brave and creative manner. Millie will start to unfold and care for herself better.

She will discover ways in which she has constricted her world or over-stretched herself. She will reclaim her freedom. She will gain trust in the world around her as she becomes more confident. She will see new opportunities. Her therapist will facilitate this journey of discovery until Millie takes the lead.

The existential therapist keeps track of Millie's state of mind, following her moods and attitudes, feelings and intuitions to their source, till a deeply felt sense of what truly matters emerges.

The therapist is personal, direct, gentle and respectful, though sometimes also quite questioning or challenging. They will face fears and terrors and they will laugh together. The therapy is a collaborative process, where Millie learns to be alive in a more open, trusting and aware manner. Her vitality is encouraged and stimulated. Millie becomes inspired by the idea of finding new purpose in her life.

Millie learns that her troubles and doubts do not define her but are part of life. She becomes more resilient and more resolute in facing up to dangers and changes. She accepts the limits of life and does not expect herself to become perfect. She now feels able to face new difficulties in her life as her mother's decline requires her to look after mum. This time when she feels anxious about this, she welcomes the feeling as proof that she is readying herself for a new challenge and a new phase of her life.

RESEARCH

There is still not too much outcome research in existential therapy because such research is generally based on the medical model, which seeks symptom relief. There is, however, a growing body of qualitative research carried out by the many doctoral counselling psychology and existential psychotherapy students and their tutors, who use phenomenological and existential methods to investigate various human issues (e.g., Deurzen, 2014; Milton, 2010; Vos, 2019; Willig, 2001). There is also research that deals with existential concerns, showing these to be at the core of the therapeutic change process:

- Yalom (1970), in his work with groups, found existential factors to be vital to client change.
- Much of the research on person-centred therapy is relevant to existential therapy, especially where it demonstrates the importance of genuineness or authenticity on the part of the therapist (Cooper, 2016).
- Bergin and Garfield (1994) recognised a number of existential factors as determining positive outcome in psychotherapy.
- Rennie's (1992) qualitative research shows the importance of a number of existential factors.
- There is much research evidence for the importance of meaning creation in the successful processing of traumatic events (Batthyany and Russo-Netzer, 2014; Clarke, 1989).
- Recent research in positive psychology demonstrates the importance of such existential factors as authenticity (Seligman, 2002) and meaning (Baumeister, 1991).
- Some research on outcome has now been done in existential therapy and is looking promising in terms of its effectiveness and relevance (Rayner and Vitali, 2016, 2018; Vos, 2019; Vos, Craig and Cooper, 2015).

REFERENCES

Baumeister, R.F. (1991) *Meanings of Life*. New York: Guilford Press.
Batthyani, A. and Russo-Netzer, P. (2014) *Meaning in Positive and Existential Psychology*. New York: Springer.
Bergin, A. and Garfield, S. (Eds) (1994) *Handbook of Psychotherapy and Behavior Change* (4th ed.). New York: Wiley.
Bugental, J.F.T. (1981) *The Search for Authenticity*. New York: Irvington.
Clarke, K.M. (1989) Creation of meaning: an emotional processing task in psychotherapy. *Psychotherapy*, 26: 139–148.
Cohn, H. (1997) *Existential Thought and Therapeutic Practice*. London: Sage.

(Continued)

(Continued)

Cooper, M. (2016) *Existential Therapies* (2nd ed.). London: Sage.
Deurzen, E. van (2009) *Psychotherapy and the Quest for Happiness*. London: Sage.
Deurzen, E. van (2010) *Everyday Mysteries: Handbook of Existential Psychotherapy* (2nd ed.). London: Routledge.
Deurzen, E. van (2012) *Existential Counselling and Psychotherapy in Practice* (3rd ed.). London: Sage.
Deurzen E. van (2014) Structural Existential Analysis (SEA): a phenomenological research method for counselling psychology. *Counselling Psychology Review*, 29(2): 70–83.
Deurzen, E. van (2015) *Paradox and Passion in Psychotherapy* (2nd ed.). Chichester: Wiley.
Deurzen, E. van (2021) *Rising from Existential Crisis: Living Beyond Calamity*. Monmouth: PCCS Books.
Deurzen, E. van and Adams, M. (2016) *Skills in Existential Counselling and Psychotherapy* (2nd ed.). London: Sage.
Deurzen, E. van and Arnold-Baker, C. (2018) *Existential Therapy: Distinctive Features*. London: Routledge.
Deurzen, E. van, with Craig, E., Schneider, K., Längle, A., Tantam, D. and du Plock, S. (2019) *Wiley World Handbook for Existential Therapy*. London: Wiley.
Frankl, V.E. (1964 [1946]) *Man's Search for Meaning*. London: Hodder and Stoughton.
Laing, R.D. (1960) *The Divided Self*. London: Tavistock.
Längle, S. and Wurm C. (Eds) (2016) *Living Your Own Life: Existential Analysis in Action*. London: Karnac.
Mahrer, A.R. (1996) *The Complete Guide to Experiential Psychotherapy*. New York: Wiley.
May, R. (1969) *Love and Will*. New York: W.W. Norton.
May, R., Angel, E. and Ellenberger, H.F. (1958) *Existence*. New York: Basic Books.
Milton, M. (2010) *Therapy and Beyond: Counselling Psychology Contributions to Therapeutic and Social Issues*. Chichester: Wiley-Blackwell.
Rayner, M. and Vitali, D. (2016) Short term existential psychotherapy in primary care: a quantitative report. *Journal of Humanistic Psychology*, 56(4): 357–372.
Rayner, M. and Vitali, D. (2018) Existential experimentation: structure and principles for a short-term psychological therapy. *Journal of Humanistic Psychology*, 58(2): 194–213.
Rennie, D.L. (1992) Qualitative analysis of the client's experience of psychotherapy: the unfolding of reflexivity. In S. Toukmanian and D.L. Rennie (Eds), *Psychotherapy Process Research: Paradigmatic and Narrative Approaches*. Newbury Park, CA: Sage.
Sartre, J.-P. (1956 [1943]) *Being and Nothingness: An Essay on Phenomenological Ontology*. Trans. H. Barnes. New York: Philosophical Library.
Schneider, K.J. and Krug, O.T. (2017) *Existential-Humanistic Therapy* (2nd ed.). Washington, DC: American Psychological Association.
Seligman, M.E.P. (2002) *Authentic Happiness*. New York: Free.
Spinelli, E. (2014) *Practising Existential Psychotherapy: The Relational World* (2nd ed.). London: Sage.
Tillich, P. (1952) *The Courage To Be*. New Haven, CT: Yale University Press.
Vos, J. (2019) A review of research on existential-phenomenological therapies. In E. van Deurzen, with E. Craig, K. Schneider, A. Längle, D. Tantam and S. du Plock, *Wiley World Handbook of Existential Therapy*. London: Wiley.
Vos, J., Craig, M. and Cooper, M. (2015) Existential therapies: a meta-analysis of their effects on psychological outcomes. *Journal of Consulting and Clinical Psychology*, 83(1): 115–128.
Willig, C. (2001) *Introducing Qualitative Research in Psychology: Adventures in Theory and Method*. Buckingham: Open University Press.
Yalom, I.D. (1970) *The Theory and Practice of Group Psychotherapy*. New York: Basic Books.
Yalom, I.D. (1980) *Existential Psychotherapy*. New York: Basic Books.

RECOMMENDED READING

Deurzen, E. van and Adams, M. (2016) *Skills in Existential Counselling and Psychotherapy* (2nd ed.). London: Sage.

This is one of the most comprehensive, easy-to-follow manuals for existential-phenomenological therapy, which is practice-based and yet firmly rooted in philosophy.

Cooper, M. (2016) *Existential Therapies* (2nd ed.). London: Sage.

This book provides an overview of all the different forms of existential therapy and gives a good sense of how existential therapy is different from any other form of psychotherapy.

Yalom, I.D. (1980) *Existential Psychotherapy*. New York: Basic Books.

This is one of the best-known books on existential psychotherapy and is regarded as a classic on existential/humanistic psychotherapy.

5.11 FEMINIST THERAPY

LIZ BALLINGER

OVERVIEW AND KEY POINTS

This chapter describes the emergence of feminist therapy out of the Women's Liberation Movement of the 1960s. Its growth and development and wider influence on therapeutic practice are outlined. While its divergent nature is highlighted, its broad tenets and therapeutic strategies and skills are summarised. Its current research profile is sketched and potentially problematised.

- Feminist therapy provides a radical critique of the power imbalance and pathologisation that characterises orthodox therapeutic approaches.
- 'The personal is political' reflects its emphasis on the all-encompassing role of power structures within society in shaping lives and creating distress.
- The central aims of feminist therapy are the empowerment of clients and both personal and social change.
- The increasing call for evidence-based practice provides a challenge to its future development.

BRIEF HISTORY

The roots of feminist therapy lie predominantly within Europe and the United States and the emergence of so-called second-wave feminism of the 1960s. This movement identified and challenged gender-based inequality across a wide range of fronts. Its clarion call 'the personal is political' reflected its emphasis on patriarchy's all-pervasive impact on women's lives. In the therapy world, dissatisfaction with the sexist and misogynistic nature of traditional psychotherapeutic theories and practices was leading a number of practitioners to turn to humanistic approaches. Practitioners also became involved in the feminist consciousness-raising groups of the second wave. This involvement is argued to have been key to the emergence of a distinctive feminist approach to therapy from the late 1960s onwards.

While the term 'feminist therapy' is used here and elsewhere, it does not imply a single, unified therapeutic approach. The development of feminist counselling has been characterised by diversity and divergence. From the outset it operated as a grassroots movement, developing outside an organisational structure, with ideas and practice shared and developed within interactive networks of interested individuals. Such individuals were drawn from a range of theoretical backgrounds, often looking for ways to integrate feminist ideas into their existing practice.

The result has been the development of a range of viewpoints and practices both nationally and internationally. While such diversity makes it difficult to generalise, some features of its overall development can be identified. As already mentioned, many therapists, in rejecting psychoanalysis, had turned towards humanistic approaches as a more appropriate way to serve the needs of women. In America, feminist empowerment models became particularly popular, often integrating understandings and techniques from a range of approaches to help facilitate change (e.g., cognitive behavioural therapy (CBT), gestalt, psychodrama, assertiveness training). A relational-cultural school also gained ground in the US. Influenced by psychodynamic understandings, it emphasises the importance of the mother–daughter bond in women's development and the centrality of connectivity to wellbeing (Jordan, 2017). In Britain, a feminist object relations model gained a foothold, similarly focusing on the importance of the unconscious and the mother–daughter relationship in female development (Eichenbaum and Orbach, 1982, 1983, 1987). Its growing influence was both reflected and rooted in its choice as the underpinning model for England's first women's therapy centre, opened in London in 1976.

A number of other developments of note can be identified. From the mid-1980s, in reaction to the perceived devaluing of 'feminine' attributes, some therapists began to develop feminist approaches to therapy based on the valuing of such feminine qualities, values and priorities (e.g., Chaplin's (1988) Rhythm model). In parallel, the diversity-awareness of third wave feminism led other feminist therapists to stress the importance of adopting an intersectional viewpoint (i.e., understanding women not simply as products of generic patriarchy but of differing cultural, social and economic contexts). Concurrently, patriarchy's destructive effect on both sexes was being acknowledged, leading some to argue the relevance of feminist therapy for men (e.g., Mintz and Tager, 2013).

The twenty-first century ushered in further change. Developments include: the incorporation of the concept of psychological colonisation; the greater recognition of the importance of the spiritual dimension; the adoption of new technologies and settings for feminist practice; and international collaboration between therapists. As feminist therapy has further developed, it has come to identify with the wider empowerment of disenfranchised and marginalised groups across society. In addition, although not without dissent, there has been an increasing identification with an inclusive definition of gender. Brown (2018: 139) points to the 'growing number of transgender and gender-queer-identified feminist therapists' as evidence for this trend.

Feminist therapy has now evolved into a 'sophisticated postmodern, liberatory, technically integrative model of practice that uses the analysis of gender, social location and power as a primary strategy for comprehending human difficulties' (Brown, 2018: 4). Feminist principles have become integrated into the practice of therapists working across a range of theoretical perspectives, with diverse client groups and in a range of settings. Its influence is reflected in the way that a number of its practices have become the norm in general practice.

At the same time, challenges remain. Worldwide, there continues to be a lack of access to training or means of becoming accredited as a feminist practitioner. The contemporary influence of feminist therapy can be overstated. In Britain, feminist practitioners have pointed to the lack of prominence given to feminist thinking in dialogue within the counselling community (Crozier et al., 2016). While the US remains active in the development of feminist thinking and practice, Brown (2018: 136) points to how 'some texts about psychotherapy and counselling still give the topic short shrift'.

BASIC ASSUMPTIONS

Remer and Hahn Oh (2013) identify a number of assumptions that underpin Empowerment Feminist Therapy but can be extended to most contemporary feminist therapeutic approaches.

1. Women's problems are rooted in living in sexist societies that devalue them, deny them resources and discriminate against them. Such oppression is institutionalised throughout society, in 'families, religion, education, recreation, the workplace, and laws' (Worell and Remer, 2003: 65).
2. Individual lives are negatively impacted by the interaction of a range of societal oppressions, such as racism, classism, sexism, ageism, ableism and heterosexism.

3. Because oppression negatively impacts on the mental health of individuals, social change is crucial to the promotion of mental wellbeing.
4. Mental health issues are predominantly the product of the external context rather than individual pathology. Likewise, the dominant culture defines both what is normal (healthy) and not normal (illness).
5. Individuals cannot be understood outside their societal context. The cultural diversity of values and perspectives needs to be both understood and respected.

ORIGIN AND MAINTENANCE OF PROBLEMS

Traditional counselling approaches start from the premise that problems originate in the individual in, for instance, their irrational thoughts or intrapsychic conflicts. In feminist therapy the starting point for both the origin of problems and their maintenance is the societal context. Distress is seen as a product of patriarchal society rather than of individual pathology, with personal experience understood as the 'lived version of political reality' (Brown, 1994: 50).

Discrimination and oppression in wider society harm mental health and wellbeing. The greater prevalence of a range of mental health issues, such as depression, disordered eating and anxiety, in women is seen as the result of gendered and other oppressions.

As Brown (2018: 44) argues, 'patriarchal systems surrounding most human life intentionally and unintentionally systematically and structurally disempower people'. The disempowerment process is both external and internal. Psychological colonisation, a process akin to Bourdieu's symbolic violence, explains how oppressed people self-objectify and self-oppress by introjecting patriarchal norms and beliefs. Brown (2018) talks of the production of a resulting 'trance of powerlessness', cultural and personal. Feminist object relations theory points to gendered psychological development rooted in early object-relational and family patterns. Eisenbaum and Orbach (1982: 43), for example, emphasise the role of the mother–daughter relationship in perpetuating women's 'cycle of deprivation' (i.e., the way a 'girl is brought up to a life directed towards caring for others'). Socialisation into gender roles is continued within wider societal systems, such as education and the media. The origin and perpetuation of 'irrational thoughts or intrapsychic conflicts' needs to be understood within this context rather than individual pathology.

THEORY OF CHANGE

Feminist therapy concerns change rather than adjustment, growth and development rather than symptom reduction and retrenchment. The aim of therapy is to empower clients to make positive changes in their world, not to find ways of better fitting into a society that harms them. Such empowerment entails the 'liberation from internalized forms of oppression so as to become powerful in confronting external obstacles' (Brown, 2018: 38). The focus, therefore, is both personal and social transformation.

A feminist analysis of society informs practice, with an emphasis placed on the central role played by society in shaping psychological wellbeing. Helping clients understand their issues in the context of their societal origin is thus key to individual empowerment. The aim of such consciousness raising is to empower clients to make positive changes in their world. Client strengths, achievements and potential are emphasised rather than client weaknesses or deficits. The ability to accord care and respect to self as well as to be instrumental in enacting change is recognised and valorised. The role of power in diagnosis is highlighted and orthodox diagnosis problematised as oppressive due to its focus on individual pathology.

SKILLS AND STRATEGIES

The difficulty in picking out common skills and strategies within feminist practice emanates from a number of sources. Feminist therapy is characterised by its philosophical foundations rather than its techniques. Its practitioners, similarly, are characterised by their feminist viewpoints, rather than the ways they translate these into practice. However, a number of research studies have shone light on the commonalities in the practice of feminist practitioners. Hill and Balou (1998) identified five 'consensually developed feminist principles', which they used as the basis of a survey into how feminist therapists translated principles into practice. This work, along with other research studies (e.g., Israeli and Santor, 2000; McLeod, 1994; Rader and Gilbert, 2005) help to construct a picture of common features of practice 'on the ground'.

1. AN EGALITARIAN RELATIONSHIP

The focus is on serving a client rather than treating a patient. While acknowledging the power invested in the therapist's role, the aim is one of equality between therapist and client. The feminist counsellors in McLeod's (1994) study were aware of the potential for women's previous experience of therapeutic care to be subordinating and stigmatising. Addressing power differentials was a major component of feminist practice across studies. Attempts to address power imbalances included openness about therapeutic processes and procedures, the use of jargon-free language and therapist transparency. Cooperative goal-setting and ongoing negotiation are seen as key, as is the valuing of client viewpoints, concerns and agency. Strategies focus on letting go of ownership of the norms, values and understandings that underpin therapy. Clients are encouraged to identify and own their strengths. Selective self-disclosure may be used by the therapist as a means of equalising power. Transparency, information-giving, negotiation and collaboration are key strategies throughout.

2. A FOCUS ON THE SOCIOCULTURAL BASIS OF DISTRESS

A feminist analysis of society informs practice, with an emphasis placed on the central role played by society in shaping psychological wellbeing. Distress is seen as a product of patriarchal society rather than of individual pathology, with personal experience understood as the 'lived version of political reality' (Brown, 1994: 50). Foregrounding the corrosive effects of powerlessness, feminist therapy focuses on how to disrupt the 'trance of powerlessness' and bring power to the powerless. *Gender-role analysis* involves inviting clients to explore the gender-related messages they grew up with and their continuing impact on their thoughts, feelings and behaviour. *Power analysis* involves an exploration of clients' understanding of and relationship with power, their own and others. Therapists might ask direct questions about client experiences and/or filter client self-statements through these lenses (Hill and Balou, 1998). Such interventions illustrate the role of *psychoeducation* in feminist practice.

This *consciousness-raising process* is designed to empower clients by helping them understand the source of their distress and identify areas for change. Pathology is redefined to include wider environmental causes. Rather than signifying 'illness', symptoms are reframed as potentially creative ways of coping with socially induced damage.

3. VALUING WOMEN'S EXPERIENCES

While feminist therapy is now not exclusively confined to working with women, its aim remains to provide an experience antithetical to societal norms by normalising and valuing clients' experiences rather than problematising and/or devaluing them. Clients' experiences are centrally placed rather than side-lined. Empathy and respect for clients' priorities, frames of reference and lived experience is fundamental. Listening to and facilitating clients in the telling of their stories is a central activity in feminist therapy. Clients in McLeod's (1994) study spoke positively of their experience of freedom of expression, validation of their emotional needs and capabilities, the opportunity to concentrate on their own needs and feeling cared for.

4. AN INTEGRATED ANALYSIS OF OPPRESSION

The studies of the 1990s (e.g., Hill and Balou, 1998; McLeod, 1994) showed a growing recognition by therapists of the importance of other sources of oppression in women's lives, and the importance of sensitivity to them. However, it is fair to say that in the last two decades an intersectional viewpoint has become more fully integrated into the understanding of oppression and the way it is worked with. 'The personal is political' has been expanded to embrace all aspects of social identity. This extends to therapists, entailing a self-awareness that embraces an understanding of their own intersectional identities, their mixed experiences of power and privilege, and how their identities might interact with those of their clients within the therapeutic process. Social identities analysis is increasingly seen as an important complement to gender role and power analyses in feminist practice.

5. THE GOAL OF CREATING SOCIAL CHANGE

A key goal of therapy is the empowerment of clients to enact change in their lives across the personal, interpersonal and social realms. The therapist's role is to enable clients to gain the skills, knowledge and awareness to address their life issues. Meaningful change is believed to be facilitated by enabling clients to apply feminist lenses to a reflection on their lives and present experiencing, and to utilise their developed understanding to help identify meaningful goals. As mentioned earlier, therapists will call on a range of techniques to support client change, including some that other approaches might regard as outside the therapist role (e.g., assertiveness training, advocacy).

CASE STUDY

Sally is a young, white care home worker from a working-class background who has been diagnosed as suffering from depression and prescribed antidepressant medicine by her doctor. She has been encouraged by her female partner to try counselling offered at a local women's centre. She has been referred to work with Amina, a middle-aged, middle-class British Asian therapist.

Amina begins by explaining to Sally what feminist therapy entails and their mutual roles within it. She introduces herself, talks about her personal values and her recognition of the differences between them. She invites Sally to decide whether she wants to move forward with the therapy. Sally expresses a sense of ambivalence, that she's not sure that talking can help anything but is prepared to give it a try. Amina re-emphasises the collaborative nature of feminist therapy and reviewing processes.

In the early stages, Amina is focused on helping Sally to tell her story on her own terms and giving time to construct mutually agreed goals. Sally's understandings of the external context for her distress focus on the demanding nature of her work and its long hours. Her partner's job is also a demanding one; she is the leading wage earner. Sally thinks it is important to prioritise her partner's needs and wellbeing. These are all things she regards as unchangeable and she feels drained and overwhelmed. At this time her goal is just to 'feel better'. Amina shares her sense of respect for the strength and abilities Sally displays in meeting the range and weight of demands on her, and how her depressive symptoms might be her body's way of saying 'take time out'.

As the work progresses, Amina encourages Sally to explore her experiences and distress in the light of feminist understandings. She introduces literature connecting the low pay and the status of care work with its devaluation as unskilled 'women's work'. This chimes with Sally's experience. Her partner is a school teacher and Sally carries a sense of inferiority in the relationship based on her lower status work and lower pay. She starts to link her low self-esteem with her low social status, her sense of personal powerlessness with her lack of social power. She starts to understand her distress as rooted both within her gender and class-based experiences. Part of this process entails the exploration of how Sally and Amina's identities converge and diverge, helping Sally to safely access her feelings and thoughts around the impact of both privilege and oppression in her relationships with others and feelings about herself.

In further sessions, with Amina's encouragement, Sally shifts her focus to her upbringing. She explores how her parents treated her differently from her brothers, how at school she often felt ignored and invisible. Amina encourages her to explore the ongoing power of these early experiences. This feeds into an exploration of what Sally might want and feel able to change and the resources she might call on. These resources include her personal strengths, which Amina continues to encourage her to identify.

In the final sessions, the focus is constructing concrete goals. Sally has a more highly developed sense of her own strengths and entitlements and of the changes that she can make to enhance her wellbeing. Her first priority is self-care, and she plans a renegotiation of the sharing of housework. She also plans to take up assertiveness training offered at the centre. Her long-term aim is to return to education to enhance her career opportunities, either inside or outside the care sector.

RESEARCH

There is limited specific evidence demonstrating feminist therapy's effectiveness, making it vulnerable in the new evidence-based practice climate. The nature and goals of feminist therapy are in many ways opposed to the production of statistical evidence of its effectiveness, and many feminist therapists are reluctant to 'buy into' the assumptions underpinning such research. Moreover, any attempts to so engage are hampered by feminist therapy's diverse composition, as well as lack of funding and opportunity (Brown, 2018).

Feminists argue generally that a multiplicity of evidence should be utilised in any assessment of effectiveness. The bulk of support for its effectiveness comes from common factors literature, which is based on a wide range of evidence. Feminist therapy's focus on empowerment and the quality of the therapeutic relationship is consistently identified with positive outcomes in psychotherapy research. Collaborative goal-setting, tailoring the therapy to the client, and the client's active engagement in the process, have been similarly linked to positive outcome (Norcross, 2011). While these are all positive indications of feminist therapy's worth, further research is needed to strengthen its position.

REFERENCES

Brown, L.S. (1994) *Subversive Dialogues*. New York: Basic Books.
Brown, L.S. (2018) *Feminist Therapy* (2nd ed.). Washington DC: American Psychological Association.
Chaplin, J. (1988) *Feminist Counselling in Action*. London: Sage.
Crozier, J., Morris-Roberts, K., O'Neill, P. and Wright, J. (2016) Feminist ideas and counselling. *Therapy Today*, 27(1). Available online at www.bacp.co.uk/bacp-journals/therapy-today/2016/february-2016/ (accessed 21 January 2022).
Eichenbaum, L. and Orbach, S. (1982) Outside In … Inside Out. *Women's Psychology: A Feminist Psychoanalytic Approach*. Harmondsworth: Pelican.
Eichenbaum, L. and Orbach, S. (1983) *What Do Women Want?* London: Fontana.
Eichenbaum, L. and Orbach, S. (1987) *Bittersweet*. London: Century Press.
Hill, M. and Balou, M. (1998) Making therapy feminist: a practice survey. *Women & Therapy*, 21(2), 1–16.
Israeli, A.L. and Santor, D.A. (2000) Reviewing effective components of feminist therapy. *Counselling Psychology Quarterly*, 13(3), 233–247.
Jordan, J.V. (2017) *Relational-Cultural Therapy* (2nd ed.). Washington, DC: American Psychological Association.
McLeod, E. (1994) *Women's Experience of Feminist Therapy and Counselling*. Buckingham: Open University Press.
Mintz, L.B. and Tager, D. (2013) Feminist therapy with male clients: empowering men to be their whole selves. In C.Z. Enns and E.N. Williams (Eds), *The Oxford Handbook of Feminist Multicultural Counselling Psychology* (pp. 322–338). New York: Oxford University Press.
Norcross, J.C. (Ed.) (2011) *Psychotherapy Relationships that Work: Evidence-based Responsiveness* (2nd ed.). New York: Oxford University Press.
Rader, J. and Gilbert, L.A. (2005) The egalitarian relationship in feminist practice. *Psychology of Women Quarterly*, 29, 427–435.
Remer, P.A. and Hahn Oh, K. (2013) Feminist therapy in counselling psychology. In C.Z. Enns and E.N. Williams (Eds), *The Oxford Handbook of Feminist Multicultural Counselling Psychology* (pp. 304–321). New York: Oxford University Press.
Worell, J. and Remer, P. (2003) *Feminist Perspectives in Therapy: Empowering Diverse Women* (2nd ed.). Hoboken, NJ: John Wiley and Sons.

> **RECOMMENDED READING**
>
> Evans, K.M., Kincade, A.E. and Seem, S.R. (2011) *Introduction to Feminist Therapy: Strategies for Social and Individual Change*. Thousand Oaks, CA: Sage.
>
> This is an accessible introduction to feminist therapy, incorporating useful discussion of specific skills and techniques.
>
> Brown, L.S. (2018) *Feminist Therapy* (2nd ed.). Washington, DC: American Psychological Association.
>
> This is an authoritative, up-to-date account of feminist therapy by one of its leading figures.
>
> McLeod, E. (1994) *Women's Experience of Feminist Therapy and Counselling*. Buckingham: Open University Press.
>
> Although somewhat dated, this is a British study of the experience of feminist therapy from both the therapist and client viewpoint, providing analysis and critique of continuing relevance.

5.12 GESTALT THERAPY

FAISAL MAHMOOD AND EMMA FLAX

OVERVIEW AND KEY POINTS

Gestalt therapy theory rests upon an understanding that a person and their world are inseparable; that we constantly impact and are impacted by our environment. We do not exist intra-dependently or independently to our situations/field. Gestalt therapy emphasises awareness of our holistic lived experience in the here-and-now, including awareness of feelings, thoughts, sensations, behaviours, contacting styles, past experiences and future anticipations. The therapeutic relationship, which is dialogic in stance, is understood as fundamental to the therapeutic work. Gestalt therapists aim to offer dialogue, including creative experiments to enhance their clients' awareness and choice-fullness. Through therapy, clients are supported to become more aware of their intra-personal and inter-personal relational dynamics, their fixed gestalts and their choices in order to creatively move towards a position of responsibility – *response-ability/ability to respond*.

Gestalt therapy:

- is fundamentally a field theory approach and rests upon a holistic view of humans – seeing people and the world as inseparable entities
- is a humanistic-existential and phenomenological approach
- focuses on here-and-now embodied lived experiences – the past and the future are explored within the present context
- suggests that we are constantly changing and evolving – self is not a fixed entity, it is a verb, not a noun
- is interested in clients' contacting styles – how people relate to themselves, others (including the therapist) and their world
- incorporates experiments to enhance clients' awareness and to support integration of different experiences and choices.

BRIEF HISTORY

Fredrick (Fritz) Perls (1893–1970), a trained psychoanalyst and Neuropsychiatrist, and the psychologist Laura Perls (1905–1990) are the primary co-founders of Gestalt therapy. They were responsible for setting up the first training institute for Gestalt, The New York Institute for Gestalt Therapy, in the 1950s. They worked alongside the first generation of Gestaltists, including Paul Goodman, Ralph Hefferline, Isadore From, Elliot Shapiro, Richard Kitzler and Paul Weisz, all of whom contributed to the birth and further development of Gestalt therapy theory.

Recognising the input from a variety of influences, it is easy to understand how Gestalt therapy, from its outset, grew from the alchemic fusion of a range of theories and sources of inspiration, including:

> *Gestalt Psychology* from which many of the key Gestalt therapy concepts are borrowed, such as 'figure and ground', 'parts and whole', 'unfinished business', etc. Key influencing psychologists were Max Wertheimer, Kurt Koffka and Wolfgang Kohler.
> *Existentialism*, where the work of Martin Buber (1878–1965), an existential philosopher, particularly influenced the birth of Gestalt therapy. Buber's (1970) concept of 'I and thou' holds the central therapeutic relational position in Gestalt therapy.
> *Psychodrama*, pioneered by Jacob Moreno (1889–1974), had a profound influence on Fritz Perls, who incorporated Moreno's practice of inviting clients to enact their histories and associated challenges in public demonstrations of his 'hot-seat technique'.
> *Zen Buddhism and other Eastern Religions*, which Fritz became interested in through his friend Paul Weisz, and which he later studied intensively in Japan, shaped Gestalt therapy from a philosophical rather than religious perspective. Its influence can be seen through Gestalt's central emphasis on holistic awareness.

While Gestalt therapy remains true to its core origins, like any therapy theory it has also grown and evolved over time. More recent history has seen Gestalt therapy theory integrate contemporary developments and theories from a range of sources, for example:

> *Developmental Theory*, where particularly the work of Daniel Stern on child development and infant perception has had a huge impact on Gestalt training and practice. Stern (2004) offers theory on the stages of child development, which effortlessly fits with Gestalt thinking.
> *Attachment Theory*, formulated by John Bowlby, has also been integrated into much Gestalt training and practice. Bowlby's (2005) understanding of contact between a baby and mother and of attachment styles overlaps closely with the Gestalt understanding of contact and of creative adjustments.

In more recent years, there has been a growing interest in understanding trauma from a Gestalt perspective (Taylor, 2021), in diversity (Jacobs, 2014; Mahmood, 2020), organisational development (Chidac, 2018), and on working with a somatic focus (Spagnuollo Lobb, 2015).

BASIC ASSUMPTIONS

Field theory – inseparability of person and world. One of the key tenets of Gestalt therapy is that the person and person's world/situation are inseparable, mutually and constantly impacting each other such that any psychological distress or disorder belongs to this shared interaction.

Figure and ground. Figure is what we notice or become aware of, and every figure is situated in its ground (context, situation, environment, history). Gestalt therapists are interested in what becomes a figure as well as the process of figure formation. We are interested in both the content of a session (a client's 'material' or 'story') as well as the process of how and what becomes 'storied'.

Organismic self-regulation and self-actualisation. Like other humanistic approaches, Gestalt believes in the innate tendencies of humans to self-regulate, self-actualise and grow (Ellis and Smith, 2017). In an ideal situation, we respond to our emerging needs, in the form of a figure, and once our needs are satisfactorily met they disappear in the background and we move to another need. For example, we become aware of our need for food, we eat, we feel satisfied, we stop eating, we move to another need. At times, this process of self-regulation gets disrupted in response to field conditions, and we develop alternative ways to meet our needs. These alternative ways (creative adjustments) can be useful on a short-term basis but once they become rigid habits (fixed gestalts), we begin to compromise on how freely and creatively we can make contact with others/environment, and impede our process of self-actualisation.

Here-and-now. Gestalt is interested in 'what is happening right now? How are you doing it?' instead of 'why did you do that?' (Yontef, 1993: 7). Gestalt focuses on the in-between of the therapist and the client. What emerges in this co-created experience in the here-and-now leads to greater awareness about the client's (and therapist's) contacting styles, phenomenal field, phenomenological experiences and relational patterns (transference). The focus on the here-and-now should not be confused with the idea that Gestalt therapists are not/less interested in the past or future. Our position is that the past and the future are present in the thick walls of the present moment (Merleau-Ponty, 1962). We are interested in the past that is present in the present and the past that is present in the present *is* the present, not the past.

Awareness. Awareness in Gestalt is more than a cognitive technique of present-centredness and is not the same thing as mindfulness. Awareness requires a holistic response to our total situation (Wollants, 2012) and involves becoming aware of our sensation, feelings, thoughts and behaviour as we pay attention to our contact with others/environment.

Contact. One of the central tenets of Gestalt therapy, contact, refers to our ways of relating, meeting and interacting with other people and our situations. Perls, Hefferline and Goodman (1951: 131) wrote that 'every healthy contact involves awareness (perceptual figure/ground) and excitement (increased energy mobilization)'. Contact and awareness are interrelated. As such, we are in contact with many things but we only become aware of some of our contacting. 'Contact as such is possible without awareness, but for awareness contact is indispensable. The crucial question is: with what is one in contact?' (Perls et al., 1951: viii).

Dialogue. Hycner and Jacobs (1995: xi) describe the dialogical relationships as '…an attitude of genuinely feeling/sensing/experiencing the other person as *a person* (not an object or part-object), and a willingness to deeply "hear" the other person's experience without prejudgement. Furthermore, it is the willingness to "hear" what is not being spoken, and to "see" what is not visible'. Dialogic relating is more than empathy. Empathy is a client-centred and unidirectional therapeutic process in order to 'know' what is going on for the client in a specific situation. The dialogical relationship is a co-created relational encounter where the therapist is not only an observer of the client's story, but also surrenders to the process of meeting the client in the room. A good Gestalt therapist is usually bold, creative, direct, kind and willing to own their vulnerable parts in the service of the therapeutic encounter.

ORIGIN AND MAINTENANCE OF PROBLEMS

In Gestalt therapy, 'problems' cannot be located or understood intrapsychically. Instead, they are seen to reflect a disturbance of the 'total situation' (Wollants, 2012) which describes the reciprocal relations of a person and their environment.

Problems arise when there is a persistent disturbance or maladjustment in the situation which leads a person to limit their range of responses, becoming less fluid and spontaneous and instead more restricted and contorted. Often these problems arise in childhood, where, for example, a child may 'adjust' to an enduring lack of attuned care or love in their family, and the adjustment becomes the same adult's indiscriminate 'go to' contact style. These habitual, rigid patterns of relating were first described theoretically in Gestalt as 'interruptions to contact' and later 'modifications to contact' in order to reflect the creativity in these adjustment patterns.

Gestalt therapy identifies a number of mechanisms which mediate contact. Where they are used choicefully and pluralistically, they are understood to be part of healthy functioning. But where contact styles become less choiceful (without awareness), they are understood to be problematic:

- Introjection, which is likened to swallowing whole without chewing over. Children will often introject their parents' beliefs and opinions without question or reflection. Social norms can be swallowed whole without consideration.
- Projection, which is giving to another what belongs to oneself. Here, beliefs, qualities or aspects of a person's personality can be disowned and projected onto another.
- Retroflection, is a turning back on oneself. Here an impulse outwards (to shout out in anger, to coo with love) is modified and redirected inwards (critical self-talk, stroking ourselves with care).
- Confluence, which is a merging of and an inability to distinguish between self and other.
- Deflection, which is turning away from, for example feelings or information, rather than fully letting in.

THEORY OF CHANGE

When thinking around Gestalt's theory of change, we want to pull out three key facets. All three rest on the foundational belief in 'organismic self-regulation' (see key concepts) and a trust in the wisdom of the person (Perls, 1969).

PARADOXICAL THEORY OF CHANGE

> Change occurs when one becomes what he is, not when he tries to become what he is not. (Beisser, 1970: 88).

In Gestalt therapy, we understand that change will come about when 'what is' is fully accepted rather than through trying to be different. To this end, practitioners try to support awareness of 'the situation', inviting new perspectives and potentially increased choicefulness.

CHANGE THROUGH DIALOGUE

Many Gestalt therapists focus on the potential of dialogic relating (including presence, confirmation, inclusion and a surrender to the between) to support change (Yontef, 1993). This involves an appreciation of the ways in which a different relational context can change our perceptions; that we can hear/take in something different depending on who is saying it and how/where, etc. Working from a dialogic stance opens the possibility for a shift in perception around contact and the potential for change and a loosening of fixed gestalts.

CHANGE THROUGH EXPERIMENTATION

Gestalt therapists understand that change can also be supported through co-created creative experimenting, affording opportunities to 'try on' new ways of behaving or thinking which potentially allow for the germination of new creative adjustments and the loosening of fixed gestalts.

SKILLS AND STRATEGIES

The skills and strategies used in Gestalt therapy support the aim of increasing clients' awareness of themselves *in their situation* in order to facilitate and foster healthy organismic self-regulation. They are used within the crucible of a dialogic relationship. Gestalt therapists are looking to cultivate *holistic* awareness, and so the skills and strategies employed by them pay attention to sensation, thinking, feeling and behaviour, and do not value any of these more highly than the others.

PHENOMENOLOGICAL ENQUIRY

Gestalt therapy is rooted in existential-phenomenological philosophy, which means a concern with (1) staying with what is present, including how the past and the future manifest in the present (*existential*), and (2) the subjective experiencing of that present (*phenomenology*).

This translates into our therapeutic practice through the use of a phenomenological method of enquiry which aims to co-create greater awareness of the situation and how it is being experienced by both therapist and client. Phenomenological enquiry involves three main components (Spinelli, 2005):

- *Bracketing*, where the therapist will temporarily suspend their own assumptions and meaning-making so as to be as open as possible to the clients' subjective experience.
- *Describing*, where we are interested in the 'how' rather than the 'why', attending to and tracking what client and therapist sees, hears, senses, etc. without interpretation.
- *Horizontalism*, where the therapist treats all phenomena, or the absence of phenomena, non-hierarchically.

A DIALOGIC STANCE

A dialogic stance within the existential-phenomenological tradition means that, as therapists, we attune and respond to our own and our clients' subjective experiences in the 'here-and-now'. We avoid objectifying our clients, and hold an intention to remain open to genuinely experiencing the other person as a person and to hear the other person's experience without pre-judgement (Hycner and Jacobs, 1995).

Gestalt therapists develop their skill in this particular style of relating, fostering a capacity to shuttle between a more objective-leaning attitude (I–it relating) and an attitude which exalts mutual humanity and horizontalism (I–thou relating). I–it relating supports Gestalt therapists in clinical decision making, while I–thou relating supports Gestalt therapists in practicing: *presence*, fully bringing themselves to the therapeutic encounter; *inclusion*, entering the client's subjective world as fully as possible; and *confirmation*, acknowledging our client's whole being with a sense of equality, appreciation and respect (Yontef, 1993).

EXPERIMENTS

Gestalt is often thought of synonymously with bombastic demonstrations of the 'empty chair' technique made famous by Perls. In contrast, Gestalt therapists in current times place more of an emphasis on working collaboratively to devise and grade experiments which emerge from the ground of the situation and seek to raise awareness in a spirit of mutuality. Examples of experiments might be about exaggerating a gesture, finding a voice for a particular part of the body, using art, focusing on non-verbal communication, speaking 'as if' or using metaphors and images, etc. All experiments are carried out in the spirit of raising awareness. There is no such thing as a predetermined experiment or a predetermined outcome of an experiment in Gestalt, and as such there is also no such thing as a failed experiment in Gestalt therapy (Houston, 2003).

RESEARCH

There has been a growing interest in research among academics and practitioners over the past three decades or so, particularly in relation to the effectiveness of the Gestalt approach. The effectiveness of the Gestalt approach has been demonstrated in a number of studies. Strümpfel (2003) included 62 studies in their literature review, demonstrating good evidence for the effectiveness of Gestalt therapy.

Stevens et al. (2011) investigated Gestalt therapy treatment outcomes based on the CORE (Clinical Outcomes in Routine Evaluation) outcome measure, and demonstrated Gestalt therapy's effectiveness with results comparable to other modalities' improvements in a range of studies. Farahzadi and Masafi (2013) reported the effectiveness of Gestalt therapy when working with children with dysthymic disorders. Raffagnino (2019) conducted a systematic review of the empirical evidence of the effectiveness of the Gestalt approach and demonstrated efficacy of Gestalt therapy, particularly in a group therapy format when working with a range of mental health and relationship/interpersonal issues.

Elliott et al. (2021) undertook a meta-analysis of 91 studies, focusing on the efficacy of humanistic-experiential psychotherapies (emotion-focused therapy, Gestalt, person-centred therapy and psychodrama) and reported overall positive outcomes related to these approaches. They conclude that in certain situations, humanistic-experiential psychotherapies were more effective than cognitive-behaviour therapy, for example in working with relational issues, dealing with chronic health conditions, self-damaging behaviour and psychosis (Elliott et al., 2021).

CASE STUDY

Hadi, a 28-year old man originally from Somalia, presented with a history of anxiety and feeling 'burnt-out' from work. He was 14 when he moved to the UK with his family in order to live a 'better and safe life'. He experienced racism at school but did not report it, saying 'it wasn't a big deal' (deflection). He feels embarrassed when he is overheard speaking in Somali to his family, and feels very anxious in public, especially when not at work. Hadi works as a nurse in a stroke unit at his local hospital, where he is overworked and exhausted. He finds it hard to say 'no' to his bosses, who regularly ask him to work extra shifts to cover his colleagues' absences. In the therapy room, he agrees with everything I (FM) say (confluence) and often effusively expresses his gratitude and appreciation of me.

In response to his praise, one day I say 'Thank you for your appreciation. I know I am a good therapist, but I also do sometimes make mistakes and I have my own limitations. I notice that it seems important to you to say thank you and praise me. Do you know more about that?'

Hadi reflects that it is important to him that our relationship remains 'good' and that his praise is part of making sure I feel positively towards him. He goes on and uncovers his belief that when relationships turn negative, it is impossible to fix them. I reflect on this fear of permanent damage and he makes a link with his experiences of growing up in war-torn Somalia (field conditions), where damage felt permanent and it was impossible to get back to safety.

Thinking clinically, it's possible that Hadi's historic field conditions have impacted his contacting styles. That is, he may have introjected that it is safer to say yes to authority figures. In the past, this approach may have been

(Continued)

(Continued)

very effective for him to survive, but this fixed gestalt is not supporting him anymore and negatively impacts his potential to interact with others/environment in a creative and dynamic manner.

In another example, I invited him to play a Somali song (experiment) on his phone during the session and we both sat quietly and listened to the song. He cried most of this time and I was also moved to tears (dialogic stance). He had never listened to a Somali song in the UK (over 14 years) in the presence of another person.

Our work supported Hadi to be more aware of his contacting styles with himself and others, including me (therapist), and feel supported and grounded. This process supported him to continue to experiment in his life in and outside the therapy room and feel more choiceful in his responses. He learned he had the choice to say no to others and yes to his own needs!

REFERENCES

Beisser, A.R. (1970) The paradoxical theory of change. In J. Fagan and I.L. Shepherd (Eds), *Gestalt Therapy Now*. Harmondsworth: Penguin.

Bowlby, J. (2005) *A Secure Base: Clinical Applications of Attachment Theory*. Abingdon, UK: Routledge.

Buber, M. (1970) *I and Thou*. New York: Charles Scribner's.

Chidac, M. (2018) *Relational Organisational Gestalt: An Emergent Approach to Organisational Development*. Abingdon, UK: Routledge.

Elliott, R., Watson, J.C., Timulak, L. and Sharbanee, J. (2021) Research on humanistic-experiential psychotherapies: Updated review. In M. Barkham, W. Lutz, and L.G. Castonguay (Eds), *Bergin and Garfield's Handbook of Psychotherapy and Behavior Change* (7th ed.). New York: Wiley.

Ellis, M. and Smith, J. (2017) Gestalt therapy. In C. Feltham, T. Hanley and L.A. Winter (Eds), *The Sage Handbook of Counselling and Psychotherapy* (4th ed.). London: Sage.

Farahzadi, M. and Masafi, S. (2013) Effectiveness of gestalt and cognitive-behavioural play therapy in decreasing dysthymic disorder. *Procedia Social and Behavioral Sciences*, 84, 1642–1645.

Houston, G. (2003) *Brief Gestalt Therapy*. London: Sage.

Hycner, R.A. and Jacobs, L. (1995) *The Healing Relationship in Gestalt Therapy*. New York: Gestalt Journal Press.

Jacobs, L. (2014) Learning to love white shame and guilt: skills for working as a white therapist in a racially divided country. *International Journal of Psychoanalytic Self Psychology*, 9, 297–312.

Mahmood, F. (2020) 'Can I please have White skin too?' In Y. Ade-Serrano and O. Nkansa Dwamena (Eds), *Applied Psychology and Applied Professions Working with Ethnic Minorities*. Leicester: The British Psychological Society.

Merleau-Ponty, M. (1962) *Phenomenology of Perception*. Trans. C. Smith. London: Routledge & Kegan Paul.

Perls, F. (1969) *Gestalt Therapy Verbatim*. Boulder, CO: Real People Press.

Perls, F., Hefferline, R. and Goodman, P. (1951) *Gestalt Therapy: Excitement and Growth in the Human Personality*. New York: Julian.

Raffagnino, R. (2019) Gestalt therapy effectiveness: a systematic review of empirical evidence. *Open Journal of Social Sciences*, 7, 66–83.

Spagnuolo Lobb, M. (2015) The body as a 'Vehicle' of our being in the world: somatic experience in gestalt therapy. *British Gestalt Journal*, 24, 21–31.

Spinelli, E. (2005) *The Interpreted World: An Introduction to Phenomenological Psychology* (2nd ed.). London: Sage.

Stern, D.N. (2004) *The Present Moment: In Psychotherapy and Everyday Life*. New York: W.W. Norton.

Steven, C., Stringfellow, J., Wakelin, K. and Waring, J. (2011) The UK gestalt psychotherapy CORE research project: the findings. *The British Gestalt Journal*, 20(2), 22–27.

Strümpfel, U. (2003) What is the current state of research on Gestalt therapy? Overview: Findings of therapy process and evaluation research. *Gestalt Therapy*, 17(2), 48–68.

Taylor, M. (2021) *Deepening Trauma Practice: A Gestalt Approach to Ecology and Ethics*. London: Open University Press.

Wollants, G. (2012) *Gestalt Therapy: Therapy of the Situation*. London: Sage.

Yontef, G. (1993) *Awareness, Dialogue and Process*. Goulsboro, ME: The Gestalt Journal Press.

RECOMMENDED READING

Joyce, P. and Sills, C. (2018) *Skills in Gestalt Counselling and Psychotherapy* (4th ed.). London: Sage.

This is an accessible introductory book with good clinical examples.

Mann, D. (2021) *Gestalt Therapy: 100 Key Points and Techniques* (2nd ed.). Abingdon, UK: Routledge.

A very useful reference book, it includes 100 short chapters on a range of key concepts and techniques.

Mackewn, J. (1997) *Developing Gestalt Counselling*. London: Sage.

This is a good introduction to the key theoretical concepts and clinical practice applications.

5.13 GENDER, SEX AND RELATIONSHIP DIVERSITY THERAPY

DOMINIC DAVIES AND SILVA NEVES

OVERVIEW AND KEY POINTS

Previously, this model might have been called *Gay Affirmative Therapy*. Many readers will be more familiar with the acronym LGBT+ (lesbian, gay, bisexual and trans) applying to the group we describe. However, we prefer Gender, Sex and Relationship Diversity (GSRD) as a term that encompasses the increasing alphabet soup of LGBTIQQAA and extends it. GSRD encompasses the long-established although frequently demonised identities and practices of BDSM/Kink to the more emerging sexual identities of Digisexuality and includes a wide range of consensual and ethical forms of non-monogamous relationship styles. For a full description of the current iteration of GSRD check out: https://pinktherapy.org/GSRD_EN/

- GSRD therapy is an emerging pluralistic model of therapy that integrates core biopsychosocial research and theories about Gender, Sex and Relationship Diverse people.
- All therapists are likely to need additional training in GSRD therapy to work ethically and improve their clinical practice. Pink Therapy offers such specialist training at (www.pinktherapy.org)

- All the major UK mental health professional organisations now mandate additional training to eradicate the practice of conversion 'therapy' for sexuality and gender diverse people.
- GSRD therapy is rooted in social justice alongside Feminist and Black psychology.

BRIEF HISTORY

DD: When I compiled the first British textbook on working with lesbian, gay and bisexual clients in 1996, I never thought I'd contribute to creating a new therapeutic approach. In the first of what became the Pink Therapy trilogies, I shared Maylon's view:

> Gay affirmative psychotherapy is not an independent system of psychotherapy. Rather it represents a special range of knowledge which challenges the traditional view that homosexual desire and fixed homosexual orientations are pathological. Gay affirmative therapy uses traditional psychotherapeutic methods but proceeds from a non-traditional perspective. This approach regards homophobia as opposed to homosexuality, as a major pathological variable in the development of certain symptomatic conditions among gay men. (Maylon, 1982: 26, cited in Davies and Neal, 1996: 25)

But a great deal has happened over my 40 years as a therapist working with these populations. We would claim that working with Gender, Sex and Relationship Diverse (GSRD) clients is one of the most rapidly changing areas of psychology, with a plethora of research and literature on all aspects and identities in GSRD happening across the world.

In earlier editions of this *Handbook*, this chapter was placed in working with 'special populations', but the editors have moved the chapter to 'Theories and Approaches' this time around. We feel this coming of age is appropriate, although probably not without dissenters, who might argue that there is nothing unique or different about working with GSRD clients.

Of course, a therapist who practises cultural humility and engages their client at relational depth (Mearns and Cooper, 2017) may do good work with some GSRD clients. On the other hand, there is now a significant body of research into specific biopsychosocial aspects of each of those identities and groups that comprise GSRD. To be an effective therapist with most GSRD clients, one will need additional training. Furthermore, if you are practising in the UK, your professional membership body is likely to be a signatory to the *Memorandum of Understanding on Conversion Therapy version 2* (Pink Therapy, 2021), which states:

> 16 Those with a responsibility for training will work to ensure that training prepares therapists to have sufficient levels of cultural competence such that they can work effectively with gender and sexually diverse clients.
>
> 17 Training organisations are advised to refer to the latest guidelines from professional associations who are signatory organisations on working with gender and sexually diverse clients when reviewing their curriculum on equality and diversity issues.

Since the BACP [British Association of Counselling and Psychotherapy] (2018), the BPS [British Psychological Society] (2019) and RCPscyh [Royal College of Psychiatrists] (2018) are signatories, and all have extensive guidelines for working with GSRD clients, all therapists have a clear obligation to engage with specific GSRD training.

Many therapists with additional training in GSRD therapy now refer to themselves as 'Pink Therapists' or practise something *they* call 'Pink Therapy' as a modality. There are an increasing number of therapists in the UK who have an almost exclusively GSRD-oriented therapy practice. Pink Therapy lists such practitioners at www.pinktherapy.com and has an accreditation scheme to recognise those with specialist training.

BASIC ASSUMPTIONS

GSRD THERAPY

Therapists practising GSRD will need to follow these assumptions, and be well trained in these skills and strategies:

- **Practice a commitment to social justice**. Because the roots of GSRD therapy are planted in the same soil as feminist therapy and other anti-oppressive therapies, the practitioner will be aware of their various privileges and intersectionalities (Turner, 2021) and can name the differences and similarities in the therapeutic relationship. In the same way that white therapists should always acknowledge their whiteness when working with an ethnically diverse client, the GSRD therapist will be willing to name their differences and similarities with their GSRD client and explore the meaning of these similarities and differences.

Therapists might also need to develop advocacy skills and be willing to stand up for and alongside GSRD communities on healthcare and human rights issues. One example of this might be supporting trans clients with access to healthcare.

- **Integration of core GSRD theories** including Minority Stress theories (Meyer, 2003; Pachankis et al., 2020), Microaggression theory (Nadal, 2013; Torino et al., 2018) and the importance of fostering micro-affirmations. They will also draw upon trauma-informed approaches to heal and promote resilience.
- **Gaining knowledge of contemporary sexology**, of different identities, lifestyles, practices and communities will lead them to adopt a non-pathologising approach and locate the cause of much of the internalised oppression, distress and damage externally.
- **Demonstrate cultural humility and cultural competence**, encouraging the development of The Self by encouraging a reflexive approach to developing personal values and self-knowledge for life regarding cultural scripts they might want to challenge or follow in what Barker (2018) refers to as 'Re-writing the Rules'. Therapists may need to offer psychoeducation based on their prior training in cultural competence and sexological knowledge about different communities and practices. Therapists with shared lived experiences might benefit some clients entering their community in seeking social support or local insider knowledge, although by no means is lived experience a prerequisite for working with these clients. Cultural humility positions clients as co-therapists and draws on their learning about their lifestyle, identity and community. Therapists failing to adopt an affirmative stance need to be mindful of colluding with clients' negative self-concept of brokenness. A constructionist stance helps acknowledge the oppressive social context and move towards self-acceptance.
- **Understanding of specific adverse effects of oppression** and helping the client alleviate isolation and find belonging and community through developing a support network – families of choice (see in particular Barker's excellent guide for BACP; Barker, 2019).
- **Trauma-informed care**, enhancing resilience and promoting self-esteem, and reducing the symptoms of complex trauma and post-traumatic stress (for survivors of abuse, attacks, discrimination and conversion therapy).
- An infographic of these core requirements can be found at: https://pinktherapy.org/core_requirements/

ORIGIN AND MAINTENANCE OF PROBLEMS

Life often revolves around binary frameworks and thinking: hetero and homo, male and female, healthy and unhealthy. We usually take it for granted that this is just how life is. It is perceived as 'normal' for a man and a woman to get married, be monogamous, have children, etc. Couples who eschew any of these steps also frequently experience microaggressions. Perhaps we have not yet come across someone who is not comfortable with their assigned sex at birth or someone who enjoys being tied up and spanked during sex. Our society operates through these normative and binary lenses: cisgenderism, heteronormativity, mononormativity and body-negative, sexual shaming cultures, religious persecution, ableism and racism. These can all lead to trauma, internalised oppression and negative core beliefs. Our paths through life are heavily influenced by intersectionality (Freeman-Coppadge and Langroudi, 2021). In certain contexts, a person's identity might confer advantages or privileges, yet in other contexts, these intersections result in a loss of power and status. So intersections of gender, race, age and class can impact the opportunities and lives of GSRD people.

THEORY OF CHANGE

As there are no entry-level training programmes in GSRD therapy, our model combines well alongside many other theoretical approaches, perhaps unsurprisingly with a long tradition of adopting a non-pathologising stance, such as person-centred therapy, which has appealed to significant numbers of GSRD therapists in the United Kingdom (Rogers, 1951). Also, Davies (1998) published a paper on the six conditions and LGB clients. The core theories of the person-centred approach are consistent with our understanding of the theory of mind and change (see elsewhere in this volume). But many other modalities are also highly effective with GSRD clients; Pink Therapy volume 2 (Davies and Neal, 2000) covered many of these models in some depth. Most GSRD therapists now operate from an integrative and pluralistic base, often incorporating humanistic and behavioural models. We would see the integration of person-centred, social constructionist/systemic and behavioural approaches as particularly practical. However, we know of practitioners outside these approaches who also work effectively with gender, sex and relationship diversity by following the basic GSRD assumptions above.

CASE STUDY

A 32-year-old white British cis gay man, Bradley, came to therapy saying he felt lost and lonely. He described being unable to build long-term relationships. He felt 'desperate' to find a steady partner, but anxious when meeting people. He met his partners on Grindr, a hook-up app that shows the nearest men online looking for sex. He also said that his sex life was unsatisfying, finding it hard to feel much pleasure from the experience because he found it challenging to be fully present. Bradley mentioned that he had no close gay friends. He socialised with a few heterosexual friends from his university days. Although Bradley thought they were 'OK people', Bradley reported never feeling fully understood. He avoided talking about himself and parts of his life that were important to him, like loneliness and gay identity. As the years passed, Bradley noticed his heterosexual friends were becoming more judgemental. As they started to settle down with partners, they made him feel bad for 'still being single' and some implied he might have a problem. One day, Bradley watched a programme about LGBT people being hunted in Chechnya. Even though he had no connection to this part of the world, he started sobbing and shaking, and he did not know why. This event was the catalyst to his seeking a GSRD-trained therapist.

Trauma-informed: One of the first things the GSRD therapist did was validate how utterly appalling these camps were and, using psychoeducation, explained the phenomenon of vicarious trauma. His therapist said: 'Of course, you would be upset seeing other LGBT people being hunted and killed. This affects LGBT people across the world.' And they explored what Bradley might want to do with his distress and anger.

Understanding the adverse effects of oppression can be obvious, such as blatant homophobia. But it is much harder to identify it when it is more covert due to heteronormativity and mononormativity. Bradley's heterosexual friends, although not overtly homophobic, were demonstrating micro-invalidations and implied judgement on his life and lifestyle based on their heterosexual lens. Bradley mentioned that when his friends started to raise families, they became much less available. The GSRD therapist validated the loss and allowed a space for Bradley's grief. Bradley had not considered that he might be experiencing loss.

Cultural humility and cultural competence: When asked about his childhood, Bradley said that it was 'OK'. Yet, knowledge about LGBTQIA+ populations is valuable to allow Bradley not to gloss over it. It is unlikely that he encountered any difficulties growing up in a heteronormative world. When asked further questions, Bradley identified some experiences that were not overtly homophobic but were covertly so. For example, he remembered his father preferring his older brother because they shared 'manly' hobbies like football and being disinterested in Bradley because he chose creative pursuits like drawing. He was significantly bullied at school for being 'camp', but he thought he couldn't talk to his parents about it because they responded with: 'you are a lad, defend yourself'. Examining this, Bradley started making connections between his childhood experiences and his attachment style. It made sense as an adult to want relationships and fear them, expecting rejection.

Contemporary sexology: The GSRD therapist explored what Bradley meant about 'wanting a relationship'. He had only considered the vision of a monogamous relationship so far because he thought it was the only way to be in a relationship (mononormativity). After an affirmative exploration, Bradley imagined various relational aspects of himself. He and the therapist also explored the difference between being present sexually in solo sex versus partnered sex. When the GSRD therapist offered the knowledge that partnered sex is often more anxiety-provoking than solo sex, Bradley learnt to normalise and manage his anxieties instead of criticising himself for it. This helped him to be more in the here-and-now when having sex with others.

Community: When the therapeutic relationship was strong, the GSRD therapist encouraged Bradley to expand his circle of friends. Rather than leaving his current friendships, he considered adding new people, with a specific focus on people from the LGBTQIA+ communities. Bradley was not sure that 'making gay friends'

> would resolve his issues, but he gave it a go and connected with gay men through the 'Meet-Up' website rather than a hook-up app. He started going to the theatre with gay men; he joined a gay hiking group. Feeling the difference in the quality of interactions from his new gay male friends, compared to his heterosexual friends, was pivotal for him. He noticed his body feeling much more relaxed in the presence of other gay men. He gradually re-created his friendship circle, contributing to better emotional health and higher self-esteem. Later, Bradley translated these profound relational experiences to his dating life. His anxious attachment slowly changed, and he successfully found a good romantic partner.

RESEARCH

Fundamental theories which inform GSRD therapy are Meyer's Minority Stress Theory (Meyer, 2003). Meyer is an epidemiological psychiatrist, and he suggested that there were specific forms of chronic stress that affected LGB people. These accounted for the elevated prevalence of mental health problems due to stigmatised social status and stress along a distal–proximal continuum. Examples of distal minority stress might include reading about violent assaults in the media, and proximal instances might involve microaggressions, which are subtle forms of discrimination that might be conscious or unconsciously directed towards GSRD people. These microaggressions paved the way for Microaggression theory (Nadal, 2013). Meyer also attributed the burden of concealment of identity as a co-factor in poor mental health and the internalisation of negative beliefs about same-sex attraction. Meyer's theory has subsequently been extended to apply to other GSRD identities.

In a large international study, Pachankis and his colleagues (2020) offered a missing piece to Meyer's earlier theory of Minority Stress. They demonstrated that gay and bisexual men are subject to intragroup competition theory, an evolutionary theory of mate selection that suggests that sexual benefits accrue to high-status men. Competition among men is standard, and low-status men are at particular risk of stress, exclusion and associated mental health symptoms. They also applied Social Field Theory, which states that by sharing the same gender as their desired partners, gay and bisexual men can measure themselves using the same social and sexual capital standards they use to size up their potential partners. The final hypothesis tested was the theory of precarious manhood (Vandello et al., 2008), which suggests that gay and bisexual men might go to great lengths to defend their masculine status, even when such defences come at a cost to their social and mental health.

In working with GSRD clients, it can be helpful to adopt a strengths-based approach (Gates and Kelly, 2017), which itself is informed by knowledge of the different lifespan and developmental processes (D'Augelli and Patterson, 1995). Odets (2020) applied Erikson's Eight developmental stages to gay men, which is also worth considering.

Intersectionality theory has significantly impacted our understanding of working with different groups and individuals (for more on this, see Freeman-Coppadge and Langroudi, 2021). 'Intersectionality' is a term first coined by Crenshaw (1989), who described how Black feminists experienced life differently from white feminists – how in certain contexts, a person's identity might confer advantages or privileges, yet in other contexts, these intersections result in a loss of power and status. A deaf, Black lesbian will experience her intersecting identities differently depending on whether she is among cisgender heterosexual Black people, the local Deaf club, or socialising with hearing white lesbians on a Pride march. Another example would be a middle-aged cis-male submissive, whose primary kink is being an adult baby, who will experience a lack of legal protections for his kink identity and a significant loss of status among most of his heterosexual peers if his kink were to be discovered. Thus, he is likely to be experiencing minority stress effects due to the concealment of his kink practices.

REFERENCES

Barker, M.-J. (2018) *Re-writing the Rules* (2nd ed.). Abingdon, UK: Routledge.
Barker, M.-J. (2019) *BACP Good Practice across the Counselling Professions: 001 Gender, Sexual, and Relationship Diversity (GSRD)*. Lutterworth: British Association of Counselling and Psychotherapy. Available at www.bacp.co.uk/media/5877/bacp-gender-sexual-relationship-diversity-gpacp001-april19.pdf
British Association of Counselling and Psychotherapy (BACP) (2018) *Ethical Framework for the Counselling Professions*. Lutterworth: BACP.
British Psychological Society (2019) *Guidelines for Psychologists Working with Gender, Sexuality and Relationship Diversity* (2nd ed.). Leicester: BPS. Available at www.bps.org.uk/guideline/guidelines-psychologists-working-gender-sexuality-and-relationship-diversity
Crenshaw, K.W. (1989) *Demarginalizing the Intersection of Race and Sex: A Black Feminist Critique of Antidiscrimination Doctrine, Feminist Theory and Antiracist Politics*. Chicago, IL: University of Chicago Legal.
Davies, D. (1998) The six necessary and sufficient conditions applied to working with lesbian, gay and bisexual clients. *The Person-Centered Journal*, 5(2), 111–120.
Davies, D. and Neal, C. (1996) *Pink Therapy: A Guide for Counsellors Working with Lesbian, Gay and Bisexual Clients*. New York: McGraw-Hill.
Davies, D. and Neal, C.E. (Eds) (2000) *Therapeutic Perspectives on Working with Lesbian, Gay and Bisexual Clients*. Maidenhead: Open University Press.
D'Augelli, A.R. and Patterson, C.J. (1995) *Lesbian, Gay, and Bisexual Identities over the Lifespan Psychological Perspectives*. Oxford: Oxford University Press.
Freeman-Coppadge, D.J. and Langroudi, K.F. (2021) Beyond LGBTQ-affirmative therapy: fostering growth and healing through intersectionality. In K.L. Nadal and M.R. Scharrón-del Río (Eds), *Queer Psychology*. New York: Springer.
Gates, T. and Kelly, B. (2017) Affirming Strengths-Based Models of Practice. *Social Work Practice with the LBGTQ Community*, NY: OU Press.
Malyon, A.K. (1982) Biphasic aspects of homosexual identity formation. *Psychotherapy: Theory, Research and Practice*, 19(3), 335–340. https://doi.org/10.1037/h0088444
Mearns, D. and Cooper, M. (2017) *Working at Relational Depth in Counselling and Psychotherapy*. London: Sage.
Meyer, I.H. (2003) Prejudice, social stress and mental health in lesbian, gay and bisexual populations: conceptual issues and research evidence. *Psychological Bulletin*, 129(5), 674–697.
Nadal, K.L. (2013) *That's So Gay! Microaggressions and the Lesbian, Gay, Bisexual, and Transgender Community*. Washington, DC: American Psychological Association.
Odets, W. (2020) *Out of the Shadows: Reimagining Gay Men's Lives*. Harmondsworth: Penguin.
Pachankis, J.E., Clark, K.A., Burton, C.L., Hughto, J.M.W., Bränström, R. and Keene, D.E. (2020) Sex, status, competition, and exclusion: intraminority stress from within the gay community and gay and bisexual men's mental health. *Journal of Personality and Social Psychology*, 119(3), 713–740. https://doi.org/10.1037/pspp0000282
Pink Therapy (2021) *Memorandum of Understanding on Conversion Therapy*. Pink Therapy, December version. Available at https://pinktherapy.org/MOU2/
Rogers, C. (1951) *Client-Centred Therapy*. Boston, MA: Houghton-Mifflin.
Royal College of Psychiatrists (2018) *Position Statement on Supporting Transgender and Gender Diverse People*. London: RCP. Available at www.rcpsych.ac.uk/pdf/PS02_18.pdf
Torino, G.C., Rivera, D.P., Capodilupo, C.M., Nadal, K.L. and Sue, D.W. (2018) *Microaggression Theory: Influence and Implications*. New York: Wiley.
Turner, D. (2021) *Intersections of Privilege and Otherness in Counselling & Psychotherapy*. Abingdon, UK: Routledge.
Vandello, J.A., Bosson, J.K., Cohen, D., Burnaford, R.M. and Weaver, J.R. (2008) Precarious manhood. *Journal of Personality and Social Psychology*, 95, 1325–1339. http://dx.doi.org/10.1037/a0012453

> **RECOMMENDED READING**
>
> Nichols, M. (2021) *The Modern Clinician's Guide to Working with LGBTQ+ Clients*. Abingdon, UK: Routledge.
>
> Margie Nichols is a key pioneer working with LGBTQ+ clients with over 40 years of experience. Her book embraces current thinking on working with a wide range of clients.
>
> Vincent, B. (2018) *Transgender Health: A Practitioner's Guide to Binary and Non-Binary Trans Patient Care*. London: Jessica Kingsley Publishers.
>
> Ben Vincent's comprehensive book embraces everything from language to service provision to biopsychosocial care for trans and non-binary clients.
>
> Boyd, C. and Whitman, J. (Eds) (2021) *Homework Assignments and Handouts for LGBTQ+ Clients: A Mental Health and Counseling Handbook*. Abingdon, UK: Routledge.
>
> This new book contains an enormous range of exercises and homework for therapists working with LGBTQ+ clients across the widest range of lifespan issues. It can also be good for groupworkers and trainers.

5.14 INTERPERSONAL PSYCHOTHERAPY

ELIZABETH ROBINSON AND CATHERINE EDMUNDS

OVERVIEW AND KEY POINTS

Interpersonal psychotherapy (IPT) is a brief, time-limited therapy initially developed for the treatment of depression but has been adapted to treat other disorders. Interpersonal therapists link the client's experience of depression to the interpersonal context. Therapy focuses on different interpersonal problem areas with two related aims: to improve the interpersonal functioning in a given area and to reduce depressive symptoms.

- A here-and-now focus targets depression in the interpersonal context.
- Goals and strategies are used to deal with interpersonal problem areas.
- The optimistic stance of the therapist helps the client celebrate their achievements and deal with their depression.
- The client is encouraged to make the most of their own social network to ease symptoms and improve interpersonal functioning.

BRIEF HISTORY

Interpersonal psychotherapy was developed as a treatment for depression. Researchers from the Boston New Haven Collaborative Project drew from interpersonal theories of depression (Meyer, 1957; Sullivan, 1953) and attachment theories (Bowlby, 1969) when they developed and manualised (Klerman et al., 1984) interpersonal psychotherapy (IPT), which was compared to antidepressant medication in clinical trials in the 1970s. The researchers found that both treatments were effective, although IPT took longer to take an effect (Klerman et al., 1974; Weissman et al., 1979). Research and development in IPT for depression continued in adolescent and old age groups: both were considered to be effective interventions (Mufson et al., 2004; Reynold et al., 1996). IPT is currently recommended by the National Institute for Health and Care Excellence (NICE) as a treatment for moderate and severe depression based on the research evidence. IPT has also been adapted for use in other mental health problems, including eating disorders (Fairburn et al., 1996), social anxiety disorder (Lipstiz, 2012) and post-traumatic stress disorder (Markowitz et al., 2015). IPT can be delivered as an individual therapy, by telephone (Miller and Weissman, 2002) or in groups (Wilfey et al., 2000).

BASIC ASSUMPTIONS

Interpersonal psychotherapy (IPT) is a manualised (Klerman et al., 1984), time-limited, supportive and structured therapy which is used primarily for the treatment of depression. IPT has a dual focus, to reduce depressive symptoms by dealing with the associated interpersonal problems. Depression is framed by the therapist as a medical illness which is not the client's fault and is treatable. 'Sick role work' in IPT helps the therapist work with the client to look at ways they can make changes to help with their recovery. This may include increasing, varying or moderating activity and optimising support from others. It may be appropriate in some circumstances to assist the client in temporarily relinquishing work activities (Wilfey et al., 2000). The IPT therapist helps the client explore and understand the interpersonal context of their current depression. This may be due to disharmony or dissatisfaction in one or a number of relationships, social isolation, bereavement or a loss or change in a role. Once a link is made between the interpersonal context (problem area) and the depression there are specific techniques (Klerman et al., 1984) to help the client work towards interpersonal changes in order to move forward and ease their depression. The therapist helps the client optimise their current support network throughout this process.

ORIGIN AND MAINTENANCE OF PROBLEMS

IPT is delivered over 16 weekly sessions and involves three phases: an initial, middle and end. The *initial phase* (sessions 1 to 4) explores the origin and maintenance of problems by identifying details of the client's depression and relating it to the interpersonal context. The therapist explores with the client links between interpersonal events and their mood. An overview of the therapy is provided at the start of the process, setting a framework for treatment. The therapist initially confirms a diagnosis of depression using diagnostic criteria (American Psychiatric Association, 2013), and reinforces that depression is a condition that is treatable. Measurements of the severity of depression are taken at the start of the process using either clinician-rated scales, such as the Hamilton depression scale (Hamilton, 1960), which was recommended in the IPT manual (Klerman et al., 1984), or, in many clinical services in the UK, a self-rated measure, the Patient Health Questionnaire (PHQ9) (Kroenke and Spitzer, 2002), is widely used. At this stage, the therapist will work together with the client to consider what steps they can take to actively help with their recovery. They may need to alter some expectations of themselves in the short term (reduce workload at home/work if appropriate), add in other activities (such as pursuing a pleasurable activity as an antidepressant) and look to see how they can access help/support that facilitate their recovery. This is known as a 'sick role work' (Klerman et al., 1984). A history of current and previous episodes of depression is gathered, considering the interpersonal context at the time.

An interpersonal inventory then gives valuable insight into the client's interpersonal world. The inventory is used to identify helpful relationships, which may provide a positive resource to build on, as well as negative relationships, which may serve as an emotional drain and contribute to the current depression. Detailed information gained about each relationship might include: frequency of contact, level of satisfaction, expectations, disagreements or disharmony and what the client may like to change. It may draw attention to any specific interpersonal issue, such as relationship struggles or changes (i.e., separation), or grief, which gives further context to the client's experiences of their current depression.

At the end of the initial phase, the therapist offers an interpersonal formulation (Markowitz and Swartz, 2007). Drawing upon the information obtained from the history, time line and interpersonal inventory, a link is made between the onset and maintenance of the current depressive episode and the client's social and interpersonal situation. This is a collaborative approach whereby the therapist seeks to reach agreement with the client regarding the possible focal area. The four potential focal areas in IPT are: role transition, role dispute, interpersonal sensitivities and complicated bereavement. Having identified one or a maximum of two linked focal areas with the client, achievable goals, linked to the focal area, are agreed and a treatment contract is set between the therapist and client.

THEORY OF CHANGE

The *middle phase* of IPT (sessions 5 to 12) forms the main focus of treatment, targeting an interpersonal problem area that is fuelling the client's depression. Having identified one or two focal areas with the client during formulation at the end of the initial phase, specific treatment approaches for the particular focal area are implemented. The IPT manual clearly defines strategies for each focal area (Klerman et al., 1984). The aim for the therapist is to work with the client to increase their interpersonal functioning and help them address the interpersonal problem area, which in turn reduces depressive symptoms.

The four problem areas used in IPT are outlined below.

ROLE DISPUTE

Interpersonal disputes are common and may manifest in various ways. The client may be in open dispute or disagreement with an individual or group of individuals, which could include friends, family or work colleagues. Non-reciprocal role expectations may contribute to the role dispute and associated depression.

ROLE TRANSITION

This is a broad area and can involve any changes in role, such as promotion, demotion, retirement or redundancy, separation, divorce, moving house, getting married, having a baby or receiving a diagnosis of a medical illness. It is important to identify the existing role that is a struggle to the client and how adapting to that particular role leads to or maintains the current depressive episode.

COMPLICATED BEREAVEMENT

The client has experienced a death of a loved one and for whatever reason has not been able to grieve for this loss. Typically, the therapist will identify with the client how they may not have effectively worked through the mourning process and how this has led to ongoing symptoms of depression.

INTERPERSONAL DEFICIT/SENSITIVITIES

There are some individuals who have limited or no satisfying or rewarding interpersonal relationships, which leads to social isolation and depression. Alternatively, any client who has relationships that are transient, superficial or disruptive can also result in social isolation and depression.

Once the IPT therapist has collaboratively identified and agreed the problem area, they will work through the strategies highlighted in the IPT manual, with the aim of reducing depressive symptoms and increasing interpersonal functioning. Specific goals linked to the focal area will be worked towards during this process.

SKILLS AND STRATEGIES

ROLE DISPUTE

The client may have a disputed relationship with their partner that is fuelling the depression. The therapist will explore with the client the differences in expectations that both parties hold, how the communication works, what works well and where things may go off track. Specific techniques, such as communication analysis, provide an opportunity to review the quality and nature of the interaction, and inform the client what role they play in the disputed relationship. Work may then focus on helping the client review their expectations in the relationship and look at alternative ways of communicating in order to address the dispute.

ROLE TRANSITION

The client may be struggling in adjusting to a role change, such as a relationship split, which is maintaining their depressive symptoms. The therapist helps the client mourn this relationship by starting with an exploration of what they liked/disliked about the lost relationship, in so doing obtaining lots of detail about this part of the client's experience. The therapist encourages a realistic evaluation of this relationship, facilitating a processing of emotions. Further work is undertaken to explore how the split took place, such as: was this unexpected? How much choice did the client have? How quickly did this happen? Again, work targeting the expression and facilitation of emotional processing gives way to allow the client to move on. Finally, opportunities in their current situation are explored, namely, how can they make the most of this current situation?

COMPLICATED BEREAVEMENT

The client may have lost a significant relationship, such as the death of a parent, which led to the ongoing depression. The aim of the work is to help the client start to mourn this loss in order to ease their depression. Exploration of the relationship covers a broad range of aspects of the relationship, including things they missed, enjoyed, treasured – the happy moments as well as the things they may not miss, or were perhaps frustrated with. There is a need to ensure this is a balanced review so that the client is not led to idealise their loved one as a 'saint', which would keep them stuck in the mourning process. Events leading up to and surrounding the death are also sensitively explored. Much of the work is geared towards facilitating affect release and encouraging the mourning process. This is done both inside and outside sessions where the client is encouraged to use social support to help them manage their loss.

INTERPERSONAL DEFICIT/SENSITIVITIES

The client may struggle in a number of relationships and a lack of sufficient quality relationships may be isolating and maintain their depression. The therapist reviews the client's current and past relationships to identify positive ones (that can be used as an example) and relationship struggles. Areas of difficulty and repeating patterns are identified and alternative options for getting relationships started or keeping them going are explored. The development of new social and communication skills is important, and opportunities to practise these skills both within and outside the session are provided. Encouragement and support also play a large part in allowing the client to increase interpersonal interaction.

Throughout all of the problem areas in IPT, the therapist engages the client to consider how they can source help and support from others outside the sessions to help deal with the interpersonal problem area, and, as a consequence, their depression.

The *end phase* of IPT (sessions 13 to 16) continues alongside the middle-phase strategies. Preparing for the end of therapy is a key task, exploring how the client feels (modelling healthy endings), evaluating the course of therapy and identifying as well as celebrating their achievements. Given that depression is a recurrent condition (Kupfer et al., 1992), IPT proactively manages future risk, with the therapist helping the client to look forward to consider what they need to do to maintain improvements once therapy has ended. This may run concurrently with advice on the need for prophylactic antidepressant medication, depending on the assessed level of risk. The IPT therapist provides advice on how to deal with a potential subsequent episode, ensuring the client is confident about how to access health services. Identification of the client's symptom signature at the start the initial phase of treatment provides information to recognise early warning signs of a further episode.

RESEARCH

IPT has been found to be effective in treating depression across all age groups: adults, old age and adolescents (Mufson et al., 2004; Reynolds et al., 1996; Weissman et al., 1979), including young children (8–12 years old) where there is a modification to engage the parent in the therapy throughout (Deitz et al., 2015). The National Institute of Health and Care Excellence (NICE) recommend IPT as a treatment for moderate or severe depression in adults and adolescents (NICE, 2010, 2015). IPT alone has been found to minimise the risk of a recurrent episode, although combining IPT and medication is superior in highly recurrent depression in both adults (Frank et al., 2000) and older-age adults. However, it is notable that the latter group tends to demonstrate a slower response to treatment and earlier relapse (Reynolds et al., 1999). Additionally, IPT has helped to improve compliance with medication (Miller et al., 2001), and has been combined with medication therapy for chronic treatment-resistant depression (Murray et al., 2010; Schramm et al., 2007).

IPT has demonstrated efficacy in postpartum depression (Spinelli and Endicott, 2003), with improvements in social adjustment and mother–infant bonding reported (O'Hara et al., 2000).

IPT can be delivered by telephone (Miller and Weissman, 2002) and in groups, in a range of cultures (Verdeli et al., 2003; Zlotnick et al., 2001). It is also manualised to be delivered in groups for adults (Wilfey et al., 2000) and for adolescents as a preventative programme for depression (Young, Mufson and Schueler, 2016).

IPT has been tested and delivered over fewer sessions (8) using brief model (IPT – B) with depressed mothers (Swartz, Grote and Graham, 2014) and adolescents (Mufson, Yanes-Lukin and Anderson, 2015), demonstrating feasibility and efficacy. Interpersonal counselling (IPC) was developed for milder depression and stress/distress in primary care settings, allowing non-mental health professionals to use a more scripted approach, which has been helpful in reducing symptoms (Matzuzaka et al., 2017, Menchetti et al., 2014).

IPT has been used in eating disorders (Fairburn et al., 1996), social phobia, social anxiety disorder and panic disorder (Lipstiz, 2012), and has been manualised as a non-exposure-based alternative to treating post-traumatic stress disorder (Markowitz, 2016).

REFERENCES

American Psychiatric Association (2013). *Diagnostic and Statistical Manual of Mental Disorders* (5th ed.). DSM-5. Washington, DC: American Psychiatric Association.

Bowlby, J. (1969). *Attachment and Loss. Volume 1: Attachment*. London: Hogarth Press.

Dietz, L.J., Weinberg, R.J., Brent, D.A. and Mufson, L. (2015). Family-based interpersonal psychotherapy for depressed preadolescents: examining efficacy and potential treatment mechanisms. *Journal of American Academy of Child and Adolescent Psychiatry*, 54(3): 191–9. doi: 10.1016/j.jaac.2014.12.011

Fairburn, C.G., Norman, P.A., Welch, S.L., O'Connor, M.E., Doll, H.A. and Peveler, P.C. (1996). A prospective study of outcome in bulimia nervosa and the long term effects of three psychological treatments. *Archives of General Psychiatry*, 52: 304–312.

Frank, E., Grochocinski, V.J., Spanier, C.A., Buysse, D.J., Cherry, C.R., Houck, P.R., Stapf, D.M. and Kupfer, D.J. (2000). Interpersonal psychotherapy and antidepressant medication: evaluation of a sequential treatment strategy in women with recurrent major depression. *Journal of Clinical Psychiatry*, 61(1): 51–57.

Hamilton, M. (1960). A rating scale of depression. *Journal of Neurology, Neurosurgery and Psychiatry*, 23: 56–62.

Klerman, G.L., Dimascio, A., Weissman, M., Prusoff, B. and Paykel, E.S. (1974). Treatment of depression by drugs and psychotherapy. *American Journal of Psychiatry*, 131(2): 186–191.

Klerman, G.L., Weissman, M.M., Rounsaville, B.J. and Chevron, E. (1984). *Interpersonal Psychotherapy for Depression*. New York: Basic Books.

Kroenke, K. and Spitzer, R.L. (2002). The PHQ-9: a new depression diagnostic and severity measure. *Psychiatric Annals*, 32(9): 509–515.

Kupfer, D.J., Frank, E., Perel, J.M., Cornes, C., Mallinger, A.G., Thase, M.E., McEachran, A.B. and Grochocinski, V.J. (1992). Five-year outcome for maintenance therapies in recurrent depression. *Archives of General Psychiatry*, 49: 769–773.

Lipstiz, J.L. (2012). Interpersonal psychotherapy for social anxiety disorder. In J.C. Markowitz and M.M. Markowitz (Eds) (2016), *Interpersonal Psychotherapy for Posttraumatic Stress Disorder*. Oxford: Oxford University Press.

Markowitz, J.C. (2016). *Interpersonal Psychotherapy for Posttraumatic Stress Disorder*. Oxford: Oxford University Press.

Markowitz, J.C., Petkova, E., Neria, Y., Ven Meter, P.E., Zhao, Y., Hembree, E., Lovell, K., Biyanova, T. and Marshall, R.D. (2015). Is exposure necessary? A randomised clinical trial of interpersonal psychotherapy for PTSD. *American Journal of Psychiatry*, 172: 1–11.

Markowitz, J.C. and Schwartz, H.A. (2007). Case formulation in interpersonal psychotherapy of depression. In T.D. Eells (Ed.), *Handbook of Psychotherapy Case Formulation* (2nd ed., pp. 221–250). New York: Guilford Press.

Matzuzaka, M., Wainberg, M., Parla, A.N., Hoffmann, E.V., Coimbra, B.M., Braga, R.F., Sweetland, A.C. and Mello, M. (2017). Task shifting interpersonal counselling for depression: a pragmatic randomised controlled trial in primary care. *BMC Psychiatry*, 17: 225.

Menchetti, M., Rucci, P., Bortollotti, B., Bombi, A., Scocco, P., Kraemer, H. and Beradi, D. (2014). Moderators of remission with interpersonal counselling or drug treatment in primary care patients with depression: randomised controlled trial. *British Journal of Psychiatry*, 204: 144–150.

Meyer, A. (1957). *Psychobiology: A Science of Man*. Springfield, IL: Charles C. Thomas.

(Continued)

(Continued)

Miller, L. and Weissman, M. (2002). Interpersonal psychotherapy delivered over the telephone to recurrent depressives: a pilot study. *Depression and Anxiety*, 16: 114–117.

Miller, M.D., Cornes, C., Frank, E., Ehrenpreis, L., Silberman, R., Schilernitzauer, M.A., Tracey, B., Richards, V., Wolfson, L., Zaltman, J., Bensasi, S. and Reynolds, C.F. (2001). Interpersonal psychotherapy for late-life depression past, present and future. *Journal of Psychotherapy Practice and Research*, 10: 231–238.

Mufson, L., Pollack Dorta, K., Wickranaratne, P., Nomura, Y., Olfson, M. and Weissman, M.M. (2004). A randomised effectiveness trial of interpersonal psychotherapy for depressed adolescents. *Archives of General Psychiatry*, 61: 577–584.

Mufson, L., Yanes-Lukin, P. and Anderson, G. (2015). A pilot study of brief IPT-A delivered in primary care. *General Hospital Psychiatry*, 37(5): 481–484.

Murray, G., Michalak, E.E., Axler, A., Yaxley, D., Hayashi, B., Westrin, A., Ogrodniczuk, J.S., Tam, E.M., Yatham, L.N. and Lam, R.W. (2010). Relief of chronic or resistant depression (Re-ChORD): a pragmatic, randomized, open-treatment trial of an integrative program intervention for chronic depression. *Journal of Affective Disorders*, 123(1–3): 243–248.

National Institute for Health and Care Excellence (NICE) (2010). *The Treatment and Management of Depression in Adults* (Updated Edition). National Clinical Practice Guideline 90. National Collaborating Centre for Mental Health. Commissioned by the National Institute of Health and Clinical Excellence. London: The British Psychological Society and The Royal College of Psychiatrists.

National Institute for Health and Care Excellence (NICE) (2015). *Depression in Children and Young People: Identification and Management*. London: NICE.

O'Hara, M.W., Stuart, S., Gorman, L.L. and Wenzel, A. (2000). Efficacy of interpersonal psychotherapy for postpartum depression. *Archives of General Psychiatry*, 57: 1039–1045.

Reynolds, C.F., Frank, E., Dew, M.A., Houck, P.R., Miller, M., Mazumdar, S., Perel, J.M. and Kupfer, D.J. (1999). Treatment of 70+ year-olds with recurrent major depression. *American Journal of Geriatric Psychiatry*, 7(1): 64–69.

Reynolds, C.F., Frank, E., Perel, J.M., Mazumdar, S., Dew, M.A., Begley, A., Houck, P.R., Hall, M., Mulsant, B., Shear, M.K., Miller, M.D., Cornes, C. and Kupfer, D.J. (1996). High relapse rates after discontinuation of adjunctive medication in elderly persons with recurrent major depression. *American Journal of Psychiatry*, 152: 1418–1422.

Schramm, E., Van Calker, D., Dykierek, P., Lieb, K., Kech, S., Zobel, I., Leonhart, R. and Berger, M. (2007). An intensive treatment programme of interpersonal psychotherapy plus pharmacotherapy for depressed inpatients: acute versus long term results. *American Journal of Psychiatry*, 164: 768–777.

Spinelli, M.G. and Endicott, J. (2003). Controlled clinical trial of interpersonal psychotherapy versus parenting education program for depressed pregnant women. *American Journal of Psychiatry*, 160(3): 555–562.

Sullivan, H.N. (1953). *The Interpersonal Theory of Psychiatry*. New York: W.W. Norton.

Swartz, H., Grote, N. and Graham, P. (2014). Brief interpersonal therapy (IPT-B): overview and review of evidence. *American Journal of Psychotherapy*, 68(4): 443–462.

Verdeli, H., Clougherty, C., Bolton, P., Speelman, E., Ndogoni, L., Bass, J., Neugebauer, R. and Weissman, M. (2003). Adapting group IPT for a developing country: an experience in rural Uganda. *World Psychiatry*, 2(2): 112–120.

Weissman, M.M., Prusoff, B.A., Dimasccio, A., Neu, C., Goklaney, M. and Klerman, G.L. (1979). The efficacy of drugs and psychotherapy in the treatment of acute depressive episodes. *American Journal of Psychiatry*, 136(4B): 555–558.

Wilfey, D.E., Mackenzie, K.R., Welch, R.R., Ayres, V.E. and Weismann, M.M. (2000). *Interpersonal Psychotherapy for Groups*. New York: Basic Books.

Young, J.F., Mufson, L. and Schueler, C.M. (2016). *Preventing Adolescent Depression: Interpersonal Psychotherapy – Adolescent Skills Training*. Oxford: Oxford University Press.

Zlotnick, C., Johnson, S.L., Miller, I.W., Pearlstein, T. and Howard, M. (2001). Postpartum depression in women receiving public assistance: pilot study of an interpersonal therapy oriented group intervention. *American Journal of Psychiatry*, 158(4): 638–640.

> **RECOMMENDED READING**
>
> Markowitz, J.C. and Weissman, M.M. (2018). *The Guide to Interpersonal Psychotherapy* (updated and expanded ed.). Oxford: Oxford University Press.
>
> This is the fifth update of the IPT manual. It outlines many case examples of IPT in mood disorders and non-mood disorders, including eating disorders, trauma-related disorders, social anxiety disorder and borderline personality disorder. It also outlines how IPT has been used in diverse populations, including adolescents, old-age depression, medically ill patients, developing countries and in low-income groups. The delivery of IPT in groups, conjoint sessions, by telephone, internet and in an inpatient setting is presented.
>
> Markowitz, J.C. (2016). *Interpersonal Psychotherapy for Posttraumatic Stress Disorder*. Oxford: Oxford University Press.
>
> This new manual provides an overview of how to use IPT for post-traumatic stress disorder (PTSD) as a non-exposure-based therapy. This is a good alternative in a therapist's armamentarium, given not all clients would wish to deal with exposure techniques. It covers a pocket guide to IPT, how it is adapted for this treatment population and how to deal with challenging/difficult situations. There is a patient handout included too.
>
> Markowitz, J.C. (2021). *In the Aftermath of the Pandemic. Interpersonal Psychotherapy for Anxiety, Depression, and PTSD*. Oxford: Oxford University Press.
>
> This is an accessible treatment manual that is helpful to address the psychological consequences of the Covid-19 pandemic and other large-scale disasters. There is a description of IPT techniques used to help the client deal with difficulties in depression, PTSD and anxiety. There are many clinical examples throughout.

5.15 JUNGIAN ANALYTICAL PSYCHOLOGY

RUTH WILLIAMS

OVERVIEW AND KEY POINTS

Analytical psychology is the term coined by Carl Gustav Jung to distinguish his approach from that of Sigmund Freud, with whom he had a close working association. Their first meeting famously lasted 13 hours. There was clearly a great excitement on the part of both men on establishing a truly deep connection with each other. Freud initially saw Jung as his natural heir in the field of psychoanalysis and encouraged him to take on leading roles in the profession.

- Clinically, the cornerstone of the work is the process of individuation.
- One of the unique features of Jung's approach was to talk about archetypes, which he saw as belonging to what he called the collective unconscious, a layer of the mind which connects us to ancient mythical images and symbols which can be analysed in the work.
- Dreams too are central to Jungian analysis. They can be seen as individual vignettes or often come in series so that a narrative might develop over time, making it important to notice the changes.

- Terms such as synchronicity, introversion, extroversion – all in common parlance now – were introduced by Jung.

BRIEF HISTORY

Analytical psychology is also referred to as Jungian analysis or psychotherapy or sometimes Jungian psychoanalysis.

Jung was born on 26 July 1875, the son of a Swiss Pastor. His disappointment in his father, whose faith he saw as rooted in dogma rather than personal experience, was critical in forming Jung's view of what we might now think of as the need for personal authenticity. His mother came from one of the oldest patrician families in Basel and he went on to marry wealthy heiress Emma Rauschenbach on Valentine's Day in 1903.

Jung worked as a psychiatrist at the Burgholzli clinic in Zurich (1900–1909) under the well-known psychiatrist Eugene Blueler (who invented the term schizophrenia, previously known as *Dementia Praecox*). During this period Jung developed the Word Association Test, which involved a list of one hundred words being given to a subject to elicit the spontaneous association to each word. Meaning was ascribed to the association itself as well as the response time to the so-called stimuluswords. When clusters of similar responses arose, these were seen as being significant and led Jung to formulate his theory of complexes. The Word Association Test is not used in contemporary practice.

On its publication in 1900, Jung read Freud's *The Interpretation of Dreams*, which he recognised as having been produced by a kindred spirit. On meeting Freud in 1906, a deep affinity was established between the two men. Freud saw Jung as his natural heir and in Freud, Jung saw a paternal figure. The relationship broke down on Jung's publication of his *Psychology of the Unconscious* (1916) when it became clear that Jung's ideas had significantly diverged from those of his mentor. The irreconcilable differences concerned whether there could be libido that was not exclusively sexual. Jung saw libido as being more broadly defined, a notion that sometimes erroneously gives rise to the notion that Jungian analysis is not concerned with sex. The trauma of this rift with Freud presaged a period of crisis for Jung, during which he developed many of his most original and creative ideas, using nature, creative media and dreams to explore his own psyche. These explorations are now available following the long-awaited publication of *The Red Book* (Jung, 2009), which gives an intimate insight into Jung's personal development in both written and artistic form. *The Red Book* presents Jung's own Active Imaginations (see definition below), giving direct access to the innermost workings of his mind in the most experimental form. Of this period Jung states:

> The years when I was pursuing my inner images were the most important of my life – in them everything essential was decided. It all began then; the later details are only supplements and clarifications of the material that burst forth from the unconscious, and at first swamped me. It was the *prima materia* for a lifetime's work. (Jung, 1995 [1963]: 199)

Some of these events are covered in abridged form in *Memories, Dreams, Reflections* (written by Jung in collaboration with Aniela Jaffe) (1995 [1963]), which is often an inspirational starting point for people encountering Jung for the first time.

In 2011 David Cronenberg released his take on the relationship between Jung and Freud in a film entitled *A Dangerous Method*, named after John Kerr's 1993 book about the relationship between Freud, Jung and Sabina Spielrein, who was a patient of both men but who is more famous for her supposed relationship with Jung than for her intellectual contribution to the field. (She became an analyst in her own right and published a number of papers, most notably one entitled 'Destruction as the Cause of Coming into Being', originally published in German in *Jahrbuch* in 1912 and finally published in English in the *Journal of Analytical Psychology* in 1994 (Vol. 39: 155–186)). The film is not entirely factual but gives an entertaining account of events.

Jung's erudition expanded the field of his psychology to include religion (Eastern and Western), and the ancient art of alchemy, which he used as a metaphorical device to illustrate his ideas by drawing on a set of ancient woodcut images from a medieval treatise entitled the *Rosarium Philosophorum* (rose garden of the philosophers), which he uses to illustrate the nature of [the transference] relationship in an utterly original way.

His interest in the esoteric has attracted a wide gamut of seekers and has been influential in what was once known as New Age thinking (see Tacey, 2001).

Jung's ideas have been widely applied to great effect in cultural studies, in the arts and popular culture, perhaps especially in film.

The International Association for Analytical Psychology, with member organisations throughout the world, regulates the training and professional aspects of Jungian analysis. In Britain, there are five affiliated societies, with distinct features ranging from the Developmental (Society of Analytical Psychology and British Jungian Analytic Association), which incorporates Kleinian ideas in regard to early human development, to the Classical (Independent Group of Analytical Psychologists and Guild of Analytical Psychologists), which pays particular heed to myth and fairy tale and thus tends to look at the personal through the lens of the collective unconscious, to the Association of Jungian Analysts, which holds the middle position between these approaches, having respect for both ends of this spectrum. The history of the divisions between these societies and an in-depth account of the differences may be found in Kirsch (2000). (This is a comprehensive account of the history of the profession and all its shifting fortunes by someone who has been involved from the earliest days, his parents having both been analysed by Jung himself.) See also Samuels (1985: Chapter 1) for an account of the 'Schools of Analytical Psychology', where Samuels systematically delineates the features of each school which, in part, includes consideration of frequency of sessions.

There is a third strand called 'archetypal psychology', which is an important off-shoot developed by James Hillman (1978) but which has not taken root as a clinical discipline.

BASIC ASSUMPTIONS

Individuation is the term used to describe the process of becoming oneself, striving towards greater wholeness; fulfilling one's potential. It is quite distinct from individualism, which is about being overly self-reliant or self-centred in a somewhat narrow way. Individuation is the process by which a person becomes a separate psychological individual, distinct from all others. This is an ongoing lifelong process which includes the spiritual dimension. Contemporary Murray Stein, based in Zurich, regards individuation as one of the four essential pillars of Jungian analysis (alongside the analytic relationship, working with dreams and using Active Imagination) (Stein, 2022).

Jung's model of the psyche consists of a *personal* and *collective unconscious*, the former being made up of the personal complexes, the latter of *archetypes*.

Archetypes may be seen as potentials. They are often referred to in the form of characters (Trickster, Hero, Mother/Father, Puer or Puella (eternal child), or Witch, for instance). These are all facets of personality to which we each have access and which vary in accordance with individual and cultural context. Archetypes are seen as deriving from radically differing origins by Jungian writers, ranging from the biological/evolutionary (Stevens, 1982, 2003), poetic (Hillman, 1983, 1994), developmental/neuroscientific (Knox, 2001, 2003) and most recently via emergence (Hogenson, 2004) (see below), to name but a few.

The collective unconscious connects us to ancient mythical images and symbols which may be analysed in clinical work. Of course modern man often sees or experiences these images in modern dress so that the images become accessible to their place in time. A brilliant example of this is that of the rap poet Kate Tempest in their *Brand New Ancients* (2013). Tempest writes of myth in a totally modern idiom. (More recently, Tempest was commissioned by the National Theatre to write a modern version of Sophocles' *Philoctetes* (1980). Their re-imagining of this play was called *Paradise* (Dir: Rickson, 2021).

Psychological types – The terms *introvert* and *extrovert* both originated with Jung and are now in common usage to describe people whose principal mode of being tends to be more internally or externally focused. Jung formulated a system whereby he saw people as falling predominantly into one of four types: feeling, thinking, intuition, sensation. Although it sounds quite restrictive and overdetermined, in fact this system can be used in quite a subtle fashion to enhance understanding. A person may need to give precedence to another facet of their personality to compensate (a Jungian term) for one-sidedness and this model might help gain insight into where a person needs to develop. It is also helpful in understanding interpersonal conflicts and where people(s) clash along the axis of different psychological types. This system gave rise to personality tests that are still used in commercial settings and (more rarely) in a clinical context.

Jung saw life as a 'continual balancing of Opposites' (1949: par. 1417). If a person is too 'nice', it is probable something less nice is being held at bay and needs to be balanced out in order for that person to become more rounded or authentic.

The *Shadow* is often referred to in this context in that it contains all the elements one does not wish to identify with or admit as part of oneself. This usually means those qualities or thoughts will burst through, like the return of the repressed.

Anima (meaning soul) and *Animus* (the feminine form) are the Latin names Jung used to describe the part of ourselves which represents the internalised aspects of the opposite sex to the gender of the individual (cf. below regarding gender). These images are sometimes seen or imagined as idealised images of the beloved or desired object in dreams or waking life and can be experienced as the external person being one's 'soul mate'.

Persona is sometimes seen as a mask. It is the face one presents to the world and is not necessarily 'false'.

Self is sometimes spelt with a capital 's' in Jung's writings to emphasise the distinction from the ordinary usage of the word self. It is seen as the centre of being, sometimes with spiritual connotations. Coming more into the 'Self' is seen as an achievement in terms of *individuation*, Self being seen as the sum of all the parts.

ORIGIN AND MAINTENANCE OF PROBLEMS

One factor which might account for analytical psychology being sometimes seen as less mainstream than psychoanalysis is that Jung has been accused of being anti-semitic. It is true that he wrote some things (regarding race, for instance) which were unwise and ill-considered, especially in the context of his time. These matters have been taken seriously by later generations of Jungians, who have re-evaluated Jung's work from this perspective both as historical corrective but also as necessary reparation (see Samuels, 1993: 287–316).

There have likewise had to be revisions to Jung's writing in regard to gender. Jung's wife, Emma (who was also a practising analyst), wrote *Two Essays* on *Animus and Anima* (1931) which show a more nuanced perspective than Jung's own writing in this area. See also Wehr (1987), Samuels (1989: Chapter 6) and Young-Eisendrath (2004), for instance.

There are also two new areas of study that have arisen in recent years and which contribute to the field of analytical psychology enormously. One is emergence theory and the other is the cultural complex.

The cultural complex has been developed by Singer and Kimbles as an idea only since 2000. They are building on Jung's own theory of complexes (which relates to the personal level) and extrapolating those ideas on to the individual, societal and the archetypal realm. They identify cultural complexes to be at the heart of conflicts between many groups in terms of politics, economics, sociology, etc. (Singer, 2004: 20) as well as being deeply embedded in 'tribal memories, patterned behaviours in the form of rituals and strong beliefs' (Singer, 2010: 234).

Emergence theory is based on the idea that phenomena can arise without any precursor. As such, it is at the cutting edge of attempts to explore the origin of archetypes (Hogenson, 2004).

THEORY OF CHANGE

The process of change and transformation in any psychotherapy is usually a slow one. Grappling with entrenched psychological trauma or patterns of being requires investment of time (and money, if formally undertaken with an analyst or therapist), as well as deep personal application. Some see the process of *individuation* as a working through of karmic tasks. The psyche (as defined in Jungian terms as encompassing the whole person) may transform through dreams or by using creative media such as art, sand tray or dance/bodywork, etc. (see Schaverien, 1991, 1995). Talking is usually the main tool in analysis. A relationship is formed with the therapist/analyst which becomes the vessel in which the issues arise and can be worked through. It was in this context that Jung used the alchemical metaphor mentioned above to elucidate the process of analysis. The alchemists were striving to turn one substance into another, which entailed various stages of transformation. This can be seen to mirror the psychic stages of transformation undergone during the course of an analysis or psychotherapeutic journey. In psychoanalytic terms, this refers to the transference, which is the framework within which matters arise and which provides the arena for working through and thus change. This is an arduous process in which one is gripped by 'real' feelings, being in a 'real' relationship. This involves coping with the vicissitudes of need and dependency. By 'working through' is meant coping with the emergence of unconscious material with a view to integrating it and gaining ways of going forward, incorporating hitherto unwanted parts of oneself. This expansion is usually felt as an enhancement of the personality and an ability to cope with and enjoy life.

SKILLS AND STRATEGIES

Dreams are central to Jungian analysis and psychotherapy. Their symbolic contents encapsulate a situation in a way words alone cannot.

The numinous is a concept unique to Jungian analysis. It refers to the mysterious, gripping, some would say spiritual, elements we all touch on in life at times and which may be encountered in dreams and synchronicities, for instance. Jung wrote 'the approach to the numinous is the real therapy and inasmuch as you attain to the numinous experiences you are released from the curse of pathology' (1945: 377).

Active Imagination was a method Jung developed during his personal crisis. In this he used creativity to identify and work problems through. This is sometimes used in contemporary practice where a flexible and open mind can facilitate exploration.

Synchronicity is the term Jung introduced to describe the co-incidence of two events which he saw as having an a-causal link. In other words, that it is not just coincidence that something happens, but that something else happens which connects the two in an inexplicable but meaningful way. The term has of course entered common parlance. Genuine synchronicities – somewhat rare as they are – can contribute to our understanding in a clinical setting as well as outside. A dramatic example taken from Main (2007: 1–2) is as follows:

> An analyst on vacation suddenly had a strong visual impression of one of her patients she knew to be suicidal. Unable to account for the impression as having arisen by any normal chain of mental associations, she immediately sent a telegram telling the patient not to do anything foolish. Two days later she learned that, just before the telegram arrived, the patient had gone into the kitchen and turned on the gas valve with the intention of killing herself. Startled by the postman ringing the doorbell, she turned the valve off; and even more struck by the content of the telegram he delivered, she did not resume her attempt.

RESEARCH

The very issue of providing research in the field of psychotherapy is somewhat contentious inasmuch as the work is not easily quantifiable. It is a highly subjective experience. Under pressure to conform to standards set by executive bodies, much effort is being put into finding ways of conducting research that does justice to the work. This has become increasingly important at a time when there has been governmental pressure to statutorily regulate the profession, and in a climate where economics has been the guiding principle in the Improving Access to Psychological Therapies (IAPT) initiative. With the IAPT programme there has been a risk of losing the essential meaning of 'therapy', shifting the focus from the 'care of souls' to a manualised practice that can be evaluated in numerical form.

Jung himself regarded his life's work to be indivisible from his life and research (Stevens, 1990).

The first Chair in Analytical Psychology was endowed in Dallas, United States of America, at the Texas A&M University in 1985. In Britain, the first Chair in Analytical Psychology was created in 1995 at the University of Essex. This is now a thriving department with pioneering research programmes in analytical psychology at BA, Masters and Doctoral level, attracting students from around the world.

REFERENCES

Freud, S. (1900) The Interpretation of Dreams. In *The Standard Edition of the Complete Psychological Works of Sigmund Freud*. London: Hogarth Press.
Hillman, J. (1978) *The Myth of Analysis: Three Essays in Archetypal Psychology*. New York: Harper Torch.
Hillman, J. (1983) *Archetypal Psychology: A Brief Account*. Woodstock, CT: Spring Publications.
Hillman, J. (1994) *Healing Fictions*. Woodstock, CT: Spring Publications.
Hogenson, G.B. (2004) Archetypes: Emergence and the Psyche's Deep Structure. In J. Cambray and L. Carter (Eds), *Analytical Psychology: Contemporary Perspectives in Jungian Analysis*. Hove and New York: Brunner-Routledge.
Jung, C.G. (1916) *Psychology of the Unconscious*. London: Kegal, Paul, Trench, Trubner & Co.
Jung, C.G. (1945) 'Letter to P.W. Martin', dated 20 August 1945. In *C.G. Jung Letters* (Vol. 1). London: Routledge & Kegan Paul.
Jung, C.G. (1949) Foreword to Neumann: Depth Psychology and a New Ethic. In *The Symbolic Life* (Collected Works, Vol. 18). London: Routledge.
Jung, C.G. (2009) *The Red Book*. London and New York: W.W. Norton.
Jung, C.G., with Jaffe, A. (1995 [1963]) *Memories, Dreams, Reflections*. London: Fontana Press.

(Continued)

(Continued)

Jung, E. (1931) *Animus and Anima: Two Essays*. Woodstock, CT: Spring Publications.

Kerr, J. (1993) *A Most Dangerous Method: The Story of Jung, Freud and Sabina Spielrein*. New York: Alfred A. Knopf.

Kirsch, T. (2000) *The Jungians: A Comparative and Historical Perspective*. London and Philadelphia, PA: Routledge.

Knox, J. (2001) Memories, fantasies, archetypes: an exploration of some connections between cognitive science and analytical psychology. *The Journal of Analytical Psychology*, 46(4), 613–635.

Knox, J. (2003) *Archetype, Attachment, Analysis: Jungian Psychology and the Emergent Mind*. Hove: Brunner-Routledge.

Main, R. (2007) *Revelations of Chance: Synchronicity as Spiritual Experience*. New York: SUNY Press.

Samuels, A. (1985) *Jung and the Post-Jungians*. London and New York: Routledge.

Samuels, A. (1989) *The Plural Psyche: Personality, Morality and the Father*. London and New York: Tavistock/Routledge.

Samuels, A. (1993) *The Political Psyche*. London and New York: Routledge.

Schaverien, J. (1991) *The Revealing Image: Analytical Art Psychotherapy in Theory and Practice*. London and New York: Tavistock/Routledge.

Schaverien, J. (1995) *Desire and the Female Therapist: Engendered Gaze in Psychotherapy and Art Therapy*. London and New York: Routledge.

Singer, T. (2004) Archetypal defences of the group spirit. In T. Singer and S.L. Kimbles (Eds), *The Cultural Complex: Contemporary Jungian Perspectives on Psyche and Society*. Hove: Routledge.

Singer, T. (2010) The transcendent function and cultural complexes: a working hypothesis. *Journal of Analytical Psychology*, 55(2), 234–241.

Spielrein, S. (1994 [1912]) 'Destruction as the Cause of Coming into Being', *Journal of Analytical Psychology*, 39: 155–186.

Stein, M. (2022) *Four Pillars of Jungian Psychoanalysis.* Asheville, NC: Chiron Publications.

Stevens, A. (1982) *Archetypes: A Natural History of the Self*. New York: William Morrow & Co.

Stevens, A. (1990) *On Jung*. London and New York: Routledge.

Stevens, A. (2003) *Archetype Revisited: An Updated Natural History of the Self*. Toronto: Inner City Books.

Tacey, D. (2001) *Jung and the New Age*. Hove: Brunner-Routledge.

Tempest, K. (2013) *Brand New Ancients*. London: Picador.

Wehr, D. (1987) *Jung and Feminism: Liberating Archetypes*. Boston, MA: Beacon Press.

Young-Eisendrath, P. (2004) *Subject to Change: Jung, Gender and Subjectivity in Psychoanalysis*. Hove: Routledge.

RECOMMENDED READING

Bair, D. (2003) *Jung: A Biography.* London: Little Brown & Co.

This book is an exhaustive and lengthy biography of Jung, the man.

Samuels, A. (1985) *Jung and the Post-Jungians*. London and New York: Routledge.

This book is a brilliant overview of the field, including contemporary developments, from a leading clinician.

Goss, P. (2015) *Jung: A Complete Introduction*. London: John Murray Learning.

This book is a simple introduction to Jungian analysis.

5.16 LACANIAN THERAPY

LIONEL BAILLY

OVERVIEW AND KEY POINTS

Lacanian Therapy is a psychoanalytically informed treatment aimed at individuals with disabling anxiety, failing coping strategies and problematic personality traits.

- Lacanian Therapy is a psychological therapy nested in a theoretical model in which humans are 'speaking beings', the unconscious is structured as a language and symptoms can be seen as having a metaphoric value.
- The overarching goal in Lacanian Therapy is to move away from the ego, understood as a fiction, to discover more of the subject and the truth of one's desire.
- Desire results from the impossibility of a subject to properly articulate what it needs. The therapy helps a patient identify what their objects, around which desire is organised, are. These imaginary objects, called 'the object cause of desire', are closely linked with anxiety.
- Therapists don't provide advice or guidance as they are sure to be mistaken, but are empty mirrors in which the patients can start to see themselves for what they are.

BRIEF HISTORY

In the middle decades of the twentieth century, Jacques Lacan created a model of psychoanalysis by revisiting the works of Freud in the light of developments in fields of study such as linguistics, philosophy, anthropology and mathematics.

Jacques Lacan was born in Paris on 13 April 1901. He studied medicine and psychiatry and was trained in psychiatric asylums, where he acquired a wide clinical experience, including of severe psychosis. After having worked with some of the most brilliant proponents of organic psychiatry, he found in psychoanalysis the most helpful theoretical model for understanding and treating the complex patients he was dealing with. In 1938, he became a psychoanalyst of the Société Psychanalytique de Paris. Lacan believed that Freudian theory was not a perfect edifice but a work in progress, and wanted to contribute towards what he saw as a developing model. His attitude towards the development of theory was modern in that he was willing to examine any body of science that could clarify or shed new light on the phenomena he was trying to explain, and consequently he drew inspiration from biological psychiatry, genetic psychology, philosophy, structural linguistics, anthropology and even mathematics. The richness of the result has attracted students in fields far from psychoanalysis or psychiatry. His use of variations on the standard psychoanalytic treatment was sufficiently controversial for Lacan to be banned from the International Psychoanalytic Association in 1962. In 1963, he created his own school of psychoanalysis. The new organisation proved a success, and the influence and membership of Lacanian analytic institutions has continued to grow to the present day. Jacques Lacan died in Paris on 9 September 1981.

BASIC ASSUMPTIONS

Lacan's view is that the characteristic that sets human beings apart from other animals is language: we are speaking beings. If speech is what makes us human, then the fundamentals of the human psyche should be found in the particularities and structure of spoken language. Lacan made the hypothesis of a structural mirroring between what we say, the way we think and what we are – and this also applies to the unconscious, which is structured like a language. Slips of the tongue, bungled actions and also symptoms encountered in psychopathology follow this linguistic structure and can be seen as having a metaphoric value.

The ego is a fiction, 'an imaginary narrative' that the infant starts to construct as soon as he/she is able to recognise itself in the mirror, and the building blocks of the edifice are signifiers (the spoken word). The ego is not based on a perception–consciousness system or organised by the reality principle, but exists instead by dint of *méconnaissance* (obliviousness) – the obliviousness or blindness of the subject to itself.

Drawing upon Freud's idea that thought and meaning are coded in ideational representatives, Lacan pinpointed these by means of Saussurian linguistics as being signifiers – the acoustic image of words. Lacan emphasised the detachable quality of signifiers from what they signify, and that it is the signifier attached to an anxiogenic thought that becomes repressed into the unconscious, so that the anxious affect becomes displaced onto other, less terrifying signifiers (which might thereby acquire an irrationally worrying nature). The unconscious for Lacan is therefore a world of repressed signifiers, and the task of analysis is to retrieve these and restore them to consciousness in the authentic signifying chain. The patient is the only person in possession of the unconscious knowledge, and it is by paying careful attention to the patient's discourse – especially to slips of the tongue, dreams, repetitive speech, irrational narrative or neurotic preoccupations – that the analyst is able to hear the manifestations of the unconscious. The patient has no feeling of responsibility for these manifestations, which seem to him to come from somewhere else, which Lacan calls the Other (*le grand autre*). The place occupied by this Other is that from which language and laws derive.

The unconscious discourse of the patient is directed by 'master signifiers' – the foundation stones of the individual's psychological structure. These signifiers 'orient' or give direction to the patient's preoccupations and unconscious narratives. One of the main tasks of analysis is to bring into consciousness these master signifiers, so that the patient becomes aware of how they influence his/her emotions and thoughts.

Lacan builds upon Freud's Oedipus complex to arrive at the subtler formulation known as the paternal metaphor to explain how a child separates psychically from its mother and accepts its status as a less-than-perfect being. In order to explain its mother's absences and preoccupations, the child must postulate an object s/he desires more than him/herself. This imaginary object is called the phallus. Castration is not a real physical threat, but the child's reluctant acceptance that s/he does not have what it takes to keep mother's perfect attention, and the consequent hypothesis that this most desirable object must exist 'somewhere out there' in the real world. The name-of-the-father is the first signifier that the child can accept as a representative of what mother finds more interesting than him/herself; it is a metaphor and the child's acceptance of it involves an important intellectual act. For Lacan, the child's submission to this formulation initiates him/her into the ability to think metaphorically, with the flexibility of signifier substitutions that this allows, and is a keystone in the construction of the psyche.

Lacan saw desire as a condition that plays a structuring role in the subject. Desire results from the impossibility that a subject can properly articulate what it needs – the 'gap between demand and need'. The articulation of need must pass through the gates of language, and what cannot squeeze through and is left behind constitutes desire. The objects, around which desire is organised, are imaginary objects called 'the object cause of desire', and this has a genetic link with the original imagined perfect object, the phallus. The object cause of desire, or object 'a', is closely linked with anxiety, in that it appears in the place of a primordial experience of loss.

For Lacan, it is not the biological reality of sex that determines our gender identity; he saw gender as the result of a process of identification, and of a process he calls 'sexuation'. This has to do with how a subject situates itself in relation to the phallus and symbolic castration, and also to his/her identification with the mother.

ORIGINS AND MAINTENANCE OF PROBLEMS

Like Sigmund and Anna Freud, Lacanians think that 'human behaviour and its aberrations [are] being determined not by overt factors but by the pressure of instinctual forces emanating from the unconscious mind' (Freud, n.d.). Besides the classical analytical views on the origin of psychopathology, the Lacanian model suggests some specific types of difficulties.

The mirror stage represents a moment at which the baby perceives itself as a unit, and also the first time the child thinks of itself as 'I' in relation to an image that he understands as representing himself. The failure to perceive oneself in this way is seen in autistic pathologies in children. In addition, the intellectual perception of oneself is an alienating experience as the image is never as perfect as the imagined self, and splits the psyche into the part that identifies with the image and the part that becomes the active agent in building a narrative about the imaginary (from image) self.

The discourse that is built upon the image is the ego, which Lacan sees as a fiction maintained and nurtured throughout one's life with the help of denegation and obliviousness (*méconnaissance*). This fictional ego can be the source of the patient's discontent and request for therapeutic help.

The ego and the subject both develop in the discourse of the Other – a way of saying that the discourse, attitudes and beliefs of the main figures in a child's development have a profound structuring effect upon the subject. The individual's master signifiers, which also derive from the Other, have a crucial role in the construction of the psychological structure of an individual and can be at the root of a subject's failure and sufferings.

The submission to the paternal metaphor allows the child to situate itself within the law, to move away from an enmeshed relationship with his/her mother and to drop his/her infantile omnipotence. For Lacan, the foreclosure of the paternal metaphor leads to the development of a psychotic structure, while other pathological modalities of dealing with it can lead to neurosis or perversion.

The subject's relationship with his object cause of desire defines the individual's unique way in which s/he seeks enjoyment, and both the nature of these objects and the specificity of the relationship can be the source of psychopathology.

THEORY OF CHANGE

Lacan was preoccupied with what exactly 'curing' means. Is it simply the disappearance of a symptom, or does one aim to change the underlying personality structure that produced it and in which it is inscribed? Is this at all achievable, and if it is, is it desirable? If it is neither achievable nor desirable, then where should curing stop – at what boundary line? Lacan clarified his position about patients and symptoms by saying that while it is reasonable that individuals expect their symptoms to disappear following an analytical treatment, the symptom has a defensive quality and it might not always be prudent to try to suppress the use of certain aspects of it. In this way, enjoyment and desire remain possible for the subject.

The Lacanian analyst knows that at some point during the course of the treatment, the patient will be faced with the decision to be cured of his/her symptom or not to be. This decision, if the treatment has been successful, could be an enlightened choice, made in the light of self-knowledge.

A patient looking to boost his/her self-esteem, or to be reassured that they are really all right and just need to rethink some of their 'coping strategies', should not go to a Lacanian analyst. Lacanians do not 'strengthen' or 'support' the ego but will try to help the patient dismantle it in order to come face-to-face with his/her own subject, to recognise the truth of his/her desire and the modalities of his/her enjoyment and to emerge from treatment with an altered ego that is closer to the fullness of the subject.

SKILLS AND STRATEGIES

As in most other forms of psychotherapy, free association is the first rule. The patient is asked to say anything that comes to mind, even if it appears superficial or unrelated to what has been discussed, and is encouraged to remember and talk about their dreams. The therapist pays particular attention to the discourse of the patient, the words used, the structure of the sentences, any unusual use of a word, patterns and repetitions, etc.

The place of counter-transference in Lacanian analysis is different from that in most other schools. Lacan recognised that the therapist experiences feelings towards his patient, but suggested that he must know not only not to give into them, but also how to make adequate use of them in his technique. If the analyst does not act on the basis of these feelings, it is not because his/her training analysis has drained away his/her passions, but because it has given him/her a desire which is even stronger than those passions: the desire to remain focused upon the treatment of the patient.

Lacanians use sessions of variable duration, including short sessions. The ending of the session is a meaningful act, too important to leave to mere form. One should not end a session just because the allotted time is up, especially if the analysand is in the middle of some interesting discourse. Conversely, it may be useful to be able to end the session just at the point that the analysand says something important – so that it can 'hang in the air' for further reflection until the next time; more words will often obfuscate the realisation that was emerging. In many ways, the end of the session emphasises some particularly important aspect and works almost as an interpretation.

CASE STUDY

A 30-year-old woman comes to see a therapist, explaining that she is gay and wants to have a baby. She has been in homosexual relationships since she was a teenager and is satisfied with her sexuality. Her family and colleagues at work know of her sexual orientation and it has never been a problem. Now that she wants a baby, people have suggested she should find a sperm donor but she does not want to become pregnant that way. She says: 'I want my children to be conceived like I have been conceived. I want them to grow up like I grew up, with a father and a mother. I want to be a real mother.' She is perfectly aware that this wish clashes with what her life has been, her sexual orientation and choice of love objects. The therapy focused on the object of her desire, the place the signifiers 'real mother' meant in her psyche and the exploration of the construction of her gender and sexual identity.

RESEARCH

There has been no quantitative research on the outcome of psychotherapy in a Lacanian theoretical framework. In addition, a Lacanian approach would lead to questioning the ability of quantitative research to assess and measure the 'improvement' of a patient, as this can't be equated with a mere reduction in symptomatology. It is not that research is impossible, but that the impact of therapy on the individual's psyche is of a complexity far beyond the reach of symptom rating scales.

REFERENCE

Freud, A. (n.d.) (www.freud.org.uk/education/topic/40053/annafreud).

RECOMMENDED READING

Bailly, L. (2009) *Lacan: A Beginner's Guide*. Oxford: One World.

This book is an introduction to Lacanian theory that allows beginners to understand some of the key concepts without being overwhelmed by the complexity of Lacan's thinking and his rather difficult style.

Lacan, J. (1982) Guiding remarks for a congress on feminine sexuality. From *Écrits* (trans. J. Rose). In J. Mitchell and J. Rose (Eds), *Feminine Sexuality*. New York: W.W. Norton.

This article introduces readers to Lacan's original and modern take on gender and sexuality.

Fink, B. (2019) On the value of the Lacanian approach to analytic practice. *International Journal of Psychoanalysis*, 100(2), 315–332.

This article is for anybody who wants a deeper understanding of Lacanian clinical work.

5.17 MINDFULNESS BASED COGNITIVE THERAPY

ADAM J. SCOTT AND KATE ADAM

OVERVIEW AND KEY POINTS

This chapter will explore mindfulness based cognitive therapy (MBCT), an evidence-based and integrative form of cognitive-behavioural therapy (CBT) used to treat a range of psychological issues. As MBCT was originally developed to work with clients experiencing recurrent episodes of major depression, the chapter will focus on this psychological presentation. The key points of the chapter are as follows:

- MBCT is part of the third wave of CBT.
- MBCT argues that *rumination* and *experimental avoidance* are two thought processes which make clients vulnerable to recurrent depressive episodes.
- MBCT makes use of cognitive therapy and mindfulness techniques to enable clients to become self-aware, so they can learn to de-centre from distressing thoughts, feelings, bodily sensations and behaviours.
- MBCT has a growing evidence base and is recommended by the National Institute for Health and Care Excellence (NICE) as a treatment for major recurrent depression.

BRIEF HISTORY

MBCT is informed by mindfulness meditation practices and cognitive therapy theory (Segal, Williams and Teasdale, 2018). Mindfulness is a form of meditation found in most world faiths, although mindfulness practices used within counselling and psychotherapy tend to be Buddhist in nature. It is important to remember that mindfulness within religious practice differs from that within counselling and psychotherapy, the former focusing on enlightenment, devotion and worship and the latter on psychological wellbeing.

Mindfulness is used in three main ways in the field of counselling and psychotherapy: (1) as a self-help tool (Williams and Penman, 2011), (2) as a technique within an eclectic approach to therapy or (3) as an integrative form of CBT, such as MBCT and compassion focused therapy and dialectical behaviour therapy (Mansell, 2018). MBCT is an integrative approach based on John Kabat-Zinn's (1990) mindfulness based stress reduction (MBSR). MBSR was developed for clients experiencing chronic pain, mental health issues and other life-limiting illnesses. Using Buddhist meditative practices (mindfulness), this approach encourages clients to accept the discomfort they experience rather than resisting it. Interestingly, through acceptance comes an alleviation of their psychological and physical distress. Segal, Williams and Teasdale (2018) further developed MBSR into MBCT by integrating it with aspects of cognitive therapy in order to effectively help those experiencing recurrent depressive episodes.

BASIC ASSUMPTIONS

MBCT is an integrative approach underpinned by assumptions of CBT (Crane, 2017). Sanders (2010) outlines these as follows:

- Collaboration – it is essential clients feel they are playing an active role in therapy, whether MBCT is used within a group or individual setting. Collaboration is facilitated through group discussion and tasks to complete at home.
- Formulation – MBCT does not necessitate the creation of a written formulation, but it does require the client to learn to formulate their presenting problem with MBCT theory in mind.
- Structured, psychoeducational and focused – MBCT is a psychoeducation group or one-to-one therapy programme designed to treat specific mental health issues (i.e., depression, anxiety, psychosis, etc.).
- Time-limited – MBCT groups are designed to last for eight weeks, although if used in individual therapy may last longer.

- Cognitive and behavioural – MBCT is integrative in nature and draws from a number of therapeutic sources, namely mindfulness meditation, but is firmly grounded in cognitive therapy theory and practice.

- Homework – MBCT requires all clients to carry out tasks at home and reflect on these in the therapy sessions. This homework is a central part of the therapeutic process.

ORIGIN AND MAINTENANCE OF PROBLEMS

CASE STUDY

INTRODUCING JEREMY

Jeremy is a 45-year-old man who has come to therapy because he is experiencing recurrent episodes of depression. He first had a depressive episode when he was 27 after a particularly stressful time at work and a relationship breakdown. He currently experiences between two to three episodes of depression a year. These are moderate in nature and generally last from two and six weeks. While he can work when feeling depressed, he finds it difficult due to the symptoms he experiences – lack of concentration, waking in the night worrying, tiredness and low motivation. Jeremy takes antidepressants and has had person-centred therapy in the past, which he found helpful. Jeremy has been referred for MBCT because his GP told him it may help to better manage his depression.

Thought patterns are central to MBCT's understanding of why people are vulnerable to mental health concerns such as recurrent depression (McCartney et al., 2021). The approach argues there are two ways of thinking which can trigger and maintain depressive episodes. The first is called *rumination* and the second *experimental avoidance* (Crane, 2017). While the term *rumination* may be unfamiliar, the experience of a negative ruminative is a common one. Most people have experienced waking up in the middle of the night worrying about something, and once they begin to worry about one thing, another worry is triggered, and so on, which culminates in a cycle of worry which is difficult to escape from. Therefore, *rumination* can be experienced as a spiral of distressing emotions, thoughts and sensations in our bodies and behaviours. This common experience can lead to a poor night's sleep, although, for people like Jeremy, with previous experience of a pathological depression, *rumination* may trigger a further episode of depression.

Depressive rumination is distressing and when Jeremy experiences it, he seeks to escape his uncomfortable thoughts, feelings, bodily sensations and behaviours. MBCT defines this as *experiential avoidance* (Crane, 2017). When awoken in the night with worry, Jeremy tries to avoid his worries by forcing himself to stop thinking about the issue he is worrying about, or by engaging in an internal dialogue which seeks to resolve his concerns through problem-solving. Unfortunately, these actions usually lead to frustration, further distress and even strengthen the ruminative pattern. During the day Jeremy tries to use coping strategies to distract himself from his distressing experiences – he tends to spend longer at work when he begins to feel down so that he is distracted from his *ruminations*, a behaviour which can work in the short term but soon exacerbates his problems. MBCT theory suggests Jeremy can learn to manage *depressive rumination* by (a) becoming aware of what triggers *rumination*, (b) recognising when he is ruminating and (c) *de-centre* or detach from the negative thoughts feelings, bodily sensations and behaviours by learning to observe and accept them rather than avoid or fight them (Segal et al., 2018).

PROCESS OF CHANGE

MBCT suggests that in order to learn to *de-centre*, clients need to be able to recognise the two *modes of mind* – the *being mode* and the *doing mode* (Crane, 2017). The *doing mode of mind* is most useful for problem-solving, analysing and comparing current problems with things that happened in the past or predicting what might happen in the future (Segal et al., 2018). However, it becomes less useful when allied with *depressive rumination*. For example, Jeremy works in a busy marketing agency and when a large contract is near completion he often has to work extra hours. This can lead to him being overwhelmed (feeling), to think that he does not have the ability to do his work (thought), to have stress-related headaches (bodily sensations) and to begin to isolate himself from others so he has more time to work (behaviours). He can use the *doing mode* to problem-solve this situation by thinking 'I know I am feeling overwhelmed but this contract will be finished soon and if I just put in another couple of day's work everything will be fine'. However, there are times when this type of problem-solving does not help and Jeremy feels he cannot 'switch off' and he begins to get caught in the *doing mode* which promotes *depressive rumination*. During these stressful times at work, Jeremy can wake up at night and begin to worry, thinking about times in the past when he felt he could not cope with stress at work and being fearful that he may be getting depressed. As we have already said, the fact that Jeremy tries to problem-solve these thoughts can lead him into a spiral of worry that he finds difficult to get out of. The problem with these ruminative patterns is they can become automatic, which means Jeremy may not be aware he is engaging in them. MBCT calls this lack of awareness the *automatic pilot* (Segal et al., 2018).

We all have an *automatic pilot* which governs thinking, feeling or behaviour processes that have become routine. For example, leaving the house and walking to the bus and then thinking 'did I lock the front door?' The reason we cannot remember locking the door is because we do it automatically and without self-awareness. It is important to note the *automatic pilot* is not a problem which we need to eradicate as it has a positive function in our lives, such as helping us with complex activities like driving a car. However, MBCT encourages people to be aware of our *automatic pilot* because by becoming aware of it clients can recognise when they are caught in negative patterns of thoughts which can leave them vulnerable to further episodes of depression.

In MBCT theory, the *being mode* of mind stands alongside the *doing mode*. In the *being mode* of mind, we experience a sense of homeostasis, for example, sitting on a park bench on a spring morning, the sweet smell of new flowers, the warm sunshine on your skin, the sound of birds singing and the experience of being at peace. Mindfulness is an aspect of the *being mode* and can be defined as 'paying attention … on purpose in the present moment with curiosity and kindness … to things as they are' (Kabat-Zinn, 1994: 4). Most importantly, by becoming mindful we can shift from the *doing* to the *being* mode of mind. Similarly, Jeremy can shift from the doing to the being mode by using mindfulness when he is overwhelmed by work stress, by observing and de-centring from the distressing thoughts, emotions, bodily sensations and behaviours he is experiencing.

In summary, by bringing together cognitive therapy with mindfulness mediation, MBCT teaches clients to learn to increase their self-awareness in order to recognise potential triggers to depressive rumination and experiential avoidance. Through this self-awareness and with training in mindfulness, the client has the opportunity to respond differently to their automatic thought processes and learn to *de-centre* before they spiral into psychological distress.

SKILLS AND STRATEGIES

This section will provide a brief overview of the eight sessions of the MBCT group intervention from Jeremy's perspective. It is based on the sessions outlined by Segal, Williams and Teasdale (2018). Each session has a clear structure and a number of elements, which include an *in vivo* mindfulness practice, discussion on a set topic and homework being set and reflected upon.

SESSION 1

In the first session Jeremy is introduced to the group in order to build rapport. He is taught about the automatic pilot and its impact on his wellbeing. The therapist introduced mindfulness by inviting the group to take a raisin and mindfully explore its appearance, texture, smell and taste as though they had never seen one before. The group also completed their first body scan, a similar exercise to the raisin meditation but this time they focused on the sensations in different parts of their bodies. Jeremy found both these exercises helpful as introductions to mindfulness, particularly in becoming aware of how distracted his mind could be when trying to focus. The group was asked to practise these exercises each day before the next session.

SESSION 2

The group discussed their homework from last week and Jeremy spoke about his growing awareness of the *chatter* in his mind when trying to meditate. The group explored the impact this *chatter* could have on their thoughts, feelings, bodily sensations and behaviours, and were introduced to the concept of *de-centring* by noticing and letting go. The therapist practised another mediation with them called the *10 minute sitting meditation*. This was added to their homework, as was a task which required the group to keep a diary of pleasant experiences.

SESSION 3

The group reviewed their homework and discussed relevant issues. Jeremy was enjoying the meditation homework even though it was challenging at times. The therapist introduced a new exercise called mindful movement. This involved using mindfulness alongside basic yoga, stretching and walking. As he had reported struggling with some of these, he found the technique of being aware of his breath, as an anchor in the present, very helpful. This exercise was added to the group's homework for the week.

SESSION 4

In this session the group focused on staying present when their minds are caught by some thoughts while avoiding others. They learned that mindfulness facilitates taking a broader perspective and relating differently to our emotions, body sensations, thoughts and behaviours. The group explored depression and Jeremy formulated an understanding around what may have contributed to the development of his difficulties. He recognised that his relationship breakdown and stress at work had impacted on the development of his depression, although the real issue was how his thoughts were subsequently interpreting interactions and experiences in the present. The homework for next week involved practising mediations and breathing spaces.

SESSION 5

In this session the group learned to allow experiences to be as they are, without judgement, by using skills like acceptance, holding, allowing and letting be. This attitude towards experiences facilitated Jeremy to see more clearly and evaluate how he best cared for himself. He recognised that a situation at work where he had an increased workload due to a contract coming to an end was causing him significant anxiety. He realised that the anxiety he was experiencing could be a 'normal' response for people in this situation, which did not mean he was necessarily getting depressed. He decided to focus on how best to look after himself during this time instead of getting caught up in negative ruminative patterns. The session also included sitting meditation and an expanded breathing space, which formed part of Jeremy's homework.

SESSION 6

This session focused on the idea that *thoughts are not facts* and explored how depressive thoughts can affect our ability to relate to our experiences – acknowledging thought patterns empowered the group members to decide whether or not they wished to engage with particular thoughts. The therapist encouraged the group to be aware that the end of therapy was approaching and to integrate mindfulness practice into their daily life. Jeremy discussed with the group his feeling that he has more control of his depression rather than being an inactive passenger of it, although he also said he was struggling to take the time needed to complete his meditative exercises. The group discussed some ways he could address this.

SESSION 7

The group learned the importance of being proactive in managing their depression and reflected on self-care skills. They discussed the impact of activity on mood and the importance of planning mindfulness and positive activities into their lives. Jeremy recognised that going for a pint with friends or walking his dog, rather than just watching TV after work, led him to feel more positive. The therapist facilitated a discussion on recognising signs of relapse and depressive symptoms. Jeremy identified thoughts where he believed others criticising him could lead to getting caught in depressive emotions and behaviours. Using the breathing space, he was able to explore these further and continued to consolidate his progress though his homework.

SESSION 8

The final session focused on *using what has been learned to deal with future moods*. It reviewed the journey the group and the individuals in it had made. The group discussed how to continue the mindfulness practices and maintain their learning. Jeremy shared that he and others were looking to attend yoga classes and perhaps set up a weekly space for mindfulness meditations. The group made practical plans for the future, during which Jeremy wrote a list to remind himself why it was important to sustain his mindfulness practice. He also recognised that since starting the group he enjoyed life more and that acceptance was something he wanted to continue to work on. He recorded he was most motivated to stay healthy by wanting to have a good relationship with his partner and being around friends and family. The session closed with a meditation.

RESEARCH

The effectiveness of MBCT has been extensively explored in the research literature as an evidence-based treatment of recurrent major depression (McCartney et al., 2021). There is also an evidence base for the use of MBCT with other mental health issues, such as bipolar disorder, anxiety disorders, psychosis, as well as people living with chronic pain and cancer survivors (Nissen et al., 2020; Pei et al., 2021; Xuan et al., 2020). Research suggests that mindfulness based approaches are an effective tool for the development of resilience and wellbeing in non-clinical populations (Janssen et al., 2018; Querstret et al., 2020). New emerging studies suggest that MBCT can be effectively offered via the internet (Moulton-Perkins et al., 2022; Nissen et al., 2020).

REFERENCES

Crane, R. (2017). *Mindfulness-based cognitive therapy* (2nd ed.). London: Routledge.
Janssen, M., Heerkens, Y., Kuijer, W., van der Heijden, B. and Engels, J. (2018). Effects of mindfulness-based stress reduction on employees' mental health: a systematic review. *PLoS One*, 13(1), e0191332. 10.1371/journal.pone.0191332
Kabat-Zinn, J. (1990). *Full catastrophe living*. New York: Delacorte.
Kabat-Zinn, J. (1994). *Wherever you go, there you are*. London: Piatkus.
Mansell, W. (2018). What is CBT really and how can we enhance the impact of effective psychotherapies such as CBT? In D. Loewenthal and G. Proctor (Eds), *Why not CBT? Against and for CBT revisited* (pp. 343–361). Monmouth: PCCS Books.
McCartney, M., Nevitt, S., Lloyd, A., Hill, R., White, R. and Duarte, R. (2021). Mindfulness-based cognitive therapy for prevention and time to depressive relapse: systematic review and network meta-analysis. *Acta Psychiatrica Scandinavica*, 143(1), 6–21. doi: 10.1111/acps.13242
Moulton-Perkins, A., Cavanagh, K., Masheder, J., Strauss, C. and Taravajra. (2022). Delivering mindfulness groups by video conferencing. In H. Wilson (Ed.), *Digital delivery of mental health therapies: A guide to the benefits and challenges and making it work* (pp. 226–239). London: Jessica Kingsley Publishers.
Nissen, E. R., O'Connor, M., Kaldo, V., Højris, I., Borre, M., Zachariae, R. and Mehlsen, M. (2020). Internet-delivered mindfulness-based cognitive therapy for anxiety and depression in cancer survivors: a randomized controlled trial. *Psycho-Oncology*, 29(1), 68–75. doi: 10.1002/pon.5237
Pei, J., Ma, T., Nan, R., Chen, H., Zhang, Y., Gou, L. and Dou, X. (2021). Mindfulness-based cognitive therapy for treating chronic pain a systematic review and meta-analysis. *Psychology, Health & Medicine*, 26(3), 333–346. doi: 10.1080/13548506.2020.1849746
Querstret, D., Morison, L., Dickinson, S., Cropley, M. and John, M. (2020). Mindfulness-based stress reduction and mindfulness-based cognitive therapy for psychological health and well-being in nonclinical samples: a systematic review and meta-analysis. *International Journal of Stress Management*, 27(4), 394–411. 10.1037/str0000165
Sanders, S. (2010). Cognitive behavioural approaches. In R. Woofle, S. Strawbridge, B. Douglas and W. Dryden (Eds), *Handbook of counselling psychology* (3rd ed., pp. 105–129). London: Sage.
Segal, Z. V., Williams, J. M. G. and Teasdale, J. D. (2018). *Mindfulness-based cognitive therapy for depression: A new approach to preventing relapse* (2nd ed.). New York: Guilford Press.
Williams, M. and Penman, D. (2011). *Mindfulness: Finding peace in a frantic world*. London: Piatkus.
Xuan, R., Li, X., Qiao, Y., Guo, Q., Liu, X., Deng, W., Hu, Q., Wang, K. and Zhang, L. (2020). Mindfulness-based cognitive therapy for bipolar disorder: a systematic review and meta-analysis. *Psychiatry Research*, 290, 113116. doi: 10.1016/j.psychres.2020.113116

> **RECOMMENDED READING**
>
> Segal, Z. V., Williams, J. M. G. and Teasdale, J. D. (2018). *Mindfulness-based cognitive therapy for depression: A new approach to preventing relapse* (2nd ed.). New York: Guilford Press.
>
> This is an updated version of a core text accessible to students and clinicians. It introduces the reader to MBCT's development, current theory, practice and relevant research. Its exploration of MBCT theory and research is engaging and provides an excellent grounding for practitioners. It is also practical in nature and provides a step-by-step overview of how to conduct the eight sessions of the MBCT group programme. The fact that it provides handouts for each session and access to downloadable audio mindfulness meditations makes it a must-have for those considering running an MBCT group.
>
> Crane, R. (2017). *Mindfulness-based cognitive therapy* (2nd ed.). London: Routledge.
>
> This is an excellent reference text in the 'CBT Distinctive Features Series'. It provides a brief overview of the theory and structure of the approach. It is suitable for those exploring MBCT for the first time and for more experienced practitioners who want a text for quick reference.
>
> Williams, M. and Penman, D. (2011). *Mindfulness: Finding peace in a frantic world.* London: Piatkus.
>
> This self-help book is structured around the eight-week MBCT programme but applies it to an individual setting. It is written in a clear and understandable way, which makes it suitable to recommend to clients. The book comes with a CD of mindfulness meditations to guide clients in mindfulness practices and has a supporting website (www.franticworld.com) where clients can access free online meditations. It remains an excellent resource for counsellors and psychotherapists wanting to structure one-to-one therapy around MBCT.

5.18 MULTIMODAL THERAPY

STEPHEN PALMER

OVERVIEW AND KEY POINTS

Multimodal therapy is a technically eclectic therapeutic approach as it uses techniques taken from many different psychological theories and systems. The techniques and strategies are applied systematically, based on data from client qualities, specific techniques and the therapist's clinical skills (Palmer, 2015). Multimodal therapy is a technically eclectic and systematic therapeutic approach.

- Human problems are multilevelled and multilayered. Few problems have a single cause or simple solution.
- The dimensions of personality are Behaviour, Affect, Sensations, Images, Cognitions, Interpersonal and Drugs/biology, known by the acronym, BASIC ID.
- The multimodal approach postulates that unless the seven BASIC ID modalities are assessed, therapy is likely to overlook significant concerns.

BRIEF HISTORY

During the 1950s Arnold Lazarus undertook his formal clinical training in South Africa. The main focus of his training was underpinned by Rogerian, Freudian and Sullivanian theories and methods. He attended seminars by Joseph Wolpe about conditioning therapies and reciprocal inhibition and in London he learned about the Adlerian orientation. He believed that no one system of therapy could provide a complete understanding of either human development or the human condition. In 1958, he became the first psychologist to use the terms 'behavior therapist' and 'behavior therapy' in an academic article.

Lazarus conducted follow-up inquiries into clients who had received behaviour therapy and found that many had relapsed. However, when clients had used both behaviour and cognitive techniques, more durable results were obtained. In the early 1970s he started advocating a broad but systematic range of cognitive-behavioural techniques, and his follow-up inquiries indicated the importance of breadth if therapeutic gains were to be maintained. This led to the development of multimodal therapy, which places emphasis on seven discrete but interactive dimensions or modalities which encompass all aspects of human personality.

BASIC ASSUMPTIONS

People are essentially biological organisms (neurophysiological and biochemical entities) who behave (act and react), emote (experience affective responses), sense (respond to olfactory, tactile, gustatory, visual and auditory stimuli), imagine (conjure up sights, sounds and other events in the mind's eye), think (hold beliefs, opinions, attitudes and values) and interact with one another (tolerate, enjoy or suffer in various interpersonal relationships). These dimensions of personality are usually known by the acronym BASIC ID, derived from the first letters of each modality, namely Behaviour, Affect, Sensations, Images, Cognitions, Interpersonal and Drugs/biology.

Modalities may interact with each other: for example, a negative image or cognition may trigger a negative emotion. Modalities may exist in a state of reciprocal transaction and flux, connected by complex chains of behaviour and other psycho-physiological processes.

The multimodal approach rests on the assumption that unless the seven modalities are assessed, therapy is likely to overlook significant concerns. Clients are usually troubled by a multitude of specific problems which can be dealt with by a similar multitude of specific interventions or techniques.

People have different thresholds for stress tolerance, frustration, pain, and external and internal stimuli in the form of sound, light, touch, smell and taste. Psychological interventions can be used to modify these thresholds but often the genetic predisposition has an overriding influence in the final analysis.

People tend to prefer some of the BASIC ID modalities more than others. They are referred to as 'cognitive reactors' or 'imagery reactors' or 'sensory reactors', depending upon which modality they favour.

Human personalities stem from interplay among social learning and conditioning, physical environment and genetic endowment. Therefore, each client is unique and may need a personalised therapy.

People usually benefit from a psychoeducational approach to help them deal with or manage their problems.

Although the therapist and client are equal in their humanity (the principle of parity), the therapist may be more skilled in certain areas in which the client needs to develop to achieve their goal(s). It is not automatically assumed that clients know how to deal with their problems or have the requisite skills, and the therapist may need to model or teach the client various skills and strategies.

No one theory has all the answers when helping clients. Multimodal therapy is underpinned by a broad social and cognitive learning theory, while drawing on group and communications theory and general systems theory. However, multimodal therapists can choose not to apply these theories obsessively to each client.

Technically speaking, 'multimodal therapy' *per se* does not exist; multimodal counsellors and psychotherapists, as technical eclectics, draw from as many other approaches or systems as necessary. To be accurate, there is a multimodal assessment format and a multimodal framework or orientation.

ORIGIN AND MAINTENANCE OF PROBLEMS

Human problems are multilevelled and multilayered. Few problems have a single cause or simple solution.

According to Lazarus, psychological disturbances are the product of one or more of the following:

- conflicting or ambivalent feelings or reactions
- misinformation
- missing information which includes ignorance, *naïveté* and skills deficits

- maladaptive habits, including conditioned emotional reactions
- issues pertaining to low self-esteem and lack of self-acceptance
- inflexible and rigid thinking styles and attitudes
- unhelpful core schemas
- tendency to cognitively or imaginally 'awfulise' events and situations
- unhelpful beliefs maintaining a low frustration tolerance (e.g., 'I can't stand it-itis')
- information-processing errors (cognitive distortions)
- interpersonal inquietude, such as misplaced affection, undue dependency or excessive antipathy
- biological dysfunctions.

People avoid or defend against discomfort, pain or negative emotions, such as shame, guilt, depression and anxiety. This is known as 'defensive reactions' and should not be confused with psychodynamic concepts.

The principal learning factors which are responsible for behavioural problems and disorders are conditioned associations (operant and respondent); modelling, identification and other vicarious processes; and idiosyncratic perceptions.

Non-conscious processes are often involved in learning. Stimuli that can influence feelings, conscious thoughts/images and behaviours may go unrecognised by the person concerned.

Interactions between two or more people involve communications and meta-communications (i.e., communication about their communication). Communication can disintegrate when individuals are unable to stand back from the transaction, thereby failing to examine the content and process of ongoing relationships.

People may have a genetic predisposition or vulnerability to certain disorders or distress.

THEORY OF CHANGE

A good therapeutic relationship, a constructive working alliance and adequate rapport are usually necessary but often insufficient for effective therapy. The therapist–client relationship is considered as the soil that enables the strategies and techniques to take root. The experienced multimodal therapist hopes to offer a lot more by assessing and treating the client's BASIC ID, endeavouring to 'leave no stone (or modality) unturned'.

Usually an active-directive approach to therapy is taken. However, this depends upon the issues being discussed and upon the client concerned.

The process of change commences with the counsellor explaining the client's problems or issues in terms of the seven modalities, that is the BASIC ID, and then negotiating a counselling programme which uses specific techniques or interventions for each specific problem. This is usually undertaken in the first or second session and the completed modality profile is developed (see Table 5.18.1).

Multimodal therapists take Paul's (1967: 111) mandate very seriously: '*What* treatment, by *whom*, is most effective for *this* individual with *that* specific problem and under *which* set of circumstances?' In addition, *relationships of choice* are also considered.

Positive, neutral or negative change in any one modality is likely to affect functioning in other modalities.

The approach is psychoeducational and the therapist ensures that the client understands why each technique or intervention is being recommended. Bibliotherapy is frequently used to help the client understand the methods applied and to correct misinformation and provide missing information. A multimodal self-help coaching book provides details of many multimodal techniques and how to develop a modality profile (Palmer, Cooper and Thomas, 2003).

The approach is technically eclectic as it uses techniques and methods taken from many different psychological theories and systems, without necessarily being concerned with the validity of their theoretical principles.

Multimodal therapists often see themselves in a coach/trainer–trainee or teacher–student relationship as opposed to a doctor–patient relationship, thereby encouraging self-change rather than dependency.

Flexible interpersonal styles of the therapist which match client needs can reduce attrition (i.e., dropout) rates and help the therapeutic relationship. This approach is known as being an 'authentic chameleon'. The term 'bespoke therapy' has been used to describe the custom-made emphasis of the approach.

Table 5.18.1 John's full modality profile (or BASIC ID chart)

Modality	Problem	Proposed programme/treatment
Behaviour	Eats/walks fast, always in a rush, hostile, competitive; indicative of type A behaviour	Discuss advantages of slowing down; disadvantages of rushing and being hostile; teach relaxation exercise; dispute self-defeating beliefs
	Avoidance of giving presentations	Exposure programme; teach necessary skills; dispute self-defeating beliefs
	Accident proneness	Discuss advantages of slowing down
Affect	Anxious when giving presentations; guilt when work targets not achieved	Anxiety management; dispute self-defeating thinking
	Frequent angry outbursts at work	Anger management; dispute irrational beliefs
Sensation	Tension in shoulders	Self-message; muscle relaxation exercise
	Palpitations	Anxiety management (e.g., breathing relaxation technique); dispute catastrophic thinking
	Frequent headaches	Relaxation exercise and biofeedback
	Sleeping difficulties	Relaxation or self-hypnosis tape for bedtime use; behavioural retraining; possibly reduce caffeine intake
Imagery	Negative images of not performing well	Coping imagery focusing on giving adequate presentations
	Images of losing control	Coping imagery of dealing with difficult work situations and with presentations; 'step-up' imagery (Palmer and Dryden, 1995)
	Poor self-image	Positive imagery
Cognition	I must perform well otherwise it will be awful and I couldn't stand it	Dispute self-defeating and irrational beliefs; coping statements; cognitive restructuring; ABCDE paradigm
	I must be in control	
	Significant others should recognise my work	(REBT) bibliotherapy
	If I fail, then I am a total failure	Coping imagery (Palmer and Dryden, 1995)
Interpersonal	Passive/aggressive in relationships; manipulative tendencies at work; always puts self first; few supportive friends	Assertiveness training
		Discuss pros and cons of behaviour
		Friendship training (Palmer and Dryden, 1995)
		Improve sleeping and reassess; refer to GP
Drugs/biology	Feeling inexplicably tired	Refer to GP; relaxation exercises
	Taking aspirins for headaches	
	Consumes 10 cups of coffee a day	Discuss benefits of reducing caffeine intake
	Poor nutrition and little exercise	Nutrition and exercise programme

Lazarus summed up briefly the main hypothesised ingredients of change when using the multimodal approach:

- *Behaviour*: positive reinforcement; negative reinforcement; punishment; counter-conditioning; extinction
- *Affect*: admitting and accepting feelings, abreaction
- *Sensation*: tension release, sensory pleasuring
- *Imagery*: coping images, changes in self-image
- *Cognition*: greater awareness, cognitive restructuring, modification of unhelpful core schema and information-processing errors
- *Interpersonal*: non-judgemental acceptance, modelling, dispersing unhealthy collusions
- *Drugs/biology*: better nutrition and exercise, substance abuse cessation, psychotropic medication when indicated.

SKILLS AND STRATEGIES

Therapists should practise humility; Lazarus stresses that therapists should know their limitations and other therapists' strengths. The therapist tries to ascertain whether a judicious referral to another therapist may be necessary to ensure that the client's needs are met. In addition, a referral to other health practitioners, such as medical doctors or psychiatrists, may be necessary if the client presents problems of an organic or a psychiatric nature.

Therapists take a flexible interpersonal approach with each client to maximise therapeutic outcome and reduce attrition rates.

Techniques and interventions are applied systematically, based on client qualities, therapist qualities, therapist skills, therapeutic alliance and technique specificity (Palmer, 2015). For example, research data will suggest various techniques that can be applied for a specific problem, although the therapist may only be proficient in using several of them, while the client may only be able to tolerate one or two of the suggested interventions due to having a low tolerance to pain or frustration. Finally, a poor therapeutic alliance may increase the chances of attrition (dropout) occurring if a high-anxiety-provoking technique is applied.

A wide range of cognitive and behavioural techniques are used in multimodal therapy. In addition, techniques are taken from other therapies, such as gestalt therapy (e.g., the empty chair). Table 5.18.2 illustrates the main techniques used in therapy.

A 24-page Multimodal Life History Inventory (MLHI-3) (Lazarus, 2019) is often, but not invariably, used to elicit information about each of the client's modalities, general historical information and expectations about therapy and the therapist. The client usually completes the MLHI-3 as an in-between session assignment after the first meeting. If the client is not up to undertaking the task due to inadequate skills or severe depression, the therapist can use the inventory questions as a guide in a therapy session (Palmer and Dryden, 1995).

Second-order BASIC ID is a modality profile which focuses solely on the different aspects of a resistant problem. It is undertaken when the interventions or techniques applied to help a specific problem do not appear to have resolved it.

To obtain more clinical information and general goals for therapy, a structural profile is drawn up (Lazarus, 1989). This can be derived from the MLHI-3 or by asking clients to rate subjectively, on a scale of 1 to 7, how they perceive themselves in relation to the seven modalities. The counsellor can ask a range of questions that focus on the seven modalities:

- *Behaviour*: How much of a 'doer' are you?
- *Affect*: How emotional are you?
- *Sensation*: How 'tuned in' are you to your bodily sensations?
- *Imagery*: How imaginative are you?
- *Cognition*: How much of a 'thinker' are you?
- *Interpersonal*: How much of a 'social being' are you?
- *Drugs/biology*: To what extent are you health conscious?

Then, in the session, the therapist can illustrate these scores graphically by representing them in the form of a bar chart on paper (see Figure 5.18.1). Then clients are asked in what way they would like to change their profiles while in therapy. Once again, the client is asked to rate subjectively each modality on a score from 1 to 7 (see Figure 5.18.2).

Tracking is another procedure regularly used in multimodal therapy. Here, the 'firing order' of the different modalities is noted for a specific problem. Therapy interventions are linked to the sequence of the firing order of the modalities. This is particularly useful for dealing with panic attacks.

Table 5.18.2 Frequently used techniques in multimodal therapy and training

Modality	Techniques and interventions	Modality	Techniques and interventions
Behaviour	Behaviour rehearsal		Positive self-statements
	Behavioural experiments		Problem-solving training
	Empty chair		Rational proselytising
	Exposure programme		Self-acceptance training
	Fixed role therapy		Thought stopping
	Modelling	Interpersonal	Assertion training
	Paradoxical intention		Communication training
	Psychodrama		Contracting
	Reinforcement programmes		Fixed role therapy
	Response prevention/cost		Friendship/intimacy training
	Risk-taking exercises		Graded sexual approaches
	Self-monitoring and recording		Paradoxical intentions
	Sleep hygiene programme		Role-play
	Stimulus control		Social skills training
	Shame attacking exercise	Drugs/biology	Alcohol reduction programme
Affect	Anger expression/management		Blood pressure reduction programme
	Anxiety management		Cholesterol (LDL) lowering programme
	Feeling identification		Lifestyle changes (e.g., exercise, nutrition)
Sensation	Biofeedback		Referral to physicians or other specialists
	Hypnosis		Stop smoking programme
	Meditation		Weight reduction and maintenance programme
	Mindfulness training		
	Relaxation training		
	Sensate focus training		
	Threshold training		
Imagery	Anti-future shock imagery		
	Associated imagery		
	Aversive imagery		
	Camera Check of Perceptions		
	Compassion-focused imagery		
	Coping imagery		
	Goal-focused imagery		
	Imagery rescripting		
	Implosion and imaginal exposure		
	Motivation imagery		
	Positive imagery		
	Rational emotive imagery		
	Relaxation imagery		
	Time projection imagery		
	Trauma-focused imagery		
Cognition	Bibliotherapy		
	Challenging faulty inferences		
	Cognitive rehearsal		
	Coping statements		
	Correcting misconceptions		
	Defusion techniques		
	Disputing irrational beliefs		
	Focusing		

Source: adapted from Palmer (1996: 55–56)

Multimodal therapists deliberately use a 'bridging' procedure to initially 'key into' a client's preferred modality, before gently exploring a modality (e.g., affect/emotion) that the client may be intentionally or unintentionally avoiding (Lazarus, 1997; Palmer, 2015).

RESEARCH

Many of the techniques used are taken from behaviour and cognitive therapy. These approaches, and, more recently, the techniques that are applied to specific problems and disorders, have been shown to be more effective than other forms of therapy. Specific research is still being undertaken in multimodal therapy (e.g., Mikaeili et al., 2015).

Controlled outcome studies have supported the benefits of multimodal assessment and counselling programmes. In addition, Kwee's (1984) outcome study on 84 hospitalised clients suffering from phobias or obsessive-compulsive disorders resulted in substantial recoveries and durable follow-ups. The MLHI was also evaluated, and results indicated that participants consistently evaluated it as more helpful, comprehensive and efficient compared to the Integral Intake, which is another initial assessment inventory (see Marquis, 2002).

The application of the multimodal approach to group counselling for new parents (Fitch and McCullough, 2018), and also the field of coaching are developing areas for research (Palmer, 2008; Palmer and Gyllensten, 2008). This includes multimodal health coaching (Palmer, 2008; Rose, Palmer and O'Riordan, 2010).

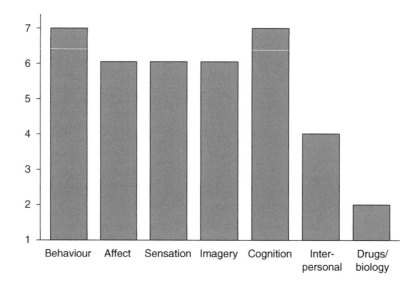

Figure 5.18.1 Natalie's structural profile

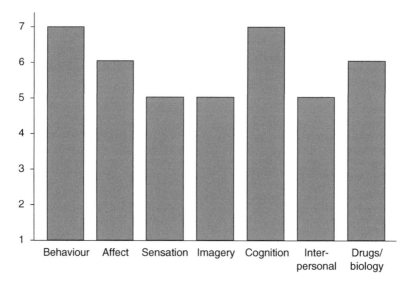

Figure 5.18.2 Natalie's desired structural profile

REFERENCES

Fitch, T. and McCullough, G. (2018) Multimodal counselling group for new parents. In D. Viers (Ed.), *The Group Therapist's Notebook. Homework, Handouts, and Activities for Use in Psychotherapy*. New York: Routledge.

Kwee, M.G.T. (1984) *Klinische Multimodale Gegragtstherapie*. Lisse: Swets and Zeitlinger.

Lazarus, A.A. (1981) *The Practice of Multimodal Therapy: Systematic, Comprehensive and Effective Psychotherapy*. New York: McGraw Hill.

Lazarus, A.A. (1997) *Brief but Comprehensive Psychotherapy: The Multimodal Way*. New York: Springer.

Lazarus, C.N. (2019) *MLHI-3: Multimodal Life History Inventory*. Champaign, IL: Research Press.

Marquis, A. (2002) *Mental health professionals' comparative evaluations of the Integral intake, the life-style introductory interview, and the multimodal life history inventory*. Unpublished PhD Dissertation, University of North Texas.

Mikaeili, N., Hajloo, N., Narimani, M. and Pournikdast, S. (2015) Effectiveness of multi-modal Lazarus and multi-modal spiritual – religious, of physical symptoms and quality life in patients with functional dyspepsia. *Journal of Asian Scientific Research*, 5(12): 534–544.

Palmer, S. (1996) The multimodal approach: theory, assessment, techniques and interventions. In S. Palmer and W. Dryden (Eds), *Stress Management and Counselling: Theory, Practice, Research and Methodology*. London: Cassell.

Palmer, S. (1997) Modality assessment. In S. Palmer and G. McMahon (Eds), *Client Assessment*. London: Sage.

Palmer, S. (2008) Multimodal coaching and its application to workplace, life and health coaching. *The Coaching Psychologist*, 4(1): 21–29.

Palmer, S. (2015) Multimodal therapy. In S. Palmer (ed.), *The Beginner's Guide to Counselling and Psychotherapy*. London: Sage.

Palmer, S., Cooper, C. and Thomas, K. (2003) *Creating a Balance: Managing Stress*. London: British Library.

Palmer, S. and Dryden, W. (1995) *Counselling for Stress Problems*. London: Sage.

Palmer, S. and Gyllensten, K. (2008) How cognitive behavioural, rational emotive behavioural or multimodal coaching could prevent mental health problems, enhance performance and reduce work related stress. *The Journal of Rational Emotive and Cognitive Behavioural Therapy*, 26(1): 38–52.

Paul, G.L. (1967) Strategy of outcome research in psychotherapy. *Journal of Consulting Psychology*, 331: 109–118.

Rose, S., Palmer, S. and O'Riordan, S. (2010) A HEALTHY development from the multimodal approach to coaching. *The Coaching Psychologist*, 6(2): 88–96.

RECOMMENDED READING

Lazarus, A.A. (1989) *The Practice of Multimodal Therapy: Systematic, Comprehensive and Effective Psychotherapy*. Baltimore, MD: Johns Hopkins University Press.

This edition of the book by Lazarus provides an excellent overview to multimodal therapy. Lazarus's approach comes alive in each chapter.

Lazarus, A.A. (1997) *Brief but Comprehensive Psychotherapy: The Multimodal Way*. New York: Springer.

In this book Lazarus describes how multimodal therapy can be a brief therapeutic intervention without losing the thoroughness of the approach.

Palmer, S. and Dryden, W. (1995) *Counselling for Stress Problems*. London: Sage.

Palmer and Dryden demonstrate how the multimodal approach can be applied to a wide range of stress-related problems. For each modality it includes a range of techniques, with the indications and contraindications for their use. It contains many real case studies.

5.19 NARRATIVE THERAPY

FIONA STIRLING AND JOHN MCLEOD

OVERVIEW AND KEY POINTS

Narrative therapy uses stories to understand people's identities, explore problems and their effects, and facilitate constructive change and development in individuals, families and communities. This chapter introduces the key assumptions and skills of the narrative therapy tradition and its application in a variety of contexts. The chapter aims to help readers understand:

- the meaning and development of narrative practice, and how it can be a powerful device for change
- the philosophical roots which make the approach distinct, and the impact this has on understanding people and the problems they have
- how narrative tools such as collaboration, externalisation and documentation of preferred stories help people
- how narrative practice is researched and disseminated.

BRIEF HISTORY

David Epston and Michael White, the founders of narrative therapy, originally trained in family therapy in the 1980s; a time when the field of psychology and psychotherapy saw a growing interest in narrative perspectives, centred on the idea that storytelling represented a fundamental human means of communication and sense-making (McLeod, 1997). Although the 'narrative turn' within psychology, philosophy and the social sciences had a significant impact on many approaches to therapy, narrative therapy represents one of its most tangible legacies. Training is now available internationally, alongside a thriving global network of events and conferences, which have seen it referred to more broadly as 'narrative practice', to encourage application in a range of contexts. This growth is intentionally fostered by groups such as the Dulwich Centre in Adelaide, Australia (of which Michael White was co-director), to celebrate the value of diverse collaboration and innovation. Because of its philosophical and politically-aware roots (Denborough, 2019), narrative therapy contributes a distinctive dimension to other therapy approaches with which it has been integrated. Narrative therapy has been combined with experiential, emotion-focused ways of working (Angus and Greenberg, 2011; Angus and McLeod, 2004; Seo et al., 2015), cognitive-behavioural therapy (CBT) (Ikonomopoulos, Smith and Schmidt, 2015), expressive arts therapies (Baştemur and Baş, 2021), and various systemic family therapy approaches (Sundet and McLeod, 2016). Online working prompted by the 2020 Covid-19 pandemic created powerful and playful digital adaptations of the approach, emphasising the core values of collaboration, curiosity and creativity (Vermeire and van den Berge, 2021). An important aspect of practice has been an openness to learning from, and working with, indigenous and minority culture healing traditions (Denborough, 2018; Drahm-Butler, 2015).

BASIC ASSUMPTIONS

Narrative therapy assumes stories are the basic way people make sense of experiences, and that people are active agents with a wealth of resources. The theoretical basis is influenced by the poststructuralist ideas of philosopher Michel Foucault and other postmodern writers critical of the assumption within contemporary psychology that cognitive, biological and emotional structures within the individual person are the source of human action and decision-making. These writers propose an alternative way of making sense of people, in terms of relationships and connections between individuals and participation in a shared language which incorporates and conveys layers of historical meaning. Within this perspective, stories play a crucial role in mediating between the person and the culture within which he or she lives their life, and individuals are characterised by beliefs, values, wishes and dreams which inform their living. As a result, narrative counselling and psychotherapy are based on a complex set of ideas or assumptions about the role of narrative in human communication, identity and meaning making. These ideas are as follows.

Stories are the basic way people make sense of experience. Relating a story conveys the intentionality and purpose of the teller and their understanding of relationships and the social world, expresses feelings and communicates a moral evaluation of what has happened. The person is not the problem story they tell, rather they have a relationship with it.

It is a mistake to regard human beings as self-contained individuals. We tell personal tales but do so by drawing on a cultural stock of narrative forms. Born into the story of our family and community, and the story of who we are (e.g., the story behind our name), we grow up adopting narrative templates provided by myths, films, novels and other cultural resources to give shape and meaning to our individual life narrative (and absorb accompanying normalising judgements).

A story is something created *between* people, with personal experience and reality co-constructed through the process of telling stories. Whether told in the presence of a real or implied audience, the stories we tell are a situated performance, a version of events created at a particular time and place to have a specific effect. As the narrativisation of experience is open-ended, there are always other stories that can be told about the same events/experiences.

The concept of *voice* refers to the way in which a story is told, and any narrative represents a weaving together of multiple voices. For example, the story of someone's life, or episodes in that life, can be narrated through an official, psychiatric/medical voice, a personal and vulnerable voice, or the harsh critical voice of an angry parent. One task of therapy is to disentangle these voices. The concept of voice also conveys something of the embodied nature of storytelling, by drawing attention to the physical qualities of *how* the story is told, in terms of volume, tone, rhythm and the use of speech forms such as metaphor, repetition and contrast.

It is useful to distinguish between oral and literary (written) forms of narration. Writing down a story tends to produce a more logically structured version, which can function as a permanent record. People attribute authority and legitimacy to written stories. Oral versions, by contrast, are generally more relational, improvised, emotionally involving and transient.

People are social beings with a basic need to tell their story. Holding back involves a process of physiological inhibition that can have negative effects on health. Telling one's story promotes a sense of knowing and being known, leading to social inclusion. Having it heard celebrates their unique insider knowledge and resists the idea that only specially trained experts are capable of facilitating insight and change.

ORIGIN AND MAINTENANCE OF PROBLEMS

These underlying assumptions suggest a distinctive perspective on the origins and maintenance of the problems that can lead people to seek therapy, detailed below.

The experience of being *silenced* is emotionally painful and problematic for most people. Silencing can be a consequence of the social isolation resulting from situations such as bereavement, emigration/exile, illness and disability. Silencing can also be produced through purposeful oppression of persons, for example those who have been sexually, physically or emotionally abused by family members or those who are members of political, ethnic, religious or sexual orientation minority categories. 'Problems' can be understood as being those areas of personal experience around which the person is not able, or willing, to engage in conversation.

The social transmission of normalising judgements limits the life narrative templates available within a culture, community or family, making it difficult or impossible to reconcile with the circumstances of actual lived experience. For example, the *dominant narratives* within a culture may prescribe gender, age or social class 'scripts' which lead to a sense of personal failure.

The trajectory of some lives may contribute to the production of narratives which are *incomplete* or *incoherent*. For example, when a person has experienced trauma, they may end up with a 'fractured' life narrative in which crucial elements of the trauma event are too hard to disclose, and as a result are not included in the stories they tell about their life.

People may develop personal stories that are almost wholly *problem saturated*, resulting in negative identity conclusions. This tendency can be exacerbated by over-involvement with mental health ideologies, leading to disempowerment and hopelessness due to limited agency and internalisation of the problem story.

THEORY OF CHANGE

The change process in narrative therapy involves collaborative construction of opportunities for stories to be told, leading to a phase of reflection, and then the possibility that the story might be modified or changed.

White and Epson (1990) use the term *reauthoring* to characterise this change process.

People find it helpful to tell their story when what they have to say is accepted and valued by others. The basic experience of another person becoming an *outsider witness* to one's account of troubles is meaningful and worthwhile.

Articulating a life narrative with support and without interruption or competition allows a person to consider whether there are any parts of it they might seek to articulate in different ways. Intentional beliefs, values, hopes and dreams will emerge through this process, establishing a preferred way of being in the world.

The opportunity to tell and re-tell different versions of a life story usually produces narratives of strength, resourcefulness and courage, which may eventually replace the more habitual problem-saturated accounts the person has brought into therapy.

The notion of *externalising* the story conveys the idea that the person creates the stories he or she tells (and therefore can tell different stories).

Narrative therapy methods involve constructing more satisfying or coherent life narratives through a process of broadening the narrative horizon. The person may find stories of current troubles make sense when understood in the light of earlier 'chapters' in the life story, or through exploration of wider cultural and political discourses previously concealed to them.

People seeking to change aspects of their life story may search for examples of more suitable narrative forms they can live within, perhaps through literary sources, meeting new people, or learning from fellow members of a therapy or self-help group.

The act of narrating a life in a changed way may necessitate disrupting or deconstructing habitual narratives. This process can be facilitated by the use of figurative and concrete language and different modes of telling (e.g., writing). Therapists encourage the telling of vivid, emotionally resonant personal stories rather than bland, abstract reports. By creating rich stories, a person's feelings and emotions can become connected to meaning, and then to action.

Telling a different story can require recruiting new audiences and challenging the ways pre-existing audiences/communities promote problem-saturated narratives. Connecting with others who have experienced similar struggles outside therapy allows communities of insider knowledge to be co-constructed, increasing the voice of marginalised groups and opportunities for social justice.

SKILLS AND STRATEGIES

The skills and strategies employed in narrative therapy can be understood as comprising two broad dimensions: a poststructuralist worldview from which the client is regarded as a person with strengths and resources, and the use of specific narrative interventions. Narrative therapy practice requires sensitivity and awareness in relation to language use and narrative forms, and genuine curiosity about the stories through which people create and maintain their identities and relationships. In narrative therapy, the role of the therapist includes being both witness to, and co-editor of, the stories told. The client–therapist relationship is not regarded as being the centre of the therapy process (as it would be in psychodynamic or person-centred therapy). Instead, the aim is to 'de-centre' the therapy relationship, in ways that invite the client to become aware of how they relate to other people in their everyday life. The narrative therapy worldview is critical of oppression and inequality in society. Narrative therapists seek to minimise the therapeutic experience functioning as a means of reinforcing dominant cultural narratives. One of the ways they do this is by adopting a *not-knowing* stance, honouring the teller as the expert on their own story. Users of therapy are considered consultants to the therapeutic process and asked for advice on what is helpful, and 'official' psychiatric language is resisted in favour of the client's naming preferences. Collaborative sense-making best describes any process resembling 'traditional' formulation.

The second dimension of narrative practice concerns specific interventions or procedures developed within the narrative therapy tradition, which all practitioners will interpret in their own way (Morgan, 2000). Some narrative-informed therapists use techniques based on writing, such as a letter written to clients or documents written by clients, rather than relying solely on spoken dialogue. The purpose is to exploit the value of a communication format that is permanent and allows re-authored stories to be recorded and reread. Most narrative therapists make use of the technique of *externalising* the problem, based on inviting the client to find a way of talking about their problem as something separate. This strategy opens up a space for exploring the influence of the person on the problem, and the problem on the person. It also enables invitation to the client to consider times when they were problem free (unique exceptions) and to build alternative narratives around previously silenced or disregarded 'glittering moments'.

Narrative therapists use the skill of drawing attention to what is *absent but implicit* as a means of enabling clients to appreciate that there are always multiple stories that can be told about any experience or event (Carey, Walther and Russell, 2009; Young, 2020). For example, when a client talks about how depressed they are, or how they have consistently failed in some area of their life, the therapist may invite them to consider the personal strengths and resources that are absent in their story but are nevertheless implied in their actions. White (2007) offers the phrase 'loitering with intent' to describe this facilitation of explorations which allow multiple, and possibly contradictory, effects of a given experience to emerge.

Preferred stories, meanings, identities and strengths can be documented and explored using techniques such as the Tree of Life, where clients are invited to draw a tree in which various elements (roots, trunk, leaves, etc.) represent different personal strengths and relationships (Denborough, 2018; Ncube, 2006). The Tree of Life technique is an example of incorporating indigenous and traditional metaphors and practices into therapy. A recent version of the Tree of Life has expanded this activity to encompass ecological awareness (Nicholas, 2021).

To help an emerging reauthored story extend into everyday life, it is important to recruit new audiences. Some narrative therapists will invite family or community members into therapy sessions to act as *outsider witnesses* to the client's new story or will encourage the client to seek external opportunities to recruit friends, family and work colleagues as witnesses. Where the social pressure and control of the dominant narrative is particularly strong, the therapist may facilitate the creation of support groups of people engaged in similar reauthoring 'projects'. The Covid-19 pandemic saw examples of this flourish online, such as the digital document 'From us to you: Stories to support the community amid the Covid-19 crisis from mental health service users, survivors and ex-patients' (Randall, Kennedy and Daya, 2020), a multi-storied collective testimony which reauthored difficult experiences of navigating psychiatric care into a shared wisdom for coping with panic, worry and isolation during the pandemic.

CASE STUDY

Ali sought help from a counsellor because of panic attacks and general anxiety. In their first meeting, the counsellor asked questions that had the effect of inviting Ali to experiment with a different way of talking about their difficulties: 'I allowed the *fog of panic* to take over my life', rather than 'I panicked'. This opened up further conversations around the characteristics of the 'fog' and whether there might have been occasions when Ali had been able to resist or outwit the 'fog'. The counsellor showed great curiosity around these moments of success and asked what had made them possible. She then invited Ali to identify people in their life who would not have been surprised about these accomplishments. Ali recalled a close friend who 'is always on my side'. Over the next few sessions, a process unfolded where Ali became more aware of their own resources in relation to the 'fog' and how to use counselling to celebrate and reflect on their successes around 'just letting fog pass me by'. After each session the counsellor sent Ali an email documenting and reinforcing the new story they were beginning to construct about who Ali was and what they stood for, and encouraged them to find audiences for this story within their circle of family, friends and work colleagues.

RESEARCH

Narrative therapy theory and practice is informed by a critical philosophical, ethical and sociological perspective that is not consistent with many of the assumptions of mainstream research in counselling and psychotherapy. For example, studies that rely on psychiatric diagnostic categories may have the effect of disseminating and supporting a 'language of deficit' that labels and excludes individuals. As a result, the narrative therapy community has been cautious in its engagement with the need for research evidence to support the development of the approach.

However, a broad-based narrative therapy research literature is available. Participatory action research studies have documented the efforts of particular groups of people to overcome specific problems (e.g., Denborough, 2008) and to communicate what they have learned to others who are engaged in similar struggles. Qualitative research has explored client and therapist experience of various aspects of narrative therapy in practice (Chimpén-López and Arriazu Muñoz, 2021; Keeling and Nielson, 2005; O'Connor et al., 2004; Young and Cooper, 2008). Process analysis of narrative practice has been conducted using coding of therapy session transcripts (Ramey, Young and Tarulli, 2010; Santos, Gonçalves and Matos, 2011). Systematic case studies of narrative therapy have been published by Ikonomopoulos, Smith and Schmidt (2015) and Palgi and Ben-Ezra (2010). Quantitative studies of the effectiveness of narrative therapy for depression, using standard outcome measures, have levels of improvement similar to CBT (Lopes et al., 2014; Vromans and Schweitzer, 2011). Taken together, these studies provide credible support for the therapeutic processes included in narrative therapy, and for the effectiveness of the approach as a whole.

REFERENCES

Angus, L.E. and Greenberg, L.S. (2011) *Working with narrative in emotion-focused therapy: Changing stories, healing lives.* Washington, DC: American Psychological Association.

Angus, L.E. and McLeod, J. (Eds) (2004) *Handbook of narrative and psychotherapy: Practice, theory and research.* Thousand Oaks, CA: Sage.

Baştemur, Ş. and Baş, E. (2021) Integration of narrative therapy with expressive art practices. *Current Approaches in Psychiatry,* 13(1), 146–169.

Carey, M., Walther, S. and Russell, S. (2009) The absent but implicit: A map to support therapeutic enquiry. *Family Process,* 48, 319–331.

Chimpén-López, C. and Arriazu Muñoz, R. (2021) Narrative therapy for anorexia nervosa: Using documents of resistance. *Australian and New Zealand Journal of Family Therapy,* 42(3), 276–291.

Denborough, D. (2008) *Collective narrative practice: Responding to individuals, groups, and communities who have experienced trauma.* Adelaide, Australia: Dulwich Centre Publications.

Denborough, D. (2018) *Do you want to hear a story? Adventures in collective narrative practice.* Adelaide, Australia: Dulwich Centre Publications.

Denborough, D. (2019) *Political dictionary for the field of narrative practice.* Adelaide, Australia: Dulwich Centre Publications.

Drahm-Butler, T. (2015) Decolonising identity stories: Narrative practice through Aboriginal eyes. In B. Wingard, C. Johnson and T. Drahm-Butler (Eds), *Aboriginal narrative practice: Honouring storylines of pride, strength and creativity* (pp. 25–48). Adelaide, Australia: Dulwich Centre Publications.

Ikonomopoulos, J., Smith, R.L. and Schmidt, C. (2015) Integrating Narrative Therapy within rehabilitative programming for incarcerated adolescents. *Journal of Counseling and Development,* 93, 460–470.

Keeling, M.L. and Nielson, L.R. (2005) Indian women's experience of a narrative intervention using art and writing. *Contemporary Family Therapy,* 27, 435–455.

Lopes, R.T., Gonçalves, M.M., Fassnacht, D.B., Machado, P.P.P. and Sousa, I. (2014) Long-term effects of psychotherapy on moderate depression: A comparative study of narrative therapy and cognitive-behavioral therapy. *Journal of Affective Disorders,* 167, 64–73.

McLeod, J. (1997) *Narrative and psychotherapy.* London: Sage.

Morgan, A. (2000) *What is narrative therapy? An easy to read introduction.* Adelaide, South Australia: Dulwich Centre Publications.

Ncube, N. (2006) The Tree of Life Project: Using narrative ideas in work with vulnerable children in Southern Africa. *International Journal of Narrative Therapy and Community Work,* (1), 3–16.

Nicholas, E. (2021) Seeing the forest for the trees: Exploring the forest aspect of the tree of life process to sustain and nourish socioecological activism. *International Journal of Narrative Therapy & Community Work,* (1), 1–9.

O'Connor, T.S., Davis, A., Meakes, E., Pickering, R. and Schuman, M. (2004) Narrative therapy using a reflecting team: An ethnographic study of therapists' experiences. *Contemporary Family Therapy*, 26, 23–39.

Palgi, Y. and Ben-Ezra, M. (2010). Prepared and still surprised. *Pragmatic Case Studies in Psychotherapy*, 6(1), 43–48. https://doi.org/10.14713/pcsp.v6i1.1015

Ramey, H.L., Young, K. and Tarulli, D. (2010) Scaffolding and concept formation in narrative therapy: A qualitative research report. *Journal of Systemic Therapies*, 29, 74–91.

Randall, R., Kennedy, H. and Daya, I. (2020) *From us to you: Stories to support the community amid the COVID-19 crisis from mental health service users, survivors and ex-patients [pdf].* Available at https://dulwichcentre.com.au/wp-content/uploads/2020/03/Lived-wisdom-on-panic.pdf (accessed 23 February 2022).

Santos, A., Gonçalves, M.M. and Matos, M. (2011) Innovative moments and poor outcome in narrative therapy. *Counselling and Psychotherapy Research*, 11, 129–139.

Seo, M., Kang, H.S., Lee, Y.J. and Chae, S.M. (2015) Narrative therapy with an emotional approach for people with depression: Improved symptom and cognitive-emotional outcomes. *Journal of Psychiatric and Mental Health Nursing*, 22, 379–389.

Sundet, R. and McLeod, J. (2016) Narrative approaches and pluralism. In M. Cooper and W. Dryden (Eds), *Handbook of pluralistic counselling and psychotherapy.* London: Sage.

Vermeire, S. and Van den Berge, L. (2021) Widening the screen: Playful responses to challenges in online therapy with children and families. *Journal of Family Therapy*, 43(2), 329–345.

Vromans, L.P. and Schweitzer, R. (2011) Narrative therapy for adults with major depressive disorder: Improved symptom and interpersonal outcomes. *Psychotherapy Research*, 21, 4–15.

White, M. (2007) *Maps of narrative practice*. New York: W.W. Norton.

White, M. and Epston, D. (1990) *Narrative means to therapeutic ends*. New York: W.W. Norton.

Young, K. (2020) Multi-story listening: Using narrative practices at walk-in clinics. *Journal of Systemic Therapies*, 39(3), 34–45.

Young, K. and Cooper, S. (2008) Toward co-composing an evidence base: The narrative therapy re-visiting project. *Journal of Systemic Therapies*, 27, 67–83.

RECOMMENDED READING

Combs, G. and Freedman, J. (2012) Narrative, poststructuralism, and social justice: Current practices in narrative therapy. *Counseling Psychologist*, 40, 1033–1060.

This is a classic overview of theory and practice in narrative therapy from two leading figures.

White, M. (2007) *Maps of narrative practice*. New York: W.W. Norton.

This is a practical guide with case examples.

Morgan, A. (2000) *What is narrative therapy? An easy to read introduction*. Adelaide, South Australia: Dulwich Centre Publications.

This book is an accessible starting point, along with many other resources available through the Dulwich Centre website (http://dulwichcentre.com.au)

5.20 PERSON-CENTRED THERAPY

KEITH TUDOR

OVERVIEW AND KEY POINTS

Person-centred therapy (PCT) is the therapeutic manifestation and application of the broader person-centred approach to life. Initially developed by Carl Rogers, PCT:

- is a form of therapy that centres on the whole person and being of the client, which, therefore, includes their context
- emphasises the view that therapy *is* the relationship between therapist and client, and, indeed, has contributed to thinking about the nature of the therapeutic relationship across therapeutic modalities
- offers a critical perspective on diagnosis and transference
- has always been informed by practice-based research
- has influenced the development of humanistic psychology.

BRIEF HISTORY

'Person-centred therapy' (PCT) or 'client-centred therapy' (CCT) was originally developed by Carl Rogers and his colleagues in the USA from the late 1930s onwards. For a short while the approach now known as PCT was referred to as 'relationship therapy' and 'non-directive therapy', terms that fell into disuse, although PCT has been reclaimed as a relational therapy by Ellingham (2011), Tudor and Worrall (2006) and Tudor (2022, in press); and 'non-directivity' as a concept and a principled attitude has remained at the centre of PCT and has been the subject of some revival (see Levitt, 2005). A key date in the history of PCT is 10 December 1940, when Rogers spoke at the University of Minnesota on 'Some newer concepts of psychotherapy'. Then CCT was further expanded by Rogers and his colleagues at the University of Chicago, including the development of a theory of personality and behaviour, as well as a more detailed description of the characteristics of person-centred therapy (see Rogers, 1951).

Between 1953 and 1954, and based on his research, Rogers formulated his now famous hypothesis of certain necessary and sufficient conditions of therapeutic personality change (published in 1957 and 1959). These papers established Rogers and his colleagues as innovators in the field of therapy, and stimulated a great deal of debate and research, for a summary of which see Patterson (2000 [1984]) and Tudor and Merry (2002) – research which finds expression in more recent research into 'common factors' across therapeutic modalities. Rogers himself identified more with an emerging 'third force' of psychology (i.e., humanistic psychology), and is widely recognised as one of its founders; and PCT became established as one of the most influential of the humanistic approaches to therapy. Mearns and Thorne (2000: 27), however, have suggested that, in 'its forsaking of mystique and other "powerful" behaviours of therapists', PCT is as different from many humanistic therapies as it is from other traditions, such as behaviourism and psychoanalysis. In the later years of his life Rogers became interested in the wider application of the principles of person-centred psychology (PCP) to education and learning; groups, group facilitation and conflict resolution; and politics. He also became more open to and interested in mystical experiences, which led Rogers to speculate about the importance of 'presence', and others to consider the interface between PCT and spirituality, notably Thorne (2000 [1991], 2002, 2008, 2012). Person-centred *therapy* is now viewed as one application of what has become more broadly referred to as the 'person-centred *approach*' (PCA), for an outline and development of which see Embleton Tudor et al. (2004).

Although its influence in the USA has diminished in recent decades, currently PCT is widely practised and studied in Europe, Japan and South America, and there is a thriving World Association of Person-Centered and Experiential Psychotherapy and Counseling (www.pce-world.org), which has individual and organisational members in over 30 countries, holds a regular (biennial) world conference (to date, 15) and publishes a quarterly journal, *Person-Centered and Experiential Psychotherapies*. English-language publications have been fostered by the presence of PCCS Books (www.pccs-books.co.uk), which, in a period of 30 years, has published over 60 books on person-centred psychology and its various manifestations, including PCT. There is also a considerable and growing international literature, including publications and journals in Dutch, French, German, Italian, Japanese, Portuguese and Spanish.

BASIC ASSUMPTIONS

There are a number of basic assumptions which underlie PCT. Here they are clustered under three core principles (see Sanders, 2000; Tudor and Worrall, 2006).

1. THAT THE HUMAN ORGANISM TENDS TO ACTUALISE

The view that the human organism, as other organisms, tends to actualise (i.e., to maintain, enhance and reproduce the experiencing organism) represents the sole motivational construct in PCP. The theory of actualisation is a natural science theory, not a moral theory. While no specific moral values are implied by the theory, two values implicit in the person-centred approach to the person are fluidity (as distinct from fixity or rigidity) and creativity (see Rogers, 1967 [1954], 1967 [1961]).

One function of the fact that we tend to actualise is that we differentiate a portion of our experience into an awareness of self and the organisation of a self-concept. The self-concept or self-structure is a fluid but consistent pattern of perceptions of the 'I', 'me' – and 'we' – in relation to the environment, personal and social values, goals and ideals. One aspect of organismic actualising, self-actualising, appears after the development of the self-concept and acts to maintain that concept. Self-actualising – or, more commonly, 'self-actualisation' – does not always result in optimal functioning because each person, whether psychologically healthy or unhealthy, is self-actualising to the extent that each has a self-structure to maintain and enhance. Thus, if an aspect of someone's self-concept is to be pleasing, then they may act socially to support that, at the expense of their organismic direction.

Awareness of self is termed 'self-experience'. When any self-experience is evaluated by others as being more or less worthy of positive regard, a person's self-regard becomes vulnerable to these external judgements. When self-experiences become sought after or avoided because they are more or less deserving of self-regard, the individual is said to have acquired conditions of worth, which are the basis of person-centred theories of psychopathology (see Bozarth, 1996; Joseph and Worsley, 2005; Tudor and Worrall, 2006).

It is clear that the root metaphor of PCT is the organism, not the self, and that, as a biological/social reality, the organism is prior to conceptualisations and theories of the self.

2. IN ORDER TO SUPPORT GROWTH AND CHANGE, THE THERAPIST/FACILITATOR NEEDS TO EMBRACE AND EMBODY A NON-DIRECTIVE APPROACH AND ATTITUDE

This follows from the first assumption. If you think that the fact that the organism tends to actualise is an expression of an inherent and trustworthy directionality, then, as a therapist or facilitator, you would tend to support the client's direction.

The view of human nature underlying this approach is positive, constructive and co-creative. It does not, however, deny the capacity for harmful, destructive and anti-social behaviour. It focuses, rather, on the potential for positive, personal and social change to occur throughout life; and takes the view that environmental influences, particularly those concerning relationships with others, including therapeutic and facilitative relationships, are critical factors in determining either positive or negative self-concepts and, hence, healthy or unhealthy functioning. PCP recognises that the outward and, indeed, inward manifestations of harmful behaviour can have serious and extreme consequences. In response, the practice of PCT understands or attempts to understand, and helps the client to understand, the motivation and needs which underlie their behaviour – and, generally, views behaviour as a needs-driven expression of a unitary theory of motivation (see Rogers, 1951, 1963).

3. THAT, TOGETHER, THERAPIST AND CLIENT CO-CREATE CERTAIN FACILITATIVE CONDITIONS WHICH PROMOTE GROWTH, CHALLENGE AND CHANGE

In PCP, people are regarded as trustworthy, creative, social, contactful, congruent or integrated in themselves, and in relationships, loving, understanding, receptive and resourceful. Given the right conditions, we are able to admit all experiencing into awareness without distortion or denial (which are the two defence mechanisms postulated in PCP [Rogers, 1951]). Everyone has the capacity to rediscover their organismic valuing process and direction in a relationship in which power and control are shared between therapist and client, and this capacity can be nurtured in a climate of facilitative psychological attitudes or conditions (described below). This climate can exist within a therapeutic setting or elsewhere, for example, in couples, groups, families, tribes, communities, schools and workplaces.

ORIGIN AND MAINTENANCE OF PROBLEMS

Disturbance exists whenever there is antagonism between a person's tendency to actualise in one direction and their self-actualisation, which may lie in another direction. Incongruence exists to the extent that these two tendencies diverge.

At the beginning of life, a person is fully congruent, that is, able to allow all experiencing into awareness without distortion or denial. Later – and developmental studies show that this can take place *in utero* – the person encounters threat, disruption, disapproval, rejection and, as a result, becomes anxious in the face of the continuing need for positive regard from significant others. The formation of the person's self-concept becomes conditioned by these negative experiences, conditions of worth become internalised and the person seeks protection from further negative experiences. The conditioned self-concept can become so reinforced that the person becomes completely alienated from any sense of themselves and their organismic direction – which is why 'psychopathology' is best understood in terms of alienation (see Tudor and Worrall, 2006). The dichotomy between the self-concept and experiencing leads to increasingly distorted perception. A condition of incongruence now exists, and the person's psychological functioning is disturbed.

Disturbance is maintained through the continuation of a high degree of reliance on the evaluations of others for a sense of self-worth or self-esteem. Anxiety, threat and confusion are created whenever incongruence is experienced between the self-concept, with its internalised conditions of worth, and actual experience. Whenever such anxiety arises, or is threatened, the person will continue to default to defences of distortion or denial of experiencing. If experiences are extremely incongruent with the self-concept, a person's defence system may be unable to prevent such experiences from overwhelming the self-concept. Resulting behaviour may be destructive, disorganised and chaotic.

THEORY OF CHANGE

Effective therapy occurs in a relationship in which the therapist holds certain attitudes or conditions, and the client receives/perceives or, more precisely, engages with how they receive/perceive these – or not. In addition, Rogers identified certain client conditions which prefigure more recent concerns about the relational, dialogic and co-creative nature of therapy – and, indeed, factors common to all therapies. Indeed, as noted above, Rogers first referred to his work as 'relationship therapy'.

The therapist's conditions (from Rogers, 1959: 213) are:

1. 'That two persons are in contact', a condition which requires both therapist and client to be actively present, both in a social sense of meeting and agreeing to work together (or not) and in a more psychological sense. Clearly some more disturbed clients are less contactful or contactable and, with advances in the theory and practice of 'pre-therapy' (Prouty, 1994), this condition is currently receiving more attention in PCT.
2. The therapist is congruent within the relationship, that is, is authentic, genuine or real, putting up no professional façade. This includes the therapist admitting into awareness all experience of the relationship so that such experiencing is available for direct communication to the client, when appropriate. This condition is more about experiencing than self-disclosing. It is not necessary for the therapist directly to communicate any particular experience of the relationship, except when the failure to do so impedes the practitioner's ability to experience unconditional positive regard and to understand the client empathically, in which circumstances it may become necessary for the therapist to communicate their experiencing.
3. The therapist experiences unconditional positive regard for the client, that is, they maintain a positive, non-judgemental and accepting attitude.
4. The therapist experiences an empathic understanding of the internal, subjective frame of reference of the client.

There is a difference between Rogers' two formulations of these hypotheses (published in 1957 and in 1959) about the extent to which the therapist should communicate these last two conditions.

The requirements of a client, which we may refer to as the 'client's conditions' (see Tudor, 2000, 2011) are:

1. 'That two persons are in contact' (as above).
2. That, by virtue of being vulnerable or anxious, they are in some way incongruent or (as discussed above) experiencing a discrepancy between organismic and self-actualising tendencies.
3. That they perceive the therapist's unconditional positive regard and empathic understanding 'at least to a minimal degree' (whether the therapist directly or explicitly communicates this or not). In one paper, Rogers (1967 [1958]) refers to this as the 'assumed condition', by which, in effect, all therapy is evaluated or assessed.

As discussed (above), a major characteristic of PCT is that it is non-directive. In other words, the therapist has no specific goals for the client and, classically, does not suggest that the client attend to any particular form of experiencing. The therapist refrains from interpreting the client's experience, but, rather, focuses on non-judgemental acceptance and understanding of that experience.

Change in the present is encapsulated in moments of therapeutic movement which consist of experiences of profound self-acceptance and integration. Typically, such moments have the following characteristics: they are immediate and consist of total experiences, and, generally, not thoughts or intellectual understandings, although these may follow or accompany the experience; they are new in that, while they may have been experienced before, at least, in part, they have never been experienced completely or with awareness combined with appropriate physiological reactions; they are self-accepting in that they are owned as a part of the self; and they are integrated into the self-structure without distortion.

SKILLS AND STRATEGIES

In person-centred theory and practice, being in contact, congruent, acceptant and understanding are conceptualised more as qualities of the therapist – and of the relationship – than as skills, strategies or techniques. It is, moreover, unhelpful to conceptualise PCT in terms of behavioural strategies, since the therapist's only intention is to maintain and enhance a way of relating with the client, based on the conditions described above, and 'strategies' suggest a certain direction based on the therapist's frame of reference. A skilled therapist is one who can communicate their contactfulness, authenticity, positive regard and empathic understanding in ways that the client experiences as non-threatening, as experiencing these conditions without threat enables the client to become increasingly free of the need to deny her/his experience and/or distort her/his perceptions.

Although opinions among person-centred and especially experiential therapists vary, many would agree that it is possible, even within the strictest theoretical understanding of PCT, to utilise techniques associated with other forms of counselling and psychotherapy *providing* that such techniques, as Rogers (1957: 102) put it, 'serve as channels for fulfilling one of the conditions'. Clearly, such techniques would not be imposed by the therapist; would be used only when requested by the client to further a particular purpose; and, in any case, the client should retain control over the extent of their use. The use of such techniques by classical person-centred practitioners, however, is minimal.

CASE STUDY

In the last session of what had been two years of regular, more or less weekly therapy, Kay summarised her experience. She told her therapist how important his consistency, calmness and caring had been. She went on to describe a number of other qualities that she had valued: his kindness, warmth, gentleness, experience, realness (in showing her, at times, what he was feeling and thinking) and mindfulness (perceived in how she felt he had held her in mind between sessions), as well as what she had experienced as a certain protectiveness. While her description was about and true of the therapist, clearly it was also naming qualities that she valued and found important. Some people regard all feedback as projection (and use that to reject the feedback). I consider and suggest that all feedback is, rather, reflective of a co-created relationship and the client's experience of that relationship.

(Continued)

(Continued)

The projective nature and quality of feedback, however, does not make it any the less true or useful. In this sense, from a person-centred perspective, and especially with reference to the importance of the sixth, central and assumed condition, Kay was describing those aspects of her therapist's unconditional positive regard and empathic understanding – and, behind that, his authenticity and contactfulness – that she had experienced and found important. That the evaluation and assessment of PCT is – or should also be – person-centred places the client at the centre of such evaluation (see Duncan, Miller and Sparks, 2004), a process which also means that acceptance and empathy are more particularly and usefully described and specified by the client.

RESEARCH

Rogers himself was one of the leading pioneers of research into counselling and psychotherapy (see Rogers and Dymond, 1954), conducting a major research study of psychotherapy with schizophrenics (Rogers et al., 1967). Partly because of its longevity, PCT itself has both been the subject of and generated more research than many other approaches. In the 1950s, using the Q-sort technique, Rogers and Dymond (1954) showed that person-centred therapy results in changes to the self-concept, whereby the perceived self becomes closer to the ideal self, and the self as perceived becomes more comfortable and adjusted.

Research evidence that the therapeutic conditions are both necessary and sufficient is not unequivocal, although much of it suffers from inadequate methodology and the possibility of poorly reported and discussed results. For a useful summary of four decades of research evidence, see Bozarth (1993). Most research strongly supports the hypothesis that the conditions are necessary for effective counselling, whether this is person-centred or not; research which forms the basis of the mainstream view in therapy that the therapeutic relationship is the key factor in successful outcome, and that Rogers' conditions describe significant 'common factors' across theoretical orientations.

Two independent studies, based on randomised, controlled assessments (Friedli et al., 1997; King et al., 2000), have concluded that person-centred, non-directive psychotherapy/counselling more than holds its own in comparison with other forms of therapy and helping. The book *Person-Centered and Experiential Therapies Work* (Cooper, Watson and Hölldampf, 2010) offers a useful review of research on person-centred counselling, psychotherapy and related practice; the international journal *Person-centered and Experiential Psychotherapies* publishes peer-reviewed articles on research; and, for a number of years, high-quality research into person-centred, experiential and humanistic-existential approaches to therapy has been conducted in the Counselling Unit at the University of Strathclyde.

REFERENCES

Bozarth, J. D. (1993). Not necessarily necessary, but always sufficient. In D. Brazier (Ed.), *Beyond Carl Rogers* (pp. 92–105). London: Constable.

Bozarth, J. D. (1996). A theoretical reconceptualization of the necessary and sufficient conditions for therapeutic personality change. *The Person-Centered Journal*, 3(1), 44–51.

Cooper, M., Watson, J. C. and Hölldampf, D. (Eds) (2010). *Person-centered and experiential therapies work: A review of the research on counseling, psychotherapy and related practices*. Monmouth: PCCS Books.

Duncan, B. L., Miller, S. D. and Sparks, J. A. (2004). *The heroic client: A revolutionary way to improve effectiveness through client-directed, outcome-informed therapy*. San Francisco, CA: Jossey-Bass.

Ellingham, I. (2011). Carl Rogers' fateful wrong move in the development of Rogerian relational therapy: Retitling 'relationship therapy' 'non-directive therapy'. *Person-Centered & Experiential Psychotherapies*, 10(3), 181–197.

Embleton Tudor, L., Keemar, K., Tudor, K., Valentine, J. and Worrall, M. (2004). *The person-centred approach: A contemporary introduction*. Basingstoke: Palgrave.

Friedli, K., King, M., Lloyd, M. and Horder, J. (1997). Randomised controlled assessment of non-directive psychotherapy versus routine general practitioner care. *Lancet*, *350*, 1662–1665.

Joseph, S. and Worsley, R. (2005). Psychopathology and the person-centred approach: Building bridges between disciples. In S. Joseph and R. Worsley (Eds), *Person-centred psychopathology: A positive psychology of mental health* (pp. 1–8). Monmouth: PCCS Books.

King, M., Lloyd, M., Sibbald, B., Gabbay, M., Ward, E., Byford, S. and Bower, P. (2000). Randomised controlled trial of non-directive counselling, cognitive behaviour therapy and usual general practitioner care in the management of depression as well as mixed anxiety and depression in primary care. *Health Technology Assessment*, *4*(19).

Levitt, B. E. (Ed.) (2005). *Embracing non-directivity: Reassessing person-centered theory and practice in the 21st century* (pp. i–iii). Monmouth: PCCS Books.

Mearns, D. and Thorne, B. (2000). *Person-centred therapy today: New Frontiers in theory and practice*. London: Sage.

Patterson, C. H. (2000 [1984]). Empathy, warm and genuineness in psychotherapy: A review of reviews. In C. H. Patterson, *Understanding psychotherapy: Fifty years of client-centred theory and practice* (pp. 161–173). Monmouth: PCCS Books.

Prouty, G. (1994). *Theoretical evolutions in person-centered/experiential therapy: Applications to schizophrenic and retarded psychoses*. New York: Praeger.

Rogers, C. R. (1951). *Client-centered therapy*. London: Constable.

Rogers, C. R. (1957). The necessary and sufficient conditions of therapeutic personality change. *Journal of Consulting Psychology*, *21*, 95–103.

Rogers, C. R. (1959). A theory of therapy, personality and interpersonal relationships, as developed in the client-centered framework. In S. Koch (Ed.), *Psychology: A study of science. Vol. 3: Formulation of the person and the social context* (pp. 184–256). New York: McGraw-Hill.

Rogers, C. R. (1963). The actualizing tendency in relation to 'motive' and to consciousness. In M. Jones (Ed.), *Nebraska Symposium on motivation, 1963* (pp. 1–24). Lincoln, NB: University of Nebraska Press.

Rogers, C. R. (1967 [1954]). Toward a theory of creativity. In C. R. Rogers, *On becoming a person* (pp. 347–359). London: Constable.

Rogers, C. R. (1967 [1958]). A process conception of psychotherapy. In C. R. Rogers, *On becoming a person* (pp. 125–159). London: Constable.

Rogers, C. R. and Dymond, R. F. (Eds) (1954). *Psychotherapy and personality change*. Chicago, IL: University of Chicago Press.

Rogers, C. R., Gendlin, E. T., Kiesler, D. J. and Truax, C. B. (Eds) (1967). *The therapeutic relationship and its impact: A study of psychotherapy with schizophrenics*. Madison, WI: University of Wisconsin Press.

Sanders, P. (2000). Mapping the person-centred approaches to counselling and psychotherapy. *Person-Centred Practice*, *8*(2), 62–74.

Thorne, B. (2000 [1991]). *Person-centred counselling: Therapeutic and spiritual dimensions*. London: Whurr.

Thorne, B. (2002). *The mystical power of person-centred therapy*. London: Whurr.

Thorne, B. (2008). *Person-centred counselling and Christian spirituality: The secular and the holy*. London: Whurr.

Thorne, B. (2012). *Counselling and spiritual accompaniment: Bridging faith and person-centred therapy*. Chichester: Wiley-Blackwell.

Tudor, K. (2000). The case of the lost conditions. *Counselling*, *11*(1), 33–37.

Tudor, K. (2011). Rogers' therapeutic conditions: A relational reconceptualisation. *Person-Centered & Experiential Psychotherapies*, *10*(3), 165–180.

Tudor, K. (2022, in press). There and back again: Re-envisioning 'relationship therapy' as the centre of a contemporary, cultural, and contextual person-centred therapy. *Person-Centered and Experiential Psychotherapies*.

Tudor, K. and Merry, T. (2002). *Dictionary of person-centred psychology*. London: Whurr.

Tudor, K. and Worrall, M. (2006). *Person-centred therapy: A clinical philosophy*. London: Routledge.

> **RECOMMENDED READING**
>
> The journal *Person-Centered and Experiential Psychotherapies* (2002–present).
>
> This peer-reviewed journal 'seeks to create a dialogue among different parts of the person-centered and experiential tradition, to support, inform, and challenge each other and to stimulate their creativity and impact in a broader professional, scientific and political context' (www.pce-world.org/pcep-journal.html). The journal has established and maintained a consistently high quality of articles which advance this tradition.
>
> Tudor, K. and Worrall, M. (2006). *Person-centred therapy: A clinical philosophy*. London: Routledge.
>
> Part of a series of books on 'Advancing Theory in Therapy', this book examines the roots of person-centred thinking, especially with regard to existential, phenomenological and organismic philosophy and psychology. It demonstrates how recent research in areas such as neuroscience supports the philosophical premises of PCT and updates Rogers' original vision of a therapy based on relationship.
>
> Lago, C. and Charura, D. (Eds) (2016). *Person-centred counselling and psychotherapy: Origins, developments and contemporary applications*. Maidenhead: Open University/McGraw Hill.
>
> Bringing together 34 authors from a number of different countries, the book covers the history and development of the person-centred approach, contributions to its theory and practice, including new theoretical paradigms and practice, research, as well as differences, diversity, its position, and the future.

5.21 PERSONAL CONSTRUCT THERAPY

DAVID WINTER

OVERVIEW AND KEY POINTS

Personal construct theory was developed in the clinical sphere by George Kelly, and while its applicability is by no means limited to this field, it has provided a basis for a particular form of constructivist counselling and psychotherapy. The theory considers that each of us constructs our world but that people who present psychological problems have become stuck in constructions that are not revised despite being invalidated. The aim of personal construct counselling and psychotherapy is therefore to help them to engage in a process of reconstruction. This generally involves the exploration of the client's construing, perhaps using personal construct assessment techniques such as the self-characterisation or the repertory grid, and the facilitation of experimentation with construing. The flexibility of the approach makes it applicable to various client groups across the life span, and it has a good evidence base. Key points include:

- Personal construct counselling and psychotherapy are derived from George Kelly's personal construct theory.
- It was the first example in a psychological theory of what has come to be termed a constructivist approach.
- The theory asserts that people construct their worlds and, when their constructions are invalidated, reconstruct them, but that this process becomes blocked in people with psychological problems.

- Personal construct counselling and psychotherapy use a range of techniques to facilitate the process of reconstruction.
- This approach to counselling and psychotherapy has a good evidence base.

BRIEF HISTORY

Personal construct counselling and psychotherapy are based directly on George Kelly's *The Psychology of Personal Constructs* (1991), set out in two volumes published in 1955. Kelly's first degrees were in physics and mathematics, followed by postgraduate degrees in sociology, education and, eventually, psychology. He spent much of his academic life at Ohio State University, and overlapped there with Carl Rogers for a short time. In his theory of personal constructs, Kelly aimed to encompass the person's experiencing of the world in its entirety, and his holistic view of the person did not make distinctions between cognition, emotion and motivation. The theory had a mixed reception on its publication as it was explicitly contrary to the current climate expressed in the psychology of behaviourism, on the one hand, and psychoanalytic theories on the other. Its influence, both as a theory of personality and as an approach to counselling and psychotherapy, was felt first in Great Britain and spread into Europe before being taken up in any substantial way in its birthplace, the United States of America. (See Fransella (1995) for more details of the man and his theory, and Walker and Winter (2007) and Winter and Reed (2016) for details of how personal construct psychology has been developed and applied since Kelly introduced it.)

Early critics of the theory insisted that it explained 'cognitions' very well but did not deal adequately with emotions. In spite of arguments to the contrary, not least the fact that Kelly himself rejected such terms, in 1980 Walter Mischel called George Kelly the first cognitive psychologist. He said: 'There is reason to hope that the current moves towards a hyphenated cognitive-behavioral approach will help fill in the grand outlines that Kelly sketched years before anyone else even realised the need' (Mischel, 1980: 86). The argument about this issue continues today, but suffice it to say that many personal construct psychologists would not be happy with the not uncommon classification of personal construct theory in textbooks as cognitive-behavioural, instead considering that it has more in common with humanistic, integrative or narrative approaches.

Of great influence has been George Kelly's philosophy of *constructive alternativisim*, which underpins the theory throughout. That philosophy is seen as one of the main precursors of the movement of *constructivism*, which has swept through psychology as well as psychotherapy and counselling (Chiari and Nuzzo, 2010; Neimeyer, 2009) in recent years. The philosophy sees reality as residing within the individual. While 'true' reality may indeed be 'out there', we, as individuals, are only able to place our own personal interpretations on that external reality.

Personal construct counselling and psychotherapy are practised around the world, but are not as popular as some other approaches. One reason, perhaps, is the fact that the personal construct approach is based on a very complex theory about how all individuals experience their worlds.

BASIC ASSUMPTIONS

Constructive alternativism states that there are always alternative ways of looking at events. This means that no one needs to be the victim of their past since that past is always capable of being seen in a different way – it can be *reconstrued*. However, we can trap ourselves by our past if we construe it as fixed. The philosophy gives a positive and optimistic view of life since there is always the possibility of change – no matter how difficult that change may be. We have created the person we now are, and so can re-create ourselves.

Personal constructs are essentially discriminations. We see some events, or people, or behaviours as being alike and, thereby, different from others. These dichotomous personal constructs are formed into a system, and it is through that system of personal constructs that we peer at the world of events milling around us.

We place an interpretation on an event by applying certain of our repertoire of personal constructs to it and, thereby, predict an outcome. You see someone smiling at you across the street and predict, perhaps, that he is about to cross the road to say hello. You act accordingly.

Behaviour is the experiment we conduct to test out our current prediction of a situation. The man does cross the street and you put out your hand to shake his only to find he is smiling at someone behind you. In the language of personal construct theory, you have been invalidated.

The theory is couched in the language of science. Kelly suggested we might look at each person 'as if' we were all scientists. We have theories (personal construct systems), make predictions from those theories, and then test them out by behaving. No sooner have we conducted one behavioural experiment than the answer leads us into another situation and another cycle of construing.

'Negative' feelings are experienced when we become aware that our current ways of construing events are not serving us well. We become aware that the current situation means we are going to have to change how we see our 'self' – we are threatened; or we become aware that we cannot make sense of what is happening and, until we do, we experience anxiety; or we become aware that we have behaved in a way which does not fit with our view of who we are, and feel guilty. Sometimes, when our constructions are invalidated, we attempt to change the world to make it fit with them, rather than vice versa, and show 'hostility' in Kelly's sense of this term.

Personal construct therapists use various ways of helping the client to find alternative possibilities of construing events and life that will enable them to conduct more productive behavioural experiments, but the client is the expert and has the answers. However, those answers may well not be available to conscious awareness.

Construing takes place at different levels of cognitive awareness. The lowest level is what is termed *preverbal*, that is, discriminations that have been made before the acquisition of language.

An essential feature of personal construct theory is its reflexivity. It accounts for the construing of the counsellor and therapist as well as that of the client.

ORIGIN AND MAINTENANCE OF PROBLEMS

A person presents with a psychological problem when their way of construing and predicting events is not working well. Predictions and behavioural experiments are being invalidated but the person is not able to modify those predictions and behaviours in the light of experience. Kelly provided a set of 'diagnostic constructs', mostly relating to the structure or process of, or transitions in, construing, which can be used to understand an individual client's predicament. Unlike the constructs of a psychiatric diagnostic system, they are applicable to the construing of any person, not just those presenting with psychological problems.

THEORY OF CHANGE

Since each person is a form of motion, change is the norm. The person with a psychological problem is seen as being 'stuck'. The goal of therapy and counselling is to help the person 'get on the move again'. At the most superficial level, this might involve the client changing the use of their existing constructs, but more fundamental changes include modification of these constructs or their replacement by new constructs (see Fransella and Dalton (2000) for more detail of the change process).

A collaborative therapist–client relationship, which Kelly saw as analogous to that between a research supervisor and their student, is necessary to facilitate change. As part of this, the therapist uses the 'credulous approach'. He or she takes at face value everything the client relates – even if it is known to be a lie. Credulous listening helps the therapist get a glimpse into the client's world. A therapeutic plan cannot be drawn up, and certainly not put into action, until the practitioner has some idea of what certain changes may mean to the client. The therapist essentially provides a climate of sufficient validation to enable the client to risk experimentation with, and the possibility of some invalidation of, their construing.

Somewhere in the client's construing system are the reasons why he or she cannot get on with the business of living. The therapist uses the diagnostic constructs provided by personal construct theory to make a temporary diagnosis or *formulation* (Winter and Procter, 2013) of why the client has the problem.

That theoretical diagnosis leads to the therapeutic plan of action. It may, for instance, focus on the *looseness* of the client's construing process. In such a case, the client cannot make enough sense of events to conduct meaningful behavioural experiments. Another client may be thought to be resisting any change because that change has some unacceptable implications. For instance, being *anxious all the time* may be seen as indicating that one is a *sensitive*, *thoughtful* and *caring* person whereas being *anxiety-free* means one is the opposite.

The focus of the process of change is mostly in the here and now. It is how the client construes things now that is important. Sometimes, the client links the present with a past event. In that case, the counsellor considers, with the client, that past event. But there is nothing in the theory that makes it mandatory to explore the past with the client.

SKILLS AND STRATEGIES

Personal construct counselling and psychotherapy are largely value-free. There is little in personal construct theory that dictates how a person should be. Therefore, the therapist or counsellor needs to be able to suspend his or her own personal construct system of values. Without that ability, it is not possible to step into the client's shoes and look at the world through the client's eyes, because the therapist's personal values get in the way. In the place of a personal system of constructs, the therapist peers through the system of professional, diagnostic constructs provided by personal construct theory. That means the therapist needs to be well versed in the use of theoretical constructs.

Kelly (1991 [1955]) suggests the personal construct practitioner needs several other skills, including creativity and good verbal ability. The need for creativity stems from the fact that the theory is eclectic in terms of tools available to the counsellor or therapist. The aim is to help the client find alternative ways of dealing with personal events and any means may be used to attain that goal. Kelly (1991 [1955]: 600–601) put it like this:

> Creation is therefore an act of daring, an act of daring through which the creator abandons those literal defenses behind which he might hide if his act is questioned or its results proven invalid. The … [therapist] who dares not try anything he cannot verbally defend is likely to be sterile in a [counselling/ psychotherapy] relationship.

Kelly described two specific tools that allow the exploration of the client's construing:

- *Self-characterisation* – stems from Kelly's first principle: 'If you want to know what is wrong with a person, ask him, he may tell you'. It consists of a sketch written by the client, in the third person, describing him/herself in a sympathetic way. The client is free to say whatever he or she likes.
- *Repertory grid technique* – is a method which can assess both the content and the structure of the client's personal construct system, by such means as indicating the strength of mathematical relationships between personal constructs, between the elements to which they may be applied, and between constructs and elements. It was a way Kelly suggested personal construct psychologists could 'get beyond the words'. This technique has been widely used in counselling and psychotherapy, for example, as a means of identifying the client's dilemmas, which may then be the focus of therapy (Feixas and Saúl, 2005). However, as with all else, its use is by no means a requirement (see Fransella, Bell and Bannister (2004) for details on how to use this technique, and Caputi et al. (2011), Bell (2016), and Procter and Winter (2020) for developments of this and numerous other personal construct assessment methods).

A specific therapeutic technique developed by Kelly for use with some, but by no means all, clients is *fixed-role therapy*. It involves the therapist or counsellor writing a sketch of a new character whom the client is invited to become for a week or more. This character is not the opposite of the client, but rather will involve the elaboration of some new theme which might be valuable for the client to explore. The client must agree that the character portrayed is understandable and acceptable. The new role that the client plays shows him or her that making changes to oneself also produces changes in how others respond to one, how one feels, and so forth. Most importantly, it shows we can re-create ourselves (see Epting, Germignani and Cross, 2005). Fixed-role therapy is but one of many ways by which the personal construct counsellor or psychotherapist may facilitate the client's experimentation. Since personal construct counselling and psychotherapy are technically eclectic, several of these techniques may be borrowed from other therapeutic models but the reasons for their selection and mode of action will be conceptualised in personal construct theory terms.

Fixed-role therapy was one of the techniques used with a client, Tom, who presented with difficulties in interpersonal relationships, including in being assertive (Winter, 1987). Repertory grid technique and other personal construct assessment methods revealed the dilemmas underlying these difficulties, not least that he contrasted being *assertive* with being *reasonable*, and associated extraversion and assertiveness with various characteristics that, for him, were undesirable, such as being *demanding*, *aggressive* and *selfish*. Exploration of the origins of this pattern of construing led him to consider his childhood relationship with his mother, who was generally very silent but at times when she expressed her opinions became verbally and physically abusive towards him and his father. It was suggested to Tom that his way of construing assertiveness was perfectly understandable as a way of anticipating his mother's behaviour when he was a child, but that it perhaps could be limited to his construing of her at that time, giving him freedom to experiment with ways of being more assertive and extraverted without the possible negative implications that were previously associated with these ways of behaving. Part of this experimentation involved fixed-role therapy using a sketch of a character which elaborated themes of showing a lively curiosity in other people, and a commitment to everything that he does. Since his self-characterisation had indicated that his construing and behaviour were dominated by a relentless and unproductive focus on finding a girlfriend, the fixed-role sketch deliberately avoided any mention of this particular concern. Post-treatment assessment revealed not only clinically significant changes on measures of symptoms and social difficulties, but also changes on grid measures indicative of more favourable self-construing and resolution of his dilemmas concerning extraversion and assertiveness.

Over the years, personal construct counselling and psychotherapy have been employed with a wide range of client groups throughout the age range, and in individual, couple, family and group settings (Winter, 1992; Winter and Viney, 2005). This has included the development of an approach which is both personal and relational, considering not only the construct systems of individuals but also those of families, groups and societies (Procter and Winter, 2020).

RESEARCH

The evidence base for personal construct counselling and psychotherapy includes research, mostly using the repertory grid, into changes in construing resulting from personal construct interventions, and evidence that the outcome of this form of counselling and psychotherapy is comparable to that of other major therapeutic approaches (Metcalfe, Winter and Viney, 2007; Winter, 2005). This is in addition to considerable research evidence of features of construing associated with particular psychological problems (Procter and Winter, 2020; Winter, 1992).

ACKNOWLEDGEMENT

When this chapter was originally published in the *Handbook*, it was written by Fay Fransella. After her death, I have modified and updated the chapter in subsequent editions, but it still retains some of her original contribution.

REFERENCES

Bell, R.C. (2016). Methodologies of assessment in personal construct psychology. In D.A. Winter and N. Reed (Eds), *Wiley Handbook of Personal Construct Psychology*. Chichester: Wiley-Blackwell.

Caputi, P., Viney, L.L., Walker, B.M. and Crittenden, N. (Eds) (2011). *Personal Construct Methodology*. Chichester: Wiley-Blackwell.

Chiari, G. and Nuzzo, M.L. (2010). *Constructivist Psychotherapy: A Narrative Hermeneutic Approach*. London: Routledge.

Epting, F., Germignani, M. and Cross, M.C. (2005). An audacious adventure: personal construct counselling and psychotherapy. In F. Fransella (Ed.), *The Essential Practitioners' Handbook of Personal Construct Psychology*. Chichester: Wiley.

Feixas, G. and Saúl, L.A. (2005). Resolution of dilemmas by personal construct psychotherapy. In D.A. Winter and L.L. Viney (Eds), *Personal Construct Psychotherapy: Advances in Theory, Practice and Research*. London: Whurr.

Fransella, F. (1995). *George Kelly*. London: Sage.

Fransella, F., Bell, R. and Bannister, D. (2004). *A Manual for Repertory Grid Technique* (2nd ed.). Chichester: John Wiley & Sons.

Fransella, F. and Dalton, P. (2000). *Personal Construct Counselling in Action* (2nd ed.). London: Sage.

Kelly, G.A. (1991 [1955]). *The Psychology of Personal Constructs* (Volumes I and II). New York: Routledge. (Originally published by W.W. Norton in 1955.)

Metcalfe, C., Winter, D. and Viney, L. (2007). The effectiveness of personal construct psychotherapy in clinical practice: a systematic review and meta-analysis. *Psychotherapy Research*, 17: 431–442.

Mischel, W. (1980). George Kelly's appreciation of psychology: a personal tribute. In M.J. Mahoney (Ed.), *Psychotherapy Process: Current Issues and Future Directions*. New York: Plenum Press.

Neimeyer, R.A. (2009). *Constructivist Psychotherapy*. London: Routledge.

Procter, H. and Winter, D.A. (2020). *Personal and Relational Construct Psychotherapy*. Basingstoke: Palgrave Macmillan.

Walker, B.M. and Winter, D.A. (2007). The elaboration of personal construct psychology. *Annual Review of Psychology*, 58: 453–477.

Winter, D.A. (1987). Personal construct psychotherapy as a radical alternative to social skills training. In R.A. Neimeyer and G.J. Neimeyer (Eds), *Personal Construct Therapy Casebook*. New York: Springer.

Winter, D.A. (1992). *Personal Construct Psychology in Clinical Practice: Theory, Research and Applications*. London: Routledge.

Winter, D.A. (2005). The evidence base for personal construct psychotherapy. In F. Fransella (Ed.), *The Essential Practitioners' Handbook of Personal Construct Psychology*. Chichester: John Wiley & Sons.

Winter, D.A. and Procter, H.G. (2013). Formulation in personal and relational construct psychotherapy. In L. Johnstone and R. Dallos (Eds), *Formulation in Psychology and Psychotherapy*. London: Routledge.

Winter, D.A. and Reed, N. (Eds) (2016). *Wiley Handbook of Personal Construct Psychology*. Chichester: Wiley-Blackwell.

Winter, D.A. and Viney, L.L. (Eds) (2005). *Personal Construct Psychotherapy: Advances in Theory, Practice and Research*. London: Whurr.

RECOMMENDED READING

Procter, H. and Winter, D.A. (2020). *Personal and Relational Construct Psychotherapy.* Basingstoke: Palgrave Macmillan.

This book provides a comprehensive account, illustrated by numerous examples, of developments in personal construct psychotherapy and of its extension into the relational sphere.

Caputi, P., Viney, L.L., Walker, B.M. and Crittenden, N. (Eds) (2011). *Personal Construct Methodology*. Chichester: Wiley-Blackwell.

This book describes personal construct assessment methods, including those originally devised by Kelly and subsequent developments.

Fransella, F. and Dalton, P. (2000). *Personal Construct Counselling in Action* (2nd ed.). London: Sage.

This is a clear introduction to personal construct counselling and psychotherapy.

5.22 PLURALISTIC THERAPY

CHRISTINE KUPFER, JOHN MCLEOD AND MICK COOPER

OVERVIEW AND KEY POINTS

Pluralistic counselling and psychotherapy, as a form of practice, is a collaborative integrative approach that recognises that there are multiple valid perspectives on what is helpful for clients and that different therapeutic concepts and methods can be suitable and effective for different clients at different times.

Key points include:

- Pluralistic therapists see clients as co-therapists rather than passive help-seeker; they try to support clients to find out and express what they want from therapy and how this can be achieved.
- This means collaboratively discovering and agreeing on goals, tasks and methods, while considering clients' difficulties, resources, insights and preferences.
- Decisions and understandings are made explicit – where possible and desirable – through dialogue, metacommunication and feedback.
- The intention is to co-create a therapy process that draws on the ideas and experiences of both the client and therapist.

BRIEF HISTORY

From the middle of the twentieth century, counselling and psychotherapy proliferated into hundreds of competing therapeutic approaches. While this creative diversity brought much growth to the field and reflected the complexity of client experiences, it also led to the development of 'schools', whose adherents often become entrenched in the 'rightness' of their model, sometimes even putting the model's truth claims above individual client needs and preferences.

While research and training programmes tend to be school-based, many practitioners use techniques and interventions from more approaches than the one in which they were originally trained. However, it has been argued that choosing interventions or concepts eclectically, or on an *ad hoc* basis, can lead to 'confusion, fragmentation and discontent' (Prochaska and Norcross, 2018: 1).

Pluralistic counselling and psychotherapy comprises a metatheoretical framework for therapy that has the potential to draw on the most valuable features of established models and approaches, without either risking unsystematic eclecticism or becoming schoolist itself. To do so, it offers a set of meta-strategies that can be adopted by therapists from a wide range of backgrounds and draws on research evidence around what works in therapy.

Pluralistic counselling and psychotherapy has been developed by Cooper and McLeod (2007, 2011) and further articulated in Cooper and Dryden (2016), McLeod (2018), and Smith and de la Prida (2021). It has been informed by postmodernist thought and shares a suspicion of 'grand narratives' such as all-encompassing psychological theories. It is also aligned to contemporary sensitivities towards valuing difference (e.g., cultural, neurodiversity, gender- and sexuality-related, etc.).

BASIC ASSUMPTIONS

Pluralism is a philosophical construct that refers to the idea that any problem in the social realm has a multiplicity of reasonable and plausible answers. A pluralistic stance implies that a person is willing to accept the validity of other answers to a question, even while adopting a specific position. Pluralistic therapy values diversity and integrates various psychological concepts (and ideas derived from other disciplines) not through disengaged tolerance but through dialogue and active curiosity. It addresses plurality and multiplicity on a variety of levels: plural ways of making sense of what is problematic for a client and the origins, maintenance and solution of these problems; plurality of clients' preferences, needs and resources and how these can change over time; contexts and cultural issues that might provide help or hindrance; a diversity of forms of therapeutic relationships, which might include collaborating with other therapists or people from other professions; and even internal plurality, when different parts of the self or internal voices want or believe different things.

Pluralism assumes that knowledge about what can be helpful comes from multiple types and sources, including the client's life experience, the therapist's learning and their personal and therapeutic experience, and wider contexts. Pluralistic therapists appreciate these multiple perspectives even if they are outside their current assumptions (McLeod, 2018), and tolerate the co-existence of seemingly opposing views as well as of 'the co-existence of knowing and not-knowing' (Cooper and McLeod, 2011: 141). The individual client's perspective (which includes their needs, preferences, values, methods and goals) is regarded as highly significant, and pluralistic therapists are actively curious in supporting clients in selecting how to best address their specific concerns (Norcross and Cooper, 2021). They recognise that when clients begin therapy, they are already in an ongoing process of making sense of what is happening to them and of working towards change and a more satisfying life. Therefore, pluralistic therapists honour and integrate clients' significant knowledge and resources and see the client as active agent and co-therapist, rather than as passive recipient. Through this endeavour, counselling becomes a highly collaborative process.

In responding to the needs of their clients, pluralistic therapists are required to possess a solid foundation of counselling skills and self-awareness, an overview and critical appreciation of a range of therapy approaches, in-depth practical knowledge of at least one approach, and commitment to a process of ongoing lifelong learning about therapy.

Pluralism can either refer to a specific form of therapeutic *practice*, which integrates concepts and methods from across a wide range of therapeutic orientations (as will be detailed below), or to a general *perspective* on therapy (Thompson, Cooper and Pauli, 2017). Single orientation practitioners might only practise one approach but also hold a pluralistic perspective by recognising the value of alternative ideas and methods, as opposed to being dogmatically entrenched in their worldview.

ORIGIN AND MAINTENANCE OF PROBLEMS

Within the counselling and psychotherapy literature, and the wider stock of cultural knowledge, there exists a multiplicity of ideas and theories around the origins of personal, emotional and behavioural problems. A pluralistic stance implies that any of these accounts, or a combination of them, may be valid in any particular case. For example, if a person seeks counselling because of fearfulness around meeting other people, it may be that this pattern is due to previous trauma (being humiliated in front of peers at school), lack of social skills (growing up in a reclusive family), biological factors (genetic predisposition to neuroticism), and so on. A therapist who works pluralistically seeks to keep an open mind about the possible origins of their clients' problems. Some pluralistic therapists use the very general and holistic term 'problems in living' as their starting point. In pluralistic therapy, clients and therapists aim to share ideas about the origins of the client's problems and strive to work together to evaluate and test out which explanations seem most relevant.

Similarly, a pluralistic approach holds that there may be a multiplicity of factors contributing to the maintenance of these problems. Clients will likely have done their best to resolve their problems before seeking help from a therapist, yet their coping strategies may have been ineffective, may not have been pursued vigorously enough or may require to be modified. By inviting discussions with the client on how they think their problems are being maintained, and their sense of what might help, a pluralistic therapist seeks to identify ways of making a difference that are grounded in the client's worldview and life experience, rather than externally imposed.

THEORY OF CHANGE

From a pluralistic perspective, there are many processes of change that may be relevant within therapy and that may be activated through the work that the client and therapist do together. The counselling and psychotherapy theoretical literature includes descriptions of a wide range of different change processes: insight, altering patterns of behaviour through reinforcement, acquiring new social or cognitive skills, developing new relationships, working through the impact of trauma and loss, beginning or ending medication, participation in exercise or spiritual activity, making changes to life situations (e.g., leaving home, starting a new job), and more. It is likely that several of these change processes will occur at the same time, no matter which therapy intervention is used. For example, training the client in relaxation skills as a means of counteracting anxiety may also be interpreted by the client in terms of greater connectedness with – and trust of – a therapist who cares about them, or as a shift in how clients perceive themselves. Ultimately, the aim of pluralistic therapy is to facilitate the client in engaging with the change processes or mechanisms that make a difference for them. Changes might happen in one session for some clients and may require a lot of time for others; they might be large or small; and they might happen in the therapy room or in everyday life.

SKILLS AND STRATEGIES

Pluralistic practitioners, with appropriate training, may use skills and strategies drawn from a wide range of established theories of counselling/psychotherapy and models of counselling skills (Cooper and Dryden, 2016; McLeod and McLeod, 2022). For example, the skill of empathic reflection is well defined within person-centred counselling, and the strategy of using a case formulation to structure planned cognitive and behavioural change is similarly well defined within the CBT literature. However, working pluralistically also requires the development of specific meta-strategies, which will be discussed below.

CAPACITY TO DECONSTRUCT EXISTING THERAPY APPROACHES

Pluralistic therapists appreciate that there is no single theory that sufficiently explains the complexity of human experience, and that existing therapy approaches consist of assemblages of ideas and practices that often reflect the personal interests of the founders of the approach and the socio-historical context in which the approach was first developed. Mainstream therapy approaches are viewed as comprising bundles of ideas and practices that have the potential to be dismantled and used separately. For example, empathic reflection is a core skill within person-centred counselling but can be used to facilitate many different types of therapeutic change processes. This kind of conceptual flexibility and resourcefulness is essential if pluralistic therapy is to be responsive to the specific preferences of a client. Pluralistic therapists seek to develop a wide range of working knowledge about different therapy approaches – acknowledging, all the time, that a 'complete' knowledge of the therapeutic field is never wholly possible.

Hence, pluralistic therapists are willing to acknowledge when an approach with which they are not sufficiently familiar might be useful for a client and will then collaborate with other professionals or refer clients on if needed.

ENABLING CLIENTS TO PARTICIPATE ACTIVELY IN THERAPY

Consistent with empirical research, pluralistic therapists challenge the view that clients are only receivers of help and instead recognise and encourage them as active participants or co-therapists who can offer much to the therapeutic process. A key skill in pluralistic therapy involves assisting clients to become aware of and communicate their own preferences and views. Therapists do this through collaboratively assessing a client's situation and co-creating a case formulation, through regular feedback, and by drawing out strategies and cultural resources that the client has used before and found helpful, so that they can be utilised further in the therapeutic process. Persistent exploration and gathering feedback after trying out various things help to discover which perspectives and methods a client finds most helpful.

It is important to provide clients with information about how they can be involved in the therapy process, during intake or assessment, and through written materials. They also need information about the broader 'therapy menu' that is potentially available to them, and to encourage them to express what they would like to try out and work with.

SHARED DECISION-MAKING AS A PROCESS

Shared decision-making is an important feature of pluralistic therapy. It means taking opportunities within therapy to engage in conversations with clients about key choice points in the therapy process, such as their goals, the immediate tasks that need to be accomplished in order to achieve these goals, and the methods or activities that might help them in making progress (Di Malta, Oddli and Cooper, 2019). To do this, a therapist needs to have genuine curiosity and interest in learning from the client, engage in an ongoing process of exploration of the client's understandings and preferences, be able to offer further perspectives and build meaning-bridges between views, and be open to trying things out. Therapists also need to pursue their own process of continuing development and learning in therapeutic methods.

Collaborative decisions are made based on suggestions from both client and therapist (McLeod, 2018).

The pluralistic commitment to collaboration and dialogue, as a means of weaving together the knowledge and experience of the therapist with that of the client, is no easy matter and a process rather than a single event that takes place at the start of therapy. It takes time for clients to articulate what they want and how they want to achieve this. The focus of therapy may change over time when clients uncover or re-prioritise issues. Shared decision-making takes the form of moment-by-moment meta-communication of intentions and responses, and conversations facilitated by completion of feedback measures. For many pluralistic therapists, a key stage in shared decision-making involves the development of a collaborative case formulation in which the client and therapist map out, on a large sheet of paper, their ideas about the nature of the client's problem and goals for therapy, how the problem has developed, relevant strengths and resources, and possible ways forward (McLeod and McLeod, 2016). Clients' goals are made explicit and become shared agreements, which are then broken down into manageable tasks that can be tackled on a step-by-step basis.

ACTIVATING CLIENT STRENGTHS AND CULTURAL RESOURCES

Pluralistic therapy takes account of the substantial evidence that is available around the value to mental health and wellbeing of cultural resources such as creative or outdoor activities, reading, sports, spiritual practice, voluntary work, and many other activities. The client has previous experience in their life of making use of such resources to promote connection with others, meaning in life and self-esteem. Part of the process of pluralistic therapy therefore involves reviewing the relevance of resources that may be applicable in the resolution of current problems in living and devising strategies for activating these resources. This can take the form of engaging with these resources outside the therapy session and talking about it with the therapist, of co-participating in the activities with the client or of collaborating with others (e.g., joint meetings with client's activity facilitator; cf. McLeod, 2018).

ROUTINE MONITORING OF WHAT WORKS

To successfully construct therapy around what works for each particular client, it is important to know if clients move towards their goals and if they find the activities and the therapeutic relationship helpful. Therefore, clients can be invited on a weekly basis to complete an outcome scale, such as the Clinical Outcomes in Routine Evaluation (CORE) questionnaires or individualised goal rating scales (Cooper and Xu, 2022). Other instruments that assess whether the client is getting what they want from therapy include the Helpful Aspects of Therapy scale, which measures the client's perception of the therapeutic alliance, or the Inventory of Client Preferences (Cooper and Norcross, 2016). These instruments might offer clients a language to convey their experience and help counter their inhibition to share their views. The aim is to use such instruments as reflective 'conversational tools' to supplement and extend what emerges from review sessions and the ongoing feedback that clients offer to their therapists.

CASE STUDY

Silvia was a single woman of 70 who had retired following a successful professional career. As an unexpected consequence of a minor surgical procedure, she suddenly became blind. Silvia became increasingly depressed and socially isolated. Six sessions of pluralistic counselling had a significant impact on her sense of wellbeing, acceptance of her condition, and hope for the future. During therapy, her counsellor regularly sought Silvia's views on what would be helpful, and whether the activities they were pursuing in therapy sessions were making a difference for her. Overall progress across therapy was monitored using a verbally administered version of the CORE outcome questionnaire. A range of therapeutic tasks were explored: (1) feeling that someone else understood what she was going through; (2) being able to express emotions around the loss of sight; (3) finding a new identity; (4) finding ways to cope with fear, loss, dependency and other people's perceptions; (5) exploring the

(Continued)

(Continued)

possibility of a positive future without sight; (6) making sense of things; and (7) finding ways to become more socially connected. Some sessions involved intensive exploratory listening and meaning-making, whereas other phases of therapy involved planning for behaviour change. Important change events within therapy included a decision to find ways to re-engage in hill-walking, and an appreciation of how she could make better use of the presence and support of her live-in carer. This case demonstrates how careful and deliberate alignment of therapy with the needs, interests and resources of the client, following pluralistic principles, can lead to meaningful and significant change within a limited number of sessions. A more detailed account of this case can be found in Thurston, McLeod and Thurston (2013).

RESEARCH

A growing body of research indicates that collaboration and attuning therapeutic interventions to clients' individual wants lead to improved outcomes, client satisfaction and reduced drop-outs (see meta-analysis by Swift et al., 2018; also Antoniou et al., 2017; Berg, Sandahl and Clinton, 2008; Walls, McLeod and McLeod, 2016). As research has shown that there is surprisingly little overlap between what therapists intuitively *think* that their client prefers, finds useful or finds significant and what the client *actually* thinks (Cooper, et al., 2015; Timulak, 2010), pluralistic therapy uses meta-communication to make explicit what is implicit and offers systematic tools for feedback to support shared decision-making, which have been shown to enhance outcomes (Lambert, 2017; Solstad, Castonguay and Moltu, 2019).

The pluralistic approach to therapy was specifically developed as a framework that could incorporate the widest possible range of findings on what clients might find helpful in therapy. Clients' ideas and preferences have primacy, yet research can inform therapists, for example, to select which other perspectives and methods to offer to clients.

Pluralistic therapy recognises that while much research has been carried out to find out which therapy is most effective, no single approach has been shown to be overall better than others (Frost, Baskin and Wampold, 2020; Luborsky, Singer and Luborsky, 1975), and cross-theoretical factors such as 'feeling understood' have been shown to be most helpful (Timulak, 2010). Furthermore, research results, particularly of larger studies, need to be read critically. Often, people with lived experience find that truth claims made in research studies do not apply to them, as their context or experience varies from that of the sample (McLeod, 2021; McPherson et al., 2020). From a pluralistic point of view, it is therefore important to consider the clients' perspectives on research and to go beyond theoretical and scientific perspectives and include personal, cultural and practical ways of knowing. A pluralistic framework pluralises what counts as evidence, and how this is gathered (Smith et al., 2021).

REFERENCES

Antoniou, P., Cooper, M., Tempier, A. and Holliday, C. (2017). Helpful aspects of pluralistic therapy for depression. *Counselling and Psychotherapy Research*, 17(2), 137–147.

Berg, A.L., Sandahl, C. and Clinton, D. (2008). The relationship of treatment preferences and experiences to outcome in generalized anxiety disorder (GAD). *Psychology and Psychotherapy: Theory, Research and Practice*, 81, 247–259.

Cooper, M. and Dryden, W. (Eds) (2016). *Handbook of Pluralistic Counselling and Psychotherapy*. London: Sage.

Cooper, M. and McLeod, J. (2007). A pluralistic framework for counselling and psychotherapy: implications for research. *Counselling and Psychotherapy Research*, 7, 135–143.

Cooper, M. and McLeod, J. (2011). *Pluralistic Counselling and Psychotherapy*. London: Sage.

Cooper, M. and Norcross, J.C. (2016). A brief, multidimensional measure of clients' therapy preferences: the Cooper-Norcross Inventory of Preferences (C-NIP). *International Journal of Clinical and Health Psychology*, 16, 87–98.

Cooper, M., Wild, C., van Rijn, B., Ward, T., McLeod, J., Cassar, S. and Sreenath, S. (2015). Pluralistic therapy for depression: acceptability, outcomes and helpful aspects in a multisite study. *Counselling Psychology Review*, 30(1), 6–20.

Cooper, M. and Xu, D. (2022). The Goals Form: reliability, validity, and clinical utility of an idiographic goal-focused measure for routine outcome monitoring in psychotherapy. *Journal of Clinical Psychology*.

Di Malta, G., Oddli, H.W. and Cooper, M. (2019). From intention to action: a mixed methods study of clients' experiences of goal-oriented practices. *Journal of Clinical Psychology*, 75(10), 1770–1789.

Frost, N.D., Baskin, T.W. and Wampold, B.E. (2020). Comparative clinical trials in psychotherapy: have large effects been replicated? *Epidemiology and Psychiatric Science*, 29, 128.

Lambert, M.J. (2017). Maximizing psychotherapy outcome beyond evidence-based medicine. *Psychotherapy and Psychosomatics*, 86(2), 80–89.

Luborsky, L., Singer, B. and Luborsky, L. (1975). Comparative studies of psychotherapies: is it true that everyone has won and all must have prizes? *Archives of General Psychiatry*, 32(8), 995–1008.

McLeod, J. (2018). *Pluralistic Therapy: Distinctive Features*. London: Routledge.

McLeod, J. (2021). Why it is important to look closely at what happens when therapy clients complete symptom measures. *Philosophy, Psychiatry, and Psychology*, 28(2), 133–136.

McLeod, J. and McLeod, J. (2016). Assessment and formulation in pluralistic counselling and psychotherapy. In M. Cooper and W. Dryden (Eds), *Handbook of Pluralistic Counselling and Psychotherapy* (pp. 15–27). London: Sage.

McLeod, J. and McLeod, J. (2022). *Counselling Skills: Theory, Research and Practice* (2nd ed.). London: Open University Press.

McPherson, S., Rost, F., Sidhu, S. and Dennis, M. (2020). Non-strategic ignorance: considering the potential for a paradigm shift in evidence-based mental health. *Health*, 24, 3–20.

Norcross, J.C. and Cooper, M. (2021). *Personalizing Psychotherapy: Assessing and Accommodating Patient Preferences*. Washington, DC: American Psychological Association.

Prochaska, J. and Norcross, J. (2018). *Systems of Psychotherapy: A transtheoretical analysis* (9th ed). New York: Oxford University Press.

Smith, K. and de la Prida, A. (2021). *The Pluralistic Therapy Primer: A Concise Introduction*. Monmouth: PCCS Books.

Smith, K., McLeod, J., Blunden, N., Cooper, M., Gabriel, L., Kupfer, C., McLeod, J., Murphie, M.C., Oddli, H.W., Thurston, M. and Winter, L.A. (2021). A pluralistic perspective on research in psychotherapy: harnessing passion, difference and dialogue to promote justice and relevance. *Frontiers in Psychology*, 3728.

Solstad, S.M., Castonguay, L.G. and Moltu, C. (2019). Patients' experiences with routine outcome monitoring and clinical feedback systems: a systematic review and synthesis of qualitative empirical literature. *Psychotherapy Research*, 29(2), 157–170.

Swift, J.K., Callahan, J.L., Cooper, M. and Parkin, S.R. (2018). The impact of accommodating client preference in psychotherapy: a meta-analysis. *Journal of Clinical Psychology*, 74(11), 1924–1937.

Thompson, A., Cooper, M. and Pauli, R. (2017). Development of a therapists' self-report measure of pluralistic thought and practice: the Therapy Pluralism Inventory. *British Journal of Guidance and Counselling*, 45(5), 489–499.

Thurston, M., McLeod J. and Thurston, A. (2013). Counselling for sight loss: using systematic case study research to build a client informed practice model. *British Journal of Visual Impairment*, 31, 102–122.

Timulak, L. (2010). Significant events in psychotherapy: an update of research findings. *Psychology and Psychotherapy: Theory, Research and Practice*, 83(4), 421–447.

Walls, J., McLeod, J. and McLeod, J. (2016). Client preferences in counselling for alcohol problems: a qualitative investigation. *Counselling and Psychotherapy Research*, 16(2), 109–118.

> **RECOMMENDED READING**
>
> McLeod, John (2018). *Pluralistic Therapy: Distinctive Features.* London: Routledge.
>
> This book provides an introduction to key aspects of pluralistic therapy.
>
> Gibson, A., Cooper, M., Rae, J. and Hayes, J. (2020). Clients' experiences of shared decision making in an integrative psychotherapy for depression. *Journal of Evaluation in Clinical Practice*, 26(2), 559–568.
>
> This article shows how clients experience shared decision making and what helps them to overcome difficulties in contributing.
>
> *Pluralistic Practice: Celebrating Diversity in Therapy.* https://pluralisticpractice.com/
>
> This website describes pluralistic practice and training paths, offers updates on research and publications, and includes an active blog from a wide range of contributors.

5.23 PSYCHOANALYTIC THERAPY

JESSICA YAKELEY

OVERVIEW AND KEY POINTS

Psychoanalytic therapy is an exploratory psychological treatment based on psychoanalytic principles and ideas that were established by Sigmund Freud at the beginning of the twentieth century and subsequently expanded and elaborated by numerous psychoanalytic thinkers and practitioners since then. Influential psychoanalysts who have shaped psychoanalytic practice and discourse include Anna Freud, Melanie Klein, Donald Winnicott and Wilfred Bion in Britain, and Heinz Hartmann, Heinz Kohut and Otto Kernberg in the United States. There are now many different 'schools' of psychoanalysis, each advocating variations in psychoanalytic theory and technique. However, many of Freud's basic psychoanalytic concepts continue to unite these different approaches, including the existence of a dynamic unconscious, resistance, transference, countertransference, defence mechanisms, free association and the repetition compulsion. This chapter focuses on Freud's original ideas and their influence on contemporary psychoanalytic thinking and practice.

The key points of psychoanalytic therapy are as follows:

- It focuses on the patient's 'internal world' of unconscious fantasies, wishes, motivations, conflicts and defences.
- It embraces a developmental perspective in which the adult personality is shaped by significant relationships and events in childhood.
- It aims to effect long-standing personality change by addressing the psychological mechanisms underlying the patient's more overt symptoms and behaviours.
- It is usually less structured, more intensive and longer term than other psychotherapy modalities, such as cognitive-behavioural treatment.
- It was originally developed by Freud for the treatment of neuroses, but has widened its scope to treat people with a range of psychological conditions, personality difficulties and relationship problems.

BRIEF HISTORY

Sigmund Freud is one of a handful of remarkable thinkers whose ideas helped shape the twentieth century and which continue to be influential today. Originally a neurologist in Vienna working with patients suffering from hysteria, Freud experimented with hypnosis, abreaction and catharsis before discovering the 'talking cure'. Freud initially believed that neurotic symptoms were the result of the 'damming up' of affect resulting from painful childhood experiences, and if patients could be encouraged to talk about them, they would be cured. Freud particularly focused on his patients' dreams, proposing that the dream represented an attempt by the dreamer to fulfil a wish, which was usually an erotic wish. Like dreams, Freud saw neurotic symptoms as meaningful, representing compromise formations between repressed sexual impulses and the censoring agents of the mind. As he developed his thinking further, he began to see neurosis not just as the result of real trauma or childhood seduction, but due to conflicts over unconscious fantasies of infantile sexual gratification stemming from early childhood.

Freud's ideas were ahead of his time, and his theory of infantile sexuality shocked his colleagues and the wider society of early twentieth-century Europe in which he lived. However, through extensive treatment of patients, as well as his own self-analysis, he continued to develop a methodology of treatment in which to test his theories of the mind, attracting a growing body of followers. Despite influential critics and controversies, Freud's ideas have endured for over a century, permeating diverse fields of thought, including education, the social sciences, literary theory, philosophy and the media. Psychoanalysis, as invented by Freud, continues today as a therapeutic treatment, a body of theoretical knowledge and as a method of investigation of the human mind.

BASIC ASSUMPTIONS

Although psychoanalysis has evolved considerably since Freud, many of his basic tenets remain central to contemporary theory and practice. Key notions include unconscious mental activity, psychic determination and the idea that childhood experiences are critical in shaping the adult personality.

THE UNCONSCIOUS AND MODELS OF THE MIND

Part of our mind is unconscious and can never be fully known to us, but is revealed through the analysis of dreams, slips of the tongue (which Freud called *parapraxes*) and patterns of speech, which provide a window into the underlying unconscious feelings, fantasies and desires that motivate our conscious thoughts and manifest behaviour. In Freud's first *topographical model*, the mind was divided into three systems: the conscious, the preconscious and the unconscious. In the *preconscious*, mental contents can easily be brought to conscious awareness by shifting awareness, whereas the mental contents of the *unconscious* are unacceptable to the conscious mind and are therefore kept from conscious awareness by the forces of *repression* but emerge in the guise of symptoms.

In Freud's second model of the mind, the *structural model*, the psychical apparatus is divided into three parts: id, ego and superego. The *id* is a reservoir of unconscious, unorganised, instinctual sexual and aggressive drives, which are unacceptable to the social, moral and ethical values of conscious civilised thought, and must therefore be kept at bay. The id is governed by primary process thinking under the domination of the pleasure principle – the inborn tendency of the organism to avoid pain and seek pleasure via the release of tension. In the lawless world of the id, opposites co-exist, wishes are fulfilled, negatives do not exist and there is no concept of time. The *ego* mediates between the conflicting demands of id, superego and reality. It is the executive organ of the psyche, controlling motility, perception, contact with reality and, via the defence mechanisms, which are located in the unconscious part, the ego modulates the drives coming from the id. The *superego* evolves from part of the ego as the heir to the Oedipus complex, with the internalisation by the child of parental standards and goals to establish the individual's moral conscience.

PSYCHIC DETERMINISM

Freud believed that although we may think we have control over our lives and operate through free choice, our conscious thoughts and actions are actually shaped and controlled by unconscious forces. For example, our chosen vocation, choice of partner or even hobbies are not randomly selected, but are unconsciously determined by our childhood experiences. Moreover, Freud proposed that a single symptom or behaviour was multi-determined, in that it could contain multiple complex meanings and serve several functions in responding to the demands of both reality and the unconscious needs of the internal world.

DRIVE THEORY AND LIBIDO

An instinct is a hereditary pattern of behaviour, specific to a species, that unfolds in a predetermined fashion during development and is resistant to change. Freud took this biological concept to embed his psychological theory of the mind in biology with his theory of the drives. For Freud, all instincts had a *source* in a part of the body or bodily stimulus; an *aim*, to eliminate the state of tension deriving from the source; and an *object* (often another person), which was the target of the aim. Freud described libido as 'the force by which the sexual instinct is represented in the mind' (Freud, 1917a: 136). The association with sexuality is misleading, as Freud considered libido to include the notion of pleasure as a whole. In Freud's final theory of the instincts, he proposed two opposing instincts – the life instinct (Eros) and the death instinct (Thanatos). Initially aimed at self-destruction, the death instinct is later turned against the outside world and underlies aggression.

DEVELOPMENTAL STAGES

Freud believed that children were influenced by sexual drives and proposed a developmental trajectory in which the early manifestations of infantile sexuality were associated with bodily functions such as feeding and bowel control. Psychosexual development consists of libidinal energy shifting from oral to anal to phallic to genital erotogenic zones respectively, where each corresponding stage of development is characterised by particular functions and objectives but builds upon and subsumes the accomplishments of the preceding stage. Failure to negotiate the emotional demands of each stage is linked to complex character traits in adult life. For example, excessive oral gratifications or deprivations can result in pathological narcissism and dependence on others, whereas developmental arrest at the anal stage can lead to miserliness or sadism.

THE OEDIPUS COMPLEX

Freud named the Oedipus complex after the Greek tragedy in which Oedipus unknowingly killed his father and married his mother. Freud proposed that the Oedipus complex was a normal stage of development occurring between the ages of 3 and 5 years, where the boy is attracted to his mother and develops feelings of rivalry and jealousy for his father. The equivalent constellation in the little girl is called the *Electra complex*. Castration anxiety refers to the boy's fear that his father will castrate him for his desire for the mother. Resolution of the Oedipus complex results in the formation of the superego. Freud proposed that failure to negotiate the Oedipus complex lies at the heart of neurotic illness and results in deficits in the capacity to enjoy healthy loving and sexual relations.

ORIGINS AND MAINTENANCE OF PROBLEMS

CONFLICT

Freud believed that neurotic illness was the result of *conflict* between the instinctual drives and the external world, or between different parts of the mind. This conflict between the ego and id can result in neurotic symptoms as unacceptable sexual and aggressive thoughts and feelings break through the ego's censorship barrier and are converted into substitute compromise formations to prevent them from fully entering consciousness. Conflict between the ego and superego can give rise to feelings of low self-esteem, shame and guilt due to the ego's failure to live up to the high moral standards imposed by the superego.

ANXIETY AND DEFENCE MECHANISMS

The notion of anxiety is also central to Freud's formulations regarding the origin of neurosis. In Freud's earlier model, anxiety is a direct expression of undischarged sexual energy or libido. He later revised his theory of anxiety to see anxiety as an affect experienced by the ego as a signal when faced with danger. This led Freud to the concept of defence mechanisms, manoeuvres of the ego that protect it from both internal sources of danger, anxiety and unpleasure (such as the sexual and aggressive drives) and external threats, especially those related to experiences of loss.

Freud proposed that different mental states result from different constellations of anxiety and defence mechanisms. In *neurosis*, the primary defence mechanism is repression, the pushing out of consciousness of thoughts and wishes that do not fit in with one's view of one's self. In *perversion*, the ego is split via the defence mechanism of disavowal, which allows contradictory beliefs to be held simultaneously so that the perverse person may hold a circumscribed delusional belief (such as the paedophile who believes children enjoy sexual intercourse) but the rest of the personality appears intact and functioning normally. In *psychosis*, repression fails completely and the person is overwhelmed by unconscious or id contents, and creates a delusional world via primitive defence mechanisms such as projection and omnipotence to make sense of such chaos.

TRAUMA

Massive trauma can also overwhelm the ego, breaking through its defences and rendering it helpless and unable to function. Freud coined the term *repetition compulsion* to describe a person's unconscious tendency in adult life to repeat past traumatic behaviour, in an attempt to resolve feelings of helplessness and conflict. Freud later explained this as a manifestation of the death instinct.

RESISTANCE

Freud described the antagonism of the patient to the therapist's attempt, which is frequently encountered, despite their distress and disability, to achieve insight and change as *resistance*, which represented a compromise between the forces that were striving towards recovery and the opposing ones. Resistances to treatment can take overt and covert forms, such as missing appointments, being late to sessions, being silent or not hearing interpretations. Resistance can be seen as a defence mechanism that arises during treatment to avoid experiencing the psychic pain associated with previously repressed unpleasant impulses and affects that the therapy is attempting to uncover and explore.

THEORY OF CHANGE

CONSCIOUSNESS

Freud's changing views of therapeutic action reflected his evolving conceptualisation of his models of the mind. His initial simple model of catharsis, in which therapy worked by releasing damned-up affects, reflected a model of the mind in which traumas had aroused unacceptable feelings and thoughts that had to be pushed from consciousness to maintain psychic stability. Freud's mechanism of change at this time was to 'transform what is unconscious into what is conscious' (Freud, 1917b: 293).

STRENGTHENING OF THE EGO

Freud's development of his topographical model of the mind led to his emphasis on the interpretation of defence and resistance as techniques to allow the unconscious mental contents into consciousness. When his structural model took priority over the topographical, his positioning of the Oedipal complex as the developmental crisis at the centre of all neuroses, and the increasing attention to ego defences, therapeutic effect now depended on the alteration and redistribution of energy between the three mental agencies of ego, id and superego, and in particular the strengthening of the ego.

TRANSFERENCE

Freud himself recognised the central role of the transference in effecting therapeutic change, in providing a window into the patient's unconscious fantasy life. Transference is the displacement by the patient of early wishes and feelings towards people from the past, particularly the patient's parents, onto the figure of the therapist. The safety of the analytic situation allows the patient to experience those unconscious wishes and fears as they arise in relation to the analyst, to appreciate their irrationality and origins from the past and to provide the opportunity of working through. Since Freud, increasing emphasis has been placed on the role of the transference and its interpretation in effecting therapeutic change, which includes superego modification with the introduction of a more benign superego.

RELATIONAL EXPERIENCE

While verbal interpretations of the meaning of the transferential experience are important, there has also been a shift to believing that the relational affective experience in itself is a mutative factor. This involves the internalisation of a new relationship with the therapist, who is reliable and not retaliatory, which may be very different from the relationships the patient has previously experienced.

SKILLS AND STRATEGIES

THE ANALYTIC SETTING

In psychoanalytic treatment, patients are encouraged to lie on the couch, with the analyst sitting behind them. The relative sensory deprivation and inability to see the analyst's facial expressions facilitates the patient in being able to focus on his inner thoughts and feelings, which he is encouraged to express in free association. The reclining position is also helpful in inducing a certain degree of regression and dependency that is necessary in order to establish and work through the patient's neurotic difficulties. The boundaries of the setting or parameters of treatment are important in creating a safe environment in which therapy can occur. These boundaries include consistency of the physical environment in which the therapy takes place, the reliability of regular 50-minute sessions that begin and end on time, and clearly defined interpersonal boundaries between patient and therapist, in which the therapist minimises self-disclosure and maintains confidentiality.

FREE ASSOCIATION

Free association is the cornerstone of classical Freudian psychoanalytic technique. The patient is encouraged to say whatever is in his mind, without censoring his thoughts, however embarrassing, disturbing or seemingly trivial these may be. The psychoanalyst's task, through a corresponding type of evenly suspended listening that Freud called *free-floating attention*, is to discover the unconscious themes that underlie the patient's discourse via the patient's slips of the tongue, associative links and resistances to speaking about certain topics that the patient himself is unaware of.

SPECTRUM OF INTERVENTIONS

The analyst intervenes in the form of verbal communications, which can be categorised along a spectrum that moves from the supportive to interpretative as the therapy progresses. Thus the analyst may initially make *empathic comments*; moving to *clarifications* – questioning or rephrasing to elucidate what the patient means; via *confrontations*, where the analyst will point out inconsistencies in the patient's account or draw his attention to subjects he may be avoiding; to *interpretations*.

INTERPRETATIONS

An interpretation offers a new formulation of unconscious meaning and motivation for the patient. Many contemporary psychoanalysts view transference interpretations in the 'here-and-now' or affective interchange of the analytic session as the most mutative intervention. However, more classical Freudian analysts may wait longer before interpreting the transference, holding back until the patient himself is aware of the feelings he has towards the analyst. The Freudian analyst also focuses attentively on details of the patient's past life to make reconstructive interpretations that can help the patient understand how his current difficulties have been influenced by his history. Exploration and interpretation about the patient's current external life (extra-transference interpretations) may also be helpful without minimising the importance of his internal world and unconscious fantasies.

COUNTERTRANSFERENCE

Countertransference describes the unconscious emotional reactions that the therapist has towards the patient, and is a result of both unresolved conflicts in the therapist as well as contributions or projections from the patient. Freud originally saw countertransference as a resistance to treatment, but contemporary analysts see it as a source of useful information about the patient and his internal object relations, which determine the patient's pattern of relating to others.

INTENSITY AND DURATION OF TREATMENT

Psychoanalytic therapy aims to effect long-lasting characterological change, not just alleviation of the patient's symptoms, and therefore tends to be long term, lasting years rather than months. This allows sufficient time for the *working-through* of difficulties – the integration of cognitive and affective understanding and the consolidation of new ways of functioning and relating to others. Psychoanalysis is also an intensive treatment, with the patient being seen four to five times per week, whereas in psychoanalytic psychotherapy the patient is seen once to three times a week, often face-to-face, rather than lying on the couch.

CASE STUDY

Ben was a 30-year-old man presenting with depression and anxiety following his girlfriend ending their relationship because of Ben's refusal to move out of the house where he lived with his mother. He was referred by his General Practitioner (GP) to his local mental health service and, following assessment, was offered weekly psychoanalytic psychotherapy with a female therapist. Significant events in Ben's history were his father leaving the family home when he was 5 years old, and his mother becoming severely depressed and hospitalised for several months, during which Ben and his siblings were looked after by their grandparents.

> At the start of the therapy, Ben appeared anxious and found silences difficult, so the therapist initially limited her interventions to empathic comments and clarifications of what his current difficulties entailed. As Ben became more engaged and able to talk more spontaneously about what was on his mind, the therapist began to explore with him how his childhood experiences of loss had impacted on his adult relationships. However, she began to feel irritated with Ben's passivity and compliant attitude towards her, which she suspected concealed more aggressive feelings that he could not admit into conscious awareness. Having reflected on the possible meaning of her countertransferential feelings, and following Ben missing the session after she had unexpectedly cancelled a session due to illness, she suggested that Ben's absence might be connected to feelings of resentment that she had not been there the previous week (a transference interpretation). Ben initially denied this, saying that he had felt too depressed to come, which had nothing to do with her. However, when Ben missed another session after the therapist returned from her planned leave, he admitted that he felt a bit annoyed and upset that his therapist had better things to do than see him. Over time, Ben was able to understand that his experience (in the transference) of his therapist as a rejecting, unavailable object was based on an unconscious identification with his mother as a depressed and abandoned victim of his father. As Ben worked through these difficult feelings in relation to his therapist, he was able to access previously unconscious feelings of anger towards his mother for being emotionally unavailable to him after his father left. By the end of therapy he felt he had a more balanced understanding of his parents' difficulties and their influence on his development, was able to move out of his mother's house and establish a relationship with his father that was less dominated by anger and resentment.

RESEARCH

Although it is difficult to conduct outcome research on intensive psychoanalytic treatments, there is an accumulating body of empirical evidence supporting the efficacy of psychoanalytic psychotherapy. Meta-analyses, which pool the results of many different independent studies, including randomised controlled trials of long-term psychoanalytic psychotherapy (Leichsenring et al., 2013), show that the effect sizes for psychoanalytic therapy are as large as those reported for other evidence-based therapies, such as cognitive-behavioural therapy, and that psychoanalytic psychotherapy is efficacious in common mental disorders, including depression, anxiety, personality disorders, eating disorders and post-traumatic stress disorder (Leichsenring et al., 2015). Moreover, patients who receive psychoanalytic therapy maintain therapeutic gains and continue to improve after cessation of treatment. The widespread scepticism regarding the scientific nature of psychoanalytic therapy is not justified, and may reflect biases in the dissemination of research findings (Shedler, 2010).

REFERENCES

Freud, S. (1917a) A difficulty in the path of psycho-analysis. In *The Standard Edition of the Complete Psychological Works of Sigmund Freud, Volume XVII.* London: Hogarth Press.

Freud, S. (1917b) Introductory lectures on psycho-analysis. In *The Standard Edition of the Complete Psychological Works of Sigmund Freud, Volume XVI.* London: Hogarth Press.

Leichsenring, F., Abbass, A., Luyten, P., Hilsenroth, M. and Rabung, S. (2013) The emerging evidence for long-term psychodynamic therapy. *Psychodynamic Psychiatry*, *41*(3), 361–384.

Leichsenring, F., Luyten, P., Hilsenroth, M. J., Abbass, A., Barber, J. P., Keefe, J. R., Leweke, F., Rabung, S. and Steinert, C. (2015) Psychodynamic therapy meets evidence-based medicine: a systematic review using updated criteria. *The Lancet: Psychiatry*, *2*(7), 648–660.

Shedler, J. (2010) The efficacy of psychodynamic psychotherapy. *American Psychologist*, 65, 98–109.

> **RECOMMENDED READING**
>
> Lemma, A. (2016) *Introduction to the Practice of Psychoanalytic Psychotherapy* (2nd ed.). Chichester: Wiley Blackwell.
>
> This is an accessible guide to the theory and technique of psychoanalysis and psychoanalytic psychotherapy with case studies and practice guidelines.
>
> Gay, P. (1988) *Freud: A Life for Our Time*. London: J.M. Dent.
>
> This biography of Sigmund Freud incorporates new material discovered since the publication of that of Ernest Jones in 1953 (Jones, E. (1953) *The Life and Work of Sigmund Freud*. London: Penguin Books).
>
> Greenson, R. (1967) *The Technique and Practice of Psychoanalysis*. New York: International Universities Press.
>
> This is a clear, readable and comprehensive textbook that remains relevant to psychoanalytic practice today.

5.24 *PSYCHODYNAMIC INTERPERSONAL THERAPY*

RICHARD J. BROWN, SARA BARDSLEY AND VANESSA HERBERT

OVERVIEW AND KEY POINTS

Psychodynamic interpersonal therapy (PIT) is a brief, largely jargon-free type of relational therapy that is easy to learn and does not require extensive knowledge of psychodynamic theory. It has theoretical roots in person-centred counselling and a number of psychodynamic traditions but is a distinct form of therapy in its own right. Key points include the following:

- PIT takes the form of an in-depth, two-way conversation focusing on the client's feelings as they emerge in the session, with a view to helping them understand and resolve emotional and interpersonal problems in their lives.
- PIT has a good evidence base, with randomised controlled trials suggesting it is efficacious as a treatment for depression, deliberate self-harm, personality disturbance and functional ('medically unexplained') symptoms.
- PIT is recognised as an efficacious treatment within the CORE competence frameworks for psychoanalytic/psychodynamic therapy and for persistent physical health problems.

BRIEF HISTORY

The conversational model (as PIT was originally known) was developed in the 1970s and 1980s by British psychiatrist and psychotherapist Robert Hobson and his Australian collaborator Russell Meares. The term PIT was adopted later when the model was manualised and evaluated as a brief intervention in clinical trials in the United Kingdom; the original name is still used in Australia, where the approach is often used as a treatment for complex trauma and personality disorders (Meares, 2012).

Hobson and Meares were influenced by a range of clinical and theoretical perspectives, such as attachment theory, interpersonal psychology, psychoanalysis, person-centred counselling and existential psychotherapy, as well as non-clinical traditions, including theology, the philosophy of Ludwig Wittgenstein, and romantic poets such as Wordsworth, Blake and Coleridge. His combination and application of these influences constitutes a unique approach to psychotherapy, a comprehensive account of which is documented in Hobson's influential book, *Forms of Feeling* (Hobson, 1985).

BASIC ASSUMPTIONS

Traditional psychodynamic concepts, such as the avoidance of painful feelings arising from emotional conflict and the re-enactment of problematic patterns of relating, are central to PIT, although Hobson's description of these concepts in *Forms of Feeling* (1985) relies very little on formal psychodynamic theory and terms, making it particularly accessible. PIT also assumes that the 'how' of therapy is often more important than the 'what', and that slavish adherence to theoretical models can often undermine the central therapeutic task, which is to develop an emotional connection with the client to help them solve their personal problems.

PIT assumes that thought and action are motivated by intrinsic needs that serve to maintain physical and emotional homeostasis, and that stress and anxiety arise when those needs are not met. Two needs that are afforded particular importance in this respect are the need to maintain relationships with other people and the need to maintain autonomy and a positive, coherent sense of self. How we manage the conflict that often arises between these needs has an important bearing on our wellbeing. According to Hobson, negotiating a successful balance between these needs (so-called *aloneness-togetherness*) requires us to relate to and value ourselves and others as unique, experiencing, feeling beings, that is, as 'persons' rather than 'objects' ('I–thou' and 'I–it' forms of relating respectively; Buber, 1937). When we are unable to do this, often because of difficulties in our early relationships, emotional disturbance can arise. PIT assumes that this can be addressed by understanding and optimising the balance between aloneness and togetherness during the therapy, which often involves focusing on and 'staying with' avoided feelings as they arise in the moment.

PIT assumes that helping the client to relate more as a person requires the therapist to be able to do so themselves, which means being genuine (i.e., 'yourself'), humble, emotionally present and responsive to the other person's feelings, without disregarding one's own. The model also assumes that it is easy for even well-meaning therapists to relate to their clients in ways that are counter-therapeutic, including responding in a subtly intrusive, derogatory, invalidating or opaque manner (Meares and Hobson, 1977). Being alert to this possibility is regarded as a crucial task, as is repairing ruptures in the therapeutic relationship when such instances inevitably arise.

ORIGIN AND MAINTENANCE OF PROBLEMS

According to this approach, unhelpful experiences in early attachment relationships may give rise to problems in relationships with the self and/or others, including (1) a tendency to perceive threats to attachments; (2) a tendency to see attachments as a threat to oneself; (3) problems regulating affect and engaging in reflective processing; and (4) problems representing the mental states of self and/or others. These experiences undermine the individual's ability to relate (both to themselves and other people) in adaptive ways, rendering them vulnerable to painful and conflicting feelings in relationships, particularly when there is a threat to their self-worth/autonomy and/or their relatedness with others. Emotional problems are said to arise when the individual manages the anxiety generated by these feelings by disowning the feelings or engaging in other avoidance activities (defences in traditional psychodynamic theory) that keep them from awareness where this is not needed. These well-intentioned avoidance activities typically include unhelpful patterns of relating that reflect how the individual learnt to cope with their early relationships, but which are no longer optimal. These activities maintain symptoms in various ways, such as by preventing the underlying issues from being recognised and dealt with, by preventing the individual's needs from being met, by exposing the individual to unhealthy relationships and by compromising the individual's sense of self.

This model provides a basis for formulation in PIT, and a key goal of the assessment is to arrive at a basic, shared understanding that incorporates some or all of these elements. As an exploratory therapy, however, the process of formulation is seen as an intrinsic aspect of PIT that continues throughout the work, with a deeper, more nuanced understanding of the client's problems (and therefore possible solutions to them) emerging over time.

THEORY OF CHANGE

The aim of PIT is to create a sense of safety so that the individual's anxieties can be tolerated, allowing them to hold the disowned material (and the relational context to which it pertains) in awareness and talk about it as it arises in the moment. This fosters a process of 'symbolical transformation' (akin to the concept of emotional processing in other traditions), whereby the nature, meaning and origins of the disowned material are understood, accepted and mastered. In so doing, new 'forms' (or mental representations) of feeling are developed that reduce the need for further avoidance activities. This renders the client more able to relate to themselves and others as persons and to test this out in the therapy and elsewhere, thereby improving their self-esteem and interpersonal relationships. Subsequent theoretical writings by Meares (2000, 2005) have focused on the development of the self through this process, although these ideas are not fundamental to how the model is understood and practised in the UK.

SKILLS AND STRATEGIES

Arguably, the personal qualities and interpersonal skills of the therapist are more important than detailed knowledge of theoretical concepts in PIT, as long as the therapist has a good understanding of the basic model and the purpose of the therapeutic conversation. There is also a specific set of core skills that are central to appropriate practice of the model. One of the strengths of PIT is that the basic interventions that characterise this approach are clearly defined, easy to learn and comparatively simple to apply (see, for example, Guthrie et al., 2004; Shaw et al., 2001). In this section, we describe some of the main interventions, using examples that might apply in the hypothetical case, *Jean*.

CASE STUDY

Jean is 46 and is coming to therapy for help with depression, which started when her youngest son left home two years ago. Jean's husband, David, is 10 years older than her and they got married the year after she left school at 16, having the first of their three children not long after that. Jean has dedicated her life since then to looking after them. Jean says she has 'the perfect marriage', describing David as 'wonderful, the ideal man ... he's always provided for me and the kids'. She explains how proud she is of his successful company and how he is 'always going abroad to do some deal or another'. There are tears in Jean's eyes when the therapist wonders what it is like for her when he's out of the country; after a long pause, she says (in a far from convincing voice) 'it's good, it really allows me to concentrate on the children'.

Jean was the oldest of seven children and spent a lot of time looking after her siblings when she was growing up, particularly after her father, whom she 'adored', died when she was 12. When the therapist asks how she reacted to his death, she says 'I never really cried when he died ... Mum was in such a state and the kids needed looking after ... I guess I just had to put a lid on it'. Jean quickly changes the subject. Jean says she has 'a lot to be thankful for' and can't understand why she is depressed. She describes getting angry at herself for 'being selfish' and 'burdening people'.

Later in the therapy, the therapist has to cancel two sessions due to illness. When they finally meet again, the therapist wonders what it was like for her while they were away. Jean wells up and replies 'It must take its toll hearing about everyone's problems all the time...'. She seems subdued and upset and the therapist feels that it is difficult to connect with her.

The overarching strategies in PIT are to develop a personal connection and emotionally vivid 'mutual feeling language' with the client regarding their problems, with an appropriate balance of aloneness-togetherness. Feelings are focused on the 'here and now' as they arise and are felt in the therapy (rather than in an abstract sense). To that end, the therapist is alert to cues pointing to the client's emotional experience during the therapy session, including what is both explicit and implicit in the language, expression and behaviour of both participants. Hobson refers to this as a focus on the 'minute particulars' of therapy. The tears in Jean's eyes, the long pause and the unconvincing tone of her voice point to more mixed feelings about her husband's absence than the verbal content of her narrative alone, for example.

Where appropriate, the therapist will seek to amplify the feelings in question by noticing the cues and tentatively 'wondering about' what the client is experiencing, with a view to bringing any feelings on the edge of awareness into focus. They may also offer an informed guess or *understanding hypothesis* about what is happening for them in that moment, based on the available cues and their knowledge of the client (e.g., 'When you were talking about David then, I noticed there were tears in your eyes and you paused … I wonder if part of you feels a bit upset about him going away sometimes'). This process is seen as a central part of empathising with clients and can be used as an adjunct to other types of treatment, such as cognitive-behaviour therapy (CBT) (Guthrie, Hughes and Brown, 2018). The client is then encouraged to 'stay with' and talk about any feelings that have emerged (e.g., 'that sounds important … maybe we could just stay with that upset feeling'), in a two-way, mutual conversation that evolves over time into a shared understanding of the client's emotional experience in relationships. First-person pronouns ('I', 'we' and 'you') are used to foster an explicit discussion of the relationship between client and therapist if the client can tolerate this.

In PIT, the style of the therapist's conversation is tentative and invites negotiation (e.g., 'This might not be quite right but I wonder if…'), communicating a wish to understand the client's difficulties and to be corrected if misunderstandings occur. A distinctive component of PIT is the use of statements (e.g., 'I wonder what's going on inside right now'), which are considered to be less anxiety-provoking and probing than questions (e.g., 'How do you feel about that?'). Statements aim to create a starting point for exploration of the person's difficulties, while providing a space for correction. Wherever possible, the client's specific words and phrases are used; in particular, their metaphors and other figurative language are picked up and used to amplify and explore feelings, with a view to broadening the client's understanding of them (e.g., 'put a lid on it you say… like a pressure cooker maybe… I wonder whether you get to let off steam too'). Detailed questioning, jargon and expert pronouncements are explicitly proscribed: the emphasis is on a shared experience within therapy, and client and therapist perspectives being of equal value.

Over time, the therapist begins to make statements that suggest parallels between what is happening in that moment and feelings in other relationships in the client's life, both currently and in the past. These are *linking hypotheses* (e.g., 'I don't know … you seem a bit upset … I wonder if it felt quite difficult me being away … a bit like when David goes away'). In so doing, previously unrelated aspects of experience can be joined up and patterns discerned. Eventually, therapist and client may begin to develop *explanatory hypotheses*, which describe possible reasons for difficulties in relationships both within and outside the therapy (e.g., 'I guess it feels really hard to say you're upset and cross with me … like it might hurt me or what we're doing in some way … just like you had to put your upset and grief to one side when your Dad died … maybe you felt you had to protect your Mum … in case you lost her too'). This provides an opportunity for conflicts, disowned feelings and avoidance activities to be acknowledged, owned and explored. Such hypotheses bear some resemblance to the transference interpretations seen in other psychodynamic therapies, but are used more sparingly and collaboratively in PIT.

In PIT, the therapist's intuitive sense of how 'connected' they are with their client is seen as a potentially useful indicator of what is happening in the therapy, and as a possible starting point for exploration. The PIT therapist may notice a possible disconnection from Jean following the unplanned break in therapy, for example, and offer an understanding hypothesis about it (e.g., 'I'm not sure, it feels like there's a bit of a distance between us today'). The therapist is also alert to the client's anxiety levels throughout, with a view to promoting meaningful exploration (which is inevitably anxiety-provoking) while ensuring that the process is tolerable for the client. This requires the therapist to use their understanding of the client, the model and their general clinical skills to determine what is safe and appropriate for that individual.

RESEARCH

There is good evidence from randomised controlled trials that PIT is an effective treatment for depression (Barkham et al., 1996; Guthrie et al., 1999; Shapiro et al., 1995), functional ('medically unexplained') symptoms (Creed et al., 2003; Creed et al., 2005a, 2005b, 2005c; Creed et al., 2008; Guthrie et al., 1991; Hamilton et al., 2000; Hyphantis et al., 2009; Mayor et al., 2010; Sattel et al., 2012), deliberate self-harm (Guthrie et al., 2001; Guthrie et al., 2003) and borderline personality disorder (Korner et al., 2006; Stevenson and Meares, 1992; Stevenson, Meares and D'Angelo, 2005). PIT has not been evaluated as a treatment for other mental health problems and is therefore not normally offered as a 'frontline' therapy in these cases. However, PIT may be offered where other treatments (such as CBT) have not worked or are not suitable, where the presenting problems seem particularly amenable to an exploratory interpersonal approach, or where the client expresses a particular preference for a more emotion- or interpersonally-focused treatment.

Process studies have shown that the focus on interpersonal difficulties in PIT is associated with improvements in self-esteem and social adjustment (Kerr et al., 1992). There is also evidence that staying with feelings helps clients to vividly experience and express emotions that are usually suppressed (Mackay, Barkham and Stiles, 1998). The quality of the therapeutic alliance in PIT is associated with improvements on a variety of therapy outcome measures, including symptoms of depression, general symptoms and interpersonal difficulties (Stiles et al., 1998).

REFERENCES

Barkham, M., Rees, A., Shapiro, D. A., Stiles, W. B. et al. (1996). Outcome of time-limited psychotherapy in applied settings: replicating the Second Sheffield Psychotherapy Project. *Journal of Consulting and Clinical Psychology*, 64, 1079–1085.

Buber, M. (1937). *I and Thou.* Edinburgh: T. and T. Clark.

Creed, F., Fernandes, L., Guthrie, E., Palmer, S., Ratcliffe, J., Read, N., Rigby, C., Thompson, D., Tomenson B. and North of England IBS Research Group (2003). The cost-effectiveness of psychotherapy and paroxetine for severe irritable bowel syndrome. *Gastroenterology*, 124(2), 303–317.

Creed, F., Guthrie, E., Ratcliffe, J., Fernandes, L., Rigby, C., Tomenson, B., Read, N. and Thompson, D. G. (2005a). Reported sexual abuse predicts impaired functioning but a good response to psychological treatments in patients with severe irritable bowel syndrome. *Psychosomatic Medicine*, 67, 490–499.

Creed, F., Guthrie, E., Ratcliffe, J., Fernandes, L., Rigby, C., Tomenson, B., Read, N. and Thompson, D. G. (2005b). Does psychological treatment help only those patients with severe irritable bowel syndrome who also have concurrent psychiatric disorder? *Australian and New Zealand Journal of Psychiatry*, 39, 807–815.

Creed, F., Ratcliffe, J., Fernandes, L., Palmer, S., Rigby, C., Tomenson, B., Guthrie, E., Read, N. and Thompson, D. G. (2005c). Outcome in severe irritable bowel syndrome with and without accompanying depressive, panic and neurasthenic disorders. *British Journal of Psychiatry*, 186, 507–515.

Creed, F., Tomenson, B., Guthrie, E., Ratcliffe, J., Fernandes, L., Read, N., Palmer, S. and Thompson, D. G. (2008). The relationship between somatisation and outcome in patients with severe irritable bowel syndrome. *Journal of Psychosomatic Research*, 64(6), 613–620.

Guthrie, E., Creed, F., Dawson, D. and Tomenson, B. (1991). A controlled trial of psychological treatment for the irritable bowel syndrome. *Gastroenterology*, 100, 450–457.

Guthrie, E., Hughes, R. and Brown, R. J. (2018). PI-E: An empathy skills training package to enhance therapeutic skills of IAPT and other therapists. *British Journal of Psychotherapy*, 34, 408–427.

Guthrie, E., Kapur, N., Mackway-Jones, K., Chew-Graham, C., Moorey, J., Mendel, E., Marino-Francis, F., Sanderson, S., Turpin, C., Boddy, G. and Tomenson, B. (2001). Randomised controlled trial of brief psychological intervention after deliberate self-poisoning. *British Medical Journal*, 323, 135–138.

Guthrie, E., Kapur, N., Mackway-Jones, K., Chew-Graham, C., Moorey, J., Mendel, E., Marino-Francis, F., Sanderson, S., Turpin, C. and Boddy, G. (2003). Predictors of outcome following brief psychodynamic-interpersonal therapy for deliberate self-poisoning. *Australian and New Zealand Journal of Psychiatry*, 37, 532–536.

Guthrie, E., Margison, F., Mackay, H., Chew-Graham, C., Moorey, J. and Sibbald, B. (2004). Effectiveness of psychodynamic interpersonal therapy training for primary care counsellors. *Psychotherapy Research*, 14(2), 161–175.

Guthrie, E., Moorey, J., Margison, F., Barker, H., Palmer, S., McGrath, G., Tomenson, B. and Creed, F. (1999). Cost-effectiveness of brief psychodynamic-interpersonal therapy in high utilizers of psychiatric services. *Archives of General Psychiatry*, 56, 519–526.

Hamilton, J., Guthrie, E., Creed, F., Thompson, D., Tomenson, B., Bennett, R., Moriarty, K., Stephens, W. and Liston, R. (2000). A randomised controlled trial of psychotherapy in patients with chronic functional dyspepsia. *Gastroenterology*, 119, 661–669.

Hobson, R. F. (1985). *Forms of Feeling: The Heart of Psychotherapy*. London: Routledge.

Hyphantis, T., Guthrie, E., Tomenson, B. and Creed, F. (2009). Psychodynamic interpersonal therapy and improvement in interpersonal difficulties in people with severe irritable bowel syndrome. *Pain*, 145, 196–203.

Kerr, S., Goldfried, M., Hayes, A., Castonguay, L. and Goldsamt, L. (1992). Interpersonal and intrapersonal focus in cognitive-behavioral and psychodynamic-interpersonal therapies: a preliminary analysis of the Sheffield Project. *Psychotherapy Research*, 2(4), 266–276.

Korner, A., Gerull, F., Meares, R. and Stevenson, J. (2006). Borderline personality disorder treated with the conversational model: a replication study. *Comprehensive Psychiatry*, 47, 406–411.

Mackay, H. C., Barkham, M. and Stiles, W. B. (1998). Staying with the feeling: an anger event in psychodynamic-interpersonal therapy. *Journal of Counseling Psychology*, 45, 279–289.

Mayor, R., Howlett, S., Grunewald, R. and Reuber, M. (2010). Long-term outcome of brief augmented psychodynamic interpersonal therapy for psychogenic non-epileptic seizures: seizure control and healthcare utilization. *Epilepsia*, 51, 1169–1176.

Meares, R. (2000). *Intimacy and Alienation: Memory, Trauma and Personal Being*. London: Brunner-Routledge.

Meares, R. (2005). *The Metaphor of Play*. London: Brunner-Routledge.

Meares, R. (2012). *Borderline Personality Disorder and the Conversational Model*. New York: W.W. Norton.

Meares, R. and Hobson, R. F. (1977). The persecutory therapist. *British Journal of Medical Psychology*, 50, 349–359.

Sattel, H., Lahmann, C., Gündel, H., Guthrie, E., Kruse, J., Noll-Hussong, M., Ohmann, C., Ronel, J., Sack, M., Sauer, N., Schneider, G. and Henningsen, P. (2012). Brief psychodynamic interpersonal psychotherapy for patients with multisomatoform disorder: randomised controlled trial. *British Journal of Psychiatry*, 100, 60–67.

Shapiro, D., Rees, A., Barkham, M. and Hardy, G. (1995). Effects of treatment duration and severity of depression on the maintenance of gains after cognitive-behavioural and psychodynamic-interpersonal psychotherapy. *Journal of Consulting and Clinical Psychology*, 63(3), 378–387.

Shaw, C. M., Margison, F. R., Guthrie, E. A. and Tomenson, B. (2001). Psychodynamic interpersonal therapy by inexperienced therapists in a naturalistic setting: a pilot study. *European Journal of Psychotherapy, Counselling and Health*, 4(1), 87–101.

Stevenson, J. and Meares, R. (1992). An outcome study of psychotherapy for patients with borderline personality disorder. *American Journal of Psychiatry*, 149, 358–362.

Stevenson, J., Meares, R. and D'Angelo, R. (2005). Five-year outcome of outpatient psychotherapy with borderline patients. *Psychological Medicine*, 35, 79–87.

Stiles, W. B., Agnew-Davies, R., Hardy, G. E., Barkham, M. and Shapiro, D. A. (1998). Relations of the alliance with psychotherapy outcome: Findings in the Second Sheffield Psychotherapy Project. *Journal of Consulting and Clinical Psychology*, 66, 791–802.

> **RECOMMENDED READING**
>
> Barkham, M., Guthrie, E., Hardy, G. and Margison, F. (2016). *Psychodynamic Interpersonal Therapy: A Conversational Model.* London: Sage.
>
> This book is a detailed manual and comprehensive overview of PIT research, teaching and practice.
>
> Hobson, R. F. (1985). *Forms of Feeling: The Heart of Psychotherapy.* London: Routledge.
>
> This is a classic presentation of the theoretical and practical aspects of the model from its founder. It is core reading for all PIT therapists, novices and experts alike.
>
> Meares, R. and Hobson, R. F. (1977). The persecutory therapist. *British Journal of Medical Psychology, 50,* 349–359.
>
> In this paper, Hobson and Meares argue that a core task for all therapists is to be alert to, and minimise, the various subtle ways that we can unwittingly damage our clients.

5.25 PSYCHODYNAMIC THERAPY

DWIGHT TURNER

OVERVIEW AND KEY POINTS

Psychodynamic therapy has been around for well over 100 years. Psychotherapy is so well established that it is very much seen as the forefather to all the other forms of psychotherapy. Psychodynamic psychotherapy was originated by Sigmund Freud in the 1890s and has evolved since that time through a number of theorists, such as Melanie Klein, Albert Adler, Carl Jung, Donald Winnicott and Jack Lacan, before moving on to more contemporary names, such as Jessica Benjamin and others.

Some of the core areas to consider when we explore psychodynamic psychotherapy are the following:

- Sigmund Freud's early work considered drive theories and how these forces were related to the sexual drives and active through us at all times.
- Psychodynamic psychotherapy works with ideas of early life and patterns of attachment, which may or may not have been forged within a family.
- Ways of working psychodynamically are very different from those of working within a person-centred or humanistic or existentialist framework. The psychodynamic therapist acts as the blank screen, which, although perhaps a cliché of psychotherapy, becomes relevant when working with the projections and transferences raised by the client's unconscious early life material.
- Sigmund Freud's work was the forerunner to our understanding of how early life processes become unconscious and how psychotherapists using terminology such as transference, countertransference and projection work with these unconscious processes to enable the client to discover and recognise more of themselves.
- The importance of Freud's ideas and of psychodynamic ways of working form an incredibly important baseline for the work we all do as practitioners. This brief chapter therefore offers some of the background and key areas of consideration when studying psychodynamic psychotherapy.

BRIEF HISTORY

The psychodynamic approach is one of the earliest approaches in psychology, originating in the latter part of the nineteenth century and into the early twentieth century. Its main figure and ascribed creator is Sigmund Freud. Sigmund Freud was an Austrian neurologist who developed a clinical method for evaluating and treating pathologies in the psyche by utilising the unconscious relationship between a client and psychoanalyst. Born to Jewish parents in 1856 in the town of Freiberg, which at that point was in the Austrian Empire, Freud died in September 1939 in Hampstead, London.

Psychodynamic theory has evolved considerably from its early nineteenth-century origins, and it was Freud himself who gathered some of the greatest psychological thinkers of his age to assist him in developing psychodynamic theories. Some of the earliest theorists to utilise Freud's ideas, and to build upon them, included Melanie Klein, Albert Adler, Carl Jung, Anna Freud, Donald Winnicott, John Bowlby and Jacque Lacan. Freud's work has been attributed as being the forerunner and grounding of many of the other theories and ways of working between clients and therapists that exist to this day.

BASIC ASSUMPTIONS

There are a number of basic assumptions that are ascribed to psychodynamic psychotherapy. The first assumption is that links are made between the client's presenting issue in the therapy space and their history. What this means is that whatever is manifested between the client and the therapist in the therapeutic space in the moment will have its origins in the relationship between the client and their parent or caregiver from earlier on in their life (Bowlby, 1988).

The second assumption is that the work between client and therapist is therefore always in the unconscious and is based on the client's and the therapist's transference and countertransference. Freud's belief is that the unconscious mind exists, and part of the malaise attributed to any client is their desire to repair any unconscious wounds they may still hold from the past in the present. For example, should a client have a difficulty in building relationships with their partners, this difficulty or struggle may also appear in the therapy space between client and therapist (Ogden, 2004). A psychodynamic psychoanalytic psychotherapist would therefore be looking to consider how this struggle to form a relationship in the present moment is also a mirror or reflection of their difficulties in creating a relationship between them and their caregiver when they were a child. For example, where there might have been some sort of trauma, their past relationships might have been tainted by developmental or attachment trauma (Bowlby, 1988).

A third basic assumption emerges from Freud's ideas of drive theory. For Freud, drive theory was a core component of many of the behaviours and ways of being attributed to human beings in the present day. A final basic assumption, originating with Sigmund Freud, involves the creation of the id, ego and super-ego as being core components of a client's psyche that govern both how we are in the world and the drives that push us to becoming more whole and complete in the world (Kahn and Liefooghe, 2014).

THE ORIGIN AND MAINTENANCE OF PROBLEMS

Psychodynamic psychotherapy, as previously stated, recognises that the origin of many of the client's problems may sit in their early life experiences and that it is through the exploration of these experiences that the client starts to understand the unconscious drives which have motivated them. For example, in the case of a female client, although slightly clichéd, exploring her early life attachment pattern with her father led to her recognising that she had chosen a partner who was similarly unavailable to her in varying ways. The client's father was an alcoholic who had spent much of her childhood with his attention turned away from her and her siblings and towards the disease of alcoholism. Her mother, by comparison, was unable to manage both her and her three siblings and was instead for much of the time focused on the father to make sure that he was contained and stable. Psychodynamically, this led to her feeling doubly abandoned by her parents and also distrusting of anyone as she grew up, in particular anyone male.

For the client to form a relationship with her former partner, Brian, whom she met when she was aged 25, was a major moment for her. Prior to this, there had been a string of transient partners, both male and female, so when Brian emerged, she did all that she could to push him away and keep him at a distance. His persistence and groundedness eventually won her over to such an extent that she found herself able for the first time to trust somebody in the relationship.

The importance of recognising how a psychodynamic lens sits over a case like this is essential. We have already mentioned the early life attachment pattern which had led the client to being unable to form a secure attachment base with a new partner. It is also important to recognise that in the relationships that she did form, and given her fear of abandonment, instead of being left by any of her subsequent partners, that she would choose to do the leaving herself.

When viewed though through the lens of drive theory, the drive to connect, to relate and to love, otherwise known as Eros, was consistently at war with the drive to destroy and ruin anything that she had invested in, otherwise known as Thanatos. These patterns, it could also be argued, led to what one could term as 'a complex', a term originally devised by Freud in conjunction with Carl Jung (Freud and Strachey, 1924). A complex, in this instance, is where a pattern of behaviour repeats itself and, whereas Carl Jung took a more hopeful position around a complex (some of which will be discussed later), for Freud and the early psychodynamic theorists, complexes were very much about the unconscious trying to reawaken within the client's psyche the felt experience and the distress endured by the original wounding.

THEORY OF CHANGE

For a psychodynamic psychotherapist, it is important to be able to build a strong enough relationship with the client that will enable the conditions for change to occur.

The first of these conditions is the ability to construct and provide a good enough level of containment within the therapy. A term often used by Bion (1985), 'containment' was originally coined as a means of understanding the process that a parent, predominantly the mother, undertakes in managing the emotional welfare and landscape of their child. For the psychodynamic psychotherapist, building a positive enough relationship and container is an essential component of working with and holding the projections and the unconscious processes within psychodynamic psychotherapy.

This process, which may take several sessions to achieve, should provide the conditions that allow the client to be able to express their feelings and experiences honestly and allow them to gently start bringing a sense of awareness of what they have undergone prior to attending counselling and psychotherapy. The therapist's work in holding projections and providing a safe enough, secure and contained enough space for the clients to explore their outer, and therefore their inner, world should then be met by a psychodynamic therapist's ability to utilise their position, the theories and their own understanding of the unconscious processes occurring within this space. This then leads the therapist to better inform the client about what is happening within the space, so that the client gains a greater understanding of who they are, both within the therapy and therefore outside it.

It is often said that when a client enacts something or acts out something tricky within the psychotherapy, that they are more often than not going to be doing the same in their wider lived environment. A psychodynamic psychotherapist therefore recognises that what is said by the client, what is experienced by the client and what is enacted in their relationship with the client are all simple facets of the client's outer world environment and experiences.

THE GOALS OF PSYCHODYNAMIC THERAPY

The goals of psychodynamic psychotherapy involve the therapist working with the client's unconscious material and helping them to make it conscious. When a presenting issue appears in the therapeutic space, the therapist's role is to understand both its presentation in the present day and its link to the past through the transferential relationship that the client builds with the therapist. Once this relationship is established, the aim is then to help the client to recognise where their problems have come from and to bring clarity and understanding to how they might approach their positioning in a different fashion.

Another core aspect of the work of a psychodynamic psychotherapist is to help the client understand the defence mechanisms the client has employed in order to defend against any conscious realisation or understanding of their problem. This is done together, through an exploration of the unconscious transferential and countertransferential relationship between client and therapist (Pavlovic and Pavlovic, 2012).

Of the techniques used to bring this deeper level of understanding, the therapeutic alliance is where the structure, container and relationship all create the base on which the work between client and therapist occurs. Sigmund Freud, in conjunction with Carl Jung, also developed free association techniques (Jacobs, 2003). While the term free association is very much used in the modern day, in its original form it was used as a way of moving beyond a mental understanding of one's malaise. By asking the client to explore the meaning of a series of words or phrases, the therapist assists the client to bring for the their projections onto said words, revealing aspects of themselves they had previously hidden. The technique was designed to ascertain the more unconscious and deeper understanding of the decisions and structures and ways of being that we employ in order to either manage or avoid the drives which motivate us. Defence and transference interpretation was another early method of working within psychodynamic psychotherapy. All of these together, under the auspices of early Freudians, were used as a means of exploring some of the early-life presenting material of the client.

To briefly bring these ideas together, the following case study will highlight some of the basic assumptions that are most common in psychodynamic psychotherapy.

CASE STUDY

Margaret was a 35-year-old working-class woman from London and a mother of two children under the age of 5. Her presenting issue was that her partner of some 10 years had left her suddenly to begin a new relationship. This break-up had left her feeling devastated and unable to cope, so much so that her mother had had to move across town and into her home to support her and the children in her time of need. The client had sought out psychotherapy, and in our work together we looked at some of what might have been triggered by the trauma of this sudden departure.

Viewing this client work through the lens of psychodynamic therapy, it is worth exploring some of the basic assumptions that are central to understanding how we work as psychodynamic psychotherapists. As stated, when working with adult clients, the feelings and the behaviours that have brought them into therapy are rooted in their early life experiences. Thus, for any client presenting with an issue around their relationship with their partner, especially when they fear a partner leaving them, one of the routes to discovering the cause behind the malaise can be based on the idea that a parent or caregiver may have departed early or was unavailable to them in some other way, such as through addiction.

Exploring Margaret's early life therefore began with a thorough assessment of her presenting issues, her past relational experiences, and her attachment patterns with her parents and caregivers. For Margaret, what quickly became apparent was that she had been sent to boarding school at the age of 7. Although she enjoyed her time at school, the emotions raised by the separation from her parents and siblings was a particularly difficult one for her. When she expressed these feelings at school, she was often told that she was being ungrateful and that these feelings should not exist at all.

The second assumption here is that each behaviour has a cause behind it and, in particular, one rooted in the unconscious. While working with Margaret, my experience of her was that she would often put on a brave face on any difficult experiences she expressed, for example regarding the separation from her partner. This relational incongruousness meant that in my countertransference I was often left feeling much of the pain and the sadness, not only of her current separation, but also of the child within Margaret who had missed her family so much and been forced to bottle up such difficult and challenging feelings. Our work involved me gently reflecting back to Margaret some of these emotions, or any that she could contain, while occasionally managing to hold and sit with others on her behalf.

The third assumption is that the unconscious, as posited in early psychodynamic theory, has within it certain drives which act upon us quite powerfully. This can be the instinctual drive to self-sabotage, which is part of the death instinct, for example. Another basic assumption is that these drives actually help to form parts of our personality. They give us a sense of who we are and our place in the world and in society.

The next aspect of this is the recognition that there is an ongoing battle between the unconscious part of our self, which wishes to be known, and our egoic sense of self, which has been formed in our early years. The drives which motivate this are very much provoked from within the unconscious. In the case of Margaret, the fact that she had chosen a partner who would ultimately suddenly leave her, just as she had been left by her family, became apparent after a time. Through our exploration of the coincidence presented by this unconscious narrative, Margaret realised that this choice, while rooted in her unconscious, gave her the opportunity finally to process, to recognise, and even to express this longing to her family. In this instance, Margaret spoke to her remaining family, who felt much the same as she did, and this deepened the relationship between them all.

(Continued)

> (Continued)
>
> It is also important to recognise that Freud's drives were apparent in this client example. The death drive otherwise, termed Thanatos, was present in the choice and the destruction of the previous relationship, while the life drive, or love drive, which is termed Eros, was also present in the repairing of her relationship with her family. These two drives, as posited by Freud, were apparent in this client example from an early age.

RESEARCH

The importance of Sigmund Freud's work should not be underestimated. Freud, although often derided in the modern era of psychotherapy, had a number of good ideas which, to this day, form the bedrock of the profession we all study or work within. His relationship with Carl Jung, which foundered on the rocks of the rivalry, contained within their parent–child relationship, had sufficient influence on Jung that he went on to adapt and reject some of the earlier psychodynamic theories and to develop his own Jungian means of understanding the psychology of his clients.

Freud's work was built on by Melanie Klein, who specifically worked with children, with her ideas then being reinvented and redeveloped by Donald Winnicott and John Bowlby. Exploring psychodynamic theories through more modern lenses has led to critiques of Freud's work by feminists such as Judith Butler, academics such as Stephen Frosh, and post-colonial theorists such as Edward Said (Butler, 2003; Frosh, Phoenix and Pattman, 2003; Said, 2003). While contemporary theorists such as Jessica Benjamin have also developed some of his ideas, bringing them into the twenty-first century, issues such as those pertaining to the LGBTQ community have been explored in light of some of the early prejudices embedded within psychodynamic psychotherapy (Benjamin, 1998; Newcomb and Mustanski, 2010). His ideas have influenced thinking around trauma and neuroscience, and Freud's work also influenced my studies of privilege and otherness, which have built on Freud's exploration of the experiences of immigrants fleeing conflict in Europe and the rise of Nazism (Freud, 1930; Sletvold, 2013).

Freud's ideas therefore form the bedrock for many contemporary ideas and theories which permeate counselling and psychotherapy today and still hold much sway in their power and presence.

REFERENCES

Benjamin, J. (1998). *Shadow of the Other*. London: Routledge.
Bion, W. (1985). Container and contained. *Group Relations Reader*, 2, 127–133.
Bowlby, J. (1988). *A Secure Base: Parent–Child Attachment and Healthy Human Development*. New York: Basic Books. https://doi.org/10.1097/00005053-199001000-00017
Butler, J. (2003). Violence, mourning, politics. *Studies in Gender and Sexuality*, 4(1), 9–37. https://doi.org/10.1080/15240650409349213
Freud, S. (1930). *Civilisation and its Discontents*. London: Penguin.
Freud, S. and Strachey, J. (1924). The dissolution of the Oedipus complex *[Der Untergang Des Ödipuskomplexes]*, *Int. Z. Psychoanal* 10(13), 245–252.
Frosh, S., Phoenix, A. and Pattman, R. (2003). Taking a stand: using psychoanalysis to explore the positioning of subjects in discourse. *The British Journal of Social Psychology / The British Psychological Society*, 42(Pt 1), 39–53. https://doi.org/10.1348/014466603763276117
Jacobs, M. (2003). *Sigmund Freud: Key Figures in Counselling and Psychotherapy* (2nd ed.). London: Sage.
Kahn, S. and Liefooghe, A. (2014). Thanatos: Freudian manifestations of death at work. *Culture and Organization*, 20(1), 53–67. https://doi.org/10.1080/14759551.2013.853064

Newcomb, M. E. and Mustanski, B. (2010). Internalized homophobia and internalizing mental health problems: a meta-analytic review. *Clinical Psychology Review*, *30*(8), 1019–1029. https://doi.org/10.1016/j.cpr.2010.07.003

Ogden, T. H. (2004). On holding and containing, being and dreaming. *The International Journal of Psycho-Analysis*, *85*(Pt 6), 1349–1364. www.ncbi.nlm.nih.gov/pubmed/15801512

Pavlovic, R. Y. and Pavlovic, A. M. (2012). Dostoevsky and psychoanalysis: *The Eternal Husband (1870) by Fyodor Dostoevsky (1821–1881)*. *British Journal of Psychiatry*, *200*(3), 181–181. https://doi.org/10.1192/bjp.bp.111.093823

Said, E. (2003). *Freud and the Non-European*. London: Verso.

Sletvold, J. (2013). The ego and the id revisited Freud and Damasio on the body ego/self. *The International Journal of Psycho-Analysis*, *94*(5), 1019–1032. https://doi.org/10.1111/1745-8315.12097

RECOMMENDED READING

Jacobs, M. (2017). *Psychodynamic Counselling in Action*. London: Sage.

An excellent, well-written and fun introduction not only to psychodynamic counselling but to the profession as a whole, this text covers each of the key stages in building a therapeutic relationship with our clients.

Howard, S. (2018). *Psychodynamic Counselling in a Nutshell* (3rd ed.). London: Sage.

The strength of this primer lies in the extensive use of case studies, which show just how psychodynamic therapy works in practice.

Howard, S. (2017). *Skills in Psychodynamic Counselling and Psychotherapy* (2nd ed.). London: Sage.

An excellent introductory text with brief yet accessible synopses of the main ideas and themes within psychodynamic therapy, this is an excellent primer for any student new to the modality

5.26 SCHEMA THERAPY

KONSTANTINA KOLONIA AND HELEN KYRITSI

OVERVIEW AND KEY POINTS

Schema therapy is an integrative and unifying approach to treatment that combines elements of cognitive-behavioural therapy with psychodynamic, gestalt and interpersonal therapies, to create a sound theoretical and therapy model. It is designed specifically for people whose psychological difficulties are stemming from early childhood experiences and which are chronic and 'difficult to treat'.

- It focuses on unmet core emotional needs in childhood and the development of self-defeating, self-perpetuating and resistant-to-change emotional and cognitive patterns (early maladaptive schemas).

- The goal is to help individuals challenge and modify these negative patterns of thinking, feeling and behaving and build up the individual's healthy side so those unmet needs can be met in adulthood in an adaptive manner.
- Schema therapy goes beyond an intellectual understanding of clients' problems to actually achieving in-depth emotional change.
- The therapist–client relationship is vital for schema healing.
- Limited re-parenting and empathic confrontations are key relational tools.

BRIEF HISTORY

TRANSITION FROM CBT TO SCHEMA THERAPY

Schema therapy (ST) is an innovative and evidence-based psychotherapy that was developed by Jeffrey Young (1999 [1990]) and is specifically designed to address the issues that face cognitive-behavioural therapy (CBT) when working with challenging and complex clients, who often present with vague yet pervasive and chronic problems, difficulties in establishing and maintaining relationships and highly avoidant and rigid patterns of coping.

It places greater emphasis on the therapeutic relationship; aims to help clients gain access to and connect with their feelings, thoughts and memories, which can otherwise be inaccessible; addresses both current issues as well as childhood origins; and focuses on coping styles and core themes (Rafaeli, Bernstein and Young, 2011). ST is broader than CBT and psychodynamic models with regards to a conceptual model as well as a range of treatment strategies, and has been proven successful in treating Cluster B and Cluster C personality disorders as well as eating disorders and substance misuse, and can be used with individuals, couples and groups.

BASIC ASSUMPTIONS

One of the basic assumptions of schema therapy is that all human beings have *core emotional needs* that are present from childhood. Young, Klosko and Weishaar (2003) hypothesised that these include:

- secure attachment to others (e.g., need for safety, nurturance, stability and acceptance)
- freedom to express one's valid emotions and needs
- autonomy, competence and a sense of identity
- spontaneity and play
- realistic limits where the emergence of self-control is nurtured.

The schema therapy model works on the premise that getting a child's emotional needs met early on in his/her life is of paramount importance for the development of a psychologically healthy individual with the ability to meet those core emotional needs in adaptive ways in adulthood (Rafaeli et al., 2011).

ORIGINS AND MAINTENANCE OF PROBLEMS

EARLY MALADAPTIVE SCHEMAS

According to Young (1999 [1990]), early maladaptive schemas (EMS) refer to dysfunctional, extremely rigid and enduring themes or patterns that develop usually within the first seven years of a child's life, and which are then elaborated further throughout adulthood. They are themes or patterns that provide a template for how a person perceives themselves and others, and they consist of feelings, thoughts, memories and bodily sensations.

SCHEMA ACQUISITION

Young et al. (2003) postulate that EMS develop when children's core emotional needs are not met in a profound and consistent manner. They propose four types of *early childhood experiences* that can lead to the development of maladaptive schemas:

1. *Toxic frustration of needs* refers to experiences where there is a total absence of healthy experiences or too little of it, if any.
2. *Traumatisation or victimisation* reflects experiences of abuse and trauma.
3. *Too much of a good thing* occurs when there is parental failure to set realistic limits, overprotection or over-involvement.
4. *Selective internalisation or identification with significant others* – the child selectively identifies with and internalises some aspects (e.g., thoughts, feelings and/or behaviours) of significant others.

They also argue that two other important factors that are considered as contributing in maladaptive schema acquisition are the child's *emotional temperament* and the child and family's *cultural influences* (Young et al., 2003).

SCHEMA PERPETUATION

Because schemas are held as unconditional beliefs about oneself, they are by their nature self-perpetuating. 'Schema perpetuation' is the term that is given to the process by which an individual acts in ways that maintain and even strengthen his/her schemas. Schema perpetuation occurs through three main mechanisms (Young, 1999 [1990]):

Cognitive distortions. Cognitive distortions are the mechanism by which the client tends to make sense of life experiences by attending to information that confirms the schemas and avoids or discards information that is contrary to the schemas.

Self-defeating patterns. Self-defeating patterns, like 'self-fulfilling prophecies', can occur on a behavioural, affective and interpersonal level. Clients might detach from painful emotions, thus preventing them from being able to make conscious changes. Their actions and behaviours might be such that they reinforce them to remain in unhealthy situations or relationships that trigger and perpetuate their schemas.

Coping styles. In order to cope with the threat of the schemas, the unmet emotional needs and the corresponding painful emotions, clients develop certain coping styles early in childhood. These coping styles start off as adaptive and healthy ways of survival for the child, but become maladaptive in adulthood, resulting in schema perpetuation, even when the life circumstances have changed. In schema therapy, behaviours are not part of the schemas but part of the coping responses, which are driven by the schemas. Coping mechanisms, although primarily behavioural, can also include emotional and cognitive strategies.

There are three maladaptive coping styles: schema surrender, schema avoidance and schema overcompensation (Young et al., 2003). Clients may use different coping styles to manage different schemas or they might switch between coping styles to manage the same schemas at different times.

1. *Schema surrender* refers to the process of passively accepting that the schemas are true and therefore giving in to the messages that they provide. Clients will behave in such a way that will confirm the schemas.
2. *Schema avoidance* is the attempt to avoid any situation that might trigger the schemas. At an extreme level, avoidance will also include thoughts and feelings, resulting in the client becoming at times emotionally disconnected and detached.
3. *Schema overcompensation* can be perceived as the healthiest of the three coping styles, as clients attempt to fight their schemas in order to meet their core emotional needs. Unfortunately, clients tend to display 'over-the-top' behaviours that go to the opposite extreme and result in chasing unobtainable standards or driving others away, ultimately maintaining and reinforcing the schemas (Young et al., 2003).

SCHEMA HEALING

The goal of schema therapy is *schema healing*, where therapist and client work together as allies to fight the schemas, using cognitive, behavioural, experiential and interpersonal strategies. This will result in reducing the intensity of the painful emotions associated with childhood memories, diminishing the conviction with which schemas are held, and replacing the maladaptive coping styles with healthier behaviours that will enable clients to finally meet their core emotional needs and build healthier interpersonal relationships (Young et al., 2003).

SCHEMA MODES

Clients with personality disorders often present with rapid changes to their mood, behaviour and choice of coping style, while a number of different schemas might be triggered all at once. This poses a particular challenge in the traditional schema therapy approach, as it is impractical to attempt to trace the moment-to-moment changes as they are happening both within the therapy session and outside. To overcome this difficulty, the concept of schema modes was developed (Young et al., 2003) to represent the temporary emotional states (a manifestation of emotional and coping responses) that the client finds themselves in, in response to a number of schemas being triggered.

In schema mode therapy, the client is supported to identify their predominant schema modes, make links with their childhood origins and develop a plan for dealing with each schema mode accordingly. Young et al. (2003) have developed specific mode models for borderline and narcissistic personality disorders, whereas other models (e.g., for forensic populations) are under development.

SKILLS AND STRATEGIES

Schema therapy is divided in two phases where different skills and strategies are employed: the assessment and education phase and the schema change phase.

ASSESSMENT AND EDUCATION

The first phase of schema therapy is the assessment and education.

Schema therapists' initial evaluation briefly assesses the client's presenting symptoms and difficulties, goals for therapy as well as suitability for schema therapy. Clients presenting with psychotic experiences, an acute and severe Axis I disorder, current drug or alcohol abuse that is severe enough to be therapy-interfering or a major crisis are not considered suitable while those problems are still ongoing and need to be addressed first by other evidence-based approaches.

Once suitability for schema therapy has been established, then the assessment phase takes place over a number of sessions, aiming to collect information on the client's dysfunctional life patterns by using various assessment methods. The focus of this process is on understanding the client's early maladaptive schemas, ways of coping and predominant modes as well as the developmental origins of those (Young et al., 2003).

The main assessment methods used in the schema assessment phase are the following:

- *Focused life history*. Attention is paid on gaining an intellectual understanding of the client's symptoms, onset and triggers (historical and current) of psychological difficulties as well as of their EMS and coping styles.
- *Schema inventories*. There are four self-report inventories that are widely used and can be administered early on to further inform the assessment phase.
- *Self-monitoring*. The self-monitoring tools that are used are similar to the ones employed in other evidence-based approaches (e.g., CBT) and they aim to gather information on the client's thoughts, feelings and behaviours that arise in response to everyday events.
- *Imagery assessment*. It is used to help the client to express strong emotions that are often associated with their schemas and heavily informs schema therapy interventions in the change phase.
- *Therapy relationship*. The therapy relationship is used as a vehicle to initially understand those dysfunctional patterns that are also played out in the client's everyday life and later 're-parent' and teach healthier ways of relating to self and others (Rafaeli et al., 2011).

Psychoeducation is a parallel and integral part of the assessment phase. The therapist's role is to educate the client about the schema therapy model by making them aware of their core emotional needs, their schemas and modes, the developmental origins of those and their coping styles.

All the information gathered from the assessment and education phase conclude in *a written case conceptualisation* which is shared with the client and it is updated and informed throughout therapy as needed.

THEORY OF CHANGE

The skills and interventions acquired in the change phase have a mixture of cognitive, experiential and behavioural strategies.

COGNITIVE TECHNIQUES

Cognitive strategies are often the first step in schema therapy as the clients need to challenge cognitive distortions and the validity of the schemas on a cognitive level. The therapist guides the client to develop a healthier understanding of their difficulties and discover that the origin of their schemas lies in emotional deprivation and unmet emotional needs early in childhood, within the context of which the schemas were taught (Young et al., 2003).

EXPERIENTIAL TECHNIQUES

Emotion-focused techniques are considered to be one of the pivotal elements for the efficacy of schema therapy as they are thought to produce change at the deepest level possible (Kellogg and Young, 2006). The rationale of using these techniques is to evoke the strong feelings that are often associated with the early maladaptive schemas of the client and challenge and heal those on an emotional level. The schema therapist aims to create new and healing experiences through limited re-parenting and modelling of new adaptive ways to meet unmet childhood needs associated with his/her client's schemas (Rafaeli et al., 2011). The three central experiential techniques used are: (i) imagery; (ii) role plays/chair work; and (iii) letter writing.

(i) Imagery. Guided imagery is a powerful tool that is used to help the client actually 'feel' their schemas and connect with those childhood memories that have led to their development. The focus is to help the client understand that although changing adverse past experiences is not possible, imagery can help in altering the meaning attached to such experiences both on a cognitive and an affective level.

In a typical imagery exercise the therapist invites the client to revisit a negative childhood memory and play it out in his/her mind as if it was happening in the here and now. The client's interactions with others are explored and his/her thoughts and feelings are experienced and expressed. Imagery re-scripting then follows to challenge schemas affectively and meet the child's needs. Initially, the re-scripting is taking place by the therapist modelling a healthy adult, but at a later stage in therapy the client's healthy adult part is invited to meet the child's needs (Arntz and Van Genderen, 2009).

(ii) Role plays/chair work. Another widely used experiential technique is role play. It can be focused on past or present experiences from the client's life and interactions with others. The therapist guides the client to play various roles and to carry out dialogues between them. The aim is to develop and strengthen the client's healthy adult part and consequently weaken his/her early maladaptive schemas. The gestalt chair work technique is often used in schema therapy to conduct dialogues among the different modes of the patient (Kellogg, 2015).

(iii) Letter writing. Clients are also encouraged to write letters describing how they were wronged by significant others (in most cases the parent/s) and expressing their memories, thoughts and feelings. They are supported by the therapist to express what they needed from them that they did not get, both in the past and in the here and now, and to assert their rights. The letters are usually read out to the therapist and are not sent to whomever they are addressed. The rationale of why the letter is not to be sent is discussed, especially at times when the client feels otherwise, and potential ramifications are considered (Ohanian and Rashed, 2012).

BEHAVIOURAL PATTERN-BREAKING TECHNIQUES

Behavioural pattern-breaking techniques are the final and more crucial component of the change phase in schema therapy as they are focused on replacing the existing schema-driven patterns of behaviour with healthier, more adaptive ways of coping. Depending on the need, the schema therapist can use either traditional behavioural techniques (e.g., relaxation, social skills training, etc.) and/or incorporate the other schema strategies, such as imagery and dialogues, to get the client to alter his/her unhealthy coping styles (Rafaeli et al., 2011).

THERAPEUTIC RELATIONSHIP

The therapeutic relationship is considered to be one of the most key ingredients for any successful psychological intervention. However, in schema therapy, the therapeutic relationship has an even more important role as it provides an 'antidote' to the client's schemas and it serves to begin to meet their core emotional needs. As such, the therapist plays a much more active role in the therapy, becoming a 'role model' of the 'healthy adult' or 'good parent', which in turn gets internalised by the client to help fight against the schemas.

There are two important elements of the therapeutic relationship that stand out in schema therapy: (i) limited re-parenting and (ii) empathic confrontation.

(i) Limited re-parenting. Limited re-parenting is an interpersonal technique which aims to provide clients with the appropriate core emotional needs that were not met in childhood by their parents, within the limits of the therapeutic relationship (Young et al., 2003). As such, the therapist is encouraged to express care, warmth, acceptance, encouragement, which is genuinely felt towards the clients, and to create a space that provides safety and stability.

(ii) Empathic confrontation. Empathic confrontation (Young et al., 2003) aims to tackle the schemas and maladaptive coping styles as they get re-enacted within the therapeutic relationship, as well as outside the therapy room. The therapist shows empathy and understanding of the client's difficulties but gently confronts the dysfunctional behaviours and coping styles in order for them to change.

RESEARCH

The popularity that schema therapy gained over the last couple of decades was followed by the need for rigorous research.

A significant number of experimental studies have been conducted on both schemas and schema modes (e.g., Lobbestael, 2012b; Sieswerda, 2012). The effectiveness of schema therapy has been explored in outcome studies and its efficacy is well documented in the scientific literature (for a summary on effectiveness studies, see Bamelis et al., 2012).

The body of empirical evidence in support of schema therapy includes randomised controlled trials (RCT) on the effectiveness of schema therapy with clients with a number of diagnoses, including borderline personality disorder (Giesen-Bloo et al., 2006), with a Cluster C personality disorder (PD) diagnosis (avoidant, dependent and obsessive-compulsive personality disorder diagnosis) (Bamelis et al., 2014), and with violent PD offenders (Bernstein et al., 2021) as well as an RCT on group schema therapy (Farrell, Shaw and Webber, 2009).

In more recent years, there has been an expansion of schema therapy with published manuals targeting a wide range of client groups, including those diagnosed with an eating disorder (Simpson and Smith, 2019), working with couples (Simeone-DiFrancesco, Roediger and Stevens, 2015), children and adolescents (Loose et al., 2020) and groups (Farrell and Shaw, 2012).

Studies focusing on the application and clinical effectiveness of the model with other personality disorders and diagnoses, such as OCD (Basile et al., 2017), bipolar affective disorder (Hawke, Provencher and Parikh, 2013) and substance misuse (Kersten, 2012), is ongoing.

REFERENCES

Arntz, A. and Van Genderen, H. (2009) *Schema Therapy for Borderline Personality Disorder*. Chichester: Wiley.

Bamelis, L., Bloo, J., Bernstein, D. and Arntz, A. (2012) Effectiveness studies. In M. Van Vreeswijk, J. Broersen and N. Nadort (Eds), *The Wiley Blackwell Handbook of Schema Therapy Theory, Research, and Practise*. Chichester: Wiley.

Bamelis, L., Evers, M.A.A., Spinhoven, P. and Arntz, A. (2014) Results of a multicenter randomized controlled trial of the clinical effectiveness of schema therapy for personality disorders. *American Journal of Psychiatry*, 171, 305–322.

Basile, B., Tenore, K., Luppino, O.I. and Mancini, F. (2017) Schema therapy mode model applied to OCD. *Clinical Neuropsychiatry*, 14(6), 407–414.

Bernstein, D.P., Keulen-de Vos, M., Clercx, M., de Vogel, V., Kersten, G.C.M. et al. (2021) Schema therapy for violent PD offenders: a randomized clinical trial. *Psychological Medicine*, 1–15.

Farrell, J.M. and Shaw, I.A. (2012) *Group Schema Therapy for Borderline Personality Disorder: A Step-by-step Treatment Manual with Patient Workbook*. Chichester: Wiley-Blackwell.

Farrell, J.M., Shaw, I.A. and Webber, M.A. (2009) A schema-focused approach to group psychotherapy for outpatients with borderline personality disorder: a randomized controlled trial. *Journal of Behavior Therapy and Experimental Psychiatry*, 40(2), 317–328.

Giesen-Bloo, J., van Dyck, R., Spinhoven, P., van Tilburg, W., Dirksen, C., van Asselt, T., Kremers, I., Nadort, M. and Arntz, A. (2006) Outpatient psychotherapy for borderline personality disorder: randomised trial of schema-focused therapy versus transference-focused psychotherapy. *Archives of General Psychiatry*, 63(6) 649–658.

Hawke, L.D., Provencher, M.D. and Parikh, S.V. (2013) Schema therapy for bipolar disorder: a conceptual model and future directions. *Journal of Affective Disorders*, 148(1), 118–122.

Kellogg, S.H. (2015) *Transformational Chair Work: Using Psychotherapeutic Dialogues in Clinical Practise*. Lanham, MD: Rowman & Littlefield.

Kellogg, S.H. and Young, J.E. (2006) Schema therapy for borderline personality disorder. *Journal of Clinical Psychology*, 62, 445–458.

Kersten, T. (2012) Schema therapy for personality disorders and addiction. In M. Van Vreeswijk, J. Broersen and N. Nadort (Eds), *The Wiley Blackwell Handbook of Schema Therapy Theory, Research, and Practice*. Chichester: Wiley.

Lobbestael, G. (2012) Experimental studies of schema modes. In M. Van Vreeswijk, J. Broersen and N. Nadort (Eds), *The Wiley Blackwell Handbook of Schema Therapy Theory, Research, and Practice*. Chichester: Wiley.

Loose, C., Graf, P., Zarbock, G. and Holt, R.A. (2020) *Schema Therapy for Children and Adolescents: A Practitioner's Guide*. Brighton: Pavilion Publishing and Media.

Ohanian, V. and Rashed, R. (2012) Schema therapy. In W. Dryden (Ed.), *Cognitive Behavioural Therapies*. London: Sage.

Rafaeli, E., Bernstein, D. and Young, J. (2011) *Schema Therapy: The CBT Distinctive Features Series*. London: Routledge.

Sieswerda, S. (2012) Experimental studies for schemas. In M. Van Vreeswijk, J. Broersen and N. Nadort (Eds), *The Wiley Blackwell Handbook of Schema Therapy Theory, Research, and Practice*. Chichester: Wiley.

Simeone-DiFrancesco, C., Roediger, E. and Stevens, B. (2015) *Schema Therapy with Couples: A Practitioner's Guide to Healing Relationships*. Chichester: Wiley-Blackwell.

Simpson, S. and Smith, E. (Eds) (2019) *Schema Therapy for Eating Disorders: Theory, Practice and Group Treatment Manual*. Abingdon, UK: Routledge.

Young, J. (1999 [1990]) *Cognitive Therapy for Personality Disorders: A Schema-focused Approach*. Sarasota, FL: Professional Resources Press.

Young, J., Klosko, J. and Weishaar, M. (2003) *Schema Therapy: A Practitioner's Guide*. New York: Guilford Press.

RECOMMENDED READING

Arntz, A. and Jacob, G. (2013) *Schema Therapy in Practice: An Introductory Guide to the Schema Mode Approach*. Chichester: Wiley.

This book is recommended to those who are interested in extending their knowledge and practice of the schema mode approach to Axis I and personality disorders other than that of borderline personality disorder.

Arntz, A. and Van Genderen, H. (2009) *Schema Therapy for Borderline Personality Disorder*. Chichester: Wiley.

This book offers a comprehensive review of the conceptual model of borderline personality disorder, a treatment model and techniques specific to treating such clients.

Young, J., Klosko, J. and Weishaar, M. (2003) *Schema Therapy: A Practitioner's Guide*. New York: Guilford Press.

This books provides an in-depth overview of the schema therapy approach to treating complex presentations, including detailed protocols for borderline and narcissistic personality disorders.

5.27 THE SKILLED HELPER MODEL

VAL WOSKET AND PETER JENKINS

OVERVIEW AND KEY POINTS

Since it first emerged on the counselling scene in the mid-1970s, the skilled helper model developed by Gerard Egan (1928–2019) has been continuously revised and expanded. Egan has had a major influence on counselling practice and training across the globe over the past five decades. Strongly influenced by Jesuit and social catholic activism, with its powerful mantra, 'See. Judge. Act.', he was actively involved in social justice work throughout his life, including for Civil Rights and in the Vietnam war protests.

The skilled helper model evolved from Egan's early writings on interpersonal skills in group and individual contexts and moved through presenting a sequential process model of individual counselling to the development of change agent models and skills within the broader field of organisational change. Latest editions of *The Skilled Helper* are co-authored with Robert Reese. In this chapter we will consider the model as it applies to the field of one-to-one counselling. Key elements of the approach include:

- a three-stage model for helping clients to change
- an evolving evidence base, which underpins the model
- use of client goals to effect change
- a 'deficit', rather than a 'pathology', model of client difficulties.

BRIEF HISTORY

Early and enduring influences on the skilled helper model include the work of Rogers and Carkhuff, which provide its person-centred values and principles. The model's cognitive-behavioural elements are closely informed by figures such as Bandura, Beck, Ellis, Seligman and Strong. While a three-stage map of the helping process has remained a constant during the various editions of the model, significant adjustments have been made to take account of emerging research and developments in integrative practice. There has been an evident shift from problem management to opportunity development to reflect developments in positive psychology. Later editions addressed shadow-side elements of the helping process and evidenced greater emphasis on relationship, dialogue, difference and diversity. In its current iteration (Reese and Egan, 2021) local examples from a range of cultures, including South Africa, are included and there is new content on the global Covid-19 pandemic.

The skilled helper model has been expanded and updated for counsellors working in the United Kingdom by Val Wosket (2006), in consultation with Gerard Egan. Wosket's approach illustrates how the model can be used to develop a personally authentic style of counselling. The model is 'dejargoned' and translated from the American idiom into terminology more familiar to therapists (and their clients) in the UK. How the model can be applied to supervision and training is discussed and a number of guidelines and exercises are included. This version of the skilled helper model considers how it can evolve and adapt to fit a range of client issues and counselling contexts that include single session formulation, working in the long term with complex issues, such as trauma and abuse, and working with unconscious and dissociated processes.

Stated in simple terms, the three stages of the skilled helper model (Reese and Egan, 2021) are concerned with:

1. Problem definition.
2. Goal setting.
3. Action planning.

The model is integrative in that it provides an overarching framework for the helping process but without an over-reliance on theory. It is derivative in that it draws on person-centred values and principles and cognitive-behavioural approaches. Egan himself described the model as atheoretical – meaning it moves beyond theory in searching for a framework that is built on pragmatism (what has been shown to work). At its best, the model provides a shared map that helps clients participate more fully in the helping process.

BASIC ASSUMPTIONS

Egan's emphasis on positive psychology involves taking the view that managing problems is more a proactive than a reactive process. As such, problem management is considered to provide opportunities for clients to learn effective, life-enhancing skills. Two core functions of the skilled helper model are: (1) providing a 'geographical' map for the terrain of helping and (2) outlining the tasks of helping and how these tasks interrelate. Egan described the three principal goals of helping encompassed by the model as follows:

- GOAL 1: Life-enhancing Outcomes. Help clients manage their problems in living more effectively and developing unused or underused resources and opportunities more fully.
- GOAL 2: Learning Self-help. Help clients become better at helping themselves in their everyday lives.
- GOAL 3: Developing a Prevention Mentality. Help clients develop an action-oriented prevention mentality in their lives. (Egan, 2014: 9–12)

In the service of these three goals for the helping process, counsellors need to be both skill learners and skill trainers.

The key values that underpin the culture of helping in the skilled helper model are client empowerment and the Rogerian core qualities of respect, genuineness and empathy. Client empowerment is linked to the three goals of helping outlined above. According to Egan, helpers do not *empower* clients as such, 'rather they help clients discover, acquire, develop, and use the power they have at the service of constructive life change' (Egan, 2014: 58). Egan suggested that helpers think of themselves as consultants and facilitators, who provide as much, or as little, assistance as the client needs in order to better manage the problem situations in their lives. Minimum intervention is considered to be the optimum way of working.

ORIGIN AND MAINTENANCE OF PROBLEMS

Egan's view of the person comprised a 'deficit' rather than a pathology model. The problems that clients bring to counselling arise, in most part, from their difficulties in harnessing energy and resources (both internal and external) to realise their best potential. The healthy and functional personality is someone who has the necessary knowledge, skills and resources to successfully complete developmental tasks and to handle upsets and crises when they occur. The individual's ability to accomplish life's challenges will be affected by external limiting factors in the environment such as economic and social constraints, racism and oppression and dysfunctional family environments.

Psychological disturbance is mainly attributed to:

- being out of community (i.e., isolated or alienated from key social systems)
- the inability to successfully negotiate developmental tasks
- being out of touch with developmental resources (intrapersonal, interpersonal and environmental).

The helper is dealing with unique human beings at particular points in their lives. Pathologising clients, through general diagnostic labels, is seen as unhelpful and perpetuates a remedial, rather than a positive psychology, approach. Psychiatry and psychoanalysis have been too much focused on the individual at the expense of the social and cultural context in which the individual exists. Egan argued that the horizons of the helper need to be expanded to include these systems and settings.

People become estranged from their capacity to realise their full potential through factors such as passivity, learned helplessness and their experience of undermining social systems and environmental conditions. Skills and knowledge have to be acquired at each stage of development in order for the individual to accomplish increasingly complex tasks and fulfil new roles. Helpers need to be accomplished skill trainers, or act as points of referral to external sources of information and skills that clients may need to make progress through developmental impasses. For instance, the counsellor might spend time helping the client to develop and practise the interpersonal skills of assertiveness and conflict management to help them move out of established patterns of passivity or deference to others.

THEORY OF CHANGE

Counselling is seen as a social-influence process. People are capable of realising their potential and rising above 'the psychopathology of the average' when they are given optimum amounts of supportive challenge within a strong therapeutic relationship. Helpers aim to be directive of the *process*, but not the *content*, of therapy. The model is collaborative and designed to be 'given away' to clients so that the process is shared with them and owned by them. The client is considered to be the expert on himself or herself and the counsellor acts as consultant to, and facilitator of, the client's process. The quality of the therapeutic relationship importantly mediates the effectiveness of the change process, but is not an end in itself. Reluctance and resistance are seen as natural aspects of the change process.

Change comes about through *action*. Action can be understood as both *internal* (an inner shift or change in thinking or feeling) and *external* (observable action in behavioural terms) and as happening both within and between sessions. This dynamic process is illustrated by an approach using single session formulation, influenced by the skilled helper model, in the highly pressurised context of student counselling (Jenkins, 2020). In this composite example, the therapist (Peter) was working to help the client to identify unhelpful thinking patterns, drawn from key experiences, contributing to high levels of social anxiety and attendant behaviours. The focus of action included small steps towards change, which were either already in progress, or easily achievable. As Egan remarked, in this kind of therapeutic interaction, 'Clarity in terms of specific experiences, behaviors and feelings is sought not for its own sake, but...to move the whole process forward' (Egan, 1990: 161).

SKILLS AND STRATEGIES

The first stage of the counselling process is about helping clients to construct a coherent personal narrative or story. Stories may consist of both problems and missed opportunities. The counsellor enables the client to tell their story through the active listening skills of attending (verbal and non-verbal), listening, reflecting back (content, thoughts and feelings), summarising and clarifying. These communication skills help to convey the key quality of empathy, through which the counsellor demonstrates their understanding and acceptance of the client.

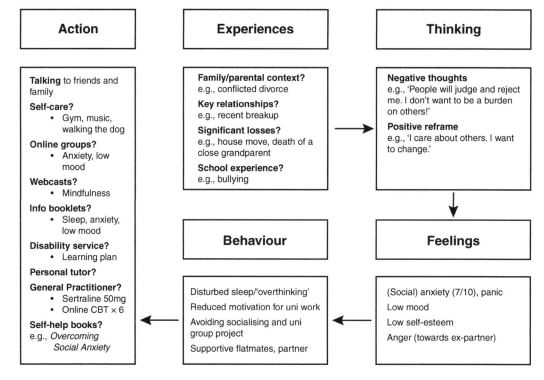

Figure 5.27.1 Adaptation of the skilled helper model as single session formulation

(Adapted from Jenkins, 2020: 22, reprinted with permission of BACP)

In order to elicit as clear a story as possible, the counsellor encourages the client to give concrete examples of behaviours, experiences and feelings. Empathic challenges are introduced to invite the client to begin to explore possible blindspots and to develop new perspectives on their situation. Through a balance of support and challenge, the counsellor helps the client search for what is termed 'leverage' or 'value'. The helper does this through using the skills of advanced empathy, immediacy, probing, questioning, summarising and clarifying.

The second stage of the counselling process is about helping the client to gain a clearer view of what they need and want. Where people have difficulty managing problems, this is frequently down to a tendency to link problems to actions, as in 'What do I *do* about this?', rather than to link action to outcomes, as in 'What do I *need to do* to get what I want?' An axiom that Egan continuously emphasised is that *goals*, not problems or strategies, should drive *action*.

The second stage involves helpers assisting their clients first to see options for a better future, variously termed the 'preferred scenario' or 'preferred picture', and then to turn these into workable objectives that can drive action. The additional skills needed by the helper here are those related to goal setting, including future-oriented questioning, goal shaping and working with reluctance and resistance to generate hope and commitment.

The third stage of the helping process is concerned with enabling the client to identify and implement strategies for action that will result in positive and sustainable outcomes. Here, the helper assists the client in achieving their identified goals, using the skills of creative and divergent thinking, force field analysis and sequential action planning.

Although this brief summary is presented in a linear fashion, it is important to emphasise that, in skilled hands, the model is rarely applied in this fashion. The truly skilled helper learns to offer the stages of the model in a flexible and fluid manner, where steps frequently overlap and merge into one another, as counsellor and client move back and forth, in the ebb and flow of the helping process.

CASE STUDY

The skilled helper model is sometimes considered suitable only for time-limited, problem management work. This composite case study shows how the model may be used in long term in-depth therapy with a client with a severe dissociative disorder.

My work with Eva was very complex and took place under medical supervision. Prior to approaching the agency in which I (Val) worked, Eva's chief way of managing triggering events in her life was to become so mentally unwell as to require frequent hospitalisation. To begin with, Eva made only silent telephone calls to the agency. Gradually and hesitatingly she began to speak, often sounding younger or older than her actual age, and on these occasions she would say she was not Eva and use other names for herself. This alerted me to the possibility of her dissociative condition.

Our early work over the phone was about establishing our relationship and building trust. One day she told me that as we were speaking there was a little bird perched on her windowsill that looked as if it wanted to come in. I took this as a point of leverage to encourage her, not for the first time, to come into the agency for an initial meeting. This time she agreed to do so, although this took careful contracting and some challenging of her strengths and blindspots. I asked her if she (or a part of her) had ever felt unsafe or threatened by me when we spoke on the phone. After mulling this over she said that she hadn't, but that didn't mean I was a safe person. I replied that she was right to be cautious and would need to work out for herself whether I seemed a safe person or not. She agreed to an initial meeting on the understanding that she could leave at any time if she did not feel safe.

Very gradually Eva was able to let me know the extent of the ritual abuse she had suffered as a child and which had led to her developing dissociative identity disorder. My overarching way of working with her followed the phased approach recommended in the treatment guidelines of the International Society for the Study of Trauma and Dissociation. This is an integrative approach that blends psychodynamic, embodied, relational and cognitive-behavioural elements (see Wosket, 2017). The skilled helper model sits well within this approach as it provides structure, safety and containment, and a framework for thinking about process and outcomes.

(Continued)

(Continued)

The steps and stages of the model acted as cogs and ratchets to sustain progress and keep the work moving forward. The model gave me a map and a set of strategies to return to when faced with the question 'What the hell do I do now?' – a question that often came up for me in chaotic and dissociative phases of the work. 'Where do I think we are in the model?, where does Eva seem to be?, and where do we need to be?' were useful orientation questions that helped me to realise when, for example, we needed to go back to relationship building or hearing another layer of her story at points where I had been thinking we might be ready for action.

During one session when she was feeling particularly suicidal and despairing, Eva told me that she had not eaten for several days. Pushing on with trauma resolution work was not an option at this point and would have been dangerous. Instead, cognitive work using goal setting and action planning was more manageable for her. I helped her weigh up the costs and consequences of not eating, to think about what might be the benefits of eating something, what she might eat if she decided to, and how this could happen. By the end of the session she had resolved to buy a sandwich from the nearest shop and she came back to eat it in the waiting room where she felt safe, before going home. Cumulatively, small steps such as this added up to keeping her safe and grounded. They gave her both a sense of hope and also, importantly, some manageable things to do while we tackled the overarching tasks of trauma resolution and integration of her dissociative parts.

Eva's preferred scenario changed many times as our work proceeded. It started with 'not to exist' and moved on to 'just to be normal'; 'I want you to adopt me' evolved into 'I want you to stick around and not abandon me'. Very slowly she became more open to reality testing these scenarios and to turning them into workable goals. Not existing became 'finding a way and a reason to live'; wanting to be normal evolved into 'doing my work and taking my medication'; wanting to be parented became 'learning to take care of mysel(ves) and let others support me'. While we did need to do a good deal of in-depth, specialised trauma resolution work, this would not have been possible without the safe container of the skilled helper model.

Over the 10 years we worked together, Eva gained several undergraduate and higher degrees that led, eventually, to a prestigious university research post. She developed a network of supportive friends and gained a partner. At the end of our work she asked if she could occasionally update me on how she was doing. In the years that followed she sent me photographs of her doctoral award ceremony, her wedding and her children.

RESEARCH

As with any integrative model that is largely mediated by the way the individual therapist adapts and applies it, the skilled helper model is not accessible to outcome research in the way that a more singular approach might be. The model is not a set of treatment techniques that exists in any useful way independently of the practitioner who uses it.

The skilled helper's approach to skills is clearly indebted to the crucial earlier research by Truax and Carkhuff (1967), which signalled a departure from the classical person-centred paradigm in concluding that the core conditions do not account for *all* perceived differences in counsellor effectiveness (Truax and Carkhuff, 1967: 114). Later studies have confirmed the positive impact of problem-solving therapies within primary care (Mynors-Wallis et al., 2000) and in social work training (Riggall, 2016).

Wosket's (2006) publication on the skilled helper model engages in-depth with the critical debate around the perceived lack of research activity relating to the model. She argues that Egan 'developed a process for counselling that makes use of sequential patterns in problem management that have been empirically validated by researchers' (Wosket, 2006: 171) and discusses at length research elements underpinning the model. This publication includes a wealth of qualitative data on the client's experience of the model, through a range of clinical case studies that show its application to different contexts and client populations.

One discussion of recent research appears to strongly validate Egan's core message, i.e., that empathy on its own is not enough to ensure meaningful and lasting change, without also helping to develop and reinforce the client's own skills in problem management (Jackson, 2021). Egan himself was at pains to point out the bedrock of research upon which the various components of the model are founded. He drew extensively on research into cognitive dissonance theory, social learning, motivation and positive psychology. That the skilled helper model has remained highly influential in the training and supervision of therapists, social workers and coaches in the UK and beyond (Page and Wosket, 2015; Wosket, 2006) attests to its enduring popularity as a pragmatic and adaptable framework, for both students and established practitioners.

REFERENCES

Egan, G. (1990) *The Skilled Helper: A Systematic Approach to Effective Helping* (4th ed.) Belmont, CA: Brooks/Cole.

Egan, G. (2014) *The Skilled Helper: A Problem Management and Opportunity-Development Approach to Helping* (10th ed.). Belmont, CA: Brooks/Cole Cengage.

Jackson, C. (2021) The big issue: What works and why. *Therapy Today*, 32(7), 22–26. Available at www.bacp.co.uk/bacp-journals/therapy-today/2021/september-2021/the-big-issue/

Jenkins, P. (2020) Single-session formulation: An alternative to the waiting list. *University and College Counselling*, 8(4), 20–25. Available at www.bacp.co.uk/bacp-journals/university-and-college-counselling/november-2020/single-session-formulation/

Mynors-Wallis, L., Gath, D., Day, A. and Baker, F. (2000) Randomised controlled trial of problem solving treatment, antidepressant medication, and combined treatment for major depression in primary care. *British Medical Journal*, 320(7226), 26–30.

Page, S. and Wosket, V. (2015) *Supervising the Counsellor and Psychotherapist: A Cyclical Model* (3rd ed.). London: Brunner-Routledge.

Reese, R. and Egan, G. (2021) *The Skilled Helper: A Client Centred Approach* (3rd ed.). Andover: Cengage Learning EMEA.

Riggall, S. (2016) The sustainability of Egan's skilled helper model in students' social work practice. *Journal of Social Work Practice*, 30(1), 81–93.

Truax, C. and Carkhuff, R. (1967) *Toward Effective Counseling and Psychotherapy.* New York: Aldine.

Wosket, V. (2006) *Egan's Skilled Helper Model: Developments and Applications in Counselling*. London: Routledge.

Wosket, V. (2017) *The Therapeutic Use of Self: Counselling Practice, Research and Supervision (Classic ed.).* Abingdon, UK: Routledge.

RECOMMENDED READING

Egan, G. (2006) *Essentials of Skilled Helping: Managing Problems, Developing Opportunities*. Pacific Grove, CA: Brooks/Cole.

This book represents Egan's succinct translation of the model for an international audience, emphasising the cross-cultural value of problem-management approaches.

Reese, R. and Egan, G. (2021) *The Skilled Helper: A Client Centred Approach* (3rd ed.). Andover: Cengage Learning EMEA.

This is the latest updating of Egan's classic three-stage model of problem management, comprising a blend of cognitive, humanistic and solution-focused approaches.

Wosket, V. (2006) *Egan's Skilled Helper Model: Developments and Applications in Counselling*. London: Routledge.

This book provides a balanced and incisive overview of the skilled helper model, making it more accessible and relevant to a UK readership.

5.28 SOLUTION-FOCUSED BRIEF THERAPY

GUY SHENNAN

OVERVIEW AND KEY POINTS

Solution-focused brief therapy (SFBT) was first developed in the early 1980s by a group of therapists in the United States. The version described here is the one predominantly used today in the United Kingdom. Its starting point is to develop a forward-facing orientation based on the client's hopes from the therapy. The major therapeutic activity then consists of helping the client to describe in detail the effects of their hopes being realised and any progress they are already making towards this 'preferred future', and to consider how they are making this progress. In short, a solution-focused brief therapist:

- focuses on hopes rather than problems
- assumes that people are already moving towards the realisation of their hopes
- does not try to solve problems or find solutions, but elicits descriptions of preferred futures and progress being made towards them
- is not gathering or analysing information or trying to understand the client
- asks questions that connect with the client's answers and help the client to continue to think and talk in ways that become useful to them.

BRIEF HISTORY

The original SFBT blueprint was developed at the Brief Family Therapy Center in Milwaukee in the early 1980s, by therapists from the brief/strategic and family therapy traditions (de Shazer et al., 1986). Like most therapists, their starting point had been to focus on the client's problems, which they viewed interactionally rather than as situated within the client, and believed to be maintained by actions the client was taking in unsuccessful attempts to resolve them. In this view of problem causation or maintenance they were following the Mental Research Institute (MRI) brief therapists in Palo Alto (Watzlawick, Weakland and Fisch, 1974), by, in short, focusing on what the client was doing that was not working. The therapists often worked as a team, with one therapist conducting the session and the others observing via a one-way screen or monitor. The conductor's role was to elicit information from the client, in particular about what was not working, so that the observing team could develop an appropriate task for the client that would encourage them to do something different, leading to problem resolution.

The shift from this problem focus to a solution focus was gradual, though one incident was pivotal (Lipchik et al., 2012). The team sometimes gave the client the task of writing down all that they wanted to change. During one session a team member suggested asking the family to list instead what they observed happening between sessions that they did not want to change. At the next session the family reported positive changes that had taken place, which encouraged the team to continue giving similar tasks.

These crystallised into the 'formula first session task', one modification being to invite the client to notice anything happening that they wanted to continue to happen, rather than to list what they did not want to change. In an exploratory study, the team routinely gave this task at the end of each first session, and found that, whatever problems a client had come with, they could almost always identify something that was working, and that focusing on this appeared to contribute to positive changes (Korman, De Jong and Jordan, 2020). This influenced the focus of the therapy sessions, as the team began to ask clients about these 'exception' times. Shifting from what was not working to what was working, the team engaged clients in 'change talk' rather than 'problem talk' ever earlier in the work (Gingerich, de Shazer and Weiner-Davis, 1988).

The other major focus of the approach developed from the goal orientation of brief therapy and the focus on what needed to happen for therapy to end. One technique devised to establish the work's endpoint was the 'miracle question' (de Shazer, 1988). As this developed into a whole framework of questions, clearly reaching beyond simple goal-setting, a focus on 'preferred futures' came to join the focus on what was working as the twin pillars of the approach.

BASIC ASSUMPTIONS

The most basic assumption of SFBT is that if someone has decided to talk to a person in a helping role, they must hope something will come from this. Every client is motivated for something, although it will often not be clear to them at the outset what this is. As the brief therapist, John Weakland once said that therapy is 'two people talking together, trying to figure out what the hell one of them wants' (de Shazer, 1999: 35). So, establishing the client's hopes is a co-constructive process, which the solution-focused therapist begins by asking: What are your best hopes from our work together?

Another assumption of SFBT is that change can occur rapidly. In fact, it is assumed that change is inevitable (de Shazer, 1985), and is happening all the time. Furthermore, it is assumed that there will be some positive change happening, there are always exceptions to problems and the client is an active agent of change. The task of the solution-focused therapist, then, is to help to highlight and amplify positive change that is already underway.

It is also assumed that the activities a solution-focused therapist engages in are helpful. However, it is not the therapist's questions that lead to change, but the thinking and talking by the client that the questions generate. In other words, it is assumed that talking about preferred futures and progress being made towards them are helpful things to do.

ORIGIN AND MAINTENANCE OF PROBLEMS

SFBT is distinctive in not being based on a theory about problem aetiology. The Milwaukee team had been influenced by the MRI idea that problems arise and are maintained by the mishandling of ordinary life difficulties. This can normalise problems and minimise the pathologising and blame that can be associated with locating their cause. As the team moved towards a solution focus, they took this normalising and depathologising a step further, seeing problems as just 'damned bad luck' (de Shazer, 1985: 18).

In SFBT's early days, its movement was away from the problems that brought the client to therapy, by focusing on exceptions to these problems. As the future focus increased in importance, the movement turned towards the client's hopes. This has been accompanied by a focus on instances of these hopes being realised, rather than on exceptions to problems, so any focus by the therapist on problems has become less necessary. Clients will still feel the need to talk of their problems, and the therapist must listen and show they have heard. However, they will be curious not about how the problems developed, but about how the client is getting through them and what they hope for instead.

When a client wants to understand their problems' causes, a solution-focused therapist will ask what they hope such an understanding will lead to, which usually paves the way for a focus on a preferred future and progress being made towards it.

THEORY OF CHANGE

The founders of SFBT stressed the pragmatic nature of its development (de Shazer et al., 2021), claiming it was not based on theory, or at least on a 'grand theory', but on many hours of 'disciplined observation' of what works in therapy. However, to talk of observing what works invites questions about the meaning and criteria of 'working' here. It cannot relate to an eventual positive outcome of the therapy, as this will not be known until later. When the developers of SFBT talked of something working, their initial criterion appeared to be the client being able to report positive changes in concrete terms. Their theory of change then became evident in questions that encouraged the client to focus on positive changes. What 'worked' within a session was whatever the therapist did that facilitated 'change talk' rather than 'problem talk' (Gingerich et al., 1988). So, SFBT has a language-based theory of change, based on the idea that how we talk about ourselves influences how we think of ourselves and who we can become.

Additionally, talking about future preferences is seen to engender hope. Once a client can articulate a wish and describe a desired future in detail, their sense of possibility grows, leading to increased hope. When the client is encouraged to talk about times they have already achieved at least some of this, hope can be transformed into expectation.

SKILLS AND STRATEGIES

Generally stated, the solution-focused brief therapist engages in three activities with the client:

- Asking questions
- Listening – with a constructive ear
- Responding – echoing and summarising.

Questions serve different purposes, including to seek information, which then guides the therapist's formulations or interpretations, or the setting of between-session tasks. The solution-focused brief therapist, however, asks questions not to gather information but to lead the client to talk in ways that become useful. Each question is constructed so that it both fits within the solution-focused framework and connects with the client's previous answer, thus helping the client to incrementally build their descriptions of a preferred future and progress towards this.

Listening closely to the client is essential in ensuring that the next question connects with the previous answer, and 'listening with a constructive ear' (Lipchik, 1988) helps the question fit within the solution-focused framework. What a therapist listens for is determined by their therapeutic orientation, and the constructive ear of the solution-focused therapist is alert for the client's hopes, signs of their emerging and anything the client is doing that fits with their realisation.

This process of asking a question, listening to the answer, constructing a question that connects with that answer, listening to the next answer and so on, elicits descriptions of preferred futures and progress that are built from the client's words, which are centred in the process. When the therapist engages in the third activity listed above, responding, it is therefore important that they do so mainly by simply echoing or summarising the client's words.

Excerpts from the first session with Sonia, aged 18, who was referred by a young people's advice worker, will illustrate this, and the three parts of the solution-focused framework.

1. SETTING A DIRECTION TOWARDS A DESIRED OUTCOME

The therapist's initial questions aimed to develop a forward-facing orientation:

Therapist: What are your best hopes from our work together?

Sonia: Well, I've got a few problems with anxiety. And since I got pregnant I've had really bad depression…

As Sonia continued to list her difficulties, the therapist listened, then acknowledged the tough time Sonia was going through, and asked:

Therapist: And how would you know that coming here had been useful to you?

Sonia: I'm stressed a lot, and I like having someone to talk to when I'm low and when I'm depressed, so that someone can help me. I just want help.

Therapist: If this does prove to be helpful, what will tell you, what will you notice about yourself that will tell you this has proved to be helpful?

Sonia: I wish that I didn't feel so anxious. I hope that I can get help with feeling anxious all the time…

A direction for the work was emerging, away from anxiety. The therapist's next question helps point this direction towards something positively desired rather than away from a problem no longer wanted:

Therapist: What would you like to be feeling instead?

Sonia: I just want to feel happy.

The therapist was not concerned by the generality of a desire to be happy. What this opening exchange had constructed was a shift in orientation, so that the work could now proceed with client and therapist looking towards something wanted rather than looking back to the problems Sonia has come with.

2. DESCRIBING A PREFERRED FUTURE

Therapist: Suppose when you wake up tomorrow, you find anxiety isn't a problem for you and you're able to feel happy as you'd like to – what's the first thing you'd notice about yourself?

Sonia: I'd have a clear head. I wouldn't be thinking so much about my problems. Because problems make you anxious. When you don't think, you're not anxious, are you?

Therapist: So what might you be thinking about instead, if you woke up feeling how you'd like to?

Sonia: I'd be more into taking more care of my little girl, more into taking care of myself and getting into my hobbies and interests as well, and not letting my relationship get the best of me.

The therapist proceeded to help Sonia to describe in detail the differences she might notice in these areas of her life, which would both accompany and indicate the realisation of her hopes from the therapy. Situating these descriptions as soon as tomorrow helped to ensure they were connected to Sonia's current life situation. The therapist's questions were designed to help Sonia both 'zoom in' to the smallest details she would notice in herself – What's the first thing you would do tomorrow if you were taking care of yourself more? – and to 'zoom out' – Where else tomorrow would you notice these differences?

Making descriptions interactional, so that clients consider themselves from others' perspectives and the effects they might have on those others, enhances their emotional content:

Therapist: What would your little girl notice about you?

Sonia: That I'd be playing with her more. And I'd be much more patient if she starts crying and I don't know what the reason is. I'd have more energy to be patient with her.

Therapist: Playing more, and patient, right. What sorts of things would you play?

Sonia: Oh, I'd sing to her, I'd read books to her, I'd make her stand up, I already do, but I feel I would do more than I do right now. I'd play with her, I'd make her feel she's walking around everywhere.

Therapist: Would she enjoy you doing those things with her?

Sonia: I'm sure she would.

Therapist: How would you know?

Sonia: She'd look up at me when I walked her around, and smile.

3. DESCRIBING PROGRESS TOWARDS AND INSTANCES OF THE PREFERRED FUTURE

A shift from preferred futures to instances when they are already happening can be facilitated by listening out for mentions of the latter. While Sonia was describing her future self being more assertive with her partner, by asking him not to phone her while working a night shift, she added: 'Because when I had depression I couldn't sleep all night, and it's only recently I've started to sleep well, and I'd like to continue sleeping well.'

The therapist's curiosity about Sonia's having started to sleep well showed itself in these questions, typically asked in such circumstances:

> How did you do that? How have you managed to start sleeping well? What differences has it made?

A common way to elicit instances and details of progress made is to use scaling questions. The therapist introduced a scale to Sonia in this way:

> Think of a scale from 0 to 10, where 10 is that things are just like you've described tomorrow, you're able to be happy, anxiety isn't a problem, so all that stuff's happening for you, and 0 the furthest you have been from that…

Sonia said she was at 4. The solution-focused therapist notes that 4 is higher than 0, which opens up a range of questions, beginning with those that elicit descriptions of the progress made:

> What tells you it's 4 and not 0? What's different? What are you doing now that you weren't doing at 0? Who else has noticed differences and what have they noticed?

These can be augmented by questions similar to those asked of Sonia about sleeping well, about her agency in bringing about the changes signified by being at 4. These have been usefully divided into 'strategy' questions – How did you do that? – and 'identity' questions – What qualities do you have that enabled you to make that change? (Ratner, George and Iveson, 2012).

The scale can also be used to make achieving progress seem more possible, by asking about a 'good enough' point, and by helping the client to 'think small' by asking about one point up the scale.

FIRST AND FOLLOW-UP SESSIONS

The structure of a first session can be discerned in the excerpts with Sonia above: a focus on the preferred future first, and then on progress being made towards it. Follow-up sessions typically reverse the order, so that progress is asked about first: What's better, since we met? This is detailed as described above, before a return to the future, often punctuated by a scale: Thinking of the scale we used last time, with 10 being your hopes realised, and 0 the opposite, where are you now? How would you know you were moving further up the scale?

'IT'S WORSE'

If a client says that they are at 0 on the scale, or that nothing is better since last time, the solution-focused therapist will acknowledge the client's difficulties while at the same time holding open the possibility of change. This might include coping questions – How are you managing to keep going? – listening for exceptions to the problems and asking how the client has prevented things from becoming even worse. Future-focused questions can then be returned to cautiously: Suppose you started to get back on track, what's the first, tiny signs you might notice?

RESEARCH

A growing body of publications reporting research into SFBT is summarised on the website of the European Brief Therapy Association (EBTA). Their latest update (EBTA, 2021) refers to 325 outcome studies, including 143 randomised controlled trials showing benefit from solution-focused approaches with 92 showing benefit over existing treatments, and 100 comparison studies, of which 71 favour solution-focused therapy.

EBTA also list a number of meta-analyses and systematic reviews. Of particular note are two reviews carried out by American academics. Reviewing 43 controlled studies, where the outcomes were indicated by observed changes in the client, Gingerich and Peterson (2013: 266) concluded that: 'SFBT is an effective treatment for a wide variety of behavioral and psychological outcomes and, in addition, it appears to be briefer and less costly than alternative approaches'. Since then, Kim, Jordan, Franklin and Froerer (2019) have found a growth of experimental design studies of SFBT with diverse populations, which show favourable results.

REFERENCES

de Shazer, S. (1985). *Keys to Solution in Brief Therapy*. New York: W.W. Norton.
de Shazer, S. (1988). *Clues: Investigating Solutions in Brief Therapy.* New York: W.W. Norton.
de Shazer, S. (1999). John Weakland: master of the fine art of 'doing nothing'. In W. Ray and S. de Shazer (Eds), *Evolving Brief Therapies: In Honor of John Weakland* (pp. 30–43). Galena, IL: Geist & Russell Companies.
de Shazer, S., Berg, I. K., Lipchik, E., Nunnally, E., Molnar, A., Gingerich, W. and Weiner-Davis, M. (1986). Brief therapy: focused solution development. *Family Process*, 25(2), 207–221.
de Shazer, S., Dolan, Y., Korman, H., Trepper, T., McCollum, E. and Berg, I. K. (2021). *More than Miracles: The State of the Art of Solution-focused Brief Therapy* (Classic ed.). New York: Routledge.
EBTA (2021). *SF Evaluation List*. European Brief Therapy Association. Available at http://u0154874.cp.regruhosting.ru/evaluationlist/ (accessed 5 January 2022).
Gingerich, W., de Shazer, S. and Weiner-Davis, M. (1988). Constructing change: a research view of interviewing. In E. Lipchik (Ed.), *Interviewing* (pp. 21–32). Rockville, MD: Aspen.
Gingerich, W. and Peterson, L. (2013). Effectiveness of solution-focused brief therapy: a systematic qualitative review of controlled outcome studies. *Research on Social Work Practice*, 23(3), 266–283.
Kim, J., Jordan, S., Franklin, C. and Froere, A. (2019). Is solution-focused brief therapy evidence-based? An update 10 years later. *Families in Society*, 100(2), 127–138.
Korman, H., De Jong, P. and Smock Jordan, S. (2020). Steve de Shazer's theory development. *Journal of Solution Focused Practices*, 4(2), Article 5, 47–70. Available at digitalscholarship.unlv.edu/journalsfp/vol4/iss2/5/ (accessed 5 January 2022).
Lipchik, E. (1988). Interviewing with a constructive ear. *Dulwich Centre Newsletter*, Winter, 3–7.
Lipchik, E., Derks, J., Lacourt, M. and Nunnally, E. (2012). The evolution of solution-focused brief therapy. In C. Franklin, T. Trepper, W. Gingerich and E. McCollum (Eds), *Solution-focused Brief Therapy: A Handbook of Evidence-based Practice*. New York: Oxford University Press.
Ratner, H., George, E. and Iveson, C. (2012). *Solution Focused Brief Therapy: 100 Key Points and Techniques*. Hove: Routledge.
Watzlawick, P., Weakland, J. and Fisch, R. (1974). *Change: Principles of Problem Formation and Problem Resolution*. New York: W.W. Norton.

> **RECOMMENDED READING**
>
> Shennan, G. (2019). *Solution-focused Practice: Effective Communication to Facilitate Change* (2nd ed.). London: Bloomsbury.
>
> This book is a systematic account of the version of SFBT predominant in the UK, as reflected in the accreditation criteria of the UK Association for Solution Focused Practice.
>
> de Shazer, S., Dolan, Y., Korman, H., Trepper, T., McCollum, E. and Berg, I. K. (2021). *More than Miracles: The State of the Art of Solution-focused Brief Therapy* (Classic ed.). New York: Routledge.
>
> With a new preface, this book is the final work of the original developers of SFBT, which presents their later thinking and practice.
>
> Ratner, H., George, E. and Iveson, C. (2012). *Solution Focused Brief Therapy: 100 Key Points and Techniques*. Hove: Routledge.
>
> This is an accessible book by a group who introduced the approach to many in the UK.

5.29 TRANSACTIONAL ANALYSIS

CHARLOTTE SILLS AND KEITH TUDOR

OVERVIEW AND KEY POINTS

Transactional analysis (TA) proposes theories of communication and relationship, personality, health and psychopathology, and child development, all of which provide the basis for a theory of clinical practice. Its theories can be applied to individuals, couples, and systems such as groups and organisations.

Key points of this chapter include:

- a brief history of TA
- its theory of personality development, life 'scripts' and patterns of relating
- skills and strategies, including a case study
- a comment on research.

BRIEF HISTORY

TA was founded by Eric Berne, a Canadian medical doctor and psychiatrist who also trained as a psychoanalyst. TA has its theoretical roots in the psychoanalytic tradition and is influenced by social theory and the cognitive-behavioural approach to psychotherapy. While Berne himself acknowledged the existential influence on TA, it also draws on humanistic values about human worth and potential. Berne was particularly influenced by Paul Federn, who was his training analyst in New York, and whose system of ego psychology was seminal in Berne's development of the ego state theory of personality. In 1947, Berne moved to California and became an analysand of Eric Erikson, from whom he learned about sequential life stages and the importance of social influences in development. In the early 1950s Berne began to take a more critical view of psychoanalysis and its conceptualisation of the unconscious. His break with psychoanalysis came in 1956 when his application for membership of the San Francisco Psychoanalytic Institute was rejected.

He established a series of weekly meetings of mental health professionals interested in TA: the San Francisco Social Psychiatry Seminar, which, in 1960, became an incorporated educational body and led to the foundation in 1964 of the International Transactional Analysis Association (ITAA). In 1961 Berne published *Transactional Analysis in Psychotherapy*, which drew together all his previous writings on TA and still represents a complete view of TA personality, psychotherapy and communication theory. The publication in 1964 of Berne's *Games People Play* marked a blossoming of public interest in TA, especially in the USA, as demonstrated by the passage into common usage of TA terms such as 'OK' (as in 'I'm OK, You're OK'), psychological 'games' (mutual transferential processes) and 'strokes' (units or gestures of recognition).

Since Berne's death, a number of different traditions within TA have emerged (see Tudor and Hobbes, 2007), and it is possible to train for qualification and certification in education and organisational applications as well as counselling and psychotherapy. To date, there are over 10,000 members of the various TA organisations in over 90 countries, 45 of which have their own national organisation(s). Two international organisations – the ITAA, and the European Association for TA (EATA) – coordinate international certifying examinations which accredit practitioners, teachers and supervisors in the four fields of application.

BASIC ASSUMPTIONS

Berne founded his work on aspirational values:

- People are born with a basic drive for growth and health – in TA terms: 'OKness', which is encapsulated in the phrase 'I'm OK, You're OK', representing mutual respect for self and other, and a conviction and faith in human nature to live harmoniously if given the right conditions. In his last book, Berne (1975 [1972]) added to the two-person I–You, the third 'They', thereby acknowledging the wider social context of such life positions and pointing to a total life direction or destiny, and, beyond that, planetary OKness (see Tudor, 2016).
- Similarly, Berne asserted that there is a third drive, alongside Freud's instinctual drives – *thanatos* (death instinct) and *eros* (sexual instinct) – namely, *physis*, which describes the creative life instinct. In his work and writing, Berne also referred to *vis medicatrix naturae* or the curative power of nature.
- A general goal in life for people is autonomy, a word that has a particular meaning in TA. Berne defined autonomy as the release or recovery of our capacity for awareness, spontaneity and intimacy. In this sense, he described a social goal not only for individuals but also for groups, organisations, communities and societies.
- Everyone has the capacity to think – and, therefore, to take responsibility for their actions.
- People decide their own destiny and, therefore, these decisions can be changed. These decisions may be cognitive and conscious in the ordinary sense of the word; they can also be unconscious, preverbal, embodied or visceral 'decisions' about ourselves and life.

ORIGIN AND MAINTENANCE OF PROBLEMS

In common with most approaches to psychological therapy, TA recognises that the past influences the present. In TA this process is called *script* or 'life plan', which starts with the interplay between psychobiological hungers (Berne, 1963, 1966) – the needs and desires with which the infant comes into the world – and the experiences of early life. From the first moment, we are shaped by experiences and events, and, importantly, the relationships that we see around us and in which we are involved. We internalise these early relationships (as *ego states*) and we form conclusions (*script decisions*), consciously and non-consciously – about ourselves, others and the world. This forms our personality and becomes the filter (*frame of reference*) through which we interpret our experiences later in our lives. In the present, as we engage with people and events, we respond with internal experience (thoughts, feelings, embodied adaptations, relational expectations, and so on) and then behaviour (*transactions, games*), all of which arise from our frame of reference and also reinforce it by bringing about repeating outcomes and patterns of relating. Some of these learned ways of being can be fluid, adaptable and effective; others are fixed and limiting.

Whether as a result of trauma or lack of environmental support, script beliefs and adaptations become the only way we know of getting our needs met to function and survive.

TA has a wealth of concepts to help people understand the process by which all this happens and how they have become who they are. Here, we introduce just a few of them.

THE STRUCTURE OF THE PERSONALITY

An ego state is a state of being: a set of feelings, thoughts, images, sensations and behaviour that represent the way a person is relating to themselves and others, and experiencing and making sense of their world. Also known as self-states, they are the building blocks of our personalities according to TA. Berne identified three types of ego state: Parent, Adult, and Child (see Figure 5.29.1).

The Parent and Child ego states represent past influences. The Parent ego state 'is a set of feelings, attitudes, and behavior patterns which resemble those of a parental figure' (Berne, 1975 [1961]: 75). In other words, in our early development, we are shaped by significant figures, such as parents, grandparents, older siblings or, later, teachers, etc. We absorb the ways of being of these significant others and these states become part of our personality. 'The Child ego state is a set of feelings, attitudes and behavior patterns which are relics of the individual's own childhood' (ibid.: 77). This ego state represents responses to what was happening to us and, through repetition, gives us a sense of 'I': i.e., identity formed from the repeated experiencing of oneself in relation to the world. The Adult ego state is characterised by autonomous, here-and-now responses: feelings, attitudes and behaviours. It is sometimes known as the 'Integrated Adult' or 'integrating Adult' as part of its function is to integrate influences from the past into the present. There have been and are lively debates within TA about the nature of ego states, for further discussions of which, see Sills and Hargaden (2003) and Tudor (2010). Importantly, Berne emphasised the need for *both* observable *and* subjective verification of intuitive diagnosis – thus requiring the collaboration of both therapist and client.

PSYCHOPATHOLOGY

This involves the *contamination* (unaware influence) of the Adult by one or more archaic ego states; *exclusion* of an ego state (a form of dissociation), for example that of the traumatised child; or *symbiosis*, a co-dependent relationship that is created based on script decisions by two (or more) individuals.

HERE-AND-NOW MANIFESTATIONS OF SCRIPT

Internal experience. TA has a number of concepts that describe the process of viewing the world through a scripted frame of reference, including '*discounting*' (ignoring or minimising) some aspects of ourselves, others or the situation, while exaggerating others, and re-experiencing familiar *racket* feelings that accompany equally familiar thoughts and conclusions about self, others and life.

Manifestation in relationships. Berne gave the name '*transaction*' to an interaction or relational interchange. All communication can be analysed in terms of transactions between ego states. This helps to understand how human beings engage with each other, both in achieving real contact and intimacy, and also in repeating old patterns of relating (*games*) that reinforce people's entrenched script positions. In analysing transactions, Berne (1966) identified three rules of communication, which shine a light on the subtlety of both conscious and unconscious relating.

1. When we communicate or transact from complementary ego states (i.e., between Parent and Parent, Adult and Adult, Child and Child, and Parent and Child), communication can continue

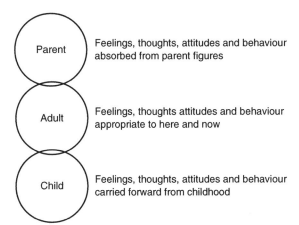

Figure 5.29.1 Structural diagram of a personality

indefinitely. As Berne (1966: 223) put it: 'As long as the vectors are parallel, communication can proceed indefinitely.'
2. A break in communication is described as a crossed transaction. When a transaction is crossed (i.e., a person responds to a communication from an ego state that is not the one that was addressed), there is a break in communication and one or both individuals will need to shift ego states in order to re-establish a connection. While crossed transactions can be problematic in perpetuating miscommunication, they can be therapeutic (e.g., when a therapist or a client 'crosses' an unhelpful, repetitive communication).
3. The ulterior transaction describes an exchange where, belying apparently straight-forward conversation, an unspoken interchange takes place at the level of right brain to right brain communication (Schore, 2019). As Berne (1966: 227) puts it: 'The behavioral outcome of an ulterior transaction is determined at the psychological and not at the social level.' The ulterior transaction is likely to be driven by script.

Game is the name Berne gave to describe repeating patterns of interaction with others in which script beliefs are enacted relationally and lead to a 'pay-off' or reinforcement of the script, usually for everybody involved. The word 'game' is not intended to imply pleasure or fun – *au contraire*, games are the most painful ways we relate to others, leading to an unconscious mutual confirmation of our scripts. In classical TA, practitioners sought to avoid playing such games with their clients, instead using clear contracts and constant vigilance. They challenged clients about their patterns and invited here-and-now self-responsibility. Nowadays, relational transactional analysts recognise that sometimes it is only through games that the unconscious processes of our deepest wounds and strongest defences are revealed (Stuthridge and Sills, 2015, 2020). We therefore welcome such games in the consulting room as being and representing the source of important understanding and learning.

THEORY OF CHANGE

Berne, a medical doctor, defined change in terms of 'cure', which he viewed as a progressive process involving four stages from social/behavioural self-control and symptom relief through to '*script cure*'.

Berne also viewed TA as a social psychiatry which, for him, was the study of the psychiatric aspects of transactions. Others in TA have emphasised the impact of the social and political world (see Tudor, 2020). Thus, in recent years, the understanding of change, cure and, indeed, health and learning, is generally considered in the context of cultural and social attitudes, pressures and circumstances, and much more in the context of a mutually influencing relationship.

SKILLS AND STRATEGIES

TA originally took an actionistic approach to change and 'treatment', focusing largely on material that was amenable to conscious cognitive awareness and changeable behaviour. Based on the contractual method and their diagnosis of the client, TA practitioners negotiated, defined and followed a mutually-agreed treatment plan. Working usually in a group, the role of the therapist was to observe the client's here-and-now words, gestures, facial expressions as well as content closely, and to help the client to see how their script was playing out in the present. Berne (1966) offered a precise sequence of 'operations', starting with inquiring into the situation, then raising awareness of script beliefs and patterns, and, finally, interpreting deeper unconscious processes.

Developments in TA have reflected changes in the wider field of psychotherapy. These include narrative or constructivist approaches that take account of new understandings in relation to memory and meaning-making. These include psychoanalytic TA (Moiso and Novellino, 2000), and two approaches to relational TA (Hargaden and Sills, 2002; Tudor and Summers, 2014). Both these approaches are 'relational' in that they view human personality as essentially shaping and being shaped by processes of relating from birth (even conception) onwards. Further, as they recognise that change and growth happen in relationship, they work with patterns of relating as they emerge in the therapeutic relationship.

In relational therapy, the relationship between therapist and client is the vehicle in which the client can express their self-experience and patterns of relating, including sometimes deeply unconscious or unsymbolised processes, which often emerge as games (Stuthridge and Sills, 2015, 2020). The 'relational turn' in psychotherapy in general is reflected and well articulated in TA in these and other publications (see Cornell and Hargaden, 2005; Fowlie and Sills, 2011) and in the development of an International Association for Relational TA (www.relationalta.com).

Apart from a few early TA authors (e.g., Cassius, 1977; Childs-Gowell, 1975; Cornell, 1975; Steere, 1982), transactional analysts have largely minimised the importance of the body both as a resource and support and as a container of script and trauma. Stuthridge (2006) offers a model of trauma as disturbance in the integrating capacity of the Adult, and other articles in the TA literature address specific traumatised client groups. Caizzi (2012) describes working with embodied trauma in victims of violence. Stuthridge and Sills (2020) also touch on this in their view and description of third-degree games. The gaps in our articulation of working with trauma and the body are being addressed. In particular, Novak (2008, 2022 – in press) not only introduces a way of thinking about and working with trauma, but also offers an integration of embodied therapy with psychoanalysis and TA in a talking therapy that directly engages with embodied trauma.

CASE STUDY

James was one of those clients that therapists usually dread! As he explained on the phone, he was being 'sent' by his wife, who had told him that if he didn't 'get his act together' she would leave him. As I (Charlotte) waited for him to arrive for his first appointment, I expected to meet a good deal of ambivalence in a man who had come to therapy under threat. However, I was interested that he appeared meekly and enthusiastically committed to his development – smiling appreciatively at me, nodding his agreement and managing to curl his two-metre height into a chair so that he could still look up at/to me. I provisionally 'diagnosed' a Child ego state and took care to meet him with a blend of complementary transactions (to establish an empathic connection) and crossed ones (to establish empathic understanding) as, together, we made sense of the situation.

James's wife suffered from anxiety, which was made tolerable if she could feel fully in charge of things. James sympathised with his wife, whom he loved very much, and did his best to make their life together predictable. However, he was a man of thoughts and dreams rather than action, and he often made small mistakes – from forgetting to buy the sausages on his way home to forgetting that they had agreed to have supper with friends. These mistakes were greeted with enraged fury by his wife, who, it appeared, covered her anxiety with a rigid and punishing Parent ego state. The pair were playing a painful script-reinforcing game by which she confirmed that the world was unsafe and she could not rely on anyone, and he confirmed that no matter how hard he tried, he could never be good enough. His most recent mistake was forgetting to do his taxes and finding unexpectedly that he had a large tax bill to pay. This had caused his precipitation into therapy.

We analysed the relational pattern and James began to experiment with having more Adult conversations with his wife, making clear agreements with her about what he would do and when. Things improved, but weren't transformed: when he reported their interaction, it sounded as if the agreements they made still represented a Child–Parent dynamic.

After a while, I began to notice that James had developed the habit of arriving five minutes late and apologising. Twice he forgot to pay. I felt annoyed and talked with him about the importance of boundaries – but there was an uncomfortable feeling in my stomach. It felt familiar to me, to be trying to get someone to do something (my son probably), and I also heard in my words the voice my own mother had used whenever *I* was forgetful.

I took a different tack and began to explore what might be going on between us. I wondered aloud whether I had become another demanding woman in his life, and how that felt. Gradually, James began to access the deeper levels of rage, fear, guilt and resentment that had their origins in his childhood with a demanding mother who had died when he was 7 years old. As his feelings emerged – to be received, accepted and named between us – something loosened for him in his relationship with his wife. Slowly he started to build a different sort of connection with her in which they could both be vulnerable.

RESEARCH

Although Berne (1966) argued that research and therapy be clearly separated, he nevertheless pre-figured the more recent concept of the reflective practitioner who is more aware of research. Berne's own writing, as well as that of other TA practitioners, reflects a broad concern in TA to observe the external manifestations of internal, phenomenological realities, and to operationalise the conclusions.

It follows that most TA concepts are amenable to research: the life script through questionnaires; passivity and discounting through the discount matrix; the stroke economy through the stroking profile, etc. (for an explanation of these and other TA concepts, see Lapworth and Sills, 2011; Stewart and Joines, 2012). In the last 20 years, research articles have appeared in the *Transactional Analysis Journal* and the *EATA News* on self-esteem in a self-reparenting programme; the impact of TA in enhancing adjustment in college students; ego states; the effects of TA psychotherapy on self-esteem and quality of life; stress among high school students; functional fluency; the use of TA in treatment centres for addiction and in groupwork; and others. Ohlsson (2010a, 2010b) provided a reference list of TA research published in TA journals since the 1960s. The last decade has produced a good deal more research (see International Transactional Analysis Association (ITAA), 2022) and relational TA has been the springboard for some qualitative action research (van Rijn et al., 2008). Finally, TA research has been systematically reviewed by Vos and van Rijn (2021, 2022 – in press). The research indicates that, overall, psychopathology, behaviour and general wellbeing is improved by TA psychotherapy.

REFERENCES

Berne, E. (1963). *The structure and dynamics of organizations and groups*. New York: Grove Press.
Berne, E. (1964). *Games people play*. New York: Grove Press.
Berne, E. (1966). *Principles of group treatment*. New York: Grove Press.
Berne, E. (1975 [1961]). *Transactional analysis in psychotherapy*. Chicago, IL and London: Souvenir Press.
Berne, E. (1975 [1972]). *What do you say after you say hello?* London: Corgi.
Caizzi, C. (2012). Embodied trauma: Using the subsymbolic mode to access and change script protocol in traumatized adults. *Transactional Analysis Journal*, *42*(3), 165–175.
Cassius, J. (1977). Bioenergetics and TA. In M. James (Ed.), *Techniques in transactional analysis* (pp. 272–282). Reading, MA: Addison-Wesley.
Childs-Gowell, E. (1975). Transactional analysis and the body: Sensory stimulation techniques. *Transactional Analysis Journal*, *5*, 148–150.
Cornell, B. and Hargaden, H. (Eds) (2005). *From transactions to relations: The emergence of a relational tradition in transactional analysis*. Scarborough, ON: Haddon Press.
Cornell, W. (1975). Wake Up 'Sleepy': Reichian techniques and script intervention. *Transactional Analysis Journal*, *5*(2), 144–147.
Fowlie, H. and Sills, C. (2011). *Relational transactional analysis: Principles in practice*. London: Karnac.
Hargaden, H. and Sills, C. (2002). *Transactional analysis: A relational perspective*. Hove: Brunner-Routledge.
International Transactional Analysis Association (ITAA) (2022). *Research instruments*. Pleasanton, CA: ITAA. Available at www.itaaworld.org/research-instruments
Lapworth, P. and Sills, S. (2011). *An introduction to transactional analysis* (rev. ed.). London: Sage.
Moiso, C. and Novellino, M. (2000). An overview of the psychodynamic school of transactional analysis and its epistemological foundations. *Transactional Analysis Journal*, *30*(3), 182–191.
Novak, E. T. (2008). Combining traditional ego state theory and relational approaches to transactional analysis in working with trauma and dissociation. *Transactional Analysis Journal*, *43*(3), 186–196.
Novak, E. T. (2022, in press). *Physical touch in psychoanalytic psychotherapy: Transforming trauma through embodied practice*. Abingdon, UK: Routledge.
Ohlsson, T. (2010a). Scientific evidence base for transactional analysis in the year 2010 Annex 1 – The big list: References to transactional analysis research 1963–2010. *International Journal of Transactional Analysis Research*, *1*(1), 12–23.

Ohlsson, T. (2010b). Scientific evidence base for transactional analysis in the year 2010 Annex 2 – The psychotherapy list: References to research on transactional analysis psychotherapy effects 1963–2010. *International Journal of Transactional Analysis Research*, *1*(1), 24–29.

Schore, A. N. (2019). *Right brain psychotherapy*. New York: W.W. Norton.

Sills, C. and Hargaden, H. (Eds) (2003). *Ego states*. Belper, UK: Worth Publishing.

Steere, D. (1982). *Bodily expressions in psychotherapy*. Hove: Brunner-Mazel.

Stewart, I. and Joines, V. (2012). *TA today (2nd ed)*. Derby: Lifespace.

Stuthridge, J. (2006). Inside Out: A Transactional Analysis Model of Trauma. *Transactional Analysis Journal*, *36*(4), 270–283. https://doi.org/10.1177/036215370603600403

Stuthridge, J. and Sills, C. (2015). Psychological games and intersubjective processes. In R. Erskine (Ed.), *Transactional analysis in contemporary psychotherapy* (pp. 185–208). London: Karnac.

Stuthridge, J. and Sills, C. (2020). Psychological games in the consulting room. *International Journal of Psychotherapy*, *23*(3), 27–40.

Tudor, K. (2010). The state of the ego: Then and now. *Transactional Analysis Journal*, *40*(3&4), 261–277.

Tudor, K. (2016). 'We are': The fundamental life position. *Transactional Analysis Journal*, *46*(2), 164–176.

Tudor, K. (2020). Transactional analysis and politics: A critical review. Transactional analysis and politics [Special issue]. *Psychotherapy and Politics International*, *18*(3).

Tudor, K. and Hobbes, R. (2007). Transactional analysis. In W. Dryden (Ed.), *The handbook of individual therapy* (5th ed., pp. 256–286). London: Sage.

Tudor, K. and Summers, G. (2014). *Co-creative transactional analysis*. London: Karnac.

van Rijn, B., Sills, C., Hunt, J., Shivanath, S., Gildebrand, K. and Fowlie, H. (2008). Developing clinical effectiveness in psychotherapy training: action research. *Counselling and Psychotherapy Research*, *8*(4), 261–268.

Vos, J. and van Rijn, B. (2022). The Effectiveness of Transactional Analysis Treatments and Their Predictors: A Systematic Literature Review and Explorative Meta-Analysis. *Journal of Humanistic Psychology*, https://doi.org/10.1177/00221678221117111

Vos, J. and van Rijn, B. (2021). The evidence-based conceptual model of transactional analysis: A focused review of the research literature. *Transactional Analysis Journal*, *51*(2), 160–201.

RECOMMENDED READING

Berne, E. (1975 [1972]). *What do you say after you say hello?* London: Corgi.

Berne's last and by far the most readable of his nine books. In it he brings together his development of TA over some 20 years, together with his interest in cross-cultural psychology, and uses independent (Martian) thinking and fairy tales to illustrate 'the psychology of human destiny' from cradle to grave.

Lapworth, P. and Sills, C. (2011). *An introduction to transactional analysis* (rev. ed.). London: Sage.

Drawing on the best of traditional TA theory and revitalising some TA theory that is not always presented in an introductory book, this revised edition presents a contemporary and vibrant TA, with many practical and useful examples aimed at enhancing the development of relational skills and thinking.

Cornell, W. F., de Graaf, A. Newton, T. and Thunisson, M. (Eds) (2015). *Into TA: A comprehensive textbook on transactional analysis*. London: Karnac.

If you are after a well-written and concise overview of the foundations of TA theory, this book comprises chapters by leading authors in the four fields of transactional analysis application: psychotherapy, counselling, education and organisation.

PART VI

LIFESPAN, MODALITIES AND TECHNOLOGY

6.1 COUNSELLING CHILDREN

KATHRYN GELDARD AND REBECCA YIN FOO

OVERVIEW AND KEY POINTS

An introduction to counselling children is provided in this chapter. First, differences between counselling children and counselling young people or adults are highlighted before varying approaches to counselling children are identified. An integrative model of counselling children is then introduced to provide a framework for drawing on approaches that best fit a particular stage of the counselling process. The chapter concludes with an exploration of the research base for counselling children.

- Counselling children is different from counselling young people or adults, therefore an alternative approach is required.
- Counselling children can include non-directive play therapy, creative and expressive therapies, gestalt therapy, time-limited play therapy, cognitive-behavioural therapy and family therapy.
- The 'sequentially planned integrative counselling for children' (SPICC) model is designed to draw on various approaches that best fit each stage of the counselling process.
- There is a growing research base for the effectiveness of counselling children.

INTRODUCTION

Whereas many young people and adults seek counselling of their own volition, children are usually accompanied by their parents or other significant adults, who are also involved in the therapeutic process. Additionally, children live in families or multigenerational groups and their emotions and behaviours occur within, and likely result in consequences for, the system in which they live. Therefore, both intrapersonal issues of the child, along with systemic issues involving parents/caregivers and the family/group, are considered.

Adults are generally comfortable and able to explore and resolve their issues in a conversational relationship with a counsellor. In comparison, many children cannot share troubling issues using only conversational strategies. Media and activity can, therefore, engage the child, enable them to talk about troubling issues and help the child find resolution.

Although many children engaging in counselling have underlying emotional concerns, they are commonly brought to counselling only after adults notice behavioural changes. For successful therapeutic outcomes, both emotional and behavioural issues are addressed.

In addition to the ethical and legal parameters that apply to adults, confidentiality with children is confounded by the rights of the parents'/caregivers' access to information also. If a child is to talk freely, they must have some confidence that the information they share is treated respectfully and not disclosed without good reason (British Psychological Society, 2017).

Considering the differences highlighted above, it can be helpful to develop professional skills under a supervisor who is trained and experienced in working with children. Additionally, ongoing supervision is essential to ensure good practice.

WAYS OF WORKING

Several therapeutic approaches can be used when counselling children, including:

- non-directive play therapy
- creative and expressive therapy
- gestalt therapy
- time-limited play therapy
- cognitive-behavioural therapy
- family therapy.

Each of these approaches has advantages and limitations. The literature suggests that there is not one preferred way of working that is suitable for all children. Whatever approach is used, several goals can usefully be achieved when counselling children. These include:

- To help the child gain mastery over issues and events.
- To enable the child to feel empowered.
- To help the child develop problem-solving and decision-making skills.
- To build the child's self-concept and self-esteem.
- To improve the child's communication skills.
- To help the child develop insight.

NON-DIRECTIVE PLAY THERAPY

Non-directive play therapy (NDPT) is one means of encouraging self-expression, when facilitated by the therapist (Axline, 1989 [1947]; Landreth, 2012; Ray et al., 2001). NDPT is used to support the child's developing self within safe boundaries provided by the setting and the counsellor's emotional holding and containment (McMahon, 2009). The counsellor observes the child as they play without direction with media including children's toys, toy furniture, and materials such as clay, paint and crayons. The counsellor's observations might include mood or affect, intellectual functioning, thinking processes, speech and language, motor skills, play, and the relationship with the counsellor. Central to this approach is that the child brings their concerns to therapy rather than the counsellor identifying issues (Wilson and Ryan, 2006).

CREATIVE AND EXPRESSIVE THERAPY

Through their early attachment experiences, children develop unconscious internal working models (IWMs) of their social world (Johnson, Dweck and Chen, 2007). Creative strategies that address the physiology of emotion, and hence target IWMs, may be useful when working with children (Gantt and Tinnin, 2009; Harris, 2009; Wright, Crawford and Del Castillo, 2009). Sand play and symbol work are creative therapeutic tools that can access and allow expression of the child's inner world, and hence reveal unconscious processes and dilemmas, bringing them into a representational form that allows resolution. Margaret Lowenfeld pioneered this approach, using objects as symbols in a sand tray to encourage non-verbal expression less influenced by rational thinking (Ryce-Menuhin, 1992; Schaefer and O'Connor, 1994). Many counsellors use sand tray to engage the child and enable them to talk openly, explore their issues, and express emotion (Sweeney, Homeyer and Drewes, 2009).

GESTALT THERAPY

Oaklander (1988, 2011) and Blom (2006) combine the use of gestalt therapy principles with media when working with children. Oaklander uses fantasy and/or metaphor and believes that usually the fantasy process will be the same as the life process in the child. She therefore works indirectly/projectively in bringing out what is hidden or avoided. Although this works well for some children, some may have difficulty making the connection between fantasy and real life. Other counsellors use gestalt therapy in a more direct way. As the child engages with media and/or activity, they will use gestalt techniques to raise awareness while the child tells their story (e.g., Blom, 2006).

TIME-LIMITED PLAY THERAPY

This approach uses ideas from brief psychodynamic therapy (Sloves and Belinger-Peterlin, 1986). A brief assessment of the child's issues is made before the counsellor selects a central theme to work with across 12 sessions. Counselling focuses on empowerment, adaptation, strengthening the ego and the future rather than the past. This form of therapy is directive and interpretative. It is particularly effective, for example, with children experiencing recent post-traumatic stress disorder and adjustment disorders, and for children who have lost a parent to a chronic medical condition (Christ et al., 1991), but not for others (Schaefer and O'Connor, 1994).

COGNITIVE-BEHAVIOURAL THERAPY

Described by Beck (1995) and developed more recently (Friedberg, McClure and Garcia, 2009) as cognitive-behavioural therapy (CBT), this educational model describes the connection between thoughts, emotions and behaviours. Current thoughts underlying the child's emotions and behaviours are explored with the aim of replacing unhelpful thoughts with more adaptive ones. Media and activity, such as worksheets, drawing and role-playing, are useful in helping the child explore their current thoughts and behaviours and practise new ways of thinking and behaving.

CBT is a short-term, cost-effective approach that can be useful in enabling many children to gain a level of control over emotions and behaviours. One limitation is that it does not directly target emotions or encourage emotional release. Also, the approach requires a certain level of language, cognitive and emotional development. Without this, the child will not understand the educational model and may not be able to interrupt emotional outbursts by making changes to their thinking. Consequently, it is not suitable for very young children.

CBT is often used with behavioural psychotherapy where incentives are used to reinforce positive behaviour and there are consequences for undesirable behaviour. Behaviour therapy can be used with children of all ages.

FAMILY THERAPY

This approach is discussed by Dallos in Chapter 6.5, this volume. Some counsellors believe it is sufficient to explore and resolve a child's emotional and behavioural problems within the context of the family system. This can be very effective for some children. However, many children who are troubled by emotional issues and/or thoughts that are highly personal may not be able to talk about these easily in the family context.

ECLECTIC AND INTEGRATIVE COUNSELLING

Some counsellors like to use a particular therapeutic approach, but others prefer to practise flexibly, selecting a method of working to meet the needs of a particular child. This 'prescriptive approach' was initially proposed by Millman and Schaefer (1977) and developed further by Schaefer (2001). An alternative is an integrative approach incorporating ideas from several therapeutic frameworks. The counsellor, for example, selects and makes use of strategies from multiple therapeutic approaches with the goal of meeting a child's needs as they arise. Both approaches can have positive outcomes. However, the process of counselling might be compromised by the inappropriate selection and/or sequence of strategies used. An alternative is an integrative model where strategies from particular therapeutic approaches are intentionally used at certain points in the therapeutic process.

THE SPICC MODEL

The 'sequentially planned integrative counselling for children' (SPICC) model is an integrative approach we developed and use ourselves (Geldard, Geldard and Yin Foo, 2017). Before using the SPICC model, we suggest family therapy to gain a full understanding of family dynamics and the child in the context of the family system. Sometimes after family therapy we discover that the problem has been resolved. At other times, the child with the presenting problem, or another child in the family, may experience emotional distress requiring individual counselling using the SPICC model.

The SPICC model involves the following sequence of stages: joining with the child, enabling the child to tell their story, raising the child's awareness so they get in touch with and express emotions, helping the child to cognitively restructure, helping the child to look into options and choices, and enabling the child to rehearse and experiment with new behaviours. The SPICC model is described below in the context of 8-year-old Sarah, whose parents have noticed a change in behaviour following the arrival of a new sibling.

SAND PLAY WORK

In the initial stage the counsellor joins with and engages the child using media and/or activity. A counsellor might use symbols in the sand tray, or with older children, who are cognitively able to use a projective technique, miniature animals to represent family members. In the sand tray, the child can be encouraged to use objects as symbols to make a picture in the sand of their world and/or family as they perceive it. The activity component enables the child to feel relaxed rather than pressured to talk. As the picture in the sand tray develops, the counsellor can explore its meaning with the child and help the child talk about their life. Sarah may choose to create a picture in the sand tray with symbols representing herself and her parents in one section of the sand tray and another symbol representing her new sibling separated from the group or even buried in the sand. During this stage, it is important for the counsellor to non-judgementally accept Sarah's story of what life is like for her with a new sibling.

USE OF GESTALT THERAPY

Once a trusting relationship has been established, the counsellor can use media and/or activity together with gestalt therapy awareness-raising techniques to help the child connect with troubling emotions. The use of media and/or activity maintains the child's interest, allows them to anchor their story, and ensures the child has time to process thoughts rather than feel pressured to talk. As the child's awareness is raised, the counsellor might encourage the release of troubling emotions through the use of media such as clay, or an activity such as painting and drawing. For Sarah, the counsellor may invite her to create a baby using clay or express her feelings about her new sibling through painting.

USE OF COGNITIVE-BEHAVIOURAL THERAPY AND BEHAVIOUR THERAPY

The next stage is to explore any unhelpful thoughts and behaviours in order to restructure unhelpful thinking patterns using CBT. Change is unlikely and emotional distress will probably recur if this stage is overlooked. Similarly, the child can be encouraged to explore their options and choices regarding current and future behaviour. The new behaviour can be reinforced using a behaviour therapy approach with the parents'/caregivers' cooperation. During this stage, the counsellor may invite Sarah to share her thoughts about her new sibling and support her in changing any unhelpful thinking patterns, for example, looking for evidence against the thought that her parents don't love her anymore.

INTEGRATION OF INDIVIDUAL AND FAMILY WORK

During the individual counselling process with the child there may be times when it is useful for the child to share information with their parents or family. Towards the end of the therapeutic process, re-engaging the whole family in family therapy can help changes be reinforced and supported and remaining problems addressed. For Sarah, it may be helpful to share her thoughts, feelings and experiences related to having a new sibling with her parents. Systemic changes can then be explored and implemented by the family. Sarah's parents could, for example, explore ways they can show Sarah that she is, indeed, still loved, such as setting aside regular one-on-one time with her.

RESEARCH

A number of review articles and books have now been published summarising the research into the effectiveness of counselling children (e.g., Lin and Bratton, 2015; Midgley et al., 2009). Play therapy methods have been criticised as not being evidence based (Lillard et al., 2013), but meta-analyses of treatment outcomes do support an evidence base for play therapy (see Bratton et al., 2005; Leblanc and Ritchie, 2001; Lin and Bratton, 2015). Familiarising ourselves with this research can enhance our counselling practice. Review studies have found moderate to large effect sizes supporting the effectiveness of counselling children across behavioural, cognitive-behavioural and play therapy approaches. Bratton and Ray (2000) found self-concept, behavioural adjustment, social skills, emotional adjustment, intelligence and anxiety/fear were topics demonstrating the most significance regarding the efficacy of play therapy. Furthermore, counselling children is effective across a range of challenges, including 'global behavioral problems, internalizing behavior problems, externalizing behavioral problems, caregiver–child relationship stress, self-efficacy, academic performance, and other presenting issues' (Lin and Bratton, 2015: 52).

REFERENCES

Axline, V.M. (1989 [1947]) *Play Therapy*. London: Ballantine Books.
Beck, J.S. (1995) *Cognitive Therapy: Basics and Beyond*. New York: Guilford Press.
Blom, R. (2006) *The Handbook of Gestalt Play Therapy: Practical Guidelines for Child Therapists*. London: Jessica Kingsley Publishers.
Bratton, S. and Ray, D. (2000) What the research shows about play therapy. *International Journal of Play Therapy*, 9(1), 47.
Bratton, S., Ray, D., Rhine, T. and Jones, L. (2005) The efficacy of play therapy with children: A meta-analytic review of treatment outcomes. *Professional Psychology: Research and Practice*, 36, 376–390.
British Psychological Society (2017) *Practice Guidelines* (3rd ed.). Leicester: BPS.

(Continued)

(Continued)

Christ, G.H., Siegel, K., Mesagno, F. and Langosch, D. (1991) A preventative intervention program for bereaved children: problems of implementation. *Journal of Orthopsychiatry*, *61*(2), 168–178.

Friedberg, R.D., McClure, J. and Garcia, J.H. (2009) *Cognitive Therapy Techniques for Children and Adolescents: Tools for Enhancing Practice*. New York: Guilford Press.

Gantt, L. and Tinnin, L.W. (2009) Support for a neurobiological view of trauma with implications for art therapy. *The Arts in Psychotherapy*, *36*(3), 148–153.

Geldard, K., Geldard, D. and Yin Foo, R. (2017) *Counselling Children: A Practical Introduction* (5th ed.). London: Sage.

Harris, D.A. (2009) The paradox of expressing speechless terror: Ritual liminality in the creative arts therapies' treatment of posttraumatic distress. *The Arts in Psychotherapy*, *36*(2), 94–104.

Johnson, S.C., Dweck, C.S. and Chen, F.S. (2007) Evidence for infants' internal working models of attachment. *Psychological Science*, *18*(6), 501–502.

Landreth, G.L. (2012) *Play Therapy: The Art of the Relationship* (3rd ed.). New York: Bruner-Routledge.

Leblanc, M. and Ritchie, M. (2001) A meta-analysis of play therapy outcomes. *Counselling Psychology Quarterly*, *14*, 149–163.

Lillard, A. S., Lerner, M. D., Hopkins, E. J., Dore, R. A., Smith, E. D. and Palmquist, C. M. (2013). The impact of pretend play on children's development: A review of the evidence. *Psychological Bulletin*, *139*(1), 1–34. https://doi.org/10.1037/a0029321

Lin, Y.-W. and Bratton, S.C. (2015) A meta-analytic review of child-centered play therapy approaches. *Journal of Counseling & Development*, *93*(1), 45–58.

McMahon, L. (2009) *The Handbook of Play Therapy and Therapeutic Play* (2nd ed.). New York: Routledge/Taylor.

Midgley, N., Anderson, J., Grainger, E., Nesic-Vuckovic, T. and Urwin, C. (Eds) (2009) *Child Psychotherapy and Research: New Approaches, Emerging Findings*. London: Routledge.

Millman, H.L. and Schaefer, C.E. (1977) *Therapies for Children*. San Francisco, CA: Jossey-Bass.

Oaklander, V. (1988) *Windows to Our Children*. New York: Center for Gestalt Development.

Oaklander, V. (2011) Gestalt play therapy. In C.E. Schaefer (Ed.), *Foundations of Play Therapy* (2nd ed., pp. 171–186). Hoboken, NJ: Wiley.

Ray, D., Bratton, S., Rhine, T. and Jones, L. (2001) The effectiveness of play therapy: Responding to the critics. *International Journal of Play Therapy*, *10*(1), 85–108.

Ryce-Menuhin, J. (1992) *Jungian Sandplay: The Wonderful Therapy*. New York: Routledge/Chapman and Hall.

Schaefer, C.E. (2001). Prescriptive play therapy. *International Journal of Play Therapy*, *10*(2), 57.

Schaefer, C.E. and O'Connor, K.J. (Eds) (1994) *Handbook of Play Therapy*. Vol. 2: *Advances and Innovations*. New York: Wiley.

Sloves, R. and Belinger-Peterlin, K. (1986) The process of time-limited psychotherapy with latency-aged children. *Journal of the American Academy of Child Psychiatry*, *25*(6), 847–851.

Sweeney, D.S., Homeyer, L.E. and Drewes, A. (2009) Blending play therapy with cognitive behavioral therapy: Evidence-based and other effective treatments and techniques. In D. Sweeney and L. Homeyer (Eds), *Sandtray Therapy* (pp. 297–318). Hoboken, NJ: Wiley.

Wilson, K. and Ryan, V. (2006) *Play Therapy: A Non-directive Approach for Children and Adolescents*. Oxford: Elsevier Health Sciences.

Wright, M.O., Crawford, E. and Del Castillo, D. (2009) Childhood emotional maltreatment and later psychological distress among college students: The mediating role of maladaptive schemas. *Child Abuse & Neglect*, *33*, 59–68.

> **RECOMMENDED READING**
>
> Geldard, K., Geldard, D. and Yin Foo, R. (2017) *Counselling Children: A Practical Introduction* (5th ed.). London: Sage.
>
> The book outlines an integrative and practical approach to working with children.
>
> Geldard, K. and Geldard, D. (2001) *Working with Children in Groups: A Handbook for Counsellors, Educators and Community Workers*. New York: Palgrave Macmillian.
>
> For those wanting to extend their skills to supporting children in a group environment, this book is a useful introduction.
>
> Midgley, N., Anderson, J., Grainger, E., Nesic-Vuckovic, T. and Urwin, C. (Eds) (2009) *Child Psychotherapy and Research: New Approaches, Emerging Findings*. London: Routledge.
>
> This book provides an overview of the current research into counselling children.

6.2 COUNSELLING YOUNG PEOPLE

KATHRYN GELDARD AND REBECCA YIN FOO

OVERVIEW AND KEY POINTS

This chapter describes the principles and practices for counselling young people in the stage known as adolescence. To help young people effectively, a counselling approach designed to fit with their developmental stage and typical communication processes is required. This approach enables a collaborative working relationship to be developed with the young person. The chapter concludes by exploring the evidence base for counselling young people.

- Two major challenges young people face are the process of individuation and developing a personal identity, and re-evaluating constructs about their world.
- Using typical adolescent communication processes is important when counselling young people.
- A proactive counselling approach draws on symbolic, creative, behavioural, psychoeducational, mindfulness and technological strategies to create an effective environment and counselling relationship.
- There is growing research evidence for the effectiveness of counselling young people.

INTRODUCTION

THE ADOLESCENT STAGE OF DEVELOPMENT

Young people experience biological, cognitive, psychological, social, moral and spiritual changes during adolescence. Two major challenges are the need for young people to individuate and establish a personal identity, and re-evaluate constructs about their world.

INDIVIDUATION AND PERSONAL IDENTITY

Whereas a child is primarily joined with parents and family, during adolescence a young person develops a level of relative independence, depending on cultural influences, and increased capacity to engage in adult society (Nelson and Nelson, 2010). This process of socialisation balances individuation with formation of personal identity, and integration with society (Fadjukoff and Pulkkinen, 2006). Unless balance is achieved, personal crises which may require counselling are likely.

RE-EVALUATION OF CONSTRUCTS

Constructivist theory explains how we try to make sense of the world by forming constructs based on personal experiences (Fransella et al., 2007). These constructs will be revised and replaced as new information emerges via new, previously unmet experiences during adolescence (Kelly, 1955; Winter, 2003).

As young people are continually revising their constructs, a counsellor can actively listen to explore, understand and respect these constructs. The counsellor can then offer therapeutic strategies which fit with the young person's constructs. The narrative therapy works of White and Epston (Becvar, 2008) highlight the value of this process when working with young people.

WAYS OF WORKING

ESTABLISHING AND MAINTAINING A THERAPEUTIC ALLIANCE

The quality of the therapeutic relationship is critical in influencing outcomes and client satisfaction (Safran and Muran, 2000). It is desirable that the counselling relationship be an authentic person-to-person relationship, accepting and understanding, warm and empathic.

Acceptance and understanding are particularly important because young people can feel criticised by adults. They are unlikely to talk freely if they believe negative judgements are being made. Counsellors are likely to help the young person experience positive outcomes from counselling if they are able to accept and validate the young person's story and constructs without judgement.

A counsellor can enhance their opportunity to establish and maintain a positive working relationship with a young person by:

- making use of typical adolescent communication processes
- using a proactive approach.

MAKING USE OF TYPICAL ADOLESCENT COMMUNICATION PROCESSES

Young people are generally reluctant to talk to adults about sensitive issues (Boldero and Fallon, 1995; Gibson-Cline, 1996). Making use of strategies commonly employed by young people when they communicate can be helpful. When young people meet with peers, they usually engage in some of the following behaviours (Geldard, Geldard and Yin Foo, 2020; Seiffge-Krenke, Kiuru and Nurmi, 2010):

- validate other's views, if possible
- frequently digress, move away from a topic, then return to it
- disclose information about themselves and assume others will self-disclose
- be very direct about what they like and do not like and use direct closed questions to get information
- match and exaggerate other's emotional expressions
- use praise when relevant
- give and receive advice.

As counsellors, we can learn from, and use, these communication processes when appropriate, as illustrated below in the context of 15-year-old Max who was referred for counselling by his mother following the death of his older brother by suicide.

BELIEVING AND ACCEPTING THE YOUNG PERSON'S CONSTRUCTS

Generally, young people will validate each other's points of view by sharing their beliefs, attitudes and constructs, examining these together, and possibly revising them (Geldard, 2006). Even if we do not agree, counsellors can validate and accept a young person by letting them know that their beliefs, attitudes and constructs are understood. This creates the opportunity to collaboratively explore, review and revise their constructs within a genuine, open and honest relationship. For Max, it was important for the counsellor to acknowledge that he viewed his mother's response to his brother's death as stressful.

POSITIVELY JOINING IN DIGRESSIONS

Young people tend to frequently digress from a topic and talk about something else, before returning to it. We believe this digression and then returning to a topic has useful purposes.

Because young people are continually revising their constructs, they are often deconstructing and reconstructing many different ideas. Digression enables them to deal with new thoughts without putting them on hold.

Digression also allows a young person some respite from discussing troubling issues. After a less intense conversation, they may feel ready to return to discussing more uncomfortable issues. Similarly, young people may worry about getting in touch with, or feeling overwhelmed by, emotion. Allowing young people to digress away from intense emotions from time to time can foster safety in the counselling environment.

Sometimes a young person will become distracted and withdraw from the counselling process. This distraction may serve the same purpose as digression, as such, the counsellor can use distraction to introduce a digression. For example, if the young person becomes absorbed with their shoes or clothing, the counsellor might say, 'I had some shoes/a shirt like that, but mine weren't very comfortable. What are yours like?' Consequently, a low-key conversation will develop that is likely helping the young person to relax, regain energy and develop a closer connection with the counsellor. The counsellor can then encourage a return to important issues by using, for example, a transitional question such as 'Earlier we were talking about … would you like to tell me more about that?' During the session attended by Max, at one point the conversation turned to future goals. By following Max's lead, the counsellor was able to support a sense of hope for Max about his future. The counsellor then used a transitional question to return to Max's current experiences of grief.

APPROPRIATE USE OF SELF-DISCLOSURE

Most counsellors working with adults believe counsellor self-disclosure should be strictly limited or non-existent. However, we believe there are good reasons for appropriate self-disclosure when working with young people.

Appropriate counsellor self-disclosure enables young people to self-disclose to us more comfortably. When a counsellor shares personal information, the young person is implicitly invited to relate as an equal to another person with feelings and experiences potentially similar to their own. However, it is not appropriate or ethical for self-disclosure to lead to undesirable closeness and over-involvement.

Generally, counsellor self-disclosure avoids the counsellor's own problems, unless these are minor, resolved and useful for joining or demonstrating depth of understanding. For example, Max's counsellor was able to help normalise the strong desire to differentiate from his mother by sharing their own experiences as an adolescent and their mother's challenges in accepting this increasing separation. This allowed Max to disclose more information. When using self-disclosure, the focus must always remain on the young person's issues.

When counsellors continue by acknowledging that full understanding is impossible because two experiences will never be identical, the young person is able to talk more about their own personal experience and avoid matching their responses inappropriately to the counsellor's.

BEING DIRECT

Most young people are direct about what they like and dislike. To foster a counselling relationship, compared to when working with adults, young people respond positively to counsellors who are open and direct about their values and beliefs. When accompanied by acknowledgement and a mutual respect for the young person's values and beliefs, directly sharing provides an opportunity for modelling confidence in identity.

Young people typically make use of direct closed questions during peer conversations. Similarly, many young people like a direct approach during counselling. In contrast, adults prefer more circumspect questioning, allowing them to reveal the information they choose. During the session with Max, the counsellor was able to challenge Max by asking directly about the conflicting information he had discussed regarding similarities to his brother.

MATCHING AND EXAGGERATING

Young people typically match and exaggerate each other's emotional expressions. As counsellors, we can learn from the lively, energetic and dynamic communication of young people and become energised when communicating with them. Throughout the session with Max, the counsellor worked to identify and match his communication style, becoming more subdued while talking about tough emotions and using humour and exaggeration, following Max's lead when he laughed.

USE OF PRAISE

Most young people use praise naturally when communicating with peers. Similarly, counsellors can endorse a young person's beliefs or behaviour using positive feedback in a genuine, but not patronising, way. The counsellor used praise throughout the session to highlight Max's strengths and resilience.

GIVING ADVICE

Typically, when young people are uncertain about what to do, they ask peers, rather than parents, for advice. Young people want to make their own decisions without parental direction. When asking for advice, it is unlikely they, or their friend, will expect advice to be followed (Geldard, 2006), whereas adults usually expect their advice to be taken. Advice-giving, then, for young people, involves sharing ideas about possible solutions.

Empowering adult clients to find their own solutions is generally preferred to advice-giving. This is also true for young people who don't want to be told what to do. However, young people also expect counsellors to give advice (Gibson-Cline, 1996) and to have experience and knowledge they do not that may be useful for construct formation. When a young person seeks advice, we can join with them and offer to collaboratively explore their situation, possible solutions and consequences. Towards the end of the session, the counsellor joined with Max to identify ways he could compromise to ease tension between himself and his mother.

USING A PROACTIVE APPROACH

When compared with counselling children or adults, counselling young people requires more spontaneous flexibility. Young people are generally less engaged in counselling which is predictable and follows a process sequentially through stages. They may have difficulty articulating their challenges, possibly moving between subjects and seemingly disconnected parts of their world. Counsellors may therefore find themselves using strategies that enable young people to draw their ideas and beliefs together to form constructs, therefore make sense of their world.

The counsellor may also benefit from finding ways to explore topics that are like those young people use. This may result in counselling behaviour that is proactively spontaneous, creative, flexible and opportunistic, while continually attending to the counselling relationship. Being proactive involves taking responsibility by introducing new direction and counselling strategies when appropriate, while also offering the young person *choice* about what they say and do. Balancing choice with being proactive enables the young person to avoid feeling controlled when the counsellor takes initiative by focusing the process.

Preferably, the counselling relationship is not predominantly intense or serious. Balancing discussion between serious matters and pleasant, friendly conversation and/or humour can be a useful technique when working with young people (Radomska, 2007; Yuan, Zhang and Chen, 2008).

Figure 6.2.1 illustrates a proactive process for counselling young people. The central feature involves supporting the therapeutic alliance by attending to the relationship and collaboratively addressing the issues presented. While focusing on these primary counselling functions, the counsellor can proactively introduce counselling skills, as described in Geldard, Geldard and Yin Foo (2021), and parallel typical adolescent communication processes. Additionally, the counsellor can introduce, at appropriate times, symbolic, creative, behavioural, psychoeducational, mindfulness or technological strategies, as described in Geldard, Geldard and Yin Foo (2020).

SYMBOLIC, CREATIVE, BEHAVIOURAL PSYCHOEDUCATIONAL, MINDFULNESS AND TECHNOLOGICAL STRATEGIES

Symbolic strategies include metaphor, ritual, symbols, sand tray and miniature animals. These strategies can support a young person to talk about sensitive issues in a non-threatening way. Additionally, they may enable a young person to get more fully in touch with their experience and therefore re-evaluate their constructs. Creative strategies involve art, role-play, journals, relaxation, imagination and dream work. These strategies appeal to many young people, who like using artistic expression. Behavioural strategies are useful for addressing issues involving self-regulation, unhelpful beliefs, anger management, assertiveness training, lifestyle goals and decision-making. Psychoeducational strategies can be

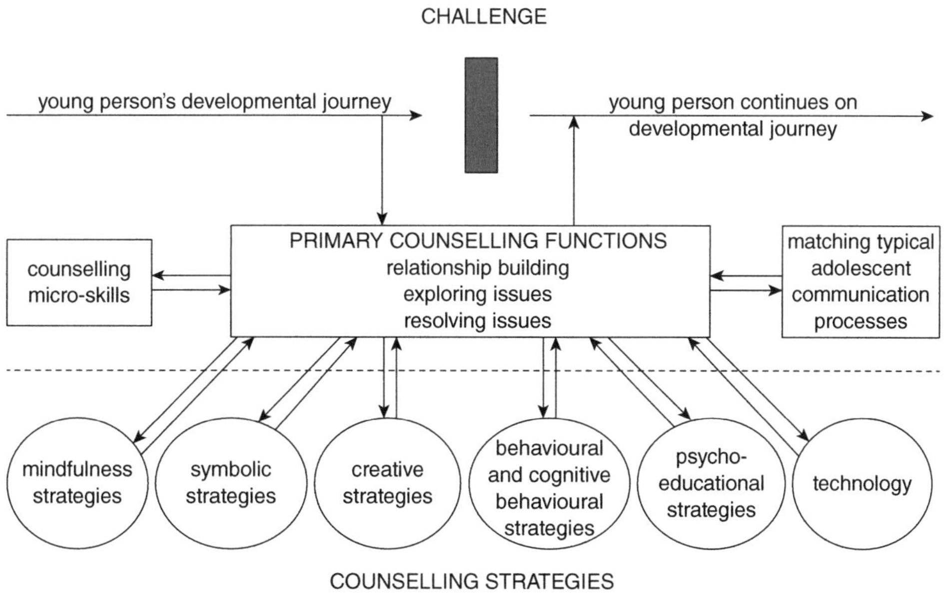

Figure 6.2.1 The proactive counselling process

used to enable the young person to share information, explain relationships and/or behaviour, and examine ways to change behaviour. Mindfulness practices have been found to decrease feelings of anxiety and reduce levels of distractibility and inattention. Finally, technology has become an everyday part of contemporary life. Video conferencing, the internet, computer games and online chats have been used to support the counselling process (Geldard et al., 2020).

During a counselling session, one or more strategies may be utilised. The counsellor can proactively select and introduce relevant strategies at particular times. Being proactive involves taking responsibility for orchestrating the counselling process to fulfil the primary counselling functions, while allowing the young person freedom to explore and resolve issues. Counselling strategies are selected in response to the young person's cognitive, emotional, somatic, verbal and non-verbal behaviours and the presenting issues.

MAKING EACH SESSION COMPLETE IN ITSELF

Many young people come to see a counsellor during a crisis but do not believe it is helpful to continue following the crisis. Young people often return when a new crisis occurs, particularly if they had positive experiences of counselling previously. Furthermore, because of their developmental stage, young people may be unreliable with keeping appointments. Hence, it is useful to assume each appointment with a young person may be the last. Achieving a level of completion in single-session therapy (SST) is therefore a useful goal when counselling young people. Indeed, SST appears to be an empirically supported and cost-effective therapy for young people with a range of mental health problems (e.g., Perkins and Scarlett, 2008).

RESEARCH

There is a large and growing research base for the effectiveness of counselling young people (e.g., Midgley, Hayes and Cooper, 2017). The research covers multiple approaches, including 'cognitive-behavioural; psychoanalytic; humanistic; and creative therapies', and presenting issues, including 'behavioural problems and conduct disorders; emotional problems including anxiety, depression and post-traumatic stress; medical illness; school-related issues; self-harming practices and sexual abuse' (Pattison and Harris, 2006: 233). While there is evidence for the effectiveness of all counselling approaches for young people, this evidence varied according to the presenting issue. For example, there was a larger body of research supporting cognitive-behaviour therapy. Therefore, this approach was found to be effective across a range of issues. This doesn't mean other approaches are less effective, just that more research is needed to build the evidence base.

REFERENCES

Becvar, D.S. (Ed.) (2008) The legacy of Michael White. *Contemporary Family Therapy: An International Journal*, *30*(3), 139–140.

Boldero, J. and Fallon, B. (1995) Adolescent help-seeking: What do they get help for and from whom? *Journal of Adolescence*, *18*(2), 193–209.

Fadjukoff, P. and Pulkkinen, L. (2006) Identity formation, personal control over development, and well-being. In L. Pulkkinen, J. Kaprio and R. Rose (Eds), *Socioemotional Development and Health from Adolescence to Adulthood* (pp. 265–285). New York and Cambridge: Cambridge University Press.

Fransella, F., Dalton, P., Weselby, G. and Dryden, W. (2007) Personal construct therapy. In W. Dryden (Ed.), *Handbook of Individual Therapy* (5th ed., pp. 173–194). Thousand Oaks, CA: Sage.

Geldard, K. (2006) *Adolescent Peer Counselling*. Doctoral dissertation, Queensland University of Technology, Brisbane, Australia.

Geldard, K., Geldard, D. and Yin Foo, R. (2020) *Counselling Adolescents: The Proactive Approach for Young People* (5th ed.). London: Sage.

Geldard, K., Geldard, D. and Yin Foo, R. (2021) *Basic Personal Counselling: A Training Manual for Counsellors* (9th ed.). South Melbourne, Vic: Cengage.

Gibson-Cline, J. (1996) *Adolescence: From Crisis to Coping. A Thirteen Nation Study*. Oxford: Butterworth-Heinemann.

Kelly, G.A. (1955) *The Psychology of Personal Constructs*. New York: W.W. Norton.

Midgley, N., Hayes, J. and Cooper, M. (2017) *Essential Research Findings in Child and Adolescent Counselling and Psychotherapy*. London: Sage.

Nelson, T. and Nelson, J.M. (2010) Evidence-based practice and the culture of adolescence. *Professional Psychology: Research and Practice*, *41*(4), 305–311.

Pattison, S. and Harris, B. (2006) Counselling children and young people: A review of the evidence for its effectiveness. *Counselling and Psychotherapy Research*, *6*(4), 233–237.

Perkins, R. and Scarlett, G. (2008) The effectiveness of single session therapy in child and adolescent mental health. Part 2: An 18-month follow-up study. *Psychology and Psychotherapy: Theory, Research and Practice*, *81*(2), 143–156.

Radomska, A. (2007) Understanding and appreciating humour in late childhood and adolescence. *Polish Psychological Bulletin*, *38*(4), 189–197.

Safran, J.D. and Muran, J.C. (2000) *Negotiating the Therapeutic Alliance: A Relational Treatment Guide*. New York: Guilford Press.

Seiffge-Krenke, I., Kiuru, N. and Nurmi, J.-E. (2010) Adolescents as 'producers of their own development': Correlates and consequences of the importance and attainment of developmental tasks. *European Journal of Developmental Psychology*, *7*(4), 479–510.

Winter, D.A. (2003) The constructivist paradigm. In R. Woolfe and W. Dryden (Eds), *Handbook of Counselling Psychology* (2nd ed., pp. 241–259). London: Sage.

Yuan, L., Zhang, J. and Chen, M. (2008) Moderating role of sense of humor to the relationship between stressful events and mental health. *Chinese Journal of Clinical Psychology*, *16*(6), 576–578.

> **RECOMMENDED READING**
>
> Geldard, K., Geldard, D. and Yin Foo, R. (2020) *Counselling Adolescents: The Proactive Approach for Young People* (5th ed.). London: Sage.
>
> This book provides an overview of working with young people within a proactive counselling framework.
>
> Geldard, K. (Ed.) (2009) *Practical Interventions for Young People at Risk*. London: Sage.
>
> This book provides more specific information about supporting young people with a range of presenting issues.
>
> Midgley, N., Hayes, J. and Cooper, M. (2017) *Essential Research Findings in Child and Adolescent Counselling and Psychotherapy*. London: Sage.
>
> For an overview of the research base when counselling young people, readers are directed to this book.

6.3 COUNSELLING OLDER PEOPLE

ANNE HAYWARD AND KEN LAIDLAW

OVERVIEW AND KEY POINTS

Common mental health conditions such as depression and anxiety can be a feature of later life but older people are not expected to experience these as a consequence of ageing. While negative appraisals of ageing are commonly held, for many other older people, later life brings better emotional stability and increased life satisfaction, even in the face of challenges. As such, understanding an appropriate developmental context and frame of reference is important for therapists working with older clients. This chapter introduces therapists to ideas about ageing that will improve engagement, create openness to the possibilities of change and enhance outcome. Key points include:

- Psychotherapy and counselling with older people is efficacious for common mental health conditions; outcome may be enhanced if counsellors seek to become more knowledgeable about normal ageing so that expectation of change is enhanced.
- Older clients may possess 'lifeskills' as a result of having faced and overcome life experiences and events that therapists may not yet have experience and 'lifeskills' may be a resource that can be drawn upon in therapy to enhance treatment outcome.
- A timeline exercise (a specific means of asking a client to provide an idiosyncratic autobiographical account of their life to date) may be beneficial for clients and therapists in appreciating the emotional and psychological strengths possessed by clients when attempting to empower clients to manage presenting problems more effectively.
- As ageing sometimes brings challenges, models such as selection, optimisation with compensation (SOC) may be useful to support clients to proactively and intentionally allocate psychological resources to prevent the further loss of function. SOC can be used in psychotherapy when older clients have realistic age-related challenges that require adjustment and adaptation (e.g., loss of physical function).

INTRODUCTION

Depression is often under-recognised and incorrectly diagnosed in later life, leading to under-treatment (Pocklinton, 2017). Psychological problems in later life are often seen as secondary to physical health problems, with research also suggesting that mental health problems in later life are poorly treated as a result (Frost et al., 2019). Evidence suggests that depression appears to be less common in older people and especially so when compared with working-age adults (Rodda, Walker and Carter, 2011).

Levy (2009) suggests that negative stereotypes about ageing are often so ingrained that they become internalised belief structures which operate unconsciously in our clients and ourselves and, as such, negative beliefs about ageing may not be questioned. An example includes inadvertently colluding with ideas suggesting that older people are too old to change, do not want therapy, and are inevitably doomed to experience low quality of life as a consequence of ageing. The application of gerontological theories to counselling may provide a useful antidote to this.

Gerontology, the multidisciplinary science of ageing, explores the physical, cognitive, emotional and social changes associated with the process of ageing. The usefulness of gerontology for therapists in working with older people is it provides factual information that can challenge and debunk common myths and misconceptions which many therapists may be unaware of themselves. For example, gauging clients' self-perceptions of ageing experiences and expectations at the start of therapy may assist in understanding their sense of possibility for change and growth (Konardt et al., 2021).

Data also suggests that levels of happiness are higher in older people and lower in adults of working age. Recent data has shown that the nadir period for happiness may be mid-life rather than later life, providing a challenge for all those who see depression as an inevitable outcome of ageing. Blanchflower (2020) presents compelling worldwide data demonstrating a U-shaped curve for life satisfaction and happiness. Therapists are encouraged to consult the NHS/Age UK *Older Adults Positive Practice Guide* (https://babcp.com/Therapists/Older-Adults-Positive-Practice-Guide) to enhance their preparedness when working with older people. One must also remember that ageing is less a state and more of a process for most people (Wahl, 2020) and there are as many experiences of ageing as there are older people. Thus, counsellors who work from a person-centred approach may find their clients to be socialised into treatment more comfortably.

Carstensen (2021) provides a good overview of the body of research on socio-emotional selectivity theory (SST) spanning a number of decades, demonstrating that as people age, they come to recognise the existence of finite time-horizons, where, having lived longer than is left remaining, priorities and goals change. As a result, people preferentially and selectively place greater emphasis on emotional stability and balance, which may suggest that older people will place greater value on counselling as it engenders emotional regulation. Mather and Carstensen (2005) also demonstrate a 'positivity effect' in memory where older adults selectively recall positive stimuli. Dicker (2019), reviewing current research into the positivity effect, suggests that this attentional bias may be employed in the treatment of late-life depression where, atypical to older age, positive recall is often difficult. In a study of people aged 60–80 years old positive imagery retraining, a cognitive technique, increased responses of pleasantness and effected structural brain changes, indicating a positive influence on affect and experience (Murphy et al., 2017). Dicker suggests such findings can engender effective interventions to promote positivity and optimism for the well-being of older clients.

Combining theories about ageing, such as selection, optimisation with compensation (SOC) (Baltes and Carstensen, 2003), which suggests that older people proactively invest in strategies to minimise loss of valued roles and goals, with person-centred approaches in counselling and psychotherapy may bring about an enhanced client experience and better treatment outcomes.

An age-appropriate approach to counselling is respectful of the skills and competences that older clients possess (Laidlaw, 2015). Consistent with this approach is a valuing of the 'lifeskills' clients develop over a lifetime. This simple idea recognises that older people will have lived longer than their counsellor and will have likely faced and overcome adversities over their lifetime (e.g., loss of spouse, changes to physical health and independence, role change) that the therapist may not yet have faced. This notion of lifeskills can be used to build a strong therapeutic relationship and to make use of the hard-earned form of wisdom from experience to empower our clients to better manage their current difficulties. Wisdom is often erroneously thought of as an outcome of age. However, this is unfortunately not the case (Bangen, Meeks and Jeste, 2013).

Research suggests that wisdom may be something people have to work to develop, reflecting an increase in competence in the fundamental pragmatics of human life (Staudinger and Glück, 2011). In reality, wisdom is rare and does not develop automatically. Baltes and Staudinger (2000) note that wisdom can be adjudged by how an individual deals with the recognition and management of uncertainty. Contemporary theories of wisdom suggest that this may be more likely to develop after one has engaged in a challenging and honest process of review and reflection: 'Wisdom-fostering forms of self-reflection require that individuals explore their own role in the occurrence of negative life events, confront and examine negative feelings, and do the effortful work of finding meaning in the difficult experience' (Weststrate and Glück, 2017: 810). Combining wisdom with lifeskills uses past experience as a teacher for how to deal with problems in the here and now (Laidlaw, 2021). This is the basis of our approach, termed 'wisdom enhancement', using timelines and lifeskills to support people to reflect on difficult life experiences in a structured way, in order to reflect on what may have come out of difficult experiences from the past and how this new learning may equip our clients to better deal with current difficulties. In this approach, developed by Laidlaw (2015), timelines are the means by which wisdom enhancement is enacted in person-centred psychological approaches.

WAYS OF WORKING

This is a case study of an older adult with Generalised Anxiety Disorder (GAD), which is the most common late-life anxiety and may be present for decades before detection and/or health-seeking (Lenze et al., 2005). GAD is denoted by excessive worry towards events where there is an actual or perceived lack of information to establish certainty. For older adults, health and ageing are concerns frequently surrounded with uncertainties about future outcomes.

Lynda, aged 67 years, was referred to our clinic because of panic attacks and GAD. Her main concern was that she had experienced a panic attack 18 months previously, and since then had frequent episodes of derealisation. Her panic attack had resulted in hospital admission to investigate her heart functioning, but no medically significant problems were detected. However, Lynda remained vigilant about her raised heart rate, 'jelly legs' and feelings of 'a bubble head'. When these symptoms arose, she interpreted them as evidence of either an imminent heart attack, onset of a stroke or possible madness. These episodes resulted in an escalating list of coping strategies, such as withdrawing from friendships, hobbies and shared social events with her husband, while simultaneously increasing control of household management and repeated checking for the personal safety of her family.

Lynda and her counsellor developed a shared conceptualisation of her panic attacks and worry cycles. Progress in understanding and controlling panic symptoms was reflected in a reduction in scores on standardised mood measures. Her counsellor encouraged her to engage in understanding the extent of her chronic worry and to continue with her sessions.

Standard CBT behavioural experiments and cognitive restructuring for GAD plus brief relaxation and mindfulness techniques were reducing negative affect and Lynda approached between-session tasks with care and thoroughness. However, by session eight she became significantly depressed, as she thought 'I can't cope if it happens again. I must be crazy if it's not a medical thing. It's my fault how I handle things.' The counsellor suggested to Lynda that they use a timeline to gain greater understanding of how she had managed challenging and ambiguous events in the past.

Timelines, as outlined by Laidlaw (2015), can be an effective technique to focus clients' attention towards recall of past successful strategies and to manage current problems in the here and now. Review of the timeline through directed Socratic questions (Laidlaw, 2021) allows the counsellor to simultaneously work with the client to reduce negative affect and increase positive affect. A fuller description of aims within the technique related to gerontological theories are explained by Laidlaw (2021). However, the explicit aim of using a timeline is to encourage clients to become more compassionate towards themselves and to recognise resilience in managing setbacks.

> The therapist can ask the client to put all notable life events from life on this timeline. The completion of the timeline is left to the client, although they can be based on overall life events, adverse life events, turning points (high or low), or a combination of all three. (Laidlaw, 2015: 149)

When using a timeline, the counsellor may ask the client what they observe from it in terms of how they perceive they have coped over their lifetime. For example, a counsellor may ask a client: 'Looking back at this timeline, what do you learn from dealing with setbacks? What does that tell you?'

It became evident from Lynda's timeline that she had successfully managed many distressing situations (see Figure 6.3.1). Lynda became aware of the contrast between her confidence in handling events at work and at home, since her retirement, a few years earlier. For example, reviewing her abrupt retirement from work she observed: 'It was a hasty decision because I felt old and incompetent. But I can see now I was valued.' Throughout her working life she had handled challenges and staff relations effectively. Now, at home, caring for her widowed mother, she felt life to be unpredictable, stressful and filled with grief for the loss of her father. From the timeline, she became aware that she was fearful about the development of dementia in herself and her family: 'I never let myself think about it. We don't talk about it. I haven't thought about things in this way before.'

In the following weeks Lynda reflected on her anxious predictions of becoming ill: 'It's like looking for the perfect insurance policy, that would guarantee everything will be ok, always!' Also, she reconsidered how to share the care of her mother: 'I've been so exhausted trying to do everything myself. It isn't feasible and my husband and son are so concerned for me. It makes sense now we lay it out like this.' Sharing of household responsibilities, including her mother's welfare, which had been the norm when she went out to work, were renegotiated and encouraged by her husband and son. Towards the end of therapy she had started to re-engage with friends and reminisce with her family about her father's life, both the happy and sad times. At the same time, scores on anxiety and depression measures had declined sharply by the end of therapy.

RESEARCH

There is strong evidence for the efficacy of psychotherapy with older people (Cuijpers et al., 2014a, 2014b, 2020; Gould, Coulson and Howard, 2012a, 2012b; Holvast et al., 2017: Kishita and Laidlaw, 2017). While a lot of evidence comes from academic research settings, more 'naturalistic' evidence can be found from Improving Access to Psychological Therapy (IAPT) services reporting national figures. These indicate that when older people do access therapy, they report good recovery rates and reduced attrition when compared to rates reported for working-age adults accessing IAPT (Chaplin et al., 2015; Pettit et al., 2017). In a more scientific approach, Cuijpers et al. (2014c) conducted a meta-analysis to examine the efficacy of psychotherapy (mainly CBT) for chronic worry (Generalised Anxiety Disorder). This included research into psychotherapy with older people and thus allows us to extrapolate results. The meta-analysis found low to moderate heterogeneity between studies and positive outcomes of psychotherapy for GAD, indicating a positive trend which continued at long-term assessment in favour of CBT. This finding was in contradiction to recent meta-analyses by Covin et al. (2008) and by Gould et al. (2012b), suggesting that CBT was less efficacious with older people. Kishita and Laidlaw (2017) explicitly addressed the question of CBT efficacy for GAD when subgroups of older people and working-age adults *are compared using the same metrics in a single integrative meta-analysis*. In this innovative study, Kishita and Laidlaw (2017) reported no statistically significant treatment differences between older people and working-age adults. Overall, however, effect sizes were moderate for older people (0.6) and large for working-age adults (0.9). Kishita and Laidlaw (2017) suggest differential outcome may be related to the poor adaptation of treatment protocols for use with older people that enable the CBT therapist to provide a treatment that is more properly age- and developmentally appropriate. While the majority of studies adopted standard CBT protocols with simplified procedural modifications, such as the use of mnemonic aids or simplifying homework forms, these modifications added little to improving treatment outcome, suggesting that a more robust approach to age-appropriate CBT may be necessary.

Kadri, Gracey and Leddy (2022) researched post traumatic growth (PTG) in older adults. PTG describes positive psychological changes developed in response to prior trauma or highly challenging life stressors. This personal growth is marked by an increased appreciation of life and of personal relationships, valuing personal strengths, openness to change and, often, a focus on spiritual matters. Kadri et al. (2022) found older adults experienced substantial levels of PTG following a lifetime of challenges and often traumatic experiences. They found that social support and recognition of older adults changing perspective was a key factor in developing the positive adaptions of PTG.

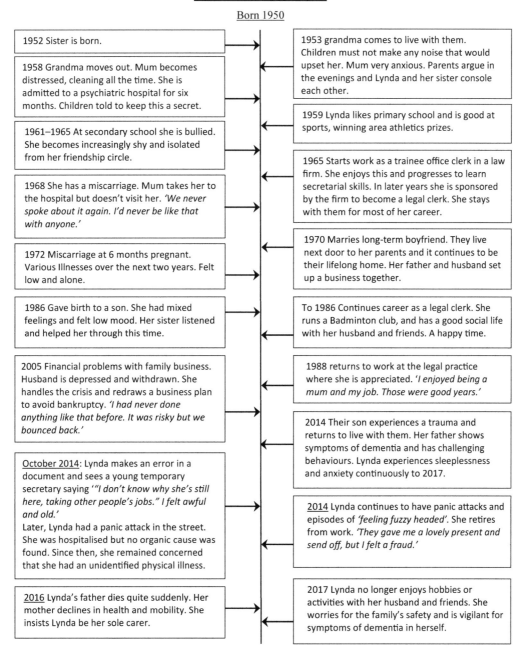

Figure 6.3.1 Timeline of Lynda Green

REFERENCES

Baltes, M.M., and Carstensen, L.L. (2003) The process of successful aging: selection, optimization, and compensation. In U.M. Staudinger and U. Lindenberger (Eds), *Understanding Human Development*. Boston, MA: Springer.

Baltes, P.B., and Staudinger, U.M. (2000) Wisdom: a metaheuristic (pragmatic) to orchestrate mind and virtue toward excellence. *American Psychologist*, 55, 122–136.

Bangen, K.J., Meeks, T.W., and Jeste, D.V. (2013) Defining and assessing wisdom: a review of the literature. *Americam Journal of Geriatric Psychiatry*, 21, 1254–1266.

Blanchflower, D. (2020) Is happiness U-shaped everywhere? Age and subjective well-being in 145 countries. *Journal of Population Economics*, 34, 575–624.

Carstensen, L.L. (2021) Socioemotional selectivity theory: the role of perceived endings in human motivation. *The Gerontologist*, 61, 1188–1196.

Chaplin, R., Farquharson, L., Clapp, M., and Crawford, M. (2015) Comparison of access, outcomes and experiences of older adults and working age adults in psychological therapy. *International Journal of Geriatric Psychiatry*, 30, 178–184.

Covin, R., Ouimet, A.J., Seeds, P.M., and Dozois, D.J. (2008) A meta-analysis of CBT for pathological worry among clients with GAD. *Journal of Anxiety Disorders*, 22(1), 108–116. doi: 10.1016/j.janxdis.2007.01.002

Cuijpers, P., Karyotaki, E., Eckshtain, D., et al. (2020c). Psychotherapy for Depression Across Different Age Groups: A Systematic Review and Meta-analysis. *JAMA Psychiatry*, 77(7), 694–702. doi:10.1001/jamapsychiatry.2020.0164

Cuijpers, P., Karyotaki, E., Pot, A.M., and Park, M. (2014a) Managing depression in older age: psychosocial interventions. *Maturitaas*, 79(2), 160–169.

Cuijpers, P., Karyotaki, E., Weitz, E., Andersson, G., Hollon, S.D., and van Straten, A. (2014b) The effects of psychotherapies for major depression in adults on remission, recovery and improvement: a meta-analysis. *Journal of Affective Disorders*, 159, 118–126. doi: 10.1016/j.jad.2014.02.026

Cuijpers, P., Sijbrandij, M., Koole, S., Huibers, M., Berking, M., and Andersson, G. (2014c) Psychological treatment of generalized anxiety disorder: a meta-analysis. *Clinical Psychology Review*, 34(2), 130–140. doi: 10.1016/j.cpr.2014.01.002

Dicker, E.E. (2019) *Research roundup: Healthy ageing and the positivity effect: identifying the regulatory mechanisms behind positivity bias in older adults*. Washington, DC: American Psychological Association Services. Available at www.apaservices.org/practice/ce/expert/healthy-aging (accessed 25 May 2022).

Frost, R., Beattie, A., Bahnu, C., Walters, K., and Ben-Shlomo, Y. (2019) Management of depression and referral of older people to psychological therapies: a systematic review of qualitative studies. *British Journal of General Practice*, 69(680), e171–e181. doi:10.3399/bjgp19X701297

Gould, R.L., Coulson, M.C., and Howard, R.J. (2012a) Cognitive behavioral therapy for depression in older people: a meta-analysis and meta-regression of randomized controlled trials. *Journal of the American Geriatrics Society*, 60(10), 1817–1830.

Gould, R.L., Coulson, M.C., and Howard, R.J. (2012b) Cognitive behavioral therapy for anxiety disorders in older people: a meta-analysis and meta-regression of randomized controlled trials. *Journal of the American Geriatrics Society*, 60(2), 218–229.

Holvast, F., Massoudi, B., Voshaar, R.C.O., and Verhaak, P.F. (2017) Non-pharmacological treatment for depressed older patients in primary care: a systematic review and meta-analysis. *PLoS One*, 12(9), e0184666

Kadri, A., Gracey, F., and Leddy, A. (2022) What factors are associated with posttraumatic growth in older adults? A systematic review. *Clinical Gerontologist*, 9 February, 1–18. doi: 10.1080/07317115.2022.2034200

Kishita, N. and Laidlaw, K. (2017) Cognitive behavior therapy for generalized anxiety disorder: is CBT equally effective in adults of working age and older adults? *Clinical Psychology Review*, 52, 124–136.

Kornadt, A.E., Kessler, E.-M., Wurm, S., Bowen, C.E., Gabrian, M., and Klusmann, V. (2020) Views on ageing: A lifespan perspective. *European Journal of Ageing*, 17(4), 387–401. https://doi.org/10.1007/s10433-019-00535-9

Laidlaw, K. (2015) *Cognitive Behaviour Therapy for Older People: An Introduction.* London: Sage.

Laidlaw, K. (2021) CBT with older people. In A. Wenzel (Ed.), *The American Psychological Association's Handbook of Cognitive Behavioral Therapy. Vol. 2: Applications.* Washington, DC: American Psychological Association.

Lenze, E.J., Mulsant, B.H., Mohlman, J., Shear, M.K., Dew, M.A., Schulz, R., Miller, M.D., Tracey, B., and Reynolds, C.F. (2005) Generalized anxiety disorder in late life: lifetime course and comorbidity with major depressive disorder. *The American Journal of Geriatric Psychiatry*, 13, 77–80.

Levy, B.R. (2009) Stereotype embodiment: a psychosocial approach to aging. *Current Directions in Psychological Science*, 18, 332–336.

Mather, M., and Carstensen, L.L. (2005) Ageing and motivated cognition: the positivity effect in attention and memory. *Trends in Cognitive Sciences*, 9, 496–502.

Murphy, S.E., O'Donoghue, M.C., Blackwell, S.E., Nobre, A.C., Browning, M., and Holmes, E.A. (2017) Increased rostral anterior cingulate activity following positive mental imagery training in healthy older adults. *Social Cognitive and Affective Neuroscience*, 12(12), 1950–1958.

NHS and Age UK (n.d.) *Older Adults Positive Practice Guide.* London: NHS/Age UK. Now included in the NHS-E IAPT Manual, hosted on the BACP website at https://babcp.com/Therapists/Older-Adults-Positive-Practice-Guide

Pettit, S., Qureshi, A., Lee, W., Stirzaker, A., Gibson, A., Henley, W., and Byng, R. (2017) Variation in referral and access to new psychological therapy services by age: an empirical quantitative study. *British Journal of General Practice*, 67(660), e453–e459.

Pocklington, C. (2017) Depression in older adults. *British Journal of Medical Practitioners*, 10(1), a1007.

Rodda, J., Walker, Z., and Carter, J. (2011) Depression in older adults. *BMJ-British Medical Journal*, 343(8), d5219.

Staudinger, U.M., and Glück, J. (2011) Intelligence and wisdom. In R.J. Sternberg and S.B. Kaufman (Eds), *The Cambridge Handbook of Intelligence* (pp. 827–846). Cambridge: Cambridge University Press. https://psycnet.apa.org/doi/10.1017/CBO9780511977244.041

Wahl, H.-W. (2020) Aging successfully: possible in principle? Possible for all? Desirable for all? *Integrative Psychological & Behavioral Science*, 54(2), 251–268.

Weststrate, N.M., and Glück, J. (2017) Hard-earned wisdom: exploratory processing of difficult life experience is positively associated with wisdom. *Developmental Psychology*, 53, 800–814.

RECOMMENDED READING

Laidlaw, K. (2015) *Cognitive Behaviour Therapy for Older People: An Introduction.* London: Sage.

This 'Counselling older people' chapter reflects on how the gerontological theory of wisdom can be used within traditional CBT to augment treatment outcome. For the readers who wish to learn more about this topic, we recommend reading this book.

Steffen, A.M., Thompson, L.W., and Gallagher-Thompson, D. (2022) *Treating Later-life Depression: A Cognitive-behavioral Therapy Approach. Clinician Guide* (2nd ed.). New York: Oxford University Press.

This book is a must have textbook on applying CBT with older people.

NHS and Age UK (n.d.) *Older Adults Positive Practice Guide.* London: NHS/Age UK. Now included in the NHS-E IAPT Manual, hosted on the BACP website at https://babcp.com/Therapists/Older-Adults-Positive-Practice-Guide

This guide was supported by Age UK and NHS-E and was overseen by an expert reference chaired by Professor Ken Laidlaw. It is intended to be a resource for clinicians, GPs and service managers to identify and overcome internal and external barriers to older people accessing psychological therapies and counselling.

6.4 COUPLE THERAPY

CATE CAMPBELL

OVERVIEW AND KEY POINTS

Sex and couple therapists are seeing a wider range of relationship presentations than ever before. They consequently need to be familiar with different kinds of relationships (together-apart, polyamorous, same sex, asexual, for instance), requiring extensive knowledge and skills. Relationships provide a form of personal development, in which couples can re-enact and repair the wounds of much earlier attachments. Relationships can, thus, provide space and support for growth or become anti-developmental battlegrounds where each partner's motivation is to defend themselves rather than to cooperate.

- The most toxic relationships can be the most stable.
- Technology has made it easier to develop new relationships, but can feel oppressive as couples remain so constantly in touch.
- Conflict must be addressed and safety assessed as the first priority in couple therapy.
- Not all relationships can, or should, be fixed.
- Most couple therapies aim to improve the couple dynamic.

INTRODUCTION

The divorce rate began to rise following World War I when women had acquired more rights in marriage, socially and politically. Huge numbers had also been empowered by wartime employment and domestic independence, and were consequently unsettled by the return of their husbands and loss of their jobs. In 1938, this resulted in the establishment of the Marriage Guidance Council, later rebranded as Relate, by clergyman Herbert Gray.

Further disruption to family life in World War II led to major research into couple relationships, led by former army psychiatrist Henry Dicks. A major finding was that relationships are a form of self-development and that couples experience unconscious attraction to one another when they have the potential to help heal each other's earlier psychological wounds. Typically, partners initially find each other very different from, say, their overbearing father. Later in the relationship, similarities emerge and the hope of overcoming them this time can keep couples endlessly locked into defensive battle. They use the psychological strategy of projection, whereby unwanted parts of themselves are attributed to their partner or even evoked in their partner (projective identification). Changing the dynamic between the partners was Dicks' (1967/2015) focus in couple counselling, which is done by helping the couple to recognise what's happening, own their own vulnerabilities, stop and reject projections.

Family therapy was evolving at around the same time, also producing couple counselling, which explored the patterns of thought and behaviour between partners and how these could be perturbed to produce change. A systemic focus also encouraged couples to appreciate how their different life experiences and the external events creating pressure on the relationship could be more influential than the quality of the relationship itself. Reframing events in ways that challenge partners' assumptions, or even just hypothesising about alternative ways of thinking, can be revelatory.

More recent behavioural approaches have also sought to change couple dynamics and interactions. In the 1970s and 1980s, couples researcher John Gottman confirmed that many relationships are characterised by couples misunderstanding one another and discounting what they hear (e.g., Gottman, 1979). Going on to set up a 'love lab', where couples were observed living together, he established that the ratio of positive to negative interactions between a couple could predict the longevity of the relationship. A particular danger was the presence of what he called 'The Four Horsemen of the Apocalypse' – criticism, defensiveness, contempt and stonewalling – which the therapy aims to overcome and replace with mutuality and respect. Significantly, Gottman found gay and lesbian couples to be kinder, more self-validating and to use more humour, while straight couples were more negative and displayed more physiological arousal.

Around 42–43% of marriages now end in divorce, but divorce figures have fallen slightly overall in England and

Wales, except among the over-65 age group where they increased in 2020 (ONS, 2022). At the time of writing, countries with the harshest lockdowns during the coronavirus pandemic appear to have had the steepest jump in divorce applications, with a surge each time lockdowns eased. This is similar to the rise in people contacting relationship therapists following the summer and Christmas holidays when couples' issues become more obvious.

Technology has exacerbated couples' dissatisfaction with one another. Relationships which begin online can often be disappointing in real life, but partners hold out for the connection they experienced virtually. There are more expectations that couples should remain in touch throughout the day, and they are more able to monitor each other's online activity, so disputes arise when a partner believes they're being neglected. It's also much easier to look up old flames, start new relationships and engage in online sex. As a result, couples in therapy are often recovering from affairs where there has been no in-person sex or no sex at all. The pseudo-intimacy of online chat can, however, increase feelings of attachment and belief that a love affair is underway. Many partners say such emotional affairs are harder to bear than sexual relationships, which can be dismissed as merely 'physical'.

SPLIT AGENDA

It isn't always possible or desirable for a relationship to continue, whatever the cause of conflict. Frequently, therapy is about helping the couple to separate, remain friends and co-parent effectively and safely. Sometimes therapy is attempted as a last resort, for one partner to fix the other or just so that couples can say they have tried everything.

A partner may attend therapy to end the relationship because the other isn't hearing or can't accept the relationship is over, leading to emotional scenes as the reality sinks in. Partners may initially need to be seen separately as either or both may be experiencing bewilderment, grief and guilt.

WAYS OF WORKING

The priority when couples initially present is to ascertain what they want to change, whether they are safe to work with together and how to stabilise them. A solution-focused approach in the first session helps to establish this. For instance, asking what has changed since a couple booked the session immediately reveals their attitude to the process. Some partners are unwilling to change themselves and bring the other to be fixed, hoping *they* will be validated. Difficulty identifying what they want to change, or wildly differing views about this, offers information about how/whether they communicate (McKergow, 2021). Asking what small change could make a difference demonstrates their flexibility, resilience and potential engagement with the change process (Miller and Rollnick, 2012).

With many couples, it's quickly evident that there is considerable blame and arguing, so reducing conflict is a priority. Exploring the most recent argument, including what each partner was intending and believed the other meant, can reveal misunderstandings and provide meaning. The way partners trigger one another is also important to establish. Having an individual session with each partner allows them to tell the story of their relationship from their own point of view and without interruption from the other. It also allows privacy to explore safety, discuss sensitive issues and consider alternative viewpoints without the partner feeling they have lost face or backed down in front of the other. This can mean the therapist is aware of secrets, such as affairs or plans to end the relationship, which the other partner may not know about. It is important to discuss how this will be managed, as knowing will inevitably change the therapist's perspective. In practice, speaking about the secret in their individual session leads many partners to reveal it to the other, so their situation may have changed considerably when they return for a session together.

Where domestic abuse is revealed, it is usually dangerous to work with the couple together and safety becomes the priority, so all therapists working with couples should be trained in management of relationship abuse. It is worth noting that sometimes the most reasonable partners, who seem deeply concerned about the other's mental health, can be the most controlling. A clue is their inability to fully take responsibility for any problems themselves and a partner who seems numb, confused or chaotic.

There are numerous therapeutic approaches that therapists adopt in couple therapy. Some of the most commonplace are introduced below.

PSYCHODYNAMIC APPROACHES

Where there is ongoing conflict, it can be helpful to continue seeing each partner individually with a joint appointment every third session. This allows time to coach couples in managing their anxiety so they can walk away from an argument, despite an overwhelming need to be heard and urge for immediate dispute resolution. Psychoeducation about couple dynamics and the likelihood of projective identification can be helpful, particularly when combined with body scanning exercises to notice somatic evidence of mood changes and triggers (Campbell, 2018). Very early and traumatic memories are 'remembered' by the body rather than cognitively. Consequently, domestic situations often provoke frightening or painful bodily reactions which actually relate to historic situations, often within the family of origin. Partners, however, attribute their reactions to each other – not realising that, for instance, their insistence the laundry is folded in a particular way is due to the repercussions in their family of origin if it was not. This situation can then be unconsciously replayed with the partner and, sometimes, with the children too.

In joint sessions, couples are able to discuss and celebrate their progress, quickly recognising that attributing all the blame to the partner also gives away volition. They are then increasingly able to appreciate they are on the same side, cooperating in creating and maintaining a life that suits them both. This may mean renegotiating space, togetherness and separation as well as ways to both ask for what they need without shame and manage refusals kindly on both sides. Couples who value spontaneity may be reluctant to plan, but considerable distress and resentment arises from conflicting expectations. Learning to check expectations before an event – whether this is a night out or who will be doing the school run – can avoid arguing and disappointment.

'Imago Therapy' (Hendrix, 2020) is a psychodynamic approach which aims to reduce relationship conflict and power struggles by making couples aware of their triggers while listening and communicating, so partners behave more empathically towards each other. They will, for instance, participate in exercises which demonstrate that their current relationship complaints reflect the emotional deficits from their childhoods, and become aware of relationship dynamics which replay the past.

ATTACHMENT

Awareness of attachment behaviours is helpful to couple therapists. Partners with avoidant/dismissive attachment can appear securely attached, but may be somatising distress beneath a calm exterior. After an initial enthusiastic interest in sex, they may avoid any form of intimacy, particularly as the relationship becomes closer, and experience shame around showing emotion. This can be hard for an anxious/preoccupied partner whose focus is on being loved and wanted, despite finding this uncomfortable. Constantly seeking evidence of being loved/not loved, they may imagine scenarios which will make them feel better or prove they are cared for, becoming upset and angry when they don't occur. How well they manage relationships (and therapy) may depend on their ability to mentalise, which involves the ability to think about the thinking of oneself and others. Although they may see themselves as empathic, and talk constantly about feelings, empathy may actually be limited, and they may have difficulty listening, paying more attention to what's in their head than what is actually happening. They can become upset rapidly during therapy sessions, so it is important the therapist remains calm and focuses on managing the arousal rather than the content of the session (Asen and Fonagy, 2021). Similarly, when couples report arguments, asking how they resolved them, and managed their own feelings, is more useful than discussing the row's causes. These clients and those with a disorganised attachment style may all find it difficult to ask for what they need, and so use sideways strategies or magical thinking.

A disorganised style is often associated with childhood abuse, neglect or loss, making intimacy difficult. Someone may be outright mean or, confusingly, extremely solicitous in order to control the behaviour of the other, which is something to look out for. Indeed, although pathologising and labelling is not advisable, a general awareness of attachment behaviours helps couple therapists to understand the inconsistencies they may encounter, depending on whether someone's attachment defences have been triggered. This is another reason for seeing the couple separately as well as together, as they may initially be too triggered by their partner's presence to benefit from couple sessions.

'Emotionally focused therapy' (Johnson, 2020) works in a short-term, structured way with couples' attachment injuries and further attachment damage they have caused one another. The couple are helped to rely less on one another for validation while having consideration for each other, acknowledging their own imperfections and settling on the same side.

SYSTEMIC THERAPIES

Expectations are not just about short-term events; each partner brings scripts about the rules for living from their past, usually assuming these are shared by their partner. Systemic approaches can help couples explore the contexts affecting them. Genograms – family trees which reveal not just who people are but how they think and behave – can help to reveal differences in core attitudes and expectations which have never been recognised or discussed, family alliances, disputes and beliefs. General genograms are illuminating, but exploring specific themes, such as family, religion, class, vulnerability or finance, can offer additional insight into why some aspects of a couple's life are such minefields. Systemic questions use the language of difference and comparison, requiring people to think in new ways about their situation. This is particularly effective at disrupting habitual narratives, broadening the way couples think and addressing difficult topics. For instance:

- Which of you is more likely to sabotage the plans we've discussed?
- Were you arguing more or less before you changed jobs?
- What will happen if you keep arguing?
- What would your children advise if they could see you now?
- When you cry, what does your partner do?
- What might be lost if you didn't argue?

Clients are often surprised by these questions and also by the therapist's curiosity and overt hypothesising about their situation. Therapists will often point out that many ideas we believe are 'right' and unchangeable are actually social constructions, not 'truths'. The idea of The One True Love is often referred to by people in relationship therapy, for instance. However, this romantic idea originated in eighteenth-century novels and is linked to religious ideas about fidelity, as if these were natural bedfellows. It is a cause of much distress to couples that their relationship isn't as perfect as fiction leads us to believe it should be. If their love was strong enough, they reason, the relationship would work. Discussion of where such fixed beliefs come from can reassure couples that their relationships are not the disaster they imagine.

CASE STUDY

Marianna and Kurt attended therapy in crisis following Kurt's affair. Marianna experienced this as a severe attachment injury, as she had recently had a stillbirth at 25 weeks' gestation following four years of gruelling fertility treatment. It would have been easy to focus on this, but the therapist explored both partner's experiences, learning they had both found treatment dehumanising, which had taken its toll on their relationship. Kurt revealed he felt unable to express this or grieve openly when the pregnancy ended. Exploring his attitude to emotion, it emerged he felt breaking down in front of Marianna would be worse than avoiding her. He feared she would see him as weak, as would family and friends, news which Marianna was unaware of and which saddened her. *She* had thought Kurt was avoiding her because he blamed her for the miscarriage, and they had become more estranged.

Kurt subsequently began confiding in a female work colleague, and then felt reluctantly obliged to repay her with the affair. Although Marianna found this hard to understand, therapy helped them both to challenge taken-for-granted ideas which made them feel like failures and to recognise their resilience and strong bond, allowing them to both grieve and move forward together.

Similarly, feminist therapies explore how power, both in the relationship and other contexts, is affecting clients, acknowledging social constructions and interrogating unhelpful beliefs in either partner. Although unequal treatment and women's sense of responsibility for many emotional and practical aspects of the relationship would likely emerge, feminist therapies can be used to explore anyone's issues, as the focus is on context and intersectionality through a social constructionist lens.

TRANSACTIONAL ANALYSIS

Transactional Analysis (TA) (Lapworth and Sills, 2011) argues that we play out 'scripts' from our early life through different relationships and in different ego states. Therapy aims to help couples recognise and manage the resulting patterns and respond from an appropriate ego state, rather than reproducing historical voices or experiences. The couple's dynamics are framed as games, whereby they collude to avoid change. The Drama Triangle (Karpman, 1968) can be used to explore most games, noting the way couples move around the triangle in the roles of victim, persecutor or rescuer. They may enact this between them or recruit a third person or context, such as a child, in-law, work, hobby, illness, addiction or sex.

REFERENCES

Asen, E. and Fonagy, P. (2021) *Mentalization-Based Treatment with Families*. New York: Guilford Press.
Campbell, C. (2018) *Love and Sex in a New Relationship*. Abingdon, UK: Routledge.
Dicks, H. (1967/2015) *Marital Tensions*. New York: Routledge.
Gottman, J. (1979) *A Couple's guide to communication*. London: Research Press.
Hendrix, H. (2020) *Getting the Love You Want*. London: Simon and Schuster.
Johnson, S.M. (2020) *The Practice of Emotionally Focused Couple Therapy* (3rd ed.). New York: Routledge.
Karpman, S.B. (1968) Fairy tales and script drama analysis. *Transactional Analysis Bulletin*, 7, 39–43.
Lapworth, P. and Sills, C. (2011) *An Introduction to Transactional Analysis*. London: Sage.
McKergow, M. (2021) *The Next Generation of Solution Focused Practice*. Abingdon, UK: Routledge.
Miller, W.R. and Rollnick, S. (2012) *Motivational Interviewing: Helping People Change* (3rd ed.). New York: Guilford Press.
ONS (2022) *Divorce Statistics: 2020*, 1 February. London: Office for National Statistics. Available at www.ons.gov.uk/Peoplepopulationandcommunity/birthsdeathsandmarriages/divorce/bulletins/divorcesinenglandandwales/2000 (accessed 15 February 2022).

RECOMMENDED READING

Martin, B. (2021) *The Art of Giving and Receiving*. Eugene, OR: Luminare Press.

This book uses the Wheel of Consent to facilitate sex and intimacy in couples, facilitating ways for them to jointly agree how they want to be together.

Perel, E. (2007) *Mating in Captivity* London: Hodder and Stoughton.

This book discusses the way couples can become so familiar that sex loses its appeal, and how to restore intimacy.

Scheinkman, M. and Fishbane, M.D. (2004) The Vulnerability Cycle: working with impasses in couple therapy. *Family Process*, 43(3), 279–299. www.kfr.nu/wp-content/uploads/2012/08/Vulnerablility-Cycle.pdf (accessed 19 February 2022).

This paper provides a detailed explanation of ways to reveal couples' underlying vulnerabilities and patterns of behaviour which maintain their stuckness, offering a variety of interventions to promote healing and change.

6.5 SYSTEMIC FAMILY THERAPY

RUDI DALLOS

OVERVIEW AND KEY POINTS

Family therapy embraces a variety of therapeutic approaches devoted to promoting changes in the dynamics of families, but the most prevalent and influential of these models is 'systemic' family therapy. The founding conceptual framework for family therapy derived from cybernetics and systems theories developed in the 1950s. The distinguishing feature of this approach is the view that problems typically displayed by individuals are seen to arise from the transactional processes in the family or other intimate relational system in which the person is immersed. Systemic family therapy includes the idea that not only family dynamics but relationships, for example between the family members and the school situation, processes within therapeutic/clinical teams, mental health units (e.g., residential therapeutic settings), dynamics between organisations (e.g., social services) and mental health, may also play a significant role in the development and maintenance of problems.

- Family therapy sees problems as caused by and maintained by relational processes.
- Family therapy involves working with family members and not just individuals.
- 'Family' is used in a broad sense and can include all significant relationships.
- Family therapy is usually, but not invariably, conducted by teams.
- The founding conceptual ideas of family therapy drew on cybernetic and systems theory.

INTRODUCTION

There have been extensive debates about whether a systemic view implies that families are seen to 'cause' problems, and many family therapists prefer to by-pass this debate and instead adopt a pragmatic view that promoting changes in family dynamics can help ameliorate problems, such as anorexia, self-harm, depressions, anxiety and psychosis. The most obvious difference between family therapy and other forms of therapy is that the target interventions are aimed predominantly at altering family relationships rather than individuals. Consistent with this, family therapists spend most of their time working with groups of people rather than individuals. Of course, some other forms of therapy, such as group therapies, also involve working with groups of people. However, family therapy aims to focus on natural groups of people, such as families, who have spent considerable time with each other. This exposure to each other over time is seen as leading to the development of patterned, repetitive and predictable forms of interaction, and it is these patterns – what goes on between rather than what goes on within people – that are the focus of interest.

THERAPEUTIC ASSUMPTIONS AND PRACTICE

Systemic family therapy was one of the first of the therapeutic approaches to employ live supervision of the therapeutic work. Originally this was done with a team observing the session from behind an observation screen or on video. Alternatively, there could be an ongoing process (in-room consultation) with a colleague in the room with the family regularly offering advice. This emphasis on live supervision was based on the recognition of the complexity of working with the whole family at the same time, and also on the idea that there needed to be some removal from the interaction in the room to be able to detect some of the family patterns maintaining the problems. The therapist would be consulted regularly by the team via telephone or an earpiece, and given suggestions: for example, to ask the family to enact how the problems occur at home, to change seats, to engage in role-play or sculpt, for one person to speak more or less, to explore certain areas more, such as their attempted solutions to the problems, and so on. After about 40 minutes, the therapist generally took a break to talk with the team and then returned with some substantive interventions, such as a reframe: for example, describing their intentions in a more positive way or suggesting 'homework' tasks, such as the parents changing roles in relation to a child – who puts her to bed, or gets her up for school, etc.

FROM PATTERNS AND PROCESSES TO BELIEFS AND NARRATIVES

The central concept of systemic family therapy is that family members are mutually influencing each other through their communications at both verbal and non-verbal levels. Over time families are seen to develop predictable patterns of interaction and this is necessary for them to be able to coordinate their activities and manage the demands of life, education, work, leisure and intimacy. They also need to be able to change and adapt to challenges and unexpected demand and crises. One guiding idea has been that the demands for change escalate at critical transitional points in the life of a family, such as the birth of a child, the death of a member, marriages, starting school, and so on (Carter and McGoldrick, 1988). This may coincide with a family experiencing some distress and crises such that they cannot manage the transition and instead it becomes avoided by developing a symptom. For example, illness in a parent at a point when a child is about to leave home may mean that the child feels unable to go, is less able to engage in friendships and romantic relationships and may subsequently become depressed or withdrawn. Unfortunately, this may become embedded into the family dynamic such that it becomes increasingly difficult for the child to manage the transition and the focus becomes more and more on 'their' depression rather than a recognition that problems were triggered by the difficulties the family was facing in making the changes. This had been described as the family becoming 'stuck', and perversely the dynamics serve to maintain a symptom.

Family therapy has seen a gradual shift from an emphasis on patterns of actions to an emphasis on the construction of meanings and their creation in families and between the family and the therapist. Inherent in this was a change in the perceived role of the therapist as less responsible for promoting changes in patterns of actions and more like a consultant who works alongside a family to co-create some new, more productive ways of the family seeing their situation. Furthermore, this represented a move towards an increased sensitivity to therapeutic relationships. Rather than trying to adopt an 'objective' stance, the therapist is encouraged to be continually reflective – to monitor their perceptions, beliefs, expectations, needs and feelings, especially in terms of how these may in turn have an influence on the family. Earlier approaches largely adopted a *functionalist* view of problems: families were seen as interacting systems in which symptoms functioned to preserve stability and viability of the family (Minuchin, 1974). In a perverse way, painful and distressing symptoms, rather than threatening family life and stability, were often seen as holding families together: symptoms were seen as distracting from or diverting conflicts, anxieties and fears (often unconsciously held) from other areas of the family's experience. This view was challenged on the grounds that the function of a symptom was not there to be 'discovered', but was the therapist's hypothesis. In turn, how difficulties were handled – the attempted solutions – was seen as linked to the wider belief system of the family.

A typical view in families is that the source of their problems lies in one member and may represent a form of diagnosable condition, similar to a form of 'illness', for example anorexia, attention deficit disorder, psychosis, depression, and so on. Once established, such assumptions can become increasingly painful to confront. For example, if the child's symptoms become severe, the parents may feel guilty and blameworthy when the therapist attempts to focus on their relationships. This may be perceived by parents to suggest the implication that their conflicts have in a sense been the cause of the problems. Other processes can also be seen to operate in families, for example, young children may discover the power that a symptom of illness confers, such as being able to avoid school and unpleasant duties, and gaining sympathy and attention. Therefore, a child may start to collude with this state of affairs and continue to display symptoms, in part because of the apparent advantages he or she gains (Haley, 1976). This in turn can serve to confirm for the whole family, including the child, the beliefs that the child is the source of the problems. A frequent dynamic is also that the parents hold different beliefs and disagree on how to treat the child (e.g., discipline versus sympathy), which leads to contradictory stances towards their child or to a position where they feel frozen and unable to make decisions regarding how to solve the problems.

CONTEMPORARY PRACTICE OF FAMILY THERAPY

Most family therapists and teams now adopt approaches which are less focused on assuming responsibility for attempting to alter processes and patterns of behaviours in families to a more collaborative approach than the early pioneers. Although teams and observation screens are still used, there are attempts to be more transparent in the process of family therapy. A key feature of contemporary practice is the use of *reflecting teams* (Andersen, 1987; White and Epston, 1990). Instead of consulting in relative secret with an anonymous supervision team, the discussions between the therapist and the team are held openly in front of the family, so that the team members share their thoughts and concerns with the family and also voice any personal connections that team members have with what they have heard about the family. Through the team's discussion, the family is invited to consider alternative stories and explanations regarding their lives together. This may allow different family members who are holding opposing views to feel understood and perhaps enable them to move on to more constructive stories. Importantly, the reflecting team enables family members to hear and perhaps internalise a different conversation rather than simply be asked to accept a different explanation. In turn, the family members are invited to reflect back on the reflecting team discussion regarding what they found helpful, interesting, useful and less helpful. The guiding idea is that family members may connect with the stories in different ways and be able to choose what they found to be helpful. More implicitly, it communicates the idea that there are multiple ways of seeing events, helping to free up some of the family's more rigid ways of thinking that they may have developed as a result of their sense of anxiety, failure and desperation.

ATTACHMENT THEORY

Although ideas from attachment theory were an early influence on family therapy, they have resurfaced as being relevant. It has been argued that Bowlby (1969, 1988) was one of the innovators of family therapy in that he was one of the first to suggest that therapy should involve working jointly with members of a family. In addition, attachment theory incorporates concepts from systems theory in describing the bond between a parent and a child as a self-corrective feedback system. Although clearly relevant to family therapy, it is only relatively recently that attachment-based family therapies have come to hold a significant place in the family therapy movement. Some key contributions it offers are to consider how family difficulties may have been prompted by attachment disruptions, parents separating, a child losing a bond with her father following a divorce. Alongside a consideration of current attachment dynamics in the family, there is a focus on transgenerational processes, for example, the parents own childhood attachment disruptions. Importantly, the emphasis is also on how life events, such as a bereavement, illness or accident, may have temporarily unbalanced the family attachment system, but that this has become stuck around the anxiety and insecurity that has been experienced (Dallos, 2006; Dallos and Vetere, 2021; Marvin and Stewart, 1990).

Attachment-based family therapies emphasise that these attachment issues drive relational patterns. A core theme in assisting families is to help them to feel secure and safe in the therapeutic situation. This involves the family therapist becoming a transitional attachment figure, like a parent or uncle to the family. From this 'secure base' they are more able to understand and be able to manage the emotional conflicts and stresses that may adversely shape their interactions and disrupt their attempts to solve their problems (Bowlby, 1988). This includes parents becoming aware of how their own attachment experiences may be shaping their parenting, marital dynamics and emotional coping strategies. Key to this is the idea that parents' attempts to apply 'corrective scripts' – to do things differently and better than their parents had with them – may, despite their best intentions, be causing problems (Byng-Hall, 1995). For example, a father may attempt to be more emotionally available for his daughter than his own parents had been for him, but this may unfortunately serve to make it difficult for his daughter to also stay emotionally connected to her mother after their divorce.

FAMILIES AND WIDER SYSTEMS

Systemic family therapy adopts a broader focus than on the dynamics of the immediate family (Campbell and Draper, 1985; Dallos and Draper, 2015). A central idea is that families are involved in and influenced by a variety of different contexts. Importantly, this includes a consideration of wider cultural contexts in terms of differences in cultural values about family life, gender roles and expectations about the relationships across the generations. What may initially appear to be family problems may, for example, be helpfully seen as confusions and conflicts related to cultural values and expectations. As an example, second-generation Asian children may feel powerful conflicts between adopting the values of western, British culture and maintaining a connection and loyalty to their Asian cultures. The parents may feel a sense of betrayal or disloyalty to a child who appears to have rejected their values, and this can be played out as an interpersonal conflict in the family. The young person may, in turn, be critical and disappointed that their parents do not understand or try to help them with their dilemmas.

WAYS OF WORKING

A consideration of wider systems is also related to thinking about the various external systems that a family is involved with and the relationships and processes between these systems. For example, a family may be concerned about how a child is experiencing school, their relationships with other children and the staff. Likewise, the school staff may have concerns about the family, and wish or need to involve them in decisions that need to be made about a child in the school situation. In some cases, some difficulties in communication may occur between a family and a school, with misunderstandings possibly aggravating difficulties that a child is displaying. A common scenario is where a child displays significant problems at home. For example, Jonathan, aged 13, was reported by his parents to show frequent outbursts of anger at home but appeared to be well behaved at school. His teachers noticed that at times he seemed preoccupied and upset about things at home, so they contacted his parents. However, this had the unfortunate consequence of making the parents feel inadequate and to blame, and had an effect of aggravating the situation. One consequence of this escalating process was that they turned to child mental health services to try to gain a diagnosis of attention deficit hyperactivity disorder (ADHD) for their son. They also became angry with what they felt were accusations from the school, which in turn generated concern in the school. School staff eventually contacted social services because they feared that Jonathan might be at 'risk' or harm. Consequently, the involvement of social services further fuelled the problems and led the parents to feel as though they were being blamed more by the school and social services and to become more angry and committed to seeking a diagnosis.

A systemic perspective can assist in considering how various systems interact and how processes are escalating in unhelpful ways. In the example above, it might be that family therapy is at the centre of initiating some change in how these various systems are interacting. However, it might also be the case that social services or the school are able to apply such a perspective and initiate some changes. A starting point can be to develop a multi-context systemic formulation. This can include a visual mapping of the various professional and family systems that are involved (see Figure 6.5.1 for an example).

An initial mapping can start to reveal which systems are involved and also to consider the relationships between them. For example, that the school and social services have started to develop frequent communication and the school and family have a more difficult conflictual relationship. It also became apparent in this example that the extended family has little communication with any of the professional systems. In this case, the maternal grandparents were closely involved with Jonathan and his parents, and when they were invited to attend for a family session it transpired that they were strongly advising the parents to seek a diagnosis of ADHD. The parents in fact were concerned about their own parenting abilities, but also about some bullying at school, which they felt Jonathan had kept a secret from the school and which they felt the school was not taking seriously enough.

Pursuing an analysis of the interplay of different systems can start to reveal that there are potential difficulties in various parts of such a network of systems and also in misunderstandings that have led to an escalation of negative processes between the different parties. Here the social services agency had recently received a critical report of their work, and were anxious to avoid the 'risk' of child abuse and possible further negative allegations. Partly as a consequence of this, their communication with the school was fuelled by some anxiety and concerns about the parents, which escalated rather than contained and resolved the situation. The role of a family therapy team in such a multiple system may be to help contain anxieties, as much in the professional systems as within the family. In some cases, this can involve initiating a meeting with representatives from the various agencies, such as school staff, social services and colleagues in mental health services. This is an increasingly important role that family therapy teams hold.

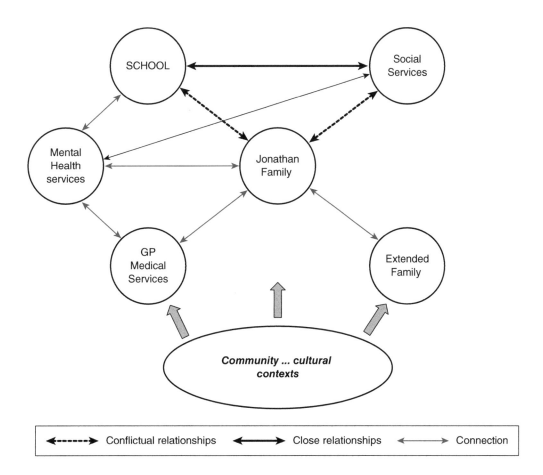

Figure 6.5.1 Mapping of family and professional systems

At the same time, they need to be skilful in reassuring the family so that they are not seen, as in this example, simply to be colluding with other professional to further blame the family.

RESEARCH

Systemic family therapy has developed in various ways from a focus on family patterns to a consideration of beliefs and the influence on families of wider cultural ideas. The developments have been supported by research evidence, which has established the effectiveness of family therapy. For example, it is the recommended treatment for young people suffering with a range of problems, including eating disorders, depression, couples problems and psychosis, and a recent major trial has shown its electiveness in helping families with a young person who is self-harming (Dallos and Draper, 2015). We are conducting a major study to examine the effectiveness of an integration of attachment and systemic family therapy (SAFE) for families with a child who has a diagnosis of autism (McKenzie et al., 2021). Our study indicated that families did find the approach helpful, especially in helping them to manage the so-called 'meltdowns' or escalating conflictual processes associated with autism.

There has been considerable integration and assimilation across various forms of therapy, so, for example, systemic ideas are included in some individual therapies and, likewise, systemic therapy has continually drawn on ideas from attachment theory and psychodynamic theory. Systemic therapy has also expanded to consider not only family dynamics, but also the relationships between and within services. Not infrequently, work with families has shown that confusions and conflicts between the professionals with whom they are involved can contribute significantly to 'stuckness' or even the escalation of their problems. Thinking about problems in such a multilevel way in terms of complex interacting systems continues to be an important area of development in systemic family therapy.

REFERENCES

Andersen, T. (1987) The reflecting team: dialogue and meta-dialogue in clinical work. *Family Process*, 26(4): 415–428.
Bowlby, J. (1969) *Attachment and Loss* (Vol. 1). London: Hogarth Press.
Bowlby, J. (1988) *A Secure Base: Parent-Child Attachment and Healthy Human Development*. New York: Basic Books.
Byng-Hall, J. (1995) *Rewriting Family Scripts*. New York and London: Guilford Press.
Campbell, D. and Draper, R. (Eds) (1985) *Applications of Systemic Family Therapy*. London: Grune & Stratton.
Carter, E. and McGoldrick, M. (1988) *The Changing Family Life Cycle: A Framework for Family Therapy* (2nd ed.). New York: Gardner.
Dallos, R. (2006) *Attachment Narrative Therapy*. Maidenhead: Open University Press/McGraw-Hill.
Dallos, R. and Draper, R. (2015) *An Introduction to Family Therapy* (4th ed.). Maidenhead: Open University Press/McGraw-Hill.
Dallos, R. and Vetere, A. (2021) *Working Systemically with Attachment Narratives* (2nd ed.). London: Routledge.
Haley, J. (1976) *Problem Solving Therapy*. San Francisco, CA: Jossey-Bass.
Marvin, R. and Stewart, R. (1990) A family systems framework for the study of attachment. In M. Greenberg, D. Cicchetti and E. Cummings (Eds), *Attachment in the Pre-school Years*. Chicago, IL: University of Chicago Press.
McKenzie, R., Dallos, R., Vassallo, T., Myhill, C., Gude, A., and Bond, N. (2021) Family experience of SAFE: a new intervention for families of children with a diagnosis of autism spectrum disorder. *Contemporary Family Therapy*, [Online] 18 February, 1–12. doi: 10.1007/s10591-021-09568-8
Minuchin, S. (1974) *Families and Family Therapy*. Cambridge, MA: Harvard University Press.
White, M. and Epston, D. (1990) *Narrative Means to Therapeutic Ends*. New York: W.W. Norton.

RECOMMENDED READING

Byng-Hall, J. (1995) *Rewriting Family Scripts*. New York and London: Guilford Press.

This is seminal text that offers an interesting integration of systemic family therapy concepts and the idea of stories/scripts across the generations. It has powerful and clear illustrations of practice.

Dallos, R. and Vetere, A. (2021) *Working Systemically with Attachment Narratives* (2nd ed.). London: Routledge.

This is the author's own integration of systemic family with concepts from attachment theory. This approach adds the important dimension of emotional connections and attachment across the generations.

Dallos, R. and Draper, R. (2015) *An Introduction to Family Therapy* (4th ed.). Maidenhead: Open University Press/McGraw-Hill.

This book offers a comprehensive overview of the field of family therapy. It offers a history of the movement, which is summarised in terms of four key phases of developments. The main techniques are illustrated with case studies. There is also an extensive overview of the evidence base for family therapy.

6.6 GROUP THERAPY

STEPHEN PAUL

OVERVIEW AND KEY POINTS

We live in relation to others and our external environment. Our self-concept is formed and develops through our experiences with others. We learn to value ourselves in relation with others.

Many of the life problems people bring to therapy evolve from trauma experienced in relation to others. People play out their relational patterns, often developed from childhood, in relation to others. Group therapy provides an environment to explore and heal the trauma of our interpersonal relations in a setting which can mirror the dynamics of the original situation. A skilled group therapist can help group members to work through issues and patterns, as they arise, in a safe and securely boundaried setting.

Group therapy can be particularly helpful for:

- those whose problems are interpersonal in nature and/or rooted in relation to a number of others
- those who are able to give and receive feedback and be empathic to others
- those who are isolated
- those who are not comfortable with one-to-one therapeutic relationships.

INTRODUCTION

Group therapy developed from the beginning of the twentieth century. Initially, it was the only therapy available for those people who could not afford individual therapy. The foundation of group work is credited to Pratt (see Paul, 2008, 2012). He established an outpatient tuberculosis therapy programme for those who could not afford individual treatment. He used encouragement, support and the didactic delivery of practical information to help attendees (a formula now developed in modern Weight Watchers programmes).

After the First World War, Marsh developed group methods for the first time in a residential psychiatric setting. Concurrently, Lazell worked with groups of mentally disturbed combatants using a didactic-instructional approach. Freudian insights into the human psyche led to the understanding of transference (Wender, 1936) and free association (Schilder, 1936) in groups. Burrow (1927) coined the term 'group analysis', noting that in groups individuals behaved as they believed others wanted them to behave. Maintaining these social images impeded spontaneity and maintained rigid ways of behaving.

Around the same time, Moreno (1958) developed psychodrama. He introduced role-playing, working with group members to re-enact past experiences and resolve repressed feelings. Moreno introduced the term 'group psychotherapy' in 1932.

In the United Kingdom, Bion (1959) formulated classical group analysis. Foulkes (1964) worked under Goldstein alongside Perls, the founder of gestalt therapy (Perls, Hefferline and Goodman, 1959). Goldstein (1939) discovered that individual neurones always functioned as part of a network. This led Foulkes to postulate that the individual is a nodal point within the network of relationships in any group and that psychoanalysis needs to view all the relationships in which the individual is involved. There are no rigid delineations between the individual and the environment, the inner and the outer.

During the 1950s, Rogers (1970) developed encounter groups. He criticised the psychoanalytic concept of 'homeostasis' – that is, that the person is a closed adaptive system with no potential for growth. He believed that the desire for change and growth is the healthy result of inner sickness. Maslow (1964) introduced 'synergy': the idea that an individual has more potential for development in a healthy group than alone.

The 1960s saw the development of family therapy (Slipp, 1993): the 'disturbed' family member was a symptom of a dysfunction in the family unit as a whole. Laing (1985) popularised the therapeutic community approach based on existential philosophy and family systems theory as an alternative to psychiatric treatment. It was not an individual's perception of the world that was faulty, but that social pressure led to the falsification of the self. Psychotic behaviour was, literally, a sane response to an insane situation.

Yalom (1981) initially explored existential approaches to group work. His later writings are now considered within an interpersonal, relational frame.

Cognitive and behavioural groups have been mostly developed in mental health settings. Task-focused group work has been used. The outcomes of such groups were more measurable quantitatively and thus lend themselves to research. A mushrooming of evidence-based practice research in this field and the development of wide-ranging group approaches for a variety of psychological problems have greatly enhanced the use of CBT in health service practice.

In the modern era, a more theoretically generic interpersonal approach to group therapy has also developed (Paul and Charura, 2014; Yalom and Leszcz, 2021). This approach is often used by therapists from different disciplines who work relationally and are not explicitly trained within a traditional core model of group therapy.

A PERSONAL REFLECTION

Through over 40 years' practice as a therapist and trainer, I have noticed that many competent individual therapists:

- have trouble relating in therapeutic groups
- have difficulty with 360° perception
- are often fearful or hesitant about communicating in a group.

Considering that so many life problems evolve from trauma experienced in relation to others, it is paradoxical that many practitioners struggle with group dynamics. Of course this may be partly due to the training of individual therapists, which is focused on one-to-one dynamics.

There are significant differences between individual and group therapies (see Table 6.6.1). These include:

1. The therapist–client relationship is not central in group therapy. Therapist training, with its focus on the unidimensional therapeutic relationship, may lead the therapist to be blind to other communications that take place in a group.
2. The group has a unique pattern of dynamics related exponentially to the number of members. Complex process issues may predominate and the group therapist needs to be able to work with process issues at an individual and group level.
3. There may be different levels of intrapsychic, interpersonal and intragroup relationships in play at any one time. The therapist needs to be aware of and competent to work with them.
4. Boundary issues are often of added importance as the therapist works with the group. Clients often test boundaries and challenge the therapist in quite different ways to individual therapy.
5. Social phenomena occur in groups which are not necessarily pathological or interpretable psychotherapeutically (e.g., groupthink, conformity, influence, cognitive dissonance, etc.) (summarised in Paul, 2008). There is a real potential for stereotyping to take place in groups, which a therapist needs to be aware of and be able to work with.
6. There are a number of 'experts' who may question the therapist or offer their own therapeutic insights and support to each other.

The group context, therefore, is often a challenging one for individually trained therapists who find themselves working with groups.

WAYS OF WORKING

The role and functions of the therapist may be very different, depending on the therapeutic model used. I summarise some of the key ways of working here using an example of a group for people suffering from depression.

> All prospective group members have been referred via medical services. They report having significant debilitating depression. Optimum group size is 8–12 members with two therapists. A group session will be one and a half hours and the group is contracted for 10 weeks. All members will have been met before the group starts to determine suitability and to agree contracts.

PSYCHOANALYTIC THERAPY

Modern psychoanalytic group therapy is based on the work of Foulkes (1964), who saw the individual as a social being whose psychological disturbances have their roots in relationships. In different situations,

Table 6.6.1 Summary of differences for therapists between individual and group therapy

Individual		Group	
	Therapist–client relationship central		Variety of relationships possible
	Content issues may predominate		Process issues may be more central in activating live material in the group
	One relationship processes all outside material		Group can replicate outside experiences
	Therapist trained typically in self-focused therapy		Therapist trained in interpersonal dynamics
	Therapist may hold more expert power and have more influence over interactions		Plethora of interactions that the therapist has to work with. Therapist may have less personal influence or power as expert
	Feedback to therapist only from one person		Therapist open to feedback at any time from any member about any things
	Research indicates *Therapeutic Relationship* most important in-therapy factor		Research indicates *Cohesiveness* most important factor

people behave in ways which seek to reduce their anxieties based on self-perceptions they believe to be true. In a group, there is a 'group tension', the conflict between the individual's and the group's needs. Individuals take up roles in groups as a result of this. Foulkes believed that, unlike classical psychoanalysis, interpretation was not to be used by the leader alone but that group members could have important insights to make about others in the group. The role of the therapist is as a conductor, who makes subtle, informing contributions. Foulkes believed in working with the healthy functioning of group members, which enables the group to move towards maturation and gradually lessens the influence of what he called 'neurotic' forces (after Lewin, 1939). The conductor encourages free-floating group discussion. As the culture of the group develops through open personal communications between members, the group matrix is formed. Group members respond in their own subjective ways, sharing their feelings with the group. The open sharing of all feelings creates a resonance in the group, each member resonating to the content.

The conductor's role is to help identify underlying causes of disturbance and to make links for members of the processes in the group and their own personal material.

> In our therapy group, the conductor will facilitate the building up of cohesiveness in the group and help members to explore common themes. Sharing by members of their own struggles will help other members to resonate with their own issues and enable some release of tensions. In some cases, the causes of the problems, such as abandonment, may have to be visited again and again in the group for the underlying conflicts to be released.

EXISTENTIAL THERAPY

In the existential approach, the subjective experience of the individual is at its core. The freedom of each individual to choose how to respond to life's limitations, the intersubjectivity of living, and the focus on authenticity are all underlying themes.

There can be said to be three aims of group therapy:

1. Enabling members to become authentic with themselves.
2. Broadening members' perspectives on themselves and their environment.
3. Enabling members to find meaning for their lives (van Deurzen-Smith, 1990).

The therapeutic relationship is a focus for corrective emotional experiences and therapy is a partnership (Corey, 2022). Change comes through relationship with others. The therapist works to foster meaningful interpersonal relationships. S/he will also work with members in confronting and working through existential life issues, which are common in some way to all members, and to help find meaning and authenticity (Yalom and Leszcz, 2005).

> In our therapeutic group, the therapist encourages open and frank sharing between members to help them accept the causes of the depressive states they find themselves in, to realise that such states are common reactions to life's events and, through the group, to see and understand that we all have to face up to such limits and challenges. Through realising this, and the realisation that all members are in the same situation, members are helped to find more helpful ways of responding to the challenges they face.

PERSON-CENTRED THERAPY

The work of Rogers (1970) is central to the development of humanistic group therapy. The facilitative conditions are seen as central to the development of the group. The therapist models congruence, unconditional positive regard and empathy, and communicates them through her/his interactions with group members. The therapist is present in the group, is willing to take part as an equal member of the group and to share his/her struggles with group issues as appropriate (Paul, 2008). When growthful opportunities are present, members of the group choose these opportunities. Obstacles as previously experienced will dissolve away or be overcome. The group becomes a safe place to explore personal incongruities in relationship with others (see Paul, 2016).

> In our therapeutic group, the therapist models the therapeutic conditions in his/her relations to others and this helps to create an environment in which members can communicate authentically with each other. Feelings of depression are caused by an inner disempowerment and distortion of innate motivation. As personal incongruities are revealed, explored and resolved, members are able to be more accessing of their inner motivation and make growthful and enhancing life choices.

COGNITIVE-BEHAVIOURAL APPROACHES

Cognitive-behavioural therapy (CBT) in groups was originally developed to facilitate the treatment of individuals in groups. Group processes and dynamics were not considered important or helpful to the task in hand. However, the importance of establishing a climate of trust and respect is indicated and particular therapist characteristics are linked with successful outcomes: respect for others, a non-judgemental attitude, warmth, humour, congruence and authenticity (Lazarus, 1989). A key component of CBT approaches is modelling (Bandura, 1986). The behaviour of the therapist is therefore an important element. More recently, CBT group therapists recognise and work with group dynamic processes in their work (White, 2000). Many CBT programmes are psychoeducational and didactic in nature. CBT programmes are therefore concerned with working with individuals in the group with a focus on individual targets. Members may take part in role-plays, exercises and collaborative problem-solving.

> Members of our therapeutic group will have agreed goals and will be encouraged to challenge and change unhealthy thinking and behaviour patterns. A typical group session will include a warm-up, introduction of new material, practice, review and setting of homework tasks. Members may take part in role-plays, exercises and collaborative problem-solving.

INTERPERSONAL/RELATIONAL APPROACHES

The prolific contributions of Yalom (and Leszcz, 2021) have been important in the development of interpersonal and relational approaches to group therapy. Therapy works through *interpersonal learning* (see Yalom's curative factors – Table 6.6.3 below), the group as *social microcosm* and the *here-and-now* focus of the group. The therapist works with the relationships between members and the therapist, relationships between group members themselves, and relationships between group members and the group. The therapist processes individual (intrapsychic), interpersonal and group-as-a-whole phenomena.

With the flourishing research on the importance of the therapeutic relationship, a relational paradigm has developed (see Paul and Charura, 2014) in which the focus of therapy is relational and that a range of theoretical perspectives can assist the therapist in the task of working with the individual in making sense of the individual in her/his social relationships. The therapeutic relationship itself is considered 'central to change' (Paul and Pelham, 2000: 110).

RESEARCH

A comprehensive summary of research into group therapies can be found in Burlingame and Strauss (2021).

Research tends to fall into two approaches to group therapy. First, interpersonal group therapy, as exemplified by Yalom (and Leszcz, 2021) and Rogers (1970), and relational approaches. Many practitioners with no formal group therapy training work in this way. It is probably the case that it is generally the most practised approach to group therapy overall. The focus is more on the process and interpersonal relationships in the here-and-now. The second type of group therapy is the more structured kind, with a focus on goals. This approach lends itself more to quantifiable research than the first by its very nature, which compounds the problem researchers have in comparing effectiveness.

Table 6.6.2 summarises Johnson's (2008) review of effective group therapy treatments.

Table 6.6.2 Effective group therapy treatments (updated from Johnson, 2008)

Type of approach	Methods	Success
Alcohol abuse and dependence		
Community reinforcement approach	Social groupwork using CBT	Some evidence of general success
Cue exposure treatment	Desensitisation to stimuli	Well-established
Project CALM (treating alcoholism in the family unit)	Groupwork with couples	Some evidence of general success
Social skills training	Developing communication skills	Probably proven effective
Anxiety disorders		
CBT for generalised anxiety disorder	CBT in groups	Too few studies to indicate generalised success
Exposure and response prevention for obsessive compulsive disorder	Behaviour therapy in groups	Probably proven effective
CBT for panic disorder and agoraphobia	CBT in groups	Probably proven effective
Depression		
Cognitive therapy	Includes CBT	Well-established
Behaviour therapy	In groups	Too few studies to indicate generalised probability
Interpersonal therapy		Well-established
Eating disorders		
CBT for binge eating disorder	In groups	Well-established
Interpersonal therapy for binge eating disorder		Probably proven effective
CBT for bulimia nervosa	In groups	Too few studies to indicate generalised probability

Yalom questions those approaches which rely on technique and are driven by goals of efficiency rather than effectiveness. For him, the 'interactional focus is the engine of group therapy' (Yalom with Leszcz, 2005: xvi). The therapeutic factors developed by Yalom have been recognised as a benchmark in group therapy research (Bednar and Kaul, 1994; Burlingame, Mackenzie and Strauss, 2004). Variously described, these are outlined in Table 6.6.3.

Cohesiveness is identified by Burlingame et al. (2004: 683) in their summary of group therapy research as 'the therapeutic relationship in group psychotherapy':

- Cohesion is positively associated with reductions in symptom distress and/or improvement in interpersonal functioning.
- All therapists need to foster cohesiveness in all its elements in the group.
- Cohesion is positively associated with outcome in groups of different theoretical orientations.
- Group leaders who focus on member interaction, irrespective of theoretical orientation, achieve higher cohesiveness–outcome links versus groups without this focus. It is important to encourage member interaction.
- Group cohesiveness builds over time.

Meta-summaries of research do concur that group members who experience acceptance, belonging and support, *regardless of therapeutic model*, typically report more improvement (Burlingame, Fuhriman and Johnson, 2002). Attributes such as warmth, openness and empathy have been associated with increased cohesion and better outcomes.

Burlingame and Strauss (2021) note a research focus on group therapy outcomes in medical settings and with severe mental illness, and less so on the process of therapy. However, cohesion and therapeutic alliance remain key indicators of outcome (Alldredge et al., 2021; Rosendahl et al., 2021). Research into online therapy (Arrow, Yap and Chester, 2021; Burlingame and Strauss, 2021) looks promising but it is still in an 'embryonic stage'.

We can summarise thus:

- Group therapy works as a whole.
- There is no significant evidence to suggest that one modality is better than any other.
- Modality-based intervention may pathologise normal behaviours.
- Therapists should check recent research into group therapy with the client group they are working with.
- Therapists may be more effective working in a way which they are comfortable with rather than trying to 'fit' into a modality.
- Cohesiveness is central to group therapy and the therapeutic relationship is central to outcome.
- Many social factors may affect group members. Therapists should not pathologise them and be mindful of the human rights of members of therapy groups.
- A group leader is in a position of power and needs to be mindful of this.

Table 6.6.3 Yalom's curative factors

Interpersonal input	Learning through the input of others in the group
Catharsis	Letting out feelings in the group
Cohesiveness	A sense of belonging and feeling accepted in the group
Self-understanding	Linking past experiences to present thoughts and feelings
Interpersonal output	Learning how to behave in relation to helpful advice from others in the group
Existential factors	Coming to terms with the fact that some things cannot be changed but have to be faced up to and that literally we are all in the same life situation and can find mutual support in this
Instillation of hope	The realisation that as others in the group can improve so the group member can
Altruism	The gains to self-esteem through helping others in the group
Family re-enactment	The group somehow recreates the family experience and can help members to understand behaviour patterns from their past
Guidance identification	Getting helpful advice from others in the group

REFERENCES

Alldredge, C. T., Burlingame, G. M., Yang, C., & Rosendahl, J. (2021) Alliance in group therapy: A meta-analysis. *Group Dynamics: Theory, Research, and Practice*, *25*(1), 13–28.

Arrow, K., Yap, K., & Chester, A. (2021) Group climate in online group cognitive behaviour therapy predicts treatment outcomes. *Clinical Psychologist*, *25*(2), 153–163.

Bandura, A. (1986) *Social Foundations of Thought and Action: A Social Cognitive Theory*. Englewood Cliffs, NJ: Prentice-Hall.

Bednar, R. L., & Kaul, T. (1994) Experiential group research. In A. E. Bergin & S. L. Garfield (Eds), *Handbook of Psychotherapy and Behavior Change* (pp. 631–663). New York: Wiley.

Bion, W. R. (1959) *Experiences in Groups*. New York: Basic Books.

Burlingame, G. M., Fuhriman, A., & Johnson, J. (2002) Cohesion in group psychotherapy. In J. Norcross (Ed.), *A Guide to Psychotherapy Relationships that Work* (pp. 71–88). Oxford: Oxford University Press.

Burlingame, G. M., Mackenzie, K. R., & Strauss, B. (2004) Small-group treatment: Evidence for effectiveness and mechanisms of change. In M. J. Lambert (Ed.), *Bergin and Garfield's Handbook of Psychotherapy and Behaviour Change* (5th ed., pp. 647–696). New York: Wiley.

Burlingame, G. M., & Strauss, B. (2021) Efficacy of small group treatments: Foundation for evidence based practice. In M. Barkham, W. Lutz, & L. G. Castonguay (Eds), *Bergin and Garfield's Handbook of Psychotherapy and Behavior Change* (50th Anniversary ed., pp. 582–624). New York: Wiley.

Burrow, T. (1927) *The Social Basis of Consciousness*. New York: Harcourt Brace and World.

Corey, G. (2022) *Theory and Practice of Group Counseling* (10th ed.). Belmont, CA: Wadsworth.

Foulkes, S. H. (1964) *Therapeutic Group Analysis*. New York: International Universities Press.

Goldstein, K. (1939) *The Organism: A Holistic Approach to Biology Derived from Pathological Data in Man*. New York: American Book Company.

Johnson, J. (2008) Using research-supported group treatments. *Journal of Clinical Psychology: In Session*, *64*(11), 1206–1224.

Laing, R. D. (1985) *Wisdom, Madness and Folly: The Making of a Psychiatrist*. London: Macmillan.

Lazarus, A. A. (1989) Multimodal therapy. In R. J. Corsini & D. Wedding (Eds), *Current Psychotherapies* (4th ed.). Itasca, IL: Peacock.

Lewin, K. (1939) Field theory and experiment in social psychology: Concepts and methods. *American Journal of Sociology*, *44*(6), 868–896.

Maslow, A. H. (1964) Synergy in society and the individual. *Journal of Individual Psychology*, *20*, 153–164.

Moreno, J. L. (1958) Fundamental rules and techniques of psychodrama. In J. H. Masserman & J. L. Moreno (Eds), *Progress in Psychotherapy*. New York: Grune and Stratton.

Paul, S. (2008) The relationship in group therapy. In S. Haugh & S. Paul (Eds), *The Therapeutic Relationship: Perspectives and Themes* (pp. 230–246). Ross-on-Wye: PCCS Books.

Paul, S. (2012) Group counselling and therapy. In C. Feltham & I. Horton (Eds), *The Sage Handbook of Counselling and Psychotherapy* (3rd ed., pp. 617–625). London: Sage.

Paul, S. (2016) Group therapy and therapeutic groups. In C. Lago & D. Charura (Eds), *Person-centred Counselling and Psychotherapy Handbook: Origins, Developments and Contemporary Considerations*. Maidenhead: Open University/McGraw-Hill.

Paul, S., & Charura, D. (2014) The relationship in group therapy. In D. Charura & S. Paul (Eds), *The Therapeutic Relationship Handbook* (pp. 131–145). Maidenhead: Open University Press.

Paul, S., & Pelham, G. (2000) A relational approach to therapy. In S. Palmer & R. Woolfe (Eds), *Integrative and Eclectic Counselling and Psychotherapy* (pp. 110–126). London: Sage.

Perls, F., Hefferline, R., & Goodman, P. (1959) *Gestalt Therapy: Excitement and Growth in the Human Personality*. Harmondsworth: Penguin.

Rogers, C. (1970) *Carl Rogers on Encounter Groups*. New York: Harper & Row.

(Continued)

(Continued)

Rosendahl, J., Alldredge, C. T., Burlingame, G. M., & Strauss, B. (2021) Recent developments in group psychotherapy research. *American Journal of Psychotherapy*, 74(2), 52–59.

Schilder, P. (1936) The analysis of ideologies as a psychotherapeutic method, especially in group treatment. *American Journal of Psychiatry*, 93(3), 601–617.

Slipp, S. (1993) Family therapy and multiple family therapy. In H. Kaplan & B. Sadock (Eds), *Comprehensive Group Psychotherapy* (3rd ed., pp. 270–283). Baltimore, MD: Williams and Wilkins.

van Deurzen-Smith, E. (1990) *Existential Therapy*. London: Society for Existential Analysis Publications.

Wender, L. (1936) The dynamics of group psychotherapy and its application. *Journal of Nervous and Mental Disease*, 84, 55.

White, J. (2000) Introduction. In J. White & A. Freeman (Eds), *Cognitive-behavioural Group Therapy for Specific Problems and Populations*. Washington, DC: American Psychological Association.

Yalom, I. D. (1981) *Existential Psychotherapy*. New York: Basic Books.

Yalom, I. D., with Leszcz, M. (2005) *The Theory and Practice of Group Psychotherapy* (5th ed.). New York: Basic Books.

Yalom, I. D., & Leszcz, M. (2021) *The Theory and Practice of Group Psychotherapy* (6th ed.). New York: Basic Books.

RECOMMENDED READING

Corey, G. (2022) *Theory and Practice of Group Counseling* (10th ed.) Belmont, CA: Wadsworth/Thomson.

This is generic text that reviews the theory and practice of the different modalities. It is useful in helping to understand the different ways of working.

Tudor, K. (1999) *Group Counselling*. London: Sage.

Tudor covers the key considerations in the practice of group therapy. This book is a useful reference guide.

Yalom, I. D., & Leszcz, M. (2021) *The Theory and Practice of Group Psychotherapy* (6th ed.). New York: Basic Books.

This is a classic exposition. Every group therapist should have a copy.

6.7 ELECTRONICALLY DELIVERED TEXT THERAPY

KATE ANTHONY AND STEPHEN GOSS

OVERVIEW AND KEY POINTS

On revision of this chapter for the new edition of this *Handbook*, I note that text-based therapies have been usurped by the immediate presumed need for visual contact during therapy sessions during the global events of 2020. It should not quite be considered a lost art just yet, however, not least because preparation for future events that may affect the ability to use live streaming video successfully is wise in a world where cyberattacks are a real threat. The chapter in this *Handbook* relating to electronically delivered therapies is testament to the acceptance of online therapy and counselling since the start of the Coronavirus pandemic.

This chapter describes the most essential elements that practitioners need to be aware of before considering an online presence. It will concentrate on the practical use of *text* (via email, chat, forums and mobile phone texting (Short Message Service: SMS)) for conducting an individual client–practitioner therapeutic relationship. Key points include:

- Text-based therapies have become an established, if somewhat forgotten, part of the therapy world.
- There are specific skills, such as enhanced writing techniques, that are needed to work online with clients.
- Research in this area commonly demonstrates the effectiveness of working through text-based media.

INTRODUCTION

Twenty-five years on from the first appearance of commercial websites that offered email and chat for therapeutic communication, many publications have provided a wealth of information and literature around the topic. Perhaps the most comprehensive of these, for further textbook reading, are Hsiung (2002), Goss and Anthony (2003), Kraus, Zack and Stricker (2004), Derrig-Palumbo and Zeine (2005), Anthony and Goss (2009), Evans (2009), Jones and Stokes (2009), Anthony and Merz Nagel (2010), Kraus, Stricker and Speyer (2010), Goss, Anthony, Stretch and Merz Nagel (2016), Anthony and Merz Nagel (2022) and see Goss, Merz Nagel and Anthony (Chapter 6.10, this volume).

As well as the work of international experts in the field, publishing literature and collaborating on research projects, the area of electronically delivered therapy (and in particular the ethical and legal side of it) has been addressed by some mental health organisations worldwide. Professional bodies such as the British Association for Counselling and Psychotherapy (BACP) (ACTO, 2021; Anthony and Goss, 2009; Anthony and Jamieson, 2005; BACP, 2020; Goss et al., 2001; Hill and Roth, 2014), the National Board of Certified Counselors (2001), and the American Counseling Association (1999) have addressed and published guidelines for their members who wish to offer an online presence. The International Society for Mental Health Online (ISMHO) was formed in 1997 and offers suggested principles for working online; the Association for Counselling and Therapy Online (ACTO) was formed in 2006 for practitioners and offers competencies revised in 2020, including for those working with children and young people.

WAYS OF WORKING

TYPES OF ELECTRONICALLY DELIVERED THERAPY

Before embarking on this method of delivery, practitioners should carefully consider their innate writing style and enjoyment of it.

> **Using block-text email (asynchronous) for therapy**. This is most people's understanding of using email for therapeutic use: the exchanging back and forth of emails between two people within a contract, which is (usually) short term and (usually) weekly, and which utilises encryption software for privacy and confidentiality.

Using narrative dynamic email (asynchronous) for therapy. This type of email is where the practitioner inserts his/her responses *within* the client's email using different fonts and/or colours, and the client reciprocates in the same way, usually for a small number of exchanges before the dynamic text becomes too unwieldy and a new narrative is required. Again, it is (usually) short term and (usually) weekly and utilises encryption software for privacy and confidentiality. This style of communication is less widely used.

Using chat rooms (synchronous) for therapy. This method involves a dialogue between client and practitioner in real time, using an encrypted internet chat room or encrypted instant messaging software. The contracted sessions are usually weekly, and often incorporate a weekly exchange of asynchronous email (this is a useful function to allow the client to expand upon actual descriptive situations that would otherwise take up valuable time within the sessions).

Using forums (asynchronous) for therapy. More secure than any other form of electronically delivered therapy within this context, forums are held on the internet behind a password protected access system so that client and therapist visit a website to view and post responses to each other.

Using mobile phone texting (asynchronous) for therapy. Mobile phone texting (SMS) is often reserved for making and cancelling in-room appointments but is increasingly used as part of the therapeutic process and is useful if used with care within a boundaried relationship. It is also used for crisis intervention by organisations such as Samaritans (Goss and Ferns, 2016).

THE ESSENTIAL CONCEPTS OF ONLINE TEXTUAL THERAPY

The first aspect of working with text that may seem obvious but bears clarifying is that it is a distance method of communication. There are obvious benefits to those who cannot access therapy, for example because of disability or geographical reasons, but apart from practical reasons, it is important to understand the 'disinhibition effect' (Suler, 2004) that often makes for a more open and honest relationship. The ability for the client to reveal much more when working at a certain perceived distance is significant. It also means that the level of disclosure is likely to occur at a much faster pace than it usually does in an in-room relationship or even within other methods of distance therapy, such as the telephone. The intensity of disinhibition is peculiar to using typed text over the internet for communication, and should not be underestimated, particularly when taking care of the self and the client. Many clients find that a one-off outpouring of emotion and narrative, due to disinhibition that affords a cathartic experience, means that they feel better and can disappear back into cyberspace – a particularly distressing experience for the practitioner. For the most part, though, the disinhibition effect is a positive empowering experience, and one that is important to clients who cannot reveal sensitive information due to shame, embarrassment or being unable to 'look someone in the eye' while doing so.

The distance of the client also means that self-revelation of practitioner material, where appropriate within the work, can be a useful tool to facilitate a second aspect of working online – the concept of presence, described by Lombard and Ditton (1997) as 'the perceptual illusion of non-mediation'. This is described in my original research as occurring when 'the media used (in this case the computer and keyboard) is unimportant and you are interacting with another person in a separate space' (Anthony, 2000: 626). In this way, the medium used to conduct a therapeutic relationship is very secondary to the therapeutic relationship taking place as a mutual journey towards the client's recovery. Despite the lack of any body language, so often cited as the reason that online work via text can never be 'real' therapy, the practitioner is able to enter the client's mental constructs of their world through their text, respond in a similar manner, and so develop a rapport that transcends the hardware used to support the communication as *well* as the 'white noise' that a physical presence can induce.

Finally, we must consider how all this building of the therapeutic relationship can occur without the gestures, vocal interventions and eye contact that make up the traditional in-room relationship. The quality of the practitioner's written communication and their ability to convey the nuances of body language that facilitate the client's growth (empathic facial expressions, for example) are paramount when working online. The use of text to replicate body language takes many forms online, as does the use of netiquette (a combination of 'net' and 'etiquette'), but both aspects are integral to the success of the communication and therefore the client's recovery. Both of these aspects are also sometimes considered facile within the conventional profession, and yet their contributions to the online therapeutic relationship being established, developed and maintained are vital. While in no way exhaustive, the following should give the reader some insight into what is possible within the remit of using typed text:

- There are different ways of communicating in an appropriate manner, depending on the context of that communication. Danet (2001) identified two types of textual communication: business and personal. However, in Goss and Anthony (2003) I propose how a third definition is necessary because the 'therapeutic textual communication' is at once both a business transaction (contracted between therapist and client) and a personal communication (because of the nature of the content).
- One rule of netiquette that it is essential to be aware of is that the use of CAPITALISATION for an entire sentence or block of text is shouting and is usually disrespectful and rude.
- There are many ways of emphasising certain words where necessary, such as *italicizing*, **bold**, underlining, _underscoring_, and *asterisks*.
- Overuse of exclamation marks generally makes the text difficult to read and is considered poor form.
- There are thousands of emoticons that are used to convey facial expressions. Most are supplied in email and chat software and some have to be (or are preferred to be) created using keyboard characters and read by imagining holding the head to the left (this does not apply in Asian countries – a cultural issue practitioners should be aware of). Some of the more frequently used in online therapeutic work are:

    ☺ or :o) or :) smiles (smileys)
    ☹ or :o(or >:o{ frowns
    ;) or ;o) winks (winkies)
    The winky, in particular, is essential to indicate irony or a non-serious statement.

- Abbreviations and acronyms are also widely used. Some of the more frequently used in online therapeutic work (and more generally) are:

    LOL - laugh out loud
    BTW - by the way
    PFT, k? - pause for thought, OK?
    The latter is particularly useful for the client to use silence within a synchronous text session.

- Emotional bracketing is also used to clarify emotion. As well as being able to hug your client by using parentheses, as in ((((Kate)))), some other uses are:

    <<crying>>
    [[sigh]]

- Automatic signature files, greetings and sign-offs also need careful consideration and the use of personal style *within the appropriate context of the communication*.

MOBILE/SMS TEXT MESSAGING

Growing research evidence (Benda et al., 2020; Ben-Zeev et al., 2020; Sindahl, Fukkink and Helles, 2020) suggests that it is possible to create helpful therapeutic services based on short message service (SMS) interactions (Blake-Buffini and Gordon, 2015), commonly referred to as mobile phone text messages or texts. This is a popular means of communication with many clients, especially younger populations (Haxell, 2015; Ling, 2007) for whom many digital health support options are often seen as particularly appropriate (Liverpool et al., 2020). The UK Samaritans' SMS service, for example, received 413,000 messages from over 7,500 unique mobile numbers in its first 36 months alone (Goss and Ferns, 2016). In the UK, a national support texting service, using volunteers, was launched with royal backing in 2019, although the service clarifies it should not be considered therapy (https://giveusashout.org/about-us/faq/#faq-11).

In addition to providing ready access to professional interventions, text messaging offers a psychologically and physically involving activity, itself of value, for example for people who self-harm. Mobile devices can also act as a platform for other interventions (Preziosa et al., 2009), are accessible during peak stress periods (e.g., during a suicide attempt), or can be well suited to semi-automated interventions, such as post-therapy follow-up (e.g., Hennemann, Farnsteiner and Sander, 2018), symptom monitoring (e.g., Elliott, 2008), which is increasingly demonstrated to be acceptable via widespread technologies such as smartphones (Walsh, Golden and Priebe, 2016) or reinforcing treatment protocol adherence or health information (e.g., Bertrand et al., 2006). Mobile-phone-based services are of particular relevance for emerging economies, typified by poor mental health care provision but burgeoning mobile phone availability (e.g., Hoefman and Apunyu, 2010).

As well as the above facets of using typed text for therapeutic communication, there is, of course, a wealth of both practical and ethical considerations that need to be considered when setting up an online presence to work with clients. In-depth analysis of these facets is available in Anthony and Goss (2009) and Anthony and Merz Nagel (2022).

Training in online work is now considered essential (Anthony and Goss, 2009; Anthony and Merz Nagel, 2010; Gehl, Anthony and Merz Nagel, 2016), and there are a variety of online trainings available in the form of long or modular courses, such as those of the Online Therapy Institute (www.onlinetherapyinstitute.com).

The world of technological development is one that moves and develops extremely quickly, and it is well known that the counselling and psychotherapy profession in particular has been playing catch-up with the arrival of technology for therapeutic use over the last 20 years. What is certain, however, is that the profession had to get up to speed quickly and urgently during early 2020, and although most practitioners turned to video during this period, it would be a tragedy if the art of electronically delivered text therapy were lost.

REFERENCES

ACTO (Association for Counselling and Therapy Online) (2021) *Competences for Online Therapy*. Available at www.acto.org.uk/about/acto-competences-online-therapy/ (accessed 12 January 2022).

American Counseling Association (1999) *Ethical Standards for Internet Online Counselling*. Alexandria, VA: ACM. Available at http://ct.counseling.org/2006/12/ct-online-ethics-update

Anthony, K. (2000) Counselling in cyberspace. *Counselling Journal*, 11(10), 625–627.

Anthony, K. and Goss, S. (2009) *Guidelines for Online Counselling and Psychotherapy* (3rd ed.). Lutterworth: British Association for Counselling and Psychotherapy.

Anthony, K. and Jamieson, A. (2005) *Guidelines for Online Counselling and Psychotherapy* (2nd ed.). Rugby: British Association for Counselling and Psychotherapy.

Anthony, K. and Merz Nagel, D. (2010) *Therapy Online: A Practical Guide*. London: Sage.

Anthony, K. and Merz Nagel, D. (2022) *Coaching Online: A Practical Guide*. Abingdon, UK: Routledge.

Benda, N.C., Alexopoulos, G.S., Marino, P., Sirey, J.A., Kiosses, D. and Ancker, J.S. (2020). The Age Limit Does Not Exist: A Pilot Usability Assessment of a SMS-Messaging and Smartwatch-Based Intervention for Older Adults with Depression. *AMIA Annu Symp Proc.* 25, 2020, 213–222.

Ben-Zeev, D., Buck, B., Mellor, S., Hudenko, W. and Hallgreen, K. (2020) Augmenting evidence-based care with a texting mobile interventionist: a pilot randomized controlled trial. *Psychiatric Services*, 71(12), 1218–1224.

Bertrand, J.T., O'Reilly, K., Denison, J., Anhang, R. and Sweat, M. (2006) Systematic review of the effectiveness of mass communication programs to change HIV/AIDS related behaviors in developing countries. *Health Education Research*, 21(4), 567–597.

British Association for Counselling and Psychotherapy (BACP) (2020) *BACP Competences for Telephone and E-counselling*. Lutterworth: BACP.

Buffini, K. and Gordon, M. (2015) One-to-one support for crisis intervention using online synchronous instant messaging: evaluating working alliance and client satisfaction, *British Journal of Guidance & Counselling*, 43(1), 105–116, DOI: 10.1080/03069885.2014.987723

Danet, B. (2001) *Cyberpl@y*. London: Berg.

Derrig-Palumbo, K. and Zeine, F. (2005) *Online Therapy: A Therapist's Guide to Expanding Your Practice*. New York: W.W. Norton.

Elliott, J. (2008) Monitoring mental health by text. *BBC WorldNews America*, 31 December. Available at www.news.bbc.co.uk/2/hi/health/7797155.stm

Evans, J. (2009) *Online Counselling and Guidance Skills: A Practical Resource for Trainees and Practitioners*. London: Sage.

Gehl, N., Anthony, K. and Merz Nagel, D. (2016) Online training for online mental health. In S. Goss, K. Anthony, L. Stretch and D. Merz Nagel (Eds), *Technology in Mental Health: Applications in Practice, Supervision and Training* (2nd ed.). Springfield, IL: C.C. Thomas.

Goss, S. and Anthony, K. (2003) *Technology in Counselling and Psychotherapy: A Practitioner's Guide*. Basingstoke: Palgrave Macmillan.

Goss, S., Anthony, K., Palmer, S. and Jamieson, A. (2001) *Guidelines for Online Counselling and Psychotherapy*. Rugby: British Association for Counselling and Psychotherapy.

Goss, S., Anthony, K., Stretch, L. and Merz Nagel, D. (Eds) (2016) *Technology in Mental Health: Applications in Practice, Supervision and Training* (2nd ed.). Springfield, IL: C.C. Thomas.

Goss, S. and Ferns, J. (2016) Using cell/mobile phone SMS to enhance client crisis and peer support. In S. Goss, K. Anthony, L. Stretch and D. Merz Nagel (Eds), *Technology in Mental Health: Applications in Practice, Supervision and Training* (2nd ed.). Springfield, IL: C.C. Thomas.

Haxell, A.J. (2015) On becoming textually active at Youthline, New Zealand. *British Journal of Guidance & Counselling*, 43(1), 144–155. https://doi.org/10.1080/03069885.2014.922163

Hennemann, S., Farnsteiner, S. and Sander, L. (2018) Internet- and mobile-based aftercare and relapse prevention in mental disorders: A systematic review and recommendations for future research. *Internet Interv.* 24(14), 1–17. doi: 10.1016/j.invent.2018.09.001

Hill, A. and Roth, A. (2014) *The Competences Required to Deliver Psychological Therapies 'at a Distance'*. Lutterworth: British Association for Counselling and Psychotherapy.

Hoefman, B.A.S. and Apunyu, B. (2010) Using SMS for HIV/AIDS education and to expand the use of HIV testing and counseling services at the AIDS Information Centre (AIC) Uganda. *M4D 2010: Proceedings of the 2nd International Conference on M4D Mobile Communication Technology for Development*. Kampala, Uganda, November, pp. 40–48.

Hsiung, R.C. (Ed.) (2002) *e-Therapy*. New York: W.W. Norton.

Jones, G. and Stokes, A. (2009) *Online Counselling: A Handbook for Practitioners*. Basingstoke: Palgrave Macmillan.

Kraus, R., Stricker, G. and Speyer, C. (Eds) (2010) *Online Counseling* (2nd ed.). San Diego, CA: Elsevier.

Kraus, R., Zack, J. and Stricker, G. (Eds) (2004) *Online Counseling*. San Diego, CA: Elsevier.

Ling, R. (2007) Children, youth and mobile communication. *Journal of Children and Media*, 1(1), 60–67.

Liverpool, S., Mota, C.P., Sales, C.M.D., Čuš, A., Carletto, S., Hancheva, C., Sousa, S., Cerón, S.C., Moreno-Peral, P., Pietrabissa, G., Moltrecht, B., Ulberg, R., Ferreira, N. and Edbrooke-Childs J. (2020) Engaging children and young people in digital mental health interventions: systematic review of modes of delivery, facilitators, and barriers. *Journal of Medical Internet Research*, 22(6), e16317. doi: 10.2196/16317

Lombard, M. and Ditton, T. (1997) At the heart of it all: the concept of presence. *Journal of Computer-Mediated Communication*, 3(2). doi/10.1111/j.1083-6101

National Board of Certified Counselors (2001) *The Practice of Internet Counseling*. Greensboro, NC: NBCC. Available at www.nbcc.org/Assets/Ethics/nbcccodeofethics.pdf

Preziosa, A, Grassi, A., Gaggioli, A. and Riva, G. (2009) Therapeutic applications of the mobile phone, *British Journal of Guidance & Counselling*, 37(3), 313–325, DOI: 10.1080/03069880902957031

Sindahl, T.N., Fukkink, R.G. and Helles, R. (2020) SMS counselling at a child helpline: counsellor strategies, children's stressors and well-being. *British Journal of Guidance & Counselling*, 48(2), 263–275.

Suler, J. (2004) The online disinhibition effect. *CyberPsychology and Behavior*, 7, 321–326 Available at http://users.rider.edu/~suler/psycyber/disinhibit.html

Walsh, S., Golden, E. and Priebe, S. (2016) Systematic review of patients' participation in and experiences of technology-based monitoring of mental health symptoms in the community. *BMJ Open*, 6, e008362. doi: 10.1136/bmjopen-2015-008362

> **RECOMMENDED READING**
>
> Goss, S., Anthony, K., Stretch, L. and Merz Nagel, D. (Eds) (2016) *Technology in Mental Health: Applications in Practice, Supervision and Training* (2nd ed.). Springfield, IL: C.C. Thomas.
>
> The second edition of this 2010 edited textbook includes 40 updated chapters on all available technologies used in the profession in 2016. It also includes a new section on clinical supervision and training. Authors are selected from experts worldwide, giving a true international flavour to the book.
>
> Anthony, K. and Merz Nagel, D. (2010) *Therapy Online: A Practical Guide.* London: Sage.
>
> Anthony, K. and Merz Nagel, D. (2022) *Coaching Online: A Practical Guide.* London: Sage.
>
> These textbooks focus on the use of text in online work and are written by the two leading experts in online therapy and counselling. *Therapy Online* also includes a full case study between a counsellor and a client from online assessment, through email, mobile SMS, chat, telephone and videoconferencing to closure of the therapeutic online relationship.
>
> Anthony, K. (2014) Training therapists to work effectively online and offline within digital culture. *British Journal of Guidance & Counselling*, 43(1), 36–42.
>
> A peer-reviewed paper analysing the author's considerable experience in the training of practitioners to use online methods of delivery.

6.8 VIDEOCONFERENCING THERAPY

ZEHRA ERSAHIN

OVERVIEW AND KEY POINTS

This chapter aims to provide an overview of the current state of the videoconferencing therapy literature, with an emphasis on its developing context and evidence base, in supporting practitioners navigating their way to safe and good practice. It will concentrate on the essential elements of therapeutic alliance and telepresence while engaging in therapy through videoconferencing, ethical considerations, and prospective areas of research in a rapidly changing world. Key points include:

- Videoconferencing therapy has become an established part of counselling and psychotherapy, and relevant work is essential for accessible and continuing services.
- The construct of the therapeutic alliance while videoconferencing may differ from its in-person counterparts, and requires practitioners to consider adapting their ways of working in accordance with the professional guidelines.
- Research evidence demonstrates therapeutic work in videoconferencing is effective in addressing common mental health issues, outcomes are

comparable to face-to-face equivalents, and good therapeutic alliance is achievable online.

INTRODUCTION

Videoconferencing therapy (or video-therapy) is a relatively new resource in conducting individual, family and group interventions online. It is an extension of audio-therapy approaches that have been traditionally delivered through telephone and, while this simpler form of tele-psychology has been available for almost half a century, notable advancements in internet technology since the 1990s have transformed the therapeutic settings accordingly. Smith and colleagues (2022: 93) define video-therapy as the 'synchronous, client–therapist interactions through video platforms which are structured in the same way as in-room counselling and psychotherapy'.

The first use of videoconferencing dates to the 1960s, where a two-way television system with a camera mounted on a cart above the television screen was set up to trial a group therapy session (Wittson, Affleck and Johnson, 1961). The study's preliminary findings were promising, indicating that therapist and client attributes were more predictive of session ratings than the television technique itself.

Since then, the terminology changed significantly (e.g., e-therapy, i-therapy, telepsychiatry), with technological developments leading to significant shifts in therapeutic settings in a more hybrid global context. Even before the Covid-19 pandemic, the last two decades witnessed increasing numbers of therapists and service providers adapting their work to different media – often led by client motivations in reaching out to services that attempt to overcome issues of accessibility, equality and population-specific needs (e.g., older adults, prisoners).

Research examining videoconferencing therapy also highlights some shortcomings. For instance, services note difficulties in recruiting trained, technologically competent staff and highlight the complexity in exchanging materials with clients remotely (e.g., Poletti et al., 2020). Such outcomes instigate debate and lead to polarised reactions about whether videoconferencing therapy is effective, safe or whether sufficient levels of therapeutic alliance can be achieved online (e.g., Berger, 2017). Hence, videoconferencing therapy did not attract much research attention for a while. The reader will notice that the fourth edition of this *Handbook* covers the topic of videoconferencing only under the chapter of 'Wider Uses of Technologies in Therapy' (Anthony, Goss and Merz Nagel, 2017) with a short introduction to the concept.

Despite these concerns, the Covid-19 pandemic led practitioners to use videoconferencing technologies almost immediately, without much training – in response to meeting the demands the pandemic placed on mental health services. Hanley (2021) suggests that the necessity to provide accessible continuing services led practitioners to consider online therapeutic interactions in a different light, with the prolonged crisis working as an 'evolutionary catalyst' (Hanley, 2021: 494) for developments in the online counselling and psychotherapy world.

Furthermore, concerns related to access, cost and therapeutic viability (Simpson et al., 2021) subsided as research gained more insight into the working dynamics of the medium. Andersson (2018) suggests that there have been over 200 randomised control studies examining internet-delivered psychotherapies in the last decade, and an abundance of books and research articles are published. The most comprehensive of these are Kraus, Strickler and Speyer (2010), Tuerk and Shore (2015), Goss et al. (2016) and Weinberg and Rolnick (2020). Videoconferencing, in this light, has proven to be a relatively straightforward resource for offering appointments with clients via applications such as Skype, Zoom, Google-Meet, VSee and so on. The level of technological knowledge is a key element in choosing the most convenient, simple, clear and efficient tool for meeting. Another key element in this transition has been to find a space for safe practice. As this is an uncharted territory for most, leading professional organisations such as American Psychological Association (APA, 2013), British Psychological Society (BPS, 2020) and British Association for Counselling and Psychotherapy (BACP, 2022a, 2022b) to revise or develop guidelines to ensure their members are working competently, while understanding ethical liabilities.

WAYS OF WORKING

There are several principles that have been trialled and developed for providing accessible, safe and effective videoconferencing services. These include promoting service quality, safeguarding client privacy and security, adapting therapy interventions on screen, identifying ways to enhance the therapeutic relationship and/or supporting practitioners with remote supervision.

Among models of therapy, cognitive behavioural therapy (CBT) has a long-standing relationship with remote therapy, starting with computerised CBT. CBT is well defined with its interventions and treatment protocols, which could explain why its adoption to remote work had an earlier start. Even though relational therapies also showed interest in videoconferencing, their techniques arguably prove more difficult to translate to the remote medium. This had an impact on how they approached videoconferencing, often with mixed attitudes (e.g., Lemma, 2017). The terminology therapy models prefer for 'videoconferencing therapy' differs, resonating with their understanding/experience of what telepresence and practice means, and in what ways their skillset as well as therapeutic orientation informs their online practice. The comprehensive volume by Weinberg and Rolnick (2020) provides detailed accounts on different modalities.

THERAPEUTIC RELATIONSHIP

In comparison to other available technologies, therapeutic relationships via videoconferencing are deemed closest to in-person equivalents. Notably, they also enable the observation of non-verbal input that promotes familiarity, connectedness and comfort. But, in contrast, the need for establishing mutual regulation has implications for practitioners in considering the increased distance, with a 'reduced window of access' into the individual's psychological state (Smith et al., 2022: 95). To start with, therapists cannot see the whole person and insights from smell, pheromones, breathing and several motor movements are absent online. Therefore, establishing a relationship that ensures a level of safety, trust and attachment requires the practitioner to significantly adapt their way of working.

Simpson and colleagues (2021) outline an in-depth list of key skills for developing a strong therapeutic alliance in videoconferencing therapy (with key references). Some of the core suggestions are:

- providing a rationale for videoconferencing therapy, considering suitability and beneficence
- rethinking technical and therapeutic induction in online practice through information sheets or in-person support, and taking client competence, interruptions and delays into account
- aiming to improve mutual regulation by taking into account posture, facial expressions, voice tone, bodily gestures and rhythming
- addressing concerns related to virtual presence in order to improve communication, taking into account perceptions of safety, privacy, intimacy and self-monitoring
- being aware about sharing control, responsibility and power
- maintaining boundaries via a therapeutic contract, considering session preparation, timing, payment and other mediums of communication
- organising risk management pathways, taking into account environmental, situational or other health-related issues, such as self-harm and abuse.

SAFE PRACTICE VIA VIDEOCONFERENCING

The expanding role of videoconferencing in the provision of therapeutic services requires careful ethical considerations. With an increasing number of mental health practitioners utilising these tools, practice guidelines intend to educate and equip practitioners with good practices and to protect them from liability.

These guidelines are underpinned by each organisation's relevant ethical principles and codes of conduct, and are guided by evidence-based practices and theories. One important aspect to these guidelines is that they all emphasise that videoconferencing is not intended to replace local guidance or other therapeutic encounters. Issues that require particular attention are data security, confidentiality, online participation/connectivity, telepresence, client consent, equity of access and choice, risk assessment and cybersupervision.

These issues also involve consideration of legal requirements, insurance, telecommunication technologies and relevant competence, intra/interagency policies and other external opportunities and challenges of a particular professional context. Practitioners are liable and responsible to appropriately balance their course of action when one set of considerations conflict with the other (American Psychological Association, 2013). Detailed accounts of information are accessible on the websites of professional organisations and practitioners are encouraged to have regular access to professional training and clinical supervision. The volume by Stokes (2018) and a chapter by Pennington, Patton and Katafiasz (2020) serve as a learning resource in cybersupervision.

One final remark is about the self-care of professionals, considering the boundary violations the medium exposes therapists to, or the cognitive load of interacting through technology for extended time periods. The following case study offers a brief account of a psychotherapist's first remote-only experience of offering videoconferencing therapy.

CASE STUDY

Peter contacted Michael during the Covid-19 lockdown with low self-esteem and anxiety issues. After arranging for a consultation session on the phone, Michael texted the electronic copy of the informed consent form he adapted for videoconferencing in supervision. In their first session on Zoom, Michael was able to sense Peter's rigid body posture, conveying discomfort, even though his body from the chest down and his hands were out of sight on the camera. His tone of voice, his discourse throughout the session was already giving away the message he voiced out later: 'I hold back'.

Michael initiated a conversation about how restrictive the remote environment could be and explained that the nature of the work needs collaboration in the face of distractions, safety issues, misunderstandings or failures of connection. The conversation continued with Peter asking further questions and it helped him to relax and feel comfortable in this new medium. The space Michael offered helped Peter communicate about his preference for connecting from his secure-home base.

Even though Peter was often quiet, Michael did not feel him to be absent as he was responding with his eyes, gestures and body posture, assuring Michael that he was present in the moment. At times, Michael was fascinated with Peter's use of the screen as he would lean into the screen in search of meanings and start a conversation, which he would never have tried in person. Peter often reflected that the medium gave him control over his presence with another person almost nose-to-nose yet with boundaries. He felt empowered.

RESEARCH

Videoconferencing therapy is rapidly becoming a medium of great research interest. In a systematic review and meta-analysis of the outcome evidence base, in which videoconferencing CBT (VCBT) was directly compared to control groups including in-person treatment, results indicated VCBT is effective for individuals with diagnoses of a variety of difficulties, including depression, chronic pain, generalised anxiety disorder, obsessive-compulsive disorder (OCD) and hypochondriasis (Matsumoto, Hamatani and Shimizu, 2021).

Another comprehensive review by Norwood and colleagues (2018) explored outcome equivalence and working alliance in studies comparing videoconferencing therapy with in-person treatment/control groups. Again, results indicated effective outcomes for videoconferencing therapy for the treatment of eating disorders, depression and insomnia, PTSD and anxiety disorders. Despite the effective outcomes, videoconferencing working alliance scores were inferior to in-person delivery. However, it could be argued this is partially due to the analyses being based on in-person working alliance scales, as the construct of online therapeutic alliance may differ from in-person counterparts (e.g., Watts et al., 2020). Another factor that might explain inconsistent outcomes is associated with therapists' competence in technology, which has an impact on client ratings of therapeutic alliance.

The nature of the work targeting specific client groups may also affect the process-related outcomes. For instance, practitioners report feeling at ease while communicating with young people through videoconferencing (e.g., Himle et al., 2012), which is consistent with research evidence of youngsters' preference for online, text-based therapies (e.g., Ersahin and Hanley, 2017). Individuals residing in rural areas also report feeling less scrutinised and self-conscious when exploring issues regarding shame, abuse, disability or body-image disorders through videoconferencing (e.g., Simpson and Morrow, 2010). Research focusing on other potentially vulnerable groups, including older adults (e.g., Christensen et al., 2020), refugees (e.g., Hassan and Sharif, 2019), and offenders (e.g., Kip et al., 2018), has found videoconferencing to be the favourable option for accessing therapy at times.

CONCLUSION

While the existing research evidence on videoconferencing therapy heavily favours the notion that in-person human contact is imperative to the success of psychotherapy, going forward, it's very likely that the technological advancements made in this field, and the inherent practicality would keep videoconferencing therapy as a developing medium with a high potential.

These developments are also in line with the stance of the pluralistic approach (Cooper and McLeod, 2011), in stepping outside the precepts and methods of therapy models by incorporating the knowledge, the goals and expectations that clients bring into therapy – including their preferences over the videoconferencing space.

Overall, it is imperative to further identify the competencies associated with good practice in videoconferencing therapy. These will help to guide and inform mental health practitioners. Further, a broader evidence base is urgently required in the territory of:

- implementing/incorporating professional training modules into existing counselling and psychotherapy courses
- risks associated with exacerbating ethnic and minority inequalities in access to mental health care via videoconferencing
- client perspectives and experiences on videoconferencing therapy, expanding research to underrepresented groups, including non-clinical client groups
- process and outcome studies on different modalities – other than CBT
- further understanding of the construct of online therapeutic alliance that is formed in videoconferencing, including specific strategies and models in establishing telepresence.

REFERENCES

American Psychological Association (2013) *Diagnostic and Statistical Manual of Mental Disorders* (5th ed.). DSM-5. Washington, DC: American Psychiatric Association.

Andersson, G. (2018) Internet interventions: Past, present and future. *Internet Interventions*, 12: 181–188.

Anthony, K., Goss, S. and Merz Nagel, D. (2017) Wider uses of technology in therapy. In C. Feltham, T. Hanley and L.A. Winter (Eds), *The SAGE Handbook of Counselling and Psychotherapy* (4th ed., pp. 639–644). London: Sage.

Berger, T. (2017) The therapeutic alliance in internet interventions: A narrative review and suggestions for future research. *Psychotherapy Research*, 27(5): 511–524.

British Association for Counselling and Psychotherapy (2022a) *Working Online in the Counselling Professions*. Lutterworth: BACP.

British Association for Counselling and Psychotherapy (2022b) *Counsellors' Guide: The competences for humanistic counselling with children and young people (4-18 years) (3rd ed.)* Lutterworth: BACP. www.bacp.co.uk/media/15874/bacp-cyp-competences-counsellors-guide-2022.pdf

British Psychological Society (2020). *Effective Therapy Via Video: Top Tips*. DCP Digital Healthcare Sub-Committee. Leicester: British Psychological Society.

Christensen, L.F., Moller, A.M., Hansen, J.P., Nielsen, C.T. and Gildberg, F.A. (2020) Patients' and providers' experiences with video consultations used in the treatment of older patients with unipolar depression: A systematic review. *Journal of Psychiatric and Mental Health Nursing*, 27(3): 258–271.

Cooper, M. and McLeod, J. (2011) *Pluralistic Counselling and Psychotherapy*. London: Sage.

Ersahin, Z. and Hanley, T. (2017) Using text-based synchronous chat to offer therapeutic support to students: A systematic review of the research literature. *Health Education Journal*, 76(5): 531–543.

Goss, S., Anthony, K., Stretch, L. and Merz Nagel, D. (Eds) (2016) *Technology in Mental Health: Applications in Practice, Supervision and Training*. Springfield, IL: C.C. Thomas.

Hanley, T. (2021) Researching online counselling and psychotherapy: The past, the present and the future. *Counselling & Psychotherapy Research*, 21: 493–497.

Hassan, A. and Sharif, K. (2019) Efficacy of telepsychiatry in refugee populations: A systematic review of the evidence. *Cureus*, 11(1): e3984.

Himle, M.B. et al. (2012) A randomized pilot trial comparing videoconference versus face-to-face delivery of behavior therapy for childhood tic disorders. *Behaviour Research and Therapy*, 50(9): 565–570.

Kip, H., Bouman, Y.H.A., Kelders, S.M. and van Gemert-Pijnen, J.E.W.C. (2018) eHealth in treatment of offenders in forensic mental health: A review of the current state. *Frontiers in Psychiatry*, 9: 42.

Kraus, R., Stricker, G. and Speyer, C. (Eds) (2010) *Online Counseling* (2nd ed.). San Diego, CA: Elsevier.

Lemma, A. (2017) *The Digital Age on the Couch*. New York: Routledge.

Matsumoto, K., Hamatani, S. and Shimizu, E. (2021) Effectiveness of videoconference-delivered cognitive behavioral therapy for adults with psychiatric disorders: Systematic and meta-analytic review. *Journal of Medical Internet Research*, 23(12): e31293.

Norwood, C., Moghaddam, N.G., Malins, S. and Sabin-Farrell, R. (2018) Working alliance and outcome effectiveness in videoconferencing psychotherapy: A systematic review and noninferiority meta-analysis. *Clinical Psychology & Psychotherapy*, 25(6): 797–808.

Pennington, M., Patton, R. and Katafiasz, H. (2020) Cybersupervision in psychotherapy. In H. Weinberg and A. Rolnick (Eds), *Theory and Practice of Online Therapy* (pp. 79–95). Abingdon, UK: Routledge.

Poletti, B., Tagini, S., Brugnera, A., Parolin, L., Ferrucci, R., Compare, A. et al. (2020) Telepsychotherapy: A leaflet for psychotherapists in the age of COVID-19. A review of the evidence. *Counnselling Psychology Quarterly*, 3–4: 352–367.

Simpson, S. and Morrow, E. (2010) Using videoconferencing for conducting a therapeutic relationship. In K. Anthony, D. Merz Nagel and S. Goss (Eds), *The Use of Technology in Mental Health: Applications, Ethics and Practice*. Springfield, IL: C.C. Thomas.

Simpson, S., Richardson, L., Pietrabissa, G., Castelnuovo, G. and Reid, C. (2021) Videotherapy and therapeutic alliance in the age of COVID-19. *Clinical Psycholology & Psychotherapy*, 28: 409–421.

Smith, K., Moller, N., Cooper, M., Gabriel, L., Roddy, J. and Sheehy, R. (2022) Videocounselling and psychotherapy: A critical commentary on the evidence base. *Counselling & Psychotherapy Research*, 22: 92–97.

Stokes, A. (Eds) (2018) *Online Supervision: A Handbook for Practitioners*. London: Routledge.

Tuerk, P.W. and Shore, P. (Eds) (2015) *Clinical Videoconferencing in Telehealth: Program Development and Practice*. Cham, Switzerland: Springer International.

Watts, S., Marchand, A., Bouchard, S., Gosselin, P., Langlois, F., Belleville, G. et al. (2020) Telepsychotherapy for generalized anxiety disorder: Impact on the working alliance. *Journal of Psychotherapy Integration*, 30: 208–225.

Weinberg, H. and Rolnick, A. (2020) *The Theory and Practice of Online Therapy. Internet-delivered Interventions for Individuals, Groups, Families, and Organizations*. New York: Routledge.

Wittson, C.L., Affleck, D.C. and Johnson, V. (1961) Two-way television in group therapy. *Mental Hospitals*, 2: 22–23.

RECOMMENDED READING

Weinberg, H. and Rolnick, A. (2020) *The Theory and Practice of Online Therapy. Internet-delivered Interventions for Individuals, Groups, Families, and Organizations*. New York: Routledge.

This comprehensive resource offers 22 chapters on conducting therapy via videoconferencing tools in different modalities, and explores the dynamics and concerns associated.

Kraus, R., Stricker, G. and Speyer, C. (2010) *Online Counseling: A Handbook for Mental Health Professionals* (2nd ed.). San Diego, CA: Elsevier.

The second edition of this 2004 edited textbook offers practical insight into how practitioners can translate their work to the online medium. It discusses online behaviour and communication, relevant skillsets and aspects of technological, ethical, legal and multicultural issues. The book provides a specific chapter on videoconferencing therapy.

Tuerk, P.W. and Shore, P. (Eds) (2015) *Clinical Videoconferencing in Telehealth: Program Development and Practice*. Cham, Switzerland: Springer International.

This work provides evidence-based practical information to administrators and clinicians in a step-by-step format. It includes checklists, templates and other tools to equip mental health professionals for service development and therapeutically sound practice.

6.9 COUNSELLING BY TELEPHONE

MAXINE ROSENFIELD

OVERVIEW AND KEY POINTS

Counselling by phone is sometimes considered 'old technology', yet people use mobile phones every day and clients are able to access phone counselling wherever they might be and at times to suit them. The skills required to work effectively by phone are among the highest order skills a counsellor can attain:

- Counselling effectively with a stranger with no visual cues.
- Counselling with no background knowledge, except perhaps a brief referral.
- Counselling skilfully, being aware of and appropriately responding to nuances, silences, slight audible changes in voice tone or pitch, words used that might be at odds with information provided.
- Holding a clear contract and its inherent boundaries negotiated by voice alone, although a final version should be signed by the client before sessions commence for legal and insurance purposes.

INTRODUCTION

As the United Kingdom moves its landline phone network from analogue to digital platforms, the numbers of households making calls on a landline is falling. According to Alsop (2020), the number of households using a landline for calls dropped from 83% in 2016 to 73% in 2020. At the same time, mobile phone usage in the UK continues to rise. In 2019, 55.5 million people owned a mobile phone, of which 87% were smartphones. Smartphone ownership in the 16–24 year-old age range was at 96% in 2021 (Struger, 2021). This makes the phone a very accessible mode for counselling.

As this chapter will highlight, working as a counsellor by telephone is significantly different from in-person and internet-based work. It is essential to examine the standards and ethical considerations that should be taken into account to ensure that clients receive the best possible service from their counsellors and that the counsellors develop high-quality practice.

Telephone counselling is not the same as one-off crisis interventions on a helpline; nor is it the same as an education-based telephone programme such as for quitting smoking. While a phone-based programme might teach a modified cognitive-behavioural therapy (CBT) approach, this is not considered true telephone counselling in the context of working with a range of issues involving a deeper exploration of the client's past and present challenges. It is holding this depth of relationship that necessitates the highly specialised skill base and clear contracts that keep both parties safe (Rosenfield, 2013: 47–65).

WAYS OF WORKING

Telephone counselling has many advantages over in-person or visual internet counselling, such as by Skype or Zoom. The lack of the impact of any visual impressions, assumptions or prejudices that occur when client and counsellor see each other in a formal counselling room causes both parties to focus on each other's voice tones and words. The anonymity of the medium is liberating for many clients and counsellors. The intensity of the interaction further enhances the development of the relationship, because there is less opportunity for distractions during the session while both parties are focused on words and voice tone alone. This often enables a deeper therapeutic relationship to be established sooner than would occur in much in-person or visual internet counselling. Silences are nuanced and form an essential part of the process.

The entire process of counselling in this medium is generally accelerated so that fewer sessions are indicated for the client to gain insight, awareness, understanding and/or empowerment. In my contracts, I suggest six sessions, with a review often at session four, as clients may experience their most emotionally challenging sessions during sessions two and three. Further blocks of four to six sessions can be negotiated, ensuring regular reviews by both parties.

Telephone counselling is an excellent example of a pluralistic approach to counselling. It can utilise aspects of psychodynamic orientations, person-centred approaches, brief therapeutic interventions and other humanistic methods of working. Cognitive-behavioural techniques may be used alongside interpretative psychotherapeutic modalities.

There is no doubt that transference and countertransference occur, triggered by words, subject matter, voice tones, pitch and accents. Psychoeducation, goal-setting and action-planning may be as much a part of some sessions as exploring the emotional aspects of the client's situation. Much effective counselling by telephone can focus on helping the client to draw on their own strengths.

When someone contracts for telephone counselling sessions, they lose some of their anonymity and confidentiality. As with helpline work, a point of crisis may be the trigger for the person to seek counselling but, unlike talking to someone on a helpline, the client is not anonymous. The client has to agree a contract for the work and therefore provide some personal details which they might not reveal if they are calling a helpline for a one-off call.

Telephone counselling is an excellent medium for challenging the inherent power relationship between counsellor and client. Both parties have to work with the unknown in ways that in-person or visual internet counselling does not present. Further, it can be argued that ultimate power lies with the client, who can choose to hang up at any time. The counsellor who has completed at least undergraduate study in counselling is going to have the theoretical knowledge, and therefore likely to hold 'academic' power in the relationship, but in practice, the client and counsellor work more 'collegially' than in any other counselling mode.

ACCESSIBILITY AND FINANCIAL CONSIDERATIONS OF TELEPHONE COUNSELLING

Many people have relatively easy access to a telephone, but for a one-hour counselling session finding a place that is private, quiet and uninterrupted may be more difficult. As long as the phone has reliable sound quality, the mobile may be the choice for many clients. It is good for the counsellor at the assessment session to stress the importance of the client being in a suitable, private, safe space for their sessions. Headsets or earpieces attached to the phone provide good quality audio and voice quality.

The cost of calls between a private counsellor and client, whether on a landline or mobile, can impact on the consideration of both parties to enter into a therapeutic relationship, although many mobile phone plans include 'unlimited' calls. Technology has also come to the aid of this potential financial constraint. The use of Voice over Internet Protocol (VoIP) enables people to talk at low cost over internet networks, although there may be data limitations for heavy usage. Software such as Skype or Zoom enable users to make voice calls over the internet. Apps such as WhatsApp and Viber use end-to-end encryption to ensure conversations are private.

Telephone counselling makes it unnecessary for the client to travel to see a counsellor. When the client has access to a phone and a quiet space, the session can take place without the client or counsellor having to be in the same location for each session. It is therefore a very accessible medium for someone who has limited mobility, who is unwell, who is caring for someone and unable to leave for a few hours, or otherwise has limited time in their schedule.

During the Covid-19 pandemic many more people used the phone for counselling than might have chosen to do previously. Both clients and counsellors had to rapidly adapt, often without counsellors taking additional training to work by phone. Lin et al. (2021) found that therapists felt less able to be effective using telehealth modes, particularly those who had little prior experience and training in these modes.

The cost of any phone call is likely to be less than the cost in time and travel to visit a counsellor, making telephone work more financially accessible in many cases. Clients can choose to work by telephone with counsellors who are not geographically accessible to them. This enables people to find a specific counsellor for a specific purpose. Some counsellors and clients work together when one party is outside their own country. Payments can be easily made electronically and instantly, ensuring that the counsellor receives their fee immediately as a session ends, as they might in in-person counselling.

From the counsellor's perspective, the telephone can be liberating, enabling them to operate from any environment that is quiet and where they are uninterrupted. It may also mean that the counsellor can work with a wider variety of clients at a greater range of times.

For telephone group work, the teleconference can bring together people from all over the country, or indeed the world, as long as each individual can be in a quiet, private place. This can lead to groups being created for people who are linked through rarer situations, specific illnesses, age or any other common theme.

CONTRACTING

Privacy and phone technology to be considered for contracting have already been addressed in this chapter, and other regular counselling contact matters are addressed elsewhere in this book. What follows are additional phone-specific matters for consideration.

- It is usual to back up any verbal consent with written documents sent to the client by mail or email, signed and returned before a first session occurs.
- The length of each session should be fixed at no longer than an hour and no less than 30 minutes to enable some discussion, reflection and processing.
- It needs to be established who calls whom, and therefore who pays, if there is any cost for the call.
- Methods of payment – how much, when and how it will be received – need to be settled.
- What is considered a late start or no-show, and what happens in these instances, needs to be set out.
- It is important to establish what types of notes or other means of recording the sessions are acceptable and legal.
- Issues about confidentiality and technology use (e.g., is the use of a loudspeaker acceptable?) need to be decided.
- It needs to be established what the client might do to 'leave the room' in a practical sense after the session ends.
- It needs to be decided what will happen if the technology fails – if the phone lines drop out or, if using VoIP, the internet crashes?

ETHICAL ISSUES

Ethical issues include the counsellor explicitly adhering to existing codes of conduct, such as those produced by professional counselling associations, which may include comments about the use of technology in counselling. There is also an ethical consideration regarding payment. It is possible for a counsellor to purchase a premium rate tariff telephone line. In this case, the client calling the counsellor pays more than the cost of a regular phone call and the 'profit' could constitute all or part of the counsellor's fee. If the counsellor who operates anything other than a freephone service, calls the client, the counsellor's phone number will be itemised on the client's telephone bill, unless the counsellor applies the 'one off' or permanent number blocking. This may be an important consideration for a vulnerable client, such as one in a family where violence is a problem or whose phone is accessed by others in their family or community.

Mixing in-person sessions and telephone sessions is not acceptable for telephone counselling. This is because the mixing of the modes will affect the transference issues/power relationship/dynamics of the relationship, with visual assumptions or judgements or prejudices changing the phone relationship thereafter. If a counselling relationship starts in-person and then moves to the phone, rapport has already been established. Both parties have knowledge about each other that they do not have if the relationship has never been visual. If it starts on the phone, counselling should remain on the phone to avoid contamination of the rapport and nuanced work that the mode provides.

SETTLING INTO A SESSION

It is important to have some 'settling in' comments to enable the client to feel as comfortable as possible to start talking in session. The counsellor takes responsibility for leading this so that the client is welcomed and encouraged to talk. Often a welcome followed by a pause and then a simple open question such as 'what is it that has brought you to counselling?' or 'what's been happening since last time we spoke?' is enough. For a first session, it can be useful to start with a few 'safe' comments about the sessions, reiterating parts of the contract, and including a reminder of how long each session will last. The counsellor should make explicit any strategies for re-contacting if technology fails for any reason, taking responsibility for trying to re-contact the client. This gives the counsellor control over this aspect of the contact. The counsellor has scheduled an hour and can only re-try for that time period. If for some reason the counsellor and client are not able to get back in contact during the hour, the counsellor could call, text, email or leave a voicemail later to re-establish contact and suggest another time to talk.

The first few minutes of any session are crucial for establishing the bond between client and counsellor, and particular attention needs to be paid to the sounds, the tone and pitch of voice, the way the client presents.

This indicates where 'they are at', emotionally speaking, and enables the counsellor to respond empathically and appropriately, following the client's agenda.

IN PRACTICE: WORKING WITH REBECCA

Rebecca chose to meet me from her car, which she had parked in a public car park. Her concerns were her partner's attitude since she had a miscarriage three months ago, when she was 11 weeks pregnant. She was blamed for the miscarriage: 'no one in his family ever had one before' and he said she was 'a failure'. Rebecca was grieving her loss and felt vulnerable. Her partner was telling her she was 'unattractive as she had put on weight and it wasn't even a real pregnancy'.

My validation of her reality, that it was OK to grieve, enabled her to release some pent up emotion that oscillated between tears and anger. By the end of the first session Rebecca said she felt calmer and explored strategies for challenging her partner's accusations. When I was summarising and wrapping up the session, she revealed something she had never told anyone: she had had one glass of wine at 10 weeks pregnant and thought this must be the reason for the miscarriage. She said it was a relief to say this out loud, a classic 'hand on the door handle' moment as there was no time left to explore further.

Over four sessions Rebecca and I explored guilt, her current and previous intimate relationships, identified patterns of behaviour in different relationships – with her partner, professionally and with her parents and siblings – and how these patterns had evolved since childhood. Grief was present in each session but with less intensity. She employed self-care strategies and we discussed and explored changing behaviours in all areas of her life.

She commented frequently that the phone enabled her to talk freely and openly. She felt heard and that she could 'say the unsayable'. She regularly commented that she could not imagine talking in this way with this intensity if she could see me. The car was a safe and private space and after each session she would go for a walk; leaving the car was leaving the session and the walk helped her switch off from the session before going back to her home.

TRAINING AND SUPERVISION

One assumption throughout this chapter is that the counsellor should hold at least a full graduate diploma or degree in counselling, psychology or social work and have at least a year's experience of in-person counselling practice before they commence telephone work. This ensures their core skills are somewhat developed.

Telephone supervision is useful to reflect on the mode of working. The issues relating to skills transfer and voice tones are the same as for the client–counsellor relationship, and not all supervisors can, or should, adapt to the phone. At the very least, a supervisor might ask a fellow supervisor to do an objective assessment for voice tone, manner and style before promoting themselves to work in this mode (Rosenfield, 2013).

As a result of the Covid-19 pandemic, Rowen, Giedgowd and Baran (2022), explored the supervision alliance and the use of phone-only supervision in training clinics that had moved to phone-only counselling services. Supervisees, all novice practitioners, reported finding phone-only supervision as effective as in-person supervision with respect to the supervisory relationship and the support that can be provided. These were, however, practitioners who had already established in-person relationships with their supervisors.

In 2005, a roundtable discussion about the use of the phone for psychoanalytic supervision highlighted several aspects of the relationship between analyst and supervisor, including that process and relational fit were more important than the mode. Margaret Fulton warned psychoanalysts not to focus exclusively on what is lost when the phone is used for supervision, noting that there can be gains due to heightened acuity to auditory cues (Manosevitz, 2006).

There is little published elsewhere that focuses solely on supervision by phone. Most research that mentions the phone does so as a small part of broader research about telehealth or telepsychology, and focuses mainly on comparing in-person with videoconference or visual internet sessions (Jordan and Shearer, 2019; Tarlow et al., 2020).

It is simplistic to assume that a good in-person counsellor will have, or be able to develop, the necessary skills for telephone counselling and it is unprofessional to assume that trained counsellors or therapists can develop a telephone practice without ever receiving qualitative feedback about their voice, style and manner, which would be assessed during a telephone counselling training course.

Telephone group counselling requires additional skills, often learned 'on the job'. Counsellors with previous experience of running in-person therapy groups may have the necessary core skills, but additional specific training is needed to ensure professionalism and skill in managing participants in an audio-only group.

A SKILLS CHECKLIST FOR THE TRAINED COUNSELLOR STARTING TELEPHONE WORK

- How do you sound?
- Is your accent pronounced or could it be off-putting to the client group you seek to attract?
- Are you able to work with silence on the phone? Be aware that a silence of a few seconds on the phone often seems like minutes and the usual counselling/therapeutic interpretations of silence and methods of responding to silence need to be adapted for successful work on the phone.
- How skilled would you be at handling distress with no visual clues?
- Are you confident at interrupting the client's flow if needs be because the session is almost over or because you believe the client is stuck and you wish to move the session on?

RESEARCH

There is limited published research on telephone counselling; there is plenty about helpline work or about specific CBT-based programmes, but these are not true phone counselling. Often the research will contrast phone and internet counselling, such as King et al. (2006: 175), who concluded that the phone was more beneficial: 'thought to be due to the greater communication efficiency of the phone enabling more counselling to be undertaken in the time available'.

Countertransference during telephone counselling is discussed by Christogiorgos et al. (2010). The paper considers countertransference phenomena, which may become apparent when working by phone, originating from the same factors that are experienced in a traditional psychotherapeutic framework.

There is much scope for research to be carried out into phone counselling, supervision and the training of practitioners. What little research there is often dates from the 1980s, 1990s and early 2000s as internet counselling has become the favoured alternative to in-person counselling. Covid-19 has reignited some interest in phone therapy out of necessity. The phone still has a significant role to play in effective therapy and supervision with appropriately skilled and trained counsellors.

REFERENCES

Alsop, T. (2020) Households with a landline telephone in the UK. *Statistica.com*. Available at www.statista.com/statistics/386778/share-of-calls-enabled-landlines-in-uk-households/The number of calls (accessed 5 March 2022).

Christogiorgos, S., Vassilopoulou, V., Florou, A., Xydou, V., Douvou, M., Vgenopoulou, S. and Tsiantis, J. (2010) Telephone counselling with adolescents and countertransference phenomena: particularities and challenges. *British Journal of Guidance & Counselling*, 38(3): 313–325.

Jordan, S.E. and Shearer, E. (2019) An exploration of supervision delivered via clinical video telehealth (CVT). *Training and Education in Professional Psychology*, 13(4): 323–330.

King, R., Bambling, M., Reid, W. and Thomas, I. (2006) Telephone and online counselling for young people: a naturalistic comparison of session outcome, session impact and therapeutic alliance. *Counselling and Psychotherapy Research*, 6(3): 175–181.

Lin, T., Stone, S. J., Heckman, T. G., and Anderson, T. (2021). Zoom-In to Zone-Out: Therapists Report Less Therapeutic Skill in Telepsychology Versus Face-to-Face Therapy During the COVID-19 Pandemic. *Psychotherapy*, 58(4) 449-459. https://doi.org/apa.org/fulltext/2022-10707-003.html

Manosevitz, M. (2006) Supervision by telephone: an innovation in psychoanalytic training – a roundtable discussion. *Psychoanalytic Psychology*, 23(3): 579–582.

Rowen, J., Giedgowd, G. and Baran, D. (2022) Effective and accessible telephone-based psychotherapy and supervision. *Journal of Psychotherapy Integration*, 32(1): 3–18. https://doi.org/10.1037/int0000257

Rosenfield, M. (2013) *Telephone Counselling: A Handbook for Practitioners*. Basingstoke: Palgrave Macmillan.

Struger, M. (2021) How many people own a smartphone in the UK? *Cybercrew* [Blog]. Available at https://cybercrew.uk/blog/how-many-people-own-a-smartphone-in-the-uk/ (accessed 5 March 2022).

Tarlow, K.R., McCord, C.E., Nelon, J.L. and Bernhard, P.A. (2020) Comparing in-person supervision and telesupervision: a multiple baseline single-case study. *Journal of Psychotherapy Integration*, 30(2): 383–393.

RECOMMENDED READING

Rosenfield, M. (1997) *Counselling by Telephone*. London: Sage.

An introductory text for those counselling by telephone.

Rosenfield, M. (2013) *Telephone Counselling: A Handbook for Practitioners*. Basingstoke: Palgrave Macmillan.

A practitioner-focused text aimed at developing skills in telephone counselling.

Lin, T., Stone, S.J., Heckman, T.G. and Anderson, T. (2021) Zoom-in to zone-out: therapists report less therapeutic skill in telepsychology versus face-to-face therapy during the COVID-19 pandemic. *Psychotherapy*, 58(4): 449–459. https://doi.org/10.1037/pst0000398

This research paper highlights the importance for practitioners to be trained to work in different media.

6.10 WIDER USES OF TECHNOLOGIES IN THERAPY

STEPHEN GOSS, DEEANNA MERZ NAGEL AND KATE ANTHONY

OVERVIEW AND KEY POINTS

This chapter briefly considers a small sampling of technologies of relevance to therapy, either as an adjunct to it or to support client development and self-help, such as:

- Computerised cognitive-behavioural therapy (CCBT)
- Videoconferencing
- Blogging
- Virtual worlds and avatar therapy.

INTRODUCTION

Mental health care's 'digital revolution' (Martinez and Farhan, 2019) leaves every therapist with a responsibility to appreciate the role and experience of technology in their client's lives. Even those who prefer not to use technologies in therapy have *at least* to understand the ramifications of technologically mediated relationships for their clients, lest they fail to appreciate that such things are real and not merely 'virtual' (Anthony, 2001). This applies throughout the world, including in regions with relatively low levels of personal income (Carter et al., 2021).

Technological mediation in therapy is not for every client or every therapist. Where it is used, adaptation to individual needs and preferences is likely to be significant in facilitating access and usage (Treanor et al., 2021). Dangers exist – such as therapists working online with victims of domestic violence who are unable to ensure privacy (Merz Nagel and Anthony, 2012) or inadequately trained therapists who are unaware of the clinical impact of the online disinhibition effect (Anthony and Merz Nagel, 2013) – as evidenced in specialist guidance (Anthony and Goss, 2009; Merz Nagel and Anthony, 2009a) and more recent competency requirements (ACTO, 2020; British Association for Counselling and Psychotherapy, 2021).

Developments in technologically mediated psychological support have frequently been led by clients rather than therapists, who often have strongly polarised reactions to the concept (Goss and Anthony, 2003; Goss and Hooley, 2015). The Covid-19 pandemic in 2020 marked a notable shift in the field. Practitioners rushed to set up online systems for their work during periods of lockdown and national caution about meeting offline, often without maintaining the training and competence standards that had been considered the required minimum. The normalisation of technological mediation of therapy during the pandemic should not be underestimated: 40% of surveyed practitioners felt they could now embrace such methods post-pandemic (TMN – Therapy Meets Numbers, 2020), with 60% of those indicating they would continue to make online work a key part of their core provision, even should the pandemic conditions disappear. Other natural disasters, such as Hurricane Katrina in the United States (Kim, 2016) and some terrorist actions, also create a communication need and technology can help to meet it. It is particularly relevant for those who are unable or reluctant to access services face to face or for specific or acute needs, as in suicide prevention (Goss and Ferns, 2016).

This chapter briefly considers a small sampling of technologies of assistance in providing therapy, either as an adjunct to it or to support client development and self-help. Telephones, email and internet chat are considered in other chapters in this volume.

WAYS OF WORKING

COMPUTERISED COGNITIVE-BEHAVIOURAL THERAPY

Computerised cognitive-behavioural therapy (CCBT) was previously among the most successful psychotherapeutic applications of technology, with a strong and growing evidence base (Cavanagh and Grist, 2016; Kaltenthaler, Cavanagh and McCrone, 2016). Lv et al. (2021) demonstrated the usefulness of CCBT during the Covid-19 pandemic, concluding it to be an effective alternative to in-room work, although meta-reviews increasingly report the need for selective caution as 'one size does not fit all' (Treanor et al., 2021: 1). CCBT benefits from being tailored to individual needs.

CCBT distils key elements of cognitive-behavioural therapy (CBT) into software for clients, who have usually been previously screened by a professional. Clients undertake tasks, such as identifying, monitoring and evaluating negative thought patterns, and are guided through strategies like graded exposure, problem solving and behavioural experiments.

CCBT varies from single-session anonymous use software to complex systems facilitating sophisticated relationships with the user. CCBT may require no therapist input, be an adjunct to therapy or be support via technology or in person. Good programs actively monitor risk (such as suicidality) and provide appropriate alerts to the user, the responsible practitioner or both.

Among numerous others, examples of CCBT include *Beating the Blues* and *FearFighter*. It is generally considered that CCBT became accepted in 2009, when NICE Guidelines were published endorsing CCBT for mild-to-moderate depression (NICE, 2006, 2009).

BLOGGING AND PODCASTING

A web log or 'blog' contains a series of articles ordered chronologically. Most are interactive to some degree, allowing responses that facilitate conversations between readers and authors, fostering distinctive communities focused around the blog's themes (Merz Nagel and Anthony, 2009b). Podcasting is a similar means of self-publishing recorded items (usually audio or video) often centred on recurrent interests and topics. Podcasting also noticed a surge in popularity during the pandemic, both for listeners and creators (Quah, 2021).

Some blogs are overtly psychoeducational or designed to keep practitioners informed (e.g., http://onlinetherapyinstitute.com/blog/ or www.psychcentral.com/blog). Others are more personal, and may be no less useful for that. Reflective writing has long been known to have therapeutic potential (Adams and Merz Nagel, 2013; Pennebaker, 1997). Electronic formats, like blogging, may offer specific additional advantages (Hyland et al., 1993) if done with sufficient attention to self-protection. Tan (2008) reported that around 50% of blogs are kept at least partly for the therapeutic effects experienced by the author.

Privacy issues easily arise, however. Practitioners should be aware of the potential for clients to blog or create podcasts or other forms of public discussion about their therapy. Whether practising via technology or not, it is wise to include discussion of such issues in contracting with clients to ensure adequate protection of privacy for both parties (Anthony and Goss, 2009; Grohol, 2016; Merz Nagel and Anthony, 2009b; see also www.onlinetherapyinstitute.com/ethical-training/).

VIRTUAL AND AUGMENTED REALITY, VIRTUAL EXPOSURE THERAPY AND AVATAR THERAPY

Virtual and augmented reality environments allow users to experience synthetically created environments with which they can interact and, often, communicate with other users. Virtual reality recreates the physical world through, typically, a headset and headphones to provide a fully immersive experience whereas augmented reality provides the experience of the immediate physical environment with added digital features. For example, an augemented reality user may see themselves and their surroundings through a head-set mounted camera that adds a stimulus such as, say, a large spider that appears to be sitting on the user's knee – and can move to generate increasingly strong fear stimuli.

Virtual worlds may be limited, like a single room or set of objects, or extensive, like the infinitely expandable world of *Second Life*, within which relationships, businesses – and therapy – can all flourish. Virtual worlds with a community of users – massively multiplayer online (MMO) environments – can offer vastly increased social opportunities (Deeley, 2008; Live2Give, 2005) with an equality not restricted by the users' gender, race or disability, including social skills deficits (Merz Nagel, 2009).

Avatars – the digital representation of the user – can express one's actual or ideal self or different 'configurations of self' (Mearns and Thorne, 2000) – a child, a different gender or even an animal – in what has been termed 'avatar therapy' (Anthony and Lawson, 2002). It is possible to construct conversations with deceased family members (Merz Nagel and Anthony, 2010), allowing clients to process 'unfinished business', or to address other parts of their selves, extending familiar 'empty chair' techniques (Ivey and Ivey, 1999).

While security issues may require virtual worlds, including *Second Life*, to be combined with more thoroughly encrypted services to allow properly private conversations, some, such as NeuroVR Editor (Riva and Repetto, 2016) or PRO REAL (Quigley, 2021), have been created with therapeutic levels of safety and benefit in mind (Riva and Repetto, 2016).

Clinical applications include virtual exposure therapy, in which clients address problematic situations within the safety of a virtual environment, which are increasingly shown to be promising (Deng et al., 2019; Eshuis et al., 2021), with some notable variations and some variation in the quality of research undertaken. Examples of areas in which virtual or augmented reality has been applied include sexual disorders (Optale, 2003), stress management (Villani, Riva and Riva, 2007) and arachnophobia (Emmelkamp et al., 2001). The client – or an avatar representing them – is placed in a simulation of the feared situation and thus experiences responding to the feared situation in a safe environment. Behavioural rehearsal, it should be noted, has potential for negative effects when conducted without a safe therapeutic frame: examples have been noted of suicidal behaviours being rehearsed in *Second Life*, leading to increased suicidality in the everyday physical world as well as escapism within a virtual world, which may also increase dysfunctional or suicidal behaviours within the physical world (Alvarez, 2021; Subudhi, Das and Sahu, 2020).

ASSISTIVE TECHNOLOGIES

Assistive technologies for psychological therapies have been available for a long time (Goss and McGillivray, 2007) but have, arguably, made more progress in medical settings in which diagnostic predictability is more achievable (Castelnuovo et al., 2015). However, as tools to support both delivery of, and access to, mental health care, assistive technologies are likely to continue to become increasingly important, especially with the development of artificially intelligent systems (Martinez and Farhan, 2019). An example is *Limbic AI*, which automates intake and initial screening, grouping clients by presenting issue and, crucially, level of risk. Improved efficiency at intake can significantly reduce waiting times, provide interim automated psychological support while waiting for therapy itself to start and it can be accessed at any time. Reported improvements in client experience, engagement and reduced drop out may improve outcomes, while features such as auto-translation may increase access for BAME communities (Harper, 2021). It is crucial that software tools are trusted (Asan, Bayrak and Choudhury, 2020) and well designed for their purpose to avoid creating an additional burden as staff integrate them with existing practices (NHS Digital, 2019). However, by removing some of the burden from practitioners, and introducing highly scalable triage and support processes, such assistive technologies can also reduce staff burnout by freeing time and boosting service capacity (Harper, 2021).

CONCLUSION

New technologies will continue to proliferate. This chapter has only been able to consider a sample of what is already available. Proper training and preparation are prerequisites to ensure client safety and optimal use as new technologies emerge (Anthony, 2015; Merz Nagel and Anthony, 2009a). A recent review (Stoll, Müller and Trachsel, 2020) indicated the top ethical concerns regarding the delivery of online psychotherapy were as follows: (1) privacy, confidentiality and security issues; (2) therapist competence and need for special training; (3) communication issues specific to the technology; (4) research gaps; and (5) emergency issues. These concerns can be mitigated with proper training that includes due diligence of the therapist regarding ethical and legal concerns. It should be noted that the top ethical reasons in support of the delivery of online psychotherapy included: (1) increased access to psychotherapy and service availability and flexibility; (2) therapy benefits and enhanced communication; (3) advantages related to specific client characteristics (e.g., a remote location); (4) convenience, satisfaction, acceptance, and increased demand; and (5) economic advantages. Post-pandemic, hybrid practice will likely be the norm for most practitioners. In 2019, hybrid practice among psychiatrists was reported as the preferred model to deliver psychiatric and psychotherapeutic care (Yellowlees and Shore, 2019). It would stand to reason that this preferred model of care will follow suit for counsellors and other mental health professionals, particularly since we have practised online work these past few years more than in previous years before the pandemic. More extensive discussion of these technologies, and others, such as social networking, telehealth, the use of film and media and technologically facilitated training and supervision, can be found in Goss et al. (2016), Goss and Anthony (2009) and Anthony and Merz Nagel (2010). Additional up-to-date discussion can also be found at www.onlinetherapyinstitute/blog.

REFERENCES

ACTO (Association for Counselling and Therapy Online) (2021) *ACTO Therapy Competencies*. Available at https://acto-org.uk/acto-recommended-competences-for-counselling-and-psychotherapy-online/ (accessed 27 October 2021).

Adams, K. and Merz Nagel, D. (2013) The benefits of therapeutic writing. *Therapeutic Innovations in Light of Technology*, 3(4): 15–20.

Alvarez, M.F. (2021) 'Closed world, wounds open. Open world, wounds closed': metacultural commentaries on digital media and youth suicide in Jan Komasa's Suicide Room. *Mortality*, 1–14.

Anthony, K. (2001) Online relationships and cyberinfidelity. *Counselling Journal*, 12(9): 38–39. Available at http://onlinetherapyinstitute.com/2011/03/14/from-the-archives-online-relationships-and-cyberinfidelity/

Anthony, K. (2015) Training therapists to work effectively online and offline within digital culture. *British Journal of Guidance & Counselling*, 43(1): 36–42.

Anthony, K. and Goss, S. (2009) *Guidelines for Online Counselling and Psychotherapy Including Guidelines for Online Supervision* (3rd ed.). Lutterworth: British Association for Counselling and Psychotherapy.

Anthony, K. and Lawson, M. (2002) *The use of innovative avatar and virtual environment technology for counselling and psychotherapy*. Available at http://onlinetherapyinstitute.com/wp-content/uploads/2012/08/BTexact.avatar.pdf

Anthony, K. and Merz Nagel, D. (2010) *Therapy Online: A Practical Guide*. London: Sage.

Anthony, K. and Merz Nagel, D. (2013) Appreciating cyberculture and the virtual self within. *Self & Society*, 40(3): 25–28.

Asan, O., Bayrak, A.E. and Choudhury, A. (2020) Artificial intelligence and human trust in healthcare: focus on clinicians. *Journal of Medical Internet Research*, 22(6): e15154. doi: 10.2196/15154

British Association for Counselling and Psychotherapy (BACP) (2021) *Online and Phone Therapy (OPT) Competence Framework*. Lutterworth: BACP. Available at www.bacp.co.uk/media/10849/bacp-online-and-phone-therapy-competence-framework-feb21.pdf

Carter, H., Araya, R., Anjur, K., Deng, D. and Naslund, J. (2021) The emergence of digital mental health in low-income and middle-income countries: a review of recent advances and implications for the treatment and prevention of mental disorders. *Journal of Psychiatric Research*, 133: 223–246.

Castelnuovo, G., Mauri, G., Simpson, S., Colantonio, A. and Goss, S.P. (2015) New technologies for the management and rehabilitation of chronic diseases and conditions. *Biomedical Research International*. doi:10.1155/2015/180436

Cavanagh, K. and Grist, R. (2016) The use of computer-aided cognitive behavioural therapy (CCBT) in therapeutic settings. In S. Goss, K. Anthony, L. Stretch and D. Merz Nagel (Eds), *Technology in Mental Health: Applications in Practice, Supervision and Training* (2nd ed.). Springfield, IL: C.C. Thomas.

Deeley, L. (2008) Is this a real life, is this just fantasy? *TimesOnline*, 24 March. Available at women.timesonline.co.uk/tol/life_and_style/women/body_and_soul/article1557980.ece

Deng, W., Hu, D., Xu, S., Liu, X., Zhao, J., Chen, Q. and Li, X. (2019) The efficacy of virtual reality exposure therapy for PTSD symptoms: a systematic review and meta-analysis. *Journal of Affective Disorders*, 257: 698–709. doi 10.1016/j.jad.2019.07.086

Emmelkamp, P.M., Bruynzeel, M., Drost, L. and van der Mast, C.A.P.G. (2001) Virtual reality treatment in acrophobia: a comparison with exposure *in vivo*. *CyberPsychology & Behavior*, 4(3): 335–340.

Eshuis, L.V., van Gelderen, M.J., van Zuidena, M., Nijdam, M., Vermetten, E., Olff, M. and Bakkera, A. (2021) Efficacy of immersive PTSD treatments: a systematic review of virtual and augmented reality exposure therapy and a meta-analysis of virtual reality exposure therapy. *Journal of Psychiatric Research*, 43: 516–527.

Goss, S. and Anthony, K. (Eds) (2003) *Technology in Counselling and Psychotherapy: A Practitioner's Guide*. London: Palgrave Macmillan.

Goss, S. and Anthony, K. (2009) Developments in the use of technology in counselling and psychotherapy. *British Journal of Guidance & Counselling*, 37(3): 223–230.

Goss, S., Anthony, K., Stretch, L. and Merz Nagel, D. (Eds) (2016) *Technology in Mental Health: Applications in Practice, Supervision and Training* (2nd ed.). Springfield, IL: C.C. Thomas.

Goss, S. and Ferns, J. (2016) Using cell/mobile phone SMS to enhance client crisis and peer support. In S. Goss, K. Anthony, L. Stretch and D. Merz Nagel (Eds), *Technology in Mental Health: Applications in Practice, Supervision and Training* (2nd ed.). Springfield, IL: C.C. Thomas.

Goss, S. and Hooley, T. (2015) Symposium on online practice in counselling and guidance. *British Journal of Guidance & Counselling*, 43(1): 1–7.

Goss, S. and McGillivray, S. (2007) *Assistive technologies in counselling and psychotherapy: a systematic review of the literature*. Invited paper. Dublin: Trinity College Dublin, European Science Foundation special symposium.

Grohol, J. (2016) Using websites, blogs and wikis within mental health. In S. Goss, K. Anthony, L. Stretch and D. Merz Nagel (Eds), *Technology in Mental Health: Applications in Practice, Supervision and Training* (2nd ed.). Springfield, IL: C.C. Thomas.

Harper, R. (2021) With AI, we're amplifying the powers of the clinician. *The Psychologist*, 34(September): 58–59.

Hyland, M., Kenyon, C.A., Allen, R. and Howarth, P. (1993) Diary keeping in asthma: comparison of written and electronic methods. *British Medical Journal*, 306(6876): 487–489.

Ivey, A.E. and Ivey, M.B. (1999) *Intentional Interviewing and Counseling*. Pacific Grove, CA: Brooks/Cole.

Kaltenthaler, E., Cavanagh, K. and McCrone, P. (2016) Evaluating the role of electronic and web-based (e-CBT) CBT in mental health. In S. Goss, K. Anthony, L. Stretch and D. Merz Nagel (Eds), *Technology in Mental Health: Applications in Practice, Supervision and Training* (2nd ed.). Springfield, IL: C.C. Thomas.

(Continued)

(Continued)

Kim, T.J. (2016) The role in behavioral telehealth in mental health. In S. Goss, K. Anthony, L. Stretch and D. Merz Nagel (Eds), *Technology in Mental Health: Applications in Practice, Supervision and Training* (2nd ed.). Springfield, IL: C.C. Thomas.

Live2Give (2005) All About Live2Give. *Braintalk* [Blog], January. Available at braintalk.blogs.com/live2give/2005/01/all_about_live2.html

Lv, Z., Li, J., Zhang, B., Zhang, N. and Wang, C. (2021) The effect of computerized cognitive behavioral therapy on people's anxiety and depression during the 6 months of Wuhan's lockdown of COVID-19 epidemic: a pilot study. *Frontiers in Psychology*, 12. doi: 10.3389/fpsyg.2021.687165

Martinez, C. and Farhan, I. (2019) *Making the Right Choices: Using Data-driven Technology to Transform Healthcare*. London: Reform. Available at https://reform.uk/sites/default/files/2019-07/Using%20data-driven%20technology%20to%20transform%20mental%20health%20services.pdf (accessed 21 December 2021).

Mearns, D. and Thorne, B. (2000) *Person-centred Therapy Today*. London: Sage.

Merz Nagel, D. (2009) People with Asperger's syndrome learn social skills in *Second Life*. *Telehealth World*, 2(1): 1–8. Available at www.telehealthworld.com/images/Spring09.pdf

Merz Nagel, D. and Anthony, K. (2009a) *Ethical Framework for the Use of Technology in Mental Health*. Online Therapy Institute. Available at www.onlinetherapyinstitute.com/id43.html

Merz Nagel, D. and Anthony, K. (2009b) Writing therapies using new technologies: the art of blogging. *Journal of Poetry Therapy*, 22(1): 41–45.

Merz Nagel, D. and Anthony, K. (2010) Conclusion: innovation and the future of technology in mental health. In K. Anthony, D. Merz Nagel and S. Goss (Eds), *The Use of Technology in Mental Health: Applications, Ethics and Practice*. Springfield, IL: CC Thomas.

Merz Nagel, D. and Anthony, K. (2012) Offering online interventions to victims of domestic violence. *Employee Assistance Report*, 15(10).

NHS Digital (2019) *Improving Access to Psychological Therapies self-referral process research*. London: NHS Digital. Available at https://digital.nhs.uk/publication-system/statistical/improving-access-to-psychological-therapies-key-performance-indicators-iapt-kpis/iapt-self-referral-process-research (accessed 21 December 2021).

NICE (2006) *Guidance on the Use of Computerised Cognitive Behavioural Therapy for Anxiety and Depression*. Technology Appraisal no. 97. London: National Institute for Health and Clinical Excellence.

NICE (2009) *Depression: Management of Depression in Primary and Secondary Care*. Guidance CG90. London: National Institute for Health and Clinical Excellence.

Optale, G. (2003) Male sexual dysfunctions and multimedia immersion therapy. *CyberPsychology & Behavior*, 6(3): 289–294.

Pennebaker, J.W. (1997) Writing about emotional experiences as a therapeutic process. *Psychological Science*, 8(3): 162–166.

Quah, N. (2021) Yes, podcast listenership is still on the rise. *Vulture* [Podcast], 16 March. Available at www.vulture.com/2021/03/podcast-listenership-download-data-on-the-rise.html (accessed 27 October 2021).

Quigley, C.A. (2021) ProReal®: the 'good enough' online alternative to face-to-face Dramatherapy. *Dramatherapy*, 41(2): 90–99.

Riva, G. and Repetto, C. (2016) Using virtual reality immersion therapeutically. In S. Goss, K. Anthony, L. Stretch and D. Merz Nagel (Eds), *Technology in Mental Health: Applications in Practice, Supervision and Training* (2nd ed.). Springfield, IL: C.C. Thomas.

Subudhi, R., Das, S. and Sahu, S. (2020) Digital escapism. *Horizon: Journal of Humanities and Social Sciences Research*, 2(S): 37–44.

Stoll, J., Müller, J.A. and Trachsel, M. (2020) Ethical issues in online psychotherapy: a narrative review. *Frontiers in Psychiatry*, 10: 993.

Tan, L. (2008) Psychotherapy 2.0: MySpace® blogging as self-therapy. *American Journal of Psychotherapy*, 62(2): 143–163.

TMN – Therapy Meets Numbers (2020) Are we embracing a new way of working? *Therapy Meets Numbers*. Available at https://therapymeetsnumbers.com/are-we-embracing-a-new-way-of-working/ (accessed 27 October 2021).

Treanor, C., Kouvonen, A., Lallukka, T. and Donnelly, M. (2021) Acceptability of computerized cognitive behavioral therapy for adults: umbrella review. *JMIR Mental Health*, 8(7): e23091. doi: 10.2196/23091 (accessed 8 December 2021).

Villani, D., Riva, F. and Riva, G. (2007) New technologies for relaxation: the role of presence. *International Journal of Stress Management*, 14(3): 260–274.

Yellowlees, P. and Shore, J. (2019) Hybrid practitioners and digital treatments. In L.W. Roberts (Ed.), *Textbook of Psychiatry* (7th ed.). Washington, DC: American Psychiatric Association Publishing.

RECOMMENDED READING

Goss, S., Anthony, K., Stretch, L. and Merz Nagel, D. (Eds) (2016) *Technology in Mental Health: Applications in Practice, Supervision and Training* (2nd ed.). Springfield, IL: C.C. Thomas.

The second edition of this wide-ranging edited textbook includes 40 updated chapters on all available technologies used in the profession in 2016, including a new section on clinical supervision and training.

Anthony, K. and Merz Nagel, D. (2010) *Therapy Online: A Practical Guide*. London: Sage.

This textbook focuses on the use of text in online work and is written by the two leading experts in online therapy and counselling. It also includes a full case study between a counsellor and a client from online assessment through email, mobile SMS, chat, telephone and videoconferencing to closure of the therapeutic online relationship.

Therapeutic Innovations in Light of Technology (*TILT*) Archives. Available at https://issuu.com/onlinetherapyinstitute/docs

TILT magazine is a quarterly publication from the Online Therapy Institute provided free of charge to all readers. It focuses on the use of technology in mental health and coaching. Archives of the online magazine are available for free download, including features, articles, book reviews and a regular research digest.

PART VII

SETTINGS

7.1 WORKING IN SCHOOLS

SHIRA BARAM

OVERVIEW AND KEY POINTS

The landscape that school-based (SB) counsellors and psychotherapists work in is slowly changing. Many schools across the UK do not offer a counselling service to their students as standard, but political pushes have the potential to change this in the future. As such, currently, there is no uniformity across the four nations in respect of provision for school-based counselling (SBC). Some key points of this chapter are:

- The challenges faced by those working in schools is diverse and wide-ranging – from employment opportunities to the level of severity of the emotional and mental wellbeing issues they will deal with.
- The importance of understanding the benefits and challenges of using routine outcome measures (ROMs) in their work.
- Equality, diversity and inclusivity (EDI) – the client base is diverse in this setting, and therefore we must be aware of our competencies and limitations.
- Location – there may be different rules, regulations and requirements for SBC and those working with children and young people (CYP), depending on the where they are based in the UK.

INTRODUCTION

The call for SBC provision in all schools in the UK has fluctuated over time, but has been increasing over the last few decades (Hanley, Noble and Toor, 2017). In 2015, the Department for Education published its report *Counselling in Schools: A Blueprint for the Future*. This is under review as much has changed since its publication in respect of mental health needs, issues around safeguarding, EDI and GDPR (General Data Protection Regulation). Currently, however, there is no uniformity across the four nations, with England lagging behind in respect of SBC provision in comparison to Scotland, Wales and Northern Ireland (NI), which have legislated/approved funding for SBC for those aged 10–18. Across the UK, forward planning is still needed to ensure consistent and continued funding and support for SBC.

Many counsellors and psychotherapists seeking to work with CYP have usually completed a training course that is predominantly focused on therapeutic work with adults. Governing bodies all highlight the need for those working with this client base to be operating within their CYP competency framework and standards (British Association for Counselling and Psychotherapy (BACP), 2019; Counselling and Psychotherapy in Scotland (COSCA), 2014; UK Council of Psychotherapy (UKCP), 2019), resulting in increasing calls for specific CYP accredited counselling training courses. Those working with CYP have a greater ethical, legal and professional duty to their clients and it is essential to have a good understanding of these areas.

In the changing landscape of mental health provision, SBC may find themselves competing with psychological wellbeing practitioners (PWP) and Education Mental Health Practitioners (EMPHs) due to school budget constraints and local mental health policies. SBCs often find themselves having to educate policy makers and head teachers to the value, economically, emotionally and educationally, of the importance of our service (Wright et al., 2020).

The House of Commons Health Select Committee (2014) recognised the importance of SBC. Schools have enormous potential to address emerging mental health issues in children and young people and the impact of the Covid-19 pandemic has highlighted the significant gaps in mental health provision for this age group as well as the long-term effects of the pandemic. Government statistics show that one in six of those aged 6–19 now experience a mental health issue (Newlove-Delgado et al., 2021; Vizard et al., 2020), which is an increase from 2017 statistics (Centre for Mental Health, 2021). CYP have been directly affected by the pandemic in areas of bereavement, social isolation, anxiety, relationship issues with their family and peers, and domestic abuse as well as stress and worry associated with exams, educational attainment and achievement. The pandemic has directly impacted on young people's mental health, with 51% of those surveyed saying their mental health has got much worse since March 2020 (Mind, 2021).

WAYS OF WORKING

School-based counselling is defined as 'a form of psychological therapy that provides young people with an empathic, non-judgemental and supportive relationship to find their own answers to their problems' (Hill, Roth and Cooper, 2014). There are various ways of working with younger clients, with the way individuals work being influenced by the age of the client base – for instance, non-directive play therapy has been demonstrated to be highly effective for primary-aged children and more directed-play therapy can benefit all children. In contrast, for those in secondary schools, creative and solution-based therapy and traditional humanistic talking therapies are viewed to be beneficial. The use of art and creative techniques alongside metaphor and symbols to allow CYP to process their feelings and experiences is also very powerful. As such, practitioners may find themselves using an integrative approach when working with CYP.

The benefits of SBC are that it offers child-centred therapy free at the point of access, at convenient times for our client base, without the need for CYP to meet specific criteria. It also allows early intervention via a simpler and less onerous referral system than statutory-funded CYP Mental Health (MH) services.

A whole-school approach in relation to SBC is advocated (Department of Health, 2015; Luxmoore, 2014; Public Health England, 2021) so as to provide a holistic and collaborative multidisciplinary approach. School-based counsellors commonly work with child and adolescent mental health services (CAMHS), other statutory CYP MH services, teachers and school pastoral teams. Those working in this setting should therefore familiarise themselves with the contracts and policies for each. Many schools will also expect counsellors to help develop appropriate health and wellbeing strategies, policies to reduce MH stigma or specific areas of concern (e.g., sexual harassment and abuse and bullying (Ofsted, 2021)).

ROUTINE OUTCOME MEASURES

It is important practitioners familiarise themselves with validated and approved CYP routine outcome measures (ROMs) so that they can use these effectively and consistently. For example, the Strengths and Difficulties Questionnaire (SDQ), Young Person's Clinical Outcomes in Routine Evaluation (YP-CORE) and Goal-Based Outcomes (GBO) are validated and approved tools that are used regularly in this setting. The use of ROMs enables practitioners and the CYP to measure and track progress (for more information on their use, see Lyons – Chapter 3.6, this volume). In addition, many schools or budget funders will require you to demonstrate effectiveness and ROMs can be used to provide validated evidence.

SAFEGUARDING

Practitioners must follow the school/academy's safeguarding policies/processes, therefore familiarising themselves with these before they start working therapeutically is essential. If unsure, each local council website will have links to CYP safeguarding policy. It is a requirement to keep safeguarding knowledge and understanding up to date, so it is recommended that practitioners check to see if this training is offered by their education employer. Further, the guidelines on how often this training should be refreshed depends on which nation you are practising in. Additional courses related to radicalisation (e.g., PREVENT) should also be attended (Department for Education, 2015; Home Office, 2015; NHS England, 2017).

EQUALITY, DIVERSITY AND INCLUSIVITY

School-based counsellors are located in a unique environmental microcosm, unlike any other setting individuals may experience in their lifetime. For this reason, equality, diversity and inclusivity is of great importance not just for the SB counsellor, but for those they work with. Being aware and sensitive to the challenges many CYP face and school-specific issues (e.g., school-based bullying and sexual harassment and abuse (House of Commons, 2016; Ofsted, 2021)) as well as an awareness of the practitioner's own personal perceptions and views is important (Equality Act 2010; HM Government, 2010). Being familiar with the protected characteristics is vital as practitioners frequently work with individuals from different ethnic, religious and cultural backgrounds from themselves, so being sensitive, understanding and aware of views towards mental health in your client's culture and community is important. Having a good understanding of learning difficulties and/or disabilities, such as autism and dyslexia, can also be very helpful as 70% of children with autism have at least one mental health issue (Centre for Mental Health, 2021; Simonoff et al., 2008) and many SB counsellors may find themselves identifying learning difficulties early, enabling schools to make the relevant referrals and obtain support.

CYP are significantly impacted by domestic violence and abuse. They are not passive, but rather they 'live with it and experience it directly, just as adults do' (Callaghan et al., 2018) and often display behaviour directly linked to what they have experienced (e.g., truancy, high anxiety, anger, self-harm, self-blame, low sense of self, depression and difficulties with recognising appropriate and healthy behaviours), resulting in referrals to SBC.

Homophobic, biphobic and transphobic bullying has a significant effect on LGBT CYP (Government Equalities Office, 2018a; Robinson, Espelage and Rivers, 2013). Many respondents of the LGBT+ National Survey (Government Equalities Office, 2018b) stated that they had been 'outed' without their consent, resulting in emotional and psychological consequences. SB counsellors might be the first person a CYP discloses to, so providing a safe, non-judgemental, empathic environment is essential, especially if CYP sexual orientation is considered incompatible to their religious beliefs.

CASE STUDY

Molly was considered to be at high risk of potential harm in her household due to witnessing and experiencing a traumatic episode of domestic violence that resulted in police involvement. In this instance, her father was verbally and physically abusive towards her mother. During the sessions with the school counsellor, Molly shared the effects of witnessing the aggressive and abusive behaviour and their frustrations at how family members supported their father and 'took their side'. They were candid and honest about how this made them feel, talking about their fears and worries, which often made sleeping at night difficult, and their anxiety about sharing with family members their sexual orientation due to negative comments made by their father about LGBTQ+. During one session, Molly discussed their anxiety and concerns that their mother might allow their father back into their home, and the fears they had about bringing this up with their mum.

With support from the counsellor, they were able to disclose these concerns to the safeguarding officer in the school, who on their behalf spoke to their mum. Even though Molly acknowledged to the SB counsellor that the result wasn't quite what they had hoped for, the fact that they had been listened to, heard and believed by the school and their mum was very powerful and beneficial for them.

ADOPTED CHILDREN

If adoption or adoption-related issues are the primary focus of the referral, only those counsellors registered as an adoption support agency (ASA) with Ofsted (or Regulation and Quality Improvement Authority (RQIA) in Northern Ireland) or those who are working under an ASA may work with issues related to adoption. SB counsellors working in Scotland and Wales should follow the laws of their nation (see the BACP Good Practice in Action guides related to adoption and the counselling professions for further guidance and information). If during the therapy, adoption or issues related to adoption are raised but are not the primary focus, guidance from Ofsted and your nation's appropriate organisation should be sought alongside advice from your governing body.

ETHICAL REQUIREMENTS

All governing bodies stipulate in their code of conduct and ethical framework that you must have regular supervision with someone more qualified than yourself, who is registered as a supervisor and has experience of working with CYP. This is an important part of ethical practice and can support safeguarding procedures.

The Education or Health Departments for England, Scotland, Wales and Northern Ireland may have their own specific requirements, so it is important that practitioners keep up to date with this information. Further, being familiar with Gillick competency is also important and, for those providing SBC in Scotland, understanding the Age of Legal Capacity (Scotland) Act published in 1991 is essential.

RESEARCH

The evidence base for SBC is very encouraging. Randomised controlled trials (RCT) into the benefits of SBC in secondary schools found that individuals experienced a significant reduction in psychological distress, which was above the effects of existing school pastoral care provision. Higher levels of improved self-esteem and achievement of personal goals were also reported (Cooper et al., 2021). An evaluation of SBC found that it offers CYP a boundaried and safe space to talk about things that mattered to them within a secure, empathic, non-judgemental and confidential area (Cooper, 2013). Additionally, students and school staff value SBC as it is seen as improving wellbeing as well as educational attainment (Cooper, 2013). There have been four small-scale RCTs that have also identified the effectiveness of SBC in relation to improvements in prosocial behaviour and a reduction in depressive symptoms (Cooper et al., 2010), a reduction in psychological distress (McArthur, Cooper and Berdondini, 2013; Pybis et al., 2015) and greater improvement in self-esteem compared to those who had usual school care (Pearce et al., 2017). The benefits for primary school children have also been researched and reveal that a reduction in mental health difficulties has been found that is maintained longer term, notably six months after counselling ended (Finning et al., 2021). Likewise, research into parent/carers' and users' views of SBC has found that they have a positive perception of this and its benefits (Longhurst et al., 2021).

In contrast, CYP counsellors and psychotherapists recognise that more research into SBC is needed, specifically related to accessibility for black and minority ethnic groups (Duncan et al., 2020), for those with protected characteristics, for those with learning difficulties/disabilities, and into the effects of the Covid-19 pandemic. Additionally, the emphasis on the requirement for RCTs by NICE in England can be seen as restrictive as it does not acknowledge the valuable contribution that non-RCT research or qualitative research contributes to SBC, which includes the voices of CYP regarding their experiences, views and the perceived benefits of SBC.

REFERENCES

British Association for Counselling and Psychotherapy (BACP) (2019) *Competencies for Work with Children and Young People (4–18 years): Core Competencies for Working for Work with Children and Young People*. Lutterworth: BACP.

Callaghan, J., Alexander, J., Sixsmith J., and Chiara Fellin, L. (2018) Beyond 'witnessing': children's experiences of coercive control in domestic violence and abuse. *Journal of Interpersonal Violence*, 33, 1551–1581.

Centre for Mental Health (2021) *Children and Young People's Mental Health: The Facts*. London: CMH.

Cooper, M. (2013) *School-Based Counselling in UK Secondary Schools: Review and Critical Evaluation*. Strathclyde: University of Strathclyde.

Cooper, M., Rowland, N., McArthur, K., Pattison, S., Cromarty, K., and Richards, K. (2010) Randomised controlled trial of school-based humanistic counselling for emotional distress in young people: feasibility study and preliminary indications of efficacy. *Child Adolescence Psychiatry Mental Health*, 4, 12.

Cooper, M., Stafford, M.R., Saxon, D., Beecham, J., Bonin, E., Barkham, M., Bower, P., Cromarty, K., Duncan, C., Pearce, P., Rameswari, T., and Ryan, G. (2021) Humanistic counselling plus pastoral care as usual versus pastoral care as usual for the treatment of psychological distress in adolescents in UK state schools (ETHOS): a randomised controlled trial. *Lancet Child and Adolescent Health*, 5, 178–189.

(Continued)

(Continued)

Counselling and Psychotherapy in Scotland (COSCA) (2014) *Competencies for Counselling Children and Young People* [Online]. Available at www.cosca.org.uk/application/files/5015/2119/6587/Counselling_competencies06-24-15.pdf (accessed 14 February 2022).

Department for Education (2015) *Counselling in Schools: A Blueprint for the Future*. London: DoE.

Department of Health (2015) *Future in Mind: Promoting, Protecting and Improving Our Children and Young People's Mental Health and Wellbeing*. London: Department of Health.

Duncan, C., Rayment, B., Cooper, M., and Kenrick, J. (2020) Counselling for young people and young adults in the voluntary and community sector: an overview of the demographic profile of clients and outcomes. *Psychology and Psychotherapy: Theory, Research and Practice*, 93(1), 36–53.

Finning, K., White, J., Toth, K., Golden, S., Melendez-Torres, G. J., and Ford, T. (2021) Longer-term effects of school-based counselling in UK primary schools. *European Child & Adolescent Psychiatry*, 14 May. [Online]. Available at https://link.springer.com/article/10.1007/s00787-021-01802-w#article-info (accessed 14 February 2022).

Government Equalities Office (2018a) *LGBT Action Plan: Improving the lives of Gay, Lesbian, Bisexual and Transgender People*. London: GEO. [Online]. Available at https://assets.publishing.service.gov.uk/government/uploads/system/uploads/attachment_data/file/721367/GEO-LGBT-Action-Plan.pdf (accessed 14 February 2022).

Government Equalities Office (2018b) *National LGBT Survey 2017: Summary Report*. London: GEO. [Online]. Available at https://assets.publishing.service.gov.uk/government/uploads/system/uploads/attachment_data/file/722314/GEO-LGBT-Survey-Report.pdf (accessed 14 February 2022).

Hanley, T., Noble, J., and Toor, N. (2017). Policy, Policy Research on School-Based Counselling in the United Kingdom. In: Carey, J., Harris, B., Lee, S., Aluede, O. (eds) *International Handbook for Policy Research on School-Based Counseling*. Springer, Cham. https://doi.org/10.1007/978-3-319-58179-8_23

Hill, A., Roth, T., and Cooper, M. (2014) *The Competencies Required to Deliver Effective Humanistic Counselling for Young People*. Lutterworth: British Association for Counselling and Psychotherapy.

HM Government (2010) *Equality Act 2010*. London: HMSO. Available at www.legislation.gov.uk (accessed 20 May 2016).

Home Office (2015) *Prevent Duty Guidance For England, Scotland and Wales*. Updated 1 April 2021 [Online]. Available at www.gov.uk/government/publications/prevent-duty-guidance (accessed 14 February 2022).

House of Commons (2016). *Sexual harassment and sexual violence in schools*. London: House of Commons

House of Commons Health Committee (2014) *Children's and Adolescents Mental Health and CAMHS: The Third Report of Session 2014–15. HC 342 House of Commons*. London: HMSO.

Longhurst, P., Sumner, A., Smith, S., Eilenberg, J., Duncan, C., and Cooper, M. (2021) They need somebody to talk to: parents and carers perceptions of school-based humanistic counselling. *Counselling and Psychotherapy Research*, 22(3), 667–677.

Luxmoore, N. (2014) *School Counsellors Working with Young People and Staff: A Whole-School Approach*. London: Jessica Kingsley Publishing.

McArthur, K., Cooper, M., and Berdondini, L. (2013) School-based humanistic counselling for psychological distress in young people: pilot randomized controlled trial. *Psychotherapy Research*, 23(3), 355–365.

Mind (2021) *Coronavirus: The Consequences for Mental Health*. London: Mind.

Newlove-Delgado, T., Williams, T., Robertson, K., McManus, S., Sadler, K., Vizard, T., Cartwright, C., Mathews, F., Norman, S., Marcheselli, F., and Ford, T. (2021) *Mental health of children and young people in England, 2021: wave 2 follow up to the 2017 survey*. London: NHS Digital [Online]. Available at https://digital.nhs.uk/data-and-information/publications/statistical/mental-health-of-children-and-young-people-in-england/2021-follow-up-to-the-2017-survey (accessed 11 November 2021).

NHS England (2017) *Guidance for Mental Health Services in Exercising Duties to Safeguard People from the Risk of Radicalisation*. London: NHS England.

Ofsted (2021) *Research and Analysis: Review of Sexual Abuse in Schools and Colleges*. London: Ofsted.

Pearce, P., Sewell, R., Cooper, M., Osman, S., Fugard, A.J.B., and Pybis, J. (2017) Effectiveness of school-based humanistic counselling for psychological distress in young people: pilot randomized controlled trial with follow-up in an ethnically diverse sample. *Psychology and Psychotherapy*, 90, 138–155.

Public Health England (2021) *Children & Young People's Mental Health Coalition, Promoting Children & Young People's Mental Health and Wellbeing: A Whole School or College Approach*. London: PHE.

Pybis, J., Cooper, M., Hill, A., Cromarty, K., Levesley, R., Murdoch, J., and Turner, N. (2015) Pilot randomised controlled trial of school-based humanistic counselling for psychological distress in young people: outcomes and methodological reflections. *Counselling and Psychotherapy Research*, 15, 241–250.

Robinson, J.P., Espelage, D., and Rivers, I. (2013) Developmental trends in peer victimisation and emotional distress in LGB and heterosexual youth. *Paediatrics*, 131(3), 423–430.

Simonoff, E., Pickles, A., Charman, T., Chandler, S., Loucas, T., and Baird, G. (2008) Psychiatric disorders in children with autism spectrum disorders: prevalence, comorbidity, and associated factors in a population derived sample. *Journal of American Academy of Child Adolescent Psychiatry*, 47(8), 921–929.

UKCP (2019) *UKCP Standards of Education and Training: The Minimum Core Criteria, Child Psychotherapy*. [Online]. Available at www.psychotherapy.org.uk/media/a1ippruq/ukcp-child-psychotherapy-standards-of-education-and-training-2019.pdf (accessed 14 February 2022).

Vizard, T., Sadler, K., Ford, T., Newlove-Delgado, T., McManus, S., Marcheselli, F., Davis, J., Williams, T., Leach, C., Mandalia, D., and Cartwright, C. (2020) *Mental health of children and young people in England, 2020: Wave 1 follow up to the 2017 survey NHS Digital* 2020. [Online]. Available at https://digital.nhs.uk/data-and-information/publications/statistical/mental-health-of-children-and-young-people-in-england/2020-wave-1-follow-up (accessed 11 November 2021).

Wright, B., Garside, M., Allgar, V., Hodkinson, R., and Thorpe, H. (2020) A large population-based study of the mental health and wellbeing of children and young people in the North of England. *Clinical Child Psychology and Psychiatry*, 25(4), 877–890.

RECOMMENDED READING

CYP Competencies framework for your governing body (i.e., COSCA, BACP, UKCP, Play Therapy UK (PTUK)).

These are freely available resources that outline the competencies for working with these age groups (see the reference list for more details).

Hanley, T., Lennie, C., and Humphrey, N. (2013) *Adolescent Counselling Psychology: Theory, Research and Practice*. London: Routledge.

A text advocating a pluralistic, research-informed approach to working with young people and young adults.

Luxmoore, N. (2014) *School Counsellors Working with Young People and Staff: A Whole-School Approach*. London: Jessica Kingsley Publishing.

An excellent overview of topics to be aware of when working in the school setting.

7.2 WORKING IN COLLEGES AND UNIVERSITIES

KIRSTEN AMIS

OVERVIEW AND KEY POINTS

This chapter provides an overview of what it is like to work in colleges and universities. It provides a brief reflection on the context in which student counsellors work before outlining some key areas for practitioners to be aware of. These include:

- Professional and ethical issues can sometimes get complex in these settings. Specifically, the limits of where the counsellor's roles begin and end are often defined by the specific setting.
- Students can attend counselling for a wide variety of issues. While many issues overlap with other settings, some are distinct to the educational setting.
- There is not a single approach that is used in all student counselling services. Many do, however, make use of short-term integrative models.
- Other important issues include managing waiting lists, referral processes and potentially supporting trainees.

INTRODUCTION

AN HISTORICAL OVERVIEW

Counselling services have been long established in colleges and universities in the United Kingdom and typically sit within a wider student support network of services. Early professional standards of the Association for Student Counselling helped inform the early work of the British Association for Counselling (later, with psychotherapy added) and, as such, student counselling has been an important influencing factor in the wider development of counselling in the UK.

THE INSTITUTIONAL SETTING

Counsellors are employed by universities, colleges (both higher and further education), sixth form colleges, community-based education and also for distance learning organisations. This variety is a key area to understand as counsellors working in universities and colleges may experience very different working environments. Universities tend to have large, embedded mental wellbeing departments, colleges often have a lone counsellor working alongside generic student support services, and community-based or distance learning centres may offer remote therapy delivered by an external service. It is also possible that counsellors may be employed to work therapeutically with staff rather than students. Often, this is in addition to employee assistance programme (EAP) alternatives, ensuring staff have a choice between internal or external support.

STUDENT SUPPORT STRUCTURES

If the counselling service sits within a wider wellbeing team with mental health advisors, psychologists and psychiatrists, colleagues can provide support. However, if a lone counsellor is placed in a generic student support department, there is less opportunity to discuss and explore clinical issues. It is rare to find a student support manager who acknowledges and accepts that counsellors must adhere to their ethical framework in addition to legislation, policies and procedures. Tensions can arise regarding areas such as boundaries and confidentiality.

In these more generic teams, it is apparent that there is little parity of esteem between psychological challenges and physical or cognitive challenges in most colleges and universities. While a student diagnosed with dyslexia may access support throughout their studies, a student with a diagnosis of depression might not. The ideal model would be to offer counselling support to a student for as long as they feel it is necessary, but this is not a realistic option in the majority of services offering between one and eight sessions due to the demand for appointments outstripping availability.

PROFESSIONAL AND ETHICAL ISSUES

BOUNDARIES, GDPR AND CONFIDENTIALITY

As mentioned previously, there is the potential for boundaries to become blurred if they are not carefully managed. These are examples of fairly common occurrences:

- A new student is referred to the counselling service by a lecturer. The lecturer approaches the counsellor to ask if they are attending.
- A student asks you to write a letter to their lecturer confirming that they are attending counselling to gain a submission extension.
- A young, upset student brings a friend and asks if they can stay during the session.

To manage these situations professionally, it is important to be confident in maintaining privacy, confidentiality and the procedures and protocols of the service. Luckily, counsellors should be able to follow the guidance safely when considering the range, importance and relevance of our personal and professional values, in addition to our principles and personal moral qualities in the context of ethical practice. Having awareness of current, relevant laws and recognised models of ethical decision making will make this process more structured and systematic.

Notwithstanding the wide age range in the student population, student counsellors are likely to be working with a generally younger client group, so evaluating risk and following safeguarding protocols are a core part of their work. Being part of a wellbeing or counselling team can be a significant help for student counsellors. It gives them an opportunity to discuss situations with others. Professional networks can offer this assistance for lone counsellors.

FITNESS TO STUDY OR PRACTISE

All students have the potential to experience a crisis or deterioration in their mental health at some point in their studies, which can significantly impair their capacity to study effectively. For students enrolled on courses which involve a healthcare placement (e.g., medicine), they are required to undertake a 'fitness to practise' or 'fitness to study' assessment. Counsellors are usually very clear that they do not see themselves as having a role in assessing, and therefore determining, an individual student's fitness to study or practise. However, increasingly, services or individual counsellors are being approached for their professional opinion. The tension arises from counsellors valuing the confidentiality of counselling and respecting the individual student's right to explore their mental health distress in the privacy of therapy as opposed to the institution's duty of care in determining fitness to practise. The role of professional organisations and associations, such as the British Association for Counselling and Psychotherapy (BACP), is key in offering advice and guidance in these situations, through their *Ethical Framework* (BACP, 2018) or through the BACP's University and College Division (www.bacp.co.uk/bacp-journals/university-and-college-counselling/). Objective guidance can help us navigate any potential of dual roles.

ETHICS AND COMPETENCE

To ensure we are aware of factors necessary to work ethically with students, BACP developed evidence-based competences for counselling within colleges and universities (BACP, 2016). This is useful for evaluating practice, identifying areas of strength and for development, as well as decision making in the context of educational settings. The framework provides a thorough overview of the areas of knowledge a counsellor should have to work competently in these settings. If you are likely to work in these settings, then it is essential that you consider these points.

PLACING WITHIN THE INSTITUTION

Although many college and university managers would prefer to outsource counselling, Wallace (2014) identifies embedding the service within the institution as offering the following contributions:

- Involvement in Freshers' weeks and mental health awareness days.
- Offering consultancy and support to departments and faculties to plan and deliver programmes that develop students' life and employability skills, such as assertiveness, confidence building and emotional resilience.
- Sitting on working groups and committees to ensure that mental health awareness contributes to the development of university values, strategic plans, policies and procedures.

- Collaborating in joint projects with other related services, such as mental health advisers, chaplains, disability advisers, student union officers and occupational health.
- Delivering staff training, such as helping skills, and offering consultation and signposting when students are in distress.
- Liaising with external agencies where appropriate, such as GPs and community support groups.

This links closely with the culture and ethos of the institution, how supportive management are, and the availability of ring-fenced funding. Without these, services can find themselves under threat, making evidence of effectiveness crucial. Challenging environmental and employment situations often force us to work creatively, introducing another area where the support and encouragement of colleagues is invaluable.

The day-to-day tasks of a student counsellor can include the following:

- Managing the application process, interviewing, appointment and ongoing support of counsellors.
- Ensuring all counsellors receive regular external counselling supervision (either provided by the service or the counsellor takes responsibility for their own).
- Monitoring and supporting the counsellors.
- Collating a comprehensive set of statistics to monitor the overall effectiveness of the service.
- Liaising with external agencies (such as securing student placements).
- Processing and/or liaising with social workers, the NHS, GPs, court referrals, etc.
- Prompt crisis intervention for students experiencing immediate difficulties (e.g., a suicide attempt, a panic attack or even physical fighting).
- Developing and updating all documentation for counsellors.
- Maintaining the professionalism and high standard of the service to meet the needs of the university or college.
- Conducting counselling sessions with students.
- Regular meetings with staff (service administrator, student support services, management).
- Developing relevant policies and procedures in keeping with current legislation and institution guidelines.
- Monitoring and adhering to national standards (e.g., mental health targets).
- Supporting under 24 year olds in line with government youth employment strategies (e.g., Opportunities for All, Skills Development Scotland, Certificate for Work Readiness, etc.).
- Working in partnership with external agencies to provide specific support for affected students.
- Of course, there are many more tasks involved, which will differ from service to service depending upon the remit of the department. (Amis, 2013: 7–8)

For the counselling service to be valued and considered necessary, it is important to generate evidence of its effectiveness. Establishing clear links between students attending counselling and achieving a positive academic outcome has become a requirement for the majority of services. This is especially relevant with vulnerable students who may otherwise be less successful on their course.

ASSESSMENT AND OUTCOME MEASURES

A range of generic measurement tools are widely used in counselling services based in tertiary education. These include CORE-OM, WEMWBS, PHQ-9, GAD-7, although there are others. In addition to these, a made-to-measure tool known as Counselling Impact on Academic Outcomes (CIAO) was developed specifically for working with students (Wallace, 2011) Some services have developed bespoke assessment and outcome measurement tools to meet their own needs. One such tool was developed collaboratively by the College Counsellors' Network, Scotland (CCNS). There are two key aspects, which relate to 'learning' and 'life' (see below for an overview of the questions asked). 'Learning' helps to view the client in the context of their studies whereas the 'life' section in focused on therapeutic aspects.

THE COLLEGE COUNSELLORS' NETWORK TOOL

LEARNING

ATTENDANCE

- How regularly are you attending your classes?
- Are you missing any due to the way you are feeling?
- Are your lecturers happy with your attendance?

SUPPORT

- Do you feel adequately supported?
- Are you accessing support elsewhere, either within the college or from an external organisation?
- Are you accessing learning support?
- Do you let your lecturers know when you struggle?
- Is your GP aware of your situation?
- Do you get help at home from friends and family?

CONTROL

- Do you feel in control of your situation or are there areas where you feel out of control?

POSITIVE LEARNING OUTCOMES

- Are you meeting your learning goals?
- Are you happy with your results?
- Are you finding the course is at the right level for you?

CONCENTRATION

- How well are you able to keep your mind on your studies?
- Do you find it hard to concentrate?

EMPLOYABILITY

- Do you feel you are learning skills and coping mechanisms which will help you find work or help you be successful in a current or future job?

AUTONOMY

- Are you able to make decisions in your own life?
- Do your feel you have choices available to you?

HOW COUNSELLING IS HELPING

- Is talking to a counsellor in college/university helping you stay on your course?
- Is it providing you with any skills or confidence to progress with successful learning?

(Continued)

(Continued)

LIFE

EMPOWERMENT

- How capable and supported do you feel in choosing what you would like to do in the future?

HEALTH

- Do you feel healthy? This might cover a wide range of health issues, including anxiety, mood, physical health, fitness, fear, etc.

RISK

- Are you at risk from others?
- Are you at risk from your own decisions and behaviours? For example, do you drink a lot of alcohol, take non-prescribed drugs, have unsafe sex, travel home on your own from a night out, not tell people where you're going, overwork?

SUICIDAL IDEATION

- Have you considered ending your life?
- Are you currently considering ending your life?

RELATIONSHIPS

- How happy are you with your relationships? This could include family members, friends, other students in your classes.
- Are you confident with your interpersonal skills?
- Do you feel you are able to communicate effectively with others or do you find it hard to explain yourself?

RESILIENCE

- How strong and capable do you feel in your life and learning?
- Do you have strong coping mechanisms in place that work well for you or do you find that you often or sometimes feel out of your depth?

EMOTIONAL AWARENESS

- Are you able to identify how you feel and communicate this to others?
- Are you sometimes embarrassed or ashamed of how you feel?

PRESENTING ISSUES

Working with students brings a range of contextual challenges which differ from working with clients in other sectors. Wallace (2011) offers an overview of the role of counsellors in colleges and universities:

- Supporting students with pre-existing mental health issues, of whom there are arguably increasing numbers due to the inclusion of a range of mental health diagnoses under the Disability Discrimination Act.
- Supporting students who experience age- and stage-related psychological issues (e.g., leaving home, relationships).
- Supporting students who experience university/college study-related issues (e.g., exam anxiety, procrastination, failure, lack of attendance, considering

leaving, etc). These are likely to be interlinked with the point above, but may be important to separate out to create a more student-specific case.
- Supporting students in serious crisis (e.g., suicide, self-harm, attack, substance misuse-induced state).
- Preventing psychological crises through offering support to individuals and groups of students when a traumatic situation occurs at university/college (e.g., the suicide attempt of a peer in halls of residence).

While we may work with generic issues, such as low mood, anxiety, relationship issues and suicidal ideation, more circumstantial issues may arise. Examples of these may include exam/assessment stress, living away from home for the first time and the challenges that come with major transitions.

Studying under the pressure of family or own expectations can result in a range of physical, psychological and emotional symptoms that paradoxically impede reaching the client's potential. Living away from home for the first time can be daunting and highly stressful, but is one of the areas where the university or college can often offer practical support in addition to counselling. Accompanying concerns can include loneliness, lack of confidence, homesickness and financial struggles.

There are several scenarios where change can bring challenge whether that is a young student transitioning from school into tertiary education or a more mature student transitioning into education from employment. This can be particularly challenging for looked-after young people. Equally, issues can arise near the end of the course, as students become nervous about leaving their course to progress to higher level study or employment.

Another presenting concern can relate to cultural variation. International and English to speakers of other Languages (ESOL) students may be challenged, not just by language difference but also by cultural and social difference. This may result in a sense of not fitting in, isolation or seeking out speakers of their first language.

In addition to these areas, the potentially wide age range of students bears consideration. However, the majority of students tends to be younger than 24 years of age, so consideration of developmental stages may help when engaging in therapeutic work. A focus on resilience, autonomy and the confidence to act on their own initiative may be appropriate.

WAYS OF WORKING

The practicalities of working in an educational setting also bear consideration. In addition to the therapeutic and professional issues, there are also day-to-day factors. Many services have recently adopted hybrid working, with a blend of in-person and remote methods on offer.

Many institutions encourage a preventative model alongside counselling support. This might include self-help areas in the library and preventative work, such as groups on avoiding exam stress or burnout, encourages students to be proactive by empowering them to increase their resilience. Offering a range of resources also enables students to try alternatives while they are waiting for counselling. Competence in group facilitation is helpful, whether that is therapeutic groups or groups aimed at preparing students for academic, personal or psychological challenges.

In some colleges and universities, counsellors are asked to deliver input to students or staff. This may be on a range of mental health topics, such as how to support someone who is struggling. Guidance on sign-posting is often requested too. However, in larger institutions, there are others in the wider mental wellbeing team who may take this role.

THERAPEUTIC APPROACHES

To manage waiting times, sessions are usually restricted to short-term work rather than unlimited therapy. This can be challenging, particularly if your training is in long-term work, and the use of a therapeutic framework (e.g., Egan's three stage model) may be encouraged. Other models include the Cardiff Model (Cowley and Groves, 2015), single session work or solution-focused approaches. This is further complicated by semesters and academic holidays. Many counsellors have contracts which only cover term time, so there is a need to factor in possible breaks as well as endings.

MANAGING WORKING WAITING LISTS

An area of frustration can be the dichotomy between the need for early intervention while experiencing significant waiting lists. Although these may not be as long as waiting lists for counselling in statutory services, counsellors can still feel a pressure to engage with students when they first approach the service. This is often overcome by offering clinical assessments to determine the level of risk, need and urgency for each case. The management of waiting lists varies between institutions but can include reducing the number or frequency of sessions, offering a single session or holding session, increasing the number of counselling trainees on placement and accessing external services to supplement internal provision.

REFERRALS

The method of accepted referrals can also impact on demand as well as clients who do not attend (DNAs). Only accepting self-referrals can increase attending rates and reduce DNAs, but is not always appropriate for the service.

THE ENVIRONMENT

Whether the service is based in a private, fit-for-purpose department with a reception area and administrators or is a case of borrowing an office on a busy corridor across several campuses, it is the welcome, accessibility and atmosphere that reassures the client. Reducing the institutionalism of the space can have an impact on the relationship – think lamps rather than overhead lighting, plants, curtains rather than blinds, in fact any aspect that changes the feel of the room.

As well as the accommodation, the promotion and marketing of the service should be considered carefully to balance awareness with privacy. Getting this right will have an impact on referrals, access, attendance and acceptance in the institution.

SUPPORTING TRAINEES ON PLACEMENT

Working in an educational setting raises a question regarding the support offered to counselling trainees on placement. Are services that support students better prepared to support trainees? We know placement opportunities can be hard to find, so providing training placements may be a way of offering more appointments, keeping the service fresh and establishing links with local training courses. Although there are usually reports to write, this can be weighed against the positive experience of supporting someone who has recently passed their readiness to practise assessment.

To conclude, counselling in a college or university setting provides a wide range of diverse clients, working opportunities and the satisfaction of supporting students during their studies. It offers a variety that makes every day different, whether that is professional development, collaborative working or personal connection.

REFERENCES

Amis, K. (2013) *Challenges in Counselling: Student Counselling*. London: Hodder Education.

BACP's University and College Counselling Division. Available at www.bacp.co.uk/bacp-journals/university-and-college-counselling/

British Association for Counselling and Psychotherapy (2016) *The Competencies Required to Deliver Effective Counselling in Further and Higher Education*. Lutterworth: BACP.

British Association for Counselling and Psychotherapy (2018) *Ethical Framework for the Counselling Professions*. Lutterworth: BACP.

Cowley, J. and Groves, V. (2015) The Cardiff Model of short-term engagement. In D. Mair (Ed.), *Short-term Counselling in Higher Education: Context, Theory and Practice* (pp. 108–127). London: Routledge.

Wallace, P. (2011) The value of an in-house counselling service in FE and HE. *University and College Counselling*. May, 30–33.

Wallace, P. (2014) The positive wider impact of counselling provision in colleges and universities. *University and College Counselling*. September, 22–25.

RECOMMENDED READING

Amis, K. (2013) *Challenges in Counselling: Student Counselling*. London: Hodder Education.

This book is a useful introduction to working as a student counsellor.

Mair, D. (2015) *Counselling in Higher Education: Context, Theory and Practice*. London: Routledge.

This is another useful overview of student counselling. In particular, this text focuses on work in higher education.

The BACP University and College Counselling Division: www.bacp.co.uk/bacp-journals/university-and-college-counselling/

This is a useful network of individuals interested in working in this setting.

7.3 WORKING WITH THE MEDIA

ELAINE KASKET

OVERVIEW AND KEY POINTS

Historically the opportunities for psychotherapists or counsellors to offer their knowledge and expertise to the public were limited. If you did not publish self-help books, author or contribute to articles in the popular press, or appear on radio or television, you would live your professional life free from mass media attention. With the advent of the digital age, you can utilise blogging, social media and other internet platforms to directly reach the public, and any media contributions are stored and accessible online over the longer term. Today's practitioners must understand the benefits and vicissitudes of media work and act ethically and responsibly. This chapter covers the following key points:

- Reflections on the media landscape for practitioners.
- Classification of media work from 'high control' to 'low control' scenarios.
- Ethical guidance for media work.
- Decision-making guidelines for engaging in media work.
- Research on psychotherapy and the media.
- Useful recommended readings.

INTRODUCTION

Most psychotherapists and counsellors carry out the bulk of their therapeutic activities in the private sphere, one client at a time. The confidentiality of that space stands in stark contrast to the exposing world of mass and social media, in which a comment on Twitter, a quote for a news story, or a sound bite from a live broadcast can flash around the world and be received by an audience of millions. When practitioners use the media to extend their therapeutic reach and influence the wider world, they need a particular set of skills, a hefty measure of caution, and an awareness of the potential ethical pitfalls. Done well, media work can inform, educate and assist the public, destigmatise mental health issues, and demystify and promote psychotherapy.

Over the last decades, the media landscape has changed in ways that are hugely salient for therapy.

Reality TV is often so strange and stressful for its participants that psychologists are employed for off-screen support as well as on-screen commentary. Programmes like A&E's *Hoarders* and Channel 4's *House of Agoraphobics* feature mental health professionals treating people struggling with sometimes severe psychiatric conditions. Bravo's *The Real Housewives of New York* and Channel 4's *Made in Chelsea* portray characters' actual therapy sessions. TV shows like VH1's *Couples Therapy* and podcasts such as Esther Perel's *Where Should We Begin?* put the therapeutic process front and centre. Long-running talk shows such as CBS's *Dr. Phil* in the United States have shaped the public's perception of how psychotherapy works and what mental health professionals do, as have popular fictional programmes that show 'shrinks' in action, such as HBO's *The Sopranos* and *In Treatment*.

As it has become more acceptable to discuss mental health issues, the psychological/psychotherapeutic perspective has become sought after and valued. Consequently, many practitioners may find themselves being approached for expert commentary or even to engage in on-screen practice. Nor is a journalist, publisher, producer or casting agent a necessary player; practitioners can disseminate information to the public themselves, using the internet as their vehicle.

In short, there is no shortage of opportunity in the media for psychotherapeutic practitioners. The European Federation of Psychologists Association (EFPA) argues that the media are now so powerful in people's lives that practitioners have a *responsibility* to offer their insights and expertise via these channels (British Psychological Society, 2021). So how can you share your wealth of knowledge with the world ethically and responsibly?

WAYS OF WORKING

When considering a media opportunity, first think about its *purpose*. What is your involvement and contribution in service of? Educating your audience? Providing a psychological perspective on an issue, event or trend? Shedding light on someone's behaviour, perhaps a public figure (something warned against in most ethical codes)? Providing treatment or caring for participants on a programme? Promoting yourself? Advancing the reputation and/or accessibility of psychology or psychotherapy? Entertaining people? Unsurprisingly, the wisdom of proceeding depends a lot on the meaning of and intent behind participation, for both you and anyone involved in your appearance. You might also wish to think about media opportunities on a 'control spectrum'.

High control. Any situation where you retain maximum editorial power over your words is a relatively 'high control' scenario. Imagine that, like podcast host and author Dr Esther Perel, you work with couples who are struggling. You could pitch a regular column to *Psychologies* magazine, for example; they would provide some editorial input, but in your contract you could insist upon final approval. You could publish a book on couples work, and although your publisher or editor may push for certain changes, you would largely retain your authorial voice. Independent of any editorial input, you could self-publish and sell via Amazon or your own website, write a blog, record podcasts, or launch an educational video series on a platform like YouTube, Vimeo, SkillShare or Udemy. Using social media allows you to mostly control your own feed, so perhaps you could use Twitter for research, tips and helpful links; Clubhouse to get a conversation going; or Instagram to build your brand and visually promote your messages.

Even in these relatively high-control scenarios, however, there are caveats. While you might retain control over the content of your book, a publisher could try to sell more copies by insisting on a sensationalist cover with extravagant claims, such as 'Cure Your Anxiety for Good!'. You may craft the material on your blog or social media carefully, but readers can post undermining remarks if comments are enabled. Your psychoeducational videos might be helpful and informative, but it's the life mission of trolls to say, 'Can you believe this idiot?!' Whenever you enter a public forum in the modern world, you invite interaction and comment, and control is never absolute.

Medium control. Medium-control media work includes live interviews or call-in programmes broadcast via television or radio or livestreamed on the web. In live broadcasts, you need not fear the distorting potential of others' editing, but this does not mean you will end up communicating what and how you want. Even when questions are provided in advance and you have prepared, limitations of format and involvement of other people – interviewers, fellow interviewees, callers or audience members – can influence your input significantly. Before appearing live on the BBC, I was once advised that I should get my core message across clearly within the first 20 seconds and should keep it 'upbeat' as it was breakfast television. I had not had my coffee, the line of questioning was unexpected, my topic was complex, and speaking about death made 'upbeat' a challenge. I could choose my responses, but I felt far from being fully in control of my message.

Pre-recorded audio and video interviews are another example of medium-control scenarios. The decisions about what segments of your interview to use are almost always made without you. I have done two-hour interviews from which a 10-second segment was plucked, and I have never been able to control or predict the contexts into which my pre-recorded contributions would be placed. Even when one collaborates closely with producers, directors and/or editors – for example, in a television series where a psychotherapeutic practitioner is a central player – other people will ultimately decide precisely how the practitioner and their input are portrayed.

Low control. I would classify any situation in which a print journalist translates your words as 'low control'. Imagine a journalist interviews you on the phone, tapping away in the background as you speak. Even if they transcribe your words exactly, in the finished piece you may discover rampant paraphrasing, rigorous editing, decontextualised comments and innocent errors or misunderstandings. Other examples of low-control scenarios include the (relatively uncommon) 'ambush' interview, in which you are neither prepared for the interview situation nor the questions asked, and situations where you or your work is referenced without the writer's consulting you.

The first time there was a press release about one of my conference papers, I thought I had complete control; I had, after all, approved the text of the release as being accurate. I had not realised journalists worldwide would take the release and write articles implying they had interviewed me directly, most of which were rife with misunderstandings and misrepresentations of my research findings and their implications. While I could control my conference presentation and the text in the press release, I lost the reins from there. To restore a sense of ownership over my work, I began maintaining my own blog so the public could get more accurate information 'from the horse's mouth'.

ETHICAL DECISION-MAKING ABOUT MEDIA WORK

For those practitioners who dip their toes into the rewarding but potentially murky waters of media work, there are multiple sources of guidance, some of which are listed in the 'Recommended reading' section of this chapter. The 'meta-code' of media ethics compiled by the European Federation of Psychologists' Association (EFPA) lists seven elements that should form the basis of any ethical guidance around media work, and these could be argued to apply to any type of mental health professional. Practitioners should:

1. Show respect for all persons involved.
2. Avoid diagnosis statements about any person in public.
3. Be careful not to bring into the public any personal data about persons with whom the [practitioner] has (had) a professional relationship.
4. Be careful not to go beyond [their] field and degree of competence.
5. Aim at empowering the audience.
6. Be aware that [they] are representing the community of [practitioners].
7. Be sensitive to the potential effects on third parties, like relatives and other acquaintances.

(European Federation of Psychologists' Associations, 2010, in British Psychological Society, 2021)

The British Psychological Society (BPS) has translated these into three broad pillars that support ethical media work: respecting the autonomy, dignity and privacy of contributors and other persons; supporting high standards of integrity; and being socially responsible.

However thorough a set of guidelines is, you need a decision-making system. Shahid (n.d.) suggests considering the following three areas when deciding whether to pursue a media invitation:

1. *Competence*: Do you have research and/or clinical competence in the area you are being requested to speak about?
2. *Time constraints*: Do you have sufficient time to review the literature, gain background on the relevant players, and gather your thoughts on the topic?
3. *Control over final product*: Do you have the ability to review and/or edit the piece before it is disseminated?

To these I would add a fourth: Are you able to assess and be satisfied about the goals, motivations and psychological 'savviness' of the interviewer, production company or journalist, and the safeguarding of both participants and likely audience? The BPS's 2021 document *Psychology and Media Productions: Guidance for Commissioners and Producers* is not just for those commissioners and producers, but for you. By using their checklists, including 'Key safeguarding questions for producers' and 'Identifying risks in productions and vulnerabilities of individual children', you can better distinguish a responsible production from one that could be both individually and societally harmful.

Even when you follow guidance, it can be difficult to spot the risks, particularly if you are inexperienced. The British Association for Counselling and Psychotherapy's (BACP) Press Office (www.bacp.co.uk/about-us/press-office/) and the British Psychological Society's Communications Team (www.bps.org.uk/about-us/communications) connect the press with members of their respective professional bodies, inform press what their professionals can and cannot do, provide support and advice on specific situations, and signpost members to media training. The BACP's general guidelines on what to do before and during media interviews are excellent and address press, TV and radio scenarios (www.bacp.co.uk/about-us/press-office/member-resources/interview-guidelines/).

To illustrate the ethical considerations and decision-making process, I offer an example from my own experience, when the producer of a well-known reality television series approached me. In the next season, she explained, one of the main characters would be seeking professional help for his relationship issues. While this would purportedly be an actual therapeutic process, a camera crew would sometimes be in the consulting room, and segments of his recorded therapy sessions would weave through the show. The producer repeatedly emphasised the 'exposure' and 'free advertising' I would get as the on-screen therapist for a well-known reality TV star.

When done well and ethically, seeing or hearing real therapeutic sessions can be extremely beneficial for audiences. However, capturing live therapy is particularly high risk and should never be done without careful consideration and a high level of practitioner control over the use of the material. I certainly have clinical competence to see people with relationship issues, but I spotted several problems. This was clearly a 'low control' scenario, in which I would be pulled into a 'structured reality' format with no say over editing. The production company had no concept that recording and broadcasting therapy might be unethical. Despite the producer's suggestions that it would educate a million viewers about psychotherapy, the spirit of this programme was pure escapist entertainment.

Filming can also, of course, interfere with how the therapeutic process would ordinarily go, including whether therapy happens at all. In contrast with the producer's claims when we spoke, the star in question said in several subsequent published interviews that therapy was the production company's idea, not his. The producer had also told me she was selecting a therapist for him based partly on the 'telegenic' qualities of the practitioner and consulting room. From the start, therefore, therapy was inextricably bound up with entertainment and considerations of plot and character. Unable to see how this enterprise could be accomplished ethically or to the advancement of the profession, I declined, and ever since I have limited myself to expert contributions within my areas of research and scholarship.

RESEARCH

Research indicates that media portrayals can significantly affect viewers' perceptions of psychology and psychotherapy. For example, one study found that people's perceptions of actual psychotherapy were significantly constructed by its portrayals on fictional comedy and drama programmes, and that these portrayals were associated with negative attitudes towards psychotherapy, lower intentions to seek services and greater reluctance to disclose to a therapist (Vogel, Gentile and Kaplan, 2008). The researchers remark that '[when] portrayals [of psychotherapy] are inaccurate or misleading, they could have direct and indirect implications on people's mental health' (p. 292). Remember that they were studying people's attitudes in response to *fictional* comedy and drama, and imagine how much more damaging it can be when *real* practitioners are untrustworthy, unethical, misleading and/or overly self-promoting in the media.

In addition, remember that psychotherapeutic practitioners who work with the media or take a public stance on various issues will inevitably see this reflected in their general online presence, which incorporates contributions to news and other media stories, postings on social media platforms, blogs and other websites, and various other disclosures both inadvertent and intentional, personal and professional. Of the 332 psychotherapist clients who participated in one study, nearly half used online information about their therapist to decide whether to move forward with treatment (Kolmes and Taube, 2016) – all the more reason to acknowledge and consider the potential effects of our public pronouncements on the private therapeutic work we do.

Psychotherapeutic practitioners who choose to do media work shoulder a fourfold burden of responsibility: they are accountable to themselves, their clients, the public and the profession. In this era of mass data storage and easy retrieval, the public commentary we make proliferates and persists in various online locations, for better or worse. That errant tweet or that interview segment for which you were drastically unprepared may be perpetually linked to your name in internet searches. On the flip side, while you may only see hundreds or thousands of face-to-face psychotherapy clients during your career, you might help literally millions of suffering people through a viral blog post or what you said on that national radio programme. After a recent BBC World Service interview recorded and broadcast from London, I received emotional and grateful emails with personal stories from listeners in Texas and Delhi. As a practitioner, there is much you can do beyond individual therapy sessions to heal, help and be a force for good in the world. With ethical awareness, education, preparation and media training, you can undertake that mission confidently, safely and well.

REFERENCES

British Psychological Society (2021) *Psychology and media productions: Guidance for commissioners and producers*. Leicester: BPS. Available at https://www.bps.org.uk/guideline/psychology-and-media-productions-guidance-commissioners-and-producers (accessed 1 February 2022).

Kolmes, K. and Taube, D. O. (2016) Client discovery of psychotherapist personal information online. *Professional Psychology: Research and Practice*, 47(2), 147–154.

Shahid, S. (n.d.) The nuts and bolts of media involvement. In *The ethics of psychology and the media: Print, internet and TV* [open access PowerPoint presentation]. Available at www.adaa.org/sites/default/files/McGrath%20348.pdf. (accessed 1 February 2022).

Vogel, D. L., Gentile, D. A. and Kaplan, S. A. (2008) The influence of television on willingness to seek therapy. *Journal of Clinical Psychology*, 64(3), 276–295.

RECOMMENDED READING

Atcheson, L. (2010) Counselling psychology and the media: the highs and lows. In M. Milton (Ed.), *Therapy and beyond: Counselling psychology contributions to therapeutic and social issues* (pp. 277–292). Chichester, UK: Wiley Blackwell.

This chapter highlights critical considerations when working with print media, and with live and pre-recorded radio and television. It also features a helpful list of 'dos and don'ts'.

Scott, S., Krotoski, A., Baffour, F., Pilgrim, D., Viding, E., Chivers, T., Riaz, H., Challenger, A., Bratton, L., Loveday, C., John, O., Frith, U., French, C., Kinderman, P., Aiken, M., Burnett, D., Byron, T., McVey, C., and Hammond, C. (2018) Psychologists in the media: Opportunities and challenges (A special feature). *The Psychologist*, 31(4), 36–51. Available at https://thepsychologist.bps.org.uk/volume-31/april-2018/psychologists-and-media-opportunities-and-challenges (accessed 1 February 2022).

This is a fantastic compendium of experiences and helpful guidances from practitioners of every stripe about all sorts of situations, which is worth its weight in gold.

McGarrah, N. A., Alvord, M. K., Martin, J. N., and Haldenman, D. C. (2009) In the public eye: The ethical practice of media psychology. *Professional Psychology: Research and Practice*, 40(2), 172–180.

This series of pieces on working with the media will help you think clearly through the ethical pitfalls and how to avoid them.

7.4 WORKING WITH NEUROSCIENCE AND NEUROPSYCHOLOGY

DAVID GOSS

OVERVIEW AND KEY POINTS

Neuroscience, subsequently neuropsychology, has undergone rapid developments over the last few decades. In this chapter, I present several ideas and reflections for psychotherapists to consider when working with neuropsychology information and client populations. Key points for the chapter include:

- Neuropsychology integrates neuroscience and psychology to develop theory and interventions which can serve a range of client populations, particularly people affected by neurological conditions.
- Neuropsychological research can be used to support and develop the role of empathy in psychotherapy, to help psychoeducate clients and to provide an evidence base for interventions.
- Psychotherapists may benefit from being mindful of the challenges involved when utilising neuropsychological information, including the risk of losing sight of a client's subjective sense of self through biological pathology, as well as ensuring they work within ethical knowledge and competency boundaries.
- A range of psychotherapeutic models can be used when working with a neurological client population.

INTRODUCTION

DEFINING NEUROPSYCHOLOGY

The fields of neuropsychology and neuroscience can often be referred to as one of the same. However, there is also a distinction between them. Neuropsychology is a profession which serves people with neurological conditions (British Psychological Society, n.d.). The World Health Organisation (WHO) defines a neurological condition as:

> [D]iseases of the central and peripheral nervous system. … These disorders [conditions] include epilepsy, Alzheimer disease and other dementias, cerebrovascular diseases including stroke, migraine and other headache disorders, multiple sclerosis, Parkinson's disease, neuroinfections, brain tumours, traumatic disorders of the nervous system such as brain trauma, and neurological disorders as a result of malnutrition. (World Health Organisation, 2014)

This somewhat differs from neuroscience, a general branch of scientific enquiry, which can be related to all research and client populations (Bear, Connors and Paradiso, 2007; Cozolino, 2017). However, there are people who define neuropsychology in a looser sense, as a discipline which bridges psychology (emotion, cognition, perception and behaviour) and neuroscience (chemical, electrical, structural and cellular underpinnings of the central nervous system) (Hallett, 1993), thus making neuropsychology applicable to all client populations.

As such, the working definition of neuropsychology for this chapter is a discipline which integrates neuroscience and psychology to develop theory and interventions which can serve a range of client populations, particularly those affected by neurological conditions. As such, this chapter will present information on how integrating information from neuroscience and psychology can support counsellors and psychotherapists in all aspects of their work, with a case study for those working with neurological populations.

THE ARRIVAL OF NEUROPSYCHOTHERAPY

The development of research techniques has led to a neuroscience revolution these last few decades and psychotherapy has subsequently increased its integration with neuroscience during this time. *Neuropsychotherapy* (Grawe, 2007), *Interpersonal Neurobiology* (Siegel, 2011, 2020) and *Neuropsychoanalysis* (Solms and Turnbull, 2011) are disciplines geared towards understanding and integrating the mechanisms of biology, neurology, psychology and social interaction, to develop holistic therapeutic practices and understanding of our species.

THE BENEFIT OF NEUROPSYCHOLOGY TO PSYCHOTHERAPY

Neuroimaging technologies such as functional magnetic resonance imaging (fMRI) and electroencephalogram (EEG) (for more details see Eysenck and Keane, 2010: 7–14) allow us to obtain information about the brain's structure and functioning. This information can be used to support and enhance psychotherapeutic interventions. For example, neuroimaging has demonstrated the brain's ability to reproduce new neurons (neurogenesis) and reorganise neural networks throughout its lifetime, a concept known as *neuroplasticity* (Begley, 2007). This restructuring is at the heart of learning and memory development (Clark and Beck, 2010). Additional research demonstrates that the expression (activation) of many genes depends on a person's environment and social experiences (Szyf, McGowan and Meaney, 2008), a concept known as *epigenetics*. The concepts of neuroplasticity and epigenetics provide scientific evidence for the long-held psychotherapeutic notions that a person's environment contributes greatly to their personality, and that psychotherapy can help restructure maladaptive brain networks. Neuroimaging has been used to demonstrate the effects of different psychotherapies on areas of the brain related to symptoms such as depression, obsessive-compulsive disorder and social phobia (Peres and Nasello, 2008; Weingarten and Strauman, 2015).

WAYS OF WORKING

ADVANTAGES

In addition to harnessing support for the profession, practitioners can use neuropsychological theory to support and enhance a variety of interventions. Examples of how neuropsychology can be used for interventions include:

- *Developing empathy for clients* – One of the tenets of psychotherapy is promoting a safe and empathic therapeutic relationship. Neuroscience has provided neural evidence of empathy (Gallese, 2001; Gallese et al., 1996). Informed with evidence that we each have neurons which attempt to mirror that of another person, a therapist can not only build security and support for a client by empathising with them, but they can also model emotional regulation within the therapy setting, which the client can in turn attempt to mirror. This advocates the importance of therapists continually working on understanding their own internal processes, aiding their own ability to feel and self-regulate distressing emotions, which can in turn help their clients (Coutinho, Silva and Decety, 2014).
- *Psychoeducation for clients* – Neuropsychological information can be used to psychoeducate clients as to why they may be experiencing certain changes in their personality and functioning. This can help the client make sense of their experience and may also help carers, friends and family develop increased understanding and empathy for the client.
- *Evidence base for intervention* – Neuropsychology has helped provide support for individual modalities of therapy. For example, efforts have been made to develop models of the brain that help provide information on psychodynamic phenomena such as repression (Bazan and Snodgrass, 2012), dreaming (Zellner, 2013) and the dynamic unconscious (Berlin, 2011; Solms and Zellner, 2012). The existence of unconscious processes such as repression has been supported through studies with neurological patients suffering with anosognosia, a condition in which people deny the existence of impairment (Vuilleumier, 2004). More recently, event related potentials (ERPs) have been promoted as a potential method of comparing and understanding the neural impact of psychotherapies known to be effective for specific presentations (Matsen, Perrone-McGovern and Marmarosh, 2020).

CHALLENGES

- *Losing the self through biological pathology* – Fuchs (2004: 483) proposed that 'a reductionist biological concept of mental life may gradually lead to a self-alienation … we are beginning to regard ourselves not as persons having wishes, motives or reasons, but as agents of our genes, hormones and neurones'. Ivey (2011) suggested that many psychotherapists worry about the medical model and that by focusing on neuroscience, we focus on pathology. However, Ivey, D'Andrea and Ivey (2012) argue that neuroscience places a high value on environmental impacts and therefore reinforces psychotherapy's psychosocial wellness model. The majority of therapeutic models focus on client empowerment and motivation for change (Ryan et al., 2011). The psychotherapist should be cautious of clients becoming overly dependent and/or downhearted about biological issues, as they may lose the motivation and self-autonomy required for change. This is where competency and integrity are crucial. If a therapist is attuned to concepts such a brain plasticity and other elements which demonstrate how a client can overcome certain deficits, they will then be better placed to use neurobiological information to help and psychoeducate a client's development, while also recognising the realistic limits as to what can be achieved (Goss, 2015).

- *Therapist competency, ethics neuroenchantment* – Ivey et al. (2012) suggest that psychotherapists often are not aware of the positive neurological impact of the client relationships they form (Goleman, 2007; Siegel, 2011), largely due to the lack of training and theoretical textbooks on offer for integrating neuropsychology and psychotherapy. Developing more theory and training around neuropsychology is vital to ensuring that therapists practise in a safe and ethical manner. This is particularly relevant as contemporary fascination with brain science could lead to overestimating tentative (or sometimes incorrect) evidence as unquestionable fact – a phenomenon recently labelled as neuroenchantment (Coutinho, Perrone-McGovern and Gonçalves, 2017).

Below is a case study which outlines some of the factors which psychotherapists may consider when working with a client in a neuropsychological setting. I have used a client with an acquired brain injury (ABI) as this can often be a complex neurological presentation, due to the extent and location variability of brain injuries. However, the reflections discussed below can be applied to many neurological presentations, although it is important to note that each client will differ in how they respond to a condition and individual formulations are vital.

CASE STUDY

Client – Casey is a 30-year-old woman who suffered an ABI as a result of a car crash. Casey sometimes struggles to speak, has difficulty concentrating and often displays sudden bursts of emotion.

Psychotherapist considerations – By consulting with neurologist reports and through the client's narrative, it appeared that Casey suffered an ABI to the front and left-hand side of her brain. The areas effected correlate with Casey's presentation. Broca's area is located towards the front of the left-hand side of the brain and has been shown to be involved in speech production and comprehension (Wallentina, Gravholtc and Skakkebæk, 2015), thus damage to this area would understandably affect speech. Adjacent to this area of the brain is the dorsolateral prefrontal cortex. This area of the brain has been shown to be involved in selective attention (Forster et al., 2015), therefore, damage to this area would understandably affect concentration. The front part of the brain, particularly the prefrontal cortex (the very front of the brain) consists of several areas which are involved in emotion regulation (Wager et al., 2008), so damage to this area would understandably affect emotion display.

POTENTIAL INTERVENTIONS

Person-centred: A common first step in this type of work is allowing Casey to vent/grieve/mourn what has happened to her, processing the things she has lost (which may include her job, partner, friends, independence, etc.). Casey may have thought about what has happened, but it is only by voicing these thoughts out loud and connecting them with the deeper emotions within that she may be able to fully acknowledge what has happened – this is one of the key benefits of psychotherapy.

Cognitive-behaviour therapy (CBT): A first step in CBT could be normalising Casey's symptoms, providing psychoeducation on her injury and subsequent difficulties. It is likely that one or all of Casey's symptoms (i.e., speech, attention, emotion) will be causing her distress, leading to feelings of anxiety and depression. For example, her speech difficulties may lead her to feel embarrassed and anxious of social situations in case people judge her, so she avoids going out and talking to people, which leads to her feeling isolated and depressed without an outlet to discuss these emotions. In Casey's situation, CBT allows us to formulate that she is embarrassed about her speech difficulties for the reasons outlined above. In this instance, CBT can be used for multiple purposes, including understanding and working on her social anxiety and developing her social skills. This type of work can be undertaken through gradual exposure, using therapy as a catalyst for Casey to begin feeling comfortable talking about her difficulties, which can then be extended to her engaging in social groups with friends, ABI support groups or groups related to her hobbies and interests. Socialising and developing a sense of purpose in life are two things which have been shown to be neurologically relevant in reducing depression (Panksepp and Biven, 2012). Third-wave CBT interventions, such as mindfulness, can also be used. Mindfulness has been shown to develop emotional and attentional brain regions, including the frontal lobe (Santarnecchi et al., 2014). Through the notion of plasticity, Casey can begin to redevelop these areas of her brain and recruit additional brain networks to help with her emotion and attention regulation.

Psychodynamic: Some clients may respond to an ABI or neurological condition in an overly maladaptive response in comparison to other people. For example, I have worked with clients who experience a neurological condition which leads to them having issues regulating their emotion, but they are not overly affected by this and they grow accustomed to the change. However, for some clients, an inability to control emotions can cause them high levels of distress. In the example of Casey, she explains that she never used to really show emotion, so she finds it extremely embarrassing when she starts crying all of a sudden, leading to isolation, anxiety and depression. This information may come about through Casey's explanation, or it may first be spotted in transference and unconscious processes. For example, the therapist may notice that Casey demonstrates defences when becoming emotional, even cancelling sessions following displays of emotion in front of the therapist. When this is explored, it materialises that Casey was not allowed to demonstrate any emotion when she was younger, as her parents told her this was a sign of weakness. As such, the psychotherapist and Casey may then work on this, exploring past and present to allow Casey to feel more comfortable with displaying emotion.

RESEARCH

Research supporting the use of psychotherapy in neuropsychological populations is often tailored to specific conditions (Lai et al., 2019). For example, mindfulness-based therapy and Acceptance and Commitment Therapy (ACT) have been shown to improve wellbeing for people with epilepsy (Dewhurst, Novakova and Reuber, 2015; Tang, Poon and Kwan, 2015). Psychotherapy has been shown to be beneficial in outcome and cost-effectiveness for people presenting with functional neurological disorders, that is, symptoms which resemble manifestations of organic disorders of the nervous system but are medically unexplained (Reuber et al., 2007). Klonoff (2010) presents a range of evidence and discussion for undertaking psychotherapy with clients who have experienced a brain injury, as well as how to support family members (Klonoff, 2014).

REFERENCES

Bazan, A. and Snodgrass, M. (2012). On unconscious inhibition: instantiating repression in the brain. In A. Fotopoulou, D. Pfaff and M. A. Conway (Eds), *From the couch to the lab: Trends in psychodynamic neuroscience* (pp. 307–337). New York: Oxford University Press.

Bear, M. F., Connors, B.W. and Paradiso, M. A. (Eds) (2007). *Neuroscience: Exploring the Brain* (3rd ed.). Baltimore, MD: Lippincott Williams & Wilkins.

Begley, S. (2007). *The plastic mind*. London: Constable & Robinson.

Berlin, H. A. (2011). The neural basis of the dynamic unconscious. *Neuropsychoanalysis*, *13*, 5–31.

British Psychological Society (BPS) (n.d.). *Careers: Neuropsychology* [web page]. Available at http://careers.bps.org.uk/area/neuro

(Continued)

(Continued)

Clark, D. A. and Beck, A. T. (2010). Cognitive theory and therapy of anxiety and depression: convergence with neurobiological findings. *Trends in Cognitive Sciences*, *14*(9), 418–424.

Coutinho, J. F., Perrone-McGovern, K. and Gonçalves, O. F. (2017). The use of neuroimaging methodology in counselling psychology research: promises, pitfalls, and recommendations. *Canadian Journal of Counselling and Psychotherapy*, *4*, 327–348.

Coutinho, J. F., Silva, P. O. and Decety, J. (2014). Neurosciences, empathy, and healthy interpersonal relationships: recent findings and implications for counseling psychology. *Journal of Counseling Psychology*, *61*(4), 541–548.

Cozolino, L. (2017). *The neuroscience of psychotherapy: Healing the social brain* (3rd ed.). New York: W.W. Norton.

Dewhurst, E., Novakova, B. and Reuber, M. (2015). A prospective service evaluation of acceptance and commitment therapy for patients with refractory epilepsy. *Epilepsy & Behavior*, *46*, 234–241.

Eysenck, M. W. and Keane, M. T. (2010). *Cognitive psychology: A student's handbook* (6th ed.). Brighton: Psychology Press.

Forster, S., Elizalde, A. O. N., Castle, E. and Bishop, S. J. (2015). Unraveling the anxious mind: anxiety, worry, and frontal engagement in sustained attention versus off-task processing. *Cerebral Cortex*, *25*(3), 609–618.

Fuchs, T. (2004). Neurobiology and psychotherapy: an emerging dialogue. *Current Opinion in Psychiatry*, *17*(6), 479–485.

Gallese, V. (2001). The 'shared manifold' hypothesis: from mirror neurons to empathy. *Journal of Consciousness Studies*, *8*(5–7), 33–50.

Gallese, V., Fadiga, L., Fogassi, L. and Rizzolatti, G. (1996). Action recognition in the premotor cortex. *Brain*, *119*(2), 593–609.

Goleman, D. (2007). *Social intelligence*. London: Arrow Books.

Goss, D. (2015). The importance of incorporating neuroscientific knowledge into counselling psychology: an introduction to affective neuroscience. *Counselling Psychology Review*, *30*, 52–63.

Grawe, K. (2007). *Neuropsychotherapy: How the neurosciences inform effective psychotherapy*. New York: Psychology Press.

Hallett, S. (1993). Neuropsychology. In G. Morgan and S. Butler (Eds), *Seminars in basic neurosciences* (pp. 151–186). London: Royal College of Psychiatrists. Available at www.rcpsych.ac.uk/pdf/semBasNeuro_chapter5.pdf

Ivey, A. E. (2011). Neuroscience and counseling: central issue for social justice leaders. *Journal for Social Action in Counseling and Psychology*, *3*, 103–116.

Ivey, A. E., D'Andrea, M. J. and Ivey, M. B. (2012). *Theories of counseling and psychotherapy: A multicultural perspective*. London: Sage. Available at www.sagepub.com/upm-data/40557_2.pdf

Klonoff, P. S. (2010). *Psychotherapy after brain injury: Principles and techniques*. New York: Guilford Press.

Klonoff, P. S. (2014). *Psychotherapy for families after brain injury*. New York: Springer.

Lai, S.-T., Lim, K.-S., Low, W.-Y. and Tang, V. (2019). Positive psychological interventions for neurological disorders: a systematic review. *The Clinical Neuropsychologist*, *33*(3), 490–518.

Matsen, J., Perrone-McGovern, K. and Marmarosh, C. (2020). Using event related potentials to explore processes of change in counseling psychology. *Journal of Counseling Psychology*, *67*, 500–508.

Panksepp, J. and Biven, L. (2012). *The archaeology of mind: Neuroevolutionary origins of human emotions*. New York: W.W. Norton.

Peres, J. and Nasello, A. (2008). Psychotherapy and neuroscience: towards closer integration. *International Journal of Psychology*, *43*(4), 943–957.

Reuber, M., Burness, C., Howlett, S., Brazier, J. and Grünewald, R. (2007). Tailored psychotherapy for patients with functional neurological symptoms: a pilot study. *Journal of Psychosomatic Research*, *63*(6), 625–632.

Ryan, R. M., Lynch, M. F., Vansteenkiste, M. and Deci, E. L. (2011). Motivation and autonomy in counseling, psychotherapy, and behavior change: a look at theory and practice. *The Counseling Psychologist*, *39*(2), 193–260.

Santarnecchi, E., D'Arista, S., Egiziano, E., Gardi, C., Petrosino, R., Vatti, G., Reda, M. and Rossi, A. (2014). Interaction between neuroanatomical and psychological changes after mindfulness based training. *PLoS One*, *9*(10), 1–9.

Siegel, D. J. (2011). *Mindsight: Transform your brain with the new science of kindness*. London: One World Publications.

Siegel, D. J. (2020). *The developing mind: How relationships and the brain interact to shape who we are* (3rd ed.). New York: Guilford Press.

Solms, M. and Turnbull, O. H. (2011). What is neuropsychoanalysis? *Neuropsychoanalysis*, *13*(2), 1–13.

Solms, M. and Zellner, M. R. (2012). The Freudian unconscious today. In A. Fotopoulou, D. Pfaff and M. A. Conway (Eds), *From the couch to the lab: Trends in psychodynamic neuroscience* (pp. 209–218). New York: Oxford University Press.

Szyf, M., McGowan, P. and Meaney, M. (2008). The social environment and the epigenome. *Environmental and Molecular Mutagenesis*, *49*, 46–60.

Tang, V., Poon, W. S. and Kwan, P. (2015). Mindfulness-based therapy for drug resistant epilepsy: an assessor-blinded randomized trial. *Neurology*, *85*(13), 1100–1107.

Vuilleumier, P. (2004). Anosognosia: the neurology of beliefs and uncertainties. *Cortex*, *40*, 9–17.

Wager, T. D., Davidson, M. L., Hughes, B. L., Lindquist, M. A. and Ochsner, K. N. (2008). Prefrontal-subcortical pathways mediating successful emotion regulation. *Neuron*, *59*(6), 1037–1050.

Wallentina, M., Gravholtc, C. H. and Skakkebæk, A. (2015). Broca's region and Visual Word Form Area activation differ during a predictive stroop task. *Cortex*, *73*, 257–270.

Weingarten, C. P. and Strauman, T. J. (2015). Neuroimaging for psychotherapy research: current trends. *Psychotherapy Research: Journal of the Society for Psychotherapy Research*, *25*(2), 185–213.

World Health Organisation (WHO). (February 2014). *What are neurological disorders?* [web page]. Geneva: WHO. Available at www.who.int/features/qa/55/en/

Zellner, M. R. (2013). Dreaming and the default mode network: some psychoanalytic notes. *Contemporary Psychoanalysis*, *49*(2), 226–232.

RECOMMENDED READING

McHenry, B., Sikorski, A. M. and McHenry, J. (2014). *A counselor's introduction to neuroscience*. New York: Routledge.

This book provides an introduction to neuroscience information that may be relevant to counsellors.

Cozolino, L. (2017). *The neuroscience of psychotherapy: Healing the social brain* (3rd ed.). New York: W.W. Norton.

This book offers a thorough exploration of how neuroscience can be used by psychotherapists across a variety of contexts and methods.

Klonoff, P. S. (2010). *Psychotherapy after brain injury: Principles and techniques*. New York: Guilford Press.

This book presents a range of evidence and discussion for undertaking psychotherapy with clients who have experienced a brain injury.

7.5 PRIVATE PRACTICE

GARETH WILLIAMS

OVERVIEW AND KEY POINTS

This chapter's aim is to support people who are interested in developing a sustainable private practice – one that is rewarding, inspiring and in alignment with their values. The approach here rests on an understanding of the importance of core values in our work; how they infuse it with a sense of purpose, and how purpose naturally motivates us, can make our goals more attainable and protect us from demoralisation and burnout.

Towards the end of the chapter, we consider a series of practical matters relevant to anyone working in private practice. Our approach will not be to provide answers but to encourage practitioners to respond to these matters from a grounding in their values and sense of purpose.

The key points of the chapter are:

- Consciously aligning our work with our values brings a greater sense of purpose and motivation.
- Purposefulness enhances resilience, commitment and the likelihood of achieving one's goals.
- Explicitly formulating a vision and mission statement for our work provides a compass for navigating the inevitable challenges we will encounter.
- A number of significant challenges to working in private practice, both inner and outer, are presented.

INTRODUCTION

> If you have your why ... then you can get along with almost any how. (Nietzsche)

The British Association for Counselling and Psychotherapy's (BACP) *Ethical Framework* (2018) outlines the fundamental values of the profession, as listed below. Against the background of this professional commitment, we are going to put our focus on our personal values – the ones that feel most important to us. There may be areas of overlap with the values expressed by the BACP, but the point here is to clarify our core values, what really matters most to us, in a way that feels authentic and alive.

BACP FUNDAMENTAL VALUES

Respecting human rights and dignity
Alleviating symptoms of personal distress and suffering
Enhancing people's wellbeing and capabilities
Improving the quality of relationships between people
Increasing personal resilience and effectiveness
Facilitating a sense of self that is meaningful to the person(s) concerned within their personal and cultural context
Appreciating the variety of human experience and culture
Protecting the safety of clients
Ensuring the integrity of practitioner–client relationships
Enhancing the quality of professional knowledge and its application
Striving for the fair and adequate provision of services

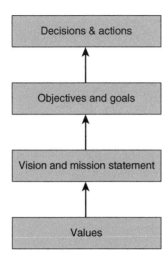

Figure 7.5.1 A values-based approach to practice

A visual overview of this approach is shown in Figure 7.5.1: values inform the vision of our work and guide us to a mission statement; vision and mission lead us to goals and objectives; goals and objectives shape our decisions and give rise to actions.

This chapter is intended to be useful to practitioners whatever their therapeutic orientations. What follows constitutes an extended reflection on how our core values, along with the unique configuration of our interests, experience and training, can guide us in establishing a private practice.

VALUES

> Principles or standards of behaviour; one's judgement of what is important in life. (*Oxford English Dictionary*)

> What makes life meaningful are the connections with closely held values through daily life actions. (Hayes, Strosahl and Wilson, 2012: 92)

This chapter proceeds from the hypothesis that living your life in alignment with your core values will bring inevitable enrichment and success. To live your life in a way that truly matters to you is its own reward – financial gain and social status may accompany it, but these will be incidental, not defining features. Clarity about our values can enhance our sense of purpose (Dahl et al., 2009) and 'purpose provides a bedrock foundation that allows a person to be more resilient to obstacles, stress, and strain' (Kashdan and McKnight, 2009: 303).

How are we to recognise what really matters to us? Can we be honest and clear enough with ourselves?

Many schools of therapy have recognised how mixed and multiple we can be (Rowan, 1990). One part of me wants 'x', while another part wants 'y', and yet another 'z'! Our motivations can be equally mixed, with some of them less than congruent with the intention to facilitate growth and healing. Gandhi is commonly paraphrased as saying 'be the change you want to see in the world'. So the point here is *what do we really want to stand for? What do we deeply wish our lives to contribute to?*

Although the process of knowing oneself is endless, mindfulness, inner work, personal therapy and supervision can enable us to venture into the world of private practice with a relatively clear sense of why and what we want to do.

CLARIFYING VALUES

There are a number of ways to help clarify one's values. One exercise involves imagining you are approaching the end of your life and, looking back, you feel contentment that you lived your life in tune with what really mattered to you. Next, you reflect upon what you prioritised – what you took a stand on throughout your life – that led to this sense of contentment.

Another means of clarification involves sorting through a list of cards, each one labelled with a particular value. The cards can be sorted into piles: 'those that really matter to me' (core values); 'those that somewhat matter'; and 'those that are less important to me'. A list of example values are listed below.

This kind of reflection calls for significant time and focus. It might be helpful to explicitly undertake this kind of reflection with a supervisor, coach, therapist, etc. Rather than constituting a purely cognitive exercise, it calls for a more holistic approach, involving attention to what Gendlin (1981) described as the 'felt sense'.

From a position of clarity about what really matters to us, we can then proceed to reflect upon how these values could be expressed through our work. We can do this by formulating a vision and a personal mission statement.

VISION AND PERSONAL MISSION STATEMENT

Creating a vision and a personal mission statement makes one's sense of purpose explicit. Mission and vision express our values and the direction we are committed to proceeding in.

EXAMPLES OF VALUES

Acceptance	Faith	Love
Authenticity	Friendship	Nature
Appreciation of beauty	Fun	Open mindedness
Bravery	Generosity	Optimism
Citizenship	Gratitude	Patience
Compassion	Growth	Peace
Community	Happiness	Pleasure
Contribution	Health	Respect
Cooperation	Humility	Responsibility
Creativity	Humour	Service
Duty	Independence	Spirituality
Doing your best	Integrity	Trust
Diversity	Justice	Wisdom
Equality	Kindness	
Fairness	Learning	

PERSONAL MISSION STATEMENT

It is common practice for organisations to have a mission statement and, over the past few decades, it has become *more* frequent for leaders and entrepreneurs to formulate a personal one. As Covey (2004: 137) points out, writing and/or reviewing your personal mission statement 'forces you to think through your priorities deeply, carefully, and to align your behaviour with your beliefs'. An example of the values and personal mission statement of a particularly well-known businessman, Richard Branson, is illustrated below.

The process of formulating a mission statement can take a few days, a few weeks or even months. Essentially, it requires us to ask 'what really fits for me, what is my mission?' We can live this inquiry by intentionally being receptive to what touches or inspires us as we go through our days. Gathering a collection of notes, quotes and ideas may prove useful as resource material in composing the statement.

Metaphorically, we gather ingredients for a 'mission soup', out of which a statement is crafted. A good mix includes core values, passionate interests, talents and experience (we might reflect on past successes and/or ask peers and supervisors for feedback), and any particular client groups with whom we are particularly drawn to working (e.g., people suffering with anxiety, the elderly, young people, etc.).

AN EXAMPLE OF VALUES AND A PERSONAL MISSION STATEMENT (EXCERPTED FROM *MOTIVATED MAGAZINE*, 2011)

What values ... did your parents pass on to you that you still follow today?

My parents are extremely kind, thoughtful, and loving people. They believe you should treat others as you would wish to be treated yourself. My mum taught me never to be afraid of failure – it's just a learning curve. My wonderful dad taught me to listen and to value other people's advice and opinions.

Do you have a personal mission statement?

Have fun in your journey through life and learn from your mistakes.

In business, know how to be a good leader and always try to bring out the best in people. It's very simple: listen to them, trust in them, believe in them, respect them, and let them have a go!

The more authentic and honest we can be with ourselves, the more potent the process and the product promises to be. Once we have gathered our ingredients, we can experiment with different wording, once again attending to the 'felt sense' of fit (Gendlin, 1981).

VISION

Our vision describes what we want to achieve in the long term. It expresses our dreams for how our values, put into action, can come to fruition.

Some questions we can ask ourselves include the following: If my core values were free to express themselves through me, what would they do? If they were free to make the best use of my abilities, experience, knowledge and so on, to what would they lead me? Contemplating such questions reveals aspirations and generates values-congruent ideas.

From a standpoint of vision, we can generate values-congruent goals and objectives.

OBJECTIVES AND GOALS

Objectives and goals that emerge from vision and mission are fuelled by intrinsic motivation. Such motivation arises from within, rather than being driven by external rewards such as money. Intrinsic motivation is more likely to be sustainable; values-congruent goals are more likely to be achieved (see the work of Ryan and Deci, for example, Deci and Ryan, 2002; Ryan and Deci, 2008).

As we use the terms here, goals express the outcomes we are aiming for, usually in the longer term. Objectives are steps on the path to achieving these goals. Objectives and goals shape our day-to-day decisions and actions.

SMARTNESS

SMART is an acronym meaning specific, measurable, achievable, realistic and timeframe – the five guides to setting goals and objectives. Rather than holding tight to SMART as a formula and insisting that all goals must satisfy all the criteria, we can remain creative and flexible, both in terms of formulation and implementation.

For example, I might formulate a goal to become a provider of online counselling services, with the specific objectives of: (1) raising my profile in the internet search engines, (2) working with more online clients in the coming year, and (3) giving my website a makeover.

My goal and objectives seem realistic and achievable to me, but I could probably use some help with goal (1). I could also be more specific about a timetable for goals (1) and (2). Although I can easily measure goal (2), with my current skillset, it is not easy to do so with goal (1). For goal (3), measurement is not really an issue, as I am going to use my own subjectivity to guide me in designing the new look of my website.

'THE PATH'

Once we have clarity related to our values, vision and mission to give us a sense of direction and a set of goals and objectives, we can set to work putting it into action. This can be envisaged as setting out on what Castaneda (1968) described as 'a path with heart'.

Traditionally, in Yogic teachings, the symbol of the heart was two overlapping triangles – one pointing up, the other pointing down (Figure 7.5.2). Mythologist Joseph Campbell (1991) taught that the upward triangle represents the direction of our values and vision, and the download triangle represents inertia, difficulties and life challenges. The path with heart is the meeting of these two. Likewise, with any creative endeavour – painting, music, cooking a meal, a relationship, a project – there is the inevitable meeting of the inspiration with the limitations of the materials, skills or the actual situation.

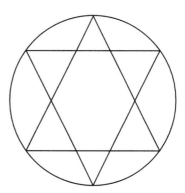

Figure 7.5.2 Yogic symbol of the heart

For example, making a work of art, there's an innate constraint on the creative impulse due to the materials themselves: the canvas has a particular size, only certain brushes and paints are available. These limitations, however, are not only obstructions; they are also the very medium for the expression of the vision.

Rather than situational, economic and psychological difficulties being nothing more than impediments, the meeting of our vision with the challenges *is* the path. Willingness to travel this path, with its inevitable hardships, requires courage. 'Courage' derives from the Latin 'cor', meaning heart.

INNER CHALLENGES

Life is characterised by ups and downs and, sooner or later, anyone who travels the path of private practice will meet obstacles.

Many of these obstacles are internal. Common ones include:

1. *Expectations and the inner critic* – A frequent source of difficulty for practitioners are expectations that we should be 'sorted out', be paragons of health and wellbeing. 'You're not good enough', says the inner critic. Getting caught up in such narratives can feel very demoralising.
2. *Fear of failure* – This can be an obstacle at any point on the path: it can arise when we try to clarify our values, when we begin the process of envisioning a mission statement, or when we think about objectives and implementing a plan. It can take the form of avoidance, procrastination and self-doubt.
3. *Assumptions and inflexibility* – Knowing 'how it should be' and attachment to doing things the 'right way' can place a significant limit on our potential for creativity and responsiveness.
4. *Ambition* – If we are too invested in achievement, we can overlook the small steps taken in line with our core values, gradual change may be missed, and small victories unnoticed.
5. *Impatience* – Setting up and developing a private practice can take considerable time. Setbacks, as we have already considered, are inevitable. This calls for patience.

OUTER CHALLENGES

What follows is a list of areas particularly relevant to setting up a private practice. Each area is presented as a collection of questions for consideration.

1. PROMOTION

How can I promote myself in line with my vision and mission? Do I want certain images to represent my work? Do I promote myself as an individual, a service, a project? What do I call myself? What kind of words am I going to use on any promotional material? Do I want a logo? Are there certain client groups I want to reach out to? What message do I hope to convey? Which of my colleagues, peers or mentors might I consult for feedback?

Is it worth paying a web designer to design a site for me or might it be better to register with an established online counselling directory? Perhaps I could do both?

How are potential clients going to contact me?

2. INSURANCE AND TAX

What insurance do I need? Public liability? Public indemnity? Are there special packages available? Might I be eligible for a discount based on BACP or United Kingdom Council for Psychotherapy (UKCP) membership? Do I want to shop around for the best offer or take whatever I can find?

Do I feel confident to take care of my own taxes? Am I able to be sufficiently organised? Perhaps I could pay someone to take care of my accounts?

3. PREMISES

If I am planning to work from home, am I insured for this? Are there any health and safety issues? Does it feel OK for me to have my work take place in my home? Do I have a space that is confidential? Is it welcoming enough? Warm enough? Does it have the right kind of decor to fit my practice?

Do I want or need to work online? If so, have I got sufficient information technology (IT) skills? Is my equipment fit for the task? Is the space I use suitably confidential?

Is there a therapy centre nearby where I could hire a room? Might I benefit from the centre's presence and publicity?

4. RECORD KEEPING

What records will I keep? Where will I store them? For how long? Are there current legal and/or professional requirements that I need to be aware of?

5. PROVISION FOR ILLNESS OR DEATH

What if I become incapacitated in an accident or due to illness? What if I die? If I work in an agency, there are colleagues who can step into the vacuum and help the situation? Working privately, what provision can I make for this?

6. ASSESSMENTS

What kind of assessments am I going to use? Are they congruent with my approach to therapy? What purpose will assessment serve? How much time am I going to spend on these measures?

7. CONTRACTS

Am I going to have a printed pro forma? What will it say? Will I want a signature? Or would I prefer a verbal contract?

8. TIME MANAGEMENT

Am I well enough able to manage my time? Can I balance my work and personal life in a way that works for me?

Do I want to work full-time in private practice? Part-time? Perhaps it is better for me to develop a portfolio approach – working privately as well as for a local organisation, employee assistance scheme, general practitioner (GP) surgery, etc.

What other opportunities might there be for me besides working as a counsellor? Teaching? Supervision? Could I write something for the local newspaper about an issue I care about? Am I open to creative possibilities?

9. ISOLATION

How will I be, working in relative isolation? Would it suit me better to work in a team? Is my supervision supportive enough? Is there a peer group I could join? Would some personal therapy be helpful?

Is it possible to team up with other practitioners? Would that suit me better? Are there like-minded people out there whose vision might align with mine? Would I benefit from collaborating with people who have complementary skills?

10. PROFESSIONAL DEVELOPMENT

How will I take care of my ongoing professional development? Supervision? What training could I benefit from? Shall I try something new, perhaps something I'm really interested in? What will help me stay fresh?

How will I keep informed of developments in the field? What areas of research will I attend to?

11. FEES

What am I going to charge people for my services? Is there some kind of standard charge locally? Will I operate a sliding scale? Will I accept donations, or work for free with clients who have no or very little financial income?

12. IS PRIVATE PRACTICE FOR ME?

Are my values and strengths best served by working in private practice? Do I have enough experience at this time? Could I benefit from being part of an organisation for a while, and then gradually start building up something private?

CONCLUSION

Our core values can steer us through the complexities and the inevitable ups and downs of private practice. Creating a vision and a mission statement for one's practice enables the generation of values-congruent goals and objectives which, in turn, lead to actions and decisions in alignment with purpose. Working purposefully, we can be more resilient and our practices can be more sustainable and rewarding.

REFERENCES

British Association for Counselling and Psychotherapy (2018) *Ethical Framework for the Counselling Professions.* Lutterworth: BACP.

Campbell, J. (1991) *A Joseph Campbell Companion.* New York: Harper Collins.

(Continued)

(Continued)

Castaneda, C. (1968) *The Teachings of Don Juan: A Yaqui Way of Knowledge*. Berkeley, CA: University of California Press.

Covey, S. (2004) *The 7 Habits of Highly Effective People*. London: Simon & Schuster.

Dahl, J.C., Plumb, J.C., Stewart, I. and Lundgren, T. (2009) *The Art and Science of Valuing in Psychotherapy: Helping Clients Discover, Explore, and Commit to Valued Action Using Acceptance and Commitment Therapy*. Oakland, CA: New Harbinger.

Deci, E.L. and Ryan, R.M. (2002) *Handbook of Self-determination Research*. New York: The University of Rochester Press.

Gendlin, E.T. (1981) *Focusing*. New York: Bantam.

Hayes, S., Strosahl, K. and Wilson, K. (2012) *Acceptance and Commitment Therapy: The Process and Practice of Mindful Change*. New York: Guilford Press.

Kashdan, T.B. and McKnight, P.E. (2009) Origins of purpose in life: Refining our understanding of a life well lived. *Psychological Topics*, 18(2), 303–316.

Motivated Magazine (2011) Sir Richard Branson: On a mission to mentor. *Motivated Magazine*, 4 May, http://motivated online.com/sir-richard-branson-on-a-mission-to-mentor/

Rowan, J. (1990) *Subpersonalities: The People Inside Us*. London: Routledge.

Ryan, R.M. and Deci, E.L. (2008) A self-determination theory approach to psychotherapy: The motivational basis for effective change. *Canadian Psychology*, 49(3), 186–193.

RECOMMENDED READING

Bor, R. and Stokes, A. (2011) *Setting Up in Independent Practice: A Handbook for Counsellors, Therapists and Psychologists*. Basingstoke: Palgrave Macmillan.

Thistle, R. (1998) *Counselling and Psychotherapy in Private Practice*. London: Sage.

These books offer a comprehensive resource about the nuts and bolts of establishing a private practice.

British Association for Counselling and Psychotherapy – Private Practice Division. Available at www.bacp.co.uk/bacp-divisions/bacp-private-practice/

The BACP's Private Practice Division produces a quarterly journal for counsellors and psychotherapists working independently.

7.6 WORKING IN PRIMARY CARE

ZUBEIDA ALI AND SATINDER PANESAR

OVERVIEW AND KEY POINTS

Counselling in primary care is influenced by the specific setting in which it takes place – that of healthcare funded by the National Health Service (NHS). It thus retains the core elements of counselling as a modality while being carried out in a fast-changing and influential arena driven by government policy. This chapter covers those distinctive features with particular reference to:

- The context of primary care counselling and how it has changed over the past few years as governments across the four nations have striven to make psychological therapies more accessible and evidence-based.
- The development of the evidence-based psychological intervention, Counselling for Depression (CfD) in NHS England's Improving Access to Psychological Therapies (IAPT) services.
- Elements that might influence the future for counselling in NHS-funded services.

INTRODUCTION

Counselling, along with psychotherapy, has been defined as an umbrella term that covers a range of talking therapies. The British Association for Counselling and Psychotherapy (BACP) website states 'counsellors offer a safe and confidential space to talk to a trained professional about issues and concerns to help explore thoughts, feelings and behaviours to develop a better understanding of self and others' (BACP, 2022). Around 90% of patient interaction is with primary care services, in particular, general practitioners (GP) (Health and Social Care Information Centre, 2016).

'Primary care' in the NHS is described by the National Association of Primary Care (2015) as having four central features: it is the first point of contact for all new health needs; it provides person-centred, continuous lifetime care; it provides comprehensive care for all needs that are common in a population; and it offers coordinated and integrated care when a person's need is sufficiently uncommon as to require special services from another sector (secondary or tertiary care). This will be further influenced by the recent introduction of *The NHS Long Term Plan* (NHS, 2021), which has referenced an Integrated Care System (ICS) from April 2021, enabling joined up working across the NHS, local services and other partners.

Put together, counselling *in* primary care means something unique: a specialism that retains the core purpose of 'enhancing wellbeing' while being shaped by the specific setting in which it takes place, with its distinctive features. We will detail those features later in this chapter, but to start, it is important to mention the historical context of counselling in primary care, and how this has evolved, especially over the past few years.

Historically, counselling has been the most widely available primary care psychological therapy, with practitioners working in a range of modalities and often in an integrative way. Provision across the United Kingdom was patchy, and while some managed primary care counselling services existed, counsellors often worked independently and in isolation, mainly employed by fund-holding GPs.

The move over the past few years to make psychological therapies more accessible, accountable, cost-efficient and equitable has led to massive changes in provision. This change has occurred particularly in NHS England, with the introduction of the Improving Access to Psychological Therapies (IAPT) programme, which supports the NHS in implementing National Institute for Health and Care Excellence (NICE), guidelines for common mental health problems, such as anxiety and depression (NICE, 2005a, 2005b, 2009, 2011, 2013, 2022). These guidelines, which correspond to specific diagnoses, make recommendations on psychological treatments combined, where appropriate, with medication – traditionally the only treatment available for health problems, including psychological health. To be included in the guidelines, psychological therapies need to be supported by positive findings in randomised controlled trials (RCTs), which are viewed as the 'gold standard' of evidence. While the implementation of IAPT has formally introduced psychological therapies to the NHS, there have been limitations to the development of an array of such therapies, which will be explained in detail later.

In Scotland, national policy and guidance are placing increasing emphasis on randomised control trials (RCT) too. The development of *The Matrix: A Guide for the Delivery of Psychological Therapies in Scotland* (NHS Education for Scotland, 2011), in parallel with Scottish Intercollegiate Guidelines Network's (SIGN) *Guidelines for the Non-pharmaceutical Management of Depression* (SIGN, 2010), signalled the intention of the Scottish Executive Health Department (SEHD) to prioritise provision of SIGN-recommended therapies for specific diagnoses. However, *The Matrix* was withdrawn in February 2020. A number of advisory groups have been established to work on this and, in addition, to developing a new guideline on complex and multi-diagnostic psychological presentations, to be released sometime in the future.

The devolved governments in Northern Ireland and Wales have also published strategies for the development of psychological therapy provision (Department of Health, Social Services and Public Safety (Northern Ireland), 2010; Welsh Government, 2012), indicating the move towards the use of specific therapies for specific diagnoses being echoed across the four nations.

These developments are therefore important to counselling in primary care, as they dictate which therapy modalities are commissioned. Commissioning in primary care is basically the process of assessing needs, planning and prioritising, purchasing and monitoring health services to get the best health outcomes. This can be different in each of the four UK nations because of political devolution.

WAYS OF WORKING

Following the publication of *Talking Therapies: A Four-year Plan of Action* (Department of Health, 2011b) to support the cross-governmental mental health strategy *No Health without Mental Health* (Department of Health, 2011a), the focus broadened to offering continuing professional development (CPD) to therapists from other NICE recommended modalities.

This resulted in further developments, by BACP and partners in higher education, of the Person Centred Experiential Counselling for Depression (PCE CfD) training programme for counsellors wishing to become IAPT-compliant. PCE CfD is now recognised as a form of evidence-based psychological therapy within the IAPT programme, with its own framework of competences (Roth, Hill and Pilling, 2010) and a CfD textbook (Murphy, 2019). The therapy itself is intended as an 'add-on' for experienced and accredited counsellors already working within IAPT teams. This training was welcomed by the profession as it ensured the place of counselling as an evidence-based intervention giving counsellors the opportunity to be considered with the rest of the IAPT multidisciplinary workforce. PCE CfD is now widely used in IAPT services to treat depression, along with a range of other evidence-based modalities. Until this time, NHS counsellors in IAPT teams remained non-compliant.

The job title of 'counsellor' is now largely treated as distinct from other roles in primary care psychological services, and counsellors now find themselves in multi-modality teams which include psychological wellbeing practitioners (PWPs) trained in the use of CBT-informed skills for brief interventions, CBT therapists, IPT therapists, CTfD therapists, and DIT therapists. The settings in which counselling takes place have grown and are now being provided in a variety of other community settings, including GP surgeries. Counselling is also now offered via other platforms, particularly since the Covid-19 pandemic of 2020, supported by the development by BACP of its telephone and e-counselling competence framework (BACP, 2021).

The recent introduction of the IAPT model is the advent of 'stepped care' (Improving Access to Psychological Therapies, 2021), which is also supported by NICE and SIGN (Scotland). As a modality, counselling is most usually placed at step 3 'high-intensity level', along with CBT, IPT, DIT and CTfD, whereas guided CBT, which is based self-help, is found at the 'low-intensity' step 2.

Taking all the above into consideration, what makes a primary care counsellor's role different from that of counsellors working in non NHS-funded settings? In addition to promoting wellbeing, a counsellors' day-to-day job is more likely to be defined by a governance framework, which includes adherence to policies, guidelines and/or commissioned targets that relate to the provider of such services, population needs and cost-effectiveness. In IAPT services in England, counselling is offered only to treat depression as a primary diagnosis. This incorporates clients with a range of presenting problems, including relationships difficulties, problems with adjustment (bereavement, parenthood, retirement, illness diagnosis, unresolved grief), sexual abuse, or people for whom another form of therapy hasn't been successful for them (based on Clark, Layard and Smithies, 2008) or who opt for counselling as an informed choice as opposed to being 'signposted following an IAPT assessment supported by an evidence-based approach'.

While BACP guidelines suggest no more than 20 actual client contacts a week for a full-time counsellor (depending on the experience of the counsellor and the complexity of the work), this may be adjusted in line with service protocols to make up for attrition rates in order to meet the required number of actual in-person contacts. The course of in-person therapy is time-limited, and session numbers are likely to be between six and 10 over 8–12 weeks (IAPT, 2021).

Collecting therapy outcome data is a requirement in any NHS-funded service to indicate to commissioners what they are paying for – and so measurement is part of a primary care counsellor's role on a day-to-day basis. In IAPT services, clients will be expected to complete the minimum data set (MDS) of clinical outcome questionnaires at each appointment (IAPT, 2021). The rationale is that data will be lost if a client drops out of treatment unplanned, which affects data completeness (a minimum of two sets of data is required at discharge) and is required to measure recovery. Services aim to meet the target of a 50% recovery rate, and clients are deemed to have reached recovery if their scores have reduced from above to below a certain clinical threshold. Thus, services rely on having scores at the start and end of therapy (known as paired data).

In addition, all therapists, including counsellors, are now expected to 'cluster' patient problems. These clusters focus mainly on severity and level of need (as opposed to the types of problem experienced) and form the basis of the mental health payment by results (PbR) national tariff payment system, whereby provider services are allocated a certain amount of money to treat each patient (tariff) depending on their cluster. The system used in IAPT services in England is HoNOS (Health of the Nation Outcome Scales) and therapists are required to assign people at first assessment to a 'care cluster' that indicates their need for care (IAPT, 2021).

Public protection and patient safety play a part in counselling services whether they are NHS-funded or not. However, this may be intensified when working in NHS-funded psychological therapy services. Counsellors in primary care are expected to be familiar with carrying out a mental health assessment, including a risk assessment and management plan. As a consequence, they are required to have a good knowledge of onward referral pathways, particularly in crisis management and secondary care, which has resulted in integrated pathways between IAPT and these teams. This is in addition to adherence to procedures regarding confidentiality, and corresponding knowledge of social care agencies with a statutory duty to disclose issues surrounding the protection of children and vulnerable adults. In 2016, NHS England published *Implementing the Five Year Forward View for Mental Health*, which committed to parity of esteem for mental and physical health. It sets out the standards that IAPT services are required to develop and deliver through integration with physical healthcare services for long-term health conditions (LTCs).

Supervision recommendations within the IAPT programme supports ethical and effective practice and must be aligned to the standards set out in the IAPT Manual (IAPT, 2021). Counsellors will receive clinical supervision, which is generally provided in-house by a supervisor who is a trained counsellor and trained clinical supervisor. Supervision training will be supplemented by specific IAPT supervision training to ensure fidelity to models such as PCE CfD. In IAPT services, supervision is also offered for case load management, focusing on IAPT targets such as Recovery and compliance with local policies (e.g., cancellation and non-attendance) to support the philosophy of the IAPT model of improving access. Frequency of supervision varies across services. All services, however, should provide the BACP-recommended minimum of 1.5 hours of supervision per month.

What training and experience is required for a counsellor in primary care?

In NHS England, jobs in counselling are banded through the Agenda for Change (A4C), which means they are scored against national job profiles. Entry-level counselling posts are banded at 5, progressing to band 6 for post-entry level and band 7 for a senior counsellor. Jobs are advertised on the NHS job site (www.jobs.nhs.uk) or the BACP website (www.bacp.co.uk) (members only).

Nearly all person specifications for NHS B5 or B6 counsellor posts cite 'registration with a professional body, working towards BACP accreditation' or 'actively seeking BACP accreditation', unless the role is a senior or leadership role where accreditation is a requirement.

Primary care counsellors may also choose to belong to a specialist division, such as BACP Healthcare, for practitioners who work in healthcare settings, either within the public, private and/or third sector across the UK (www.bacphealthcare.org.uk).

Training as part of the Diploma qualification tends to be non-specific in terms of primary care counselling. Additionally, as Health Eduction England (HEE) have not included counselling training in their workforce expansion plan, newly-trained counsellors face challenges in trying to acquire the specific experience relevant to a job within NHS. PCE CfD training is usually only provided to counsellors already in IAPT services (it is one of the criteria in order to access ring-fenced HEE funding). More recently, training providers have started to offer places to anyone wishing to fund their own training, which is helping to increase the numbers of non-NHS counsellors trained in an IAPT-compliant modality.

While there is graduate training available in the form of university modules, and some trained counsellors gain employment in another role, such as a PWP, before applying for a counselling job, it is more common that trainee counsellors look to acquire healthcare experience, training and development, availing themselves where possible of the very limited numbers of NHS counselling placements opportunities. These opportunities have unfortunately been reducing as increasing numbers of NHS talking therapy services adopt the IAPT model and focus on HEE-funded trainee PWP and CBT initiatives to meet key performance indicators. BACP's *Accreditation of Training Courses* (BACP, 2016), unofficially known as the '*Gold Book*', sets out the standards that accredited courses should meet, and also covers the governance of trainee placements, although these are not specific to NHS placements.

There has been a significant and positive development recently as a result of much lobbying by BACP with regards to the expansion of HEE's workforce programme. The *IAPT High Intensity Psychotherapeutic Counselling Training pilot* (www.hee.nhs.uk/our-work/mental-health/improving-access-psychological-therapies) will be observed with much interest by the profession as it will open up new opportunities for counsellors if the pilot is a success.

RESEARCH

In England, all NICE guidelines are periodically reviewed so that fresh evidence can be taken into account: the presence of humanistic counselling in the guidance is seen as important to the future commissioning of counselling in NHS-funded services.

The advantages of evaluating humanistic counselling are evident in terms of feeding into the next phases of guideline development and informing commissioners. More evidence is needed if counselling is going to feature more strongly in future NICE and SIGN guidance, and also be part of psychological therapy provision strategy in Northern Ireland and Wales. A third consultation by NICE is underway on the Depression in Adults updated draft guideline, which was launched in November 2021, and publication is awaited. The BACP has lobbied and challenged NICE on their over-reliance on data collected from RCTs and recommended their use of other sources of evidence from the 'real world', such as client experiences and client evaluation of the counselling received. While the BACP accept that NICE's reputation and clinical guidelines remain influential, it continues to lobby and generate such evidence. It has funded an RCT to compare PCE CfD to a CBT treatment for depression (originated by Beck et al., 1987) to see whether PCE CfD has equivalent outcomes to Beckian cognitive therapy (University of Sheffield, 2016). Early findings are extremely positive.

REFERENCES

Beck, A.T., Rush, A.J., Shaw, B.F. and Emery, G. (1987) *Cognitive Therapy of Depression*. New York and Oxford: Guilford Press.
British Association for Counselling and Psychotherapy (BACP) (2016) *Accreditation of Training Courses*. Lutterworth: BACP. Available at https://www.bacp.co.uk/media/1502/bacp-course-accreditation-criteria.pdf

British Association for Counselling and Psychotherapy (BACP) (2021) *Online and Phone Therapy (OPT) Competence Framework*. Lutterworth: BACP. Available at www.bacp.co.uk/media/10849/bacp-online-and-phone-therapy-competence-framework-feb21.pdf

British Association for Counselling and Psychotherapy (BACP) (2022) [Website]. Available at https//www.bacp.co.uk

Clark, D.M., Layard, R. and Smithies, R. (2008) *Improving Access to Psychological Therapy: Initial Evaluation of the Two Demonstration Sites*. LSE Centre for Economic Performance Working Paper no. 1648. London: LSE Centre for Economic Performance.

Department of Health (DH) (2011a) *No Health without Mental Health. A Cross-government Mental Health Outcomes Strategy for People of All Ages: A Call to Action*. London: Department of Health.

Department of Health (DH) (2011b) *Talking Therapies: A Four-year Plan of Action*. London: Department of Health.

Department of Health, Social Services and Public Safety (Northern Ireland) (2010) *A Strategy for the Development of Psychological Therapy Service*. Belfast: Department of Health (Northern Ireland).

Health and Social Care Information Centre (2016) [Website]. Available at www.hscic.gov.uk/primary-care

Murphy, D. (2019) *Person-centred Experiential Counselling for Depression*. London: Sage, in association with British Association for Counselling and Psychotherapy (BACP).

Improving Access to Psychological Therapies (IAPT) (2021) *Improving Access to Psychological Therapies Manual*. London: NHS. Available at www.england.nhs.uk/publication/the-improving-access-to-psychological-therapies-manual/

National Association of Primary Care (2015) *Primary Care*. [Website]. Available at www.napc.co.uk/primary-care-home

NHS England (2016) *Implementing the Five Year Forward View for Mental Health*. London: NHS England.

National Institute for Health and Care Excellence (NICE) (2022) *Depression in Adults: Treatment and Management*. NICE Guideline CG222. London: NICE.

National Institute for Health and Clinical Excellence (NICE) (2005a) *Post-traumatic Stress Disorder: Management*. NICE Guidelines CG26. London: NICE.

National Institute for Health and Clinical Excellence (NICE) (2005b) *Obsessive-compulsive Disorder and Body Dysmorphic Disorder: Treatment*. NICE Guidelines CG31. London: NICE.

National Institute for Health and Clinical Excellence (NICE) (2009) *Depression in Adults (update). Depression: The Treatment and Management of Depression in Adults*. NICE Guidelines CG 90. London: NICE/National Collaborating Centre for Mental Health.

National Institute for Health and Clinical Excellence (NICE) (2011) *Generalised Anxiety Disorder and Panic Disorder in Adults: Management*. NICE Guidelines CG113. London: NICE.

National Institute for Health and Clinical Excellence (NICE) (2013) *Social Anxiety Disorder: Recognition, Assessment and Treatment*. NICE Guidelines CG159. London: NICE.

NHS Education for Scotland (2011) *The Matrix: A Guide for the Delivery of Psychological Therapies in Scotland*. Edinburgh: NHS Education for Scotland.

NHS (2021) *Long Term Plan*. London: NHS. Available at www.longtermplan.nhs.uk

Roth, A.D., Hill, A. and Pilling, S. (2010) *The Competences Required to Deliver Effective Humanistic Psychological Therapies*. London: Research Department of Clinical, Educational and Health Psychology, University College London.

Scottish Intercollegiate Guidelines Network (SIGN) (2010) *Non-pharmaceutical Management of Depression in Adults*. Edinburgh: SIGN/Healthcare Improvement Scotland.

University of Sheffield (2016) *Mental Health Research*. [Website]. Available at www.shef.ac.uk/scharr/sections/hsr/mh/mhresearch/practiced/info

Welsh Government (2012) *A Strategy for Mental Health and Wellbeing in Wales*. Cardiff: Welsh Government.

> **RECOMMENDED READING**
>
> Sanders, P. and Hill, A. (2014) *Counselling for Depression: A Person-centred and Experiential Approach to Practice*. London: Sage, in association with the British Association for Counselling and Psychotherapy (BACP).
>
> Murphy, D. (2019) *Person-centred Experiential Counselling for Depression*. London: Sage, in association with British Association for Counselling and Psychotherapy (BACP).
>
> These textbooks for Counselling for Depression (CfD) are essential for counsellors undertaking the training and also useful for trainees on Diploma courses who would like to know what is involved in the approach.
>
> NHS England's IAPT programme (www.england.nhs.uk/mental-health/adults/iapt).
>
> The website of NHS England's IAPT programme, featuring guidance documents, learning resources and examples of materials.

7.7 SHORT-TERM THERAPY

ALEX COREN

OVERVIEW AND KEY POINTS

The majority of clinical encounters today are brief. Frequently, this is by default rather than design due to factors such as managerial, as opposed to clinical, decisions on the length of therapy and client drop out. Problems of definition occur when brief therapy is defined by the number of sessions offered. It is perhaps more helpful to view short-term therapy as a modality which operates to a specific time frame – is time aware and time limited – and places time as the central organising factor of the work. Some time-limited therapies are not particularly brief but what distinguishes them is the open acknowledgement that the therapeutic frame needs to incorporate, and use, time as a therapeutic resource. Rather than conceptualising the issue in terms of brief or long term, it is more helpful to distinguish between time-limited and open-ended therapies.

General features of short-term therapy would include:

- Short-term therapy is time-limited – it has a mutually agreed ending – as opposed to being open-ended.
- It is helpful to distinguish between what can be termed a short-term consultation or conversation, which may be in the region of four to six sessions, or even a single session, and planned, focal short-term therapy, which can involve treatments which stretch over some months. Anything from one to 30 sessions has been put forward as 'brief'. Typically, 12–16 sessions are considered optimal for short-term interventions, depending on modality and assessment variables.
- Activity – short-term therapy involves an active and collaborative therapist.

- Most short-term therapies involve the collaborative articulation of a focus which assists in providing a therapeutic framework or scaffolding to the intervention.
- Many short-term approaches include a relational approach where the therapeutic relationship, the client's relational history and current relational patterns can be used to facilitate therapeutic change.
- Short-term therapies range on a continuum from manualised, protocol-driven interventions to process-led relational approaches, depending on the therapeutic modality.

INTRODUCTION

It is significant that, originally, most psychological interventions were brief and highly focused. Over time, these were supplanted in favour of the increasing length of treatments, making therapy longer and the clinician more passive and less time-sensitive (for a description of the history of brief interventions, see Coren, 2010).

Contemporary short-term therapists (Barkham et al., 2017; Coren, 2010, 2014, 2016; Della Selva, 2004; Lemma, Target and Fonagy, 2011; Levenson, 2012, 2017; Mander, 2000; Messer and Warren, 1998; Smith, 2006; Stadter, 2004) advocate that the therapist is active, establishes a therapeutic focus, and has a confidence in outcome – albeit with limited goals – which is conveyed to the client. Material is proactively elicited, and a mutually empowering therapeutic relationship forms the basis of the work. This is not dissimilar to the early psychological, including Freudian, clinical interventions.

It was through the work of Davanloo (1980), Malan (1979), and the behavioural and humanistic modalities of the mid-twentieth century that shorter-term therapies became more widespread. The work of Horowitz (1997), Budman and Gurman's Interpersonal, Developmental, Existential (IDE) therapy (2002), James Mann (1992), Klerman's Interpersonal Therapy (Klerman et al., 1994), as well as cognitive analytic therapy (Ryle and Kerr, 2001) and more recent developments in cognitive behavioural therapy (Bond and Dryden, 2005; Bor et al., 2003; Brosnan and Westerbrook, 2015; Curwen and Palmer, 2000; Gilbert, 2022; Hays et al., 2016; Wills and Sanders, 1997) have all contributed to short-term interventions. Humanistic or client-centred approaches have also addressed the issue of short-term interventions (Tudor, 2008), as has Systems Theory (Gustafson, 2005). Solution-focused therapy (de Shazer, 1985; Kim, 2013; Macdonald, 2007), a very brief intervention, rather than focusing on pathology, looks at how clients solve problems and attempts to generalise these successful strategies to other areas of their lives. Single-session interventions (Dryden, 2018; Talmon, 1993), and the two-plus-one Model (Barkham, 1989) have also provided the framework for many time-limited approaches. These theories have all had an impact on the practice of integrative time-aware therapy. Existential therapy (Strasser and Strasser, 1997), Transactional Analysis (Tudor, 2002) Art Therapy (Hughes, 2016) and Gestalt Therapy (Houston, 2003) are among modalities which have articulated discrete short-term models, and short-term models have been applied to, among others, attachment theory (Wake, 2000), narrative therapy (Schauer, 2011; White, 2011), self-psychology (Smith, 2015) and relational therapies (Barkham, 2017; Holmquist, 2022).

The progressively more widespread acceptance of psychological interventions, and the increasing demand for them, has led to a variety of therapeutic modalities articulating short-term models of practice. Developments in public, private and voluntary sectors, employment assistance programmes, general practice, education and coaching have all contributed to their popularity. The rise of both an evidence base which suggests the efficacy of short-term approaches (and the suggestion that major therapeutic change happens early in therapy) and the increasing influence of the managed care, insurance- and employer-led approaches, has led to the increasing popularity of short-term interventions. New technology (email, virtual, Skype counselling, etc.) has also contributed to the growth of short-term therapies, as has the impact of the Improving Access to Psychological Therapy (IAPT) programme and the National Institute for Health and Care Excellence (NICE) guidelines. It is worth noting, however, that the NICE guidelines suggest that 12–16 sessions are the optimum number of sessions for many clinical populations, which contrasts with many contemporary clinical contexts where 4–6 sessions are frequently the maximum offered. The danger then exists that short-term interventions are seen as a response to managing clinical demands, or are practised at the behest of management diktats, rather than as the treatment of choice, based on clinical assessment, for many populations. We are seeing this in the increasingly 'one size fits all' approach to the number of sessions offered in many contexts.

MODELS

There are a variety of modality-led models of short-term-therapy but they can grouped into two different categories:

- Those that use the time frame as non-negotiable and offer a specific number of sessions (either by number or by date). Examples would include Mann's 12-session model, Cognitive Analytic Therapy's 16 sessions and Dynamic Interpersonal Therapy's 16 sessions.
- Therapies that use time more flexibly, either by spreading a number of sessions over time, offering reviews at the end of a time-limited course of counselling, or offering blocks of therapy – often referred to as 'life span', 'intermittent' or 'top up' therapy – may suit the client's developmental needs over time.

Within these categories, modalities also differ between the more structured, protocol- or manual-led short-term therapies and those that are more unstructured and process led.

Clinical assessment is important in guiding the clinician as to length of treatment and number of sessions offered. Increasingly, clinicians are agreeing on the assessment criteria which are indicated for short-term approaches. In general, these are clients presenting with mild-to-moderate problems, motivation, psychological readiness and the ability to form a therapeutic alliance. While it has been assumed that clients with long-standing personality issues, multiple problems, substance and alcohol abuse, developmentally early deprivation, and reluctant attenders would be contraindicated for time-limited approaches, it is now thought that these clients might need more sessions than the former group but could still benefit from a time-aware approach. Increasingly, relational short-term therapy, among other brief approaches (Town et al., 2012), is being formulated in such a way that it can be significantly effective for clients with personality disorders or deeper-seated problems (Farber, 2020; Levenson, 2017).

Increasingly, attachment style (see Holmes, 2014) is also likely to have a bearing on the number of sessions offered and the length of treatment, with those who are securely attached needing fewer sessions than those exhibiting more insecure attachment patterns. Clinicians also need to be mindful in distinguishing between those clients who would benefit from an emotionally expressive approach and those who require a more supportive therapeutic intervention.

WAYS OF WORKING

KEY PRINCIPLES

The clinician has to have a commitment to, and belief in, short-term therapy. In cases where there is a profound ambivalence towards short-term work on behalf of the clinician for whatever reason (e.g., management, or context, prescription of session numbers), a short-term approach is unlikely to be successful. The clinician needs to believe that something of real value can be achieved in a limited time. Equally, a joint clinician/client agreement on time and focus is important for short-term therapy to be helpful. Short-term therapy is collaborative and relational and, in this sense, empowering for the client. The establishment of an early working/therapeutic alliance is central to short-term approaches. This can involve therapeutic hope, the early identification of resistances (relational obstacles) and any transferential material (often in the 'here and now' which makes it very accessible) that need to be promptly identified and addressed. While working in the transference, as traditionally defined, is often not applicable to short-term work, the 'here and now' relational experience assumes greater significance and the use of symbols and metaphors can be of major importance. Therapeutic collaboration is the basis for the establishment of a sound working alliance in short-term work.

The establishment of a central organising focus provides the framework for many short-term therapies. This involves high levels of therapeutic activity on the part of the therapist and a collaborative agreement on a therapeutic focus to be articulated and worked with from the beginning of counselling. Some modalities may find this easier than others to implement. Frequently, the focus is an interpersonal one and is apparent in the client's history, present(ing) problem and, interestingly, in the therapeutic alliance (see Malan's Therapeutic Triangle (1979) and Coren's concept of Idiom (2010)). The focus can be related to therapeutic content (an issue or difficulty) or process (relational history, self-regulation, affects, etc.). It can also be in evidence in the client's transference to time (too short or too long) and become a 'navigational beacon' (Stadter, 2004) for the counselling.

The establishment of a focal framework for the work will inevitably lead to 'selective attention' and 'benign neglect' of some therapeutic material on behalf of the clinician. One of the functions of the focus is to prevent the clinician being overwhelmed by clinical material and to enable both client and clinician to identify core issues which are marbled throughout the sessions and recur over time (Smith, 2006).

Working with time, especially in relation to endings, assumes great significance in short-term work. Therapist resistance to ending can contribute to termination difficulties and needs to be acknowledged and addressed. The end needs to be kept in mind from the beginning of therapy – often by counting down sessions – and the client's feelings about limited time needs to be constantly kept in mind. However, clinicians need to be led by their clients – some clients may consider 4–6 sessions long term. Realism needs to be factored into endings, which need to give space for a therapeutic review and the articulation of both successes and disappointments. Modalities differ as to whether follow-up sessions – and 'goodbye letters – are offered or not.

Some short-term models are applications of existing open-ended therapeutic modalities, while others are specifically geared to brief interventions. This means that traditional theoretical models may need to be adapted or even sometimes abandoned, and that the short-term intervention needs to be suited to the client's problem rather than the client's difficulty being shoehorned into a favoured theoretical model.

A certain flexibility based on a pragmatic approach may be required and the therapist may need to use techniques from other modalities in the service of the client. Examples would include the 'miracle question' (de Shazer, 1985), where clients are asked how things would be different if they were magically transformed. Asking clients for exceptions to the presenting problem can be helpful in providing the hope of generalising from the positive to more problematic areas of their lives, as can paradoxical injunctions, where clients are asked to escalate a problem.

Since the goals of short-term therapy are modest and not generic personality or characterlogical change – although one can be surprised by the ripple effect of brief interventions – different clinical paradigms and therapeutic techniques are required, and the clinician needs to develop a short-term state of mind. This can be very different from their training. It is a source of some debate currently whether discrete short-term therapy training alone can suffice for time-limited work (and might be advantageous) or whether the counsellor's experience of, and comfort with, the process of open-ended therapies are a necessary prerequisite to be able to work effectively with a short-term therapeutic alliance. Binder (2004; Binder and Betan, 2013) has written about the competencies needed by the clinician for successful short-term work. While short-term approaches have traditionally been described in terms of working with adult populations, an increasing literature is also speaking to the use of short-term, structured and process-led therapies in the field of working with children and adolescents (Briggs and Lyon, 2012; Feardon et al., 2006).

CASE STUDY

Having been depressed and on antidepressant medication for some time, Bill was referred to a counsellor by his GP. He was bewildered by this suggestion and thought he would be seen for a few minutes and given advice, not unlike his experience of consulting his GP. He was a somewhat withdrawn and hostile young man, suspicious of the motives of others and had limited, and unsatisfactory, relationships since his childhood, which he described as uneventful but unhappy. In answer to the magic question, Bill said he would be sociable, have lots of friends, be happy and in a relationship. A short-term, process-led contract of six sessions was agreed with Bill. This involved:

- Initial psychoeducation about the counselling process – that they would meet at the same time for 50 minutes for six weeks to try to shed some light on the reasons Bill was feeling as he was, and what was preventing him being able to live a life more in line with the answer he gave to his magic question.

(Continued)

(Continued)

- An agreed focus for Bill's depression. This was broken down into sub foci which included its association with his sadness and anger at the lack of satisfying relationships, and their possible origins in the past, but most importantly, their current manifestations in Bill's life, and, as came to be evident, their replication in the therapeutic relationship. Thus, they were able to be expressed in the 'here and now'. (The 'here and now' tends to assume greater importance in short-term work than the 'there and then'. The past tends only to become significant to the extent in which it casts a shadow over the present difficulties.)
- The counsellor explained that they would expect Bill to talk about the things he felt were important to him as well as anything that came into his mind in the context of the general focus, while the counsellor would help Bill to think about them by commenting on Bill's thoughts and adding some of his own. More protocolled therapies may have approached this issue differently.
- The counsellor maintained an active and collaborative stance with Bill, frequently linking therapeutic material to the focus and asking for Bill's comments and reflections, while continually ensuring that both parties were aware of the time frame and how that might affect the therapeutic alliance and process.
- Sessions were counted down at the end of each one. Bill was relieved and felt safe that the length of therapy was clear and transparent. Both Bill and the therapist felt that more regular sessions were not indicated, although a follow-up was arranged two months after ending.

RESEARCH

Short-term work is often the treatment of choice for clients. Evidence suggests that clients tend to have rather more limited temporal expectations of counselling than their clinicians. Top-up/intermittent therapy is also claimed to be more efficacious than open-ended therapy and deals with one of the concerns about short-term work, which is the danger of relapse, particularly in relation to more severe and long-standing difficulties.

There are a considerable number of time-limited therapies that are developing a sound and rigorous evidence base. These include Intensive Dynamic Psychotherapy (ISTDP) (Abbas et al., 2008, 2012, 2014; Della Selva, 2004; Malan and Della Selva, 2006; Neborsky et al., 2012; Osimo and Stein, 2012), Accelerated Experiential Dynamic Psychotherapy (AEDP) (Fosha, 2000), time-limited dynamic psychotherapy (Betan and Binder, 2017; Levenson, 1995, 2002, 2012), and Interpersonal Therapy (IPT) (Klerman et al., 1994). Short-term therapies originating in the UK with a sound evidence base include Psychodynamic Interpersonal Therapy (PIT), which is based on the seminal work of Hobson (1982) and Guthrie (1999), Dynamic Interpersonal Therapy (DIT) (Haliburn, 2017; Lemma, Target and Fonagy, 2011), and Brief Psychoanalytic Therapy (Hobson, 2016). The increasing use of structured therapies within IAPT are also contributing to this, and there is growing evidence that many clients who have received short-term counselling have experienced considerable benefit from it (Roth and Fonagy, 2005).

REFERENCES

Abbas, A., Town, J., and Driessen, E. (2012) Intensive short-term dynamic psychothereapy: systematic review and meta-analysis of outcome research. *Harvard Review of Psychiatry*, 20(2), 97–108.

Abbas A. et al. (2014) Short-term psychodynamic psychotherapies for common mental disorders. *Cochrane Database of Systematic Reviews Review – Intervention*, July 1(7), CD004687. doi: 10.1002/14651858.CD004687.pub4.

Barkham, M. (1989) Exploratory therapy in two-plus-one sessions I: rationale for a brief psychotherapy model. *British Journal of Psychiatry*, 6(1), 81–88.

Barkham, M., Guthrie, E., Hardy, G., and Margison, F. (2017) *Psychodynamic Interpersonal Therapy: A Conversational Model*. London: Sage.

Berne, E. (1964) *Games People Play: Basic Handbook of Transactional Analysis*. New York: Ballantine.

Betan, E., and Binder, J. (2017) Psychodynamic therapies in practice: time limited dynamic psychotherapy. In A. Consoli et al. (Eds), *Comprehensive Textbook of Psychotherapy: Theory and Practice* (2nd ed.). Oxford: Oxford University Press.

Binder, J. (2004) *Key Competencies in Brief Dynamic Psychotherapy*. New York. Guilford Press.

Binder, J., and Betan, E. (2013) *Core Competencies in Brief Dynamic Psychotherapy*. London: Routledge.

Bond, F., and Dryden, D. (2005) *Handbook of Brief Cognitive Behaviour Therapy*. Chichester, UK: Wiley & Sons.

Bor, R. et al. (2003) *Doing Therapy Briefly*. London: Palgrave.

Briggs, S., and Lyon, L. (2012) Time-limited psychodynamic psychotherapy for adolescents and young adults. In A. Lemma (ed) *Contemporary Developments in Adult and Young Adult Therapy: The Work of the Tavistock and Portman Clinics*, (Vol. 1). Tavistock Clinic Series. London: Karnac.

Brosnan, L., and Westerbrook, D. (2015) *The Complete CBT Guide to Depression and Low Mood*. London: Robinson.

Budman, S. H. and Gurman, A.S. (2002) *Theory and Practice of Brief Therapy*. New York, NY: Guildford Press.

Coren, A. (2010) *Short Term Psychotherapy: A Psychodynamic Approach*. Basingstoke: Palgrave.

Coren, A. (2014) Learning and teaching (briefly). *Psychodynamic Practice*, 20(1), 40–53.

Coren, A. (2016) Short term therapy: therapy lite? In D. Mair (Ed.), *Short Term Counselling in Higher Education: Context Theory and Practice* (pp. 29–44). London: Routledge.

Curwen, B., and Palmer, S. (2000) *Brief CBT*. London: Sage.

Davanloo, H. (Ed.) (1980) *Short Term Dynamic Psychotherapy*. London: Jason Aronson.

Della Selva, P. (2004) *Intensive Dynamic Short Term Therapy*. London: Karnac.

de Shazer, S. (1985) *Keys to Solution in Brief Therapy*. New York: W.W. Norton.

Dryden, W. (2018) *Single-Session Therapy (SST): 100 Key Points and Techniques*. Abingdon, UK: Routledge.

Farber, E. (2020) Interpersonal psychotherapy and brief psychodynmaic therapies. In S. Messer and N. Kaslow (Eds), *Essential Psychotherapies: Theories and Practice* (4th ed.). New York: Guilford Press.

Feardon, P. et al. (2006) Short Term Mentalisation and Relational Therapy (SMART): an integrative family therapy for children and adolescents. In J. Allen and P. Fonagy (Eds), *Handbook of Mentalisation-based Treatments*. Chichester, UK: Wiley & Sons.

Fosha, D. (2000) *The Transforming Power of Affect: A Model for Accelerated Change*. New York: Basic Books.

Gilbert, P. (Ed.) (2022) *Compassion Focused Therapy: Clinical Practice and Applications*. Abingdon, UK: Routledge.

Gustafson, J.P. (2005) *Very Brief Psychotherapy*. New York: W.W. Norton.

Guthrie, E. (1999) Psychodynamic interpersonal therapy. *Advances in Psychiatric Treatment*, 5, 135–145.

Haliburn, J. (2017) *An Integrated Approach to Short-term Dynamic Interpersonal Psychotherapy: A Clinician's Guide*. Abingdon, UK: Routledge.

Hays, S. et al. (2016) *Acceptance and Commitment Therapy: The Process and Practice of Mindful Change* (2nd ed.). New York: Guilford Press.

Hobson, R.F. (1982) *A Conversational Model of Psychotherapy: A Training Method*. London: Tavistock.

Hobson, R.P. (2016) *Brief Psychoanalytic Therapy*. Oxford: Oxford University Press.

Holmes, J. (2014) *The Search for a Secure Base: Attachment Theory and Psychotherapy*. Abingdon, UK: Routledge.

Holmquist, R. (2022) *Principles and Practices of Relational Psychotherapy*. Abingdon, UK: Routledge.

Horowitz, M.J. (1997) *Stress Response Syndromes: PTSD Grief and Adjustment Disorders*. New York: Aronson.

Houston, G. (2003) *Brief Gestalt Therapy*. London: Sage.

Hughes, R. (2016) *Time Limited Art Therapy: Developments in Theory and Practice*. Abingdon, UK: Routledge.

(Continued)

(Continued)

Kim, J. (2013) *Solution-Focused Brief Therapy: A Multicultural Approach.* London: Sage.

Klerman, G.L. et al. (1994) *Interpersonal Psychotherapy of Depression.* New York: Aronson.

Lemma, A., Target, M., and Fonagy, P. (2011) *Brief Dynamic Interpersonal Therapy: A Clinicians Guide.* Oxford: Oxford University Press.

Levenson, H. (1995) *Time Limited Dynamic Psychotherapy.* New York: Basic Books.

Levenson, H. (2012) Time limited dynamic psychotherapy: an integrative perspective. In M. Dewin, B. Steenbarger and R. Greenberg (Eds), *The Art and Science of Brief Psychotherapy.* Arlington, VA: American Psychiatric Association.

Levenson, H. (2017) *Brief Dynamic Therapy.* Arlington, VA: American Psychiatric Association.

Macdonald, A. (2007) *Solution Focused Therapy: Theory, Research and Practice.* London: Sage.

Malan, D. (1979) *Individual Psychotherapy and the Science of Psychodynamics.* London: Butterworth.

Malan, D., and Della Selva, P. (2006) *Lives Transformed: A Revolutionary Method of Dynamic Psychotherapy.* London: Karnac.

Mander, G. (2000) *A Psychodynamic Approach to Brief Therapy.* London: Sage.

Mann, J. (1992) Time limited psychotherapy. In P. Crits-Cristoph and J. Barber (Eds), *Handbook of Short Term Dynamic Psychotherapy.* New York: Basic Books.

Messer, S., and Warren, C. (1988) *Models of Brief Psychodynamic Therapy: A Comparative Approach.* NewYork: Guilford Press.

Neborsky, R. et al. (2012) *Mastering Intensive Short Term Dynamic Therapy: A Road Map to the Unconscious.* London: Karnac.

Osimo, F., and Stein, M. (2012) *Theory and Practice of Experiential Dynamic Psychotherapy.* London: Routledge.

Roth, A., and Fonagy, P. (2005) *What Works for Whom? A Critical Review of Psychotherapy Research.* New York: Guilford Press.

Ryle, A., and Kerr, I. (2001) *Introducing Cognitive Analytic Therapy.* London: Wiley.

Schauer, M. (2011) *Narrative Exposure Therapy: A Short-Term Treatment for Traumatic Stress Disorders* (2nd ed.). Oxford: Hogrefe.

Smith, J.D. (2006) Form and forming a focus in Brief Dynamic Psychotherapy. *Psychodynamic Practice*, 12(3), 261–280.

Smith, J.D. (2015) Creative restorations: holding a mirror to the self in brief dynamic therapy. *Psychodynamic Practice*, 21(4).

Stadter, M. (2004) *Object Relations Brief Therapy: The Therapeutic Relationship in Short Term Work.* New York: Aronson.

Strasser, F., and Strasser, A. (1997) *Existential Time Limited Therapy: The Wheel of Existence.* London: Wiley.

Talmon, M. (1993) *Single Session Solutions.* Reading, MA: Addison-Wesley.

Town, J. et al. (2012) Short-term psychodynamic psychotherapy for personality disorders: a critical review of randomized controlled trials. *Journal of Personality Disorders*, 25(6).

Tudor, K. (2008) *Brief Person Centered Therapies.* London: Sage.

Tudor, K. (Ed.) (2002) *Transactional Analysis Approaches to Brief Therapy: What do you say between saying hello and goodbye?.* London: Sage.

Wake, L. (2010) *The Role of Brief Therapy in Attachment Disorders.* London: Karnac.

White, M. (2011) *Narrative Practice: Continuing the Conversation.* New York: W.W. Norton.

Wills, F., and Sanders, D. (1997) *Cognitive Therapy: Transforming the Image.* London: Sage.

RECOMMENDED READING

Coren, A. (2010) *Short Term Psychotherapy: A Psychodynamic Approach*. London: Palgrave.

This book provides a generic overview of the field of brief interventions, which includes a time-specific model for short-term work and a discussion of the strengths and limitations of the approach in contemporary therapeutic contexts and settings.

Lemma, A., Target, M., and Fonagy, P. (2011) *Brief Dynamic Interpersonal Therapy: A Clinicians Guide*. Milton Keynes: Open University Press.

This book outlines a brief model of therapy which seeks to integrate both process- and protocol-based interventions in an approachable and practical fashion.

Barkham, M., Guthrie, E., Hardy, G., and Margison, F. (2017) *Psychodynamic Interpersonal Therapy: A Conversational Model*. London: Sage.

This is a practical manual which covers the theory of the short-term conversational model, the foundational and advanced clinical skills involved, and its implementation in a wide range of settings.

7.8 WORKPLACE THERAPY

CHARLOTTE CONN AND AASHIYA PATEL

OVERVIEW AND KEY POINTS

Workplace therapy refers to psychological support offered to employees. This can range from in-house counselling, external counselling and any practice pertaining to psychological wellbeing. This chapter will include:

- An exploration of the need for and implementation of workplace therapy.
- An outline of how counsellors work within workplace therapy settings and ethical considerations.
- A case study illustrating the intricacies of a counsellor working within an EAP setting and another outlining how an employee may access workplace therapy.
- Consideration of research evidence exploring the effectiveness of workplace therapy and the impact on employee performance.

INTRODUCTION

Psychological wellbeing is a core area of interest across several fields, including the workplace. Workplace therapy, otherwise known as workplace counselling, is the provision of psychological and emotional support for employees in an attempt to address or improve emotional and behavioural issues. The initiative to provide psychological support for employees in the western world can be traced back to the 1940s when employers in America began providing alcohol dependency related support to their employees to combat absenteeism and low productivity (Bophela and Govender, 2015).

Due to employees often citing workplace stress as the reason for their absence, it becomes incumbent upon employers to put measures in place to address this. In fact, the latest estimates from the UK Labour Force Survey (LFS) show that between 2018 and

2019 new work-related ill health cases cost Britain £10.6 billion. Additionally, recent data suggests that between 2019 and 2020 work-related stress, anxiety and depression were attributed to 51% of all work-related ill-health cases, resulting in a total of 17.6 million days lost. These figures demonstrate an increase in work-related stress, anxiety and depression in the UK workforce when compared to the previous period. However, it is understood that work-related stress is not the sole reason for employee absenteeism, and factors in employees' personal lives also contribute to sickness and low performance. It is no surprise, then, that the need to reduce absenteeism and maintain workforce productivity is echoed in the modern-day workforce through the implementation of employee assistance programmes (EAP) as well as the provision of in-house workplace therapy.

Many organisations offer EAPs to their employees as part of the staff benefits package. From an employer's perspective, the provision of an EAP is highly cost effective as it is inexpensive to run yet supports the retainment and productivity of employees. EAPs act as a central hub for employee wellbeing, with the intention of supporting employees from a holistic angle. Of course, one of the core services provided is counselling, although EAPs also offer a wider range of support, including advice from financial advisers, legal advocates, medical professionals as well as self-help guides, incident de-briefs and managerial support helplines. These services are free to use for employees and are confidential, which means employers are typically not notified when an employee accesses any of the pre-approved EAP support services.

The counselling provision itself usually consists of a telephone helpline that employees have access to on an *ad-hoc* basis. They may use this service to speak to a qualified counsellor for a variety of reasons (e.g., emergency support, to self-refer themselves for scheduled therapy or for some one-off counselling support). If an employee calls to make a self-referral for sessional support, they will be taken through a telephone assessment of their needs and then referred for the most suitable type of therapy by the counsellor. This can be a range of modalities, such as humanistic counselling, cognitive behavioural therapy, trauma-focused therapy or eye movement desensitisation and reprocessing therapy (EMDR). The employee is given the option for the modality in which they would like the therapy to be delivered (e.g., attend these sessions face-to-face, via secure video software or over the phone).

It is important to note that the types of therapy and support employees have access to is determined by the EAP package that employers' purchase. Therefore, in some instances, they may not have access to the type of therapy the counsellor thinks is most suitable. For example, an employee's assessment may indicate they would benefit from trauma-focused therapy. However, if this is not part of the package the employers have purchased, it may not be available to the employee regardless of it being something the EAP offers. Additionally, there is no limit to the number of times an employee can call the helpline for one-off or emergency support, although if they choose to refer themselves for therapy, the number of sessions employees receive is pre-approved by the employer. Typically, the therapy is delivered within a six-session model which refreshes each year. Therefore, if an employee has completed six sessions of therapy but then begins to struggle sometime later, they must wait until a year has passed since the initial six sessions to be re-referred for more. The alternative would be either to use the helpline on an *ad-hoc* basis, meaning they are not guaranteed to speak to the same counsellor each time, or to breach confidentiality and ask the employer to approve additional sessions, thus incurring an additional cost for the organisation.

WAYS OF WORKING

The determining factor for the diverse ways in which workplace therapy works often depends on the number of employees within the workplace, as this will inform the cost versus the demand of the service. The two main inferences of workplace therapy are in-house and EAP counsellors. Simply put, the in-house counsellor is internal to the organisation and usually works within the workplace alongside human resources, whereas EAP counsellors are external to the workplace organisation and are usually outsourced, away from the workplace. Despite the plethora of options for workplace therapies, the aim of the counselling is one thing they all have in common: to improve staff wellbeing and decrease staff absence.

Counsellors may work full-time within an EAP service, which could include a range of activities such as working on the helplines, completing assessments and conducting scheduled counselling sessions. In contrast, private counsellors, who gain referrals from EAP services, are usually only used for scheduled counselling sessions. In-house counsellors are less common in the current climate due to the emergence of technological accessibility and demands for stricter client confidentiality. However, some do still exist within large corporations (Hartwell et al., 1996). The emergence of EAPs has opened up a horizon of opportunities. For example, counsellors working in private practice can build their client portfolio by accepting referrals externally from workplaces.

As stated above, there are various levels and packages of employee assistance programmes, depending on how much the workplace invests in the employee benefits. The EAP service will influence how the counsellor works with them. If the EAP service provides 24/7 telephone counselling, the counsellor is likely to work mixed shifts, where they will provide both immediate support to callers on the helpline as well as structured sessional support to self-referred clients. A typical day's work would depend on the number of incoming calls to the helpline, which is also influenced by the time of day. Each call could vary from a couple of minutes to an hour, depending on the level of risk and client need. If late at night, the calls may be fewer but may present higher risks, so the counsellor must be confident with triaging and breaching confidentiality where necessary. During these shifts, the counsellor must be competent to work autonomously as access to managerial support may be limited.

As mentioned above, the employee will be able to call this helpline as often as they want confidentially, and this may challenge the counsellor's usual modality of counselling. In a helpline format, the counsellor will usually work with a solution-focused approach to provide immediate support, and therefore extra training is required to adapt to the EAP demands. The competence of an EAP counsellor has to be managed and concepts such as goal setting and focused targets may be utilised throughout the call.

In other cases, the person positioned to assess the employee's needs may recommend the employee has scheduled counselling sessions. This usually means an allotted number of sessions scheduled on a particular day/time. If the counsellor works privately but receives referrals from an EAP service, then the counsellor will work within their own availability and will have an agreement with the EAP service as to which mode and approach they provide (e.g., person-centred or cognitive behavioural therapy over the telephone, online or face to face). The counsellor will usually work an allotted number of sessions agreed with the workplace and, compared to other counsellors running their own private practice, they will work in a goal-oriented fashion to help the client maintain in or return to work.

More recently, single session therapy has become popular due to long waiting lists for mental health support (Dryden, 2019). This therapy still comes under the assessed and referred counselling umbrella, but allows for the EAP to offer an hour of therapy for the client to explore their presenting issues with a counsellor. This is effective for employees who require support at the 'point of need' within a scheduled time. If after the single session, the counsellor or client feel more support is required, they can then be referred for further scheduled counselling sessions.

When considering counselling ethics, the usual boundaries of counselling are maintained, particularly around confidentiality. However, counsellors within a workplace have an extra consideration of the 'third party' in the therapeutic relationship, the employer. Clinical information is often collected by the employer to assess the employee's engagement with the EAP. This can range from psychometric scores assessed at the start and end of therapy, the employee's engagement with the sessions, as well as their therapeutic progress. This can cause potential confidentiality issues for the counsellors if it is not contracted correctly with the client from the start.

CASE STUDY

Ji-Hoon is a prison officer working in a high security prison who has been on sick leave since an incident occurred with an inmate. His employers offer an EAP service as part of the staff wellbeing package, so he calls the helpline and is greeted by a qualified counsellor who proceeds to explain how the service works and to ask some questions regarding the purpose of his call. He is initially nervous as he does not want to tell the counsellor that he

(Continued)

(Continued)

is off work due to a serious incident exacerbated by what he believes is poor management. However, once the counsellor explains that no information is relayed back to his employers, Ji-Hoon explains his reasons for calling.

The counsellor explains that she will conduct an assessment with him over the phone and will then refer him for the most suitable support available. During the assessment he discloses that aside from the effects on his mental health from the incident at work, he is also struggling financially due to debts he has incurred. At the end of the assessment the counsellor recommends him for six sessions of trauma-focused therapy. She explains that this has already been pre-approved by the employers as part of the EAP package and he can decide how he would like the sessions to be conducted. Ji-Hoon feels online video counselling will be best for him as he will not have to travel and so chooses this option. The counsellor adds that she can forward his details to a colleague who can offer free debt-related advice if he wishes. Ji-Hoon accepts and so later that day he receives a call from the debt advisor and goes on to start his online therapy sessions the following week.

Once he has completed his sessions, the therapist advises that they will need to complete a closure form and he will then be discharged. The therapist explains that although Ji-Hoon has used up his six sessions for the year, he can still access the helpline for *ad-hoc* emotional support or other financial and legal advice.

CASE STUDY

Bethany is a private counsellor working within the EAP service for large healthcare organisations. Bethany receives a referral from the occupational therapist detailing the client's needs and provides an initial assessment. This includes a CORE-10 measurement, which indicates the client is suffering a high level of psychological stress. The client is allocated six face-to-face sessions with the counsellor and on the third session a midway review is completed where Bethany and her client set a focus and goal for the remaining sessions. On the sixth session, Bethany completes the CORE-10 with her client again to track the client's progress and assess the level of therapeutic change/effect. If the client is scoring similarly to the first CORE-10 and they want additional sessions, these may be applied for through the EAP service. Where this is the case, Bethany will have to notify her client that she is requesting additional sessions and will have to provide some information about the session's content as a rationale for requesting the additional sessions. This may include a section where the counsellor is to detail how engaged the client has been with the service.

RESEARCH

Exploration into the effectiveness of workplace therapy has been in focus over recent decades. Analysing the usefulness of EAP provision not only assesses the efficacy of the services provided, but also whether the provision of such services is of financial benefit to organisations. There are several parameters that the literature investigates, and these include organisational outcomes such as absenteeism, presenteeism and levels of functioning, as well individual outcomes such as improvements in personal health, life satisfaction and prevalence of depressive symptoms.

When considering the effectiveness of workplace therapy through the provision of EAPs, studies have often concentrated on absenteeism, meaning an employee being off sick or absent from work due to ill-health, and presenteeism, which pertains to the 'degree in which personal problems impinge on productivity in work' (Sharar and Lennox, 2014: 2). Interestingly, research suggests that presenteeism may be a better indicator of the EAP impact on employees as there are significantly more organisational costs associated with presenteeism than absenteeism (Hargrave et al., 2008). Joseph, Walker and Fuller-Tyszkiewicz (2018) conducted a systematic review evaluating the effectiveness of EAP programmes and concluded that, overall, the literature suggests that the utilisation of EAPs enhances both organisational and individual outcomes for employees. For example, McLeod (2010) found that as well as an alleviation in psychological problems, employees moderately improved their attitudes to work. Moreover, workplace counselling has also enhanced existing employee skills. Millar (2002) found police officers and support staff who had received counselling for work-related issues felt the counselling had helped. Unexpectedly, the study also uncovered that the employees felt counselling had improved their existing skills, such as active listening. Furthermore, Richmond et al. (2014) found a decrease in presenteeism in employees after an EAP intervention, and the results indicated that EAP interventions were particularly helpful for employees who screened positive for depression prior to receiving the support.

It is evident from the plethora of literature investigating the efficacy of workplace therapy that access to it benefits both the organisation and the individual. Nevertheless, the literature highlights that what indicates the effectiveness of workplace therapy can be subjective. For example, employers may consider an improvement in presence and functioning at work as an indicator of effectiveness, whereas employees may believe that general life satisfaction or overall wellbeing are more reliable measures. It has also been suggested that the majority of EAP research was conducted in North America, which suggests further scope for expansion of research in other countries (Joseph et al., 2018). Finally, a limited incorporation of control groups in the body of literature raises the question of whether the provision of workplace therapy through EAPs is more effective in improving outcomes than having no intervention at all.

REFERENCES

Bophela, N., & Govender, P. (2015). Employee assistance programs (EAPs): tools for quality of work life. *Problems and Perspectives in Management*, 13(2), 506–514.

Dryden, W. (2019). *Single-Session Therapy: 100 Key Points and Techniques*. Abingdon, UK: Routledge.

Hargrave, G. E., Hiatt, D., Alexander, R., & Shaffer, I. A. (2008). EAP treatment impact on presenteeism and absenteeism: implications for return on investment. *Journal of Workplace Behavioral Health*, 23(3), 283–293.

Hartwell, T. D., Steele, P., French, M. T., Potter, F. J., Rodman, N. F., & Zarkin, G. A. (1996). Aiding troubled employees: the prevalence, cost and characteristics of Employee Assistance Programs in the United States. *American Journal of Public Health*, 86, 804–808.

Joseph, B., Walker, A., & Fuller-Tyszkiewicz, M. (2018). Evaluating the effectiveness of employee assistance programmes: a systematic review. *European Journal of Work and Organizational Psychology*, 27(1), 1–15. https://doi.org/10.1080/1359432X.2017.1374245

McLeod, J. (2010). The effectiveness of workplace counselling: a systematic review. *Counselling and Psychotherapy Research: Linking Practice with Research*, 10(4), 238–248.

Millar, A. (2002). Beyond resolution of presenting issues: clients' experiences of an in-house police counselling service. *Counselling and Psychotherapy Research*, 2, 159–166.

Richmond, M. K., Shepherd, J. L., Pampel, F. C., Wood, R. C., Reimann, B., & Fischer, L. (2014). Associations between substance use, depression, and work outcomes: an evaluation study of screening and brief intervention in a large Employee Assistance Program. *Journal of Workplace Behavioral Health*, 29(1), 1–18. doi:10.1080/15555240.2014.866470

Sharar, D. A., & Lennox, R. (2014). The workplace effects of EAP use: pooled results from 20 different EAPs with before and after WOS 5-item data. *EASNA Research Notes*, 4(1), 1–5. Retrieved from http://hdl.handle.net/10713/5139

RECOMMENDED READING

British Association for Counselling and Psychotherapy (n.d.). *BACP Workplace*. Lutterworth: BACP. Retrieved 19 March 2022 from www.bacp.co.uk/bacp-divisions/bacp-workplace/

The BACP workplace division website includes resources which support practitioners who work with employees, employers and EAPs.

Coles, A. (2013). *Counselling in the Workplace*. London: McGraw-Hill Education.

This book will help anyone who wants to further explore the context of workplace counselling. Coles has a wealth of experience researching and working with counsellors, managers and organisations who are involved in workplace therapy.

Franklin, L. (2003). *An Introduction to Workplace Counselling: A Practitioner's Guide*. London: Macmillan Education.

This book is aimed to be used as an introduction into the world of workplace counselling. Franklin takes a facilitative approach to guide counsellors on understanding issues surrounding workplace therapy while they navigate through the professional workplace landscapes.

7.9 WORKING IN FORENSIC SETTINGS

JENIKA PATEL AND SUNIL LAD

OVERVIEW AND KEY POINTS

This chapter provides an overview of the mental health problems that forensic populations experience and how they can be compounded and maintained by the criminal justice system. It addresses some of the challenges of delivering therapeutic care in forensic settings.

- The cultural norms within prisons promote control, security and cohesion, making it difficult for individual emotional needs to be met safely.
- Defensive stances, of aggression and violence, are commonly used to manage vulnerability.
- Balancing the conflicts of security and care is essential when working in forensic settings for good outcomes for individuals.

INTRODUCTION

England and Wales have the highest rate of imprisonment in western Europe, with approximately 80,000 people in prison currently (Prison Reform Trust, 2019). The types of prisons vary according to categories (A–D) of security, with Category A prisons being the most secure, housing those deemed the highest risk to society, while Category D prisons are open, where residents are able to move freely and spend time in the community prior to their release. Those admitted to secure hospitals are detained and sectioned under the Mental Health Act 1983 in high, medium and low secure hospitals. Within both settings the security level has an influence on searching, restrictions and how the environment operates, impacting on the therapeutic milieu; these differ between hospital and prison environments. The adult prison population houses both males and females from the age of 18 to the elderly.

The clinical needs of the prison population are vast. First, suicide rates are much higher than in the community, with men in prison being 3.7 times more likely to die from suicide compared to other populations (Kaur, Manders and Windsor-Shellard, 2019). Research by Pope (2018) found that females engaged in a greater frequency of self-harm incidents, while the incidents in males were more severe, with associated injuries and the lethality of the method.

Within the literature, researchers have connected adverse childhood experiences (ACEs) to offending behaviours (Fox et al., 2015), following the landmark study conducted by Felitti et al. (1998). They identified seven ACEs: physical abuse, sexual abuse, emotional neglect, mental illness, substance misuse, witnessing violence against mother or witnessing criminal behaviour in the household. These traumas are likely to impact unhelpfully on areas of a person's life if exposure is frequent and accumulative before the age of 18. Although the ACE questionnaire provides a retrospective account of early life adversity, is subject to reporting bias and does not capture the severity, chronicity or age at which exposure to one or more of these experiences occurred, it remains strong in its predicative capacity to determine psychiatric and medical disorders (Anda et al., 2006). Studies have found that a high proportion of people accessing forensic services have had contact with the care system, experiencing abandonment and abuse (Reingle et al., 2014; Piquero et al., 2011).

Despite the extent of mental health challenges experienced by those housed in prisons and secure hospitals, there remains an emphasis on security, punishment and rehabilitation of the offender. The provision of therapeutic care can be perceived as undermining this ethos, making therapeutic work challenging. Forensic settings can often re-traumatise those accessing services. Re-traumatisation fundamentally means to be traumatised again, because a person experiences something in the present that evokes similar emotional and physiological responses as the original event (Bloom and Farragher, 2010). However those accessing forensic settings may not be aware that their current distress is embedded in past events. Memories, thoughts and feelings can manifest incoherently and can be triggered by a range of sensory experiences, leading to responses such as mistrust, aggression and paranoia. This can be equally, if not at times more distressing and confusing for people.

In prisons, examples of re-traumatisation can include restraint, physical assault and seclusion, which can often mimic past experiences of powerlessness, violation, lack of safety and loss of choice. While re-traumatisation can be unintentional and unanticipated, it remains because forensic settings fail to acknowledge the role of trauma in people's lives and people's consequent need for safety, mutuality, collaboration and empowerment. This lack of understanding may reinforce a person's need for coping strategies such as illicit drug use or self-harm, overt acts of aggression and general engagement in behaviours that are considered anti-social, which prevent good outcomes in therapy.

WAYS OF WORKING

To break this cycle, care and understanding for the reasons behind these behaviours is required. Time needs to be spent on navigating the balance between effective security and providing good care. Therapists are required to work within multi-disciplinary teams, to explore processes both conscious and unconscious of staff and residents, which may be at play, causing disruptions and instability. They are required to work alongside other professionals to deliver psychological interventions and guide clinical discussions based on assessment, formulation and intervention (McGauley et al., 2018).

The therapist has to hold in mind parallel processes and the punitive and hierarchical structure in which prisons operate. Often hostile and aggressive stances can serve to protect and preserve a person in prison. This stance is frequently adopted because of fear – showing vulnerability is often interpreted as weakness. If a person is 'weak', they are at risk of being exploited and harmed.

Additional challenges of working therapeutically come from recognising that people in forensic settings hold both the victim and perpetrator stances. Exploring these positions takes risk and courage; in a setting not conducive in developing safety, this can feel shaming and threatening. Having a therapeutic relationship in which emotional regulation can be demonstrated and developed is a starting point in therapy. Understanding the role of repression, denial, dissociation and other forms of avoidance, which are developed as a way of protecting individuals in challenging and hostile environments, is required. If these defences are not acknowledged and addressed safely, there is the potential of causing harm within the therapeutic process, which could lead to instability in a person's presentation, reinforcing or increasing risk behaviours. This means that there are many different considerations to make when offering therapy in forensic settings.

This imbalance of power needs attention; residents are unable to move freely in the prison. Therapists, in contrast, have their own keys, can freely walk around the prison and have access to personal information, including offence details. Having awareness of the power imbalance is necessary to prevent boundary breaches.

In working with the forensic population therapists may come into contact with people who have committed offences against children, sexual offences or behaviour involving sadism. Being aware of their thoughts and feelings are vital when working in this setting and may challenge the core conditions of being non-judgemental. Utilising supervision and support to explore feelings around the offences committed that may impede the therapeutic alliance or evoke fears of personal safety need to be addressed (Davies, 2015).

In forensic settings, any therapist disclosing personal information may be at risk of being threatened, or their personal safety being compromised. This lack of disclosure may make it difficult to develop a therapeutic relationship, as suspicion and mistrust develop on both parties (Crewe, 2012).

Overall, there are complex interactions between organisations and people who are imprisoned. Organisations are often seen as being insufficient in responding to survivors of trauma. Those within the criminal justice system feel unsafe, and use aggression as a way of coping with this. Staff may be directly impacted by this aggression, which then leads to hostile and wary attitudes towards those accessing services, resulting in more punitive and risk management measures. In this way, 'parallel processes' emerge, whereby service users, practitioners and organisations come to mirror each other (Bloom and Covington, 2008). Becoming 'trauma-informed' has the potential to break these processes and create environments that foster safety and engagement, where trauma is recognised as a shared experience. This has the potential for generating relationships where positive interactions can develop, through trauma-informed care.

CASE STUDY

Jack is a 28 year-old white male referred by wing staff to psychological services because he was isolating in his cell and not coming out for work and exercise. Jack reported a very difficult and troubled childhood where he witnessed his mother being assaulted. When he was 8 years old, his mother took her own life, and he was taken into foster care.

Jack would frequently witness violence between his foster carers. When Jack was 14 his paternal grandmother died in a house fire. Jack felt a huge amount of guilt that he was not able to care for her. He had few friends, and he would spend his days smoking cannabis and drinking alcohol. He would avoid people when he was feeling paranoid. He could become easily angered if he did not like what others were saying about him, and this would lead to aggression. One day, under the influence of cannabis and alcohol, and following an argument with his partner, he was arrested by the police and became violent, which led to imprisonment.

In therapy he presented with symptoms of anxiety and low mood, reporting that he was scared to associate with other residents in case he harmed them. He expressed high levels of agitation at the prospect of leaving his cell. He reported that he was not eating regularly and had lost weight, his sleep patterns were disrupted and often he would sleep during the day. Sometimes he would become paranoid that residents were talking about him, although this was not common. Jack agreed initially to meet with a therapist. However, his reluctance and ambivalence were clear from the outset. He was mistrusting of what could be offered and was also scared that if therapy 'did not work', what was there left to try?

In the room, there was a large window looking out into the corridor, with no blinds. This meant that people would frequently walk past the room and look in, including officers and other residents. This made the reality of working in a prison more evident – that privacy was compromised because of the need for security officers to be able to see into a room at any given time.

As Jack engaged in therapy, his therapist realised that he had felt let down. His early life had been unpredictable and uncertain, and he had learnt to manage his feelings through drugs and alcohol. He had witnessed violence at an early age, and he had learnt this strategy to protect himself from harm too.

Within therapy, the theme of hopelessness was in the room, almost tangibly so, and it was important to be aware of this and be able to tolerate the discomfort of this hopelessness. The therapist was aware of the risk of boundaries becoming blurred due to the sadness of his life and a need to rescue Jack from distress. The therapist processed these feelings in supervision to ensure that boundaries did not become blurred and containment was offered. Jack's therapist worked collaboratively to understand how early life experiences had contributed to the development of Jack's beliefs and sense of self-identity.

Within therapy, the focus was placed on normalising his thoughts and feelings by developing a shared understanding of why he behaved in the way he did, and the role that violence and aggression had played in his life. Jack began to learn that a lot of what had happened to him was not his fault, as this is what he believed. He learned about the role of different emotions and their function, and strategies for acknowledging and managing them. The work was structured, and the meaning-making process was collaborative. Jack steadily developed confidence in himself to socialise with others, and he started to exercise. Therapeutic space was held for him to explore the unease and discomfort he frequently felt, the fear he had of hurting others. He was clear in telling the therapist that some things he did not feel comfortable sharing. On one occasion, Jack was found with a mobile phone. He did not talk about this in therapy sessions, or how he came to be holding it. In prisons, phone are prohibited for security reasons. This made his therapist realise that there were aspects of his prison life that Jack did not bring to the session, as he was fully aware that any issues that comprise security would have to be disclosed.

There was a delicate balance in allowing Jack to feel safe in being vulnerable, yet not to feel overwhelmed by it in a highly unsafe environment. Within therapy he had also shared how processes had triggered previous negative experiences where he did not have autonomy or choice, for example having to open his mouth so that a member of staff could check whether medication had been swallowed. He found this process dehumanising. This made him adamant that he did not wish to take medication. It took time to build trust. His experiences began to be normalised in the context of the things that had happened to him and in the prison environment.

Over time, Jack spent less time isolating himself from others, began to engage in the regime, and shared interests with others. Overall, Jack felt more confident that he would be able to cope with things better on release. He reported having a better understanding of why he was feeling the way he was, how he had learnt to numb his feelings through cannabis and alcohol, and how he felt safe in developing trust with another human being.

RESEARCH

There is little research that has been conducted in working therapeutically in forensic settings away from risk and reoffending. Therapeutic communities have been found to be effective, especially for those with problems with substances (Richardson and Zini, 2021). Due to a growing recognition of trauma, a meta-analysis by Malik et al. (2021) revealed that individual therapy led to greater reductions in PTSD symptoms. The challenges of working in this setting as well as confounds in treatments may make conducting research in this area very difficult.

REFERENCES

Anda, R.F., Felitti, V.J., Bremner, J.D., Walker, J.D., Whitfield, C.H., Perry, B.D., Dube, S.R. and Giles, W.H. (2006). The enduring effects of abuse and related adverse experiences in childhood. *European Archives of Psychiatry and Clinical Neuroscience, 256*(3), 174–186.

Bloom, B.E. and Covington, S. (2008). Addressing the mental health needs of women offenders. *Women's Mental Health Issues across the Criminal Justice System*, January, 160–176.

(Continued)

(Continued)

Bloom, S.L. and Farragher, B. (2010). *Destroying Sanctuary: The Crisis in Human Service Delivery Systems*. Oxford: Oxford University Press.

Crewe, B. (2012). *The Prisoner Society: Power, Adaptation and Social Life in an English Prison*. Oxford: Oxford University Press.

Davies, J. (2015). *Supervision for Forensic Practitioners*. Abingdon, UK: Routledge.

Felitti, V.J., Anda, R.F., Nordenberg, D., Williamson, D.F., Spitz, A.M., Edwards, V. and Marks, J.S. (1998). Relationship of childhood abuse and household dysfunction to many of the leading causes of death in adults: the Adverse Childhood Experiences (ACE) study. *American Journal of Preventive Medicine*, 14(4), 245–258.

Fox, B.H., Perez, N., Cass, E., Baglivio, M.T. and Epps, N. (2015). Trauma changes everything: examining the relationship between adverse childhood experiences and serious, violent and chronic juvenile offenders. *Child Abuse & Neglect*, 46, 163–173. https://doi.org/10.1016/j.chiabu.2015.01.011

Kaur, J., Manders, B. and Windsor-Shellard, B. (2019). Drug-related deaths and suicide in prison custody in England and Wales: 2008 to 2016. *Office for National Statistics* [Release], 25 July. London: Office for National Statistics.

Malik, N., Facer-Irwin, E., Dickson, H., Bird, A. and MacManus, D. (2021). The effectiveness of trauma-focused interventions in prison settings: a systematic review and meta-analysis. *Trauma, Violence, & Abuse*. [Online first], 28 October. https://doi.org/10.1177/15248380211043890

McGauley, G., Humphrey, M., Parry, E. and Oyebode, F. (2018). *Advances in Psychiatric Treatment*. Cambridge: Cambridge University Press.

Piquero, A.R., Shepherd, I., Shepherd, J.P. and Farrington, D.P. (2011). Impact of offending trajectories on health: disability, hospitalisation and death in middle-aged men in the Cambridge study in delinquent development. *Criminal Behaviour and Mental Health*, 21(3), 189–201.

Pope, L. (2018). *Self-harm by Adult Men in Prison: A Rapid Evidence Assessment (REA)*. London: Her Majesty's Prison and Probation Service.

Prison Reform Trust (2019). *Prison: The Facts*. Bromley Briefings Summer 2019. London: Prison Reform Trust.

Reingle, J.M., Jennings, W.G., Connell, N.M., Businelle, M.S. and Chartier, K. (2014). On the pervasiveness of event-specific alcohol use, general substance use, and mental health problems as risk factors for intimate partner violence. *Journal of Interpersonal Violence*, 29(16), 2951–2970.

Richardson, J. and Zini, V. (2021). Are prison-based therapeutic communities effective? Challenges and considerations. *International Journal of Prisoner Health*, 17(1), 42–53.

RECOMMENDED READING

Vossler, A.E., Havard, C.E., Pike, G.E., Barker, M.J.E. and Raabe, B.E. (2017). *Mad or Bad: A Critical Approach to Counselling and Forensic Psychology*. Thousand Oaks, CA: Sage.

This book explores the tensions and differences in values, cultures and practices both in the field of counselling psychology and forensic psychology, debating the interface of mental health and the criminal justice system.

Drennan, G. and Alred, D. (2012). *Secure Recovery:* Approaches to Recovery in Forensic Mental Health Settings. Cullompton, UK: Willan.

This book addresses the challenges of recovery-based mental healthcare provision in forensic settings and prison-based therapeutic communities. It is a valuable resource for aspiring practitioners working across forensic and mental health settings.

> Adshead, G. (2012). *Professional and Therapeutic Boundaries in Forensic Mental Health Practice*. London: Jessica Kingsley Publishers.
>
> This text provides an introduction to the challenges of implementing professional and therapeutic boundaries within forensic settings from multiple professional perspectives, including psychotherapy, considering theoretical and clinical issues.

7.10 COACHING

ZSÓFIA ANNA UTRY AND STEPHEN PALMER

OVERVIEW AND KEY POINTS

In the previous edition we argued that coaching could offer an evidence-based personal and organisational coping/learning/developmental solution in a volatile, uncertain, complex and ambiguous (VUCA) world that requires us to continuously reflect and learn and un-learn to succeed in personal and work environments. Since then, life has become even more VUCA. While the associated challenges resulting from Brexit mostly concern the UK and the European Union's population, the outcomes of long-term systemic exclusion of different minority groups are now also more in the public consciousness. Climate change and the still ongoing Covid-19 pandemic places further challenges on everybody around the globe. While systemic coaching used to be a specialism, now coaches cannot ignore the impact of multiple layers and their intersections in their clients' and coachees', and in their own lives. This chapter will explore how coaching as a profession is responding to new and significantly bigger challenges. It will cover:

- The role of coaching in society and its current status quo.
- Evolving ways of coaching and new topics.
- A case study: coaching a person with a diverse cognitive profile.
- An update on the development in coaching research.

INTRODUCTION

In principle, coaching is not owned by one group or discipline, and the setup is inherently democratic, where two equal persons meet in a shared space with a mutually agreed goal. Coaching was established in the western business world by filling the space where counselling and therapy did not go (Western, 2012). Over time, it moved beyond the work domain (see the life coaching industry), but also integrated personal life questions back into work-related practice (see work–life balance coaching and positive psychology coaching).

We can say that coaching in general is a dialogue-based service which aims to facilitate a coachee's personal development and support them to achieve their personal and professional goals. The caveat is that coaching services are not generally offered to people who are suffering from high levels of distress or clinical disorders such as anxiety or depression (Utry and Palmer, 2017), but there are exceptions. For example, a person who has become depressed about being made redundant may still benefit from receiving career coaching in order to assist them in obtaining another job.

The understanding of coaching from a practice point of view will depend on the context in which it is used. There are people who think about coaching as a profession, while there are others who think about it as an activity and just as part of a job role (e.g., managers and leaders using coaching skills) (International Coaching Federation (ICF), 2020). Professional coaches tend to have a deeper level of training than those who just use coaching skills (ICF, 2020).

Coaching as a profession has been continuously evolving and growing in recognition across the world, although most of the responses informing the latest International Coaching Federation Global Survey still came from North America and western Europe (ICF, 2020). It was estimated that the number of coaching practitioners grew by 33% between 2015 and 2019, indicating that coaching is continuously growing in popularity as a profession. Most coaches are Gen X and Baby boomers, and only one in 10 coaches are likely to belong to the Millennial generation. The estimated global income from coaching was US$2.949 billion in 2019, suggesting a 21% increase since 2015. Some coaching service providers (Bearne, 2021) can still remind us to the 'wild west of coaching' era (Sherman and Freas, 2004), but those coaches, leaders and managers who engaged in the ICF survey predominantly agreed on the high importance of coaching-specific training and accreditation by recognised professional bodies that promote ethical practice (ICF, 2020).

Most coaching assignments are business related (65%), but coaches tend to offer additional services in consulting, training and facilitation. Typically, a coachee is a manager or leader between the ages of 35 and 44, and a coaching contract is likely to last for several months. People interested in the widespread organisational application of coaching largely think that initiatives to achieve a 'coaching culture' (Clutterbuck and Megginson, 2005) in an organisation are likely to meet obstacles, such as limited support from senior leaders, an inability to measure the impact of coaching, and a lack of budget for coaching activities (ICF, 2020).

A growing number of professional coaches and bodies are concerned with what it means to coaching as a profession to have a social impact. It is recognised that coaching itself is practised in a democratic spirit, although professional coaching services are not equally accessible to and inclusive of all, thus maintaining or further growing the gap between privileged and less privileged groups and populations. There is stronger ecological crisis awareness among coaches now too. Initiatives like the Climate Coaching Alliance (see www.climatecoachingalliance.org) encourage practitioners to apply a systemic view when working with leaders, and to address the deep and difficult questions of climate change with them.

WAYS OF WORKING

Coaching remains an eclectic or integrative field of practice. However, there is greater interest and need for training in evidence-based coaching approaches. Many universities across the world now offer post-graduate level training in coaching.

Typical coachees want to work on different transitions in their lives (such as career or personal life changes), to improve in executive or leadership roles, and/or they experience dissatisfaction with one or more aspects of their lives (e.g., with work–life imbalance or unhealthy lifestyle). Irrespective of specialism, coaching practitioners expect that life vision and enhancement coaching will dominate in the future (ICF, 2021).

Team coaching (Widdowson and Barbour, 2021) has increased in popularity as a more effective learning and problem-solving approach for leadership teams in large organisations. Now individual coaching in organisations can be seen as potentially more counterproductive from a whole organisation perspective (Clutterbuck, 2021).

In-person coaching is not the norm anymore. Since the Covid-19 pandemic 83% of coaches have increased their use of audio and video platforms (ICF, 2021). However, this trend was increasing anyway, as an earlier survey suggested (ICF, 2020).

Not surprisingly, the coaching profession has started to expand to include nature in the coaching conversations, and to explore the possibility of facilitating connections with our natural environment to achieve an ecologically aware perspective shift in both individuals and organisations. This is referred to as eco-coaching or ecopsychology coaching (International Centre for Ecopsychology, 2021).

Following the recent social unrest related to racial and ethnic inequity and injustices, businesses, including coaching businesses and professional bodies, started to pay more attention to diversity and inclusion issues, both within the profession and in working with coachees (e.g., Shah, 2020). While this area is not well researched at the moment, early evidence suggests (Bernstein, 2019) that coaches are more likely to avoid difficult conversations with Black coachees out of fear of being seen as prejudiced, in so doing depriving Black leaders from developmental opportunities.

Another area of inclusion, called neurodiversity (Singer, 2017), has become topical in corporate environments in the recent years (Doyle, 2020). Workplace strategy coaching aims to help people with diverse cognitive profiles to find and implement workplace adjustments to maintain and progress in their jobs.

CASE STUDY

The coachee is in their late 30s. They have been in full-time self-employment for nearly four years but, when work has been slow, they have had to diversify their workload and do less satisfying and focused part-time projects to make ends meet. Over the years they have tried selling many different products but none of them has led to a sufficiently sustainable income. The coachee values their independence and creativity highly, and has been educated in economics and the performing arts. They have managed to keep their business afloat over the years, and they are working towards a more significant sales breakthrough at this point.

The coachee reports chronic time management issues and difficulties in staying on task, starting too many other tasks while feeling they have not completed any of them. They feel 'enslaved' by unanticipated administrative tasks in their business and that having a PA would be 'a dream come true'. They also fear being potentially overwhelmed in their business.

They have contracted for four one-hour coaching sessions over a two-month period, leading up to the Christmas rush. The coachee wants to work towards a lifestyle reform in the new year, that will allow them to 'have a life' and not just work.

The coach aims to create a relaxed, non-demanding space for the coaching sessions. A number of stress-inducing thoughts have been identified over the course of the coaching contract, such as 'I'm nearly 40 and I haven't achieved anything', or 'If anything happens to me...', or 'You can only achieve success with hard work', or 'I cannot waste my time', or 'Customers want me to be available 24/7'. However, it is difficult to keep the focus of the coachee on one thought for long enough to really unpick it.

Over the four sessions, the coachee reports more significant work–life balance issues alongside an increased workload and more unexpected challenges, such as equipment breakdowns. But as time moved on, positive feedback from the market helps the coachee to experience a sense of satisfaction and enthusiasm for working.

By the last two sessions the coachee is reporting less anxiety and is planning how they might expand the small business into a company with employees to help. They are also considering different ways to enhance the quality of their life, such as using habit trackers (tools to monitor whether individuals do, or do not, engage in particular habits).

When asked how the coaching process has been helpful, the coachee says that they have found it useful to talk things through, as normally they 'didn't get proper attention' from others. They feel calmer and more self-aware after the coaching sessions. They also associate their challenging behaviours with ADHD, and that the coaching process has increased their self-acceptance and decreased their self-criticism. All this has helped them to engage in more short breaks over this period, as they have realised that 'It's OK to have some rest'.

RESEARCH

Early research into coaching was found to be limited in quality (Kampa-Kokesch and Anderson, 2001). Passmore and Fillery-Travis argued (2011) that organisations expected to see evidence to back up the claims of the coaching industry, and that coaching training need to be based on evidence-based practices to give the best to coachees too.

Between 2014 and 2020, five meta-analyses (Theeboom, Beersma and van Vianem, 2014; Sonesh et al., 2015; Jones, Woods and Guillaume, 2016; Burt and Talati, 2017; Graßmann, Schölmerich and Schermuly, 2020) and five systematic reviews (Lai and McDowall, 2014; Blackman, Moscardo and Gray, 2016; Grover and Furnham, 2016; Athanasopoulou and Dopson, 2018; Bozer and Jones, 2018) were published in the coaching research field. The reviewed studies mainly investigated coaching effectiveness in organisational settings (leadership, executive, business and workplace coaching, delivered by internal and external coaches), but some in the personal/life and career domains as well.

Across these studies it was found that coaching had a positive impact on workplace learning and performance. Theeboom et al. (2014) showed that employees' coping mechanisms and wellbeing improved significantly. The professional helping relationship (working alliance) was also identified (Graßmann et al., 2020; Lai and McDowall, 2014; Sonesh et al., 2015) as a key factor in achieving positive process experience and positive outcomes through coaching. The research in the reviewed studies is limited as the studies were not consistent or rigorous in the way that 'coaching' was defined and the coaching model constructs that were applied.

Lai and Palmer's (2019) literature review excluded non-psychological coaching approaches and focused only psychologically informed studies. They examined psychological coaching approaches in their integrated literature review with the aim of helping organisations to select and evaluate executive coaches successfully. Cognitive-behavioural, solution-focused, GROW (Goals, Reality, Options and Will) based, and strengths-based approaches to coaching were found to show evidence of effectiveness. This study was also concerned with the contextual or process factors in coaching, and not just outcomes. Building trust, transparency and rapport, and facilitating learning were identified as essential skills and factors in effective coaching. Scientifically validated outcome measures were also recommended to use in organisational coaching settings to promote an evidence-based practice.

Wang, Lai, Xu, and McDowall (2021) published a meta-analysis of contemporary psychologically informed coaching approaches. This study demonstrated that coaching had a significant positive effect on coachee's goal-attainment, self-efficacy, mental health, resilience, positive moods, and reduced stress and psychopathologies. No difference was found between the different approaches (cognitive-behavioural, solution-focused, GROW, or Positive Psychology coaching), but integrative practice seemed somewhat, but not significantly, more effective than single orientation approaches.

Thus, there is robust research evidence which suggests that coaching works, and that coaching has established itself as an independent research field. However, the theoretical diversity in coaching practice makes it hard to gather statistical results, and the quality of the evidence would be improved by better research methodologies and evaluation design (Lai and Palmer, 2019). It was also argued that existing research neglected the social complexity of coaching (Wang et al., 2021). Future research should therefore focus on the role of the social and political environment where the coaching takes place to gain a fuller understanding of what makes coaching successful.

REFERENCES

Athanasopoulou, A. and Dopson, S. (2018) A systematic review of executive coaching outcomes: is it the journey or the destination that matters the most? *The Leadership Quarterly*, 29(129), 70–88.

Bearne, S. (2021) Online job coaches 'are exploiting the unemployed during pandemic'. *The Guardian*, 18 April. Available at: www.theguardian.com/money/2021/apr/18/online-job-coaches-are-exploiting-the-unemployed-during-pandemic (accessed 1 September 2021).

Bernstein, A.F. (2018) *Race Matters in Coaching: An Examination of Coaches' Willingness to Have Difficult Conversations with Leaders of Color.* PhD thesis, Columbia University. Available at https://doi.org/10.7916/d8-ks03-ve37 (accessed 10 November 2021).

Blackman, A., Moscardo, G. and Gray, D.E. (2016) Challenges for the theory and practice of business coaching: a systematic review of empirical evidence. *Human Resource Development Review*, 15(4), 459–486.

Bozer, G. and Jones, R.J. (2018) Understanding the factors that determine workplace coaching effectiveness: a systematic literature review. *European Journal of Work and Organizational Psychology*, 27(3), 342–361.

Burt, D. and Talati, Z. (2017) The unsolved value of executive coaching: a meta-analysis of outcomes using randomised control trial studies. *International Journal of Evidence-Based Coaching and Mentoring*, 15(2), 17–24.

Clutterbuck, D. (2021) *Is coaching in danger of becoming part of the problem, instead of part of the solution?* Paper presented at the Special Group in Coaching Psychology Annual Conference, 9–10 May [virtual conference].

Clutterbuck, D. and Megginson, D. (2005) *Making Coaching Work: Creating a Coaching Culture.* London: Chartered Institute of Personnel and Development.

Doyle, N. (2020) Neurodiversity at work: a biopsychosocial model and the impact on working adults. *British Medical Bulletin*, 135(1), 108–125. Available at https://academic.oup.com/bmb/article/135/1/108/5913187 (accessed 10 November 2021).

Graßmann, C., Schölmerich, F. and Schermuly, C. (2020) The relationship between working alliance and client outcomes in coaching: a meta-analysis. *Human Relations*, 73(1), 35–58.

Grover, S. and Furnham, A. (2016) Coaching as a developmental intervention in organisations: a systematic review of its effectiveness and the mechanisms underlying it. *PLoS One*, 11(7), e0159137.

International Centre for Ecopsychology (2021) *Ecopsychology Coaching and Ecocoaching*. Available at www.ecopsychology.info/ecopsychology-coaching (accessed 14 December 2021).

International Coaching Federation (2020) *2020 ICF Global Coaching Study: Executive Summary*. Available at https://coachfederation.org/app/uploads/2020/09/FINAL_ICF_GCS2020_ExecutiveSummary.pdf (accessed 13 December 2021).

International Coaching Federation (2021) *Covid-19 and the Coaching Industry: 2021 ICF Global Snapshot Survey Results*. Available at https://coachingfederation.org/app/uploads/2021/05/2021ICF_COVIDStudy_Part2_FINAL.pdf (accessed 13 December 2021).

Jones, R., Woods, S. and Guillaume, Y. (2016) The effectiveness of workplace coaching: a meta-analysis of learning and performance outcomes from coaching. *Journal of Occupational and Organizational Psychology*, 89(2), 249–277.

Kampa-Kokesch, S. and Anderson, M. Z. (2001) Executive coaching: a comprehensive review of the literature. *Consulting Psychology Journal: Practice and Research*, 53(4), 205–228.

Lai, Y.-L. and McDowall, A. (2014) A systematic review (SR) of coaching psychology: focusing on the attributes of effective coaching. *International Coaching Psychology Review*, 9(2), 120–136.

Lai, Y.-L. and Palmer, S. (2019) Psychology in executive coaching: an integrated literature review. *Journal of Work-Applied Management*, 11(2), 143–164. Available at https://doi.org/10.1108/JWAM-06-2019-0017 (accessed 14 October 2021).

Passmore, J. and Fillery-Travis, A. (2011) A critical review of executive coaching research: a decade of progress and what's to come. *Coaching: An International Journal of Theory, Research and Practice*, 4(2), 70–88.

Shah, S. (2020) Why we need more diversity in coaching. *People Management*, 14 July. Available at www.peoplemanagement.co.uk/voices/comment/why-we-need-more-diversity-in-coaching#gref (accessed 10 October 2021).

Sherman, S. and Freas, A. (2004) The wild west of executive coaching. *Harvard Business Review*, 82(10), 82–90. Available at https://hbr.org/2004/11/the-wild-west-of-executive-coaching (accessed 31 May 2021).

Singer, J. (2017) *NeuroDiversity: The Birth of an Idea*. Kindle: Judy Singer.

Sonesh, S.C., Coultas, C.W., Lacerenza, C.N., Marlow, S.L., Benishek, L.E. and Salas, E. (2015) The power of coaching: a meta-analytic investigation. *Coaching: An International Journal of Theory, Research and Practice*, 8(2), 73–95.

Theeboom, T., Beersma, B. and van Vianen, A.E.M. (2014) Does coaching work? A meta-analysis on the effects of coaching on individual level outcomes in an organizational context. *The Journal of Positive Psychology*, 9(1), 1–18.

Utry, Z.A. and Palmer, S. (2017) Coaching. In C. Feltham, T. Hanley and L.A. Winter (Eds), *The SAGE Handbook of Counselling and Psychotherapy* (pp. 548–552). London: Sage.

Wang, Q., Lai, Y.-L., Xu, X. and McDowall, A. (2021) The effectiveness of workplace coaching: a meta-analysis of contemporary psychologically informed coaching approaches, *Journal of Work-Applied Management*, 14(1), 77–101. [Online first], 21 June. https://doi.org/10.1108/JWAM-04-2021-0030 (accessed 15 October 2021).

Western, S. (2012) *Coaching and Mentoring: A Critical Text*. London: Sage.

Widdowson, L. and Barbour, P.J. (2021) *Building Top-Performing Teams: A Practical Guide to Team Coaching to Improve Collaboration and Drive Organizational Success*. London: Kogan Page.

RECOMMENDED READING

Palmer, S. and Whybrow, A. (2019) *Handbook of Coaching Psychology: A Guide for Practitioners* (2nd ed.). Abingdon, UK: Routledge.

This is a comprehensive read for professionals interested in the psychology of coaching.

Hawkins, P. and Turner, E. (2020) *Systemic Coaching: Delivering Value Beyond the Individual*. Abingdon, UK: Routledge.

This is a future-oriented book on systemic coaching, looking at the whole picture of where coaching takes place, not just the individual.

Stelter, R. (2019) *The Art of Dialogue in Coaching: Towards Transformative Change*. Abingdon, UK: Routledge.

This value- and meaning-oriented book on coaching is mindful of the social complexities and relations effecting both coaches and coachees in the twenty-first century.

POSTSCRIPT: HOW MIGHT COUNSELLING AND PSYCHOTHERAPY CHANGE OVER THE COMING YEARS?

As we end this edition of the *Handbook*, it is customary to project forward and consider the challenges for the fields of counselling and psychotherapy. Given the way that things turned out over the past few years, maybe this is unwise. Neither of us would have predicted when we wrote the postscript in 2016 that, in 2022, we would be sitting here now in the midst of an ongoing global pandemic, having experienced lockdowns and the changes to living (and counselling and psychotherapy as a result) that we have seen since Covid-19 was first noted in 2019. We probably also would not have predicted all the other social, economic and political turbulence currently being experienced globally.

So, for this edition of the *Handbook*, we discussed various possibilities we could write about in terms of future directions in counselling and psychotherapy. We discussed the increasing role of the political, and therapists' engaging with social justice and community work. We discussed being responsive in our work to new technologies and learning to work in new ways. We talked about whether the issue of professionalisation of the counselling and psychotherapy professions will be resolved, about working with new difficulties like long covid, and increasing populations of refugees and asylum seekers, displaced as part of new and ongoing wars. We talked about the importance of counselling and psychotherapy responding to the climate and ecological crises.

Instead of predicting, or even highlighting the importance of any of these issues, however, we are choosing to end the fifth edition of *The SAGE Handbook of Counselling and Psychotherapy* by embracing the unknown and the unpredictability. Rather, we simply want to highlight that whatever happens globally, we can only see the role of counselling and psychotherapy increasing, adapting and proving ever important for individuals and communities alike.

INDEX

Note: Page numbers in *italic* indicate figures and in **bold** indicate tables.

AAT *see* animal-assisted therapy (AAT)
    Abram, David, 373
abstinence violation effect, 223
Acceptance and Commitment Therapy (ACT), 89, 216, 241–2, 254–5, 272, 332–7, *335*
access to therapy, 36, 101, 561–2
    see also Improving Access to Psychological Therapy (IAPT) services
ACEs *see* adverse childhood experiences (ACEs)
ACT *see* Acceptance and Commitment Therapy (ACT)
Action Plans, 356
Active Imagination, 422, 425
active listening, 137
actualisation theory, 451
Adaptive Information Processing (AIP) model, 379
addiction, 220
    'sex addiction', 80, 82
    see also drug-related problems
adjustment and resource provision, 15
Adler, Alfred, 3, 4, 481
adolescents
    counselling, 35, 36, 517–22, *521*
    school-based counselling (SBC), 25, 574–7
    student counselling services, 25, 580–6
adopted children, 576
adoption counselling, 175
Adult ego state, 505, *505*
adverse childhood experiences (ACEs), 259, 486, 623
    see also child sexual abuse
affect regulation
    alcohol-related problems and, 221
    child sexual abuse and, 315, 317
    domestic abuse and, 328, 329
affirmation model of disability, 48–9
aftercare, 180
age, 34–7
ageing *see* older people
ageism, 35, 36, 37
agoraphobia, 295
AIDS, 80
Ainsworth, Mary, 339–40
AIP *see* Adaptive Information Processing (AIP) model
alcohol-related problems, 220–5, **545**
allied professions, 5, 21–2
aloneness-togetherness, 475

analytical psychology, 421–5
animal-assisted therapy (AAT), 373
Animus and *Anima*, 423–4
anorexia *see* eating disorders
anorgasmia, 309
anosognosia, 593
anti-psychotics, **204**
antidepressants, 201, 203, **204**
anxiety
    eco-anxiety, 40
    in existential therapy, 392
    generalised anxiety disorder (GAD), 226, 227, 229, 525–6, *527*, **545**
    group therapy, **545**
    obsessive-compulsive disorder (OCD), 282–7, **545**
    older people, 525–6, *527*
    panic disorder, 227, 228–30, **545**
    phobias, 294–8
    in psychoanalytic therapy, 470–1
approaches *see* therapeutic approaches
arbitrary inference, 354
archetypes, 423
art therapy, 375, 611
asexuality, 82
assault, sexual *see* sexual violence
assessment, 86–7, 97–102
    adult sexual violence, 214–15, 216
    alcohol-related problems, 220–1
    child sexual abuse, 313–15
    chronic physical health problems, 239–40
    depression, 251–3
    domestic abuse, 326–7
    drug-related problems, 246, 247–8
    eating disorders, 257–9
    Eye Movement Desensitisation and Reprocessing (EMDR) and, 381
    generalised anxiety disorder (GAD), 226
    grief, 233–4
    hearing voices, 264–6
    low self-esteem, 269–71
    obsessive-compulsive disorder (OCD), 282–4
    online, 101, 102
    panic disorder, 227
    personality disorders, 288–90
    phobias, 294–5

post-traumatic stress disorder (PTSD), 300, 303–4
primary care counselling, 607
questionnaires, 102
risk assessment, 102, 104, 107
schema therapy, 488
sex and relationship problems, 307–10
short-term therapy, 612
stress, 276–7
suicide and self-harm, 319–21, **320**
assistive technologies, 567–8
attachment-based family therapies, 537
attachment-based psychoanalytic psychotherapy, 338–42, *339*
attachment issues
    alcohol-related problems and, 222
    couple therapy and, 532
    depression and, 252, 253
    short-term therapy and, 612
attachment theory, 339–40, 342, 404, 537
attendance management, 139
attention training, 363
attributional style, 253
augmented reality, 567
autism, 52, 576
automatic pilot, 433
automatic thought diaries, 356
autonomy, 5, 504
avatars, 567
awareness
    in Gestalt therapy, 405, 406
    self-awareness, 16–17, 65, 191–2, 433

BACP *see* British Association for Counselling and Psychotherapy (BACP)
Bakhtin, Mikhail, 345
BASIC ID modalities, 277–8, **279**, 436, 437, 438–40, **439**, **441**, *442*
Beck, Aaron, 211, 332, 352, *353*, 354, 355, 356
behavioural couples therapy (BCT), 222
behavioural pattern-breaking techniques, 489
behavioural rehearsal, 368
behaviourism, 332, 366
being mode of mind, 432, 433
benzodiazepines, 203, **204**, 246
bereavement and loss, 233–6, 417, 418
Berne, Eric, 503–6, 508
bibliotherapy, 248, 438
binge eating disorder *see* eating disorders
Binswanger, Ludwig, 392
biomedical model, 203
biomedical model of disability, 47
Bion, Wilfred, 468, 482, 541
biophilia, 373, 374
biopsychosocial approach, 81, 240, 288, 361, 409
bisexuality *see* Gender, Sex and Relationship Diversity (GSRD) therapy; sexuality

black-and-white thinking, 354, 368
blogging, 566–7
body scan, 273, 381
borderline personality disorder (BPD), 288, 289, 290–1
    cognitive analytic therapy (CAT), 346, 347, 350
    dialectical behaviour therapy (DBT), 291, 365–70, **368**
    schema therapy, 490
Boss, Medard, 392
Bourdieu, Pierre, 75, 77
Bowlby, John, 222, 339, 404, 481, 484, 537
BPD *see* borderline personality disorder (BPD)
BPS *see* British Psychological Society (BPS)
bracketing, 406
brain
    child sexual abuse and, 314
    Eye Movement Desensitisation and Reprocessing (EMDR) and, 379, 380
    neuroplasticity, 593
    obsessive-compulsive disorder (OCD) and, 284
brief therapy, 88, 210, 610–14
    interpersonal psychotherapy (IPT), 415–19, 614
    psychodynamic interpersonal therapy (PIT), 474–8, 614
    single-session therapy (SST), 521, 611, 619
    solution-focused brief therapy (SFBT), 498–502, 611
British Association for Counselling and Psychotherapy (BACP), 4, 5, 21, 153
    complaints, 166, 167
    data protection guidance, 199
    ethical framework, 5–6, 10, 117, 161–2, 172, 581, 598
    measures, 116–17, 119, *122*
    media ethics, 590
    membership, 24
    online guidance, 549
    primary care counselling, 605, 606, 607, 608
    social media guidance, 196, 199
    working with interpreters, 130
British Psychological Society (BPS), 4, 22, 69, 290
    code of ethics, 6, 10, 159, 161
    drug treatments, 203
    formulation guidelines, 110, 112
    media ethics, 589, 590
    working with interpreters, 130
Buber, Martin, 404
Buddhism, 241, 272, 431
    see also Zen
Bugental, James, 392
Buhler, Charlotte, 3
bulimia *see* eating disorders

Caldicott Guardians, 125, 126
Care Act 2014, 180
Care Quality Commission (CQC), 126
case conceptualisation
    emotion-focused therapy (EFT), 387

Eye Movement Desensitisation and Reprocessing (EMDR), 379–80
schema therapy, 488
see also formulation
case studies
Acceptance and Commitment Therapy (ACT), 336
adult sexual violence, 217
alcohol-related problems, 224
assessment, 98–9, 102
child sexual abuse, 315–17
chronic physical health problems, 240–2
coaching, 629
compassion focused therapy (CFT), 362–4
counselling children, 514–15
couple therapy, 533
depression, 254
dialectical behaviour therapy (DBT), 369
domestic abuse, 326, 328–9, 576
drug-related problems, 250
eating disorders, 260–1
emotion-focused therapy (EFT), 388–9
existential therapy, 394–5
Eye Movement Desensitisation and Reprocessing (EMDR), 382–3
family therapy, 538–9, *539*
feminist therapy, 401
forensic settings, 624–5
Gender, Sex and Relationship Diversity (GSRD) therapy, 412–13
Gestalt therapy, 407–8
grief, 234–6
hearing voices, 267–8
Lacanian Therapy, 430
law, 171, 173
low self-esteem, 270–1
measures, 119
mindfulness based cognitive therapy (MBCT), 432–5
narrative therapy, 447
neuropsychology, 594–5
obsessive-compulsive disorder (OCD), 285–6
older people, 525–6, *527*
panic disorder, 228
person-centred therapy (PCT), 453–4
personal construct therapy, 459–60
personality disorders, 290–1
phobias, 297
pluralistic therapy, 465–6
post-traumatic stress disorder (PTSD), 302
psychoanalytic therapy, 472–3
psychodynamic interpersonal therapy (PIT), 476
psychodynamic therapy, 483–4
race, culture and ethnicity, 70–1
referrals, 87
risk, 106
ruptures in therapeutic relationship, 139

school-based counselling (SBC), 576
sex and relationship problems, 310–11
short-term therapy, 613–14
skilled helper model, 495–6
social media, 197, 198, 199
solution-focused brief therapy (SFBT), 500–2
stress management, 278, **279**, 280
suicide and self-harm, 322–3
telephone counselling, 563
transactional analysis (TA), 507
unplanned endings, 144, 145
videoconferencing therapy, 557
working with interpreters, 132
workplace therapy, 619–20
young people, 518–20
castration anxiety, 470
CAT *see* cognitive analytic therapy (CAT)
catastrophising, 354
CBT *see* cognitive behavioural therapy (CBT)
CCBT *see* computerised cognitive-behavioural therapy (CCBT)
CFT *see* compassion focused therapy (CFT)
chair work, 235, 362, 489
empty chair dialogue, 349, 387, 388–9, 407, 567
two chair dialogues, 387, 388
change
as goal of therapy, 17
social change, 400
stages of change model, 247–8
see also theories of change
charity model of disability, 47–8, 56–7
chat rooms, 550
'Cheshire West' case, 181, 182
Child ego state, 505, *505*
child protection and safeguarding, 107, 109, 125, 172, 326, 575
child sexual abuse, 259, 309, 313–17, 328, 623
children
counselling, 35, 36, 512–15
school-based counselling (SBC), 25, 574–7
Children Act 1989, 177
chronic physical health problems, 238–42
Circle of Security model, 338, *339*
class, 74–7
'clearing a space' task, 387
client-centred therapy (CCT) *see* person-centred therapy (PCT)
client–therapist relationship *see* therapeutic relationship
clients
attendance, 139
class base, 76
feedback, 102, 119, 137–8, 142, 186–7, 218
goals, 14–18, 89
perceptions of therapeutic alliance, 142, 184, 465
climate crisis, 9, 39–42, 628
clinical supervision *see* supervision
coaching, 627–30
coercive or controlling behaviour, 326–7

cognitive analytic therapy (CAT), 110, 143, 216, 345–50, *346*, *348*
cognitive behavioural models
    low self-esteem, 270–1
    panic disorder, 228–9
cognitive behavioural therapy (CBT), 352–7, *353*
    alcohol-related problems, 222 3
    assessment, 87
    child sexual abuse, 315, 316
    chronic physical health problems, 242
    computerised cognitive-behavioural therapy (CCBT), 566
    counselling children, 513–14, 515
    depression, 253
    eating disorders, 259, **545**
    group therapy, 544, **545**
    low self-esteem, 271–2
    mindfulness based cognitive therapy (MBCT), 431–5
    in neuropsychological settings, 594–5
    obsessive-compulsive disorder (OCD), 284
    for older people, 525, 526
    phobias, 297
    post-traumatic stress disorder (PTSD), 301
    in primary care settings, 25, 606, 608
    psychosexual therapy, 311–12
    relapse prevention, 143
    schema therapy and, 486
    stress management, 277
    trauma-focused, 217, 316
    videoconferencing therapy, 555–6, 557
cognitive distortions, 487
cognitive fusion, 334
cognitive rehearsal, 356
cognitive restructuring, 242, 271, 349
cohesiveness, 546
Collaborative Empiricism, 356
collective unconscious, 423
College Counsellors' Network tool, 582–4
colleges *see* student counselling services
Collins, Patricia Hill, 30
combined wisdom approach, 206
communication
    adolescent processes, 518–20
    interpreters, 129–33
    metacommunication, 138, 139, 466
    transactional analysis of, 505–6
community care law, 180
Community Treatment Orders (CTOs), 177, 179
compassion fatigue, 133, 218
compassion focused therapy (CFT), 191, 272–3, 359–64, *360*
compassionate leadership, 191
complaints, 165–9, 174
complexes, theory of, 422, 424, 482
complicated bereavement, 417, 418
complicated grief, 233
comprehensive distancing, 332
computerised cognitive-behavioural therapy (CCBT), 566

confidentiality, 88, 123–5, 172–3, 174–5, 619
confirmation bias, 210
conflict, in psychoanalytic therapy, 470
confluence, 405
confrontation ruptures, 138
consent *see* informed consent
constructive alternativisim, 457
constructivism, 456, 457, 518
contact, in Gestalt therapy, 405
contemporary sexology, 80–1, 411, 412
continuing bonds, 234
continuing professional development (CPD)
    interpreters, 133
    neurodivergence, 58
    primary care counselling, 606, 608
    race, culture, and ethnicity, 71
    supervision, 192
    see also personal and professional development
contracting, 88–9, 172–3, 562
controlling or coercive behaviour, 326–7
conversion therapies, 80, 82, 175
coping skills training, 223
coping styles, 487, 488, 489
core conflictual relationship theme (CCRT), 93
core emotional needs, 486
core skills
    active listening, 137
    attendance management, 139
    beginning therapy, 86–9
    complaints, 165–9, 174
    contracting, 88–9, 172–3, 562
    critical thinking, 208–11
    ending therapy, 142–5, 349–50, 613
    ethics-in-practice, 159–64
    goal setting, 89
    integrating research and practice, 184–7
    in middle phase of therapy, 136–40
    notetaking, 126–7
    paraphrasing, 137
    personal and professional development, 147–51
    psychopharmacology knowledge, 201–6, **204**
    recordkeeping, 126, 174
    reflecting feelings, 137
    relapse prevention, 143
    research skills, 185–6
    reviewing, 137–8
    social media use, 156, 196–9
    using measures, 116–19, *122*
    working with interpreters, 129–33
    see also assessment; formulation
Coroners and Justice Act 2009, 180
cost–benefit analysis, 356
counselling and psychotherapy
    allied professions, 5, 21–2
    definitions, 2

development of, 3–4
goals, 14–18, 89
social and political context, 8–12
values, 5–6, 598–601, *599*
see also core skills; employment settings; therapeutic approaches; therapy process; training
counselling psychology, 4, 22, 68, 193
countertransference, 83, 342, 429, 472, 561, 564
couple therapy, 222, 385, 389, 530–4
Covid-19 pandemic
depression and, 251
divorce and, 531
eating disorders and, 259
impacts on children, 574, 575
inequality and, 74
Long Covid, 10, 240–1
narrative therapy and, 444, 447
obsessive-compulsive disorder (OCD) and, 284
psychological impacts, 10
technology use, 6, 101, 156, 444, 447, 555, 561, 563, 564, 566, 628
CPD *see* continuing professional development (CPD)
creative and expressive therapy, 513
credulous listening, 209, 458
Crenshaw, Kimberley, 30, 51, 413
Criminal Justice Act 2003, 177
Criminal Procedure (Insanity) Act 1964, 177, 180
crisis intervention and management, 15–16
crisis plans, 108–9
Critical Race Theory (CRT), 69
critical thinking skills, 208–11
cross-cultural understandings, 63–4
CTOs *see* Community Treatment Orders (CTOs)
cultural competence, 411, 412
cultural complexes, 424
cultural humility, 411, 412
cultural resources, 465
culture, 67–72
cure, as goal of therapy, 16

DABS *see* Dual Attention Bilateral Stimulation (DABS)
Daseinsanalysis, 391, 392
data protection, 123–5, 174–5, 199
DBT *see* dialectical behaviour therapy (DBT)
de Beauvoir, Simone, 31
decathexis, 234
decision making, as goal of therapy, 16
decolonisation, 11, 63–4
defence mechanisms, 16, 469, 470–1, 482
deflection, 405
delayed ejaculation, 309
depression, 251–5
group therapy, **545**
interpersonal psychotherapy (IPT), 415–19
mindfulness based cognitive therapy (MBCT), 431–5
older people, 524

primary care counselling, 605–8
short-term therapy, 613–14
depressive rumination, 432–3
Deprivation of Liberty Safeguards, 181
describing, in Gestalt therapy, 406
desire, 428
developmental stages, 470
developmental theory, 404
diagnosis, 112–13
Diagnostic and Statistical Manual of Mental Disorders (DSM-5), 80, 83, 233, 252, 288–9, 295, 300, **301**, 303, 308, 366
dialectical behaviour therapy (DBT), 216, 291, 332, 365–70, **368**
dialogic stance, 406
dialogue
empty chair, 349, 387, 388–9, 407, 567
in Gestalt therapy, 405, 406
risk exploration, 107–8
Socratic questioning, 356, 362, 392, 394
two chair, 387, 388
dichotomous thinking, 354
Dicks, Henry, 530
digital mental health technologies, 230
disability, 45–9, 56–7
discrimination
ageism, 35, 36, 37
classism, 76, 77
racial, 67–8, 69
religious, 64
sexism, 51, 52–4
see also feminist therapy
disenfranchised grief, 234
distress tolerance, 235, 291, 328, 369
divorce, 530–1
doing mode of mind, 432–3
domestic abuse, 325–9, 531, 576
Domestic Abuse Act 2021, 326
Drama Triangle, 534
dream interpretation, 296, 424, 429, 469
drive/excitement system, 361
drive theory, 470, 481, 482
drug-related problems, 245–50
drug treatments, 201–6
adverse effects, 203, **204**, 205
erectile difficulty, 308
models of drug action, 202–3
withdrawal reactions, 203, **204**, 205–6
DSM *see Diagnostic and Statistical Manual of Mental Disorders* (DSM-5)
Dual Attention Bilateral Stimulation (DABS), 378, 380–1
Dual Process Model (DPM), 234
duty of care, 173

EAPs *see* employee assistance programmes (EAPs)
early childhood experiences, 486
early ejaculation, 309
early maladaptive schemas, 486

eating disorders, 257–61, 370, **545**
EBP *see* evidence-based practice (EBP)
eco-anxiety, 40
eco-coaching, 628
ecosystemic thinking, 373–4
ecotherapy, 372–6
Education Mental Health Practitioners (EMPHs), 574
educational settings
    school-based counselling (SBC), 25, 574–7
    student counselling services, 25, 580–6
EFC *see* experience-focused counselling (EFC)
EFT *see* emotion-focused therapy (EFT)
egalitarian relationship, 399–400
Egan, Gerard, 492–3, 494, 496–7
ego, 427–8, 429, 469, 471, 481
ego states, 505–6, *505*
either-or thinking, 210
Electra complex, 470
electronically delivered text therapy, 549–52
Ellis, Albert, 211, 352
email-based therapies, 549–50
EMDR *see* Eye Movement Desensitisation and Reprocessing (EMDR)
emergence theory, 424
emoticons, 551
emotion-focused therapy (EFT), 316, 317, 385–9, 532
emotion regulation, 291, 356, 369, 370
emotional reasoning, 354
empathic attunement, 342, 387
empathic confrontation, 489
empathy, 52, 191, 593
employee assistance programmes (EAPs), 15, 26, 617–21
employment settings, 23–7
    coaching, 627–30
    colleges and universities, 25, 580–6
    forensic settings, 622–5
    media work, 587–91
    National Health Service (NHS), 25–6, 605–8
    neuropsychology, 592–5
    primary care, 25, 605–8
    private practice, 26, 598–603
    schools, 25, 574–7
    short-term therapy, 610–14
    voluntary agencies and third sector, 24–5
    workplace therapy, 15, 26, 617–21
empty chair dialogue, 349, 387, 388–9, 407, 567
ending therapy, 142–5, 349–50, 613
environmental crisis, 9, 39–42, 628
epigenetics, 593
Epston, David, 444
Equality Act 2010, 10, 30, 130
equality, diversity and inclusivity, 575–6
Equine Assisted Growth and Learning Association (EAGALA) model, 285
equine therapy, 373
erectile difficulty, 308–9

Erikson, Eric, 503–4
ERPs *see* event related potentials (ERPs)
ethical codes and frameworks, 5–6, 10, 117, 159, 161–2, 163, 164, 172, 576–7, 581, 598
ethical issues, 159–64
    assessment, 102
    confidentiality, 88, 123–5, 172–3, 174–5, 619
    drug treatments, 202
    ethical dilemmas, 162–4
    informed consent, 117, 172–3, 202
    media work, 589–90
    relational ethics, 160
    religion and spirituality, 64–5
    school-based counselling (SBC), 576–7
    social media, 198–9
    student counselling services, 581
    telephone counselling, 562
    workplace therapy, 619
ethnicity, 51, 67–72, 628
European Brief Therapy Association (EBTA), 502
European Convention on Human Rights (ECHR), 177, 181
European Court of Human Rights (ECtHR), 177
European Federation of Psychologists' Association (EFPA), 588, 589
event related potentials (ERPs), 593
evidence-based practice (EBP), 6, 16, 117, 184, 593
existential therapy, 41, 391–5, 543–4, 611
existentialism, 392, 404, 406
experience-focused counselling (EFC), 267–8
experiential avoidance, 333–4, 337, 361, 432, 433
experiential focusing, 387
experiential techniques, 488–9
experiments, in Gestalt therapy, 406, 407
explanatory hypotheses, 477
exposure therapies
    generalised anxiety disorder (GAD), 229
    grief, 234, 235
    imaginal, 229, 298
    obsessive-compulsive disorder (OCD), 284–5
    phobias, 297, 298
    post-traumatic stress disorder (PTSD), 301
    virtual reality, 298, 567
    in vivo, 298
Eye Movement Desensitisation and Reprocessing (EMDR), 216, 235, 301, 310, 378–83

false equivalence, 210
family therapy, 259, 514, 515, 530, 535–40, *539*
Federn, Paul, 503
feedback
    client, 102, 119, 137–8, 142, 186–7, 218
    in supervision, 155
fees, 88–9
female orgasmic disorder, 309
feminism, 10, 30, 51, 52, 53, 397
feminist therapy, 53–4, 397–402, 533–4

field theory, 404
figure and ground, 404
Fisher, Andy, 373
fitness to study or practise assessments, 581
fixed-role therapy, 459–60
follow-up appointments, 143
Fonagy, Peter, 340
forensic settings, 622–5
formulation, 110–14, 138
    adult sexual violence, 215–16
    alcohol-related problems, 221
    best practice, 110, 112
    child sexual abuse, 314
    climate-related distress, 41
    cognitive behavioural therapy (CBT), 355–6
    compassion focused therapy (CFT), 362–3
    eating disorders, 260
    interpersonal psychotherapy (IPT), 416–17
    mindfulness based cognitive therapy (MBCT), 431
    personal construct therapy, 458
    personality disorders, 290
    pluralistic therapy, 464, 465
    post-traumatic stress disorder (PTSD), 304
    psychodynamic interpersonal therapy (PIT), 475
    psychosexual therapy, 311
    skilled helper model, 494, *494*
    suicide and self-harm, 321–2
    in teams, 113
    see also case conceptualisation
fortune telling, 354
forums, online, 550
Foster Report, 3
Foulkes, S. H., 541, 543
Frankl, Victor, 392
free association, 296, 429, 472, 482–3
free-floating attention, 472
Freud, Anna, 3, 428, 468, 481
Freud, Sigmund, 3, 4, 5, 32, 93, 234, 296, 421, 422, 428, 468–71, 480, 481, 482, 484
From, Isadore, 404
functional contextualism, 332, 333
further education *see* student counselling services

GAD *see* generalised anxiety disorder (GAD)
games
    therapeutic, 230
    in transactional analysis, 506
gardening, therapeutic, 374
GDPR *see* General Data Protection Regulation (UK-GDPR)
gender, 50–4
    see also intersectionality
gender aware therapy, 53–4
    see also feminist therapy
gender-based violence, 51
gender identity, 51–2, 310, 428
    see also Gender, Sex and Relationship Diversity (GSRD) therapy
gender-role analysis, 400
Gender, Sex and Relationship Diversity (GSRD) therapy, 409–13
general adaptation syndrome, 276
General Data Protection Regulation (UK-GDPR), 124–5, 199
generalised anxiety disorder (GAD), 226, 227, 229, 525–6, *527*, **545**
genetic factors
    depression, 252
    obsessive-compulsive disorder (OCD), 284
    phobias, 295–6
genograms, 533
Gestalt psychology, 404
Gestalt therapy, 385, 392, 403–8, 513, 514–15, 611
Gilbert, Paul, 359
goal-based outcome measures, 116, 575
goals
    clients', 14–18, 89
    private practice, 601–2
    psychodynamic therapy, 482–3
    skilled helper model, 493
    of supervision, 154
Goldman, Rhonda, 385
Goldstein, Kurt, 541
Goodman, Paul, 404
Gottman, John, 530
Greenberg, Leslie, 385–6
grief, 233–6, 417
group therapy, 541–6, **543**, **545**, **546**, 561–2, 563–4
GSRD therapy *see* Gender, Sex and Relationship Diversity (GSRD) therapy
guardianship orders, 179

habitus, 75, 77
hallucinogens, 246
Hanisch, Carol, 10
harm minimisation, 248–9
Hartmann, Heinz, 468
Hayes, Steven, 332, 334
Health and Care Professions Council (HCPC), 2, 4, 6, 10, 22, 166, 175, 196
health, physical
    chronic physical health problems, 238–42
    personality disorders and, 289
    socio-economic status and, 75
hearing voices, 263–8
Hefferline, Ralph, 404
here-and-now focus
    Gestalt therapy, 405, 406
    group therapy, 544, 545
    humanistic approaches, 253
    person-centred therapy (PCT), 93
    psychoanalytic therapy, 472
    psychodynamic interpersonal therapy (PIT), 476–7

working with depression, 253
see also mindfulness
High Intensity Cognitive Behavioural Therapists, 21, 22
higher education *see* student counselling services
Hillman, James, 423
HIV, 80
Hobson, Robert, 474–5, 476–7
Homicide Act 1957, 177, 180
homophobia, 53, 64, 81, 412, 576
homosexuality *see* Gender, Sex and Relationship Diversity (GSRD) therapy; sexuality
horizontalism, 406
horses, 285, 373
Hoxter, Hans, 3
Human Rights Act 1998, 181–2
human rights model of disability, 49, 56

IAPT *see* Improving Access to Psychological Therapy (IAPT) services
ICD *see International Classification of Diseases* (ICD-11)
id, 469, 481
identity
    gender, 51–2, 310, 428
    intersectional, 9, 30–3
    religious, 64
    social class and, 75, 76
imagery
    compassion focused therapy (CFT), 363–4
    schema therapy, 489
imaginal exposure therapies, 229, 298
Imago Therapy, 532
Improving Access to Psychological Therapy (IAPT) services, 21, 25, 117, 119, *122*, 425, 526, 605–8, 611
in vivo exposure therapies, 298
Independent Mental Health Advocates, 179
individuation, 423, 424, 518
inequality
    gender, 51, 52–4
    health, 75
    material and social, 74–5
    racial, 69
infertility counselling, 175
Information Commissioner's Office (ICO), 124
information disclosure, 123–5, 174–5
informed consent, 117, 172–3, 202
insecure attachment, 252, 327, 339–40, 612
insight and understanding, as goal of therapy, 16
institutional racism, 69
International Classification of Diseases (ICD-11), 80, 233, 282, 289, 291, 300, **301**, 366
International Coaching Federation (IFC), 628
internet
    blogging, 566–7
    counselling young people, 521
    couples' relationships and, 531
    online assessment, 101, 102
    online pornography, 309–10
    online supervision, 156
    social media, 156, 196–9
    text-based therapies, 549–52
    therapist's online presence, 590–1
    videoconferencing therapy, 554–8
interpersonal deficit/sensitivities, 417, 418
interpersonal effectiveness, 291, 369
interpersonal group therapy, 544–5, 546, **546**
interpersonal inventories, 416
interpersonal psychotherapy (IPT), 415–19, 614
interpreters, 129–33
intersectionality, 9, 30–3, 51, 68, 75, 400, 411, 413
intersex people, 51–2
intragroup competition theory, 413
introjection, 405
invalidating environments, 367
IPT *see* interpersonal psychotherapy (IPT)
irrational primacy effect, 210
IT systems, 126

Jaspers, Karl, 392
Johnson, Sue, 385
Jordan, Martin, 373
Jung, Carl, 4, 32, 421–5, 481, 482, 484
Jung, Emma, 424
Jungian analytical psychology, 421–5

'keep safe' plans, 108–9
Kelly, George, 456, 457–8, 459
Kernberg, Otto, 468
Key, David, 373
Kitzler, Richard, 404
Klein, Melanie, 3, 4, 221, 468, 481, 484
Koffka, Kurt, 404
Kohler, Wolfgang, 404
Kohut, Heinz, 221–2, 468

Lacan, Jacques, 427–8, 481
Lacanian Therapy, 427–30
Laing, R.D., 392, 541–2
law, 10, 171–5
    confidentiality, 123–5, 172–3, 174–5
    contracts, 172–3
    conversion therapies, 175
    data protection, 123–5, 174–5, 199
    domestic abuse, 326
    drug-related problems, 246
    duty of care, 173–4
    equality, 10, 30, 130
    handling risk, 174
    information disclosure, 123–5, 174–5
    liability, 173–4
    mental health law, 177–82

sexual violence, 214–15
statutory regulation of therapists, 175
therapeutic relationship, 172–4
Lazarus, Arnold, 277, 279, 436–8, 440
leadership, 190–4
learning theory of phobia development, 296
letter writing
compassionate, 273
goodbye letters, 143, 349–50
meaning-oriented grief therapy, 235
reformulation letters, 143, 347, 348–9
schema therapy, 489
LGBTQ+ people *see* Gender, Sex and Relationship Diversity (GSRD) therapy; sexuality
Liberty Protection Safeguards, 181
libido, 422, 470
limited re-parenting, 489
Linehan, Marsha, 366–7
linking hypotheses, 477
listening, 137
Logotherapy, 391, 392
loss model of disability, 48
lying and deception, drug users, 246–7

Maastricht Interview, 265, 267
Macy, Joanna, 373
Mahrer, Alvin, 392
Main, Mary, 340
marker-driven therapy, 387
Maslow, Abraham, 3, 541
maximisation, 354
May, Rollo, 3, 392
MBCT *see* mindfulness based cognitive therapy (MBCT)
MBSR *see* mindfulness based stress reduction (MBSR)
MBT *see* mentalisation-based treatment (MBT)
meaning discovery, as goal of therapy, 17
meaning-oriented grief therapy, 234–5
Meares, Russell, 474–5, 476
measures, 116–19, *122*
of chronic physical health problems, 240
of depression, 416
pluralistic therapy, 465
questionnaires in assessment, 102
school-based counselling (SBC), 575
of self-esteem, 270
student counselling services, 582–4
of therapeutic alliance, 93–4, 119, *122*, 142, 184, 465
of trauma symptoms, 315
validity and reliability, 117
media work, 589–90
Medical Foundation for the Victims of Torture, 374
medical model, 203
medical model of disability, 47, 56
medications *see* drug treatments
medicine walk, 375

Mental Capacity Act 2005, 177, 180–1
mental health
racial inequality and, 69
social and political context, 9–10
socio-economic status and, 75
Mental Health Act 1983, 130, 177–9
mental health crisis, 107
mental health law, 177–82
Mental Health Units (Use of Force) Act 2018, 180
mentalisation-based treatment (MBT), 291
mentoring, 192–3
metacommunication, 138, 139, 466
methodological pluralism, 185
Microaggression Theory, 411, 413
microaggressions, 58, 69, 138, 411, 413
mind
Freud's models of, 469, 471
modes of, 432–3
mind reading, 354
mindfulness, 431
in Acceptance and Commitment Therapy (ACT), 332, 334, 335
chronic physical health problems, 242
in cognitive analytic therapy (CAT), 349
in compassion focused therapy (CFT), 363
in dialectical behaviour therapy (DBT), 332, 366, 368–9
domestic abuse, 328
low self-esteem, 272
in neuropsychological settings, 595
for young people, 521
mindfulness based cognitive therapy (MBCT), 431–5
mindfulness based stress reduction (MBSR), 431
minimisation, 354
Minority Stress Theory, 81, 411, 413
mission statement, 599–601
mobile phones
telephone counselling, 560–4
text messaging, 550, 551–2
mood stabilisers, **204**
moral model of disability, 46–7
Moreno, Jacob, 404, 541
motivated reasoning, 210
motivational interviewing (MI), 224
mourning, 342, 417, 418
see also grief
multimodal therapy, 277–8, **279**, 436–42, **439**, **441**, *442*
multiple self states model (MSSM), 346

Narrative Exposure Therapy, 261, 301
narrative therapy, 444–8
National Health Service and Community Care Act 1990, 180
National Health Service (NHS), 21, 25–6, 126, 180, 605–8
see also Improving Access to Psychological Therapy (IAPT) services

National Institute for Health and Care Excellence (NICE), 16, 25, 221, 259, 290, 319, 350, 378, 416, 418, 577, 605, 606, 608, 611
Natural Growth Project, 374
nature therapy, 372–6
NDPT *see* non-directive play therapy (NDPT)
Negative Automatic Thoughts (NATS), 354, 355
Negative Cognitive Triad, 352, *353*, 355
neurodivergence/neurodiversity, 52, 56–60, 628
neuroimaging, 593
neuroplasticity, 593
neuropsychology, 592–5
neurosis, 470
NHS *see* National Health Service (NHS)
NICE *see* National Institute for Health and Care Excellence (NICE)
non-binary gender, 51–2
non-directive approach, 296, 450, 451, 453
non-directive play therapy (NDPT), 513
notetaking, 126–7
numinous, 424–5

object relations theory, 92, 339, 345, 398, 399
obsessive-compulsive disorder (OCD), 282–7, **545**
Oedipus complex, 428, 469, 471
older people, 34–7, 523–6, *527*
organisational change, 17
organismic self-regulation, 404, 405–6
origin and maintenance of problems
    Acceptance and Commitment Therapy (ACT), 333–4
    attachment-based psychoanalytic psychotherapy, 340–1
    cognitive analytic therapy (CAT), 346–7
    cognitive behavioural therapy (CBT), 354–5
    compassion focused therapy (CFT), 361
    dialectical behaviour therapy (DBT), 367
    ecotherapy, 374
    emotion-focused therapy (EFT), 386
    existential therapy, 393
    Eye Movement Desensitisation and Reprocessing (EMDR), 379–80
    feminist therapy, 399
    Gender, Sex and Relationship Diversity (GSRD) therapy, 411
    Gestalt therapy, 405
    interpersonal psychotherapy (IPT), 416–17
    Jungian analytical psychology, 424
    Lacanian Therapy, 428–9
    mindfulness based cognitive therapy (MBCT), 432
    multimodal therapy, 437–8
    narrative therapy, 445
    person-centred therapy (PCT), 452
    personal construct therapy, 458
    pluralistic therapy, 463
    psychoanalytic therapy, 470–1
    psychodynamic interpersonal therapy (PIT), 475

    psychodynamic therapy, 481–2
    schema therapy, 486–7
    skilled helper model, 493
    solution-focused brief therapy (SFBT), 499
    transactional analysis (TA), 504–6
otherness, 30–1
outcome measures, 116–19, *122*
    of chronic physical health problems, 240
    pluralistic therapy, 465
    school-based counselling (SBC), 575
    student counselling services, 582–4
outcome research, 142, 184–5
overdoses, 248–9

panic attacks, 227, 228, 295
panic disorder, 227, 228–30, **545**
Panic Focused Psychodynamic Psychotherapy (PFPP), 296
paraphrasing, 137
Parent ego state, 505, *505*
paternal metaphor, 428, 429
patient reported outcome measures (PROMs), 240
patriarchal society *see* feminist therapy
PCT *see* person-centred therapy (PCT)
Perls, Fredrick, 404, 541
Perls, Laura, 404
Person Centred Experiential Counselling for Depression (PCE CfD), 606, 608
person-centred therapy (PCT), 385, 392, 450–4
    assessment, 86, 87
    group therapy, 544
    with GSRD clients, 411
    in neuropsychological settings, 594
    phobias, 296
    therapeutic relationship, 93
persona, 424
personal and professional development, 21, 147–51
    see also continuing professional development (CPD)
personal construct theory, 345, 456, 457–8
personal construct therapy, 456–60
'personal is political', 10, 397, 400
personal mission statement, 599–601
personality
    BASIC ID modalities, 277–8, **279**, 436, 437, 438–40, **439**, **441**, *442*
    ego states, 505–6, *505*
    obsessive-compulsive disorder (OCD) and, 284
    personality change as goal of therapy, 17
    psychological types, 423
    trait theories, 190, 291–2
personality disorders, 288–92, 487
    see also borderline personality disorder (BPD)
perversion, 470
phenomenological enquiry, 406
phenomenology, 394, 395, 406
phobias, 294–8

Pink Therapy, 410
PIT *see* psychodynamic interpersonal therapy (PIT)
Plotkin, Bill, 373
pluralistic therapy, 462–6, 561
podcasting, 566–7
points of contact model, 185–6
Police and Criminal Evidence Act (PACE) 1984, 180
police powers, 179–80
Polyvagal Theory, 285
pornography, 309–10
post-traumatic growth (PTG), 233–4, 305, 526
post-traumatic stress disorder (PTSD), 3, 300–5
    climate crisis and, 40
    diagnostic criteria, 300, **301**
    domestic abuse and, 326
    Eye Movement Desensitisation and Reprocessing (EMDR), 301, 378, 382–3
    grief and, 233
    relational approach, 301–5, *303*
    sexual violence and, 215, 218
postcolonial perspective, 63–4
poverty, 51, 53, 75
power, 11
    access to therapy and, 36
    intersectionality and, 31, 33
    race and, 69
power analysis, 400
Power Threat Meaning Framework, 11, 325, 327
practice-based evidence (PBE), 350
pragmatic truth criterion, 333
precarious manhood theory, 413
preconscious, 469
preference theory, 278–80
premature ejaculation, 309
Prentice, Hilary, 373
primary care counselling, 25, 605–8
prison settings, 622–5
private practice, 26, 598–603
privilege, 31
proactive approach, 520, *521*
problem solving, 16, 229, 277, 314, 628
procedural sequence model (PSM), 345
procedural sequence object relations model (PSORM), 345
process-experiential therapy, 385
process measures, 94, 116–19, *122*
process research, 184
professional knowledge studies, 186
Professional Standards Authority (PSA), 167, 175
projection, 405
Prolonged Exposure Therapy, 235, 301
prolonged grief disorder (PGD), 233
psychiatric drugs *see* psychopharmacology
psychic determinism, 469
psycho-emotional model of disability, 48

psychoanalytic therapy, 88, 89, 234, 296, 468–73, 542–3
    see also attachment-based psychoanalytic psychotherapy; Lacanian Therapy
psychodrama, 404, 541
psychodynamic interpersonal therapy (PIT), 474–8, 614
psychodynamic therapy, 41, 92–3, 250, 253, 480–4, 531–2, 595
    see also Lacanian Therapy; psychoanalytic therapy
psychoeducation, 15
    adult sexual violence, 216, 217
    child sexual abuse, 315–16
    cognitive analytic therapy (CAT), 349
    cognitive behavioural therapy (CBT), 355
    compassion focused therapy (CFT), 362
    depression, 253
    domestic abuse, 327, 328
    eating disorders, 260
    feminist therapy, 400
    generalised anxiety disorder (GAD), 229
    multimodal therapy, 437
    neuropsychological information, 593
    panic disorder, 229–30
    schema therapy, 488
    sex and relationship problems, 309, 311
    telephone counselling, 561
    young people, 520–1
psychological contact, 87–8
psychological types, 423
Psychological Wellbeing Practitioners (PWPs), 21–2, 574, 606, 608
psychopharmacology, 201–6
    adverse effects, 203, **204**, 205
    models of drug action, 202–3
    withdrawal reactions, 203, **204**, 205–6
psychosexual development, 470
psychosexual therapy, 311–12
psychosis, 470–1
PTG *see* post-traumatic growth (PTG)
PTSD *see* post-traumatic stress disorder (PTSD)
PWPs *see* Psychological Wellbeing Practitioners (PWPs)

questionnaires, assessment, 102

race, 51, 67–72, 628
    see also intersectionality
racism, 51, 67–8, 69–70
randomised controlled trials (RCTs), 185, 301, 337, 350, 366, 369, 383, 385, 454, 473, 477, 490, 502, 555, 577, 606
rape *see* sexual violence
rapid eye movement (REM) sleep, 380
rational emotive behavioural therapy (REBT), 277, 352
RCTs *see* randomised controlled trials (RCTs)
re-traumatisation, 218
reality testing, 356
Reality TV, 588

REBT *see* rational emotive behavioural therapy (REBT)
reciprocal roles, 345, 346–7, *346*, 349
recordkeeping, 126, 174
Reese, Robert, 492
referrals, 86–7, 145, 586
reflecting feelings, 137
reflecting teams, 537
reflective listening, 137
reflexive practice, 140
reformulation letters, 143, 347, 348–9
relapse prevention, 143
    alcohol-related problems, 223
    panic disorder, 230
relational approaches
    ecotherapy, 374, 375
    group therapy, 545
    post-traumatic stress disorder (PTSD), 301–5, *303*
    transactional analysis, 506–7
    see also psychodynamic interpersonal therapy (PIT)
relational ethics, 160
relational frame theory (RFT), 332, 333–4
relationship problems, 307–12
    child sexual abuse and, 314
relaxation training, 229
reliability of measures, 117
religion, 62–5
religious model of disability, 46–7
repertory grid technique, 459
repetition compulsion, 471
repression, 469
research
    gender bias in, 52–3
    integrating into practice, 184–7
    outcome, 142, 184–5
    process, 184
    skills, 185–6
research evidence
    Acceptance and Commitment Therapy (ACT), 336–7
    attachment-based psychoanalytic psychotherapy, 342
    coaching, 629–30
    cognitive analytic therapy (CAT), 350
    cognitive behavioural therapy (CBT), 356–7
    compassion focused therapy (CFT), 364
    complaints, 166–7
    counselling children, 515
    counselling older people, 526
    counselling young people, 521–2
    dialectical behaviour therapy (DBT), 369–70
    ecotherapy, 375–6
    emotion-focused therapy (EFT), 389
    existential therapy, 395
    Eye Movement Desensitisation and Reprocessing (EMDR), 383
    family therapy, 539–40
    feminist therapy, 401–2
    forensic settings, 625
    formulation, 113
    Gender, Sex and Relationship Diversity (GSRD) therapy, 413
    Gestalt therapy, 407
    group therapy, 545–6, **545**, **546**
    interpersonal psychotherapy (IPT), 418–19
    interpreters, 133
    Jungian analytical psychology, 425
    Lacanian Therapy, 430
    measures, 116–18
    media work, 590–1
    mindfulness based cognitive therapy (MBCT), 435
    multimodal therapy, 441–2
    narrative therapy, 447–8
    neuropsychology, 595
    person-centred therapy (PCT), 454
    personal construct therapy, 460
    pluralistic therapy, 466
    primary care counselling, 608
    psychoanalytic therapy, 473
    psychodynamic interpersonal therapy (PIT), 477–8
    psychodynamic therapy, 484
    schema therapy, 490
    school-based counselling (SBC), 577
    short-term therapy, 614
    skilled helper model, 496–7
    social media usage, 199
    solution-focused brief therapy (SFBT), 502
    supervision, 154–5, 156
    systemic therapies, 539–40
    telephone counselling, 564
    therapeutic relationship, 92–4
    transactional analysis (TA), 508
    videoconferencing therapy, 557
    workplace therapy, 620–1
research-informed practice, 184–7
resistance to treatment, 471
responsiveness, 92
Restorative Retelling, 235–6
retroflection, 405
reviewing therapeutic work, 137–8
RFT *see* relational frame theory (RFT)
Rice, Laura, 385
risk, 104–9
    assessment, 102, 104, 107
    crisis plans, 108–9
    legal obligations, 174
    mitigation, 108
Robertson, James, 339
Rogers, Carl, 3, 5, 11, 87–8, 93, 139, 184, 296, 385, 450–4, 541, 544, 545
role dispute, 417

role play, 356, 489, 541
role transition, 417
roles, reciprocal, 345, 346–7, *346*, 349
Roszak, Theodore, 372–3
rumination, 361, 432–3
Rust, Mary-Jayne, 373
Ryle, Anthony, 345

safeguarding, 107, 109, 125, 172, 326, 575
sand play work, 514
Sartre, Jean-Paul, 392
SBC *see* school-based counselling (SBC)
schema therapy, 485–90
schemas, 354–5
Schneider, Kirk, 392
school-based counselling (SBC), 25, 574–7
Scope of Practice and Education (ScoPEd) framework, 2
Scottish Intercollegiate Guidelines Network (SIGN), 606, 608
SDR *see* sequential diagrammatic reformulation (SDR)
Second Life, 567
secure hospital settings, 622–5
Seed, John, 373
selection, optimisation with compensation (SOC) model, 523, 524
self, 148–9, 254
    child sexual abuse and, 314–15, 316–17
    in existential therapy, 392
    in Jungian analytical psychology, 424
    see also ego
self-actualisation, 5, 16–17, 404, 451, 452
self-awareness, 16–17, 65, 191–2, 433
self-care, 556
self-characterisation, 459
self-concept, 451, 452
self-defeating patterns, 487
self-disclosure, 518
self-esteem, low, 269–73
self-experience, 451
self-harm *see* suicide and self-harm
self-medication, 221, 250
self-reflection, 140, 148, 150
self-regulation, organismic, 404, 405–6
self-states *see* ego states
Sensate Focus, 82
sense of self, child sexual abuse and, 314–15, 316–17
sequential diagrammatic reformulation (SDR), 347–8, *348*, 349
sequentially planned integrative counselling for children (SPICC) model, 514–15
session frequency, 88, 472
Sewell Race Report, 69
'sex addiction', 80, 82
sex and relationship problems, 307–12
sexism, 51, 52–4
    see also feminist therapy

sexology, contemporary, 80–1, 411, 412
sexual abuse in childhood, 313–17
sexual violence, 214–18
sexuality, 79–83, 175, 576
sexuation, 428
SFBT *see* solution-focused brief therapy (SFBT)
Shapiro, Elliot, 404
Shapiro, Francine, 378–9
shell shock, 3
short-term therapy, 88, 210, 610–14
    interpersonal psychotherapy (IPT), 415–19, 614
    psychodynamic interpersonal therapy (PIT), 474–8, 614
    single-session therapy (SST), 521, 611, 619
    solution-focused brief therapy (SFBT), 498–502, 611
'sick role work', 416
Sieghart Report, 3
silencing, 445
single-session therapy (SST), 521, 611, 619
skilled helper model, 491–7, *494*
skills and strategies
    Acceptance and Commitment Therapy (ACT), 334–6, *335*
    attachment-based psychoanalytic psychotherapy, 341–2
    cognitive analytic therapy (CAT), 347–50, *348*
    cognitive behavioural therapy (CBT), 356
    compassion focused therapy (CFT), 362–4
    dialectical behaviour therapy (DBT), 368–9
    ecotherapy, 374–5
    emotion-focused therapy (EFT), 387
    existential therapy, 394–5
    Eye Movement Desensitisation and Reprocessing (EMDR), 380–3
    feminist therapy, 399–400
    Gender, Sex and Relationship Diversity (GSRD) therapy, 410–11
    Gestalt therapy, 406–7
    interpersonal psychotherapy (IPT), 417–18
    Jungian analytical psychology, 424–5
    Lacanian Therapy, 429
    mindfulness based cognitive therapy (MBCT), 433–5
    multimodal therapy, 440–1, **441**, *442*
    narrative therapy, 446–7
    person-centred therapy (PCT), 453
    personal construct therapy, 459–60
    pluralistic therapy, 464–5
    psychoanalytic therapy, 471–2
    psychodynamic interpersonal therapy (PIT), 476–7
    psychodynamic therapy, 482–3
    schema therapy, 488–9
    skilled helper model, 494–5
    solution-focused brief therapy (SFBT), 499–502
    transactional analysis (TA), 506–7
    see also core skills
Skinner, B.F., 332
SMART, 601

smartphone apps, 230
SMS text messaging, 550, 551–2
social and political context, 8–12
social behaviour and network therapy (SNBT), 222
social change, 17, 400
social class, 74–7
Social Field Theory, 413
social justice, 11, 191–2
    age, 34–7
    climate and environmental crisis, 9, 39–42, 628
    disability, 45–9, 56–7
    gender, 50–4
    Gender, Sex and Relationship Diversity (GSRD) therapy and, 410–11
    intersectionality, 9, 30–3, 51, 68, 75, 400, 411, 413
    neurodivergence, 52, 56–60, 628
    race, culture and ethnicity, 51, 67–72, 628
    religion and spirituality, 62–5
    sexuality, 79–83, 175, 576
    social class, 74–7
social media, 156, 196–9
social model of disability, 48, 57
social phobias, 295
social shaping, 361
socialisation, 399, 518
socio-emotional selectivity theory, 524
sociocultural basis of distress, 400
Socratic questioning, 356, 362, 392, 394
solo/vision quest, 374–5
solution-focused brief therapy (SFBT), 498–502, 611
soothing breathing, 273, 363
soothing system, 361
specific phobias, 294–5
SPICC *see* sequentially planned integrative counselling for children (SPICC) model
Spielrein, Sabina, 422
spirituality, 62–5
SST *see* single-session therapy (SST)
stages of change model, 247–8
statutory regulation, 175
Steele, Howard, 340
Steele, Miriam, 340
stereotypes
    ageist, 35, 36, 37
    classist, 77
    disability, 45, 47, 48
    gender, 52, 53
Stern, Daniel, 404
stimming, 59
stimulants, **204**, 246
stories *see* narrative therapy
Strange Situation tool, 339–40
strengths-based approaches, 413
stress, 275–80, **279**

see also post-traumatic stress disorder (PTSD)
structural bias, 51
structural model of the mind, 469, 471
student counselling services, 25, 580–6
Subjective Units of Disturbance (SUD) scale, 381
suffocated grief, 234
suicide and self-harm, 318–24
    bereavement due to, 234–6
    dialectical behaviour therapy (DBT), 365–70, **368**
    personality disorders and, 289
    risk of, 105, 106, 319–21, **320**
superego, 469, 481
supervision, 138–9, 153–7, 192
    culturally informed, 71, 72
    primary care counselling, 606
    religion and spirituality, 65
    self-reflection, 140
    supervisor training, 155–6
    technology use, 156
    telephone, 563
    trainee placements, 20–1
    working alliance, 153, 154
supportive therapy, 15
symbolic strategies, 520
symptom amelioration, as goal of therapy, 16
synchronicity, 425
systematic evocative unfolding, 387
systemic change, 17
systemic therapies, 533, 535–40, *539*

TA *see* transactional analysis (TA)
team coaching, 628
team formulation, 113
technology, 565–8
    assistive technologies, 567–8
    augmented reality, 567
    avatars, 567
    blogging, 566–7
    coaching, 628
    computerised cognitive-behavioural therapy (CCBT), 566
    counselling young people, 521
    couples' relationships and, 531
    digital mental health technologies, 230
    IT systems, 126
    online assessment, 101, 102
    online pornography, 309–10
    podcasting, 566–7
    social media, 156, 196–9
    in supervision, 156
    telephone counselling, 560–4
    text-based therapies, 549–52
    videoconferencing therapy, 554–8
    virtual reality exposure therapy (VRET), 298, 567
    virtual worlds, 567

telephone counselling, 560–4
text-based therapies, 549–52
theories of change
    Acceptance and Commitment Therapy (ACT), 334
    attachment-based psychoanalytic psychotherapy, 341
    cognitive analytic therapy (CAT), 347
    cognitive behavioural therapy (CBT), 355–6
    compassion focused therapy (CFT), 362
    dialectical behaviour therapy (DBT), 367–8, **368**
    ecotherapy, 374
    emotion-focused therapy (EFT), 386–7
    existential therapy, 393–4
    Eye Movement Desensitisation and Reprocessing (EMDR), 380
    feminist therapy, 399
    Gender, Sex and Relationship Diversity (GSRD) therapy, 411
    Gestalt therapy, 405–6
    interpersonal psychotherapy (IPT), 417
    Jungian analytical psychology, 424
    Lacanian Therapy, 429
    mindfulness based cognitive therapy (MBCT), 432–3
    multimodal therapy, 438–40, **439**
    narrative therapy, 445–6
    person-centred therapy (PCT), 452–3
    personal construct therapy, 458
    pluralistic therapy, 463–4
    psychoanalytic therapy, 471
    psychodynamic interpersonal therapy (PIT), 476
    psychodynamic therapy, 482–3
    schema therapy, 488–9
    skilled helper model, 493–4, *494*
    solution-focused brief therapy (SFBT), 499
    transactional analysis (TA), 506
therapeutic alliance, 92, 101, 136
    client perceptions of, 142, 184, 465
    cognitive behavioural therapy (CBT), 355, 356
    interpreters and, 130, 131, 132
    measures of, 93–4, 119, *122*, 142, 184, 465
    multimodal therapy, 440
    psychodynamic interpersonal therapy (PIT), 478
    psychodynamic therapy, 482
    psychometric concepts, 93–4
    research into, 184
    ruptures, 94, 138–9, 167
    videoconferencing therapy, 556
    with young people, 518
    see also therapeutic relationship
therapeutic approaches
    Acceptance and Commitment Therapy (ACT), 89, 216, 241–2, 254–5, 272, 332–7, *335*
    for adult sexual violence, 216–18
    for alcohol-related problems, 221–4, **545**
    attachment-based psychoanalytic psychotherapy, 338–42, *339*
    for child sexual abuse, 315–17
    for chronic physical health problems, 241–2
    cognitive analytic therapy (CAT), 110, 143, 216, 345–50, *346*, *348*
    compassion focused therapy (CFT), 191, 272–3, 359–64, *360*
    for counselling children, 512–15
    couple therapy, 222, 385, 389, 530–4
    creative and expressive therapy, 513
    for depression, 253–5, 415–19, 431–5
    dialectical behaviour therapy (DBT), 216, 291, 332, 365–70, **368**
    for domestic abuse, 327–9
    for drug-related problems, 248–50
    for eating disorders, 259–61
    ecotherapy, 372–6
    emotion-focused therapy (EFT), 316, 317, 385–9, 532
    existential therapy, 41, 391–5, 543–4, 611
    experience-focused counselling (EFC), 267–8
    Eye Movement Desensitisation and Reprocessing (EMDR), 216, 235, 301, 310, 378–83
    family therapy, 259, 514, 515, 530, 535–40, *539*
    feminist therapy, 397–402, 533–4
    Gender, Sex and Relationship Diversity (GSRD) therapy, 409–13
    for generalised anxiety disorder (GAD), 229, 525–6, *527*, **545**
    Gestalt therapy, 385, 392, 403–8, 513, 514–15, 611
    for grief, 234–6
    group therapy, 541–6, **543**, **545**, **546**, 561–2, 563–4
    for hearing voices, 266–8
    interpersonal psychotherapy (IPT), 415–19
    Jungian analytical psychology, 421–5
    Lacanian Therapy, 427–30
    for low self-esteem, 271–3
    meaning-oriented grief therapy, 234–5
    mentalisation-based treatment (MBT), 291
    mindfulness based cognitive therapy (MBCT), 431–5
    multimodal therapy, 277–8, **279**, 436–42, **439**, **441**, *442*
    narrative therapy, 444–8
    non-directive play therapy (NDPT), 513
    for obsessive-compulsive disorder (OCD), 284–7, **545**
    for older people, 525–6
    for panic disorder, 229–30, **545**
    personal construct therapy, 456–60
    for personality disorders, 289–92
    for phobias, 296–8
    pluralistic therapy, 462–6, 561
    for post-traumatic stress disorder (PTSD), 300–5, 378, 382–3
    preference theory, 278–80
    psychoanalytic therapy, 88, 89, 234, 296, 468–73, 542–3
    psychodynamic interpersonal therapy (PIT), 474–8
    psychodynamic therapy, 41, 92–3, 250, 253, 480–4, 531–2, 595
    psychosexual therapy, 311–12
    schema therapy, 485–90

for sex and relationship problems, 310–12
skilled helper model, 491–7, *494*
social behaviour and network therapy (SNBT), 222
solution-focused brief therapy (SFBT), 498–502
for stress, 277–80
for suicide and self-harm, 321–3
systemic therapies, 533, 535–40, *539*
time-limited play therapy, 513
transactional analysis (TA), 310, 503–8, *505*, 534, 611
virtual reality exposure therapy (VRET), 298, 567
for young people, 518–21, *521*
see also cognitive behavioural therapy (CBT); exposure therapies; mindfulness; person-centred therapy (PCT); short-term therapy
therapeutic games, 230
therapeutic gardening, 374
therapeutic relationship, 91–4
age and, 36–7
assessment and, 101
attachment-based psychoanalytic psychotherapy, 341
child sexual abuse, 316
cognitive analytic therapy (CAT), 349
cognitive behavioural therapy (CBT), 355, 356
countertransference, 83, 342, 429, 472, 561, 564
drug treatments and, 205
ending therapy and, 142, 143, 144
feminist therapy, 399–400
group therapy, 544–5, 546
legal aspects, 172–4
managing and maintaining, 136–7
meaning-oriented grief therapy, 234–5
multimodal therapy, 438
narrative therapy, 446
person-centred therapy (PCT), 452–3
personal construct therapy, 458
pluralistic therapy, 464–5
post-traumatic stress disorder (PTSD), 301–5
research into, 184
resistance to treatment, 471
responsiveness, 92
ruptures, 94, 138–9, 167
schema therapy, 488, 489
social class and, 77
text-based therapies, 550–1
transference, 36, 92–3, 296, 424, 471, 561
videoconferencing therapy, 556, 557
with young people, 518
see also therapeutic alliance
therapy process
attendance management, 139
beginning therapy, 86–9
complaints, 165–9, 174
confidentiality, 88, 123–5, 172–3, 174–5
contracting, 88–9, 172–3, 562
ending therapy, 142–5, 349–50, 613

ethics-in-practice, 159–64
fees, 88–9
goal setting, 89
length of, 88
middle phase, 136–40
notetaking, 126–7
psychological contact, 87–8
recordkeeping, 126, 174
referrals, 86–7, 145, 586
relapse prevention, 143
research into, 184
reviewing, 137–8
session frequency, 88
using measures, 116–19, *122*
working with interpreters, 129–33
see also assessment; formulation
thinking
black-and-white, 354, 368
critical, 208–11
dichotomous, 354
ecosystemic, 373–4
either-or, 210
third sector, 24–5
threat system, 361
Tillich, Paul, 392
time-limited play therapy, 513
topographical model of the mind, 469, 471
Totton, Nick, 373
tragedy model of disability, 47–8
training, 19–22
allied professions, 21–2
assessment, 21
beginning, 19–20
counselling training, 20–1
in educational settings, 586
interpreters, 133
neurodivergence, 58
personal development, 21, 150, 151
primary care counselling, 606, 608
psychotherapy training, 21
race, culture, and ethnicity, 71
recordkeeping, 126
safeguarding, 125
self-reflection, 150
supervised placements, 20–1
supervisors, 155–6
telephone counselling, 563–4
trans people, 51–2, 80, 81, 175, 576
see also Gender, Sex and Relationship Diversity (GSRD) therapy
transactional analysis (TA), 310, 503–8, *505*, 534, 611
transactional theories of stress, 276–7
transcendental experience, 17
transference, 36, 92–3, 296, 424, 471, 561
see also countertransference

INDEX **649**

transference interpretations, 472, 477, 483
transphobia, 81, 576
trauma
    child sexual abuse, 259, 309, 313–17, 328, 623
    domestic abuse, 325–9, 531, 576
    post-traumatic growth (PTG), 233–4, 305, 526
    racial, 70
    re-traumatisation, 218
    repetition compulsion, 471
    sexual violence, 214–18
    vicarious, 218
    see also post-traumatic stress disorder (PTSD)
trauma-based enactments, 342
trauma-focused therapies, 217, 316, 618
trauma-informed approaches
    domestic abuse, 325, 327, 328
    eating disorders, 260–1
    in forensic settings, 624
    formulation, 112
    Gender, Sex and Relationship Diversity (GSRD) therapy, 411, 412
Trauma Symptom Inventory (TSI), 315
Tree of Life technique, 447
true self, 148
two chair dialogues, 387, 388
Two-Track Model of Bereavement (TTMB), 234

unconditional positive regard, 41, 93, 139, 191, 209, 296, 356, 374, 452, 453
unconscious, 340, 393, 423, 427, 469, 471, 481, 593
understanding hypotheses, 477
United Kingdom Council for Psychotherapy (UKCP), 2, 3, 6, 10, 21, 24, 110, 163, 164, 166, 196
universal design, 59
universities *see* student counselling services
unplanned endings, 143–5

vaginismus, 309
Validity of Cognition (VOC) scale, 381
validity of measures, 117
values, 5–6, 598–9, *599*
vicarious trauma, 218
videoconferencing therapy, 554–8
violence
    domestic abuse, 325–9, 531, 576
    gender-based, 51
    risk of, 106–7
    sexual, 214–18
    symbolic, 77
virtual reality exposure therapy (VRET), 298, 567
virtual worlds, 567
vision and mission statement, 599–601
vision quest, 375
voice, 445
voluntary agencies, 24–5
VRET *see* virtual reality exposure therapy (VRET)
Vygotsky, Lev, 345, 347

waiting lists, 585–6
Weisz, Paul, 404
Wertheimer, Max, 404
Wesley, Simon, 179
White, Michael, 444
Wilson, Edward O., 373
Winnicott, Donald, 468, 481, 484
wisdom, 524–5
withdrawal ruptures, 138
Wolpe, Joseph, 437
Word Association Test, 422
working alliance
    in supervision, 153, 154
    see also therapeutic alliance
workplace therapy, 15, 26, 617–21
worry, 226, 227, 229
Wosket, Val, 492, 496

Yalom, Irvin, 392, 542, 544, 545, 546, **546**
Yogic teachings, 601, *601*
Young, Jeffrey, 486–7
young people
    counselling, 35, 36, 517–22, *521*
    school-based counselling (SBC), 25, 574–7
    student counselling services, 25, 580–6

Z-Drugs, **204**
Zen, 366, 367, 404
zone of proximal development (ZPD), 347